KOREAN
STANDARD DICTIONARY

KOREAN
STANDARD DICTIONARY

Jeyseon Lee
Kangjin Lee

HIPPOCRENE BOOKS, INC.
New York

For information, address:
HIPPOCRENE BOOKS, INC.
171 Madison Avenue
New York, NY 10016
www.hippocrenebooks.com

Library of Congress Cataloging-in-Publication Data

Lee, Jeyseon.
  Korean-English, English-Korean standard dictionary / Jeyseon Lee, Kangjin Lee.
    p. cm.
  ISBN-13: 978-0-7818-1234-4 (alk. paper)
  ISBN-10: 0-7818-1234-8
    1. Korean language--Dictionaries--English. 2. English language--Dictionaries--Korean. I. Yi, Kang-jin, 1964- II. Title.

PL937.E5L436 2008
495.7'321--dc22

                                                    2008013648

Printed in the United States of America.

Contents

Introduction:
About the Korean Language

Korean is the native language of 67 million people living on the Korean peninsula, as well as the heritage language of 5.6 million Diaspora Koreans.

The Korean language consists of seven geographically based dialects. Despite the differences in dialects, Korean is relatively homogeneous, with strong mutual intelligibility among speakers from different areas. This is because the mass media and formal education are based on standard speech and strongly contribute to the standardization of the language.

The closest sister language of Korean is Japanese. However, they are not mutually intelligible and their relationship is very weak. Some scholars claim that Korean and Japanese are remotely related to the Altaic languages, such as native Manchu, Mongolian, and the Turkic languages.

Although Korean and Japanese are geographically, historically, and culturally close to China, Korean and Japanese are not part of the same language family as Chinese, and therefore are not grammatically similar to Chinese. However, both Korean and Japanese have borrowed a large number of Chinese words and characters throughout the course of their long historical contact with various Chinese dynasties, and those borrowed Chinese words and characters have become an integral part of the Korean and Japanese vocabularies.

Since the end of World War II, Korean people have been in contact with many foreign countries and have borrowed thousands of words, the majority from English. During the 35-year occupation of Korea by Japan, a considerable number of Japanese words were also borrowed.

The Korean vocabulary has three components: native words and affixes (approximately 35 percent), Sino-Korean words (approximately 60 percent), and loanwords (approximately 5 percent). Native words denote daily necessities (food, clothing, and shelter), locations, basic actions, activities, states of being, lower-level numbers, body parts, natural objects, animals, and so forth.

Due to their ideographic and monosyllabic nature, Chinese characters are easily combined and recombined to coin new terms as new cultural objects and concepts are created. Most institutional terms, traditional cultural terms, personal names, and place names are Sino-Korean words. There are 14,000 loanwords in Korean, almost 9 percent from English. Most of those loanwords are commonly used, facilitating, to a certain extent, cross-cultural communication.

Korean is often called a situation-oriented language in that contextually or situationally understood elements, including subject and object, are omitted more frequently than not. Therefore, inserting the pronoun "you" or "I" in expressions such as 안녕하세요? (annyeong- ha-se-yo?) / How are you?, or 고맙습니다 (go-map-sum-nida) / thank you, would sound awkward in normal contexts.

Korean is a "macro-to-micro" language. The larger context of something is presented first, followed by gradually smaller contexts, ending with the individual context. For example, when referring to someone by name, Koreans say or write the family name first and the given name second, which may be followed by a title. An address is given by first indicating the country, followed by, in descending order, the province, city, street, house number, and, finally, the name of the addressee. Koreans indicate a date with the year first, the month second, and the day last.

Korean may be called an honorific language, in that one uses different words and phrases depending on the status of the person being discussed or to whom one is speaking. Differences such as age, family relationship, and social status are systematically encoded in the structure and use of Korean. A small number of commonly used words have two forms, one plain and one honorific. The honorific forms are used with an adult of equal or greater status, such as an elder, whereas the plain forms are reserved for another of lesser status. There are also humble verbs used to express deference to an elder or one of greater status.

Korean has an extensive set of address and reference terms that are sensitive to degrees of social stratification and distance between the speaker and addressee and between the speaker and referent. The most frequently used terms for a social superior or an adult distant equal are composed of an occupational title followed by the gender-neutral honorific suffix –님 (nim), such as 교수님 (gyo-su-nim) / Professor.

This may be preceded by the full or family name. There are several titles. The most frequently used among younger co-workers or when speaking to a child or adolescent is the gender-neutral noun –씨 (ssi). This noun is affixed to one's full or given name. When speaking or referring to child, use either the given name alone or the full name without a title. When addressing a child by a given name, the name is followed by a particle. When the name ends with a consonant, the particle is 아 (a). When it ends with a vowel, the particle is 야 (ya).

In Korean, first person pronouns—the English "I" and "we"— have both plain and humble forms. The plain singular form is 나 (na) and the plain plural is 우리 (u-ri), while the humble singular is 저 (jeo) and the humble plural is 저희 (jeo-hui). The humble forms are used when speaking with an elder or an adult of higher social status. Second person pronouns, the equivalent of the English "you", are used only when speaking with children. The singular form is 너 (neo) and the plural is 너희 (neo-hui). When speaking with an adult, one must address them with their name and title. For example: 김선생님 (gim-seon-saeng-nim) / you, teacher Kim.

Korean is currently written using both Chinese characters and the Korean phonetic alphabet known as 한글(hanguel/hangul). Chinese characters were used exclusively in written Korean until 1443, when King Sejong the Great, the fourth king of the 조선 (jo-seon) Dynasty, created 한글 with his court scholars. 한글 has continued to enjoy increasing favor over Chinese characters. The latter's contemporary usage is largely restricted to newspapers and scholarly books, and even there it is limited. Chinese characters, however, are very useful in differentiating between words with identical pronunciation and 한글 spelling.

There are considerable differences between the Korean and English languages. Such differences range from pronunciation and grammar to vocabulary principles and writing systems to underlying traditions and culture. These differences make Korean one of the most challenging languages for a native English speaker to learn. We hope this book will help to make it one of the most rewarding.

Korean Alphabet & Pronunciation Guide

The Letters of the 한글 (Hangul/han-geul) Alphabet and Their Pronunciation

The current 한글 alphabet has 40 characters: 19 consonants, 8 vowels, and 13 diphthongs. A diphthong combines two separate vowel sounds. In English, examples include the "ou" sound in the word "out" and the "eo" sound in the word "people."

Korean allows a three-way voiceless contrast (plain, aspirate, and tense) in plosive consonants, and a two-way (plain and tense) or no contrast in fricative consonants. In addition to these consonants, Korean has the liquid consonant *l*, which is pronounced as *r* in initial position or between vowels, and three nasal consonants. The Korean consonant chart is illustrated below.

There are four kinds of consonants in Korean: plosive, fricative, liquid, and nasal. Plosive consonants have three kinds of contrasts: plain, aspirate, and tense. Twelve consonants are plosive, with four in each contrast. There are 3 fricative consonants, two using the plain contrast and the other using the tense contrast. The one liquid consonant is *l*, although it is pronounced as *r* when it begins a word or appears between two vowels. There are three nasal consonants, but they are not distinguished by contrasts. A pronunciation chart, which also indicates the proper tongue position when making the consonant sounds, appears below:

	Lips	Gum Ridge	Hard Palatal	Soft Palatal	Throat
PLOSIVE					
Plain	ㅂ [p/b] <u>b</u>aby	ㄷ [t/d] <u>d</u>ay	ㅈ [ch/j] an<u>g</u>el	ㄱ [k/g] <u>b</u>egin	
Aspirate	ㅍ [p'] <u>p</u>ublic	ㅌ [t'] a<u>t</u>omic	ㅊ [ch'] a<u>ch</u>ieve	ㅋ [k'] a<u>k</u>in	
Tense	ㅃ [pp] <u>sp</u>oon	ㄸ [tt] <u>st</u>ate	ㅉ [tch] pi<u>zz</u>a	ㄲ [kk] <u>sk</u>ate	
FRICATIVE					
Plain		ㅅ [s/sh] <u>sh</u>eep			ㅎ [h] <u>h</u>ome
Tense		ㅆ [ss] a<u>ss</u>ign			
LIQUID		ㄹ [l/r] <u>l</u>eaf <u>r</u>adio			
NASAL	ㅁ [m] <u>m</u>e	ㄴ [n] <u>n</u>ow		ㅇ [ng] so<u>ng</u>	

Consonants change sounds depending on their position in a word. The 한글 spellings, however, do not change. In standard Korean, there are 8 vowels and 13 diphthongs. The vowels are grouped into categories of front and back. Back vowels are further categorized as round and unround. (All front vowels are unround.) The Korean vowel chart, which indicates both these divisions and the tongue position during pronunciation, is below:

Tongue Position	Front		Back	
	Unround	Round	Unround	Round
High	ㅣ [i] beet		― [û] good	ㅜ [u] buoy
Mid	ㅔ [e] bet		ㅓ [ô] mother	ㅗ [o] awkward
Low	ㅐ [ae] at		ㅏ [a] father	

There are two semi-vowels, *y* and *w*, and they combine with 8 vowels to make 13 diphthongs. The Korean diphthong chart is represented below.

	ㅏ	ㅓ	ㅗ	ㅜ	―	ㅣ	ㅔ	ㅐ
y	ㅑ [ya] yacht	ㅕ [yô] young	ㅛ [yo] yawn	ㅠ [yu] yukon	ㅢ [ûi]		ㅖ [ye] yet	ㅒ [yae] yak
w	ㅘ [wa] wander	ㅝ [wô] wonder			ㅟ [wi] win	ㅚ [we] west	ㅞ [we] west	ㅙ [wae] wangle

Syllable Blocks in Korean

한글 han-geul letters are combined into syllable blocks. The syllable blocks are constructed out of what is referred to as consonant, vowel, and dipthong positions. A square syllable block has the initial consonant position followed by a vowel or diphthong position. In the final consonant position, one or two consonants may occur. If a syllable does not begin with a consonant, the syllable block must have the letter ㅇ in the initial consonant position. The letter ㅇ is silent and functions as a zero consonant in the initial position of a syllable block.

If the vowel letter in the syllable block contains one or two long vertical strokes, it is written to the right of the initial consonant letter (e.g. 나 [na], 계 [gye]). If the vowel letter in the syllable block contains only a long horizontal stroke, the vowel letter is written below the initial consonant letter (e.g. 무 [mu], 교 [gyo]). If a diphthong letter contains a long horizontal stroke and a long vertical stroke, the initial consonant letter occurs in the upper left corner (e.g. 귀 [gwi], 놔 [nwa]). When a syllable ends with consonants, they occur beneath the vowel letter (e.g. 봤 [bwat], 김 [gim], 흙 [heuk, heulk]). Final consonants can be all single consonant letters and the following two-letter combinations: ㄲ (kk), ㅆ (ss), ㄳ (ks), ㄵ (nj), ㄶ (nh), ㄺ (lk), ㄻ (lm), ㄼ (lp), ㄽ (ls), ㄾ (lt'), ㄿ (lp'), ㅀ (lh), ㅄ (ps). When writing the letters in syllable blocks, they should be balanced to fill the space.

To demonstrate the construction of a word in written Korean, let us consider the word 한글 (han-geul). It has two syllable blocks, 한 (han) and 글 (geul). In the first syllable block, ㅎ (h), ㅏ (a), and ㄴ (n) combine like this:

한 (han)

In the second syllable block, the letters ㄱ (g), ㅡ (eu), and ㄹ (l) combine to form:

글 (gul)

Note how, in accordance with the rules outlined above, the initial consonant ㅎ (h) in 한 (han) appears with ㅏ (a) to its right and the final consonant ㄴ (n) below. With the syllable block 글 (geul), note how the initial consonant ㄱ (g) is placed first, with the vowel ㅡ (eu), which is written as a horizontal stroke, below it, and the final consonant ㄹ (l) appearing below the vowel.

The Romanization of Korean

(Korean Ministry of Culture and Tourism proclamation No. 2000-8)

1. Basic principles of romanization

(1) Romanization is based on standard Korean pronunciation.
(2) Symbols other than Roman letters are avoided to the greatest extent possible.

2. Summary of the romanization system

(1) Vowels are transcribed as follows:

Simple Vowels
ㅏ *a* / ㅓ *eo* / ㅗ *o* / ㅜ *u* / ㅡ *eu* / ㅣ *i* / ㅐ *ae* / ㅔ *e* / ㅚ *oe* / ㅟ *wi*

Diphthongs
ㅑ *ya* / ㅕ *yeo* / ㅛ *yo* / ㅠ *yu* / ㅒ *yae* / ㅖ *ye* / ㅘ *wa* / ㅙ *wae* / ㅝ *wo* / ㅞ *we* / ㅢ *ui*

Note 1: ㅢ is transcribed as *ui*, even when pronounced as ㅣ.

Note 2: Long vowels are not reflected in romanization.

(2) Consonants are transcribed as follows:

Plosives (Stops)
ㄱ *g, k* / ㄲ *kk* / ㅋ *k* / ㄷ *d, t* / ㄸ *tt* / ㅌ *t* / ㅂ *b, p* / ㅃ *pp* / ㅍ *p*

Affricates and Fricatives

ㅈ *j* / ㅉ *jj* / ㅊ *ch* / ㅅ *s* / ㅆ *ss* / ㅎ *h*

Nasals and Liquids

ㄴ *n* / ㅁ *m* / ㅇ *ng* / ㄹ *r, l*

Note 1: The sounds ㄱ, ㄷ, and ㅂ are transcribed respectively as *g*, *d*, and *b* when they appear before a vowel. They are transcribed as *k*, *t*, and *p* when followed by another consonant or forming the final sound of a word.

Note 2: ㄹ is transcribed as *r* when followed by a vowel, and *l* when followed by a consonant or when appearing at the end of a word. ㄹㄹ is transcribed as *ll*.

3. Special provisions for romanization

(1) When Korean sound values change as in the following cases, the results of those changes are romanized.

    1) The case of assimilation of adjacent consonants
    2) The case of the epenthetic [inserted within the body of a word] ㄴ and ㄹ
    3) Cases of palatalization
    4) Cases where ㄱ, ㄷ, ㅂ and ㅈ are adjacent to ㅎ

However, aspirated sounds are not reflected in case of nouns where ㅎ follows ㄱ, ㄷ, and ㅂ.

Note: Tense (or glottalized) sounds are not reflected in cases where morphemes [the smallest part of a word that has meaning] are compounded.

(2) When there is the possibility of confusion in pronunciation, a hyphen "-" may be used.

(3) The first letter is capitalized in proper names.

(4) Personal names are written by family name first, followed by a space and the given name. In principle, syllables in given names are not separated by hyphen, but the use of a hyphen between syllables is permitted.

    1)   Assimilated sound changes between syllables in given names are not transcribed.

    2)   Romanization of family names will be determined separately.

(5) Administrative units, such as 도 *do*, 시 *si*, 군 *gun*, 구 *gu*, 읍 *eup*, 면 *myeon*, 리 *ri*, 동 *dong*, and 가 *ga* are transcribed respectively as *do, si, gun, gu, eup, myeon, ri, dong,* and *ga,* and are preceded by a hyphen. Assimilated sound changes before and after the hyphen are not reflected in romanization.

Note: Terms for administrative units such as 시 *si*, 군 *gun*, 읍 *eup* may be omitted.

(6) Names of geographic features, cultural properties, and manmade structures may be written without hyphens.

(7) Proper names such as personal names and those of companies may continue to be written as they have been previously.

(8) When it is necessary to convert romanized Korean back to *hangul* in special cases such as in academic articles, romanization is done according to *hangul* spelling and not pronunciation. Each *hangul* letter is romanized as explained in section 2 except that ㄱ, ㄷ, ㅂ and ㄹ are always written as *g, d, b* and *l*. When ㅇ has no sound value, it is replaced by a hyphen. It may also be used when it is necessary to distinguish between syllables.

Pronunciation Rules

Rule 1. Resyllabification

When a syllable in a word ends with a consonant and the next syllable begins with a vowel, the consonant, when pronounced, is part of the latter syllable. For example, 한글은 (han-geul-eun) is pronounced han-geu-reun. In this case, the sound of ㄹ changes from *l* to *r* because ㄹ now appears between two vowels. Similarly, when a syllable block ends in a double consonant, the second consonant is pronounced before the vowel as part of the latter syllable, so the Korean word for 읽어요 (ilk-eo-yo) "read," is pronounced il-geo-yo.

Rule 2. Final closure in syllable pronunciation

At the end of a word or before a consonant, all Korean consonants are pronounced without releasing air. As a result, consonants at the end of words or preceding other consonants change sounds. For example, 꽃 (kkoch) is pronounced kkot and 꽃도 (kkoch-do) is pronounced kkot-do. The change of ㅊ to ㄷ happens here because the speech organs responsible for the articulation of the word-final and pre-consonantal ㅊ are not released. The sound of ㅊ (ch') becomes *t* because one does not release air when pronouncing it in these and similar words. The only consonant sounds that occur at the end of a word or before another consonant are the seven simple consonants: ㅂ (p/b), ㄷ (t/d), ㄱ (k/g), ㅁ (m), ㄴ (n), ㅇ (ng), and ㄹ (l/r). The sound changes are illustrated below.

ㅂ, ㅃ, ㅍ → ㅂ

ㄷ, ㄸ, ㄸ, ㅅ, ㅆ, ㅈ, ㅉ, ㅊ, ㅎ → ㄷ

ㄱ, ㄲ, ㅋ → ㄱ

ㅁ → ㅁ

ㄴ → ㄴ

ㅇ → ㅇ

ㄹ → ㄹ

Rule 3. Nasal assimilation

All plosive and fricative consonants become corresponding nasal consonants when preceding a nasal consonant. For example, 앞문 (ap-mun)
"front gate" is pronounced am-mun and 일학년 (il-hak-nyeon) "first
grade/first year" is pronounced il-hang-nyeon. The chart below fully
illustrates the changes.

ㅂ, ㅃ, ㅍ → ㅁ
ㄷ, ㄸ, ㄸ, ㅅ, ㅆ, ㅈ, ㅉ, ㅊ, ㅎ → ㄴ
ㄱ, ㄲ, ㅋ → ㅇ

Rule 4. ㄴ to ㄹ assimilation

When ㄹ (l/r) and ㄴ (n) appear together in a word, the *n* sound is
usually replaced by the *l/r* sound, as in the Korean word for "seven
years," 칠년 (chil-lyeon). When *l/r* is followed by the vowel ㅣ (i)
or the semivowel ㅑ (ya) in certain compound words, another *l/r* is
inserted between them, as in the Korean word for "liquid medicine,"
물약 (mul-lyak).

Rule 5. Tensification

When a plain plosive consonant (ㅂ (p/b), ㄷ (t/d), ㅈ (ch/j), ㄱ (k/g))
or the fricative consonant ㅅ (s/sh) is preceded by a plosive or fricative consonant (ㅂ, ㄷ, ㅈ, ㄱ, ㅍ[p'], ㅌ[t'], ㅊ[ch'], ㅋ[k'], ㅃ[pp],
ㄸ[tt], ㅉ[tch], ㄲ[kk], ㅅ, ㅎ[h], ㅆ [ss]) it becomes a corresponding
tense consonant, as in the words 학생 (hak-ssaeng) "students," 없다
(eop-tta) "not exist," and 학교 (hak-kkyo) "school."

Rule 6. Aspiration and the weakening of ㅎ

When the fricative consonant ㅎ (h) is preceded or followed by a plain
plosive consonant (ㅂ [p/b], ㄷ [t/d], ㅈ [ch/j], ㄱ [k/g]), it merges
with the consonant to produce a corresponding aspirate consonant

(ㅍ [p'], ㅌ [t'], ㅊ [ch'], ㅋ [k']), as in the words for 좋다 (jo-ta) 'to be good,' 입학 (i-pak) 'entering school,' and 착하다 (cha-ka-da) 'to be kind.'

Rule 7. Double consonant reduction

As indicated in Rule 1, the second of the two consonants at the end of a syllable is, when pronounced, carried over to the following syllable if the latter syllable does not begin with a consonant. However, one of the two consonants becomes silent at the end of a word or before a consonant, as in the words for "price," 값 (gap) and 값도 (gap-tto). In English, up to three consonants may be combined in a syllable, but not even two may be combined in Korean. It is difficult to predict which of two consonants will become silent. The silent consonant is usually the second one, but there are exceptions.

Rule 8. Palatalization

When a word ending in ㄷ (t/d) or ㅌ (t') is followed by a suffix beginning with the vowel ㅣ (i) or the semivowel ㅕ (yeo), the ㄷ and ㅌ are pronounced, respectively, *ch/j and ch'*, as in the words for 닫혀요 (da-chyeo-yo) "to be closed," and 붙이다 (bu-chi-da) "to attach." This change is technically called "palatalization" because the original consonants, which are pronounced using the gum-ridge, are articulated with the hard palate.

Abbreviations

abbr.	abbreviation
adj.	adjective (including noun-modifier in Korean)
adv.	adverb
coll.	colloquial
conj.	conjunction
cop.	copula, i.e., linking verb
count.	counter
dat.	dative/indirect object particle
dir.	direction
e.g.	for example
fut.	future tense
hon.	honorific
loc.	location
n.	noun
num.	number
obj.	object/object particle
part.	particle
pl.	plural
pren.	pre-noun/noun modifier
pres.	present tense
pron.	pronoun
pst.	past tense
sing.	singular
subj.	subject/subject particle
top.	topic/topic particle
v.	verb (including both active verb and descriptive verb in Korean)
v. stem	verb stem
v. intr.	intransitive verb, i.e., cannot have an object
v. tr.	transitive verb, i.e., can have an object

Korean-English Dictionary

ㄱ

가 ga *part.* subject particle; 정호가 학교에 갑니다 Jeong-ho-ga hak-gyo-e gam-ni-da Jungho goes to school

가게 ga-ge *n.* shop, store

가격 ga-gyeok *n.* price

가곡 ga-gok *n.* classical-style song

가공하다 ga-gong-ha-da *v.* process, manufacture

가구 ga-gu *n.* furniture; 가구점 ga-gu-jeom *n.* furniture store

가급적 ga-geup-jeok *adv.* as ... as possible; 가급적 일을 빨리 끝내도록 하자 ga-geup-jeok il-eul ppal-li kkeun-nae-do-ro-ka-ja Let's finish this job as soon as possible

가까워지다 ga-kka-wo-ji-da *v.* get near to, approach; become intimate

가까이 ga-kka-i *adv.* near, close to; nearly, almost

가까이하다 ga-kka-i-ha-da *v.* associate with, make friends with

가깝다 ga-kkap-da *v.* be close

가꾸다 ga-kku-da *v.* grow, cultivate; take care of

가끔 ga-kkeum *adv.* once in a while; sometimes

가난뱅이 ga-nan-baeng-i *n.* poor man, the poor

가난하다 ga-nan-ha-da *v.* be poor

가냘프다 ga-nyal-peu-da *v.* be slender, be slim

가느다랗다 ga-neu-da-ra-ta *v.* be thin, be slender

가늘다 ga-neul-da *v.* be thin, be slender

가능성 ga-neung-sseong *n.* possibility, chance

가능하다 ga-neung-ha-da *v.* be possible

가다 ga-da *v.* go, proceed; be out, go out; die; go by, pass; last long, keep; 그는 매일 회사에 간다 geu-neun mae-il hoe-sa-e gan-da He goes to work everyday; 요즘 시간이 빨리 간다 yo-jeum si-gan-i ppal-li gan-da Time passes so fast these days; 이 건전지는 오래 간다 i geon-jeon-ji-neun o-rae gan-da This battery lasts a long time

가다가 ga-da-ga *adv.* sometimes, occasionally

가담하다 ga-dam-ha-da *v.* side with, stand by

가동하다 ga-dong-ha-da *v.* operate, run

가두다 ga-du-da *v.* shut in, lock in

가득 ga-deuk *adv.* full, filled with

가득하다 ga-deu-ka-da *v.* be filled with, be full of

가뜩이나 ga-tteug-i-na *adv.* in addition to, what is worse

가라앉다 ga-ra-an-tta *v.* sink, settle down; cool down; quiet down

가라앉히다 ga-ra-an-chi-da *v.* sink; calm oneself, keep cool; cool off; relieve

가락 ga-rak *n.* tune, melody

가락지 ga-rak-ji *n.* a traditional set of twin rings usually made of jade or gold

가랑이 ga-rang-i *n.* fork; crotch; legs

가랑잎 ga-rang-nip *n.* dried fallen leaves

가래 ga-rae *n.* phlegm; 가래침 ga-rae-chim *n.* spit, spittle

가래톳 ga-rae-tot *n.* swelling of the lymphatic gland

가량 ga-ryang *n.* about, almost

가려내다 ga-ryeo-nae-da *v.* sort out, pick out

가렵다 ga-ryeop-da *v.* be itchy, feel itchy

가령 ga-ryeong *conj.* if

가로 ga-ro *n.* width; 가로세로 ga-ro-se-ro *n.* length and breadth

가로등 ga-ro-deung *n.* street light, street lamp

가로막다 ga-ro-mak-da *v.* interrupt, obstruct

가로젓다 ga-ro-jeot-da *v.* shake one's head from side-to-side

가로채다 ga-ro-chae-da *v.* snatch

가루 ga-ru *n.* flour; powder; 가루비누 ga-ru-bi-nu *n.* detergent *(powder)*

가르다 ga-reu-da *v.* divide; discriminate

가르치다 ga-reu-chi-da *v.* teach

가리개 ga-ri-gae *n.* twofold screen

가리다 ga-ri-da *v.* select, discriminate; hide, screen

가리마 ga-ri-ma *n.* part in one's hair

가리키다 ga-ri-ki-da *v.* point to

가마니 ga-ma-ni *n.* sack, bale

가마솥 ga-ma-sot *n.* iron pot

가만두다 ga-man-du-da *v.* leave alone, leave as is

가만있다 ga-man-it-da *v.* remain still, keep silent

가만히 ga-man-hi *adv.* quietly; secretly; silently

가망 ga-mang *n.* hope, prospect, probability

가면 ga-myeon *n.* mask, disguise

가명 ga-myeong *n.* pen name, alias

가뭄 ga-mum *n.* drought; 가뭄 들다 ga-mum deul-da *v.* be in a period of drought

가발 ga-bal *n.* wig

가방 ga-bang *n.* bag, sack

가버리다 ga-beo-ri-da *v.* be gone

가볍다 ga-byeop-da *v.* be light; 가벼워지다 ga-byeo-wo-ji-da *v.* become lighter

가보 ga-bo *n.* family treasure, heirloom

가보다 ga-bo-da *v.* have been to a place

가불하다 ga-bul-ha-da *v.* pay in advance

가사 ga-sa *n.* lyrics

가속도 ga-sok-do *n.* acceleration

가수 ga-su *n.* singer

가스 kka-sseu *n.* gas

가스레인지 kka-sseu-re-in-ji *n.* gas range

가슴 ga-sum *n.* chest *(body part)*

가슴둘레 ga-seum-dul-le *n.* girth, bust

가습기 ga-seup-gi *n.* humidifier

가시 ga-si *n.* thorn, spine; eyesore

가시덤불 ga-si-deom-bul *n.* thorn bush

가야금 ga-ya-geum *n.* Korean 12-string musical instrument

가엾다 ga-yeop-da *v.* be poor, be pitiful

가요 ga-yo *n.* song, ballad

가운 kka-un *n.* gown, robe

가운데 ga-un-de *n.* center, middle

가위 ga-wi *n.* scissors

가위눌리다 ga-wi-nul-li-da *v.* have a nightmare

가위바위보 ga-wi-ba-wi-bo *n.* rock-paper-scissors

가을 ga-eul *n.* fall, autumn

가입하다 ga-i-pa-da *v.* join, subscribe

가장 ga-jang *adv.* the most; *n.* head of family

가재 ga-jae *n.* crawfish

가전제품 ga-jeon-je-pum *n.* electric home appliance

가정 ga-jeong *n.* home, family

가정생활 ga-jeong-saeng-hwal *n.* family life

가정환경 ga-jeong-hwan-gyeong *n.* home background, home environment

가져가다 ga-jyeo-ga-da *v.* take along, take, carry

가져 놓다 ga-jyeo-da no-ta *v. phr.* bring and put on

가져오다 ga-jyeo-o-da *v.* bring, take along

가족 ga-jok *n.* family

가족관계 ga-jok-gwan-gye *n.* family relationship

가족사진 ga-jok-sa-jin *n.* family photo

가죽 ga-juk *n.* leather

가지 ga-ji *n.* branch, twig; eggplant; kind, variety, sort; 이 나무에는 나무에 가지가 많다 i na-mu-e-neun ga-ji-ga man-ta There are lots of branches in this tree; 나는 가지 요리를 좋아한다 na-neun ga-ji yo-ri-reul jo-a-han-da I like eggplant dishes; 책방에 여러가지 한국어 책이 있다 chaek-bang-e yeo-reo-ga-ji han-gug-eo chaeg-i it-da There are many kinds of Korean books in the bookstore

가지가지 ga-ji-ga-ji *adj.* variety of, all sorts of

가지고 가다 ga-ji-go ga-da *v. phr.* take, carry away

가지고 놀다 ga-ji-go nol-da *v. phr.* play with

가지고 오다 ga-ji-go o-da *v. phr.* bring

가지다 ga-ji-da *v.* have, possess

가짜 ga-jja *n.* imitation, fake

가축 ga-chuk *n.* domestic cattle, livestock

가축병원 ga-chuk-byeong-won *n.* animal hospital

가치 ga-chi *n.* value, merit

가치관 ga-chi-gwan *n.* one's values

가파르다 ga-pa-reu-da *v.* be steep

각가지 gak-ga-ji *adj.* various kinds, all sorts

각각 gak-gak *adv.* each, all; *adj.* every

각국 gak-guk *n.* every country, each nation

각기 gak-gi *adv.* each, individually

각목 gang-mok *n.* square wooden club, square wooden stick

각선미 gak-seon-mi *n.* beautiful shape of leg, nice leg line

각자 gak-ja *n.* each one, every one; *adv.* each; respectively

각종 gak-jong *adv.* every kind, various kinds

간 gan *n.* liver; courage

간격 gan-gyeok *n.* space, interval

간결하다 gan-gyeol-ha-da *v.* be concise, be terse, be brief

간단하게 gan-dan-ha-ge *adv.* briefly, simply

간단하다 gan-dan-ha-da *v.* be simple

간단히 gan-dan-hi *adv.* simply, briefly

간략하다 gal-lya-ka-da *v.* be concise, be simple, be brief

간략히 gal-lya-ki *adv.* concisely, simply, briefly

간섭 받다 gan-seop bat-da *v.* be interfered with, be intervened

간섭하다 gan-seo-pa-da *v.* interfere, intervene

간소하다 gan-so-ha-da *v.* be simple, be plain

간식 gan-sik *n.* snack

간신히 gan-sin-hi *adv.* barely; 시험에 간신히 붙었다 si-heom-e gan-sin-hi but-eot-da He barely passed the exam

간암 gan-am *n.* liver cancer

간염 gan-yeom *n.* hepatitis

간장 gan-jang *n.* soy sauce; liver

간절히 gan-jeol-hi *adv.* earnestly, sincerely

간접적으로 gan-jeop-jeog-eu-ro *adv.* indirectly

간지럼 gan-ji-reom *n.* tickle

간지럽다 gan-ji-reop-da *v.* be ticklish, feel ticklish

간첩 gan-cheop *n.* spy, secret agent

간판 gan-pan *n.* store signboard

간편하다 gan-pyeon-ha-da *v.* be convenient, be simple

간호사 gan-ho-sa *v.* nurse

간호원 gan-ho-won *n.* nurse

간호하다 gan-ho-ha-da *v.* nurse, tend, care for

간혹 gan-hok *adv.* sometimes, occasionally

갇히다 ga-chi-da *v.* be shut in, be kept indoors

갈다 gal-da *v.* change, replace; sharpen, grind

갈등 gal-tteung *n.* conflict

갈라놓다 gal-la-no-ta *v.* estrange; part, divide

갈라지다 gal-la-ji-da *v.* be divided; crack

갈림길 gal-lim-kkil *n.* forked road

길매기 gal-mae-gi *n.* gull

갈비 gal-bi *n.* barbecued spare ribs

갈비찜 gal-bi-jjim *n.* steamed short ribs

갈빗대 gal-bit-dae *n.* ribs, rib-bone

갈색 gal-ssaek *adj.* light brown

갈수록 gal-ssu-rok *adv.phr.* as time goes by

갈아입다 gal-a-ip-da *v.* change clothes

갈아타다 gal-a-ta-da *v.* change vehicles; transfer

갈증나다 gal-jjeung na-da *v.* feel thirsty

갈치 gal-chi *n.* hairtail *(fish)*

갉아먹다 galg-a-meok-da *v.* nibble, gnaw

감각 gam-gak *n.* sense, feeling

감격하다 gam-gyeo-ka-da *v.* be deeply moved

감귤 gam-gyul *n.* tangerine, mandarin orange

감기 gam-gi *n.* cold; 감기 걸리다 gam-gi geol-li-da catch a cold

감기다 gam-gi-da *v.* be rolled; shut one's eyes; 줄이 감겨있다 jul-i gam-gyeo-it-da The strings are rolled; 졸려서 눈이 감긴다 jol-lyeo-seo nun-i gam-gin-da My eyes are shut because I am so sleepy

감기약 gam-gi-yak *n.* cold medicine

감나무 gam-na-mu *n.* persimmon tree

감다 gam-tta *v.* wind, roll, wash, close one's eye(s)

감동 gam-dong *n.* impression, deep emotion, excitement

감동받다 gam-dong-bat-da *v.* be impressed

감동하다 gam-dong-ha-da *v.* feel emotion, be impressed

감사하다 gam-sa-ha-da *v.* be thankful, thank

감상하다 gam-sang-ha-da *v.* enjoy, appreciate

감색 gam-saek *adj.* navy blue

감소하다 gam-so-ha-da *v.* diminish, decrease

감시하다 gam-si-ha-da *v.* watch, keep watch

감싸다 gam-ssa-da *v.* protect, cover, shelter, shield

감염 gam-yeom *n.* infection

감옥 gam-ok *n.* jail

감자 gam-ja *n.* potato

감전되다 gam-jeon-doe-da *v.* receive an electric shock

감정 gam-jeong *n.* feeling, emotion

감쪽같다 gam-jjok-gat-da *v.* be perfect in, be just like before

감추다 gam-chu-da *v.* hide, conceal

감탄스럽다 gam-tan-seu-reop-da *v.* admire, wonder

감탄하다 gam-tan-ha-da *v.* admire, wonder

감히 gam-hi *adv.* boldly, daringly

갑갑하다 gap-ga-pa-da *v.* be boring, be tedious; feel bored

갑자기 gap-ja-gi *adv.* suddenly

갑작스럽다 gap-jak-seu-reop-da *v.* be sudden, be abrupt, be unexpected

갑절 gap-jeol *n.* double, twice

갑판 gap-pan *n.* deck

값 gap *n.* price, cost

값지다 gap-ji-da *v.* be costly, be expensive

갓 gat *n.* Korean hat; *affix.* fresh, brand-new; just, exactly

갓난아기 gan-nan-a-gi *n.* newborn baby

갔다오다 gat-da o-da *v.* go and come back, come back

강 gang *n.* river

강가 gang-kka *n.* river bank, riverside

강간하다 gang-gan-ha-da *v.* rape, violate

강강술래 gang-gang-sul-lae *n.* Korean circle dance

강남 gang-nam *n.* area south of the Han river *(district of Seoul)*

강단 gang-dan *n.* lecture platform

강당 gang-dang *n.* lecture hall

강대국 gang-dae-guk *n.* powerful country

강도 gang-do *n.* intensity, degree of strength; burglar, robber

강릉 gang-neung *n.* Gang Reung *(Korean province)*

강물 gang-mul *n.* river water

강변도로 gang-byeon-do-ro *n.* riverside road

강북 gang-guk *n.* area north of the Han river *(district of Seoul)*

강사 gang-sa *n.* speaker, lecturer

강수량 gang-su-ryang *n.* rainfall

강습 gang-seup *n.* short training course

강아지 gang-a-ji *n.* puppy

강연하다 gang-yeon-ha-da *v.* lecture, talk

강연회 gang-yeon-hoe *n.* lecture

강요 gang-yo *n.* enforcement, exaction

강우량 gang-u-ryang *n.* rainfall

강원도 gang-won-do *n.* Gang Won province

강의 gang-ui *n.* lecture; 강의를 듣다 gang-ui-reul deul-da *v.* listen to a lecture; take a course

강의실 gang-ui-sil *n.* lecture room

강의하다 gang-ui-ha-da *v.* lecture, give a lecture

강점 gang-jjeom *n.* one's strength, strong point

강조하다 gang-jo-ha-da *v.* stress, emphasize, accentuate

강철 gang-cheol *n.* steel

강추위 gang-chu-wi *n.* spell of cold dry weather

강풍 gang-pung *n.* strong wind

강하다 gang-ha-da *v.* be strong

갖고가다 gat-go ga-da *v.* take, carry away

갖고오다 gat-go o-da *v.* bring

갖다놓다 gat-da no-ta *v.* bring and put down

갖다주다 gat-da ju-da *v.* bring, take; bring over

갖다 gat-da *v.* have, hold

갖추다 gat-chu-da *v.* get ready, prepare

같다 gat-da *v.* be the same; 나와 내 동생은 키가 같다 na-wa nae dong-saeng-eun ki-ga gat-da My sister and I are the same height.

같이 ga-chi *adv.* together

갚다 gap-da *v.* pay back; revenge; 빌린 돈을 갚았다 bil-lin don-eul gap-at-da I paid back the money that I borrowed; 적에게 원수를 갚았다 jeog-e-ge won-su-reul gap-at-da I took revenge on my enemy

개 gae *n.* dog; items

개고기 gae-go-gi *n.* dog meat

개구리 gae-gu-ri *n.* frog

개그맨 gae-geu-maen *n.* comedian

개다 gae-da *v.* clear up, become clear; fold up

개미 gae-mi *n.* ant

개발하다 gae-bal-ha-da *v.* develop, improve

개성 gae-seong *n.* personality, individuality

개시 gae-si *n.* start, opening

개시하다 gae-si-ha-da *v.* begin, open

개업식 gae-eop-sik *n.* opening ceremony

개업하다 gae-eo-pa-da *v.* open business, begin business

개운하다 gae-un-ha-da *v.* be refreshed, feel refreshed

개월 gae-wol *count.* months

개인 gae-in *n.* individual, private person

개인생활 gae-in-saeng-hwal *n.* personal life, private life

개인용 gae-in-nyong *adj.* for individual usage

개인적 gae-in-jeok *adj.* private, individual; 개인적으로 gae-in-jeog-eu-ro *adv.* privately, individually

개장 gae-jang *n.* opening

개조하다 gae-jo-ha-da *v.* remodel, reconstruct, reorganize

개찰구 gae-chal-gu *n.* ticket gate

개천절 gae-cheon-jeol *n.* Foundation Day of Korea *(national holiday)*

개학식 gae-hak-sik *n.* opening ceremony of the school year

객관적 gaek-gwan-jeok *adj.* objective

갱년기 gaeng-nyeon-gi *n.* menopause

거기 geo-gi *n.* there; 거기 가만히 계세요 geo-gi ga-man-hi gye-se-yo Please stay still there

거꾸로 geo-kku-ro *adv.* topsy-turvy, inside out

거나 geo-na *part.* or; 주말에는 집에서 자거나 음악을 들어요 ju-mal-e-neun jib-e-seo ja-geo-na eum-ag-eul deul-eo-yo On the weekend I sleep or listen to music at home

거리 geo-ri *n.* street, road; distance

거문고 geo-mun-go *n.* Korean harp

거미 geo-mi *n.* spider

거미줄 geo-mi-jul *n.* spider web

거북 geo-buk *n.* tortoise, turtle

거북하다 geo-bu-ka-da *v.* be uncomfortable

거세다 geo-se-da *v.* be rough, be wild, be violent, be fierce

거스름돈 geo-seu-reom-tton *n.* change *(coins)*

거실 geo-sil *n.* living room

거울 geo-ul *n.* mirror

거위 geo-wi *n.* goose

거의 geo-ui *adv.* almost

거절 geo-jeol *n.* refusal, rejection

거절하다 geo-jeol-ha-da *v.* refuse, decline, reject

거지 geo-ji *n.* beggar

거짓말 geo-jin-mal *n.* lie

거짓말쟁이 geo-jin-mal-jaeng-i *n.* liar

거짓말하다 geo-jin-mal-ha-da *v.* tell a lie

거치다 geo-chi-da *v.* pass by, go through

거칠다 geo-chil-da *v.* be coarse, be rough

거품 geo-pum *n.* bubble, foam; 거품 내다 geo-pum nae-da *v.* form bubbles, make bubbles

걱정 geok-jeong *n.* worry

걱정되다 geok-jeong-doe-da *v.* worry

걱정하다 geok-jeong-ha-da *v.* worry

건강 geon-gang *n.* health

건강하다 geon-gang-ha-da *v.* be healthy

건강해지다 geon-gang-hae-ji-da *v.* become healthy

건강히 geon-gang-hi *adv.* healthily

건국 geon-guk *n.* establishment of a country

건너 geon-neo *adv.* across, the opposite side of; 길을 건너 학교가 있다 gil-eul geon-neo hak-gyo-ga it-da There is a school across the road

건너가다 geon-neo-ga-da *v.* go over, go across

건너다 geon-neo-da *v.* cross

건너오다 geon-neo-o-da *v.* come over, cross over

건너편 geon-neo-pyeon *n.* the other side

건널목 geon-neol-mok *n.* road crossing, railway crossing

건네 받다 geon-ne bat-da *v.* be received; be handed over

건네다 geon-ne-da *v.* carry across, take over; hand over, deliver

건네주다 geon-ne-ju-da *v.* pass over, carry across

건더기 geon-deo-gi *n.* solid ingredients; 내 국에는 건더기가 많이 없다 nae gug-e-neun geon-deo-gi-ga man-i cop-da There is not much solid food in my soup

건드리다 geon-deu-ri-da *v.* touch, meddle with, provoke

건망증 geon-mang-jjeung *n.* forgetfulness

건물 geon-mul *n.* building

건방지다 geon-bang-ji-da *v.* be impertinent, be impudent

건설하다 geon-seol-ha-da *v.* construct, build, establish

건의하다 geon-ui-ha-da *v.* propose, recommend

건전지 geon-jeon-ji *n.* electric cell, battery

건져주다 geon-jeo-ju-da *v.* take out of water; help out of, rescue from

건조기 geon-jo-gi *n.* dry season; dry machine, dryer

건조하다 geon-jo-ha-da *v.* be dry

건지다 geon-ji-da *v.* take out of water; help out; take back

건축 geon-chuk *n.* construction, building

건축물 geon-chung-mul *n.* construction, building, structure

건축학 geon-chu-kak *n.* architecture

걷다 geot-da *v.* walk; collect, gather; roll up

걸다 geol-da *v.* hang, hook, suspend; speak to; provoke; lock; 옷을 걸었다 os-eul geol-eot-da I hung up my clothes; 옆 사람에게 말을 걸었다 yeop sa-ram-e-ge mal-eul geol-eot-da I spoke to a person beside me; 시비 걸지 마 si-bi geol-ji-ma Don't

provoke a fight; 문을 걸었다 mun-eul
geol-eot-da I locked the door

걸레 geol-le *n.* floor cloth; floor wipe *(for
cleaning)*

걸레질하다 geol-le-jil-ha-da *v.* wipe with a
damp cloth

걸리다 geol-li-da *v.* take time; hang, be
suspended; be caught; be involved, catch

걸어다니다 geol-eo da-ni-da *v.* walk

걸어가다 geol-eo-ga-da *v.* walk

걸어오다 geol-eo-o-da *v.* come by foot

걸음 geol-eum *n.* step, walking, stepping; 걸
음을 멈추다 geol-eum-eul meom-chu-da
stop walking; 걸음을 재촉하다 geol-eum-
eul jae-cho-ka-da walk faster

걸치다 geol-chi-da *v.* extend, spread; stretch
over; slip on, throw on

걸터앉다 geol-teo-an-tta *v.* straddle

걸핏하면 geol-pi-ta-myeon *adv.* too often

검다 geom-tta *v.* be black, be dark

검문소 geom-mun-so *n.* checkpoint

검사 geom-sa *n.* public prosecutor

검사하다 geom-sa-ha-da *v.* inspect, examine

검색하다 geom-sae-ka-da *v.* refer to,
search, check

검정 geom-jeong *adj.* black color; *n.* official
approval, authorization

겁 geop *n.* fear, fright

겁나다 geom-na-da *v.* be frightened,
be scared

겁내다 geom-nae-da *v.* fear, be scared of

겁쟁이 geop-jaeng-i *n.* coward, chicken

겉 geot *n.* surface, face; the outside

겉껍질 geot-kkeop-jil *n.* husk, crust, shell

겉모습 geon-mo-seup *n.* outward appearance

게 ge *n.* crab

게다가 ge-da-ga *adv.* over there, besides; on
top of that

게시판 ge-si-pan *n.* bulletin board

게으르다 ge-eu-reu-da *v.* be idle, be lazy

게으름뱅이 ge-eu-reum-baeng-i *n.* idler

게임 kke-im *n.* game

겨드랑이 gyeo-deu-rang-i *n.* armpit

겨우 gyeo-u *adv.* barely

겨울 gyeo-ul *n.* winter

겪다 gyeok-da *v.* undergo, suffer, experience

견디다 gyeon-di-da *v.* bear, endure, stand

결과 gyeol-gwa *n.* result

결국 gyeol-guk *adv.* after all, finally, in the
end; 결국 그렇게 됐구나 geol-guk geu-
reo-ke dwaet-gu-na It finally turned out
that way/It worked out that way in the end

결근하다 gyeol-geun-ha-da *v.* be absent from
one's job

결론 gyeol-lon *n.* conclusion; 결론 내리다
gyeol-lon nae-ri-da *v.* conclude

결말 gyeol-mal *n.* end, close, conclusion

결석 gyeol-sseok *n.* absence

결석하다 gyeol-sseo-ka-da *v.* be absent,
stay away

결승 gyeol-sseung *n.* finals

결심 gyeol-ssim *n.* determination, resolution

결심하다 gyeol-ssim-ha-da *v.* decide,
determine, be resolute

결점 gyeol-jjeom *n.* fault, weakness

결정 gyeol-jjeong *n.* decision

결정되다 gyeol-jjeong-doe-da *v.* be decided

결정하다 gyeol-jjeong-ha-da *v.* decide

결코 gyeol-ko *adv.* never, by no means

결혼 gyeol-hon *n.* marriage, wedding

결혼식 gyeol-hon-sik *n.* wedding ceremony

결혼식장 gyeol-hon-sik-jang *n.* wedding hall

결혼하다 gyeol-hon-ha-da *v.* marry

겸손하다 gyeom-son-ha-da *v.* be modest

겹겹이 gyeop-gyeob-i *adv.* in many folds,
one over another, layer after layer

겹치다 gyeop-chi-da *v.* overlap

경계 gyeong-gye *n.* boundary, border; guard,
caution, watch

경고하다 gyeong-go-ha-da *v.* warn against,
give warning

경기 gyeong-gi *n.* game, match contest;
business condition, economic situation

경기장 gyeong-gi-jang *n.* sports field

경력 gyeong-nyeok *n.* career, personal history

경마 gyeong-ma *n.* horse racing

경보장치 gyeong-bo-jang-chi *n.* alarm

경복궁 gyeong-bok-gung *n.* Gyeung Bok
palace

경부고속도로 gyeong-bu-go-sok-do-ro *n.*
Gyeong Bu expressway

경비 gyeong-bi *n.* expenses, expenditure;
defense, guard

경비원 gyeong-bi-won *n.* security guard

경사 gyeong-sa *n.* slant, slope; happy event

경사지다 gyeong-sa-ji-da *v.* incline, slant, slope

경상도 gyeong-sang-do *n.* Gyeong Sang (*Korean province*)

경솔하다 gyeong-sol-ha-da *v.* be careless, be thoughtless

경영학 gyeong-yeong-hak *n.* management

경우 gyeong-u *n.* circumstance, situation, case

경유하여 gyeong-yu-ha-yeo *adv.* by way of, through

경음악 gyeong-eum-ak *n.* light music

경쟁 gyeong-jaeng *n.* competition

경쟁률 gyeong-jaeng-nyul *n.* acceptance rate (*of school or job admission*)

경쟁하다 gyeong-jaeng-ha-da *v.* compete, contest

경제 gyeong-je *n.* economy

경제사정 gyeong-je-sa-jeong *n.* financial situation

경제적 gyeong-je-jeok *adj.* economic, financial, economical

경제학 gyeong-je-hak *n.* economics

경주 gyeong-ju *n.* Gyeong Ju (*Korean province*); race, run

경찰 gyeong-chal *n.* police officer

경찰관 gyeong-chal-gwan *n.* police officer

경찰서 gyeong-chal-sseo *n.* police station

경찰차 gyeong-chal-cha *n.* police car

경치 gyeong-chi *n.* scene, scenery; 경치가 좋다 gyeong-chi-ga jo-ta The view is fine

경쾌하다 gyeong-kwae-ha-da *v.* be light, be cheerful

경품 gyeong-pum *n.* free gift

경품권 gyeong-pum-kkwon *n.* gift coupon

경향 gyeong-hyang *n.* tendency, trend

경험 gyeong-heom *n.* experience

경험하다 gyeong-heom-ha-da *v.* experience

경호원 gyeong-ho-won *n.* bodyguard

곁 gyeot *n.* side, beside

계곡 gye-gok *n.* valley

계급 gye-geup *n.* class, rank, grade

계단 gye-dan *n.* stairs

계란 gye-ran *n.* egg

계량기 gye-ryang-gi *n.* gauge, measure

계산기 gye-san-gi *n.* calculator

계산서 gye-san-seo *n.* check, bill

계산하다 gye-san-ha-da *v.* calculate; pay

계속 gye-sok *adv.* continuously

계속되다 gye-sok-doe-da *v.* continue

계속하다 gye-so-ka-da *v.* continue

계시다 gye-si-da *v.* stay, exist (*hon.*); 할아버지가 저기 계시다 hal-a-beo-ji-ga jeo-gi gye-si-da Grandfather is there

계약 gye-yak *n.* contract, agreement

계절 gye-jeol *n.* season

계층 gye-cheung *n.* social stratum

계피 gye-pi *n.* cinnamon

계획 gye-hoek *n.* plan, project

계획세우다 gye-hoek-se-u-da *v.* make a plan

계획표 gye-hoek-pyo *n.* written schedule

계획하다 gye-hoe-ka-da *v.* plan, make a plan

고가도로 go-kka-do-ro *n.* high-level road

고개 go-gae *n.* head, neck; ridge; crest; 고개 돌리다 go-gae dol-li-da *v.* turn one's head

고객 go-gaek *n.* customer, client

고구려 go-gu-ryeo *n.* Go Gu Ryeo (*ancient Korean kingdom, 37 B.C.-668*)

고구마 go-gu-ma *n.* sweet potato

고국 go-guk *n.* one's homeland

고급 go-gup *adj.* high rank

고기 go-gi *n.* meat, fish

고기압 go-gi-ap *n.* high pressure

고난 go-nan *n.* trouble, hardship

고단하다 go-dan-ha-da *v.* be tired, be exhausted

고달프다 go-dal-peu-da *v.* be tired, be exhausted

고동색 go-dong-saek *n..* brown; 고드름 go-deu-reum *n.* icicle

고등어 go-deung-eo *n.* mackerel

고등학교 go-deung-hak-gyo *n.* high school

고등학생 go-deung-hak-saeng *n.* high school student

고래 go-rae *n.* whale

고려 go-ryeo *n.* Go Ryeo (*ancient Korean kingdom, 918-1392*)

고르다 go-reu-da *v.* choose, select

고름 go-reum *n.* pus; coat string (*in Korean costume*)

고릴라 go-ril-la *n.* gorilla

고마워하다 go-ma-wo-ha-da *v.* be thankful, be grateful

고맙다 go-map-da *v.* be thankful, be grateful

고모 go-mo *n.* paternal aunt

고모부 go-mo-bu *n.* husband of one's paternal aunt

고무 go-mu *n.* rubber

고무신 go-mu-sin *n.* shoes made of rubber

고무장갑 go-mu-jang-gap *n.* pair of rubber gloves

고무줄 go-mu-jul *n.* elastic cord

고무풍선 go-mu-pung-seon *n.* toy balloon

고물상 go-mul-ssang *n.* antique shop

고민 go-min *n.* agony, anguish

고민하다 go-min-ha-da *v.* worry

고백하다 go-bae-ka-da *v.* confess, admit

고부간 go-bu-gan *n.* between mother-in-law and daughter-in-law; 우리집 고부간은 사이가 좋다 u-li-jip go-bu-gan-eun sa-i-ga jo-ta The relationship between mother-in-law and dauther-in-law is good in my family

고사리 go-sa-ri *n.* fern

고상하다 go-sang-ha-da *v.* be elegant

고생하다 go-saeng-ha-da *v.* suffer, have hard time

고속도로 go-sok-do-ro *n.* highway, expressway

고속버스 go-sok-ppeo-sseu *n.* express bus; 고속버스 터미널 go-sok-ppeo-sseu teo-mi-neol *n.* express bus terminal

고아 go-a *n.* orphan

고아원 go-a-won *n.* orphanage

고양이 go-yang-i *n.* cat

고요하다 go-yo-ha-da *v.* be quiet, be silent

고유하다 go-yu-ha-da *v.* be peculiar, be characteristic, be inherent

고자질하다 go-ja-jil-ha-da *v.* tattle, squeal

고작 go-jak *adv.* at most, at best

고장 go-jang *n.* defect, break down; district; 고장 나다 go-jang na-da *v.* be out of order, be broken

고전 go-jeon *n.* classics

고전음악 go-jeon-eum-ak *n.* classical music

고전적 go-jeon-jeok *adj.* classic, classical

고조선 go-jo-seon *n.* Go Jo Seon *(first Korean kingdom, 108 B.C.)*

고졸 go-jol *n.* high school graduate

고지서 go-ji-seo *n.* written notice

고집 go-jip *n.* stubbornness

고집불통 go-jip-bul-tong *n.* stubborn person

고추 go-chu *n.* red-pepper

고추잠자리 go-chu-jam-ja-ri *n.* red dragonfly

고추장 go-chu-jang *n.* red-pepper paste

고춧가루 go-chut-ga-ru *n.* red-pepper powder

고층아파트 go-cheung-a-pa-teu *n.* high-rise apartment

고치다 go-chi-da *v.* cure, fix, repair, remand, correct

고통 go-tong *n.* pain, suffering, anguish

고통스럽다 go-tong-seu-reop-da *v.* be painful, be distressing

고함 go-ham *n.* shout, yell

고향 go-hyang *n.* hometown

고혈압 go-hyeol-ap *n.* high blood pressure; 고혈압 환자 go-hyeol-ap hwan-ja *n.* hypertensive

곡 gok *n.* tune, music, song

곡괭이 gok-gwaeng-i *n.* hoe, pick

곡선 gok-seon *n.* curve

곡식 gok-sik *n.* grain, cereals

곤두서다 gon-du-seo-da *v.* stand on one's head

곤란하다 gol-lan-ha-da *v.* be difficult, be hard

곤충 gon-chung *n.* insect, bug

곧 got *adv.* soon, at once

곧바로 got-ba-ro *adv.* at once, straight

곧잘 got-jal *adv.* fairly well, well enough, frequently

곧장 got-jang *adv.* directly, straight

골내다 gol lae-da *v.* be angry, get angry

골고루 gol-go-ru *adv.* evenly among all, equally

골동품 gol-ttong-pum *n.* antiques, curios

골목 gol-mok *n.* alley, lane, side street

골아 떨어지다 gol-a tteol-eo-ji-da *v.* fall into a deep sleep

골짜기 gol-jja-gi *n.* valley

골치아프다 gol-chi a-peu-da *v.* worry about, be troubled

골칫거리 gol-chit-geo-ri *n.* headache, nuisance

골키퍼 kkol-ki-peo *n.* goalkeeper

골탕먹다 gol-tang-meok-da *v.* suffer a big loss, be cheated

골프 gol-peu *n.* golf; 골프 치다 gol-peu chi-da *v.* play golf

골프장 gol-peu-jang *n.* golf course

곪다 gom-tta *v.* form pus, boil, fester

곰 gom *n.* bear; 곰 인형 gom in-hyeong *n.* teddy bear

곰곰이 gom-gom-i *adv.* musing over, considering carefully

곰팡이 gom-pang-i *n.* mold

곱게 gop-ge *adv.* beautifully, nicely

곱다 gop-da *v.* be pretty

곱빼기 gop-ppae-gi *n.* double measure, double serving *(food)*

곱상하다 gop-sang-ha-da *v.* be neat and beautiful

곱슬곱슬하다 gop-seul-gop-seul-ha-da *v.* be curly, be curled

곳 got *n.* place

곳곳 got-got *adv.* on all sides, in several places

공 gong *n.* ball; zero

공간 gong-gan *n.* space, room

공개하다 gong-gae-ha-da *v.* open to the public

공격하다 gong-gyeo-ka-da *v.* attack

공경하다 gong-gyeong-ha-da *v.* respect

공공기관 gong-gong-gi-gwan *n.* public institute

공공생활 gong-gong-saeng-hwal *n.* communal life

공공시설 gong-gong-si-seol *n.* public facilities

공과금 gong-gwa-gum *n.* public utilities charges

공교롭게 gong-gyo-rop-ge *adv.* unexpectedly, accidentally

공군 gong-gun *n.* air force

공군사관학교 gong-gun-sa-gwan-hak-gyo *n.* air force academy

공기 gong-gi *n.* air, atmosphere

공동주택 gong-dong-ju-taek *n.* attached house

공무원 gong-mu-won *n.* public servants

공부벌레 gong-bu-ppeol-le *n.* bookworm

공부하다 gong-bu-ha-da *v.* study

공사 gong-sa *n.* construction

공사중 gong-sa-jung *adj.* under construction

공산당 gong-san-dang *n.* communist party

공산주의 gong-san-ju-i *n.* communism

공상과학 gong-sang-gwa-hak *n.* science fiction

공손하다 gong-son-ha-da *v.* be polite, be respectful

공업 gong-eop *n.* industry

공연 gong-yeon *n.* public performance

공연시간 gong-yeon-si-gan *n.* performance schedule

공연하다 gong-yeon-ha-da *v.* perform, present

공원 gong-won *n.* park

공인중개사 gong-in-jung-ga-sa *n.* licensed real estate agent

공장 gong-jang *n.* factory

공정하다 gong-jeong-ha-da *v.* be fair, be impartial

공주 gong-ju *n.* princess; Gong Ju *(province in Korea)*

공중 gong-jung *n.* the air, the sky, space; the public

공중도덕 gong-jung-do-deok *n.* public morality

공중전화 gong-jung-jeon-hwa *n.* public phone; 공중전화 카드 gong-jung-jeon-hwa ka-deu *n.* phone card

공짜 gong-jja *n.* free of charge

공짜로 gong-jja-ro *adv.* for nothing, free

공책 gong-chaek *n.* notebook

공치기 gong-chi-gi *n.* ball game

공터 gong-teo *n.* empty lot

공통점 gong-teong-jjeom *n.* common feature

공평하다 gong-pyeong-ha-da *v.* be fair, be impartial

공포 gong-po *n.* fear, scare

공항 gong-hang *n.* airport

공해 gong-hae *n.* pollution

공휴일 gong-hyu-il *n.* holiday

과 gwa *part.* and, with; *n.* department; lesson, number of lessons, chapter; 형과 동생 hyeong-gwa dong-saeng male's older brother and younger brother; 영문학과 yeong-mun-hak-gwa Dept. of English language and literature; 제7과 je-chil-gwa Lesson 7; 열두과 yeol-ttu-gwa 12 chapters

과거 gwa-geo *n.* the past

과격하다 gwa-gyeo-ka-da *v.* be radical

과녁 gwa-nyeok *n.* target

과로 gwa-ro *n.* overwork, excessive labor

과로하다 gwa-ro-ha-da *v.* work too hard, overwork oneself

과목 gwa-mok *n.* subject, course

과수원 gwa-su-won *n.* fruit garden

과식하다 gwa-si-ka-da *v.* overeat

과실 gwa-sil *n.* fruit; fault
과외 gwa-oe *n.* extracurricular work
과음하다 gwa-eum-ha-da *v.* drink too much
과일 gwa-il *n.* fruit
과자 gwa-ja *n.* cookie
과장님 gwa-jang-nim *n.* head of department
과장하다 gwa-jang-ha-da *v.* exaggerate, overstate
과학 gwa-hak *n.* science
과학자 gwa-hak-ja *n.* scientest
관 gwan *n.* crown; coffin; pipe
관객 gwan-gaek *n.* spectator, audience
관계 gwan-gye *n.* relationship, connection, influence; 관계 있다 gwan-gye it-da *v.* have a relationship, be connected
관공서 gwan-gong-seo *n.* government and public offices
관광 gwan-gwang *n.* tourism; 관광 코스 gwan-gwang ko-sseu *n.* a series of tour sites
관광객 gwan-gwang-gaek *n.* tourist
관광단지 gwan-gwang-dan-ji *n.* big size tour sites, big size tourist attractions
관광지 gwan-gwang-ji *n.* tour sites, tourist attractions
관광하다 gwan-gwang-ha-da *v.* sightsee, tour
관대하다 gwan-dae-ha-da *v.* be generous
관람 gwal-lam *n.* viewing, inspection
관람가 gwal-lam-ga *n.* viewing allowed, admission allowed
관람불가 gwal-lam-bul-ga *n.* viewing not allowed, admission not allowed
관람하다 gwal-lam-ha-da *v.* see, inspect, view
관련되다 gwal-lyeon-doe-da *v.* be related to, be connected with
관련하다 gwal-lyeon-ha-da *v.* be related to, be connected with
관리 gwal-li *n.* management, administration, control, supervision; government official, public official
관리비 gwal-li-bi *n.* management expenses
관리사무소 gwal-li-sa-mu-so *n.* superintendent's office
관리인 gwal-li-in *n.* administrator
관리하다 gwal-li-ha-da *v.* manage, control, administrate
관세 gwan-sse *n.* customs
관습 gwan-seup *n.* custom, convention

관심 gwan-sim *n.* concern, interest; 관심을 끌다 gwan-sim-eul kkeul-da *v.* draw interest
관심사 gwan-sim-sa *n.* matter of concern and interest
관절 gwan-jeol *n.* joint
관절염 gwan-jeol-lyeom *n.* arthritis
관점 gwan-jjeom *n.* point of view
관제탑 gwan-je-tap *n.* control tower
관중 gwan-jung *n.* spectators, audience
관직 gwan-jik *n.* government service, government post
관찰하다 gwan-chal-ha-da *v.* observe, watch
관현악 gwan-hyeon-ak *n.* orchestra
괄호 gwal-ho *n.* parenthesis
광견병 gwang-gyeon-ppyeong *n.* rabies
광경 gwang-gyeong *n.* spectacle
광고 gwang-go *n.* advertisement
광고란 gwang-go-ran *n.* advertisement column
광고문안 gwang-go-mun-an *n.* advertisement description, written advertisement
광고지 gwang-go-ji *n.* flyer
광고회사 gwang-go-hoe-sa *n.* advertisement company
광대뼈 gwang-dae-ppyeo *n.* cheekbone
광물 gwang-mul *n.* mineral
광범위하다 gwang-beom-wi-ha-da *v.* be extensive
광복절 gwang-bok-jeol *n.* Korean Independence Day
광산 gwang-san *n.* mine
광장 gwang-jang *n.* plaza
광주리 gwang-ju-ri *n.* round basket
광화문 gwang-hwa-mun *n.* Gwang Hwa Gate in Seoul *(historical site)*
괜찮다 gwaen-chan-ta *v.* be all right, be OK
괴로움 goe-ro-um *n.* trouble, distress, suffering
괴롭다 goe-rop-da *v.* be painful, be distressing
괴롭히다 goe-ro-pi-da *v.* afflict, worry, annoy
괴물 goe-mul *n.* monster
괴짜 goe-jja *n.* odd person
굉장하다 goeng-jang-ha-da *v.* be grand, be magnificent
굉장히 goeng-jang-hi *adv.* very much; extremely, very

교과서 gyo-gwa-seo *n.* textbook

교내 gyo-nae *n.* at school, on campus

교대하다 gyo-dae-ha-da *v.* take turns

교도소 gyo-do-so *n.* jail

교문 gyo-mun *n.* school entrance

교사 gyo-sa *n.* teacher, instructor

교수 gyo-su *n.* professor, faculty; instruction, teaching

교수님 gyo-su-nim *n.* professor *(hon.)*

교실 gyo-sil *n.* classroom

교외 gyo-oe *n.* the suburbs

교육 qyo-yuk *n.* education

교육학 gyo-yu-kak *n.* education

교장 gyo-jang *n.* principal

교제하다 gyo-je-ha-da *v.* date, associate with

교직원 gyo jig won *n.* school personnel

교차로 gyo-cha-ro *n.* intersection, cross street

교토 kyo-to *n.* Kyoto, Japan

교통 gyo-tong *n.* traffic

교통방송 gyo-tong-bang-song *n.* traffic news broadcast

교통사고 gyo-tong-sa-go *n.* traffic accident

교통수단 gyo-tong-su-dan *n.* transportation

교통순경 gyo-tong-sun-gyeong *n.* traffic policeman

교통위반 gyo-tong-wi-ban *n.* traffic offense

교통질서 gyo-tong-jil-sseo *n.* traffic order

교통편 gyo-tong-pyeon *n.* transportation

교포 gyo-po *n.* ethnic Korean living abroad

교환 gyo-hwan *n.* exchange, interchange, trade

교환교수 gyo-hwan-gyo-su *n.* visiting professor

교환하다 gyo-hwan-ha-da *v.* exchange, trade

교환학생 gyo-hwan-hak-saeng *n.* exchange students

교황 gyo-hwang *n.* pope

교황청 gyo-hwang-cheong *n.* papal court

교회 qyo-hoe *n.* church

교회당 gyo-hoe-dang *n.* chapel

교훈 gyo-hun *n.* edification, instruction

구 gu *n.* nine

구간 gu-gan *n.* block, section

구걸하다 gu-geol-ha-da *v.* go begging

구경 gu-gyeong *n.* sightseeing

구경거리 gu-gyeong-kkeo-ri *n.* attraction

구경꾼 gu-gyeong-kkun *n.* sightseer, spectator

구경하다 gu-gyeong-ha-da *v.* look around, sightsee

구구단 gu-gu-dan *n.* multiplication table

구급약 gu-gum-nyak *n.* emergency treatments

구급차 gu-geup-cha *n.* ambulance

구기다 gu-gi-da *v.* wrinkle, crumple

구김살 gu-gim-ssal *n.* rumple, fold

구내매장 gu-nae-mae-jang *n.* storage inside a school or inside a company

구내식당 gu-nae-sik-dang *n.* cafeteria, dining hall

구덩이 gu-deong-i *n.* pit

구독료 gu-dong-nyo *n.* subscription rates

구두 gu-du *n.* dress shoes

구두쇠 gu su soe *n.* stingy person, miser

구두약 gu-du-yak *n.* shoe polish

구두창 gu-du-chang *n.* sole of shoe

구렁이 gu-reong-i *n.* big snake

구렁텅이 gu-reong-teong-i *n.* pit, depth

구레나룻 gu-ren-na-ru *n.* whiskers

구루마 gu-ru-ma *n.* wagon, cart

구르다 gu-reu-da *v.* roll over; tumble; stamp on

구름 gu-reum *n.* cloud; 구름 끼다 gu-reum kki-da *v.* get cloudy

구름다리 gu-reum-da-ri *n.* overpass, land bridge

구리 gu-ri *n.* copper

구린내 gu-rin-nae *n.* bad smell

구멍 gu-meong *n.* hole, opening

구멍가게 gu-meong-kka-ge *n.* small shop

구명대 gu-myeong-dae *n.* life vest

구명정 gu-myeong-jeong *n.* life boat

구미에 맞다 gu-mi-e mat-da *v.phr.* suit one's taste

구박하다 gu-ba-ka-da *v.* ill-treat, mistreat

구별하다 gu-byeol-ha-da *v.* distinguish

구부러뜨리다 gu-bu-reo-tteu-ri-da *v.* bend, crook

구부러지다 gu-bu-reo-ji-da *v.* bend, bow, curve

구부리다 gu-bu-ri-da *v.* bend, curve

구분하다 gu-bun-ha-da *v.* divide, classify

구불구불하다 gu-bul-gu-bul-ha-da *v.* be crooked, be winding

구석 gu-seok *n.* corner, recess

구석구석 gu-seok-gu-seok *adv.* every nook and cranny

구석기시대 gu-seok-gi-si-dae *n.* stone age, paleolithic era

구석지다 gu-seok-ji-da *v.* be secluded, be recessed

구성 gu-seong *n.* organization, composition, constitution

구속하다 gu-so-ka-da *v.* restrict, restrain

구수하다 gu-su-ha-da *v.* taste good; be pleasant; be delightful

구슬 gu-seul *n.* bead, precious stone

구슬프다 gu-seul-peu-da *v.* be sad, be sorrowful

구식 gu-sik *n.* old-fashioned, old-style

구실 gu-sil *n.* duty, obligation; excuse, pretense

구어체 gu-eo-che *n.* spoken language, colloquial style

구역 gu-yeok *n.* zone, district, division

구역질하다 gu-yeok-jil-ha-da *v.* feel nausea, feel sick

구연동화 gu-yeon-dong-hwa *n.* orally-narrated fairy tale

구월 gu-wol *n.* September

구인광고 gu-in-gwang-go *n.* wanted poster

구입하다 gu-i-pa-da *v.* purchase

구절 gu-jeol *n.* subject and object *(words forming a complete sentence)*

구정 gu-jeong *n.* New Year's Day *(lunar calendar)*

구정물 gu-jeong-mul *n.* slops, sewage

구제하다 gu-je-ha-da *v.* relieve, help

구조대 gu-jo-dae *n.* relief squad

구조신호 gu-jo-sin-ho *n.* signal for help

구조하다 gu-jo-ha-da *v.* save, rescue

구좌 gu-jwa *n.* account, bank account

구직광고 gu-jik-gwang-go *n.* job wanted advertisement

구직자 gu-jik-ja *n.* job hunter, job seeker

구체적 gu-che-jeok *adj.* concrete, definite

구충제 gu-chung-je *n.* insecticide

구치소 gu-chi-so *n.* detention house

구태여 gu-tae-yeo *adv.* intentionally, deliberately

구하다 gu-ha-da *v.* rescue, save; buy, purchase; look for, seek; 여동생을 구해 주세요 yeo-dong-saeng-eul gu-hae ju-se-yo Please save my little sister; 드디어 그 가방을 구했다 deu-di-eo geu ga-bang-eul gu-haet-da Finally, I bought the bag; 룸메이트를 구합니다 rum-me-i-teu-reul gu-ham-ni-da I am looking for a roommate

국 guk *n.* soup

국가 guk-ga *n.* state, nation, country

국가적 guk-ga-jeok *adj.* national, state

국경 guk-gyeong *n.* border, boundary

국경선 guk-gyeong-seon *n.* borderline

국경일 guk-gyeong-il *n.* national holiday

국군 guk-gun *n.* national army

국기 guk-gi *n.* national flag

국내 gung-nae *n.* inside country

국내선 gung-nae-seon *n.* domestic flight

국력 gung-nyeok *n.* national power

국립 gung-nip *n.* national establishment

국립공원 gung-nip-gong-won *n.* national park

국명 gung-myeong *n.* name of a country

국물 gung-mul *n.* soup, broth

국민 gung-min *n.* people, citizen

국보 guk-bo *n.* national treasure

국사 guk-sa *n.* history of a nation

국산 guk-san *n.* domestic product, home products

국산품 guk-san-pum *n.* domestic product, home products

국수 guk-su *n.* noodle

국어 gug-eo *n.* national language; mother tongue

국자 guk-ja *n.* ladle, dipper

국적 guk-jeok *n.* nationality, citizenship

국제공항 guk-je-gong-hang *n.* international airport

국제선 guk-je-seon *n.* international flight

국제적 guk-je-jeok *adj.* international

국제적으로 guk-je-jeog-eu-ro *adv.* internationally

국제전화 guk-je-jeon-hwa *n.* international call

국토 guk-to *n.* territory, domain

국화 gu-kwa *n.* chrysanthemum

국회 gu-koe *n.* national assembly

국회의사당 gu-koe-ui-sa-dang *n.* national assembly building

국회의원 gu-koe-ui-won *n.* member of national assembly

군것질 gun-geot-jil *n.* eating between meals, snacking

군고구마 gun-go-gu-ma *n.* roasted sweet potato

군대 gun-dae *n.* troops, army

군데 gun-de *n.* place, spot

군데군데 gun-de-gun-de *adv.* here and there; 이 집은 군데군데 고칠 곳이 있다 i jib-eun gun-de-gun-de go-chil-gos-i it-da The house needs repairs here and there

군밤 gun-bam *n.* roasted chestnut

군복 gun-bok *n.* military uniform

군사분계선 gun-sa-bun-gye-seon *n.* military demarcation line; Joint Security Area

군살 gun-sal *n.* flab, excess fat

군소리 gun-so-ri *n.* unnecessary remark

군의관 gun-ui-gwan *n.* army surgeon

군인 gun-in *n.* military personnel

군중 gun-jung *n.* crowd

군침돌다 gun-chim dol-da *v.* to make one's mouth water

군침흘리다 gun-chim heul-li-da *v.* slobber, dribble, drool

굳다 gut-da *v.* harden, get stiff; solidify, stiffen, firm up; secure

굳세다 gut-se-da *v.* be strong, be firm

굳은살 gud-eun-sal *n.* hardened skin, callus

굳이 guj-i *adv.* firmly, positively

굴 gul *n.* cave; oyster

굴뚝 gul-ttuk *n.* chimney

굴리다 gul-li-da *v.* roll; run; neglect

굵기 gul-kki *n.* thickness

굵다 guk-da *v.* be thick, be deep, be heavy, be bold

굶기다 gum-gi-da *v.* let somebody go hungry

굶다 gum-tta *v.* starve, go hungry

굶주리다 gum-ju-ri-da *v.* be hungry, starve

굽다 gup-da *v.* be crooked, be bent; bake, broil, roast

굽히다 gu-pi-da *v.* bend, bow, stoop, curve

굿 gut *n.* exorcism

궁궐 gung-gwol *n.* royal palace

궁금하다 gung-geum-ha-da *v.* be curious; wonder

궁둥이 gung-dung-i *n.* buttocks, hips

궁리하다 gung-ni-ha-da *v.* deliberate, consider

궁전 gung-jeon *n.* royal palace

궁지 gung-ji *n.* difficult situation; 궁지에 몰리다 gung-ji-e mol-li-da *v.* be pushed to the wall

궁합 gung-hap *n.* marital harmony as predicted by a fortuneteller

궂은일 guj-eun-nil *n.* misfortune, disaster

권 gwon *n.* volume(s)

권력 gwol-lyeok *n.* power

권리 gwol-li *n.* a right (*legal*)

권세 gwon-se *n.* power, influence, authority

권위 gwon-wi *n.* authority

권총 gwon-chong *n.* pistol, gun

권투 gwon-tu *n.* boxing

권하다 gwon-ha-da *v.* recommend; ask; offer

궤짝 gwe-jjak *n.* box

귀 gwi *n.* ear

귀걸이 gwi-geol-i *n.* earring

귀공자 gwi-gong-ja *n.* young noble

귀국하다 qwi-qu-ka-da *v.* return to one's home country

귀금속 gwi-geum-sok *n.* precious metal

귀뚜라미 gwi ttu ra mi *n.* cricket

귀머거리 gwi-meo-geo-ri *n.* deaf person

귀신 gwi-sin *n.* ghost, demon

귀양가다 gwi-yang-ga-da *v.* go into exile, be exiled to a distant place

귀여워하다 gwi-yeo-wo-ha-da *v.* be affectionate to, treat with love, caress

귀엽다 gwi-yeop-da *v.* be lovely, be cute

귀족 gwi-jok *n.* nobleman; the nobility

귀중품 gwi-jung-pum *n.* valuables

귀찮게하다 gwi-chan-ke ha-da *v.* bother

귀찮다 gwi-chan-ta *v.* be annoying; be bothersome

귀찮아하다 gwi-chan-a-ha-da *v.* feel bothered

귀퉁이 gwi-tung-i *n.* corner, angle

귀하다 gwi-ha-da *v.* be noble; be rare; be lovable; be precious

귓구멍 gwit-gu-meong *n.* ear canal

귓속말 gwit-song-mal *n.* whisper

규격 gyu-gyeok *n.* standard, norm

규모 gyu-mo *n.* scale, scope

규칙 gyu-chik *n.* rule, regulation

규칙적 gyu-chik-jeok *adj.* regular

규칙적으로 gyu-chik-jeog-eu-ro *adv.* regularly

균 gyun *n.* germ

균형 gyun-hyeong *n.* balance

귤 gyul *n.* Orange (*fruit*)

그 geu *adj.* that; 그 동안 geu dong-an *adv.* during that time; 그 이후로 geu i-hu-ro *adv.* since then; 그 중 geu jung *adv.* among the rest, among them; 그 후 geu hu *adv.* after that, afterwards

그건 그렇고 geu-geon geu-reo-ko *adv.phr.* by the way

그까짓 geu-kka-jit *adj.* that kind of, trivial, not very important

그나마 geu-na-ma *adv.* even so, still

그냥 geu-nyang *adv.* as is, as one finds it, in that condition; all the way; just because, without any special reason; 너무 피곤해서 세수도 안하고 그냥 잤어 neo-mu pi-gon-hae-seo se-su-do an-ha-go geu-nyang jass-eo I was so tired that I just went to sleep without even washing my hands and face

그네 geu-ne *n.* swing

그늘 geu-neul *n.* shade

그다지 geu-da-ji *n.* so much, in that way

그대로 geu-dae-ro *adv.* like that, as is

그때 geu-ttae *n.* then, at that time

그래 geu-rae *adv.* well, so, therefore; yes

그래도 geu-rae-do *adv.* nevertheless, but, still, even so

그래서 그런지 geu-rae-seo geu-reon-ji *adv. phr.* not sure but guess that's why

그래서 geu-rae-seo *conj.* so; 어제는 너무 아팠다. 그래서 직장에 못 갔다. eo-je-neun neo-mu a-pat-da geu-rae-seo jik-jang-e mot gat-da I was so sick yesterday. So I couldn't go to work

그래프 geu-rae-peu *n.* graph, diagram

그랬더니 geu-raet-deo-ni *adv.* then

그러나 geu-reo-na *conj.* but, still, however

그러니까 geu-reo-ni-kka *conj.* therefore, hence, consequently

그러다가 geu-reo-da-ga *adv.* while doing…, being in that state for a while and…

그러더니 geu-reo-deo-ni *adv.* then

그러던 어느 날 geu-reo-deon eo-neu nal *adv.phr.* one day since…

그러면 geu-reo-myeon *conj.* if so

그러므로 geu-reo-meu-ro *conj.* therefore, hence

그러자 geu-reo-ja *conj.* then, thereon

그런 식 geu-reon sik *n.* that way

그런대로 geu-reon-dae-ro *adv.* such as it is

그런데 geu-reon-de *conj.* by the way, but then

그런데도 geu-reon-de-do *adv.* in spite of, for all that

그럼 geu-reom *conj.* then, if then, if so; indeed, of course; that's right

그렇게 geu-reo-ke *adv.* so, like that, that way

그렇고 말고 geu-reo-ko mal-go *adv.phr.* indeed, of course

그렇다 geu-reo-ta *v.* be so

그렇다면 geu-reo-ta-myeon *adv.* then, so then

그렇지 않으면 geu-reo-chi an-eu-myeon *adv.phr.* otherwise, unless

그렇지만 geu-reo-chi-man *conj.* but, however

그룹 geu-rup *n.* group

그릇 geu-reut *n.* container, vessel

그리 geu-ri *adv.* that way

그리고 geu-ri-go *conj.* and; 주말에 잠을 많이 잤다. 그리고 밀린 집안일도 했다 ju-mal-e jam-eul man-i jat-da geu-ri-go mil-lin jib-an-nil-do haet-da I slept a lot over the weekend and I also did housework that I've been putting off

그리다 geu-ri-da *v.* draw a picture

그리스 geu-ri-sseu *n.* Greece

그림 geu-rim *n.* picture, drawing

그림물감 geu-rim-mul-kkam *n.* pigment, paint

그림엽서 geu-rim-yeop-seo *n.* picture postcard

그림자 geu-rim-ja *n.* shadow

그림책 geu-rim-chaek *n.* picture book

그립다 geu-rip-da *v.* be longed for; be missed, be beloved

그만 geu-man *adv.* without doing anything further, to that extent; little; unavoidably; unintentionally, by mistake; 실수로 그만 문을 잠갔다 sil-ssu-ro geu-man mun-eul jam-gat-da I locked the door by mistake; 일 그만 하고 이제 집에 가자 il geu-man ha-go i-je jib-e ga-ja To that extent let's stop work here and go home; 아이들 키가 다 그만 하다 a-i-deul ki-ga da geu-man-ha-da To that extent the kids' height is pretty much the same; 참지 못하고 그만 화를 냈다 cham-jji mo-ta-go geu-man hwa-reul naet-da I couldn't take it anymore and unavoidably lost my temper

그만두다 geu-man-du-da *v.* stop, quit, cease

그만이다 geu-man-i-da *v.* be enough, be neither more nor less

그만큼 geu-man-keum *adv.* that much, to that extent

그물 geu-mul *n.* *(fishing)* net

그믐 geu-meum *n.* the last day of the month

그믐날 geu-meum-nal *n.* the last day of the month

그사이 geu-sa-i *n.* meanwhile

그야말로 geu-ya-mal-lo *adv.* indeed, truly

그어놓다 geu-eo-no-ta *v.* draw a line and keep it, to maintain a boundary

그저그렇다 geu-jeo geu-reo-ta *v.* be so-so; 요즘 경기가 그저그렇다 yo-jeum gyeong-gi-ga geu-jeo geu-reo-ta Business is so-so these days

그저 geu-jeo *adv.* without any reason

그저께 geu-jeo-kke *n.* day before yesterday

그전 geu-jeon *n.* former days, the past

그제 geu-je *n.* day before yesterday

그제야 geu-je-ya *adv.* for the first time, only when

그쯤 geu-jjeum *adv.* that much; around there

그치다 geu-chi-da *v.* stop, cease, end

그토록 geu-to-rok *adv.* so, such, to such an extent

극단 geuk-dan *n.* drama troupe

극복하다 geuk-bo-ka-da *v.* overcome

극성스럽다 geuk-seong-seu-reop-da *v.* be flourishing

극장 geuk-jang *n.* theater; 극장 표 geuk-jang pyo *n.* theater/movie ticket

극적 geuk-jeok *adj.* dramatic

근거 geun-geo *n.* basis, base

근교 geun-gyo *n.* suburbs

근대 geun-dae *n.* modern times, the modern age

근무 geun-mu *n.* service, work, duty

근무시간 geun-mu-ssi-gan *n.* service time, working time, time on duty

근무하다 geun-mu-ha-da *v.* do one's duty, be on duty

근시 geun-si *n.* near-sighted

근심 geun-sim *n.* anxiety, concern

근육 geun-yuk *n.* muscles

근육통 geun-yuk-tong *n.* muscular pain

근처 geun-cheo *n.* nearby

글 geul *n.* writing, script; piece of writing

글러브 geul-leo-beu *n.* gloves

글쎄 geul-sse *adv.* well, let me see; 글쎄... 오늘은 시간이 좀 없는데 내일 만나자 geul-sse o-neul-eun si-gan-i jom eopm-neun-de nae-il man-na-ja Well ... I am a little busy today, so let's meet tomorrow

글씨 geul-ssi *n.* letter, character

글읽기 geul-il-kki *n.* reading

글자 geul-jja *n.* letter, character

글짓기 geul-jit-gi *n.* composition

긁다 geuk-da *v.* scratch; rake; offend

긁히다 geul-ki-da *v.* be scratched; be offended

금 geum *n.* gold; line, fold; 금 가다 geum ga-da *v.* crack, split; 금 긋다 geum geut-da *v.* draw a line

금강산 geum-gang-san *n.* Mt. Geum Gang in North Korea

금고 geum-go *n.* strong box, vault

금년 geum-nyeon *n.* this year

금덩이 geum-tteong-i *n.* gold nugget

금메달 geum-me-dal *n.* gold medal

금반지 geum-ban-ji *n.* gold ring

금발 geum-bal *n.* golden hair

금방 geum-bang *adv.* immediately, just now, moments ago, in a short time; 금방 갈 게요 geum-bang gal-kke-yo I will leave immediately; 그 사람 금방 갔어요 geu sam-ram geum-bang gass-eo-yo He left moments ago

금붕어 geum-bung-eo *n.* goldfish

금성 geum-seong *n.* gold star

금세 geum-se *adv.* in a moment, at once

금속활자 geum-so-kwal-jja *n.* printing type made of metal

금액 geum-aek *n.* amount of money

금연 geum-yeon *n.* smoking prohibited; no smoking

금요일 geum-yo-il *n.* Friday

금융 geum-yung *n.* finance

금은방 geum-eun-ppang *n.* jeweler's shop

금전등록기 geum-jeon-deung-nok-gi *n.* cash register

금주 geum-ju *n.* this week; no drinking; 금주에는 비가 많이 오겠습니다 geum-ju-e-neun bi-ga man-i o-gess-eum-ni-da It is going to be raining a lot in this week; 건강이 안좋으니까 금주하세요 geon-gang-i an jo-eu-ni-kka geum-ju-ha-se-yo

Since your health is poor, please stop
drinking

금지하다 geum-ji-ha-da *v.* prohibit, ban

금하다 geum-ha-da *v.* suppress, abstain

급기야 geup-gi-ya *adv.* in the end, after all

급료 geum-nyo *n.* salary

급성 geup-seong *adj.* acute

급소 geup-so *n.* vital spot

급속히 geup-so-ki *adv.* rapidly

급정거 geup-jeong-geo *n.* sudden stop

급체 geup-che *n.* urgent stomach upset

급하다 geu-pa-da *v.* be in a hurry, be urgent

급히 geu-pi *adv.* hastily, in a hurry

굿다 geut-da *v.* draw a line

긍정적 geung-jeong-jeok *adj.* affirmative

기간 gi-gan *n.* period, term

기계 gi-gye *n.* machine, machinery

기계공학 gi-gye-gong-hak *n.* mechanical
engineering

기관 gi-gwan *n.* steam boiler; organ (*body
part*); engine; institute, school; 증기 기관
을 사용하는 배는 이제 많지 않다 jeung-
gi gi-wan-eul sa-yong-ha-neun bae-neun
i-je man-chi-an-ta There are not many
steamboats these days; 자동차 사고 때문
에 내장 기관이 많이 상했다 ja-dong-cha
sa-go ttae-mun-e nae-jang gi-gwan-i man-i
sang-haet-da He received serious organ
injuries in the car accident; 기관 고장
으로 기차가 제시간에 출발하지 못했
다 gi-gwan go-jang-eu-ro gi-cha-ga je-si-
gan-e chul-bal-ha-ji mo-taet-da The train
couldn't depart on schedule due to engine
trouble; 요즘 미국에 한국어 교육기관
들이 많다 yo-jeum mi-gug-e han-gug-eo
gyo-yuk-gi-gwan-deul-i man-ta There are a
lot of Korean language schools in America
these days

기교 gi-gyo *n.* art, technique

기구 gi-gu *n.* tools; balloon

기껏 gi-kkeot *adv.* to the best of one's ability

기껏해야 gi-kkeo-tae-ya *adv.* at most, at best

기념 gi-nyeom *n.* commemoration

기념식 gi-nyeom-sik *n.* commemoration
ceremony

기념일 gi-nyeom-il *n.* commemoration day,
aniversary

기념품 gi-nyeom-pum *n.* memento, souvenir

기념하다 gin-nyeom-ha-da *v.* commemorate,
be in memory of

기능 gi-neung *n.* skill, capability; function

기다 gi-da *v.* crawl, creep

기다랗다 gi-da-ra-ta *v.* (*length*) be rather long

기다리다 gi-da-ri-da *v.* wait

기대 gi-dae *n.* expectation, anticipation

기대다 gi-dae-da *v.* rely upon, lean on

기대되다 gi-dae-doe-da *v.* be expected, be
anticipated

기대하다 gi-dae-ha-da *v.* expect, look forward

기도하다 gi-do-ha-da *v.* pray

기독교 gi-dok-gyo *n.* Christianity

기둥 gi-dung *n.* pillar, post, pole

기러기 gi-reo-gi *n.* wild goose

기록하다 gi-ro-ka-da *v.* record, write down

기르다 gi-reu-da *v.* look after, take care of,
raise; grow

기름 gi-reum *n.* oil; fat; gas

기린 gi-rin *n.* giraffe

기막히다 gi-ma-ki-da *v.* stifle, feel choked;
be stunned, be struck dumb

기말 gi-mal *n.* end of a term, end of a
semester

기말시험 gi-mal-si-heom *n.* final exam

기발하다 gi-bal-ha-da *v.* be clever

기본 gi-bon *n.* basis, foundation

기부하다 gi-bu-ha-da *v.* contribute, donate

기분 gi-bun *n.* feeling; one's sense of being;
기분 좋다 gi-bun jo-ta *v.* feel good

기뻐하다 gi-ppeo-ha-da *v.* be pleased,
be happy

기쁘게하다 gi-ppeu-ge ha-da *v.* make
someone happy

기쁘다 gi-ppeu-da *v.* be happy

기사 gi-sa *n.* driver; news article; engineer;
오늘 택시기사들 모임이 있습니다 o-
neul taek-si gi-sa-deul mo-im-i iss-eum-ni-
da Taxi drivers have a meeting today; 신
문기사 봤어요 Sin-mun-gi-sa bwass-eo-yo
Have you read the news article; 건축학
과를 졸업하면 건축기사 자격증을 받
는다 geon-chu-kak-kkwa-reul jol-eo-pa-
myeon geon-chuk-gi-sa ja-gyeok-jeung-eul
ban-neun-da When you graduate from
the dept. of civil construction, you get a
construction engineer license

기사거리 gi-sa-kkeo-ri *n.* news item

기상대 gi-sang-dae *n.* meteorological observatory

기색 gi-saek *n.* look, mood, countenance

기생충 gi-saeng-chung *n.* parasite

기선 gi-seon *n.* large ship, steamship

기성복 gi-seong-bok *n.* factory-made clothing

기세 gi-se *n.* spirit, ardor

기숙사 gi-suk-sa *n.* dormitory

기술 gi-sul *n.* skill, technique, ability

기슭 gi-seuk *n.* edge

기압 gi-ap *n.* air pressure

기어 qi-eo *n.* gear

기어다니다 gi-eo-da-ni-da *v.* crawl around

기어오르다 gi-eo-o-reu-da *v.* climb up

기어이 gi-eo-i *adv.* by all means

기억 gi cok *n.* memory; 기억에 난다 gi-eog-e nam-tta *v.* remember, bear in mind, recollect, memorize

기억나다 gi-eong-na-da *v.* remember, bear in mind, recollect, memorize

기억력 gi-eong-nyeok *n.* memory

기억상실 gi-eok-sang-sil *n.* loss of memory

기억하다 gi-eo-ka-da *v.* remember

기업 gi-eop *n.* enterprise, business

기업가 gi-eop-ga *n.* entrepreneur

기여하다 gi-yeo-ha-da *v.* contribute

기온 gi-on *n.* temperature

기와 gi-wa *n.* roof tile

기와집 gi-wa-jip *n.* tile-roofed house

기왕 gi-wang *adv.* already, since

기운 qi-un *n.* strength, force; vigor, energy

기울다 gi-ul-da *v.* tilt, incline, lean; decline; go down

기웃기웃 gi-ut-gi-ut *adv.* peeking around

기원전 gi-won-jeon *n.* B.C.; 불교는 B.C. 2000; 년쯤 성립되었다 bul-gyo-neun bi-ssi i-cheon-nyeon-jjeum seong-nip-doe-eot-da Buddhism was established around 2000 B.C.

기이하다 gi-i-ha-da *v.* be strange

기자 gi-ja *n.* reporter

기장 gi-jang *n.* pilot

기저귀 gi-jeo-gwi *n.* diaper

기적 gi-jeok *n.* miracle

기준 gi-jun *n.* standard, criteria

기증하다 gi-jeung-ha-da *v.* contribute, donate

기차 gi-cha *n.* train; 기차를 놓치다 gi-cha-reul no-chi-da *v.* miss a train

기차소리 gi-cha-sso-ri *n.* whistling sound of a train

기차역 gi-cha-yeok *n.* train station

기차표 gi-cha-pyo *n.* train ticket

기찻길 gi-chat-gil *n.* railway, railroad track

기체 gi-che *n.* gas, vapor

기초 gi-cho *n.* foundation

기초반 gi-cho-ban *n.* beginner's class

기초적 gi-cho-jeok *adj.* fundamental

기초하다 gi-cho-ha-da *v.* be based on; 대통령은 헌법에 기초하여 국가를 통치한다 dea-tong-nyeong-eun heon-ppeob-e gi-cho-ha-yeo guk-ga-reul tong-chi-han-da The President governs the nation based on the Constitution

기침 gi-chim *n.* cough

기타 gi-ta *n.* guitar; and so forth (etc.); 기타 치다 gi-ta chi-da *v.* play the guitar

기타치기 gi-ta-chi-gi *n.* guitar playing

기한 gi-han *n.* period, time limit, term

기형아 gi-hyeong-a *n.* deformed child

기호 gi-ho *n.* sign, mark, symbol

기혼 gi-hon *n.* be married

기회 gi-hoe *n.* chance, opportunity

기후 gi-hu *n.* weather, climate

긴 팔 옷 gin pal ot *n.phr.* long-sleeve shirts

긴장하다 gin-jang-ha-da *v.* be nervous, be tense, be strained

길 gil *n.* road, street; 길 막히다 gil ma-ki-da have traffic congestion *v.* have heavy traffic; 길 잃다 gil il-ta *v.* take the wrong road; 길을 물어보다 gil-eul mul-eo-bo-da *v.* ask directions

길거리 gil-kkeo-ri *n.* street, road

길다 gil-da *v.* be long

길들이다 gil-deul-i-da *v.* tame, domesticate

길목 gil-mok *n.* corner, turn

길어지다 gil-eo-ji-da *v.* extend, become longer

길이 gil-i *n.* length

길쭉하다 gil-jju-ka-da *v.* be long and slender

김 gim *n.* nori *(seaweed wrap for sushi)*, dried seaweed; steam, vapor

김장 gim-jang *n.* kimchi prepared for the winter

김장하다 gim-jang-ha-da *v.* make kimchi for the winter

김치 gim-chi *n.* kimchi *(traditional Korean food)*; 김치 담그다 gim-chi dam-geu-da *v.* make kimchi; 김치 독 gim-chi ttok *n.* ceramic kimchi jar

깃 git *n.* collar; feather

깃발 git-bal *n.* flag, banner

깊다 gip-da *v.* be deep; be late; be profound; 웅덩이가 아주 깊다 ung-deong-i-ga a-ju gip-da The ditch is very deep; 밤이 깊었으니 이제 집에 가자 bam-i gip-eoss-eu-ni i-je jib-e ga-ja It's late so let's go home now; 그 철학자의 견해는 아주 생각이 깊다geu cheol-hak-ja-ui gyeon-hae-neun a-ju saeng-gag-i gip-daThe philosopher's comment was profound

깊숙이 gip-sug-i *adv.* deep, far

깊숙하다 gip-su-ka-da *v.* be deep; be retired

깊어지다 gi-peo-ji-da *v.* deepen; thicken

깊이 gi-pi *n.* depth; *adv.* deeply, profoundly

까다 kka-da *v.* husk, peel off; hatch; reduce

까다롭게 kka-da-rop-ge *adv.* critically, harshly; with difficulty

까다롭다 kka-da-rop-da *v.* be particular, be hard to please; be complicated, be troublesome

까마득하게 kka-ma-deu-ka-ge *adv.* completely; far-away, far off

까맣다 kka-ma-ta *v.* be black

까매지다 kka-mae-ji-da *v.* get dark, become blackened

까지 kka-ji *part.* until, by; up to; 밤 1시까지 일했다 bam han-si-kka-ji il-haet-da I worked until 1:00am; 9시까지 오세요 a-hop-si-kka-ji o-se-yo Please come here by 9:00; 한시간에 50불까지 줄 수 있어요 han-si-gan-e o-sip-bul-kka-ji jul ssu iss-eo-yo I can pay you up to 50 dollars per hour

까치 kka-chi *n.* magpie

깎다 kkak-da *v.* discount, peel

깜빡 kkam-ppak *adv.* completely, in an instant

깜짝 kkam-jjak *adv.* startling; 깜짝 놀라다 kkam-jjak nol-la-da *v.* surprise suddenly, startle suddenly

깡충깡충 kkang-chung-kkang-chung *adv.* jumping up and down

깨 kkae *n.* sesame

깨끗이 kkae-kkeus-i *adv.* cleanly, neatly

깨끗하다 kkae-kkeu-ta-da *v.* be clean

깨다 kkae-da *v.* wake up, break

깨닫다 kkae-dat-da *v.* recognize, realize, perceive

깨어나다 kkae-eo-na-da *v.* return to consciousness, recover oneself

깨우다 kkae-u-da *v.* wake someone up

깨지다 kkae-ji-da *v.* be broken, get broken

꺼내다 kkeo-nae-da *v.* pull out, take out

꺼지다 kkeo-ji-da *v.* go out, be put out; cave in, sink

꺾다 kkeok-da *v.* break off, snap

꺾이다 kkeokk-i-da *v.* be broken; turn, make a turn; be folded; be discouraged; 나무 가지가 꺾였다 na-mu ga-ji-ga kkeokk-eot-da The tree branches were broken; 여기서부터 길이 많이 꺾이니까 조심해서 운전하세요 yeo-gi-seo-bu-teo gil-i man-i kkeokk-i-ni-kka jo-sim-hae-seo un-jeon-ha-se-yo From this point the road turns sharply, please drive carefully; 아버지의 말을 듣고 나는 용기가 꺾였다 a-beo-ji-ui mal-eul deut-go na-neun yong-gi-ga kkeokk-yeot-da When I heard what my father told me, I was discouraged

껌 kkeom *n.* chewing gun

껍데기 kkeop-de-gi *n.* husks, hulls, shell

껍질 kkeop-jil *n.* bark, nutshell, skin, peel

껑충 kkeong-chung *adv.* with a jump, with a leap

껑충거리다 kkeong-chung-geo-ri-da *v.* jump, leap

께 kke *part. (hon.)* to (a person); 이선생님께 편지하세요 i-seon-saeng-nim-kke pyeon-ji-ha-se-yo Please send a letter to Mr. Lee

께서 kke-seo *part. (hon.)* subject particle; 이선생님께서 전화하셨어요 i-seon-saeng-nim-kke-seo jeon-hwa-ha-syeoss-eo-yo Mr. Lee called on the telephone

껴안다 kkyeo-an-tta *v.* hug, hold to one's breast

껴입다 kkyeo-ip-da *v.* wear a shirt underneath one's outer clothes

꼬리 kko-ri *n.* tail, tag

꼬부라지다 kko-bu-ra-ji-da *v.* bend, curve, become crooked

꼬불거리다 kko-bul-geo-ri-da *v.* wind, zigzag

꼬불꼬불 kko-bul-kko-bul *adv.* zigzag, winding

꼬이다 kko-i-da *v.* go wrong, become perverse; be snarled

꼬집다 kko-jip-da *v.* pinch

꼬챙이 kko-chaeng-i *n.* spit, skewer, spear

꼬투리 kko-tu-ri *n.* pod, legume; cause, lead

꼭 kkok *adv.* exactly; tightly; surely; patiently; as if

꼭대기 kkok-dae-gi *n.* the top

꼭지 kkok-ji *n.* knob, handle

꼴 kkol *n.* shape, appearance, condition, situation, clothes; 꼴 보기 싫다 kkol bo-gi sil-ta *v.* hate to see; 꼴사납다 kkol-sa-nap-da *v.* be ugly, be disgusting

꼴불견 kkl-bul-gyeon *n.* unsightliness

꼴찌 kkol-jji *n.* the last, the bottom, the tail end

꼼꼼하다 kkom-kkom-ha-da *v.* be careful, meticulous

꼼짝못하다 kkom-jjak mo-ta-da *v.* cannot move at all; be cowed, be intimidated

꼽다 kkop-da *v.* count on one's fingers

꼿꼿이 kkot-kkos-i *adv.* straight, erect; hard and dry, stiff

꽁꽁 kkong-kkong *adv.* frozen hard; 얼음이 꽁꽁 얼었다 eol-eum-i kkong-kkong eol-eot-da The ice is frozen solid

꽁초 kkong-cho *n.* cigarette-butt

꽂다 kkot-da *v.* stick into, put into, pin, prick

꽂히다 kko-chi-da *v.* get inserted, be stuck, be pinned

꽃 kkot *n.* flower

꽃가게 kkot-ga-ge *n.* flower shop

꽃꽂이 kkot-kkoj-i *n.* flower arrangement

꽃바구니 kkot ba-gu-ni *n.* flower basket

꽃병 kkot-byeong *n.* flower vase

꽃잎 kkon-nip *n.* petal

꽃집 kkot-jip *n.* flower shop

꽃피다 kkot-pi-da *v.* bloom

꽉 kkwak *adv.* tightly, firmly; closely; to the full; patiently

꽤 kkwae *adv.* substantially, fairly, pretty

꽥꽥 kkwaek-kkwaek *adv.* ring-ring, bang-bang (*screaming or shouting sound*)

꽹과리 kkwaeng-gwa-ri *n.* gong

꾀 kkoe *n.* wit, trick, scheme

꾀병 kkoe-byeong *n.* feigned illness

꾸기다 kku-gi-da *v.* wrinkle, crumple

꾸러미 kku-reo-mi *n.* bundle, package, bale

꾸물거리다 kku-mul-geo-ri-da *v.* wriggle

꾸미다 kku-mi-da *v.* decorate, ornament, make up, touch up; invent, prepare

꾸중듣다 kku-jung-deut-da *v.* get a scolding

꾸지람 kku-ji-ram *n.* scolding, rebuke

꾸짖다 kku-jit-da *v.* scold, rebuke, chide

꾹 kkuk *adv.* tightly, firmly, hard; patiently

꿀 kkul *n.* honey, nectar

꿀꺽 kkul-kkeok *adv.* gulp

꿀벌 kkul-beol *n.* honeybee, bee

꿈 kkum *n.* dream

꿈꾸다 kkum-kku-da *v.* dream

꿈쩍않다 kkum-jjeok an-ta *v.* be unperturbed, keep cool and calm; remain motionless, safe and sound

꿍 kkung *adv.* with a thud, with a boom

꿩 kkwong *n.* peasant

꿰다 kkwe-da *v.* thread, string; pierce, thrust

꿰매다 kkwe-mae-da *v.* sew, stitch, mend

끄다 kkeu-da *v.* put out, extinguish, blow out

끄덕이다 kkeu-deog-i-da *v.* nod, make a slight movement

끄떡없다 kkeu-tteog-eop-da *v.* be safe, be secure, be immune from

끄르다 kkeu-reu-da *v.* undo, untie, unfasten

끄집어내다 kkeu-jib-eo-nae-da *v.* take out, pull out, pick out; start a conversation

끈 kkeun *n.* strip, string, cord

끈기 kkeun-gi *n.* endurance, patience; adhesiveness, stickiness

끈끈하다 kkeun-kkeun-ha-da *v.* be sticky, be adhesive; be humid

끈질기다 kkeun-jil-gi-da *v.* be strong and sticky, be strongly adhesive

끊기다 kkeun-gi-da *v.* be cut, be broken, be stopped

끊다 kkeun-ta *v.* hang up; quit, give up; cut, break

끊어지다 kkeun-eo-ji-da *v.* break down; break off, discontinue; have done with; run out

끊임없이 kkeun-im-eops-i *adv.* constantly, ceaselessly, endlessly

끌다 kkeul-da *v.* pull, draw; attract, arouse; lead; drag; prolong, delay, extend; 줄을 끌어 당기세요 jul-eul kkeul-eo dang-gi-se-yo Please pull the rope; 귀여운 아기는 언

제나 사람들의 시선을 끈다 gwi-yeo-un
a-gi-neun eon-je-na sa-ram-deul-ui si-seon-
eul kkeun-da A cute baby always attract
people's attention; 가방을 그렇게 끌고
다니면 금방 더러워져요 ga-bang-eul
geu-reo-ke kkeul-go da-ni-myeon geum-
bang deo-reo-wo-jyeo-yo If you drag your
bag like that, it will get dirty soon; 날짜
를 너무 오래 끌지 마세요 nal-jja-reul
neo-mu o-rae kkeul-ji ma-se-yo Please do
not delay too long

끌려가다 kkeul-lyeo-ga-da v. be drawn, be
pulled, be dragged

끌어내다 kkeul-eo-nae-da v. take out,
bring out

끌어당기다 kkeul-eo-dang-gi-da v. draw
near, pull up

끌어안다 kkeul-eo-an-tta v. hug, draw closer
to one's breast

끌어올리다 kkeul-eo-ol-li-da v. pull up, lift up

끓다 kkeul-ta v. boil, simmer; burn, glow;
rumble; surge

끓이다 kkeul-i-da v. boil, heat; cook

끔찍하다 kkeum-jji-ka-da v. be horrible, be
terrible; be wholehearted, be sincere

끙끙거리다 kkeung-kkeung-geo-ri-da v.
grumble, moan

끝 kkeut n. end, conclusion; the tip, the point

끝까지 kkeut-kka-ji adv. to the last, to the end

끝끝내 kkeut-kkeun-nae adv. to the last, to
the end

끝나다 kkeun-na-da v. finish, be over

끝내 kkeun-nae adv. to the last, to the end

끝내놓다 kkeun-nae-no-ta v. make an end of,
finish, get through

끝내다 kkeun-nae-da v. make an end of,
finish, get through

끝마치다 kkeun-ma-chi-da v. make an end
of, finish, get through

끝말 kkeun-mal n. last syllable of a word

끝없다 kkeud-eop-da v. be endless, be
boundless

끝없이 kkeud-eops-i adv. endlessly,
boundlessly

끝에 kkeut-e adv. at the end, at the final

끝으로 kkeut-eu-ro adv. finally, in conclusion, at the end

끝장 kkeut-jang n. end, conclusion; settlement, termination

끼니 kki-ni n. meal, diet

끼니때 kki-ni-ttae n. meal time

끼다 kki-da v. wear (glasses, gloves, a ring);
smoke, be foggy; become dirty, be stained;
fold; hold; be involved; 그는 안경을 낀
다 geu-neun an-gyeong-eul kkin-da He
wears glasses; 오늘 안개가 끼었다 o-neul
an-gae-ga kki-eot-da It is foggy today;
그릇에 때가 끼었다 geu-reus-e ttae-ga
kki-eot-da This plate got dirty; 나도 끼어
도 돼 Na-do kki-eo-do dwae Is it OK if I
get involved with the group

끼리 kki-ri affix. among, between

끼리끼리 kki-ri-kki-ri adv. in-group, exclusively among themselves

끼우다 kki-u-da v. put between, insert, hold
between

끼이다 kki-i-da v. be put between; be
sandwiched between

끽해야 kki-kae-ya adv. at the most, at the best

낌새 kkim-sae n. secret; delicate signs; hint

ㄴ

나 na pron. I, me

나가다 na-ga-da v. advance, progress, go
forward; go out, get out; work, join,
enter; 경제가 앞으로 한걸음 더 나가다
gyeong-je-ga ap-eu-ro han-geol-eum deo
na-ga-da The economy advances one step
forward; 주말에는 친구와 함께 교외로
나가기로 했다 ju-mal-e-neun chin-gu-wa
ham-kke gyo-oe-ro na-ga-gi-ro haet-da
I decided to go to the country side with
my friend over the weekend; 북한은 요
즘 국제사회로 나가고 있다 bu-kan-eun
yo-jeum guk-je-sa-hoe-ro na-ga-go it-da
Currently North Korea is joining the
international community

나그네 na-geu-ne n. traveler, passenger

나날이 na-nal-i *adv.* day by day, day after day

나누다 na-nu-da *v.* divide, separate; share; classify

나누어주다 na-nu-eo-ju-da *v.* divide, share

나뉘다 na-nwi-da *v.* be divided, be apart, be separated

나다 na-da *v.* be born; come out; break; appear

나들이 na-deul-i *n.* going out

나라 na-ra *n.* country, nation

나란히 na-ran-hi *adv.* in a line, side by side; evenly, uniformly, in order

나루터 na-ru-teo *n.* ferry

나르다 na-reu-da *v.* carry, convey, transport

나른하다 na-reun-ha-da *v.* languish, feel tired

나머지 na-meo-ji *n.* the rest, the remainder

나무 na-mu *n.* tree, plant; wood, timber; firewood

나무기러기 na-mu-gi-reo-gi *n.* wild goose made of wood *(traditional Korean wood carvings)*

나무라다 na-mu-ra-da *v.* blame, admonish

나물 na-mul *n.* seasoned vegetables

나뭇가지 na-mut-ga-ji *n.* tree branch

나방 na-bang *n.* moth

나붙다 na-but-da *v.* be put up, be posted

나비 na-bi *n.* butterfly

나비넥타이 na-bi-nek-ta-i *n.* bow tie

나빠지다 na-ppa-ji-da *v.* grow worse, go bad

나쁘게 na-ppeu-ge *adv.* badly, ill

나쁘다 na-ppeu-da *v.* be bad, wrong; be inferior, poor

나사 na-sa *n.* screw

나서다 na-seo-da *v.* leave, get out of; turn up, be found; intrude, meddle in; 진주는 정장을 하고 집을 나섰다 jin-ju-neun jeong-jang-eul ha-go jib-eul na-seot-da Jin-ju left her house wearing a suit; 넌 이번엔 좀 나서지 마 neon i-beon-en jom na-seo-ji ma Please do not meddle this time

나아지다 na-a-ji-da *v.* become better, be improved

나오다 na-o-da *v.* come out; appear, emerge; originate

나와있다 na-wa-it-da *v.* to be coming to work; come out; appear, emerge; originate

나이 na-i *n.* age; 나이 들다 na-i deul-da *v.* get old, become old; 나이 들어 보이다 na-i deul-eo bo-i-da *v.* look old

나이테 na-i-te *n.* ring *(of a tree)*

나일론 na-il-lon *n.* nylon

나중에 na-jung-e *adv.* later

나침반 na-chim-ban *n.* compass

나타나다 na-ta-na-da *v.* appear, turn up; be revealed; be described; come to light

나타내다 na-ta-nae-da *v.* show, display, reflect; express; represent, symbolize

나팔 na-pal *n.* trumpet

나폴레옹 na-pol-le-ong *n.* Napoleon

나풀거리다 na-pul-geo-ri-da *v.* flap gently, flutter lightly

나흘 na-heul *n.* four days

낙관적 nak-gwan-jeok *adj.* optimistic

낙서하다 nak-seo-ha-da *v.* scribble, doodle

낙엽 nag-yeop *n.* fallen leaves

낙천적 nak-cheon-jeok *adj.* optimistic

낙타 nak-ta *n.* camel

낙하산 na-ka-san *n.* parachute

낚시 nak-si *n.* fishing; 낚시 가다 nak-si ga-da *v.* go fishing

낚시꾼 nak-si-kkun *n.* angler, fisherman

낚시질하다 nak-si-jil-ha-da *v.* fish, angle

낚시터 nak-si-teo *n.* place to do angling, fishing place

낚싯대 nak-sit-dae *n.* fishing rod

낚싯줄 nak-sit-jul *n.* fishing line

난간 nan-gan *n.* railing, handrail

난로 nal-lo *n.* stove, fireplace

난롯가 nal-lot-ga *n.* the fire side

난리 nal-li *n.* war, revolt, disturbance, riot

난민 nan-min *n.* the destitute, refugees

난방 nan-bang *n.* heating, heated room

난방장치 nan-bang-jang-chi *n.* heating system

난시 nan-si *n.* astigmatism

난장판 nan-jang-pan *n.* scene of confusion and disorder, turmoil

난쟁이 nan-jaeng-i *n.* dwarf

난처하다 nan-cheo-ha-da *v.* be hard to deal with, be difficult

난초 nan-cho *n.* orchid, iris

난폭하다 nan-po-ka-da *v.* be violent

날 nal *n.* day, date; edge, blade

날개 nal-gae *n.* wings

날다 nal-da *v.* fly, take wings

날달걀 nal-dal-gyal *n.* uncooked egg

날려보내다 nal-lyeo-bo-nae-da *v.* let fly, set free; waste, blow

날로 nal-lo *adv.* raw, uncooked; every day, day by day; 고기를 날로 먹었다 go-gi-reul nal-lo meog-eot-da He ate the meat raw; 사는게 날로 어려워진다 sa-neun-ge nal-lo eo-ryeo-wo-jin-da Living is getting harder every day

날리다 nal-li-da *v.* fly, make fly; lose, waste; wave, flutter, flap; 연을 날린다 yeon-eul nal-lin-da He flies a kite; 카지노에서 돈을 다 날렸다 ka-ji-no-e-seo don-eul da nal-lyeot-da He lost all his money in a Casino; 태극기가 바람에 날린다 tae-geuk-gi-ga ba-ram-e nal-lin-da The Korean flag is waving in the wind

날마다 nal-ma-da *adv.* every day, daily

날쌔다 nal-ssae-da *v.* be quick, swift

날씨 nal-ssi *n.* weather

날씬하다 nal-ssin-ha-da *v.* be slim; be thin

날씬해지다 nal-ssin-hae-ji-da *v.* become slim, become thin

날아가다 nal-a-ga-da *v.* fly away, take wing; be gone

날아다니다 nal-a-da-ni-da *v.* fly about

날아오르다 nal-a-o-reu-da *v.* fly high, take off

날짜 nal-jja *n.* date; days

날카롭다 nal-ka-rop-da *v.* be sharp, be pointed

낡다 nal-tta *v.* be old, be worn, be old-fashioned, be out-of-date

남 nam *n.* another person, other people

남극 nam-geuk *n.* South Pole

남기다 nam-gi-da *v.* leave behind, save, spare; make profit

남김없이 nam-gim-eops-i *adv.* entirely, without exception

남녀 nam-nyeo *n.* men and women

남녀공학 nam-nyeo-gong-hak *n.* coeducation

남녀노소 nam-nyeo-no-so *n.* men and women of all ages

남녀평등 nam-nyeo-pyeong-deung *n.* equality of the sexes

남다 nam-tta *v.* remain, be left over; make a profit

남다르다 nam-da-reu-da *v.* be peculiar, be different from others

남달리 nam-dal-li *adv.* in a different way than other

남대문 nam-dae-mun *n.* the South Gate *(historic site in Korea)*

남동 nam-dong *n.* southeast

남동생 nam-dong-saeng *n.* younger brother

남동풍 nam-dong-pung *n.* southeaster, southeasterly wind

남들 nam-deul *n.* others

남매 nam-mae *n.* brother and sister

남모르다 nam-mo-reu-da *v.* be unknown to others, hidden, secret

남몰래 nam-mol-lae *adv.* secretly

남미 nam-mi *n.* South America

남반구 nam-ban-gu *n.* Southern Hemisphere

남부 nam-bu *n.* southern part, the south

남부끄럽다 nam-bu-kkeu-reop-da *v.* be ashamed, be disgraceful, be shameful

남부럽잖다 nam-bu-reop-jan-ta *v.* be well-to-do, be well off, be wealthy, be rich

남북 nam-buk *n.* north and south

남북한 nam-bu-kan *n.* North and South Korea

남산 nam-san *n.* Mt. Nam *(in Seoul)*

남색 nam-saek *n.* indigo, deep blue

남서 nam-seo *n.* southwest

남성 nam-seong *n.* male

남성적 nam-seong-jeok *adj.* masculine, manly

남아돌다 nam-a-dol-da *v.* be in excess, be superabundant, have too many

남아메리카 nam-a-me-ri-ka *n.* South America

남아있다 nam-a-it-da *v.* remain, be left over

남아프리카 nam-a-peu-ri-ka *n.* South Africa

남자 nam-ja *n.* man, male

남자답다 nam-ja-dap-da *v.* be manly

남자친구 nam-ja-chin-gu *n.* boyfriend

남존여비 nam-jon-nyeo-bi *n.* male dominance *(over women)*

남짓 nam-jit *affix.* slightly over, approximately, about

남쪽 nam-jjok *n.* south

남태평양 nam-tae-pyeong-nyang *n.* South Pacific Ocean

남편 nam-pyeon *n.* husband

남학생 nam-hak-saeng *n.* male student

남한 nam-han *n.* South Korea

남해안 nam-hae-an *n.* south coast

남향 nam-hyang *n.* southern exposure, facing south

남향집 nam-hyang-jjip *n.* southern exposure (*for a house*), house facing to the south

납 nap *n.* lead *(metal)*

납기일 nap-gi-il *n.* pay day

납부하다 nap-bu-ha-da *v.* pay, deliver

납작 nap-jak *adv.* flat, low

납작코 nap-jak-ko *n.* flat nose, flat-nosed person

납작하다 nap-ja-ka-da *v. be* flat; be low; be thin

납치하다 nap-chi-ha-da *v.* kidnap, hijack

낫 nat *n.* sickle, scythe

낫다 nat-da *v.* be better, be superior; recover from illness, get well

낭떠러지 nang-tteo-reo-ji *n.* cliff, bluff

낭만적 nang-man-jeok *adj.* romantic

낭비하다 nang-bi-ha-da *v.* waste, use to no purpose

낮 nat *n.* daytime

낮다 nat-da *v.* be low; be poor

낮잠 nat-jam *n.* nap; 낮잠 자다 nat-jam ja-da *v.* take a nap

낮추다 nat-chu-da *v.* lower, make low

낯 nat *n.* face, visage; 낯을 들다 na-chul deul-da *v.* show one's face

낯붉히다 nat-bul-ki-da *v.* become red in the face

낯익다 nan-nik-da *v.* be familiar, be acquainted

낱개 nat-gae *n.* piece, each piece

낱낱이 nan-na-chi *adv.* individually, one by one

낱말 nan-mal *n.* word, vocabulary

낳다 na-ta *v.* bear, give birth, breed

내 nae *pron.* I; my

내가다 nae-ga-da *v.* take out, remove

내걸다 nae-geol-da *v.* hang out, display; stand for, advocate; risk

내과 nae-kkwa *n.* internal medicine, internal treatment

내기 nae-gi *n.* betting, bet

내기하다 nae-gi-ha-da *v.* bet, make a bet

내내 nae-nae *adv.* all along, all the time, from start to finish, throughout a time period

내년 nae-nyeon *n.* next year, the coming year

내놓다 nae-no-ta *v.* put out, take out; expose, show; publish; present; serve

내다 nae-da *v.* hand in, turn in; pay; publish; produce

내다보다 nae-da-bo-da *v.* look out, see outside from inside; foresee, forecast

내달 nae-dal *n.* next month

내던지다 nae-deon-ji-da *v.* throw out; abandon

내려가다 nae-ryeo-ga-da *v.* go down

내려놓다 nae-ryeo-no-ta *v.* set down, take down, bring down

내려다보다 nae-ryeo-da-bo-da *v.* look down, overlook

내려앉다 nae-ryeo-an-tta *v.* come down to an inferior seat; collapse, fall down; 상석에 계시던 아버지께서 할아버지가 들어오시자 내려앉으셨다 sang-seong-e gye-si-deon a beo ji-kke-seo hal-a-beo-ji-ga deul-eo-o-si-ja nae-ryeo-anj-eu-syeot-da My father moved from the highest seat to a lower seat when my grandfather came in

내려오다 nae-ryeo-o-da *v.* come down, get off

내려주다 nae-ryeo-ju-da *v.* drop

내려치다 nae-ryeo-chi-da *v.* strike from above

내리다 nae-ri-da *v.* get off, get out of; take off; descend, come down, hand down; drop, go down; take down, set down, pull down; grant; 차에서 내렸다 cha-e-seo nae-ryeot-da He got out of the car; 이 반지는 우리 집안 여자들에게 대대로 내려왔다 i ban-ji-neun u-ri jib-an yeo-ja-deul-e-ge dae-dae-ro nae-ryeo-wat-da This ring has been handed down by the women in my family for generations; 비가 와서 기온이 많이 내려갔다 bi-ga wa-seo gi-on-i man-i nae-ryeo-gat-da Because of the rain, the temperature dropped a lot; 커튼을 좀 내려 주세요 keo-teun-eul jom nae-ryeo-ju-se-yo Please pull down the curtain

내리막 nae-ri-mak *n.* downward slope, downhill

내밀다 nae-mil-da *v.* protrude, jut out, project; push out, stick out

내뱉다 nae-baet-da *v.* spit out; spur

내버려두다 nae-beo-ryeo-du-da *v.* leave as is, leave alone

내버리다 nae-beo-ri-da *v.* throw away, cast away, dump

내보내다 nae-bo-nae-da *v.* let out, let go out; expel, evict; fire

내복 nae-bok *n.* underwear

내복약 nae-bong-nyak *n.* internal use

내부 nae-bu *n.* the inside, the inner part

내비치다 nae-bi-chi-da *v.* be transparent; hint, insinuate

내뻗다 nae-ppeot-da *v.* put forth, spread out

내뿜다 nae-ppum-tta *v.* gush out, spout, jet, blow up

내성적 nae-seong-jeok *adj.* introverted; *n.* introvert

내세우다 nae-se-u-da *v.* make stand; nominate, designate; stand on, insist

내오다 nae-o-da *v.* take out, remove

내외 nae-oe *n.* the interior and exterior; home and abroad

내용 nae-yong *n.* contents, substance

내의 nae-ui *n.* underwear

내일 nae-il *n.* tomorrow

내장 nae-jang *n.* internal organs

내적 nae-jjeok *adj.* inner, internal

내젓다 nae-jeot-da *v.* wave, swing, shake, wag

내주 nae-ju *n.* next week, the coming week

내주다 nae-ju-da *v.* take out and give to somebody, give away

내쫓기다 nae-jjot-gi-da *v.* be driven out, be dismissed

내쫓다 nae-jjot-da *v.* drive out, expel, discharge, evict

내팽개치다 nae-paeng-gae-chi-da *v.* throw out, toss away

내한하다 nae-han-ha-da *v.* visit Korea

내향적 nae-hyang-jeok *adj.* introverted; *n.* introvert

내후년 nae-hu-nyeon *n.* the year after next

냄비 naem-bi *n.* pot, cook-pot, pan, saucepan

냄새 naem-sae *n.* smell, scent, fragrance, stink; 냄새 나다 name-sae na-da *v.* have an aroma, give off a smell; 냄새 맡다 name-sae mat-da *v.* sniff, smell, get a whiff of

냅킨 naep-kin *n.* napkin

냇가 naet-ga *n.* riverside, riverbank

냇물 naen-mul *n.* water of a stream

냉국 naeng-kkuk *n.* soup served cold

냉동식품 naeng-dong-sik-pum *n.* frozen food

냉동실 naeng-dong-sil *n.* freezer

냉동피자 naeng-dong-pi-ja *n.* frozen pizza

냉동하다 naeng-dong-ha-da *v.* refrigerate, deep-freeze

냉면 naeng-myeon *n.* cold noodle soup

냉방 naeng-bang *n.* air conditioning, air cooling system

냉방장치 naeng-bang-jang-chi *n.* air conditioner

냉수 naeng-su *n.* cold water

냉장고 naeng-jang-go *n.* refrigerator

냉장하다 naeng-jang-ha-da *v.* keep cold, keep on ice

냉전 naeng-jeon *n.* cold war

냉정하다 naeng-jeong-ha-da *v.* be cold-hearted, self-possessed

냉채 naeng-chae *n.* cold vegetable dishes

냉커피 naeng-keo-pi *n.* iced coffee

너그럽게 neo-geu-reop-ge *adv.* generously, broadmindedly

너그럽다 neo-geu-reop-da *v.* be broad-minded, be generous

너덜너덜하다 neo-deol-leo-deol-ha-da *v.* be tattered, be worn-out

너도나도 neo-do-na-do *pron.* everyone

너머 neo-meo *n.* beyond, the other side

너무 neo-mu *adv.* too much

너무나 neo-mu-na *adv.* too much

너무하다 neo-mu-ha-da *v.* be unreasonable, be too hard, be too bad

너저분하다 neo-jeo-bun-ha-da *v.* be shabby and untidy, be dirty, be nasty

너희 neo-hi *pron.* you, you all, you people

넉넉하다 neog-neo-ka-da *v.* be enough, be sufficient; be rich; be big-minded

넋 neok *n.* soul, spirit, ghost

널다 neol-da *v.* spread out, stretch, hang out to dry

널따랗다 neol-tta-ra-ta *v.* be rather wide, be extensive

널뛰기 neol-ttwi-gi *n.* seesaw, seesawing

널리 neol-li *adv.* widely, broadly, extensively; on a large scale, all over

널어놓다 neol-eo-no-ta *v.* spread out, hang out

넓다 neol-tta *v.* be wide, be spacious, be vast

넓이 neolb-i *n.* width

넓적다리 neop-jeok-da-ri *n.* thigh

넓적하다 neop-jeo-ka-da *v.* be flat

넓히다 neol-pi-da *v.* widen, enlarge, expand

넘기다 neom-gi-da *v.* bring across, pass over; throw down, fall; pass, spend; transfer, turn over; 무사히 올해를 넘겼다 mu-sa-hi ol-hae-reul neom-gyeot-da We made it through this year safely; 이 문제는 다음 정부에게 넘기십시오 i mun-je-neun da-eum jeong-bu-e neom-gi-sip-si-o Please hand this issue down to the next administration; 공을 나한테 넘기세요 gong-eul na-han-te neom-gi-se-yo Please pass the ball to me

넘다 neom-tta *v.* cross, go across; exceed, pass; overflow, run over; jump, hop

넘어가다 neom-eo-ga-da *v.* cross, go across, go over; sink, go down; fall into; fall down

넘어뜨리다 neom-eo-tteu-ri-da *v.* throw down, blow down, tip down; defeat, beat; overthrow, undermine

넘어오다 neom-eo-o-da *v.* fall, come down; vomit, throw up; be transferred; cross, cross over, go across; come over, surrender

넘어지다 neom-eo-ji-da *v.* fall down, collapse; be defeated, go bankrupt

넘치다 neom-chi-da *v.* overflow, run over; exceed, pass, be more than

넝쿨 neong-kul *n.* vine, runner *(plants)*

넣다 neo-ta *v.* put in, bring in; set in, insert; include, count; accommodate, admit; send; 국에 소금을 넣었다 gug-e so-geum-eul neo-eot-da I put some salt in the soup; 컴퓨터에 시디를 넣으면 프로그램이 돌아간다 keom-pyu-teo-e ssi-di-reul neo-eu-myeon peu-ro-geu-raem-i dol-a-gan-da When you insert a CD in your computer, the program starts; 이번에 나온 책까지 다 넣으면 모두 100권이다 I-beon-e na-on chaek-kka-ji da neo-eu-myeon mo-du baek-gwon-i-da Including those published this time, there are 100 books total; 아이를 사립학교에 넣었다 a-i-rul sa-ri-pak-gyo-e neo-eot-da I sent my kid to a private school

넣어주다 neo-eo-ju-da *v.* put in, bring in; set in, insert; include, count; accommodate, admit; send

네 ne *pron.* you, your; *n.* four; *adv.* yes; 네 책이 어떤거니 ne chaeg-i eo-tteon-geo-ni Which one is your book; 사과가 네개 있다 sa-gwa-ga ne-gae it-da There are four apples; 네, 그렇게 하겠습니다 ne geu-reo-ke ha-gess-eum-ni-da Yes, I will do it that way

네거리 ne-geo-ri *n.* four-way intersection, crossroads

네다섯 ne-da-seot *n.* four or five

네모 ne-mo *n.* square, rectangle

넥타이 nek-ta-i *n.* necktie

넥타이핀 nek-ta-i-pin *n.* necktie pin

넷 net *n.* four

넷째 net-jjae *n.* the fourth

녀석 nyeo-seok *n.* fellow, boy, guy

년 nyeon *n.* years; bitch*(profanity)*

노끈 no-kkeun *n.* string, cord

노년기 no-nyeon-gi *n.* old age

노동 no-dong *n.* labor

노동력 no-dong-nyeok *n.* manpower, labor force

노동자 no-dong-ja *n.* laborer

노동하다 no-dong-ha-da *v.* labor, work

노란색 no-ran-saek *adj.* yellow color

노랗다 no-ra-ta *v.* be yellow

노래 no-rae *n.* song; 노래 부르다 no-rae bu-reu-da *v.* sing a song

노래방 no-rae-bang *n.* karaoke room

노래자랑 no-rae-ja-rang *n.* amateur singing contest

노래하다 no-rae-ha-da *v.* sing a song

노려보다 no-ryeo-bo-da *v.* glare at, look angrily at

노력 no-ryeok *n.* effort

노력하다 no-ryeo-ka-da *v.* strive, endeavor, exert oneself

노름 no-reum *n.* gambling

노름하다 no-reum-ha-da *v.* gamble

노릇 no-reut *n.* role, function, duty

노벨상 no-bel-ssang *n.* Nobel prize

노선도 no-seon-do *n.* route map

노약자 no-yak-ja *n.* old/weak people

노여워하다 no-yeo-wo-ha-da *v.* be offended, be given offense

노예 no-ye *n.* slave, slavery

노이로제 no-i-ro-je *n.* neurosis

노인 no-in *n.* old people

노점 no-jeom *n.* street stall, roadside stand

노처녀 no-cheo-nyeo *n.* old maid, spinster

노천극장 no-cheon-geuk-jang *n.* open-air
theater

노총각 no-chong-gak *n.* old bachelor

노출하다 no-chul-ha-da *v.* expose, disclose

노크하다 no-keu-ha-da *v.* knock

노트 no-teu *n.* note

노트하다 no-teu-ha-da *v.* take notes

노티나다 no-ti na-da *v.* look old for one's age

노폐물 no-pye-mul *n.* waste matter

녹다 nok-da *v.* melt, thaw; dissolve

녹색 nok-saek *n.* green, green color

녹슬다 nok-seul-da *v.* gather rust, get rusty;
weaken, become dull

녹용 nog-yong *n.* antlers of a young stag
(*ingredient in traditional medicine*)

녹음 nog-eum *n.* sound recording

녹음기 nog-eum-gi *n.* recorder

녹음하다 nog-eum-ha-da *v.* record

녹이다 nog-i-da *v.* melt, fuse; dissolve, liquefy

녹차 nok-cha *n.* green tea

녹초가 되다 nok-cho-ga doe-da *v.phr.* be
exhausted, be dog-tired

녹화 no-kwa *n.* video recording

녹화하다 no-kwa-ha-da *v.* record on
video tape

논 non *n.* rice field, paddy field

논농사 non-nong-sa *n.* rice farming

논두렁 non-ttu-reong *n.* ridge between
rice fields

논리적 nol-li-jeok *adj.* logical

논문 non-mun *n.* thesis, dissertation, paper

논밭 non-bat *n.* paddy field

놀 nol *n.* glow

놀다 nol-da *v.* play; enjoy oneself, amuse
oneself

놀라게하다 nol-la-ge ha-da *v.* surprise
somebody

놀라다 nol-la-da *v.* be surprised, be startled,
be frightened; wonder at, marvel at

놀라움 nol-la-um *n.* surprise, astonishment,
horror, wonder

놀랍다 nol-lap-da *v.* be surprised, be frightened; be wonderful, be marvelous

놀러가다 nol-leo ga-da *v.* go out to play; go
to play

놀리다 nol-li-da *v.* laugh at; tease

놀림 nol-lim *n.* teasing, bantering

놀이 nol-i *n.* play, game, sports, pleasure

놀이공원 nol-i-gong-won *n.* amusement park

놀이기구 nol-i-gi-gu *n.* amusement park rides

놀이동산 nol-i-dong-san *n.* amusement park

놀이터 nol-i-teo *n.* playground

농구 nong-gu *n.* basketball

농구선수 nong-gu-seon-su *n.* basketball
player

농구하다 nong-gu-ha-da *v.* play basketball

농담 nong-dam *n.* joke

농담하다 nong-dam-ha-da *v.* joke, jest

농번기 nong-beon-gi *n.* busy time on the
farm (*season for planting and harvesting*)

농부 nong-bu *n.* farmer, peasant

농사 nong-sa *n.* farming

농사짓다 nong-sa-jit-da *v.* farm, cultivate

농산물 nong-san-mul *n.* agricultural
products, farm products

농수산물 nong-su-san-mul *n.* agricultural
and marine products

농악 nong-ak *n.* a sort of rural folk music

농약 nong-yak *n.* fertilizer

농어민 nong-eo-min *n.* farmers and
fishermen

농어촌 nong-eo-chon *n.* farming and fishing
villages

농업 nong-eop *n.* agriculture, farming

농업협동조합 nong-eop-hyeop-dong-jo-hap
n. agricultural cooperative

농작물 nong-jang-mul *n.* crops, harvest, farm
products

농장 nong-jang *n.* farm, ranch

농촌 nong-chon *n.* farm village

농한기 nong-han-gi *n.* slow season (*rest
time for farmers between harvest and next
sowing*)

높낮이 nom-naj-i *n.* high and low,
unevenness

높다 nop-da *v.* be high, be tall; be noble; be
expansive; be loud; 건물이 높다 geon-
mul-i nop-da The building is high; 신분
이 높은 사람 sin-bun-i no-peun sa-ram A
noble man; 가격이 높다 ga-gyeog-i nop-
da The price is high; 소리가 높다 so-ri-ga
nop-da The sound is loud

높이 no-pi *n.* height, elevation, loudness,
tone; *adv.* high, highly, loudly

높이다 no-pi-da *v.* raise, elevate, lift,
improve, boost

높임말 no-pim-mal *n.* honorific term, honorific words

놓다 no-ta *v.* put down, lay down; construct, install; inject

놓아두다 no-a-du-da *v.* leave as is, let alone

놓아주다 no-a-ju-da *v.* let go, set free, release

놓이다 no-i-da *v.* get put, be placed; feel relieved, feel at rest

놓치다 no-chi-da *v.* fail to catch, miss, let slip, let escape

뇌 noe *n.* brain, brains

뇌물 noe-mul *n.* bribe

누가 nu-ga *pron.* who (combination of 누구 and subject particle 가); 누가 선생님이세요 nu-ga seon-saeng-nim-i-se-yo Who is the teacher

누구 nu-gu *pron.* who, whose, whom; 누구 찾으세요 nu-gu chaj-eu-se-yo Who are you looking for/Whom do you seek

누구나 nu-gu-na *adv.* anyone

누군가 nu-gun-ga *adv.* whoever

누그러지다 nu-geu-reo-ji-da *v.* get milder, soften, cool down

누나 nu-na *n.* older sister (of a boy/man)

누님 nu-nim *n.* (hon.) older sister (of a boy/man)

누더기 nu-deo-gi *n.* tattered clothes, rags

누드 nu-deu *n.* nude

누룽지 nu-rung-ji *n.* scorched rice, hardened rice at bottom of stone rice bowl

누르다 nu-reu-da *v.* press down, push down, weigh down, suppress, oppress

누명쓰다 nu-myeong sseu-da *v.* be dishonored, be stigmatized

눅눅하다 nung-nu-ka-da *v.* be damp, be moist, be wet

눈 nun *n.* eye; snow, bud; 눈 나빠지다 nun na-ppa-ji-da eyesight is getting bad; 눈 오다 nun o-da *n.* snow; 눈 축제 nun chuk-je *n.* snow festival; 눈에 띄다 nun-e tti-da *v.* catch one's attention; 눈에 선하다 nun-e seon-ha-da *v.* be vivid, be distinct

눈감다 nun-gam-tta *v.* close one's eyes; die

눈곱 nun-kkop *n.* discharge from the eyes

눈금 nun-kkeum *n.* scale, gradation

눈길 nun-kkil *n.* line of vision; attention; snowy road

눈꺼풀 nun-kkeo-pul *n.* eyelid

눈동자 nun-ttong-ja *n.* pupil of the eye

눈뜨다 nun-tteu-da *v.* open one's eyes, wake up, be awakened

눈물 nun-mul *n.* tear; 눈물 흘리다 nun-mul heul-li-da *v.* shed tears, cry; 눈물이 나다 nun-mul-i na-da *v.* well up (with tears)

눈병 nun-ppyeong *n.* eye disease, sore eyes

눈보라 nun-bo-ra *n.* snowstorm

눈부시다 nun-bu-si-da *v.* be dazzling, be glaring; be brilliant, be gorgeous

눈빛 nun ppit *n.* glitter of one's eyes; expression in one's eyes (for reading another's intent or personality)

눈사람 nun-ssa-ram *n.* snowman

눈사태 nun-sa-tae *n.* avalanche

눈송이 nun-ssong-i *n.* snowflake

눈싸움 nun-ssa-um *n.* snowball fight; staring match

눈썹 nun-sseop *n.* eyebrow

눈앞 nun-ap *n.* before one's face, under one's nose; just ahead, close at hand

눌리다 nul-li-da *v.* be squeezed, be pressed, be pushed; be repressed, be oppressed

눕다 nup-da *v.* lie down, lay oneself down

눕히다 nu-pi-da *v.* make someone lie down

뉘우치다 nwi-u-chi-da *v.* regret, repent

뉴스 nyu-sseu *n.* news

느글거리다 neu-geul-geo-ri-da *v.* feel sick, feel nausea

느긋하다 neu geu-ta-da *v.* be relaxed, be comfortable, be carefree

느껴지다 neu-kkyeo-ji-da *v.* feel, be realized; be impressed, be moved

느끼다 neu-kki-da *v.* feel, realize, experience; be impressed, be moved

느끼하다 neu-kki-ha-da *v.* be too fat, be too rich

느낌 neu-kkim *n.* touch, feel

느닷없이 neu-dad-eops-i *adv.* suddenly, abruptly, all of sudden

느리다 neu-ri-da *v.* be slow, be sluggish

느림보 neu-rim-bo *n.* slow poke, dawdler

느릿느릿 neu-rin-neu-rit *adv.* slowly, sluggishly

느티나무 neu-ti-na-mu *n.* zelkova tree, willow tree

늑대 neuk-dae *n.* wolf

늑장부리다 neuk-jang-bu-ri-da *v.* slow up work, linger, dawdle

는 neun *part. (topic particle)*; 이 비행기는 한국으로 간다 i bi-haeng-gi-neun han-gug-eu-ro gan-da This airplane goes to Korea

늘 neul *adv.* always

늘다 neul-da *v.* increase, gain, grow; improve, make progress, advance

늘리다 neul-li-da *v.* increase, add, multiply; extend, enlarge; stretch

늘씬하다 neul-ssin-ha-da *v.* be slender, be slim

늘어가다 neul-eo-ga-da *v.* go on increasing, continue to increase

늘어놓다 neul-eo-no-ta *v.* scatter about, put in disorder; arrange, line up, display; talk away, rattle on

늘어뜨리다 neul-eo-tteu-ri-da *v.* hang down, suspend, dangle

늘이다 neul-i-da *v.* lengthen, extend, stretch, make longer

늙다 neuk-da *v.* be old, grow old

능력 neung-nyeok *n.* ability, capability, brain power, capacity

능률 neung-nyul *n.* efficiency

능률적 neung-nyul-jjeok *adj.* efficient

능숙하다 neung-su-ka-da *v.* be skilled, be skillful, be experienced

능청스럽다 neung-cheong-seu-reop-da *v.* be deceitful, be cunning, be sly, be wily

늦가을 neut-ga-eul *n.* late fall

늦게 neut-ge *adv.* late

늦겨울 neut-gyeo-ul *n.* late winter

늦다 neut-da *v.* be late; be behind, be delayed

늦더위 neut-deo-wi *n.* late summer heat

늦어지다 neuj-eo-ji-da *v.* become late, be delayed

늦잠 neut-jam *n.* late rising, morning sleep; 늦잠 자다 neut-jam ja-da *v.* rise late, sleep in

늦장마 neut-jang-ma *n.* late rainy season

늦추다 neut-chu-da *v.* relax; ease; slack, slacken, slow down; postpone, delay, extend

늦추위 neut-chu-wi *n.* late winter chill, late freeze

늪 neup *n.* swamp, marsh, bog

니코틴 ni-ko-tin *n.* nicotine

ㄷ

다 da *adv.* all, everything; almost, nearly; completely

다가가다 da-ga-ga-da *v.* step up to, go near, approach

다가서다 da-ga-seo-da *v.* step up to, go near, approach

다가앉다 da-ga-an-tta *v.* move one's seat closer, sit closer

다가오다 da-ga-o-da *v.* approach, come near

다녀가다 da-nyeo-ga-da *v.* drop in for a short visit

다녀오다 da-nyeo-o-da *v.* drop in; get back; be back

다니다 da-ni-da *v.* attend, come and go; attend; work in, work at

다달이 da-dal-i *adv.* every month, monthly

다되다 da-doe-da *v.* be all done, be all worn out

다듬다 da-deum-tta *v.* trim; nip; sort out; refine, polish

다락 da-rak *n.* attic, loft

다람쥐 da-ram-jwi *n.* squirrel, chipmunk

다르다 da-reu-da *v.* be different, be extraordinary, be uncommon; be disagree, not correspond

다름아니라 da-reum-a-ni-ra *adv.* be nothing but

다름없다 da-reum-eop-da *v.* be similar, be like, be the same, not be different

다름없이 da-reum-eops-i *adv.* equally, similarly, alike, in the same way

다리 da-ri *n.* leg; bridge; mediation

다리다 da-ri-da *v.* iron, press

다리미 da-ri-mi *n.* clothes iron

다리미질하다 da-ri-mi-jil-ha-da *v.* iron, press

다림질 da-rim-jil *n.* ironing

다림질하다 da-rim-jil-ha-da *v.* iron, press

다만 da-man *adv.* only, merely, simply, just

다목적 da-mok-jeok *adj.* multipurpose

다발 da-bal *count.* bundle, bunch

다방 da-bang *n.* tea house

다섯 da-seot *n.* five

다소 da-so *adv.* more or less, to some degree

다수 da-su *n.* large number; majority

다수결 da-su-gyeol *n.* decision by majority

다스 da-sseu *count.* dozen

다스리다 da-seu-ri-da *v.* rule over, govern, administer

다시 da-si *adv.* again, repeatedly

다시는 da-si-neun *adv.* again, any more

다시마 da-si-ma *n.* kelp

다양하게 da-yang-ha-ge *adv.* variously, diversely

다양하다 da-yang-ha-da *v.* be various, diverse

다음 da-eum *adj.* next, following; second

다음가다 da-eum-ga-da *v.* be second to, come after

다음날 da-eum-nal *n.* the following day

다음달 da-eum-ttal *n.* next month

다음부터 da-eum-bu-teo *adv.* from next time, from now on; 다음부터 그러지 마 da-eum-bu-teo geu-reo-ji ma Don't do that from now on

다음해 da-eum-hae *n.* next year

다이너마이트 da-i-neo-ma-i-teu *n.* dynamite

다이빙 da-i-bing *n.* diving

다이아몬드 da-i-a-mon-deu *n.* diamond

다이어트 da-i-eo-teu *n.* diet

다이어트하다 da-i-eo-teu-ha-da *v.* be on a diet

다이얼 da-i-eol *n.* dial

다정하게 da-jeong-ha-ge *adv.* affectionately, friendly, intimately

다정하다 da-jeong-ha-da *v.* be affectionate, be warm-hearted; be intimate, friendly

다지다 da-ji-da *v.* chop up, mince; harden

다짐하다 da-jim-ha-da *v.* pledge, swear, assure

다치다 da-chi-da *v.* be injured; get hurt

다큐멘터리 da-kyu-men-teo-ri *n.* documentary

다투다 da-tu-da *v.* fight, have a conflict, quarrel, argue; compete, struggle

다하다 da-ha-da *v.* become exhausted, be used up, terminate, be out; finish, accomplish, run out of

다행이다 da-haeng-i-da *v.* be lucky, be fortunate

다행히 da-haeng-hi *adv.* fortunately

다혈질 da-hyeol-jjil *n.* sanguine temperament

닦다 dak-da *v.* wipe, brush; polish, shine

닦이다 dakk-i-da *v.* be polished, be shined, be wiped

단 dan *count.* bunch, bundle

난계 dan-gye *n.* step, phase, stage

단골 dan-gol *n.* regular customer

단군 dan-gun *n.* Dan Gun *(founding father of the Korean nation)*

단군신화 dan-gun-sin-hwa *n.* myth(s) concerning Dan Gun

단단하다 dan-dan-ha-da *v.* be hard, be solid, be firm

단단히 dan-dan-ho *adv.* hard, solidly; tightly, firmly; greatly, severely

단독주택 dan-dok-ju-taek *n.* detached house

단백질 dan-baek-jil *n.* protein

단번에 dan-beon-e *adv.* only once, once and for all

단색 dan-saek *n.* single color

단순하다 dan-sun-ha-da *v.* be simple

단숨에 dan-sum-e *adv.* at a stretch, at a breath, at a stroke

단시간에 dan-si-gan-e *adv.* in brief

단시일에 dan-si-il-e *adv.* in short time

단식하다 dan-si-ka-da *v.* fast, abstain from food

단어 dan-eo *n.* word, vocabulary

단위 dan-wi *n.* unit, module

단일국가 dan-il-guk-ga *n.* one nation

단적으로 dan-jjeog-eu-ro *adv.* directly, flatly, plainly

단절하다 dan-jeol-ha-da *v.* be broken off

단점 dan-jjeom *n.* weak point, defect

단정하다 dan-jeong-ha-da *v.* be proper, be upright, be chaste; conclude, judge

단조롭다 dan-jo-rop-da *v.* be monotonous

단지 dan-ji *adv.* simply, merely, just

단짝 dan-jjak *n.* intimate friend

단체 dan-che *n.* organization, community, association

단추 dan-chu *n.* button, stud

단춧구멍 dan-chut-gu-meong *n.* button hole

단층집 dan-cheung-jjip *n.* single-story house

단칸방 dan-kan-ppang *n.* single room

단팥죽 dan-pat-juk *n.* sweet red-bean soup

단편소설 dan-pyeon-so-seol *n.* short story

단풍 dan-pung *n.* tinged autumn leaves; 단풍 들다 dan-pung deul-da *v.* turn autumnal colors

단풍나무 dan-pung-na-mu *n.* maple tree

닫다 dat-da *v.* shut, close

닫히다 da-chi-da *v.* be shut, be closed

달 dal *n.* month, months; moon; 달 구경 dal gu-gyeong enjoying *n.* the moon, moonlight party (*also known as harvest festival or January festival*)

달걀 dal-gyal *n.* egg

달걀형 dal-gyal-hyeong *n.* oval

달구지 dal-gu-ji *n.* wagon, oxcart

달다 dal-da *v.* be sweet, be sugary; attach, put up, hang out; weigh, measure

달라고 하다 dal-la-go ha-da *v.phr.* request to give

달라붙다 dal-la-but-da *v.* stick to

달라지다 dal-la-ji-da *v.* change, be amended

달래다 dal-lae-da *v.* calm down, pacify, soothe

달러 dal-leo *n.* dollar

달려가다 dal-lyeo-ga-da *v.* run, rush, dash

달려들다 dal-lyeo-deul-da *v.* attack, jump at

달려오다 dal-lyeo-o-da *v.* come running, hasten to

달력 dal-lyeok *n.* calendar

달리 dal-li *adv.* differently, in a different way, distinctively

달리기 dal-li-gi *n.* race

달리다 dal-li-da *v.* run, rush; sag; be tired; hang, be attached; depend on

달마다 dal-ma-da *adv.* every month

달밤 dal-ppam *n.* moonlit night

달빛 dal-ppit *n.* moonlight, moonshine

달아나다 dal-a-na-da *v.* run away, get away, escape, flee

달아보다 dal-a-bo-da *v.* weigh, check the weight

달콤하다 dal-kom-ha-da *v.* be sweetish, be sugary, be honeyed

달팽이 dal-paeng-i *n.* snail

닭 dak *n.* chicken

닭고기 dalk-go-gi *n.* chicken (*meat*)

닮다 dam-tta *v.* resemble, be alike

닳다 dal-ta *v.* wear out, be worn

담 dam *n.* wall, fence

담그다 dam-geu-da *v.* soak; pickle, preserve

담기다 dam-gi-da *v.* be put in, be dished up; be included

담다 dam-tta *v.* put into, fill, dish up

담담하다 dam-dam-ha-da *v.* be plain; be light; be unconcerned

담당자 dam-dang-ja *n.* person in charge, person who undertakes the job

담당하다 dam-dang-ha-da *v.* undertake

담배 dam-bae *n.* cigarette; 담배 피우다 dam-bae pi-u-da *v.* smoke a cigarette

담배꽁초 dam-bae-kkong-cho *n.* half-smoked cigarette

담뱃갑 dam-baet-gap *n.* cigarette case

답 dap *n.* answer

답답하다 dap-da-pa-da *v.* be stuffy; feel frustrated, feel closed in

답장 dap-jang *n.* reply letter, answer; 답장 쓰다 dap-jang sseu-da *v.* write a reply (*letter*)

닷새 dat-sae *n.* five days

당근 dang-geun *n.* carrot

당분 dang-bun *n.* sugar

당분간 dang-bun-gan *adv.* for the time being, until further notice

당시 dang-si *adv.* at that time, in those days

당신 dang-sin *pron.* you; dear, darling

당연하다 dang-yeon-ha-da *v.* be fair, reasonable, natural

당장 dang-jang *adv.* on the spot, immediately, at once

당첨되다 dang-cheom-doe-da *v.* win the prize

당초에 dang-cho-e *adv.* at first, initially, originally

당하다 dang-ha-da *v.* experience; encounter, come upon; keep up with, stand

당황스럽다 dang-hwang-seu-reop-da *v.* be confused, lose one's head

당황하다 dang-hwang-ha-da *v.* be confused, lose one's head; be embarrassed

닿다 dat-da *v.* reach, touch; arrive at, get to; have connection with, get in touch with

대 dae *affix.* versus

대가 dae-kka *n.* price, cost

대가족 dae-ga-jok *n.* extended family, large family

대강 dae-gang *adv.* roughly, cursorily

대개 dae-gae *adv.* mostly, generally, almost, mainly

대견하다 dae-gyeon-ha-da *v.* confront, stand face to face

대관령 dae-gwal-lyeong *n.* Dae Gwan (*mountain ridge in Korea*)

대굴대굴 dae-gul-dae-gul *adv.* rolling continuously (*gaining momentum*)

대궐 dae-gwol *n.* royal palace

대규모 dae-gyu-mo *n.* large scale

대극장 dae-geuk-jang *n.* auditorium, big size hall

대나무 dae-na-mu *n.* bamboo

대낮 dae-nat *n.* the middle of the day, high noon

대다 dae-da *v.* place, put, lay, moor; feel, touch; 배를 여기에 대세요 bae-reul yeo-gi-e dae-se-yo Please moor your boat here; 손을 대지 마세요 son-eul dae-ji ma-se-yo Don't touch

대다수 dae-da-su *n.* large majority, the greater part

대단하다 dae-dan-ha-da *v.* be wonderful, be great, be intense, be serious

대단히 dae-dan-hi *adv.* very much, greatly, seriously

대답 dae-dap *n.* answer

대답하다 dae-da-pa-da *v.* answer, reply

대답해주다 dae-da-pae-ju-da *v.* answer, reply

대대로 dae-dae-ro *adv.* generation after generation

대대적으로 dae-dae-jeog-eu-ro *adv.* on a large scale

대덕과학연구단지 dae-deok-gwa-hak-yeon-gu-dan-ji *n.* Dae Deok Science Complex in Korea

대도시 dae-do-si *n.* big city

대로 dae-ro *part.* like, as, according to; as soon as, immediately after; 들은 대로 쓰세요 deul-eun dae-ro sseu-se-yo Please write what you hear; 끝나는 대로 올게 kkeun-na-neun dae-ro ol-kke I will come immediately after I finish

대륙 dae-ryuk *n.* continent

대륙성 dae-ryuk-seong *adj.* continental

대만원 dae-man-won *n.* full house, crowded audience

대머리 dae-meo-ri *n.* bald head, baldheaded person

대문 dae-mun *n.* gate, front gate

대번에 dae-beon-e *adv.* at once, immediately, directly

대법원 dae-beob-won *n.* Supreme Court

대보다 dae-bo-da *v.* compare with, measure

대보름 dae-bo-reum *n.* the 15th of the first lunar month

대부분 dae-bu-bun *adv.* mostly, mainly; greater part, most

대사관 dae-sa-gwan *n.* embassy

대서양 dae-seo-yang *n.* Atlantic Ocean

대신 dae-sin *adv.* instead of, by way of compensation

대신하다 dae-sin-ha-da *v.* take the place of, act as a substitute

대야 dae-ya *n.* basin, washbasin, washbowl

대여섯 dae-yeo-seot *n.* five or six

대왕 dae-wang *n.* the Great King; 세종대왕이 한글을 만드셨다 se-jong-dae-wang-i han-geul-eul man-deu-syeot-da The Great King Se-jong invented the Korean alphabet

대웅전 dae-ung-jeon *n.* main temple

대위 dae-wi *n.* captain, first lieutenant

대이동 dae-i-dong *n.* massive movement, mass exodus

대인 dae-in *n.* adult

대자연 dae-ja-yeon *n.* Mother Nature

대장 dae-jang *n.* general, admiral; leader, captain

대전 dae-jeon *n.* Dae Jeon (*city in Korea*)

대접하다 dae-jeo-pa-da *v.* treat, treat to

대조하다 dae-jo-ha-da *v.* contrast

대주다 dae-ju-da *v.* supply, provide

대중 dae-jung *n.* public, popular

대중교통 dae-jung-gyo-tong *n.* public transportation

대중음악 dae-jung-eum-ak *n.* pop music

대청소 dae-cheong-so *n.* general cleaning, house cleaning; Spring cleaning

대체로 dae-che-ro *adv.* generally

대추 dae-chu *n.* jujube

대출 dae-chul *n.* lending, loan

대출인 dae-chul-in *n.* borrower

대출하다 dae-chul-ha-da *v.* lend out, loan out, check out

대충 dae-chung *adv.* almost, nearly, roughly

대통령 dae-tong-nyeong *n.* president *(of a country)*

대포 dae-po *n.* cannon

대표 dae-pyo *n.* representative; representation

대표작 dae-pyo-jak *n.* masterpiece

대표적 dae-pyo-jeok *adj.* representative

대표하다 dae-pyo-ha-da *v.* represent, stand for

대하다 dae-ha-da *v.* face, confront

대학 dae-hak *n.* university

대학교 dae-hak-gyo *n.* university, college

대학로 dae-hang-no *n.* college avenue, college street

대학생 dae-hak-saeng *n.* university student, college student

대학생활 dae-hak-saeng-hwal *n.* college life

대학원 dae-hag-won *n.* graduate school

대학원생 dae-hag-won-saeng *n.* graduate student

대합실 dae-hap-sil *n.* waiting place in a station/terminal

대항하다 dae-hang-ha-da *v.* oppose; rival; cope with

대해서 dae-hae-seo *part.* about, in regard to

대형 dae-hyeong *n.* large size

대화 dae-hwa *n.* conversation

대화하다 dae-hwa-ha-da *v.* talk, have a talk with

대회 dae-hoe *n.* great meeting, general meeting, convention, tournament

댁 daek *n.* your house, *(hon.)* your family

댄스 daen-sseu *n.* dance

댄스뮤직 daen-sseu-myu-jik *n.* dance music

댐 ttaem *n.* dam

더 deo *adv.* more; 더 이상 deo i-sang *adv.* any more

더군다나 deo-gun-da na *adv.* moreover, further, besides

더러워지다 deo-reo-wo-ji-da *v.* get dirty

더럽다 deo-reop-da *v.* be dirty

더럽히다 deo-reo-pi-da *v.* make unclean, stain; dishonor, disgrace

더미 deo-mi *n.* heap, pile

더욱 deo-uk *adv.* more, all the more

더위 deo-wi *n.* the heat, hot weather; heatstroke; 더위 먹다 deo-wi meok-da *v.* be affected by the heat

더하다 deo-ha-da *v.* get worse, grow harder; add up, sum up

덕분에 deok-bun-e *adv.* thanks to

덕수궁 deok-su-gung *n.* Deok Su *(palace in Seoul)*

덕택에 deok-taeg-e *adv.* due to, owing to

던져두다 deon-jeo-du-da *v.* put to one side, leave; lay aside

던져버리다 deon-jeo-beo-ri-da *v.* throw, toss, pitch

던지다 deon-ji-da *v.* throw, toss, pitch

덜 deol *adv.* less, incompletely

덜다 deol-da *v.* lighten, mitigate; subtract, remove

덜렁대다 deol-leong-dae-da *v.* be restless; conduct oneself flippantly

덤 deom *n.* extra, anything thrown in

덤불 deom-bul *n.* thicket, bush

덥다 deop-da *v.* be hot, be heated

덧니 deon-ni *n.* snaggletooth

덧붙이다 deot-bu-chi-da *v.* add to, append, attach

덩굴 deong-gul *n.* vine

덩어리 deong-eo-ri *n.* lump, mass; cluster, clump

덫 deot *n.* trap, snare

덮개 deop-gae *n.* bedding; lid

덮다 deop-da *v.* cover, conceal, shut, close

덮밥 deop-bap *n.* bowl of rice topped with...; 불고기 덮밥 하나 주세요 bul-go-gi deop-bap ha-na ju-se-yo Please give me a dish of rice with bulgogi

덮어두다 deop-eo-du-da *v.* pass over, unnoticed; keep secret

덮여있다 deop-yeo-it-da *v.* be covered, be veiled

덮이다 deop-i-da *v.* be covered, be veiled

데 de *n.* spot, place, point

데굴데굴 de-gul-de-gul *adv.* tumbling down *(rolling down without stop)*

데다 de-da *v.* be burnt, get scorched

데려가다 de-ryeo-ga-da *v.* take a person with; 아픈 사람을 병원에 데려갔다 a-peun sa-ram-eul byeong-won-e de-ryeo-gat-da I took a sick person to the hospital

데려다가 de-ryeo-da-ga *adv.* having brought

데려오다 de-ryeo-o-da *v.* bring a person along; 배우자를 데려와도 됩니다 bae-u-ja-reul de-ryeo-wa-do doem-ni-da You can bring your spouse along with you

데리고가다 de-ri-go ga-da *v.* bring someone to some place

데리고 de-ri-go *part.* bringing someone; 아이를 데리고 학교에 갔다 a-i-reul de-ri-go hak-gyo-e gat-da I went to school with my kid

데모 de-mo *n.* demonstration

데모하다 de-mo-ha-da *v.* demonstrate

데뷔하다 de-bwi-ha-da *v.* make one's debut

데우다 de-u-da *v.* warm, heat, reheat

데이터 de-i-teo *n.* data

데이터베이스 de-i-teo-be-i-sseu *n.* database

데이트 de-i-teu *n.* date, going out

데이트하다 de-i-teu-ha-da *v.* date, go out

도 do *part.* also, too; *n.* degree; 그 사람도 미팅에 올거예요 geu sa-ram-do mi-ting-e ol-kkeo-ye-yo He will also come to the meeting; 오늘 기온이 50도이다 o-neul gi-on-i o-sip-do-i-da Today's temperature is 50°F

도구 do-gu *n.* instrument, tool

도깨비 do-kkae-bi *n.* goblin

도끼 do-kki *n.* ax

도넛 do-neot *n.* doughnut

도대체 do-dae-che *adv.* on earth, in the world

도둑 do-duk *n.* thief, bugler

도둑질하다 do-duk-jil-ha-da *v.* steal, rob

도려내다 do-ryeo-nae-da *v.* scoop out, cut out

도로 do-ro *n.* road, way, street

도리어 do-ri-eo *adv.* on the contrary, instead, rather

도마 do-ma *n.* chopping board

도마뱀 do-ma-baem *n.* lizard

도망가다 do-mang-ga-da *v.* run away, escape

도망치다 do-mang-chi-da *v.* run away, escape

도박하다 do-ba-ka-da *v.* gamble, play for money

도배하다 do-bae-ha-da *v.* to wallpaper

도봉산 do-bong-san *n.* Mt. Do Bong *(in Seoul)*

도서 do-seo *n.* islands; books, publications

도서관 do-seo-gwan *n.* library

도시 do-si *n.* city

도시락 do-si-rak *n.* lunch; lunch package

도시생활 do-si-saeng-hwal *n.* city life

도심지 do-sim-ji *n.* downtown

도와드리다 do-wa-deu-ri-da *v. (hon.)* help, assist

도와주다 do-wa-ju-da *v.* help, assist

도움 do-um *n.* help, aid, assistant, support

도움되다 do-um-doe-da *v.* be helpful, be of help to

도자기 do-ja-gi *n.* ceramic ware, pottery

도장 do-jang *n.* stamp, seal; drill hall

도저히 do-jeo-hi *adv.* not at all, by any possibility

도적 do-jeok *n.* thief, bugler

도중에 do-jung-e *adv.* on the way

도착 do-chak *n.* arrival

도착하다 do-cha-ka-da *v.* arrive

도청 do-cheong *n.* provincial office

도청소재지 do-cheong-so-jae-ji *n.* the seat of a provincial office

도토리 do-to-ri *n.* acorn

도표 do-pyo *n.* chart, diagram

독 dok *n.* poison; jar, vat

독감 dok-gam *n.* influenza

독립 dong-nip *n.* independence

독립기념일 dong-nip-gi-nyeom-il *n.* Independence Day

독립문 dong-nim-mun *n.* Dok Rip Gate *(historic site in Seoul)*

독립운동 dong-nip-un-dong *n.* independence movement

독립하다 dong-ni-pa-da *v.* become independent

독불장군 dok-bul-jang-gun *n.* an assertive man

독서 dok-seo *n.* reading books

독서하다 dok-seo-ha-da *v.* read books

독수리 dok-su-ri *n.* eagle

독신 dok-sin *n.* bachelorhood

독약 dog-yak *n.* poison, poisonous drug

독일 dog-il *n.* Germany

독자 dok-ja *n.* reader, subscriber

독재 dok-jae *n.* dictatorship

독재자 dok-jae-ja *n.* dictator

독창 dok-chang *n.* solo *(vocal)*

독창성 dok-chang-sseong *n.* originality

독특하다 dok-teu-ka-da *v.* be peculiar, be unique

독하다 do-ka-da *v.* be strong; be firm; be spiteful; be poisonous

돈 don *n.* money; 돈 내다 don nae-da *v.* pay with money; 돈 찾다 don chat-da *v.* withdraw money from the bank

돈까스 don-kka-sseu *n.* pork cutlet

돈주머니 don-jju-meo-ni *n.* moneybag

돈지갑 don-jji-gap *n.* coin purse

돋보기 dot-bo-gi *n.* glasses *(for the elderly)*

돌 dol *n.* first birthday; anniversary; stone, rock

돌고래 dol-go-rae *n.* dolphin, porpoise

돌기둥 dol-gi-dung *n.* stone pillar

돌다 dol-da *v.* turn, go round; circulate

돌담 dol-ttam *n.* stone wall

돌대가리 dol-dae-ga-ri *n.* stupid person

돌덩이 dol-tteong-i *n.* piece of stone, pebble, rock

돌려놓다 dol-lyeo-no-ta *v.* change direction, turn around

돌려보내다 dol-lyeo-bo-nae-da *v.* return, give back, send back

돌려주다 dol-lyeo-ju-da *v.* return, give back, send back

돌리다 dol-li-da *v.* turn, revolve, spin; change; pass round, hand round

돌림병 dol-lim-ppyeong *n.* contagious disease

돌멩이 dol-meng-i *n.* stone, a piece of stone

돌무더기 dol-mu-deo-gi *n.* stone pile, pile of stone

돌무덤 dol-mu-deom *n.* stone grave

돌보다 dol-bo-da *v.* take care of, look after

돌부처 dol-bu-cheo *n.* stone Buddha

돌아가다 dol-a-ga-da *v.* go back, return; go round, make a detour; work, operate

돌아가시다 dol-a-ga-si-da *v.* pass away, die

돌아다니다 dol-a-da-ni-da *v.* wander about, patrol; prevail

돌아다보다 dol-a-da-bo-da *v.* look back, look back upon, retrospect; take notice of

돌아서다 dol-a-seo-da *v.* turn one's back on, turn against; turn on one's heels

돌아앉다 dol-a-an-tta *v.* sit with one's back to

돌아오다 dol-a-o-da *v.* return, come back; come around; go around; fall on

돌잔치 dol-jan-chi *n.* celebration of a baby's first birthday

돌팔이 dol-pal-i *n.* quack *(doctor)*

돌하루방 dol-ha-ru-bang *n.* stone statue in Jeju island

돕다 dop-da *v.* help, aid; give relieve

돗자리 dot-ja-ri *n.* mat, matting

동갑 dong-gap *n.* the same age

동굴 dong-gul *n.* cave, cavern

동그라미 dong-geu-ra-mi *n.* circle

동그랗다 dong-geu-ra-ta *v.* be round, circle

동급생 dong-geup-saeng *n.* classmate

동기 dong-gi *n.* motive; the same class; siblings; 동기가 뭐니 dong-gi ga mwo-ni What is your motive; 그와 나는 대학 동기다 geu-wa na-neun dae-hak dong-gi-da He and I are in the same university class; 저는 동기간이 많습니다 jeo-neun dong-gi-gan-i man-seum-ni-da I have many siblings

동남아시아 dong-nam-a-si-a *n.* Southeast Asia

동네 dong-ne *n.* neighborhood, village

동대문 dong-dae-mun *n.* East Gate *(historic site in Korea)*

동료 dong-nyo *n.* companion, colleague

동메달 dong-me-dal *n.* copper medal

동물 dong-mul *n.* animal

동물원 dong-mul-won *n.* zoo

동복 dong-bok *n.* winter clothes

동부 dong-bu *n.* east coast; eastern part

동사무소 dong-sa-mu-so *n.* district office

동상 dong-sang *n.* bronze statue; frostbite

동생 dong-saeng *n.* younger sibling

동서 dong-seo *n.* east and west

동서남북 dong-seo-nam-buk *n.* north, south, east, and west *(the four directions)*

동시에 dong-si-e *adv.* at the same time; at a time

동식물 dong-sing-mul *n.* animals and plants

동아리 dong-a-ri *n.* group, companions

동안 dong-an *adv.* during, while; interval, space, span, period

동양 dong-yang *n.* the East

동양사 dong-yang-sa *n.* Asian history

동양학 dong-yang-hak *n.* Asian studies

동양화 dong-yang-hwa *n.* Asian brush painting

동요 dong-yo *n.* children's song

동유럽 dong-yu-reop *n.* Eastern Europe

동작 dong-jak *n.* action, movement, motions, behavior, gestures

동전 dong-jeon *n.* coin, copper coin

동점 dong-jjeom *n.* the same grade, the same point, tie

동지 dong-ji *n.* winter solstice

동짓달 dong-jit-dal *n.* 11th month of the lunar calendar

동쪽 dong-jjok *n.* the east

동창 dong-chang *n.* fellow student, schoolmate

동창모임 dong-chang-mo-im *n.* alumni reunion, alumni meeting

동창생 dong-chang-saeng *n.* fellow student, schoolmate

동창회 dong-chang-hoe *n.* alumni meeting, alumni reunion

동치미 dong-chi-mi *n.* turnips pickled in salt water

동트다 dong-teu-da *v.* the day break

동포 dong-po *n.* brothers, fellow countrymen

동해 dong-hae *n.* the East Sea

동해안 dong-hae-an *n.* east coast

동향 dong-hyang *n.* eastern exposure, facing east

동호회 dong-ho-hoe *n.* club, society of people *(who share a hobby)*

동화 dong-hwa *n.* fairy tale

동화책 dong-hwa-chaek *n.* fairy tale book

돛 dot *n.* sail, canvas

돛단배 dot-dan-bae *n.* sailing boat

돛대 dot-dae *n.* mast, stick

돼지 dwae-ji *n.* pig

돼지고기 dwae-ji-go-gi *n.* pork

되게 doe-ge *adv.* extremely, very, severely

되다 doe-da *v.* become, get, grow; turn into; consist of

되도록 doe-do-rok *adv.* as much as possible, as much as you can

되돌려주다 doe-dol-lyeo-ju-da *v.* return, give back, send back

되돌리다 doe-dol-li-da *v.* restore; put back

되돌아가다 doe-dol-a-ga-da *v.* turn back, retrace one's steps; go back

되돌아오다 doe-dol-a-o-da *v.* come back, retrace one's steps

되살아나다 doe-sal-a-na-da *v.* revive, restore

되어가다 doe-eo-ga-da *v.* be turning out

되풀이하다 doe-bul-i-ha-da *v.* repeat, do over again

된장 doen-jang *n.* soy bean paste (*soup ingredient*)

된장국 doen-jang-kkuk *n.* soy bean paste soup

된장찌개 doen-jang-jji-gae *n.* soy bean paste stew

두 du *adj.* two; 두 번째 du beon-jjae the second time

두고가다 du-go ga-da *v.* leave behind, forget

두고오다 du-go o-da *v.* mislay, misplace, leave behind, forget

두고두고 du-go-du-go *adv.* many times, from time to time

두근거리다 du-geun-geo-ri-da *v.* palpitate, throb

두근두근 du-geun-du-geun *adv.* palpitating, throbbing

두꺼비 du-kkeo-bi *n.* toad

두껍다 du-kkeop-da *v.* be thick, be heavy

두께 du-kke *n.* thickness

두다 du da *v.* put, place, lay, deposit; keep store; leave

두드러기 du-deu-reo-gi *n.* rash, hives

두드리다 du-deu-ri-da *v.* beat, hit, strike, knock

두들기다 du-deul-gi-da *v.* beat, hit, strike

두려워하다 du-ryeo-wo-ha-da *v.* be afraid of, be scared of

두루마기 du-ru-ma-gi *n.* Korean overcoat

두루마리 du-ru-ma-ri *n.* roll of paper

두리번거리다 du-ri-beon-geo-ri-da *v.* look around

두말하다 du-mal-ha-da *v.* repeat a word, say again; break one's word

두부 du-bu *n.* tofu

두세 du-se *adj.* two or three

두통 du-tong *n.* headache

두통거리 du-tong-kkeo-ri *n.* source of constant anxiety

둔하다 dun-ha-da *v.* be dull, slow, stupid; blunt

둘 dul *n.* two

둘러보다 dul-leo-bo-da *v.* give a look around, look around

둘러싸다 dul-leo-ssa-da *v.* surround, besiege

둘러싸이다 dul-leo-ssa-i-da *v.* be surrounded, be besieged

둘러앉다 dul-leo-an-tta *v.* sit in a circle

둘레 dul-le *n.* circumference, girth

둘째 dul-jjae *n.* the second, number two; 저는 둘째 아들입니다 jeo-neun dul-jjae a-deul im-ni-da I am the second oldest son

둥그렇다 dung-geu-reo-ta *v.* be round, circular, globular

둥글다 dung-geul-da *v.* be round, circular, globular

둥둥 dung-dung *adv.* rub-a-dub; floating

둥실둥실 dung-sil-dung-sil *adv.* buoyantly, floating

둥지 dung-ji *n.* nest

뒤 dwi *n.* the back, behind; the future; end, conclusion

뒤꿈치 dwi-kkum-chi *n.* heels

뒤늦다 dwi-neut-da *v.* be too late, be behind time

뒤덮다 dwi-deop-da *v.* cover with, veil, overspread

뒤덮이다 dwi-deo-pi-da *v.* be covered, be overspread

뒤돌아보다 dwi-dol-a-bo-da *v.* turn one's head, look back

뒤따라 dwi-tta-ra *adv.* following

뒤지다 dwi-ji-da *v.* search for, look for

뒤집다 dwi-jip-da *v.* turn over; reverse, switch; overthrow, overturn

뒤집히다 dwi-ji-pi-da *v.* be turned inside out, be turned over; be overturned; be reversed

뒤쫓다 dwi-jjot-da *v.* follow up, pursue, run after

뒤통수 dwi-tong-su *n.* back side of head

뒷걸음질하다 dwit-geol-eum-jil-ha-da *v.* step backward, step back

뒷마당 dwin-ma-dang *n.* backyard

뒷문 dwin-mun *n.* back door

뒷줄 dwit-jul *n.* back row

뒹굴다 dwing-gul-da *v.* toss about in one's bed, tumble about

드나들다 deu-na-deul-da *v.* keep coming in and going out

드디어 deu-di-eo *adv.* at last, finally, eventually

드라마 deu-ra-ma *n.* drama

드라이버 deu-ra-i-beo *n.* screwdriver

드라이브 deu-ra-i-beu *n.* drive

드라이아이스 deu-ra-i-a-i-sseu *n.* dry ice

드라이클리닝 deu-ra-i-keul-li-ning *n.* dry cleaning

드럼 deu-reom *n.* drum

드레스 deu-re-sseu *n.* dress

드리다 deu-ri-da *v. (hon.)* give, offer

드물다 deu-mul-da *v.* be rare, unusual, uncommon

드시다 deu-si-da *v. (hon.)* eat

든든하다 deun-deun-ha-da *v.* be strong, be firm; be secure

듣다 deut-da *v.* listen; take a course

들 deul *n.* field; *part. (noun plural marker);* 들에 꽃이 많이 피었다 deul-e kkoch-i man-i pi-eot-da A lot of flowers bloom in the field; 사람들이 많다 sa-ram-deul-i man-ta There are a lot of people

들꽃 deul-kkot *n.* wild flower

들다 deul-da *v.* be included, be among; *(hon.)* eat, *(hon.)* have; lift, hold, take; cite, name, mention, state; cost

들러리 deul-leo-ri *n.* best man, bridesmaid

들려있다 deul-lyeo-it-da *v.* be held

들려주다 deul-lyeo-ju-da *v.* tell, inform, read to

들르다 deul-leu-da *v.* stop by, drop in

들리다 deul-li-da *v.* be heard, be audible, reach one's ear; be lifted, be raised

들어가다 deul-eo-ga-da *v.* enter, go in, get in, step in; join, be employed; contain, include

들어오다 deul-eo-o-da *v.* come in, enter, walk in

들어주다 deul-eo-ju-da *v.* grant

들여다보다 deul-yeo-da-bo-da *v.* look into, peep into; look hard, gaze at

들짐승 deul-jjim-seung *n.* wild animals

들창코 deul-chang-ko *n.* turned-up nose

들키다 deul-ki-da *v.* be found out, be discovered, be caught

들판 deul-pan *n.* field, plain

등 deung *n.* the back; grade, class; *adv.* etc.; 등
에 지다 deung-e ji-da *v.* carry on the back

등기우편 deung-gi-u-pyeon *n.* registered mail

등대 deung-dae *n.* lighthouse

등록하다 deung-no-ka-da *v.* register, enroll

등불 deung-ppul *n.* lamplight, lamp

등산 deung-san *n.* hiking, mountain climbing

등산가다 deung-san-ga-da *v.* go hiking

등산하다 deung-san-ha-da *v.* go hiking

등잔 deung-jan *n.* oil lamp

디자이너 di-ja-i-neo *n.* designer

디자인 di-ja-in *n.* design

따님 tta-nim *n. (hon.)* daughter

따다 tta-da *v.* pick up, pluck; open, cut out;
obtain

따뜻이 tta-tteus-i *adv.* warmly, kindly

따뜻하다 tta-tteu-ta-da *v.* be warm; be kind

따라읽다 tta-ra il-tta *v.* repeat out loud (*a
word or phrase*)

따라하다 tta-ra-ha-da *v.* repeat

따라가다 tta-ra-ga-da *v.* go with, follow;
obey; keep up with

따라서 tta-ra-seo *adv.* therefore

따라오다 tta-ra-o-da *v.* follow, come with,
keep up with

따라주다 tta-ra-ju-da *v.* pour in, fill

따로 tta-ro *adv.* separately, apart; addition-
ally, in addition; especially, in particular

따르다 tta-reu-da *v.* accompany, follow,
go after; be followed by, be attended by;
obey, yield; comply with; pour in, fill

따르면 tta-reu-myeon *part.* according to

따오다 tta-o-da *v.* pick off and bring

딱 ttak *adv.* accurately, exactly, precisely,
tightly; firmly; definitely; wide

딱딱하다 ttak-tta-ka-da *v.* be hard, be solid;
be strict, be rigid, be stiff

딱지 ttak-ji *n.* scab, crust; label, tag; ticket;
딱지를 떼다 ttak-ji-reul tte-da *v.* get a
ticket

딴 ttan *adj.* another, other, separate, different

딸 ttal *n.* daughter

딸기 ttal-gi *n.* strawberry

딸꾹질하다 ttal-kkuk-jil-ha-da *v.* hiccup, have
hiccups

딸랑거리다 ttal-lang-geo-ri-da *v.* jingle

땀 ttam *n.* sweat, perspiration; 땀 흘리다
ttam heul-li-da *v.* sweat; 운동을 하면

땀을 많이 흘린다 un-dong-eul ha-myeon
ttam-eul man-i heul-lin-da When I exercise
I sweat a lot

땀나다 ttam-na-da *v.* sweat

땀내다 ttam-nae-da *v.* induce perspiration,
work up a sweat

땀방울 ttam-ppang-ul *n.* beads of sweat

땅 ttang *n.* the earth, land, the ground;
territory; real estate; bang, with bang; 땅
파다 ttang pa-da *v.* dig the soil, dig into
the ground

땅굴 ttang-kkul *n.* tunnel

땅바닥 ttang-ppa-dak *n.* the ground

땅콩 ttang-kong *n.* peanut

때 ttae *n.* time, hour; when; occasion, season,
case; dirt, filth, stain; 비가 올 때는 밖에
나가지 마세요 bi-ga ol-ttae-neun bakk-e
na-ga-ji ma-se-yo Please do not go out
when it is raining; 옷에 때가 많다 os-e
ttae-ga man-ta These clothes have a lot
of stains

때때로 ttae-ttae-ro *adv.* occasionally, from
time to time

때리다 ttae-ri-da *v.* strike, hit, beat, knock,
tap; attack, denounce

때마침 ttae-ma-chim *adv.* at the right
moment, just in time

때문에 ttae-mun-e *part.* because of, on
account of, thanks to; 비 때문에 모임이
취소됐다 bi-ttae-mun-e mo-im-i chwi-so-
dwaet-da Because of the rain, the meeting
has been cancelled; 그분 때문에 우리
가 이겼다 geu-bun ttae-mun-e u-ri-ga
i-gyeot-da Thanks to him, we won

때우다 ttae-u-da *v.* substitute; solder *(metal)*

떠나다 tteo-na-da *v.* leave, start, depart;
break off, part from

떠내려가다 tteo-nae-ryeo-ga-da *v.* be
washed away, drift away

떠다니다 teo-da-ni-da *v.* float in the sky, drift

떠들다 tteo-deul-da *v.* make noise; speak
loudly

떠밀다 tteo-mil-da *v.* thrust aside, shove into

떠오르다 tteo-o-reu-da *v.* rise up, be up,
come across one's mind; rise to the surface

떠있다 tteo-it-da *v.* rise to the surface,
float up

떡 tteok *n.* Korean rice-cake

떡국 tteok-guk *n*. rice-cake soup

떡볶이 tteok-bokk-i *n*. rice-stick with vegetables

떨다 tteol-da *v*. tremble, quake, shake, thrill, vibrate

떨리다 tteol-li-da *v*. tremble, shiver, quake, shake

떨어뜨리다 tteol-eo-tteu-ri-da *v*. drop something, throw down; miss

떨어지다 teol-eo-ji-da *v*. fall, drop, crash, come down; be short of, run out; be worn out

떼 tte *n*. group, crowd, herd; impossible demand, persistent demand

떼다 tte-da *v*. take off, remove; draw apart, separate; break

떼어내다 tte-eo-nae-da *v*. take off, remove; draw apart, separate; break

떼어놓다 tte-eo-no-ta *v*. draw apart, separate

또 tto *adv*. again, repeatedly; also, too

또다시 tto-da-si *adv*. again, once more, afresh

또래 tto-rae *n*. of the same age group

또한 tto-han *adv*. too, also, as well; moreover, further

똑같다 ttok-gat-da *v*. be the same

똑같이 ttok-ga-chi *adv*. equally, evenly, impartially

똑딱거리다 ttok-ttak-geo-ri-da *v*. tick-tock, click-clock

똑똑 ttok-ttok *adv*. rapping, knocking; dripping, dropping

똑똑하다 ttok-tto-ka-da *v*. be clear, be distinct; be smart, be bright

똑똑히 ttok-tto-ki *adv*. clearly, distinctly; brightly, smartly, intelligently

똑바로 ttok-ba-ro *adv*. straight, in a straight line, directly; honestly, frankly

똑바르다 ttok-ba-reu-da *v*. be straight, be upright, be erect

뚜껑 ttu-kkeong *n*. lid, cover, cap

뚜렷하다 ttu-ryeo-ta-da *v*. be distinctive, be vivid, be clear

뚝 ttuk *adv*. suddenly, unexpectedly; with a snap; with a thump

뚫다 ttul-ta *v*. bore, punch, make a hole; excavate; penetrate

뚫리다 ttul-li-da *v*. be pierced, get opened

뚫어지다 ttul-eo-ji-da *v*. bore, drill, be bored, be drilled

뚱뚱보 ttung-ttung-bo *n*. corpulent fellow, fatty

뚱뚱하다 ttung-ttung-ha-da *v*. be fat, corpulent

뚱보 ttung-bo *n*. corpulent fellow, fatty

뛰다 ttwi-da *v*. run, dash, rush; jump, leap; beat, pulsate

뛰어가다 ttwi-eo-ga-da *v*. run, dash, rush

뛰어나가다 ttwi-eo-na-ga-da *v*. run forward, run out

뛰어나다 ttwi-eo-na-da *v*. be outstanding

뛰어내리다 ttwi-eo-nae-ri-da *v*. jump down

뛰어넘다 ttwi-eo-neom-tta *v*. jump over; skip over

뛰어들다 ttwi-eo-deul-da *v*. jump into, rush into, run into

뛰어오다 ttwi-eo-o-da *v*. run along the way, come running

뛰쳐나가다 ttwi-cheo-na-ga-da *v*. run forward, run out

뛰쳐나오다 ttwi-cheo-na-o-da *v*. run along the way, come running

뜨개질 tteu-gae-jil *n*. knitting, knit work

뜨겁다 tteu-geop-da *v*. be hot, be heated, be burning

뜨다 tteu-da *v*. float, keep afloat; rise, come up; open; be awake

뜯다 tteut-da *v*. take away

뜯어보다 tteud-eo-bo-da *v*. open a package or letter and look inside

뜯어지다 tteud-eo-ji-da *v*. be torn; become ripped

뜻대로 tteut-dae-ro *adv*. as one likes, in one's own ways, just as wished

뜻밖에 tteut-bakk-e *adv*. quite unexpected, unlooked for

뜻밖의 tteut-bakk-ui *adj*. unexpected, surprising

뜻하다 tteu-ta-da *v*. plan, intend, determine; mean, signify

띄우다 ttui-u-da *v*. fly, let fly; float

ㄹ

라디오 ra-di-o *n.* radio

라면 ra-myeon *n.* ramen, instant noodles

라벨 ra-bel *n.* label

라스트신 ra-seu-teu-ssin *n.* last scene

라운지 ra-un-ji *n.* lounge

라이벌 ra-i-beol *n.* rival

라이터 ra-i-teo *n.* lighter

라이트 ra-i-teu *n.* light; right

라인 ra-in *n.* line

라켓 ra-ket *n.* racket

라틴 ra-tin *n.* Latin

란제리 ran-je-ri *n.* lingerie

랑 rang *part.* and, or, and so on; together with; 가게에서 옷이랑 신발을 샀다 ga-ge-e-seo os-i-rang sin-bal-eul sat-da I bought clothes and shoes at the store; 친구랑 쇼핑간다 chin-gu-rang shyo-ping-gan-da I'm going shopping with my friend

램프 raem-peu *n.* lamp

랩 raep *n.* lab; rap music

랭킹 raeng-king *n.* ranking

러닝메이트 reo-ning-me-i-teu *n.* running mate

러닝셔츠 reo-ning-syeo-cheu *n.* sweatshirt

러시아 reo-si-a *n.* Russia

러시아어 reo-si-a-eo *n.* Russian language

러시아워 reo-si-a-wo *n.* rush hour

런던 reon-deon *n.* London

레모네이드 re-mo-ne-i-deu *n.* lemonade

레몬 re-mon *n.* lemon

레스토랑 re-seu-to-rang *n.* restaurant

레슨 re-sseun *n.* lesson

레슬링 re-sseul-ling *n.* wrestling

레이더 re-i-deo *n.* radar

레이스 re-i-sseu *n.* race; lace

레이저 re-i-jeo *n.* laser

레인지 re-in-ji *n.* cooking stove

레일 re-il *n.* rail, railway line, railroad track

레저 re-jeo *n.* leisure

레저산업 re-jeo-san-eop *n.* leisure industry

레크리에이션 센터 re-keu-ri-e-i-syeon ssen-teo *n.* recreation center

렌즈 ren-jeu *n.* lens

렌터카 ren-teo-ka *n.* rental car

로 ro *part.* by, by means of, with; from, because of; to, forward; as, in the position; 볼펜으로 쓰세요 bol-pen-eu-ro sseu-se-yo Please write with a ball-point pen; 그이유로 우리는 헤어졌다그 이유로 geu i-yu-ro u-ri-neun he-eo-jeot-da That's the reason we separated; 서울로 가세요 seo-ul-lo ga-se-yo Please go to Seoul; 나는 도서관 사서로 일한다 na-neun do-seo-gwan sa-seo-ro il-han-da I am working as a librarian

로마 ro-ma *n.* Rome

로마법 ro-ma-ppeop *n.* Roman Law

로마신화 ro-ma-sin-hwa *n.* Roman mythology

로맨스 ro-maen-sseu *n.* romance, love affair

로맨틱 ro-maen-tik *adj.* romantic

로봇 ro-bot *n.* robot

로부터 ro-bu-teo *part.* from, out of; 친구 로부터 편지가 왔다 chin-gu-ro-bu-teo pyeon-ji-ga wat-da I got a letter from a friend

로비 ro-bi *n.* lobby

로빈 훗 ro-bin hut *n.* Robin Hood

로서 ro-seo *part.* as, for

로션 ro-syeon *n.* lotion

로써 ro-sseo *part.* with, by means of; as, for, with; as a consequence of

로열티 ro-yeol-ti *n.* royalty

로켓 ro-ket *n.* rocket

로큰롤 ro-keun-nol *n.* rock 'n roll

로프 ro-peu *n.* rope

롤러 블레이드 rol-leo beul-le-i-deu *n.* roller blade

롤러 스케이트 rol-leo seu-ke-i-teu *n.* roller skate

롤러 스케이트장 rol-leo seu-ke-i-teu-jang *n.* roller skating rink

루비 ru-bi *n.* ruby

룸메이트 rum-me-i-teu *n.* roommate

류머티즘 ryu-meo-ti-jeum *n.* rheumatism

르네상스 reu-ne-ssang-sseu *n.* Renaissance

를 reul *part. (object particle)*; 사과를 사세요 sa-gwa-reul sa-se-yo Please buy apples

리듬 ri-deum *n.* rhythm

리본 ri-bon *n.* ribbon

리사이틀 ri-ssa-i-teul *n.* recital

리셉션 ri-ssep-syeon *n.* reception

리스트 ri-seu-teu *n.* list
리어카 ri-eo-ka *n.* bicycle-drawn cart, pedi-cab
리터 ri-teo *n.* liter
리포트 ri-po-teu *n.* report

리허설 ri-heo-seol *n.* rehearsal
린스 rin-sseu *n.* conditioner; 린스 하다 rin-sseu ha-da *v.* apply conditioner
릴레이 ril-le-i *n.* relay race
립스틱 rip-seu-tik *n.* lipstick

□

마 ma *n.* linen
마개 ma-gae *n.* stopper, cork, plug
마구 ma-gu *adv.* carelessly, at random; hard, much
마구간 ma-gu-kkan *n.* stable, barn
마귀 ma-gwi *n.* evil spirit, devil, demon
마귀할멈 ma-gwi-hal-meom *n.* witch
마네킹 ma-ne-king *n.* mannequin
마녀 ma-nyeo *n.* witch
마누라 ma-nu-ra *n.* wife *(one's own)*
마늘 ma-neul *n.* garlic; 마늘 빵 ma-neul ppang *n.* garlic bread
마다 ma-da *part.* each, every, all
마당 ma-dang *n.* yard, garden
마당발 ma-dang-bal *n.* wide-sized foot; someone who knows a lot of people
마디 ma-di *n.* joint, knot; tune
마라톤 ma-ra-ton *n.* marathon
마련이다 ma-ryeon-i-da *v.* be supposed to do, be natural to do
마련하다 ma-ryeon-ha-da *v.* prepare
마루 ma-ru *n.* floor
마룻바닥 ma-rut-ba-dak *n.* floor
마르다 ma-reu-da *v.* be slim; be dry, wither; be thirsty
마른걸레 ma-reun geol-le *n.* dry floor cloth *(type of handle-less mop)*
마른반찬 ma-reun-ban-chan *n.* dried side dishes for meal
마른안주 ma-reun-an-ju *n.* dried snack for drinking
마리 ma-ri *count. (counter word for animals)*
마무리하다 ma-mu-ri-ha-da *v.* finish, complete, conclude
마법 ma-beop *n.* magic, black arts
마법사 ma-beop-sa *v.* magician, wizard
마부 ma-bu *n.* horse keeper
마사지 ma-ssa-ji *n.* massage

마술 ma-sul *n.* magic, black arts
마스크 ma-seu-keu *n.* mask
마시다 ma-si-da *v.* drink, swallow; breathe in, inhale, inspire
마약 ma-yak *n.* drugs
마약중독 ma-yak-jung-dok *n.* drug addiction
마을 ma-eul *n.* village
마음 ma-eum *n.* mind, heart, nature; consideration; attention; 마음 놓다 ma-eum no-ta *v.* set one's heart at ease, feel at rest; relax one's attention, be inattentive; 마음 좋다 ma-eum jo-ta *v.* be goodhearted; 마음에 들다 ma-eum-e deul-da *v.* like, love; 마음을 쓰다 ma-eum-eul sseu-da *v.* pay attention, feel sympathy; 마음이 곧다 ma-eum-i got-da *v.* have a rightful heart, be virtuous; 마음이 편해지다 ma-eum-i pyeon-hae-ji-da *v.* feel comfortable
마음껏 ma-eum-kkeot *adv.* to one's heart's content, to the full; with one's whole heart
마음대로 ma-eum-dae-ro *adv.* as one pleases, at one's convenience, of one's free will
마음먹다 ma-eum-meok-da *v.* intend to, mean to, think of; be determined, make up one's mind
마음속 ma-eum-ssok *n.* one's mind, one's heart
마음씨 ma-eum-ssi *n.* mind, temper, disposition
마이크 ma-i-keu *n.* microphone
마일 ma-il *n.* mile
마주보다 ma-ju-bo-da *v.* look at each other, look at each other face to face
마주서다 ma-ju-seo-da *v.* stand face to face, stand right opposite
마주앉다 ma-ju-an-tta *v.* sit face to face
마주잡다 ma-ju-jap-da *v.* hand in hand

마주치다 ma-ju-chi-da *v.* meet with, be faced by, come across

마중나가다 ma-jung na-ga-da *v.* go out to greet someone

마중나오다 ma-jung na-o-da *v.* come out to greet someone

마중하다 ma-jung-ha-da *v.* come/go out to greet someone

마지막 ma-ji-mak *n.* the last, the end

마지막으로 ma-ji-mag-eu-ro *adv.* finally, last

마지못해 ma-ji-mo-tae *adv.* against one's will, reluctantly

마차 ma-cha *n.* carriage, coach, cab

마찬가지 ma-chan-ga-ji *n.* the same, identical, equal, alike

마치 ma-chi *adv.* as if, just like

마치다 ma-chi-da *v.* finish, complete

마침 ma-chim *adv.* coincidently, opportunely

마침내 ma-chim-nae *n.* finally, at last, eventually

마흔 ma-heun *n.* forty

막 mak *adv.* just, just now, about to; carelessly, at random, severely; *n.* curtain; 지금 막 도착했다 ji-geum mak do-cha-kaet-da He arrived just now; 물건을 막 던지지 마세요 mul-geon-eul mak deon-ji-ji ma-se-yo Please do not toss the products carelessly; 막을 올리세요 mag-eul ol-li-se-yo Please raise the curtain

막걸리 mak-geol-li *n.* raw rice wine, undistilled sake

막국수 mak-guk-su *n.* noodle dish

막내 mang-nae *n.* youngest child, the lastborn

막내딸 mang-nae-ttal *n.* youngest daughter

막다 mak-da *v.* block, obstruct; close; screen off; defend, prevent

막다른 골목 mak-da-reun gol-mok *n.phr.* blind alley

막다른 집 mak-da-reun jip *n.phr.* house at the end of a blind alley

막대기 mak-dae-gi *n.* stick, rod, bar

막아내다 mag-a-nae-da *v.* ward off, keep away

막차 mak-cha *n.* the last train/bus

막판 mak-pan *n.* the last round, the final scene, the last moment

막히다 ma-ki-da *v.* be blocked, be congested, be held up, be stopped

만 man *part.* only, alone; *n.* ten-thousand

만끽하다 man-kki-ka-da *v.* have enough, enjoy full

만나다 man-na-da *v.* meet, interview, see

만남 man-nam *n.* meeting

만년필 man-nyeon-pil *n.* fountain pen

만두 man-du *n.* dumpling

만들다 man-deul-da *v.* make, create, manufacture, build

만약 man-yak *adv.* if, in case; 만약 내가 대통령이 되면 man-yak nae-ga dae-tong-nyeong-i doe-myeon If I am elected as President

만우절 man-u-jeol *n.* April Fool's Day

만원 man-won *n.* full house

만일 man-il *adv.* if, in case, suppose

만져보다 man-jeo-bo-da *v.* feel, touch, finger

만족하다 man-jo-ka-da *v.* be satisfied, be pleased

만지다 man-ji-da *v.* feel, touch, finger

만큼 man-keum *part.* as...as, so...so; how much/many; so...that, so as...to, enough... to; 아인슈타인만큼 똑똑하다 a-in-shyu-ta-in-man-keum ttok-tto-ka-da He is as smart as Einstein; 얼만큼 잤어 eol-man-keum jass-eo How much did you sleep; 목숨을 버릴만큼 너를 사랑해 mok-sum-eul beo-ril-man-keum neo-reul sa-rang-hae I love you so much that I would sacrifice my life

만화 man-hwa *n.* cartoon, comic book

만화영화 man-hwa-yeong-hwa *n.* animated film, cartoon

많다 man-ta *v.* be many, be much, be plenty; be frequent, to occur often

많아야 man-a-ya *adv.* at most

많이 man-i *adv.* much, many, plenty, in abundance; frequently, often

맏딸 mat-ttal *n.* the eldest daughter

맏아들 mad-a-deul *n.* the eldest son

말 mal *n.* words, talk, conversation, language, speech; end; horse; 말 되다 mal doe-da *v.* be reasonable, be sensible; 말을 막다 mal-eul mak-da *v.* stop someone's speech; 말이 통하다 mal-i tong-ha-da *v.* be able to communicate

말고 mal-go *part.* not...but..., instead of..., except; 커피 말고 물을 마시세요 keo-pi mal-go mul-eul ma-si-se-yo Please drink water, not coffee

말기 mal-gi *n.* last stage, the end

말다 mal-da *v.* cease, stop, not to do; roll up paper

말다툼하다 mal-da-tum-ha-da *v.* dispute, quarrel

말대꾸하다 mal-dae-kku-ha-da *v.* retort, talk back

말동무 mal-ttong-mu *n.* someone to talk to, someone with whom to chat

말라죽다 mal-la juk-da *v.* wither, dry up

말리다 mal-li-da *v.* dry; rolled up; make somebody stop doing something

말버릇 mal-ppeo-reut *n.* manner of speaking, way of talking

말복 mal-bok *n.* last heat wave (*in lunar calendar*)

말솜씨 mal-ssom-ssi *n.* one's ability to talk, speech skill

말실수하다 mal-ssil-ssu ha-da *v.* have a slip of the tongue, use improper language

말썽 mal-sseong *n.* trouble, dispute

말썽거리 mal-sseong-kkeo-ri *n.* cause of trouble, matter of complaint

말씀 mal-sseum *n. (hon.)* speech, talk, words

말씀하시다 mal-sseum-ha-si-da *v. (hon.)* speak, talk

말씨 mal-ssi *n.* speech style, way of speaking

말없이 mal-eops-i *adv.* without any words; without causing any trouble; without leave

말조심하다 mal-jo-sim-ha-da *v.* be careful of one's speech, watch what one says

말투 mal-tu *n.* one's way of talking, style of speech

말하다 mal-ha-da *v.* talk, speak, chat, mention

말하자면 mal-ha-ja-myeon *adv.* so to speak

말해주다 mal-hae-ju-da *v.* talk to someone, give information to someone

맑다 mal-tta *v.* be clear, be clean, be pure

맛 mat *n.* taste, flavor

맛보다 mat-bo-da *v.* taste, try the flavor of; experience

맛사지 크림 mat-sa-ji keu-rim *n.* massage cream

맛없다 mad-eop-da *v.* not taste good, unsavory

맛있다 mas-it-da *v.* be tasty, be delicious

망가뜨리다 mang-ga-tteu-ri-da *v.* break down, destroy, ruin, spoil

망가지다 mang-ga-ji-da *v.* break, be broken, be damaged

망년회 mang-nyeon-hoe *n.* year-end party, New Year's Eve party

망보다 mang-bo-da *v.* keep watch, look out for

망설이다 mang-seol-i-da *v.* hesitate, be hesitant

망신당하다 mang-sin-dang-ha-da *v.* disgrace oneself, humiliate oneself

망원경 mang-won-gyeong *n.* telescope, spyglass

망치 mang-chi *n.* hammer

망치다 mang-chi-da *v.* ruin, spoil, destroy

망하다 mang-ha-da *v.* go to ruin, be ruined, perish

맞다 mat-da *v.* be correct, be right; fit, suit; meet; agree with; receive; greet; be exposed; get hit

맞닿아있다 mat-da-a-it-da *v.* touch each other, come in contact with each other

맞먹다 man-meok-da *v.* be a match for, be equal to

맞벌이부부 mat-beol-i-bu-bu *n.* working couple

맞벌이하다 mat-beol-i-ha-da *v.* work together for a living (*in a marriage*)

맞붙다 mat-but-da *v.* stick together

맞서다 mat-seo-da *v.* stand opposite each other; stand against, hold out against

맞선 mat-seon *n.* marriage meeting, blind date

맞은편 maj-eun-pyeon *n.* the opposite side, the other side

맞이하다 maj-i-ha-da *v.* go to meet, greet, welcome

맞장구치다 mat-jang-gu chi-da *v.* chime in with others, echo another's words

맞추다 mat-chu-da *v.* put together, assemble; set right, correct; adjust, adapt; order

맞춰보다 mat-chwo-bo-da *v.* correct, adjust

맞히다 ma-chi-da *v.* hit the mark, guess right

맡기다 mat-gi-da *v.* leave something with a person, entrust, deposit

맡다 mat-da *v.* keep, take charge of, be entrusted with; get, obtain, receive; smell, scent

매 mae *n.* whip, rod; hawk, falcon

매끄럽다 mae-kkeu-reop-da *v.* be smooth, be sleek, be slippery

매끈하다 mae-kkeun-ha-da *v.* be smooth, be sleek

매너 mae-neo *n.* manners

매년 mae-nyeon *n.* every year

매다 mae-da *v.* tie, bind, knot, fasten

매달 mae-dal *n.* every month

매달다 mae-dal-da *v.* bind up, hang, suspend

매달리다 mae-dal-li-da *v.* be hung, be suspended, be tied down

매듭 mae-deup *n.* knot, tie, joint

매력 mae-ryeok *n.* charm, fascination, attractiveness

매맞다 mae-mat-da *v.* get flogged, be whipped, be hit, be beaten

매미 nae-mi *n.* cicada

매번 mae-beon *adv.* every time, very often, always

매우 mae-u *adv.* very, so, most, much

매일 mae-il *n.* everyday

매장 mae-jang *n.* store, shop; deposits; burial; 석유 매장량이 얼마나 됩니까 seog-yu mae-jang-nyang-i eol-ma-na doem-ni-kka How much is in the petroleum reserves

매점 mae-jeom *n.* booth, stand, stall

매주 mae-ju *n.* every week

매진 mae-jin *n.* sold out

매진되다 mae-jin-doe-da *v.* be sold out, run out of, sell out

매체 mae-che *n.* medium, media

매트 mae-teu *n.* mat

매표소 mae-pyo-so *n.* ticket booth

매표원 mae-pyo-won *n.* ticket vendor, box office employee

매해 mae-hae *n.* every year

맥주 maek-ju *n.* beer

맨 끝 maen kkeut *n.phr.* the very end

맨 뒤 maen dwi *n.phr.* the very last, the tail

맨 먼저 maen meon-jeo *n.phr.* at the very first, first of all

맨 아래 maen a-rae *n.phr.* the bottom

맨 앞 maen ap *n.phr.* the head, the very front

맨 위 maen wi *n.phr.* the top, the best

맨 처음 maen cheo-eum *n.phr.* at the very first, the very first, the original

맨발 maen-bal *n.* barefoot

맨손 maen-son *n.* empty hands; hands

맵다 maep-da *v.* be spicy, be hot; be severe, be strict, be intense; 한국음식이 맵다 han-gug-eum-sig-i maep-da Korean food is spicy; 이번 겨울 추위는 아주 맵다 i-beon gyeo-ul chu-wi-neun a-ju maep-da This winter is severely cold

맹세하다 maeng-se-ha-da *v.* swear, pledge

맹장염 maeng-jang-nyeom *n.* appendicitis

맺다 maet-da *v.* knot, tie; bear, produce; form, contract; conclude

머리 meo-ri *n.* head; hair; brain; mind; 머리 감다 meo-ri gam-tta *v.* shampoo, wash one's hair; 머리 빗다 meo-ri bit-da *v.* comb one's hair; 머리가 좋다 meo-ri-ga jo-ta *v.* be smart, be brilliant

머리방 meo-ri-bang *n.* hair salon

머리카락 meo-ri-ka-rak *n.* hair

머릿속 meo-rit-sok *n.* brains

머물다 meo-mul-da *v.* stay, stop, remain

머플러 meo-peul-leo *n.* muffler

먹고살다 meok-go sal-da *v.* live, make a living, earn one's living

먹고싶다 meok-go sip-da *v.* want to eat

먹구름 meok-gu-reum *n.* black cloud, rain cloud

먹다 meok-da *v.* eat, take

먹이 meog-i *n.* feed, food

먹이다 meog i da *v.* let someone eat, serve, treat, feed

먹히다 meo-ki-da *v.* be eaten, be swallowed

먼저 meon-jeo *adv.* first, ahead, first of all, above all; ago, previously

먼지 meon-ji *n.* dust, mote

멀다 meol-da *v.* be far, be distant, be remote

멀리 meol-li *adv.* far, far away, in the distance

멀미 meol-mi *n.* nausea, motion sickness

멀미하다 meol-mi-ha-da *v.* have nausea, get sick

멈추게하다 meom-chu-ge ha-da *v.* make somebody or something stop

멈추다 meom-chu-da *v.* stop, cease

멋 meot *n.* stylishness, dandyism; taste, charm, elegance; 멋 내다 meon nae-da *v.* dress stylishly, try to look pretty

멋대로 meot-dae-ro *adv.* in one's own way, selfishly

멋없다 meod-eop-da *v.* be unattractive; be unstylish

멋있다 meos-it-da *v.* be attractive; be stylish

멋쟁이 meot-jaeng-i *n.* dandy

멋지다 meot-ji-da *v.* be full of beauty, be splendid

멍들다 meong-deul-da *v.* get a bruise, have bruised

멍멍 meong-meong *adv.* bowwow (*a dog's bark*)

멍청이 meong-cheong-i *n.* stupid person, fool

멍청하다 meong-cheong-ha-da *v.* be stupid, be dull, be dumb

멍하다 meong-ha-da *v.* stay stunned, be out of mind

메뉴 me-nyu *n.* menu

메다 me-da *v.* shoulder, carry on one's shoulder

메달 me-dal *n.* medal; 메달을 따다 me-dal-eul tta-da *v.* win a medal

메모 me-mo *n.* memo, memorandum

메모판 me-mo-pan *n.* memo board

메모하다 me-mo-ha-da *v.* take a memo

메스껍다 me-seu-kkeop-da *v.* feel nauseous, feel sick

메시지 me-ssi-ji *n.* message

메아리 me-a-ri *n.* echo

메일 me-il *n.* mail

멕시코 mek-si-ko *n.* Mexico

멜로디 mel-lo-di *n.* melody

멜빵 mel-ppang *n.* shoulder strap

멤버 mem-beo *n.* member

며느리 myeo-neu-ri *n.* daughter-in-law

며칠 myeo-chil *n.* several days; what day of the month, how many days

면 myeon *n.* cotton; *part.* if, in case; 오늘 떠나면 너무 늦겠다 o-neul tteo-na-myeon neo-mu neut-get-da If you depart today, it will be too late

면도칼 myeon-do-kal *n.* razor

면도하다 myeon-do-ha-da *v.* shave oneself, get a shave

면적 myeon-jeok *n.* area, size

면접 myeon-jeop *n.* interview

면접관 myeon-jeop-gwan *n.* interviewer

면접시험 myeon-jeop-si-heom *n.* oral exam, interview

면허증 myeon-heo-jjeung *n.* license, permission

명 myeong *count.* (*counter word for people*)

명단 myeong-dan *n.* list of names

명동 myeong-dong *n.* Myeong Dong (*famous shopping area in Seoul*)

명랑하다 myeong-nang-ha-da *v.* be bright, be clear, be cheerful, be light-hearted

명령 myeong-nyeong *n.* order, command, instruction

명령하다 myeong-nyeong-ha-da *v.* order, command, instruct

명물 myeong-mul *n.* special product, specialty

명성 myeong-seong *n.* fame, reputation

명예 myeong-ye *n.* honor, distinction, fame

명작 myeong-jak *n.* masterpiece

명절 myeong-jeol *n.* traditional national holiday, festival days

명필 myeong-pil *n.* excellent handwriting; noted calligrapher

명함 myeong-ham *n.* name card, business card

몇 myeot *adj.* how many, what; several, some; 몇 번 myeot beon *adv.* how often, several times; 오늘 몇 사람이 와요 o-neul myeot-sa-ram-i wa-yo How many people are going to come today; 그 사람을 몇번 만났다 geu sa-ram-eul myeot-beon man-nat-da I met him several times

몇몇 myeon-myeot *adv.* some, several

모 mo *n.* wool

모국 mo-guk *n.* mother country

모국어 mo-gug-eo *n.* mother tongue

모금 mo-geum *n.* gulp, drop

모기 mo-gi *n.* mosquito

모기장 mo-gi-jang *n.* mosquito net

모녀 mo-nyeo *n.* mother and daughter

모니터 mo-ni-teo *n.* monitor

모닥불 mo-dak-bul *n.* bonfire, campfire

모델 mo-del *n.* model

모두 mo-du *pron.* all, everyone; *adv.* in all, all together

모든 mo-deun *adj.* all, every, each and every

모래 mo-rae *n.* sand, grit

모래밭 mo-rae-bat *n.* sand box

모레 mo-re *n.* day after tomorrow

모르는 사람 mo-reu-neun sa-ram *n.* someone one does not know, person with whom you are unacquainted, stranger

모르다 mo-reu-da *v.* unable to tell; be unaware of, not understand; not feel

모범 mo-beom *n.* model, example, pattern

모범적 mo-beom-jeok *adj.* model, exemplary

모서리 mo-seo-ri *n.* corner, edge

모셔놓다 mo-syeo-no-ta *v.* accompany a senior person

모습 mo-seup *n.* features, appearance, figure, image

모시다 mo-si-da *v.* accompany; treat; take; serve, honor *(hon.)*

모아두다 mo-a-du-da *v.* collect and keep

모양 mo-yang *n.* shape, form, appearance, looks

모여살다 mo-yeo sal-da *v.* live together

모으다 mo-eu-da *v.* collect; get together; focus; accumulate

모이다 mo-i-da *v.* get together, come together

모임 mo-im *n.* meeting, gathering

모자 mo-ja *n.* hat, cap; mother and son

모자라다 mo-ja-ra-da *v.* be insufficient

모조리 mo-jo-ri *adv.* all, utterly

모직 mo-jik *n.* woolen fabric

모집 mo-jip *n.* invitation, collection, recruitment

모집광고 mo-jip-gwang-go *n.* recruiting advertisement

모집하다 mo-ji-pa-da *v.* recruit, invite, collect, raise

모처럼 mo-cheo-reom *adv.* at long last, after a long time

모터 mo-teo *n.* motor

모델 mo-tel *n.* motel

모토 mo-to *n.* motto

모퉁이 mo-tung-i *n.* corner, turning

모피 mo-pi *n.* fur, skin

모험 mo-heom *n.* adventure, risk

목 mok *n.* neck; throat; 목 아프다 mok a-peu-da *v.* have a sore throat

목걸이 mok-geol-i *n.* necklace, neckwear

목격하다 mok-gyeo-ka-da *v.* witness, observe

목도리 mok-do-ri *n.* muffler

목록 mong-nok *n.* list, index, catalogue, contents

목마르다 mong-ma-reu-da *v.* be thirsty

목사님 mok-sa-nim *n.* pastor, minister

목소리 mok-so-ri *n.* voice, tone

목숨 mok-sum *n.* life

목요일 mog-yo-il *n.* Thursday

목욕 mog-yok *n.* bath; 목욕 캡 mog-yok kaep *n.* bath cap

목욕탕 mog-yok-tang *n.* bathroom; bath house

목욕하다 mog-yo-ka-da *v.* take a bath, bathe

목장 mok-jang *n.* ranch *(cattle)*

목적 mok-jeok *n.* purpose, aim, object

목적지 mok-jeok-ji *n.* one's destination

목축 mok-chuk *n.* ranching *(cattle)*

목표 mok-pyo *n.* mark, target, goal, aim

몫 mok *n.* share, portion

몬순 mon-sun *n.* monsoon

몰다 mol-da *v.* drive, urge on

몰라보다 mol-la-bo-da *v.* fail to recognize

몰래 mol-lae *adv.* secretly, in secret

몰려다니다 mol-lyeo-da-ni-da *v.* move about in crowds

몰려오다 mol-lyeo-o-da *v.* come in flocks

몰리다 mol-li-da *v.* flock, swarm; be driven after; be driven to the wall; gather together

몰아내다 mol-a-nae-da *v.* expel, turn out, kick out, eject

몰아넣다 mol-a-neo-ta *v.* drive into; drive into a corner

몰아치다 mol-a-chi-da *v.* put all to one side; do all one's work at once

몸 mom *n.* body, figure

몸매 mom-mae *n.* one's figure

몸무게 mom-mu-ge *n.* weight

몸살 mom-sal *n.* body ache

몸조리 mom-jo-ri *n.* taking care of one's health

몸소리하다 mom-jo-ri-ha-da *v.* take good care of one's health

몸조심하다 mom-jo-sim-ha-da *v.* take care of one's health

몹시 mop-si *adv.* awfully, terribly, very, extremely

못 mot *adv.* cannot, will not; *n.* peg, screw, nail

못 본 척하다 mot bon cheok ha-da *v.phr.* pretend not to see, neglect

못되다 mot-doe-da *v.* be under, be short of; be bad, be evil, be wicked

못마땅하다 mon-ma-ttang-ha-da *v.* be unsatisfactory, be disagreeable

못보다 mot-bo-da *v.* overlook, fail to notice

못살게굴다 mot-sal-ge gul-da *v.* tease, tease badly

못생기다 mot-saeng-gi-da *v.* look ugly, look plain

못쓰다 mot-sseu-da *v.* be bad, be wrong; not be supposed to do something; be inferior, be poor

못지않게 mot-ji-an-ke *adv.* not inferior to, as good as, no less than

못하다 mo-ta-da *v.* be unable to do; be inferior, be below

몽고 mong-go *n.* Mongolia; 몽고군 mong-go-gun *n.* Mongolian army

몽둥이 mong-dung-i *n.* stick, club

묘 myo *n.* grave, tomb

묘비 myo-bi *n.* tombstone, gravestone

묘지 myo-ji *n.* graveyard, cemetery

무 mu *n.* radish

무가당 mu-ga-dang *adj.* sugarless

무겁다 mu-geop-da *v.* be heavy; be serious

무게 mu-ge *n.* weight

무관심하다 mu-gwan-sim-ha-da *v.* be unconcerned about, be unmindful of

무궁화 mu-gung-hwa *n.* Rose of Sharon (*national flower of Korea*)

무궁화호 mu-gung-hwa-ho *n.* local train

무기 mu-gi *n.* arms, weapon

무너뜨리다 mu-neo-tteu-ri-da *v.* pull down, tear down, break down, destroy

무너지다 mu-neo-ji-da *v.* collapse, fall down, be destroyed

무늬 mu-nui *n.* design, figure, pattern

무당 mu-dang *n.* shaman

무대 mu-dae *n.* stage, arena

무더기 mu-deo-gi *n.* pile, heap

무더위 mu-deo-wi *n.* humidity, sultry weather

무덤 mu-deom *n.* grave, tomb

무덥다 mu-deop-da *v.* be sultry, be muggy

무뚝뚝하다 mu-ttuk-ttu-ka-da *v.* be blunt, be abrupt

무료 mu-ryo *n.* free of charge; gratis

무료로 mu-ryo-ro *adv.* free, free of charge

무릎 mu-reup *n.* knee, lap; 무릎 꿇다 mu-reup kkeul-ta *v.* bend one's knees, go down on one's knees

무면허 mu-myeon-heo *n.* unlicensed

무사하다 mu-sa-ha-da *v.* be safe, be peaceful

무사히 mu-sa-hi *adv.* safely

무서움 mu-seo-um *n.* fear, horror, terror

무서워하다 mu-seo-wo-ha-da *v.* be afraid, fear, be frightened

무섭게 mu-seop-ge *adv.* awfully, terribly, frightfully

무섭다 mu-seop-da *v.* be scared, be afraid

무술 mu-sul *n.* martial arts

무스 mu-sseu *n.* mousse

무슨 mu-seun *adj.* what; 무슨 색깔을 좋아하세요 mu-seun saek-kkal-eul jo-a-ha-se-yo What color do you like

무시하다 mu-si-ha-da *v.* ignore, disregard

무심코 mu-sim-ko *adv.* unintentionally, by chance, unconsciously

무안해지다 mu-an-hae-ji-da *v.* be ashamed, feel ashamed

무언가 mu-eon-ga *n.* something

무엇 mu-eot *pron.* what, which, something, anything; 무엇을 찾으세요 mu-eos-eul chaj-eu-se-yo What are you looking for

무역 mu-yeok *n.* trade, commerce

무역항 mu-yeo-kang *n.* commerce port, trading port

무역회사 mu-yeo-koe-sa *n.* trading company

무용 mu-yong *n.* dance

무용수 mu-yong-su *n.* dancer

무작정 mu-jak-jeong *adv.* without any definite plan, aimlessly

무조건 mu-jo-kkeon *adv.* unconditional, unconditionally

무좀 mu-jom *n.* athlete's foot

무지개 mu-ji-gae *n.* rainbow

무직 mu-jik *n.* unemployed

무질서 mu-jil-sseo *n.* disorder, confusion

무척 mu-cheok *adv.* very much

무턱대고 mu-teok-dae-go *adv.* for no good reason

무형문화재 mu-hyeong-mun-hwa-jae *n.* intangible cultural properties (*skills, songs, dances, etc.*)

묵다 muk-da *v.* stay; get old

묶다 muk-da *v.* bind, tie, fasten

묶음 mukk-eum *n.* bundle, bunch

묶이다 mukk-i-da *v.* be fastened, be bound, be tied by

문 mun *n.* gate, door
문구 mun-gu *n.* stationary
문구류 mun-gu-ryu *n.* stationary
문득 mun-tteuk *adv.* suddenly, unexpectedly
문밖 mun-bak *n.* outside the door
문방구 mun-bang-gu *n.* stationary, writing materials; stationary store
문방구점 mun-bang-gu-jeom *n.* stationary store
문법 mun-ppeop *n.* grammar
문병가다 mun-byeong ga-da *v.* visit a sick person
문자 mun-jja *n.* letters, character, alphabet
문자메시지 mun-jja-me-ssi-ji *n.* text message *(cell phone)*
문장 mun-jang *n.* sentence; 이 문장은 너무 길다 i mun-jang-eun neo-mu gil-da This sentence is too long
문제 mun-je *n.* problem, question
문지르다 mun-ji-reu-da *v.* rub, scrub
문학 mun-hak *n.* literature
문화 mun-hwa *n.* culture, civilization
문화재 mun-hwa-jae *n.* cultural assets
묻다 mut-da *v.* bury; conceal; stick to; ask, question
묻히다 mu-chi-da *v.* smear, cover; be buried, be concealed
물 mul *n.* water
물가 mul-kka *n.* cost of living, prices; shore, beach, water's edge
물감 mul-kkam *n.* dyes, color
물건 mul-geon *n.* merchandise, goods, stuff
물걸레 mul-geol-le *n.* wet mop, damp house cloth
물결 mul-kkyeol *n.* wave
물결치다 mul-kkyeol-chi-da *v.* wave
물고기 mul-kko-gi *n.* fish
물기 mul-kki *n.* moisture
물꼬러미 mul-kkeu-reo-mi *adv.* with a blank look
물놀이 mul-nol-i *n.* water rippling, water babbling; waterside excursion
물다 mul-da *v.* bite; pay, pay for
물러가다 mul-leo-ga-da *v.* move backward, fall back
물러나다 mul-leo-na-da *v.* fall back, retreat, retire, leave

물러서다 mul-leo-seo-da *v.* step back, move off
물렁물렁하다 mul-leong-mul-leong-ha-da *v.* be soft, be tender, be juicy
물렁하다 mul-leong-ha-da *v.* be soft, be tender, be juicy; be yielding, be flabby
물려받다 mul-lyeo-bat-da *v.* inherit, take over
물려주다 mul-lyeo-ju-da *v.* hand over, transfer
물론 mul-lon *adv.* of course
물리다 mul-li-da *v.* be bitten; be fed up, get sick
물리학 mul-li-hak *n.* physics
물방울 mul-ppang-ul *n.* drop of water
물병 mul-ppyeong *n.* water bottle
물비누 mul-bi-nu *n.* liquid soap
물빨래 mul-ppal-lae *n.* machine wash or hand wash with water; dry cleaning not required
물수건 mul-ssu-geon *n.* wet towel
물안경 mul-an-gyeong *n.* diver's goggles
물약 mul-lyak *n.* liquid medicine
물어가다 mul-eo-ga-da *v.* take something away
물어뜯다 mul-eo-tteut-da *v.* bite, tear off
물어보다 mul-eo-bo-da *v.* ask, inquire, question
물엿 mul-lyeot *n.* molasses
물위 mul-wi *n.* surface of the water
물장난하다 mul-jang-nan-ha-da *v.* play in water
물주다 mul-ju-da *v.* give water; water a plant
물질적 mul-jjil-jjeok *adj.* material, physical
물집 mul-jjip *n.* blister; 물집이 생기다 mul-jjib-i saeng-gi-da *v.* form a blister, get a blister
물통 mul-tong *n.* water pail
묽다 mul-tta *v.* be watery
뭉뚝하다 mung-tteu-ka-da *v.* be stumpy, be blunt
뭉치 mung-chi *count.* bundle, lump *(counter word for paper, cloth, etc.)*
뭐하러 mwo-ha-reo *adv.* for what, why, for what purpose; 뭐하러 왔어 mwo-ha-reo wass-eo Why did you come here
뮤지컬 myu-ji-keol *n.* musical
미국 mi-guk *n.* America
미국사람 mi-guk-sa-ram *n.* American

미국인 mi-gug-in *n.* American

미군 mi-gun *n.* US Armed Forces, American military

미끄러지다 mi-kkeu-reo-ji-da *v.* slide, glide, slip

미끄럼 mi-kkeu-reom *n.* slide, sliding

미끄럽다 mi-kkeu-reop-da *v.* be slippery, be slick

미끼 mi-kki *n.* bait

미나리 mi-na-ri *n.* Korean parsley, water dropwort (*oenanthe stolonifera DC*)

미남 mi-nam *n.* good-looking man, handsome man

미녀 mi-nyeo *n.* beautiful woman

미니스커트 mi-ni-seu-keo-teu *n.* miniskirt

미래 mi-rae *n.* future

미련하다 mi-ryeon-ha-da *v.* be stupid, be clumsy

미루다 mi-ru-da *v.* postpone, put off, delay

미리 mi-ri *adv.* in advance, beforehand

미만 mi-man *part.* under, below, less than; 다섯살 미만은 돈을 받지 않는다 da-seot-sal mi-man-eun don-eul bat-ji an-neun-da No charge for children under age five

미모 mi-mo *n.* beautiful face, good looks

미사일 mi-sa-il *n.* missile

미성년 mi-seong-nyeon *n.* minor, under age

미성년자 mi-seong-nyeon-ja *n.* minority, under age

미소 mi-so *n.* smile; 미소 짓다 mi-so jit-da *v.* wear a smile

미술 mi-sul *n.* art

미술가 mi-sul-ga *n.* artist

미술관 mi-sul-gwan *n.* art museum

미술전 mi-sul-jeon *n.* art exhibition

미식축구 mi-sik-chuk-gu *n.* football

미신 mi-sin *n.* superstition

미안하다 mi-an-ha-da *v.* be sorry, be regrettable

미안해하다 mi-an-hae-ha-da *v.* regret, be sorry about

미역 mi-yeok *n.* brown seaweed

미역국 mi-yeok-guk *n.* seaweed soup

미용사 mi-yong-sa *n.* hairstylist

미움 mi-um *n.* hate, hatred

미워하다 mi-wo-ha-da *v.* hate, loathe

미인 mi-in *n.* beautiful woman

미장원 mi-jang-won *n.* beauty shop

미제 mi-je *n.* made in USA

미지근하다 mi-ji-geun-ha-da *v.* be tepid, not be warm enough

미쳐 mi-cheo *adv.* as far as, to that extent, far enough

미치다 mi-chi-da *v.* go mad, become insane; be crazy about; bequeath, leave

미터 mi-teo *n.* meter

미풍양속 mi-pung-yang-sok *n.* good morals and manners

미혼 mi-hon *n.* single, unmarried

미화 mi-hwa *n.* dollar *(US currency)*

믹서기 mik-seo-gi *n.* blender

민박 min-bak *n.* taking lodging in a private house

민속무용 min-song-mu-yong *n.* folk dance

민속음악 min-sog-eum-ak *n.* folk music

민속촌 min-sok-chon *n.* Folk village *(tour site)*

민족 min-jok *n.* people, ethnic group

민주주의 min-jok-ju-ui *n.* democracy

민주화 min-ju-hwa *n.* democratization; 민주화 운동 min-ju-hwa un-dong *n.* democratization movement

믿다 mit-da *v.* trust, believe in, be sure of

믿음 mid-eum *n.* trust, confidence; faith, belief

믿음직하다 mid-eum-ji-ka-da *v.* be reliable, be dependable

밀가루 mil-kka-ru *n.* wheat flour

밀다 mil-da *v.* push, shove

밀려오다 mil-lyeo-o-da *v.* beat upon, rush for

밀리다 mil-li-da *v.* be delayed, be behind; be pushed, be shoved; fall behind

밀림 mil-lim *n.* dense forest, dense undergrowth

밀물 mil-mul *n.* the flow, the tide

밀어올리다 mil-eo ol-li-da *v.* push up

밀어내다 mil-eo-nae-da *v.* push out, force out

밀짚모자 mil-jjim-mo-ja *n.* straw hat

밀치다 mil-chi-da *v.* push roughly, shove

밀크 mil-keu *n.* milk

밉다 mip-da *v.* be hateful; dislike; not be pretty, not be beautiful, be ugly

밑 mit *n.* the base, the bottom, below, under

밑바닥 mit-ba-dak *n.* the bottom, the base

ㅂ

바가지 ba-ga-ji *n.* gourd; dipper

바가지쓰다 ba-ga-ji-sseu-da v. pay through the nose, pay too much

바겐세일 ba-geon-sse-il *n.* bargain sale, discount sale

바구니 ba-gu-ni *n.* wicker basket

바깥 ba-kkat *n.* outside

바깥쪽 ba-kkat-jjok *n.* outside, the exterior

바꾸다 ba-kku-da v. switch, change, exchange; replace; alter

바꾸어주다 ba-kku-eo-ju-da v. change, exchange

바꿔놓다 ba-kkwo-no-ta v. replace, substitute

바꿔주다 ba-kkwo-ju-da v. change, exchange

바뀌다 ba-kkwi-da v. be changed, be transformed, be revised

바나나 ba-na-na *n.* banana

바느질하다 ba-neu-jil-ha-da v. sew, do needlework

바늘 ba-neul *n.* needle

바다 ba-da v. sea, ocean

바닥 ba-dak *n.* flat part; the bottom; the end; floor; the lowest; 요즘 주식가격이 바닥이다 yo-jeum ju-sik-ga-gyeog-i ba-dag-i-da Stock prices have bottomed out lately; 네 점수가 제일 바닥이다 ne jeom-su-ga je-il ba-daq-i-da You have the lowest score; 바닥에 앉지 마세요 ba-dag-e an-jji ma-se-yo Please do not sit on the floor

바닷가 ba-dat-ga *n.* beach

바닷물 ba-dan-mul *n.* seawater

바둑 ba-duk *n.* Ba Duk (*Korean board game played with black and white stones aka 'Go'*)

바라다 ba-ra-da v. desire, wish, want, hope

바라보다 ba-ra-bo-da v. see, look at, watch, gaze

바람 ba-ram *n.* wind, breeze; 바람 불다 ba-ram bul-da v. be windy

바람개비 ba-ram-gae-bi *n.* pinwheel

바람나다 ba-ram-na-da v. have a secret love affair; be fickle

바람둥이 ba-ram-dung-i *n.* fickle person, playboy/playgirl

바람맞다 ba-ram-mat-da v. be stood up, be kept waiting in vain

바람맞히다 ba-ram-ma-chi-da v. stand someone up

바람에 ba-ram-e *part.* as a result of, because of

바래다주다 ba-rae-da ju-da v. see a person home

바래다 ba-rae-da v. fade, discolor, bleach in the sun

바로 ba-ro *adv.* right there; directly; exactly; at once, immediately

바르다 ba-reu-da v. apply, put on (*for make-up or skin care products*)

바바리코트 ba-ba-ri-ko-teu *n.* raincoat, trench coat

바보 ba-bo *n.* fool, stupid person

바비큐 ba-bi-kyu *n.* barbecue

바빠지다 ba-ppa-ji-da v. become busy

바쁘다 ba-ppeu-da v. be busy; be urgent

바위 ba-wi *n.* rock

바이러스 ba-i-reo-sseu *n.* virus

바이어 ba-i-eo *n.* buyer

바이올린 ba-i-ol-lin *n.* violin

바지 ba-ji *n.* pants

바짝 ba-jjak *adv.* completely; closely

바캉스 ba-kang-sseu *n.* vacation

바퀴 ba-kkwi *n.* wheel; round; cockroach

바탕 ba-tang *n.* background

바티칸 ba-ti-kan *n.* Vatican

박 bak *n.* gourd

박다 bak-da v. hammer; thrust in

박람회 bang-ram-hoe *n.* exhibition, exposition

박물관 bang-mul-gwan *n.* museum

박사 bak-sa *n.* doctor; expert

박수 bak-su *n.* handclapping, applause; 박수 치다 bak-su chi-da v. clap one's hands, applaud

박자 bak-ja *n.* beat, rhythm

박쥐 bak-jwi *n.* bat (*animal*)

박히다 ba-ki-da v. be nailed to, be stuck

밖 bak *n.* the outside, the exterior; the rest, the others

밖에 bakk-e *part.* nothing but, only

반 ban *n.* class; half; group

반가워하다 ban-ga-wo-ha-da v. be gladdened by, take pleasure in

반갑게 ban-gap-ge *adv.* gladly, with pleasure

반갑다 ban-gap-da *v.* be glad, be happy, be pleased

반값 ban-kkap *n.* half-price

반나절 ban-na-jeol *n.* six hours, half of the day time

반년 ban-nyeon *n.* half a year

반달 ban-dal *n.* half-moon; half a month

반대 ban-dae *n.* reverse, opposite, contrary

반대로 ban-dae-ro *adv.* reversely, oppositely

반대하다 ban-dae-ha-da *v.* be against, be opposed to; reverse

반도 ban-do *n.* peninsula

반도체 ban-do-che *n.* semiconductor

반드시 ban-deu-si *adv.* by all means, without fail, for sure, necessarily

반딧불 ban-dit-bul *n.* firefly

반만년 ban-man-nyeon *n.* 5000 years; half a myriad

반말 ban-mal *n.* plain speech

반면에 ban-myeon-e *adv.* in contrast, on the other hand

반바지 ban-ba-ji *n.* shorts

반반 ban-ban *n.* half-and-half, fifty-fifty

반복하다 ban-bo-ka-da *v.* repeat

반소매 ban-so-mae *n.* half-sleeve, half-length sleeve

반액 ban-aek *n.* half-price

반절 ban-jeol *n.* half

반주 ban-ju *n.* accompaniment; aperitif

반지 ban-ji *n.* ring; 반지 끼다 ban-ji kki-da *v.* wear a ring

반짝 ban-jjak *adv.* lightly, easily; high

반짝이다 ban-jjag-i-da *v.* shine, glitter, twinkle

반찬 ban-chan *n.* side dish

반창고 ban-chang-go *n.* plaster

반칙 ban-chik *n.* foul, violation

반코트 ban-ko-teu *n.* half-coat (*coat that reaches to the knees*)

반팔 ban-pal *n.* short-sleeve shirts

반하다 ban-ha-da *v.* fall in love with; be charmed by

반환 ban-hwan *n.* return, restoration

받다 bat-da *v.* receive, accept; take; undergo, go through; catch

받들다 bat-deul-da *v.* esteem, treat with deference

받아적다 bad-a-jeok-da *v.* write down, take down

받아들이다 dad-a-deul-i-da *v.* accept, take in, adopt

받치다 bat-chi-da *v.* support, prop up, hold up

발 bal *n.* foot; screen, blind

발가락 bal-kka-rak *n.* toe

발걸음 bal-kkeol-eum *n.* step, pace

발견되다 bal-gyeon-doe-da *v.* be discovered, be detected

발견하다 bal-gyeon-ha-da *v.* discover, find, detect

발꿈치 bal-kkum-chi *n.* heel

발달 bal-ttal *n.* development, progress, advancement

발달하다 bal-ttal-ha-da *v.* develop, make progress, advance

발등 bal-tteung *n.* instep of a foot

발레 bal-le *n.* ballet

발레리나 bal-le-ri-na *n.* ballerina

발렌타인 데이 bal-len-ta-in de-i *n.* Valentine's Day

발맞추다 bal-mat-chu-da *v.* keep pace with

발명 bal-myeong *n.* invention

발명되다 bal-myeong-doe-da *v.* be invented

발명품 bal-myeong-pum *n.* invention; device

발명하다 bal-myeong-ha-da *v.* invent, devise

발목 bal-mok *n.* ankle

발바닥 bal-ppa-dak *n.* sole of the foot

발소리 bal-sso-ri *n.* sound of footsteps

발음 bal-eum *n.* pronunciation

발음하다 bal-eum-ha-da *v.* pronounce

발자국 bal-jja-guk *n.* footprint, track

발전 bal-jjeon *n.* development, growth

발전소 bal-jjeon-so *n.* power plant

발전하다 bal-jjeon-ha-da *v.* develop, prosper

발톱 bal-top *n.* toenail, claw

발표 bal-pyo *n.* announcement

발표하다 bal-pyo-ha-da *v.* announce, make known, express

밝기 bal-kki *n.* luminosity

밝다 bal-tta *v.* be bright, be light; be promising; be sharp, be keen; dawn

밝은 색 balg-eun saek *adj.* light color, bright color

밝히다 bal-ki-da *v.* light up, lighten; make clear, clarify

밟다 bal-tta *v.* step on; follow, trail after; go through

밤 bam *n.* night, evening; chestnut; 밤이 깊다 bam-i gip-da It is late at night; 밤이 새다 bam-i sae-da *v.* day breaks, becomes dawn

밤낮 bam-nat *n.* night and day; *adv.* always, day in and day out

밤낮으로 bam-naj-eu-ro *adv.* night and day, always, day in and day out

밤늦다 bam-neut-da *v.* be late at night

밤마다 bam-ma-da *adv.* nightly, every night

밤사이 bam-sa-i *n.* nighttime

밤새 bam-sae *adv.* all night, all through the night

밤새다 bam-sae-da *v.* stay up all night

밤새도록 bam-sae-do-rok *adv.* all night long

밤새우다 bam-sae-u-da *v.* stay up all night

밤색 bam-saek *adj.* brown, chestnut color

밤중에 bam-jjung-e *adv.* at midnight, in the middle of the night

밥 bap *n.* meal, food; boiled rice, rice

밥그릇 bap-geu-reut *n.* rice bowl

밥맛 bam-mat *n.* appetite

밥상 bap-sang *n.* dinner table

밥주걱 bap-ju-geok *n.* spatula

밥짓다 bap-jit-da *v.* cook rice

밥하다 ba-pa-da *v.* cook rice; fix a meal

방 bang *n.* room; 방 정리하다 bang jeong-ni-ha-da *v.* clean one's room, organize one's room

방값 bang-kkap *n.* room rent

방귀 bang-gwi *n.* fart

방귀뀌다 bang-gwi-kkwi-da *v.* break wind, fart

방금 bang-geum *adv.* just now

반긋 bang-geut *adv.* with a smile

방망이 bang-mang-i *n.* club, mallet

방면 bang-myeon *n.* direction, field; aspect, phase; 수원 방면으로 가는 지하철을 타세요 su-won bang-myeon-eu-ro ga-neun ji-ha-cheol-eul ta-se-yo Please take the subway that heads in the direction of Su-Won; 이 방변으로는 내가 전문가다 i bang-myeon-eu-ro-neun nae-ga jeon-mun-ga-da I am an expert in this field.

방문 bang-mun *n.* door; visit

방문객 bang-mun-gaek *n.* visitor

방문하다 bang-mun-ha-da *v.* visit

방바닥 bang-ppa-dak *n.* floor

방법 bang-beop *n.* method, way

방부제 bang-bu-je *n.* antiseptic

방사능 bang-sa-neung *n.* radioactivity

방사선 bang-sa-seon *n.* radiation

방석 bang-seok *n.* cushion

방세 bang-sse *n.* rent (*for a room*)

방송 bang-song *n.* broadcasting, broadcast

방송국 bang-song-guk *n.* broadcasting station

방송되다 bang-song-doe-da *v.* be broadcast

방송하다 bang-song-ha-da *v.* broadcast

방식 bang-sik *n.* form, method, process

방울 bang-ul *n.* bell; drop (*liquid*)

방충망 bang-chung-mang *n.* moth-proof screen

방패 bang-pae *n.* shield

방학 bang-hak *n.* vacation

방학하다 bang-ha-ka-da *v.* go on vacation; close for vacation

방해되다 bang-hae-doe-da *v.* be disturbed, be interrupted

방해하다 bang-hae-ha-da *v.* obstruct; disturb, interrupt

방향 bang-hyang *n.* direction

밭 bat *n.* field; farm; garden

밭농사 ban-nong-sa *n.* dry field farming, upland agriculture

배 bae *n.* stomach, abdomen; pear; boat, ship; double; 배 아프다 bae a-peu-da *v.* have a stomachache

배경 bae-gyeong *n.* background, setting

배고프다 bae-go-peu-da *v.* be hungry

배구 bae-gu *n.* volleyball

배꼽 bae-kkop *n.* belly button

배낭 bae-nang *n.* rucksack, pack, knapsack

배달 bae-dal *n.* delivery

배달하다 bae-dal-ha-da *v.* deliver, distribute

배드민턴 bae-deu-min-teon n. badminton

배멀미 bae-meol-mi *n.* seasickness

배부르다 bae-bu-reu-da *v.* to have a full stomach

배우 bae-u *n.* actor, actress

배우다 bae-u-da *v.* learn, take lessons, study

배우자 bae-u-ja *n.* spouse

배웅하다 bae-ung-ha-da *v.* see off, give a send-off

배추 bae-chu *n.* cabbage, Chinese cabbage

배탈 bae-tal *n.* upset stomach, stomachache

배탈나다 bae-tal-la-da *v.* have an upset stomach, have a stomachache

배터리 bae-teo-ri *n.* battery

배트 bae-teu *n.* bat

배편 bae-pyeon *n.* shipping service

백 baek *n.* hundred; background, patronage; 백 년 baek nyeon *n.* century

백곰 baek-gom *n.* polar bear

백과사전 baek-gwa-sa-jeon *n.* encyclopedia

백두산 baek-du-san *n.* Mt. Baek Du *(historical and tourist site in Korea)*

백록담 baeng-nok-dam *n.* crater of the Mt. Halla in Jeju Island *(historical and tourist site in Korea)*

백만 baeng-man *n.* million

백만장자 baeng-man-jang-ja *n.* millionaire

백미러 ppaeng-mi-reo *n.* rearview mirror

백성 baek-seong *n.* the people *(citizens)*

백악관 baeg-ak-gwan *n.* the White House

백열등 baeg-yeol-tteung *n.* incandescent electric lamp

백의민족 baeg-ui-min-jok *n.* the Korean people; the white-clad folk *(euphemism for the Korean people)*

백인 baeg-in *n.* white man, Caucasian

백일 baeg-il *n.* hundred days; the one hundredth day *(celebration for newborn babies)*

백제 baek-je *n.* a kingdom during the Three Kingdom Period *(Korean historical period, 18 B.C.-660)*

백포도주 baek-po-do-ju *n.* white wine

백화점 bae-kwa-jeom *n.* department store

밴드 baen-deu *n.* band, strap; belt; brass band

뱀 baem *n.* snake

뱀장어 baem-jang-eo *n.* eel

뱃놀이 baen-nol-i *n.* boating, boat ride

뱃살 baet-sal *n.* abdominal muscle

뱃속 baet-sok *n.* the stomach

뱉다 baet-da *v.* spit out

버드나무 beo-deu-na-mu *n.* willow

버럭 beo-reok *adv.* suddenly

버릇 beo-reut *n.* habit; characteristic; manners

버릇없다 beo-reu-deop-da *v.* be ill-mannered, ill-behaved

버리다 beo-ri-da *v.* throw away, cast aside, abandon, discard, give up; spoil, ruin

버선 beo-seon *n.* Korean socks

버섯 beo-seot *n.* mushroom

버스 ppeo-sseu *n.* bus

버스정류장 ppeo-sseu-jeong-nyu-jang *n.* bus stop

버스터미널 ppeo-sseu-teo-mi-neol *n.* bus terminal

버스표 ppeo-sseu-pyo *n.* bus ticket

버터 beo-teo *n.* butter

번 beon *count.* a time; number of numerical order

번갈아 beon-gal-a *adv.* alternately, by turns

번개 beon-gae *n.* a flash of lightning; 번개 치다 beon-gae chi-da *v.* lighten

번번이 beon-beon-i *adv.* every and each time, always

번역하다 beon-yeo-ka-da *v.* translate into; 한국어를 영어로 번역했다 han-gug-eo-reul yeong-eo-ro beon-yeo-kaet-da I translated a Korean passage into English

번지 beon-ji *n.* house number

번지다 beon-ji-da *v.* spread, run

번지수 beon-ji-ssu *n.* house number

번째 beon-jjae *count.* ordinal number

번쩍 beon-jjeok *adv.* in a flash, in a breath; easily; 번쩍 들다 beon-jjeok deul-da *v.* lift easily

번쩍거리다 beon-jjeok-geo-ri-da *v.* glitter, glisten, twinkle, flash, sparkle

번쩍이다 beon-jjeog-i-da *v.* glitter, glisten, twinkle, flash, sparkle

번호 beon-ho *n.* number

번호판 beon-ho-pan *n.* number plate, license plate

벌 beol *count.* classifier for clothes; *n.* bee; punishment, penalty

벌금 beol-geum *n.* fine, penalty

벌꿀 beol-kkul *n.* honey

벌다 beol-da *v.* earn, make money

벌떡 beol-tteok *adv.* suddenly, abruptly; 벌떡 일어나다 beol-tteok il-eo-na-da *v.* stand up suddenly, stand up abruptly

벌레 beol-le *n.* insect, bug

벌리다 beol-li-da *v.* open, widen; stretch out; lay out

벌받다 beol-bat-da *v.* be punished, take the penalty

벌벌 beol-beol *adv.* trembling, shivering, shaking

벌써 beol-sseo *adv.* already, yet

벌어지다 beol-eo-ji-da *v.* get wider; happen; get serious; break out

벌주다 beol-ju-da *v.* punish, penalize

벌집 beol-jjip *n.* beehive, honeycomb

벌판 beol-pan *n.* plain, field; wilderness

범위 beom-wi *n.* scope, range, extent, limits

범인 beom-in *n.* criminal, offender

범퍼 beom-peo *n.* bumper

법 beop *n.* law

법관 beop-gwan *n.* lawyer

법대 beop-dae *n.* law school

법률 beom-nyul *n.* law

법원 beob-won *n.* court of justice

법학 beo-pak *n.* law

벗겨지다 beot-gyeo-ji-da *v.* come off, be taken off; get undressed; fall off; fade; get removed

벗기다 beot-gi-da *v.* undress, take off; peel, skin; remove

벗다 beot-da *v.* take off, remove

벙어리 beong-eo-ri *n.* dumb person

벙어리장갑 beong-eo-ri-jang-gap *n.* mitten

벚꽃놀이 beot-kkon-nol-i *n.* picnic under the cherry blossoms

베개 be-gae *n.* pillow

베끼다 be-kki-da *v.* copy, make a copy of

베다 be-da *v.* rest one's head on; cut, chop, saw, carve, slash, slice; 베개를 베었다 be-gae-reul be-eot-da I rested my head on the pillow; 나무를 베었다 na-mu-reul be-eot-da I cut down the tree

베란다 be-ran-da *v.* porch

베스트셀러 be-seu-teu-ssel-leo *n.* best seller

베어먹다 be-eo-meok-da *v.* cut off and eat

베이지색 be-i-ji-saek *n.* tan

베일 be-il *n.* veil

베짱이 be-jjang-i *n.* grasshopper

벤치 ben-chi *n.* bench

벨 bel *n.* bell, doorbell; 벨 소리 bel sso-ri *n.* bell sound, ringing

벨트 bel-teu *n.* belt

벼락공부하다 byeo-rak-gong-bu-ha-da *v.* cram, study for an exam in a short time

벼락부자 byeo-rak-bu-ja *n.* overnight millionaire

벼락치기 byeo-rak-chi-gi *n.* hasty preparation

벼락치다 byeo-rak-chi-da *v.* strike *(lightning)*

벼랑 byeo-rang *n.* cliff

벼룩시장 byeo-ruk-si-jang *n.* flea market

벼슬 byeo-seul *n.* official rank, government post

벽 byeok *n.* wall, partition; habit, characteristic; 벽을 칠했다 byeog-eul chil-haet-da I painted the wall; 그 남자는 주벽이 있다 geu nam-ja-neun ju-byeog-i it-da He has a habit of being quarrelsome when under the influence of alcohol

벽걸이 byeok-geoi-l *n.* wall tapestry, wall hanging

벽난로 byeong-nal-lo *n.* hearth, fireplace

벽돌 byeok-dol *n.* brick

벽보 byeok-bo *n.* poster

벽시계 byeok-si-gye *n.* wall clock

벽장 byeok-jang *n.* wall closet

벽지 byeok-ji *n.* wall paper

벽화 byeo-kwa *n.* wall painting, mural, fresco

변경되다 byeon-gyeong-doe-da *v.* be changed, be modified

변경하다 byeon-gyeong-ha-da *v.* change, modify, alter

변기 byeon-gi *n.* chamber pot

변덕 byeon-deok *n.* fickleness, caprice

변덕꾸러기 byeon-deok-kku-reo-gi *n.* capricious person, moody person

변덕스럽다 byeon-deok-seu-reop-da *v.* be capricious, fickle

변두리 byeon-du-ri *n.* outskirts of a district

변명하다 byeon-myeong-ha-da *v.* explain oneself, defend oneself

변비 byeon-bi *n.* constipation

변장하다 byeon-jang-ha-da *v.* disguise oneself, wear a disguise

변천 byeon-cheon *n.* change, transition

변하다 byeon-ha-da *v.* change, become different

변호사 byeon-ho-sa *n.* lawyer

변화 byeon-hwa *n.* change, alteration

변화하다 byeon-hwa-ha-da *v.* change, alter

별 byeol *n.* star

별것 byeol-geot *n.* something peculiar

별꼴 byeol-kkol *n.* spectacle, sight

별나다 byeol-la-da *v.* be peculiar, strange

별다르다 byeol-da-reu-da *v.* be extraordinary

별로 byeol-lo *adv.* not really, not particularly

별명 byeol-myeong *n.* nickname

별미 byeol-mi *n.* delicacy, exquisite flavor

별별 byeol-byeol *adj.* of various and unusual sorts, various kinds of

별빛 byeol-ppit *n.* starlight

별소리 byeol-so-ri *n.* unreasonable remarks, extraordinary remark

별수없다 byeol-su-eop-da *v.* have no special means, have no secret key

별안간 byeol-an-gan *n.* suddenly, all at once

별일 byeol-lil *n.* special event, special incident, unusual occurrence

별장 byeol-jjang *n.* vacation home

별표 byeol-pyo *n.* asterisk

병 byeong *n.* bottle; sickness, illness, disease; 병 걸리다 byeong geol-li-da *v.* get a disease; 병 나다 byeong na-da *v.* be taken ill, get sick; 병 생기다 byeong saeng-gi-da *v.* contract a disease; 병이 낫다 byeong-i nat-da *v.* get cured

병균 byeong-gyun *n.* germ, virus

병들다 byeong-deul-da *v.* become sick, become diseased

병따개 byeong-tta-gae *n.* bottle opener

병마개 byeong-ma-gae *n.* bottle cap, cork

병명 myeong-myeong *n.* the name of a disease

병실 byeong-sil *n.* ward

병아리 byeong-a-ri *n.* chick

병원 byeong-won *n.* hospital

병자 byeong-ja *n.* sick person, patient

병풍 byeong-pung *n.* folding screen

병환 byeong-hwan *n.* (hon.) disease

볕 byeot *n.* sunshine

볕들다 byeot-deul-da *v.* be sunny

보고 bo-go *part.* to (*a person*); *n.* report

보고서 bo-go-seo *n.* report, paper

보고하다 bo-go-ha-da *v.* report, inform

보관하다 bo-gwan-ha-da *v.* keep; take charge of

보글보글 bo-geul-bo-geul *adv.* simmering

보기 bo-gi *n.* example; a way of looking at things

보나마나 bo-na-ma-na *adv.* needless to say, no doubt

보내다 bo-nae-da *v.* spend, pass time; send, transmit

보내주다 bo-nae-ju-da *v.* send

보너스 bo-neo-sseu *n.* bonus

보다 bo-da *v.* look at, see; consider; read; look after; rather than; 나를 봐 na-reul bwa Look at me; 책을 봐 chaeg-eul bwa Read a book; 나는 사과보다 배를 더 좋아해 na-neun sa-gwa-bo-da bae-reul deo jo-a-hae I like pears more than apples

보다못해 bo-da-mo-tae *adv.* being unable to stand by and watch, being more than one can bear to see

보도 bo-do *n.* sidewalk; news, report

보드카 bo-deu-ka *n.* vodka

보디가드 bo-di-ga-deu *n.* bodyguard

보라색 bo-ra-saek *adj.* purple; violet

보람 있다 bo-ram it-da *v.* be fruitful, be worthwhile

보름 bo-reum *n.* fifteen days; fifteenth day of a lunar calendar

보름달 bo-reum-ttal *n.* full moon

보리 bo-ri *n.* barley

보리차 bo-ri-cha *n.* barley tea

보물 bo-mul *n.* treasure, jewel, valuables

보살상 bo-sal-ssang *n.* statue of Buddhist saint

보살펴주다 bo-sal-pyeo-ju-da *v. hon.* take care of, look after

보살피다 bo-sal-pi-da *v.* take care of, look after

보석 bo-seok *n.* jewel, gemstone, precious stone

보수 bo-su *n.* compensation, reward; mending, repair

보수적 bo-su-jeok *adj.* conservative

보슬비 bo-seul-bi *n.* drizzle

보신탕 bo-sin-tang *n.* soup of dog's meat

보아주다 bo-a-ju-da *v.* take care of, look after

보약 bo-yak *n.* tonic, restorative herbal medicine

보여주다 bo-yeo-ju-da *v.* show, display

보온병 bo-on-byeong *n.* thermos

보이다 bo-i-da *v.* be seen, be visible; look, seem; show, display

보일러 bo-il-leo *n.* boiler, heating system

보자기 bo-ja-gi *n.* wrapping cloth

보장하다 bo-jang-ha-da *v.* guarantee

보조개 bo-jo-gae *n.* dimple

보존하다 bo-jon-ha-da *v.* preserve, conserve, maintain

보채다 bo-chae-da *v.* fret, make a fuss

보청기 bo-cheong-gi *n.* hearing aid

보태다 bo-tae-da *v.* add, supplement

보통 bo-tong *adv.* usually, commonly; normally

보트 bo-teu *n.* boat

보편적인 bo-pyeon-jeog-in *adj.* universal

보험 bo-heom *n.* insurance; 보험 들다 bo-heom deul-da *v.* insure an item

보호자 bo-ho-ja *n.* protector, guardian

보호하다 bo-ho-ha-da *v.* protect, guard, look after

복 bok *n.* blessing, fortune; 복 받다 bok bat-da *v.* be blessed

복구되다 bok-gu-doe-da *v.* be restored to normal, be returned to the former condition

복권 bok-gwon *n.* lottery; 복권이 맞나 bok-gwon-i mat da *v.* win the lottery

복날 bong-nal *n.* the dog days of summer (*three hottest days in lunar calendar*)

복더위 bok-deo-wi *n.* heat wave during the dog days

복덕방 bok-deok-bang *n.* real estate office

복도 bok-do *n.* hallway

복사하다 bok-sa-ha-da *v.* reproduce, copy

복숭아 bok-sung-a *n.* peach

복습 bok-seup *n.* review

복습하다 bok-seu-pa-da *v.* review, go over

복싱 bok-sing *n.* boxing

복용 bog-yong *n.* (*the act of*) taking medicine

복용하다 bog-yong-ha-da *v.* take medicine

복잡하다 bok-ja-pa-da *v.* be crowded

복통 bok-tong *n.* stomachache

볶다 bok-da *v.* fry, roast, pan-broil

볶음밥 bokkeum-bap *n.* fried rice

본국 bon-guk *n.* one's home country

본뜨다 bon-tteu-da *v.* copy from a model, imitate

본보기 bon-bo-gi *n.* example, model

본분 bon-bun *n.* station in life, one's position

본업 bon-eop *n.* main occupation

본인 bon-in *n.* oneself; 본인을 만나세요 bon-in-eul man-na-se-yo Please meet the man himself

본체만체 하다 bon-che-man-che ha-da *v.* neglect

본토 bon-to *n.* mainland

볼 bol *n.* cheek

볼링 bol-ling *n.* bowling

볼만하다 bol-man-ha-da *v.* be worth seeing, be worthy of notice

볼일 bol-lil *n.* business, errand

볼트 bol-teu *n.* volt

볼펜 bol-pen *n.* ballpoint pen

봄 bom *n.* spring

봄철 bom chool *n.* spring, springtime

봉급 bong-geup *n.* salary, wages

봉사 bong-sa *n.* service; blind man; 무료봉사 mu-ryo-bong-sa Free service; 그 남자는 봉사네은 bong-sa-da He is blind

봉사하다 bong-sa-ha-da *v.* service, serve

봉사활동 bong-sa-hwal-ttong *n.* community service activities

봉오리 bong-o-ri *n.* bud

봉우리 bong-u-ri *n.* peak, summit, top

봉투 bong-tu *n.* envelope

봐두다 bwa-du-da *v.* see, have an audience with

뵙다 boep-da *v. hon.* see, meet

부군 bu-gun *n.* another person's husband

부근 bu-geun *n.* neighborhood

부끄럼 bu-kkeu-reom *n.* shyness; shame, disgrace

부끄럽다 bu-kkeu-reop-da *v.* be shameful, be disgraceful; be shy, be bashful

부녀자 bu-nyeo-ja *n.* woman, lady

부닥치다 bu-dak-chi-da *v.* face, confront; encounter, meet with

부담하다 bu-dam-ha-da *v.* assume the cost of, pay, defray

부대 bu-dae *n.* bag, sack; corps, force

부동산 bu-dong-san *n.* real estate

부두 bu-du *n.* wharf, pier

부둣가 bu-dut-ga *n.* pier, wharf side

부드럽다 bu-deu-reop-da *v.* be soft, be tender

부딪치다 bu-dit-chi-da *v.* collide with, bump against

부딪히다 bu-dit-chi-da *v.* be crashed into, be bumped against

부러뜨리다 bu-reo-tteu-ri-da *v.* break, snap

부러워하다 bu-reo-wo-ha-da *v.* envy, be
envious of
부러지다 bu-reo-ji-da *v.* be broken, snap
부럽다 bu-reop-da *v.* be jealous, be envious
부르다 bu-reu-da *v.* call, call out; name, brand
부모님 bu-mo-nim *n.* parents
부부 bu-bu *n.* husband and wife
부분 bu-bun *n.* part, portion, section
부사장 bu-sa-jang *n.* vice president of a
company
부산 bu-san *n.* Busan *(city)*
부서지다 bu-seo-ji-da *v.* break, be broken,
break down, become out of order
부수다 bu-su-da *v.* break, smash, destroy,
demolish
부스러기 bu-seu-reo-gi *n.* small fragments,
crumbs
부스러지다 bu-seu-reo-ji-da *v.* break, fall to
pieces, crumble
부업 bu-eop *n.* side business, subsidiary work
부엉이 bu-eong-i *n.* owl
부엌 bu-eok *n.* kitchen
부엌용품 bu-eong-nyong-pum *n.* kitchen
utensils
부여 bu-yeo *n.* Bu Yeo *(ancient Korean tribe,
1 B.C.-300)*
부유하다 bu-yu-ha-da *v.* be wealthy, be rich
부인 bu-in *n.* another person's wife; woman,
lady; denial, disapproval
부자 bu-ja *n.* rich man; father and son; 부자
되다 bu-ja doe-da *v.* become rich
부작용 bu-jag-yong *n.* side effect
부적 bu-jeok *n.* charm
부전공 bu-jeon-gong *n.* minor, second major
부족 bu-jok *n.* tribe; shortage, lack
부족하다 bu-jo-ka-da *v.* be lacking, not be
good enough, be short of, lack
부지런하다 bu-ji-reon-ha-da *v.* be diligent,
be hardworking
부채 bu-chae *n.* fan, folding fan
부채질하다 bu-chae-jil-ha-da *v.* fan, use a fan
부채춤 bu-chae-chum *n.* fan dance
부처 bu-cheo *n.* Buddha
부처님 bu-cheo-nim *n. hon.* Buddha
부츠 bu-cheu *n.* boots
부치다 bu-chi-da *v.* mail, send mail; fan; fry,
griddle
부침개 bu-chim-gae *n.* flat cake, pancake

부케 bu-ke *n.* bouquet
부탁 bu-tak *n.* request
부탁하다 bu-ta-ka-da *v.* ask a favor, request,
make a request
부터 bu-teo *part.* from, since; beginning
with, starting from
부통령 bu-tong-nyeong *n.* vice president of
a country
부풀다 bu-pul-da *v.* swell up, expand
부피 bu-pi *n.* volume
부하 bu-ha *n.* follower, subordinate
북 buk *n.* drum; north
북경 buk-gyeong *n.* Beijing (*Peking*) in China
북극 guk-geuk *n.* North Pole
북녘 bung-nyeok *n.* north *(direction)*
북대서양 buk-dae-seo-yang *n.* the North
Pacific Ocean
북돋우다 buk-dod-u-da *v.* encourage,
strengthen
북동 buk-dong *n.* northeast
북미 bung-mi *n.* North America
북반구 buk-ban-gu *n.* Northern Hemisphere
북부 buk-bu *n.* northern part
북새통 buk-sae-tong *n.* confusion
북서 buk-seo *n.* northwest
북적거리다 buk-jeok-geo-ri-da *v.* bustle, be
crowded
북쪽 buk-jjok *n.* north
북한 bu-kan *n.* North Korea
북한산 bu-kan-san *n.* Mt. Buk Han in Seoul
분 bun *count. hon.* minutes; person; *n.*
powder; anger
분노 bun-no *n.* anger
분단되다 bun-dan-doe-da *v.* be divided, be
cut into halves
분단하다 bun-dan-ha-da *v.* divide into
sections, cut into pieces
분량 bul-lyang *n.* quantity
분명하다 bun-myeong-ha-da *v.* be clear, be
obvious, be evident
분명히 bun-myeong-hi *adv.* clearly,
distinctively
분수 bun-su *n.* fountain; fraction
분실물 bun-sil-mul *n.* missing article, lost
property
분야 bun-ya *n.* field
분위기 bun-wi-gi *n.* atmosphere,
surroundings

분유 bun-yu *n*. powdered milk

분필 bun-pil *n*. chalk

분홍색 bun-hong-saek *adj*. pink

분다 but-da *v*. swell, grow sodden; rise, increase

불 bul *n*. fire, flame; light; lamp; 불 나다 bul-la-da *v*. a fire breaks out; 불 들어오다 bul deul-eo-o-da the light/power is on; 불 나가다 bul na-ga-da the light/power is out; 불 붙이다 bul bu-chi-da *v*. light, light a fire

불가능 bul-ga-neung *n*. impossibility

불가능하다 bul-ga-neung-ha-da *v*. be impossible

불가리아 bul-ga-ri-a *n*. Bulgaria

불가사리 bul-ga-sa-ri *n*. starfish

불경 bul-gyeong *n*. Buddhist scriptures; disrespect

불고기 bul-go-gi *n*. marinated beef

불공평하다 bul-gong-pyeong-ha-da *v*. be unfair, be biased

불교 bul-gyo *n*. Buddhism

불구자 bul-gu-ja *n*. the handicapped, the disabled

불국사 bul-guk-sa *n*. Bul Guk temple in Gyeong Ju

불길 bul-kkil *n*. flame, blaze

불꽃 bul kkot *n*. flame, blaze, spark

불꽃놀이 bul-kkon-nol-i *n*. fireworks

불다 bul-da *v*. blow

불당 bul-ttang *n*. Buddhist temple

불도저 bul-do-jeo *n*. bulldozer

불독 bul-dok *n*. bulldog

불량품 bul-lyang-pum *n*. inferior goods

불러내다 bul-leo-nae-da *v*. call a person out, call up

불러오다 bul-leo-o-da *v*. summon, send for a person

불리다 bul-li-da *v*. be called, be invited; fill, enrich oneself

불리하다 bul-li-ha-da *v*. be disadvantageous, be unfavorable

불만 bul-man *n*. dissatisfaction; 불만을 품다 bul-man-eul pum-tta *v*. have a grudge

불면증 bul-myeon-jjeung *n*. insomnia

불법 bul-ppeop *n*. illegality, unlawfulness

불붙다 bul-but-da *v*. catch fire

불상 bul-ssang *n*. image of Buddha

불쌍하다 bul-ssang-ha-da *v*. be poor, be pitiable, be pitiful, be pathetic

불쌍히 bul-ssang-hi *adv*. pitifully, poorly

불쑥 bul-ssuk *adv*. suddenly, unexpectedly, abruptly

불안하다 bul-an-ha-da *v*. be uneasy, be anxious, be insecure

불어 bul-eo *n*. French language

불여우 bul-lyeo-u *n*. red fox

불장난하다 bul-jang-nan-ha-da *v*. play with fire

불조심하다 bul-jo-sim-ha-da *v*. be careful not to start a fire

불지르다 bul-ji-reu-da *v*. set fire to, set on fire

불쾌지수 bul-kwae-ji-su *n*. Discomfort Index

불쾌하다 bul-kwae-ha-da *v*. be unpleasant, be uncomfortable

불타다 bul-ta-da *v*. burn, be in flames

불편하다 bul-pyeon-ha-da *v*. be inconvenient, be uncomfortable

불평 bul-pyeong *n*. dissatisfaction, complaint

불평등 bul-pyeong-deung *n*. inequality

불평하다 bul-pyeong-ha-da *v*. vent one's dissatisfaction, complain of, grumble

불행하다 bul-haeng-ha-da *v*. be unhappy, be unfortunate

붉다 bul-tta *v*. be red, be crimson

붉히다 bul-ki-da *v*. blush, turn red

붐 bum *n*. boom

붐비다 bum-bi-da *v*. be crowded, be congested

붓 but *n*. writing brush

붓글씨 but-geul-ssi *n*. calligraphy

붓다 gut-da *v*. be swollen; pour, fill

붕괴 bung-goe *n*. collapse, breakdown

붕대 bung-dae *n*. bandage, dressing

붙다 but-da *v*. stick, adhere, cling

붙들다 but-deul-da *v*. catch, seize, grasp; arrest, capture

붙들리다 but-deul-li-da *v*. be caught, be arrested

붙어있다 but-eo-it-da *v*. stick, adhere, cling

붙여놓다 bu-cheo-no-ta *v*. stick, affix, attach, apply

붙이다 bu-chi-da *v*. stick, affix, attach, apply; give a name

붙잡다 but-jap-da *v.* catch, hold, grasp

붙잡히다 but-ja-pi-da *v.* be caught, be arrested

브래지어 beu-rae-ji-eo *n.* brass

브레이크 beu-re-i-keu *n.* brake

브로치 beu-ro-chi *n.* brooch

블라우스 beul-la-u-sseu *n.* blouse

블라인드 beul-la-in-deu *n.* blind

비 bi *n.* rain, rainfall; broom; monument; 비 맞다 bi mat-da *v.* get caught in the rain; 비 오다 bi o-da *v.* rain

비겁하다 bi-geo-pa-da *v.* be cowardly

비관적 bi-gwan-jeok *adj.* pessimistic

비교적 bi-gyo-jeok *adj.* relatively

비교하다 bi-gyo-ha-da *v.* compare with

비구름 bi-gu-reum *n.* rain cloud

비극적 bi-geuk-jeok *adj.* tragic

비기다 bi-gi-da *v.* end in a tie, tie

비난하다 bi-nan-ha-da *v.* criticize, blame

비누 bi-nu *n.* soap

비능률적 bi-neung-nyul-jjeok *adj.* inefficient

비닐 bi-nil *n.* vinyl

비다 bi-da *v.* be empty, be vacant, be unoccupied, be free; be hollow

비둘기 bi-dul-gi *n.* dove, pigeon

비듬 bi-deum *n.* dandruff, scurf

비디오 bi-di-o *n.* video

비디오카메라 bi-di-o-ka-me-ra *n.* video camera

비로소 bi-ro-so *adv.* for the first time

비록 bi-rok *adv.* if, even if, even though

비롯하여 bi-ro-ta-yeo *part.* including; headed by; as well as

비료 bi-ryo *n.* fertilizer

비만 bi-man *n.* fatness, corpulence

비명 bi-myeong *n.* scream

비무장지대 bi-mu-jang-ji-dae *n.* DMZ (*demilitarized zone*)

비밀 bi-mil *n.* secret, mystery

비밀금고 bi-mil-geum-go *n.* secret safe-deposit box

비밀번호 bi-mil-beon-ho *n.* PIN number

비바람 bi-ba-ram *n.* rain and wind, rainstorm

비비다 bi-bi-da *v.* rub, chafe; mix

비빔국수 bi-bim-guk-su *n.* noodles with assorted mixtures

비빔밥 bi-bim-ppap *n.* boiled rice with assorted mixtures

비상경보 bi-sang-gyeong-bo *n.* alarm signal

비상벨 bi-sang-bel *n.* alarm

비상사태 bi-sang-sa-tae *n.* state of emergency

비상시 bi-sang-si *n.* emergency

비상용 bi-sang-nyong *adj.* for emergency use

비서 bi-seo *n.* secretary

비서실 bi-seo-sil *n.* secretary's office

비석 bi-seok *n.* tombstone

비스듬하다 bi-seu-deum-ha-da *v.* be slightly tilted, be a bit askew

비스킷 bi-seu-kit *n.* cracker, biscuit

비슷비슷하다 bi-seut-bi-seu-ta-da *v.* be much the same, be alike

비슷하다 bi-seu-ta-da *v.* be similar, be alike, resemble

비싸다 bi-ssa-da *v.* be expensive, be costly

비올라 bi-ol-la *n.* viola (*instrument*)

비옷 bi-ot *n.* raincoat

비용 bi-yong *n.* expense, cost, expenditure

비우다 bi-u-da *v.* empty, vacate

비웃다 bi-ut-da *v.* laugh scornfully, ridicule, mock

비웃음 bi-us-eum *n.* sneer, jeer, mock, scorn

비워두다 bi-wo-du-da *v.* empty, vacate

비원 bi-won *n.* Bi Won (*old palace garden in Seoul*)

비율 bi-yul *n.* ratio, percentage, rate

비자 bi-ja *n.* visa

비전 bi-jeon *n.* vision

비좁다 bi-jop-da *v.* be narrow, be cramped

비지땀 bi-ji-ttam *n.* heavy sweat

비집다 bi-jip-da *v.* push open, spread apart

비추다 bi-chu-da *v.* shed light; light up, flash on; reflect, mirror; hold a thing up to the light

비치다 bi-chi-da *v.* shine; be reflected, be mirrored; fall upon; hint; show through, be seen

비켜서다 bi-kyeo-seo-da *v.* stand aside, step back

비키니 bi-ki-ni *n.* bikini

비키다 bi-ki-da *v.* get out of the way, step aside

비타민 bi-ta-min *n.* vitamin

비탈길 bi-tal-kkil *n.* slope, uphill road

비틀거리다 bi-teul-geo-ri-da *v.* stagger, reel, totter

비틀다 bi-teul-da *v.* twist, screw, wrench

비틀리다 bi-teul-li-da *v.* be twisted

비틀비틀 bi-teul-bi-teul *adv.* staggeringly, totteringly, reelingly

비틀어지다 bi-teul-eo-ji-da *v.* get twisted

비하다 bi-ha-da *v.* compare to, compare with

비행기 bi-haeng-gi *n.* airplane

비행기표 bi-haeng-gi-pyo *n.* airplane ticket

비행소년 bi-haeng-so-nyeon *n.* juvenile delinquent

비행장 bi-haeng-jang *n.* airport

비행접시 bi-haeng-jeop-si *n.* flying saucer

비행하다 bi-haeng-ha-da *v.* fly, make a flight

빈 병 bin byeong *n.* empty bottle

빈대떡 bin-dae-tteok *n.* green-bean pancake

빈민굴 bin-min-gul *n.* slum, ghetto

빈방 bin-bang *n.* empty room, vacant room

빈부 bin-bu *n.* wealth and poverty; the rich and the poor

빈자리 bin-ja-ri *n.* vacant seat

빈칸 bin-kan *n.* blank column, blank space

빈터 bin-teo *n.* vacant lot, open space

빈틈 bin-teum *n.* gap, crack; blind side

빌다 bil-da *v.* ask, beg; wish, pray; apologize, ask pardon

빌딩 bil-ding *n.* building

빌려쓰다 bil-lyeo-sseu-da *v.* borrow and use

빌려가다 bil-li-da *v.* borrow

빌려주다 bil-lyeo-ju-da *v.* lend, loan; rent out

빌리다 bil-li-da *v.* borrow

빗 bit *n.* comb

빗기다 bit-gi-da *v.* comb someone's hair

빗나가다 bin-na-ga-da *v.* turn away; miss; deviate

빗다 bit-da *v.* comb

빗맞다 bin-mat-da *v.* miss the mark; go wrong

빗물 bin-mul *n.* rainwater

빗방울 bit-bang-ul *n.* raindrop

빗자루 bit-ja-ru *n.* sweeper, broom

빗줄기 bit-jul-gi *n.* great sheets of rain

빙 pping *adv.* round, in a circle

빙그레 bing-geu-re *adv.* with a gentle smile

빙글빙글 bing-geul-bing-geul *adv.* gliding around and around smoothly; smilingly

빙빙 bing-bing *adv.* round and round

빙상경기 bing-sang-gyeong-gi *n.* ice sports

빙수 bing-su *n.* shaved ice with syrup, snow cone

빙판 bing-pan *n.* icy road, frozen road

빙하 bing-ha *n.* glacier

빚 bit *n.* debt, loan

빚내다 bin-nae-da *v.* borrow money

빚쟁이 bit-jaeng-i *n.* moneylender, loan shark

빚지다 bit-ji-da *v.* get into debt

빛 bit *n.* light; ray, beam; flash; luster; color, tint; look, expression

빛깔 bit-kkal *n.* color, tint

빛나다 bin-na-da *v.* shine, be bright, glitter, gleam, twinkle

빛내다 bin-nae-da *v.* light up, cause to shine

빠뜨리다 ppa-tteu-ri-da *v.* throw into; tempt; trap; omit, exclude; lose; drop

빠르다 ppa-reu-da *v.* be fast, be swift, be rapid, be speedy, be quick; be early; be soon

빠른우편 ppa-reun u-pyeon *n.* express mail

빠져나가다 ppa-jeo na-ga-da *v.* escape, slip out, get off, slip away

빠져나오다 ppa-jeo na-o-da *v.* escape, slip out, get off, slip away

빠지다 ppa-ji-da *v.* fall into; be drowned; give oneself up; indulge; come off; fall out; be omitted, be missing

빠짐없이 ppa-jim-eops-i *adv.* wholly, in full, without omission

빤히 ppan-hi *adv.* fixedly, intently

빨간색 ppal-gan-saek *adj.* red color

빨갛다 ppal-ga-ta *v.* be red

빨개지다 ppal-gae-ji-da *v.* be reddened, turn red

빨다 ppal-da *v.* sip; suck; smoke; absorb; wash, launder, do laundry

빨대 ppal-ttae *n.* straw

빨래 ppal-lae *n.* laundry

빨래비누 ppal-lae-ppi-nu *n.* detergent

빨래하다 ppal-lae-ha-da *v.* do laundry, wash laundry

빨리 ppal-li *adv.* quickly

빨아내다 ppal-a-nae-da *v.* suck out, absorb, draw out

빨아들이다 ppal-a-deul-i-da *v.* inhale, suck in; soak up

빨아먹다 ppal-a-meok-da *v.* suck, sip

빳빳하다 ppat-ppa-ta-da *v.* be stiff, be straight; be firm; be willful

빵 ppang *n.* bread; bang, pop; 빵 가루 ppang kka-ru *n.* flour

빵꾸 ppang-kku *n.* hole, blowout

빵빵 ppang-ppang *adv.* pop-pop, bang-bang

빵집 ppang-jjip *n.* bakery

빻다 ppa-ta *v.* grind, to make into powder

빼고 ppae-go *part.* except

빼내다 ppae-nae-da *v.* pull out, extract; select, pick out

빼놓다 ppae-no-ta *v.* exclude, leave out, omit; set aside

빼다 ppae-da *v.* pull out, take out, extract; subtract; remove; cancel

빼먹다 ppae-meok-da *v.* forget, leave out; cut a class

빼앗기다 ppae-at-gi-da *v.* be taken away, be robbed of, be deprived of; be fascinated, be captivated

빼앗다 ppae-at-da *v.* snatch, take away, rob, deprive; fascinate, captivate

빽빽이 ppaek-ppaeg-i *adv.* compactly, tightly, densely

빽빽하다 ppaek-ppae-ka-da *v.* be closely packed

뺏기다 ppaet-gi-da *v.* be robbed of, have something taken from; 돈을 나쁜 사람에게 뺏겼다 don-eul na-ppeun sa-ram-e-ge ppaet-gyeot-da A bad person took my money

뺏다 ppaet-da *v.* take, snatch

뺨맞다 ppyam mat-da *v.* get slapped

뻐근하다 ppeo-geun-ha-da *v.* feel heavy; feel stiff; have a dull pain

뻔뻔하다 ppeon-ppeon-ha-da *v.* be brazen-faced

뻔하다 ppeon-ha-da *v.* be obvious, clear, evident; ...을 뻔하다 eul ppeon-ha-da *adv.* almost, nearly

뻗다 ppeot-da *v.* spread, stretch, extend

뻗치다 ppeot-chi-da *v.* stretch, extend, reach; hold out

뻣뻣하다 ppeot-ppeo-ta-da *v.* be straight, be stiff

뻥 ppeong *adv.* bang, pop

뼈 ppyeo *n.* bone, rib; the gist, main points, essential parts; mettle; spirit; grit

뼈다귀 ppyeo-da-gwi *n.* bone

뼈대 ppyeo-dae *n.* frame, physique

뼈마디 ppyeo-ma-di *n.* joint of bones, joints

뽀뽀 ppo-ppo *n.* kiss

뽐내다 ppom-nae-da *v.* affect, put on airs, boast

뽑다 ppop-da *v.* select, pick out; pluck out, pull out

뽑히다 ppo-pi-da *v.* be taken out; be singled out

뾰족하다 ppyo-jo-ka-da *v.* be pointed, sharp

뿌리 ppu-ri *n.* root

뿌리다 ppu-ri-da *v.* be driven into; sprinkle, spray, scatter

뿐 ppun *part.* only, alone, merely; 뿐만 아니라 ppun-man a-ni-ra *adv.* besides, moreover, in addition, what is more, not only that

뿔 ppul *n.* horn, antler

뿜다 ppum-tta *v.* spout, gush out; burst; shoot up

삐다 ppi-da *v.* sprain, dislocate

삐뚤어지다 ppi-ttul-eo-ji-da *v.* become crooked, slant; be cross, be in a bad mood

삐삐 ppi-ppi *n.* beeper, pager; *adv.* screeching, bawling; gaunt, haggard

삑 ppik *adv.* whistling

人

사 sa *n.* four

사가다 sa-ga-da *v.* go with something bought, buy something and bring it with you

사각형 sa-ga-kyeong *n.* square

사거리 sa-geo-ri *n.* intersection

사건 sa-kkeon *n.* event, incident, affair, happening

사격하다 sa-gyeo-ka-da *v.* shoot, fire at, fire on

사계절 sa-gye-jeol *n.* four seasons

사고 sa-go *n.* accident, mishap, trouble; 사고 나다 sa-go na-da *v.* have an accident *(unintentional)*; 사고 내다 sa-go nae-da *v.* cause an accident

사공 sa-gong *n.* boatman

사과 sa-gwa *n.* apple; apology; 사과 세개 주세요 sa-gwa se-gae ju-se-yo Please give me three apples; 제 사과를 받아 주세요 je sa-gwa-reul bad-a-ju-se-yo Please accept my apology

사과하다 sa-gwa-ha-da *v.* apologize

사교적 sa-gyo-jeok *adj.* social

사귀다 sa-gwi-da *v.* make friends with, keep company with, get acquainted with

사글세 sa-geul-sse *n.* monthly rent

사납다 sa-nap-da *v.* be fierce, be violent, be wild

사내 sa-nae *n.* boy, lad

사내아이 sa-nae-a-i *n.* boy, lad

사냥 sa-nyang *n.* hunting

사냥개 sa-nyang-kkae *n.* hunting dog

사냥꾼 sa-nyang-kkun *n.* hunter

사냥하다 sa-nyang-ha-da *v.* hunt

사다 sa-da *v.* buy, purchase

사다리 sa-da-ri *n.* ladder

사당 sa-dang *n.* shrine; troupe of singing and dancing people; 사당에서 제사를 지낸다 sa-dang-e-seo je-sa-reul ji-naen-da We perform our ancestor worship rituals before the shrine; 내일 남사당패 공연이 있다 transliteration There will be a singing and dancing troupe performance tomorrow

사돈 sa-don *n.* relative by marriage

사들이다 sa-deul-i-da *v.* buy, purchase

사라지다 sa-ra-ji-da *v.* disappear, vanish, be gone, be lost

사람 sa-ram *n.* person, people

사랑 sa-rang *n.* love, affection, passion

사랑니 sa-rang-ni *n.* wisdom teeth

사랑스럽다 sa-rang-seu-reop-da *v.* be lovable, be lovely, be charming

사랑하다 sa-rang-ha-da *v.* love

사로잡다 sa-ro-jap-da *v.* catch alive, capture

사로잡히다 sa-ro-ja-pi-da *v.* be taken alive, be captured

사르르 sa-reu-reu *adv.* softly, gently

사립학교 sa-ri-pak-gyo *n.* private school

사막 sa-mak *n.* desert

사망하다 sa-mang-ha-da *v.* die, pass away

사먹다 sa-meok-da *v.* buy food and eat, eat out

사모님 sa-mo-nim *n.* another person's wife

사무실 sa-mu-sil *n.* office

사물 sa-mul *n.* objects, things, matters

사방 sa-bang *n.* four directions, all directions, everywhere

사방팔방 sa-bang-pal-bang *adv.* everywhere, every direction, all directions

사범대학 sa-beom-dae-hak *n.* college of education

사뿐사뿐 sa-ppun-sa-ppun *adv.* with soft steps, lightly

사사건건 sa-sa-kkeon-kkeon *adv.* in all cases, each and every event

사생활 sa-saeng-hwal *n.* private life

사서 sa-seo *n.* librarian

사서함 sa-seo-ham *n.* mailbox

사설 sa-seol *n.* editorial

사소하다 sa-so-ha-da *v.* be trivial, be insignificant

사슬 sa-seul *n.* chain, chains

사슴 sa-seum *n.* deer

사시사철 sa-si-sa-cheol *n.* four seasons

사실 sa-sil *n.* fact, truth

사실은 sa-sil-eun *adv.* in fact, actually

사양하다 sa-yang-ha-da *v.* decline, refuse, hold back

사업 sa-eop *n.* enterprise, business

사업가 sa-eop-ga *n.* businessman

사오다 sa-o-da *v.* come with something bought, buy something and bring it with you

사용 sa-yong *n.* use, application

사용자 sa-yong-ja *n.* user

사용중 sa-yong-jung *n.* being in use, being occupied

사용하다 sa-yong-ha-da *v.* use, make use of

사우나 ssa-u-na *n.* sauna

사원 sa-won *n.* personnel, employee of a company

사월 sa-wol *n.* April

사위 sa-wi *n.* son-in-law

사윗감 sa-wit-gam *n.* potential son-in-law

사이 sa-i *n.* relationship, connections; space, interval, distance apart; 사이 좋게 sa-i jo-ke *adv.* on good terms, in peace, like good friends; 사이 좋다 sa-i jo-ta *v.* be on intimate terms, be on good terms with

사이다 sa-i-da *n.* 7-Up, Sprite *(clear lemon-lime soda)*

사이렌 ssa-i-ren *n.* siren

사이사이 sa-i-sa-i *n.* spaces, intervals

사이에 sa-i-e *adv.* between

사이즈 ssa-i-jeu *n.* size

사인 ssa-in *n.* signature, autograph; signal, sign

사자 sa-ja *n.* lion

사장님 sa-jang-nim *n.* president of a company

사적 sa-jeok *n.* historical relics

사적 sa-jjeok *adj.* private, personal

사전 sa-jeon *n.* dictionary

사정 sa-jeong *n.* circumstances, situation

사정없이 sa-jeong-eops-i *adv.* mercilessly, ruthlessly

사주다 sa-ju-da *v.* buy something for a person

사주팔자 sa-ju-pal-jja *n.* fate, destiny, fortune

사직공원 sa-jik-gong-won *n.* Sa Jik Park *(in Seoul)*

사진 sa-jin *n.* picture, photo; 사진 찍다 sa-jin jjik-da *v.* take a picture; 사진 찍히다 sa-jin jji-ki-da *v.* have a picture taken

사진기 sa-jin-gi *n.* camera

사철 sa-cheol *n.* four seasons

사촌 sa-chon *n.* cousin

사춘기 sa-chun-gi *n.* puberty

사치스럽다 sa-chi-seu-reop-da *v.* be luxurious, be extravagant

사치품 sa-chi-pum *n.* luxuries

사탕 sa-tang *n.* candy

사투리 sa-tu-ri *n.* dialect

사파리 ssa-pa-ri *n.* safari

사팔뜨기 sa-pal-tteu-gi *n.* cross-eyed person

사표 sa-pyo *n.* written resignation

사학 sa-hak *n.* private school; history, historical study

사항 sa-hang *n.* matter, item, article, particulars

사형 sa-hyeong *n.* death penalty

사화산 sa-hwa-san *n.* extinct volcano

사회 sa-hoe *n.* society, community; head of a meeting; chairmanship

사회적 sa-hoe-jeok *adj.* social

사회학 sa-hoe-hak *n.* sociology

사회학자 sa-hoe-hak-ja *n.* sociologist

사흘 sa-heul *n.* three days

산 san *n.* mountain, hill; acid; 산이 높다 san-i nop-da The mountain is high; 산성이

강하다 san-seong-i gang-ha-da The acid is very potent

산간벽지 san-gan-byeok-ji *n.* isolated place in the mountains

산골 san-kkol *n.* secluded place in the mountains

산골짜기 san-kkol-jja-gi *n.* valley, gorge

산기슭 san-kki-seuk *n.* foot of a mountain

산길 san-kkil *n.* mountain path, mountain road

산꼭대기 san-kkok-dae-gi *n.* mountaintop, summit

산더미 san-tteo-mi *n.* great mass, huge amount, heap

산돼지 san-ttwae-ji *n.* wild boar

산들바람 san-deul-ba-ram *n.* gentle breeze

산들산들 san-deul-san-deul *adv.* gently, softly

산등성이 san-tteung-seon-i *n.* mountain ridge

산딸기 san-ttal-gi *n.* wild berries

산뜻하다 san-tteu-ta-da *v.* be clean, be clear, be fresh, be neat, be tidy

산모 san-mo *n.* woman who delivered a child, woman who gave birth

산모퉁이 san-mo-tung-i *n.* the spur of a hill, the corner of a mountain foot

산밑 san-mit *n.* foot of a mountain

산보하다 san-ppo-ha-da *v.* walk, stroll

산봉우리 san-ppong-u-ri *n.* mountain peak

산부인과 san-bu-in-kkwa *n.* obstetrics and gynecology

산불 san-ppul *n.* forest fire

산비둘기 san-ppi-dul-gi *n.* ring dove, wild pigeon

산비탈 san-ppi-tal *n.* steep mountain slope

산사태 san-sa-tae *n.* landslide, landfall

산산이 san-san-i *adv.* in pieces; in all directions

산산조각 san-san-jjo-gak *n.* bits and pieces, broken pieces

산삼 san-sam *n.* wild ginseng

산새 san-ssae *n.* wild birds, mountain birds

산소 san-so *n.* grave, tomb; oxygen; 한국사람들은 설날에 산소에 간다 han-guk-sa-ram-deul-eun seol-lal-e san-so-e gan-da Koreans visit their ancestors' graves on New Year's Day *(lunar calendar)*; 높은 산에는 산소가 부족하다 nop-eun san-se-neun san-so-ga bu-jo-ka-da There is not enough oxygen in the high mountains

산속 san-ssok *n.* deep in the mountains

산신 san-sin *n.* mountain god *(generic term)*

산신령 san-sil-lyeong *n.* the guardian spirit of a mountain, god of a mountain

산양 san-nyang *n.* antelope

산업 san-eop *n.* industry

산울림 san-ul-lim *n.* echo

산유국 san-yu-guk *n.* oil-producing country

산장 san-jang *n.* mountain villa

산적 san-jeok *n.* Korean-style kebab; bandit; 한국에서는 설날에 산적을 많이 만든다 han-gue-e-seo-neun seol-lal-e san-jeog-eul man-i man-deun-da People usually cook Korean-style kebab on New Year's Day *(lunar calendar)*; 옛날에는 산에 산적들이 많았다 yet-nal-e-neun san-e san-jeog-deul-i man-at-da In the old days, there were many bandits in the mountains

산지기 san-ji-gi *n.* forest ranger

산짐승 san-jjim-seung *n.* mountain animal

산채로 san-chae-ro *adv.* alive

산책 san-chaek *n.* walk, stroll; 산책 나가다 san-chaek na-ga-da *v.* go out to walk, go out for a stroll

산책하다 san-chae-ka-da *v.* take a walk, stroll

산타클로스 ssan-ta-keul-lo-sseu *n.* Santa Claus

산토끼 san-to-kki *n.* hare, wild rabbit

산허리 san-heo-ri *n.* a hillside

산호 san-ho *n.* coral

살 sal *count.* years of age; *n.* flesh, meat, muscle; frame, spoke; 살 빼다 sal ppae-da *v.* lose weight

살결 sal-kkyeol *n.* skin complexion, skin texture

살그머니 sal-geu-meo-ni *adv.* in secret, secretly

살금살금 sal-geum-sal-geum *adv.* furtively, sneakingly

살다 sal-da *v.* live, be alive; get along, make a living; dwell, inhabit

살려내다 sal-lyeo-nae-da *v.* rescue from danger, death

살려주다 sal-lyeo-ju-da *v.* save, rescue

살리다 sal-li-da *v.* save one's life, rescue, spare; make good use of

살림 sal-lim *n.* household; housekeeping

살림살이 sal-lim-sal-i *n.* housekeeping; household

살며시 sal-myeo-si *adv.* secretly, in secret; gently, softly

살살 sal-sal *adv.* gently, softly, lightly

살아가다 sal-a-ga-da *v.* lead a life, get along, keep on living

살아계시다 sal-a-gye-si-da *v. hon.* be alive; 부모님이 아직 살아계시다 bu-mo-nim-i a-jik sal-a-gye-si-da My parents are still alive

살아나다 sal-a-na-da *v.* revive, flame up again; escape death; be relieved from hardship

살얼음 sal-eol-eum *n.* thin ice

살인 sal-in *n.* homicide, murder

살인하다 sal-in-ha-da *v.* commit murder

살짝 sal-jjak *adv.* in secret, by stealth; softly, gently

살찌다 sal-jji-da *v.* gain weight

살충제 sal-chung-je *n.* insecticide

살펴보다 sal-pyeo-bo-da *v.* look around, watch for

살피다 sal-pi-da *v.* look over carefully, take a good look at; judge

삶 sam *n.* life, living

삶다 sam-tta *v.* boil, cook

삼 sam *n.* three; ginseng

삼각관계 sam-gak-gwan-gye *n.* love triangle

삼각형 sam-ga-kyeong *n.* triangle

삼거리 sam-geo-ri *n.* three-way intersection

삼계탕 sam-gye-tang *n.* boiled chicken soup with ginseng *(traditional Korean dish)*

삼국시대 sam-guk-si-dae *n.* Period of the Three Kingdoms *(57 BC – 668)*

삼다 sam-tta *v.* adopt, use a thing as

삼대 sam-dae *n.* three generations; third generation

삼면 sam-myeon *n.* three sides; third page

삼복 sam-bok *n.* the period of summer heat

삼복더위 sam-bok-deo-wi *n.* the midsummer heat

삼월 sam-wol *n.* March

삼일절 sam-il-jjeol *n.* anniversary of the Independence Movement of March 1st, 1919

삼천리 강산 sam-cheol-li gang-san *n.phr.* Korean peninsula *(poetic)*

삼촌 sam-chon *n.* uncle

삼층 sam-cheung *n.* three stories, the third floor

삼층밥 sam-cheung-bap *n.* three-layered cooked rice *(implies that somebody is not good at cooking)*

삼키다 sam-ki-da *v.* swallow, gulp down

삼팔선 sam-pal-sseon *n.* 38th parallel *(demilitarized zone)*

삼한사온 sam-han-s-on *n.* a cycle of three cold days and four warm days

삽 sap *n.* shovel, scoop

삽시간에 sap-si-gan-e *adv.* in a moment, in a flash

상 sang *n.* table; prize, reward; 상 타다 sang ta-da *v.* win a prize, be awarded a prize; 상 주다 sang ju-da *v.* give a prize

상가 sang-ga *n.* shopping center, shopping district

상관하다 sang-gwan-ha-da *v.* be related to; interfere in, participate in

상금 sang-geum *n.* prize money, award, reward

상냥하다 sang-nyang-ha-da *v.* be gentle, sweet, kind

상다리 sang-tta-ri *n.* table legs

상담 sang-dam *n.* consultation, counsel

상담소 sang-dam-so *n.* consultation office

상담하다 sang-dam-ha-da *v.* consult, take counsel

상대 sang-dae *n.* business school; counterpart

상대방 sang-dae-bang *n.* counterpart

상대편 sang-dae-pyeon *n.* the other party

상대하다 sang-dae-ha-da *v.* face, confront each other; keep company with; act counterpart to; 다음에 우리가 상대할 팀은 아주 강하다 da-eum-e u-ri-ga sang-dae-hal tim-eun a-ju gang-ha-da The next team we'll face is very strong; 저 사람은 상대하기 정말 힘들다 jeo sa-ram-eun sang-dae-ha-gi jeong-mal him-deul-da It is really difficult to keep company with that person

상류사회 sang-nyu-sa-hoe *n.* upper-class *(social class)*

상보다 sang-bo-da *v.* set the table

상사병 sang-sa-ppyeong *n.* lovesickness

상상하다 sang-sang-ha-da *v.* imagine, suppose

상수도 sang-su-do *n.* waterworks

상식 sang-sik *n.* common sense, good sense

상아 sang-a *n.* ivory

상어 sang-eo *n.* shark

상업 sang-eop *n.* trade, commerce, business

상여금 sang-yeo-geum *n.* reward, bonus, premium

상영시간 sang-yeong-ssi-gan *n.* the running time of a movie

상영중 sang-yeong-jung *n.* now showing

상영하다 sang-yeong-ha-da *v.* show, project, screen *(film)*

상원 sang-won *n.* the Senate *(congress)*

상원의원 sang-won-ui-won *n.* senator

상위 sang-wi *n.* higher rank, superior position

상의 sang-ui *n.* jacket, shirts, blouse; discussion; 상의를 입었다 sang-ui-reul ib-eot-da He/she wore a jacket; 상의가 필요하다 sang-ui-ga pil-yo-ha-da We need to discuss it

상의하다 sang-ui-ha-da *v.* consult, counsel, discuss

상인 sang-in *n.* merchant, dealer, storekeeper

상자 sang-ja *n.* box, case

상장 sang-jjang *n.* certification of merit, honorary certificate

상점 sang-jeom *n.* store, shop

상징 sang-jing *n.* symbol

상징하다 sang-jing-ha-da *v.* symbolize

상처 sang-cheo *n.* wound, injury, cut, bruise

상체 sang-che *n.* upper body

상추 sang-chu *n.* lettuce

상쾌하다 sang-kwae-ha-da *v.* be refreshing, fresh

상태 sang-tae *n.* condition, situation

상패 sang-pae *n.* medal, medallion

상표 sang-pyo *n.* trademark, brand

상품 sang-pum *n.* prize; article of commerce, goods; high-quality article

상품번호 sang-pum-beon-ho *n.* bar code

상하다 sang-ha-da *v.* be damaged, be injured, be hurt

상한선 sang-han-seon *n.* maximum

상행선 sang-haeng-seon *n.* train heading to Seoul

상형문자 sang-hyeong-mun-jja *n.* hiero-glyphic character

상황 sang-hwang *n.* conditions, situation, circumstances

샅샅이 sat-sa-chi *adv.* everywhere, all over

새 sae *n.* bird; *adj.* new, fresh; 새 집 new house

새겨지다 sae-gyeo-ji-da *v.* be engraved, be carved

새기다 sae-gi-da *v.* engrave, carve; take something to heart, memorize

새까맣다 sae-kka-ma-ta *v.* be deep black, be coal black

새끼 sae-kki *n.* young animal

새끼손가락 sae-kki-son-kka-rak *n.* little finger

새다 sae-da *v.* day break, leak, escape, be disclosed

새댁 sae-daek *n.* newly-wed woman

새로 sae-ro *adv.* newly, afresh; 새로 생기다 sae-ro saeng-gi-da *adv.* newly open, newly started, recently transpired

새롭다 sae-rop-da *v.* be new, fresh, vivid

새마을호 sae-ma-eul-ho *n.* first-class (*express*) train in Korea

새벽 sae-byeok *n.* dawn

새빨갛다 sae-ppal-ga-ta *v.* be crimson, be deep red

새빨개지다 sae-ppal-gae-ji-da *v.* turn red, blush deeply

새삼스럽게 sae-sam-seu-reop-ge *adv.* anew, again

새색시 sae-saek-si *n.* bride

새싹 sae-ssak *n.* sprout, bud

새앙쥐 sae-ang-jwi *n.* mouse

새우 sae-u *n.* shrimp, prawn

새우다 sae-u-da *v.* stay up all night

새집 sae-jip *n.* new house; bird's nest

새총 sae-chong *n.* slingshot

새출발하다 sae-chul-bal-ha-da *v.* make a fresh start

새치 sae-chi *n.* premature gray hair

새치기하다 sae-chi-gi-ha-da *v.* break in, cut in

새콤하다 sae-kom-ha-da *v.* be acidic, be sour

새털 sae-teol *n.* feather, down

새파랗다 sae-pa-ra-ta *v.* be deep blue; be pale; be young; 놀라서 얼굴이 새파랗다 nol-la-seo eol-gul-i sae-para-ta Because he is shocked, his face is pale; 새파랗게 젊은 녀석 sae-pa-ra-ke jeolm-eun nyeo-seok very young person

새하얗다 sae-ha-ya-ta *v.* be snow-white, be pure white

새해 sae-hae *n.* New Year

색 saek *n.* color 무슨 색 좋아해 mu-seun saek jo-a-hae What color do you like

색 ssaek *n.* sack 이 색에다가 넣어 i ssaeg-e-da-ga neo-eo Put the things into this sack

색깔 saek-kkal *n.* color

색다르다 saek-da-reu-da *v.* be different, be unusual, be uncommon

색동저고리 saek-dong-jeo-go-ri *n.* a Korean traditional jacket with sleeves of many-colored stripes

색맹 saeng-maeng *n.* color blindness

색안경 saeg-an-gyeong *n.* tinted glasses, sunglasses

색연필 saeng-nyeon-pil *n.* colored pencil

색인번호 saeg-in-beon-ho *n.* index number; 여기에서 책을 찾으려면 색인번호를 알아야 한다 yeo-gi-e-seo chaeg-eul chaj-eu-ryeo-myeon saeg-in-beon-ho-reul al-a-ya han-da To find a book here, you need to know its index number

색종이 saek-jong-i *n.* colored paper

색칠하다 saek-chil-ha-da *v.* color, paint

샌달 ssaen-dal *n.* sandals

샌드백 ssaen-deu-baek *n.* sandbag

샌드위치 ssaen-deu-wi-chi *n.* sandwich

샌들 ssaen-dul *n.* sandals

샐러드 ssael-leo-deu *n.* salad

샐러리맨 ssael-leo-ri-maen *n.* corporate employee

샘 saem *n.* spring, fountain; jealousy; 산짐승들은 샘에서 물을 마신다 san-jjim-seung-deul-eun saem-e-seo mul-eul ma-sin-da Wild animals drink water from springs; 그 아이는 샘이 많다 geu a-i-neun saem-i man-ta That kid is always jealous

샘물 saem-mul *n.* spring water

샘플 ssaem-peul *n.* sample

생각 saeng-gak *n.* thought, idea; 생각 없이 saeng-gag eops-i *adv.* thoughtlessly; 생각이 깊다 saeng-gag-i gip-da *v.* be thoughtful; 생각이 들다 sang-gag-i deul-da *v.* be reminded of

생각나다 saeng-gang-na-da *v.* come to one's recollection; hit upon, have an idea

생각다 못해 saeng-gak-da mo-tae *adv.phr.* at wit's end

생각되다 saeng-gak-doe-da *v.* appear, be seen as

생각하다 saeng-ga-ka-da *v.* consider, think (*be of the opinion that...*), intend, expect

생각해내다 saeng-ga-kae-nae-da *v.* think out a plan, think up an excuse; devise; remember, recall

생강 saeng-gang *n.* ginger

생겨나다 saeng-gyeo-na-da *v.* come into existence; occur, happen

생기다 saeng-gi-da *v.* form, come into existence; look; occur, happen; 새 화산이 생겼다 sae hwa-san-i saeng-gyeot-da New volcanoes were formed; 그 사람 정말 잘 생겼다 geu sa-ram jeong-mal jal saeng-gyeot-da He looks really handsome; 무슨 일이 생겼다 mu-sun il-i saeng-gyeot-da Something happened

생김새 saeng-gim-sae *n.* looks, appearance

생년월일 saeng-nyeon-wol-il *n.* date of birth

생략하다 saeng-nya-ka-da *v.* omit; abbreviate

생리 saeng-ni *n.* menstruation

생리대 saeng-ni-dae *n.* menstrual pad

생맥주 saeng-maek-ju *n.* draught beer

생명 saeng-myeong *n.* life; soul

생명보험 saeng-myeong-bo-heom *n.* life insurance

생물 saeng-mul *n.* living thing, creature

생물학 saeng-mul-hak *n.* biology

생방송 saeng-bang-song *n.* live broadcasting

생사 saeng-sa *n.* life and death

생산비 saeng-san-bi *n.* production cost

생산지 saeng-san-ji *n.* production center

생산품 saeng-san-pum *n.* product

생산하다 saeng-san-ha-da *v.* produce, make, turn out

생새우 saeng-sae-u *n.* raw shrimp

생선 saeng-seon *n.* fish

생신 saeng-sin *n. hon.* Birthday; 내일이 할 아버지 생신이다 nae-il-i hal-a-beo-ji saeng-sin-i-da Tomorrow is my grandfather's birthday

생애 saeng-ae *n.* life, lifetime; living

생으로 saeng-eu-ro *adv.* raw, uncooked

생일 saeng-il *n.* birthday

생전 saeng-jeon *adv.* lifetime; during one's lifetime

생쥐 saeng-jwi *n.* mouse

생태계 saeng-tae-gye *n.* ecosystem

생화학 saeng-hwa-hak *n.* biochemistry

생활 saeng-hwal *n.* daily life, living

생활모습 saeng-hwal-mo-seup *n.* living conditions, lifestyle

생활비 saeng-hwal-bi *n.* living cost, living expenses

생활습관 saeng-hwal-seup-gwan *n.* customs, lifestyle

생활용품 saeng-hwal-lyong-pum *n.* necessary items for daily life

생활정보지 saeng-hwal-jeong-bo-ji *n.* newspapers with only classified ads

생활하다 saeng-hwal-ha-da *v.* live, exist, make a living

생후 saeng-hu *adv.* after one's birth; since one's birth

샤머니즘 sya-meo-ni-jeum *n.* shamanism (*ancient religion*)

샤워하다 sya-wo-ha-da *v.* take a shower

샤프 sya-peu *n.* mechanical pencil

샴페인 syam-pe-in *n.* champagne

샴푸 syam-pu *n.* shampoo

샴푸하다 syam-pu-ha-da *v.* shampoo

서구 seo-gu *n.* Western Europe

서기 seo-gi *n.* A.D.

서낭당 seo-nang-dang *n.* shrine of a tutelary deity

서너 seo-neo *adj.* three or four, about three

서늘하다 seo-neul-ha-da *v.* be cool, be refreshing; have a chill, feel a chill

서다 seo-da *v.* stand; stop; erect; 문 앞에 누가 서 있다 mun ap-e nu-ga seo it-da Someone is standing in front of the door; 거기 서 geo-gi seo Stop there; 우리 집앞 에 높은 건물이 섰다 u-ri jib-ap-e nop-eun geon-mul-i seot-da A tall building was erected in front of my house

서대문 seo-dae-mun *n.* the West Gate (*historic site*)

서두르다 seo-du-reu-da *v.* hurry up, hasten

서둘러 seo-dul-leo *adv.* hurriedly, hastily

서랍 seo-rap *n.* drawer

서랍장 seo-rap-jang *n.* drawer

서러움 seo-reo-um *n.* sorrow, grief

서러워하다 seo-reo-wo-ha-da *v.* grieve, feel sad

서럽다 seo-reop-da *v.* be sad, be sorrowful, be unhappy

서로 seo-ro *adv.* each other, mutually

서류 seo-ryu *n.* documents, papers

서류가방 seo-ryu-ga-bang *n.* briefcase

서른 seo-reun *n.* thirty

서리 seo-ri *n.* frost

서머타임 sseo-meo-ta-im *n.* Daylight Saving Time

서명 seo-myeong *n.* signature

서민 seon-min *n.* common people, the masses

서방 seo-bang *n.* west, the West, Western countries; husband; 요즘 서방세계에는 무슨 일이 있나 yo-jeum seo-bang-se-gye-e-neun mu-seun il-i in-na What is going on in the Western countries these days; 네 서방 요즘 잘 지내니 ne seo-bang yo-jeum jal ji-nae-ni Is your husband doing well these days

서부 seo-bu *n.* west coast; west, the West

서비스 sseo-bi-sseu *n.* service

서비스센터 sseo-bi-sseu-ssen-teo *n.* service center

서슴없이 seo-seum-eops-i *adv.* without hesitation, unhesitatingly

서양 seo-yang *n.* Western countries, the West

서양식 seo-yang-sik *n.* Western style

시예 seo-ye *n.* calligraphy

서운하다 seo-un-ha-da *v.* be sorry, be regretful, be unsatisfied

서운해하다 seo-un-hae-ha-da *v.* be sorry, be saddened by

서울 seo-ul *n.* Seoul *(capital of South Korea)*

서울역 seo-ul-lyeok *n.* Seoul train station

서유럽 seo-yu-reop *n.* Western Europe

서재 seo-jae *n.* study, library

서점 seo-jeom *n.* bookstore

서쪽 seo-jjok *n.* the west, westward

서커스 sseo-keo-sseu *n.* circus

서투르다 seo-tu-reu-da *v.* be unfamiliar; be unpracticed, be unskilled

서핑 sseo-ping *n.* surfing

서해 seo-hae *n.* Western sea

서해안 seo-hae-an *n.* Western seashore

석가탄신일 seok-ga-tan-sin-il *n.* Buddha's Birthday *(April 8ᵗʰ in the lunar calendar)*

석고붕대 seok-go-bung-dae *n.* plaster cast

석굴 seok-gul *n.* stone cave

석굴암 seok-gul-am *n.* Seok Gul cave in Gyeong Ju *(tourist destination in Korea)*

석기시대 seok-gi-si-dae *n.* Stone Age

석사 seok-sa *n.* M.A., M.S.

석사학위 seok-sa-hag-wi *n.* master's degree

석쇠 seok-soe *n.* grill, gridiron

석유 seog-yu *n.* petroleum

석탄 seok-tan *n.* coal

석탑 seok-tap *n.* stone pagoda

섞다 seok-da *v.* mix, blend

섞이다 seokk-i-da *v.* be mixed, be blended

선거 seon-geo *n.* election

선거하다 seon-geo-ha-da *v.* elect, vote

선교사 seon-gyo-sa *n.* missionary

선글라스 sseon-geul-la-sseu *n.* sunglasses

선녀 seon-nyeo *n.* fairy, nymph

선뜻 seon-tteut *adv.* quickly; gladly; 그는 선뜻 대답했다 geu-neun seon-tteot dae-da-paet-da He quickly answered; 그는 선뜻 나에게 돈을 빌려주었다 geu-neun seon-tteut na-e-ge don-eul bil-lyeo-ju-eot-da He gladly lent me money

선물 seon-mul *n.* present, gift

선물하다 seon-mul-ha-da *v.* give a present

선박 seon-bak *n.* vessel, big ship

선반 seon-ban *n.* shelf

선발되다 seon-bal-doe-da *v.* be selected, be chosen

선배 seon-bae *n.* senior, elder

선보다 seon-bo-da *v.* arrange a date; have an interview with a prospective bride

선생님 seon-saeng-nim *n.* teacher

선선하다 seon-seon-ha-da *v.* be cool, be refreshing

선수 seon-su *n.* player, athlete

선약 seon-yak *n.* previous engagement

선원 seon-won *n.* crew, crew members

선인장 seon-in-jang *n.* cactus

선입견 seon-ip-gyeon *n.* prejudice

선장 seon-jang *n.* captain, commander

선전 seon-jeon *n.* advertisement

선전하다 seon-jeon-ha-da *v.* advertise

선진국 seon-jin-guk *n.* advanced country

선착순으로 seon-chak-sun-eu-ro *adv.* by order of arrival, on a first-come, first-served basis

선천적 seon-cheon-jeok *adj.* inborn, innate, inherent

선택하다 seon-tae-ka-da *v.* choose, select

선풍기 seon-pung-gi *n.* electric fan

선하다 seon-ha-da *v.* be vivid, be fresh, be distinct

섣달그믐 seot-dal-geu-meum *n.* New Year's Eve

섣불리 seot-bul-li *adv.* carelessly; awkwardly

설 seol *n.* New Year's Day

설거지 seol-geo-ji *n.* dishwashing

설거지하다 seol-geo-ji-ha-da *v.* do the dishes

설날 seol-lal *n.* New Year's Day

설다 seol-da *v.* be unripe, be half-done; be unfamiliar, be inexperienced

설렁탕 seol-lyeontang *n.* beef and noodle soup

설마 seol-ma *adv.* by no means, impossibly; 설마, 못 믿겠어 seol-ma mot mit-gess-eo It's impossible. I can't believe it

설명 seol-myeong *n.* explanation

설명하다 seol-myeong-ha-da *v.* explain, make clear

설문지 seol-mun-ji *n.* questionnaire

설빔 seol-bim *n.* New Year's garb

설사 seol-ssa *n.* diarrhea

설사하다 seol-ssa-ha-da *v.* have diarrhea

설쇠다 seol-soe-da *v.* celebrate New Year's, observe the New Year's Day

설악산 seol-ak-san *n.* Mt. Seol Ak *(tourist destination in Korea)*

설익다 seol-ik-da *v.* be half-done, be half-cooked *(food)*

설탕 seol-tang *n.* sugar

섬 seom *n.* island

섬세하다 seom-se-ha-da *v.* be delicate, be fine

섬유소 seom-yu-so *n.* fiber

섭섭하게 seop-seo-pa-ge *adv.* regretfully, unfortunately

섭섭하다 seop-seo-pa-da *v.* be sorry, be disappointed, regret

섭씨 seop-ssi *n.* Celsius

성 seong *n.* family name; gender, sex; castle; 성이 뭐예요 seong-i mwo-ye-yo What is your family name; 산 위에 성이 있다 san wi-e seong-i it-da There is a castle on top of the mountain; 성전환자 seong-jeon-hwan-ja *n.* transgender, transsexual

성격 seong-kkyeok *n.* character, personality

성경 seong-gyeong *n.* Bible

성공 seong-gong *n.* success, achievement

성공하다 seong-gong-ha-da *v.* succeed, be successful

성급하다 seong-geu-pa-da *v.* be hasty, be impatient, be quick-tempered

성냥 seong-nyang *n.* matches

성능 seong-neung *n.* efficiency, performance

성당 seong-dang *n.* Catholic church

성명 seong-myeong *n.* full name

성묘객 seong-myo-gaek *n.* a person visiting the tombs of his/her ancestors

성묘하다 seong-myo-ha-da *v.* to visit one's ancestral graves

성별 seong-byeol *n.* sex distinction, gender difference

성분 seong-bun *n.* ingredient, component

성실하다 seong-sil-ha-da *v.* be sincere, be faithful, be truthful

성악가 seong-ak-ga *n.* vocalist

성인 seong-in *n.* adult, grownup

성장 seong-jang *n.* growth

성장하다 seong-jang-ha-da *v.* grow up

성적 seong-jeok *n.* grade

성조기 seong-jo-gi *n.* U.S. flag

성질 seong-jil *n.* nature, disposition, temper

성탄절 seong-tan-jeol *n.* Christmas

성함 seong-ham *n. hon.* name; 성함이 어떻게 되십니까 seong-ham-i eo-tteo-ke doe-sim-ni-kka May I have your name please

성형수술 seong-hyeong-su-sul *n.* plastic surgery

세 se *adj.* three

세계 se-gye *n.* the world, the earth; the universe

세계대전 se-gye-dae-jeon *n.* World War; 세계 제1차 대전 se-gye je-il-cha dae-jeon World War I

세계일주 se-gye-il-jju *n.* a tour round the world

세계적으로 se-gye-jeog-eu-ro *adv.* internationally

세관 se-gwan *n.* customs *(government)*

세균 se-gyun *n.* bacteria, germ

세금 se-geum *n.* tax
세기 se-gi *n.* century
세기말 se-gi-mal *n.* the end of a century
세놓다 se-no-ta *v.* rent, lease
세다 se-da *v.* be strong, be powerful; be severe, be rough; count, calculate; 그는 힘이 세다 geun-neun him-i se-da He is strong; 오늘 바람이 세다 o-neul ba-ram-i se-da The wind is severe today; 아이가 돈을 센다 a-i-ga don-eul sen-da The child counts money
세대 se-dae *n.* generation
세련되다 se-ryeon-doe-da *v.* be polished, be refined
세로 se-ro *n.* length
세면대 se-myeon-dae *n.* washstand
세모 se-mo *n.* triangle
세미나 sse-mi-na *n.* seminar
세배 se-bae *n.* formal bow on New Year's Day, New Year's Bow given to one's senior
세뱃돈 se-baet-don *n.* the New Year's gift of money given to one's juniors
세상 se-sang *n.* the world; society, the public; one's lifetime; 세상에는 이상한 일들이 많다 se-sang-e-neun i-sang-han il-deul-i man-ta Many strange things happen in the world; 그건 세상이 다 아는 이야기이다 geu-geon se-sang-i da a-neun i-ya-gi-i-da The public knows that whole story; 그 노인은 한 세상동안 여러가지 일을 겪었다 geu no-in-eun han se-sang-dong-an yeo-reo-ga-ji il-eul gyeokk-eot-da That old man experienced so many things in his lifetime
세상에 se-sang-e *adv.* on earth, in the world, my God
세수하다 se-su-ha-da *v.* wash face, wash up
세우다 se-u-da *v.* stop, park, stand; build, erect, establish
세워지다 se-wo-ji-da *v.* be built, be established
세월 se-wol *n.* (*long period of*) time
세일 sse-il *n.* sale
세일기간 sse-il-gi-ga *n.* discount sale period
세제 se-je *n.* detergent
세종대왕 se-jong-dae-wang *n.* the Great King Sejong (*inventor of the Korean alphabet, 1397-1450*)

세주다 se-ju-da *v.* lease, rent
세차게 se-cha-ge *adv.* strongly, heavily
세차장 se-cha-jang *n.* car wash
세탁기 se-tak-gi *n.* washing machine
세탁비누 se-tak-bi-nu *n.* laundry detergent
세탁소 se-tak-so *n.* laundromat
세탁실 se-tak-sil *n.* laundry room
세탁통 se-tak-tong *n.* laundry basket
세탁표지 se-tak-pyo-ji *n.* laundry care label
세탁하다 se-ta-ka-da *v.* do laundry
세트 sse-teu *n.* a set
센터 ssen-teo *n.* center
셀 수 없이 sel ssu eops-i *adv.phr.* countless
셈이다 sem-i-da *v.* to be as though, I would say, to suppose, (*one*) plans to, (*one*) intends to; 그가 이긴 셈이다 geu-ga i-gin sem-i-da It's just as though he won.
셋방 set-bang *n.* rented room, room for rent
셋방살이 set-bang-sal-i *n.* living in a rented room
셔츠 syeo-cheu *n.* shirt
셔터 syeo-teo *n.* shutter
소 so *n.* cow; 소 죽 so juk *n.* boiled hay and grain mixture (*cattle feed*); 소 시장 so si-jang *n.* cattle market; 농부들이 소시장에서 소를 사고 판다 nong-bu-deul-i so-si-jang-e-seo so-reul sa-go pan-da Farmers buy and sell their cows at the cattle market
소개되다 so-gae-doe-da *v.* be introduced, be recommended
소개받다 so-gae-bat-da *v.* get someone introduced, get someone recommended; be introduced, be recommended
소개하다 so-gae-ha-da *v.* introduce, recommend
소고기 so-go-gi *n.* beef
소곤거리다 so-gon-geo-ri-da *v.* whisper
소극장 so-geuk-jang *n.* small theater (*for live performances*)
소극적 so-geuk-jeok *adj.* passive, negative
소금 so-geum *n.* salt
소금물 so-geum-mul *n.* salt water
소나기 so-na-gi *n.* sudden rainfall
소나무 so-na-mu *n.* pine tree
소녀 so-nyeo *n.* young girl
소년 so-nyeon *n.* young boy
소독약 so-dong-nyak *n.* disinfectant
소독하다 so-do-ka-da *v.* disinfect, sterilize

소련 sso-ryeon *n.* Soviet Union

소련인 sso-ryeon-in *n.* citizen of the Soviet Union

소름 so-reum *n.* goose bumps, gooseflesh; 소름 끼치다 so-reum kki-chi-da *v.* shudder, shiver, thrill

소리 so-ri *n.* sound, noise; 소리 내다 so-ri nae-da *v.* make a sound

소리글자 so-ri-geul-jja *n.* phonetic symbol

소리지르다 so-ri-ji-reu-da *v.* shout, yell

소리치다 so-ri-chi-da *v.* shout, yell

소리나다 so-ri na-da *v.* sound

소매 so-mae *n.* sleeve

소매치기 so-mae-chi-gi *n.* pickpocket; the act of picking someone's pocket

소문 so-mun *n.* news, rumor, gossip

소문나다 so-mun-na-da *v.* start a rumor

소방관 so-bang-gwan *n.* fireman

소방서 so-bang-seo *n.* fire station

소방차 so-bang-cha *n.* fire truck

소비 so-bi *n.* consumption

소비자 so-bi-ja *n.* consumer

소설 so-seol *n.* novel

소설가 so-seol-ga *n.* fiction writer, novelist

소설책 so-seol-chaek *n.* novel

소수 so-su *n.* minority

소스 sso-sseu *n.* sauce

소시지 sso-si-ji *n.* sausage

소식 so-sik *n.* news, information

소아과 so-a-kkwa *n.* pediatrics

소아마비 so-a-ma-bi *n.* polio

소양댐 so-yang-ttaem *n.* So Yang dam *(tourist destination)*

소용없다 so-yong-eop-da *v.* be useless, be of no use

소원 so-won *n.* desire, wish

소인 so-in *n.* child; postmark; 입장료 소인 1500원 ip-jang-nyo so-in cheon-o-baeg-won child's entrance fee; 1500 Korean won; 우체국 소인이 안 찍혔다 u-che-guk so-in-i an jji-kyeot-da The postmark is not stamped on this letter

소주 so-ju *n.* Korean hard liquor

소중하다 so-jung-ha-da *v.* be important, be valuable, be precious

소중히 여기다 so-jung-hi yeo-gi-da *v.phr.* consider precious, valuable

소책자 so-chaek-ja *n.* pamphlet, booklet

소쿠리 so-ku-ri *n.* bamboo basket

소크라테스 sso-keu-ra-te-sseu *n.* Socrates

소파 sso-pa *n.* sofa

소포 so-po *n.* parcel, package

소품 so-pum *n.* state properties; small piece of art work

소풍 so-pung *n.* picnic; 소풍 가다 so-pung ga-da *v.* go on an outing

소프트웨어 sso-peu-teu-we-eo *n.* software

소형 so-hyeong *n.* small item

소화 so-hwa *n.* digestion; 소화가 되다 so-hwa-ga doe-da *v.* be digested

속 sok *n.* inside, interior; heart; 속 끓이다 sok kkeul-i-da *v.* agonize, suffer anxiety, worry; 속 썩다 sok sseok-da *v.* feel troubled, feel distressed, feel depressed, feel disheartened; 속 썩이다 sok sseog-i-da *v.* annoy; cause heartache

속눈썹 song-nun-sseop *n.* eyelashes

속다 sok-da *v.* be cheated, be deceived, be fooled

속달우편 sok-dal-u-pyeon *n.* express mail service

속도 sok-do *n.* speed, pace, tempo

속도제한 sok-do-je-han *n.* speed limit

속력 song-nyeok *n.* speed, rate, velocity

속마음 song-ma-eum *n.* innermost feelings, bottom of one's heart

속보이다 sok-bo-i-da *v.* disclose one's intention

속삭이다 sok-sag-i-da *v.* whisper, talk in whispers

속상하다 sok-sang-ha-da *v.* be upset, feel troubled, be distressing, be distressed; 남자친구랑 싸워서 속상하다 nam-ja-chin-gu-rang ssa-wo-seo sok-sang-ha-da I'm upset because I fought with my boyfriend

속옷 sog-ot *n.* underwear

속이다 sog-i-da *v.* deceive, cheat, trick

속임수 sog-im-su *n.* trick, deception, cheat

속치마 sok-chi-ma *n.* underskirt, slip, chemise

속타다 sok-ta-da *v.* be distressed, be vexed

속태우다 sok-tae-u-da *v.* worry, be distressed, be vexed; make nervous, cause to worry

속하다 so-ka-da *v.* belong to

손 son *n.* hand; 손 씻다 son ssit-da *v.* wash hands

손가락 son-kka-rak *n.* finger

손가락질하다 son-kka-rak-jil-ha-da *v.* point fingers at, scorn, ridicule

손녀 son-nyeo *n.* grandchildren

손님 son-nim *n.* guest, visitor; customer, client

손들다 son-deul-da *v.* raise one's hand; give in, throw up one's hand, be beaten

손등 son-tteung *n.* back of the hand

손목 son-mok *n.* wrist

손바닥 son-ppa-dak *n.* palm of the hand

손뼉치다 son-ppyeok-chi-da *v.* clap one's hands

손세탁 son-se-tak *n.* hand wash *(laundry)*

손수건 son-ssu-geon *n.* handkerchief

손아랫사람 son-a-raet-sa-ram *n.* someone younger than you, one's junior *(in age)*; 그는 손아랫사람에게 늘 자상하다 geu-neun son-a-raet-sa-ram-e-ge neul ja-sang-ha-da He is always gentle with younger people

손윗사람 son-wit-sa-ram *n.* someone older than you, one's senior *(in age)*; 그는 늘 손윗사람을 존경한다 geu-neun neul son-wit-sa-ram-eul jon-gyeong-han-da He always respects older people

손자 son-ja *n.* grandson

손잡이 son-jab-i *n.* handle, knob, grip

손전등 son-jjeon-deung *n.* flashlight

손질하다 son-jil-ha-da *v.* take care of, handle with care

손짓발짓 son-jjit-bal-jjit *n.* body language

손짓하다 son-jji-ta-da *v.* gesture, make a gesture

손톱 son-top *n.* fingernail

손톱깎이 son-top-kkakk-i *n.* nail clipper

손해 son-hae *n.* damage, harm, loss

솔방울 sol-ppang-ul *n.* pine cone

솔솔 sol-sol *adv.* softly, gently

솔잎 sol-lip *n.* pine needle

솔직하다 sol-jji-ka-da *v.* be frank; be openhearted

솜 som *n.* cotton, cotton wool

솜사탕 som-sa-tang *n.* cotton candy

솜씨 som-ssi *n.* skill, ability

솟다 sot-da *v.* gush out, flow out

송곳 song-got *n.* awl, auger

송두리째 song-du-ri-jjae *adv.* completely, thoroughly

송별회 song-byeol-hoe *n.* farewell party

송송 song-song *adv.* into small pieces, finely; full of small holes

송아지 song-a-ji *n.* calf

송이 song-i *n.* cluster, blossom, flake

송편 song-pyeon *n.* rice-cake steamed on a layer of pine needles *(traditional food for Korean harvest festival)*

솥 sot *n.* iron pot

솥뚜껑 sot-ttu-kkeong *n.* lid of an iron pot

쇠 soe *n.* iron, metal

쇠고기 soe-go-gi *n.* beef; 쇠고기 전 soe-go-gi jeon *n.* ground-beef and vegetable pancake

쇠다 soe-da *v.* celebrate, observe holiday

쇼 ssyo *n.* show

쇼핑 syo-ping *n.* shopping

쇼핑센터 syo-ping-sen-teo *n.* shopping center

쇼핑하다 syo-ping-ha-da *v.* shop, go shopping

수갑 su-gap *n.* handcuffs

수건 su-geon *n.* towel

수고하다 su-go-ha-da *v.* put forth effort, take pains, work hard

수녀 su-nyeo *n.* nun

수다스럽다 su-da-seu-reop-da *v.* be talkative

수다쟁이 su-da-jaeng-i *n.* talkative person

수단 su-dan *n.* means, ways, device

수도 su-do *n.* capital city; waterworks, running water *(utility)*

수도권 su-do-kkwon *n.* capital district *(national)*, metropolitan area around the capital city

수동적 su-dong-jeok *adj.* passive

수레 su-re *n.* wagon, cart

수력발전 su-ryeok-bal-jjeon *n.* hydroelectric power generation

수력발전소 su-ryeok-bal-jjeon-so *n.* hydro-electric power plant

수리센터 su-ri-ssen-teo *n.* repair center

수리하다 su-ri-ha-da *v.* repair, fix, mend; accept, receive; 차를 수리했다 cha-reul su-ri-haet-da He/she repaired his car; 사장이 사표를 수리했다 sa-jang-i sa-pyo-reul su-ri-haet-da The president accepted his resignation

수명 su-myeong *n.* life span

수박 su-bak *n.* watermelon; 수박 철 su-bak cheol *n.* watermelon season

수백만 su-baeng-man *n.* millions

수북이 su-bug-i *adv.* in a heap, high

수산시장 su-san-si-jang *n.* seafood market

수산업 su-san-eop *n.* fishery, marine product industry

수상교통 su-sang-gyo-tong *n.* water transportation

수상스키 su-sang-seu-ki *n.* water skis

수속절차 su-sok-jeol-cha *n.* formalities, procedure

수수께끼 su-su-kke-ki *n.* riddle, puzzle

수수료 su-su-ryo *n.* fee

수술 su-sul *n.* operation

수술하다 su-sul-ha-da *v.* have surgery

수시로 su-si-ro *adv.* at any time

수십 su-sip *n.* tens of (*20, 30, 40, etc.*); scores of

수양 su-yang *n.* cultivation of mind, mental traning

수양하다 su-yang-ha-da *v.* train one's mind

수업 su-eop *n.* class, instruction

수없이 su-eops-i *adv.* innumerably

수염 su-yeom *n.* beard, mustache, whiskers

수영 su-yeong *n.* swimming

수영복 su-yeong-bok *n.* swimsuit

수영장 su-yeong-jang *n.* swimming pool

수영하다 su-yeong-ha-da *v.* swim

수요일 su-yo-il *n.* Wednesday

수입 su-ip *n.* income; import

수입품 su-i-pum *n.* imported goods

수입하다 su-i-pa-da *v.* import

수재민 su-jae-min *n.* flood victim

수저 su-jeo *n.* spoon; spoon and chopsticks, (*traditional Korean*) utensils

수정과 su-jeong-gwa *n.* dried persimmon fruit punch

수족관 su-jok-gwan *n.* aquarium

수준 su-jun *n.* level, standard

수줍어하다 su-jub-eo-ha-da *v.* feel shy, feel timid, feel bashful

수증기 su-jeung-gi *n.* steam, vapor

수집하다 su-ji-pa-da *v.* collect

수천 su-cheon *n.* thousands

수첩 su-cheop *n.* a pocket notebook, notebook

수출 su-chul *n.* export

수출품 su-chul-pum *n.* exports, exported goods

수출하다 su-chul-ha-da *v.* export

수표 su-pyo *n.* check

수프 su-peu *n.* soup

수필 su-pil *n.* essay

수필집 su-pil-jip *n.* collection of essays

수학 su-hak *n.* mathematics

수학여행 su-hang-nyeo-haeng *n.* school trip, field trip

수화기 su-hwa-gi *n.* telephone receiver

숙녀 sung-nyeo *n.* lady, gentlewoman

숙면하다 sung-myeon-ha-da *v.* sleep well

숙모 sung-mo *n.* aunt

숙박비 suk-bak-bi *n.* lodging charge, room and board

숙박시설 suk-bak-si-seol *n.* sleeping accommodation

숙박업소 suk-bag-eop-so *n.* hospitality industry, inn, hotel

숙소 suk-so *n.* lodging, abode

숙이다 sug-i-da *v.* drop, bow, droop

숙제 suk-je *n.* homework, assignment; 숙제하다 suk-je ha-da *v.* do one's homework

순간 sun-gan *n.* moment, instant

순경 sun-gyeong *n.* police officer

순면 sun-myeon *n.* pure cotton

순모 sun-mo *n.* pure wool

순서 sun-seo *n.* order, sequence; method

순서대로 sun-seo-dae-ro *adv.* in order, sequentially

순수하다 sun-su-ha-da *v.* be pure, be genuine

순식간에 sun-sik-gan-e *adv.* in the blink of an eye

순진하다 sun-jin-ha-da *v.* be naïve, be pure, be genuine

순하다 sun-ha-da *v.* be gentle, be meek, be amiable

숟가락 sut-ga-rak *n.* spoon

술 sul *n.* liquor, alcoholic drink; 술 마시다 sul ma-si-da *v.* drink alcohol

술고래 sul-go-rae *n.* strong drinker

술래잡기 sul-lae-jap-gi *n.* tag

술안주 sul-an-ju *n.* snacks eaten with drinks

술자리 sul-jja-ri *n.* drinking party

술잔 sul-jjan *n.* shot glass, Korean wine cup; wine glass

술집 sul-jjip *n.* pub, bar

숨 sum *n.* breath, breathing, respiration

숨기다 sum-gi-da *v.* conceal, hide

숨다 sum-tta *v.* hide, take cover, disappear

숨바꼭질하다 sum-ba-kkok-jil-ha-da *v.* play hide-and-seek

숨소리 sum-sso-ri *n.* breathing sound

숨쉬다 sum-swi-da *v.* breathe, respire

숨차다 sum-cha-da *v.* be out of breath, be breathless, pant

숫자 sut-ja *n.* number

숭늉 sung-nyung *n.* scorched rice-tea, water boiled in a kettle where rice has been cooked

숭숭 sung-sung *adv.* into large pieces

숯 sut *n.* charcoal

숲 sup *n.* forest; 숲 속 sup sok *n.* forest, woods

쉬다 swi-da *v.* take rest; get hoarse; go to bed; breathe; 숨을 못 쉬겠다 sum-eul mot swi-da I cannot breathe; 이제 좀 쉬자 i-je jom swi-ja Let's rest now

쉰 swin *n.* fifty

쉴 새 없이 swil sae eops-i *adv.phr.* without time to rest, without a break

쉽게 swip-ge *adv.* easily, simply

쉽다 swip-da *v.* be easy, be simple

슈퍼마켓 syu-peo-ma-ket *n.* supermarket

스님 seu-nim *n.* monk, priest

스릴 seu-ril *n.* thrill

스무 seu-mu *adj.* twenty

스물 seu-mul *n.* twenty

스웨터 seu-we-teo *n.* sweater

스위치 seu-wi-chi *n.* switch

스치다 seu-chi-da *v.* pass by

스카프 seu-ka-peu *n.* scarf

스커트 seu-keo-teu *n.* skirt

스케이트 seu-ke-i-teu *n.* skate

스케이트장 seu-ke-i-teu-jang *n.* skating rink

스케줄 seu-ke-jul *n.* schedule

스케치북 seu-ke-chi-buk *n.* sketchbook

스쿠버다이빙 seu-keu-beo-da-i-bing *n.* scuba diving

스키 seu-ki *n.* ski; 스키 타다 seu-ki ta-da *v.* ski

스키장 seu-ki-jang *n.* ski resort

스타일 seu-ta-il *n.* style

스타킹 seu-ta-king *n.* stocking, pantyhose

스트레스 seu-teu-re-sseu *n.* stress; 스트레스 쌓이다 seu-teu-re-sseu ssa-i-da *v.* be under stress; 스트레스 풀다 seu-teu-re-sseu pul-da *v.* get rid of stress; 스트레스 풀리다 seu-teu-re-sseu pul-li-da *v.* recover from stress

스팀 seu-tim *n.* heating system; steam

스파게티 seu-pa-ge-ti *n.* spaghetti

스페인 seu-pe-in *n.* Spain

스포츠 seu-po-cheu *n.* sports

스포츠뉴스 seu-po-cheu-nyu-sseu *n.* sports news

스포츠카 seu-po-cheu-ka *n.* sports car

스프링 seu-peu-ring *n.* spring

슬리퍼 seul-li-peo *n.* slipper

슬퍼하다 seul-peo-ha-da *v.* feel sad, be distressed

슬프게 seul-peu-ge *adv.* sadly

슬프다 seul-peu-da *v.* be sad

슬픔 seul-peum *n.* sorrow, sadness

습관 seup-gwan *n.* habit

습기 seup-gi *n.* moisture, dampness

습도 seup-do *n.* humidity

승강기 seung-gang-gi *n.* elevator

승객 seung-gaek *n.* passenger

승리 seung-ni *n.* victory

승무원 seung-mu-won *n.* crewman, stewardess

승용차 seung-yong-cha *n.* passenger car

승진 seung-jin *n.* promotion, advancement

시 si *n.* poem; time, hour; o'clock; city; 그는 시를 쓴다 geu-neun si-reul sseun-da He writes a poem; 몇시예요 myeot-si-ye-yo What time is it; 다섯시예요 da-seot-si-ye-yo It's five o'clock; 전주시는 별로 크지 않다 jeon ju si neun byeol lo keu ji an ta Jeon-ji city is not very big

시가 ssi-ga *n.* cigar

시가 si-kka *n.* current price, market price

시간 si-gan *n.* hours; time (*duration*); 시간 없다 si-gan eop-da *v.* have no time; 시간 있다 si-gan it-da *v.* have some time; 시간을 지키다 si-gan-eul ji-ki-da *v.* be punctual; 시간적 여유 si-gan-jeok yeo-yu *n.* spare time

시간표 si-gan-pyo *n.* time table, schedule

시계 si-gye *n.* watch, clock

시계탑 si-gye-tap *n.* clock tower

시골 si-gol *n.* rural area, country; one's hometown

시궁창 si-gung-chang *n.* ditch, drain

시금치 si-geum-chi *n.* spinach

시기 si-gi *n.* time, times; opportunity, chance; jealousy; 지금은 시기가 좋지 않다

ji-jeum-eun si-gi-ga jo-chi an-ta It's not a good time; 시기를 잘 잡아라 si-gi-reul jal jab-a-ra Take an opportunity; 시기하지 마 si-gi-ha-ji ma Don't be jealous

시꺼멓다 si-kkeo-meo-ta *v.* be deep black

시끄럽다 si-kkeu-reop-da *v.* be clamorous, be noisy

시내 si-nae *n.* downtown, area within the city limit; brook, stream; 샌디에고 시내 구경 가자 ssaen-di-e-go si-nae gu-gyeong-ga-ja Let's go to see downtown San Diego; 시내 에 물이 말랐다 si-nae-e mul-i mal-lat-da The stream is dried up

시냇가 si-naet-ga *n.* bank of a stream

시냇물 si-naen-mul *n.* the waters of a brook

시누이 si-nu-i *n.* one's husband's sister, sister-in-law

시다 si-da *v.* be sour, be acidic, be tart

시달리다 si-dal-li-da *v.* be afflicted with, be annoyed by, suffer from

시대 si-dae *n.* period, era

시댁 si-daek *n.* the esteemed house of a woman's parents-in-law

시동 si-dong *n.* starting; 시동을 걸다 si-dong-eul geol-da *v.* start a car/machine

시동생 si-dong-saeng *n.* one's husband's younger brother, younger brother-in law

시들다 si-deul-da *v.* wither, fade; be dispirited

시들시들하다 si-deul-si-deul-ha-da *v.* be slightly wilted, have withered a little

시럽 si-reop *n.* syrup

시력 si-ryeok *n.* eyesight, vision

시루떡 si-ru-tteok *n.* steamed rice cake

시리즈 ssi-ri-jeu *n.* series

시립 si-rip *adj.* municipal

시멘트 si-men-teu *n.* cement

시무룩하다 si-mu-ru-ka-da *v.* be sullen, be displeased

시민 si-min *n.* citizen, town folk

시범 si-beom *n.* setting an example, demonstration

시범적으로 si-beom-jeog-eu-ro *adv.* by way of example

시부모 si-bu-mo *n.* parents of one's husband

시상식 si-sang-sik *n.* award ceremony

시설 si-seol *n.* establishment; equipment, facilities

시속 si-sok *n.* miles/kilometers per hour

시스템 ssi-seu-tem *n.* system

시시하다 si-si-ha-da *v.* be dull and flat, be uninteresting

시신 si-sin *n.* dead body, corpse

시아버지 si-a-beo-ji *n.* one's husband's father, father-in-law of a woman

시야 si-ya *n.* range of vision, visibility

시어머니 si-eo-meo-ni *n.* one's husband's mother, mother-in-law of a woman

시외 si-oe *n.* the outskirts of a city, the suburbs, outside the city limits

시외버스 si-oe-ppeo-sseu *n.* cross-country bus

시원섭섭하다 si-won-seop-seo-pa-da *v.* feel mixed emotions of joy and sorrow

시원시원하다 si-won-si-won-ha-da *v.* be clear and brisk, be lively

시원찮다 si-won-chan-ta *v.* be unsatisfactory; be dull

시원하다 si-won-ha-da *v.* be cool, be refreshing; feel relieved; be bright, be brisk, be active

시월 si-wol *n.* October

시인 si-in *n.* poet

시일 si-il *n.* time, days, hours; the date, the time

시작 si-jak *n.* the beginning, the start

시작하다 si-ja-ka-da *v.* start, begin

시장 si-jang *n.* market; mayor

시장보다 si-jang-bo-da *v.* go grocery shopping

시장하다 si-jang-ha-da *v.* be hungry, feel empty

시절 si-jeol *n.* occasion, season

시조 si-jo *n.* Korean sonnet

시중가격 si-jung-kka-gyeok *n.* market price

시집 si-jip *n.* one's husband's home, one's husband's family; collection of poems; 시 집 식구들이 좋다 si-jip sik-gu-deul-i jo-ta My husband's family members are very nice to me; 시집을 출판했다 si-jib-eul chul-pan-haet-da I published a collection of poems; 시집 보내다 si-jip bo-nae-da *v.* marry one's daughter off; marry one's daughter to

시집가다 si-jip-ga-da *v.* marry *(woman only)*

시집살이 si-jip-sal-i *n.* a woman's married life in the home of her husband's parents

시차 si-cha *n.* time difference

시청 si-cheong *n.* city hall; *v.* see and hear, watch; 시청 앞에서 내리세요 si-cheong ap-e-seo nae-ri-se-yo Please get off in front of City Hall; 텔레비전을 시청한다 tel-le-bi-jeon-eul si-cheong-han-da I am watching television

시청률 si-cheong-nyul *n.* program rating, an audience rating

시청자 si-cheong-ja *n.* viewer, TV audience

시청하다 si-cheong-ha-da *v.* audition

시체 si-che *n.* corpse, dead body

시치미떼다 si-chi-mi-tte-da *v.* pretend not to know

시커멓다 si-keo-meo-ta *v.* be dark, be black

시키다 si-ki-da *v.* force a person to do, order; make somebody do something

시퍼렇다 si-peo-reo-ta *v.* be deep blue; be deadly pale; be influential; 바닷물이 시퍼렇다 ba-dan-mul-i si-peo-reo-ta The ocean is deep blue; 놀라서 그사람 얼굴이 시퍼렇다 nol-la-seo geu-sa-ram eol-gul-i si-peo-reo-ta His face is deadly pale because he is so shocked

시합 si-hap *n.* match, game

시합하다 si-ha-pa-da *v.* play against, have a game

시험 si-heom *n.* test, exam; experiment; trial; 시험에 떨어지다 si-heom-e tteol-eo-ji-da *v.* fail an exam

시험보다 si-heom-bo-da *v.* take an exam

시험준비 si-heom-jun-bi *n.* test preparation

시험지 si-heom-ji *n.* test paper

시험하다 si-heom-ha-da *v.* test, experiment

식 sik *n.* style, form, type, fashion; ceremony, rituals

식곤증 sik-gon-jjeung *n.* languor, drowsiness

식구 sik gu *n.* family, member of family

식기세척기 sik-gi-se-cheok-gi *n.* dish washer, dish washing machine

식다 sik-da *v.* cool off

식당 sik-dang *n.* restaurant, cafeteria, dining room

식료품 sing-nyo-pum *n.* food items

식목일 sing-mog-il *n.* Arbor Day

식물 sing-mul *n.* plant, vegetation

식물원 sing-mul-won *n.* botanical garden

식비 sik-bi *n.* food expenses

식빵 sik-ppang *n.* bread

식사 sik-sa *n.* meal

식사습관 sik-sa-seup-gwan *n.* table manners

식사하다 sik-sa-ha-da *v.* take a meal, dine, eat

식성 sik-seong *n.* taste, preference, palate

식욕 sig-yok *n.* appetite

식은땀 sig-eun-ttam *n.* cold sweat

식전 sik-jeon *n.* before a meal

식중독 sik-jung-dok *n.* food poisoning

식초 sik-cho *n.* vinegar

식탁 sik-tak *n.* dining table

식품 sik-pum *n.* food, food items

식혜 si-kye *n.* sweet rice drink, Korean rice punch

식후 si-ku *n.* after a meal

식히다 si-ki-da *v.* cool, let a thing cool

신 sin *n.* footwear, shoes; joy, delight; God; 신을 사야 돼 sin-eul sa-ya dwae I have to buy a pair of shoes; 신났다 sin-nat-da He is joyful; 신을 믿는다 sin-eul min-neun-da I believe in God

신경 sin-gyeong *n.* nerves; 신경 쓰다 sin-gyeong sseu-da *v.* concern oneself, care, mind

신고하다 sin-go-ha-da *v.* declare, report

신기다 sin-gi-da *v.* put shoes on someone, make someone put on shoes

신기하게도 sin-gi-ha-ge-da *adv.* marvelously, magically

신기하다 sin-gi-ha-da *v.* be marvelous, be wonderful

신기해하다 sin-gi-hae-ha-da *v.* think something is marvelous or magical

신나게 sin-na-ge *adv.* excitingly

신나다 sin-na-da *v.* be excited, feel triumphant

신년계획 sin-nyeon-gye-hoek *n.* New Year's resolution

신다 sin-tta *v.* put on, wear (*footwear*)

신라 sil-la *n.* a kingdom during the Three Kingdom Period (*Korean historical period, 57 B.C.-935*)

신랑 sil-lang *n.* groom (*in a wedding*)

신랑감 sil-lang-kkam *n.* groom-to-be, eligible bachelor

신문 sin-mun *n.* newspaper

신문사 sin-mun-sa *n.* newspaper company

신발 sin-bal *n.* shoes

신발가게 sin-bal-kka-ge *n.* shoe store

신발업 sin-bal-eop *n.* footwear manufacturers

신발장 sin-bal-jjang *n.* shoe-keeping closet

신부 sin-bu *n.* bride; catholic priest; 신부가 예쁘다 sin-bu-ga ye-ppeu-da The bride is pretty; 성당에 신부님이 계신다 seong-dang-e sin-bu-nim-i gye-sin-da There is a priest inside the catholic church

신부감 sin-bu-kkam *n.* bride-to-be

신분 sin-bun *n.* social position

신분증 sin-bun-jjeung *n.* ID card

신비하다 sin-bi-ha-da *v.* be mystic, be mysterious, be miraculous

신사 sin-sa *n.* gentleman

신사복 sin-sa-bok *n.* business suit

신선 sin-seon *n.* Taoist hermit (*with super-natural powers*), a mountain wizard

신선로 sin-seol-lo *n.* brass chafing dish, Korean traditional dish with vegetables, meat and seafood in a chafing dish

신선하다 sin-seon-ha-da *v.* be fresh

신세대 sin-se-dae *n.* new generation

신식 sin-sik *n.* new style, new method

신용카드 sin-yong-ka-deu *n.* credit card

신인 sin-in *n.* rising star

신입사원 sin-ip-sa-won *n.* newly hired employee; rookie

신자 sin-ja *n.* believer (*in a religion*)

신제품 sin-je-pum *n.* new product

신중하다 sin-jung-ha-da *v.* be prudent, be discreet

신청서 sin-cheong-seo *n.* application form

신청하다 sin-cheong-ha-da *v.* apply, fill out an application

신체 sin-che *n.* body

신체검사 sin-che-geom-sa *n.* physical checkup

신하 sin-ha *n.* government officer, minister

신형 sin-hyeong *n.* new model, new style

신호 sin-ho *n.* signal

신호등 sin-ho-deung *n.* traffic light; traffic signal

신혼부부 sin-hon-bu-bu *n.* newly wed couple

신혼여행 sin-hon-yeo-haeng *n.* honeymoon

신화 sin-hwa *n.* myth, mythology

싣다 sit-da *v.* load, take on board, carry; record, publish; 차에 짐을 싣다 cha-e jim-eul sit-da to load in a car; 신문에 글을 싣다 sin-mun-e geul-eul sit-da to publish an article in a newspaper

실 sil *n.* thread, yarn

실내 sil-lae *n.* indoors

실내장식 sil-lae-jang-sik *n.* interior design

실력 sil-lyeok *n.* skill, ability

실례 sil-lye *n.* bad manners, rudeness, discourtesy

실례되다 sil-lye-doe-da *v.* act rudely

실례하다 sil-lye-ha-da *v.* be excused

실례합니다 sil-lye-ham-ni-da *v.phr.* excuse me, I beg your pardon

실리다 sil-li-da *v.* be recorded, be printed; be loaded (*for an object*)

실리콘 벨리 ssil-li-kon bel-li *n.phr.* Silicon Valley

실망하다 sil-mang-ha-da *v.* be disappointed, discouraged

실수 sil-ssu *n.* mistake, error

실수하다 sil-ssu-ha-da *v.* make a mistake

실업가 sil-eop-ga *n.* businessperson

실업자 sil-eop-ja *n.* unemployed person

실외 sil-oe *n.* outdoor

실용적 sil-yong-jeok *adj.* practical, pragmatic

실제 sil-jje *n.* the truth, fact, practice, reality, actual condition

실제로 sil-jje-ro *adv.* in fact, actually, practically

실지로 sil-jji-ro *adv.* in practice, practically, actually

실컷 sil-keot *adv.* to one's satisfaction, as much as one likes

실크 ssil-keu *n.* silk

실패하다 sil-pae-ha-da *v.* fail, end in failure, go wrong

실험하다 sil-heom-ha-da *v.* experiment, perform an experiment

싫건 좋건 sil-keon jo-keon *adv.phr.* whether one will or will not, whether willing or not

싫다 sil-ta *v.* be unlikable; not like, dislike

싫어하다 sil-eo-ha-da *v.* hate, dislike

싫증나다 sil-jjeung-na-da *v.* be tired of, get sick of

심각하다 sim-ga-ka-da *v.* be serious

심다 sim-tta *v.* plant

심리학 sim-ni-hak *n.* psychology

심보 sim-ppo *n.* mind, nature, disposition

심부름 sim-bu-reum *n.* errand; 심부름 시키다 sim-bu-reum si-ki-da make someone go on an errand

심부름센터 sim-bu-reum-ssen-teo *n.*
personal assistant service (*business that
runs errands for customers*)

심부름하다 sim-bu-reum-ha-da *v.* run an
errand

심사위원 sim-sa-wi-won *n.* judge, examiner

심사하다 sim-sa-ha-da *v.* judge, investigate,
inspect, screen

심술 sim-sul *n.* cross temper, ill nature

심술꾸러기 sim-sul-kku-reo-gi *n.* ill-natured
person

심술부리다 sim-sul-bu-ri-da *v.* be cross with,
be unkind to

심술쟁이 sim-sul-jaeng-i *n.* ill-natured person

심심하다 sim-sim-ha-da *v.* be bored, feel
bored

심야 sim-ya *n.* the dead of night, midnight

심장 sim-jang *n.* the heart *(body)*

심장마비 sim-jang-ma-bi *n.* heart failure

심지어 sim-ji-eo *adv.* even, what is more, on
top of that

심판 sim-pan *n.* referee, umpire; judgment,
trial

심하게 sim-ha-ge *adv.* seriously

심하다 sim-ha-da *v.* be severe, be keen, be
fierce

십 sip *n.* ten, the tenth

십대 sip-dae *n.* the teenage years; teenager

십만 sim-man *n.* hundred thousand

십억 sib-eok *n.* billion

십이월 sib-i-wol *n.* December

십일월 sib-il-wol *n.* November

십자가 sip-ja-ga *n.* a cross *(Christianity)*

싱가포르 sing-ga-po-reu *n.* Singapore

싱겁다 sing-geop-da *v.* taste bland

싱글벙글 sing-geul-beong-geul *adv.* smiling

싱글벙글하다 sing-geul-beong-geul-ha-da *v.*
smile, beam

싱싱하다 sing-sing-ha-da *v.* be fresh, be new,
be full of life

싱크대 ssing-keu-dae *n.* sink

싸구려 ssa-gu-ryeo *n.* inferior article, cheap
article

싸늘하다 ssa-neul-ha-da *v.* be cool, be
chilled

싸다 ssa-da *v.* be cheap, be inexpensive;
wrap up, bundle, pack up, cover

싸매다 ssa-mae-da *v.* wrap and tie up

싸우다 ssa-u-da *v.* argue, fight, have a quarrel

싸움 ssa-um *n.* struggle, fight, battle, conflict

싸움하다 ssa-um-ha-da *v.* struggle, fight,
have a quarrel

싹 ssak *n.* bud, sprout; *adv.* completely,
entirely, with clean sweep; 싹이 나왔다
ssag-i na-wat-da The sprout appeared; 집
이 싹 타 버렸다 jib-i ssak ta beo-ryeot-da
The house burned down completely

싹트다 ssak-teu-da *v.* bud, sprout, germinate

쌀 ssal *n.* raw rice, uncooked rice

쌀쌀하다 ssal-ssal-ha-da *v.* be chilly

쌈 ssam *n.* rice wrapped in leaves of lettuce
(Korean traditional dish)

쌍 ssang *n.* pair

쌍꺼풀 ssang-kkeo-pul *n.* double-folded
eyelid

쌍둥이 ssang-dung-i *n.* twins

쌍쌍이 ssang-ssang-i *adv.* by twos, in pairs

쌍안경 ssang-an-gyeong *n.* binoculars

쌓다 ssa-ta *v.* pile up, heap up; erect,
construct; accumulate

쌓이다 ssa-i-da *v.* be piled up, be heaped;
pile up

써내다 sseo-nae-da *v.* write and hand out,
turn out written material

써넣다 sseo-neo-ta *v.* fill in the blanks, fill
in the form

써보다 sseo-bo-da *v.* write; use; wear

써주다 sseo-ju-da *v.* write for someone's
sake; use for someone's sake

써지다 sseo-ji-da *v.* be written *(passive)*

썩 sseok *adv.* very much, greatly; right away,
immediately

썩다 sseok-da *v.* go bad, rot, spoil, decay

썩이다 sseog-i-da *v.* let a thing rot, corrupt,
spoil; leave unemployed, let go to waste;
make one sick at heart; 음식을 안 먹고 다
썩인다 eum-sig-eul an eok-go da sseog-
in-da They do not eat the food and let it
spoil; 기술을 안 쓰고 썩인다 gi-seul-eul
an sseu-go sseog-in-da He does not use his
skills and remains unemployed; 그는 어
머니 속을 썩인다 geu-neun eo-meo-ni
sog-eul sseog-in-da He makes his mother
sick at heart

썰다 sseol-da *v.* cut into small pieces, chop, dice, slice

썰매 sseol-mae *n.* sled, sleigh

썰물 sseol-mul *n.* ebb, ebb tide

쏘다 sso-da *v.* shoot, fire, discharge

쏘아올리다 sso-a-ol-li-da *v.* shoot up, launch

쏘이다 sso-i-da *v.* be stung; expose to the sun

쏟다 ssot-da *v.* pour out, spill, empty

쏟아지다 ssod-a-ji-da *v.* pour out, get spilt

쑤셔 넣다 ssu-syeo neo-ta *v.* thrust in, stuff into

쑤시다 ssu-si-da *v.* tingle; feel sharp pain

쑥 ssuk *adv.* (*protruded*) way out, (*sunken*) way in; with a jerk; *n.* wormwood

쑥스럽다 ssuk-sseu-reop-da *v.* be unseemly, be indecent, be improper

쑥쑥 ssuk-ssuk *adv.* growing fast

쓰다 sseu-da *v.* write; use; wear; be bitter; employ

쓰다듬다 sseu-da-deum-tta *v.* stroke, pat, pass one's hand over

쓰러뜨리다 sseu-reo-tteu-ri-da *v.* throw down, knock down

쓰러지다 sseu-reo-ji-da *v.* collapse, break down from exhaustion, fall down; be ruined

쓰레기 sseu-re-gi *n.* waste, garbage, rubbish, trash

쓰레기통 sseu-re-gi-tong *n.* trash can, garbage can, waste basket

쓰여있다 sseu-yeo-it-da *v.* be written

쓰이다 sseu-i-da *v.* be spent, cost; be used, serve

쓱 sseuk *adv.* quickly and quietly; abruptly; rapidly

쓸다 sseul-da *v.* sweep off, sweep away

쓸데없다 sseul-tte-eop-da *v.* be of no use, be useless

쓸데없이 sseul-tte-eops-i *adv.* uselessly, of no use

쓸모있다 sseul-mo-it-da *v.* be useful, be of use

쓸쓸하다 sseul-sseul-ha-da *v.* be lonely

쓸쓸히 sseul-sseul-hi *adv.* lonely

씌우다 ssi-u-da *v.* put a hat on, plate a thing with, cover

씨 ssi *n.* seed, kernel; breed, lineage; Mr., Mrs., Miss.; 씨 뿌리다 ssi ppu-ri-da *v.* plant a seed

씨디 플레이어 ssi-di peul-le-i-eo *n.* CD player

씨름 ssi-reum *n.* Korean wrestling

씨름하다 ssi-reum-ha-da *v.* wrestle

씨앗 ssi-at *n.* seed

씩웃다 ssik ut-da *v.* smile

씩 ssik *part.* each, apiece

씩씩 ssik-ssik *adv.* breathing heavily, panting

씩씩하다 ssik-ssi-ka-da *v.* be manly, be valiant, be brave

씹다 ssip-da *v.* chew

씹히다 ssi-pi-da *v.* be chewed

씻다 ssit-da *v.* wash, rinse; wipe out, wipe off

씻어놓다 ssis-eo-no-ta *v.* wash, rinse

ㅇ

아가 a-ga *n.* baby

아가미 a-ga-mi *n.* gills of a fish

아가씨 a-ga-ssi *n.* miss, young lady

아군 a-gun *n.* our troops

아궁이 a-gung-i *n.* fireplace

아기 a-gi *n.* baby

아기자기하다 a-gi-ja-gi-ha-da *v.* be sweet, be charming; be full of interest

아까 a-kka *adv.* a little while ago, a while ago, a moment ago; some time ago

아깝다 a-kkap-da *v.* be regrettable, be pitiful; be precious, be valuable

아끼다 a-kki-da *v.* spare, begrudge, be sparing of

아낌없이 a-kkim-eops-i *adv.* unsparingly, ungrudgingly, generously, without stint

아나운서 a-na-un-seo *n.* announcer

아낙네 a-nang-ne *n.* woman; wife

아날로그 a-nal-lo-geu *n.* analogue

아내 a-nae *n.* my wife

아늑하다 a-neu-ka-da *v.* be cozy, be snug, be comfortable

아는체하다 a-neun-che-ha-da *v.* pretend to know; speak in a knowing manner

아니 a-ni *adv.* not; no; why; what

아니꼽다 a-ni-kkop-da *v.* be disgusting, be sickening; be nauseated, be sick

아니나 다를까 a-ni-na-da-reul-kka *adv.phr.* just as was expected, as one expected, sure enough; 아니나 다를까 그는 나타나지 않았다 a-ni-na da-reul-kka geu-neun na-ta-na-ji an-at-da As was expected, he didn't appear

아니다 a-ni-da *v.* not be, negate; 그는 학생이 아니다 geu-neun hak-saeng-i a-ni-da He is not a student

아니라면 a-ni-ra-myeon *adv.phr.* if (*you say*) it is not; 그게 사실이 아니라면 어떤게 사실이지 geu-ge sa-sil-i a-ni-ra-myeon eo-tteon-ge sa-sil-i-ji If that is not true what is the truth

아니면 a-ni-myeon *adv.phr.* either ... or; otherwise; 너 이니면 내가 맞다 neo a-ni-myeon nae-ga mat-da Either you or I are right

아니오 a-ni-o *v.phr.* no; 아니오, 그 사람 내일 와요 a-ni-o geu sa-ram nae-il wa-yo No, he will come tomorrow

아닌게 아니라 a-nin-ge a-ni-ra *adv. phr.* sure enough, really, indeed; 아닌게 아니라 네 말이 옳다 a-nin-ge a-ni-ra ne mal-i ol-ta be sure what you say is correct

아담하다 a-dam-ha-da *v.* be nice, be elegant; be neat, be tidy

아동 a-dong *n.* child, juvenile

아드님 a-deu-nim *n.* son, *hon.* your esteemed son

아득하다 a-deu-ka-da *v.* be far away, be far off, remote, in the distance

아들 a-deul *n.* son, boy

아들녀석 a-deul-leyo-seok *n.* my son, my boy

아랍 a-rap *n.* Arab

아랑곳 않다 a-rang-got an-ta *v.* be unconcerned, take no interest

아래 a-rae *n.* the lower part; the base; under, beneath

아래위 a-rae-wi *n.* up and down, above and below, high and low; 아래위로 움직이다 a-rae-wi-ro um-jig-i-da *v.* move up and down

아래쪽 a-rae-jjok *n.* down; lower position; the south

아래층 a-rae-cheung *n.* downstairs

아랫배 a-raet-bae *n.* the belly

아랫사람 a-raet-sa-ram *n.* one's junior, one's inferior

아랫집 a-raet-jip *n.* the house just below, next door

아령 a-ryeong *n.* dumbbell

아르바이트 a-reu-ba-i-teu *n.* part-time job

아른거리다 a-reun-geo-ri-da *v.* flicker; flit; glisten; blink; haunt; come in and out of sight; glimmer; 의심의 눈초리가 그의 얼굴에 아른거린다 ui-sim-ui nun-cho-ri-ga geu-ui eol-gul-e a-reun-geo-rin-da An expression of doubt flitted across his face; 달이 나무 사이로 아른거린다 dal-i na-mu sa-i-ro a-reun-geo-rin-da The moon is glimmering through the trees

아름 a-reum *count.* the span of both arms, armful; 꽃을 한아름 샀다 kkoch-eul han-a-reum sat-da I bought an armful of flowers

아름답다 a-reum-dap-da *v.* be beautiful, be pretty, be lovely, be fine, be good-looking, be handsome, be charming

아리랑 a-ri-rang *n.* traditional Korean song "Arirang"

아리송하다 a-ri-song-ha-da *v.* be ambiguous

아마 a-ma *adv.* probably, perhaps, maybe

아마추어 a-ma-chu-eo *n.* amateur

아메리카 a-me-ri-ka *n.* America

아무 a-mu *pron.* anyone, anybody; everybody; nobody, none, no one; any; none at all; 아무 것 a-mu geot *pron.* anything; something; nothing; none; 아무 때 a-mu ttae *adv.* anytime; any day; whenever; always, all the time; 아무 말 a-mu mal *n.* any words; 아무 일 a-mu il *n.* something; anything; nothing

아무나 a-mu-na *n.* anybody

아무데 a-mu-de *n.* any place, anywhere

아무데서나 a-mu-de-seo-na *adv.* anywhere; everywhere

아무도 a-mu-do *pron.* no one, nobody

아무래도 a-mu-rae-do *adv.* anyway; anyhow; no matter what one may do; for anything; never; by any means

아무런 a-mu-reon *adv.* any sort of; whatever; in any way

아무렇게나 a-mu-reo-ke-na *adv.* in any manner one pleases, indifferently, carelessly

아무렇지도 않다 a-mu-reo-chi-do an-ta *v.*
be indifferent, be unconcerned; be safe, be
all right

아무리 a-mu-ri *adv.* however, no matter how

아무튼 a-mu-teun *adv.* anyway, no matter
what

아물다 a-mul-da *v.* heal, be healed

아버지 a-beo-ji *n.* father, dad

아부하다 a-bu-ha-da *v.* flatter, fawn

아빠 a-ppa *n.* dad, daddy

아삭거리다 a-sak-geo-ri-da *v.* be crispy

아삭아삭하다 a-sag-a-sa-ka-da *v.* be crispy,
crunchy

아쉬워하다 a-swi-wo-ha-da *v.* feel the lack
of, be inconvenienced by not having

아쉽다 a-swip-da *v.* miss; feel the lack of; be
inconvenient

아스팔트 a-seu-pal-teu *n.* asphalt

아스피린 a-seu-pi-rin *n.* aspirin

아슬아슬하다 a-seul-a-seul-ha-da *v.* be
dangerous, be risky; be critical

아시아 a-si-a *n.* Asia

아양부리다 a-yang-bu-ri-da *v.* flatter, act in a
coquettish manner

아역 a-yeok *n.* child's part in a play; child
actor

아열대 a-yeol-ttae *n.* subtropic, subtropical
zone

아예 a-ye *adv.* from the beginning; by any
means

아우성치다 a-u-seong-chi-da *v.* clamor,
scream, cry

아울러 a-ul-leo *adv.* together, along with, in
addition to

아이 a-i *n.* child, youngster; 아이 낳다 a-i
na-ta *v.* give birth

아이들 a-i-deul *n.* children

아이디어 a-i-di-eo *n.* idea

아이스크림 a-i-seu-keu-rim *n.* ice cream

아이스하키 a-i-seu-ha-ki *n.* ice hockey

아이슬란드 a-i-seul-lan-deu *n.* Iceland

아이큐 a-i-kyu *n.* IQ

아장아장 a-jang-a-jang *adv.* with toddling
steps, with short steps

아저씨 a-jeo-ssi *n.* uncle; middle-aged
man; 우리 아저씨가 어제 오셨다 uri
a-jeo-ssi-ga eo-je o-syeot-da My uncle
arrived yesterday; 아저씨, 좀 도와주세요

a-jeo-ssi jom do-wa-ju-se-yo Mister, please
help me

아주 a-ju *adv.* very much, really, utterly

아주머니 a-ju-meo-ni *n.* aunt; middle age
woman

아주버니 a-ju-beo-ni *n.* one's husband's
older brother, older brother-in-law

아지랑이 a-ji-rang-i *n.* heat haze, shimmering

아직 a-jik *adv.* yet, still; 아직 안왔어 a-jik an-
wass-eo He didn't arrive yet; 아직 일하고
있어 a-jik il-ha-go iss-eo I am still working

아직까지 a-jik-kka-ji *adv.* so far, up to now,
till now

아직도 a-jik-do *adv.* yet, still

아찔하다 a-jjil-ha-da *v.* be dizzy, feel faint

아차 a-cha *interj.* oh my, darn

아첨하다 a-cheom-ha-da *v.* flatter, fawn upon

아치 a-chi *n.* arch

아침 a-chim *n.* breakfast, morning

아침밥 a-chim-ppap *n.* breakfast

아틀리에 a-tteul-li-e *n.* atelier, studio

아파트 a-pa-teu *n.* apartment

아프다 a-peu-da *v.* be sick, feel pain

아프리카 a-peu-ri-ka *n.* Africa

아픔 a-peum *n.* pain, ache; sorrow, grief

아홉 a-hop *n.* nine

아흐레 a-heu-re *n.* nine days, ninth day of
the month

아흔 a-heun *n.* ninety

악 ak *n.* evil, vice, wickedness

악기 ak-gi *n.* musical instrument

악단 ak-dan *n.* orchestra

악담하다 ak-dam-ha-da *v.* abuse, speak ill of,
call names

악당 ak-dang *n.* villain, hooligan

악대 ak-dae *n.* musical band

악덕상인 ak-deok-sang-in *n.* dishonest dealers

악독하다 ak-do-ka-da *v.* be vicious, be harsh,
be naughty

악랄하다 ang-nal-ha-da *v.* be vicious, be
mean, be nasty

악령 ang-nyeong *n.* evil spirit

악마 ang-ma *n.* evil spirit, devil, demon

악명 ang-myeong *n.* evil reputation; 악명 높
다 ang-myeong nop-da *v.* be notorious

악몽 ang-mong *n.* bad dream, nightmare

악물다 ang-mul-da *v.* clench one's teeth

악바리 ak-ba-ri *n.* tough fellow

악법 ak-beop *n.* bad law, unjust law

악보 ak-bo *n.* musical note, music score

악선전 ak-seon-jeon *n.* vile propaganda, false propaganda

악성 ak-seong *adj.* bad, vicious

악센트 ak-sen-teu *n.* accent, stress, tone

악수 ak-su *n.* handshake

악수하다 ak-su-ha-da *v.* shake hands with

악순환 ak-sun-hwan *n.* vicious circle

악습 ak-seup *n.* bad custom; vicious habit

악쓰다 ak-sseu-da *v.* yell (*in distress*); struggle desperately

악어 ag-eo *n.* crocodile; alligator

악역 ag-yeok *n.* villain's part in a play

악연 ag-yeon *n.* bad destiny, unfortunate relation

악영향 ag-yeong-hyang *n.* bad effect, bad influence, harm

악용하다 ag-yong-ha-da *v.* abuse, misuse

악운 ag-un *n.* ill luck, bad fortune

악의 ag-ui *n.* ill will, sinister motive

악인 ag-in *n.* bad person, wicked man, villain

악조건 ak-jo-kkeon *n.* bad conditions

악질 ak-jil *n.* bad nature; inferior quality

악착같다 ak-chak-gat-da *v.* be unyielding, be tough

악착스럽다 ak-chak-seu-reop-da *v.* be unyielding, be tough

악처 ak-cheo *n.* a nagging wife

악취 ak-chwi *n.* bad smell, stink

악취미 ak-chwi-mi *n.* bad taste

악평하다 ak-pyeong-ha-da *v.* speak ill of, make a malicious remark, criticize adversely

악하다 a-ka-da *v.* be bad, be evil, be wicked, be vicious

악한 a-kan *n.* wicked fellow, villain

악화되다 a-kwa-doe-da *v.* become worse, deteriorate

안 an *adv.* not; within; less than; *n.* the inside; proposal, proposition; 저 안가요 jeo an-ga-yo I am not leaving; 3일 안에 다 해 sam-il an-e da hae Do everything in three days; 안에 아무도 없다 an-e a-mu-do eop-da No one is inside; 무슨 안이 있어요 mu-seun an-i iss-eo-yo Do you have a proposal

안간힘쓰다 an-gan-him-sseu-da *v.* hold back an urge

안감 an-kkam *n.* lining material

안개 an-gae *n.* fog, mist; 안개 끼다 an-gae kki-da *v.* be foggy

안경 an-gyeong *n.* glasses, eyeglasses; 안경 쓰다 an-gyeong sseu-da *v.* wear glasses

안경점 an-gyeong-jeom *n.* optician

안과 an-kkwa *n.* ophthalmic hospital

안구 an-gu *n.* eyeball

안기다 an-gi-da *v.* be held, hug, go into a person's arms; charge with the responsibility, lay on

안내 an-nae *n.* information, guidance

안내방송 an-nae-bang-song *n.* announcement

안내원 an-nae-won *n.* guide

안내책자 an-nae-chaek-ja *n.* brochure

안내하다 an-nae-ha-da *v.* guide, conduct, usher, lead the way

안녕하다 an-nyeong-ha-da *v.* be well, be all right, be in good health

안녕히 an-nyeong-hi *adv.* peacefully; safely

안다 an-tta *v.* hold in one's arms, embrace, hug

안달하다 an-dal-ha-da *v.* fret, worry about; be impatient

안되다 an-doe-da *v.* be sorry; must not, should not; 그 사람 너무 안됐다 geu sa-ram neo-mu an-dwaet-da I feel so sorry for him; 그러면 안돼 geu-reo-myeon an-dwae You shouldn't do that

안락사 al-lak-sa *n.* euthanasia

안마 an-ma *n.* massage

안마하다 an-ma-ha-da *v.* massage

안면있다 an-myeon-it-da *v.* be acquainted with

안목있다 an-mok it-da *v.* have an eye for, have a good eye, have a sense of discrimination

안방 an-ppang *n.* master bedroom

안보 an-bo *n.* security

안부 an-bu *n.* regards; 안부를 묻다 an-bu-reul mut-da *v.* inquire after, ask after

안부편지 an-bu-pyeon-ji *n.* letter of greeting

안색 an-saek *n.* complexion of one's face; look, expression

안성맞춤 an-seong-mat-chum *n.* the very thing wanted, the most desirable outcome, the best option

안식처 an-sik-cheo *n.* place to rest, resting place, place of retreat

안심하다 an-sim-ha-da *v.* be relieved, feel safe, rest assured

안약 an-yak *n.* eye drops, medicine for the eyes

안이하다 an-i-ha-da *v.* be easy, easygoing

안일하다 an-il-ha-da *v.* be easy, be idle, be indolent

안장 an-jang *n.* saddle

안전 an-jeon *n.* safety, security

안전벨트 an-jeon-bel-teu *n.* seat belt

안전하다 an-jeon-ha-da *v.* be safe, be secure, free from danger

안절부절 못하다 an-jeol-bu-jeol mo-ta-da *v.phr.* be restless, be anxious; be irritated

안정 an-jeong *n.* rest, repose; stability, settlement

안정하다 an-jeong-ha-da *v.* be tranquil, be at ease; be settled, stabilized

안주 an-ju *n.* appetizers served with drinks

안주머니 an-jju-meo-ni *n.* inside pocket, pocket inside one's jacket

안주인 an-jju-in *n.* the lady of the house

안주하다 an-ju-ha-da *v.* live peacefully, lead a comfortable life

안중에 없다 an-jung-e eop-da *v.phr.* be out of one's consideration

안쪽 an-jjok *n.* the inside, the inner part

안창 an-chang *n.* inner sole, shoe liner

안치다 an-chi-da *v.* get rice ready to cook, prepare rice for cooking

안타까워하다 an-ta-kka-wo-ha-da *v.* be nervous about, be anxious about; be heartbroken about; be distressed by

안타깝다 an-ta-kkap-da *v.* be heart-breaking; be distressing; be frustrating, be annoying

안테나 an-te-na *n.* antenna

안팎 an-pak *n.* the interior and exterior, the inside and outside; both sides; *adv.* more or less; around, almost

안팎에 an-pakk-e *adv.* both inside and outside

앉다 an-tta *v.* sit, take a seat, sit down; take up, hold

앉아있다 anj-a-it-da *v.* be seated

앉았다 일어났다 하다 anj-at-da il-eo-nat-da ha-da *v.phr.* keep doing and stand up

앉은뱅이 anj-eun-baeng-i *n.* disabled person

앉은키 anj-eun-ki *n.* one's height when seated

앉히다 an-chi-da *v.* make someone sit down, place someone in a seat

않을 수 없다 an-eul ssu eop-da *v.phr.* be compelled to do; be driven by dire necessity to do

알 al *n.* tablet; egg; spawn; ball; bead; 알 껍질 al kkeop-jil *n.* egg shell

알갱이 al-gaeng-i *n.* kernel, grain

알거지 al-geo-ji *n.* a person as poor as a church mouse

알곡 al-gok *n.* pure grain with no grit in it; husked grain

알기 쉽다 al-gi swip-da *v.phr.* be easy to understand, be comprehensible

알다 al-da *v.* know, be well aware of, be familiar with; understand, comprehend, grasp; recognize, realize; notice

알뜰하다 al-tteul-ha-da *v.* be prudent, be thrifty, be frugal

알랑거리다 al-lang-geo-ri-da *v.* seek to gain favor by flattery, curry favor with, flatter

알래스카 al-lae-seu-ka *n.* Alaska

알레르기 al-le-reu-gi *n.* allergy

알려주다 al-lyeo-ju-da *v.* inform

알려지다 al-lyeo-ji-da *v.* be known to; turn out, be revealed, be disclosed; become famous, win fame

알루미늄 al-lu-mi-nyum *n.* aluminum

알리다 al-li-da *v.* let a person know, inform, notify, break the news to

알림 al-lim *n.* notice, announcement

알맞다 al-mat-da *v.* be fitting, be suitable, be appropriate, be adequate

알맹이 al-maeng-i *n.* kernel; substance, contents; 땅콩 알맹이 ttang-kong al-maeng-i *n.* peanuts; 알맹이 없는 말 al-maeng-i eom-neun mal *n.* unsubstantial words

알몸 al-mom *n.* naked body, nudity

알밤 al-bam *n.* shelled chestnut

알부자 al-bu-ja *n.* rich person

알쏭달쏭하다 al-ssong-dal-ssong-ha-da *v.* be vague, be obscure, be ambiguous; be doubtful

알아내다 al-a-nae-da *v.* find out, make out, detect, discover

알아듣다 al-a-deut-da *v.* understand, catch, comprehend

알아맞히다 al-a-ma-chi-da *v.* guess right, make a good guess

알아보다 al-a-bo-da *v.* find out; check out, investigate, search

알아서 하다 al-a-seo ha-da *v.phr.* do at one's discretion, do as one thinks fit

알아주다 al-a-ju-da *v.* recognize, appreciate

알아차리다 al-a-cha-ri-da *v.* take precaution; sense, become aware of

알아채다 al-a-chae-da *v.* become aware of, notice, take notice of

알약 al lyak *n.* tablet, pill

알짜 al-jja *n.* the best thing; the essence; the gist

알짱거리다 al-jjang-geo-ri-da *v.* curry favor with, fawn upon, hang about

알코올 al-ko-ol *n.* alcohol

알통 al-tong *n.* muscles

앓는 소리 al-leun so-ri *n.phr.* moaning, groaning, complaints

앓다 al-ta *v.* be ill, be sick, suffer from

암 am *n.* cancer; stumbling block, obstacle; female

암거래 am-geo-rae *n.* black market dealing, transaction on the black market

암기하다 am-gi-ha-da *v.* memorize

암담하다 am-dam-ha-da *v.* be dark, be gloomy, be dismal

암만해도 am-man-hae-do *adv.* by all means, at all costs, at any cost, in every respect

암매장하다 am-mae-jang-ha-da *v.* bury secretly

암모니아 am-mo-ni-a *n.* ammonia

암벽 am-byeok *n.* stone wall; sheer cliff

암산하다 am-san-ha-da *v.* do in mental arithmetic

암살하다 am-sal-ha-da *v.* assassinate, murder

암석 am-seok *n.* rock, crag

암소 am-so *n.* cow

암송하다 am-song-ha-da *v.* recite, recite from memory

암수 am-su *n.* male and female

암시장 am-si-jang *n.* black market

암시하다 am-si-ha-da *v.* hint, suggest, imply

암암리에 am-am-ni-e *adv.* tacitly

암자 am-ja *n.* monk's cell, small Buddhist temple

암초 am-cho *n.* reef, submerged rock

암컷 am-keot *n.* female animal

암탉 am-tak *n.* hen

암팡지다 am-pang-ji-da *v.* be bold, be dauntless

암표 am-pyo *n.* illegally sold ticket, scalped ticket

암표상 am-pyo-sang *n.* illegal ticket-broker, scalper

암호 am-ho *n.* code, password

암흑 am-heuk *n.* darkness

압도적으로 ap-do-jeog-eu-ro *adv.* overwhelmingly, overpoweringly

압도하다 ap-do-ha-da *v.* overwhelm, overpower, surpass

압력 am-nyeok *n.* pressure, stress

압록강 am-nok-gang *n.* Amnok River (*river between North Korea and China*); Yalu River

압박하다 ap-ba-ka-da *v.* oppress; suppress; press

압수하다 ap-su-ha-da *v.* seize, take over

압정 ap-jeong *n.* thumb tack, push pin

압축하다 ap-chu-ka-da *v.* press; condense; constrict

앙갚음하다 ang-gap-eum-ha-da *v.* take revenge on, repay

앙금 ang-geum *n.* deposit; sediment

앙상하다 ang-sang-ha-da *v.* be haggard, be gaunt

앙숙 ang-suk *n.* bad terms, bad relationship

앙심 ang-sim *n.* grudge, enmity, malice; 앙심 품다 ang-sim pum-tta *v.* bear a grudge against, have a grudge against

앙증스럽다 ang-jeung-seu-reop-da *v.* be disproportionately small, be tiny, be little

앙칼지다 ang-kal-ji-da *v.* be fierce, be tenacious

앙코르 ang-ko-reu *n.* encore

앞 ap *n.* the front; the future; presence; the former; 앞 못보다 ap mot-bo-da *v.* be blind, unable to see what is going on

앞길 ap-gil *n.* the road ahead; outlook; promise

앞날 am-nal *n.* the future, the days ahead

앞당기다 ap-dang-gi-da *v.* move a date up, advance, make earlier

앞두다 ap-du-da *v.* have (*a period or a distance*) to go

앞뒤 ap-dwi *n.* before and behind, the front and the rear; order, sequence

앞마당 am-ma-dang *n.* front yard

앞머리 am-meo-ri *n.* forehead

앞문 am-mun *n.* the front gate

앞서 ap-seo *adv.* before, previously, already, in advance, beforehand

앞서가다 ap-seo-ga-da *v.* go ahead, go in advance of, go first, go before, take the lead

앞서다 ap-seo-da *v.* go before, precede, go in advance of, take the lead

앞서서 ap-seo-seo *adv.* prior to, earlier than

앞세우다 ap-se-u-da *v.* make a person lead, place a person at the head

앞으로 ap-eu-ro *adv.* from now on, in the future

앞일 am-nil *n.* the future, the time to come

앞자리 ap-ja-ri *n.* front seat

앞잡이 ap-jab-i *n.* police spy, paid informer

앞장서다 ap-jang-seo-da *v.* go ahead, lead

앞장세우다 ap-jang-se-u-da *v.* make a person lead, place a person at the head

앞줄 ap-jul *n.* front row

앞지르다 ap-ji-reu-da *v.* pass, get ahead of, leave behind

앞집 ap-jip *n.* the house in front of yours

앞차 ap-cha *n.* an earlier departing car/train; the car/train ahead

앞치마 ap-chi-ma *n.* apron

애걸하다 ae-geol-ha-da *v.* implore, beg, appeal

애교 ae-gyo *n.* charms; courtesy; 애교있다 ae-gyo it-da *v.* be charming, attractive

애국가 ae-guk-ga *n.* patriotic song, national anthem

애국심 ae-guk-sim *n.* patriotism, nationalism

애꾸눈 ae-kku-nun *n.* one-eyed person; a blind eye

애당초 ae-dang-cho *adv.* from the very first time, the beginning

애매하다 ae-mae-ha-da *v.* be vague, be obscure, be equivocal; be wrongly accused, be falsely charged

애먹다 ae-meok-da *v.* have bitter experience, have a hard time of it, be troubled

애먹이다 ae-meog-i-da *v.* harass, annoy, give a person trouble, bother

애벌레 ae-beol-le *n.* larva

애석하다 ae-seo-ka-da *v.* grieve, lament, mourn

애송이 ae-song-i *n.* very young person; novice

애써 ae-sseo *adv.* as much as possible, as much as one can

애쓰다 ae-sseu-da *v.* make efforts, take pains, work hard

애완동물 ae-wan-dong-mul *n.* pet

애용하다 ae-yong-ha-da *v.* use regularly, patronize

애원하다 ae-won-ha-da *v.* entreat, implore, appeal

애인 ae-in *n.* boyfriend/girlfriend, lover, sweetheart

애절하다 ae-jeol-ha-da *v.* be sad, be touching, be pathetic

애정 ae-jeong *n.* love, affection, devotion

애지중지하다 ae-ji-jung-ji-ha-da *v.* value highly, treasure, prize

애착 ae-chak *n.* attachment, affection

애처롭다 ae-cheo-rop-da *v.* be pitiful, be sorrowful

애초에 ae-cho-e *adv.* at first, at the start

애타다 ae-ta-da *v.* be worried, be troubled, be nervous

애태우다 ae-tae-u-da *v.* be anxious, worry, concern; annoy

애프터서비스 ae-teu-teo-sseo-bi-sseu *n.* warranty

액땜하다 aek-ttaem-ha-da *v.* forestalling an impending misfortune by undergoing one of lesser degree

액세서리 aek-se-seo-ri *n.* accessories

액센트 aek-sen-teu *n.* accent, stress

액션 aek-syeon *n.* action

액수 aek-su *n.* sum, amount

액자 aek-ja *n.* picture frame

액체 aek-che *n.* liquid, fluid

앨범 ael-beom *n.* album

앳되다 aet-doe-da *v.* look young, look childlike

앵무새 aeng-mu-sae *n.* parrot, parakeet

야간 ya-gan *n.* night, night time

야경 ya-gyeong *n.* night view, night scene

야광 ya-gwang *n.* luminous

야구 ya-gu *n.* baseball

야구장 ya-gu-jang *n.* baseball stadium

야구하다 ya-gu-ha-da *v.* play baseball

야근하다 ya-geun-ha-da v. work the night shift

야단맞다 ya-dan-mat-da v. be scolded thoroughly

야단법석 ya-dan-beop-seok n. spree; racket

야단치다 ya-dan-chi-da v. scold, rebuke

야단하다 ya-dan-ha-da v. be uproarious, be in a commotion

야당 ya-dang n. opposition party (politics)

야만인 ya-man-in n. savage, barbarian

야망 ya-mang n. personal ambition, aspiration

야무지게 ya-mu-ji-ge adv. firmly, securely, steadily

야무지다 ya-mu-ji-da v. be stout, be sturdy

야박하다 ya-ba-ka-da v. be hard-hearted, be cold-hearted, be unkind

야비하다 ya-bi-ha-da v. be vulgar, be mean, be coarse

야산 ya-san n. hill, hillock

야생동물 ya-saeng-dong-mul n. wild animal

야심 ya-sim n. ambition, aspiration

야심하다 ya-sim-ha-da v. be late at night

야영하다 ya-yeong-ha-da v. camp out

야옹 ya-ong adv. meow

야외 ya-oe n. the fields; the open air; the suburbs

야유회 ya-yu-hoe n. picnic

야자수 ya-ja-su n. coconut tree

야채 ya-chae n. vegetable

야채수프 ya-chae-su-peu n. vegetable soup

야하다 ya-ha-da v. be gaudy, be too gaudy, be tacky

야행성 ya-haeng-sseong adj. nocturnal

약 affix. about, approximately; n. drug, medicine; anger; anxiety; irritation; 약 먹다 yak meok-da v. take medicine; 약 오르다 yak o reu da v. get angry, be offended, get irritated; 약 올리다 yak ol-li-da v. make a person angry, make a person mad

약간 yak-gan adv. a little; a little bit

약과 yak-gwa n. easy thing, sure thing; Korean wheat flour cake

약국 yak-guk n. drugstore, pharmacy

약다 yak-da v. be clever, be smart, be sharp

약대 yak-dae n. a school of pharmacy

약도 yak-do n. direction map, outline map, sketch map

약방 yak-bang n. drugstore, pharmacy

약사 yak-sa n. pharmacist

약삭빠르다 yak-sak-ppa-reu-da v. be tactful; be shrewd

약속 yak-sok n. appointment; promise; 약속을 지키다 yak-sog-eul ji-ki-da v. keep one's promise/appointment

약속하다 yak-so-ka-da v. promise, make a promise

약손 yak-son n. comforting hand

약솜 yak-som n. surgical cotton, sanitary cotton

약수터 yak-su-teo n. mineral spring

약용식물 yag-yong-sing-mul n. medicinal plant, medicinal herb

약장 yak-jang n. medicine cabinet

약점 yak-jeom n. weak point, weakness

약초 yak-cho n. medicinal plant, medicinal herb

약품 yak-pum n. drugs, chemicals, medicines

약하다 ya-ka-da v. be weak, be feeble, be delicate, be light

약학 ya-kak n. pharmacology

약혼하다 ya-kon-ha-da v. be engaged, engage oneself

약효 ya-kyo n. potency of a medicine

얄밉다 yal-mip-da v. be offensive, be mean and nasty; provoke

얇다 yal-tta v. be thin

얌전하다 yam-jeon-ha-da v. be gentle, be well-behaved, be modest, be decent; be excellent, be nice, be fine

얌체 yam-che n. selfish person; shameless fellow

양 yang n. sheep, ram, lamb; quantity, amount

양계장 yang-gye-jang n. chicken farm

양국 yang-guk n. both two countries

양녀 yang-nyeo n. foster daughter, adopted daughter

양념 yang-nyeom n. spices and condiments, dressing materials

양념하다 yang-nyeom-ha-da v. season

양동이 yang-dong-i n. metal bucket

양력 yang-nyeok n. solar calendar

양로원 yang-no-won n. nursing home

양말 yang-mal n. socks

양면 yang-myeon n. double-sided, double-faced

양미간 yang-mi-gan *n.* the space between the eyebrows

양반 yang-ban *n.* the nobility, noble people; scholar-official class (*of old Korea*)

양배추 yang-bae-chu *n.* cabbage

양보 yang-bo *n.* yield

양보하다 yang-bo-ha-da *v.* make a concession, concede, yield

양복 yang-bok *n.* Western-style suit, suit

양부모 yang-bu-mo *n.* foster parents, adoptive parents

양분 yang-bun *n.* nutrient, nourishment

양산 yang-san *n.* parasol

양상치 yang-sang-chi *n.* lettuce

양손 yang-son *n.* both hands

양식 yang-sik *n.* Western-style food; Western-style; food, bread; raising seafood, farming seafood

양식집 yang-sik-jip *n.* Western-style restaurant; Western-style house

양심 yang-sim *n.* conscience

양어장 yang-eo-jang *n.* fish-farm

양옥집 yang-ok-jip *n.* Western-style house

양자 yang-ja *n.* foster child, adopted child

양장 yang-jang *n.* Western-style garment

양젖 yang-jeot *n.* goat milk

양지바르다 yang-ji-ba-reu-da *v.* be sunny (*weather*)

양쪽 yang-jjok *n.* both sides, either side

양초 yang-cho *n.* candle

양치기 yang-chi-gi *n.* shepherd

양치질하다 yang-chi-jil-ha-da *v.* brush teeth

양탄자 yang-tan-ja *n.* rug, carpet

양털 yang-teol *n.* wool

양파 yang-pa *n.* onion

양화점 yang-hwa-jeom *n.* shoe store

얕다 yat-da *v.* be shallow, be superficial

얕보다 yat-bo-da *v.* look down upon, make light of

얕잡아보다 yat-jab-a-bo-da *v.* make a low estimate of, to hold in low esteem; neglect

얘기 yae-gi *n.* talk, conversation; story

어귀 eo-gwi *n.* entrance, entry

어긋나다 eo-geun-na-da *v.* be at cross purposes with; go amiss, go wrong with; conflict with from, be contrary to

어기다 eo-gi-da *v.* run counter to, go against, break, violate

어깨 eo-kkae *n.* shoulder

어깨동무하다 eo-kkae-dong-mu-ha-da *v.* put arms around each other's shoulders

어느 eo-neu *adj.* which, what; 어느 것 eo-neu geot *adj.* which; 어느 날 eo-neu nal *adv.* one day; 어느 때 eo-neu ttae *adv.* what time, when; 어느 세월에 eo-neu se-wol-e *adv.* when; 어느 정도 eo-neu jeong-do *adv.* to some degree, to a certain extent; 어느 쪽 eo-neu jjok which side; whichever; either or; 어느 틈에 eo-neu teum-e *adv.* in so little time, in no time, so soon

어느덧 eo-neu-deot *adv.* before you know it; unnoticed

어느새 eo-neu-sae *adv.* in no time, so soon, quickly

어댑터 eo-daep-teo *n.* adopter

어두운 색 eo-du-un saek *adj.* dark color

어두워지다 eo-du-wo-ji-da *v.* become dark, get dark

어두컴컴하다 eo-du-keom-keom-ha-da *v.* be very dark

어둠 eo-dum *n.* darkness

어둡다 eo-dup-da *v.* be dark, gloomy; be ignorant of

어디 eo-di *adv.* where, what place; 어디 가나 eo-di ga-da *adv.* wherever you go

어디까지 eo-di-kka-ji *adv.* how far, to what extent

어디까지나 eo-di-kka-ji-na *adv.* anywhere; to the ends of the earth

어디선가 eo-di-seon-ga *adv.* somewhere

어딘가 eo-din-ga *adv.* somehow, in some way, in some respects

어떤 eo-tteon *adj.* some; certain; any, every; what kind of

어떻게 eo-tteo-ke *adv.* how, in what manner, by what means; 어떻게 되다 eo-tteo-ke doe-da *v.* be managed somehow; 어떻게 하다 eo-tteo-ke ha-da *v.* do somehow, manage to do

어떻다 eo-tteo-ta *v.* be the manner in which something is done

어떻든지 eo-tteo-teun-ji *adv.* at any rate, in any case, regardless

어려움 eo-ryeo-um *n.* difficulty, hardship

어려워하다 eo-ryeo-wo-ha-da *v.* feel constrained; be ill at ease; be afraid of

어련히 eo-ryon-hi *adv.* naturally, surely, certainly

어렴풋이 eo-ryeom-pus-i *adv.* dimly, faintly, vaguely

어렵다 eo-ryeop-da *v.* be difficult, be hard; be needy, be poor; feel ill at ease

어렸을 때 eo-ryeoss-eul ttae *adv.phr.* when someone was young

어른 eo-reun *n.* adult, grown-up; one's senior

어른스럽다 eo-reun-seu-reop-da *v.* be gentle, be meek, be well-behaved

어리광부리다 eo-ri-gwang-bu-ri-da *v.* act babyishly, behave like a spoilt child

어리다 eo-ri-da *v.* be young, be immature, be childish

어리둥절하다 eo-ri-dung-jeol-ha-da *v.* become confused, be at a loss

어리벙벙하다 eo-ri-beong-beong-ha-da *v.* be confounded, bewildered

어리석다 eo-ri-seok-da *v.* be foolish, be silly, be stupid

어리숙하다 eo-ri-su-ka-da *v.* be a bit foolish, look a little stupid

어린아이 eo-rin-a-i *n.* young child, young kid

어린이 eo-rin-i *n.* young child, young kid

어릴 적 eo-ril jeok *adv.phr.* when someone was young

어림없다 eo-rim-eop-da *v.* be far from; be beyond; be impossible

어마어마하다 eo-ma-eo-ma-ha-da *v.* be pompous; be grand, be magnificent, be tremendous

어머니 eo-meo-ni *n.* mother

어물거리다 eo-mul-geo-ri-da *v.* prevaricate, equivocate

어민 eo-min *n.* fisherman

어버이 eo-beo-i *n.* parents

어부 eo-bu *n.* fisherman

어색하다 eo-sae-ka-da *v.* be at a loss for words, feel awkward

어서 eo-seo *adv.* please, kindly; in a hurry, quickly

어선 eo-seon *n.* fishing boat

어설프다 eo-seol-peu-da *v.* be sloppy, be careless

어수룩하다 eo-su-ru-ka-da *v.* be naïve, be simple-hearted, be unsophisticated

어수선하다 eo-su-seon-ha-da *v.* be chaotic, be out of order, be in disorder

어슬렁거리다 eo-seul-leong-geo-ri-da *v.* hang about, wander about, loiter

어시장 eo-si-jang *n.* fish market

어안이 벙벙하다 eo-an-i beong-beong-ha-da *v.phr.* be dumbfounded, be struck dumb

어업 eo-eop *n.* fishery, the fishing industry

어울리다 eo-ul-li-da *v.* look good, match well, go well with

어이없다 eo-i-eop-da *v.* be struck dumb, be dumbfounded

어제 eo-je *n.* yesterday

어젯밤 eo-jet-bam *n.* last night

어중간하다 eo-jung-gan-ha-da *v.* be about halfway, be about midway

어지럼 eo-ji-reom *n.* dizziness; giddiness

어지럽다 eo-ji-reop-da *v.* be dizzy; feel giddy; be in disorder; be troubled

어지르다 eo-ji-reu-da *v.* scatter, put in disorder; litter

어째서 eo-jjae-seo *adv.* why, for what reason

어쨌든 eo-jjaet-deun *adv.* anyhow, anyway, at any rate, in any case

어쩌나 eo-jjeo-na *adv.* what to do, how to handle

어쩌다가 eo-jjeo-da-ga *adv.* by chance, by accident; once in a while, from time to time

어쩌면 eo-jjeo-myeon *adv.* maybe, perhaps; how; what

어쩌자고 eo-jjeo-ja-go *adv.* for what reason

어쩐지 eo-jjeon-ji *adv.* somehow, without knowing why

어쩔 수 없다 eo-jjeol su eop-da *v.phr.* be unavoidable, be urgent, be inevitable

어쩔 줄 모르다 eo-jjeol jul mo-reu-da *v.phr.* to not know what to do

어찌나 eo-jji-na *adv.* too; so, very, awfully; 값이 어찌나 비싼지 살 수 없다 gaps-i eo-jji-na bi-ssan-ji sal ssu eop-da The price is too high for me to buy it

어차피 eo-cha-pi *adv.* anyhow, anyway, in any case, at any rate

어처구니없다 eo-cheo-gu-ni eop-da *v.* be dumbfounded, be taken aback

어촌 eo-chon *n.* fishing village

어치 eo-chi *affix.* fixed quantity; worth, value

어항 eo-hang *n.* fish bowl

억 eok *n.* hundred million

억누르다 eong-nu-reu-da *v.* press down with force, suppress, oppress, control, keep under

억대 eok-dae *n.* several hundred million

억세다 eok-se-da *v.* be strong, be tough, be firm; be stiff, be rigid

억수같이 eok-su-ga-chi *adv.* so much, an extreme amount of

억울하다 eog-ul-ha-da *v.* suffer unfairness; feel victimized

억지로 eok-ji-ro *adv.* by force, against one's will

억지부리다 eok-ji-bu-ri-da *v.* insist on having one's own way, persist stubbornly

억척스럽다 eok-cheok-seu-reop-da *v.* be unyielding, be stout-hearted

언니 eon-ni *n.* older sister of a female

언덕 eon-deok *n.* hill, hillock; slope

언뜻 eon-tteut *adv.* in an instant, in a flash; by chance, by accident

언어 eon-eo *n.* language, speech, words

언어학 eon-eo-hak *n.* linguistics

언제 eon-je *adv.* when, what time, how soon; someday, some time; any moment; every moment

언제까지 eon-je-kka-ji *adv.* how long, until when; by what time, how soon

언제나 eon-je-na *adv.* always; usually

언제든지 eon-je-deun-ji *adv.* at any time, whenever; always, all the time

언제부터 eon-je-bu-teo *adv.* from what time, since when, how long

언제쯤 eon-je-jjeum *adv.* about what time, when, how soon

언젠가 eon-jen-ga *adv.* someday, some time; once, at one time, before

얹다 eon-tta *v.* put on, place on, load

얻다 eont-da *v.* get, acquire, obtain, earn, gain

얻어내다 eod-eo-nae-da *v.* obtain, acquire, gain, receive

얻어맞다 eod-eo-mat-da *v.* receive a blow, be struck

얼굴 eol-gul *n.* face; look, expression

얼굴빛 eol-gul-ppit *n.* complexion, color; look, expression

얼다 eol-da *v.* freeze, be frozen; get nervous

얼떨결에 eol-tteol-kkyeol-e *adv.* in the confusion of the moment

얼떨떨하다 eol-tteol-tteol-ha-da *v.* be confused, be upset, lose one's head; be at a loss

얼렁뚱땅 eol-leong-ttung-ttang *adv.* trickily, flatteringly, playing false

얼룩 eol-luk *n.* stain; spot; speckle

얼룩얼룩하다 eol-lug-eol-lu-ka-da *v.* be spotted, be dappled, be mottled

얼른 eol-leun *adv.* quickly, rapidly, immediately

얼마 eol-ma *adv.* how much; to some extent, in some degree; 얼마 남지 않다 eol-ma nam-jji an-ta there is not much left; 얼마 전 eol-ma jeon *adv.* some time ago; 얼마 후 eol-ma hu *adv.* after a while

얼마나 eol-ma-na *adv.* how much, how long, how far

얼마든지 eol-ma-deun-ji *adv.* any amount, without limit, as much as one wants

얼버무리다 eol-beo-mu-ri-da *v.* speak ambiguously, equivocate

얼빠지다 eol-ppa-ji-da *v.* lose one's senses, be dull-headed

얼빼다 eol-ppae-da *v.* drive a person out of his mind; take a person aback

얼어붙다 eol-eo-but-da *v.* freeze up, be frozen hard

얼얼하다 eol-eol-ha-da *v.* smart with pain; taste spicy

얼음 eol-eum *n.* ice

얼큰하다 eol-keun-ha-da *v.* taste rather spicy, taste peppery, be heavily seasoned; be rather tipsy, be intoxicated

얽매이다 eong-mae-i-da *v.* be bound, be tied; be restricted; be occupied with

얽히다 eol-ki-da *v.* be entangled, be involved, get complicated

엄격하다 eom-kkyeo-ka-da *v.* be strict, be stern

엄마 eom-ma *n.* mom, mommy

엄밀히 eom-mil-hi *adv.* strictly; closely; exactly

엄벌에 처하다 eom-beol-e cheo-ha-da *v.phr.* punish severely

엄살꾸러기 eom-sal-kku-reo-gi *n.* fussy person

엄살부리다 eom-sal-bu-ri-da *v.* exaggerate pain; make a big fuss

엄지발가락 eom-ji-bal-kka-rak *n.* big toe

엄지손가락 eom-ji-son-kka-rak *n.* thumb

엄청나다 eom-cheong-na-da *v.* be huge, be enormous

엄하다 eom-ha-da *v.* be severe, be strict, be harsh

업다 eop-da *v.* carry on one's back, shoulder

업무 eom-mu *n.* business, duty

업신여기다 eop-sin-yeo-gi-da *v.* despise, scorn, look down upon

업종 eop-jong *n.* types of business, types of industry

업히다 eo-pi-da *v.* ride on a person's back, be carried on a person's back

없다 eop-da *v.* not exist, not have

없애다 eops-ae-da *v.* remove, get rid of; waste, lose

없어지다 eops-eo-ji-da *v.* lose, be lost, be gone; run out, be used up; disappear, vanish, go away

없이 eops-i *part.* without

엇갈리다 eot-gal-li-da *v.* cross paths, miss each other on the way

엇비슷하다 eot-bi-seu-ta-da *v.* be nearly the same

엉겁결에 eong-geop-gyeol-e *adv.* unexpectedly, all of sudden, suddenly

엉금엉금 eong-geum-eong-geum *adv.* crawling, creeping

엉덩방아 eong-deong-bang-a *n.* fall on one's backside

엉덩이 eong-deong-i *n.* the buttocks; the hips

엉뚱하다 eong-ttung-ha-da *v.* be extraordinary, be extravagant; be unreasonable

엉망 eong-mang *n.* mess, bad shape, wreck

엉성하다 eong-seong-ha-da *v.* be sparse, be loose, be coarse; be unfamiliar; be unsatisfactory

엉엉 울다 eong-eong ul-da *v.phr.* cry bitterly

엉클어지다 eong-keul-eo-ji-da *v.* get tangled, be entangled, be complicated

엉큼하다 eong-keum-ha-da *v.* be full of deep-seated ambition

엉터리 eong-teo-ri *n.* a fake, a cheat

엊그제 eot-geu-je *adv.* a few days ago; *n.* the day before yesterday

엎다 eop-da *v.* turn upside-down; overturn; overthrow

엎드리다 eop-deu-ri-da *v.* lie flat on the ground, prostrate oneself

엎어놓다 eop-eo-no-ta *v.* put a thing face down

엎어지다 eop-eo-ji-da *v.* be turned over; be overthrown

엎지르다 eop-ji-reu-da *v.* spill, slop

에 e *part.* static location particle (*in, at, on*); destination particle (*to*); 집에 개가 있다 jib-e gae-ga it-da I have a dog at my house; 집에 가자 jib-e ga-ja Let's go home

에게 e-ge *part.* to (*a person*); 친구에게 편지를 쓴다 chin-gu-e-ge pyeon-ji-reul sseun da I am writing a letter to my friend

에너지 e-neo-ji *n.* energy

에는 e-neun *part.* as for, to, at, in; 내 생각에는 nae saeng-gag-e-neun in my opinion; 일요일에는 il-yo-il-e-neun on Sunday

에다 e-da *part.* into, onto, upon; 벽에다 그림을 건다 byeog-e-da geu-rim-eul geon-da I hang a picture on the wall

에도 e-do *part.* to, at, also, even, either; 그는 주말에도 일을 한다 geu-neun ju-mal-e-do il-eul han-da He works even on weekends

에만 e-man *part.* just to, only; 나는 주말에만 TV를 본다 na-neun ju-mal-e-man tel-le-bi-jeon-eul bon-da I watch television only on the weekends

에서 e-seo *part.* location of action particle (*in, at*); 나는 도서관에서 공부한다 na-neun do-seo-gwan-e-seo gong-bu-han-da I study at the library

에서도 e-seo-do *part.* even at…, at … also; 나는 전에 한국에서도 살았다 na-neun jeon-e han-gug-e-seo-do sal-at-da I also used to live in Korea

에서만 e-seo-man *part.* only at…, just in…; 나는 평생 한국에서만 살았다 na-neun pyeong-saeng han-gug-e-seo-man sal-at-da I've lived only in Korea whole my life

에스컬레이터 e-seu-kal-le-i-teo *n.* escalator

에스키모 e-seu-ki-mo *n.* Eskimo

에어컨 e-eo-keon *n.* air conditioner

에워싸다 e-wo-ssa-da *v.* surround, enclose, encircle

에티켓 e-ti-ket *n.* etiquette, good manners

에펠탑 e-pel-tap *n.* Eiffel Tower

엑스레이 ek-seu-re-i *n.* X-ray

엑스포 ek-seu-po *n.* expo

엔지니어 en-ji-ni-eo *n.* engineer

엔진 en-jin *n.* engine

엘리베이터 el-li-be-i-teo *n.* elevator

여가 yeo-ga *n.* leisure, spare time

여가활동 yeo-ga-hwal-ttong *n.* leisure time activities

여간 아니다 yeo-gan a-ni-da *phr.* be uncommon, be unusual, be extraordinary

여겨지다 yeo-gyeo-ji-da *v.* be considered

여관 yeo-gwan *n.* inn

여권 yeo-kkwon *n.* passport; women's rights

여기 yeo-gi *n.* here, this place

여기저기 yeo-gi-jeo-gi *adv.* here and there, in places

여남은 yeo-nam-eun *adj.* more than ten

여느 때 yeo-neu ttae *n.phr.* ordinary times; 여느 때처럼 yeo-neu ttae-cheo-reom *adv.* as usual

여당 yeo-dang *n.* the administration party, government party

여덟 yeo-deol *n.* eight

여동생 yeo-dong-saeng *n.* younger sister

여드레 yeo-deu-re *n.* eight days

여드렛날 yeo-deu-ren-nal *n.* the eighth day of the month

여드름 yeo-deu-reum *n.* pimple, acne

여든 yeo-deun *n.* eighty

여러 yeo-reo *adj.* many, several; 여러 가지 yeo-reo ga-ji *adj.* various, all kinds of, several, diverse; 여러 날 yeo-reo nal *adv.* many days, several days; 여러 달 yeo-reo dal *adv.* many months, several months; 여러 번 yeo-reo beon *adv.* often, frequently, several times, again and again, over and over; 여러 해 yeo-reo hae *adv.* many years, several years

여러모로 yeo-reo-mo-ro *adv.* in various ways, one way or another

여러분 yeo-reo-bun *n.* all of you, ladies and gentlemen, everybody

여론 yeo-ron *n.* public opinion, public sentiment

여름 yeo-reum *n.* summer

여름방학 yeo-reum-ppang-hak *n.* summer vacation

여리다 yeo-ri-da *v.* be soft, tender, fragile

여보 yeo-bo *n.* Honey, Dear

여보세요 yeo-bo-se-yo *v.phr.* hello (*to get another's attention*); hello (*common expression for answering the telephone*)

여분 yeo-bun *n.* extra, excess, leftovers

여생 yeo-saeng *n.* the rest of one's life, one's remaining years

여성 yeo-seong *n.* women

여신 ywo-sin *n.* goddess

여왕 yeo-wang *n.* queen

여우 yeo-u *n.* fox; cunning fellow; conniving woman

여유 yeo-yu *n.* time to spare; reserve, surplus; 여유 없다 yeo-yu eop-da *v.* have no time/money to spare; 여유 있다 yeo-yu it-da *v.* have time/money to spare

여자 yeo-ja *n.* woman, female

여자친구 yeo-ja-chin-gu *n.* girlfriend; female friend

여전하다 yeo-jeon-ha-da *v.* be unchanged, be the same, be as usual

여쭈어보다 yeo-jju-eo-bo-da *v.* ask, inform, explain *(hum.)*

여쭤보다 yeo-jjwo-bo-da *v.* ask, inform, explain *(hum.)*

여차하면 yeo-cha-ha-myeon *adv.* in case of emergency, in time of need

여태 yeo-tae *adv.* until now

여태까지 yeo-tae-kka-ji *adv.* till now, until now, by this time, so far

여하간 yeo-ha-gan *adv.* anyway, at any rate, in any case

여하튼 yeo-ha-teun *adv.* anyway, at any rate, in any case

여학생 yeo-hak-saeng *n.* female student

여행 yeo-haeng *n.* travel, tour; 여행 경비 yeo-haeng gyeong-bi *n.* travel expenses; 여행 상품 yeo-haeng-sang-pum *n.* travel package; 여행 안내 책 yeo-haeng an-nae chaek *n.* travel guide

여행가다 yeo-haeng-ga-da *v.* travel, take a trip

여행객 yeo-haeng-gaek *n.* tourist

여행사 yeo-haeng-sa *n.* travel agency

여행용 yeo-hang-nyong *adj.* for travel

여행자수표 yeo-haeng-ja-su-pyo *n.* traveler's check

여행지 yeo-haeng-ji *n.* destination, place of one's sojourn

여행하다 yeo-haeng-ha-da *v.* travel, take a trip

역 yeok *n.* train station; part in a play

역겹다 yeok-gyeop-da *v.* be disgusting, be offensive

역도 yeok-do *n.* weight lifting

역부족 yeok-bu-jok *n.* want of ability

역사 yeok-sa *n.* history

역사적 yeok-sa-jeok *adj.* historical, historic

역사적으로 yeok-sa-jeog-eu-ro *adv.* historically

역사학 yeok-sa-hak *n.* history

역설 yeok-seol *n.* paradox

역시 yeok-si *adv.* too, also; still

역전승 yeok-jeon-seung *n.* last minute victory

역전하다 yeok-jeon-ha-da *v.* be reversed, reverse

역할 yeo-kal *n.* part, role

역효과 yeo-kyo-kkwa *n.* side effect, adverse reaction

연 yeon *n.* kite; lotus; year

연간 yeon-gan *adj.* annual; *adv.* for a year

연거푸 yeon-geo-pu *adv.* continuously, one after another

연결하다 yeon-gyeol-ha-da *v.* connect, attach, interlink

연고 yeon-go *n.* ointment

연구 yeon-gu *n.* research, investigation

연구소 yeon-gu-so *n.* research institute

연구실 yeon-gu-sil *n.* office; research lab

연구하다 yeon-gu-ha-da *v.* study, research, investigate

연극 yeon-geuk *n.* stage drama, theatrical performance, play

연극공연 yeon-geuk-gong-yeon *n.* theatrical performance

연극배우 yeon-geuk-bae-u *n.* stage actor

연금 yeon-geum *n.* pension

연기 yeon-gi *n.* smoke, fume; performance, acting

연기하다 yeon-gi-ha-da *v.* postpone, put off, defer, delay

연날리기 yeon-nal-li-gi *n.* kite flying

연년생 yeon-nyeon-saeng *n.* sibling children born within a year of each other

연달아 yeon-dal-a *adv.* one after another, without a break, continuously

연두색 yeon-du-saek *adj.* light green

연락 yeol-lak *n.* connection; 연락이 오다 yeol-lag-i o-da *v.* get a contact from; 연락이 끊어지다 yeol-lag-i kkeun-eo-ji-da *v.* lose contact with

연락처 yeol-lak-cheo *n.* contact information

연락하다 yeol-la-ka-da *v.* connect, keep in touch

연령 yeol-lyeong *n.* age

연료 yeol-lyo *n.* fuel

연립주택 yeol-lip-ju-taek *n.* row house, tenement house

연말 yeon-mal *n.* end of the year

연못 yeon-mot *n.* pond

연변 yeon-byeon *n.* Yen Ben (*area in China with many ethnic Koreans*)

연보라 yeon-bo-ra *adj.* light purple

연봉 yeon-bong *n.* annual salary

연분홍 yeon-bun-hong *adj.* light pink

연상 yeon-sang *n.* older, senior

연설 yeon-seol *n.* speech, talk

연설하다 yeon-seol-ha-da *v.* deliver a speech, give a talk

연세 yeon-se *n. hon.* age

연소자 yeon-so-ja *n.* youth, young people

연속극 yeon-sok-geuk *n.* soap opera series

연수 yeon-su *n.* study and training

연습 yeon-seup *n.* practice, exercise

연습문제 yeon-seum-mun-je *n.* exercises

연습하다 yeon-seu-pa-da *v.* practice, train, drill

연애 yeon-ae *n.* dating; love

연애결혼 yeon-ae-gyeol-hon *n.* love marriage

연애하다 yeon-ae-ha-da *v.* fall in love

연예인 yeon-ye-in *n.* entertainer

연월일 yeon-wol-il *n.* year, month, and date

연이율 yeon-i-yul *n.* annual rate of interest

연인 yeon-in *n.* sweetheart

연일 yeon-il *adv./n.* every day, day after day, day by day

연장 yeon-jang *n.* tool, utensil

연장자 yeon-jang-ja *n.* elder, senior

연장하다 yeon-jang-ha-da *v.* extend, renew

연주 yeon-ju *n.* musical performance

연주하다 yeon-ju-ha-da *v.* perform, play, give a performance

연주회 yeon-ju-hoe *n.* concert, recital

연중행사 yeon-jung-haeng-sa *n.* annual event

연초 yeon-cho *n.* the beginning of the year

연출하다 yeon-chul-ha-da *v.* show, stage, present, perform

연탄 yeon-tan *n.* coal briquette

연필 yeon-pil *n.* pencil

연하 yeon-ha *n.* younger, junior

연하다 yeon-ha-da *v.* be tender, be soft, be light

연하장 yeon-ha-jjang *n.* New Year's card

연휴 yeon-hyu *n.* long holiday; consecutive holidays

열 yeol *n.* fever; ten; line

열광하다 yeol-gwang-ha-da *v.* go wild with enthusiasm, go crazy over

열기 yeol-gi *n.* heat, hot air

열나다 yeol-la-da *v.* have a fever; become enthusiastic; become hot with anger, get angry

열다 yeol-da *v.* open, unlock; lift; set up; hold; clear the way; bear fruit; grow

열대과일 yeol-ttae-gwa-il *n.* tropical fruits

열대지방 yeol-ttae-ji-bang *n.* tropical area

열람실 yeol-lam-sil *n.* reading room in the library

열량 yeol-lyang *n.* calorie; 열량이 높다 yeol-lyang-i nop-da *adj.* high in calories; 열량이 낮다 yeol-lyang-i nat-da *adj.* low in calories

열렬하다 yeol-lyeol-ha-da *v.* be ardent, be fervent, be passionate; be glowing

열리다 yeol-li-da *v.* open, be opened, be unlocked; be held; be given; take place; bear fruit; grow

열매 yeol-mae *n.* fruit, nut, berry

열무김치 yeol-mu-gim-chi *n.* young radish kimchi

열성적 yeol-sseong-jeok *adj.* warm, earnest, enthusiastic, devoted

열쇠 yeol-ssoe *n.* key

열심히 yeol-ssim-hi *adv.* diligently; ardently, passionately

열어주다 yeol-eo-ju-da *v.* open a window of opportunity, give somebody a chance

열의 yeol-ui *n.* zeal, ardor, enthusiasm

열정 yeol-jjeong *n.* passion, ardor

열정적 yeol-jjeong-jeok *adj.* passionate, ardent

열중하다 yeol-jjung-ha-da *v.* devote oneself to, be absorbed in

열차 yeol-cha *n.* train

열흘 yeol-heul *n.* ten days

얇다 yeol-tta *v.* be thin; be light, be pale; be shallow, be superficial

염가판매 yeom-kka-pan-mae *n.* bargain sale

염려 yeom-nyeo *n.* worry, fear

염려하다 yeom-nyeo-ha-da *v.* worry, be anxious about, be afraid of

염색하다 yeom-sae-ka-da *v.* dye

염소 yeom-so *n.* goat; chlorine

염증 yeom-jjeung *n.* inflammation; dislike, disgust

엽기적 yeop-gi-jeok *adj.* bizarre, strange, weird

엽서 yeop-seo *n.* postcard

엿 yeot *n.* rice jelly, taffy

엿듣다 yeot-deut-da *v.* overhear; eavesdrop

엿보다 yeot-bo-da *v.* watch for, look for; spy out; steal a glance

엿새 yeot-sae *n.* six days

영 yeong *n.* not at all; zero; spirit, soul

영광 yeong-gwang *n.* glory, honor

영구적 yeong-gu-jeok *adj.* permanent

영구차 yeong-gu-cha *n.* funeral carriage

영구히 yeong-gu-hi *adv.* eternally, permanently

영국 yeong-guk *n.* England, Britain

영동 yeong-dong *n.* Yeong-Dong districts, eastern part of Korea

영동고속도로 yeong-dong-go-sok-do-ro *n.* Yeong-Dong highway (*highway connecting Seoul to Kangwon Province*)

영락없이 yeong-nag-eops-i *adv.* without fail, for sure, certainly

영리하다 yeong-ni-ha-da *v.* be clever, be bright, be smart

영문모르다 yeong-mun mo-reu-da *v.* not know the reason, not know why

영문학 yeong-mun-hak *n.* English literature

영부인 yeong-bu-in *n.* the First Lady

영사관 yeong-sa-gwan *n.* consulate

영사기 yeong-sa-gi *n.* projector

영상 yeong-sang *n.* above freezing; image; reflection

영서 yeong-seo *n.* Yeong-Seo district, western part of Korea

영수증 yeong-su-jeung *n.* receipt

영양 yeong-yang *n.* nutrition, nourishment

영양가 yeong-yang-kka *n.* nutritive value, nutritive qualities

영어 yeong-eo *n.* English

영업시간 yeong-eop-si-gan *n.* business hours

영업용 yeong-eom-nyong *adj.* for business

영영 yeong-yeong *adv.* forever, eternally

영웅 yeong-ung *n.* hero, great man

열원히 yeong-won-hi *adv.* forever, eternally

영재 yeong-jae *n.* genius, gifted person

영주권 yeong-ju-kkwon *n.* permanent residency

영도 yeong-to *n.* territory, domain

영특하다 yeong-teu-ka-da *v.* be wise, be intelligent

영판 yeong-pan *adv.* very, awfully

영하 yeong-ha *n.* temperature below freezing

영향 yeong-hyang *n.* influence, effect, affection

영향력 yeong-hyang-nyeok *n.* influence, influencing power

영혼 yeong-hon *n.* soul, spirit

영화 yeong-hwa *n.* movie, film

영화관 yeong-hwa-gwan *n.* movie theater

영화배우 yeong-hwa-bae-u *n.* movie actor/actress

영화상영 yeong-hwa-sang-yeong *n.* movie viewing

옅다 yeot-da *v.* be light, be pale

옆 yeop *n.* the side, beside, next to

옆구리 yeop-gu-ri *n.* the side, the flank

옆모습 yeom-mo-seup *n.* profile

옆집 yeop-jip *n.* next door

예 ye *n.* example; salutation; etiquette; yes; 예를 들면 ye-reul deul-myeon *adv.* for example

예감 ye-gam *n.* presentiment, premonition

예고 ye-go *n.* advance notice, warning

예고편 ye-go-pyeon *n.* preview

예금 ye-geum *n.* deposit, money on deposit

예금하다 ye-geum-ha-da *v.* place money on deposit

예로부터 ye-ro-bu-teo *adv.* from old times

예리하다 ye-ri-ha-da *v.* be sharp, be keen, be acute

예매처 ye-mae-cheo *n.* booth for advance ticket sales, box office

예매하다 ye-mae-ha-da *v.* buy or sell ticket in advance

예민하다 ye-min-ha-da *v.* be sharp, be keen, be acute, be clever

예방 ye-bang *n.* prevention, protection

예방접종 ye-bang-jeop-jong *n.* preventive inoculation

예방하다 ye-bang-ha-da *v.* prevent

예보 ye-bo *n.* forecasting, prediction

예복 ye-bok *n.* dress suit; full dress; ceremonial dress

예쁘다 ye-ppeu-da *v.* be pretty, be beautiful, be good-looking; be charming

예사롭지 않다 ye-sa-rop-ji an-ta *v phr.* be uncommon, be out of the ordinary, be unusual

예산 ye-san *n.* budget

예상하다 ye-sang-ha-da *v.* expect, anticipate, forecast, estimate

예선 ye-seon *n.* preliminary match

예순 ye-sun *n.* sixty

예술 ye-sul *n.* art, fine arts

예습 ye-seup *n.* preparation, rehearsal

예식장 ye-sik-jang *n.* ceremony hall, marriage ceremony hall

예약 ye-yak *n.* reservation, booking

예약하다 ye-ya-ka-da *v.* reserve, book in advance

예언하다 ye-eon-ha-da *v.* foretell, predict, make a prediction

예외 ye-oe *n.* exception

예의 ye-ui *n.* manner, etiquette

예전 ye-jeon *n.* old days, former days

예절 ye-jeol *n.* manners, etiquette

예정 ye-jeong *n.* schedule, plan, previous arrangement

예정하다 ye-jeong-ha-da *v.* arrange beforehand, map out

예측하다 ye-cheu-ka-da *v.* predict, foretell, forecast

옛날 yen-nal *n.* old days, the past

옛날얘기 yen-nal-yae-gi *n.* folk tale; legend

옛모습 yen-mo-seup *n.* traces, vestiges

옛일 yen-nil *n.* things of the past, bygones

옛추억 yet-chu-eok *n.* old memories

오 o *n.* five

오각형 o-ga-kyeong *n.* pentagon

오고가다 o-go ga-da *v.* come and go, keep coming and going, go back and forth

오곡밥 o-gok-bap *n.* five-grain rice

오그라들다 o-geu-ra-deul-da *v.* curl up; shrink

오그리다 o-geu-ri-da *v.* curl up; bend out of shape

오나가나 o-na-ga-na *adv.* always, all the time; wherever you turn

오누이 o-nu-i *n.* a brother and a sister

오는 o-neun *adj.* coming, next, forthcoming

오늘 o-neul *n.* today

오다 o-da *v.* come, reach, arrive

오두막집 o-du-mak-jip *n.* hut, shed

오들오들 o-deul-o-deul *adv.* shivering, trembling

오디오 o-di-o *n.* audio

오락 o-rak *n.* entertainment, recreation, pastime, amusement

오락가락하다 o-rak-ga-ra-ka-da *v.* come and go, go back and forth

오래 o-rae *adv.* long, for a long time; 오래 전에 o-rae jeon-e *adv.* long ago, long before

오래가다 o-rae-ga-da *v.* last long, stay long

오래간만 o-rae-gan-man *n.* first time in a while

오래도록 o-rae-do-rok *adv.* for long; till late; eternally

오래되다 o-rae-doe-da *v.* be a long time since, be old, be stale

오래오래 o-rae-o-rae *adv.* for a long time; forever, eternally

오랜만에 o-raen-man-e *adv.* after a long time

오랫동안 o-raet-dong-an *adv.* for a long time, for a long while

오렌지 o-ren-ji *n.* orange (*fruit*)

오렌지주스 o-ren-ji-ju-sseu *n.* orange juice

오려내다 o-ryeo-nae-da *v.* cut out

오로지 o-ro-ji *adv.* only, solely, entirely

오르간 o-reu-gan *n.* organ (*music*)

오르내리다 o-reu-nae-ri-da *v.* go up and down, rise and fall; be talked about

오르다 o-reu-da *v.* rise, go up, climb

오르막 o-reu-mak *n.* upward slope

오른손 o-reun-son *n.* right hand

오른손잡이 o-reun-son-jab-i *n.* right handed person

오른쪽 o-reun-jjok *n.* right side

오른팔 o-reun-pal *n.* right arm; one's right-hand man

오리 o-ri *n.* duck

오리다 o-ri-da *v.* cut off, cut out, carve out

오목하다 o-mo-ka-da *v.* be pushed in, be dented

오븐 o-beun *n.* oven

오빠 o-ppa *n.* older brother of a female

오솔길 o-sol-kkil *n.* narrow path, lane, trail

오순도순 o-sun-do-sun *adv.* harmoniously, on good terms

오스트리아 o-seu-teu-ri-a *n.* Austria

오슬오슬 o-seul-o-seul *adv.* shivering

오싹하다 o-ssa-ka-da *v.* shudder, shiver, feel a thrill

오염되다 o-yeom-doe-da *v.* be contaminated, be polluted

오월 o-wol *n.* May

오이 o-i *n.* cucumber

오전 o-jeon *n.* a.m.

오전근무 o-jeon-geun-mu *n.* morning shift

오존 o-jon *n.* ozone

오죽 o-juk *adv.* indeed, very, how; 오죽 배가 고프겠니 o-juk bae-ga go-peu-get-ni You must be very hungry

오죽헌 o-ju-keon *n.* "O-Juk-Heon" Old residence of famed Korean philosopher Yi I aka Yulguk, 1536-1584 (*historical and tourist destination*)

오줌 o-jum *n.* urine; 오줌 누다 o-jum nu-da *v.* urinate; 오줌 마렵다 o-jum ma-ryeop-da *v.* feel the urge to urinate

오직 o-jik *adv.* only, merely, solely

오징어 o-jing-eo *n.* dried squid, cuttlefish

오케스트라 o-ke-seu-teu-ra *n.* orchestra

오토바이 o-to-ba-i *n.* motorcycle

오페라 o-pe-ra *n.* opera

오피스텔 o-pi-seu-tel *n.* studio

오해하다 o-hae-ha-da *v.* misunderstand, misapprehend

오후 o-hu *n.* p.m.

오히려 o-hi-ryeo *adv.* rather; unexpectedly

옥상 ok-sang *n.* the roof, the rooftop

옥수수 ok-su-su *n.* corn

온 on *adj.* all, entire, whole, total; 온 집안 on jib-an *n.* the whole family, all the family; *adv.* all over the house

온갖 on-gat *adj.* all kinds of, every kind of, various

온대지방 on-dae-jji-bang *n.* the temperate region

온도 on-do *n.* temperature

온도계 on-do-gye *n.* thermometer

온돌 on-dol *n.* Korean under-floor heating system, hypocaust

온라인 on-na-in *n.* online

온수 on-su *n.* warm water

온순하다 on-sun-ha-da *v.* be gentle; be obedient

온실 on-sil *n.* greenhouse

온종일 on-jong-il *n./adv.* all day long, the whole day

온천 on-cheon *n.* hot spring

온통 on-tong *adv.* all, wholly, entirely, altogether

온화하다 on-hwa-ha-da *v.* be mild, be gentle, be temperate

올가미 ol-ga-mi *n.* trap, snare; trick, cheat

올라가다 ol-la-ga-da *v.* go up, rise, climb; be promoted, be raised

올라서다 ol-la-seo-da *v.* get up to a higher place; rise to a higher rank

올라오다 ol-la-o-da *v.* come up

올려놓다 ol-lyeo-no-ta *v.* put a thing on a place

올리다 ol-li-da *v.* lift up, raise, elevate; offer; give

올리브유 ol-li-beu-yu *n.* olive oil

올림픽 ol-lim-pik *n.* Olympic

올바로 ol-ba-ro *adv.* uprightly, honestly

올바르다 ol-ba-reu-da *v.* be straight, be upright, be honest

올빼미 ol-ppae-mi *n.* owl

올챙이 ol-chaeng-i *n.* tadpole, polliwog

올케 ol-ke *n.* the wife of a girl's brother, sister-in-law

올해 ol-hae *n.* this year

옮기다 om-gi-da *v.* move, remove, transfer; infect, give

옮다 om-tta *v.* be infected, be catch

옳다 ol-ta *v.* be right, be proper, be reasonable, be correct, be accurate

옷 ot *n.* clothes; 옷 가게 ot ga-ge *n.* clothing store

옷걸이 ot-geol-i *n.* coat hanger, clothes rack

옷깃 ot-git *n.* the collar of a coat

옷장 ot-jang *n.* wardrobe, chest

옷차림 ot-cha-rim *n.* dress, attire; one's appearance

옹기종기 ong-gi-jong-gi *adv.* densely, thickly

옹졸하다 ong-jol-ha-da *v.* be narrow-minded, be ungenerous, be intolerant

와 wa *part.* and; with; 나는 축구와 야구를 좋아한다 na-neun chuk-gu-wa ya-gu-reul jo-a-han-da I like soccer and baseball; 나는 친구와 쇼핑을 간다 na-eun chin-gu-wa shyo-ping-eul gan-da I'm going shopping with my friend

와글거리다 wa-geul-geo-ri-da *v.* be clamorous, be noisy, be crowded, be swarmed

와글와글 wa-geul-wa-geul *adv.* in swarms, in crowds; clamorously, noisily

와들와들 wa-deul-wa-deul *adv.* shivering, trembling

와락 wa-rak *adv.* all at once, with a rush

와르르 wa-reu-reu *adv.* with a rush; crumbling, all in a heap

와이셔츠 wa-i-syeo-cheu *n.* dress shirt

왁자지껄하다 wak-ja-ji-kkeol-ha-da *v.* be noisy, be clamorous

완공되다 wan-gong-doe-da *v.* be completely established, be completely built

완구점 wan-gu-jeom *n.* toyshop

완벽하다 wan-byeo-ka-da *v.* be perfect, be complete, be ideal

완비하다 wan-bi-ha-da *v.* equip completely, furnish completely

완성하다 wan-seong-ha-da *v.* complete, finish, accomplish

완전하다 wan-jeon-ha-da *v.* be perfect, be complete, be whole

완전히 wan-jeon-hi *adv.* completely, entirely, perfectly

완행열차 wan-haeng-yeol-cha *n.* local train, slow train

왈칵 wal-kak *adv.* all at once, all of sudden

왔다갔다하다 wat-da-gat-da-ha-da *v.* come and go, stroll, loiter, wander

왕 wang *n.* king, monarch

왕관 wang-gwan *n.* crown

왕국 wang-guk *n.* kingdom, monarchy

왕궁 wang-gung *n.* king's palace
왕래하다 wang-nae-ha-da *v.* come and go; associate with
왕릉 wang-neung *n.* royal tomb
왕발 wang-bal *n.* big foot *(nickname)*
왕복 wang-bok *n.* round trip
왕복표 wang-bok-pyo *n.* round-trip ticket
왕복하다 wang-bo-ka-da *v.* go and return, run between
왕비 wang-bi *n.* queen, empress
왕새우 wang-sae-u *n.* prawn
왕자 wang-ja *n.* prince, royal prince
왕조 wang-jo *n.* dynasty
왕족 wang-jok *n.* royal family
왜 wae *adv.* why, for what reason, on what grounds
왜냐하면 wae-nya-ha-myeon *adv.phr.* because; the reason is...
외가 oe-ga *n.* one's mother's parents' home
외과 oe-kkwa *n.* surgery
외과의사 oe-kkwa-ui-sa *n.* surgeon
외교 oe-gyo *n.* diplomacy, diplomatic relations
외교관 oe-gyo-gwan *n.* diplomat, diplomatic official
외국 oe-guk *n.* foreign country
외국어 oe-gug-eo *n.* foreign language
외국인 oe-gug-in *n.* foreigner, alien
외국인등록증 oe-gug-in-deung-nok-jeung *n.* alien registration card
외국출장 oe-guk-chul-jjang *n.* business trip to a foreign country
외동딸 oe-dong-ttal *n.* only daughter
외따로 oe-tta-ro *adv.* separated, isolated, lonely
외딴 oe-ttan *adj.* isolated, separated
외래어 oe-rae-eo *n.* loan words
외로움 oe-ro-um *n.* solitude, loneliness
외로이 oe-ro-i *adv.* all alone, solitarily
외롭다 oe-rop-da *v.* be lonely, be lonesome, be all alone
외면하다 oe-myeon-ha-da *v.* turn away, look away
외모 oe-mo *n.* appearance
외박하다 oe-ba-ka-da *v.* sleep away from home, stay out
외부 oe-bu *n.* the outside, the exterior
외사촌 oe-sa-chon *n.* maternal cousin

외삼촌 oe-sam-chon *n.* maternal uncle
외상 oe-sang *n.* credit; trust, on the cuff
외손주 oe-son-ju *n.* child of one's daughter
외숙모 oe-sung-mo *n.* the wife of one's maternal uncle
외식하다 oe-si-ka-da *v.* dine out
외아들 oe-a-deul *n.* only son
외양간 oe-yang-kkan *n.* stable, cowshed
외우다 oe-u-da *v.* memorize; recite from memory
외제 oe-je *n.* of foreign manufacture, foreign-made
외출 중에 oe-chul jung-e *adv.phr.* while one is out
외출복 oe-chul-bok *n.* fancy clothes, formal clothes
외출하다 oe-chul-ha-ad *v.* go out
외치다 oe-chi-da *v.* shout out, utter, cry, exclaim, cry out, scream
외톨이 oe-tol-i *n.* loner, lonely person
외투 oe-tu *n.* overcoat
외판원 oe-pan-won *n.* salesperson
외할머니 oe-hal-meo-ni *n.* maternal grandmother
외할아버지 oe-hal-a-beo-ji *n.* maternal grandfather
외향적 oe-hyang-jeok *adj.* extroverted, extroversive
외화 oe-hwa *n.* foreign currency
외환은행 oe-hwan-eun-haeng *n.* foreign exchange bank
왼손 oen-son *n.* left hand
왼손잡이 oen-son-jab-i *n.* left handed person
왼쪽 oen-jjok *n.* left side
왼팔 oen-pal *n.* left arm
왼편 oen-pyeon *n.* the left side
요구르트 yo-gu-reu-teu *n.* yogurt
요구하다 yo-gu-ha-da *v.* request, demand, claim
요금 yo-geum *n.* fare, fee, charge
요란스러워지다 yo-ran-seu-reo-wo-ji-da *v.* become noisy, become clamorous
요란하다 yo-ran-ha-da *v.* be noisy, ne clamorous
요령 yo-ryeong *n.* the gist, the main point; the knack
요리 yo-ri *n.* cooking; dish, cuisine
요리사 yo-ri-sa *n.* cook, chef

요리조리 yo-ri-jo-ri *adv.* here and there, this way and that way

요리하다 yo-ri-ha-da *v.* cook, prepare food

요새 yo-sae *adv.* in these days, currently, recently; fortress

요소 yo-so *n.* element, important factor, essential part; important position

요술 yo-sul *n.* magic, magical practice

요약하다 yo-ya-ka-da *v.* summarize, condense, sum up, give an outline

요일 yo-il *n.* day of the week

요전 yo-jeon *n.* the other day, a few days ago, the previous time, last time

요점 yo-jjeom *n.* the main point, the gist, the substance

요즘 yo-jeum *adv.* these days, nowadays

요청하다 yo-cheong-ha-da *v.* request, demand, ask

요충지 yo-chung-ji *n.* important spot, important position

요컨대 yo-keon-dae *adv.* in short, in a word; after all

요트 yo-teu *n.* yacht

욕 yok *n.* abuse, abusive language

욕구 yok-gu *n.* desire, urge, want

욕망 yong-mang *n.* desire, ambition, wants

욕먹다 yong-meok-da *v.* be spoken ill of; be scolded; be abused

욕실 yok-sil *n.* bathroom, bath

욕신 yok-sim *n.* greed, desire, rapacity

욕심쟁이 yok-sim-jaeng-i *n.* greedy person

욕조 yok-jo *n.* bathtub

욕하다 yo-ka-da *v.* speak ill of, call names, disgrace, insult

용 yong *n.* dragon; antler

용감하다 yong-gam-ha-da *v.* be brave, be courageous, be valiant

용감히 yong-gam-hi *adv.* bravely, courageously

용건 yong kkeon *n.* business, matter of business

용기 yong-gi *n.* container; courage; 용기를 잃다 yong-gi-reul il-ta *v.* be discouraged

용도 yong-do *n.* expenses, expenditure; use, usage

용돈 yong-tton *n.* pocket money, allowance; 용돈을 타다 yong-tton-eul ta-da *v.* receive an allowance

용량 yong-nyang *n.* amount, capacity, volume, content; dose, dosage

용모 yong-mo *n.* face; look; feather

용모단정 yong-mo-dan-jeong *n.* neat look

용무 yong-mu *n.* business, matter of business

용법 yong-ppeop *n.* directions, the way to use

용산 yong-san *n.* Yong San in Seoul *(district near main train station)*

용서 yong-seo *n.* pardon, forgiveness; 용서를 빌다 yong-seo-reul bil-da *v.* beg one's pardon, apologize

용서하다 yong-seo-ha-da *v.* pardon, forgive

용수철 yong-su-cheol *n.* spring *(mechanical)*

용암 yong-am *n.* lava

용액 yong-aek *n.* solution, solvent

용어 yong-eo *n.* terminology, term, wording, vocabulary

용의자 yong-ui-ja *n.* suspect, suspected person

용지 ong-ji *n.* paper, stationary; lot, site

우거지다 u-geo-ji-da *v.* grow thick, overgrow

우겨대다 u-gyeo-dae-da *v.* hang on to; insist on one's own way, persist

우그러지다 u-geu-reo-ji-da *v.* be crushed; be dented

우글거리다 u-geul-geo-ri-da *v.* swarm, be crowded

우기다 u-gi-da *v.* demand one's own way, force, impose

우두머리 u-du-meo-ri *n.* the top, the head, chief, leader

우두커니 u-du-keo-ni *adv.* absent-mindedly, aimlessly

우뚝 u-ttuk *adv.* high, aloft

우락부락하다 u-rak-bu-ra-ka-da *v.* be rough, be wild, be harsh

우렁차다 u-reong-cha-da *v.* resound, resonant, roar

우르르 u-reu-reu *adv.* all in a group, all together, all in a heap, all over

우르릉 u-reu-reung *adv.* rolling; rumbling; booming

우리 u-ri *pron.* we, our, us; *n.* cage, pen; 우리가 이겼다 u-ri-ga i-gyeot-da We won; 돼지를 우리에 넣어라 dwae-ji-reul u-ri-e neo-eo-ra Put the pigs inside the pen

우묵하다 u-mu-ka-da *v.* be hollow; be dented

우물 u-mul *n.* well

우물거리다 u-mul-geo-ri-da *v.* mumble, murmur

우물우물 u-mul-u-mul *adv.* mumbling

우물쭈물하다 u-mul-jju-mul-ha-da *v.* hesitate, boggle

우박 u-bak *n.* hail, hailstone

우비 u-bi *n.* raincoat

우산 u-san *n.* umbrella

우선 u-seon *adv.* first of all, to begin with

우선권 u-seon-kkwon *n.* priority, preference

우세하다 u-se-ha-da *v.* be superior, be leading

우수하다 u-su-ha-da *v.* be superior, be distinguished

우스갯소리 u-seu-gaet-so-ri *n.* joke, jest

우습게 보다 u-seup-ge bo-da *v.phr.* despise, look down on, treat with contempt

우습다 u-seup-da *v.* be funny, be amusing, be ridiculous

우승 u-seung *n.* victory, championship

우승자 u-seung-ja *n.* winner

우승하다 u-seung-ha-da *v.* win a victory, win a championship

우아하다 u-a-ha-da *v.* be elegant, be refined, be graceful

우애 u-ae *n.* brotherly love

우연 u-yeon *n.* accident, chance

우연히 u-yeon-hi *adv.* accidentally, by accident, by chance

우울하다 u-ul-ha-da *v.* be gloomy, be cheerless

우유 u-yu *n.* milk

우정 u-jeong *n.* friendship

우주 u-ju *n.* universe, cosmos

우중충하다 u-jung-chung-ha-da *v.* be gloomy, be dismal

우쭐하다 u-jjul-ha-da *v.* be proud of, hold one's head high

우체국 u-che-guk *n.* post office

우체부 u-che-bu *n.* mailman; mail carrier

우체통 u-che-tong *n.* mailbox

우툴두툴하다 u-tul-du-tul-ha-da *v.* be rugged, be bumpy, be rough

우편배달 u-pyeon-bae-dal *n.* mail delivery

우편번호 u-pyeon-beon-ho *n.* zip code

우편요금 u-pyeon-nyo-geum *n.* postage

우표 u-pyo *n.* stamp

우회전하다 u-hoe-jeon-ha-da *v.* turn right

욱신거리다 uk-sin-geo-ri-da *v.* tingle, smart

운 un *n.* fortune, luck, fate, destiny, chance; 운 좋다 un jo-ta be lucky, have good luck

운동 un-dong *n.* sports, exercise; political movement, campaign; motion

운동경기 un-dong-gyeong-gi *n.* sports game

운동모자 un-dong-mo-ja *n.* sports hat, baseball cap

운동복 un-dong-bok *n.* exercise clothes

운동선수 un-dong-seon-su *n.* athlete

운동장 un-dong-jang *n.* field, playground

운동하다 un-dong-ha-da *v.* do exercise

운동화 un-dong-hwa *n.* sneakers

운명 un-myeong *n.* fate, destiny, fortune, luck

운반하다 un-ban-ha-da *v.* carry, convey, transport

운송하다 un-song-ha-da *v.* carry, transport, convey

운영하다 un-yeong-ha-da *v.* operate, manage, administer

운전면허증 un-jeon-myeon-heo-jjeung *n.* driver's license

운전사 un-jeon-sa *n.* taxi/bus driver, chauffeur

운전습관 un-jeon-seup-gwan *n.* driving habit

운전하다 un-jeon-ha-da *v.* drive, put in motion, operate

운치있다 un-chi it-da *v.* be tasteful, be elegant, be graceful

운행 시간표 un-haeng si-gan-pyo *n.phr.* timetable, schedule

울긋불긋하다 ul-geut-bul-geu-ta-da *v.* be colorful

울다 ul-da *v.* cry, weep, sob

울렁거리다 ul-leong-geo-ri-da *v.* palpitate, throb, thump, pound; roll, toss; feel nausea, feel sick

울렁울렁 ul-leong-ul-leong *adv.* palpitating, thumping; tossing, rolling

울룩불룩하다 ul-luk-bul-lu-ka-da *v.* be rough, be bumpy, be uneven

울리다 ul-li-da *v.* make a person cry, break a person's heart, move a person to tears; ring, clang

울보 ul-bo *n.* crybaby

울부짖다 ul-bu-jit-da *v.* scream, cry, yell, utter a cry; howl, roar

울상 ul-ssang *n.* tearful face, weeping eyes

울음 ul-eum *n.* crying, weeping

울음소리 ul-eum-sso-ri *n.* tearful voice, sob

울적하다 ul-jjeo-ka-da *v.* be depressed, be lonesome, be cheerless

울창하다 ul-chang-ha-da *v.* be dense, be thick

울타리 ul-ta-ri *n.* fence, hedge

울퉁불퉁하다 ul-tung-bul-tung-ha-da *v.* be uneven, be bumpy, be rugged

움직이다 um-jig-i-da *v.* move, shift, budge, change position; operate; inspire

움직임 um-jig-im *n.* movement, motion, trend

움츠리다 um-cheu-ri-da *v.* shrink back, crouch, draw in

움켜잡다 um-kyeo-jap-da *v.* grab, grasp, seize, hold tight

움켜쥐다 um-kyeo-jwi-da *v.* grab, grasp, seize, hold tight

움큼 um-keum *count.* handful

움푹움푹 um-pug-um-puk *adv.* in hollows, in pits

웃기다 ut-gi-da *v.* cause to laugh, amuse

웃다 ut-da *v.* laugh, smile, giggle; laugh at, ridicule

웃어른 ud-eo-reun *n.* one's elders

웃을 일 us-eul il *phr.* laughing matter, joke; 웃을 일이 아니다 us-eul il-i a-ni-da It is no laughing matter

웃음 us-eum *n.* laugh, laughter, smile

웃음거리 us-eum-kkeo-ri *n.* object of ridicule, laughingstock

웃음바다 us-eum-ppa-da *n.* bursting into laughter

웅덩이 ung-deon-i *n.* mud puddle; bog

웅성거리다 ung-seong-geo-ri-da *v.* make a noise, bustle, be noisy, fuss

웅장하다 ung-jang-ha-da *v.* be grand, be magnificent, be splendid

웅그리다 ung-keu-ri-da *v.* crouch, pull in a limb

워낙 wo-nak *adv.* by nature, constitutionally, originally

워크맨 wo-keu-maen *n.* portable music player

원 won *count.* won (Korean currency); *n.* circle; desire, wish

원가 won-kka *n.* prime cost

원각사 won-gak-sa *n.* Won Gak temple (*historic Buddhist temple*)

원고 won-go *n.* manuscript

원기 won-gi *n.* vigor, energy, spirit

원두막 won-du-mak *n.* look-out for a fruit field

원래 wol-lae *adv.* originally, primarily

원료 wol-lyo *n.* raw material, materials

원룸 won-num *n.* studio

원리 wol-li *n.* principle, theory, fundamentals

원만하다 won-man-ha-da *v.* be harmonious, be peaceful

원망하다 won-mang-ha-da *v.* resent, reproach, think ill of

원산지 won-san-ji *n.* the place of origin

원상복구 won-sang-bok-qu *n.* restoration to the original state

원서 won-seo *n.* application

원숭이 won-sung-i *n.* monkey, ape

원시적 won si jeok *adj.* primitive

원양어업 won-yang-eo-eop *n.* deep-sea fishery

원인 won-in *n.* cause, factor

원자력 won-ja-ryeok *n.* atomic energy; 원자력 발전소 won-ja-ryeok bal-jjeon-so *n.* atomic power plant

원장 won-jang *n.* director, superintendent

원주민 won-ju-min *n.* native people, natives

원칙 won-chik *n.* principle, general rule

원피스 won-pi-sseu *n.* dress

원하다 won-ha-da *v.* want, desire, hope for

원형 won-hyeong *n.* original form; round shape, circle

원활하다 won-hwal-ha-da *v.* be smooth, be harmonious, be peaceful

월 wol *n.* month

월간잡지 wol-gan-jap-ji *n.* monthly magazine

월경 wol-gyeong *n.* menstruation, period

월급 wol-geup *n.* salary, monthly payment

월남하다 wol-lam-ha-da *v.* come south over the DMZ border, come from North Korea to the south over the DMZ

월동준비 wol-ttong-jun-bi *n.* preparation for winter

월말 wol-mal *n.* the end of the month

월부 wol-bu *n.* monthly installment

월북하다 wol-bu-ka-da *v.* go to North Korea from South Korea, cross the DMZ into North Korea

월세 wol-sse *n.* monthly rent

월요일 wol-yo-il *n.* Monday

월초 wol-cho *n.* beginning of the month

웨딩드레스 we-ding-deu-re-sseu *n.* wedding dress

웨이터 we-i-teo *n.* waiter

웬만큼 wen-man-keum *adv.* properly, moderately, to some extent, to a certain degree

웬만하다 wen-man-ha-da *v.* be tolerable, be fairly good

웬만하면 wen-man-ha-myeon *adv.phr.* if it is tolerable, if it is not very bad

웬일 wen-nil *n.* what matter, what cause, what reason; 여긴 웬일이세요 yo-gin wen-nil-i-se-yo What brings you here

위 wi *n.* stomach; the upper side, the top side, above, over

위기 wi-gi *n.* crisis, emergency, critical moment

위대하다 wi-dae-ha-da *v.* be great, be mighty, be grand

위로하다 wi-ro-ha-da *v.* console, comfort, relieve, soothe

위반하다 wi-ban-ha-da *v.* violate, infringe, break the law, infract

위생 wi-saeng *n.* sanitation, preservation of health

위성 wi-seong *n.* satellite

위아래 wi-a-rae *n.* up and down, high and low

위암 wi-am *n.* stomach cancer

위원회 wi-won-hoe *n.* committee

위쪽 wi-jjok *n.* the upper direction

위치 wi-chi *n.* location, situation, position, place

위치하다 wi-chi-ha-da *v.* be situated, stand, lie

위하다 wi-ha-da *v.* do for the sake of, do on behalf of, respect, take good care of

위하여 wi-ha-yeo *part.* for the sake of, on behalf of

위해서 wi-hae-seo *part.* for the sake of, on behalf of

위험 wi-heom *n.* danger, risk

위험하다 wi-heom-ha-da *v.* be dangerous, be risky

윗사람 wit-sa-ram *n.* one's senior, one's elder, one's superior

윗자리 wit-ja-ri *n.* the upper seat, the seat of honor

윙크하다 wing-keu-ha-da *v.* wink

유괴하다 yu-goe-ha-da *v.* abduct, seduce, kidnap

유교 yu-gyo *n.* Confucianism

유난히 yu-nan-hi *adv.* unusually, exceptionally

유니폼 yu-ni-pom *n.* uniform

유람선 yu-ram-seon *n.* cruise ship

유래 yu-rae *n.* origin, derivation

유래하다 yu-rae-ha-da *v.* originate, be derived from

유럽 yu-reop *n.* Europe

유료 yu-ryo *adj.* requiring payment

유리 yu-ri *n.* glass

유리창 yu-ri-chang *n.* glass window

유리하다 yu-ri-ha-da *v.* be advantageous, be favorable

유머 yu-meo *n.* humor

유명하다 yu-myeong-ha-da *v.* be famous, be famed, be renowned, be well-known

유물 yu-mul *n.* relics, remains

유별나다 yu-byeol-la-da *v.* be distinctive, be different

유부남 yu-bu-nam *n.* married man

유부녀 yu-bu-nyeo *n.* married woman

유산 yu-san *n.* abortion; miscarriage; inheritance, legacy

유산하다 yu-san-ha-da *v.* miscarry; abort

유서 yu-seo *n.* written will

유선방송 yu-seon-bang-song *n.* cable broadcasting

유실물센터 yu-sil-mul-ssen-teo *n.* lost and found office

유언 yu-eon *n.* will, testament, last wishes

유엔군 yu-en-gun *n.* UN Forces

유원지 yu-won-ji *n.* amusement park, public garden

유월 yu-wol *n.* June

유익하다 yu-i-ka-da *v.* be beneficial, be useful

유일하다 yu-il-ha-da *v.* be unique

유자차 yu-ja-cha *n.* citron tea

유적 yu-jeok *n.* remains, relics, ruins

유적지 yu-jeok-ji *n.* place of remains, relics, ruins

유전 yu-jeon *n.* oil field; inheritance

유제품 yu-je-pum *n.* milk product, dairy product

유지하다 yu-ji-ha-da *v.* keep up, maintain, support

유창하다 yu-chang-ha-da *v.* be fluent

유채꽃 yu-chae-kkot *n.* rape flower (*yellow flower found on Jeju Island, Brassica napus*)

유치원 yu-chi-won *n.* kindergarten

유치원생 yu-chi-won-saeng *n.* kindergarten student

유쾌하다 yu-kwae-ha-da *v.* be cheerful, be pleasant, be delightful

유턴하다 yu-teon-ha-da *v.* make a U-turn

유학 yu-hak *n.* studying abroad; 유학 가다 yu-hak-ga-da *v.* study abroad

유학생 yu-hak-saeng *n.* student studying abroad

유행 yu-haeng *n.* fashion, vogue, fad

유행가 yu-haeng-ga *n.* popular song

유행하다 yu-haeng-ha-da *v.* be in fashion, be in vogue, be popular

유형문화제 yu-hyeong-mun-hwa-je *n.* traditional arts, cultural relics

유효기간 yu-hyo-gi-gan *n.* the available period

육 yuk *n.* six

육각형 yuk-ga-kyeong *n.* hexagon

육개장 yuk-gae-jang *n.* soup of chopped beef with various condiments

육교 yuk-gyo *n.* overpass

육군 yuk-gun *n.* the army

육이오 yug-i-o *n.* Korean War (1950-53)

육지 yuk-ji *n.* land

윤기 yun-kki *n.* luster, shine, gloss; 윤기 나 다 yun-kki na-da *v.* shine, be glossy

윷놀이 yun-nol-i *n.* Korean game played with four-sticks

으러 eu-reo *part.* in order to

으로 eu-ro *part.* by means of; toward, to

으슬으슬 eu-seul-eu-seul *adv.* shivering

은 eun *part.* topic particle; *n.* silver; 우리 집 은 샌디에고에 있다 u-ri jib-eun saen-di-e-go-e it-da my house is in San Diego; 나 는 은반지를 샀다 na-neun eun-ban-ji-reul sat-da I bought a silver ring

은근히 eun-geun-hi *adv.* politely, courteously

은박지 eun-bak-ji *n.* tinfoil

은수저 eun-su-jeo *n.* set of silver spoon and chopstick

은어 eun-eo *n.* slang; secret language; jargon

은은하다 eun-eun-ha-da *v.* be distant, be faint; be vague, be dim

은퇴하다 eun-toe-ha-da *v.* retire

은행 eun-haeng *v.* bank; 은행거래 신청서 eun-haeng-geo-rae sin-cheong-seo *n.* bank account application

은행나무 eun-haeng-na-mu *n.* gingko tree

은혜 eun-hye *n.* favors, benefits, grace

을 eul *part.* objective marker; 사촌 형을 만 났다 sa-chon hyeong-eul man-nat-da I met my older cousin

음 eum *n.* sound, note, tone; pronunciation; yin, the negative (*of 'yin and yang,' in Korean 'eum and yang'*)

음력 eum-nyeok *n.* lunar calendar

음료수 eum-nyo-su *n.* beverage, drink

음성 eum-seong *n.* voice; negative

음식 eum-sik *n.* food, foodstuffs, meal; 음식을 차리다 eum-sig-eul cha-ri-da *v.* prepare food

음식값 eum-sik-kap *n.* cost of food

음식물 eum-sing-mul *n.* foodstuffs

음식상 eum-slk-sang *n.* dining table

음식점 eum-sik-jeom *n.* restaurant

음악 eum-ak *n.* music

음악가 eum-ak-ga *n.* musician

음악감상 eum-ak-gam-sang *n.* listening to music

음악회 eum-a-koe *n.* music concert

음절 eum-jeol *n.* syllable

음주운전 eum-ju-un-jeon *n.* driving under the influence of alcohol

음치 eum-chi *n.* tone-deaf

음표 eum-pyo *n.* musical note

응급실 eung-geup-sil *n.* emergency room

응급치료 eung-geup-chi-ryo *n.* emergency treatment

응모하다 eung-mo-ha-da *v.* apply for, enter for

응시하다 eung-si-ha-da *v.* apply for an examination, take an examination

응원하다 eung-won-ha-da *v.* assist, cheer, support

응접실 eung-jeop-sil *n.* living room; reception room

의 ui *part.* possessive particle; 우리 나라 의 미래 u-ri na-ra-ui mi-rae future of our country

의견 ui-gyeon *n.* opinion, view, idea, suggestion

의과 ui-kkwa *n.* the medical department of a university, the medical school

의논하다 ui-non-ha-da *v.* discuss, consult, counsel

의대 ui-dae *n.* medical school

의도 ui-do *n.* intention, aim, purpose

의도하다 ui-do-ha-da *v.* intend, plan, aim

의롭다 ui-rop-da *v.* be righteous, be chivalrous

의료보험 ui-ryo-bo-heom *n.* medical insurance

의무 ui-mu *n.* duty, responsibility, obligation

의문 ui-mun *n.* question, doubt

의미 ui-mi *n.* meaning, sense; 의미 있다 ui-mi it-da be meaningful

의미하다 ui-mi-ha-da *v.* mean, signify, imply

의복 ui-bok *n.* clothes, garments

의사 ui-sa *n.* doctor, physician

의성어 ui-seong-eo *n.* onomatopoeic words

의식 ui-sik *n.* consciousness; ceremony, ritual

의식주 ui-sik-ju *n.* basic necessaries for survival (*food, clothing, shelter*)

의심 ui-sim *n.* doubt, suspicion

의심하다 ui-sim-ha-da *v.* doubt, be doubtful, be suspicious

의약품 ui-yak-pum *n.* medical supplies

의외 ui-oe *n.* surprise, unexpected thing, surprising thing

의자 ui-ja *n.* chair

의젓하다 ui-jeo-ta-da *v.* be dignified, be well-behaved

의족 ui-jok *n.* artificial leg

의지 ui-ji *n.* will, intention, volition

의지하다 ui-ji-ha-da *v.* lean on, look to, depend on

의하면 ui-ha-myeon *part.* according to, by; 뉴스에 의하면 오늘 날씨가 좋다 nyu-sseu-e ui-ha-myeon o-neul nal-ssi-ga jo-ta According to the news, the weather is nice today

의학 ui-hak *n.* medicine, medical science

의해서 ui-hae-seo *part.* by means of, in accordance with; 생각은 언어에 의해서 표현된다 saeng-gag-eun eon-eo-e ui-hae-seo pyo-hyeon-doen-da Thoughts are expressed through words

이 i *adj.* this; *part.* subject particle; *n.* tooth; two; 동생이 온다 dong-saeng-i on-da My brother is coming; 이 같은 i gat-eun such; like this; 이 핑계 저 핑계 하다 i ping-gye jeo ping-gye ha-da excuse this and that; 이 닦다 i dak-da *v.* brush one's teeth; 이 번 i beon *n.* number two

이갈다 i-gal-da *v.* grind one's teeth

이같이 i-ga-chi *adv.* like this, thus, in this way, in such a manner; 저희를 이같이 도와주셔서 감사합니다 jeo-hi-reul i-ga-chi do-wa ju-syeo-seo gam-sa-ham-ni-da Thank you for helping us like this

이거 i-geo *n.* this thing; 이거 얼마예요 i-geo eol-ma-ye-yo How much is this

이것저것 i-geot-jeo-geot *n.* this and that, one thing and another; 시장에서 이것저것 많이 샀다 si-jang-e-seo i-geot-jeo-geot man-i sat-da I bought a lot of diffrent things at the market.

이겨내다 i-gyeo-nae-da *v.* overcome, conquer, get over

이국적 i-guk-jeok *adj.* exotic

이기다 i-gi-da *v.* win, gain a victory

이기적 i-gi-jeok *adj.* selfish

이끌다 i-kkeul-da *v.* guide, lead

이끌리다 i-kkeul-li-da *v.* be guided, be led; be tied

이끌어가다 i-kkeul-eo-ga-da *v.* guide, lead

이끼 i-kki *n.* moss

이나 i-na *part.* or; as many as; trivial; 오빠가 세명이나 있다 o-ppa-ga se-myeong-i-na it-da I have as many as three brothers' (*euphemism for a female's older male friends*); 배고프니까 밥이나 좀 먹고 이야기하자 bae-go-peu-ni-kka bab-i-na jom meok-go i-ya-gi-ha-ja I'm hungry, so let's talk after we eat rice or whatever; 돈이 있으면 책이나 옷을 산다 don-i iss-eu-myeon chaeg-i-na os-eul san-da If I have some money I usually buy some books or clothes

이나마 i-na-ma *part.* although it is this; 작은 집이나마 있으면 좋겠다 jag-eun jib-i-na-ma iss-eu-myeon jo-ket-da I wish I had a house however small it might be

이내 i-nae *part.* within, inside; less than; *adv.* soon, at once, right away

이념 i-nyeom *n.* idea, ideology

이다 i-da *part.* be; become

이다음 i-da-eum *n.* next time

이대로 i-dae-ro *adv.* as it is, as one is

이동식 i-dong-sik *adj.* movable, portable

이든지 i-deun-ji *part.* whether...or; either...or; no matter; 여동생이든지 남동생이든지 동생이 하나 있으면 좋겠어요 yeo-dong-saeng-i-deun-ji nam-dong-saeng-i-deun-ji dong-saeng-i ha-na iss-eu-myeon jo-kess-eo-yo I would like to have a younger sibling, either a girl or a boy; 무슨 일이든지 어려운 일이 있으면 도와줄게요 mu-seun il-i-deun-ji eu-ryeo-un il-i iss-eu-myeon do-wa-jul-kke-yo I will help you if you have a difficult problem, no matter what it is

이따가 i-tta-ga *adv.* a little later, after a while

이래 i-rae *part.* since, since then, after that, after this

이래저래 i-rae-jeo-rae *adv.* with this and that, one thing or another, one way or another

이랬다저랬다 하다 i-raet-da-jeo-raet-da ha-da *v.phr.* be changeable, be fickle, be unreliable

이러다가 i-reo-da-ga *adv.* doing this way, at this rate

이러쿵저러쿵 i-reo-kung-jeo-reo-kung *adv.* this or that

이런 i-reon *adj.* such, such... as, like this, of this kind

이런저런 i-reon-jeo-reon *adj.* this and that, one thing or another; 아버지에게서 할머니에 대한 이런저런 이야기를 들었다 a-beo-ji-e-ge-seo hal-meo-ni-e dae-han i-reon-jeo-reon i-ya-gi-reul deul-eot-da I heard many stories about grandmother from my father

이렇게 i-reo-ke *adv.* thus, like this, in this way; 옷을 이렇게 입으면 더 젊어 보여요 os-eul i-reo-ke ib-eu-myeon deo jeolm-eo bo-yeo-yo If you wear it this way, you look younger

이레 i-re *n.* seven days

이력서 i-ryeok-seo *n.* resume

이론 i-ron *n.* theory

이롭다 i-rop-da *v.* be good, do good; be advantageous, be favorable

이루다 i-ru-da *v.* accomplish, achieve, realize; make, form, constitute

이루어지다 i-ru-eo-ji-da *v.* come true, be accomplished; be formed

이룩하다 i-ru-ka-da *v.* erect, build, set up, establish; accomplish, achieve

이륙하다 i-ryu-ka-da *v.* take off, take the air

이르다 i-reu-da *v.* be early; reach, arrive, come to, lead to; let a person know, inform; tattle

이른 새벽 i-reun sae-byeok *n.phr.* early morning, dawn

이름 i-reum *n.* name, title; 이름 높다 i-reum nop-da *v.* be famous

이름표 i-reum-pyo *n.* name tag, name placard

이리 i-ri *adv.* this way, this direction, this side

이리저리 i-ri-jeo-ri *adv.* here and there, this way and that, in places; 은퇴하면 이리저리 여행 다니고 싶다 eun-toe-ha-myeon i-ri-jeo-ri yeo-haeng da-ni-go sip-da I would like to travel here and there after I retire

이마 i-ma *n.* forehead

이만 i-man *adv.* this much, this only, to this extent, this far; 오늘은 이만 하지요 o-neul-eun i-man ha-ji-yo Let's just do this much today

이만큼 i-man-keum *adv.* this much, to this extent; 밥을 매일 이만큼 많이 먹어요 bab-eul mae-il i-man-keum man-i meog-eo-yo Do you eat this much rice everyday

이메일 i-me-il *n.* email

이모 i-mo *n.* one's mother's sister, maternal aunt

이모부 i-mo-bu *n.* husband of one's mother's sister, maternal uncle by marriage

이모저모 i-mo-jeo-mo *adv.* various sides, every facet of

이미 i-mi *adv.* already, yet; previously, beforehand

이미지 i-mi-ji *n.* image

이민 i-min *n.* emigration; immigration; 이민 가다 i-min ga-da *v.* emigrate; 이민 오다 i-min o-da *v.* immigrate

이발사 i-bal-ssa *n.* barber

이발소 i-bal-sso *n.* barber shop

이발하다 i-bal-ha-da *v.* cut men's hair

이번 i-beon *adj.* this time, recently, lately, present, next, recent

이별하다 i-byeol *n.* part, separate

이북 i-buk *n.* North Korea, north side of DMZ in Korea

이불 i-bul *n.* bedding, quilt

이브 i-beu *n.* eve, the previous evening; Eve *(Bible)*

이비인후과 i-bi-in-hu-kkwa *n.* ear, nose and throat *(ENT)* department *(medical)*

이빨 i-ppal *n.* teeth

이사 i-sa *n.* move *(one's home)*; 이사 가다 i-sa ga-da *v.* move out; 이사 오다 i-sa o-da *v.* move in

이사하다 i-sa-ha-da *v.* move, change residence

이산가족 i-san-ga-jok *n.* families dispersed and displaced by the Korean War

이삿짐 i-sat-jim *n.* packed boxes *(when one moves)*

이삿짐센터 i-sat-jim-ssen-teo *n.* moving company

이상 i-sang *part.* more than, over, above, upward of; *n.* abnormal condition, abnormality, disorder; ideal, the goal; 이상 없다 i-sang eop-da *v.* be normal; 이상 있다 i-sang it-da *v.* be abnormal; 열이 100도 이상 오르면 병원에 가야 한다 yeol-i baek-do i-sang o-reu-myeon byeong-won-e ga-ya han-da If your body temperature goes over 100°F, you must go to the hospital

이상하다 i-sang-ha-da *v.* be strange, be queer, be odd, be unusual, be abnormal, be suspicious

이상형 i-sang-hyeong *n.* ideal type, ideal

이성적 i-sang-jeok *adj.* rational, reasonable

이슬 i-seul *n.* dew, dewdrops

이슬람교 i-seul-lam-gyo *n.* Islam

이슬비 i-seul-bi *n.* drizzle

이야기 i-ya-gi *n.* conversation, talk, chat; 이야기 걸다 i-ya-gi geol-da *v.* talk to

이야기하다 i-ya-gi-ha-da *v.* have a talk with, talk, speak, tell, say

이야말로 i-ya-mal-lo *part.* this indeed; indeed, just, exactly; 이 책이야말로 내가 제일 좋아하는 것이다 i chaeg-i-ya-mal-lo nae-ga je-il jo-a-ha-neun geos-i-da Indeed, this is my favorite book

이어받다 i-eo-bat-da *v.* inherit, be heir to, succeed, take over

이어서 i-eo-seo *adv.* continuing, following, next

이어지다 i-eo-ji-da *v.* get joined on, be continued, be connected

이어폰 i-eo-pon *n.* earphones

이외에도 i-oe-e-do *adv.* besides, in addition

이용하다 i-yong-ha-da *v.* utilize, make use of

이웃 i-ut *n.* neighborhood, neighbor

이웃집 i-ut-jip *n.* next door

이월 i-wol *n.* February

이유 i-yu *n.* reason, cause, motive; 이유 없이 i-yu eops-i without reason, without good cause

이익 i-ik *n.* profit, gain, benefit, advantage

이자 i-ja *n.* interest

이전 i-jeon *n.* the previous, former times; *adv.* before, formerly

이제 i-je *adv.* now; 이제 와서 i-je-wa-seo now, after so long a time; now, when it is too late; now

이주하다 i-ju-ha-da *v.* move, migrate, emigrate, immigrate, transfer

이쪽 i-jjok *n.* this side; our side

이쪽으로 i-jjog-eu-ro *adv.* to this way, in this way

이차세계대전 i-cha-se-gye-dae-jeon *n.* World War II

이처럼 i-cheo-reom *adv.* like this, in this way

이층집 i-cheung-jjip *n.* two-story house

이탈리아 i-tal-li-a *n.* Italy

이태리 i-tae-ri *n.* Italy

이태원 i-tae-won *n.* E Tae Won *(tourist destination/shopping district in Seoul)*

이토록 i-to-rok *adv.* like this, so much

이튿날 i-teun-nal *n.* the next day, the day after

이틀 i-teul *n.* two days

이틀치 i-teul-chi *n.* two-day's supplies

이하 i-ha *part.* less than, under, below; *n.* the following, the rest

이해 i-hae *n.* understanding

이해시키다 i-hae-si-ki-da *v.* explain to someone, impart knowledge/understanding

이해하다 i-hae-ha-da *v.* understand, catch, grasp

이혼 i-hon *n.* divorce

이혼하다 i-hon-ha-da *v.* divorce, be divorced from

이후 i-hu *part.* after this, in the future, from now on

익다 ik-da *v.* ripen, be ripe, mature; be used to, be familiar, be experienced; be cooked, be done

익숙하다 ik-su-ka-da *v.* be familiar, be good at, be skilled, be skillful

익숙해지다 ik-su-kae-ji-da *v.* get used to, become familiar with

익히다 i-ki-da *v.* ferment, brew, cook; mature, mellow; make oneself familiar with, learn

인간 in-gan *n.* human being, mankind

인간세계 in-gan-se-gye *n.* human world

인건비 in-kkeon-bi *n.* labor cost, wages

인격 in-kkyeok *n.* personality, character

인공 in-gong *adj.* artificial, man-made

인구 in-gu *n.* population

인기 in-kki *n.* popularity, popular esteem; 인기 있다 in-kki it-da *v.* be popular

인내심 in-nae-sim *n.* patience, endurance

인도 in-do *n.* sidewalk; India; guidance

인디언 in-di-eon *n.* Indian; Native American

인력 il-lyeok *n.* gravity; manpower

인류학 il-lyu-hak *n.* anthropology

인물 in-mul *n.* man, person, individual

인사 in-sa *n.* greetings, bow, salutation

인사과 in-sa-kkwa *n.* department of human resources

인사동 in-sa-dong *n.* In Sa Dong *(tourist destination in Seoul)*

인사하다 in-sa-ha-da *v.* greet, salute, bow

인삼 in-sam *n.* ginseng, Panax *(Asian)* ginseng

인삼차 in-sam-cha *n.* ginseng tea

인상 in-sang *n.* impression, imprint; look, features; 인상 깊다 in-sang gip-da *v.* be impressive

인상적 in-sang-jeok *adj.* impressive

인상착의 in-sang-chag-i *n.* look, features, personal appearance

인상하다 in-sang-ha-da *v.* pull up, raise, increase

인색하다 in-sae-ka-da *v.* be stingy, be miserly, be tight-fisted

인생 in-sang *n.* life, human life

인쇄술 in-swae-sul *n.* printing, presswork; typography

인쇄하다 in-swae-ha-da *v.* print, put into print

인스턴트식품 in-seu-teon-teu-sik-pum *n.* instant food, precooked food

인식 in-sik *n.* recognition, understanding

인식하다 in-si-ka-da *v.* recognize, understand

인심 in-sim *n.* one's mind, one's heart; 인심이 좋다 in-sim-i jo-ta *v.* be good-hearted, be genial, be generous

인연 in-yeon *n.* destiny; tie, affinity, bond

인원 in-won *n.* the number of persons, population

인정 in-jeong *n.* warmth, affection, kindness; human nature; recognition, confirmation

인정하다 in-jeong-ha-da *v.* recognize, admit, acknowledge

인종 in-jong *n.* human race, ethnics

인천 in-cheon *n.* In Cheon *(tourist destination)*

인천국제공항 in-cheon-guk-je-gong-hang *n.* In Cheon International Airport

인터넷 in-teo-net *n.* internet

인터뷰 in-teo-byu *n.* interview

인터체인지 in-teo-che-in-ji *n.* intersection; interchange

인턴 in-teon *n.* intern

인형 in-hyeong *n.* doll, puppet, figure

일 il *n.* date, days of the month; one; work, matter, incident

일거리 il-kkeo-ri *n.* things to do, job, task

일곱 in-gop *n.* seven

일과표 il-gwa-pyo *n.* daily schedule

일교차 il-gyo-cha *n.* daily temperature range

일그러지다 il-geu-reo-ji-da *v.* be distorted, be twisted, be contorted

일기 il-gi *n.* journal, diary

일기예보 il-gi-ye-bo *n.* weather forecast

일단 il-ttan *adv.* for the moment; once; *n.* first stage, the first grade

일등 il-tteung *n.* the first class, the first rank, the first place

일등석 il-tteung-seok *n.* first-class seat

일류 il-lyu *n.* first class, first rate

일리있다 il-li it-da *v.* there is some truth in it

일반 il-ban *adj.* general, common, usual

일반석 il-ban-seok *n.* economy-class seat, general admission seat

일방적 il-bang-jeok *adj.* unilateral, one-sided

일방통행 il-bang-tong-haeng *n.* one-way

일벌레 il-beol-le *n.* workaholic

일본 il-bon *n.* Japan

일본어 il-bon-eo *n.* Japanese language

일부 il-bu *n.* part, portion, section, division

일부러 il-bu-reo *adv.* on purpose, intentionally

일부분 il-bu-bun *n.* one part, one portion

일상 il-ssang *n.* everyday, daily life

일상생활 il-ssang-saeng-hwal *n.* everyday life

일생 동안 il-ssaeng dong-an *phr.* for one's whole lifetime, throughout one's whole life

일식 il-ssik *n.* Japanese-style food; solar eclipse

일식당 il-ssik-dang *n.* Japanese restaurant

일식집 il-ssik-jip *n.* Japanese-style restaurant

일어나다 il-eo-na-da *v.* wake up, get up; stand up; happen, occur

일어서다 il-eo-seo-da *v.* stand up, rise to one's feet

일요일 il-yo-il *n.* Sunday

일월 il-wol *n.* January

일으키다 il-eu-ki-da *v.* raise, get up, set up; wake up; start; cause

일인분 il-in-bun *n.* portion for a person

일일이 il-il-i *adv.* one by one, individually, in detail

일자리 il-jja-ri *n.* job, position

일전에 il-jjeon-e *adv.* the other day, some time ago

일정 il-jjeong *n.* the day's schedule

일정하다 il-jjeong-ha-da *v.* be fixed, be uniform, be regular

일제시대 il-jje-si-dae *n.* Japanese colonial period (*1910-1945*)

일종의 il-jjong-e *adj.* a kind of, a sort of

일주하다 il-jju-ha-da *v.* go round, make a round, circle

일직선 il-jjik-seon *n.* straight line

일찍 il-jjik *adv.* early; earlier, formerly

일체 il-che *n.* all, everything; *adv.* entirely, altogether

일출 il-chul *n.* sunrise

일평생 il-pyeong-saeng *n.* one's entire life

일하다 il-ha-da *v.* work, labor

일흔 il-heun *n.* seventy

읽다 ilk-da *v.* read

잃다 il-ta *v.* lose, be deprived

잃어버리다 lil-eo-beo-ri-da *v.* lose, be deprived

임금 im-geum *n.* king, ruler; wages, pay

임금님 im-geum-nim *n.* king, ruler, emperor

임무 im-mu *n.* duty, task, mission

임시 im-si *adj.* temporary

임신하다 im-sin-ha-da *v.* be pregnant

입 ip *n.* mouth; 입에 맞다 ib-e mat-da fit to one's taste (*food*)

입고가다 ip-go ga-da *v.* go dressed in something

입고오다 ip-go o-da *v.* arrive dressed in something

입구 ip-gu *n.* entrance, gateway

입국수속 ip-guk-su-sok *n.* formalities for entry

입다 ip-da *v.* wear, put on (*clothes*)

입다물다 ip-da-mul-da *v.* be silent, keep one's mouth closed

입력하다 im-nyeo-ka-da *v.* make input

입맛 im-mat *n.* appetite, taste

입사시험 ip-sa-si-heom *n.* entrance exam to a company

입술 ip-sul *n.* lips

입양하다 ib-yang-ha-da *v.* adopt a child

입원하다 ib-won-ha-da *v.* be hospitalized, be in the hospital

입장객 ip-jang-gaek *n.* visitor to public place, attendee

입장권 ip-jang-kkwon *n.* admission ticket

입장료 ip-jang-nyo *n.* admission fee

입장하다 ip-jang-ha-da *v.* enter, get into, obtain admission

입학 i-pak *n.* entering school

입학하다 i-pa-ka-da *v.* enter a school, be admitted into a school

입히다 i-pi-da *v.* dress someone; coat, cover

잇다 it-da *v.* join, put together, connect, link; continue, keep up

잇몸 in-mom *n.* gums

있는 그대로 in-neun geu-dae-ro *adv.phr.* as it is, frankly, without exaggeration

있다 it-da *v.* stay; exist; have; stay, remain; lie, be located

잉크 ing-keu *n.* ink

잊다 it-da *v.* forget; leave behind; think no more of

잊어버리다 ij-eo-beo-ri-da *v.* forget

잎 ip *n.* leaf

ㅈ

자 ja *n.* ruler, yard stick

자가용차 ja-ga-yong-cha *n.* private car

자격 ja-gyeok *n.* qualification, requirement for eligibility

자국 ja-guk *n.* mark, scar, trace, track; 자국 나다 ja-guk na-da *v.* get marked, form a scar

자기 ja-gi *pron.* self, oneself; honey, sweetie *(colloq.)*

자기네 ja-gi-ne *pron.* his/her...; 친구가 자기네 집에서 전신을 먹자고 했다 chin-gu-ga ja-gi-ne jib-e-seo jeom-sim-eul meog-ja-go haet-da My friend suggested that we eat lunch together at his place

사기앞수표 ja-gi-ap-su-pyo *n.* cashier's check

자꾸 ja-kku *adv.* constantly, incessantly, repeatedly

자나깨나 ja-na-kkae-na *adv.* day and night

자녀 ja-nyeo *n.* children

자녀교육 ja-nyeo-gyo-yuk *n.* education of one's children

자다 ja-da *v.* sleep, fall asleep, go to sleep

자동 ja-dong *adj.* automatic, self-operating

자동발매기 ja-dong-bal-mae-gi *n.* vending machine for tickets

자동응답기 ja-dong-eung-dap-gi *n.* answering machine

자동차 ja-dong-cha *n.* automobile

자동차보험 ja-dong-cha-bo-heom *n.* car insurance

자동판매기 ja-dong-pan-mae-gi *n.* vending machine for goods

자라다 ja-ra-da *v.* grow up; increase, gain

자랑 ja-rang *n.* boast, brag; pride

자랑거리 ja-rang-jjeo-ri *n.* something one is proud of

자랑하다 ja-rang-ha-da *v.* be proud of, brag of

자루 ja-ru *n.* bag, sack; handle, shaft

자르다 ja-reu-da *v.* cut, chop, slice; refuse flatly

자리 ja-ri *n.* seat; room, space; situation; position; mark; mat

자리잡다 ja-ri-jap-da *v.* occupy a position, take one's place

자마자 ja-ma-ja *affix.* as soon as, no sooner than

자매 ja-mae *n.* sisters

자명종 ja-myeong-jong *n.* alarm clock

자물쇠 ja-mul-ssoe *n.* lock, padlock

자본주의 ja-bon-ju-i *n.* capitalism

자부심 ja-bu-sim *n.* pride, self-esteem

자상하다 ja-sang-ha-da *v.* be detailed, go over in detail, be meticulous

자석 ja-seok *n.* magnet

자세 ja-se *n.* posture, pose

자세하게 ja-se-ha-ge *adv.* in detail, closely

자세히 ja-se-hi *adv.* closely, in detail

자식 ja-sik *n.* one's children

자신 ja-sin *n.* oneself; self-confidence; 자신 없다 ja-sin eop-da *v.* lack confidence in; 자신 있게 ja-sin it-ge *adv.* confidently; 자신 있다 ja-sin it-da *v.* be confident about

자연 ja-yeon *n.* nature

자연스럽다 ja-yeon-seu-reop-da *v.* be natural

자연식품 ja-yeon-sik-pum *n.* organic food

자연적 ja-yeon-jeok *adj.* natural; spontaneous; wild

자외선 ja-oe-seon *n.* ultraviolet ray

자원 ja-won *n.* resources

자유 ja-yu *n.* freedom, liberty

자유로움 ja-yu-ro-um *n.* freedom, liberty

자유롭게 ja-yu-rop-ge *adv.* freely

자유롭다 ja-yu-rop-da *v.* be free, be unrestricted

자작자작 ja-jak-ja-jak *adv.* almost dry

자장가 ja-jang-ga *n.* lullaby

사장면 ja-jang-myeon *n.* Chinese dish of wheat noodles in black soybean paste

자전거 ja-jeon-geo *n.* bike

자정 ja-jeong *n.* midnight

지존심 ja-jon-sim *n.* self-respect, pride

자주 ja-ju *adv.* often, frequently

자주색 ja-ju-saek *adj.* purple, violet

자질구레하다 ja-jil-gu-re-ha-da *v.* be all of a small size, be petty, be trifling

자체 ja-che *n.* oneself, itself

자취 ja-chwi *n.* trace, track, trail; marks

자취하다 ja-chwi-ha-da *v.* cook for oneself, do one's own cooking

자치구 ja-chi-gu *n.* self-governing district

자치단체 ja-chi-dan-che *n.* self-governing body

자칫 ja-chit *adv.* with the slightest provocation, at the slightest oversight

자켓 ja-ket *n.* jacket

자택 ja-taek *n.* one's own house, private
residence

작가 jak-ga *n.* writer, author

작곡 jak-gok *n.* music composition

작곡하다 jak-go-ka-da *v.* compose the music

작년 jang-nyeon *n.* last year, the past year

작다 jak-da *v.* be small, be tiny, be of small
size; be petty, be trifling, be trivial; be
young, be little

작문하다 jang-mun-ha-da *v.* compose, write
a compositioin

작성하다 jak-seong-ha-da *v.* draw up, write
out, make out

작업 jag-eop *n.* work, operation

작업실 jag-eop-sil *n.* work space, studio

작용 jag-yong *n.* action, effect, function

작은아들 jag-eun-a-deul *n.* second son

작은아버지 jag-eun-a-beo-ji *n.* uncle, younger
brother of one's father, fraternal uncle

작은어머니 jag-eun-eo-meo-ni *n.* aunt, the
wife of one's father's younger brother,
paternal aunt by marriage

작은집 jag-eun-jip *n.* one's father's younger
brother's house; one's paternal uncle's
house

작품 jap-pum *n.* piece of artwork

잔 jan *n.* glasses, cup

잔돈 jan-don *n.* small change

잔디 jan-di *n.* grass, turf; 잔디 깎다 jan-di
kkak-da *v.* mow grass

잔뜩 jan-tteuk *adv.* to the greatest possible
extent, to the fullest, extremely

잔소리하다 jan-so-ri-ha-da *v.* rebuke, lecture,
nag, scold

잔액 jan-aek *n.* the balance, the remainder

잔인하다 jan-in-ha-da *v.* be cruel, be brutal

잔잔하다 jan-jan-ha-da *v.* be calm, be still,
be quiet

잔치 jan-chi *n.* feast, banquet, party

잔칫상 jan-chit-sang *n.* feast, banquet, party
table

잘 jal *adv.* well, nicely, skillfully, satisfactorily, favorably; thoroughly; 잘 지내다 jal
ji-nae-da *v.* be doing fine

잘게 jal-ge *adv.* finely, closely; to pieces

잘나다 jal-la-da *v.* be distinguished, be great;
be worthless, be useless

잘난체하다 jal-lan-che-ha-da *v.* pretend to be
outstanding, pretend to be distinguished;
be snobbish

잘되다 jal-doe-da *v.* be going well, come out
well, prosper, make good progress

잘라내다 jal-la-nae-da *v.* cut off, cut out

잘라주다 jal-la-ju-da *v.* cut something for
someone's sake

잘리다 jal-li-da *v.* be snapped, be cut

잘못 jal-mot *n.* fault, mistake, error; blame

잘못나오다 jal-mon-na-o-da *v.* be unsatisfactory in result

잘못되다 jal-mot-doe-da *v.* go wrong

잘못하다 jal-mo-ta-da *v.* make a mistake,
commit an error

잘생기다 jal-saeng-gi-da *v.* look good, be
handsome

잘하다 jal-ha-da *v.* do well, be skillful; do a
lot, do often

잠 jam *n.* sleep, nap, doze; 잠 깨다 jam kkae-
da *v.* wake up, be awakened; 잠 오다 jam
o-da *v.* be getting sleepy, become sleepy

잠가버리다 jam-ga-beo-ri-da *v.* lock, fasten

잠그다 jam-geu-da *v.* lock, fasten; soak,
immerse, sink

잠기다 jam-gi-da *v.* be locked, be fastened;
be submerged, go down; get hoarse

잠깐 jam-kkan *adv.* for a little while, for a
moment, for some time

잠깐만 jam-kkan-man *adv.* for a short time,
for a moment, for some time

잠꼬대하다 jam-kko-dae-ha-da *v.* talk in
one's sleep

잠꾸러기 jam-kku-reo-gi *n.* sleepyhead

잠들다 jam-deul-da *v.* fall asleep, go to sleep;
die, pass away

잠수하다 jam-su-ha-da *v.* dive, go under
water, submerge

잠시 jam-si *n.* a short while, for a while, for
some time; 잠시 후 jam-si hu *adv.* after a
while, a little later

잠옷 jam-ot *n.* pajamas, night clothes

잠자다 jam-ja-da *v.* sleep, go to sleep, fall
asleep, take a nap

잠자리 jam-ja-ri *n.* dragonfly; jam-jja-ri *n.*
sleeping place, bed

잠자코 jam-ja-ko *adv.* without a word, in silence

잡다 jap-da *v.* catch, grab, grip

잡수시다 jap-su-si-da *v. hon.* eat, drink, have

잡아가다 jab-a-ga-da *v.* arrest a suspect

잡아당기다 jab-a-dang-gi-da *v.* pull, draw, tug, stretch

잡아먹다 jab-a-meok-da *v.* butcher and eat; torture

잡지 jab-ji *n.* magazine, journal, periodical

잡지사 jap-ji-sa *n.* magazine publisher

잡채 jap-chae *n.* noodles with sauteed vegetables

잡히다 ja-pi-da *v.* be caught, fall into the hands of

짱 jang *count.* sheets; *n.* market, fair, intestine

장가가다 jang-ga-ga-da *v.* marry, get married (*for men only*)

장갑 jang-gap *n.* gloves, mittens

장거리전화 jang-geo-ri-jeon-hwa *n.* long distance call

장구춤 jang-gu-chum *n.* double-headed drum dance (*traditional Korean drum dance*)

장기 jang-gi *n.* Korean chess

장기 jang-kki *n.* special skill, one's favorite performance

장기간 jang-gi-gan *n.* long period, long time

장난 jang-nan *n.* game, playing; joke; 장난 삼아 jang-nan sam-a *adv.* for fun, as a joke

장난감 jang-nan-kkam *n.* toy, plaything

장난꾸러기 jang-nan-kku-reo-gi *n.* naughty boy

장난치다 jang-nan-chi-da *v.* play, frisk, get funny with

장난하다 jang-nan-ha-da *v.* play, frisk, get funny with

장남 jang-nam *n.* eldest son

장녀 jang-nyeo *n.* eldest daughter

장님 jang-nim *n.* blind person, the blind

장단점 jang-dan-jjeom *n.* merits and demerits; strengths and weaknesses

장래 jang-nae *n.* the future; *adv.* in the future, some day

장례식 jang-nye-sik *n.* funeral

장롱 jang-nong *n.* wardrobe, dresser

장마 jang-ma *n.* rainy season, rainy spell

장마철 jang-ma-cheol *n.* the rainy season

장면 jang-myeon *n.* scene, situation, spectacle

장모 jang-mo *n.* one's wife's mother, mother-in-law

장미꽃 jang-mi-kkot *n.* rose

장바구니 jang-ppa-gu-ni *n.* shopping basket

장보다 jang-bo-da *v.* go grocery shopping, go to market

장사 jang-sa *n.* business, trade

장소 jang-so *n.* place, location, spot, position, site

장수 jang-su *n.* seller, merchant, dealer; long life, longevity

장시간 jang-si-gan *n.* long hours

장식장 jang-sik-jang *n.* showcase

장식하다 jang-si-ka-da *v.* decorate, trim

장애인 jang-ae-in *n.* disabled person, the handicapped

장인 jang-in *n.* one's wife's father, father-in-law

장점 jang-jjeom *n.* merit, strong point

장치 jang-chi *n.* equipment, installation

장편소설 jang-pyeon-so-seol *n.* novel

장학금 jang-hak-geum *n.* scholarship

잦다 jat-da *v.* be frequent, be incessant

재 jae *n.* ashes

재다 jae-da *v.* measure, gauge, calculate; view

재떨이 jae-tteol-i *n.* ash tray

재래시장 jae-rae-si-jang *n.* traditional outdoor market

재료 jae-ryo *n.* raw material, material, stuff, ingredients

재미교포 jae-mi-gyo-po *n.* ethnic Korean living in America

재미붙이다 jae-mi-bu-chi-da *v.* take interest in, be interested in

재미없다 jae-mi-eop-da *v.* be boring, be unpleasant

재미있게 jae-mi-it-ge *adv.* interestingly, enjoyably

재미있다 jae-mi-it-da *v.* be fun, be interesting

재방송 jae-bang-song *n.* rebroadcast

재배하다 jae-bae-ha-da *v.* cultivate, grow, raise

재벌 jae-beol *n.* plutocracy, financial clique, the plutocrats

재봉틀 jae-bong-teul *n.* sewing machine

재빠르다 jae-ppa-reu-da *v.* be quick, be nimble, be quick-witted

재빨리 jae-ppal-li *adv.* quickly; rapidly

재산 jae-san *n.* property, fortune, estate

재생하다 jae-saeng-ha-da *v.* revive, regen-
erate, remake, recycle

재수 jae-su *n.* luck, fortune; 재수가 좋다
jae-su-ga jo-ta *v.* be lucky; 재수가 나쁘다
jae-su-ga na-ppeu-da *v.* be unlucky

재수하다 jae-su-ha-da *v.* cram to repeat a
college entrance exam

재우다 jae-u-da *v.* put a person to sleep, send
to sleep, give a person a bed, give a person
lodgings

재일교포 jae-il-gyo-po *n.* ethnic Korean
living in Japan

재작년 jae-jang-nyeon *n.* two years ago

재정 jae-jeong *n.* finances, financial affairs

재주 jae-ju *n.* ability, talent, gifts, skill

재즈 jae-jeu *n.* jazz

재질 jae-jil *n.* the quality of the material (*of
fabric, wood, stone, etc.*)

재채기하다 jae-chae-gi-ha-da *v.* sneeze

재촉하다 jae-cho-ka-da *v.* press a person for,
urge a person to do

재치 jae-chi *n.* wit, tact

재킷 jae-kit *n.* jacket

재판 jae-pan *n.* trial, hearing; reprint, second
edition

재학중 jae-hak-jung *n.* being enrolled at
school, while at school, during one's
school day

재학하다 jae-ha-ka-da *v.* be in school, attend
school

재혼하다 jae-hon-ha-da *v.* marry again,
remarry

재활용 jae-hwal-yong *n.* recycling, recycling

잽싸다 jaep-ssa-da *v.* be nimble, be agile,
be quick

쟁반 jaeng-ban *n.* tray

쟁쟁하다 jaeng-jaeng-ha-da *v.* be outstanding, be prominent, lead; linger in
one's ears, be sonorous

저 jeo *pron.* I, me *(hum.)*; *adj.* that; 저 사람
누구예요 jeo sa-ram nu-gu-ye-yo Who is
that person; 저는 이강진입니다 jeo neun
i-gang-jin-im-ni-da My name is Kang-jin
Lee (*lit.* I am Kang-jin Lee)

저고리 jeo-go-ri *n.* Korean jacket, upper
garment of traditional Korean custume

저금통장 jeo-geum-tong-jang *n.* saving
bankbook, deposit book

저금하다 jeo-geum-ha-da *v.* save money,
deposit in the bank

저기 jeo-gi *adv.* over there

저기압 jeo-gi-ap *n.* low pressure; bad temper

저녁 jeo-nyeok *n.* dinner; evening

저녁때 jeo-nyeok-ttae *n.* evening

저녁밥 jeo-nyeok-bap *n.* supper, dinner

저녁식사 jeo-nyeok-sik-sa *n.* supper, dinner

저대로 jeo-dae-ro *adv.* as it is, like that; 그냥
저대로 놔두세요 geu-nyang jeo-dae-ro
nwa-du-se-yo Just leave it as it is

저도 모르게 jeo-do mo-reu-ge *adv.phr.*
unconsciously, unwittingly

저런 jeo-reon *adj.* such, that sort of, like that;
intj. oh dear, oh my

저렴하다 jeo-ryeom-ha-da *v.* be cheap, be
inexpensive

저리 jeo-ri *adv.* that way, that direction

저마다 jeo-ma-da *adv.* each one, everyone

저만큼 jeo-man-keum *adv.* so, like that, that
much, to that extent; 벌써 저만큼 많이 컸
네 beol-sseo jeo-man-keum man-i kkeon-
ne He has already grown that much

저번 jeo-beon *n.* last time, some time ago,
the other day

저수지 jeo-su-ji *n.* reservoir

저울 jeo-ul *n.* balance, scales

저울질하다 jeo-ul-jil-ha-da *v.* weigh, scale;
compare

저자 jeo-ja *n.* writer, author

저장하다 jeo-jang-ha-da *v.* store, keep,
preserve

저절로 jeo-jeol-lo *adv.* of itself, by itself,
automatically

저지르다 jeo-ji-reu-da *v.* commit; ruin, mar

저쪽 jeo-jjok *n.* that side, over there

저축하다 jeo-chu-ka-da *v.* save, store up;
deposit

저항 jeo-hang *n.* resistance, struggle, defi-
ance, opposition

저희 jeo-hi *pron.* we, our *(hum.)*; 저희 학교
에서는 요즘 한국어가 인기예요 jeo-hi
hak-gyo-e-seo-neun yo-jeum han-gug-
eo-ga in-kki-ye-yo Currently, the Korean
language is very popular in our school

적 jeok *n.* enemy, foe, opponent, rival

적군 jeok-gun *n.* rebel army; the enemy force

적극적 jeok-geuk-jeok *adj.* positive, active, constructive

적금 jeok-geum *n.* installment savings

적나라하게 jeong-na-ra-ha-ge *adv.* frankly, plainly, openly

적다 jeok-da *v.* be small in quantity, be unplentiful; write, fill out, record

적당하다 jeok-dang-ha-da *v.* be appropriate, be proper, be suitable

적도 jeok-do *n.* equator

적령기 jeong-nyeon-gi *n.* the suitable age (*for marriage*)

적발하다 jeok-bal-ha-da *v.* disclose, expose

적성 jeok-seong *n.* aptitude, talent; 적성에 맞다 jeok-seong-e mat-da fit for one's aptitude, appropriate to one's ability

적시다 jeok-si-da *v.* wet, moisten, dampen, soak

적십자 jeok-sip-ja *n.* the Red Cross

적어도 jeog-eo-do *adv.* at least, at a minimum

적어주다 jeog-eo-ju-da *v.* write down for someone

적외선 jeog-oe-seon *n.* infrared rays

적용하다 jeog-yong-ha-da *v.* apply a rule to

적응하다 jeog-eung-ha-da *v.* be fit for, be suited to, be adapted to

적절하다 jeok-jeol-ha-da *v.* be pertinent; be adequate, be proper; be appropriate, be reasonable

적중하다 jeok-jung-ha-da *v.* hit the mark, make a good hit; guess right, make a good guess

적지 않은 jeok-ji an-eun *adv.phr.* not a few, several

적포도주 jeok-po-do-ju *n.* red wine

적합하다 jeo-ka-pa-da *v.* be suitable, be fit, be compatible

적히다 jeo-ki-da *v.* be recorded, put on record, written down

전 jeon *affix.* before, prior to; *n.* grilled food

전골 jeon-gol *n.* beef with vegetables cooked in a casserole

전공 jeon-gong *n.* major, specialty

전공하다 jeon-gong-ha-da *v.* major in, specialize in

전구 jeon-gu *n.* electric bulb, light bulb

전국 jeon-guk *n.* nationwide; whole country

전국적으로 jeon-guk-jeog-eu-ro *adv.* on a national scale

전기 jeon-gi *n.* beginning of an era; electricity; biography; 전기 나가다 jeon-gi na-ga-da There is currently no electricity

전기공학 jeon-gi-gong-hak *n.* electrical engineering

전기밥솥 jeon-gi-bap-sot *n.* electric rice-cooker

전깃줄 jeon-git-jul *n.* electrical wire

전날 jeon-nal *n.* the other day, some days ago; *adv.* previously

전달하다 jeon-dal-ha-da *v.* deliver, forward, convey

전등 jeon-deung *n.* electric light, electric lamp

전라도 jeol-la-do *n.* Jeolla province (*south-western part of Korea*)

전람실 jeol lam-sil *n.* showroom

전람회 jeol-lam-hoe *n.* exhibition

전력 jeol-lyeok *n.* electric power, electricity; all one's power, one's best effort

전류 jeol-lyu *n.* electric current

전망 jeon-mang *n.* view, prospective; 전망이 좋다 jeon-mang-i jo-ta *v.* have a good sense of a prospective happening

전망대 jeon-mang-dae *n.* observation platform

전면적 jeon-myeon-jeok *adj.* all-out, overall, general

전문 jeon-mun *n.* specialty, major

전문강사 jeon-mun-gang-sa *n.* professional lecturer, specialist

전문용어 jeon-mun-yong-eo *n.* special terms

전반기 jeon-ban-gi *n.* the first half of a year; the whole, the entirety

전반적으로 jeon-ban-jeog-eu-ro *adv.* generally, over all

전번 jeon-beon *n.* last time, the other day

전보 jeon-bo *n.* telegram

전봇대 jeon-bot-dae *n.* electric pole; telephone pole

전부 jeon-bu *adv.* all together, in all

전생애 jeon-saeng-ae *n.* one's whole life

전선 jeon-seon *n.* electric wire, electric cord, cable

전설 jeon-seol *n.* legend, myth

전세 jeon-se *n.* the lease of a house/room on a deposit basis; reservations

전세계 jeon-se-gye *n.* the whole world

전속력으로 jeon-song-nyeog-eu-ro *adv.* at full speed, as fast as one can

전시되다 jeon-si-doe-da *v.* be exhibited, be displayed

전시회 jeon-si-hoe *n.* exhibition, display

전압 jeon-ap *n.* voltage

전액 jeon-aek *n.* the total amount, the sum total

전야제 jeon-ya-je *n.* an evening of the day before an important day

전업주부 jeon-eop-ju-bu *n.* full-time housewife

전에 jeon-e *adv.* before, prior to

전연 jeon-yeon *adv.* entirely, completely, utterly

전염병 jeon-yeom-ppyeong *n.* epidemic, infectious disease

전용 jeon-yong *n.* exclusive use, private use

전원 jeon-won *n.* farms, fields, countryside; source of electricity; all members, entire staff

전자공학 jeon-ja-gong-hak *n.* electronic engineering

전자레인지 jeon-ja-re-in-ji *n.* microwave

전자상가 jeon-ja-sang-ga *n.* electronics store mall

전자수첩 jeon-ja-su-cheop *n.* electronic organizer, palm pilot

전자우편 jeon-ja-u-pyeon *n.* email

전자제품 jeon-ja-je-pum *n.* electronic appliances

전쟁 jeon-jaeng *n.* war, battle, combat

전적으로 jeon-jjeog-eu-ro *adv.* totally, wholly, entirely

전조등 jeon-jo-deung *n.* headlight

전주 jeon-jju *n.* last week

전주 jeon-ju *n.* Jeon Ju *(historical and tourist destination)*

전철 jeon-cheol *n.* electric railway

전철역 jeon-cheol-lyeok *n.* subway station

전체 jeon-che *adj.* the whole, entire, general

전축 jeon-chuk *n.* record player

전통 jeon-tong *n.* tradition, convention

전통적 jeon-tong-jeok *adj.* traditional, conventional

전파 jeon-pa *n.* electric wave, radio wave; spread, circulate

전편 jeon-pyeon *n.* the whole book/reel; the first part

전하다 jeon-ha-da *v.* pass, convey, deliver, transmit; teach, introduce, initiate; hand down, leave

전학가다 jeon-hak-ga-da *v.* change schools

전해듣다 jeon-hae deut-da *v.* overhear, be informed of

전해드리다 jeon-hae-deu-ri-da *v.* deliver, convey, pass *(hum.)*

전해주다 jeon-hae-ju-da *v.* deliver, convey, pass

전해지다 jeon-hae-ji-da *v.* it is reported, it is said that; be handed down, be transmitted; be conveyed, spread, circulate

전혀 jeon-hyeo *adv.* entirely, completely, utterly

전화 jeon-hwa *n.* telephone, phone; 전화 걸다 jeon-hwa geol-da *v.* make a phone call; 전화 끊다 jeon-hwa-kkeun-tta *v.* hang up; 전화 받다 jeon-hwa bat-da *v.* answer the phone

전화국 jeon-hwa-guk *n.* telephone company

전화기 jeon-hwa-gi *n.* telephone

전화번호 jeon-hwa-beon-ho *n.* phone number

전화번호부 jeon-hwa-beon-ho-bu *n.* telephone directory, phone book

전화비 jeon-hwa-bi *n.* telephone bill

전화하다 jeon-hwa-ha-da *v.* make a phone call

전화회사 jeon-hwa-hoe-sa *n.* telephone company

전후 jeon-hu *n.* sequence, order; before and behind, before and after; postwar days

절 jeol *n.* Buddhist temple; bow, salutation; clause

절교하다 jeol-gyo-ha-da *v.* break off with, break relations

절다 jeol-da *v.* be salted, be seasoned with salt; walk lamely, limp

절대로 jol-ttae-ro *adv.* absolutely, positively

절뚝거리다 jeol-ttuk-geo-ri-da *v.* limp, walk lamely

절뚝절뚝 jeol-ttuk-jeol-ttuk *adv.* limping, hobbling

절레절레 jeol-le-jeol-le *adv.* shaking one's head

절름발이 jeol-leum-bal-i *n.* disabled person

절반 jeol-ban *n.* half

절벽 jeol-byeok *n.* cliff, bluff

절약하다 jeol-ya-ka-da *v.* economize, dispense with, spare

절이다 jeol-i-da *v.* preserve with salt

절전 jeol-jjeon *n.* power-saving

절차 jeol-cha *n.* process, formalities, proceedings

절하다 jeol-ha-da *v.* bow, salute

젊다 jeom-tta *v.* be young, be younger

젊은이 jeolm-eun-i *n.* the youth

점 jeom *n.* point, thing; spot; viewpoint, standpoint; issue; fortune-telling

점령하다 jeom-nyeong-ha-da *v.* occupy

점박이 jeom-bag-i *n.* dappled animal, brindled animal

점보 jeom-bo *adj.* jumbo, jumbo-sized

점선 jeom-seon *n.* dotted line

점성가 jeom-seong-ga *n.* astrologer

점수 jeom-su *n.* marks, points

점심 jeom-sim *n.* lunch, afternoon

점원 jeom-won *n.* salesperson; salesperson, store clerk

점잔빼다 jeom-jan ppae-da *v.* assume a dignified air, behave in a genteel way

점잖다 jeom-jan-ta *v.* be dignified, be well-bred, be decent, be genteel

점쟁이 jeom-jaeng-i *n.* fortuneteller

점점 jeom-jeom *adv.* more and more, less and less, little by little

점찍다 jeom-jjik-da *v.* fasten one's eyes on; pick out

점차 jeom-cha *adv.* gradually, little by little, step by step

점퍼 jeom-peo *n.* sports jacket

점프하다 jeom-peu-ha-da *v.* jump

접근하다 jeop-geun-ha-da *v.* approach, come close

접다 jeop-da *v.* fold up, wrap up

접수처 jeop-su-cheo *n.* information office

접시 jeop-si *n.* plate, dish

접어 넣다 jeob-eo-neo-ta *v.* fold in, make a tuck in

접착제 jeop-chak-je *n.* adhesives

접하다 jeo-pa-da *v.* be close to, come in contact, touch; border on; receive, have, get

접히다 jeo-pi-da *v.* get folded, be furled

젓가락 jeot-ga-rak *n.* chopsticks

젓다 jeot-da *v.* stir, beat, whip; row, paddle; shake; gesticulate

정 jeong *n.* emotion, affection, passion, sympathy, heart

정가 jeong-kka *n.* regular price, normal price; fixed price

정각 jeong-gak *n.* the exact time, the appointed time, scheduled time

정감 jeong-gam *n.* feeling, emotion, sentiment

정강이 jeong-gang-i *n.* shin, shank

정거장 jeong-geo-jang *n.* railroad station, depot

정교하다 jeong-gyo-ha-da *v.* be elaborate, be exquisite, be delicate

정글 jeong-geul *n.* jungle

정기휴일 jeong-gi-hyu-il *n.* scheduled day off

정답 jeong-dap *n.* correct answer, answer

정답다 jeong-dap-da *v.* be friendly, be affectionate

정도 jeong-do *affix.* approximately, about; extent

정돈되다 jeong-don-doe-da *v.* be arranged, be put in order

정들다 jeong-deul-da *v.* become familiar, become intimate

정떨어지다 jeong-tteol-eo-ji-da *v.* fall out of love, be disgusted with

정류장 jeong-nyu-jang *n.* stopping-place, station, stop

정리 jeong-ni *n.* arrangement, adjustment

정리하다 jeong-ni-ha-da *v.* arrange, put in order

정말 jeong-mal *n.* really, seriously

정면 jeong-myeon *n.* the front, the façade

정문 jeong-mun *n.* the front gate, main entrance

정반대 jeong-ban-dae *n.* exact opposite, direct opposite

정보 jeong-bo *n.* information, news

정복하다 jeong-bo-ka-da *v.* conquer, overcome

정부 jeong-bu *n.* government

정상 jeong-sang *n.* normality; condition, circumstances; the top, the summit, the peak

정서 jeong-seo *n.* emotion, feeling, sentiment

정성 jeong-seong *n.* sincerity, earnestness, devotion; 정성이 담기다 jeong-seong-i dam-gi-da *v.* give one's best wishes

정성껏 jeong-seong-kkeot *adv.* with utmost sincerity

정수기 jeong-su-gi *n.* water purifier

정승 jeong-seung *n.* minister/cabinet/secretary *(ancient)*

정식 jwong-sik *adj.* formal, official

정신 jeong-sin *n.* mind, spirit, soul, intention, motive; 정신 없다 jeong-sin eop-da *v.* be absent-minded; be unconscious; 정신 없이 jeong-sin eops-i *adv.* mindlessly, absent-mindedly, unconsciously

정신차리다 jeong-sin-cha-ri-da *v.* recover consciousness; collect one's mind, pay attention

정열 jeong-nyeol *n.* passion, enthusiasm

정오 jeong-o *n.* high noon, midday

정원 jeong-won *n.* capacity; garden

정월 jeong-wol *n.* January

정육점 jeong-yuk-jeom *n.* butcher's shop

정의 jeong-ui *n.* justice; right; definition; 정의 내리다 jeong-ui nae-ri-da *v.* define, give a definition

정장 jeong-jang *n.* formal outfit

정전 jeong-jeon *n.* interruption of electric power, electricity failure

정전기 jeong-jeon-gi *n.* static electricity

정정당당하게 jeong-jeong-dang-dang-ha-ge *adv.* fairly and squarely

정중하게 jeong-jung-ha-ge *adv.* courteously, politely

정지 jeong-ji *n.* stop, standstill

정지하다 jeong-ji-ha-da *v.* stop, interrupt, suspend; stand still, rest

정직 jeong-jik *n.* honesty, frankness

정직하다 jeong-ji-ka-da *v.* be honest, be straightforward

정찰제 jeong-chal-jje *n.* price tag system

정체 jeong-che *n.* true character, identity, original form

정초 jeong-cho *n.* first ten days of January

정치 jeong-chi *n.* politics, administration, political affairs

정치가 jeong-chi-ga *n.* politician

정치학 jeong-chi-hak *n.* political science

정하다 jeong-ha-da *v.* decide, settle, determine, choose

정해놓다 jeong-hae-no-ta *v.* decide, settle, determine, choose

정해주다 jeong-hae-ju-da *v.* make a decision in someone's stead

정해지다 jeong-hae-ji-da *v.* be decided, be settled, be determined, be fixed

정확하다 jeong-hwa-ka-da *v.* be correct, be exact, be accurate

젖다 jeot-da *v.* get wet, get soaked, be damp, be moistened

제 je *pron.* I; my *(hum.)*; 이번이 제 차례입니다 i-beon-i je cha-rye-im-ni-da It's my turn

제각기 je-gak-gi *adv.* each, respectively, individually

제공 je-gong *n.* offer, proffer

제공되다 je-gong-doe-da *v.* be offered, be furnished

제과점 je-gwa-jeom *n.* bakery

제기 je-gi *n.* traditional Korean shuttlecock game played with the feet; 제기 차다 je-gi cha-da *v.* play Korean shuttlecock

제대로 je-dae-ro *adv.* appropriately, properly

제도 je-do *n.* system, organization

제때 je-ttae *n.* appointed time

제목 je-mok *n.* title, theme

제발 je-bal *adv.* kindly, please, by all means

제법 je-beop *adv.* quite, fairly, considerably

제비 je-bi *n.* lot, raffle; swallow

제사 je-sa *n.* religious service, ancestral memorial service

제삼자 je-sam-ja *n.* third person, outsider

제수 je-su *n.* one's younger brother's wife, sister-in-law

제스처 je-seu-cheo *n.* gesture

제시간 je-si-gan *n.* on time; in time; scheduled time, appropriate time

제안하다 je-an-ha-da *v.* propose, suggest

제약 je-yak *n.* condition, restriction, limitation; pharmacy, manufacture of medicines

제외하다 je-oe-ha-da *v.* except, make an exception, exclude

제일 je-il *adv.* the first, most, best, prime; 제일 먼저 je-il meon-jeo *adv.* first of all, before everything else

제자리 je-ja-ri *n.* the proper place, the original place

제정신 je-jeong-sin *n.* consciousness; sanity, right mind; sobriety

제주도 je-ju-do *n.* Jeju island *(tourist destination in Korea)*

제주시 je-ju-si *n.* Jeju city *(tourist destination in Korea)*

제출하다 je-chul-ha-da *v.* present, submit, offer

제품 je-pum *n.* manufactured goods

제품설명서 je-pum-seol-myeong-seo *n.* instructions for the manufacture of goods

젤리 jel-li *n.* jelly

조 jo *n.* millet; trillion

조각 jo-gak *n.* sculpture

조각조각 jo-gak-jo-gak *adv.* in pieces

조각하다 jo-ga-ka-da *v.* carve, engrave

조개 jo-gae *n.* shellfish

조건 jo-kkeon *n.* condition, term

조교 jo-gyo *n.* teaching assistant

조국 jo-guk *n.* mother country

조그맣다 jo-geu-ma-ta *v.* be small, be tiny

조금 jo-geum *adv.* a little, a dash; somewhat, slightly

조금도 jo-geum-do *adv.* not in the least, not at all, not a bit

조기 jo-gi *n.* yellow corvine *(traditional dish)*; flag at half-mast; early stage

조깅하다 jo-ging-ha-da *v.* jog

조끼 jo-kki *n.* vest; pitcher, jug

조르다 jo-reu-da *v.* tie up; strangle; importune, ask, press for, urge, request

조리다 jo-ri-da *v.* boil down

조림 jo-rim *n.* boiled dishes served with soy sauce

조마조마하다 jo-ma-jo-ma-ha-da *v.* feel nervous, be uneasy

조미료 jo-mi-ryo *n.* seasoning, condiment

조사하다 jo-sa-ha-da *v.* check, check up; investigate, research

조상 jo-sang *n.* ancestor, forefather

조선 jo-seon *n.* Chosun *(last kingdom of Korea)*

조선시대 jo-seon-si-dae *n.* Chosun period *(last monarchic period of Korea, 1392-1910)*

조선업 jo-seon-eop *n.* shipbuilding industry

조선족 jo-seon-jok *n.* ethnic Korean living in China

조심 jo-sim *n.* care, caution, precaution, prudence

조심하다 jo-sim-ha-da *v.* be careful, watch out, take precaution, look out

조약돌 jo-yak-dol *n.* pebbles, gravel

조언 jo-eon *n.* advice, counsel, suggestion; 조언을 구하다 jo-eon-eul gu-ha-da *v.* ask the advice of a person

조언하다 jo-eon-ha-da *v.* counsel, give advice

조용조용 jo-yong-jo-yong *adv.* quietly, silently; softly, gently

조용하다 jo-yong-ha-da *v.* be quiet, be silent, be calm; be soft, be gentle; be restful

조용히 jo-yong-hi *adv.* quietly, silently; softly, gently

조작하다 jo-ja-ka-da *v.* manipulate, operate; fabricate, forge

조절하다 jo-jeol-ha-da *v.* control, adjust, modulate

조정하다 jo-jeong-ha-da *v.* mediate, arbitrate, settle

조조 jo-jo *n.* early morning

조종사 jo-jong-sa *n.* pilot, aviator

조카 jo-ka *n.* nephew

조퇴하다 jo-toe-ha-da *v.* leave a school or a job place earlier than usual

조화 jo-hwa *n.* symmetry; harmony; artificial flower, imitation flower; 조화를 이루다 jo-hwa-reul i-ru-da *v.* harmonize with

존경심 jon-gyeong-sim *n.* respect, deference

존경하다 jon-gyeong-ha-da *v.* respect, honor, venerate

손댓말 jon-daen-mal *n.* honorific word, term of respect

존재하다 jon-jae-ha-da *v.* exist, be present

존중하다 jon-jung-ha-da *v.* appreciate, respect, esteem

졸다 jol-da *v.* doze off, nap, doze; get boiled down, be boiled dry

졸라대다 jol-la-dae-da *v.* badger, clamor

졸리다 jol-li-da *v.* be sleepy, feel sleepy; be tightened, be fastened

졸업 jol-eop *n.* graduation

졸업반 jol-eop-ppan *n.* graduating senior

졸업식 jol-eop-sik *n.* graduation ceremony

졸업식사 jol-eop-sik-sa *n.* speech in a graduation ceremony

졸업여행 jol-eom-nyeo-haeng *n.* field trip before graduation

졸업하다 jol-eo-pa-da *v.* graduate

졸음 jol-eum *n.* drowsiness, sleepiness

졸이다 joi-i-da *v.* boil down; feel anxious, nervous

졸졸 jol-jol *adv.* murmuring; trickling; persistently

졸지에 jol-jji-e *adv.* suddenly, abruptly

좀 jom *adv.* a little; certainly, indeed; please, kindly; 좀 더 jom deo *n.* a little more, a few more; a little longer

좀처럼 jom-cheo-reom *adv.* rarely, seldom; easily

좁다 jop-da *v.* be narrow, be small, be limited; be narrow-minded

좁아지다 job-a-ji-da *v.* become narrow

좁히다 jo-pi-da *v.* make narrow, restrict, constrain

종 jong *n.* servant, slave; bell, gong, buzzer

종각 jong-gak *n.* bell tower

종교 jong-gyo *n.* religion, faith

종교적인 jong-gyo-jeog-in *adj.* religious

종로 jong-no *n.* Jong Ro street *(tourist and shopping destination in Seoul)*

종류 jong-nyu *n.* kind, type, sort

종묘 jong-myo *n.* ancestral shrine of the royal family

종아리 jong-a-ri *n.* calf of the leg

종알거리다 jong-al-geo-ri-da *v.* mutter, grumble

종업원 jong-eob-won *n.* waiter, waitress; worker, employee

종이 jong-i *n.* paper

종이접시 jong-i-jeop-si *n.* paper plate

종이컵 jong-i-keop *n.* paper cup

종일 jong-il *adv.* all day, all day long

종전에 jong-jeon-e *adv.* formerly, before

종점 jong-jjeom *n.* terminal station

종종 jong-jong *adv.* occasionally, now and then; often

종탑 jong-tap *n.* belfry, bell tower

종합병원 jong-hap-byeong-won *n.* general hospital

좋다 jo-ta *v.* be good, be fine, be nice; be beneficial, be skilled; like, prefer

좋아지다 jo-a-ji-da *v.* become better, become finer; get to like, become fond of

좋아하다 jo-a-ha-da *v.* like, be fond of, love; be delighted, be pleased

좋지 않다 jo-chi an-ta *v.phr.* be bad, be evil, be wrong, be immoral; be harmful; be inferior; be weak; be ill

좌석 jwa-seok *n.* seat

좌우명 jwa-u-myeong *n.* favorite motto

좌회전하다 jwa-hoe-jeon-ha-da *v.* turn to the left, make a left turn

죄 joe *n.* crime, sin, blame, fault, offense

죄송하다 joe-song-ha-da *v.* feel guilty, be sorry, regret

죄짓다 joe-jit-da *v.* do a sinful thing, commit a sin, commit a crime

주가 ju-kka *n.* price of a stock

주간 ju-gan *n.* daytime, day; weekly, weekly publication; week

주고받다 ju-go-bat-da *v.* give and take, exchange

주관적 ju-gwan-jeok *adj.* subjective

주근깨 ju-geun-kkae *n.* freckles; flecks

주기적으로 ju-gi-jeog-eu-ro *adv.* periodically

주다 ju-da *v.* give, grant, donate, give away

주렁주렁 ju-reong-ju-reong *adv.* in abundance; in clusters

주로 ju-ro *adv.* mainly, usually, generally, mostly

주룩주룩 ju-ruk-ju-ruk *adv.* pouring hard, in sudden downpours

주르르 ju-reu-reu *adv.* dribbling, trickling

주름 ju-reum *n.* wrinkle, rumple, fold

주름살 ju-reum-ssal *n.* wrinkle, rumple, fold

주말 ju-mal *n.* weekend

주머니 ju-meo-ni *n.* pocket, sack, bag

주먹 ju-meok *n.* fist

주무르다 ju-mu-reu-da *v.* finger; fumble; massage; make a puppet of, have a person under control

주무시다 ju-mu-si-da *v. hon.* sleep

주문하다 ju-mun-ha-da *v.* order, request

주물럭거리다 ju-mul-leok-geo-ri-da *v.* finger; fumble; massage

주물럭주물럭 ju-mul-leok-ju-mul-leok *adv.* fingering, fumbling

주민등록증 ju-min-deung-nok-jeung *n.* citizen ID card, certificate of residence

주방 ju-bang *n.* kitchen

주변 ju-byeon *n.* circumference; surroundings

주부 ju-bu *n.* housewife

주사 ju-sa *n.* injection, inoculation; 주사 맞다 ju-sa mat-da *v.* get a shot

주사위 ju-sa-wi *n.* die, dice

주성분 ju-seong-bun *n.* main ingredient

주소 ju-so *n.* address, residence

주스 ju-sseu *n.* juice

주식 ju-sik *n.* stocks, shares; principal item of diet

주워담다 ju-wo-dam-tta *v.* pick up and put in, gather up

주워듣다 ju-wo-deut-da *v.* overhear, learn of, get wind of

주워먹다 ju-wo-meok-da *v.* grab a bite to eat; eat with one's hands

주위 ju-wi *n.* the circumference; surroundings

주유소 ju-yu-so *n.* gas station

주의사항 ju-i-sa-hang *n.* things worthy of attention, matters that demand special attention

주의점 ju-i-jjeom *n.* warnings

주의하다 ju-i-ha-da *v.* pay attention, notice; be careful, look out for

주인 ju-in *n.* host, employer, owner

주인공 ju-in-gong *n.* protagonist

주일 ju-il *n.* week

주장하다 ju-jang-ha-da *v.* assert, contend, advocate

주저앉다 ju-jeo-an-tta *v.* sit down, plump; settle down; crumble

주저앉히다 ju-jeo-an-chi-da *v.* force a person to sit down; make a person stay on

주저하다 ju-jeo-ha-da *v.* hesitate, think twice

주전자 ju-jeon-ja *n.* kettle, teakettle

주점 ju-jeom *n.* wine store, liquor store

주정하다 ju-jeong-ha-da *v.* act in a drunken and disorderly way

주제 ju-je *n.* theme, motif

주제명 ju-je-myeong *n.* theme, motif, main subject

주중 ju-jung *n.* weekdays

주차 ju-cha *n.* parking

주차금지 ju-cha-geum-ji *n.* no parking

주차위반 ju-cha-wi-ban *n.* parking violation

주차장 ju-cha-jang *n.* parking lot

주차하다 ju-cha-ha-da *v.* park

주택 ju-taek *n.* house, residence, housing

주한미군 ju-han-mi-gun *n.* US Army in South Korea

주황색 ju-hwang-saek *n.* orange (*color*)

죽 juk *adv.* in a row; all the time; far, away; ripping; droopingly, quickly; *n.* gruel

죽는소리하다 jung-neun-so-ri-ha-da *v.* shriek, scream, whine

죽다 juk-da *v.* die, pass away, wither, perish; run out; stop; go out, die out

죽어라 하고 jug-eo-ra ha-go *adv.phr.* desperately, frantically, as hard as one can

죽어지내다 jug-eo-ji-nae-da *v.* live under oppression, live in constant fear

죽은 목숨 jug-eun mok-sum *n.phr.* almost dead, person beyond the realm of hope; enslaved life

죽을 둥 살 둥 jug-eul ttung sal ttung *adv.phr.* desperately, frantically

죽을병 jug-eul-ppyeong *n.* fatal disease

죽음 jug-eum *n.* death, demise

죽이다 jug-i-da *v.* kill; murder; put to death; hold back, restrain, suppress

죽치다 juk-chi-da *v.* live in seclusion, remain indoors for a long time, stay put at home

준결승 jun-gyeol-sseung *n.* semifinal game

준비 jun-bi *n.* preparation, arrangement

준비하다 jun-bi-ha-da *v.* prepare, arrange

준우승 jun-u-seung *n.* victory in the semifinal

줄 jul *n.* line, rope, cord, string, strip; lane, row

줄거리 jul-geo-ri *n.* outline, plot; stalk, stem

줄곧 jul-got *adv.* all the time

줄기 jul-gi *n.* trunk, stem, vein

줄기차게 jul-gi-cha-ge *adv.* vigorously, strongly; incessantly, constantly

줄넘기 jul-leom-kki *n.* jumping rope

줄다 jul-da *v.* decrease, diminish, shrink, lose size

줄다리기 jul-da-ri-gi *n.* tug of war

줄무늬 jul-mu-ni *n.* stripes

줄서다 jul-seo-da *v.* form a line, stand in a line

줄어들다 jul-eo-deul-da *v.* grow smaller, shrink, diminish, decrease

줄이다 jul-i-da *v.* reduce, decrease, diminish, shorten

줄자 jul-ja *n.* measuring tape

줄줄 jul-jul *adv.* ceaselessly, profusely; smoothly, fluently

줄줄이 jul-jul-i *adv.* in row after row, all in rows

줌 jum *count.* handful, grasp, grip

줍다 jup-da *v.* pick up, gather up

중 jung *affix.* in the middle of, during, among; monk

중간 jung-gan *n.* middle, center

중고품 jung-go-pum *n.* used articles, secondhand goods

중국 jung-guk *n.* China

중국사람 jung-guk-sa-ram *n.* Chinese

중국식 jung-guk-sik *n.* Chinese-style (*housing, clothing, hair, etc.*), Chinese-style food

중국어 jung-gug-eo *n.* Chinese language

중국집 jung-guk-jip *n.* Chinese-style restaurant

중기 jung-gi *n.* the middle years of an era; metaphase

중년 jung-nyeon *n.* middle age, mid-life

중단하다 jung-dan-ha-da *v.* discontinue; interrupt, suspend

중독 jung-dok *n.* poisoning

중동 jung-dong *n.* Middle East

중력 jung-nyeok *n.* gravity, gravitation

중매 jung-mae *n.* matchmaking

중매결혼 jung-mae-gyeol-hon *n.* arranged marriage

중매쟁이 jung-mae-jaeng-i *n.* matchmaker

중반 jung-ban *n.* the middle phase

중부 jung-bu *n.* central districts, the central part of an area

중부지방 jung-bu-jji-bang *n.* central districts

중산층 jung-san-cheung *n.* middle class

중세 jung-se *n.* middle ages, medieval times

중소기업 jung-so-gi-eop *n.* small business

중순 jung-sun *n.* the second ten days of a month

중심 jung-sim *n.* the center, the focus, the core

중심지 jung-sim-ji *n.* the center, central place

중앙 jung-ang *n.* the center, the middle, the heart of a place

중앙우체국 jung-ang-u-che-guk *n.* central post office

중얼거리다 jung-eol-geo-ri-da *v.* mutter, grumble, murmur

중얼중얼 jung-eol-jung-eol *adv.* murmuring, muttering, grumbling

중에 jung-e *adv.* among, between

중에서 jung-e-seo *adv.* among, between

중요하다 jung-yo-ha-da *v.* be important

중장비 jung-jang-bi *n.* heavy equipment (*mechanical*)

중지하다 jung-ji-ha-da *v.* discontinue; suspend, stop

중턱 jung-teok *n.* the mid-slope of a mountain, halfway up a mountain

중퇴하다 jung-toe-ha-ad *v.* drop out of school

중학교 jung-hak-gyo *n.* junior high

중학생 jung-hak-saeng *n.* junior high student

중화요리 jung-hwa-yo-ri *n.* Chinese dish

중환자 jung-hwan-ja *n.* patient in critical condition

쥐 jwi *n.* rat, mouse; cramp; 쥐 죽은 듯하다 jwi jug-eun deu-ta-da *v.* be still as a stone; be silent as the grave

쥐다 jwi-da *v.* grip, clench, grasp, seize

쥐약 jwi-yak *n.* rat poison, raticide

즈음 jeu-eum *n.* the time, an occasion, when, at the time

즉 jeuk *adv.* namely, that is, so to speak; precisely, exactly, nothing but

즉시 jeuk-si *adv.* at once, immediately, instantly, without delay

즐거움 jeul-geo-um *n.* pleasure, enjoyment, delight, joy

즐거이 jeul-geo-i *adv.* pleasantly, delightfully; cheerfully

즐겁다 jeul-geop-da *v.* be joyful, be pleasant, be enjoyable

즐기다 jeul-gi-da *v.* enjoy oneself, take pleasure in, amuse oneself

증가하다 jeung-ga-ha-da *v.* increase, rise, grow, multiply

증거 jeung-geo *n.* evidence, proof, witness

증권 jeung-kkwon *n.* securities, stocks

증권회사 jeung-kkeon-hoe-sa *n.* stock company

증명하다 jeung-myeong-ha-da *v.* prove, show, witness, verify, identify

증상 jeung-sang *n.* symptoms, the condition of a patient

증서 jeung-seo *n.* deed, voucher, certificate

증세 jeung-se *n.* symptoms, the condition of a patient

증인 jeung-in *n.* witness, testifier, eyewitness

증후군 jeung-hu-gun *n.* syndrome

지가하다 ji-ga-ka-da *v.* be late, come late; recognize, realize

지갑 ji-gap *n.* wallet, purse

지게 ji-ge *n.* A-frame carrier *(traditional Korean carrier strapped to one's back)*

지겹다 ji-gyeop-da *v.* be tedious, be tiresome; be disgusting

지경이다 ji-gyeong-i-da *v.* be at the point of, be in the situation of

지구 ji-gu *n.* earth, globe; district, region, area

지그시 ji-geu-si *adv.* patiently, with patience; gently, softly, calmly, quietly

지극하다 ji-geu-ka-da *v.* be extreme, be the utmost, be exceeding

지극히 ji-geu-ki *adv.* very, extremely, exceedingly

지글지글 ji-geul-ji-geul *adv.* sizzling, simmering, seething

지금 ji-geum *n.* now

지금까지 ji-geum-kka-ji *adv.* so far, till now, all the while, all this time

지금부터 ji-geum-bu-teo *adv.* from now on, after this, hence

지금쯤 ji-geum-kkeot *adv.* by this time

지긋지긋하다 ji-geut-ji-geu-ta-da *v.* be tedious, be wearisome, be tiresome; be loathsome, be detestable, be horrible

지나가다 ji-na-ga-da *v.* go through, pass

지나다 ji-na-da *v.* pass by, go past, pass through; go on, go by, pass; expire; terminate; exceed

지나오다 ji-na-o-da *v.* pass by, pass through, go through, undergo

지나치다 ji-na-chi-da *v.* go too far, go to extremes, carry too far; pass by, go past, pass through

지난 ji-nan *adj.* last

지난날 ji-nan-nal *n.* old days, bygone days, days gone by

지난달 ji-nan-dal *n.* last month

지난번 ji-nan-beon *n.* last time, some time ago, the other day, before this

지난주 ji-nan-ju *n.* last week

지남철 ji-nam-cheol *n.* magnet

지내다 ji-nae-da *v.* spend time, live, get along; observe; hold; pursue; go through, experience; associate with, consort with

지능 ji-neung *n.* intelligence, intellect

지다 ji-da *v.* lose, be defeated; carry on the back; bear a burden, be under an obligation, incur; fall, fade and fall, be gone; set, sink

지도 ji-do *n.* map, atlas, chart

지도하다 ji-do-ha-da *v.* guide, direct, lead

지독하다 ji-do-ka-da *v.* be vicious, be venomous; be intense, be severe, be terrible

지렁이 ji-reong-i *n.* earthworm

지로 ji-ro *n.* giro *(electronic banking service)*

지루하다 ji-ru-ha-da *v.* be boring, be tedious

지르다 ji-reu-da *v.* yell, scream, cry aloud; set fire to

지름길 ji-reum-kkil *n.* shortcut, short way

지리산 ji-ri-san *n.* Ji Ri mountain *(tourist destination)*

지리적 ji-ri-jeok *adj.* geographical

지망하다 ji-mang-ha-da *v.* desire, choose, prefer

지명 ji-myeong *n.* name of a place; nomination; designation

지문 ji-mun *n.* fingerprint, finger mark

지물포 ji-mul-po *n.* paper goods store

지방 ji-bang *n.* local area, country; region; fat

지배인 ji-bae-in *n.* manager, superintendent

지배하다 ji-bae-ha-da *v.* control, rule, govern, direct

지불하다 ji-bul-ha-da *v.* pay, disburse; redeem

지붕 ji-bung *n.* roof

지사 ji-sa *n.* branch office

지상 ji-sang *n.* the ground

지시하다 ji-si-ha-da *v.* direct, instruct; indicate, point out

지식 ji-sik *n.* knowledge, information, understanding

지압 ji-ap *n.* acupressure

지어내다 ji-eo-nae-da *v.* make up, fabricate, invent

지역 ji-yeok *n.* area, region, zone

지역번호 ji-yeok-beon-ho *n.* area code

지옥 ji-ok *n.* hell

지우개 ji-u-gae *n.* eraser, wiper

지우다 ji-u-da *v.* erase, rub out, cross out; charge, lay a duty upon; make a person carry

지원하다 ji-won-ha-da *v.* apply for, volunteer; support, back up, give support

지위 ji-wi *n.* position, status, rank, post

지은이 ji-eun-i *n.* writer, author

지저귀다 ji-jeo-gwi-da *v.* twitter, chirp

지저분하다 ji-jeo-bun-ha-da *v.* be messy, be disordered, be untidy, be unclean

지적 ji-jjeok *adj.* intellectual, brainy

지적하다 ji-jeo-ka-da *v.* point out, indicate, put out a finger on

지점 ji-jeom *n.* spot, point, place, position; branch office

지중해 ji-jung-hae *n.* Mediterranean Sea

지지리 ji-ji-ri *adv.* terribly, awfully, shockingly

지지하다 ji-ji-ha-da *v.* support, prop up, stand by

지진 ji-hin *n.* earthquake; 지진 나다 ji-jin na-da *v.* have an earthquake

지출 ji-chul *n.* expenses, expenditure

지치다 ji-chi-da *v.* be exhausted, be fatigued, be worn out, be tired

지켜보다 ji-kyeo-bo-da *v.* watch, stare, witness

지켜주다 ji-kyeo-ju-da *v.* defend, protect, guard; watch

지키다 ji-ki-da *v.* defend, protect, guard; watch; keep, maintain

지팡이 ji-pang-i *n.* stick, cane, walking stick

지퍼 ji-peo *n.* zipper

지평선 ji-pyeong-seon *n.* the horizon

지폐 ji-pye *n.* paper money, bill

지푸라기 ji-pu-ra-gi *n.* piece of straw

지하 ji-ha *n.* underground

지하도 ji-ha-do *n.* underpass

지하상가 ji-ha-sang-ga *n.* underground shopping center, underground shopping district

지하철 ji-ha-cheol *n.* subway

지하철역 ji-ha-cheol-lyeok *n.* subway station

지하철표 ji-ha-cheol-pyo *n.* subway ticket

지혜 ji-hye *n.* wisdom, wits

지휘 ji-hwi *n.* command, direction, instructions

지휘하다 ji-hwi-ha-da *v.* command, conduct, direct, control

직사광선 jik-sa-gwang-seon *n.* direct sunlight

직선 jik-seon *n.* straight line

직업 jig-eop *n.* job, occupation, career

직원 jig-won *n.* agent, clerk, staff member

직장 jik-jang *n.* place of work, job

직장생활 jik-jang-saeng-hwal *n.* life in the workplace

직장인 jik-jang-in *n.* employee

직전 jik-jeon *n.* just before, just prior to

직접 jik-jeop *adv.* directly, immediately, firsthand, personally

직진하다 jik-jin-ha-da *v.* go right on, make straight for

직통 jik-tong *n.* direct communication, direct service, direct code

직할시 ji-kal-si *n.* city under the direct control of the government

직행 ji-kaeng *n.* going straight, going direct, going non-stop

직후 ji-ku *n.* immediately after

진갑 jin-gap *n.* 71st birthday

진공청소기 jin-gong-cheong-so-gi *n.* vacuum cleaner

진급하다 jin-geu-pa-da *v.* be promoted, win a promotion

진눈깨비 jin-nun-kkae-bi *n.* sleet, snow mixed with rain

진단하다 jin-dan-ha-da *v.* diagnose, make a diagnosis

진담 jin-dam *n.* serious talk, earnest talk

진도 jin-do *n.* the rate of progress

진땀 jin-ttam *n.* greasy sweat, sticky sweat; 진땀 나다 jin-ttam na-da *v.* sweat profusely; undergo terrible hardships

진로 jil-lo *n.* course, direction, path

진료 jil-lyo *n.* medical examination and treatment

진료시간 jil-lyo-si-gan *n.* consultation hours

진보적 jin-bo-jeok *adj.* progressive, up-to-date

진수성찬 jin-su-seong-chan *n.* all kinds of delicious food

진실되다 jin-sil-doe-da v. be true, be truthful, be real, be sincere, be honest, be faithful

진심으로 jin-sim-eu-reo adv. from one's heart, sincerely

진열장 jin-yeol-jjang n. showcase

진열하다 jin-yeol-ha-da v. exhibit, display

진입로 jin-im-no n. admission path

진작 jin-jak adv. on the spot, immediately, directly, promptly; earlier

진주 jin-ju n. pearl

진지 jin-ji n. hon. rice, meal

진짜 jin jja n. genuine article, real thing

진찰 jin-chal n. medical examination

진찰받다 jin-chal-bat-da v. consult doctor

진찰실 jin-chal-sil n. examining room

진찰하다 jin-chal-ha-da v. consult a patient, examine, diagnose

진창 jin-chang n. mud, muddy place

진탕 jin-tang adv. to one's heart's content, as one likes, freely

진통제 jin-tong-je n. painkiller, anodyne

진하다 jin-ha-da v. be dark; be deep, be thick, be heavy, be strong, be rich

진학하다 jin-ha-ka-da v. enter into studies, enter a school of higher grade

진행하다 jin-haeng-ha-da v. progress, make progress, proceed, go on

진화론 jin-hwa-ron n. the theory of evolution

진흙 jin-geuk n. mud, dirt, clay

진흙탕 jin-heuk-tang n. muddy water

질기다 jil-gi-da v. be tough, be durable, be tenacious, be persistent

질다 jil-da v. be soft; be watery; be muddy; be wet

질러가다 jil-leo-ga-da v. take a shortcut, cut across

질리다 jil-li-da v. become disgusted, get sick of; turn pale, lose color; be cowed, be overwhelmed

질문 jil-mun n. question, inquiry

질문하다 jil-mun-ha-da v. ask a question

질색하다 jil-ssae-ka-da v. be disgusted by, detest, loathe

질서 jil-sseo n. order, regularity, method

질질 jil-jil adv. trailing, dragging; dribbling, oozing

질투 jil-tu n. jealousy

짊어지다 jilm-eo-ji-da v. carry on the back,

carry on the shoulder; be charged with, bear

짐 jim n. load, cargo, luggage, burden, package; 짐 꾸리다 jim kku-ri-da v. pack up, package; 짐 들다 jim deul-da v. carry luggage, hold a package; 짐 풀다 jim pul-da v. unpack

짐꾼 jim-kkun n. porter

짐승 jim-seung n. beast, animal

짐작하다 jim-ja-ka-da v. guess, conjecture, infer

집 jip n. house, residence, home; nest; case, box; 집 봐주다 jip bwa ju da v. house-sit; 집 정리 jip jeong-ni v. organize one's house; 집 짓다 jip jit-da v. build a house

집값 jip-gap n. house price

집게 jip-ge n. tongs, tweezers

집게발 jip-ge-bal n. claws

집다 jip-da v. pick up, take up

집들이 jip-deul-i n. housewarming party

집보다 jip-bo-da v. house-sit

집사람 jip-sa-ram n. my wife

집세 jip-se n. rent

집안 jib-an n. family background; family, household; inside of a house; 집안이 어렵다 jib-an-i eo-ryeop-da The family's situation is difficult (usually financial)

집안일 jib-an-nil n. housework

집어넣다 jib-eo-neo-ta v. put into, bring in; set in, insert; include, count; accommodate, admit; send

집어먹다 jib-eo-meok-da v. eat with one's fingers, pick up and eat

집어주다 jib-eo-ju-da v. pass, reach; bribe

집주인 jip-ju-in n. landlord, owner of a house

집중하다 jip-jung-ha-da v. concentrate upon, centralize upon

집집마다 jip-jim-ma-da adv. every house, each house

집터 jip-teo n. house site, lot

집회 ji-poe n. meeting, assembly, gathering

집히다 ji-pi-da v. get picked up, be held between one's fingers

짓 jit n. behavior, act, conduct; motion

짓궂다 jit-gut-da v. be ill-tempered, be ill-natured, be cursed

짓누르다 jin-nu-reu-da v. weigh down, press down, put down

짓다 jit-da v. make, manufacture; build, construct; write, compose; cook, prepare; cultivate, grow; commit; show, express

징 jing n. gong

징검다리 jing-geom-da-ri n. stepping stones

징그럽다 jing-geu-reop-da v. be creepy, be hideous

짖다 jit-da v. bark, howl, croak

짙다 jit-da v. be dark, be deep, be rich, be thick, be heavy

짚다 jip-da v. feel; examine; take; use, carry; figure out, guess; put, rest

짚신 jip-sin n. straw shoes, straw sandals

짜다 jja-da v. construct, make; form, organize, plan; unite, cooperate; weave, knit; squeeze, press, compress; weep, sob; be salty

짜리 jja-ri affix. worth, value

짜임새 jja-im-sae n. structure

짜증 jja-jeung n. temper, irritability

짝 jjak n. one of a set, counterpart; adv. ripping, tearing, wide open; 짝 맞추다 jjak mat-chu-da v. match two things, make a match

짝사랑 jjak-sa-rang n. unrequited love

짝짓다 jjak-jit-da v. make a pair, make a match, mate

짝짝이 jjak-jjag-i n. unmatched pair, wrongly matched pair

짝하다 jja-ka-da v. enter into a partnership, partake

짤막하다 jjal-ma-ka-da v. be short, be choppy

짧게 jjal-kke adv. briefly, shortly

짧다 jjal-tta v. be short, be brief; be insufficient, be short of

짬뽕 jjam-ppong n. Chinese spicy noodle soup; mixture, medley

짭짤하다 jjap-jjal-ha-da v. be nice and salty, have a good salty taste

째 jjae affix. ordinal suffix; 저는 셋째입니다 jeo-neun set-jjae-im-ni-da I am the third child (in my family)

째다 jjae-da v. rip, cut open, tear

짹짹거리다 jjaek-jjaek-geo-ri-da v. tweet, twitter, chirp

쨍그랑 jjaeng-geu-rang adv. with a clink, with a clank

쩌렁쩌렁하다 jjeo-reong-jjeo-reong-ha-da v. be resonant, be sonorous

쩔렁거리다 jjeol-leong-geo-ri-da v. clink, jingle

쩔쩔매다 jjeol-jjeol-mae-da v. be at one's wit's end, be at a loss

쩝쩝 jjeop-jjeop adv. licking one's chops, smacking one's lips

쩝쩝거리다 jjeop-jjeop-geo-ri-da v. lick one's chops, smack one's lips

쩨쩨하다 jje-jje-ha-da v. be stingy, be miserly; be shabby, be worthless

쪼개다 jjo-gae-da v. split, divide; smash

쪼개지다 jjo-gae-ji-da v. split, break, divide

쪼다 jjo-da v. peck, pick up, chisel

쪼아먹다 jjo-a-meok-da v. peck at and eat, pick

쪽 jjok count. piece; n. side, direction; 교과서 37쪽 펴 보세요 gyo-gwa-seo sam-sip-chil-jjok pyeo bo-se-yo Please open your textbook to page 37; 어느 쪽으로 가야 되지 eo-neu jjog-eu-ro ga-ya doe-ji Which direction should I go

쫄깃쫄깃하다 jjol-git-jjol-gi-ta-da v. be chewy, be sticky

쫄딱 jjol-ttak adv. completely, wholly, altogether, utterly

쫓겨가다 jjot-gyeo-ga-da v. be chased, be driven

쫓기다 jjot-gi-da v. be chased, be driven, feel the pressure of business

쫓다 jjot-da v. drive away; run after, chase; follow, follow suit; catch up with, keep up with

쫓아가다 jjoch-a-ga-da v. run after, pursue; catch up with, keep up with

쫓아내다 jjoch-a-nae-da v. drive back, send away, turn away

쬐다 jjoe-da v. shine; bathe in the sun; hold up against the heat

쭈그러뜨리다 jju-geu-reo-tteu-ri-da v. press out of shape, crush, crumple

쭈그러지다 jju-geu-reo-ji-da v. be crushed, be crumpled; grow gaunt, shrivel

쭈그리다 jju-geu-ri-da v. crush; crouch, squat, bend low

쭈글쭈글하다 jju-geul-jju-geul-ha-da v. be crumpled, be rumpled, be wrinkled

쪽쪽 jjuk-jjuk *adv.* in rows, row after row; briskly, rapidly; into shreds, in pieces

쯤 jjeum *affix.* about, around

찌개 jji-gae *n.* dish served in the pot, pot stew

찌그러뜨리다 jji-geu-reo-tteu-ri-da *v.* crush, squash

찌그러지다 jji-geu-reo-ji-da *v.* be crushed, be battered

찌꺼기 jji-kkeo-gi *n.* remnants, grounds, sediments, dregs

찌다 jji-da *v.* grow fat, gain weight; be humid, be sultry; steam, cook with steam

찌르다 jji-reu-da *v.* pierce, prick; inform, report; stink, smell nasty; hurt, offend

찌푸리다 jji-pu-ri-da *v.* cloud over, get cloudy; frown, make a face

찍 jjik *adv.* sliding, sliding down; drawing a line with a stroke

찍다 jjik-da *v.* take a picture; stamp, seal; dip into; mark, dot; mark out, keep an eye on; chop, hack; punch; thrust, pierce

찍히다 ji-ki-da *v.* get imprinted; get dipped; get pointed off; get chopped; get punched; get taken; get hooked

찐득찐득하다 jjin-deuk-jjin-deu-ka-da *v.* be sticky, be adhesive

찐빵 jjin-ppang *n.* steamed bread

찔끔하다 jjil-kkeum-ha-da *v.* be startled, be alarmed; be intimidated

찔리다 jjil-li-da *v.* be stuck, be pricked, be pierced

찜 jjim *n.* steamed dish, boiled dish

찜질하다 jjim-jil-ha-da *v.* foment; apply a hot pack to

찜찜하다 jjim-jjim-ha-da *v.* feel constrained, feel ill at ease, be uncomfortable

찡그리다 jjing-geu-ri-da *v.* frown, scowl, make a wry face

찡긋하다 jjing-geu-ta-da *v.* wink at; wrinkle up one's face at; make a mouth at

찡하다 jjing-ha-da *v.* be stuffy, be blocked, be clogged

찢기다 jjit-gi-da *v.* get torn, be ripped

찢다 jjit-da *v.* tear, split, rip

찢어지다 jjij-eo-ji-da *v.* tear, rend, rip

찧다 jji-ta *v.* pound, hull, husk, ram

ㅊ

차 cha *n.* car, vehicle; tea; 차를 돌리다 cha-reul dol-li-da *v.* change the direction in which one is driving; 차가 밀리다 cha-ga mil-li-da Traffic is heavy; 차 사고 cha sa-go *n.* car accident; 차를 몰다 cha-reul mol-da *v.* drive a car

차갑다 cha-gap-da *v.* be cold

차고 cha-go *n.* garage, car shed

차곡차곡 cha-gok-cha-gok *adv.* in an orderly fashion, neatly

차근차근 cha-geun-cha-geun *adv.* compactly; carefully, minutely

차남 cha-nam *n.* one's second eldest son

차녀 cha-nyeo *n.* one's second eldest daughter

차다 cha-da *v.* kick; be cold, be chilly, be icy; fill up, be full of, be filled with; fasten on, wear

차도 cha-do *n.* road

차라리 cha-ra-ri *adv.* rather, preferably

차려입다 cha-ryeo-ip-da *v.* dress up, be dressed up

차례 cha-rye *n.* ancestor worship; order, sequence; time; round; turn; 차례 지내다 cha-rye ji-nae-da *v.* perform rites honoring one's ancestors

차례로 cha-rye-ro *adv.* one by one, one after another

차리다 cha-ri-da *v.* prepare for, make ready; pull oneself together; be wide awake

차림표 cha-rim-pyo *n.* menu

차멀미 cha-meol-mi *n.* car sickness

차멀미하다 cha-meol-mi-ha-da *v.* get carsick

차문 cha-mun *n.* car door

차바퀴 cha-ba-kwi *n.* wheel

차버리다 cha-beo-ri-da *v.* kick away, give a person a kick; reject, refuse

차별 cha-byeol *n.* distinction, discrimination

차별하다 cha-byeol-ha-da *v.* discriminate, distinguish

차분하다 cha-bun-ha-da *v.* be calm, be quiet

차비 cha-bi *n.* transportation fare, carfare

차선 cha-seon *n.* traffic lane

차이 cha-i *n.* difference, distinction

차이나타운 cha-i-na-ta-un *n.* Chinatown

차이점 cha-i-jjeom *n.* differences, points of distinction

차장 cha-jang *n.* conductor

차주전자 cha-jju-jeon-ja *n.* tea pot

차지하다 cha-ji-ha-da *v.* hold, occupy, take possession

차차 cha-cha *adv.* gradually, little by little; later on, afterwards

차창 cha-chang *n.* car window

차츰차츰 cha-cheum-cha-cheum *adv.* gradually, step by step, little by little

차트 cha-teu *n.* chart

차표 cha-pyo *n.* ticket for train/bus

착각하다 chak-ga-ka-da *v.* be under an illusion, misunderstand, misjudge

착륙하다 chang-nyu-ka-da *v.* land, make a landing

착실하다 chak-sil-ha-da *v.* be steady, be faithful

착착 chak-chak *adv.* in an orderly fashion, step by step

착하다 cha-ka-da *v.* be good-natured, be tenderhearted, be nice

찬란하다 chal-lan-ha-da *v.* be brilliant, be shining, be gorgeous

찬물 chan-mul *n.* cold water

찬밥 chan-bap *n.* cold boiled rice

찬성하다 chan-seong-ha-da *v.* approve, agree, support

찬송가 chan-song-ga *n.* hymn

찬스 chan-sseu *n.* chance, opportunity

찬장 chan-jjang *n.* pantry, cupboard

찬찬히 chan-chan-hi *adv.* staidly, calmly; carefully, cautiously; slowly

찰랑거리다 chal-lang-geo-ri-da *v.* jingle, clink, tinkle; slosh; lap

찰싹 chal-ssak *adv.* with a spank; with splashes

찰흙 chal-heuk *n.* clay

참 cham *adv.* really, very, indeed, actually

참가하다 cham-ga-ha-da *v.* participate, join, enter

참견하다 cham-gyeon-ha-da *v.* meddle in, interfere

참고 cham-go *n.* reference, information

참기름 cham-gi-reum *n.* sesame oil

참다 cham-tta *v.* endure, put up with, be patient, control oneself

참모습 cham-mo-seup *n.* one's true face, one's true character

참새 cham-sae *n.* sparrow

참석하다 chm-seo-ka-da *v.* participate, be present, attend

참신하다 cham-sin-ha-da *v.* be up-to-date, be original

참아내다 cham-a-nae-da *v.* endure, put up with, be patient, control oneself

참여하다 cham-yeo-ha-da *v.* participate in, take part in, join in

참외 cham-oe *n.* melon

참을성 cham-eul-sseong *n.* patience, forbearance

참조하다 cham-jo-ha-da *v.* refer, compare

참하다 cham-ha-da *v.* be nice and pretty; be modest; be gentle; be tidy, be fair

찻길 chat-gil *n.* street, roadway

찻숟갈 chat-sut-gal *n.* teaspoon

찻잔 chat-jan *n.* teacup

찻집 chat-jip *n.* teahouse

창 chang *n.* window; spear; 창 밖 chang bak *n.* outside the window

창가 chang-kka *n.* window side; area near window

창경궁 chang-gyeong-gung *n.* Chang Gyeong palace *(tourist destination)*

창고 chang-go *n.* warehouse, storehouse

창구 chang-gu *n.* window

창덕궁 chang-deok-gung *n.* Chang Deok palace *(tourist destination)*

창문 chang-mun *n.* window

창조하다 chang-jo-ha-da *v.* create, call into being

창턱 chang-teok *n.* windowsill

창틀 chang-teul *n.* window frame; sash

창피당하다 chang-pi-dang-ha-da *v.* become ashamed, undergo a shameful situation

창피하다 chang-pi-ha-da *v.* be ashamed, be shameful

창호지 chang-ho-ji *n.* window-paper, sliding screen paper

찾다 chat-da *v.* look for, find, seek, search; pick up; draw, take out; visit

찾아가다 chaj-a-ga-da *v.* visit

찾아내다 chaj-a-nae-da *v.* find out, discover; seek

찾아보다 chaj-a-bo-da *v.* look for, seek, search

찾아서 chaj-a-seo *part.* in search of; 잃어버린 아이를 찾아서 이리저리 다닌다 il-eo-beo-rin a-i-reul chaj-a-seo i-ri-jeo-ri da-nin-da He is wandering here and there in search of his missing child

찾아오다 chaj-a-o-da *v.* come to find, come to see; retrieve something

찾아주다 chaj-a-ju-da *v.* find something for somebody, look for something for somebody

채 chae *count.* counter for houses

채널 chae-neol *n.* channel

채소 chae-so *n.* vegetable, greens

채소가게 chae-so-ga-ge *n.* vegetable shop

채식주의자 chae-sik-ji-i-ja *n.* vegetarian

채용하다 chae-yong-ha-da *v.* employ, appoint

채우다 chae-u-da *v.* lock, fasten; fulfill, fill up, complete

채치다 chae-chi-da *v.* mince, slice, chop

채칼 chae-kal *n.* slicer, chopper

책 chaek *n.* book

책값 chaek-gap *n.* book price

책꽂이 chaek-kkoj-i *n.* bookshelf, bookcase

책받침 chaek-bat-chim *n.* notepad

책방 chaek-bang *n.* bookstore

책벌레 chaek-beol-le *n.* bookworm

책상 chaek-sang *n.* desk

책임 chaeg-im *n.* responsibility, duty, obligation; blame

책임감 chaeg-im-gam *n.* sense of responsibility; 책임감 있다 chaeg-im-gam it-da *v.* be responsible

책임지다 chaeg-im-ji-da *v.* be responsible, take the responsibility

책장 chaek-sang *n.* bookcase, bookshelf

챔피언 chaem-pi-eon *n.* champion, champ

챙기다 chaeng-gi-da *v.* take care of; gather, collect, pack, put things in order

처가 cheo-ga *n.* the house of one's wife's parents; 처가살이 cheo-ga-sal-i *n.* living at the house of one's wife's parents

처남 cheo-nam *n.* brother of one's wife, brother-in-law

처넣다 cheo-neo-ta *v.* push into, stuff, put into, sink in

처녀 cheo-nyeo *n.* maiden, maid

처럼 cheo-reom *part.* like, as, as if; 인형처럼 예쁘다 in-hyeong-cheo-reom ye-ppeu-da She is as pretty as a doll

처리하다 cheo-ri-ha-da *v.* handle, treat, manage, deal with

처마 cheo-ma *n.* eaves

처방전 cheo-bang-jeon *n.* prescription slip

처세술 cheo-se-sul *n.* art of managing in society; the secret of success in life

처음 cheo-eum *adv.* for the first time; *n.* the beginning, the first, the origin

처음에 cheo-eum-e *adv.* at the beginning, at first

처자 cheo-ja *n.* one's wife and children, one's family

처제 cheo-je *n.* younger sister of one's wife, younger sister-in-law

처지 cheo-ji *n.* situation, condition, circumstance; relation

처지다 cheo-ji-da *v.* sink, go down; hang, droop; be left behind, stay behind, remain

처형 cheo-hyeong *n.* older sister of one's wife, older sister-in-law

척 cheok *adv.* tightly, closely; droopingly, languidly; without hesitation, quickly

척척 cheok-cheok *adv.* fold by fold, in orderly fashion; coil by coil, clinging; all sticking fast, adhesively; all without delay; promptly

척척하다 cheok-cheo-ka-da *v.* be wet, be damp

척추 cheok-chu *n.* vertebra, the backbone, the spine

천 cheon *n.* thousand; cloth, fabric

천국 cheon-guk *n.* Heaven, Paradise

천년 cheon-nyeon *n.* thousand years

천대받다 cheon-dae-bat-da *v.* be mistreated

천대하다 cheon-dae-ha-da *v.* mistreat, treat with contempt

천둥 cheon-dung *n.* thunder

천둥 치다 cheon-dung chi-da *v.* thunder

천막 cheon-mak *n.* tent

천만 cheon-man *n.* ten million

천만다행 cheon-man-da-haeng *n.* being extremely fortunate, being very lucky

천만에 cheon-man-e *adv.* not at all, don't mention it; far from it, certainly not

천문대 cheon-mun-dae *n.* astronomical observatory

천문학 cheon-mun-hak *n.* astronomy

천벌 cheon-beol *n.* divine punishment, the wrath of God; 천벌 받다 cheon-beol bat-da *v.* be punished by Heaven

천부적 cheon-bu-jeok *adj.* innate, naturally gifted, inborn

천사 cheon-sa *n.* angel

천생연분 cheon-saeng-nyeon-bun *n.* marriage ties preordained by God

천성 cheon-seong *n.* nature, natural disposition, temperament; instinct

천식 cheon-sik *n.* asthma

천양지차 cheon-yang-ji-cha *n.* complete opposite, all the difference in the world

천연 cheon-yeon *adj.* natural

천연가스 cheon-yeon-kka-sseu *n.* natural gas

천연기념물 cheon-yeon-gi-nyeom-mul *n.* natural monument

천연자원 cheon-yeon-ja-won *n.* natural resources

천왕성 cheon-wang-seong *n.* Uranus

천우신조로 cheon-u-sin-jo-ro *adv.* by the grace of God

천장 cheon-jang *n.* ceiling

천재 cheon-jae *n.* genius, gifted person

천재지변 cheon-jae-ji-byeon *n.* natural disaster

천주교 cheon-ju-gyo *n.* Catholic Church

천지 cheon-ji *n.* crater lake on Mt. Baekdu (*tour site*)

천지차이 cheon-ji-cha-i *n.* huge difference

천진난만하다 cheon-jin-nan-man-ha-da *v.* be simple and innocent, be naïve, be open-hearted

천차만별 cheon-cha-man-byeol *n.* infinite variety

천천히 cheon-cheon-hi *adv.* slowly, gradually

천치 cheon-chi *n.* idiot, fool

천하다 cheon-ha-da *v.* be humble, be ignoble; be vulgar, be base

천하에 cheon-ha-e *adv.* under the sun, in the world

천하장사 cheon-ha-jang-sa *n.* strongest man on earth; winner of the Korean wrestling competition

철 cheol *n.* season; iron, steel

철강 cheol-gang *n.* iron, steel

철거하다 cheol-geo-ha-da *v.* remove, clear away

철근 cheol-geun *n.* steel reinforcement

철도 cheol-tto *n.* railroad, railway

철들다 cheol-deul-da *v.* become sensible, become wise

철렁거리다 cheol-leong-geo-ri-da *v.* jingle, clink, tinkle

철로 cheol-lo *n.* railroad, railway

철망 cheol-mang *n.* wire-gauge, wire-screen, wire-netting

철면피 cheol-myeon-pi *n.* brazenness, cheekiness

철모르다 cheol-mo-reu-da *v.* have no common sense, be simple-minded

철벅거리다 cheol-beok-geo-ri-da *v.* splash

철봉 cheol-bong *n.* iron bar; exercise bar, dumbbell

철부지 cheol-bu-ji *n.* mere child; person who has no sense

철분 cheol-bun *n.* iron (*mineral*)

철사 cheol-ssa *n.* wire, wiring

철새 cheol-ssae *n.* seasonal bird, migratory bird

철썩 cheol-sseok *adv.* with a splash; with a thud, with a slam

철썩거리다 cheol-sseok-geo-ri-da *v.* splash; spank

철썩철썩 cheol-sseok-cheol-sseok *adv.* splashing; spanking; slamming

철없다 cheol-eop-da *v.* have no sense, be thoughtless

철자법 cheol-jja-ppeop *n.* the system of spelling, writing system

철저히 cheol-jjeo-hi *adv.* completely, thoroughly

철조망 cheol-jjo-mang *n.* wire-entanglements, barbed-wire entanglements

철철 cheol-cheol *adv.* brimming over, overflowing

철철이 cheol-cheol-i *adv.* each and every season, at each season

철커덕 cheol-keo-deok *adv.* with a snap, with a click

철학 cheol-hak *n.* philosophy

첨벙 cheom-beong *adv.* with a splash

첩 cheop *n.* concubine

첩보 cheop-bo *n.* secret information, intelligence

첫 cheot *affix.* first, new beginning

첫걸음 cheot-geol-eum *n.* the first step; a start; the rudiments

첫날 cheon-nal *n.* the first day

첫눈 cheon-nun *n.* the first sight, the first glance; the first snow of the season

첫돌 cheot-dol *n.* a child's first birthday

첫마디 cheon-ma-di *n.* an opening remark, the first word

첫배 cheot-bae *n.* the first boat; the first litter

첫번 cheot-beon *n.* the first time

첫사랑 cheot-sa-rang *n.* first love; first sweetheart

첫새벽 ceot-sae-byeok *n.* break of day, daybreak, early morning

첫선 cheot-seon *n.* the first appearance

첫손자 cheot-son-ja *n.* one's first grandson

첫아들 cheod-a-deul *n.* one's first son

첫인상 cheod-in-sang *n.* one's first impression

첫째 cheot-jjae *n.* first, the foremost, number one

첫출발 cheot-chul-bal *n.* the first start, the very beginning

첫해 cheo-tae *n.* the first year

청개구리 cheong-gae-gu-ri *n.* tree frog

청교도 cheong-gyo-da *n.* Puritan

청년 cheong-nyeon *n.* young man, youth, young people, the youth

청량음료 cheong-nyang-eum-nyo *n.* soft drink

청바지 cheong-ba-ji *n.* blue jeans

청색 cheong-saek *adj.* blue, green

청소 cheong-so *n.* cleaning

청소기 cheong-so-gi *n.* vacuum cleaner

청소년 cheong-so-nyeon *n.* young boys and girls, teenagers, juveniles

청소하다 cheong-so-ha-da *v.* clean, sweep

청신호 cheong-sin-ho *n.* green light, positive sign

청와대 cheong-wa-dae *n.* the Blue House, Korean Presidential Mansion

청일점 cheong-il-jjeom *n.* the only man among the women

청자 cheong-ja *n.* celadon porcelain *(traditional art/craft)*

청중 cheong-jung *n.* audience

청진기 cheong-jin-gi *n.* stethoscope

청첩장 cheong-cheop-jang *n.* invitation card, letter of invitation

청평사 cheong-pyeong-sa *n.* Cheong Pyeong temple *(tourist destination in Korea)*

청혼하다 cheong-hon-ha-da *v.* propose a marriage

체격 che-gyeok *n.* physical constitution, physique

체계 che-gye *n.* system, organization

체계적 che-gye-jeok *adj.* systematic

체구 che-gu *n.* the body, the frame

체력 che-ryeok *n.* physical strength

체면 che-myeon *n.* one's face, honor, reputation

체온 che-on *n.* body temperature, body heat

체육 che-yuk *n.* physical education, physical exercise

체조 che-jo *n.* gymnastics

체중 che-jung *n.* body weight; 체중이 늘다 che-jung-i neul-da *v.* gain weight; 체중이 줄다 che-jung-i jul-da *v.* lose weight

체증 che-jjeung *n.* congestion; indigestion, digestive disorder

체질 che-jil *n.* physical constitution

체크하다 che-keu-ha-da *v.* check up

체하다 che-ha-da *v.* have an upset stomach, suffer from indigestion

체험 che-heom *n.* experience

체험하다 che-heom-ha-da *v.* experience, go through, undergo

체형 che-hyeong *n.* figure, form

첼로 chel-lo *n.* cello

쳐넣다 cheo-neo-ta *v.* throw in, dump into

쳐다보다 cheo-da-bo-da *v.* look at, look for

쳐들다 cheo-deul-da *v.* lift up, hold up

쳐들어가다 cheo-deul-eo-ga-da *v.* raid, invade *(carry attack to a location)*

쳐들어오다 cheo-deul-eo-o-da *v.* raid, invade *(enter a location under attack)*

쳐바르다 cheo-ba-reu-da *v.* paint thickly, coat thickly

쳐박다 cheo-bak-da *v.* drive into, ram down, wedge in; douse, duck, dip

초 cho *affix.* beginning; *count.* seconds; *n.* candle; vinegar

초가을 cho-ja-eul *n.* early fall

초가집 cho-ga-jip *n.* thatch-roofed house

초겨울 cho-gyeo-ul *n.* early winter

초고속 cho-go-sok *n.* extremely high speed

초고추장 cho-go-chu-jang *n.* vinegared red pepper paste

초기 cho-gi *n.* the early days; the first stage, the early stage

초대 cho-dae *n.* invitation

초대장 cho-dae-jjang *n.* written invitation

초대하다 cho-dae-ha-da *v.* invite

초대형 cho-dae-hyeong *adj.* extra-large, oversized

초등학교 cho-deung-hak-gyo *n.* elementary school

초등학생 cho-deung-hak-saeng *n.* elementary-school student

초록색 cho-rok-saek *adj.* green

초밥 cho-bap *n.* Japanese vinegar and rice delicacies

초보 cho-bo *n.* first steps, the first stage, the rudiments, the beginning, the beginner's course

초복 cho-bok *n.* the first period of summer doldrums

초봄 cho-bom *n.* early spring

초봉 cho-bong *n.* initial payment, the hiring rate

초상화 cho-sang-hwa *n.* portrait

초생달 cho-saeng-ttal *n.* new moon; crescent moon

초여름 cho-yeo-reum *n.* early summer

초음파 cho-eum-pa *n.* supersonic

초인종 cho-in-jong *n.* doorbell, buzzer

초저녁 cho-jeo-nyeok *n.* early evening

초점 cho-jjeom *n.* focus, focal point

초청하다 cho-cheong-ha-da *v.* invite

초콜릿 cho-kol-lit *n.* chocolate

초특급 cho-teuk-geup *n.* super-express; 초특급 열차는 서울에서 부산까지 두시간 안에 간다 cho-teuk-geup yeol-cha-neun seo-ul-e-seo bu-san-kka-ji du-si-gan an-e gan-da The super-express train takes only two hours from Seoul to Busan

초하루 cho-ha-ru *n.* the first day of the month

초하룻날 cho-ha-run-nal *n.* the first day of the month

초현대적 cho-hyeon-dae-jeok *adj.* ultramodern

촉감 chok-gam *n.* the sense of touch, feel

촌극 chon-geuk *n.* short drama performance

촌놈 chon-nom *n.* country fellow, countryman

촌뜨기 chon-tteu-gi *n.* country fellow, countryman

촌수 chon-ssu *n.* the distance of a blood relationship, the degree of kinship (*genealogy*)

촌스럽다 chon-seu-reop-da *v.* be rustic, be tacky, be boorish

촌장 chon-jang *n.* chief of a village

촌티 chon-ti *n.* touch of the country; 촌티 나다 chon-ti na-da be boorish, be countrified, be tacky

촐랑거리다 chol-lang-geo-ri-da *v.* act frivolous, behave carelessly

촐싹거리다 chol-ssak-geo-ri-da *v.* act frivolous; incite, instigate

촘촘하다 chom-chom-ha-da *v.* be dense, be thick

촛농 chon-nong *n.* melted wax running down a candlestick

촛대 chot-dae *n.* candlestick, candleholder

촛불 chot-bul *n.* candlelight

총 chong *n.* gun, rifle

총각 chong-gak *n.* bachelor, unmarried man

총격전 chong-gyeok-jeon *n.* gunfight, shooting

총계 chong-gye *n.* total

총공격 chong-gong-gyeok *n.* full-scale attack, attack in full force

총동원하다 chong-dong-won-ha-da *v.* make a general mobilization, mobilize all the resources

총리 chong-ni *n.* Prime Minister

총명하다 chong-myeong-ha-da *v.* be smart, be brilliant

총소리 chong-sso-ri *n.* gunshot

총수입 chong-su-ip *n.* gross income

총알 chong-al *n.* bullet, shot

총액 chong-aek *n.* the total amount, the sum

총영사 chong-yeong-sa *n.* general consul

총원 chong-won *n.* the whole number, all members

총장 chong-jang *n.* chancellor; the secretary-general

총점 chong-jjeom *n.* total of one's marks, total score

총지출 chong-ji-chul *n.* gross expenditure

총출동하다 chong-chul-ttong-ha-da *v.* be entirely mobilized, be all called out

총칼 chong kal *n.* gun and sword

총파업 chong-pa-eop *n.* general strike

총회 chong-hoe *n.* general meeting

촬영 chwal-yeong *n.* photography

촬영하다 chwal-yeong-ha-da *v.* take a photograph

최강 choe-gang *n.* the strongest

최고 choe-go *n.* the highest, maximum

최고급 choe-go-geup *n.* the highest grade, the top class

최근 choe-geun *adv.* lately, most recently

최대 choe-dae *n.* the largest, the biggest

최면술 choe-myeon-sul *n.* hypnotism; 최면술 걸다 choe-myeon-sul geol-da *v.* hypnotize

최상 choe-sang *n.* the best, the highest

최선 choe-seon *n.* the best; the first, the foremost

최소 choe-so *n.* the smallest, the minimum

최신 choe-sin *n.* the newest, the latest

최신식 choe-sin-sik *n.* the latest fashion, the ultramodern style

최신형 choe-sin-hyeong *n.* the newest model

최악 choe-ak *n.* the worst

최우수 choe-u-su *n.* the very best

최장 choe-jang *n.* the longest, the oldest

최저 choe-jeo *n.* the lowest, the minimum

최종 choe-jong *n.* last, final, terminal

최첨단 choe-cheom-dan *n.* the spearhead

최초 choe-cho *n.* the very first, the very beginning

최하 choe-ha *n.* the lowest, the worst

최후 choe-hu *n.* the last, the end, the conclusion; one's death

추가하다 chu-ga-ha-da *v.* add to, supplement, subjoin

추격하다 chu-gyeo-ka-da *v.* pursue, give chase

추녀 chu-nyeo *n.* eaves; protruding

추리소설 chu-ri-so-seol *n.* mystery novel

추석 chu-seok *n.* Korean harvest festival

추수 chu-su *n.* harvesting

추수감사절 chu-su-gam-sa-jeol *n.* Thanksgiving Day

추수하다 chu-su-ha-da *v.* harvest

추억 chu-eok *n.* recollection, remembrance

추워지다 chu-wo-ji-da *v.* become cold

추위 chu-wi *n.* cold weather

추천 chu-cheon-ha-da *v.* recommend

추천서 chu-cheon-seo *n.* recommendation letter

추천하다 chu-cheon-ha-da *v.* recommend, nominate

추첨하다 chu-cheom-ha-da *v.* draw lots, cast lots

추측하다 chu-cheu-ka-da *v.* guess, suppose

축 처지다 chuk cheo-ji-da *adv.phr.* droop low, sag low

축가 chuk-ga *n.* festival song, carol

축구 chuk-gu *n.* soccer; 축구 하다 chuk-gu ha-da *v.* play soccer

축구경기 chuk-gu-gyeong-gi *n.* soccer game

축대 chuk-dae *n.* stone embankment

축복 chuk-bok *n.* blessing, benediction

축복하다 chuk bo ka-da *v.* bless, call a blessing upon

축산업 chuk-san-eop *n.* livestock breeding business

축소하다 chuk-so-ha-da *v.* reduce, cut down

축음기 chug-eum-gi *n.* phonograph

축제 chuk-je *n.* festival

축축하다 chuk-chu-ka-da *v.* be slightly wet, be damp, be moist

축하인사 chu-ka-in-sa *n.* congratulatory greetings

축하하다 chu-ka-ha-da *v.* congratulate, celebrate; greet

춘천 chun-cheon *n.* Chun Cheon (*tourist destination*)

출구 chul-gu *n.* exit, way out

출국수속 chul-guk-su-sok *n.* departure process, departure formalities

출국하다 chul-gu-ka-da *v.* depart from the country

출근 chul-geun *n.* being on the job, going to work

출근하다 chul-geun-ha-da *v.* go to work, go to the office

출동하다 chul-ttong-ha-da *v.* be mobilized, be called out

출렁거리다 chul-lyeong-geo-ri-da *v.* lap, slop; splash; roll; swell

출발 chul-bal *n.* departure

출발시키다 chul-bal-si-ki-da *v.* make something or someone depart, make something or someone leave

출발하다 chul-bal-ha-da *v.* depart, start, leave, make a start

출생률 chul-ssaeng-nyul *n.* birth rate

출세하다 chul-sse-ha-da *v.* have great success in life, rise in the world

출신 chul-ssin *n.* native; graduation; origin, birth, affiliation

출입 chul-ip *n.* coming and going, going in and out, entrance and exit

출입금지 chul-ip-geum-ji *n.* no trespassing

출입하다 chul-i-pa-da *v.* go in and out, make one's entrance and exit; visit frequently

출장 chul-jjang *n.* business trip; 출장 가다 chul-jjang ga-da *v.* go on a business trip

출퇴근 chul-toe-geun *n.* commuting

출퇴근하다 chul-toe-geun-ha-da *v.* commute

출판되다 chul-pan-doe-da *v.* be published, be printed

출판사 chul-pan-sa *n.* publishing company

출판연도 chul-pan-nyeon-do *n.* year of publication

출판하다 chul-pan-ha-da *v.* publish

춤 chum *n.* dance

춤추다 chum-chu-da *v.* dance

춥다 chup-da *v.* be cold, be chilly, be feel cold

충 chung *n.* patriotism

충격 chung-gyeok *n.* shock

충고 chung-go *n.* advice

충고하다 chung-go-ha-da *v.* give advice, advise

충분하다 chung-bun-ha-da *v.* be enough, be sufficient

충분히 chung-bun-hi *adv.* enough, sufficiently, satisfactorily

충전하다 chung-jeon-ha-da *v.* electrify, charge

충청도 chung-cheong-do *n.* Chung Cheong province *(central part of South Korea)*

충치 chung-chi *n.* cavity, decayed tooth

충혈되다 chung-hyeol-doe-da *v.* become turgid with blood; be bloodshot

취미 chwi-mi *n.* hobby; 취미를 붙이다 chwi-mi-reul bu-chi-da *v.* find pleasure in

취미생활 chwi-mi-saeng-hwal *n.* hobbies

취소되다 chwi-so-doe-da *v.* be cancelled

취소하다 chwi-so-ha-da *v.* cancel, withdraw, recall

취업률 chwi-eom-nyul *n.* employment rate

취직 chwi-jik *n.* employment, getting a job

취직하다 chwi-ji-ka-da *v.* get a job, secure a position

취하다 chwi-ha-da *v.* get drunk, be drunk

층 cheung *count.* floor; 사무실이 사층에 있다 sa-mu-sil-i sa-cheung-e it-da The office is on the fourth floor

층계 cheung-gye *n.* stairs, staircase, stairway

치고 chi-go *affix.* when it comes to, as for, be that as it may; 여름치고 날씨가 별로 안 덥다 yeo-reum-chi-go nal-ssi-ga byeol-lo an deop-da The weather is not very hot considering that it is summer.

치고는 chi-go-neun *affix.* considering, seeing, as, for; 여름치고는 날씨가 별로 안 덥다 yeo-reum-chi-go-neun nal-ssi-ga byeol-lo an deop-da The weather is not very hot considering that it is summer.

치과 chi-kkwa *n.* dentistry

치과의사 chi-kkwa-ui-sa *n.* dentist

치다 chi-da *v.* play a game; play a musical instrument; strike, hit, beat, punch; attack; run over; take a test

치료 chi-ryo *n.* treatment

치료받다 chi-ryo-bat-da *v.* receive treatment, be treated for

치료하다 chi-ryo-ha-da *v.* treat, cure

치마 chi-ma *n.* skirt

치솟다 chi-sot-da *v.* rise suddenly, skyrocket, shoot up

치수 chi-ssu *n.* size

치아 chi-a *n. hon.* tooth

치약 chi-yak *n.* toothpaste

치우다 chi-u-da *v.* put things in order, tidy up; clear away, take away

치이다 chi-i-da *v.* be hit by a car, get hit, be crushed

치즈 chi-jeu *n.* cheese

치통 chi-tong *n.* toothache

칙칙폭폭 chik-chik-pok-pok *adv.* chug-chug, puff-puff

칙칙하다 chik-chi-ka-da *v.* be dark; be gaudy

친구 chin-gu *n.* friend; 친구를 사귀다 chin-gu-reul sa-gwi-da *v.* make a friend

친부모 chin-bu-mo *n.* one's birth parents

친손자 chin-son-ja *n.* the children of one's son

친절하게 chin-jeol-ha-ge *adv.* kindly, friendly

친절하다 chin-jeol-ha-da *v.* be considerate, be kind

친정 chin-jeong *n.* woman's parents' home

친척 chin-cheok *n.* relative, kinfolk

친하다 chin-ha-da *v.* be close, be friendly, be intimate with

친할머니 chin-hal-meo-ni *n.* paternal grandmother

친할아버지 chin-hal-a-beo-ji *n.* paternal grandfather

친형제 chin-hyeong-je *n.* one's siblings by blood

칠 chil *n.* seven

칠면조 chil-myeon-jo *n.* turkey

칠순 chil-ssun *n.* seventieth birthday, seventy years of age

칠십 chil-ssip *n.* seventy

칠월 chil-wol *n.* July

칠칠치 못하다 chil-chil-chi mo-ta-da *adv.phr.* be slovenly, be slack, be loose

칠판 chil-pan *n.* blackboard

칠하다 chil-ha-da *v.* paint, coat

침 chim *n.* saliva, spit; spine, needle, sting; 침 뱉다 chim baet-da *v.* spit, salivate; 침 삼키다 chim sam-ki-da *v.* gulp saliva; be tempted; 침 흘리다 chim heul-li-da *v.* drool; be tempted

침대 chim-dae *n.* bed

침략 chim-nyak *n.* invasion, raid

침략하다 chim-nya-ka-da *v.* invade, raid

침묵 chim-muk *n.* silence

침실 chim-sil *n.* bedroom

침입하다 chim-i-pa-da *v.* enter into, invade, make an invasion upon, raid

침착하다 chim-cha-ka-da *v.* be composed, be calm, be cool

침팬지 chim-paen-chi *n.* chimpanzee

칫솔 chit-sol *n.* tooth brush

칭얼거리다 ching-eol-geo-ri-da *v.* whimper, whine, fret

칭찬하다 ching-chan-ha-da *v.* praise, admire

ㅋ

카네이션 ka-ne-i-syeon *n.* carnation

카드 ka-deu *n.* card

카레 ka-re *n.* curry

카레라이스 ka-re-ra-i-sseu *n.* curried rice

카메라 ka-me-ra *n.* camera

카메라맨 ka-me-ra-maen *n.* cameraman

카세트 ka-se-teu *n.* cassette

카세트테이프 ka-se-teu-te-i-peu *n.* cassette tape

카운터 ka-un-teo *n.* register, counter, front desk

카지노 ka-ji-no *n.* casino

카톨릭 ka-tol-lik *n.* Catholic

카페 ka-pe *n.* café

카페인 ka-pe-in *n.* caffeine

카펫 ka-pet *n.* carpet

카피라이터 ka-pi-ra-i-teo *n.* copywriter

칵테일 kak-te-il *n.* cocktail

칼 kal *n.* knife, sword, blade

칼국수 kal-guk-su *n.* home-made noodles; home-made noodle soup

칼날 kal-lal *n.* blade of a knife

칼라 kal-la *n.* collar

칼럼 kal-leom *n.* column

칼로리 kal-lo-ri *n.* calorie

칼슘 kal-syum *n.* calcium

칼자국 kal-jja-guk *n.* mark or scar by knife/sword

캄캄하다 kam-kam-ha-da *v.* be dark, be pitch-black

캐나다 kae-na-da *n.* Canada

캐나다사람 kae-na-da-ssa-ram *n.* Canadian

캐다 kae-da *v.* dig, pick

캐비닛 kae-bi-nit *n.* cabinet

캐시미어 kae-si-mi-eo *n.* cashmere

캘린더 kael-lin-deo *n.* calendar

캠코더 kaem-ko-deo *n.* camcorder

캠퍼스 kaem-peo-sseu *n.* campus

캠페인 kaem-pe-in *n.* campaign

캠프 kaem-peu *n.* camp

캠프파이어 kaem-peu-pa-i-eo *n.* campfire

캠핑 kaem-ping *n.* camping

캡슐 kaep-syul *n.* capsule

캥거루 kaeng-geo-ru *n.* kangaroo

커녕 keo-nyeong *affix.* far from; much less; instead of; not at all; 만불은 커녕 천불도 없다 man-bul-eun keo-nyeong cheon-bul-do eop-da I don't have a thousand dollars, much less ten-thousand dollars

커다랗다 keo-da-ra-ta *v.* be big, be very large, be huge

커다래지다 keo-da-rae-ji-da *v.* become bigger, increase in size, become taller

커리큘럼 keo-ri-kyul-leom *n.* curriculum

커버 keo-beo *n.* cover, jacket

커브 keo-beu *n.* curve, curved line

커지다 keo-ji-da *v.* grow big, expand; become serious

커트하다 keo-teu-ha-da *v.* have a hair cut; cut; strike off, cross out

커튼 keo-teun *n.* curtain

커피 keo-pi *n.* coffee; 커피 타다 keo-pi ta-da *v.* brew coffee

커피숍 keo-pi-syop *n.* coffee shop

컨닝 keon-ning *n.* cheating on an examination

컨닝하다 keon-ning-ha-da *v.* cheat on an examination

컨디션 keon-di-syeon *n.* condition

컨테이너 keon-te-i-neo *n.* container

컬러 keol-leo *n.* color

컴컴하다 keom-keom-ha-da *v.* be dark, be black, be dim

컴퓨터 keom-pyu-teo *n.* computer; 컴퓨터 공학 keom-pyu-teo gong-hak *n.* computer science

컵 keop *n.* cup, trophy

케이블 ke-i-beul *n.* cable

케이블카 ke-i-beul-ka *n.* cable car

케이스 ke-i-sseu *n.* case

케이크 ke-i-keu *n.* cake

케첩 ke-cheop *n.* ketchup

켜다 kyeo-da *v.* light, turn on; saw; play

켜져있다 kyeo-jeo it-da *v.* be lightened, be turned on

켤레 kyeol-le *n.* a pair

코 ko *n.* nose; nasal mucus; 코 막히다 ko ma-ki-da *v.* be congested, be stuffed up

코감기 ko-gam-gi *n.* nasal congestion

코골다 ko-gol-da *v.* snore

코끝 ko-kkeut *n.* end of one's nose, tip of one's nose

코끼리 ko-kki-ri *n.* elephant

코너 ko-neo *n.* corner

코드 ko-deu *n.* cord

코르크 ko-reu-keu *n.* cork

코미디 ko-mi-di *n.* comedy

코미디언 ko-mi-di-eon *n.* comedian

코뿔소 ko-ppul-sso *n.* rhino

코스 ko-sseu *n.* course, track, fairway

코스모스 ko-sseu-mo-sseu *n.* cosmos

코치 ko-chi *n.* coach

코코아 ko-ko-a *n.* cocoa

코트 ko-teu *n.* coat; court

코팅 ko-ting *n.* coating

코피 ko-pi *n.* nosebleed

콕 kok *adv.* stinging, poking

콕콕 kok-kok *adv.* repeatedly stinging, poking

콘도 kon-do *n.* condominium

콘돔 kon-dom *n.* condom

콘서트 kon-sseo-teu *n.* concert

콘센트 kon-sen-teu *n.* wall outlet

콘크리트 kon-keu-ri-teu *n.* concrete

콘택트렌즈 kon-taek-teu-ren-jeu *n.* contact lens

콘테스트 kon-te-seu-teu *n.* contest

콘트롤 kon-teu-rol *n.* control

콜라 kol-la *n.* coke

콜록거리다 kol-lok-geo-ri-da *v.* cough

콜록콜록 kol-lok-kol-lok *adv.* coughing

콜택시 kol-taek-si *n.* car service

콤보 kom-bo *n.* combo

콤비 kom-bi *n.* combination

콤팩트 kom-paek-teu *n.* powder compact

콤플렉스 kom-peul-lek-seu *n.* complex

콧구멍 kot-gu-meong *n.* nostrils

콧물 kon-mul *n.* nasal mucus; 콧물 나오다 kon-mul na-o-da *v.* have a runny nose

콧수염 kot-su-yeom *n.* moustache

콩 kong *n.* bean

콩국수 kong-guk-su *n.* noodles served with soybean soup

콩기름 kong-gi-reum *n.* soybean oil

콩나물 kong-na-mul *n.* bean sprouts

콩쿠르 kong-ku-reu *n.* concours, contest, competition

꽉 kwak *adv.* with a thrust, thrusting hard

콸콸 kwal-kwal *adv.* gushing, in a steady stream

쾅 kwang *adv.* with a boom, with a thud

쾅쾅거리다 kwang-kwang-geo-ri-da *v.* keep booming, keep thudding

쾌감 kwae-gam *n.* pleasant sensation

쿠데타 ku-de-ta *n.* coup d'etat

쿠바인 ku-ba-in *n.* Cuban

쿠션 ku-ssyeon *n.* cushion

쿠폰 ku-pon *n.* coupon

쿡 kuk *adv.* stinging hard

쿨쿨 kul-kul *adv.* snoring

쿵 kung *adv.* with a bang, with a thud

쿵쾅거리다 kung-kwang-geo-ri-da *v.* make a din; romp about

쿵쿵 kung-kung *adv.* banging, thudding

퀴즈 kwi-jeu *n.* quiz

크게 keu-ge *adv.* greatly

크기 keu-gi *n.* size, volume

크다 keu-da *v.* be big, be large, be spacious; be loud; grow big, grow up

크래커 keu-re-keo *n.* cracker

크레디트카드 keu-re-di-teu ka-deu *n.* credit card

크레용 keu-re-yong *n.* crayon

크레인 keu-re-in *n.* crane

크레파스 keu-re-pa-sseu *n.* crayon

크리스마스 keu-ri-sseu-ma-sseu *n.* Christmas; 크리스마스 이브 keu-ri-sseu-ma-sseu i-beu *n.* Christmas Eve

크리스천 keu-ri-seu-cheon *n.* Christian

크리스털 keu-ri-seu-teol *n.* crystal

크림 keu-rim *n.* cream

큰길 keun-gil *n.* main road, main street, principal avenue

큰누나 keun-nu-na *n.* boy's oldest sister

큰딸 keun-ttal *n.* eldest daughter

큰북 keun-buk *n.* large drum

큰사위 keun-sa-wi *n.* eldest son-in-law

큰소리 keun-so-ri *n.* loud voice; yell, shout, roar; loud boasting, bragging

큰아들 keun-a-deul *n.* eldest son

큰아버지 keun-a-beo-gi *n.* father's elder brother

큰어머니 keun-eo-meo-ni *n.* father's elder brother's wife

큰언니 keun-eon-ni *n.* girl's eldest sister

큰오빠 keun-o-ppa *n.* girl's eldest brother

큰일 keun-nil *n.* important affair, serious matter, serious situation

큰일나다 keun-il-na-da *v.* be in big trouble, get into trouble

큰절 keun-jeol *n.* deep bow

큰절하다 keun-jeol-ha-da *v.* make a deep bow

큰집 keun-jip *n.* large house; house of one's eldest brother; the house of the eldest son of a family

큰형 keun-hyeong *n.* boy's eldest brother

클라리넷 keul-la-ri-net *n.* clarinet

클라이맥스 keul-la-i-maek-seu *n.* climax

클래스 keul-lae-sseu *n.* class

클래스메이트 keul-lae-sseu-me-i-teu *n.* classmate

클래식 keul-lae-sik *n.* classic

클래식음악 keul-lae-sik-eum-ak *n.* classical music

클럽 keul-leop *n.* club, society

클로버 keul-lo-beo *n.* clover

클립 keul-lip *n.* clip

큼직하다 keum-ji-ka-da *v.* be quite big

키 ki *n.* height; key; 키 작다 ki jak-da *v.* be short; 키 크다 ki keu-da *v.* be tall

키다리 ki-da-ri *n.* tall man

키스하다 ki-sseu-ha-da *v.* kiss

키우다 ki-u-da *v.* bring up, raise, nurse, breed, foster

킬로그램 kil-lo-geu-raem *n.* kilogram

킬킬거리다 kil-kil-geo-ri-da *v.* giggle

ㅌ

타고나다 ta-go-na-da *v.* be born with

타다 ta-da *v.* ride, get in, take a ride in; burn, blaze; be tanned, be sunburned; dry up; mix in, blend, mingle; 타고 가다 ta-go ga-da *v.* leave riding in a vehicle; 타고 오다 ta-go o-da *v.* arrive riding in a vehicle

타악기 ta-ak-gi *n.* percussion instrument

타오르다 ta-o-reu-da *v.* blaze, burn up

타원형 ta-won-hyeong *n.* oval

타월 ta-wol *n.* towel

타이어 ta-i-eo *n.* tire

타이틀 ta-i-teul *n.* title, championship

타입 ta-ip *n.* type

타조 ta-jo *n.* ostrich

타죽다 ta-juk-da *v.* be burned to death

탁 tak *adv.* with a bang, with a crack; with a slap, with a snap; with relief; widely; chockingly

탁구 tak-gu *n.* ping-pong

탁구치다 tak-gu-chi-da *v.* play ping-pong

탁아소 kag-a-so *n.* nursery school

탁자 tak-ja *n.* tea table

탁탁 tak-tak *adv.* speedily; in rapid succession; flapping; stifling

탁하다 ta-ka-da *v.* be muddy, be dull, be impure, be cloudy

탄내 tan-nae *n.* scorched smell

탄력성 tal-lyeok-seong *n.* elasticity

탄수화물 tan-su-hwa-mul *n.* carbohydrate

탈 tal *n.* mask, disguise; trouble; sickness; fault

탈것 tal-kkeot *n.* vehicle

탈의실 tal-ui-sil *n.* dressing room

탈지면 tal-jji-myeon *n.* absorbent cotton

탈출하다 tal-chul-ha-da *v.* escape, get away from

탈춤 tal-chum *n.* masquerade

탐내다 tam-nae-da *v.* want, desire, covet

탐정 tam-jeong *n.* detective

탐험하다 tam-heom-ha-da *v.* explore

탑 tap *n.* tower, pagoda

탑승객 tap-seung-gaek *n.* passenger

탑승하다 tap-seung-ha-da *v.* ride, board, get aboard

탕 tang *adv.* bang, boom; *n.* soup, stew

탕수육 tang-su-yuk *n.* sweet and sour pork

탕탕 tang-tang *adv.* bang-bang

태국 tae-guk *n.* Thailand

태권도 tae-kkwon-do *n.* Taekwondo, Korean martial art

태극기 tae-geuk-gi *n.* national flag of Korea

태도 tae-do *n.* attitude, manner, behavior

태백산 tae-baek-san *n.* old name for Ma Ni mountain *(tourist destination)*

태양 tae-yang *n.* sun

태어나다 tae-eo-na-da *v.* be born, come into the world

태우다 tae-u-da *v.* burn, throw into fire; scorch; worry; accommodate, give a ride

태워다 주다 tae-wo-da ju-da *v.phr.* give a person a ride, give a person a lift in one's car

태워주다 tae-wo-ju-da *v.* give a person a ride

태평양 tae-pyeong-nyang *n.* Pacific Ocean

태풍 tae-pung *n.* typhoon; 태풍이 불다 tae-pung-i bul-da A typhoon strikes

택견 taek-gyeon *n.* Korean martial art in ancient time

택시 taek-si *n.*taxi

택시비 taek-si-bi *n.* taxi fare

택하다 tae-ka-da *v.* choose, select

탤런트 tael-leon-teu *n.* TV stars *(talent)*

탬버린 taem-beo-rin *n.* tambourine

탭댄스 taep dan-sseu *n.* tap dance

탱크 taeng-keu *n.* tank

터 teo *n.* site, place; foundation, ground

터널 teo-neol *n.* tunnel

터미널 teo-mi-neol *n.* terminal

터지다 teo-ji-da *v.* explode, burst, blow up; rip; be cracked; get chopped

턱 teok *n.* chin, jaw; projection; elevated place; treat; feast

턱걸이 teok-geol-i *n.* chinning, chin-up

턱수염 teok-su-yeom *n.* mustache

턱시도 teok-si-do *n.* tuxedo

털 teol *n.* hair, fur, feather

털다 teol-da *v.* shake off, brush off; empty, clear; rob

털리다 teol-li-da *v.* get dusted; get emptied; get robbed

털실 teol-sil *n.* woolen yarn

털썩 teol-sseok *adv.* with a plop, with a thud

털어놓다 teol-eo-no-ta *v.* open one's heart, speak frankly

텅비다 teong bi-da *v.* be entirely empty, vacant

텅텅 teong-teong *adv.* being completely empty

테니스 te-ni-sseu *n.* tennis; 테니스 라켓 te-ni-sseu ra-ket *n.* tennis racket; 테니스 치다 te-ni-sseu chi-da *v.* play tennis

테러 te-reo *n.* terrorism

테마 te-ma *n.* theme

테스트 te-seu-teu *n.* test

테이블 te-i-beul *n.* table

테이프 te-i-peu *n.* tape

텐트 ten-teu *n.* tent

텔레비전 tel-le-bi-jeon *n.* television

템포 tem-po *n.* speed, tempo

토끼 to-kki *n.* rabbit

토너먼트 to-neo-meon-teu *n.* tournament

토론하다 to-ron-ha-da *v.* debate, discuss

토마토 to-ma-to *n.* tomato

토막 to-mak *n.* piece, block

토막토막 to-mak-to-mak *adv.* into pieces, piece by piece

토목공학 to-mok-gong-hak *n.* civil engineering

토박이 to-bag-i *n.* natives, aboriginals

토산물 to-san-mul *n.* local produce, rigional products

토성 to-seong *n.* Saturn

토스트 to-seu-teu *n.* toast

토실토실하다 to-sil-to-sil-ha-da *v.* be plump, be chubby

토요일 to-yo-il *n.* Saturday

토의 to-ui *n.* discussion

토큰 tto-keun *n.* token (*coin*)

토템 to-tem *n.* totem

토픽 to-pik *n.* topic

토하다 to-ha-da *v.* vomit, throw up; spit

토함산 to-ham-san *n.* Mt. To Ham (*tourist destination*)

톡 tok *adv.* protruding; popping out; with snap; prickingly; with a thud

톤 ton *count.* ton, tonnage

톱 top *n.* saw; top person, top position

통 tong *adv.* not at all; entirely; *n.* bin, pail, barrel, can

통가죽 tong-ga-juk *n.* whole skin of an animal

통계 tong-gye *n.* statistics

통과하다 tong-gwa-ha-da *v.* pass, get through

통근하다 tong-geun-ha-da *v.* commute, go to work

통나무 tong-na-mu *n.* log, pole

통닭 tong-dak *n.* whole chicken

통로 tong-no *n.* aisle, passage

통마늘 tong-ma-neul *n.* whole bulb of garlic

통신 tong-sin *n.* communication, news

통신망 tong-sin-mang *n.* communication network

통신문화 tong-sin-mun-hwa *n.* communication-related culture, communication etiquette

통신판매 tong-sin-pan-mae *n.* telemarketing; mail-order business

통역 tong-yeok *n.* interpreter; interpreting

통역사 tong-yeok-sa *n.* interpretor

통역하다 tong-yeo-ka-da *v.* interpret, translate orally

통으로 tong-eu-ro *adv.* wholly, in full, in the lump

통일 tong-il *n.* unity, unification, standardization

통일되다 tong-il-doe-da *v.* be unified, be standardized

통일하다 tong-il-ha-da *v.* unify, consolidate, standardize

통일호 tong-il-ho *n.* second-class train

통장 tong-jang *n.* bankbook

통제하다 tong-je-ha-da *v.* control, regulate, govern

통조림 tong-jo-rim *n.* canned food

통증 tong-jjeung *n.* ache, pain

통째 tong-jjae *adv.* all, wholly

통치하다 tong-chi-ha-da *v.* rule over

통쾌하다 tong-kwae-ha-da *v.* be extremely delightful, be very gratifying

통통 tong-tong *adv.* resoundingly; plumply; pounding

통통하다 tong-tong-ha-da *v.* be chubby, be plump

통틀어 tong-teul-eo *adv.* in all, all told, altogether, in total

통하다 tong-ha-da *v.* run, lead to; flow; go through; be circulated; be understood; make sense

통해 tong-hae *part.* through, by, via; 요즘
엔 이메일을 통해 소식을 주고 받는다
yo-jeum-en i-me-il-eul tong-hae so-sig-eul
ju-go ban-neun-da We exchange information via email these days

통해서 tong-hae-seo *part.* through, by, via

통화하다 tong-hwa-ha-da *v.* talk over the
telephone, speak by telephone

퇴근시간 toe-geun-ssi-gan *n.* closing time

퇴근하다 toe-geun-ha-da *v.* go home from
work, leave the office

퇴원하다 toe-won-ha-da *v.* be discharged
from the hospital, leave the hospital

퇴장 toe-jang *n.* departure, withdrawal

투덜거리다 tu-deol-geo-ri-da *v.* grumble,
complain, nag

투명하다 tu-myeong-ha-da *v.* be transparent,
be limpid, be clear

투수 tu-su *n.* pitcher

투우 tu-u *n.* bull fighting

투우장 tu-u-jang *n.* bull fighting arena,
bullring

투자 tu-ja *n.* investment

투자하다 tu-ja-ha-da *v.* invest, put money in

투표하다 tu-pyo-ha-da *v.* vote, cast a vote

투피스 tu-pi-sseu *n.* suit, two-piece dress

툭 tuk *adv.* prutruding; popping out; with a
bang; with a snap; prickingly; with a thud

툭하면 tu-ka-myeon *adv.* always; without
any reason; at the slightest provocation

퉁명스럽다 tung-myeong-seu-reop-da *v.* be
blunt; bluff

튀기다 twi-gi-da *v.* fry; pop

튀김 twi-gim *n.* fried food

튀어나오다 twi-eo-na-o-da *v.* jump out,
spring out; project, extend outward

튜브 tyu-beu *n.* tube

튤립 tyul-lip *n.* tulip

트다 teu-da *v.* sprout; crack; break open

트라이앵글 teu-ra-i-aeng-geul *n.* triangle

트랙 teu-raek *n.* track

트럭 teu-reok *n.* truck

트럼펫 teu-reom-pet *n.* trumpet

트럼프 teu-reom-peu *n.* cards

트레이너 teu-re-i-neo *n.* trainer

트레이닝 teu-re-i-ning *n.* training

트로피 teu-ro-pi *n.* trophy

트림하다 teu-rim-ha-da *v.* burp, belch

트이다 teu-i-da *v.* get cleared; be opened; be
sensible; become better

트집잡다 teu-jip-jap-da *v.* pick on, find fault
with

특기 teuk-gi *n.* special ability, specialty

특별시 teuk-byeol-si *n.* special city district
(government)

특별하다 teuk-byeol-ha-da *v.* be special, be
extraordinary, be particular, be exceptional

특산물 teuk-san-mul *n.* special product,
specialty

특색 teuk-saek *n.* specific feature, specific
character

특성 teuk-seong *n.* special quality,
characteristic

특수하다 teuk-su-ha-da *v.* be special, be
distinct, be unique

특이하다 teug-i-ha-da *v.* be peculiar, be
particular, be unique

특집 teuk-jip *n.* special edition

특집기사 teuk-jip-gi-sa *n.* feature articles,
feature story

특징 teuk-jing *n.* special feature, distin-
guishing mark, characteristic

특히 teu-ki *adv.* especially, particularly

튼튼하다 teun-teun-ha-da *v.* be healthy, be
strong

틀 tuel *n.* frame; formality; device

틀니 teul-li *n.* artificial tooth, denture

틀다 teul-da *v.* twist, wrench; switch on;
play; wind; thwart

틀리다 teul-li-da *v.* go wrong, be mistaken;
get distorted

틀림없다 teul-lim-eop-da *v.* be inarguable, be
beyond a doubt; be correct; be trustworthy; 그 사람은 언제나 틀림없다 geu
sa-ram-eun eon-je-na teul-lim-eop-da He is
always trustworthy

틀림없이 teul-lim-eops-i *adv.* without a
doubt, without any question

틈 teum *n.* crack, gap; spare time, leisure;
room, space; interval; opportunity, chance;
friction; 틈을 주다 teum-eul ju-da *v.* give
a chance, give an opportunity

틈나다 teum-na-da *v.* have spare time, have
a chance

틈틈이 teum-teum-i *adv.* at each gap; at spare moments; in the intervals

티 ti *n.* dust, grit; speck; flaw; style, manner

티눈 ti-nun *n.* corn

티셔츠 ti-syeo-cheu *n.* T-shirt

티켓 ti-ket *n.* ticket

팀 tim *n.* team

팁 tip *n.* tip, gratuity

ㅍ

파 pa *n.* green onion, scallion

파내다 pa-nae-da *v.* dig out, unearth

파다 pa-da *v.* dig, excavate, dig out, bore, drill, burrow

파도 pa-do *n.* waves, surge

파라솔 pa-ra-sol *n.* parasol

파랗다 pa-ra-ta *v.* be blue, be green, be pale

파래지다 pa-rae-ji-da *v.* turn blue, turn green, turn pale

파리 pa-ri *n.* fly; Paris

파마 pa-ma *n.* permanent

파마하다 pa-ma-ha-da *v.* get a perm

파먹다 pa-meok-da *v.* dig a thing out and eat it, eat into

파묻다 pa-mut-da *v.* bury, inter

파스 pa-sseu *n.* pain killing patch; Paraaminosalicylic acid (*PAS*)

파스텔 pa-seu-tel *n.* pastel

파업 pa-eop *n.* strike, walkout

파운데이션 pa-un-de-i-syeon *n.* foundation

파이 pa-i *n.* pie

파인애플 pa-in-ae-peul *n.* pineapple

파일럿 pa-il-leot *n.* pilot

파자마 pa-ja-ma *n.* pajama

파출부 pa-chul-bu *n.* visiting housekeeper

파출소 pa-chul-sso *n.* police branch office

파카 pa-ka *n.* padded thick sports jacket

파트너 pa-teu-neo *n.* partner

파티 pa-ti *n.* party

팍 pak *adv.* all at once; with a thud; feebly, weakly

판단하다 pan-dan-ha-da *v.* judge, decide, interpret

판매원 pan-mae-won *n.* salesperson

판매중 pan-mae-jung *n.* on sale

판사 pan-sa *n.* judge

판소리 pan-sso-ri *n.* traditional Korean singing drama, traditional Korean narrative songs

판잣집 pan-jat-jip *n.* wooden shack

판탈롱 pan-tal-long *n.* pants, slacks

판판하다 pan-pan-ha-da *v.* be flat, be even

팔 pal *n.* arm; eight

팔각정 pal-gak-jeong *n.* octagonal pavilion

팔꿈치 pal-kkum-chi *n.* elbow

팔다 pal-da *v.* sell, deal in

팔뚝 pal-ttuk *n.* forearm

팔리다 pal-li-da *v.* be sold, be in demand

팔목 pal-mok *n.* wrist

팔십 pal-ssip *n.* eighty

팔씨름 pal-ssi-reum *n.* arm wrestling

팔씨름하다 pal-ssi-reum-ha-da *v.* arm wrestle

팔아먹다 pal-a-meok-da *v.* sell, sell off

팔월 pal-wol *n.* August

팔월한가위 pal-wol-han-ga-wi *n.* August 15th (*lunar calendar*), Harvest Festival, Mid-Autumn Festival

팔일오 pal-il-o *n.* August 15th (*Gregorian calendar*), Liberation Day

팔자 pal-jja *n.* fate, fortune, destiny

팔짝 pal-jjak *adv.* jumping up suddenly

팔짱끼다 pal-jjang-kki-da *v.* fold one's arms, lock arms with

팔찌 pal-jji *n.* bracelet

팔팔 pal-pal *adv.* seething, boiling, burning

팝송 pap-song *n.* pop song

팥 pat *n.* red-beans

팥떡 pat-tteok *n.* rice cake coated with mashed red beans

팥밥 pat-bap *n.* rice cooked with red beans

팥죽 pat-juk *n.* rice gruel boiled with red beans

패다 pae-da *v.* chop, split; beat, strike

패물 pae-mul *n.* shell goods, shell ware

패션 pae-ssyeon *n.* fashion

패션디자이너 pae-ssyeon-di-ja-i-neo *n.* fashion designer

패션모델 pae-ssyeon-mo-del *n.* fashion model

패스 pae-sseu *n.* pass, season ticket; passing; 시험에 패스했다 si-heom-e pae-sseu-haet-da He passed the exam

패이다 pae-i-da *v.* be dug; be split

패하다 pae-ha-da *v.* be defeated, be beaten, lose

팩스 paek-seu *n.* fax

팩시밀리 paek-si-mil-li *n.* facsimile

팬 paen *n.* fan; 야구팬 ya-gu-paen *n.* baseball fan

팬더 paen-deo *n.* panda

팬츠 paen-cheu *n.* underpants, drawers

팬케이크 paen-ke-i-keu *n.* pancake

팬티 paen-ti *n.* panties (*term used for both female panties and male briefs*)

팸플릿 paem-peul-lit *n.* pamphlet

팻말 paen-mal *n.* notice board

팽 paeng *adv.* round, around, circling quickly

팽이 paeng-i *n.* top (*toy*)

팽이치기 paeng-i-chi-gi *n.* top spinning, playing a top

팽팽 paeng-paeng *adv.* round and round rapidly

팽팽하다 paeng-paeng-ha-da *v.* be tight, be taut; be equal, be even

퍼내다 peo-nae-da *v.* bail out, scoop out, pump out

퍼뜨리다 peo-tteu-ri-da *v.* spread, circulate, advertise

퍼레이드 peo-re-i-deu *n.* parade

퍼먹다 peo-meok-da *v.* scoop and eat

퍼붓다 peo-but-da *v.* pour upon, rain upon; pour down, rain in torrents

퍼센트 peo-sen-teu *n.* percent, percentage

퍼스트레이디 peo-seu-teu-re-i-di *n.* the First Lady

퍼지다 peo-ji-da *v.* spread out, get broader

퍽 peok *adv.* hard, firmly; with a thud; very, very much, greatly

퍽퍽하다 peok-peo-ka-da *v.* be dry and crumbling

펄럭거리다 peol-leok-geo-ri-da *v.* flap, wave

펄럭펄럭 peol-leok-peol-leok *adv.* with a flutter, flapping

펄쩍펄쩍 peol-jjeok-peol-jjeok *adv.* jumping up and down

펄펄 peol-peol *adv.* boiling, seething, burning; fluttering, flapping

펌프 peom-peu *n.* pump

펑 peong *adv.* popping, accompanied by an explosion

펑펑 peong-peong *adv.* with a rush, with force; heavily; pop pop, bang bang

페달 pe-dal *n.* pedal

페스티벌 pe-seu-ti-beol *n.* festival

페이지 pe-i-ji *n.* page

페인트 pe-in-teu *n.* paint

펜 pen *n.* pen

펜팔 pen-pal *n.* pen pal, pen-friend

펭귄 peng-gwin *n.* penguin

퍼내다 pyeo-nae-da *v.* publish, issue, bring out

펴놓다 pyeo-no-ta *v.* unfold, spread, keep open

펴다 pyeo-da *v.* open, spread, unfold, stretch, unroll

펴지다 pyeo-ji-da *v.* get unfolded, unroll, spread; get smoothed, be flattened

편 pyeon *n.* side, party

편견 pyeon-gyeon *n.* prejudice, bias

편도 pyeon-do *n.* one-way trip

편도선 pyeon-do-seon *n.* tonsils

편두통 pyeon-du-tong *n.* migraine, sick headache

편리하다 pyeol-li-ha-da *v.* be comfortable, be convenient, be handy

편물 pyeon-hi *n.* knitting

편식하다 pyeon-si-ka-da *v.* have an unbalanced diet

편안하다 pyeon-an-ha-da *v.* be peaceful, be calm, be restful, be easy, be comfortable

편의점 pyeon-ui-jeom *n.* convenience store

편지 pyeon-ji *n.* letter, note; 편지 받다 pyeon-ji bat-da *v.* receive a letter; 편지 보내다 pyeon-ji bo-nae-da *v.* send a letter

편찮다 pyeon-chan-ta *v.* be unwell; be uncomfortable

편하다 pyeon-ha-da *v.* be comfortable, be convenient, be easy, be simple

편해지다 pyeon-hae-ji-da *v.* become convenient

편히 pyeon-hi *adv.* conveniently, comfortably

펼치다 pyeol-chi-da *v.* open, spread, outstretch, extend, unroll

평가받다 pyeong-kka-bat-da *v.* be evaluated, be estimated

평균 pyeong-gyun *n.* average, the mean

평등 pyeong-deung *n.* equality, equibility

평등하다 pyeong-deung-ha-da *v.* be equal, be even

평면 pyeong-myeon *n.* plane, level

평민 pyeong-min *n.* common people

평범하다 pyeong-beom-ha-da *v.* be common, be ordinary

평상시 pyeong-sang-si *n.* normal times; normally, usually

평생 pyeong-saeng *n.* life time, one's life

평소 pyeong-so *n.* ordinary times; *adv.* usually, ordinarily

평소에 pyeong-so-e *adv.* usually, ordinarily

평안도 pyeong-an-do *n.* Pyeong An *(province)*

평원 pyeong-won *n.* plain, prairie

평일 pyeong-il *n.* weekday, ordinary time

평준화 pyeong-jun-hwa *n.* equalization

평창동 pyeong-chang-dong *n.* Pyeong Chang Dong *(Seoul district)*

평판 pyeong-pan *n.* reputation, fame, popularity

평평하다 pyeong-pyeong-ha-da *v.* be flat, be even

평화 pyeong-hwa *n.* peace, harmony

평화롭다 pyeong-hwa-rop-da *v.* be peaceful, be harmonious

평화스럽다 pyeong-hwa-seu-reop-da *v.* be peaceful, be harmonious

평화적 pyeong-hwa-jeok *adj.* peaceful, harmonious

폐 pe *n.* lungs; trouble, bother; 폐 끼치다 pe kki-chi-da *v.* cause trouble

포개다 po-gae-da *v.* pile up, heap up

포근하다 po-geun-ha-da *v.* be warm, be mild; be soft and comfortable, fluffy

포근히 po-geun-hi *adv.* comfortably, softly

포기하다 po-gi-ha-da *v.* give up, resign

포도 po-do *n.* grapes

포도주 po-do-ju *n.* wine *(made from grapes)*

포동포동하다 po-dong-po-dong-ha-da *v.* be chubby, *v.* plump

포로 po-ro *n.* war prisoner

포르투갈 po-reu-tu-kal *n.* Portugal

포수 po-su *n.* hunter

포스터 po-seu-teo *n.* poster

포옹하다 po-ong-ha-da *v.* hug, cuddle

포위하다 po-wi-ha-da *v.* surround, encircle

포장 po-jang *n.* packing, wrapping

포장마차 po-jang-ma-cha *n.* covered carriage

포장지 po-jang-ji *n.* wrapping paper

포장하다 po-jang-ha-da *v.* pack, wrap

포즈 po-jeu *n.* pose

포지션 po-ji-syeon *n.* position

포크 po-keu *n.* fork

포크댄스 po-keu-ttaen-sseu *n.* folk dance

포크송 po-keu song *n.* folk song

포탄 po-tan *n.* cannon ball

포함되다 po-ham-doe-da *v.* be included, be contained, be implied

포함하다 po-ham-ha-da *v.* include, contain, imply

폭 pok *adv.* deeply, completely; *n.* width, range

폭격 pok-gyeok *n.* bombing

폭력 pong-nyeok *n.* violence, force

폭발하다 pok-bal-ha-da *v.* explode, burst up, blow up

폭삭 pok-sak *adv.* entirely, wholly, completely, all

폭우 pog-u *n.* pouring rain, downpour

폭죽 pok-juk *n.* firecracker

폭탄 pok-tan *n.* bomb

폭파하다 pok-pa-ha-da *v.* blast, blow up, explode, demolish

폭포 pok-po *n.* waterfall

폭폭 pok-pok *adv.* piercing, repeatedly; boiling completely

폭풍 pok-pung *n.* storm, windstorm

폭풍우 pok-pung-u *n.* rainstorm

폼 pom *n.* form, way of holding oneself, carriage

퐁당 pong-dang *adv.* with a plop, with a splash

퐁퐁 pong-pong *adv.* bubbling, gurgling

표 pyo *n.* ticket, coupon, vote; table, diagram, chart, list; mark, sign

표값 pyo-kkap *n.* ticket price

표나다 pyo-na-da *v.* stand out, make a mark, leave traces

표면 pyo-myeon *n.* the surface, the face, the exterior, the outside, appearance

표시 pyo-si *n.* indication, mark

표시하다 pyo-si-ha-da *v.* indicate, manifest

표정 pyo-jeong *n.* facial expression; 표정을 짓다 pyo-jeong-eul jit-da *v.* make a facial expression, express one's feelings facially

표준 pyo-jun *n.* standard, norm

표지 pyo-ji *n.* cover

표지판 pyo-ji-pan *n.* sign board

표파는곳 pyo-pa-neun-got *n.* box office

표현 pyo-hyeon *n.* expression

표현방식 pyo-hyeon-bang-sik *n.* way of expression, how to express

표현하다 pyo-hyeon-ha-da *v.* express, represent

푯말 pyon-mal *n.* signpost

푸다 pu-da *v.* dip out, pump; scoop out, take out

푸르다 pu-reu-da *v.* be blue, be green; be sharp

푸짐하다 pu-jim-ha-da *v.* be abundant, be generous

푹 puk *adv.* deeply, soundly, carefully

푹쉬다 pul-swi-da *v.* have a complete rest, have a good quality rest

푹신하다 puk-sin-ha-da *v.* be soft

푹푹 puk-puk *adv.* with repeated force; prickly; freely; perfectly; hard; muggy; 푹푹 찌다 puk-puk jji-da *v.* be sultry; be muggy

풀 pul *n.* grass, glue; pool

풀다 pul-da *v.* untie, unbind; solve, answer; remove, resolve, relieve

풀려나다 pul-lyeo-na-da *v.* get free, get released, be set free

풀리다 pul-li-da *v.* be relieved; get loose; dissolve; warm up; get solved

풀밭 pul-bat *n.* grass field, meadow, lawn

풀벌레 pul-beol-le *n.* grass insect

풀썩 pul-sseok *adv.* rising suddenly

풀어놓다 pul-eo-no-ta *v.* undo, untie, unpack; release, set free, loose

풀어주다 pul-eo-ju-da *v.* set free, release, liberate

풀어지다 pul-eo-ji-da *v.* turn soft; go bleary

풀잎 pul-lip *n.* blade of grass

풀칠하다 pul-chil-ha-da *v.* apply paste

품 pum *n.* bosom, breast

품다 pum-tta *v.* bear in mind

품질 pum-jil *n.* quality

풋고추 put-go-chu *n.* green pepper

풋볼 put-bol *n.* football

풍경 pung-gyeong *n.* landscape, scenery, scene, view; wind-bell; 풍경소리 pung-gyeong-sso-ri *n.* sound of a wind-bell

풍기다 pung-gi-da *v.* give out; send forth; stink

풍년 pung-nyeon *n.* year of abundance, year of good harvest

풍덩 pung-deong *adv.* with a splash, with plop

풍덩거리다 pung-deong-geo-ri-da *v.* keep splashing

풍덩풍덩 pung-deong-pung-deong *adv.* with splashes

풍부하다 pung-bu-ha-da *v.* be abundant, be plentiful

풍선 pung-seon *n.* balloon

풍선껌 pung-seon-kkeom *n.* bubble gum

풍속 pung-sok *n.* customs, public manners

풍습 pung-seup *n.* customs, manners, practices

풍자하다 pung-ja-ha-da *v.* satirize

풍족하다 pung-jo-ka-da *v.* be abundant, plentiful

풍차 pung-cha *n.* windmill

프라이팬 peu-ra-i-pan *n.* frying pan

프랑스 peu-rang-sseu *n.* France

프런트데스크 peu-reon-teu de-seu-keu *n.* front desk

프로 peu-ro *n.* pro, professional

프로그래머 peu-ro-geu-rae-meo *n.* programmer

프로그램 peu-ro-geu-raem *n.* program

프로야구 peu-ro-ya-gu *n.* professional baseball game

프로젝트 peu-ro-jek-teu *n.* project

프로판가스 peu-ro-pan-kka-sseu *n.* propane gas

프로펠러 peu-ro-pel-leo *n.* propeller

프로포즈 peu-ro-po-jeu *n.* marriage proposal

프리랜서 peu-ri-ren-sseo *n.* freelance, freelancer

프리미엄 peu-ri-mi-eom *n.* premium

프린터 peu-rin-teo *n.* printer

프린트 peu-rin-teu *n.* print

플라스틱 peul-la-seu-tik *n.* plastics

플래시 peul-lae-ssi *n.* flash
플랫폼 peul-laet-pom *n.* platform, track
플루트 peul-lu-teu *n.* flute
피 pi *n.* blood
피곤하다 pi-gon-ha-da *v.* be tired
피다 pi-da *v.* blossom, bloom; burn, make a fire
피라미드 pi-ra-mi-eu *n.* pyramid
피로 pi-ro *n.* fatigue
피로하다 pi-ro-ha-da *v.* be tired, be fatigued
피뢰침 pi-roe-chim *n.* lightening rod
피리 pi ri *n.* recorder
피부 pi-bu *n.* skin
피서 pi-seo *n.* getting away from the summer, out of town avoiding the summer heat
피서객 pi-seo-gaek *n.* summer visitor
피서지 pi-seo-ji *n.* summer resort
피서하다 pi-seo-ha-da *v.* pass the summer
피아노 pi-a-no *n.* piano
피아니스트 pi-a-ni-seu-teu *n.* pianist
피어오르다 pi-eo o-reu-da *v.* go up, rise
피어나다 pi-eo-na-da *v.* burn up again, rekindle; come back to life; recover; come into bloom
피우다 pi-u-da *v.* make a fire, kindle; smoke, scent, make bloom
피임하다 pi-im-ha-da *v.* use contraceptives
피자 pi-ja *n.* pizza
피차 pi-cha *adv.* both sides, each other
피켓 pi-ket *n.* picket
피크 pi-keu *n.* peak
피클 pi-keul *n.* pickles
피하다 pi-ha-da *v.* avoid, keep out of, escape; take refuge; evade, dodge

피해 pi-hae *n.* damage, injury, harm, casualties
피해주다 pi-hae-ju-da *v.* avoid, keep out of; damage, harm
픽픽 pik-pik *adv.* weakly, feebly; smiling aimlessly
핀 pin *n.* pin
핀셋 pin-set *n.* tweezers
핀트 pin-teu *n.* focus
필기도구 pil-gi-do-gu *n.* writing equipment, pen and paper
필기시험 pil-gi-si-heom *n.* written exam
필름 pil-leum *n.* film *(camera)*
필수품 pil-ssu-pum *n.* necessary element, essential element; 컴퓨터는 이제 필수품이 되었다 keom-pyu-teo-neun i-je pil-ssu-pum-i doe-eot-da The computer is an essential device these days
필요없다 pil-yo-eop-da *v.* be unnecessary
필요하다 pil-yo-ha-da *v.* need, be necessary
필자 pil-jja *n.* writer, author
필터 pil-teo *n.* filter
필통 pil-tong *n.* pencil case, writing-brush case
핏줄 pit-jul *n.* vein, blood vessel; bloodline
핑 ping *adv.* round, circling; around, surrounding; dizzy
핑계 ping-gye *n.* excuse, apology; 핑계 대다 ping-gye dae-da *v.* make an excuse, offer an apology
핑크 ping-keu *adj.* pink
핑퐁 ping-pong *n.* table tennis, ping-pong
핑핑 ping-ping *adv.* round and round quickly

ㅎ

하계 ha-gye *n.* summer
하고 ha-go *part.* and
하기는 ha-gi-neun *adv.* in fact, in truth, indeed; 하기는 요즘엔 돈이 최고다 ha-gi-neun yo-jeum-en don-i choe-go-da In fact, money is everything nowadays
하기야 ha-gi-ya *adv.* in fact, indeed, definitely
하나 ha-na *n.* one, single, only, unique; the same; once

하나님 ha-na-nim *n.* God *(Christianity)*
하나도 ha-na-do *adv.* even one; 하나도 없다 ha-na-do eop-da *v.phr.* there is nothing, there is not a single one
하나로 ha-na-ro *adv.* with only one; into one; 컴퓨터 하나로 충분하지 않다 keom-pyu-teo ha-na-ro chung-bun-ha-ji an-ta We do not have enough with only one computer; 이거 두개를 하나로

합치자 i-geo du-gae-reul ha-na-ro hap-chi-ja Let's combine these two into one

하나마나 ha-na-ma-na *adv.* useless

하나씩 ha-na-ssik *adv.* one by one, one at each time

하느님 ha-neu-nim *n.* god

하는 수 없이 ha-neun su eops-i *v.phr.* unavoidably, reluctantly, unwillingly

하늘 ha-neul *n.* the sky, the heavens, the air

하늘나라 ha-neul-la-ra *n.* the heavens

하늘색 ha-neul-ssaek *n.* sky blue

하다 ha-da *v.* do, act, try; experience, undergo; cost; eat; wear; say; 일을 하다 il-eul ha-da *v.* do work; 전에 수영 해 봤다 jeon-e su-yeong hae-bwat-da I have been swimming before; 수박 하나에 만원이나 한다 su-bak ha-na-e man-won-i-na han-da One watermelon costs ten dollars; 식사 하러 갑시다 sik-sa-ha-reo gap-si-da Let's go to eat; 귀걸이를 했다 gwi-geol-i-reul haet-da She wore earrings

하다못해 ha-da-mo-tae *adv.* unavoidably, inevitably, at the least

하도 ha-do *adv.* extremely; very, so, insistently

하드디스크 ha-deu-di-seu-keu *n.* hard disc

하루 ha-ru *n.* day, one day, the daytime; 하루 아침 ha-ru a-chim one morning; 하루 종일 ha-ru jong-il all day long

하루라도 ha-ru-ra-do *adv.* for even one day

하루일과 ha-ru-il-gwa *n.* daily schedule, daily activities

하루하루 ha-ru-ha-ru *adv.* day after day, day by day

하룻밤 ha-rut-bam *n.* one night, overnight

하마 ha-ma *n.* hippo

하마터면 ha-ma-teo-myeon *adv.* nearly, almost, barely

하모니 ha-mo-ni *n.* harmony

하모니카 ha-mo-ni-ka *n.* harmonica

하반기 ha-ban-gi *n.* the second half of the year

하소연하다 ha-so-yeon-ha-da *v.* appeal, complain of

하수구 ha-su-gu *n.* sink-hole, outfall

하수도 ha-su-do *n.* drainage system, drain

하숙 ha-suk *n.* room and board; 하숙 하다 ha-suk ha-da *v.* live at a boarding house

하숙방 ha-suk-bang *n.* room at a boarding house

하숙비 ha-suk-bi *n.* charge for room and board

하숙집 ha-suk-jip *n.* boarding house

하순 ha-sun *n.* the last ten days of a month

하얗다 ha-ya-ta *v.* be white, be pure white

하얘지다 ha-yae-ji-da *v.* get white, turn white

하여간 ha-yeo-gan *adv.* anyway, in any case, at all events

하여튼 ha-yeo-teun *adv.* anyway, in any case, at all events

하원 ha-won *n.* House of Representatives

하의 ha-ui *n.* undergarment

하이라이트 ha-i-la-i-teu *n.* highlighter

하이웨이 ha-i-we-i *n.* highway

하이킹 ha-i-king *n.* hiking

하이테크 ha-i-te-keu *n.* hi-tech

하이힐 ha-i-hil *n.* high-heeled dress shoes

하인 ha-in *n.* servant

하자마자 ha-ja-ma-ja *adv.* as soon as, no sooner than, soon after

하지만 ha-ji-man *adv.* but, however, though

하키 ha-ki *n.* hockey

하트형 ha-teu-hyeong *n.* heart shape

하품하다 ha-pum-ha-da *v.* yawn, gape

하프 ha-peu *n.* harp

하필 ha-pil *adv.* why of all things, of all others

하행선 ha-haeng-seon *n.* down line, outbound line; down train, outbound train

학교 hak-gyo *n.* school 학교가 쉬다 hak-gyo-ga swi-da School is temporarily closed

학교생활 hak-gyo-saeng-hwal *n.* school life

학기 hak-gi *n.* semester, quarter, school term

학기말 hak-gi-mal *n.* end of semester, end of school term

학년 hang-nyeon *n.* school year, academic year

학력 hang-nyeok *n.* academic background

학문 hang-mun *n.* learning, study

학문적으로 hang-mun-jeog-eu-ro *adv.* academically, scientifically

학벌 hak-beol *n.* educational background

학부형 hak-bu-hyeong *n.* parents *(of students)*

학비 hak-bi *n.* tuition and fees

학생 hak-saeng *n.* student, pupil

학생대표 hak-saeng-dae-pyo *n.* student representative

학생증 hak-saeng-jjeung *n.* student ID

학생회관 hak-saeng-hoe-gwan *n.* student center

학습 hak-seup *n.* studying, learning

학식 hak-sik *n.* knowledge, scholarship, learning

학용품 hag-yong-pum *n.* school supplies

학원 hag-won *n.* educational institute, academy

학위 hag-wi *n.* academic degree

학자 hak-ja *n.* scholar, academic person

학점 hak-jeom *n.* unit, credit

학회 ha-koe *n.* institute, academy

한 han *affix.* one; the same; whole, entire; the peak, the extreme; about, approximately; 한 개 han gae *n.* one, a unit; 한 모금 han mo-geum *n.* a draft; a drop *(liquid)*; 한 바퀴 han ba-kwi *n.* one round, a turn; 공원을 한바퀴 돌았다 gong-won-eul ha-ba-kwi dol-at-da I walked round the whole park; 벌써 한바퀴 다 돌았다 beol-sseo han-ba-kwi da dol-at-da We already finished one whole round

한가운데 han-ga-un-de *n.* the very middle, the center

한가위 han-ga-wi *n.* August 15th *(lunar calendar)*, Harvest Festival, Mid-Autumn Festival

하가을 han-ga-ul *n.* harvesting season; the whole autumn

한가지 han-ga-ji *n.* a kind, a sort, one thing; the same

한가하다 han-ga-ha-da *v.* have spare time, have leisure

한강 han-gang *n.* Han River *(in Korea)*

한걸음 han-geol-eum *n.* one step, a pace

한겨울 han-gyeo-ul *n.* midwinter

한결 han-gyeol *adv.* remarkably, much more

한결같다 han-gyeol-gat-da *v.* be constant, be consistent

한결같이 han-gyeol-ga-chi *adv.* constantly, consistently

한계 han-gye *n.* boundary, limit, bounds, margin

한계점 han-gye-jjeom *n.* the critical point, the maximum

한고비 han-go-bi *n.* the climax, critical moment

한구석 han-gu-seok *n.* corner, secluded place

한국 han-guk *n.* South Korea

한국말 han-gung-mal *n.* Korean language

한국사 han-guk-sa *n.* Korean history

한국사람 han-guk-sa-ram *n.* Korean

한국어 han-gug-eo *n.* Korean language

한국학 han-gu-kak *n.* Korean studies

한군데 han-gun-de *n.* one place, the same place

한글 han geul *n.* Korean alphabet

한글날 han-geul-lal *n.* Hangul Day, day to celebrate creation of Korean alphabet

한꺼번에 han-kkeo-beon-e *adv.* all at once, all at one time, altogether, at the same time

한끝 han-kkeut *n.* one end, one edge, one side

한끼 han-kki *n.* one meal

한나절 han-na-jeol *n.* half a day

한낮 han-nat *n.* high noon, midday

한눈 han-nun *n.* one eye; a look, a glance, a glimpse; 한눈 팔다 han-nun pal-da *v.* look away, look aside, see off

한눈에 han-nun-e *adv.* in one glimpse

한달 han-dal *n.* one month

한더위 han-deo-wi *n.* intense heat, severe heat; the hot season

한도 han-do *n.* limit, bounds

한동안 han-dong-an *adv.* for a while

한두 han-du *affix.* one or two

한두달 han-du-dal *n.* one or two months

한때 han-ttae *adv.* once, at one time, for a while

한라산 hal-la-san *n.* Mt. Han Ra *(in Korea)*

한마디 han-ma-di *n.* a word; 한마디 하다 han-ma-di ha-da *v.* say a few words about, make a remark on

한마음 han-ma-eum *n.* one mind, accord

한문 han-mun *n.* Chinese writing system; Chinese literature; Chinese characters

한물가다 han-mul-ga-da *v.* be out of date, be past their season

한미 han-mi *n.* Korea and America

한바탕 han-ba-tang *n.* a round, a bout, an event; 한바탕 하다 han-ba-tang ha-da *v.* make a scene with a person

한반도 han-ban-do *n.* Korean peninsula

한발 han-bal *n.* one step

한밤중 han-bam-jjung *n.* midnight, middle of the night

한방 han-bang *n.* Chinese herbal medicine

한번 han-beon *n.* once, one time, one round

한복 han-bok *n.* Korean dress (*traditional*)

한복판 han-bok-pan *n.* the very middle, the center

한사코 han-sa-ko *adv.* with all one's life, to the last, persistently

한산하다 han-san-ha-da *v.* be almost empty; be inactive; be slow; be off work

한살 먹다 han-sal meok-da *v.phr.* be one year old

한상자 han-sang-ja *n.* one box

한세상 han-se-sang *n.* a lifetime, one's whole life

한숨 han-sum *n.* deep sigh, sigh of relief; breath, rest, pause; 한숨 쉬다 han-sum swi-da *v.* pause for breath; sigh

한시도 han-si-do *adv.* even for a moment

한식 han-sik *n.* Korean-style food; Korean style

한식집 han-sik-jip *n.* Korean-style restaurant; Korean-style house

한심하다 han-sim-ha-da *v.* be pitiful, be regretful, be miserable

한아름 han-a-reum *n.* an armful

한약 han-yak *n.* Chinese medicine, herbs

한없다 han-eop-da *v.* be unlimited, be boundless, be endless

한여름 han-nyeo-reum *n.* midsummer; the whole summer

한옆 han-nyeop *n.* one side

한옥 han-ok *n.* Korean-style house

한움큼 han-um-keum *n.* a handful, a grip

한의사 han-ui-sa *n.* Chinese herb doctor

한일 han-il *n.* Korea and Japan

한입 han-nip *n.* a mouthful, a bite

한자 han-jja *n.* Chinese character

한자어 han-jja-eo *n.* Sino-Korean words, Chinese loanwords

한잔 han-jan *n.* a cup, a glass, a cupful, a glassful; a glass of wine, a drink; 한잔 하다 jan-jan ha-da *v.* have a drink, drink alcohol

한잠 han-jam *n.* a sleep, a nap

한적하다 han-jeo-ka-da *v.* be quiet, be secluded, be restful

한정식 han-jeong-sik *n.* Korean formal-style food

한조각 han-jo-gak *n.* one piece

한줄기 han-jul-gi *n.* a ray, a streak; a spell

한줌 han-jum *n.* a handful

한중 han-jung *n.* Korea and China

한지 han-ji *n.* Korean paper hand-made from mulberry trees

한집안 han-jib-an *n.* a family, members of a family, relatives

한쪽 han-jjok *n.* one side, one way

한차례 han-cha-rye *n.* one round, a turn, a time

한참 han-cham *adv.* for some time, for a time, for a spell

한창 han-chang *n.* the height, the summit, the peak, the climax; 한창 때 han-chang ttae *adv.* in the midst of, at the height of, in full swing

한창이다 han-chang-i-da *v.* be in the peak time, be in the climax (*of one's life, a season or an event*)

한철 han-cheol *n.* one season

한층 han-cheung *adv.* more, still more, all the more; *n.* the first story, the first floor

한치도 han-chi-do *adv.* at all, a bit, not at all, not a bit

한턱내다 han-teong-nae-da *v.* treat to a meal or a drink, give a treat

한테 han-te *part.* (*colloq.*) to (*a person*); 친구한테 편지를 보냈다 chin-gu-han-te pyeon-ji-reul bo-naet-da I sent a letter to my friend

한테서 han-te-seo *part.* (*colloq.*) from (*a person*); 친구한테서 편지를 받았다 chin-gu-han-te-seo pyeon-ji-reul bad-at-da I have received a letter from my friend

한통속 han-tong-sok *n.* one and the same group, a party

한판 han-pan *n.* a game, a round, a bout

한패 han-pae *n.* one of the same party; confederate, fellows

한편 han-pyeon *n.* one side, one hand, the other side, meanwhile, in addition to

한평생 han-pyeong-saeng *n.* a lifetime, all one's life

한푼 han-pun *n.* a penny, a coin

할 말 hal mal *n.phr.* what one wants to say

할 수 없이 hal ssu eops-i *n.phr.* without any other choice

할 일 hal lil *n.phr.* thing(s) to do

할머니 hal-meo-ni *n.* grandmother

할아버지 hal-a-beo-ji *n.* grandfather

할인 hal-in *n.* discount, price-cutting

할인가격 hal-in-kka-gyeok *n.* discounted price

할인하다 hal-in-ha-da *v.* discount, cut off

핥다 hal-ta *v.* lick, lap

핥아먹다 halt-a-meok-da *v.* lick up, lap up

함께 ham-kke *adv.* together, in company with

함박눈 ham bang-nun *n.* large snowflakes

함부로 ham-bu-ro *adv.* at random, disorderly, thoughtlessly

함정 ham-jeong *n.* pitfall, pit, trap

합격하다 hap-gyeo-ka-da *v.* pass an exam

합계 hap-gye *n.* the sum total, the total amount

합승 hap-seung *n.* riding together; jitney cab; carpool

합창 hap-chang *n.* chorus, ensemble

합치다 hap-chi-da *v.* put together, combine, join together, merge; sum up, add up; mix, compound, combine

합하다 ha-pa da *v.* unite, put together, combine, join together, merge; sum up, add up; mix, compound, combine

핫도그 hat-do-geu *n.* hotdog

핫케이크 hat-ke-i-keu *n.* hot cake

항공 hang-gong *n.* aviation, flight

항공권 hang-gong-kkwon *n.* airline ticket

항공료 hang-gong-nyo *n.* airfare

항공사 hang-gong-sa *n.* airline

항공편 hang-gong-pyeon *n.* by plane, airline

항구 hang-gu *n.* port, harbor

항복하다 hang-bo-ka-da *v.* surrender, capitulate

항상 hang-sang *adv.* always, at all times, as a rule

항아리 hang-a-ri *n.* jar, pot

항의하다 hang-ui-ha-da *v.* protest, make a protest

항해하다 hang-hae-ha-da *v.* sail, make a voyage

해 hae *n.* sun; year; harm; 해를 주다 hae-reul ju-da *v.* cause harm to somebody

해결하다 hae-gyeol-ha-da *v.* solve a question, settle a problem

해골 hae-gol *n.* skeleton

해군 hae-gun *n.* the navy

해남 hae-nam *n.* southwest coast of Korea

해내다 hae-nae-da *v.* accomplish, achieve, fulfill

해녀 hae-nyeo *n.* woman diver *(who harvests seashells)*

해답 hae-dap *n.* solution, answer

해돋이 hae-do-ji *n.* sunrise, sunup

해롭다 hae-rop-da *v.* be harmful, be bad

해마 hae-ma *n.* sea horse

해마다 hae-ma-da *adv.* every year, each year

해바라기 hae-ba-ra-gi *n.* sunflower

해변 hae-byeon *n.* beach, seashore

해보다 hae-bo-da *v.* try, attempt; experience

해산물 hae-san-mul *n.* marine products

해삼 hae-sam *n.* sea cucumber

해석하다 hae-seo-ka-da *v.* interpret, define, translate

해설하다 hae-seol-ha-da *v.* explain, comment

해수욕장 hae-su-yok-jang *n.* swimming beach

해안 hae-an *n.* seashore, coast, seaside

해야하다 hae-ya ha-da *v.* have to, be obligatory, be required to

해열제 hae-yeol-jje *n.* fever remedy

해외 hae-oe *n.* foreign countries, overseas

해외여행 hae-oe-yeo-haeng *n.* traveling overseas

해운대 hae-un-dae *n.* Hae Un Dae *(summer resort area)*

해일 hae-il *n.* tsunami

해장국 hae-jang-kkuk *n.* beef broth with ox blood and vegetables used for curing hangovers

해적 hae-jeok *n.* pirate

해적선 hae-jeok-seon *n.* pirate ship

해주다 hae-ju-da *v.* do something for somebody; 친구를 위해 생일날 저녁을 해 주었다 chin-gu-reul wi-hae saeng-il-lal jeo-nyeog-eul hae-ju-eot-da I prepared dinner for my friend on his/her birthday

해질녘 hae-jil-lyeok *n.* sunset

해초 hae-cho *n.* seaweeds, sea plants

해치다 hae-chi-da *v.* injure, harm, hurt, cause harm, spoil, damage

해치우다 hae-chi-u-da *v.* finish up, do completely

해파리 hae-pa-ri *n.* jellyfish

해해거리다 hae-hae-geo-ri-da *v.* giggle, titter

핵 haek *n.* nucleus

핵가족 haek-ga-jok *n.* nuclear family

핵무기 haeng-mu-gi *n.* nuclear weapons

핵폭탄 haek-pok-tan *n.* nuclear bomb

핸드백 haen-deu-baek *n.* handbag

핸드폰 haen-deu-pon *n.* cell phone

핸들 haen-deul *n.* handle bar, steering wheel

핸섬하다 haen-sseom-ha-da *v.* be good-looking, be handsome

햄 haem *n.* ham

햄버거 haem-beo-geo *n.* hamburger

햇볕 haet-byeot *n.* sunbeam, sunlight

햇빛 haet-bit *n.* sunshine, sunlight

행 haeng *affix.* bound for; 신촌행 지하철 sin-chon-haeng ji-ha-cheol *n.* subway bound for sin-chon

행동 haeng-dong *n.* action, behavior, doings

행동하다 haeng-dong-ha-da *v.* act, behave, move

행복 haeng-bok *n.* happiness

행복하다 haeng-bo-ka-da *v.* be happy

행사 haeng-sa *n.* event

행여나 haeng-yeo-na *adv.* by chance, possibly

행운 haeng-un *n.* good luck, good fortune

행인 haeng-in *n.* passerby, pedestrian

행주 haeng-ju *n.* dish cloth

행진하다 haeng-jin-ha-da *v.* march, parade

행해지다 haeng-hae-ji-da *v.* be done, be performed

향긋하다 hyang-geu-ta-da *v.* be fragrant

향기 hyang-gi *n.* fragrance, perfume, aroma, scent

향기롭다 hyang-gi-rop-da *v.* be fragrant, be aromatic

향냄새 hyang-naem-sae *n.* smell fragrant, aromatic smell

향수 hyang-su *n.* homesick; fragrance, perfume

향하다 hyang-ha-da *v.* face, look out at, turn towards; proceed to, start for; lean towards

향해서 hyang-hae-seo *part.* toward; 기차가 서울을 향해서 간다 gi-cha-ga seo-ul-eul hyang-hae-seo gan-da The train goes toward Seoul

허가하다 heo-ga-ha-da *v.* permit, allow, approve

허겁지겁 heo-geop-ji-geop *adv.* in a hurry, confusedly

허락하다 heo-ra-ka-da *v.* assent to, approve, grant, allow

허름하다 heo-reum-ha-da *v.* be shabby, be poor-looking

허리 heo-ri *n.* waist

허리띠 heo-ri-tti *n.* belt

허벅지 heo-beok-ji *n.* the thigh

허비하다 heo-bi-ha-da *v.* waste, cast away

허수아비 heo-su-a-bi *n.* scarecrow, dummy, puppet

허용되다 heo-yong-doe-da *v.* be permitted, be approved, be granted, be allowed

허전하다 heo-jeon-ha-da *v.* feel empty, feel lonesome

헌 heon *adj.* old, shabby, worn-out, second-hand

헌신 heon-sin *n.* dedication; old shoes

헌차 heon-cha *n.* old car

헌혈 heon-hyeol *n.* donation of blood

헐값 heol-kkap *n.* low price

헐다 heol-da *v.* destroy, demolish

헐떡거리다 heol-tteok-geo-ri-da *v.* gasp, pant, puff

헐렁하다 heol-leong-ha-da *v.* be loose, be loose-fitting

헐레벌떡 heol-le-beol-tteok *adv.* panting and puffing

헐리다 heol-li-da *v.* be demolished, be destroyed

험상궂다 heom-sang-gut-da *v.* be sinister, be savage-looking

험악하다 heom-a-ka-da *v.* be dangerous

험하다 heom-ha-da *v.* be steep, be rugged; be stormy, be rough; be sinister, be savage-looking

헛간 heot-gan *n.* barn, open shed

헛걸음하다 heot-geol-eum-ha-da *v.* make a trip in vain; return empty-handed; make a fruitless call on a person

헛기침하다 heot-gi-chim-ha-da *v.* clear one's throat

헛디디다 heot-di-di-da *v.* miss one's step, lose one's footing, take a false step

헛소리 heot-so-ri *n.* nonsense, silly talk

헛소문 heot-so-mun *n.* groundless rumor

헛수고하다 heot-su-go-ha-da *v.* make vain efforts; work in vain; get nothing for one's pains

헝가리 heong-ga-ri *n.* Hungary

헝겊 heong-geop *n.* piece of cloth, rag

헝클어지다 heong-keul-eo-ji-da *v.* be tangled, be entangled

헤드라이트 he-deu-ra-i-teu *n.* headlight

헤드폰 he-deu-pon *n.* head set

헤매다 he-me-da *v.* wander about, walk around; be at a loss, be perplexed

헤벌어지다 he-beol-eo-ji-da *v.* be very wide; get shallow

헤어컷 he-eo keot *n.* haircut

헤어스타일 he-eo-seu-ta-il *n.* hairstyle

헤어지다 he-eo-ji-da *v.* break up, part, part from, separate, divorce; get scattered

헤엄치다 he-eom-chi-da *v.* swim, have a swim

헬리콥터 hel-li-kop-teo *n.* helicopter

헬멧 hel-met *n.* helmet, hard hat

헬스클럽 hel-sseu-keul-leop *n.* health club, fitness club

헷갈리다 het-gal-li-da *v.* be confused, be distracted; be hard to find/see

헹구다 heng-gu-da *v.* rinse away, wash out

혀 hyeo *n.* tongue

혁대 hyeok-dae *n.* leather belt

혁명 hyeong-myeong *n.* revolution

현 상태 hyeon sang-tae *n.* present state of things, present circumstances

현관 hyeon-gwan *n.* entrance, foyer

현관문 hyeon-gwan-mun *n.* entrance door

현금 hyeon-geum *n.* cash

현금지급기 hyeon-geum-ji-geup-gi *n.* ATM machine

현금카드 hyeon-geum-ka-deu *n.* debit card

현기증 hyeon-gi-jjeung *n.* vertigo, dizziness

현대 hyeon-dae *n.* the present age, modern times

현대인 hyeon-dae-in *n.* modern people

현대화 hyeon-dae-hwa *n.* updating, modernization

현대화하다 hyeon-dae-hwa-ha-da *v.* update, modernize

현명하다 hyeon-myeong-ha-da *v.* be wise, be prudent

현모양처 hyeon-mo-yang-cheo *n.* a wise mother and good wife

현미 hyeon-mi *n.* brown rice

현미경 hyeon-mi-gyeong *n.* microscope

현상 hyeon-sang *n.* the present situation, the actual state, existing state of affairs; appearance, phenomenon, happening

현상하다 hyeon-sang-ha-da *v.* develop film

현수막 hyeon-su-mak *n.* hanging banner, suspended placard

현실 hyeon-sil *n.* actuality, reality

현악기 hyeon-ak-gi *n.* string instrument

현장 hyeon-jang *n.* the actual spot, the scene of action

현재 hyeon-jae *n.* present time, currently

현찰 hyeon-chal *n.* cash

현충일 hyeon-chung-il *n.* Memorial Day

혈압 hyeol-ap *n.* blood pressure

혈액형 hyeol-ae-kyeong *n.* blood type

협동하다 hyeop-dong-ha-da *v.* cooperate, collaborate, work together

협력하다 hyeom-nyeo-ka-da *v.* cooperate, collaborate, work together

협박하다 hyeop-ba-ka-da *v.* threaten, intimidate

협조하다 hyeop-jo-ha-da *v.* help, aid; cooperate, collaborate

협회 hyeop-poe *n.* society, association, league

혓바늘 hyeot-ba-neul *n.* fuzz on the tongue

혓바닥 hyeot-ba-dak *n.* the blade of the tongue

형 hyeong *n.* a man's older brother; punishment, penalty, sentence; model, style, type

형광등 hyeong-gwang-deung *n.* fluorescent lamp

형님 hyeong-nim *n.* *(hon.)* older brother *(for men)*

형무소 hyeong-mu-so *n.* prison, jail

형부 hyeong-bu *n.* the husband of a girl's elder sister, brother-in-law

형사 hyeong-sa *n.* detective, police investigator

형수 hyeong-su *n.* the wife of one's elder brother, sister-in-law

형식 hyeong-sik *n.* form; formality

형제 hyeong-je *n.* brothers, siblings

형제자매 hyeong-je-ja-mae *n.* brothers and sisters

형체 hyeong-che *n.* form, shape, the body

형태 hyeong-tae *n.* form, shape, configuration

형편 hyeong-pyeon *n.* the situation, the state of things, the aspect of affairs; one's family circumstances, one's family situation; condition, circumstances

형편없다 hyeong-pyeon-eop-da *v.* be terrible, be bad

혜성 he-seong *n.* comet

혜택 he-taek *n.* favor, benefit

호 ho *count.* a number; an issue; size; *n.* title, pseudonym

호각 ho-gak *n.* whistle

호감 ho-gam *n.* good feeling, goodwill, favorable impression

호기심 ho-gi-sim *n.* curiosity

호남 ho-nam *n.* southwestern Korea, the Jeolla provinces

호두 ho-du *n.* walnut

호들갑을 떨다 ho-deul-gab-eul tteol-da *v.phr.* be extravagant in speech, be bubbling over

호떡 ho-tteok *n.* Chinese stuffed pancake

호랑이 ho-rang-i *n.* tiger

호루라기 ho-ru-ra-gi *n.* whistle

호르몬 ho-reu-mon *n.* hormone

호박 ho-bak *n.* zucchini, squash, pumpkin

호박전 ho-bak-jeon *n.* zucchini pancake

호수 ho-su *n.* lake

호수 hot-ssu *n.* the number of house

호숫가 ho-sut-ga *n.* edge of lake, lakeside

호스 ho-seu *n.* hose

호신술 ho-sin-sul *n.* martial art used for self-defense

호실 ho-sil *count.* room number

호우주의보 ho-u-ju-i-bo *n.* heavy rain warning

호주 ho-ju *n.* Australia

호주머니 ho-ju-meo-ni *n.* pocket

호치키스 ho-chi-ki-sseu *n.* stapler

호텔 ho-tel *n.* hotel

호화스럽다 ho-hwa-seu-reop-da *v.* be gorgeous, be luxurious

호흡 ho-heup *n.* breath, respiration

혹 hok *n.* lump, tumor, bump, hump

혹부리 hok-bu-ri *n.* a person who has a wart on his/her face

혹시 hok-si *adv.* by any chance; maybe, perhaps, probably

혼 hon *n.* sole, spirit

혼기 hon-gi *n.* marriageable age

혼나다 hon-na-da *v.* have hard time, have a bitter experience; be scolded by, get frightened

혼내다 hon-nae-da *v.* frighten a person out of his wits, startle, horrify, scare; make a person have hard time, teach a person a lesson

혼내주다 hon-nae-ju-da *v.* frighten a person out of his wits, startle, horrify, scare; make a person have hard time, teach a person a lesson

혼동하다 hon-dong-ha-da *v.* confuse; run into each other

혼란 hol-lan *n.* confusion

혼수 hon-su *n.* dowry

혼수상태 hon-su-sang-tae *n.* coma

혼자 hon-ja *adv.* alone, by oneself

혼자서 hon-ja-seo *adv.* alone, by oneself

혼혈아 hon-hyeol-a *n.* children with one parent of Korean descent and one parent of non-Korean descent

홀딱 hol-ttak *adv.* quickly, completely; easily; with a jump

홀랑 hol-lang *adv.* naked, nude

홀로 hol-lo *adv.* alone, single-handed

홀어머니 hol-eo-meo-ni *n.* widowed mother, mother who does not have husband

홈 hom *n.* flaw, speck, crack

홍길동전 hong-gil-tong-jeon *n.* The Story of Hong Gil Dong *(first novel written in Korean c. 1608-13)*

홍당무 hong-dang-mu *n.* carrot

홍삼 hong-sam *n.* ginseng steamed red

홍수 hong-su *n.* flood; 홍수 나다 hong-su na-da *v.* get flooded

홍일점 hong-il-jjeom *n.* the only woman member among the men

홍차 hong-cha *n.* black tea

홍콩 hong-kong *n.* Hong Kong

혼이불 hon-ni-bul *n.* single-layer quilt

화 hwa *n.* anger, wrath; disaster, misfortune; 화를 내다 hwa-reul nae-da *v.* be angry; 화가 풀리다 hwa-ga pul-li-da *v.* calm down

화가 hwa-ga *n.* painter, artist

화교 hwa-gyo *n.* Chinese emigrants

화끈거리다 hwa-kkeun-geo-ri-da *v.* burn, glow, flush, feel hot

화나다 hwa-na-da *v.* be angry, be mad

화내다 hwa-nae-da *v.* get angry, vent one's anger

화단 hwa-dan *n.* flower-bed, flower garden; the art world

화랑 hwa-rang *n.* art gallery; warrior youth corp in Silla Dynasty (*57 B.C.-935*)

화려하다 hwa-ryeo-ha-da *v.* be splendid, be gorgeous

화력 hwa-ryeok *n.* steam power, heating power, force of fire

화력발전소 hwa-ryeok-bal-jjeon-so *n.* steam power plant

화면 hwa-myeon *n.* screen

화목하다 hwa-mo-ka-da *v.* be friendly, be on intimate terms

화문석 hwa-mun-seok *n.* mat woven with floral pattern

화물 hwa-mul *n.* freight, cargo

화분 hwa-bun *n.* flower pot

화사하다 hwa-sa-ha-da *v.* be splendid, be luxurious

화산 hwa-san *n.* volcano

화산구 hwa-san-gu *n.* crater

화살 hwa-sal *n.* arrow

화석 hwa-seok *n.* fossil

화성 hwa-seong *n.* Mars

화씨 hwa-ssi *n.* Fahrenheit

화요일 hwa-yo-il *n.* Tuesday

화장대 hwa-jang-dae *n.* dressing table

화장실 hwa-jang-sil *n.* bathroom

화장품 hwa-jang-pum *n.* cosmetics

화장하다 hwa-jang-ha-da *v.* make oneself up; cremate

화재 hwa-jae *n.* fire; conflagration

화세 hwa-je *n.* subject of conversation

화창하다 hwa-chang-ha-da *v.* be balmy, be bright, be sunny

화채 hwa-chae *n.* fruit punch

화톳불 hwa-tot-bul *n.* bonfire

화투 hwa-tu *n.* Korean card game ('*hana-fuda*' in Japan)

화풀이하다 hwa-pul-i-ha-da *v.* satisfy one's resentment

화학 hwa-hak *n.* chemistry

화학공학 hwa-hak-gong-hak *n.* chemical engineering

화해 hwa-hae *n.* reconciliation, peacemaking, composition

화해하다 hwa-hae-ha-da *v.* be reconciled, make up with

확 hwak *adv.* with a great puff, with a gust, with a burst

확대경 hwak-dae-gyeong *n.* magnifying glass, magnifier

확률 hwang-nyul *n.* possibility

확보하다 hwak-bo-ha-da *v.* secure, ensure, assure, guarantee

확성기 hwak seong gi *n.* loud speaker

확신하다 hwak-sin-ha-da *v.* feel convinced, believe firmly

확실하다 hwak-sil-ha-da *v.* be certain, be sure, be reliable

확실히 hwak-sil-hi *adv.* certainly, for sure

확인하다 hwag-in-ha-da *v.* confirm, verify, certify

확장하다 hwak-jang-ha-da *v.* expand, extend, enlarge

환갑 hwan-gap *n.* sixtieth birthday

환경 hwan-gyeong *n.* environment, surroundings

환기하다 hwan-gi-ha-da *v.* change air, ventilate

환불하다 hwan-bul-ha-da *v.* repay, refund, reimburse

환상 hwan-sang *n.* fantasy; illusion

환상적 hwan-sang-jeok *adj.* fantastic, illusive

환송회 hwan-song-hoe *n.* farewell party

환영하다 hwan-yeong-ha-da *v.* welcome, give a reception to

환영회 hwan-yeong-hoe *n.* welcome party

환웅 hwan-ung *n.* father of Dan Gun (*considered a forefather of the Go Jo Seon kingdom*)

환율 hwan-nyul *n.* exchange rate

환인 hwan-in *n.* father of Hwan-ung, God of the Heaven

환자 hwan-ja *n.* patient

환전 hwan-jeon *n.* money exchanging, exchange of money

환전소 hwan-jeon-so *n.* money changer

환전하다 hwan-jeon-ha-da *v.* exchange money

환절기 hwan-jeol-gi *n.* change of season

환풍기 hwan-pung-gi *n.* ventilation fan

환하다 hwan-ha-da *v.* be clear, be open, be bright, be fine-looking; be evident, be obvious, be familiar

활 hwal *n.* bow *(archery)*

활달하다 hwal-ttal-ha-da *v.* be outgoing, be extroverted

활동 hwal-ttong *n.* activity, action, motion

활동적 hwal-ttong-jeok *adj.* active

활동하다 hwal-ttong-ha-da *v.* display activity, lead an active life

활력소 hwal-lyeok-so *n.* tonic, vitamin

활발하다 hwal-bal-ha-da *v.* be lively, be active, be full of life

활약하다 hwal-ya-ka-da *v.* be active, get into action, display actively

활용하다 hwal-yong-ha-da *v.* apply, utilize, put to practical use, make practical application

활주로 hwal-jju-ro *n.* airstrip, runway

활짝 hwal-jjak *adv.* extensively, widely, entirely, completely

활활 hwal-hwal *adv.* in great flames, vigorously

홧김에 hwat-gim-e *adv.* under the influence of anger, in a fit of anger

황금 hwang-geum *n.* gold

황당하다 hwang-dang-ha-da *v.* be fabulous, be nonsensical

황무지 hwang-mu-ji *n.* wilderness

황사현상 hwang-sa-hyeon-sang *n.* sandy dust phenomena *(weather)*

황제 hwang-je *n.* emperor

황태자 hwang-tae-ja *n.* crown prince

황혼 hwang-hon *n.* dusk, twilight

황홀하다 hwang-hol-ha-da *v.* be enraptured, be charmed, be raptured

휙 hwaek *adv.* with a snap, with dispatch, with swish

횃불 hwaet-bul *n.* torch, torchlight

회 hoe *n.* lime, stucco; sliced raw fish/meat; *count.* time, round; meeting, gathering; 제삼회 졸업식 je-sam-hoe jol-eop-sik the third commencement

회갑 hoe-gap *n.* one's 61st birthday

회교 hoe-gyo *n.* Islam

회담 hoe-dam *n.* conference, conversation

회복하다 hoe-bo-ka-da *v.* recover, get better, regain, restore

회비 hoe-bi *n.* membership fee

회사 hoe-sa *n.* company, corporation

회사생활 hoe-sa-saeng-hwal *n.* work life, life in the work place

회사원 hoe-sa-won *n.* company employee

회색 hoe-saek *n.* gray

회식 hoe-sik *n.* dining together

회오리 hoe-o-ri *n.* cyclone, twister

회원 hoe-won *n.* member of a society/association

회의 hoe-ui *n.* conference, meeting, assembly

회화 hoe-hwa *n.* conversation, talk, dialogue

횡단보도 hoeng-dan-bo-da *n.* crosswalk; pedestrian crossing

효 hyo *n.* filial piety, obedience to parents

효과 hyo-kkwa *n.* effect, efficiency; 효과 있다 hyo-kkwa it-da *v.* have an effect, take effect; 효과 없다 hyo-kkwa eop-da *v.* have no effect

효과적 hyo-kkwa-jeok *adj.* effective, efficient

효녀 hyo-nyeo *n.* filial daughter

효도 hyo-do *n.* filial duty, filial piety

효력 hyo-ryeok *n.* effect, virtue

효성 hyo-seong *n.* filial piety

효자 hyo-ja *n.* filial son

후 hu *affix.* after, later, next to, following; *adv.* with a puff, blowing

후계자 hu-gye-ja *n.* successor, inheritor

후기 hu-gi *n.* end of an era

후년 hu-nyeon *n.* year after next

후다닥 hu-da-dak *adv.* with a startle, with a jump, suddenly, in a hurry

후대 hu-dae *n.* future generation, after ages

후덥지근하다 hu-deop-ji-geun-ha-da *v.* be sultry, be sticky

후들거리다 hu-deul-geo-ri-da *v.* tremble, shake, shiver

후들후들 hu-deul-hu-deul *adv.* trembling, shivering

후려치다 hu-ryeo-chi-da *v.* lash, whip, thrash

후련하다 hu-ryeon-ha-da *v.* feel relieved, feel unburdened

후루룩 hu-ru-ruk *adv.* with a slurp, with a gulp

후문 hu-mun *n.* back gate

후반 hu-ban *n.* the latter half

후배 hu-bae *n.* one's junior, younger generation

후보 hu-bo *n.* candidate, candidacy

후비다 hu-bi-da *v.* scoop out, pick out

후세 hu-se *n.* the future, coming age, future generations

후손 hu-son *n.* descendants

후식 hu-sik *n.* dessert

후에 hu-e *part.* after; 저녁 식사 후에 텔레비전을 보자 jeo-nyeok sik-sa hu-e tel-le-bi-jeon-eul bo-ja Let's watch TV after dinner

후원하다 hu-won-ha-da *v.* support, give support to, back up

후유증 hu-yu-jjeung *n.* aftermath, sequel

후일 hu-il *n.* some other day, later days

후임자 hu-im-ja *n.* successor

후자 hu-ja *n.* the latter, the other

후진국 hu-jin-guk *n.* underdeveloped country

후진하다 hu-jin-ha-da *v.* go backward

후추 hu-chu *n.* black pepper

후춧가루 hu-chut-ga-ru *n.* ground black pepper

후퇴하다 hu-toe-ha-da *v.* retreat, go back

후하다 hu-ha-da *v.* be kind, be kindhearted, be hospitable, be generous

후회하다 hu-hoe-ha-da *v.* regret, repent

훅 huk *adv.* with a sip, with a gulp

훈련 hul-lyeon *n.* training, practice

훈련하다 hul-lyeon-ha-da *v.* practice, train, exercise

훈민정음 hun-min-jeong-eum *n.* original name of the Korean script 'hangul'

훈장 hun-jang *n.* mark of honor

훈훈하다 hun-hun-ha-da *v.* be comfortably warm

훌떡 hul-tteok *adv.* quickly, nimbly; entirely, perfectly

훌라춤 hul-la-chum *n.* hula dance

훌라후프 hul-la-hu-peu *n.* hula hoop

훌륭하게 hul-lyung-ha-ge *adv.* excellently, magnificently, nicely

훌륭하다 hul-lyung-ha-da *v.* be nice, be fine, be wonderful, be excellent, be superb, be magnificent; be respectable, be honorable; be admirable, be commendable

훌쩍 hul-jjeok *adv.* quickly, with a jump, at a gulp

훌쩍거리다 hul-jjeok-geo-ri-da *v.* sip; keep sniffing; sob

훑어보다 hult-eo-bo-da *v.* give a searching glance at, look carefully at

훔쳐먹다 hum-chyeo-meok-da *v.* steal and eat, swipe and eat

훔치다 hum-chi-da *v.* swipe, steal; wipe, mop

훗날 hun-nal *n.* some day, the future, another day

훤칠하다 hwon-chil-ha-da *v.* have a full well-developed figure, be strapping

훤하다 hwon-ha-da *v.* be dim; be light; be open, be sunny, be familiar

훨씬 hwol-ssin *adv.* by far

훨훨 hwol-hwol *adv.* with a flapping, gently; with great flames, vigorously

훼방하다 hwe-bang-ha-da *v.* interfere with, interrupt

훼손하다 hwe-son-ha-da *v.* damage, impair, spoil

휘감다 hwi-gam-tta *v.* wind around, coil, tie around

휘날리다 hwi-nal-li-da *v.* flap, fly, flutter

휘다 hwi-da *v.* get bent, get curved, get crooked; bend, curve, crook

휘두르다 hwi-du-reu-da *v.* brandish, flourish, wield; make a puppet of a person, have a person under perfect control

휘둥그래지다 hwi-dung-geu-rae-ji-da *v.* become wide eyed, get surprised, be startled

휘말리다 hwi-mal-li-da *v.* be rolled, get mixed up, be caught

휘몰아치다 hwi-mol-a-chi-da *v.* blow hard, blow violently

휘발유 hwi-bal-lyu *n.* gasoline

휘어잡다 hwi-eo-jap-da *v.* grasp, grab; control, keep a person under one's thumb, have a person under one's control, keep a person under control

휘어지다 hwi-eo-ji-da *v.* get bent, be curved

휘장 hwi-jang *n.* curtain, curtain screen; emblem, ensign

휘적거리다 hwi-jeok-geo-ri-da *v.* swing one's arm; 그는 늘 걸을 때 팔을 휘적거

린다 geu-neun neul geol-eul ttae pal-eul hwi-jeok-geo-rin-da He always swings his arms while he walks

휘젓다 hwi-jeot-da *v.* stir round and round, whip, beat, swing; disarrange, disturb

휘청거리다 hwi-cheong-geo-ri-da *v.* be pliant; stagger; totter

휘파람 hwi-pa-ram *n.* whistle; 휘파람 불다 hwi-pa-ram bul-da *v.* whistle, give a whistle

휘황찬란하다 hwi-hwang-chal-lan-ha-da *v.* be resplendent, brilliant

휙 hwik *adv.* with a gust, with a sweep, lightly and nimbly

휠체어 hwil-che-eo *n.* wheel chair

휩싸다 hwip-ssa-da *v.* wrap up, surround

휩싸이다 hwip-ssa-i-da *v.* get wrapped up

휩쓸다 hwip-sseul-da *v.* sweep away

휩쓸리다 hwip-sseul-li-da *v.* be swept away; be overrun, suffer a rampage

휴가 hyu-ga *n.* vacation, leave of absence

휴가비 hyu-ga-bi *n.* money to go on vacation, expenses needed to go on vacation

휴가철 hyu-ga-cheol *n.* vacation season

휴게소 hyu-ge-so *n.* resting place

휴게실 hyu-ge-sil *n.* lounge

휴대전화 hyu-dae-jeon-hwa *n.* cellular phone

휴식 hyu-sik *n.* rest

휴식하다 hyu-si-ka-da *v.* rest, take a rest

휴양지 hyu-yang-ji *n.* rest area

휴일 hyu-il *n.* weekend, holiday

휴전선 hyu-jeon-seon *n.* DMZ *(abbr. Demilitarized Zone)*

휴지 hyu-ji *n.* toilet paper, tissue; pause, suspension

휴지통 hyu-ji-tong *n.* trashcan

휴학하다 hyu-ha-ka-da *v.* temporarily stay away from school for a time

흉 hyung *n.* scar; defect, fault

흉기 hyung-gi *n.* deadly weapon

흉내 hyung-nae *n.* imitation, mock; 흉내 내다 hyung-nae nae-da *v.* imitate, copy

흉년 hyung-nyeon *n.* year of famine

흉보다 hyung-bo-da *v.* speak ill of, speak against

흉악하다 hyung-a-ka-da *v.* be brutal, be wicked, be cruel, be ugly

흉터 hyung-teo *n.* scar

흉하다 hyung-ha-da *v.* be ominous, be ill-omened, be unlucky; be ugly, be bad-looking, be terrible

흐느끼다 heu-neu-kki-da *v.* sob

흐려지다 heu-ryeo-ji-da *v.* get cloudy; 날씨가 흐려졌다 nal-ssi-ga heu-ryeo-jyeot-da The weather grew cloudy

흐르다 heu-reu-da *v.* flow, stream, run down; float, drift; overflow, run over; pass away, elapse, flow by

흐름 heu-reum *n.* flowing, stream, current

흐리다 heu-ri-da *v.* be cloudy; be muddy; be vague, be dim, be dull

흐릿하다 heu-ri-ta-da *v.* be rather cloudy, be dull, be dim, be vague, be hazy

흐물흐물하다 heu-mul-heu-mul-ha-da *v.* be overripe, very soft

흐뭇하다 heu-mu-ta-da *v.* be pleasing, be satisfying, be satisfied

흐지부지 heu-ji-bu-ji *adv.* unclearly, in secret; wastefully

흐트러지다 heu-teu-reo-ji-da *v.* scatter, disperse, get scattered, be distracted

흑설탕 heuk-seol-tang *n.* unrefined sugar

흑심 heuk-sim *n.* evil intentions, dark designs

흑인 heug-in *n.* ethnic Africans

흑흑 heuk-heuk *adv.* sobbing, with sobs

흔들거리다 heun-deul-geo-ri-da *v.* swing, sway, shake, be swayed

흔들다 heun-deul-da *v.* shake, wave, swing, wag

흔들리다 heun-deul-li-da *v.* shake, sway, rock, tremble, swing, waver

흔들의자 heun-deul-ui-ja *n.* rocking chair

흔들흔들 heun-deul-heun-deul *adv.* swinging, shakily

흔적 heun-jeok *n.* marks, traces, track, indications, evidences

흔하다 heun-ha-da *v.* be plenty, be common, be met with everywhere

흔히 heun-hi *adv.* plentifully, usually, commonly, frequently, generally

흘겨보다 heul-gyeo-bo-da *v.* leer at, glance sidewise at

흘금거리다 heul-kkeum-geo-ri-da *v.* keep looking sideways, keep leering at

흘깃 heul-kkit *adv.* with a glance

흘깃거리다 heul-kkit-geo-ri-da *v.* keep glaring at, keep looking angrily

흘러 들다 heul-leo deul-da *phr.* flow into, pour in

흘러가다 heul-leo-ga-da *v.* flow; run; float along; fly

흘러나오다 heul-leo-na-o-da *v.* flow out, run out, stream out, gush forth

흘러내리다 heul-leo-nae-ri-da *v.* fall, drop, run down; slip down

흘리다 heul-li-da *v.* spill, drop; lose; scribble; take no notice

흙 heuk *n.* earth, soil

흙더미 heuk-deo-mi *n.* heap of earth

흙먼지 heung-meon-ji *n.* dust, dust storm

흙장난하다 heuk-jang-nan-ha-da *v.* play with earth

흙탕물 heuk-tang-mul *n.* muddy water

흙투성이 heuk-tu-seong-i *n.* covered all over with mud

흠 heum *n.* flaw, scratch, bruise; defect, blemish

흠뻑 heum-ppeok *adv.* very much, completely

흠씬 heum-ssin *adv.* sufficiently, utterly, enough

흠잡다 heum-jap-da *v.* find fault with, pick out flaws, look for defects

흠집 heum-jjip *n.* flaw, scratch, bruise; defect, blemish

흡수하다 heup-su-ha-da *v.* absorb, suck in

흡연 heub-yeon *n.* smoking

흡연금지 heub-yeon-geum-ji *n.* no smoking

흥건하다 heung-geon-ha-da *v.* be full of water, have too much liquid in

흥겹다 heung-gyeop-da *v.* be lots of fun, be delightful, be exciting

흥미 heung-mi *n.* interest, zest, taste; 흥미 있다 heung-mi it-da *v.* be interested, be interesting

흥부전 heung-bu-jeon *n.* "Heung Bu" *(a Korean-style opera/old time story)*

흥분하다 heung-bun-ha-da *v.* be excited, be stimulated

흥얼거리다 heung-eol-geo-ri-da *v.* hum, sing to oneself

흥얼흥얼 heung-eol-heung-eol *adv.* humming

흥정하다 heung-jeong-ha-da *v.* strike a bargain, haggle over terms, deal, do business

흥청망청 heung-cheong-mang-cheong *adv.* with elation, merrily

흩날리다 heun-nal-li-da *v.* scatter, blow off

흩어지다 heut-eo-ji-da *v.* scatter, get scattered, break up

희귀하다 hi-gwi-ha-da *v.* be rare, be uncommon, be unusual

희다 hi-da *v.* be white, be fair

희망 hi-mang *n.* hope, wish, desire, prospect

희미하다 hi-mi-ha-da *v.* be faint, be dim, be vague, be hazy

희박하다 hi-ba-ka-da *v.* be thin, be weak, be dilute; be rare

희생하다 hi-saeng-ha-da *v.* sacrifice, victimize

희소식 hi-so-sik *n.* good news

희한하다 hi-han-ha-da *v.* be rare, be curious; scare; be uncommon

흰곰 hin-gom *n.* polar bear

흰머리 hin-meo-ri *n.* gray hair

흰밥 hin-bap *n.* white rice

흰색 hin-saek *adj.* white color

흰자위 hin-ja-wi *n.* egg white; white of the eye

히터 hi-teo *n.* heater

히트 hi-teu *n.* hit *(sports)*; success

힌트 hin-teu *n.* hint

힘 him *n.* power, physical strength, force, energy; ability, capacity; effort

힘껏 him-kkeot *adv.* with all one's might, to the best of one's ability

힘들다 him-deul-da *v.* be difficult, be tiring, be painful

힘들어하다 him-deul-eo-ha-da *v.* feel painful, feel tired

힘들이다 him-deul-i-da *v.* make an effort, take pains, elaborate

힘세다 him-sse-da *v.* be strong, be powerful

힘쓰다 him-sseu-da *v.* force with one's muscles; make an effort; help, give a hand

힘없다 him-eop-da *v.* be feeble, be weak

힘없이 him-eops-i *adv.* feebly, dejectedly

힘있다 him-it-da *v.* be full of energy, be strong, have strength; be powerful, forceful; be influential

힘자랑하다 him-ja-rang-ha-da *v.* boast of one's strength, be proud of one's strength

힘주다 him-ju-da *v.* devote one's strength to, concentrate, emphasize

힘줄 him-jjul *n.* muscle, tendon, string

힘차다 him-cha-da *v.* be powerful, be full of strength, be energetic

English-Korean Dictionary

A

a, an *art.* 한 han; 어떤 eo-tteon, 어느 eo-neu; ~ **apple** 사과 한 개 sa-gwa han gae; **There is ~ man** 저기 어떤 남자가 있다 jeo-gi eo-tteon nam-ja-ga it-da

abandon *vt.* 버리다 beo-ri-da, 단념하다 dan-nyeom-ha-da, 그만두다 geu-man-du-da

abase *vt.* 품위를 떨어뜨리다 pum-wi-reul tteol-eo-tteu-ri-da

abash *vt.* 무안하게 하나 mu-an-ha-ge ha-da, 당황하게 하다 dang-hwang-ha-ge ha-da

abate *vt.* 감소시키다 gam-so-si-ki-da, 낮추다 nat-chu-da; 배제하다 bae-je-ha-da

abbreviate *vt.* 짧게하다 jjalp-ge-ha-da, 생략하다 saeng-nya-ka-da

abbreviation *n.* 생략 saeng-nyak, 단축 dan-chuk

abdicate *vi.* 퇴위하다 toe-wi-ha-da; *vt.* 왕권을 포기하다 wang-kkwon-eul po-gi-ha-da

abdomen *n.* 배 bae, 복부 bok-bu

abdominal *adj.* 복부의 bok-bu-ui

abduct *vt.* 유괴하다 yu-goe-ha-da

abduction *n.* 유괴 yu-goe

ability *n.* 능력 neung-nyeok

able *adj.* 능력있는 neung-nyeog-in-neun, 할 수 있는 hal ssu in-neun

ablush *adj.* 얼굴을 붉힌 eol-gul-eul bul-kin, 얼굴이 홍당무가 된 eol-gul-i hong-dang-mu-ga doen

abnormal *adj.* 비정상적인 bi-jeong-sang-jeog-in

abnormality *n.* 이상 i-sang, 변칙 byeon-chik, 변태 byeon-tae; 기형 gi-hyeong, 불구 bul-gu, 비정상적인 것 bi-jeong-sang-jeog-in geot

aboard *adv.* 배에 bae-e, 배로 bae-ro; **all ~** 모두 승선해 주십시오 mo-du seung-seon-hae ju-sip-si-o

abolish *vt.* 폐지하다 pye-ji-ha-da, 철폐하다 cheol-pye-ha-da

abominate *vt.* 혐오하다 hyeom-o-ha-da, 질색하다 jil-ssae-ka-da

abortion *n.* 유산 yu-san

about *adv.* 한 han, 약 yak; 지금 막...(으)려고 하다 ji-geum mak…(eu)ryeo-go ha-da; **~ a week ago** 한 일주일 전에 ha nil-jju-il jeon-e; **We are ~ to leave** 우리는 지금 막 떠나려고 한다 u-ri-neun ji-geum mak tteo-na-ryeo-go han-da; **I am not ~ to do that** 저는 그러지 않을 것입니다 jeo-neun geu-reo-ji an-eul geos-im-ni-da; *prep.* ...에 대해 …e dae-hae, ...에 대한 …e dae-han; **a book ~ art** 예술에 대한 책 ye-sul-e dae-han chaek

above *adv.* ...위에 …wi-e; ...이상 …i-sang; 앞에서 ap-e-seo; **on the shelf ~** 저 선반 위에 jeo seon-ban wi-e; **as I stated ~** 앞에서 언급한 것과 같이 ap-e-seo eon-geu-pan geot-gwa ga-chi; *num.* **twenty-one and ~** 21이상 i-sib-il i-sang; *prep.* **It's ~ the self-help shelf** 그 책은 자기관리 섹션 서가에 있습니다 geu chaeg-eun ja-gi-gwal-li ssek-syeon seo-ga-e it-seum-ni-da; **As department manager, he is ~ me** 그 분은 과장님이시고 제 상사이십니다 geu-bun-eun gwa-jang-nim-i-si-go je sang-sa-i-sim-ni-da; **They are ~ that kind of behavior** 그 사람들은 그런 행동은 절대로 안한다 geu sa ram-deul-eun geu-reon haeng-dong-eun jeol-ttae-ro an-han-da; **~ all** *adv.* 특히 teu-ki

abroad *adv.* 외국에 oe-gug-e; 널리 neol-li; *adj.* 외국산 oe-guk-san

abrupt *adj.* 뜻밖의 tteut-bakk-ui; 가파른 ga-pa-reun

abruption *n.* 갑작스런 중단 gap-jak-seu-reon jung-dan; 분열 bun-yeol

abruptly *adv.* 갑자기 gap-ja-gi

absence *n.* 결석 gyeol-sseok, 결근 gyeol-geun; 부재 bu-jae, 방심 bang-sim

absent *adj.* 결석하다 gyeol-sseo-ka-da, 결근하다 gyeol-geun-ha-da

absent-minded *adj.* 방심한 bang-sim-han, 멍한 meong-han

absolute *adj.* *(perfect, complete)* 완전한 wan-jeon-han; *(pure, genuine)* 순수한 sun-su-han; *(unconditional, positive)* 절대의 jeol-ttae-ui; *(unconditional)* 무조건의 mu-jo-kkeon-ui

absorb *vt.* 흡수하다 heup-ssu-ha-da; 열중하게 하다 yeol-jjung-ha-ge ha-da; **He is ~ed in his work** 그 사람은 자기 일에 열중해

있다 geu sa-ram-eun ja-gi il-e yeol-jjung-hae it-da

absorbent *adj.* 흡수성의 heup-su-sseong-ui; *n.* 흡수제 heup-su-je

abstract *adj.* 추상적인 chu-sang-jeog-in

absurd *adj.* 불합리한 bul-ham-ni-han; 어리석은 eo-ri-seog-eun

abundance *n.* 풍부 pung-bu

abundant *adj.* 풍부한 pung-bu-han

abuse *n.* 남용 nam-yong; 학대 hak-dae; *vt.* 남용하다 nam-yong-ha-da; 학대하다 hak-dae-ha-da

abusive *adj.* 남용하는 nam-yong-ha-neun; 학대하는 hak-dae-ha-neun; 입버릇이 사나운 ip-beo-reus-i sa-na-un

abuzz *adj.* 윙윙거리는 wing-wing-geo-ri-neun, 떠들썩한 tteo-deul-sseo-kan; 활기 넘치는 hwal-gi neom-chi-neun

academic *adj.* 학구적인 hak-gu-jeog-in

academy *n.* 학술원 hak-sul-won, 학원 hag-won; **Academy Award** *n.* 아카데미상 a-ka-de-mi sang

accelerate *vi.* 가속하다 ga-so-ka-da

accelerator *n.* 가속기 ga-sok-gi, 엑셀러레이터 ek-sel-leo-re-i-teo

accent *n.* 액센트 aek-sen-tteu; 강조 gang-jo; 사투리 sa-tu-ri

accept *vt.* 받아들이다 bad-a-deul-i-da, 수락하다 su-ra-ka-da

acceptable *adj.* 수락할 수 있는 su-ra-kal ssu in-neun, 용인할 수 있는 yong-in-hal ssu in-neun

acceptance *n.* 수락 su-rak

access *n.* 접근 jeop-geun; *vt.* 접근하다 jeop-geun-ha-da; **I can't ~ that file** 나는 그 파일을 열 수 없다 na-neun geu pa-il-eul yeol ssu eop-da

accessible *adj.* 접근하기 쉬운 jeop-geun-ha-gi swi-un

accessory *n.* 액세서리 aek-se-seo-ri

accident *n.* 사고 sa-go; 우연 u-yeon

accidental *adj.* 우연한 u-yeon-han

accidentally *adv.* 우연히 u-yeon-hi; 사고로 sa-go-ro

accommodate *vt.* 숙박시키다 suk-bak-si-ki-da; 조절하다 jo-jeol-ha-da; 편의를 도모하다 pyeon-ui-reul do-mo-ha-da

accommodation *n.* 숙박시설 suk-bak-si-seol; 편의제공 pyeon-ui-je-gong; 적응 jeog-eung

accompany *vt.* 동반하다 dong-ban-ha-da

accomplice *n.* 공범 gong-beom

accomplish *vt.* 성취하다 seong-chwi-ha-da, 이루다 i-ru-da

accomplishment *n.* 성취 seong-chwi, 완성 wan-seong

according to *phr.* ...에 따르면 e tta-reu-myeon, ...에 의하면 e ui-ha-myeon

account *n.* 구좌 gu-jwa; 계산 gye-san; 보고(서) bo-go(-seo), 설명(서) seol-myeong(-seo); **on ~ of** ...때문에 ...ttae-mun-e; **bank ~** 은행구좌 eun-haeng-gu-jwa

accountant *n.* 회계사 hoe-gye-sa

accounting *n.* 회계학 hoe-gye-hak

accumulate *vt.* 쌓다 ssa-ta, 축적하다 chuk-jeo-ka-da

accuracy *n.* 정확도 jeong-hwak-do, 정밀성 jeong-mil-sseong

accurate *adj.* 정확한 jeong-hwa-kan

accusation *n.* 고발 go-bal; 비난 bi-nan

accuse *vt.* 고발하다 go-bal-ha-da; 비난하다 bi-nan-ha-da

accustom *vi.* 습관을 들이다 seup-gwan-eul deul-i-da; **to be ~ed to** ...에 익숙해지다 ...e ik-su-kae-ji-da

ace *n.* 에이스 e-i-sseu; **~ of hearts** 하트 에이스 ha-teu e-i-sseu

acetone *n.* 아세톤 a-se-ton

ache *n.* 통증 tong-jjeung; *vi.* 아프다 a-peu-da

achieve *vt.* 이루다 i-ru-da, 완수하다 wan-su-ha-da

achievement *n.* 업적 eop-jjeok; 완수 wan-su

acid *n.*, *adj.* 산 san; *adj.* 산성의 san-seong-ui

acidity *n.* 산도 san-do

acknowledge *vt.* 인정하다 in-jeong-ha-da; 사의를 표하다 sa-ui-reul pyo-ha-da

acknowledgement *n.* 승인 seung-in; 감사 gam-sa; 수령증명 su-ryeong-jeung-myeong

acne *n.* 여드름 yeo-deu-reum

acorn *n.* 도토리 do-to-ri

acoustic *adj.* 청각의 cheong-gag-ui, 음향의 eum-hyang-ui

acquaint *vt.* 알리다 al-li-da, 소개하다 so-gae-ha-da

acquaintance *n.* 지식 ji-sik; 면식 myeon-sik; 아는 사람 a-neun sa-ram

acquire *vt.* 습득하다 seup-deu-ka-da

acquisition *n.* 습득 seup-deuk; 습득물 seup-deung-mul

acre *n.* 에이커 e-i-keo

acrobat *n.* 곡예사 gog-ye-sa

acrobatics *n.* 곡예 gog-ye

acrophobia *n.* 고소 공포증 go-so gong-po-jjeung

across *adv.* 건너(서) geon-neo(-seo); **a bridge ~** ...위의 다리 ...wi-ui da-ri; **They walked ~** 그들은 걸어서 지나갔다 geu-deul-eun geol-eo-seo ji-na-gat-da; **to get a message ~** 메시지를 이해시키다 me-ssi-ji-reul i-hae-si-ki-da, 메시지를 전달하다 me-si-ji-reul jeon-dal-ha-da; *prep.* 건너(서) geon-neo(-seo); ...에 걸쳐 ...e geol-cheo; **~ the river** 강 건너 gang geon-neo; **to come ~** 우연히 만나게 되다 u-yeon-hi man-na-ge doe-da; **~ the entire spectrum** 전 스팩트럼에 걸쳐 jeon seu-pek-teu-reom-e geol-cheo

acryl *n.* 아크릴 a-keu-ril

act *n.* *(deed)* 행동 haeng-dong; *(of a play)* 막 mak; *vi.* *(perform)* 연기하다 yeon-gi-ha-da; *(take action)* 행동하다 haeng-dong-ha-da

action *n.* 활동 hwal-ttong; 작용 jag-yong; 동작 dong-jak; **to take ~** 조처를 취하다 jo-cheo-reul chwi-ha-da; **to take ~ against sth./sb.** ...을 상대로 소송을 제기하다 ...eul sang-dae-ro so-song-eul je-gi-ha-da

active *adj.* 활동적인 hwal-ttong-jeog-in; 적극적인 jeok-geuk-jeog-in

activity *n.* 활동 hwal-ttong

actor *n.* 배우 bae-u

actual *adj.* 현재의 hyeon-jae-ui; 실제의 sil-jje-ui

actually *adv.* 실제로 sil-jje-ro, 정말로 jeong-mal-lo, 실지로 sil-jji-ro

acute *adj.* 날카로운 nal-ka-ro-un

A.D. *abbr.* ***Anno Domini*** 서기 seo-gi

adage *n.* 격언 gyeog-eon, 속담 sok-dam

adapt *vt.* 각색하다 gak-sae-ka-da; 적응시키다 jeog-eung-si-ki-da

adapter *n.* 각색자 gak-saek-ja; 어댑터 eo-daep-teo

add *vt.* 더하다 deo-ha-da

addict *vt.* 나쁜일에 빠지다 na-ppeun-il-e ppa-ji-da; 마약중독 시키다 ma-yak-jung-dok si-ki-da; *n.* 마약중독자 ma-yak-jung-dok-ja

addictive *adj.* 습관성의 seup-gwan-sseong-ui

addition *n.* 추가 chu-ga; *(mathmatics)* 덧셈 deot-sem

additional *adj.* 추가의 chu-ga-ui, 추가적인 chu-ga-jeog-in

address *n.* *(postal)* 주소 ju-so; *(public speech)* 연설 yeon-seol; *vt.* *(to deliver a speech)* 연설히다 yeon-seol ha-da; *(to talk to sb.)* 말을 걸다 mal-eul geol-da; *(to send mail [letter or email] to sb.)* 편지를 보내다 pyeon-ji-reul bo-nae-da; **~ee** 수취인 su-chwi-in

adequate *adj.* 적당한 jeok-dang-han

adhere *vi.* 부착하다 bu-cha-ka-da; **to ~ to a schedule** 스케줄을 고수하다 seu-ke-jul-eul go-su-ha-da; **to ~ to unorthodox beliefs** 집착하다 jip-cha-ka-da

adhesive *adj.* 접착성이 강한 jeop-chak-seong-i gang-han

adjacent *adj.* 인접한 in-jeo-pan

adjective *n.* 형용사 hyeong-yong-sa

adjoin *vi.* 인접하다 in-jeo-pa-da; **~ing rooms** 붙어있는 방 but-eo-in-neun bang, 옆방 yeop-bang, 인접한 방 in-jeo-pan bang

adjust *vt.* 맞추다 mat-chu-da, 조정하다 jo-jeong-ha-da

adjustable *adj.* 조정할 수 있는 jo-jeong-hal ssu in-neun

administer *vt.* 관리하다 gwal-li-ha-da

administration *n.* 관리 gwal-li; 행정 haeng-jeong

administrative *adj.* 관리의 gwal-li-ui, 행정상의 haeng-jeong-sang-ui

admirable *adj.* 감탄할만한 gam-tan-hal-man-han

admiral *n.* 해군제독 hae-gun-je-dok

admire *vt.* 감탄하다 gam-tan-ha-da

admission *n.* 입장 ip-jang, 입학 i-pak; **~ fee** 입장료 ip-jang-nyo; **free ~** 무료입장 mu-ryo-ip-jang

admit *vt.* 허가하다 heo-ga-ha-da

admonish *vt.* 훈계하다 hun-gye-ha-da, 타이르다 ta-i-reu-da

adolescent *n.* 청년 cheong-nyeon; *adj.* 청년(기)의 cheong-nyeon(-gi)-ui

adopt *vt.* *(a new rule)* 채택하다 chae-tae-ka-da; *(a child)* 양자삼다 yang-ja-sam-tta

adoption *n.* 채택 chae-taek, 채용 chae-yong; 양자결연 yang-ja-gyeol-yeon; ~ **agency** 양자 알선기관 yang-ja al-sseon-gi-gwan

adorable *adj.* 공경할만한 gong-gyeong-hal-man-han, 귀여운 gwi-yeo-un

adore *vt.* 숭배하다 sung-bae-ha-da; 아주 좋아하다 a-ju jo-a-ha-da

adult *n.* 어른 eo-reun, 성인 seong-in; *adj.* 어른의 eo-reun-ui, 성숙한 seong-su-kan

adultery *n.* 간통 gan-tong, 부정 bu-jeong

advance *n.* *(development, progress)* 진전 jin-jeon, *(progress, improvement)* 진보 jin-bo; *vt.* *(to let go in front of)* 앞으로 내보내다 ap-eu-ro nae-bo-nae-da; *(to submit, to present)* 제출하다 je-chul-ha-da; *(to promote)* 진급시키다 jin-geup-si-ki-da; *vi.* *(to go forward)* 앞으로 나아가다 ap-eu-ro na-a-ga-da; *(to go up)* 오르다 o-reu-da; **in ~** 미리 mi-ri

advantage *n.* 유리 yu-ri, 우세 u-se; 유리한 점 yu-ri-han jeom

adventure *n.* 모험 mo-heom

adverb *n.* 부사 bu-sa

adversary *n.* 적 jeok, 상대 sang-dae

advertize *vt.* 광고하다 gwang-go-ha-da, 알리다 al-li-da; *vi.* 광고를 내다 gwang-go-reul nae-da

advertizement *n.* 광고 gang-go

advice *n.* 조언 jo-eon, 충고 chung-go

advise *vt.* 조언하다 jo-eon-ha-da, 충고하다 chung-go-ha-da; 권하다 gwon-ha-da

adviser *n.* 조언자 jo-eon-ja, 고문 go-mun

advocate *vt.* 주장하다 ju-jang-ha-da, 옹호하다 ong-ho-ha-da; *n.* 대변자 dae-byeon-ja, 주창자 ju-chang-ja

aerial *n.* 안테나 an-te-na; *adj.* 공기의 gong-gi-ui; 가벼운 ga-byeo-un; 항공기의 hang-gong-gi-ui

aerobic *n.* 에어로빅 e-eo-ro-bik, 체조 che-jo; *adj.* 호기성의 ho-gi-sseong-ui

affair *n.* 일 il, 사건 sa-kkeon

affect *vt.* 영향을 주다 yeong-hyang-eul ju-da; 감동시키다 gam-dong-si-ki-da; …은 체하다 …eun che-ha-da

affection *n.* 애정 ae-jeong, 애착 ae-chak; 감동 gam-dong; 영향 yeong-hyang

affectionate *adj.* 다정한 da-jeong-han

affiliate *vt.* 회원으로 가입시키다 hoe-won-eu-ro ga-ip-si-ki-da, 합병시키다 hap-byeong-si-ki-da; *vi.* 제휴하다 je-hyu-ha-da

affiliation *n.* 입회 ip-hoe, 가입 ga-ip, 제휴 je-hyu; 양자결연 yang-ja-gyeol-yeon

affirm *vt.* 확언하다 hwag-eon-ha-da; 확인하다 hwag-in-ha-da

affirmation *n.* 주장 ju-jang; 증언 jeung-eon

affix *vt.* 첨부하다 cheom-bu-ha-da, 도장을 찍다 do-jang-eul jjik-da, 책임을 지우다 chaeg-im-eul ji-u-da; *n.* 첨부물 cheom-bu-mul, 접사 jeop-sa

afflict *vt.* 괴롭히다 goe-ro-pi-da

affliction *n.* 고통 go-tong; 재해 jae-hae; 병 byeong

afford *vt.* …을 여유가 있다 …eul yeo-yu-ga it-da; 제공하다 je-gong-ha-da

afloat *adv.* 물위에 떠서 mul-wi-e tteo-seo; 지급능력이 있는 ji-geum-neung-nyeog-i in-neun

afoot *adv.* 걸어서 geol-eo-seo, 진행중에 jin-haeng-jung-e

afraid *adj.* 무서운 mu-seo-un; **to be ~ of** 무서워하다 mu-seo-wo-ha-da

Africa *n.* 아프리카 a-peu-ri-ka

African *n.* 아프리카 사람 a-peu-ri-ka sa-ram; *adj.* 아프리카의 a-peu-ri-ka-ui

after *adv.* …후에 …hu-e, …뒤에 …dwi-e, …다음에 …da-eum-e; **shortly ~** 잠시 후에 jam-si hu-e; **to be named ~ someone** 어떤 사람의 이름을 따서 이름 붙여지다 eo-tteon sa-ram-ui i-reum-eul tta-seo i-reum bu-chyeo-ji-da; **~ all** 결국 gyeol-guk, 역시 yeok-si

afternoon *n.* 오후 o-hu

aftershave *n.* 애프터 셰이브 로션 ae-peu-teo sye-i-beu ro-syeon

afterward *adv.* 뒤에 dwi-e, 나중에 na-jung-e, 그 후에 geu hu-e

again *adv.* 다시 da-si

against *prep.* …에 기대어 …e gi-dae-eo; …에 반대하여 …e ban-dae-ha-yeo; …에

대하여 ...e dae-ha-yeo; ~ **the law** 불법적
으로 bul-ppeop-jeog-eu-ro; ~ **the wind** 바
람을 거슬러 ba-ram-eul geo-seul-leo
age *n.* 나이 na-i, *(hon.)* 연세 yeon-se
agency *n.* 대리권 dae-ri-kkwon, 대리점 dae-
ri-jeom; 주선 ju-seon, 알선 al-sseon
agenda *n.* 안건 an-kkeon, 의사일정
ui-sa-il-jjeong
agent *n.* 대행자 dae-haeng-ja; **travel** ~ 여행
사 직원 yeo-haeng-sa jig-won
aggravate *vt.* 악화시키다 a-kwa-si-ki-da; 괴
롭히다 goe-ro pi da
aggregation *n.* 집합 ji-pap, 집합체 ji-pap-che
aggressive *adj.* 호전적인 ho-jeon-jeog-in; 진
취적인 jin-chwi-jeog-in
agile *adj.* 재빠른 jae-ppa-reun
aging *n.* 노화 no-hwa, 숙성 suk-seong
agitate *vt.* 흔들어대다 heun-deul-eo-dae-da,
동요시키다 dong-yo-si-ki-da
agitation *n.* 동요 dong-yo, 선동 seon-dong
aglow *adv.* 타올라서 ta-ol-la-seo, 흥분
하여 heung-bun-ha-yeo, 발개져서
bal-gae-jyeo-seo
ago *adj.* ...전 ...jeon; *adv.* ...전에
...jeon-e; **several years** ~ 몇년 전에
myeon-nyeon-jeon-e
agonize *vt.* 괴롭히다 goe-ro-pi-da; *vi.* 괴로
워하다 goe-ro-wo-ha-da
agony *n.* 고민 go-min; 고통 go-tong
agree *vt.* 동의하다 dong-ui-ha-da; 합치하다
hap-chi-ha-da
agreeable *adj.* 마음에 드는 ma-eum-e deu-
neun; 동조적인 dong-jo-jeog-in
agreement *n.* 동의 dong-ui; 합치 hap-chi; 협
정 hyeop-jeong
agricultural *adj.* 농업의 nong-eob-ui
agriculture *n.* 농업 nong-eop; 농학 nong-hak
ahead *adj.* ...전 ...jeon, 틀에박힌 teul-e-ba-
kin, 정직한 jeong-ji-kan, 상식적인 sang-
sik-jeog-in; **to get** ~ 앞서다 ap-seo-da; **to
go** ~ 진전하다 jin-jeon-ha-da, 진보하다
jin-bo-ha-da; ~ **of** 앞에 ap-e, 앞서 ap-seo;
adv. ...전에 ...jeon-e, ...에 앞서서 ...e
ap-seo-seo; **straight** ~ 똑바로 ttok-ba-ro
aid *n.* 원조 won-jo; *vt.* 원조하다
won-jo-ha-da
AIDS *n. abbr.* **Acquired Immunodeficiency
Syndrome** 에이즈 e-i-jeu

aim *n.* 표적 pyo-jeok; 목적 mok-jeok; *vt.*
겨냥하다 gyeo-nyang-ha-da; 목표하다
mok-pyo-ha-da
air *n.* 공기 gong-gi; **to go by** ~ 비행기로
가다 bi-haeng-gi-ro ga-da; ~ **bag** 에어백
e-eo-baek; ~**force base** 공군기지 gong-
gun-gi-ji; ~ **filter** 에어필터 e-eo-pil-teo;
~ **freight** 항공화물 hang-gong-hwa-mul;
~ **pocket** 에어포켓 e-eo-po-ket
air-condition *vt.* 냉방하다 naeng-bang-ha-
da; ~**ed** 냉방장치가 된 naeng-bang-jang-
chi-ga doen
air conditioner *n.* 에어컨 e-eo-keon
air-conditioning *n.* 냉방 naeng-bang
air force *n.* 공군 gong-gun
airline *n.* 항공사 hang-gong-sa
airmail *n.* 항공우편 hang-gong-u-pyeon
airplane *n.* 비행기 bi-haeng-gi, 항공기
hang-gong-gi
airport *n.* 공항 gong-hang, 비행장
bi-haeng-jang
aisle *n.* 통로 tong-no
alarm *n.* 경보 gyeong-bo; *vt.* 경보를 발하다
gyeong-bo-reul bal-ha-da
alarm clock *n.* 자명(종) 시계 ja-myeong-
(jong) si-gye
Alaska *n.* 알래스카 al-lae-seu-ka
album *n.* 앨범 ael-beom, 사진첩 sa-jin-cheop
alcohol *n.* 알코올 al-ko-ol; 술 sul; **rubbing** ~
소독용 알코올 so-dong-nyong al-ko-ol
alcoholic *n.* 알코올중독자 al-ko-ol jung-dok-
ja; *adj.* 알콜중독의 al-kol jung-dog-ui; 알
콜의 al-kol-ui
alcove *n.* 골방 gol-bang; 정자 jeon-ja
ale *n.* 에일 e-il
alert *n.* 경계 gyeong-gye; *vt.* 경계시키다
gyeong-gye-si-ki-da
algae *n.* 조류 jo-ryu, 바닷말 ba-dan-mal
Algeria *n.* 알제리아 al-je-ri-a
alien *n. (foreign)* 외국인 oe-gug-in; *adj.* 외
국의 oe-gug-ui; *(extraterrestrial)* 외계인
oe-gye-in; *adj.* 외계의 oe-gye-ui
align *vt.* 정렬시키다 jeong-nyeol-si-ki-da, 제
휴시키다 je-hyu-si-ki-da
alignment *n.* 정렬 jeong-nyeol, 제휴 je-hyu
alike *adj.* 비슷한 bi-seu-tan
alive *adj.* 살아있는 sal-a-in-neun; 생생한
saeng-saeng-han

alkali *n.* 알칼리 al-kal-li

all *adj.* 모든 mo-deun; **~day tour** 24시간 투어 i-sip-sa-si-gan tu-eo; **~night restaurant** 철야영업 식당 cheol-ya-yeong-eop sik-dang; **~ over** 완전히 끝나다 wan-jeon-hi kkeun-na-da; **~ right** 괜찮다 gwaen-chan-ta, 좋다 jo-ta

allegory *n.* 풍유 pung-yu, 우화 u-hwa

allergic *adj.* 알레르기의 al-le-reu-gi-ui; **to be ~ to** …에 알레르기가 있다 …e al-le-reu-gi-ga it-da

allergy *n.* 알레르기 al-le-reu-gi

alleviate *vt.* 덜다 deol-da, 완화하다 wan-hwa-ha-da, 경감시키다 gyeong-gam-si-ki-da

alley *n.* 뒷골목 dwit-gol-mok

alliance *n.* 동맹 dong-maeng

allocate *vt.* 할당하다 hal-ttang-ha-da, 배분하다 bae-bun-ha-da, 배치하다 bae-chi-ha-da

allocation *n.* 할당 hal-ttang, 배분 bae-bun, 배치 bae-chi

allow *vt.* 허락하다 heo-ra-ka-da; 인정하다 in-jeong-ha-da

allowance *n.* *(bonus)* 수당 su-dang; *(grant, supply)* 급여액 geub-yeo-aek; *(pocket money)* 용돈 yong-tton; *(deduction, subtraction)* 공제 gong-je, *(deduction, discount)* 할인 hal-in; *(consideration)* 참작 cham-jak

allude *vt.* 암시하다 am-si-ha-da, 언급하다 eon-geu-pa-da

allusive *adj.* 암시적인 am-si-jeog-in, 넌지시 말하는 neon-ji-si mal-ha-neun

ally *n.* 동맹국 dong-maeng-guk; *vt.* 동맹하다 dong-maeng-ha-da

almighty *adj.* 전능한 jeon-neung-han, 대단한 dae-dan-han; *n.* 전능자 jeon-neung-ja

almond *n.* 아몬드 a-mon-deu

almost *adv.* 거의 geo-ui

aloe *n.* 알로에 al-lo-e

aloft *adv.* 위에 wi-e; 높이 no-pi

alone *adj.* 혼자 hon-ja

along *adv.* …와 함께 …wa ham-kke, … 과 함께 …gwa ham-kke; …을 따라 …eul tta-ra,… 를 따라 … reul tta-ra

aloud *adv.* 크게 keu-ge

alphabet *n.* 알파벳 al-pa-bet

alphabetize *vt.* 철자순으로 배열하다 chol-jja-sun-eu-ro bae-yeol-ha-da

Alps *n.* 알프스산 al-peu-sseu san

already *adv.* 벌써 beol-sseo

also *adv.* 또한 tto-han

altar *n.* 제단 je-dan

alter *vt.* 바꾸다 ba-kku-da; 변하다 byeon-ha-da

alteration *n.* 수선 su-seon; 변경 byeon-gyeong

alternate *adj.* 교대의 gyo-dae-ui, 교류의 gyo-ryu-ui; *vt.* 교대하다 gyo-dae-ha-da, 교류하다 gyo-ryu-ha-da

alternative *adj.* 양자택일의 yang-ja-taeg-il-ui, 대안의 dae-an-ui

although *conj.* …이긴 하지만 …i-gin ha-ji-man

altitude *n.* 높이 nop-i, 고도 go-do

alto *n.* 알토 al-to

altogether *adv.* 다 같이 da ga-chi

aluminum *n.* 알루미늄 al-lu-mi-nyum

always *adv.* 항상 hang-sang, 늘 neul

a.m. *adj. abbr.* **ante meridiem (before noon)** 오전 o-jeon; **7:30 ~ 오전 7시 30분** o-jeon il-gop-si sam-sip-bun

amateur *n.* 아마추어 a-ma-chu-eo

amaze *vt.* 깜짝 놀라게 하다 kkam-jjak nol-la-ge ha-da

amazing *adj.* 놀랄만한 nol-lal-man-han; 두드러진 du-deu-reo-jin

Amazon *n.* 아마존강 a-ma-jon-gang

ambassador *n.* 대사 dae-sa

ambidexterous *adj.* 양손잡이의 yang-son-jab-i-ui; 두마음을 품은 du-ma-eum-eul pum-eun

ambiguous *adj.* 애매한 ae-mae-han

ambition *n.* 야망 ya-mang, 야심 ya-sim

ambitious *adj.* 야심적인 ya-sim-jeog-in

ambulance *n.* 앰뷸런스 aem-byul-leon-sseu

ambush *n.* 매복 mae-bok

amend *vt.* 고치다 go-chi-da, 수정하다 su-jeong-ha-da

amendment *n.* 변경 byeon-gyeong; 수정조항 su-jeong-jo-hang

America *n.* 아메리카 a-me-ri-ka, 미국 mi-guk

American *n.* 미국사람 mi-guk-sa-ram; *adj.* 미국의 mi-gug-ui

Americanize *vt., vi.* 미국화되다
mi-gu-kwa-doe-da

amid *prep.* ...의 한 가운데에 ...ui han
ga-un-de-e

ammonia *n.* 암모니아 am-mo-ni-a

amnesia *n.* 기억상실증 gi-eok-sang-sil-
jjeung, 건망증 geon-mang-jjeung

among *prep.* ...(의) 사이에 ...(ui) sa-i-e; ~
many people 많은 사람들 사이에 man-
eun sa-ram-deul sa-i-e

amorous *adj.* 요염한 yo-yeom-han, 호색적
인 ho-saek-jeog-in

amount *n.* 양 yang; *vi.* 총계가...에 이르다
chong-gye-ga...e i-reu-da; **Total income
-s to ten million won** 수입 총계가
1000만원에 이른다 su-ip chong-gye-ga
cheon-man-won-e i-reun-da

amphibian *n.* 양서류 yang-seo-ryu

amphibious *adj.* 양서류의 yang-seo-ryu-ui;
수륙양용의 su-ryuk-yang-yong-ui

ample *adj.* 충분한 chung-bun-han; 넓은
neolb-eun

amplifier *n.* 앰프 aem-peu, 확성기
hwak-seong-gi

amplify *vt.* 확대하다 hwak-dae-ha-da; 증폭
하다 jeung po-ka-da

amputate *vt.* 절단하다 jeol-ttan-ha-da

amputation *n.* 절단 jeol-ttan

Amsterdam *n.* 암스테르담
am-seu-te-reu-dam

amuse *vt.* 즐겁게 하다 jeul-geop-ge ha-da

amusement *n.* 오락 o-rak

anal *adj.* 항문 부근의 hang-mun bu-geun-ui,
항문의 hang-mun-ui

analogue *n.* 아날로그 a-nal-lo-geu; 비슷한
물건 bi-seu-tan mul-geon

analogy *n.* 유사 yu-sa; 유추 yu-chu

analysis *n.* 분석 bun-seok

analyze *vt.* 분석하다 bun-seo-ka-da

anarchy *n.* 무정부 상태 mu-jeong-bu sang-
tae, 무질서 mu-jil-sseo

anatomy *n.* 해부 hae-bu; 해부학 he-bu-hak

ancestor *n.* 조상 jo-sang, 선조 seon-jo

anchor *n.* 닻 dat; *vi.* 닻을 내리다 da-cheul
nae-ri-da

anchorman *n.* 앵커맨 aeng-keo-maen, 앵커
aeng-keo

anchovy *n.* 멸치 myeol-chi, 멸치류
myeol-chi-ryu

ancient *adj.* 고대의 go-dae-ui, 옛날의
yen-nal-ui

and *conj.* 그리고 geu-ri-go; ~ **so forth** 등등
deung-deung

Andes *n.* 안데스 산맥 an-de-sseu san-maek

anecdote *n.* 일화 il-hwa

anemia *n.* 빈혈 bin-hyeol

anemone *n.* 아네모네 a-ne-mo-ne

anesthesia *n.* 마취 ma-chwi

angel *n.* 천사 cheon-sa

anger *n.* 분노 bun-no; *vi.* 화내다 hwa-nae-da

angle *n.* 각 gak, 각도 gak-do; 모 mo, 모퉁이
mo-tung-i

angry *adj.* 화가 난 hwa-ga nan

anguish *n.* 번민 beon-min, 고뇌 go-noe

animal *n.* 동물 dong-mul

animate *vt.* 생명을 불어넣다 saeng-
myeong-eul bul-eo-neo-ta; 활기를 주다
hwal gi-reul ju-da

animation *n.* 생기 saeng-gi, 활기
hwal-gi; 동화 dong-hwa, 만화영화
man-hwa-yeong-hwa

ankle *n.* 발목 bal-mok

annals *n.* 연대기 yeon-dae-gi, 기록 gi-rok;
연보 yeon-bo

annex *n.* 별관 byeol-gwan; 부속서류 bu-sok-
seo-ryu; 부록 bu-rok

anniversary *n.* 기념일 gi-nyeom-il

announce *vt.* 알리다 al-li-da

announcement *n.* 발표 bal-pyo, 공표 gong-
pyo, 알림 al-lim

announcer *n.* 발표자 bal-pyo-ja; 아나운서
a-na-un-seo

annoy *vt.* 괴롭히다 goe-ro-pi da

annoyance *n.* 성가심 seong-ga-sim

annual *adj.* 연간 yeon-gan; 일년의
il-lyeon-ui

annul *vt.* 무효화하다 mu-hyo-hwa-ha-da, 취
소하다 chwi-so-ha-da

anonymous *adj.* 익명의 ing-myeong-ui, 작
자불명의 jak-ja-bul-myeong-ui

another *adj.* 또 다른 tto da-reun

answer *n.* 대답 dae-dap, 해답 hae-dap;
vt., vi. 대답하다 dae-da-pa-da, 응하다
eung-ha-da

ant *n.* 개미 gae-mi

antagonism *n.* 반대 ban-dae, 반항심 ban-hang-sim, 적대심 jeok-dae-sim

antarctic *adj.* 남극의 nam-geug-ui, 남극지방의 nam-geuk-ji-bang-ui; *n.* 남극지방 nam-geuk-ji-bang, 남극해 nam-geu-kae

Antarctica *n.* 남극대륙 nam-geuk-dae-ryuk

antecedent *adj.* 앞서는 ap-seo-neun, 이전의 i-jeon-ui; *n.* 전례 jeol-lye; 선행자 seon-haeng-ja

antenna *n.* 안테나 an-te-na

anthropology *n.* 인류학 il-lyu-hak

anti- *pref.* 반... ban...; ...반대 ...ban-dae

antibiotic *n.* 항생제 hang-saeng-je; *adj.* 항생의 hang-saeng-ui

antibody *n.* 항체 hang-che

anticipate *vt.* 예기하다 ye-gi-ha-da

anticipation *n.* 예감 ye-gam

antihistamine *n.* 항히스타민제 hang-hi-seu-ta-min-je

antique *n.* 골동품 gol-ttong-pum; *adj.* 고대의 go-dae-ui; ~ shop 골동품 가게 gol-ttong-pum ga-ge

antiseptic *n.* 방부제 bang-bu-je; *adj.* 방부의 bang-bu-ui

antonym *n.* 반의어 ban-ui-eo, 반대어 ban-dae-eo

anxiety *n.* 걱정 geok-jeong; 염원 yeom-won

anxious *adj* 걱정하는 geok-jeong-ha-neun; 염원하는 yeom-won-ha-neun

any *adj.* 어떤 eo-tteon; 아무 a-mu

anybody *pron.* 누구든지 nu-gu-deun-ji; 누군가 nu-gun-ga; 누구도 nu-gu-do

anyone *pron.* 누구든지 nu-gu-deun-ji; 누군가 nu-gun-ga; 누구도 nu-gu-do

anything *pron.* 뭐든지 mwo-deun-ji; 뭔가 mwon-ga; 아무것도 a-mu-geot-do

anytime *adv.* 언제든지 eon-je-deun-ji; 언젠가 eon-jen-ga

anywhere *adv.* 어디든지 eo-di-deun-ji; 어디엔가 eo-di-en-ga; 어디에도 eo-di-e-do

apart *adv.* 떨어져서 tteol-eo-jyeo-seo

apartment *n.* 아파트 a-pa-teu

apathetic *adj.* 냉담한 naeng-dam-han

ape *n.* 원숭이 won-sung-i

apologize *vi.* 사과하다 sa-gwa-ha-da

apology *n.* 사과 sa-gwa

apparatus *n.* 장치 jang-chi, 기구 gi-gu

apparel *n.* 의복 ui-bok, 의상 ui-sang

apparent *adj.* 또렷한 tto-ryeo-tan; 외견상의 oe-gyeon-sang-ui

appeal *vi.* 호소하다 ho-so-ha-da; 흥미를 끌다 heung-mi-reul kkeul-da; 항소하다 hang-so-ha-da

appear *vi.* 나타나다 na-ta-na-da; ...처럼 보이다 ...cheo-reom bo-i-da

appearance *n.* 출현 chul-hyeon; 외관 oe-gwan, 겉모양 geon-mo-yang; 기색 gi-saek

appendicitis *n.* 맹장염 maeng-jang-nyeom

appendix *n.* 맹장 maeng-jang; 부록 bu-rok

appetite *n.* 식욕 sig-yok, 식성 sik-seong

appetizer *n.* 애피타이저 ae-pi-ta-i-jeo, 전채요리 jeon-chae-yo-ri

applaud *vt.* 박수를 치다 bak-su-reul chi-da

applause *n.* 박수갈채 bak-su-gal-chae

apple *n.* 사과 sa-gwa

appliance *n.* 기계 gi-gye; 가전제품 ga-jeon-je-pum

application *n.* 신청 sin-cheong, 지원 ji-won

apply *vt.* 적용하다 jeog-yong-ha-da; 약을 바르다 yag-eul ba-reu-da; *vi.* 꼭 맞다 kkong mat-da; 신청하다 sin-cheong-ha-da, 지원하다 ji-won-ha-da

appoint *vt.* 임명하다 im-myeong-ha-da; 지정하다 ji-jeong-ha-da

appointment *n.* 임명 im-myeong; 지정 ji-jeong; 약속 yak-sok

appraisal *n.* 평가 pyeong-kka; 감정 gam-jeong

appreciate *vt. (to appraise, to rate)* 평가하다 pyeong-kka-ha-da; *(to appreciate one's true worth)* 진가를 인정하다 jin-kka-reul in-jeong-ha-da; *(to enjoy)* 감상하다 gam-sang-ha-da; *(to thank, to be thankful)* 고맙게 여기다 go-map-ge yeo-gi-da

appreciation *n.* 평가 pyeong-kka; 감상 gam-sang; 감사 gam-sa

approach *n.* 접근 jeop-geun; *vi.* 접근하다 jeop-geun-ha-da

appropriate *adj.* 적당한 jeok-dang-han; 특유한 teug-yu-han

approval *n.* 승인 seung-in, 찬성 chan-seong, 인가 in-ga

approve *vt.* 승인하다 seung-in-ha-da, 찬성하다 chan-seong-ha-da

approximate *adj.* 대략 dae-ryak; *vt.* ...에 접근하다 ...e jeop-geun-ha-da

apricot *n.* 살구 sal-gu

April *n.* 4월 sa-wol; **in ~** 4월에 sa-wol-e; **the month of ~** 4월달 sa-wol-ttal

apron *n.* 앞치마 ap-chi-ma

apropos *adj.* 적절한 jeok-jeol-han, 알맞은 al-maj-eun; *adv.* 적절하게 jeok-jeol-ha-ge, 때마침 ttae-ma-chim

apt *adj.* ...하기 쉬운 ...ha-gi swi-un; 적절한 jeok-jeol-han; 적성이 있는 jeok-seong-i in-neun

aptitude *n.* 적성 jeok-seong, 경향 gyeong-hyang, 소질 so-jil

aquafarm *n.* 양식장 yang-sik-jang, 양어장 yang-eo-jang

aquarium *n.* 수족관 su-jok-gwan

aquatic *adj.* 물의 mul-ui, 물속에 사는 mul-sog-e sa-neun

Arab *n.* 아랍 a-rap; *adj.* 아랍의 a-rab-ui

Arabic *n.* 아랍사람 a-rap-sa-ram, 아라비아말 a-ra-bi-a mal

arbitrary *adj.* 임의적인 im-ui-jeog-in; 독단적인 dok-dan-jeog-in

arbitrate *vt.* 중재하다 jung-jae-ha-da, 조정하다 jo-jeong-ha-da

arc *n.* 원호 won-ho, 호형 ho-hyeong, 아크 a-keu

arch *n.* 아치 a-chi

archaeological *adj.* 고고학의 go-go-hag-ui

archaeology *n.* 고고학 go-go-hak

archaic *adj.* 고풍의 go-pung-ui, 낡은 nalg-eun

archery *n.* 궁술 gung-sul, 활쏘기 hal-sso-gi

architect *n.* 건축가 geon-chuk-ga

architectural *adj.* 건축학의 geon-chu-kag-ui; 건축상의 geon-chuk-sang-ui

architecture *n.* 건축양식 geon-chug-yang-sik; 건축학 geon-chu-kak

archive *n.* 기록 보관소 gi-rok bo-gwan-so, 문서 보관소 mun-seo bo-gwan-so; 고문서 go-mun-seo, 공문서 gong-mun-seo

arctic *adj.* 북극의 buk-geug-ui; *n.* 북극지방 buk-geuk-ji-bang, 북극해 buk-geu-kae

Arctic Ocean *n.* 북극해 buk-geu-kae

area *n.* 지역 ji-yeok

arena *n.* 경기장 gyeong-gi-jang, 투기장 tu-gi-jang; 활동무대 hwal-ttong-mu-dae

Argentina *n.* 아르헨티나 a-reu-hen-ti-na

argue *vt.* 논쟁하다 non-jaeng-ha-da; 주장하다 ju-jang-ha-da

argument *n.* 주장 ju-jang; 요지 yo-ji

aria *n.* 아리아 a-ri-a, 영창 yeong-chang

arise *vi.* 일어나다 il-eo-na-da; 나타나다 na-ta-na-da

aristocratic *adj.* 귀족의 gwi-jog-ui, 귀족적인 gwi-jok-jeog-in; 배타적인 bae-ta-jeog-in; 당당한 dang-dang-han

arithmetic *n.* 산수 san-su

ark *n.* 방주 bang-ju, 궤 gwe, 상자 sang-ja

arm *n.* 팔 pal; 무기 mu-gi

armada *n.* 함대 ham-dae, 군용 비행단 gun-yong bi-haeng-dan

armchair *n.* 안락의자 al-lag-ui-ja

armed *adj.* 무장한 mu-jang-han

armful *n.* 한아름 han-a-reum

armor *n.* 갑옷 gab-ot

armpit *n.* 겨드랑이 gyeo-deu-rang-i

army *n.* 군대 gun-dae; 육군 yuk-gun

aroma *n.* 향기 hyang-gi

around *adv.* 주위에 ju-wi-e, 주변에 ju-byeon-e; *prep.* ...의 주변에 ...ui ju-byeon-e

arouse *vt.* 깨우다 kkae-u-da; 자극하다 ja-geu-ka-da

arrange *vt.* 배열하다 bae-yeol-ha-da; 정리하다 jeong-ni-ha-da; 조정하다 jo-jeong-ha-da

arrangement *n.* 배열 bae-yeol; 정리 jeong-ni; 조정 jo-jeong

arrest *n.* 체포 che-po; *vt.* 체포하다 che-po-ha-da

arrival *n.* 도착 do-chak

arrive *vi.* 도착하다 do-cha-ka-da

arrogance *n.* 거만 geo-man

arrogant *adj.* 거만한 geo-man-han

arrow *n.* 화살 hwa-sal

arrowhead *n.* 화살촉 hwa-sal-chok

arson *n.* 방화 bang-hwa, 방화죄 bang-hwa-jjoe

art *n.* 예술 ye-sul; 미술 mi-sul

artery *n.* *(blood)* 동맥 dong-maek; *(roadway)* 주요도로 ju-yo-do-ro

article *n.* *(an item)* 품목 pum-mok; *(in a newspaper)* 기사 gi-sa; *(grammar)* 문법 mun-ppeop

articulate *vt.* 또렷하게 발음하다 tto-ryeo-ta-ge bal-eum-ha-da, 명료하게 표현하다 myeong-nyo-ha-ge pyo-hyeon-ha-da; *adj.* 또렷한 tto-ryeo-tan, 명확한 myeong-hwa-kan

articulation *n.* 또렷한 발음 tto-ryeo-tan bal-eum

artifact *n.* 인공품 in-gong-pum

artificial *adj.* 인공적인 in-gong-jeog-in; 부자연스러운 bu-ja-yeon-seu-reo-un

artisan *n.* 장인 jang-in, 기술자 gi-sul-jja

artist *n.* 예술가 ye-sul-ga; 미술가 mi-sul-ga

artistic *adj.* 예술적인 ye-sul-jjeog-in; 미술의 mi-sul-ui

as *adv.* ...만큼 ...man-keum, ...와 같은 정도로 ...wa gat-eun jeong-do-ro; *conj.* ...처럼 ...cheo-reom, ...하고 있을 때 ...ho-go iss-eul ttae, ...이므로 ...i-meu-ro, ...같은 ...gat-eun; *prep.* ...으로서 ...eu-ro-sseo, ...같은 ...gat-eun, ...처럼 ...cheo-reom: ~...~... ...와 같은 정도로 ...wa gat-eun jeong-do-ro, ...와 마찬가지로 ...wa ma-chan-ga-ji-ro, ...와 같이 ...wa ga-chi, ...만큼 ...man-keum, ...처럼 ...cheo-reom; ~ **is** 있는 그대로 in-neun geu-dae-ro; ~ **far** ~ **... is concerned** ...하는 한 ...ha-neun han; ~ **for** ...에 관한한 ...e gwan-han-han; ~ **well** 게다가 ge-da-ga, 그 위에 geu wi-e; 마찬가지로 ma-chan-ga-ji-ro, ...와 같이 ...wa ga-chi

ascend *vt., vi.* 오르다 o-reu-da, 올라가다 ol-la-ga-da

aseptic *adj.* 무균의 mu-gyun-ui, 방부처치의 bang-bu-cheo-chi-ui; *n.* 방부제 bang-bu-je

ash *n.* 재 jae

ashamed *adj.* 부끄럽게 생각하는 bu-kkeu-reop-ge saeng-ga-ka-neun

ashore *adv.* 물가로 mul-kka-ro, 물가에 mul-kka-e, 육상에 yuk-sang-e

ashtray *n.* 재떨이 jae-tteol-i

Asia *n.* 아시아 a-si-a, 동양 dong-yang

aside *adv.* 곁에 gyeot-e, ...은 제쳐두고 ...eun je-chyeo-du-go, ...는 제쳐두고 ...neun je-chyeo-du-go; ~ **from** ...을제외하고...eul je-oe-ha-go, ...를 제외하고 ...reul je-oe-ha-go

ask *vt.* 물어보다 mul-eo-bo-da, 요청하다 yo-cheong-ha-da

asleep *adj.* 잠든 jam-deun; *adv.* 잠들어 jam-deul-eo

aspect *n.* 양상 yang-sang, 국면 gung-myeon

asphalt *n.* 아스팔트 a-seu-pal-teu

aspiration *n.* 포부 po-bu, 대망 dae-mang, 열망 yeol-mang

aspire *vi.* 열망하다 yeol-mang-ha-da, 동경하다 dong-gyeong-ha-da

aspirin *n.* 아스피린 a-seu-pi-rin

assassinate *vt.* 암살하다 am-sal-ha-da

assassination *n.* 암살 am-sal

assault *n.* 맹공격 maeng-gong-gyeok, 폭행 po-kaeng; 습격 seup-gyeok; *vt.* 맹공격하다 maeng-gong-gyeo-ka-da

assemble *vt.* 모으다 mo-eu-da, 조립하다 jo-ri-pa-da; *vi.* 모이다 mo-i-da

assembly *n.* 집회 ji-poe, 모임 mo-im

assent *vi.* 동의하다 dong-ui-ha-da, 찬성하다 chan-seong-ha-da

assert *vt.* 단언하다 dan-eon-ha-da

assertion *n.* 단언 dan-eon, 주장 ju-jang

assertive *adj.* 단정적인 dan-jeong-jeog-in, 독단적인 dok-dan-jeog-in

assessment *n. (imposition, incidence)* 부과 bu-gwa; *(appraisal, evaluation)* 평가 pyeong-kka; *(tax)* 세액 se-aek, 사정액 sa-jeong-aek

asset *n. (property, estate)* 자산 ja-san, 재산 jae-san; *(a strength)* 강점 gang-jjeom, *(merit, good point)* 장점 jang-jjeom

assign *vt.* 배당하다 bae-dang-ha-da; 지명하다 ji-myeong-ha-da, 선임하다 seon-im-ha-da

assignment *n. (distribution, division)* 할당 hal-ttang; *(mission, duty)* 임무 im-mu; *(task, research subject)* 연구과제 yeon-gu-gwa-je; *(designation, appointment)* 지정 ji-jeong

assimilate *vt.* 동화하다 dong-hwa-ha-da

assist *vt.* 조력하다 jo-ryeo-ka-da, 돕다 dop-da

assistance *n.* 원조 won-jo, 조력 jo-ryeok

assistant *n.* 조력자 jo-ryeok-ja, 도우미 do-u-mi

associate *n.* 동료 dong-nyo; *vt.* 가입시키다 ga-ip-si-ki-da; 연상하다 yeon-sang-ha-da; *vi.* 교제하다 gyo-je-ha-da

association *n.* 연합 yeon-hap; 교제 gyo-je; 협회 hyeo-poe; 연상 yeon-sang

assort *vt.* 분류하다 bul-lyu-ha-da, 분류하여 정리하다 bul-lyu-ha-yeo jeong-ni-ha-da; 구색을 갖추다 gu-saeg-eul gat-chu-da; *vi.* 어울리다 eo-ul-li-da, 조화하다 jo-hwa-ha-da; 교제하다 gyo-je-ha-da

assume *vt.* 추정하다 chu-jeong-ha-da; 떠맡다 tteo-mat-da

assumed *adj.* 가장한 ga-jang-han; 가정한 ga-jeong-han

assumption *n.* 가정 ga-jeong; 인수 in-su; 횡령 hoeng-nyeong; 거만 geo-man

assurance *n.* 보증 bo-jeung, 확신 hwak-sin

assure *vt.* 보증하다 bo-jeung-ha-da, 확실히 하다 hwak-sil-hi ha-da

asterisk *n.* 별표 byeol-pyo; *vt.* 별표를 붙이다 byeol-pyo-reul bu-chi-da

asteroid *n.* 소행성 so-haeng-seong; *adj.* 별모양의 byeol-mo-yang-ui

asthma *n.* 천식 cheon-sik

asthmatic *adj.* 천식의 cheon-sig-ui; *n.* 천식 환자 cheon-si-kwan-ja

astonish *vt.* 놀라게 하다 nol-la-ge ha-da

astray *adj.* 길을 잃은 gil-eul il-eun; *adv.* 길을 잃어 gil-eul il-eo

astringent *n.* 아스트린젠트 a-seu-teu-rin-jen-teu; *adj.* 수렴성의 su-ryeom-sseong-ui

astrology *n.* 점성술 jeom-seong-sul

astronaut *n.* 우주비행사 u-ju-bi-haeng-sa

astronomy *n.* 천문학 cheon-mun-hak

astute *adj.* 기민한 gi-min-han

asylum *n.* 수용소 su-yong-so, 도피처 do-pi-cheo, 보호소 bo-ho-so, 보호시설 bo-ho-si-seol

asymmetry *n.* 불균형 bul-gyun-hyeong, 비대칭 bi-dae-ching

at *prep.* ...에서 ...e-seo, ...에 ...e, ...으로 ...eu-ro, ...을 향하여 ...eul hyang-ha-yeo, ...한 상태에 ...han sang-tae-e

atheism *n.* 무신론 mu-sil-lon

atheist *n.* 무신론자 mu-sil-lon-ja

Athens *n.* 아테네 a-te-ne

atherosclerosis *n.* 동맥경화증 dong-maek-gyeong-hwa-jjeung

athlete *n.* 운동선수 un-dong-seon-su

athletics *n. pl.* 운동경기 un-dong-gyeong-gi

Atlantic Ocean *n.* 대서양 dae-seo-yang

atlas *n.* 지도책 ji-do-chaek

ATM *n. abbr.* **Automated Teller Machine** 현금자동지급기 hyeon-geum-ja-dong-ji-geup-gi

atmosphere *n.* 대기 dae-gi; 분위기 bun-wi-gi, 환경 hwan-gyeong

atom *n.* 원자 won-ja

attach *vt.* 붙이다 bu-chi-da; 애착심을 갖게 하다 ae-chak-sim-eul gat-ge-ha-da

attachment *n.* 부착 bu-chak, 부착물 bu-chang-mul; 애착 ae-chak; 압류 am-nyu

attack *n.* 공격 gong-gyeok; *vt.* 공격하다 gong-gyeo-ka-da

attain *vt., vi.* 달성하다 dal-sseong-ha-da, 도달하다 do-dal-ha-da

attempt *n.* 시도 si-do; *vt.* 시도하다 si-do-ha-da

attend *vt. (to go to)* 다니다 da-ni-da, *(to be present at)* 출석하다 chul-sseo-ka-da; *(to take care, to serve)* 시중들다 si-jung-deul-da; *(to accompany, to go with)* 수반하다 su-ban-ha-da

attendance *n.* 출석 chul-sseok; 시중 si-jung

attendant *n.* 수행원 su-haeng-won; 참석자 cham-seok-ja

attention *n.* 주의 ju-ui, 집중 jip-jung; **to pay ~ to** ...에 주의를 집중하다 ...e ju-ui-reul jip-jung-ha-da

attentive *adj.* 주의깊은 ju-ui-gi-peun; 친절한 chin-jeol-han, 정중한 jeong-jung-han

attic *n.* 다락 da-rak

attitude *n.* 태도 tae-do

attorney *n.* 변호사 byeon-ho-sa, 대리인 dae-ri-in

attract *vt.* 마음을 끌다 ma-eum-eul kkeul-da, 주의를 끌다 ju-ui-reul kkeul-da, 유인하다 yu-in-ha-da

attraction *n.* 매력 mae-ryeok, 유혹 yu-hok

attractive *adj.* 매력적인 mae-ryeok-jeog-in

attribute *n.* 속성 sok-seong, 특질 teuk-jil; *vt.* 돌리다 dol-li-da, 탓하다 ta-ta-da

auction *n.* 경매 gyeong-mae; *vt.* 경매하다 gyeong-mae-ha-da

audible *adj.* 들리는 deul-li-neun, 들을 수 있는 deu-eul ssu in-neun

audience *n.* 청중 cheong-jung, 청취자 cheong-chwi-ja

audiovisual *adj.* 시청각의 si-cheong-gag-ui; *n.* 시청각 교재 si-cheong-gak-gyo-jae

audit *n.* 회계감사 hoe-gye-gam-sa, 결산 gyeol-ssan; *vt.* 회계감사하다 hoe-gye-gam-sa-ha-da; 청강하다 cheong-gang-ha-da

audition *n. (hearing ability)* 청력 cheong-nyeok, *(the sense of hearing)* 청각 cheong-gak; *(screening, inspection)* 오디션 o-di-syeon, *(inspection, screening)* 심사 sim-sa; *vt., vi.* 오디션을 하다 o-di-syeon-eul ha-da

auditorium *n.* 청중석 cheong-jung-seok, 방청석 bang-cheong-seok; 강당 gang-dang, 공회당 gong-hoe-dang

auditory *adj.* 청각의 cheong-gag-ui, 귀의 gwi-ui; *n.* 청중석 cheong-jung-seok, 청중 cheong-jung

augment *vt.* 늘리다 neul-li-da

August *n.* 8월 pal-wol

aunt *n. (mother's sister)* 이모 i-mo, *(father's sister)* 고모 go-mo, *(father's brother's wife)* 숙모 sung-mo, *(mother's brother's wife)* 외숙모 oe-sung-mo

aurora *n.* 오로라 o-ro-ra, 극광 geuk-gwang

Australia *n.* 오스트레일리아 o-seu-teu-re-il-li-a

Australian *n.* 오스트레일리아 사람 o-seu-teu-re-il-li-a sa-ram; *adj.* 오스트레일리아의 o-seu-teu-re-il-li-a-ui

Austria *n.* 오스트리아 o-seu-teu-ri-a

authentic *adj.* 진정한 jin-jeong-han; 믿을 만한 mid-eul man-han

author *n.* 저자 jeo-ja

authority *n.* 권위 gwon-wi, 권한 gwon-han

authorization *n.* 권한 위임 gwon-han wi-im; 허가서 heo-ga-seo

authorize *vt.* 권한을 주다 gwon-han-eul ju-da, 위임하다 wi-im-ha-da

authorized *adj.* 권한을 부여받은 gwon-han-eul bu-yeo-bad-eun, 공인된 gong-in-doen

autism *n.* 자폐증 ja-pye-jjeung

autobiography *n.* 자서전 ja-seo-jeon

autocracy *n.* 독재권 dok-jae-kkwon, 독재정치 dok-jae-jeung-chi

automatic *adj.* 자동의 ja-dong-ui; ~ **transmission** 자동변속장치 ja-dong-byeon-sok-jang-chi

automation *n.* 자동조작 ja-dong-jo-jak

automobile *n.* 자동차 ja-dong-cha

autonomous *adj.* 자치적인 ja-chi-jeog-in

autonomy *n.* 자치권 ja-chi-kkwon, 자치단체 ja-chi-dan-che, 자치 ja-chi

autopsy *n.* 해부 hae-bu

autoreverse *n.* 오토리버스 o-to-ri-beo-sseu

autumn *n.* 가을 ga-eul

availability *n.* 이용가능성 i-yong-ga-neung-sseong

available *adj.* 이용가능한 i-yong-ga-neung-han; 입수가능한 ip-su-ga-neung-han

avalanche *n.* 눈사태 nun-sa-tae, 산사태 san-sa-tae

avenue *n.* 도로 do-ro; …로 …ro

average *n.* 평균 pyeong-gyun, 보통 bo-tong; *adj.* 평균의 pyeong-gyun-ui, 보통의 bo-tong-ui; **on** ~ 평균하여 pyeong-gyun-ha-yeo

aviation *n.* 비행 bi-haeng

avoid *vt.* 피하다 pi-ha-da

avoidance *n.* 기피 gi-pi, 도피 do-pi

awake *vi.* 깨다 kkae-da, 일어나다 il-eo-na-da

award *n.* 상 sang, 상품 sang-pum; *vt.* 상을 주다 sang-eul ju-da

aware *adj.* 의식하는 ui-si-ka-neun

away *adj.* 떨어진 tteol-eo-jin; 사라진 sa-ra-jin; *adv.* 떨어져서 tteol-eo-jyeo-seo; 사라져 sa-ra-jyeo

awesome *adj.* 장엄한 jang-eom-han, 황공한 hwang-gong-han

awful *adj.* 두려운 du-ryeo-un; 대단한 dae-dan-han; *adv.* 몹시 mop-si

awfully *adv.* 대단히 dae-dan-hi, 몹시 mop-si, 무섭게 mu-seop-ge

awkward *adj.* 거북한 geo-bu-kan

ax *n.* 도끼 do-kki

axis *n.* 축 chuk

axle *n.* 축 chuk

B

B.A. *n. abbr. Bachelor of Arts* 학사학위 hak-sa-hag-wi

babble *vi.* 종알거리다 jong-al-geo-ri-da, 재잘거리다 jae-jal-geo-ri-da

baby *n.* 아기 a-gi, 애 ae

baby-sitter *n.* 애 봐주는 사람 ae bwa-ju-neun sa-ram

bachelor *n.* 미혼남자 mi-hon nam-ja

back *n.* 뒤 dwi, 등 deung; *(part of something)* **In the ~ of the car** 치 뒤쪽에 cha dwi-jjog-e; *(of the body)* **~ pain** 요통 yo-tong; *adj.* 뒤의 dwi-ui, **~ door** 뒷문 dwin-mun; *adv.* 뒤에 dwi-e; **to be ~** 뒤에 있다 dwi-e it-da; *v.* **to be ~** 후퇴하다 hu-toe-ha-da; 후원하다 hu-won-ha-da; **to ~ down** 뒤로 물러나다 dwi-ro mul-leo-na-da; **to ~ up (a car, etc.)** 후원하다 hu-won-ha-da; 정체하다 jeong-che-ha-da

backbite *vt., vi.* 뒤에서 험담하다 dwi-e-seo heom-dam-ha-da

backboard *n. (sports)* 백보드 baek-bo-deu

backbone *n.* 등뼈 beung-ppyeo

backfire *n.* 맞불 mat-bul

background *n.* 배경 bae-gyeong; 경력 gyeong-nyeok

backpack *n.* 배낭 bae-nang

backseat *n.* 뒷자리 dwit ja ri, 보잘것 없는 지위 bo-jal-kkeot eom-neun ji-wi

backstage *adj.* 분장실에 있는 bun-janq-sil-se in-neun, 막후의 ma-ku-ui

backswing *n. (tennis)* 백스윙 back-seu-wing

backtalk *n.* 말대꾸 mal-dae-kku

backward *adj.* 뒤쪽의 dwi-jjog-ui; *adv.* 뒤쪽으로 dwi-jjog-eu-ro

backyard *n.* 뒷뜰 dwit-tteul

bacon *n.* 베이컨 be-i-keon

bacteria *n.* 박테리아 bak-te-ri-a

bacterial *adj.* 세균성의 se-gyun-sseong-ui

bad *adj.* 나쁜 na-ppeun

badge *n.* 배지 bae-jji

badly *adv.* 나쁘게 na-ppeu-ge; 서투르게 seo-tu-reu-ge

badminton *n.* 배드민턴 be-deu-min-teon

bag *n.* 가방 ga-bang; **paper ~** 종이 jong-i, **plastic ~** 비닐가방 bi-nil ga-bang

bagel *n.* 베이글 be-i-geul

baggage *n.* 여행용짐 yeo-haeng-nyong jim

bail *n.* 보석 bo-seok; 보석금 bo-seok-geum

bait *n.* 미끼 mi-kki

bake *vt.* 굽다 gup-da

baker *n.* 빵집 ppang-jjip; 제과업자 je-gwa-eop-ja

bakery *n.* 제과점 je-gwa-jeom, 빵집 ppang-jjip

balance *n.* 평균 pyeong-gyun, 균형 gyun-hyeong; 예금잔고 ye geum jan go

balcony *n.* 발코니 bal-ko-ni

bald *adj.* 대머리의 dae-meo-ri-ui; 무모한 mu-mo-han; *n.* 대머리 dae-meo-ri

Balkans *n.* 발칸반도 bal-kan-ban-do

ball *n.* 공 gong; 공놀이 gong-nol-i; 탄환 tan-hwan, 포환 po-hwan; 무도회 mu-do-hoe

ball-point pen *n.* 볼펜 bol-pen

ballad *n.* 발라드 bal-la-deu, 민요 min-yo

ballerina *n.* 발레리나 bal-le-ri-na

ballet *n.* 발레 bal-le

balloon *n.* 기구 gi-gu

ballot *n.* 무기명 투표 mu-gi-myeong tu-pyo, 무기명 투표용지 mu-gi-myeong tu-pyo-yong-ji, 투표총수 tu-pyo-chong-su

ballpark *n.* 야구장 ya-gu-jang

ballroom *n.* 무도장 mu-do-jang, 무도실 mu-do-sil, 댄스장 daen-sseu-jang

balmy *adj.* 향유의 hyang-yu-ui, 상쾌한 sang-kwae-han

Baltic Sea *n.* 발틱해 bal-ti-kae

bamboo *n.* 대나무 dae-na-mu

ban *n.* 금지령 geum-ji-ryeong; 파문 pa-mun, 추방 chu bang; *vt.* 금지하다 geum-ji-ha-da; 파문하다 pa-mun-ha-da

banana *n.* 바나나 ba-na-na

band *n.* 악단 ak-dan; 밴드 baen-deu; **broad~** 다중 통신망 da-jung tong-sin-mang; *(internet)* 광주파수대의 gwang-ju-pa-su-ttae-ui

band-aid *n.* 밴드 baen-deu, 반창고 ban-chang-go

bandage *n.* 붕대 bung-dae; *vt.* 붕대를 감다 bung-dae-reul gam-tta

bang *vt.* 탕 치다 tang chi-da; 발포하다 bal-po-ha-da; 두드리다 du-deu-ri-da, 쾅

닫다 kwang dat-da; *n.* 강타 gang-ta, 포성
po-seong; 앞머리 am-meo-ri
Bangladesh *n.* 방글라데시 bang-geul-la-de-si
banish *vt.* 추방하다 chu-bang-ha-da, 내쫓
다 nae-jjot-da
banister *n.* 난간 nan-gan
bank *n.* 은행 eun-haeng; 둑 ttuk, 제
방 je-bang; ~ **card** 현금카드
hyeon-geum-ka-deu
banker *n.* 은행가 eun-haeng-ga; **investment** ~ 투자전문 은행가 tu-ja-jeon-mun
eun-haeng-ga
bankrupt *n.* 파산자 pa-san-ja; *adj.* 파산한
pa-san-han; *vt.* 파산시키다 pa-san-si-ki-da
bankruptcy *n.* 파산 pa-san, 파탄 pa-tan
banner *n.* 배너 bae-neo, 기 gi
banquet *n.* 연회 yeon-hoe
baptism *n.* 세례 se-rye, 침례 chim-nye
baptize *vt.* 세례를 주다 se-rye-reul ju-da
bar *n.* 막대기 mak-dae-gi; 법정 beop-jjeong;
(pub) 술집 sul-jjip; *(bar-shaped object)* 막
대기 모양의 물건mak-dae-gi mo-yang-ui
mul-geon; **chocolate** ~ 초콜릿 cho-kol-lit;
~ **of soap** 비누 bi-nu
barbarian *n.* 야만인 ya-man-in, 미개인
mi-gae-in; *adj.* 미개인의 mi-gae-in-ui
barbecue *n.* 바비큐 ba-bi-kyu; *vt.* 바비큐하
다 ba-bi-kyu-ha-da
barber *n.* 이발사 i-bal-sa
barbershop *n.* 이발소 i-bal-sso
bare *adj.* 벌거벗은 beol-geo-beos-eun; 휑한
hweng-han; 부족한 bu-jo-kan
barefoot *adj.* 맨발의 maen-bal-ui
barely *adv.* 간신히 gan-sin-hi, 겨우 gyeo-u;
노골적으로 no-gol-jjeog-eu-ro, 드러내놓
고 deu-reo-nae-no-ko
bargain *n.* 매매 mae-mae; 바겐세일 ba-gen-
sse-il; 싼물건 ssan-mul-geon
bark *n.* *(of a dog)* 개 짖는 소리 gae jin-neun
so-ri; *(of a tree)* 나무껍질 na-mu-kkeop-jil;
vi. 컹컹짖다 keong-keong-jit-da, 호통치
다 ho-tong-chi-da
barley *n.* 보리 bo-ri
barn *n.* 헛간 heot-gan, 광 gwang
barometer *n.* 기압계 gi-ap-gye
baroque *adj.* 바로크 양식의 ba-ro-keu yang-
sig-ui, 괴상한 goe-sang-han

barrack *n.* 병영 byeong-yeong; 헛간
heot-gan
barrel *n.* 배럴 bae-reol
barren *adj.* 불모의 bul-mo-ui; 불임의
bul-im-ui
barricade *n.* 바리케이트 ba-ri-ke-i-teu, 장
애물 jang-ae-mul; *vt.* 바리케이트를 치다
ba-ri-ke-i-teu-reul chi-da
barrier *n.* 울타리 ul-ta-ri, 장벽 jang-byeok
bartender *n.* 바텐더 ba-ten-deo
barter *vt.* 교환하다 gyo-hwan-ha-da; *n.* 물물
교환 mul-mul-gyo-hwan
base *n.* 기지 gi-ji; 기초 gi-cho; *vt.* 기초를 두
다 gi-cho-reul du-da
baseball *n.* 야구 ya-gu
basement *n.* 지하실 ji-ha-sil
bashful *adj.* 수줍어하는 su-jub-eo-ha-neun,
부끄럼타는 bu-kkeu-reom-ta-neun
basic *adj.* 기초의 gi-cho-ui, 기본의
gi-bon-ui
basically *adv.* 근본적으로 geun-bon-jeog-
eu-ro, 원래 wol-lae
basin *n.* 물동이 mul-ttong-i; 웅덩이 ung-
deong-i; 분지 bun-ji
basis *n.* 기초 gi-cho
basket *n.* 바구니 ba-gu-ni
basketball *n.* 농구 nong-gu
bass *n.* *(sound)* 베이스 be-i-sseu
bat *n.* *(stick)* 방망이 bang-mang-i, 배트
bae-teu; *(animal)* 박쥐 bak-jwi
batch *n.* 한솥 han-sot, 일회분 il-hoe-bun
bath *n.* 목욕 mog-yok
bathe *vt.* 목욕시키다 mog-yok-si-ki-da; *vi.* 목
욕하다 mog-yo-ka-da
bathhouse *n.* 목욕탕 mog-yok-tang
bathroom *n.* 욕실 yok-sil, 화장실hwa-jang-sil
bathtub *n.* 욕조 yok-jo
batter *n.* 타자 ta-ja; 반죽 ban-juk; *vt.* 난타
하다 nan-ta-ha-da, 강타하다 gang-ta-ha-
da; **pancake** ~ 팬케익 반죽 paen-ke-ik
ban-juk; **The storm ~ed the coast** 폭풍이
해안을 강타했다 pok-pung-i hae-an-eul
gang-ta-haet-da
battery *n.* 배터리 bae-teo-ri, 건전지
geon-jeon-ji
battle *n.* 싸움 ssa-um, 전쟁 jeon-jaeng; *vt.* 싸
우다 ssa-u-da, 전쟁하다 jeon-jaeng-ha-da

battlefield *n.* 싸움터 ssa-um-teo, 전장 jeon-jang

bay *n.* 만 man

B.C. *abbr.* **Before Christ** 기원전 gi-won-jeon

be *vi.* 이다 i-da; 있다 it-da; ...고 있다 ...go it-da; 되다 doe-da

beach *n.* 바닷가 ba-dat-ga, 해안 hae-an

bead *n.* 구슬 gu-seul, 비드 bi-deu

beak *n.* 부리 bu-ri

beam *n.* 대들보 dae-deul-ppo; 광선 gwang-seon

bean *n.* 콩 kong

bear *n.* 곰 gom; *vt.* 참다 cham-tta; 나르다 na-reu-da; 지탱하다 ji-taeng-ha-da; 견디다 gyeon-di-da

beard *n.* 턱수염 teok-su-yeom

bearing *n.* 태도 tae-do; 관계 gwan-gye

beast *n.* 짐승 jim-seung

beat *n.* 박자 bak-ja, 비트 bi-teu; *vt.* 치다 chi-da; 뛰다 ttwi-da; 이기다 i-gi-da

beautiful *adj.* 아름다운 a-reum-da-un

beauty *n.* 미 mi, 아름다움 a-reum-da-um; 미인 mi-in

beauty shop *n.* 미장원 mi-jang-won, 미용실 mi-yong-sil

because *conj.* ...기 때문에 ...gi ttae-mun-e, ...아서 ...a-seo, ... 어서 ... eo-seo; ~ **the girl is smart** 그 여자아이가 똑똑하기 때문에 geu yeo-ja-a-i-ga ttok-tto-ka-gi ttae-mun-e

become *vi.* ... 이 되다 ... i doe-da, ... 가 되다 ... ga doe-da; ...에 어울리다 ...e eo-ul-li-da; **He became vegetarian** 그는 채식주의자가 되었다 geu-neun chae-sik-ju-ui-ja-ga doe-eot-da; **Does this skirt ~ me** 이 치마가 나한테 잘 어울려요 i chi-ma-ga na-han-te jal eo-ul-lyeo-yo

bed *n.* 침대 chim-dae

bedroom *n.* 침실 chim-sil, 방 bang

bee *n.* 벌 beol; ~**hive** 벌집 beol-jjip, 벌통 beol-tong; ~**keeping** 양봉 yang-bong

beef *n.* 쇠고기 soe-go-gi, 소고기 so-go-gi

beefsteak *n.* 비프스테이크 bi-peu-seu-te-i-keu

beep *n.* 경적 gyeong-jeok, 신호 sin-ho

beer *n.* 맥주 maek-ju; ~**house** 맥주집 maek-ju-jjip

beeswax *n.* 밀랍 mil-lap

beet *n.* 비트 bi-teu

beetle *n.* 딱정벌레 ttak-jeong-beol-le

before *prep.* ...기 전에 ...gi jeon-e; ...앞에 ...ap-e; **He is walking ~ me** 그 사람이 내 앞에 걸어간다 geu sa-ram-i nae ap-e geol-eo-gan-da

beforehand *adv.* 미리 mi-ri, 벌써 beol-sseo

beg *vi.* 간청하다 gan-cheong-ha-da; 빌다 bil-da

beggar *n.* 거지 geo-ji

begin *vi.* 시작하다 si-ja-ka-da, 시작되다 si-jak-doe-da

beginner *n.* 초보자 cho-bo-ja

beginning *n.* 처음 cheo-eum, 시작 si-jak; 시초 si-cho, 발단 bal-ttan

behalf *n.* 측 cheuk; 이익 i-ik; **on ~ of** ...을 대신하여...eul dae-sin-ha-yeo, ... 를 대신하여 ... reul dae-sin-ha-yeo, ...을 위하여...eul wi-ha-yeo, ... 를 위하여 ... reul wi-ha-yeo

behave *vi.* 행동하다 haeng-dong-ha-da; 예절바르게 행동하다 ye-jeol-ba-reu-ge haeng-dong-ha-da

behavior *n.* 행동 haeng-dong, 행위 haeng-wi

behead *vt.* 목을 베다 mog-eul be-da, 참수하다 cham-su-ha-da

behind *prep.* ...뒤에 ...dwi-e, ...보다 늦게 ...bo-da neut-ge; ~ **schedule** 예정시간보다 늦게 ye-jeong-si-gan-bo-da neut ge

behold *vi.* 보다 bo-da, 바라보다 ba-ra-bo-da

beige *n.* 베이지색 be-i-ji-saek

Beijing *n.* 베이징 be-i-jjing

being *n.* 존재 jon-jae; 존재자 jon-jae-ja, 실존 sil-jjon, 실재 sil-jjae; 생존 saeng-jon, 인생 in-saeng

belated *adj.* 늦은 neuj-eun, 구식의 gu-sig-ui, 시대에 뒤떨어진 si-dae-e dwi-tteol-eo-jin

Belgium *n.* 벨기에 bel-gi-e

belief *n.* 믿음 mid-eum; 확신 hwak-sin, 신뢰 sil-loe; 신앙 sin-ang

believe *vt.* 믿다 mit-da, 신뢰하다 sil-loe-ha-da

believer *n.* 신자 sin-ja

bell *n.* 종 jong; ~**tower** 종루 jong-nu

bellboy *n.* 호텔 종업원 ho-tel jong-eob-won

belly *n.* 배 bae, 복부 bok-bu; ~ **button** 배꼽 bae-kkop

belong *vi.* ...(의) 것이다 ...(ui) keos-i-da,
...에 속하다 ...e so-ka-da; **This ball-point
pen ~s to me** 이 볼펜은 내 것이다 i
bol-pen-eun nae geos-i-da; **We both ~ to
the same team** 우리는 둘 다 같은 팀에
속해 있다 u-ri-neun dul da gat-eun tim-e
so-kae it-da

belongings *n. pl.* 소유물 so-yu-mul, 소지품
so-ji-pum

beloved *adj.* 사랑하는 sa-rang-ha-neun, 귀
여워하는 gwi-yeo-wo-ha-neun

below *prep.* ...밑에 ...mit-e, ...아래 ...a-
rae; ...에 미치지 못하여 ...e mi-chi-ji
mo-ta-yeo

belt *n.* 벨트 bel-teu, 허리띠 heo-ri-tti;
conveyor ~ 벨트 컨베이어 bel-teu
keon-be-i-eo

bench *n.* 벤치 ben-chi

bench mark *n.* 기준 gi-jun

bend *vt.* 구부리다 gu-bu-ri-da; *vi.* 구부러지
다 gu-bu-reo-ji-da

beneath *prep.* ...밑에 ...mit-e, ...아래에
...a-rae-e; **The boat sank ~ the waves** 배
가 파도 밑에 가라앉았다 bae-ga pa-do
mit-e ga-ra-anj-at-da

benediction *n.* 축복 chuk-bok, 감사기도
gam-sa-gi-do; 축성식 chuk-seong-sik

benefaction *n.* 자비 ja-bi, 선행 seon-haeng,
자선 ja-seon, 은혜 eun-hye

beneficent *adj.* 자선심이 많은 ja-seon-sim-i
man-eun

beneficial *adj.* 유리한 yu-ri-han, 유익한
yu-i-kan

benefit *n.* 이익 i-ik; *vt.* ...에(게) 이롭다
...e-(ge) i-rop-da; *vi.* 이익을 얻다 i-ig-eul
eot-da

Bengal *n.* 벵갈 beng-gal

benign *adj.* 친절한 chin-jeol-han, 온화한
on-hwa-han

bent *adj.* 굽은 gub-eun; 마음을 쏟은 ma-
eum-eul ssod-eun

Bering Strait *n.* 베링해협 be-ring-hae-hyeop

Berlin *n.* 베를린 be-reul-lin

Bermuda Triangle *n.* 버뮤다 삼각지 beo-
mu-da sam-gak-ji

berry *n.* 딸기류 ttal-gi-ryu

beside *prep.* ...옆에 ...yeop-e; ...와 비교하
여 ...wa bi-gyo-ha-yeo; ...을 벗어나서

...eul beos-eo-na-seo; **Please sit ~ me** 제
옆에 앉으세요 je yeop-e anj-eu-se-yo

besides *prep.* ...외에도 ...oe-e-do, ...밖에
도 ...bakk-e-do ~ **that, there are a lot of
interesting things** 그 밖에도 재미있는
것들이 많이 있다 geu bakk-e-do jae-mi-
in-neun geot-deul-i man-i it-da

best *n.* 최선 choe-seon; *adj.* 가장 좋은 ga-
jang jo-eun; *adv.* 가장 좋게 ga-jang-jo-ke

best-known *adj.* 가장 잘 알려진 ga-jang jal
al-lyeo-jin

best man *n.* 신랑 들러리 sil-lang deul-leo-ri

bestow *vt.* 주다 ju-da, 수여하다 su-yeo-
ha-da; 사용하다 sa-yong-ha-da, 바치다
ba-chi-da

best seller *n.* 베스트 셀러 be-seu-teu ssel-leo

bet *n.* 내기 nae-gi; *vt.* 내기를 하다 nae-gi-
reul ha-da; 단언하다 dan-eon-ha-da

betray *vt.* 배반하다 bae-ban-ha-da; 팔다
pal-da; 누설하다 nu-seol-ha-da; 무심코
드러내다 mu-sim-ko deu-reo-nae-da

betrayer *n.* 매국노 mae-gung-no, 배신자
bae-sin-ja, 밀고자 mil-go-ja

betrayal *n.* 배반 bae-ban, 밀고 mil-go; 내통
nae-tong

better *adj.* 더 좋은 deo jo-eun; *adv.* 더 좋게
deo jo-ke

betting *n.* 내기 nae-gi

between *prep.* ...(의)사이에 ...(ui) sa-i-e;
...의 중간에 ...(ui) jung-gan-e; ...의 사이
에서 ...(ui) sa-i-e-seo

beverage *n.* 음료수 eum-nyo-su

beware *vt.* 조심하다 jo-sim-ha-da

bewilder *vt.* 당황하다 dang-hwang-ha-da,
어리둥절하다 eo-ri-dung-jeol-ha-da

bewitch *vt.* 요술을 걸다 yo-sul-eul geol-da

beyond *prep.* ...을 넘어서 ...eul neom-
eo-seo; ...을 지나서 ...eul ji-na-seo;
...의 범위를 넘어서 ...ui beom-wi-reul
neom-eo-seo

biannual *adj.* 일년에 두번의 il-nyeon-e du-
beon-ui, 반년마다의 ban-nyeon-ma-da-ui

bias *n.* 성향 seong-hyang, 편향 pyeon-
hyang, 선입견 seon-ip-gyeon; 사선
sa-seon, 바이어스 ba-i-eo-sseu; 치우침
chi-u-chim

biased *adj.* 치우친 chi-u-chin

bib *n.* 턱받기 teok-bat-gi, 턱받이 teok-ba-ji

bible *n.* 성경 seong-gyeong

bibliography *n.* 서지학 seo-ji-hak; 서적해제 seo-ji-hae-je; 관계서적 목록 gwan-gye-seo-jeok mong-nok, 저서목록 jeo-seo-mong-nok

bicentennial *adj.* 200년간 계속되는 i-baeng-nyeon-gan gye-sok-doe-neun, 200년마다의 i-baeng-nyeon-ma-da-ui

bicycle *n.* 자전거 ja-jeon-geo

bid *v.* 명령하다 myeong-nyeong-ha-da; 말하다 mal-ha-da; 값을 매기다 gaps-eul mae-gi-da; *n.* 입찰 ip-chal; 시도 si-do; 입회권유 i-poe-gwon-yu

biennial *adj.* 2년마다의 i-nyeon-ma-da-ui, 2년에 한번의 i-nyeon-e han-beon-ui

bifocal *adj.* 초점이 둘인 cho-jjeom-i dul-in; *n.* 두초점 렌즈 du-cho-jjeom len-jeu, 두초점 안경 du-cho-jjeom an-gyeong

big *adj.* 큰 keun; 위대한 wi-dae-han, 관대한 gwan-dae-han

big brother *n.* 독재자 dok-jae-ja; 독재국가 dok-jae-guk-ga

big business *n.* 재벌 jae-beol, 대기업 dae-gi-eop

bighearted *adj.* 관대한 gwan-dae-han, 친절한 chin-jeol-han, 대범한 dae-beom-han

bigmouth *n.* 수다쟁이 su-da-jaeng-i, 허풍쟁이heo-pung-jaeng-i; 입큰 물고기류 ip-keun mul-kko-gi-ryu

bigname *n.* 명사 myeong-sa, 유명인 yu-mycong-in, 인기스타 in-kki-seu-ta

bike *n.* 자전거 ja-jeon-geo

bikeway *n.* 자전거 전용도로 ja-jeon-geo jeon-yong-do-ro

bikini *n.* 비키니 수영복 bi-ki-ni su-yeong-bok

bilateral *adj.* 두 글자의 du geul-jja-ui; 양쪽면이 있는 yang-jjong-myeon-i in-neun, 좌우 양측의 jwa-u yang-cheug-ui

bilingual *adj.* 이중언어의 i-jung-eon-eo-ui, 두 나라 말을 하는 du na-ra mal-eul ha-neun; *n.* 이중언어화자 i-jung-eon-eo-hwa-ja

bill *n.* 계산서 gye-san-seo; 지폐 ji-pye; 법안 beob-an; 삐라 ppi-ra; 목록 mong-nok; 부리 bu-ri; *vt.* 계산서를 보내다 gye-san-seo-reul bo-nae-da; 표로 만들다 pyo-ro man-deul-da; 발표하다 bal-pyo-ha-da

billboard *n.* 광고 게시판 gwang-go ge-si-pan

billiards *n.* 당구 dang-gu

billion *n.* 10억 sib-eok; 막대한 수 mak-dae-han su

billionaire *n.* 억만장자 eong-man-jang-ja

bimonthly *adj., adv.* 격월의 gyeog-wol-ui, 한달씩 거른 han-dal-ssik geo-reun; 월2회의 wol i-hoe-ui

bin *n.* 통 tong

bind *vt.* 묶다 muk-da; 얽매다 eong-mae-da, 속박하다 sok-ba-ka-da

binding *adj.* 구속력있는 gu-song-nyeog-in-neun, 의무적인 ui-mu-jeog-in; *n.* 제본 je-bon, 바인딩 ba-in-ding

bingo *n.* 빙고게임 bing-go-kke-im

binocular *n.* 쌍안경 ssang-an-gyeong

biochemical *adj.* 생화학적인 saeng-hwa-hak-jeog-in, 생회학의 saeng-hwa-hag ui

biochemistry *n.* 생화학 saeng-hwa-hak

bioengineering *n.* 생체공학 saeng-che-gong-hak, 생명공학 saeng-myeong-gong-hak

biography *n.* 전기 jeon-gi, 일대기 il-ttae-gi

biological *adj.* 생물학의 saeng-mul-hag-ui

biologist *n.* 생물학자 saeng-mul-hak-ja

biology *n.* 생물학 saeng-mul-hak

bionic *adj.* 초인적인 cho-in-jeog-in, 사이보그 같은 ssa-i-bo-geu gat-eun; 생체공학의 saeng-che-gong-hag-ui

bipolar *adj.* 양극의 yang-geug-ui, 양극시의 yang-geuk-ji-ui; 상반하는 sang-ban-ha-neun

bird *n.* 새 sae

birdcage *n.* 새장 sae-jang

birdie *n. (animal)* 작은 새 jag-eun sae; *(sport term)* 버니 beo-di; *vt.* 버디를 치다 beo-di-reul chi-da

birdseed *n.* 새모이 sae-mo-i

birth *n.* 탄생 tan-saeng, 태어남 tae-eo-nam; ~ **certificate** 출생증명서 chul-ssaeng-jeung-myeong-seo; ~ **control** 피임 pi-im; **date of** ~ 생일 saeng-il

birthday *n.* 생일 saeng-il, *(hon.)* 생신 saeng-sin

birth place *n.* 출생지 chul-ssaeng-ji, 고향 go-hyang

birthrate *n.* 출생률 chul-ssaeng-nyul

biscuit *n.* 비스켓 bi-seu-ket

bisect *vt.* 양분하다 yang-bun-ha-da, 2등분 하다 i-deung-bun-ha-da

bisexual *adj.* 양성의 yang-seong-ui; 양성을 좋아하는 yang-seong-eul jo-a-ha-neun; *n.* 양성애자 yang-seong-ae-ja

bishop *n.* 주교 ju-gyo

bit *n.* 작은 조각 jag-eun jo-gak, 조금 jo-geum

bite *n.* 한 입 han nip; 묾 mum; 물린 상처 mul-lin sang-cheo; *vt.* 물다 mul-da; 자극하 다 ja-geu-ka-da

biting *adj.* 무는 mu-neun, 물어뜯는 mul-eo-tteun-neun; 날카로운 nal-ka-ro-un, 살을 에는 듯한 sal-eul e-neun-deu-tan

bitter *adj.* 쓴 sseun; 모진 mo-jin, 지독한 ji-do-kan

bitterly *adv.* 심하게 sim-ha-ge, 따끔하게 tta-kkeum-ha-ge, 지독하게 ji-do-ka-ge, 가 혹하게 ga-ho-ka-ge; 쓰게 sseu-ge

bitterness *n.* 쓴맛 sseun-mat, 실랄함 sil-lal-ham, 비통함 bi-tong-ham

biweekly *adj.* 격주의 gyeok-ju-ui; *adv.* 격주 로 gyeok-ju-ro

biyearly *adj., adv.* 2년에 한번 i-nyeon-e han-beon; 1년에 두번 il-lyeon-e du-beon

bizarre *adj.* 기괴한 gi-goe-han, 이상한 i-sang-han

blab *vt., vi.* 주책없이 떠들다 ju-chaeg-eops-i tteo-deul-da

black *adj.* 까만 kka-man; *n.* 까만색 kka-man-saek; 까만 옷 kka-man-ot

black-and-white *adj.* 흑백의 heuk-baeg-ui; 흑백이 뚜렷한 heuk-baeg-i ttu-ryeo-han

black bear *n.* 흑곰 heuk-gom

black belt *n.* 까만띠 kka-man-tti

blackberry *n.* 블랙베리 beul-laek-be-ri

blackboard *n.* 칠판 chil-pan

black hole *n.* 블랙홀 beul-lae-kol

blacklist *n.* 블랙리스트 beul-laek-li-seu-teu

blackmail *vt.* 공갈하다 gong-gal-ha-da, 약 탈하다 yak-tal-ha-da; *n.* 공갈 gong-gal, 약 탈 yak-tal

black market *n.* 암시장 am-si-jang, 암거 래 am-geo-rae; *vt.* 암거래하다 am-geo-rae-ha-da; ~er *n.* 암거래 상인 am-geo-rae sang-in

black-out *n.* 정전 jeong-jeon; *(curfew)* 등화 관제 deung-hwa-gwan-je

black pepper *n.* 후추 hu-chu

Black Sea *n.* 흑해 heu-kae

blacksmith *n.* 대장장이 dae-jang-jang-i, 제 철공 je-cheol-gong

black tea *n.* 홍차 hong-cha

bladder *n.* 방광 bang-gwang; 부레 bu-re

blade *n.* 칼날 kal-lal

blame *n.* 비난 bi-nan; *vt.* 나무라다 na-mu-ra-da, 비난하다 bi-nan-ha-da

blameless *adj.* 죄가 없는 joe-ga eom-neun, 결백한 gyeol-bae-kan

bland *adj.* 온화한 on-hwa-han, 부드러운 bu-deu-reo-un; 자극성이 적은 ja-geuk-seong-i jeog-eun; 김빠진 gim-ppa-jin, 재 미없는 jae-mi-eom-neun

blank *n.* 공백 gong-baek, 공란 gong-nan; 백 지 baek-ji; *adj.* 공백의 gong-baeg-ui, 백 지의 baek-ji-ui; 멍한 meong-han, 얼빠진 eol-ppa-jin

blank check *n.* 백지수표 baek-ji-su-pyo; 백 지위임 baek-ji-wi-im

blanket *n.* 담요 dam-nyo; *vt.* 담요로 덮 다 dam-nyo-ro deop-da, 전면을 뒤덮다 jeon-myeon-eul dwi-deop-da

blare *vt., vi.* 울려터지다 ul-lyeo-teo-ji-da, 쾅 쾅 울리다 kwang-kwang ul-li-da; 큰 소리 로 외치다 keun so-ri-ro oe-chi-da

blast *n.* 돌풍 dol-pung; 폭발 pok-bal; *vt.* 큰 소리를 내다 keun so-ri-reul nae-da, 폭발 하다 pok-bal-ha-da

blast-off *n.* 발사 bal-ssa, 이륙 i-ryuk

blaze *n.* 불길 bul-kkil; 번쩍거림 beon-jjeok-geo-rim; *vt.* 타오르다 ta-o-reu-da, 빛나다 bin-na-da, 번쩍이다 beon-jjeog-i-da; 격노 하다 gyeong-no-ha-da

bleach *n.* 표백 pyo-baek, 표백제 pyo-baek-je; *vt., vi.* 표백하다 pyo-bae-ka-da, 희게하 다 hi-ge-ha-da

bleak *adj.* 황폐한 hwang-pye-han

bleary *adj.* 눈이 흐린 nun-i heu-rin, 침침한 chim-chim-han, 희미한 hi-mi-han

bleed *vi.* 피를 흘리다 pi-reul heul-li-da

bleeding *n.* 출혈 chul-hyeol; *adj.* 출혈하는 chul-hyeol-ha-neun; 끔찍한 kkeum-jji-kan, 괴로운 goe-ro-un

blemish *n.* 흠 heum, 결점 gyeol-jjeom; *vt.* 더럽히다 deo-reo-pi-da, 손상시키다 son-sang-si-ki-da

blend *vt.* 섞다 seok-da; *vi.* 섞이다 seokk-i-da,
조화되다 jo-hwa-doe-da

blender *n.* 믹서 mik-seo

bless *vt.* 축복하다 chuk-bo-ka-da, 은총을 내
리다 eun-chong-eul nae-ri-da

blessed *adj.* 축복된 chuk-bok-doen, 축복받
은 chuk-bok-bad-eun

blessing *n.* 축복 chuk-bok

blind *adj.* 눈이 먼 nun-i meon; 맹목적인
maeng-mok-jeog-in; 알아보는 눈이 없는
al-a-bo-neun nun-i eom-neun; *n. (window
covering)* 블라인드 beul-la-in-deu

blind date *n.* 맞선 mat-seon

blindness *n.* 무분별 mu-bun-byeol; 무지 mu-ji

blind spot *n.* 맹점 maeng-jjeom, 자신이 잘
모르는 약점 ja-sin-i jal mo-reu-neun yak-
jeom, 난시청지역 nan-si-cheong-ji-yeok,
사각지대 sa-gak-ji-dae

blink *vi.* 깜빡이다 kkam-ppag-i-da

bliss *n.* 다시 없는 기쁨 da-si eom-neun
gi-ppeum

blister *n.* 물집 mul-jjip; *vt.* 물집이 생기다
mul-jjib-i saeng-gi-da

blizzard *n.* 눈보라 nun-bo-ra

bloat *vt.* 부풀게 하다 bu-pul-ge ha-da, 팽창
시키다 paeng-chang-si-ki-da; 자만심을 일
으키다 ja-man-sim-eul il-eu-ki-da

bloated *adj.* 부푼 bu-pun, 부은 bu-eun; 거만
한 geo-man-han

block *n.* 블록 beul-lok; 덩어리 deong-eo-ri;
받침 bat-chim; *vt.* 막다 mak-da, 봉쇄하다
bong-swae-ha-da

blockage *n.* 봉쇄 bong-swae, 방해 bang-hae;
방해물 bang-hae-mul

blockbuster *n.* 초대형 폭탄 cho-dae-hyeong
pok-tan; 영향력 있는 인물 yeong-
hyang-nyeog in-neun in-mul; 대히트작
dae-hi-teu-jak

blond *adj.* 금발의 geum-bal-ui; *n.* 금발
geum-bal

blood *n.* 피 pi, 혈액 hyeol-aek; ~ **pressure** 혈
압 hyeol-ap; ~ **bank** 혈액은행 hyeol-aeg-
eun-haeng; ~ **donor** 헌혈자 heon-hyeol-jja

blood group *n.* 혈액형 hyeol-ae-kyeong

bloodless *adj.* 창백한 chang-bae-kan, 핏기
없는 pit-gi-eom-neun; 피를 흘리지 않는
pi-reul heul-li-ji an-neun, 무혈의 mu-hyeol-
ui; 냉혈의 naeng-hyeol-ui, 무정한 mu-
jeong-han; 원기없는 won-gi-eom-neun

bloodshot *adj.* 충혈된 chung-hyeol-doen, 핏
발이 선 pit-bal-i seon; 혈안이 된 hyeol-
an-i doen

blood stain *n.* 핏자국 pit-ja-guk, 혈흔
hyeol-heun

blood stream *n.* 혈류 hyeol-lyu, 혈행
hyeol-haeng

bloodsucker *n.* 흡혈귀 heu-pyeol-gwi;
거머리 geo-meo-ri; 고리대금업자
go-ri-dae-geum-eop-ja

blood sugar *n.* 혈당 hyeol-ttang, 혈당량
hyeol-ttang-nyang

blood test *n.* 혈액검사 hyeol-aek-geom-sa

blood transfusion *n.* 수혈 su-hyeol

blood vessel *n.* 혈관 hyeol-gwan

bloody *adj.* 피의 pi-ui, 피가 나는 pi-ga
na-neun, 피비린내 나는 pi-bi-rin-nae
na-neun; 지독한 ji-do-kan, 엄청난
eom-cheong-nan

bloom *vi.* 꽃이 피다 kko-chi pi-da; *n.* 꽃 kkot,
개화기 gae-hwa-gi

blooming *adj.* 만발한 man-bal-han; 꽃 같은
kkot gat-eun, 활짝 꽃핀 hwal-jjak kkot-pin

blossom *n.* 개화 gae-hwa, 꽃이 핌 kkoch-i pim

blouse *n.* 블라우스 beul-la-u-sseu

blow *vt.* 불다 bul-da; 폭파하다 pok-pa-ha-
da; *vi.* 바람에 날리다 ba-ram-e nal-li-da;
울리다 ul-li-da; *n.* 강타 gang-ta, 구타
gu-ta; 타격 ta-gyeok, 쇼그 syo-keu

blow-dry *vt.* 머리를 드라이하다 meo-ri-reul
deu-ra-i-ha-da

blow hole *n.* 물뿜는 구멍 mul-ppum-neun
gu-meong, 통풍구 tong-pung-gu, 바람구
멍 ba-ram-kku meong

blowout *n.* 파열 pa-yeol, 파열된 구멍
pa-yeol-doen gu-meong; 증기분출
jeung-gi-bun-chul

blow up *n.* 파열 pa-yeol, 폭발 pok-bal; 확대
hwak-dae, 확대사진 hwak-dae-sa-jin; 발끈
화냄 bal-kkeun hwa-naem

blubber *n.* 고래기름 go-rae-gi-reum, 여분
의 지방 yeo-bun-ui ji-bang; *vt., vi.* 엉엉
울다 eong-eong-ul-da, 울면서 말하다
ul-myeon-seo mal-ha-da

blue *adj.* 파란 pa-ran

blueberry *n.* 블루베리 beul-lu-be-ri

blue blood *n.* 귀족혈통 gwi-jo-kyeol-tong, 명문가 myeong-mun-ga

blue chip *n.* 우량주 u-ryang-ju; *adj.* 확실한 hawk-sil-han, 우량한 u-ryang-han; 일류의 il-lyu-ui, 탁월한 tag-wol-han

blue collar *adj.* 작업복의 jag-eop-bog-ui, 육체 노동자의 yuk-che no-dong-ja-ui

blue jeans *n.* 청바지 cheong-ba-ji

blueprint *n.* 청사진 cheong-sa-jin, 자세한 계획 ja-se-han gye-hoek

blues *n.* 우울증 u-ul-jjeung, 우울한 기분 u-ul-han gi-bun; 블루스 beul-lu-sseu

blunt *adj.* 무딘 mu-din; 무뚝뚝한 mu-ttuk-ttu-kan

blush *vi.* 얼굴을 붉히다 eol-gul-eul bul-ki-da

board *n.* 널판지 neol-pan-ji, 판자 pan-ja; 식사 sik-sa; 위원회 wi-won-hoe; ~ **game** 보드게임 bo-deu-kke-im; **on** ~ 배 안에 bae an-e, 차 안에 cha an-e; *vt.* 판자를 치다 pan-ja-reul chi-da; 하숙시키다 ha-suk-si-ki-da

boarding house *n.* 하숙집 ha-suk-jip, 기숙사 gi-suk-sa

boarding pass *n.* 탑승권 tap-seung-kkwon

boarding school *n.* 기숙학교 gi-su-kak-gyo

boardwalk *n.* 바닷가 산책로 ba-dat-ga san-chaeng-no

boast *vt., vi.* 자랑하다 ja-rang-ha-da, 호언장담하다 ho-eon-jang-dam-ha-da, 큰소리치다 keun-so-ri-chi-da; *n.* 허풍 heo-pung, 자랑 ja-rang

boat *n.* 배 bae; ~**ing** 뱃놀이 baen-nol-i; ~**man** 뱃사공 baet-sa-gong

bobcat *n.* 살쾡이 sal-kwaeng-i

body *n.* 몸 mom; 몸통 mom-tong; 집단 jip-ttan

bodybuilding *n.* 보디빌딩 bo-di-bil-ding

bodyguard *n.* 보디가드 bo-di-ga-deu, 수행원 su-haeng-won

body language *n.* 바디랭귀지 ba-di-laeng-gwi-ji

body shop *n.* 자동차 수리센터 ja-dong-cha su-ri-ssen-teo

bog *n.* 습지 seup-ji, 수렁 su-reong

bogey *n. (sport term)* 보기 bo-gi; *vt.* 보기를 치다 bo-gi-reul chi-da

boil *n.* 끓임 kkeul-im; *vi.* 끓다 kkeul-ta; *vt.* 끓이다 kkeul-i-da

boiler *n.* 보일러 bo-il-leo; ~ **room** 보일러실 bo-il-leo-sil

boiling *adj.* 끓어 오르는 kkeul-eo o-reu-neun; 사나운 sa-na-un; 찌는듯한 jji-neun-deu-tan

bold *adj.* 대담한 dae-dam-han

bolt *n.* 볼트 bol-teu; 빗장 bit-jang; 전광 jeon-gwang

bomb *n.* 폭탄 pok-tan; *vi.* 폭발하다 pok-bal-ha-da; *vt.* 폭격하다 pok-gyeo-ka-da; ~ **proof** 방탄의 bang-tan-ui

bond *n.* 묶는 것 mung-neun geot, 속박 sok-bak, 결속 gyeol-ssok; 약정 yak-jeong, 계약 gye-yak; 채권 chae-kkwon, 차용증서 cha-yong-jeung-seo

bonded *adj.* 접착제로 붙인 jeop-chak-je-ro bu-chin; 담보가 붙은 dam-bo-ga but-eun, 공채로 보증된 gong-chae-ro bo-jeung-doen

bone *n.* 뼈 ppyeo; ~ **marrow** 골수 gol-ssu

bonnet *n.* 본네트 bon-ne-teu

bonus *n.* 보너스 bo-neo-sseu, 상여금 sang-yeo-geum

book *n.* 책 chaek

bookcase *n.* 책꽂이 chaek-kkoj-i, 책장 chaek-jang

booking *n.* 좌석예약 jwa-seog-ye-yak; 장부기입 jang-bu-gi-ip

booklet *n.* 소책자 so-chaek-ja

bookmark *n.* 서표 seo-pyo

book review *n.* 서평 seo-pyeong

bookshelf *n.* 책꽂이 chaek-kkoj-i, 서가 seo-ga

bookstore *n.* 책방 chaek-bang, 서점 seo-jeom

bookworm *n.* 독서광 dok-seo-gwang, 책벌레 chaek-beol-le

boom *n.* 쿵 울리는 소리 kung ul-li-neun so-ri; 붐 bum; *vt.* 큰 소리로 알리다 keun so-ri-ro al-li-da; 붐을 일으키다 bum-eul il-eu-ki-da

boomerang *n.* 부메랑 bu-me-rang

boost *n.* 밀어올림 mil-eo-ol-lim; 후원 hu-won, 경기부양 gyeong-gi-bu-yang; *vt.* 밀어올리다 mil-eo-ol-li-da; 후원하다 hu-won-ha-da, 경기를 부양하다 gyeong-gi-reul bu-yang-ha-da; 전압을 올리다 jeon-ab-eul ol-li-da

boot *n.* 부츠 bu-cheu

booth *n.* 매점 mae-jeom, 노점 no-jeom; 공중 전화 박스 gong-jung-jeon-hwa bak-seu

border *n.* 국경 guk-gyeong; 테두리 te-du-ri; 경계 gyeong-gye;

borderline *n.* 국경선 guk-gyeong-seon, 경계 선 gyeong-gye-seon

bore *vt., vi.* 구멍을 뚫다 gu-meong-eul tteul-ta, 꿰뚫다 kkwe-ttul-ta; 제치고 나아 가다 je-chi-go na-a-ga-da

boresome *adj.* 지루한 ji-ru-han, 진절머리나 는 jin-jeol-meo-ri-na-neun

boring *adj.* 지루한 ji-ru-han, 따분한 tta-bun-han

born *adj.* 태어난 tae-eo-nan; **I was ~ in California** 나는 캘리포니아에서 태 어났다 na-neun kael-li-po-ni-a-e-seo tae-eo-nat-da; **foreign ~** 외국출생 oe-guk-chul-ssaeng

Borneo *n.* 보루네오 bo-ru-ne-o

borrow *vt.* 빌리다 bil-li-da, 도입하다 do-i-pa-da

boss *n.* 상관 sang-gwan; 고용주 go-yong-ju

bossy *adj.* 으스대는 eu-seu-dae-neun, 두목 행세하는 du-mo-kaeng-se-ha-neun

botanical *adj.* 식물의 sing-mul-ui, 식물 학의 sing-mul-hag-ui; **~ garden** 식물원 sing-mul-won

both *adj., pron.* 양자의 yang-ja-ui, 쌍방의 ssang-bang-ui, 양쪽의 yang-jjog-ui

bother *vt.* 괴롭히다 goe-ro-pi-da, 귀찮게 하 다 gwi-chan-ke ha-da; *vi.* 걱정하다 geok-jeong-ha-da, 근심하다 geun-sim-ha-da

bothersome *adj.* 귀찮은 gwi-chan-eun, 성가 신 seong-ga-sin

bottle *n.* 병 byeong; *vt.* 병에 넣다 byeong-e neo-ta

bottleneck *n.* 병목 byeong-mok; 좁은 통 로 job-eun tong-no; 교통체증지역 gyo tong-che-jjeung-ji-yeok

bottom *n.* 밑바닥 mit-ba-dak; 기초 gi-cho

bottomless *adj.* 밑바닥이 없는 mit-ba-dag-i eom-neun, 헤아릴 수 없는 he-a-ril ssu eom-neun; 앉는 부분이 없는 an-neun bu-bun-i eom-neun

boulder *n.* 큰 바위 keun ba-wi, 표석 pyo-seok

bounce *vt.* 튀기다 twi-gi-da; *vi.* 튀다 twi-da

boundary *n.* 경계 gyeong-gye, 한계 han-gye

boundless *adj.* 무한한 mu-han-han, 한이 없 는 han-i eom-neun

bountiful *adj.* 관대한 gwan-dae-han, 풍부한 pung-bu-han

bouquet *n.* 꽃다발 kkot-da-bal, 부케 bu-kke

bourgeois *n.* 중산계급 시민 jung-san-gye-geup si-min, 자본가 ja-bon-ga, 부르주아 bu-reu-ju-a

boutique *n.* 부티크 bu-ti-kkeu

bow *vi.* 허리를 굽히다heo-ri-reul gu-pi-da, 절하다 jeol-ha-da; 굴종하다 gul-jjong-ha-da; *vi.* 미리를 숙이다 meo ri reul sug-i-da, 인사하다 in-sa-ha-da; *n.* 활 hwal; **~ tie**나 비 넥타이 na-bi nek-ta-i

bowel *n.* 창자 chang-ja, 내장 nae-jang

bowl *n.* 보울 bo-ul, 사발 sa-bal; 나무공 na-mu-gong; *vt.* 공을 굴리다 gong-eul gul-li-da

bowling *n.* 볼링 bol-ling; **~ alley** 볼링장 bol-ling-jang

box *n.* 상자 sang-ja; *vi.* 상자에 넣다 sang-ja-e neo-ta, 권투하다 gwon-tu-ha-da; *vt.* 수 먹으로 때리다 ju-meog-eu-ro ttae-ri-da

box office *n.* 극장 매표소 geuk-jang mae-pyo-so; *adj.* 인기를 끄는 in-kki-reul kkeu-neun, 흥행이 되는 heung-haeng-i doe-neun

boxer *n.* 권투선수 gwon-tu-seon-su

boxing *n.* 권투 gwon-tu, 복싱 bok-sing

boy *n.* 남자아이 nam-ja-a-i, 소년 so-nyeon

boycott *vt.* 보이코트하다 bo-i-ko-teu-ha-da, 배척하다 bae-cheo-ka-da, 불매동맹을 맺 다 bul-mae-dong-maeng-eul maet-da

boyfriend *n.* 남자친구 nam-ja-chin-gu

boyhood *n.* 소년기 so-nyeon-gi; 소년사회 so-nyeon-sa-hoe

boy scout *n.* 보이 스카우트 bo-i seu-ka-u-teu

bracelet *n.* 팔찌 pal-jji

bracket *n.* 괄호 gwal-ho; 까치발 kka-chi-bal

brag *v.* 자랑하다 ja-rang-ha-da, 허풍떨다 beo-pung-tteol-da; *n.* 자랑 ja-rang, 허풍 heo-pung

braid *n.* 노끈 no-kkeun, 꼰 끈 kkon kkeun; 땋은 머리 tta-eun meo-ri

brain *n.* 두뇌 du-noe, 뇌 noe; 지적인 사람 ji-jjeog-in sa-ram; **~ dead** 뇌사 noe-sa; **~ drain** 두뇌유출 du-noe-yu-chul

brainwash *n.* 세뇌 se-noe; *vt.* 세뇌시키다 se-noe-si-ki-da

brake *n.* 브레이크 beu-re-i-keu; *vt.* 브레이크를 걸다 beu-re-i-keu-reul geol-da

branch *n.* 가지 ga-ji; 분파 bun-pa; 지류 ji-ryu; 부문 bu-mun; *vi.* 가지를 내다 ga-ji-reul nae-da; 갈라지다 gal-la-ji-da

brand *n.* 상표 sang-pyo

brand-new *adj.* 아주 새로운 a-ju sae-ro-un, 신품의 sin-pum-ui

brandy *n.* 브랜디 beu-raen-di

brass *n.* 금관악기 geum-gwan-ak-gi; 놋쇠 not-soe, 놋그릇 not-geu-reut

brass band *n.* 취주악단chwi-ju-ak-dan, 브라스밴드 beu-ra-sseu-baen-deu

brassiere *n.* 브래지어 beu-rae-ji-eo

brave *adj.* 용감한 yong-gam-han

bravo *n.* 브라보 beu-ra-bo

brazenfaced *n.* 철면피 cheol-myeon-pi

Brazil *n.* 브라질 beu-ra-jil

Brazilian *n.* 브라질 사람 beu-ra-jil sa-ram; *adj.* 브라질의 beu-ra-jil-ui

bread *n.* 빵 ppang; 생계 saeng-gye

break *n.* 중지 jung-ji, 갈라진 틈 gal-la-jin teum; 파손 pa-son; **coffee ~** 커피 브레이크 keo-pi beu-re-i-keu; *vi.* 깨지다 kkae-ji-da; 관계가 끊어지다 gwan-gye-ga kkeun-eo-ji-da; *vt.* 깨뜨리다 kkae-tteu-ri-da, 어기다 eo-gi-da

breakdown *n.* 고장 go-jang, 파손 pa-son; 붕괴 bung-goe, 몰락 mol-lak

breakfast *n.* 아침 a-chim, 아침식사 a-chim-sik-sa

break-in *n.* 침입 chim-ip

break-up *n.* 파괴 pa-goe, 해산 hae-san, 헤어짐 he-eo-jim

breast *n.* 가슴 ga-seum; 유방 yu-bang

breast-feed *vt.* 모유로 키우다 mo-yu-ro ki-u-da

breath *n.* 숨 sum, 호흡 ho-heup; 산들거림 san-deul-geo-rim

breathe *vi.* 숨쉬다 sum-swi-da, 호흡하다 ho-heu-pa-da; 산들거리다 san-deul-geo-ri-da

breathless *adj.* 숨가쁜 sum-ga-ppeun, 숨도 못쉴 정도의 sum-do mot-swil jeong-do-ui

breathtaking *adj.* 아슬아슬한 a-seul-a-seul-han

breed *vt.* 새끼를 낳다 sae-kki-reul na-ta; 양육하다 yang-yu-ka-da; 번식시키다 beon-sik-si-ki-da

breeze *n.* 산들바람 san-deul-ba-ram

brew *vt.* 양조하다 yang-jo-ha-da; 음모를 꾸미다 eum-mo-reul kku-mi-da; *n.* 양조주 yang-jo-ju

bribe *n.* 뇌물 noe-mul; *vt.* 매수하다 mae-su-ha-da

brick *n.* 벽돌 byeok-dol; 벽돌쌓기 놀이기구 byeok-dol-ssa-ki nol-i-gi-gu; *vt.* 벽돌로 쌓다 byeok-dol-lo ssa-ta

bridal *adj.* 신부의 sin-bu-ui, 결혼식의 gyeol-hon-sig-ui

bride *n.* 신부 sin-bu

bridegroom *n.* 신랑 sil-lang

bridge *n.* 다리 da-ri; 브리지 beu-ri-ji; 콧날 kon-nal

brief *adj.* 간결한 gan-gyeol-han

briefcase *n.* 서류가방 seo-ryu-ga-bang

briefing *n.* 요약보고 yo-yak-bo-go, 브리핑 beu-ri-ping

briefly *adv.* 간단히 gan-dan-hi, 간단하게 gan-dan-ha-ge

bright *adj.* 빛나는 bin-na-neun; 머리가 좋은 meo-ri-ga jo-eun

brilliant *adj.* 빛나는 bin-na-neun; 머리가 좋은 meo-ri-ga jo-eun

brim *n.* 가장자리 ga-jang-ja-ri, 테두리 te-du-ri

bring *vt.* 가져오다 ga-jyeo-o-da; 초래하다 cho-rae-ha-da

brisk *adj.* 활발한 hwal-bal-han, 민첩한 min-cheo-pan; 상쾌한 sang-kwae-han

British *n.* 영국사람 yeong-guk-sa-ram; *adj.* 영국의 yeong-gug-ui

Briton *n.* 브리튼사람 beu-ri-teun-sa-ram

broad *adj.* 폭이 넓은 pog-i neolb-eun, 널따란 neol-tta-ran; 대강의 dae-gang-ui, 도량이 넓은 do-ryang-i neolb-eun

broadband *adj.* 넓은 지역의 neolb-eun ji-yeog-ui

broadcast *vt.* 방송하다 bang-song-ha-da; 소문을 퍼뜨리다 so-mun-eul peo-tteu-ri-da; *n.* 방송 bang-song, 방영 bang-yeong; *adj.* 방송의 bang-song-ui, 방영의 bang-yeong-ui

broaden *vt., vi.* 넓히다 neol-pi-da, 넓게하다 neol-kke-ha-da, 넓어지다 neolb-eo-ji-da

broadly *adv.* 널리 neol-li; 노골적으로 no-gol-jjeog-eu-ro

broadminded *adj.* 마음이 넓은 ma-eum-i neolb-eun, 관대한 gwan-dae-han

Broadway *n.* 브로드웨이 beu-ro-deu-we-i

broccoli *n.* 브로컬리 beu-ro-keol-li

brochure *n.* 팜플렛 pam-peul-let, 소책자 so-chaek-ja, 브로셔 beu-ro-syeo

broil *vi.* 볕이 내리쬐다 byeoch-i nae-ri-jjoe-da; 구워지다 gu-wo-ji-da; *vt.* 불에 굽다 bul-e qup-da

broke *adj.* 파산한 pa-san-han

broken *adj.* 부서진 bu-seo-jin; 낙담한 nak-dam-han; 파산한 pa-san-han

brokenhearted *adj.* 실연한 sil-yeon-han, 낙담한 nak-dam-han

broker *n.* 브로커 beu-ro-keo, 중개인 jung-gae-in

bronchitis *n.* 기관지염 gi-gwan-ji-yeom

bronze *n.* 청동 cheong-dong; 청동제품 cheong-dong-je-pum; *adj.* 청동의 cheong-dong-ui

brook *n.* 시내 si-nae, 개천 gae-cheon

broom *n.* 비 bi, 빗자루 bit-ja-ru; ~**stick** 빗자루 bit-ja-ru

broth *n.* 고깃국물 go-git-gung-mul

brother *n.* *(family member)* 형제 hyeong-je; 동포 dong-po; *(religious)* 남자신도 nam-ja-sin-do

brotherhood *n.* 형제간 hyeong-je-gan; 조합 jo-hap

brother-in-law *n.* 자형 ja-hyeong, 매부 mae-bu

brown *adj.* 갈색의 gal-ssaeg-ui; *n.* 갈색 gal-ssaek

brown sugar *n.* 흑설탕 heuk-seol-tang

browser *n.* *(computer)* 브라우저 beu-ra-u-jeo

bruise *n.* 타박상 ta-bak-sang

brunch *n.* 늦은 아침식사 neuj-eun a-chim-sik-sa, *(coll.)* 아점 a-jeom

brush *n.* 브러시 beu-reo-ssi, 솔 sol; *vt.* 솔질하다 sol-jil-ha-da; *vi.* 스치고 지나가다 seu-chi-go ji-na-ga-da

Brussels *n.* 브뤼셀 beu-rwi-ssel

brutal *adj.* 잔인한 jan-in-han, 짐승의 jim-seung-ui, 난폭한 nan-po-kan

brutality *n.* 만행 man-haeng, 잔학행위 jan-ha-kaeng-wi, 잔인성 jan-in-sseong

bubble *n.* 거품 geo-pum; *vi.* 거품이 일다 geo-pum-i il-da

bubble gum *n.* 풍선껌 pung-seon-kkeom

bucket *n.* 바께쓰 ba-kke-sseu, 물통 mul-tong

bud *n.* 싹 ssak, 꽃봉오리 kkot-bong-o-ri

Buddha *n.* 부처 bu-cheo

Buddhism *n.* 불교 bul-gyo

budget *n.* 예산 ye-san

buffalo *n.* 들소 deul-sso

bug *n.* 벌레 beol-le, 곤충 gon-chung; ~ **hunting** 곤충채집 gon-chung-chae-jip

build *vt.* 세우다 se-u-da, 짓다 jit-da; *vi.* 건축하다 geon-chu-ka-da

builder *n.* 건축업자 geon-chug-eop-ja

building *n.* 건물 geon-mul, 건축물 geon-chung-mul; 긴축 geon-chuk

buildup *n.* 강화 gang-hwa, 증강 jeung-gang, 증신 jeung-jin; 축적 chuk-jeok, 체증 che-jjeung

built *adj.* 조립된 jo-rip-doen

built-in *adj.* 붙박이의 but-bag-i-ui

built-up *adj.* 짜맞춘 jja-mat-chun, 조립한 jo-ri-pan; 건물이 빽빽이 들어선 geon-mul-i ppaek-ppaeg-i deul-eo-seon

bulb *n.* **lightbulb** 전구 jeon-gu; **plant/flower bulb** 구근 gu-geun

bulk *n.* 크기 keu-gi, 용적 yong-jeok; 대부분 dae-bu-bun

bulky *adj.* 부피가 큰 bu-pi-ga keun, 다루기 힘든 da-ru-gi him-deun

bull *n.* 황소 hwang-so

bulldog *n.* 불독 bul-dok

bulldozer *n.* 불도저 bul-do-jeo

bullet *n.* 총알 chong-al

bulletin board *n.* 게시판 ge-si-pan

bulletproof *adj.* 방탄의 bang-tan-ui

bullfight *n.* 투우 tu-u

bullhead *n.* 고집쟁이 go-jip-jaeng-i

bully *n.* 심술쟁이 sim-sul-jaeng-i, 문제아 mun-je-a

bum *n.* 부랑자 bu-rang-ja, 건달 geon-dal; *vi.* 빈둥거리다 bin-dung-geo-ri-da

bump *vt.* 충돌하다 chung-dol-ha-da, 부딪치다 bu-dit-chi-da, 마주치다 ma-ju-chi-da; *n.* 충돌 chung-dol

bumper *n.* 범퍼 beom-peo; 풍작 pung-jak, 성황 seong-hwang

bumpy *adj.* 울퉁불퉁한 ul-tung-bul-tung-han, 덜컥거리는 deol-kkeok-geo-ri-neun

bun *n.* 롤빵 rol-ppang

bunch *n.* 다발 da-bal; 한패 han-pae, 떼거리 tte-geo-ri; *vt.* 다발로 묶다 da-bal-lo muk-da; *vi.* 다발이 되다 da-bal-i doe-da, 한떼가 되다 han-tte-ga doe-da

bundle *n.* 묶음 mukk-eum, 다발 da-bal; *vt.* 다발로 꾸리다 da-bal-lo kku-ri-da

bungalow *n.* 방갈로 bang-gal-lo

bunkbed *n.* 이층침대 i-cheung-chim-dae

bunker *n.* 벙커 beong-keo

bunny *n.* 토끼 to-kki

bunt *vt., vi.* 번트하다 beon-teu-ha-da, 밀다 mil-da

buoy *n.* 부표 bu-pyo; *vt.* 띄우다 tti-u-da; 지탱하다 ji-taeng-ha-da; *vi.* 뜨다 tteu-da

burble *vi.* 거품이 일다 geo-pum-i il-da; 거품을 내며 말하다 geo-pum-eul nae-myeo mal-ha-da

burden *n.* 무거운 짐 mu-geo-un jim; 부담 bu-dam, 걱정 geok-jeong; *vt.* 짐을 지우다 jim-eul ji-u-da, 부담시키다 bu-dam-si-ki-da

burdensome *adj.* 부담되는 bu-dam-doe-neun, 짐스러운 jim-seu-reo-un, 귀찮은 gwi-chan-eun

bureau *n.* 사무소 sa-mu-so, 사무국 sa-mu-kuk, 편집국 pyeon-jip-guk

bureaucrat *n.* 관료 gwal-lyo; 관료적인 사람 gwal-lyo-jeog-in sa-ram

bureaucratic *adj.* 관료적인 gwal-lyo-jeog-in

burglar *n.* 강도 gang-do

burial *n.* 매장 mae-jang

Burma *n.* 버마 beo-ma

burn *vi.* 불타다 bul-ta-da, 그을다 geu-eul-da; 불끈하다 bul-kkeun-ha-da; *vt.* 태우다 tae-u-da, 그을리다 geu-eul-li-da; *n.* 화상 hwa-sang

burned-out *adj.* 타버린 ta-beo-rin, 식은 sig-eun

burner *n.* 버너 beo-neo, 연소기 yeon-so-gi

burning *adj.* 타고있는 ta-go-in-neun, 뜨거운 tteu-geo-un, 강렬한 gang-nyeol-han

burp *n.* 트림 teu-rim; *vt., vi.* 트림하다 teu-rim-ha-da

burst *v.* 파열하다 pa-yeol-ha-da, 폭발하다 pok-bal-ha-da, 터지다 teo-ji-da

bury *vt.* 묻다 mut-da

bus *n.* 버스 beo-sseu

bush *n.* 수풀 su-pul, 덤불 deom-bul

business *n.* 사업 sa-eop; 용건 yong-kkeon; 사무 sa-mu; ~ **school** 경영대학 gyeong-yeong-dae-hak

business card *n.* 명함 myeong-ham

business hours *n.* 영업시간 yeong-eop-si-gan

businessman *n.* 사업가 sa-eop-ga

bus station *n.* 버스 터미널 beo-sseu teo-mi-neol, 버스 종점 beo-sseu jong-jjeom

bus stop *n.* 버스 정류장 beo-sseu jeong-nyu-jang

bust *n.* 상반신 sang-ban-sin; 흉상 hyung-sang; 버스트 beo-seu-teu; *vt.* 폭발시키다 pok-bal-si-ki-da, 파열시키다 pa-yeol-si-ki-da, 파멸시키다 pa-myeol-si-ki-da; *vi.* 파열하다 pa-yeol-ha-da; 파산하다 pa-san-ha-da

bustle *vi.* 부산스레 움직이다 bu-san-seu-re um-jig-i-da; *vt.* 재촉하다 jae-cho-ka-da

busy *adj.* 바쁜 ba-ppeun

but *conj.* 그렇지만 geu-reo-chi-man; **He is very handsome ~ not kind** 그 사람은 잘생겼지만 친절하지 않다 geu sa-ram-eun jal-saeng-gyeot-ji-man chin-jeol-ha-ji an-ta

butcher *n.* 정육점 주인 jeong-nyuk-jeom ju-in

butter *n.* 버터 beo-teo

butterfly *n.* 나비 na-bi

button *n.* 단추 dan-chu; ~**hole** 단추구멍 dan-chu-kku-meong

buy *vt.* 사다 sa-da

buyer *n.* 구매자 gu-mae-ja

buzz *vi.* 윙윙거리다 wing-wing-geo-ri-da; 바쁘게 돌아다니다 ba-ppeu-ge dol-a-da-ni-da; *vt.* 시끄럽게 떠들다 si-kkeu-reop-ge tteo-deul-da

by *prep.* …의 옆에 …ui yeop-e; …에 의해 …e ui-hae; …까지 …kka-ji; ~ **the way** 그건 그렇고 geu-geon geu-reo-ko; **(to go)** ~ **bus** 버스로 (가다) beo-sseu-ro (ga-da); *(measurement)* **nine ~ eighteen feet** 가로 9피트 세로 18피트 ga-ro gu-pi-teu se-ro

sip-pal-pi-teu; **north ~ northeast**북미 동
북으로, 북미 동북의, 북미 동북에 있는
buk-mi-dong-bug-ui/eu-ro/e in-neun
bye-bye *phr.* 안녕 an-nyeong

by-product *n.* 부산물 bu-san-mul
bystander *n.* 방관자 bang-gwan-ja, 구경꾼
gu-gyeong-kkun
byte *n.* 바이트 ba-i-teu

C

cab *n.* 택시 taek-si; ~ **fare** 택시요금
taek-si-yo-geum
cabbage *n.* 양배추 yang-bae-chu
cabin *n.* 오두막 o-du-mak; 선실 seon-sil
cabinet *n.* 캐비닛 kae-bi-net, 장식장 jang-
sik-jang; 내각 nae-gak
cable *n.* 케이블 ke-i-beul; 굵은 밧줄 gulg-
eun bat-jul; 해외전보 hae-oe-jeon-bo
cable car *n.* 케이블카 ke-i-beul-ka
cable television *n.* 유선방송
yu-seon-bang-song
cacophony *n.* 불협화음 bul-heo-pwa-eum
cactus *n.* 선인장 seon-in-jang
caddie *n.* 캐디 kae-di; *vi.* 캐디로 일하다
kae-di-ro il-ha-da
cadet *n.* 사관생도 sa-gwan-saeng-do
Caesarean section *n.* 제왕절개
je-wang-jeol-gae
café *n.* 카페 ka-pe
cafeteria *n.* 식당 sik-dang
caffeine *n.* 카페인 ka-pe-in
cage *n.* 새장 sae-jang; 우리 u-ri
Cairo *n.* 카이로 ka-i-ro
cake *n.* 케이크 ke-i-keu
calcium *n.* 칼슘 kal-syum
calculate *vt.* 계산하다 gye-san-ha-da, 추정
하다 chu-jeong-ha-da
calculation *n.* 계산 gye-san
calculator *n.* 계산기 gye-san-gi
calendar *n.* 달력 dal-lyeok
calf *n.* (*cow*) 송아지 song-a-ji; (*body part*) 종
아리 jong-a-ri
call *n.* 통화 tong-hwa; 초청 cho-cheong; *vt.*
부르다 bu-reu-da; 불러오다 bul-leo-o-da;
...라고 부르다 ...ra-go bu-reu-da
call box *n.* 비상전화 bi-sang-jeon-hwa
called game *n.* (*baseball*) 콜드게임
kol-deu-kke-im
calligraphy *n.* 서예 seo-ye

calling card *n.* (*phone card*) 전화카드
jeon-hwa-ka-deu; (*business card*) 명함
myeong-ham
callus *n.* 굳은살 gud-eun sal, 못 mot
calm *adj.* 고요한 go-yo-han; 평온한 pyeong-
on-han; *vt.* 진정시키다 jin-jeong-si-ki-da,
가라앉히다 ga-ra-an-chi-da; *vi.* 진정하다
jin-jeong-ha-da, 가라앉다 ga-ra-an-tta
calorie *n.* 칼로리 kal-lo-ri
camcorder *n.* 캠코더 kaem-ko-deo
camel *n.* 낙타 nak-ta
camera *n.* 카메라 ka-me-ra; **digital ~** 디지털
카메라 di-ji-teol ka-me-ra
cameraman *n.* 카메라맨 ka-me-ra-maen
Cameroon *n.* 카메룬 ka-me-run
camouflage *n.* 위장 wi-jang; *vt.* 위장하다
wi-jang-ha-da
camp *n.* 캠프 kaem-peu; 진영 jin-yeong; 야
영지 ya-yeong-ji, 캠프장 kaem-peu-jang;
vi. 야영하다 ya-yeong-ha-da
campaign *n.* 전쟁 jeon-jaeng; 사회운동
sa-hoe-un-dong, 유세 yu-se
campfire *n.* 캠프파이어 kaem-peu-pa-i-eo,
모닥불 mo-dak-bul, 화톳불 hwa-tot-bul
campsite *n.* 캠프장 kaem-peu-jang; 야영지
ya-yeong-ji
campus *n.* 캠퍼스 kaem-peo-sseu, 교정
gyo-jeong
can *n.* 캔 kaen, 깡통 kkang-tong; *aux.* 할 수
있다 hal ssu it-da; ~ **opener** 깡통따개
kkang-tong-tta-gae
Canada *n.* 캐나다 kae-na-da
Canadian *n.* 캐나다사람 kae-na-da-ssa-ram;
adj. 캐나다의 kae-na-da-ui
canal *n.* 운하 un-ha
Canary Islands *n.* 카나리아섬
ka-na-ri-a-seom
cancel *vt.* 취소하다 chwi-so-ha-da; 삭제하다
sak-je-ha-da

cancellation *n.* 취소 chwi-so; 삭제 sak-je
cancer *n.* 암 am; 병폐 byeong-pye
candid *adj.* 정직한 jeong-ji-kan
candidate *n.* 후보자 hu-bo-ja
candle *n.* 양초 yang-cho; ~holder 촛대
    chot-dae
candy *n.* 사탕 sa-tang, 캔디 kaen-di
cane *n.* 지팡이 ji-pang-i
canned *adj.* 통조림한 tong-jo-rim-han; 미리
    준비된 mi-ri jun-bi-doen
cannon *n.* 대포 dae-po
cannon ball *n.* 포탄 po-tan; 캐논볼
    kae-non-bol
canoe *n.* 카누 ka-nu
canteen *n. (cafeteria)* 매점 mae-jeom; 간이
    식당 gan-i-sik-dang; *(flask)* 수통 su-tong
canvas *n.* 캔버스 kaen-beo-sseu
canyon *n.* 깊은 협곡 gip-eun hyeop-gok
cap *n. (hat)* 모자 mo-ja; *(lid or top)* 뚜껑
    ttu-kkeong, 캡 kaep; *vt.* 모자를 씌우다
    mo-ja-reul ssi-u-da; 덮다 deop-da
capability *n.* 능력 neung-nyeok, 재능 jae-
    neung; 가능성 ga-neung-sseong, 장래성
    jang-nae-sseong
capable *adj.* 유능한 yu-neung-han
capacious *adj.* 널찍한 neol-jji-kan, 용량
    이 큰 yong-nyang-i keun, 포용력있는
    po-yong-nyeog-in-neun
capacity *n.* 수용량 su-yong-nyang; 능
    력 neung-nyeok; 재능 jae-neung; 자격
    ja-gyeok
cape *n. (land form)* 곶 got; *(clothing)* 망토
    mang-to
capital *n. (city)* 수도 su-do; *(finance)* 자본
    ja-bon; 대문자 dae-mun-jja; ~ city 수도
    su-do, 서울 seo-ul; ~ letters 대문자 dae-
    mun-jja; *adj.* 주요한 ju-yo-han, 으뜸가는
    eu-tteum-ga-neun; 대문자의 dae-mun-jja-
    ui; 자본의 ja-bon-ui
capitalism *n.* 자본주의 ja-bon-ju-ui
capricious *adj.* 변덕스러운 byeon-deok-seu-
    reo-un; 급변하는 geup-byeon-ha-neun
capsize *vt.* 뒤집다 dwi-jip-da, *vi.* 뒤집히다
    dwi-ji-pi-da; *n.* 전복 jeon-bok
capsule *n.* 캡슐 kaep-syul
captain *n.* 장 jang; 선장 seon-jang; 대령
    dae-ryeong

caption *n.* 표제 pyo-je, 제목 je-mok; 자막
    ja-mak, 캡션 kaep-syeon; *vt.* 자막을 넣다
    ja-mag-eul neo-ta
captivate *vt.* 마음을 사로잡다 ma-eum-eul
    sa-ro-jap-da, 매혹하다 mae-ho-ka-da
capture *vt.* 사로잡다 sa-ro-jap-da; 점령하다
    jeom-nyeong-ha-da; 포착하다 po-cha-ka-
    da; *n.* 점령 jeom-nyeong, 포획 po-hoek
cappuccino *n.* 카푸치노 ka-pu-chi-no
car *n.* 차 cha, 자동차 ja-dong-cha
caramel *n.* 캐러멜 kae-reo-mel
carbohydrate *n.* 탄수화물 tan-su-hwa-mul
carbon paper *n.* 복사지 bok-sa-ji
card *n.* 카드 ka-deu
cardboard *n.* 판지 pan-ji, 마분지 ma-bun-ji
card game *n.* 카드놀이 ka-deu-nol-i
cardigan *n.* 가디건 ga-di-geon
care *n.* 걱정 geok-jeong; 주의 ju-ui; 관심
    gwan-sim; *vi.* 걱정하다 geok-jeong-ha-da,
    마음을 쓰다 ma-eum-eul sseu-da; to take
    ~ of 돌보다 dol-bo-da
career *n.* 생애 saeng-ae, 경력 gyeong-nyeok;
    출세 chul-sse, 성공 seong-gong; 전문직업
    jeon-mun-jig-eop
careful *adj.* 조심스러운 jo-sim-seu-reo-un;
    주의깊은 ju-ui-gi-peun
careless *adj.* 부주의한 bu-ju-i-han; 무관심
    한 mu-gwan-sim-han
cargo *n.* 뱃짐 baet-jim, 화물 hwa-mul; ~
    boat 화물선 hwa-mul-sseon
Caribbean Sea *n.* 카리브 해 ka-ri-beu hae
caricature *n.* 풍자만화 pung-ja-man-hwa; 풍
    자만화를 그리다 pung-ja-man-hwa-reul
    geu-ri-da
carnation *n.* 카네이션 ka-ne-i-syeon
carnival *n.* 카니발 ka-ni-bal, 사육제
    sa-yuk-je
carnivore *n.* 육식동물 yuk-sik-dong-mul
carnivorous *adj.* 육식성의 yuk-sik-seong-ui
carol *n.* 캐롤 kae-rol, 축가 chuk-ga
carousel *n.* 회전목마 hoe-jeon-mong-ma; 회
    전식 컨베이어 hoe-jeon-sik keon-be-i-eo
carpenter *n.* 목수 mok-su
carpet *n.* 양탄자 yang-tan-ja, 카페트 ka-pe-teu
car pool *n.* 카풀 ka-pul, 합승 hap-seung
carrier *n.* 운반인 un-ban-in, 배달원 bae-dal-
    won; 항공모함 hang-gong-mo-ham

carrot n. 당근 dang-geun

carry vt. 나르다 na-reu-da; 가지고 있다 ga-ji-go it-da; 따르다 tta-reu-da; 실어가다 sil-eo-ga-da; 받치고 있다 bat-chi-go it-da

carry-on n. 기내 휴대 수하물 gi-nae hyu-dae su-ha-mul

car seat n. 카시트 ka-ssi-teu

carsick adj. 차멀미하는 cha-meol-mi-ha-neun

carsickness n. 차멀미 cha-meol-mi

cart n. 손수레 son-su-re, 카트 ka-teu

cartilage n. 년골 yeon-gol, 연골조직 yeon-gol-jo-jik

carton n. 마분지 ma-bun-ji, 두꺼운 종이 du-kkeo-un jong-i

cartoon n. 만화 man-hwa

cartridge n. 카트리지 ka-teu-ri-jji; **ink ~** 잉크 카트리지 ing-keu ka-teu-ri-jji

cartwheel n. 수레바퀴 su-re-ba-kwi; 옆회전 yeo-poe-jeon

carve vt. 조각하다 jo-ga-ka-da; 새기다 sae-gi-da

carving n. 조각 jo-gak

cascade n. 작은 폭포 jag-eun pok-po; 인공 폭포 in-gong-pok-po

case n. 경우 gyeong-u; (legal) 케이스 ke-i-sseu, 사건 sa-kkeon; (object) 상자 sang-ja

case study n. 사례연구 sa-rye-yeon-gu

cash n. 현금 hyeon-geum, 지폐 ji-pye, 주회 ju-hwa; vt. 현금으로 바꾸다 hyeon-geum-eu-ro ba-kku-da; ~ **machine (ATM)** 현금 인출기 hyeon-geum-in-chul-gi

cashier n. 회계원 hoe-gye-won, 출납계원 chul-lap-gye-won

cashier's check n. 자기앞수표 ja-gi-ap-su-pyo

cashmere n. 캐시미어 kae-si-mi-eo

casino n. 카지노 ka-ji-no, 도박장 do-bak-jang

cask n. 통 tong

Caspian Sea n. 카스피해 ka-seu-pi-hae

cassette tape n. 카세트 테니프 ka-se-teu te-i-peu

cast n. 기브스 gi-beu-sseu; 배역 bae-yeok; 던지기 deon-ji-gi; 주형 ju-hyeong; vt. 기브스하다 gi-beu-sseu-ha-da; 던지다 deon-ji-da; 계산하다 gye-san-ha-da; 주조 하다 ju-jo-ha-da

castanet n. 캐스터네츠 ke-seu-teo-ne-cheu

caste n. 배타적 계급 bae-ta-jeok gye-geup, 카스트 ka-seu-teu

castle n. 성 seong

casual adj. 일상적인 il-ssang-jeog-in; 캐주 얼한 kae-ju-eol-han

casualty n. 사고 sa-go; 사상자 sa-sang-ja; 불 상사 bul-ssang-sa

casualty ward n. 응급처치실 eung-geup-cheo-chi-sil

cat n. 고양이 go-yang-i

catacomb n. 카타콤 ka-ta-kom, 지하묘지 ji-ha-myo-ji

catalog n. 카달로그 ka-dal-lo-geu, 목록 mong-nok

catapult n. 투석기 tu-seok-gi; vt. 투석기로 쏘다 tu-seok-gi-ro sso-da

catastrophe n. 대참사 dae-cham-sa, 대이변 dae-i-byeon

catch n. 포획 po-hoek; 파악 pa-ak; vt. 잡다 jap-da; 습력하다 seup-gyeo-ka-da, 이해하 다 i-hae-ha-da; 걸리다 geol-li-da

catcher n. 포수 po-su, 캐쳐 kae-cheo; 잡는 사람 jam-neun sa-ram

catch phrase n. 캐치프레이즈 kae-chi-peu-re-i-jeu, 표어 pyo-eo, 유행어 yu-haeng-eo

catch-up n. 만회하기 man-hoe-ha-gi

category n. 범주 beom-ju, 카테고리 ka-te-go-ri

catering n. 음식주문 eum-sik-ju-mun

caterpillar n. 유충 yu-chung, 애벌레 ae-beol-le

catharsis n. 카타르시스 ka-ta-reu-ssi-sseu

cathedral n. 대성당 dae-seong-dang

Catholic n. 카톨릭교도 ka-tol-lik-gyo-do, 천 주교도 cheon-ju-gyo-do; adj. 카불릭의 ka-tol-lig-ui, 천주교의 cheon-ju-gyo-ui

Catholicism n. 카톨릭 ka-tol-lik, 천주교 chon-ju-gyo

CAT scan n. abbr. **Computed Tomography Scan** 캣스켄 kaet-seu-ken

cattle n. 소 so; 가축 ga-chuk

Caucasus n. 코카서스산맥 ko-ka-sseo-sseu-san-maek

cauldron n. 큰 솥 keun sot

cauliflower n. 컬리플라워 keol-li-peul-la-wo

cause n. 원인 won-in; 주의 ju-ui; vt. 원인 이 되다 won-in-i doe-da; (of a problem; political) 일으키다 il-eu-ki-da caution *n.* 조심 jo-sim; 경고 gyeong-go

cautious *adj.* 주의깊은 ju-ui-gi-peun

cavalry *n.* 기병대 gi-byeong-dae

cave *n.* 동굴 dong-gul

caviar *n.* 캐비어 kae-bi-eo, 상어알 sang-eo-al

cavity *n.* 공동 gong-dong; 충치 chung-chi

cease *vi.* 그만두다 geu-man-du-da; 그치다 geu-chi-da

cedar *n.* 시더나무 ssi-deo-na-mu, 히말라야 삼나무 hi-mal-la-ya sam-na-mu

ceiling *n.* 천장cheon-jang; 상한선 sang-han-seon

celadon *n. (porcelain)* 청자 cheong-ja

celebrate *vt., vi.* 경축하다 gyeong-chu-ka-da; 칭찬하다 chng-chan-ha-da

celebration *n.* 경축 gyeong-chuk; 칭찬 ching-chan

celebrity *n.* 명성 myeong-seong; 명사 myeong-sa

celery *n.* 셀러리 sel-leo-ri

cell *n. (biology)* 세포 se-po; *(jail)* 감방 gam-bang; 작은 방 jag-eun bang

cellar *n.* 지하저장실 ji-ha-jeo-jang-sil, 지하실 ji-ha-sil

cello *n.* 첼로 chel-lo

cellular *adj.* 세포로 이루어진 se-po-ro i-ru-eo-jin; 구획의 gu-hoeg-ui; ~ **phone** 핸드폰 haen-deu-pon

Celsius *n.* 섭씨 seop-si

cement *n.* 시멘트 si-men-teu

cemetery *n.* 공동묘지 gong-dong-myo-ji

censor *n.* 센서 ssen-sseo; 검열관 geom-yeol-gwan, 감찰관 gam-chal-gwan; *vt.* 검열하다 geom-yeol-ha-da

censorship *n.* 검열 geom-yeol; 검열관직 geom-yeol-gwan-jik

censure *n.* 비난 bi-nan; *vt.* 비난하다 bi-nan-ha-da

census *n.* 인구조사 in-gu-jo-sa

cent *n.* 센트 ssen-teu, 전 jeon

centennial *adj.* 100년마다의 baeng-nyeon-ma-da-ui, 100년간의 baeng-nyeon-gan-ui

center *n.* 가운데 ga-un-de, 중심 jung-sim, 센터 ssen-teo, 중심지 jung-sim-ji; *v* 중심에 두다 jung-sim-e du-da, 중심에 있다 jung-sim-e it-da

centigrade *adj.* 섭씨의 seop-si-ui

centimeter *n.* 센티미터 ssen-ti-mi-teo

centipede *n.* 지네 ji-ne

central *adj.* 중부의 jung-bu-ui, 중심의 jung-sim-ui, 중심적인 jung-sim-jeog-in

century *n.* 세기 se-gi

CEO *n. abbr. Chief Executive Officer* 최고 경영자 choe-go gyeong-yeong-ja

ceramic *n.* 세라믹 sse-ra-mik, 도기 do-gi; *adj.* 세라믹의 sse-ra-mig-ui, 도기의 do-gi-ui

cereal *n. (breakfast food/flakes)* 씨리얼 ssi-ri-eol; *(grain)* 곡물 gong-mul

ceremony *n.* 의식 ui-sik; 의례 ui-rye

certain *adj.* 일정한 il-jjeong-han; 확신하는 hwak-sin-ha-neun

certainly *adv.* 확실히 hwak-sil-hi, 틀림없이 teul-lim-eops-i

certificate *n.* 증명 jeung-myeong; 증명서 jeung-myeong-seo; **birth** ~ 출생증명서 chul-ssaeng-jeung-myeong-seo

certify *vt.* 증명하다 jeung-myeong-ha-da, 보증하다 bo-jeung-ha-da

chain *n.* 체인 che-in, 사슬 sa-seul; 연쇄 yeon-swae, 일련 il-lyeon; ~ **saw** 전기톱 jeon-gi-top; ~ **store** 연쇄점 yeon-swae-jeom

chair *n.* 의자 u-ja

chairman *n.* 의장 ui-jang, 학과장 hak-gwa-jang

chalk *n.* 분필 bun-pil

chalkboard *n.* 칠판 chil-pan

challenge *n.* 도전 do-jeon; *vt.* 도전하다 do-jeon-ha-da

challenging *adj.* 도전적인 do-jeon-jeog-in

chamber *n.* 독방 dok-bang; 의원 ui-won

chameleon *n.* 카멜레온 ka-mel-le-on; 변덕쟁이 byeon-deok-jaeng-i

champagne *n.* 샴페인 syam-pe-in

champion *n.* 챔피언 chaem-pi-eon

championship *n.* 선수권 seon-su-kkwon, 선수권대회 seon-su-kkwon-dae-hoe

chance *n.* 기회 gi-hoe, 찬스 chan-sseu; 우연 u-yeon; 가망 ga-mang; *vi.* 운에 맞기고 해보다 un-e mat-gi-go hae-bo-da

chancellor *n.* 대법관 dae-beop-gwan, 장관 jang-gwan; 총장 chong-jang, 학장 hak-jang

chandelier *n.* 샹들리에 syang-deul-li-e

change *n.* 변화 byeon-hwa; *(balance due)* 거스름돈 geo-seu-reum-tton, *(coins)* 잔돈 jan-don; *vi.* 변하다 byeon-ha-da; 갈아타다 gal-a-ta-da; 갈아입다 gal-a-ip-da; *vt.* 바꾸다 ba-kku-da, 교환하다 gyo-hwan-ha-da

changeable *adj.* 변하기 쉬운 byeon-ha-gi swi-un

changing room *n.* 탈의실 tal-ui-sil

channel *n.* 경로 gyeong-no, 루트 ru-teu; 해협 hae-hyeop, 수로 su-ro

chant *n.* 찬트 chant, 영창 yeong-chang; *vt.* 영창하다 yeong-chang-ha-da

chaos *n.* 혼돈 hon-don; 무질서 mu-jil-sseo

chaotic *adj.* 혼돈된 hon-don-doen

chap *n.* 튼 곳 teun got, 튼 자리 teun ja-ri; 균열 gyun-yeol, 금 geum; *vi.* 트다 teu-da, 거칠어지다 geo-chil-eo-ji-da

chapel *n.* 교회 gyo-hoe, 예배당 ye-bae-dang

chapter *n.* 챕터 chaep-teo, 장 jang

character *n.* 특성 teuk-seong; 인격 in-kkyeok; 인물 in-mul; 문자 mun-jja

characteristic *n.* 특질 teuk-jil; *adj.* 특색을 이루는 teuk-saeg-eul i-ru-neun

charcoal *n.* 숯 sut, 목탄 mok-tan

charge *n.* 짐 jim; 책임 chaeg-im; 부담 bu-dam; 요금 yo-geum; *vt.* 짐을 싣다 jim-eul sit-da; 채우다 chae-u-da; 부과하다 bu-gwa-ha-da; 청구하다 cheong-gu-ha-da; **credit card ~** 신용카드 사용요금 sin-yong-ka-deu sa-yong-nyo-geum; **to ~ to my credit card account** 신용카드에 청구하다 sin-yong-ka-deu-e cheong-gu-ha-da

charisma *n.* 카리스마 ka-ri-seu-ma

charity *n.* 자선 ja-seon; 자선기금 ja-seon-gi-geum

charm *n.* 매력 mae-ryeok; 마력 ma-ryeok; *vt.* 매혹하다 mae-ho-ka-da; 주문을 걸다 ju-mun-eul geol-da

charming *adj.* 매력있는 mae-ryeog-in-neun; 귀여운 gwi-yeo-un; 기분좋은 gi-bun-jo-eun

chart *n.* 차트 cha-teu, 도표 do-pyo; *vt.* 차트를 만들다 cha-teu-reul man-deul-da, 도표를 만들다 do-pyo-reul man-deul-da

charter *n.* 헌장 heon-jang; 대차계약 dae-cha-gye-yak; *vt.* 전세내다 jeon-se-nae-da; 특허를 주다 teu-keo-reul ju-da

chase *n.* 추적 chu-jeok; *vt.* 쫓다 jjot-da, 추적하다 chu-jeo-ka-da

chassis *n.* 새시 sae-si; 동체골격 dong-che-gol-gyeok

chat *n.* 잡담 jap-dam; *vi.* 잡담하다 jap-dam-ha-da

chatter *n.* 수다 su-da; *vi.* 수다떨다 su-da-tteol-da, 재잘거리다 jae-jal-geo-ri-da

chauffeur *n.* 자가용 운전기사 ja-ga-yong-un-jeon-gi-sa

chauvinism *n.* 쇼비니즘 syo-bi-ni-jeum, 극단적 배타주의 geuk-dan-jeok bae-ta-ju-ui

cheap *adj.* 값싼 gap-ssan

cheat *vt.* 속이다 sog-i-da, 부정하다 bu-jeong-ha-da, 사기치다 sa gi chi da

check *n.* *(banking)* 수표 su-pyo; *(verify)* 점검 Jeom-geom; 저지 jeo-ji; *vt.* 저지하다 jeo-ji-ha-da; 검사하다 geom-sa-ha-da, 조사하다 jo-sa-ha-da; **~book** 수표책 su-pyo-chaek; **~mark** 점검하다 jeom-geom-ha-da

checkered pattern *n.* 체크무늬 che-keu-mu-ni

checkers *n.* 체커 che-keo; 바둑무늬 ba-dung-mu-ni; 검사자 geom-sa-ja

check-in *n.* 체크인 che-keu-in

checking account *n.* 당좌예금구좌 dang-jwa-ye-geum gu-jwa

checklist *n.* 체크리스드 che-keu-ri-seu-teu

checkmate *n.* 외통수 oe-tong-su; 징군 jang-gun

check-out *n.* 체크아웃 che-keu-a-ut

checkpoint *n.* 검문소 geom-mun-so

checkup *n.* 건강진단 geon-gang-jin-dan; 총점검 chong-jeom-geom

cheek *n.* 빰 ppyam

cheekbone *n.* 광대뼈 gwang-dae-ppyeo

cheer *n.* 격려 gyeong-nyeo, 환호 hwan-ho, 갈채 gal-chae; *vt.* 격려하다 gyeong-nyeo-ha-da, 갈채하다 gal-chae-ha-da

cheerful *adj.* 쾌활한 kwae-hwal-han, 유쾌한 yu-kwae-han, 기분좋은 gi-bun-jo-eun

cheerleader *n.* 치어리더 chi-eo-ri-deo

cheese *n.* 치즈 chi-jeu

chef *n.* 요리사 yo-ri-sa, 주방장 ju-bang-jang

chemical *n.* 화학약품 hwa-hang-nyak-pum; 화학제품 hwa-hak-je-pum; *adj.* 화학의 hwa-hag-ui

chemistry *n.* 화학 hwa-hak

cheque *n.* 수표 su-pyo

cherish *vt.* 소중히 여기다 so-jung-hi yeo-gi-da; 마음에 품다 ma-eum-e pum-tta

cherry *n.* 버찌 beo-jji, 체리 che-ri; *adj.* 버찌의 beo-jji-ui

chess *n.* 체스 che-sseu; ~**board** 체스판 che-sseu-pan; ~ **piece** 말 mal

chest *n.* *(container)* 가슴 ga-seum; *(body part)* 상자 sang-ja; 자금 ja-geum; ~ **of drawers** 서랍장 seo-rap-jang; ~ **pains** 가슴통증 ga-seum-tong-jjeung

chestnut *n.* 밤 bam, 밤나무 bam-na-mu

chew *vt.* 씹다 ssip-da

chewing gum *n.* 껌 kkeom

chewy *adj.* 잘 씹히지 않는 jal ssi-pi-ji an-neun, 쫄깃쫄깃한 jjol-git-jjol-gi-tan

chick *n.* 병아리 byeong-a-ri

chicken *n.* 닭 dak, 닭고기 dak-go-gi

chicken breast *n.* 새가슴 sae-ga-seum

chicken pox *n.* 수두 su-du

chief *n.* 장 jang, 추장 chu-jang

child *n.* 아이 a-i; *(pl.)* 아이들 a-i-deul

childcare *n.* 육아 yug-a, 아동보호 a-dong-bo-ho

childhood *n.* 어린시절 eo-rin-si-jeol

childish *adj.* 어린애 같은 eo-rin-sae gat-eun

Chile *n.* 칠레 chil-le

chill *n.* 냉기 naeng-gi; *vt.* 냉각하다 naeng-ga-ka-da; *adj.* 냉랭한 naeng-naeng-han, 냉담한 naeng-dam-han

chilly *adj.* 차가운 cha-ga-un; 냉담한 naeng-dam-han

chime *n.* 차임벨 cha-im-bel

chimney *n.* 굴뚝 gul-ttuk

chimpanzee *n.* 침팬지 chim-paen-jji

chin *n.* 턱 teok

China *n.* 중국 jung-guk

china *n.* 도자기 do-ja-gi, 자기 ja-gi

Chinatown *n.* 차이나타운 cha-i-na-ta-un

Chinese *n.* 중국사람 jung-guk-sa-ram; *adj.* 중국의 jung-gug-ui

Chinese character *n.* 한자 han-jja

chip *n.* 칩 chip; 조각 jo-gak, 토막 to-mak; *vt.* 잘게 썰다 jal-ge sseol-da, 잘게 쪼개다 jal-ge jjo-gae-da

chiropractic *n.* 지압요법 ji-am-nyo-ppeop, 척추교정 cheok-chu-gyo-jeong

chisel *n.* 끌 kkeul; *vt.* 끌로 깎다 kkeul-lo-kkak-da

chocolate *n.* 초콜렛 cho-kol-let

choice *n.* 선택 seon-taek; 종류 jong-nyu

choir *n.* 합창단 hap-chang-dan

choke *vt.* 숨이 막히다 sum-i ma-ki-da, 질식시키다 jil-ssik-si-ki-da

cholera *n.* 콜레라 kol-le-ra

cholesterol *n.* 콜레스테롤 kol-le-seu-te-rol

choose *vt., vi.* 선택하다 seon-tae-ka-da, 고르다 go-reu-da

chop *vt.* 찍다 jjik-da, 쪼개다 jjo-gae-da

chopping board *n.* 도마 do-ma

chopstick *n.* 젓가락 jeot-ga-rak

chore *n.* 잡일 jam-nil, jab-il, 허드렛일 heo-deu-ren-nil

chorus *n.* 합창 hap-chang

chosen *adj.* 선발된 seon-bal-doen, 선택된 seon-taek-doen

christen *vt.* 세례를 주다 se-rye-reul ju-da, 기독교도로 만들다 gi-dok-gyo-do-ro man-deul-da

Christian *n.* 기독교인 gi-dok-gyo-in; *adj.* 기독교의 gi-dok-gyo-ui

Christian name *n.* 세례명 se-rye-myeong

Christianity *n.* 기독교 신앙 gi-dok-gyo sin-ang

Christmas *n.* 크리스마스 keu-ri-sseu-ma-sseu

chronic *adj.* 만성의 man-seong-ui, 상습적인 sang-seup-jeog-in

chronological *adj.* 연대순의 yeon-dae-sun-ui

chubby *adj.* 통통한 tong-tong-han, 토실토실한 to-sil-to-sil-han

chuckle *vt.* 킬킬 웃다 kil-kil ut-da

chunk *n.* 큰 덩어리 keun deong-eo-ri

church *n.* 교회 gyo-hoe

churchman *n.* 신자 sin-ja, 성직자 seong-jik-ja

cider *n.* 사과주스 sa-gwa-ju-sseu

cigar *n.* 시가 ssi-ga

cigarette *n.* 담배 dam-bae

cinder *n.* 타다 남은 찌꺼기 ta-da nam-eun jji-kkeo-gi

cinema *n.* 영화관 yeong-hwa-gwan; 영화 yeong-hwa

cinnamon *n.* 계피 gye-pi

circle n. 원 won; 범위 beom-wi; 집단 jip-dan; 서클 sseo-keul

circuit n. 소케트 so-ke-teu; 순회 sun-hoe; 우회 u-hoe; closed ~ TV 유선 텔레비전 yu-seon tel-le-bi-jeon; closed ~ 폐회로 pye-hoe-ro

circulate vt. 돌리다 dol-li-da; 유포시키다 yu-po-si-ki-da; vi. 순환하다 sun-hwan-ha-da, 돌다 dol-da

circulation n. 순환 sun-hwan; 유통 yu-tong; 발행부수 bal-haeng-bu-ssu

circumcision n. 포경수술 po-gyeong-su-sul

circumference n. 원주 won-ju

circumstance n. 상황 sang-hwang; 환경 hwan-gyeong

circus n. 서커스 sseo-keo-sseu

cite vt. 인용하다 in-yong-ha-da

citizen n. 시민 si-min

citrus n. 감귤 gam-gyul

city n. 시 si, 도시 do-si

city hall n. 시청 si-cheong

city planning n. 도시계획 do-si-gye-hoek

civil war n. 내란 nae-ran, 내전 nae-jeon

civilian n. 일반인 il-ban-in, 민간인 min-gan-in

civilization n. 문명 mun-myeong; 문명화 mun-myeong-hwa

civilize vt. 문명화하다 mun-myeong-hwa-ha-da, 개화하다 gae-hwa-ha-da

claim n. 요구 yo-gu; 주장 ju-jang; vt. 요구하다 yo-gu-ha-da; 주장하다 ju-jang-ha-da

clam n. 대합조개 dae-hap-jo-gae

clan n. 일족 il-jjok, 대가족 dae-ga-jok

clap vt. 박수치다 bak-su-chi-da; 살짝 때리다 sal-sal ttae-ri-da

clarification n. 정화 jeong-hwa; 설명 seol-myeong, 해명 hae-myeong

clarify vt. 맑게하다 mal-kke-ha-da; 명백히 하다 myeong-bae-ki ha-da, 분명히 하다 bun-myeong-hi ha-da

clarinet n. 클라리넷 keul-la-ri-net

class n. (kind, sort) 종류 jong-nyu; (grade) 등급 deung-geup; (social) 계급 gye-geup; (school) 학급 hak-geup; (academic course) 수업 su-eop

classical adj. 고전적인 go-jeon-jeog-in

classics n. 고전작품 go-jeon-jak-pum

classification n. 분류 bul-lyu

classify vt. 분류하다 bul-lyu-ha-da

classmate n. 동급생 dong-geup-saeng, 급우 geub-u

classroom n. 교실 gyo-sil

claw n. 집게발 jip-ge-bal; 발톱 bal-top

clay n. 진흙 jin-heuk, 찰흙 chal-heuk

clean adj. 깨끗한 kkae-kkeu-tan, 순결한 sun-gyeol-han; vt. 깨끗하게 하다 kkae-kkeu-ta-ge ha-da, 청소하다 cheong-so-ha-da

cleaner n. (person) 세탁업자 se-tag-eop-ja; (material) 진공청소기 jin-gong-cheong-so-gi; 세제 se-je

cleaning n. 청소 cheong-so, 세탁 se-tak

cleanse vt. 청결하게 하다 cheong-gyeol-ha-ge ha-da, 정화하다 jeong-hwa-ha-da

clean-up n. 대청소 dae-cheong-so; 재고정리 jae-go-jeong-ni

clear adj. 맑은 malg-eun; 분명한 bun-myeong-han; 명백한 myeong-bae-kan; 명석한 myeong-seo-kan; 이해된 i-hae-doen; vt. 맑게 하다 mal-kke ha-da; 깨끗이 치우다 kkae-kkeus-i chi-u-da; 해제하다 hae-je-ha-da; 밝히다 bal-ki-da; 결말을 내다 gyeol-mal-eul nae-da

clear-cut adj. 윤곽이 뚜렷한 yun-gwag-i ttu-ryeo-tan, 선명한 seon-myeong-han, 명쾌한 myeong-kwae-han

clearance n. 정리 jeong-ni; 세관통과 se-gwan-tong-gwa; 재고정리 jae-go-jeong-ni

clearly adv. 똑똑히 ttok-tto-ki, 뚜렷하게 ttu-ryeo-ta-ge

clearance sale n. 창고정리 판매 chang-kko-jeong-ni pan-mae, 염가판매 yeom-kka-pan-mae

clergy n. 목사직 mok-sa-jik, 성직 seong-jik

clergyman n. 목사 mok-sa, 성직자 seong-jik-ja

clerk n. 사무원 sa-mu-won; 점원 jeom-won

clever adj. 영리한 yeong-ni-ha-da

click vi. 딸깍 소리를 내다 ttal-kkak so-ri-reul nae-da, 클릭하다 keul-Il-ka-da

client n. 소송 의뢰인 so-song-ui-roe-in; 고객 go-gaek

cliff n. 절벽 jeol-byeok, 낭떠러지 nang-tteo-reo-ji

cliff-hanging adj. 손에 땀을 쥐게 하는 son-e ttam-eul jwi-ge ha-neun, 아슬아슬한 a-seul-a-seul-han

climate n. 기후 gi-hu

climax *n.* 클라이맥스 keul-la-i-maek-seu, 절
정 jeol-jjeong

climb *n.* 등반 deung-ban; *vt., vi.* 오르다 o-
reu-da, 올라가다 ol-la-ga-da; 기어오르다
gi-eo-o-reu-da, 등반하다 deung-ban-ha-da

cling *vi.* 들러붙다 deul-leo-but-da; 매달리다
mae-dal-li-da

clinic *n.* 진료소 jil-lyo-so; 임상강의
im-sang-gang-ui

clip *n.* 클립 keul-lip; *vt.* 자르다 ja-reu-da; 꼭
집다 kkok jip-da, 꽉 쥐다 kkwak jwi-da

clip board *n.* 클립보드 keul-lip-bo-deu

clipper *n.* 손톱깎이 son-top-kkakk-i

clock *n.* 시계 si-gye

clockwise *adv.* 시계방향으로 si-gye-bang-
hang-eu-ro

clog *vt.* 방해하다 bang-hae-ha-da, 무겁
게 하다 mu-geop-ge ha-da; *vi.* 막히다
ma-ki-da

cloning *n.* 생물복제 saeng-mul-bok-je

close *adj.* 가까운 ga-kka-un; 닫은 dad-eun;
정밀한 jeong-mil-han; *adv.* 밀접하여
mil-jjeo-pa-yeo; 정밀히 jeong-mil-hi; *vt.*
눈을 감다 nun-eul gam-tta; 문을 닫다
mun-eul dat-da; *vi.* 닫히다 da-chi-da, 완결
하다 wan-gyeol-ha-da

close-by *adj.* 가까운 ga-kka-un, 인접한
in-jeo-pan, 근처의 geun-cheo-ui

closed *adj.* 닫힌 da-chin; 경계의
gyeong-gye-ui

closely *adv.* 밀접하게 mil-jjeo-pa-ge, 면밀히
myeon-mil-hi

closet *n.* 벽장 byeok-jang

close-up *n.* 클로즈업 keul-lo-jeu-eop

closure *n.* 폐쇄 pye-swae, 마감 ma-gam,
폐점 pye-jeom, 휴업 hyu-eop, 종결
jong-gyeol

cloth *n.* 천 cheon, 헝겊 heong-geop

clothe *vt.* 옷을 주다 os-eul ju-da; 싸다 ssa-
da, 덮다 deop-da, 옷을 입다 os-eul ip-da

clothes *n. pl.* 옷 ot, 의복 ui-bok

clothing *n.* 의복 ui-bok, 의류 ui-ryu

cloud *n.* 구름 gu-reum

cloudy *adj.* 흐린 heu-rin; 구름이 낀 gu-
reum-i kkin

clover *n.* 클로버 keul-lo-beo, 토끼풀
to-kki-pul

clown *n.* 광대 gwang-dae

club *n.* *(stick)* 곤봉 gon-bong; *(playing card,
organization)* 클럽 keul-leop

clue *n.* 실마리 sil-ma-ri, 단서 dan-seo

clumsy *adj.* 꼴사나운 kkol-sa-na-un, 모양
없는 mo-yang-eom-neun, 실수가 잦은
sil-ssu-ga jaj-eun

cluster *n.* 송이 song-i; 덩어리 deong-eo-ri;
vi. 떼를 이루다 tte-reul i-ru-da; 주렁주렁
달리다 ju-reong-ju-reong dal-li-da

clutch *n.* *(auto)* 클러치 keul-leo-chi; *vi.* 매달
리다 mae-dal-li-da, 클러치를 넣다 keul-
leo-chi-reul neo-ta; *vt.* 꼭 잡다 kkok jap-da

coach *n.* 코치 ko-chi

coal *n.* 석탄 seok-tan

coal tar *n.* 콜타르 kol-ta-reu

coalition *n.* 연합 yeon-hap, 제휴 je-hyu

coarse *adj.* 조잡한 jo-ja-pan; 야비한
ya-bi-han

coast *n.* 해안 hae-an

coastguard *n.* 연안경비대
yeon-an-gyeong-bi-dae

coastline *n.* 해안선 hae-an-seon

coast-to-coast *adj.* 전국적인 jeon-guk-jeog-in

coat *n.* 양복 상의 yang-bok-sang-ui; 외막
oe-mak, 표피 pyo-pi; 칠 chil

coated *adj.* 방수가공한 bang-su-ga-gong-
han, 겉에 바른 geot-e ba-reun

coating *n.* 코팅 ko-ting, 칠 chil

cobra *n.* 코브라 ko-beu-ra

cobweb *n.* 거미집 geo-mi-jip

Coca-Cola *n.* 코카콜라 ko-ka-kol-la

cock *n.* 콜라 kol-la; 수탉 su-tak; 건초더미
geon-cho-tteo-mi

cocktail *n.* 칵테일 kak-te-il

cocoa *n.* 코코아 ko-ko-a

cod *n.* 대구 dae-gu

code *n.* 암호 am-ho; 코드 ko-deu; 법전
beop-jeon

coed *adj.* 남녀공학의 nam-nyeo-gong-hag-ui

coexistence *n.* 공존 gong-jon

coffee *n.* 커피 keo-pi; ~ beans 커피콩 keo-
pi-kong; ~ break 커피 브레이크 keo-pi
beu-re-i-keu; ~ table 탁자 tak-ja

coffeemaker *n.* 커피메이커 keo-pi-me-i-keo

coffeepot *n.* 커피주전자 keo-pi-ju-jeon-ja

coffee shop *n.* 다방 da-bang, 카페 ka-pe,
(store, restaurant) 커피숍 keo-pi-syop

coffin *n.* 관 gwan

coherence *n.* 통일성 tong-il-sseong, 일관성 il-gwan-sseong

cohesion *n.* 결합력 gyeol-ham-nyeok, 응집력 eung-jim-nyeok

coil *n.* 코일 ko-il; 소용돌이 so-yong-dol-i

coin *n.* 동전 dong-jeon; ~ **box** 동전통 dong-jeon-tong

coincide *vi.* 동시에 일어나다 dong-si-e il-eo-na-da

coincidence *n.* 우연의 일치 u-yeon-ui il-chi; 동시 발생 dong-si-bal-ssaeng

coincidental *adj.* 우연이 일치에 의한 u-yeon-ui il-chi-e ui-han; 동시에 발생한 dong-si-e bal-ssaeng-han

coke (soda) *n.* 코크 ko-keu

cold *n.* 감기 gam-gi; 추위 chu-wi; *adj.* 추운 chu-un; 냉정한 naeng-jeong-han

cold-blooded *adj.* 냉혈의 naeng-hyeol-ui, 냉정한 naeng-jeong-han

cold cream *n.* 콜드크림 kol-deu keu rim

cold feet *n.* 공포 gong-po, 겁 geop

cold sweat *n.* 식은 땀 sig-eun ttam

cold war *n.* 냉전 naeng-jeon

collaborate *vi.* 협력하다 hyeom-nyeo-ka-da

collaboration *n.* 협력 hyeom-nyeok

collague *n.* 동료 dong-nyo

collapse *vi.* 무너지다 mu-neo-ji-da, 좌절하다 jwa-jeol-ha-da, 폭락하다 pong-na-ka-da; *n.* 붕괴 bung-goe, 좌절 jwa-jeol, 폭락 pong-nak

collar *n.* 칼라 kal-la, 깃 git

collect *vt.* 모으다 mo-eu-da; *vi.* 모이다 mo-i-da

collection *n.* 수집 su-jip; 수집품 su-jip-pum

collector *n.* 수집가 su-jip-ga; 수금원 su-geum-won

college *n.* 대학 dae-hak

collide *vi.* 충돌하다 chung-dol-ha-da

collision *n.* 충돌 chung-dol

colloquial *adj.* 일상 회화의 il-ssang hoe-hwa-ui, 구어의 gu-eo-ui

Colombia *n.* 콜롬비아 kol-lom-bi-a

colon *n.* (*punctuation*) 콜론 kol-lon; (*body part*) 결장 gyeol-jjang

colonel *n.* 육군대령 yuk-gun-dae-ryeong

colony *n.* 식민지 sing-min-ji

color *n.* 색 saek, 색깔 saek-kkal; ~**ing book** 색칠그림책 saek-chil geu-rim-chaek; ~ **TV** 컬러 텔레비전 keol-leo tel-le-bi-jeon

color-blind *adj.* 색맹의 saeng-maeng-ui

color-code *vt.* 색으로 구분하다 saeg-eu-ro gu-bun-ha-da

colorful *adj.* 화려한 hwa-ryeo-han, 다채로운 da-chae-ro-un

coloring *n.* 채색 chae-saek

column *n.* 기둥 gi-dung; 칼럼 kal-leom

coma *n.* 혼수상태 hon-su-sang-tae

comb *n.* 빗 bit; *vt.* 머리빗다 meo-ri-bit-da

combat *vi.* 싸우다 ssa-u-da, 투쟁하다 tu-jaeng-ha-da; *n.* 전투 jeon-tu, 논쟁 non-jaeng

combination *n.* 결합 gyeol-hap

combination lock *n.* 다이얼 자물쇠 da-i-eol ja-mul-ssoe

combine *vt.* 결합하다 gyeol-ha-pa-da; 연합하다 yeon-ha-pa-da

come *vi.* 오다 o-da; 일이 생기다 il-i saeng-gi-da; …하게 되다 …ha-ge doe-da

comeback *n.* 복귀 bok-gwi, 컴백 ceom-baek, 회복 hoe-bok

comedian *n.* 코메디언 ko-me-di-eon, 개그맨 gae-geu-man

comedown *n.* 몰락 mol-lak, 실추 sil-chu

comedy *n.* 코메디 ko-me-di

comet *n.* 혜성 hye-seong

comfort *n.* 위로 wi-ro; 안락 al-lak; *vt.* 위로하다 wi-ro-ha-da

comfortable *adj.* 편한 pyeon-han, 안락한 al-la-kan

comforter *n.* 이불 i-bul; 위안자 wi-an-ja

comic *n.* 만화 man-hwa; 희극성 hi-geuk-seong; *adj.* 우스운 u-seu-un, 익살스러운 ik-sal-seu-reo-un; ~ **book** 만화책 man-hwa-chaek

comic strip *n.* 연재만화 yeon-jae-man-hwa

comma *n.* 쉼표 swim-pyo

command *n.* 명령 myeong-nyeong, 지배력 ji-bae-ryeok; *vt.* 명령하다 myeong-nyeong-ha-da; 지배하다 ji-bae-ha-da

commander *n.* 지휘관 ji-hwi-gwan, 사령관 sa-ryeong-gwan

commandment *n.* 명령 myeong-nyeong; 계명 gye-myeong

commence *vi.* 시작되다 si-jak-doe-da, 시작하다 si-ja-ka-da

comment *n.* 논평 non-pyeong, 코멘트 ko-men-teu; *vt.* 논평하다 non-pyeong-ha-da, 코멘트하다 ko-men-teu-ha-da

commentary *n.* 주석서 ju-seok-seo, 비평 bi-pyeong; 시사해설 si-sa-hae-seol

commerce *n.* 상업 sang-eop, 통상 tong-sang

commercial *n.* 광고방송 gwang-go-bang-song; *adj.* 상업의 sang-eob-ui, 통상의 tong-sang-ui; **television** ~ 텔레비전 광고 방송 tel-le-bi-jeon gwang-go-bang-song

commission *n.* 수수료 su-su-ryo, 커미 션 keo-mi-syeon; 임무 im-mu; 위원회 wi-won-hoe

commit *vt.* 위탁하다 wi-ta-ka-da, 맡기다 mat-gi-da; 언질을 주다 eon-jil-eul ju-da

committee *n.* 위원회 wi-won-hoe

common *adj.* 공통의 gong-tong-ui, 보통의 bo-tong-ui; 일반의 il-ban-ui

common ground *n.* 공통기반 gong-tong-gi-ban

commonly *adv.* 일반적으로 il-ban-jeog-eu-ro, 통상 tong-sang, 보통 bo-tong

common sense *n.* 상식 sang-sik

commotion *n.* 동요 dong-yo, 소동 so-dong

communicate *vt.* 전달하다 jeon-dal-ha-da; *vi.* 통하다 tong-ha-da; 통신하다 tong-sin-ha-da

communication *n.* 통신 tong-sin, 전달 jeon-dal; 교통 gyo-tong

communication satellite *n.* 통신위성 tong-sin-wi-seong

communicative *adj.* 수다스런 su-da-seu-reon; 통신의 tong-sin-ui

communion *n.* 친교 chin-gyo; *(sacrament)* 종교단체 jong-gyo-dan-che

communism *n.* 공산주의 gong-san-ju-ui

communist *n.* 공산주의자 gong-san-ju-ui-ja; *adj.* 공산주의의 gong-san-ju-i-ui

community *n.* 일반사회 il-ban-sa-hoe, 공동사회 gong-dong-sa-hoe, 공동체 gong-dong-che

community college *n.* 전문대학 jeon-mun-dae-hak

commutation ticket *n.* 정기 승차권 jeong-gi seung-cha-kkwon

commute *vt.* 교환하다 gyo-hwan-ha-da, 대체하다 dae-che-ha-da; *vi.* 통근하다 tong-geun-ha-da

compact *n.* 콤팩트 kom-paek-teu; 계약 gye-yak; *adj.* 밀집한 mil-jji-pan; 아담한 a-dam-han

compact disc *n.* 컴팩트 디스크 keom-paek-teu di-seu-keu

companion *n.* 동료 dong-nyo, 동반자 dong-ban-ja

companionship *n.* 교우관계 gyo-u-gwan-gye, 교제 gyo-je

company *n.* 회사 hoe-sa; 동아리 dong-a-ri; 동료 dong-nyo; 교제 gyo-je

compare *vt.* 비교하다 bi-gyo-ha-da; 비유하 다 bi-yu-ha-da

comparison *n.* 비교 bi-gyo; 비유 bi-yu

compartment *n.* 간막이 gan-mag-i; 컴파트 먼트 keom-pa-teu-meon-teu

compass *n.* 나침반 na-chim-ban, 콤파스 kom-pa-sseu; 한계 han-gye

compatible *adj.* 양립하는 yang-ni-pa-neun; 호환가능한 ho-hwan-ga-neung-han

compel *vt.* 강요하다 gang-yo-ha-da

compelling *adj.* 강제적인 gang-je-jeog-in

compensate *vt.* 갚다 gap-da, 보상하다 bo-sang-ha-da

compensation *n.* 보상 bo-sang, 배상 bae-sang

compete *vi.* 경쟁하다 gyeong-jaeng-ha-da, 맞서다 mat-seo-da

competence *n.* 적성 jeok-seong

competent *adj.* 적임의 jeog-im-ui; 유능한 yu-neung-han

competition *n.* 경쟁 gyeong-jaeng, 시합 si-hap

competitive *adj.* 경쟁적인 gyeong-jaeng-jeog-in, 경쟁의 gyeong-jaeng-ui

compile *vt.* 편집하다 pyeon-ji-pa-da, 수집하 다 su-ji-pa-da

complain *vi.* 불평하다 bul-pyeong-ha-da, 하소연하다 ha-so-yeon-ha-da, 호소하다 ho-so-ha-da

complaint *n.* 불평 bul-pyeong, 불만 bul-man

complement *n.* 보완물 bo-wan-mul; *vt.* 보완 하다 bo-wan-ha-da

complementary *adj.* 보완적인 bo-wan-jeog-in

complete *adj.* 완전한 wan-jeon-han; *vt.* 완성 하다 wan-seong-ha-da

complex *adj.* 복잡한 bok-ja-pan, 어려운 eo-ryeo-un; 복합된 bo-kap-doen, 합성 의 hap-seong-ui; *n.* 합성물 hap-seong-mul, 복합체 bo-kap-che; 콤플렉스 kom-peul-lek-seu

complicate *vt.* 복잡하게 하다 bok-ja-pa-ge ha-da

complicated *adj.* 복잡한 bok-ja-pan

compliment *n.* 칭찬 ching-chan; *vt.* 칭찬하다 ching-chan-ha-da

comply *vi.* 동의하다 dong-ui-ha-da, 따르다 tta-reu-da, 응하다 eung-ha-da

component *n.* 구성요소 gu-seong-nyo-so, 성분 seong-bun; *adj.* 구성하고 있는 gu-seong-ha-go in-neun, 성분의 seong-bun-ui

compose *vt.* 조립하다 jo-ri-pa-da; 작곡하다 jak-go-ka-da; 작문하다 jang-mun-ha-da; 정돈하다 jeong-don-ha-da

composition *n.* 작곡 jak-gok; 작문 jang-mun; 구성 gu-seong

compound *n.* *(chemical)* 화합물 hwa-ham-mul; 혼합물 hon-ham-mul; 복합어 bo-kab-eo; *(buildings)* 구내 gu-nae; 포로 수용소 po-ro su-yong-so; *adj.* 복합의 bo-kab-ui, 화합의 hwa-hab-ui, 혼성의 hon-seong-ui

comprehension *n.* 이해 i-hae, 이해력 i-hae-ryeok; 함축 ham-chuk

comprehensive *adj.* 포괄적인 po-gwal-jjeog-in, 범위가 넓은 beom-wi-ga neolb-eun; 이해가 빠른 i-hae-ga ppa-reun

compress *vt.* 압축하다 ap-chu-ka-da; 집약하다 jib-ya-ka-da; *n.* 압박붕대 ap-bak-bung-dae

compressor *n.* 압축기 ap-chuk-gi

comprise *vt.* 함유하다 ham-yu-ha-da, 포함하다 po-ham-ha-da

compromise *n.* 타협 ta-hyeop, 절충 jeol-chung; *vt.* 양보하다 yang-bo-ha-da; 더럽히다 deo-reo-pi-da; *vi.* 타협하다 ta-hyeo-pa-da

computer *n.* 컴퓨터 keom-pu-teo; **personal** ~ 개인용 컴퓨터 gae-in-nyong keom-pyu-teo

computer virus *n.* 컴퓨터 바이러스 keom-pu-teo ba-i-reo-sseu

con *n.* *(opposite of pro)* 반대투표 ban-dae-tu-pyo, 반대자 ban-dae-ja

conceal *vt.* 숨기다 sum-gi-da, 비밀로 하다 bi-mil-lo ha-da

conceit *n.* 자만 ja-man

concentrate *vi.* 집중하다 jip-jung-ha-da

concept *n.* 개념 gae-nyeom, 생각 saeng-gak

concern *n.* 관계 gwan-gye; 관심 gwan-sim; 관심사 gwan-sim-sa; *vt.* 관계하다 gwan-gye-ha-da, 관심을 갖다 gwan-sim-eul gat-da

concert *n.* 음악회 eum-a-koe; 협력 hyeom-nyeok

concession *n.* 양보 yang-bo; 면허 myeon-heo

concise *adj.* 간결한 gan-gyeol-han

conclude *vt.* 끝내다 kkeun-nae-da; 조약을 맺다 jo-yag-eul maet-da; 결론을 내리다 gyeol-lon-eul nae-ri-da

conclusion *n.* 결말 gyeol-mal, 결론 gyeol-lon

concrete *n.* 콘크리트 kon-keu-ri-teu; *adj.* 구체적인 gu-che-jeog-in

condemn *vt.* 비난하다 bi-nan-ha-da; 유죄판결을 내리다 yu-joe-pan-gyeol-eul nae-ri-da; 운명지우다 un-myeong-ji-u-da

condense *vt.* 응축하다 eung-chu-ka-da, 압축하다 ap chu ka da, 요약하다 yo-ya-ka-da

condiment *n.* 조미료 jo-mi-ryo, 양념 yang-nyeom

condition *n.* 컨디션 keon-di-syeon, 상태 sang-tae; 조건 jo-kkeon, 지위 ji-wi

condolence *n.* 조의 jo-ui, 애도 ae-do

condom *n.* 콘돔 kon-dom

condominium *n.* 콘도 kon-do, 아파트 a-pa-teu

conduct *n.* 행위 haeng-wi; 지도 ji-do; *vt.* 안내하다 an-nae-ha-da; 집행하다 ji-paeng-ha-da; 지도하다 ji-do-ha-da; 행동하다 haeng-dong-ha-da; 선도하다 jeon-do-ha-da

conductor *n.* 안내자 an-nae-ja; 지휘자 ji-hwi-ja; 차장 cha-jang

cone *n.* 콘 kon, 원추체 won-chu-che, 원뿔 won-ppul

confederation *n.* 연합 yeon-hap, 동맹 dong-maeng; 연방 yeon-bang

conference *n.* 협의 hyeob-ui; 회의 hoe-ui

confess *vt.* 실토하다 sil-to-ha-da; 참회하다 cham-hoe-ha-da; 인정하다 in-jeong-ha-da; 표명하다 pyo-myeong-ha-da

confession *n.* 실토 sil-to; 참회 cham-hoe

confidence *n.* 신용 sin-yong, 신임 sin-im; 자신 ja-sin, 확신 hwak-sin; 비밀 bi-mil

confident *adj.* 확신하는 hwak-sin-ha-neun; 자신만만한 ja-sin-man-man-han

confidential *adj.* 신임하는 sin-im-ha-neun; 기밀의 gi-mil-ui
confirm *vt.* 확인하다 hwag-in-ha-da
confirmation *n.* 확인 hwag-in; 확정 hwak-jeong
conflict *n.* 충돌 chung-dol, 상충 sang-chung
conform *vt.* 따르게 하다 tta-reu-ge ha-da, 맞게 하다 mat-ge ha-da
confront *vt.* 직면하다 jing-myeon-ha-da, 맞서다 mat-seo-da
confuse *vt.* 혼동하다 hon-dong-ha-da; 혼란시키다 hol-lan-si-ki-da
confusion *n.* 혼동 hon-dong; 혼란 hol-lan; 당황 dang-hwang
congest *vt.* 혼잡하게 하다 hon-ja-pa-ge ha-da; *vi.* 충혈하다chung-hyeol-ha-da
congestion *n.* 밀집 mil-jjip, 과잉 gwa-ing, 정체 jeong-che; 충혈 chung-hyeol
Congo *n.* 콩고 kong-go
congratulate *vt.* 축하하다 chu-ka-ha-da
congratulation *n.* 축하 chu-ka; ~s 축하합니다. chu-ka-ham-ni-da
congregation *n.* 모임 mo-im; 회중 hoe-jung
congress *n.* 회의 hoe-ui; 의회 ui-hoe
conjecture *n.* 어림짐작 eo-rim-jim-jak, 추측 chu-cheuk
conjunction *n.* 결합 gyeol-hap; 접속사 jeop-sok-sa
connect *vt.* 연결하다 yeon-gyeol-ha-da
connection *n.* 연결 yeon-gyeol; 관계 gwan-gye
connotation *n.* 함축 ham-chuk, 내포 nae-po
conquer *vt.* 정복하다 jeong-bo-ka-da
conscience *n.* 양심 yang-sim
conscientious *adj.* 양심적인 yang-sim-jeog-in
conscious *adj.* 지각있는 ji-gag-in-neun; 의식하고 있는 ui-si-ka-go in-neun
consent *n.* 동의 dong-ui; *vt.* 동의하다 dong-ui-ha-da
consequence *n.* 결과 gyeol-gwa; 중대성 jung-dae-sseong
conservation *n.* 보호 bo-ho, 유지 yu-ji, 보존 bo-jon
conservative *adj.* 보수적인 j-bo-su-jeog-in; 수수한 su-su-han
conserve *vt.* 보존하다 bo-jon-ha-da
consider *vt.* 고려하다 go-ryeo-ha-da
considerable *adj.* 중요한 jung-yo-han; 적지 않은 jeok-ji-an-eun

consideration *n.* 고려 go-ryeo; 고려의 대상 go-ryeo-ui dae-sang
consist *vi.* ...(으)로 이루어지다 ...(eu)ro i-ru-eo-ji-da; ...에 존재하다 ...e jon-jae-ha-da; 양립하다 yang-ni-pa-da
consistency *n.* 일관성 il-gwan-sseong; 농도 nong-do
consolation *n.* 위로 wi-ro, 위안 wi-an
console *n.* 콘솔 kon-sol; *vt.* 위로하다 wi-ro-ha-da, 위안하다 wi-an-ha-da
consolidate *vt.* 합병하다 hap-byeong-ha-da, 통합하다 tong-ha-pa-da
consonant *n.* 자음 ja-eum; *adj.* 조화하는 so-hwa-ha-neun
consortium *n.* 협회 hyeop-hoe, 조합 jo-hap
constant *n.* 불변의 것 bul-byeon-ui geot; 불변수량 bul-byeon-su-ryang; *adj.* 변하지 않는 byeon-ha-ji an-neun; 성실한 seong-sil-han
constantly *adv.* 끊임없이 kkeun-im-eops-i, 항상 hang-sang, 자주 ja-ju
constellation *n.* 별자리 byeol-jja-ri
constipation *n.* 변비 byeon-bi
constitute *vt.* 구성하다 gu-seong-ha-da; ...(으)로 되어 있다 ...(eu)ro doe-eo it-da
constitution *n.* 구성 gu-seong, 조직 jo-jik; 체질 che-jil; 정체 jeong-che; 헌법 heon-ppeop
constrict *vt.* 조이다 jo-i-da, 압축하다 ap-chu-ka-da
construct *vt.* 짜맞추다 jja-mat-chu-da, 건설하다 geon-seol-ha-da
construction *n.* 건설 geon-seol, 건설공사 geon-seol-gong-sa; 건물 geon-mul
consul *n.* 영사 yeong-sa
consulate *n.* 영사관 yeong-sa-gwan; 영사직 yeong-sa-jik
consult *vi.* 의견을 묻다 ui-gyeon-eul mut-da, 상담하다 sang-dam-ha-da; 참고하다 cham-go-ha-da, 찾다 chat-da; *vi.* 상의하다 sang-ui-ha-da; to ~ with ...와 상담하다 ...wa sang-dam-ha-da
consultant *n.* 고문 go-mun; 컨설턴트 keon-sseol-teon-teu
consume *vt.* 소비하다 so-bi-ha-da, 소모하다 so-mo-ha-da; 소멸시키다 so-myeol-ha-da
consumer *n.* 소비자 so-bi-ja
consumption *n.* 소비 so-bi; 소모 so-mo

contact *n.* 접촉 jeop-chok; *vt.* 접촉하다 jeop-cho-ka-da

contact lens *n.* 콘텍트 렌즈 kon-tek-teu ren-jeu

contagious *adj.* 전염되는 jeon-yeom-doe-neun

contain *vt.* 내포하다 nae-po-ha-da; 감정을 억누르다 gam-jeong-eul eong-nu-reu-da

container *n.* 용기 yong-gi, 컨테이너 keon-te-i-neo

contaminate *vt.* 오염시키다 o-yeom-si-ki-da

contemporary *adj.* 동시대의 dong-si-dae-ui; 현대의 hyeon-dae ui

contempt *n.* 경멸 gyeong-myeol, 멸시 myeol-ssi; 창피 chang-pi

contend *vi.* 다투다 da-tu-da, 싸우다 ssa-u-da; 주장하다 ju-jang-ha-da

content *n.* 만족 man-jok; 내용 nae-yong; 목차 mok-cha; *adj.* 만족하는 man-jo-ka-neun

contest *n.* 논쟁 non jaeng, 경쟁 gyeong jaeng; *vt.* 논쟁하다 non-jaeng-ha-da; 겨루다 gyeo-ru-da

context *n.* 문맥 nun-maek, 전후관계 jeon-hu-gwan-gye

continent *n.* 대륙 dae ryuk

continue *vt.* 계속하다 gye-so-ka-da; 연속하다 yeon-so-ka-da

continuous *adj.* 연속하는 yeon-so-ka-da

contraceptive *n.* 피임약 pi-im-nyak; 피임봉구 pi-im-nyong-gu; *adj.* 씨임봉 pi-im-nyong

contract *n.* 계약 gye-yak; *vt.* 계약하다 gye-ya-ka-da; *vi.* 줄어들다 jul-eo-deul-da

contraction *n.* 수축 su-chuk, 위축 wi-chuk, 축소 chuk-so, 단축 dan-chuk

contractor *n.* 계약자 gye-yak-ja

contradict *vt.* 부정하다 bu-jeong-ha-da; 모순되다 mo-sun-doe-da

contrary *adj.* 반대의 ban-dae-ui; 적합치 않은 jeo-kap-chi an-eun

contrast *n.* 대조 dae-jo; 대비 dae-bi

contribute *vt.* 기부하다 gi-bu-ha-da; 기여하다 gi-yeo-ha-da; 기고하다 gi-go-ha-da

contribution *n.* 기여 gi-yeo; 기부 gi-bu; 기고 gi-go

control *n.* 통제 tong-je; 지배 ji-bae; 억제 eok-je; *vt.* 지배하다 ji-bae-ha-da; 통제하다 tong-je-ha-da; 억제하다 eok-je-ha-da

controller *n.* 관리인 gwal-li-in; 검사관 geom-sa-won

control room *n.* 관제실 gwan-je-sil, 통제실 tong-je-sil, 조정실 jo-jeong-sil

control tower *n.* 관제탑 gwan-je-tap

controversy *n.* 논쟁 non-jaeng, 논의 non-ui

convene *vt.* 모으다 mo-eu-da, 소집하다 so-ji-pa-da; 소환하다 so-hwan-ha-da

convenience *n.* 편리 pyeol-li

convenience store *n.* 편의점 pyeon-ui-jeom

convenient *adj.* 편리한 pyeol-li-han; 형편이 좋은 hyeong-pyeon-i jo-eun; 간편한 gan-pyeon-han

convent *n.* 수도원 su-do-won; 수녀원 su-nyeo-won

convention *n.* 집회 ji-poe; 협약 hyeob-yak; 관례 gwal-lye; 관습 gwan-seup

conventional *adj.* 전통적인 jeon-tong-jeog-in; 진부한 jin-bu-han; 회의의 hoe-ui-ui

conversation *n.* 대회 dae hwa; 회화 hoe hwa

converse *v.* 담화하다 dam-hwa-ha-da; *adj.* 뒤바뀐 dwi-ba-kkwin

convert *n.* 전환 jeon-hwan; 개종자 gae-jong-ja; 전향자 jeon-hyang-ja; *vt.* 전환하다 jeon-hwan-ha-da; 개종하다 gae-jong-ha-da; 전향하다 jeon-hyang-ha-da

convey *vt.* 나르다 na-reu-da; 전달하다 jeon-dal-ha-da

convince *vt.* 확신시키다 hwak-sin-si-ki-da

cook *n.* 요리사 yo-ri-sa; *vt.* 요리하다 yo-ri-ha-da; **~book** 요리책 yo-ri-chaek

cooker *n.* *(appliance)* 요리기구 yo-ri-gi-gu

cookie *n.* 쿠키 ku-ki, 과자 gwa-ja

cooking *n.* 요리(법) yo-ri(-ppeop)

cool *adj.* 시원한 si-won-han; *vt.* 차갑게 하다 cha-gap-ge ha-da; 진정시키다 jin-jeong-si-ki-da

co-op *n.* 협동조합 hyeop-dong-jo-hap

cooperate *vi.* 협력하다 hyeom-nyeo-ka-da, 협동하다 hyeop-dong-ha-da

coordinate *vt.* 조정하다 jo-jeong-ha-da; 대등하게 하다 dae-deung-ha-ge ha-da

cop *n.* 순경 sun-gyeong; 실톳 sil-tot

cope *vi.* 겨루다 gyeo-ru-da, 대항하다 dae-hang-ha-da; 대처하다 dae-cheo-ha-da

Copenhagen *n.* 코펜하겐 ko-pen-ha-gen

copier *n.* 복사기 bok-sa-gi

copper *n.* 구리 gu-ri

copy *n.* 복사 bok-sa; 사본 sa-bon; *vt.* 복사하다 bok-sa-ha-da; 베끼다 be-kki-da

copycat *n.* 모방자 mo-bang-ja

copyright *n.* 저작권 jeo-jak-kkwon; *vt.* 저작권으로 보호하다 jeo-jak-kkwon-eu-ro bo-ho-ha-da; 판권을 얻다 pan-kkwon-eul eot-da

copywriter *n.* 카피라이터 ka-pi-ra-i-teo

coral *n.* 산호 san-ho

cord *n.* 끈 kkeun, 노끈 no-kkeun

cordially *adv.* 진심으로 jin-sim-eu-ro

cordless *adj.* 무선의 mu-seon-ui

core *n.* 핵심 haek-sim

cork *n.* 코르크 ko-reu-keu

corn *n.* 옥수수 ok-su-su; 티눈 ti-nun

corn dog *n.* 핫도그 hat-do-geu

corner *n.* 구석 gu-seok, 코너 ko-neo; **on the ~/around the ~** 구석에 gu-seog-e

corner kick *n.* 코너킥 ko-neo-kik

cornflakes *n.* 콘프레이크 kon-peu-re-i-keu

corny *adj.* 곡류의 gong-nyu-ui; 진부한 jin-bu-han; 감상적인 gam-sang-jeog-in

corporation *n.* 법인 beob-in; 주식회사 ju-si-koe-sa

corpse *n.* 시체 si-che

correct *adj.* 옳은 ol-eun; *vt.* 바로잡다 ba-ro-jap-da, 정정하다 jeong-jeong-ha-da

correction *n.* 정정 jeong-jeong; **~ fluid** 리퀴드 페이퍼 li-qwi-deu pe-i-peo

correspond *vi.* 상당하다 sang-dang-ha-da; 교신하다 gyo-sin-ha-da; **to ~ with/to** ...와 교신하다 ...wa gyo-sin-ha-da

correspondence *n.* 대응 dae-eung; 일치 il-chi; 통신 tong-sin

correspondent *n.* 통신자 tong-sin-ja; 특파원 teuk-pa-won

corridor *n.* 복도 bok-do

corrupt *adj.* 타락한 ta-ra-kan, 부정한 bu-jeong-han; 순수성을 잃은 sun-su-sseong-eul il-eun; *vt.* 타락시키다 ta-rak-si-ki-da, 매수하다 mae-su-ha-da; *vi.* 타락하다 ta-ra-ka-da

corruption *n.* 부정 bu-jeong, 부패 bu-pae, 타락 ta-rak; 매수 mae-su

cosign *vt., vi.* 공동서명하다 gong-dong-seo-myeong-ha-da

cosmetic *n.* 화장품 hwa-jang-pum; *adj.* 화장용의 hwa-jang-nyong-ui

cosmopolitan *adj.* 세계주의의 se-gye-ju-ui-ui

cosmos *n.* 우주 u-ju

cost *n.* 가격 ga-gyeok; 비용 bi-yong; 대가 dae-kka; 희생 hi-saeng; *vt.* 비용이 들다 bi-yong-i deul-da; 시간을 요하다 si-gan-eul yo-ha-da

costly *adv.* 값비싼 gap-bi-ssan; 희생이 큰 hi-saeng-i keun

cost price *n.* 원가 won-kka

costume *n.* 특별한 복장 teuk-byeol-han bok-jang, 옷차림 ot-cha-rim

cot *n.* 오두막집 o-du-mak-jjip; 간이침대 gan-i-chim-dae

cottage *n.* 작은 시골집 jag-eun si-gol-jjip

cotton *n.* 솜 som; 무명 mu-myeong; 무명실 mu-myeong-sil

cotton candy *n.* 솜사탕 som-sa-tang

couch *n.* 소파 sso-pa

cough *n.* 기침 gi-chim; *vi.* 기침하다 gi-chim-ha-da; **~ drop** 기침 진정제 gi-chim jin-jeong-je

could *aux. past of* **can** ...할 수가 있었다 ...hal ssu iss-eot-da, ...할 수 있다 ...hal ssu-it-da; ...할 수 있다면 ...hal ssu it-da-myeon, ...할 수 있을텐데 ...hal ssu iss-eul-ten-de, ...할 수 있었을텐데 ...hal ssu-iss-eoss-eul-ten-de; ...해 주시겠습니까 ...hae ji-si-get-seum-ni-kka; **~ be** 아마 a-ma

council *n.* 심의회 sim-ui-hoe

counsel *n.* 충고 chung-go, 상담 sang-dam, 조언 jo-eon; *vt.* 충고하다 chung-go-ha-da, 권고하다 gwon-go-ha-da

counselor *n.* 카운슬러 ka-un-seul-leo, 상담원 sang-dam-won

count *n.* *(to tally)* 계산 gye-san, 셈 sem; *(nobleman)* 백작 baek-jak; *vt.* 계산하다 gye-san-ha-da; ...(으)로 간주되다 ...(eu)ro gan-ju-doe-da

countdown *n.* 초읽기 cho-il-kki, 카운트다운 ka-un-teu-da-un

counter *n.* 계산대 gye-san-dae; 판매대 pan-mae-dae; *adj.* 반대의 ban-dae-ui; *vt.* 대항하다 dae-hang-ha-da

counterclockwise *adv.* 시계 반대방향으로 si-gye ban-dae-bang-hyang-eu-ro

counterfeit *adj.* 모조의 mo-jo-ui, 가짜의 ga-jja-ui; *vt.* 위조하다 wi-jo-ha-da; 모조하다 mo-jo-ha-da, 흉내내다 hyung-nae-nae-da

counterplan *n.* 대안 dae-an

countless *adv.* 셀 수 없는 sel-ssu eom-neun, 무수한 mu-su-han

country *n.* 국가 guk-ga, 나라 na-ra; 시골 si-gol; 지역 ji-yeok

countryside *n.* 시골 si-gol

county *n.* 군 gun, 주 ju

coup d'etat *n.* 쿠데타 ku-de-ta

couple *n.* 커플 keo-peul; 부부 bu-bu; 한 쌍 han ssang

coupon *n.* 쿠폰 ku-pon

courage *n.* 용기 yong-gi

courageous *adj.* 용감한 yong-gam-han

course *n.* 진로 jil-lo; 진행 jin-haeng; 강의 gang-ui; 방침 bang-chim; **of ~** 물론 mul-lon

court *n.* 안뜰 an-tteul; 궁전 gung-jeon; 법정 beop-jjeong

courtesy *n.* 예의 ye-ui; 호의 ho ui

court house *n.* 법원 beob-won, 재판소 Jae-pan-so

courtyard *n.* 안뜰 an-tteul

cousin *n.* 사촌 sa-chon

cover *n.* 덮개 deop-gae; 표지 pyo-ji; *vt.* 덮다 deop-da, 덮어 가리다 deop-eo ga-ri-da, 커버하다 keo-beo-ha-da; 걸치다 geol-chi-da

coverage *n.* 적용범위 jeog-yong-beom-wi, 보상범위 bo-sang-beom-ui

cover story *n.* 커버스토리 keo beo seu-to-ri

cow *n.* 암소 am-so

coward *n.* 겁쟁이 geop-jaeng-i

cowboy *n.* 카우보이 ka-u-bo-i, 목동 mok-dong

cozy *adj.* 기분좋은 gi-bun-jo-eun, 포근한 po-geun-han; 안락한 al-la-kan

crab *n.* 게 ge

crack *n.* 갈라진 틈 gal-la-jin teum; 날카로운 소리 nal-ka-ro-un so-ri; *vt.* 금가게 하다 geum-ga-ge ha-da; *vi.* 금가다 geum-ga-da; 딱 소리가 나다 ttak so-ri-ga na-da

cracker *n.* 크래커 keu-rae-keo; 폭죽 pok-juk

cradle *n.* 요람 yo-ram

craft *n.* 기능 gi-neung, 기교 gi-gyo, 특수기술 teuk-su-gi-sul

craftsman *n.* 공예가 gong-ye-ga, 장인 jang-in

cramp *n.* 경련 gyeong-nyeon; 꺾쇠 kkeok-soe

crane *n.* *(bird)* 두루미 du-ru-mi, 학 hak; *(equipment)* 기중기 gi-jung-gi

cranky *adj.* 까다로운 kka-da-ro-un, 괴팍한 goe-pa-kan; 변덕스러운 byeon-deok-seu-reo-un

crash *n.* 충돌 chung-dol; 추락 chu-rak; *vt.* 충돌하다 chung-dol-ha-da; 추락하다 chu-ra-ka-da; 산산히 부수다 san-san-hi bu-su-da

crate *n.* 크레이트 keu-re-i-teu, 나무상자 na-mu-sang-ja

orator *n.* 분화구 bun-hwa-gu

crawl *vi.* 네발로 기다 ne-bal-lo gi-da; 서행하다 seo-haeng-ha-da; 득실거리다 deul-sil-geo-ri-da, 들끓다 deul-kkeul-ta

crayon *n.* 크레용 keu-re-yong, 크레파스 keu-re-pa-sseu

crazy *adj.* 미친 mi-chin; 열중한 yeol-jjung-han

cream *n.* 크림 keu-rim

crease *n.* 주름살 ju-reum-ssal; 접은 금 jeob-eun geum

create *vt.* 창조하나 chang-jo-ha-da, 창작하다 chang-ja-ka-da; 일으키다 il-eu-ki-da, 야기하다 y-gi-ha-da

creation *n.* 창조 chang-jo, 창작 chang-jak; 창조물 chang-jo-mul; 창작품 chang-jak-pum

creature *n.* 피조물 pi-jo-mul; 생물 saeng-mul

credential *n.* 신임장 sin-im-jjang; 자격 증명서 ja-gyeok jeung-myeong-seo

credibility *n.* 신용 sin-yong, 신빙성 sin-bing-sseong

credit *n.* 신용 sin-yong; 신용대부 sin-yong-dae-bu; 영예 yeong-ye; *vt.* 신용하다 sin-yong-ha-da; 영예가 되다 yeong-ye-ga doe-da; **on ~** 신용대부로 sin-yong-dae-bu-ro, 외상으로 oe-sang-eu-ro; **~ report** 신용조회서 sin-yong-jo-hoe-seo

credit card *n.* 크레딧 카드 keu-re-dit ka-deu

creditor *n.* 채권자 chae-kkwon-ja

creep *vi.* 살금살금 걷다 sal-sal geot-da, 살살 기다 sal-sal gi-da

creepy *adj.* 오싹하는 o-ssa-ka-neun, 소름끼치는 so-reum-kki-chi-neun; 기어 돌아다니는 gi-eo dol-a-da-ni-neun

crescent *n.* 초승달 cho-seung-ttal

crest *n.* 장식 jang-sik, 볏 byeot

crew *n.* 승무원 seung-mu-won; 선원 seon-won

crib *n.* 유아용 침대 yu-a-yong chim-dae

cricket *n.* *(insect)* 귀뚜라미gwi-ttu-ra-mi; *(sport)* 크리켓 keu-ri-ket

crime *n.* 범죄 beom-joe

criminal *n.* 범인 beom-in, 범죄자 beom-joe-ja; *adj.* 범죄의 beom-joe-ui; ~ **law** 형법 hyeong-ppeop

crippled *adj.* 절름발이의 jeol-leum-bal-i-ui; 불구의 bul-gu-ui; 무능력한 mu-neung-nyeo-kan

crisis *n.* 위기 wi-gi; 갈림길 gal-lim-kkil

crispy *adj.* 파삭파삭한 pa-sak-pa-sa-kan, 아삭아삭한 a-sag-a-sa-kan

criterion *n.* 표준 pyo-jun, 기준 gi-jun

critical *adj.* 위기의 wi-gi-ui; 결정적인 gyeol-jjeong-jeog-in; 비평의 bi-pyeong-ui

criticism *n.* 비평 bi-pyeong; 비판 bi-pan

criticize *vt.* 비평하다 bi-pyeong-ha-da; 비판하다 bi-pan-ha-da

crocodile *n.* 악어 ag-eo

crooked *adj.* 구부러진 gu-bu-reo-jin, 기형의 gi-hyeong-ui; 부정직한 bu-jeong-ji-kan

crop *n.* 수확 su-hwak; 농작물 nong-jang-mul

cross *n.* 십자가 sip-ja-ga; 십자형 sip-ja-hyeong; 잡종 jap-jong; *vt.* 교차시키다 gyo-cha-si-ki-da; 가로지르다 ga-ro-ji-reu-d

crossing *n.* 동물 횡단길 dong-mul hoeng-dan-kkil; 철도 건널목 cheol-tto geon-neol-mok

crossroad *n.* 교차로 gyo-cha-ro; 사거리 sa-geo-ri

crosswalk *n.* 횡단보도 hoeng-dan-bo-do

crossword *n.* 크로스워드 keu-ro-sseu-wo-deu; ~ **puzzle** 크로스워드 퍼즐 keu-ro-sseu-wo-deu peo-jeul

crouch *vi.* 쭈그리다 jju-geu-ri-da, 몸을 구부리다 mom-eul gu-bu-ri-da

crow *n.* 까마귀 kka-ma-gwi

crowd *n.* 군중 gun-jung; 다수 da-su; *vi.* 군집하다 gun-ji-pa-da; *vt.* 꽉 들어차다 kkwak deul-eo-cha-da

crowded *adj.* 붐비는 bum-bi-neun

crown *n.* 왕관 wang-gwan

crucial *adj.* 결정적인 gyeol-jjeong-jeog-in, 중대한 jung-dae-han; 어려운 eo-ryeo-un, 혹독한 hok-do-kan

crude *adj.* 조야한 jo-ya-han; 천연 그대로의 cheon-yeon geu-dae-ro-ui

cruel *adj.* 잔혹한 jan-ho-kan

cruise *n.* 크루즈 keu-ru-jeu; 순항 sun-hang; ~ **ship** 순항선 sung-hang-seon; **to go on a** ~ 크루즈여행을 가다 keu-ru-jeu yeo-haeng-eul ga-da

crumb *n.* 빵부스러기 ppang bu-seu-reo-gi; 작은 조각 jag-eun jo-gak

crumble *vi.* 부서지다 bu-seo-ji-da; 무너지다 mu-neo-ji-da; *vt.* 빻다 ppa-ta

crumple *vt.* 구기다 gu-gi-da; 압도하다 ap-do-ha-da

crunch *vt.* 우두둑 깨물다 u-du-duk kkae-mul-da; 저벅저벅 걷다 jeo-beok-jeo-beok geot-da

crush *vt.* 으깨다 eu-kkae-da, 눌러 뭉개다 nul-leo mung-gae-da

crust *n.* 빵껍질 ppang-kkeop-jil; 딱딱한 껍질 ttak-tta-kan kkeop-jil

crutch *n.* 크러치 keu-reo-chi, 목발 mok-bal

cry *n.* 울음소리 ul-eum-sso-ri; *(yell)* 고함 go-ham; *vt.* 울다 ul-da; 고함치다 go-ham-chi-da

crystal *n.* 크리스탈 keu-ri-seu-tal, 수정 su-jeong

cub *n.* 새끼 sae-kki; 애송이 ae-song-i

Cuba *n.* 쿠바 ku-ba

cube *n.* 정육면체 jeong-nyung-myeon-che; **ice** ~ 얼음조각 eol-eum-jjo-gak

cubicle *n.* 작은 칸막이 방 jag-eun kan-mag-i bang; 특별 열람식 teuk-byeol yeol-lam-sil; **office** ~ 사무실 칸막이방 sa-mu-sil kan-mag-i-bang

cuckoo clock *n.* 뻐꾸기 시계 ppeo-kku-gi si-gye

cucumber *n.* 오이 o-i

cue *n.* 신호 sin-ho, 암시 am-si, 단서 dan-seo; 큐 kyu

cuff *n.* 소맷부리 so-maet-bu-ri, 커프스 keo-peu-sseu; 바지 아랫단 ba-ji a-raet-dan; ~ **links** 커프링크 keo-peu-ring-keu

cul-de-sac *n.* 막다른 골목 mak-da-reun gol-mok; 궁지 gung-ji, 곤경 gon-gyeong

culinary *adj.* 부엌용의 bu-eong-nyong-ui, 조리용의 jo-ri-yong-ui

cultivate *vt.* 경작하다 gyeong-ja-ka-da; 재배하다 jae-bae-ha-da; 신장하다 sin-jang-ha-da

cultivation *n.* 경작 gyeong-jak; 재배 jae-bae; 사육 sa-yuk

cultural *adj.* 문화의 mun-hwa-ui; 교양의 gyo-yang-ui

culture *n.* 문화 mun-hwa; 교양 gyo-yang

cumulative *adj.* 누적하는 nu-jeo-ka-neun

cunning *adj.* 교활한 gyo-hwal-han, 교묘한 gyo-myo-han

cup *n.* 컵 keop

cupboard *n.* 찬장 chan-jjang

curator *n.* 박물관 관리자 bang-mul-gwan gwal-li-ja, 미술관 관리자 mi-sul-gwan gwal-li-ja

curb *n.* 재갈 jae-gal, 고삐 go-ppi; 커브 keo-beu; *vt.* 재갈을 물리다 jae-gal-eul mul-li-da; 억세하다 eok-je-ha-da, 구속하 다 gu-so-ka-da; 보도블록을 깔다 bo-do-beul-log-eul kkal-da

cure *n.* 치료 chi-ryo; *vt.* 치료하다 chi-ryo-ha-da

curfew *n.* 야간통행금지 ya-gan-tong-haeng-geum-ji

curious *adj.* 궁금한 gung-geum-han; 기묘 한 gi-myo-han

curl *n.* 곱슬머리 gop-seul-meo-ri; 컬 keol; *vt.* 곱슬거리게 하다 gop-seul-geo-ri-ge ha-da

curly *adj.* 곱슬거리는 gop-seul-geo-ri-neun

currency *n.* 유통 yu-tong; 통화 tong-hwa, 화폐 hwa-pye; ~ **exchange** 화폐교환 hwa-pye-gyo-hwan

current *adj.* 현행의 hyeon-haeng-ui, 지금 의 ji-geum-ui; *n.* 흐름 heu-reum; 경향 gyeong-hyang; *(electricity)* 전류 jeol-lyu; 해류 hae-ryu

currently *adv.* 일반적으로 il-ban-jeog-eu-ro; 시금 ji-geum

curriculum *n.* 교과과정 gyo-kkwa-gwa-jeong

curry *n.* 카레 ka-re

curse *n.* 저주 jeo-ju, 악담 ak-dam; *vt.* 저주하 다 jeo-ju-ha-da, 악담하다 ak-dam-ha-da

cursor *n.* 커서 keo-seo

curtain *n.* 커튼 keo-teun; 막 mak

curve *n.* 커브 keo-beu, 곡선 gok-seon

curvy *adj.* 구불구불한 gu-bul-gu-bul-han

cushion *n.* 쿠션 ku-syeon, 방석 bang-seok; 완충물 wan-chung-mul

cuisine *n.* 요리 yo-ri, 요리법 yo-ri-ppeop

cussword *n.* 욕 yok, 악담 ak-dam

custard *n.* 커스터드 keo-seu-teo-deu

custodian *n.* 관리인 gwal-li-in, 수위 su-wi

custody *n.* 보관 bo-gwan, 관리 gwal-li; 구 류 gu-ryu

custom *n.* 관습 gwan-seup, 풍습 pung-seup

customer *n.* 손님 son nim; service 고객 서 비스 go-gaek sseo-bi-sseu

custom-made *adj.* 주문제작의 ju-mun-je-jag-ui

customs *n.* 관세 gwan-sse; ~ **agent** 세관 se-gwan

cut *n.* 상처 sang-cheo; 절단 jeol-ttan; 단편 dan-pyeon; 지름길 ji-reum-kkil; *vt.* 베다 be-da; 깎다 kkak-da

cute *adj.* 귀여운 gwi-yeo-un

cutlet *n.* 커틀릿 keo-teul-lit

cut-off *n.* 차단장치 cha-dan-jang-chi; 절단 jeol-ttan, 차단 cha-dan

cut-out *n.* 차단 cha-dan, 도려내기 do-ryeo-nae-gi; 삭제부분 sak-je-bu-bun

cyber- *pref.* 인공지능 in-gong-ji-neung; 사 이버 ssi-beo

cycle *n.* 순환 sun-hwan; 주기 ju-gi; 자전거 ja-jeon-geo

cylinder *n.* 원통 won-tong, 원기둥 won-gi-dung

cynical *adj.* 냉소적인 naeng-so-jeog-in

Czech Republic *n.* 체코슬로바키아 che-ko-seul-lo-ba-ki-a

D

Dad (my) *n.* 아버지 a-beo-ji, 아빠 a-ppa

daily *adj.* 일상의 il-ssang-ui; 매일의 mae-il-ui

dairy *n.* 낙농장 nang-nong-jang; 우유가게 u-yu-kka-ge; *adj.* 낙농의 nang-nong-ui

dam *n.* 댐 ttaem

damage *n.* 손해 son-hae; *vt.* 손해를 입히다 son-hae-reul i-pi-da

damn *vt.* 비난하다 bi-nan-ha-da; 저주하다 jeo-ju-ha-da

damp adj. 축축한 chuk-chu-kan; n. 습기 seup-gi; 낙담 nak-dam; vt. 축축하게 하다 chuk-chu-ka-ge ha-da

dampen vt. 축이다chug-i-da; 풀죽이다 pul-jug-i-da; vi. 축축해지다 chuk-chu-kae-ji-da

dance n. 춤 chum, 댄스 daen-sseu; vi. 춤추 다 chum-chu-da

danger n. 위험 wi-heom

dangerous adj. 위험한 wi-heom-han

dangle vi. 매달리다 mae-dal-li-da, 따라다니 다 tta-ra-da-ni-da; vt. 매달다 mae-dal-da

Danube n. 다뉴브강 da-nyu-beu-gang

dare n. 대담무쌍 dae-dam-mu-ssang; vi. 감 히...하다 gam-hi...ha-da; 도전하다 do-jeon-ha-da; 위험을 무릅쓰다 wi-heom-eul mu-reup-sseu-da

daring adj. 대담한 dae-dam-han

dark n. 어둠 eo-dum, 땅거미 ttang-kkeo-mi; adj. 어두운 eo-du-un; 짙은 jit-eun

darken vt. 어둡게 하다 eo-dup-ge ha-da; 어두워지다 eo-du-wo-ji-da; 거뭇해지다 geo-mu-tae-ji-da

dark horse n. 다크호스 da-keu-ho-sseu

darkness n. 암흑 am-heuk, 어둠eo-dum; 무 지 mu-ji

darkroom n. 암실 am-sil

darling n. 사랑하는 사람 sa-rang-ha-neun sa-ram, 사랑스러운 사람 sa-rang-seu-reo-un sa-ram

darn vt. (to stitch) 꿰매다 kkwe-mae-da; (profanity) 헐뜯다 heol-tteut-da, 저주하 다 jeo-ju-ha-da; interj. 젠장jen-jang, 아 차 a-cha

dart n. 다트 da-teu; ~**board** 다트판 da-teu-pan

dash n. 돌진 dol-jjin; 충돌 chung-dol; vt. 내던지다 nae-deon-ji-da; vi. 돌진하다 dol-jjin-ha-da

dashboard n. 대시보드 dae-si-bo-deu

data n.pl. 데이터 de-i-teo, 자료 ja-ryo

data bank n. 데이터 뱅크 de-i-teo-baeng-keu

date n. (calendar) 날짜 nal-jja; (meeting) 데 이트 de-i-teu; (fruit) 데이트 de-i-teu; vt. 날짜를 적다 nal-jja-reul jeok-da; **to ~ a document** 서류에 날짜를 적다 seo-ryu-e nal-jja-reul jeok-da; ~ **line** 날짜 변경선 nal-jja byeon-gyeong-seon

daughter n. 딸 ttal

daughter-in-law n. 며느리 myeo-neu-ri

dawn n. 새벽 sae-byeok

day n. 낮 nat; 하루 ha-ru

daydream n. 공상 gong-sang

daylight n. 일광 il-gwang, 빛 bit

daylight saving time n. 섬머타임 sseom-meo-ta-im

day time n. 주간 ju-gan, 낮 nat

daze vt. 멍하게 하다 meong-ha-ge ha-da, 어 리둥절하게 하다 eo-ri-dung-jeol-ha-ge ha-da

dazzle vt. 눈부시게 하다 nun-bu-si-ge ha-da; 현혹시키다 hyeon-hok-si-ki-da

dazzling adj. 눈부신 nun-bu-sin, 현혹적인 hyeon-hok-jeog-in

dead adj. 죽은 jug-eun; 무감각한 mu-gam-ga-kan

dead end n. 막다른 골목 mak-da-reun gol-mok; 궁지 gung-ji

deadline n. 원고마감시간 won-go-ma-gam-ssi-gan, 최종기한 choe-jong-gi-han

deadly adv. 치명적인chi-myeong-jeog-in; 죽 음과 같은 jug-eum-gwa gat-eun

deaf adj. 귀머거리의 gwi-meo-geo-ri-ui, 귀 먹은 gwi-meog-eun

deal n. 분량 bul-lyang; 거래 geo-rae; 타협 ta-hyeop; vt. 분배하다 bun-bae-ha-da; vi. 나누다 na-nu-da; 장사하다 jang-sa-ha-da, 취급하다 chwi-geu-pa-da; **It's a good ~** 괜찮은 거래이다 gwaen-chan-eun geo-rae-da; **to ~ in art** 미술품을 거래하다 mi-sul-pum-eul geo-rae-ha-da; **to ~ cards** 카드를 나누다 ka-deu-reul na-nu-da

dealer n. 딜러 dil-leo; 상인 sang-in

dealership n. 대리점 dae-ri-jeom, 판매점 pan-mae-jeom; 판매권 pan-mae-kkwon

dean n. 학장 hak-jang

dear adj. 친애하는 chin-ae-ha-neun; 사랑하 는 sa-rang-ha-neun

death n. 죽음 jug-eum, 사망 sa-mang

death penalty n. 사형 sa-hyeong

debate n. 토론 to-ron; vt. 토론하다 to-ron-ha-da

debit n. 차변 cha-byeon; 차변기입 cha-byeon-gi-ip; vt. 차변에 기입하다 cha-byeon-e gi-i-pa-da; ~ **card** 데빗카드 de-bit-ka-deu

debt *n.* 빚 bit, 부채 bu-chae; **in ~** 빚이 있는 bij-i in-neun

debut *n.* 데뷰 de-byu, 첫등장 chot-deung-jang

decade *n.* 10년간 sim-nyeon-gan

decaffeinated *adj.* 디카페 di-ka-pe, 카페인 프리 ka-pe-in peu-ri, 카페인이 없는 ka-pe-in-i eom-neun

decay *n.* 부패 bu-pae; *vi.* 부패하다 bu-pae-ha-da, 썩다 sseok-da

deceit *n.* 사기 sa-gi, 속임수 sog-im-su

deceive *vt.* 사기치다 sa-gi-chi-da, 속이다 sog-i-da

decelerate *vt., vi.* 속도를 줄이다 sok-do-reul jul-i-da, 감속하다 gam-so-ka-da

December *n.* 12월 sib-i-wol

decent *adj.* 버젓한 beo-jeo-tan; 남보기 흉하지 않은 nam-bo-gi hyung-ha-ji an-eun; 상당한 신분의 sang-dang-han sin-bun-ui; 예절바른 ye-jeol-ba-reun

deception *n.* 사기 sa-gi; 속임수 sog-im-su

decide *vt., vi.* 해결히다 hae-gyeol-ha-da; 결심하다 gyeol-ssim-ha-da

decimal *adj.* 십진법의 sip-jin-ppeob-ui; 소수의 so-ssu-ui

decision *n.* 결심 gyeol-ssim, 결정 gyeol-jjeong

decisive *adj.* 결정적인 gyeol-jjeong-jeog-in

deck *n.* *(on a ship)* 갑판 gap-pan; 한벌 ahn-beol; **~ of cards** 카드 한벌 ka-deu han-beol

declaration *n.* 선언 seon-eon; 공표 gong-pyo; **customs ~** 세관 신고서 se-gwan sin-go-seo

declare *vt.* 선언히다 seon-eon-ha-da

decline *vi.* 기눌다 gi-ul-da; 쇠하다 soe-ha-da; 사절하다 sa-jeol-ha-da

decode *vt., vi.* 해독하다 hae-do-ka-da, 번역하다 beon-yeo-ka-da, 풀다 pul-da

decompose *vt.* 분해시키다 bun-hae-si-ki-da; 부패시키다 bu-pae-si-ki-da

decorate *vt.* 장식하다 jang-si-ka-da; 훈장을 주다 hun-jang-eul ju-da

decoration *n.* 장식 jang-sik; 훈장 hun-jang

decrease *vt.* 줄이다 jul-i-da; *vi.* 줄다 jul-da

dedicate *vt.* 바치다 ba-chi-da; 헌신하다 heon-sin-ha-da

dedication *n.* 봉헌 bong-heon; 헌신 hon-sin

deduction *n.* *(mathematical)* 공제 gong-je; *(logical)* 빼기 ppae-gi

deed *n.* 행위 haeng-wi; 권리증 gwol-li-jjeung

deem *vt.* 생각하다 saeng-ga-ka-da; 간주하다 gan-ju-ha-da

deep *adj.* 깊은 gi-peun

deepen *vt., vi.* 깊게하다 gip-ge-ha-da

deep-fry *vt.* 튀기다 twi-gi-da

deer *n.* 사슴 sa-seum

default *n.* 태만 tae-man; 불이행 bul-i-haeng; 기권 gi-kkwon; 디폴트 di-pol-teu; *vt.* 의무를 게을리히디 ui mu reul ge-eul-li-ha-da; 기권하다 gi-kkwon-ha-da

defeat *n.* 패배 pae-bae; 좌절 jwa-jeol; *vt.* 쳐부수다 cheo-bu-su-da

defect *n.* 결점 gyeol-jjeom, 결함 gyeol-ham

defend *vt.* 막다 mak-da, 방어하다 bang-eo-ha-da

defendant *n.* 피고 pi-go

defense *n.* 방어 bang-eo, 수비 su-bi

defer *vt.* 연기하다 yeon-gi-ha-da; 양보하다 tang-bo-ha-da; 경의를 표하다 gyeong-ui-reul pyo-ha-da

deficiency *n.* 부족 bu-jok, 결핍 gyeol-pip; 결함 gyeol-ham

define *vt.* 규정짓다 gyu-jeong-jit-da, 정의를 내리다 jeong-ui-reul nae-ri-da

definite *adj.* 뚜렷한 ttu-ryeo-tan

definitely *adv.* 면확히 myeong-hwa-ki, 확실히 hwak-sil-hi

definition *n.* 한정 han-jeong; 정의 jeong-ui

definitive *adj.* 결정적인 gyeol-jjeong-jeog-in

deflate *vt.* 공기를 빼다 gong-gi-reul ppae-da; 통화를 수축시키다 tong-hwa-reul su-chuk-si-ki-da

defuse *vt.* 발산하다 bal-ssan-ha-da, 퍼뜨리다 peo-tteu-ri-da

defy *vt.* 도전하다 do-jeon-ha-da; 문제삼지 않다 mun-je-sam-jji an-ta

degree *n.* 정도 jeong-do, 도 do

dehydrated *adj.* 수분이 빠진 su-bun-i ppa-jin, 건조된 geon-jo-doen

delay *n.* 지연 ji-yeon; *vt.* 미루다 mi-ru-da, 연기하다 yeon-gi-ha-da

delete *vt.* 생략하다 saeng-nya-ka-da, 삭제하다 sak-je-ha-da

deliberate *adj.* 계획적인 gye-hoek-jeog-in; 생각이 깊은 saeng-gag-i gip-eun

delicacy n. 섬세 seom-se; 민감 min-gam; 미묘 mi-myo

delicate adj. 섬세한 seom-se-han; 민감한 min-gam-han; 미묘한 mi-myo-han; 가냘픈 ga-nyal-peun

delicious adj. 맛있는 mas-in-neun; 상쾌한 sang-kwae-han

delight n. 기쁨 gi-ppeum, 즐거움 jeul-geo-um

deliver vt. 인도하다 in-do-ha-da; 배달하다 bae-dal-ha-da; 해방시키다 hae-bang-si-ki-da

delivery n. 인도 in-do; 배달 bae-dal; 구출 gu-chul

delude vt. 속이다 sog-i-da

demand n. 요구 yo-gu; 수요 su-yo; vt. 요구하다 yo-gu-ha-da; 묻다 mut-da

demo n. 데모 de-mo, 시위행진 si-wi-haeng-jin

democracy n. 민주주의 min-ju-ju-i

democratic adj. 민주주의의 min-ju-ju-i-ui

demolish vt. 망가뜨리다 mang-ga-tteu-ri-da, 파괴하다 pa-goe-ha-da, 헐다 heol-da

demon n. 악마 ang-ma, 귀신 gwi-sin

demonstrate vt. 증명하다 jeung-myeong-ha-da; 설명하다 seol-myeong-ha-da; 드러내다 deu-reo-nae-da; vi. 시위하다 si-wi-ha-da

demonstration n. 논증 non-jeung; 데모 de-mo; 실물교습 sil-mul-gyo-seup

den n. 굴 gul; 우리 u-ri; 분대 bun-dae

denial n. 부정 bu-jeong, 부인 bu-in

Denmark n. 덴마크 den-ma-keu

dense adj. 밀접한 mil-jjeo-pan; 조밀한 jo-mil-han

density n. 밀도 mil-tto

dent n. 움푹 패인 자국 um-puk pae-in ja-guk; vt. 움푹 패이게 하다 um-puk pae-i-ge ha-da; vi. 움푹 패이다 um-puk pae-i-da

dental adj. 치과의 chi-kkwa-ui; 이의 i-ui

dentist n. 치과의사 chi-kkwa-ui-sa

denture n. 틀니 teul-li

deny vt. 부정하다 bu-jeong-ha-da; 취소하다 chwi-so-ha-da; 거절하다 geo-jeol-ha-da

deodorant n. 방취제 bang-chwi-je; adj. 방취력있는 bang-chwi-ryeog-in-neun

depart vi. 출발하다 chul-bal-ha-da; 벗어나다 beos-eo-na-da

department n. 부분 bu-bun; 과 kkwa; 국 guk

departure n. 출발 chul-bal; 이탈 i-tal

depend vi. …에 달려있다 …e dal-lyeo-it-da; to ~ on 의지하다 ui-ji-ha-da; that ~s 그건 때와 형편에 달려있다 geu-geon ttae-wa hyeong-pyeon-e dal-lyeo-it-da

dependent n. 부양가족 bu-yang-ga-jok; adj. 의존하고 있는 ui-jon-ha-go in-neun; …나름의 …na-reum-ui

depict vt. 묘사하다 myo-sa-ha-da

deport vt. 처신하다 cheo-sin-ha-da; 추방하다 chu-bang-ha-da

deposit vt. 두다 du-da, 맡기다 mat-gi-da; n. 예금 ye-geum; 기탁 gi-tak; 창고 chang-go

depot n. 저장소 jeo-jang-so, 보관소 bo-gwan-so, 창고 chang-kko

depreciate vt. 가치를 저하시키다 ga-chi-reul jeo-ha-si-ki-da; vi. 가치가 떨어지다 ga-chi-ga tteol-eo-ji-da

depress vt. 풀이 죽게 하다 pul-i juk-ge ha-da

depressed adj. 풀이 죽은 pul- jug-eun, 우울한 u-ul-han

depression n. 우울증 u-ul-jjeung; 불경기 bul-gyeong-gi, 디프레션 di-peu-re-syeon

deprive vt. 빼앗다 ppae-at-da; 박탈하다 bak-tal-ha-da

depth n. 깊이 gip-i; 깊은 곳 gip-eun got

deputy n. 대리인 dae-ri-in; 부관 bu-gwan; 대표자 dae-pyo-ja

derive vt. 끌어내다 kkeul-eo-nae-da; …에서 시작하다 …eo-seo si-ja-ka-da

descend vi. 내리다 nae-ri-da, 내려가다 nae-ryeo-ga-da, 내려오다 nae-ryeo-o-da

descendant n. 후손 hu-son, 자손 ja-son

descent n. 하강 ha-gang; 가계 ga-gye

describe vt. 기술하다 gi-sul-ha-da; 묘사하다 myo-sa-ha-da

description n. 기술 gi-sul; 묘사 myo-sa

desert n. 사막 sa-mak; 황무지 hwang-mu-ji; vt. 버리다 beo-ri-da, 돌보지 않다 dol-bo-ji an-ta; 도망가다 do-mang-ga-da

deserve vt. …할 만하다 …hal man-ha-da

design n. 디자인 di-ja-in, 설계 seol-gye; vt. 디자인하다 di-ja-in-ha-da, 설계하다 seol-gye-ha-da

designate *vt.* 가리키다 ga-ri-ki-da; 명시하다 myeong-si-ha-da

designer *n.* 디자이너 di-ja-i-neo; **interior ~** 인테리어 디자이너 in-te-ri-eo di-ja-i-neo

desirable *adj.* 바람직한 ba-ram-ji-kan

desire *n.* 욕구 yok-gu; *vt.* 바라다 ba-ra-da

desk *n.* 책상 chaek-sang; **front ~** 프론트 데스크 peu-ron-teu de-seu-keu

despair *n.* 절망 jeol-mang, 자포자기 ja-po-ja-gi; *vi.* 절망하다 jeol-mang-ha-da, 자포자기하다 ja-po-ja-gi-ha-da; **to ~ of** 계약을 성사시키기를 포기하다 gye-yag-eul seong-sa-si-ki-gi-reul po-gi-ha-da

desperate *adj.* 자포자기의 ja-po-ja-gi-ui, 필사적인 pil-ssa-jeog-in; 절망적인 jeol-mang-jeog-in

despite *prep.* …에도 불구하고 …e-do bul-gu-ha-go

dessert *n.* 디저트 di-jeo-teu, 후식 hu-sik

destination *n.* 목적지 mok-jeok-ji

destiny *n.* 운명 un-myeong

destroy *vt.* 파괴하다 pa-goe-ha-da; 파멸시키다 pa-myeol-si-ki-da

destruction *n.* 파괴 pa-goe; 파멸 pa-myeol

detach *vt.* 떼다 tte-da, 분리하다 bul-li-ha-da

detail *n.* 세부사항 se-bu-sa-hang, 세부항목 se-bu-hang-mok, 자세한 것 ja-se-han-geot

detain *vt.* 붙들다 but-deul-da; 억류하다 eong-nyu-ha-da

detect *vt.* 발견하다 bal-gyeon-ha-da; 간파하다 gan-pa-ha-da

detection *n.* 발견 bal-gyeon; 간파 gan-pa; 검출 geom-chul

detective *n.* 형사 hyeong-sa, 탐정 tam-jeong; **~ story** 탐정소설 tam-jeong-so-seol

detergent *n.* 세제 se-je

determination *n.* 결심 gyeol-ssim, 결정 gyeol-jjeong

determine *vt.* 결심하다 gyeol-ssim-ha-da; 결정하다 gyeol-jjeong-ha-da; 결심시키다 gyeol-ssim-si-ki-da

determined *adj.* 단호한 dan-ho-han

detour *n.* 우회로 u-hoe-ro, 우회도로 u-hoe-do-ro

devastate *vt.* 황폐시키다 hwang-pe-si-ki-da

develop *vt.* 개발하다 gae-bal-ha-da; 발전시키다 bal-jjeon-si-ki-da; *vi.* 발전하다 bal-jjeon-ha-da; **to ~ a plan** 계획을 발전시키다 gye-hoeg-eul bal-jjeon-si-ki-da; **to ~ a country** 나라를 발전시키다 na-ra-reul bal-jjeon-si-ki-da; **to ~ film** 필름을 현상하다 pil-leum-eul hyeon-sang-ha-da

development *n.* 개발 gae-bal; 발전 bal-jjeon; 발달 bal-ttal

deviation *n.* 벗어남 beos-eo-nam; 탈선 tal-sseon

device *n.* 장치 jang-chi; 고안 go-an

devil *n.* 악마 ang-ma

devise *vt.* 궁리하다 gung-ni-ha-da; 고안하다 go-an-ha-da

devote *vt.* 헌신하다 heon-sin-ha-da, 노력을 기울이다 no-ryeog-eul gi-ul-i-da

devout *adj.* 독실한 dok-sil-han; 경건한 gyeong-geon-han

dew *n.* 이슬 i-seul

diabetes *n.* 당뇨병 dang-nyo-ppyeong

diabetic *adj.* 당뇨병의 dang-nyo-ppyeong-ui; *n.* 당뇨환자 dang-nyo-hwan-ja

diagnosis *n.* 진단 jin-dan

diagonal *adj.* 대각선의 dae-gak-seon-ui

diagram *n.* 도형 do-hyeong, 도표 do-pyo

dial *n.* 다이얼 da-i-eol; *vt.* 다이얼을 돌리다 da-i-eol-eul dol-li-da

dialect *n.* 방언 bang-eon, 사투리 sa-tu-ri

dialogue *n.* 대화 dae-hwa

diameter *n.* 지름 ji-reum

diamond *n.* 다이아몬드 da-i-a-mon-deu; **a three-carat ~** 3캐럿짜리 다이아몬드 sam-kae-reot-jja-ri da-i-a-mon-deu; **the queen of ~s** 다이아몬드의 여왕 da-i-a-mon-deu-ui yeo-wang; **a ~ ring** 다이아몬드 반지 da-i-a-mon-deu ban-ji; **~-shaped** 다이아몬드 모양 da-i-a-mon-deu mo-yang

diaper *n.* 기저귀 gi-jeo-gwi

diarrhea *n.* 설사 seol-ssa

diary *n.* 일기 il-gi; 일기장 il-gi-jang

dice *n.* 주사위 ju-sa-wi

dictate *vt.* 구술하다 gu-sul-ha-da; 명령하다 myeong-nyeong-ha-da

dictation *n.* 구술 gu-sul; 받아쓰기 bad-a-sseu-gi

dictator *n.* 독재자 dok-jae-ja; 명령자 myeong-nyeong-ja

dictatorship *n.* 독재권력 dok-jae-gwol-lyeok, 독재정권 dok-jae-jeong-kkwon

dictionary *n*. 사전 sa-jeon

die *n*. 주사위 ju-sa-wi; *vi*. 죽다 juk-da; 사망 하다 sa-mang-ha-da

die-hard *adj*. 완고한 wan-go-han, 끝까지 버티는 kkeut-kka-ji beo-ti-neun

diehard *n*. 완강한 저항자 wan-gang-han jeo-hang-ja, 완고한 보수주의자 wan-go-han bo-su-ju-i-ja

diesel *n*. 디젤기관 di-jel-gi-gwan; 디젤 di-jel

diet *n*. 다이어트 da-i-eo-teu; 식품 sik-pum; 규정식 gyu-jeong-sik; *vi*. 다이어트하 다 da-i-eo-teu-ha-da; 식이요법을 하다 sig-i-yo-ppeob-eul ha-da

differ *vi*. 다르다 da-reu-da

difference *n*. 차이 cha-i, 다름 da-reum

different *adj*. 다른 da-reun

differential *adj*. 차별적인 cha-byeol-jjeog-in, 특이한 teug-i-han; *n*. 차이 cha-i

differentiate *vt*. 구별짓다 gu-byeol-jit-da, 차 별하다 cha-byeol-ha-da

difficult *adj*. 어려운 eo-ryeo-un

difficulty *n*. 어려움 eo-ryeo-um, 곤란 gol-lan, 곤경 gon-gyeong

dig *vt., vi*. 파다 pa-da; 파헤치다 pa-he-chi-da

digest *vt*. 소화하다 so-hwa-ha-da; 요약하다 yo-ya-ka-da

digestion *n*. 소화 so-hwa; 이해력 i-hae-ryeok

digit *n*. 숫자 sut-ja

digital *adj*. 디지털 방식의 di-ji-teol bang-sig-ui

dignified *adj*. 위엄있는 wi-eom-in-neun

dignity *n*. 위엄 wi-eom, 존엄 jon-eom

dilate *vt*. 팽창시키다 paeng-chang-si-ki-da, 넓히다 neol-pi-da

dilemma *n*. 딜레마 dil-le-ma, 진퇴양란 jin-toe-yang-nan

diligent *adj*. 부지런한 bu-ji-reon-han

dilute *vt*. 희석하다 hi-seo-ka-da, 묽게하다 mul-kke-ha-da

dim *adj*. 흐릿한 heu-ri-tan; *vt*. 어둡게 하다 eo-dup-ge ha-da; **to ~ the lights** 불빛을 어둡게 하다 bul-ppich-eul eo-dup-ge ha-da

dimension *n*. 치수 chi-ssu; 차원 cha-won; 넓 이 neolb-i

diminish *vt*. 줄이다 jul-i-da, 감소시키다 gam-so-si-ki-da

dimple *n*. 보조개 bo-jo-gae; 잔물결 jan-mul-kkyeol

dimwit *n*. 바보 ba-bo, 멍청이 meong-cheong-i

dine *vi*. 저녁식사를 하다 jeo-nyeok-sik-sa-reul ha-da

dining room *n*. 식당 sik-dang

dining table *n*. 식탁 sik-tak

dinner *n*. 저녁식사 jeo-nyeok-sik-sa

dip *vt*. 살짝 담그다 sal-jjak dam-geu-da

diploma *n*. 졸업장 jol-eop-jang

diplomat *n*. 외교관 oe-gyo-gwan

diplomatic *adj*. 외교의 oe-gyo-ui

direct *adj*. 똑바른 ttok-ba-reun; 직접의 jik-jeob-ui; 솔직한 sol-jji-kan; *adv*. 똑바 로 ttok-ba-ro; 직접 jik-jeop; *vt*. 돌리다 dol-li-da; 지도하다 ji-do-ha-da; 겉봉을 쓰 다 geot-bong-eul sseu-da

direction *n*. 방향 bang-hyang; 지도 ji-do

directly *adv*. 곧장 got-jang; 직접 jik-jeop, 즉 시 jeuk-si

director *n*. 지도자 ji-do-ja; 관리자 gal-li-ja

directory *n*. 전화번호부 jeon-hwa-beon-ho-bu; 주소 성명록 ju-so seong-myeong-nok

dirt *n*. 진흙 jin-heuk; 쓰레기 sseu-re-gi

dirty *adj*. 더러운 deo-reo-un

dirty work *n*. 귀찮은 일 gwi-chan-eun il, 하 기 싫은 일 ha-gi sil-eun nil

disabled *adj*. 불구가 된 bul-gu-ga doen; 무 능력해진 mu-neung-nyeo-kae-jin

disadvantage *n*. 불리 bul-li, 손실 son-sil

disagree *vi*. 의견이 다르다 ui-gyeon-i da-reu-da

disagreement *n*. 의견 불일치 ui-gyeon bul-il-chi

disappear *vi*. 사라지다 sa-ra-ji-da

disappoint *vt*. 실망시키다 sil-mang-si-ki-da

disappointment *n*. 실망 sil-mang

disapproval *n*. 불찬성 bul-chan-seong, 불만 bul-man, 비난 bi-nan

disarm *vt*. 무장을 해제하다 mu-jang-eul hae-je-ha-da, 군비를 축소하다 gun-bi-reul chuk-so-ha-da

disaster *n*. 재난 jae-nan, 참사 cham-sa; **~ area** 비상 재해지구 bi-sang-jae-hae-ji-gu

discard *vt*. 버리다 beo-ri-da, 해고하다 hae-go-ha-da

discharge vt. 짐을 부리다 jim-eul bu-ri-da; 해방하다 hae-bang-ha-da; 약속을 이행하다 yak-sog-eul i-haeng-ha-da

discipline n. 훈련 hul-lyeon; 규율 gyu-yul; 학과 hak-gwa

disclose vt. 폭로하다 pong-no-ha-da, 드러내다 deu-reo-nae-da

discomfort n. 불쾌 bul-kwae, 불안 bul-an, 불편 bul-pyeon

disconnect vt. 연락을 끊다 yeol-lag-eul kkeun-ta, 떼어놓다 tteo-eo-no-ta

discontinue vt. 그만두다 geu-man-du-da, 중단하다 jung-dan-ha-da

discord n. 불일치 bul-il-chi, 불화 bul-hwa

discount n. 할인 hal-in; vt. 할인하다 hal-in-ha-da; ~ **store** 할인점 hal-in-jeom

discourage vt. 용기를 잃게하다 yong-gi-reul il-ke-ha-da, 낙담시키다 nak-dam-si-ki-da; 방해하나 bang-hae-ha-da

discover vt. 발견하다 bal-gyeon-ha-da

discovery n. 발견 bal-gyeon

discreet adj. 신중한 sin-jung-han

discrepancy n. 모순 mo-sun

discriminate vi. 구별히다 gu-byeol-ha-da; 차별대우하다 cha-byeol-dae-u-ha-da

discuss vt. 토론하다 to-ron-ha-da, 논의하다 non-ui-ha-da

discussion n. 토론 to-ron

disease n. 질병 jil-byeong, 병 byeong

disestablish vt. 폐지하다 pe-ji-ha-da

disgrace n. 창피 chang-pi; 불명예 bul-myeong-ye; 눈밖에 남 nun-bakk-e nam

disguise n. 변장 byeon-jang

disgust n. 혐오 hyeom-o

disgusting adj. 혐오스러운 hyeom-o-seu-reo-un

dish n. 접시 jeop-si; 요리 yo-ri

dishonest adj. 부정직한 bu-jeong-ji-kan

dishonesty n. 부정직 bu-jeong-jik; 불성실 bul-sseong-sil

dishonor n. 불명예 bul-myeong-ye, 망신 mang-sin

disinfect vt. 소독하다 so-do-ka-da

disinfectant n. 소독약 so-dong-nyak; 살균제 sal-gyun-je

disjoin vt., vi. 분리하다 bul-li-ha-da

disk n. 디스크 di-seu-keu; **floppy** ~ 플로피 디스크 peul-lo-pi di-seu-keu; ~ **space** 디스크 용량 di-seu-keu yong-nyang

diskette n. 디스켓 di-seu-ket

dislike vt. 싫어하다 sil-eo-ha-da; 미워하다 mi-wo-ha-da

dismiss vt. 떠나게 하다 tteo-na-ge ha-da; vi. 해산하다 hae-san-ha-da

disobey vt. 말을 안듣다 mal-eul an-deut-da, 불복종하다 bul-bok-jong-ha-da

disorder n. 무질서 mu-jil-sseo, 혼란 hol-lan; 장애 jang-ae

disorganize adj. 조직이 문란한 jo-jig-i mul-lan-han, 질서없는 jil-sseo-eom-neun

dispense vt. 분배하다 bun-bae-ha-da; 투여하다 tu-yeo-ha-da

display n. 진열 jin-yeol, 전시 jeon-si; 과시 gwa-si; vt. 보이다 bo-i-da; 전시하다 jeon-si-ha-da, 진열하다 jin-yeol-ha-da

displease vt. 불쾌하게 하다 bul-kwae-ha-ge ha-da

dispose vi. 배치하다 bae-chi-ha-da; 처분하다 cheo-bun-ha-da; **to ~ of** 처분하다 cheo-bun-ha-da

disposal n. 디스포저 di-seu-po-jeo

dispute n. 토론 to-ron; 논쟁 non-jaeng

disqualification n. 무자격 mu-ja-gyeok, 실격 sil-kkyeok

disregard n. 무시 mu-si; vt. 무시하다 mu-si-ha-da

disrespect n. 무례 mu-rye, 실례 sil-lye

disrupt vt. 붕괴시키다 bung-goe-si-ki-da; 혼란시키디 hol-lan-si-ki-da

dissatisfaction n. 불만 bul-man, 불평 bul-pyeong

dissertation n. 학위논문 hag-wi-non-mun

dissolve vt. 용해하다 yong-hae-ha-da; 해산하다 hae-san-ha-da; 해소하다 hae-so-ha-da

distance n. 거리 geo-ri; 간격 gan-gyeok

distant adj. 멀리 떨어진 meol-li tteol-eo-jin

distension n. 팽창 paeng-chang, 확대 hwak-dae

distill vt. 증류하다 jeung-nyu-ha-da

distinct adj. 독특한 dok-teu-kan; 뚜렷한 ttu-ryeo-tan

distinction n. 구별 gu-byeol; 특성 teuk-seong; 탁월 tag-wol

distinguish vt. 구별하다 gu-byeol-ha-da; 눈에 띄게 하다 nun-e tti-ge ha-da

distort vt. 찡그리다 jjing-geu-ri-da; 비틀다 bi-teul-da

distract *vt.* 마음을 흩뜨리다 ma-eum-eul heut-tteu-ri-da; 미혹케 하다 mi-hok-ke ha-da

distress *n.* 고민 go-min; 가난 ga-nan; *vt.* 괴롭히다 goe-ro-pi-da

distribute *vt.* 분배하다 bun-bae-ha-da; 살포하다 sal-po-ha-da; 분류하다 bul-lyu-ha-da

distribution *n.* 분배 bun-bae; 분포 bun-po

district *n.* 지역 ji-yeok, 지구 ji-gu

distrust *n.* 불신 bul-ssin; *vt.* 불신하다 bul-ssin-ha-da

disturb *vt.* 방해하다 bang-hae-ha-da; 혼란시키다 hol-lan-si-ki-da; 어지럽히다 eo-ji-reo-pi-da

ditch *n.* 도랑 do-rang, 개천 gae-cheon

dive *n.* 다이빙 da-i-bing

diverse *adj.* 다양한 da-yang-han

diversity *n.* 다양성 da-yang-sseong

divert *vt.* 전환하다 jeon-hwan-ha-da; 주의를 돌리다 ju-i-reul dol-li-da

divide *vt.* 나누다 na-nu-da, 분할하다 bun-hal-ha-da; **Ninety ~d by fifteen is six** 90 나누기 15는 6이다 gu-sip na-nu-gi sib-o-neun yug-i-da

diving *n.* 잠수 jam-su; 다이빙 da-i-bing; ~ **board** 대이빙대 da-i-bing-dae

division *n.* 분할 bun-hal; 분배 bun-bae; 나눗셈 na-nut-sem

divorce *n.* 이혼 i-hon; 분리 bul-li; *vt.*, *vi.* 이혼하다 i-hon-ha-da; **They ~d** 그들은 이혼했다 geu-deul-eun i-hon-haet-da

divorced *adj.* 이혼한 i-hon-han; 분리된 bul-li-doen

dizziness *n.* 현기증 hyeon-gi-jjeung

dizzy *adj.* 현기증 나는 hyeon-gi-jjeung na-neun, 어지러운 eo-ji-reo-un

DMZ *n. abbr.* **demilitarized zone** 비무장지대 bi-mu-jang-ji-dae

DNA *n. abbr.* **deoxyribonucleic acid** 유전자 yu-jeon-ja

do *vt.* 하다 ha-da, 주다 ju-da, 처리하다 cheo-ri-ha-da; *vi.* 행하다 haeng-ha-da, 처신하다 cheo-sin-ha-da, …한 형편이다 …han hyeong-pyeon-i-da; …에 쓸모가 있다 …e sseul-mo-ga it-da; ~ **it now** 지금 하십시오 ji-geum ha-sip-si-o; **It will** ~ 이거면 될 겁니다 i-geo-myeon doel kkeom-ni-da

dock *n.* 방파제 bang-pa-je, 선창 seon-chang, 도크 do-keu; 피고석 pi-go-seok; *vi.* 도크에 넣다 do-keu-e neo-ta; 도크를 설치하다 do-keu-reul seol-chi-ha-da; 도킹하다 do-king-ha-da

doctor *n.* 의사 ui-sa

document *n.* 문서 mun-seo, 서류 seo-ryu; 기록영화 gi-rong-nyeong-hwa

dog *n.* 개 gae; ~ **food** 개밥 gae-bap; **rescue** ~ 구조견 gu-jo-gyeon

doll *n.* 인형 in-hyeong; ~**house** 인형놀이집 in-hyeong-nol-i-jip

dollar *n.* 달러 dal-leo; 불 bul

dolphin *n.* 돌고래 dol-go-rae

domain *n.* 영토 yeong-to; 영역 yeong-yeok; 분야 bun-ya; 도메인 do-me-in

dome *n.* 돔 dom, 둥근천장 dung-geun cheon-jang

domestic *adj.* 가정의 ga-jeong-ui; 국내의 gung-nae-ui; 사육되는 sa-yuk-doe-neun

dominant *adj.* 지배적인 ji-bae-jeog-in, 유력한 yu-ryeo-kan

dominate *vt.* 지배하다 ji-bae-ha-da; 우세하다 u-se-ha-da

domination *n.* 지배 ji-bae; 우월 u-wol

Dominican Republic *n.* 도미니카 공화국 do-mi-ni-ka gong-hwa-guk

domino *n.* 도미노 do-mi-no

donate *vt.* 기증하다 gi-jeung-ha-da

donation *n.* 기증 gi-jeung; 기증품 gi-jeung-pum

donkey *n.* 당나귀 dang-na-gwi

donor *n.* 기증자 gi-jeung-ja

door *n.* 문 mun; ~**knob** 손잡이 son-jab-i; ~**mat** 매트 mae-teu

doorbell *n.* 초인종 cho-in-jong

doorman *n.* 문지기 mun-ji-gi

door-to-door *adv.* 집집마다 jip-jim-ma-da

dopey *adj.* 멍한 meong-han, 멍청한 meong-cheong-han

dormitory *n.* 기숙사 gi-suk-sa

dose *n.* …회분 …hoe-bun; **one** ~ 1회분 il-hoe-bun

dot *n.* 점 jeom

double *adj.* 두배의 du-bae-ui; 이중의 i-jung-ui

double-check *vt.* 재확인하다 jae-hag-in-ha-da

double-digit *adj.* 두자리 숫자의 du-ja-ri sut-ja-ui

doubt *n.* 의심 ui-sim; *vt.* 의심하다 ui-sim-ha-da

doubtful *adj.* 의심스러운 ui-sim-seu-reo-un; 확신할 수 없는 hwak-sin-hal ssu eom-neun

doubtless *adv.* 확실히 hwak-sil-hi, 틀림없이 teul-lim-eops-i

dough *n.* 반죽 ban-juk

doughnut *n.* 도우넛 do-u-neot

dove *n.* 비둘기 bi-dul-gi

down *n.* 솜털 som-teol, 다운 da-un; **a ~filled jacket** 다운자켓 da-un-ja-ket, *adv.* 아래 a-rae, 낮은 쪽으로 naj-eun jjog-eu-ro; 드러 누워서 deu-reo nu-wo-seo; 떨어져서 tteol-eo-jeo-seo; 남쪽으로 nam-jjog-eu-ro; 내려가서 nae-ryeo-ga-seo

downhill *n.* 내리막 길 nae-ri-mak-gil; 몰락 mol-lak

download *vt.* 다운로드하다 da-un-ro-deu-ha-da

downsize *vt.* 소형화하다 so-hyeong-hwa-ha-da

downstairs *adv.* 아래층으로 a-rae-cheung-eu-ro

downtown *n.* 도심지 do-sim-ji, 중심가 jung-sim-ga

doze *vi.* 졸다 jol-da

dozen *n.* 한다스 han-da-sseu

draft *n.* 도안 do-an; *(early version)* 초안 cho-an; 징병 jing-byeong; *(air)* 통풍 tong-pung; *(beer)* 생맥주 saeng-maek-ju; **bank ~** 은행 환어음 eun-haeng hwan-eo-eum

drag *vt.* 질질끌다 jil-jil-kkeul-da

dragon *n.* 용 yong

dragonfly *n.* 잠자리 jam-ja-ri

drain *n.* 배수 bae-su; 하수구 ha-su-gu; *vt.* 배수하다 bae-su-ha-da; 다 써 버리다 da sseo beo-ri-da

drama *n.* 드라마 deu-ra-ma, 연극 yeon-geuk

draw *vt.* 끌어당기다 kkeul-eo-dang-gi-da; 끌어내다 kkeul-eo-nae-da; *vi.* 접근하다 jeop-geun-ha-da; 그림을 그리다 geu-rim-eul geu-ri-da

drawing *n.* 그림 geu-rim, 스케치 seu-ke-chi

dread *n.* 공포 gong-po; *vt.* 두려워하다 du-ryeo-wo-ha-da

dream *n.* 꿈 kkum; 희망 hi-mang

dreary *adj.* 황량한 hwang-nyang-han; 울적한 ul-jjeo-kan

dress *n.* 정장 jeong-jang; 의복 ui-bok; 드레스 deu-re-ssu; *vt.* 옷을 입히다 os-eul i-pi-da; *vi.* 옷을 입다 os-eul ip-da

drift *n.* 표류 pyo-ryu, 동향 dong-hyang; *vi.* 표류하다 pyo-ryu-ha-da; *vt.* 떠내려 보내다 tteo-nae-ryeo bo-nae-da

drill *n.* 드릴 deu-ril; 훈련 hul-lyeon; *vt.* 구멍을 뚫다 gu-meong-eul ttul-ta; 훈련하다 hul-lyeon-ha-da

drink *n.* 마실 것 ma-sil kkeot, 음료수 eum-nyo-sul; *vt.* 마시다 ma-si-da

drip *vt.* 똑똑 떨어지다 ttok ttok tteol-eo-ji-da; 흠뻑 젖다 heum-ppeok jeot-da

drive *vt.* 운전하다 un-jeon-ha-da; 쫓아버리다 jjoch-a-beo-ri-da; *vi.* 돌진하다 dol-jjin-ha-da; 목표하다 mok-pyo-ha-da

driver *n.* 운전사 un-jeon-sa; 운전자 un-jeon-ja; **~'s license** 운전면허증 un-jeon-myeon-heo-jjeung

driving *adj.* 정력적인 jeong-nyeok-jeoq-in; 추진하는 chu-jin-ha-neun; **~ permit** 운전허가서 un-jeon heo-ga-seo

driving range *n.* 골프 연습장 gol-peu yeon-seup-jang

drizzle *vi.* 이슬비가 내리다 i-seul bi-ga nae-ri-da; **It's drizzling** 이슬비가 내린다 i-seul-bi-ga nae-rin-da

drop *n.* 방울 bang-ul; *vt.* 떨어뜨리다 tteol-eo-tteu-ri-da; *vi.* 떨어지다 tteol-eo-ji-da; 쓰러지다 sseu-reo-ji-da, 중퇴하다 jung-toe-ha-da

drought *n.* 가뭄 ga-mum

drown *vt.* 물에 빠뜨리다 mul-eo ppa-tteu-ri-da; *vi.* 물에 빠지다 mul-e ppa-ji-da, 익사하다 ik-sa-ha-da

drowsy *adj.* 졸리는 jol-li-neun, 자는 듯한 ja-neun-deu-tan; 나른한 na-reun-han

drug *n.* 약 yak; 마약 ma-yak

drugstore *n.* 약국 yak-guk, 약방 yak-bang

drum *n.* 드럼 deu-reom, 북 buk

drumstick *n.* 북채 buk-chae; 닭다리 dak-da-ri

drunk *adj.* 술취한 sul-chwi-han

dry *vt.* 말리다 mal-li-da; *vi.* 마르다 ma-reu-da; *adj.* 마른 ma-reun

dry cleaner *n.* 드라이클리닝 업자 deu-ra-i-keul-li-ning eop-ja; 드라이클리닝 약품 deu-ra-i-keul-li-ning yak-pum

dry-clean *vt.* 드라이클리닝하다 deu-ra-i-keul-li-ning-ha-da

dryer *n.* 건조기 geon-jo-gi

dual *adj.* 둘의 dul-ui, 이중의 i-jung-ui

Dublin *n.* 더블린 deo-beul-lin

duck *n.* 오리 o-ri; *vi.* 물속으로 처박다 mul-ssog-e cheo-bak-da

due *adj.* 만기가 된 man-gi-ga doen; 예정된 ye-jeong-doen; 합당한 hap-dang-han

duet *n.* 이중창 i-jung-chang, 이중주 i-jung-ju, 듀엣 dyu-et

dull *adj.* 무딘 mu-din; 둔한 dun-han; 지루한 ji-ru-han; 활기가 없는 hwal-gi-ga eom-neun; ~ **brown** 흐린 갈색 heu-rin gal-ssaek

dumb *adj.* 벙어리의 beong-eo-ri-ui; 말을 하지 않는 mal-eul ha-ji an-neun; 바보스러운 ba-bo-seu-reo-un

dummy *n.* 인체모형 in-che-mo-hyeong; 바보 ba-bo

dump *vt.* 내버리다 nae-beo-ri-da; 덤핑하다 deom-ping-ha-da; *n.* 쓰레기장 sseu-re-gi-jang

dung *n.* 똥 ttong, 거름 geo-reum, 비료 bi-ryo

duplex *adj.* 이중의 i-jung-ui, 복식의 bok-sig-ui

duplicate *adj.* 중복의 jung-bog-ui; 꼭 같은 kkok gat-eun; *n.* 복제 bok-je, 복제품 bok-je-pum

durable *adj.* 영구적인 yeong-gu-jeog-in

during *prep.* ...동안 ...dong-an; ...사이에 ...sa-i-e; **I was busy ~ the summer** 여름동안 바빴다 yeo-reum-ttong-an ba-ppat-da; **~ the period I was in Korea, my friends came to see me**내가 한국에 있는 사이에 친구들이 나를 만나러 왔다 nae-ga han-gug-e in-neun sa-i-e chin-gu-deul-i na-reul man-na-reo wat-da

dusk *n.* 땅거미 ttang-kkeo-mi, 황혼 hwang-hon

dust *n.* 먼지 meon-ji; *vt.* 먼지를 털다 meon-ji-reul teol-da

duster *n.* 먼지떨이 meon-ji-teol-i

dusty *adj.* 먼지투성이의 meon-ji-tu-seong-i-ui

duty *n.* 의무 ui-mu, 임무 im-mu; **on ~** 근무중인 geun-mu-jung-in

dutyfree *adj.* 무관세의 mu-gwan-sse-ui, 면세의 myeon-se-ui

DVD *n.* 디비디 di-bi-di

dwell *vi.* 살다 sal-da; 오래 머무르다 o-rae meo-mu-reu-da

dwelling *n.* 집 jip; 거주지 geo-ju-ji

dye *n.* 물감 mul-kkam, 염료 yeom-nyo; 색깔 saek-kkal; *vt.* 물들이다 mul-deul-i-da

dying *adj.* 죽어가는 jug-eo-ga-neun

dynamic *adj.* 활기있는 hwal-gi-in-neun; 동적인 dong-jjeog-in

dynamite *n.* 다이너마이트 da-i-neo-ma-i-teu

dynasty *n.* 왕조 wang-jo

E

each *adj.* 각자의 gak-ja-ui, 개개의 gae-gae-ui; **~ time** 매번 mae-beon; *adv.* 한사람마다 han-sa-ram-ma-da, 제각기 je-gak-gi; *pron.* 각자 gak-ja, 각기 gak-gi; **They are two dollars ~** 한개에 이불씩입니다 han-gae-e i-bul-ssig-im-ni-da; *pron.* **one of ~** 각각 하나씩 gak-gak ha-na-ssik; **~ other** 서로 seo-ro

eager *adj.* 열망하는 yeol-mang-ha-neun; 열심인 yeol-ssim-in

eagle *n.* 독수리 dok-su-ri

ear *n.* 귀 gwi; 이삭 i-sak

earache *n.* 귀앓이 gwi-al-i

early *adj.* 이른 i-reun; *adv.* 일찍 il-jjik; **~ in the morning** 아침 일찍 a-chim il-jjik

earn *vi.* 벌다 beol-da; 획득하다 hoek-deu-ka-da

earnest *adj.* 성실한 seong-sil-han; 진지한 jin-ji-han

earnings *n.* 소득 so-deuk, 임금 im-geum

earphone *n.* 이어폰 i-eo-pon

earplug *n.* 귀막이gwi-mag-i, 귀마개 gwi-ma-gae

earring *n.* 귀걸이 gwi-geol-i

earth *n.* 지구 ji-gu; 대지 dae-ji; 세상 se-sang

earthquake *n.* 지진 ji-jin

earthworm *n.* 지렁이 ji-reong-i

earwax *n.* 귀지 gwi-ji

east *adj.* 동쪽의 dong-jjog-ui; *adv.* 동쪽으
로 dong-jjog-eu-ro; 동쪽에 dong-jjog-e;
n. 동쪽 dong-jjok; 동양 dong-yang; 동
부지방 dong-bu-jji-bang; ~ **coast** 동해
안 dong-hae-an; **to go** ~ 동쪽으로 가다
dong-jjog-eu-ro ga-da
East Africa *n.* 동아프리카 dong-a-peu-ri-ka
East Asia *n.* 동아시아 dong-a-si-a
eastern *adj.* 동쪽의 dong-jjog-ui; 동양의
dong-yang-ui
Eastern Europe *n.* 동유럽 dong-yu-reop
easy *adj.* 쉬운 swi-un; 마음편한 ma-eum-
pyeon-han; **easily** *adv.* 쉽게 swip-ge, 편안
하게 pyeon-an-ha-ge
easygoing *adj.* 태평스러운
tae-pyeong-seu-reo-un
eat *vt.* 먹다 meok-da, 식사하다 sik-sa-ha-da;
to ~ **out** 외식하다 oe-si-ka-da
eccentric *adj.* 괴상한 goe-sang-han
echo *n.* 메아리 me-a-ri; *vi.* 울리다 ul-li-da; *vt.*
반향하다 ban-hyang-ha-da
economical *adj.* 경제적인 gyeong-je-jeog-in
economics *n.* 경제학 gyeong-je-hak
economist *n.* 경제학자 gyeong-je-hak-ja
economy *n.* 경제 gyeong-je; 절약 jeol-yak
economy class *n.* 일반석 il-ban-jeok
ecosystem *n.* 생태계 saeng-tae-gye
edge *n.* 끝 kkeut, 가장자리 ga-jang-ja-ri; 테
두리 te-du-ri; 칼날 kal-lal; *vt.* 날을 세우다
nal eul se-u-da
edible *adj.* 먹을 수 있는 meog-eul ssu
in-neun, 식용(의) sig yong(ui)
edit *vt.* 편집하다 pyeon-ji-pa-da
edition *n.* 판 pan; 간행 gan-haeng
editor *n.* 편집자 pyeon-jip-ja
editorial *n.* 사설 sa seol, 논설 non-seol
educate *vt.* 교육하다 gyo-yu-ka-da
education *n.* 교육 gyo-yuk
educational *adj.* 교육적인 gyo-yuk-jeog-in
eel *n.* 뱀장어 baem-jang-eo
effect *n.* 결과 gyeol-gwa; 효과 hyo-kkwa; 영
향 yeong-hyang
effective *adj.* 효과적인 hyo-kkwa-jeog-in
efficiency *n.* 능력 neung-nyeok, 능률
neung-nyul
efficient *adj.* 능률적인 neung-nyul-jjeog-in,
효과가 있는 hyo-kkwa-ga in-neun; 유능
한 yu-neung-han
effort *n.* 노력 no-ryeok

egg *n.* 계란 gye-ran, 달걀 dal-gyal, 알 al
eggplant *n.* 가지 ga-ji
eggshell *n.* 달걀껍질 dal-gyal-kkeop-jil, 계란
껍질 gye-ran-kkeop-jil
egocentric *adj.* 자기중심적인
ja-gi-jung-sim-jeog-in
egoist *n.* 이기주의자 i-gi-ju-i-ja
Egypt *n.* 이집트 i-jip-teu
Egyptian *n.* 이집트사람 i-jip-teu-ssa-ram;
adj. 이집트의 i-jip-teu-ui
eight *num.* 팔 pal, 여덟 yeo-deol
eighteen *num.* 십팔 sip-pal, 열여덟
yeol-yeo-deol
eighteenth *adj.* 열여덟번째의 yeol-yeo-deol-
ppeon-jjae-ui, 제십팔회 je sip-pal-hoe
eighth *adj.* 여덟번째의 yeo-deol-ppeon-jjae-
ui, 제팔회 je-pal-hoe
eighty *num.* 팔십 pal-ssip, 여든 yeo-deun
either *adj.* 어느 한쪽의 eo-neu han-jjog-ui;
pron. 어느 한쪽 eo-neu ha-jjok, 어느 한쪽
도 eo-neu jjok-do, 어느 쪽인가 eo-neu
jjog-in-ga; ~ **one (or the other)** 어느 한
쪽 eo-neu han-jjok; *adv.* -도 또한 do
tto-han; ~ **...** or **...** 둘 중 어느 한쪽도 dul
jjung eo-neu han-jjok-do, 둘 중 어느 한쪽
(이)라도 dul jjung eo-neu han-jjok-(i)-ra-do,
둘 중 어느 한쪽 (이)든 dul jjung eo-neu
han-jjok-(i)-deun
eject *vt.* 축출하다 chuk-chul-ha-da; 뿜
어내다 ppum-eo-nae-da, 배출히다
bae-chul-ha-da
elastic *n.* 고무줄 go-mu-jul; 고무밴드
go-mu-baen-deu; *adj.* 탄력성이 있는
tal-lyeok-seong-i in-neun
elbow *n.* 팔꿈치 pal-kkum-chi
elderly *adj.* 나이가 지긋한 na-i-ga ji-geu-
tan; *n.* 나이가 지긋하신 분들 na-i-ga
ji-geu-ta-sin bun-deul
elect *vt.* 선거하다 seon-geo-ha-da; 선출하다
seon-chul-ha-da
election *n.* 선거 seon-geo; 선정 seon-jeong
electric *adj.* 전기의 jeon-gi-ui; ~**al cord**
전깃줄 jeon-git-jul; ~ **eel** 전기뱀장어
jeon-gi-baem-jang-eo
electric shock *n.* 감전 gam-jeon
electricity *n.* 전기 jeon-gi; 전류 jeol-lyu
electronic *adj.* 전자의 jeon-ja-ui; 전자학의
jeon-ja-hag-ui
elegant *adj.* 우아한 u-a-han

element *n.* 요소 yo-so; 원소 won-so

elementary *adj.* 기본의 gi-bon-ui; 초
보의 cho-bo-ui; ~ **school** 초등학교
cho-deung-hak-gyo

elephant *n.* 코끼리 ko-kki-ri

elevate *vt.* 들어올리다 deul-eo-ol-li-da; 승진
시키다 seung-jin-ha-da

elevator *n.* 엘리베이터 el-li-be-i-teo

eleven *num.* 십일 sib-il, 열하나 yeol-ha-na

eleventh *adj.* 열한번째의 yeol-han-beon-
jjae-ui; 제십일회 je sib-il-hoe

eligible *adj.* 적격의 jeok-gyeog-ui, 바람직한
ba-ram-ji-kan

eliminate *vt.* 제거하다 je-geo-ha-da, 없애다
eops-ae-da

elite *n.* 엘리트 el-li-teu

El Niño *n.* 엘리뇨 el-li-nyo

else *adj.* 그밖의 geu-bakk-ui, 다른 da-reun;
what ~ 그밖에 어떤것이 있나요 geu
bakk-e eo-tteon-geos-i in-na-yo; **somebody**
~ 그 외에 다른 누군가 geu oe-e da-reun
nu-gun-ga; *adv.* 그밖에 geu bakk-e; 그렇
지 않으면 geu-reo-chi an-eu-myeon

e-mail *n.* 이메일 i-me-il, 전자우편 jeon-ja-u-
pyeon; ~ **message** 이메일 메세지 i-me-il
me-sse-ji-reul bo-nae-da; *vt.* 이메일을 보
내다jeon-ja-u-pyeon-eul b-nae-da, 전자우
편을 보내다 jeon-ja-u-pyeon-eul b-nae-da;

embargo *n.* 출입항 금지 chul-i-pang geum-
ji; 통상금지 tong-sang-geum-ji

embark *vt.* 배를 타다bae-reul ta-da, 비행기
를 타다 bi-haeng-gi-reul ta-da; 착수하다
chak-su-ha-da

embarrass *vt.* 당황하게 하다 dang-hwang-
ha-ge ha-da; 곤란에 빠뜨리다 gol-lan-e
ppa-tteu-ri-da; ~**ed**/~**ing** 당황스러운
dang-hwang-seu-reo-un

embarrassment *n.* 당황 dang-hwang; 거북
함 geo-bu-kam

embassy *n.* 대사관 dae-sa-gwan; 사절단
sa-jeol-ttan

emblem *n.* 상징 sang-jing, 문장 mun-jang

embrace *n.* 포옹 po-ong; *vt.* 껴안다 kkyeo-
an-tta; 환영하다 hwan-yeong-ha-da

embroider *vt.* 수를 놓다 su-reul no-ta; ~**ed**
수놓은 su-no-eun

embroidery *n.* 자수 ja-su

emerge *vi.* 나오다 na-o-da, 나타나다
na-ta-na-da

emergency *n.* 비상사태 bi-sang-sa-tae, 응
급사태 eung-geup-sa-tae; ~ **exit** 비상구
bi-sang-gu; ~ **room** 응급실 eung-geup-sil

emigrant *n.* 이민 i-min; 이주민 i-ju-min

emigrate *vi.* 이민가다 i-min-ga-da

emigration *n.* 이민 i-min, 이주 i-ju

eminent *adj.* 저명한 jeo-myeong-han; 뛰어
난 ttwi-eo-nan

emit *vt.* 내다 nae-da, 발하다 bal-ha-da

emotion *n.* 감동 gam-dong; 감정 gam-jeong,
정서 jeong-seo

emperor *n.* 황제 hwang-je

emphasis *n.* 강조 gang-jo; 강세 gang-se

emphasize *vt.* 강조하다 gang-jo-ha-da; 역설
하다 yeok-seol-ha-da

empire *n.* 제국 je-guk

empirical *adj.* 경험적인 gyeong-heom-jeog-in

employ *vt.* 고용하다 go-yong-ha-da

employee *n.* 고용인 go-yong-in, 종업원
jong-eob-won

employer *n.* 고용주 go-yong-ju

employment *n.* 고용 go-yong; 직업 jig-eop;
~ **agency** 직업 안내소 jig-eop an-nae-so

empty *adj.* 비어있는 bi-eo-in-neun; 공허한
gong-heo-han; *vt.* 비우다 bi-u-da

enable *vt.* 힘을 주다him-eul ju-da, 능력을
주다 neung-nyeog-eul ju-da; 가능성을 주
다 ga-neung-sseong-eul ju-da

enamel *n.* 에나멜 e-na-mel, 법랑 beom-nang

enchanting *adj* 매혹적인 mae-hok-jeog-in,
매력적인 mae-ryeok-jeog-in

enclose *vt.* 둘러싸다 dul-leo-ssa-da; 동봉하
다 dong-bong-ha-da

enclosure *n.* 둘러쌈 dul-leo-ssam; 봉입
bong-ip; 첨부별지cheom-bu-byeol-jji; 구
내 gu-nae

encore *n.* 앙콜 ang-kol, 앙코르 ang-ko-reu

encounter *n.* 우연히 만남 u-yeon-hi man-
nam, 조우 jo-u; *vt.* 우연히 만나다 u-yeon-
hi man-na-da, 마주치다 ma-ju-chi-da

encourage *vt.* 격려하다 gyeong-nyeo-ha-da

encyclopedia *n.* 백과사전 baek-gwa-sa-jeon

end *n.* 끝 kkeut, 마지막 ma-ji-mak; 결과
gyeol-gwa; 목적 mok-jeok; *vi.* 끝나다
kkeun-na-da; *vt.* 끝내다 kkeun-nae-da

endanger vt. 위험에 빠뜨리다 wi-heom-e ppa-tteu-ri-da

endangered adj. 멸종위기의 myeol-jjong-wi-gi-ui

ending n. 결말 gyeol-mal; 죽음 jug-eum; 어미 eo-mi

endless adj. 끝없는 kkeud-eom-neun

endorse vt. 승인하다 seung-in-ha-da; 양도하다 yang-do-ha-da; 배서하다 bae-seo-ha-da

endurance n. 인내 in-nae; 지구력 ji-gu-ryeok

endure vi. 견디다 gyeon di da, 참다 cham-tta, 인내하다 in-nae-ha-da

enemy n. 적 jeok

energetic adj. 정력적인 jeong-nyeok-jeog-in

energy n. 에너지 e-neo-ji; 활기 hwal-gi; 정력 jeong-nyeok

enforce vt. 시행하다 si-haeng-ha-da; 강요하다 gang-yo-ha-da

engagement n. 약속 yak-sok; 약혼 ya kon; ~ **ring** 약혼반지 ya-kon-ban-ji

engine n. 엔진 en-jin; 기관차 gi-gwan-cha; 발동기 bal-ttong-gi; ~ **room** 기관실 gi-gwan-sil

engineer n. 기사 gi-sa; 기관사 gi-gwan-sa; 공학자 gong-hak-ja

England n. 영국 yeong-guk

English n. 영국사람 yeong-guk-sa-ram; adj. 영국의 yeong-gug-ui

English Channel n. 영국해협 yeong-gu-kae-hyeop

engrave vt. 파다 pa-da; 새기다 sae-gi-da

engraving n. 조각 jo-gak; 판화 pan-hwa

enhance vt. 질을 높이다 jil-eul nop-i-da, 강화하다 gang-hwa-ha-da

enjoy vt. 즐기다 jeul-gi-da; 맛보다 mat-bo-da; 받다 bat-da; 가지고 있다 ga-ji-go lt-da

enjoyment n. 즐거움 jeul-geo-um, 기쁨 gi-ppeum; 향락 hyang-nak; 향유 hyang-yu

enlarge vt. 확대하다 hwak-dae-ha-da; 넓히다 neol-pi-da

enormous adj. 거대한 geo-dae-han

enough adj. 충분한 chung-bun-han; adv. 충분히 chung-bun-hi

enquire vt. 묻다 mut-da, 문의하다 mun-ui-ha-da

enrich vt. 풍성하게 하다 pung-seong-ha-ge ha-da, 풍부하게 하다 pung-bu-ha-ge ha-da

enroll vt. 등록하다 deung-no-ka-da, 입학하다 i-pa-ka-da

ensure vt. 책임지다 chaeg-im-ji-da; 보장하다 bo-jang-ha-da

enter vi. 들어가다 deul-eo-ga-da; 넣다 neo-ta; 시작하다 si-ja-ka-da

enterprise n. 기획 gi-hoek; 기업 gi-eop; 진취적인 정신 jin-chwi-jeog-in jeong-sin

entertain vt. 환대하다 hwan-dae-ha-da; 즐겁게 하다 jeul-geop-ge ha-da; 마음에 품다 ma-eum-e pum-tta

entertainer n. 예능인 ye-neung-in

entertaining adj. 재미있는 jae-mi-in-neun

entertainment n. 환대 hwan-dae; 연예 yeon-ye; 오락 o-rak

enthusiasm n. 열중 yeol-jjung; 열광 yeol-gwang

entire adj. 전체의 jeon-che-ui

entirely adv. 아주 a-ju, 전적으로 jeon-jjeog-eu-ro

entrance n. 입구 ip-gu; 입장 ip-jang; ~ **exam** 입학시험 i-pak-si-heom; ~ **fee** 입장료 ip-jang-nyo

entrust vt. 맡기다 mat-gi-da

entry n. 입장 ip-jang; 참가 cham-ga; 기입 gi-ip

envelop vt. 봉하다 bong-ha-da; 싸다 ssa-da

envelope n. 봉투 bong-tu

envious adj. 부러워하는 bu-reo-wo-ha-neun

environment n. 환경 hwan-gyeong; 주위 ju-wi; 주위사정 ju-wi-sa-jeong

environs n. 도시근교 do-si-geun-gyo, 교외 gyo-oe; 주변지역 ju-byeon-ji-yeok

envy n. 질투 jil-tu; 부러움 bu-reo-um; 선망의 대상 seon-mang-ui dae-sang; vt. 부러워하다 bu-reo-wo-ha-da

epidemic n. 유행병 yu haeng-ppyeong; 유행 yu-haeng; adj. 유행병의 yu-haeng-ppyeong-ui; 유행하는 yu-haeng-ha-neun

epilepsy n. 간질 gan-jil

episode n. 에피소드 e-pi-sso-deu, 일화 il-hwa

equal adj. 동등한 dong-deung-han; 같은 gat-eun; 적당한 jeok-dang-han; vt. 같다 gat-da; 필적하다 oil-jjeo-ka-da

equality n. 같음 gat-eum, 동등 dong-deung

equator n. 적도 jeok-do

equip vt. 설비하다 seol-bi-ha-da, 장비를 갖추다 jang-bi-reul gat-chu-da

equipment *n.* 장비 jang-bi, 설비 seol-bi; 준비 jun-bi; 능력 neung-nyeok

equity *n.* 공평 gong-pyeong, 정당 jeong-dang

equivalent *adj.* 동등한 dong-deung-han; ...에 상당하는 ...e sang-dang-ha-neun

era *n.* 기원gi-won; 연대 yeon-dae; 시대 si-dae

eradicate *vt.* 뿌리뽑다 ppu-ri-ppop-da

erase *vt.* 지우다 ji-u-da

eraser *n.* 지우개 ji-u-gae

erect *adj.* 똑바로 선 ttok-ba-ro seon; *vt.* 세우다 se-u-da, 설립하다 seol-li-pa-da

erode *vt.* 부식시키다 bu-sik-si-ki-da; 좀먹다 jom-meok-da

errand *n.* 심부름 sim-bu-reum; 볼일 bol-lil; 용건 yong-kkeon

error *n.* 잘못 jal-mot, 실수 sil-ssu

erupt *vi.* 화산이 폭발하다 hwa-san-i pok-bal-ha-da

escalate *vt.* 단계적으로 확대하다 dan-gye-jeog-eu-ro hwak-dae-ha-da; 차츰 올리다 cha-cheum ol-li-da

escalator *n.* 에스컬레이터 e-seu-keol-le-i-teo

escape *n.* 탈출 tal-chul, 도망 do-mang; *vt.* 탈출하다 tal-chul-ha-da, 도망하다 do-mang-ha-da; 모면하다 mo-myeon-ha-da; 벗어나다 beos-eo-na-da

escort *n.* 호위자 ho-wi-ja; 호위 ho-wi; *vt.* 호위하다 ho-wi-ha-da

especially *adv.* 특히 teu-ki, 각별히 gak-byeol-hi

essay *n.* 수필 su-pil; 소평론 so-pyeong-non

essence *n.* 엣센스 et-ssen-sseu, 본질 bon-jil, 정수 jeong-su

essential *adj.* 필수적인 pil-ssu-jeog-in; 불가결한 bul-ga-gyeol-han; 본질적인 bon-jil-jjeog-in

establish *vt.* 설립하다 seol-li-pa-da; 확립하다 hwang-ni-pa-da; 안정시키다 an-jeong-si-ki-da

estate *n.* 토지 to-ji, 부동산 bu-dong-san

estimate *n.* 평가 pyeong-kka; 판단 pan-dan; *vt., vi.* 평가하다 pyeong-kka-ha-da; 견적을 내다 gyeon-jeog-eul nae-da

etcetera *n.* 기타 gi-ta, 등등deung-deung

eternal *adj.* 영구불변의 yeong-gu-bul-byeon-ui

ethical *adj.* 윤리의 yul-li-ui; 도덕의 do-deog-ui

Ethiopia *n.* 에티오피아 e-ti-o-pi-a

ethnic *adj.* 인종의in-jong-ui, 민족의 min-jog-ui

etiquette *n.* 예의 ye-ui, 에티켓 e-ti-ket

Euro *n. (currency)* 유로화 yu-ro-hwa

Europe *n.* 유럽 yu-reop

European *n.* 유럽사람 yu-reop-sa-ram; *adj.* 유럽의 yu-reob-ui

European Union *n.* 유럽공동체 yu-reop-gong-dong-che

euthanasia *n.* 안락사 al-lak-sa

evacuate *vt.* 비우다 bi-u-da; 철수하다cheol-ssu-ha-da; 철거하다 cheol-geo-ha-da

evacuation *n.* 철수 cheol-ssu; 철거 cheol-geo; 퇴거 toe-geo

evaluate *vt.* 평가하다 pyeong-kka-ha-da

evaluation *n.* 평가 pyeong-kka-ha-da

evaporate *vt.* 증발시키다 jeung-bal-si-ki-da; *vi.* 증발하다 jeung-bal-ha-da

eve *n.* 이브 i-beu, 전야 jeon-ya; **Christmas ~** 크리스마스 이브 keu-ri-sseu-ma-sseu i-beu; **on the ~ of** ...전야에 ...jeon-ya-e

even *adv.* ...까지도 ...kka-ji-do, ...조차도 ...jo-cha-do, 한층 더 han-cheung deo; **They are open ~ on Sundays** 그 (가게)들은 일요일 저녁에도 문을 연다 geu (ga-ge)deul-eun il-yo-il jeo-nyeog-e-do mun-eul yeon-da; *adj.* 평평한 pyeong-pyeong-han, 평탄한 pyeong-tan-han, 같은 높이로 gat-eun nop-i-ro, 같은 gat-eun, 짝수의 jjak-su-ui; **an ~ number** 짝수 jjak-su; **an ~ surface** 균등한 표면 gyun-deung-han pyo-myeon, 평평한 표면 pyeong-pyeong-han pyo-myeon; *vt.* 평평하게 하다 pyeong-pyeong-ha-ge ha-da, 고르다 go-reu-da, 동등하게 하다 dong-deung-ha-ge ha-da; *vi.* 평평하게 되다 pyeong-pyeong-ha-ge doe-da, 균등해지다 gyun-deung-hae-ji-da; **We are ~** 우리는 평등하다 u-ri-neun pyeong-deung-ha-da, 우리는 비겼다 u-ri-neun bi-gyeot-da

evening *n.* 저녁 jeo-nyeok, 밤 bam; **~ paper** 석간신문 seok-gan-sin-mun; **~ school** 야간학교 ya-gan-hak-gyo

event *n.* 이벤트 i-ben-teu; 사건 sa-kkeon; 결과 gyeol-gwa; 종목 jong-mok eventually *adv.* 결과적으로 gyeol-gwa-jeog-eu-ro

ever *adv.* 일찍이 il-jjig-i, 이전에 i-jeon-e, 전혀 jeon-hyeo, 언젠가 eon-jen-ga, 이제까지 i-je-kka-ji, 언제나 eon-je-na, 도대체 do-dae-che; **more than** ~ 어느 때 보다도 더 eo-neu ttae bo-da-do deo, 여느 때 없이 yeo-neu ttae eops-i; 더욱 더 deo-uk deo, 점점 더 jeom-jeom deo

evergreen *n.* 상록수 sang-nok-su; *adj.* 늘푸른 neul-pu-reun

everlasting *adj.* 영원히 계속되는yeong-won-hi gye-sok-doe-neun, 끝없는 kkeud-eom-neun, 영원한 yeong-won-han

every *adj.* 어느 …(이)나 다 eo-neu …(i)-na da, 모든 mo-deun, 가능한 한 ga-neung-han han, 충분한 chung-bun-han, 매… mae…, …마다 …ma-da; ~ **day** 매일 mae-il

everybody *pron.* 각각 gak-gak; 누구나 nu-gu-na

everyday *adj.* 매일의 mae-il-ui, 일상의 il-ssang-ui

everyone *pron.* 각각 gak-gak; 누구나 nu-gu-na

everything *pron.* 모든 것 mo-deun geot; 무엇이나 mu-eos-i-na

everywhere *adv.* 어디에나 eo-di-e-na

evidence *n.* 증거 jeung-geo; 징후 jing-hu

evident *adj.* 분명한 bun-myeong-han; 명백한 myeong-bae-kan

evil *n.* 악 ak; 해악 hae-ak; *adj.* 나쁜 na-ppeun; 사악한 sa-a-kan; 불길한 bul-gil-han

evolution *n.* 진화 jin-hwa

exact *adj.* 정확한 jeong-hwa-kan; 꼼꼼한 kkom-kkom-han; *vt.* 강요하다 gang-yo-ha-da

exaggerate *vt.* 과장하다 gwa-ja-jang-ha-da

exaggeration *n.* 과장 gwa-jang

examination *n.* 시험 si-heom; 진찰 jin-chal; 조사 jo-sa; ~ **paper** 시험지 si-heom-ji

examine *vt.* 시험하다 si-heom-ha-da; 진찰하다 jin-chal-ha-da; 조사하다 jo-sa-ha-da

example *n.* 예 ye, 보기 bo-gi; 견본 gyeon-bon; 모범 mo-beom; **for** ~ 예를 들면 ye-reul-deul-myeon

excavation *n.* 파냄 pa-naem, 발굴 bal-gul; 발굴유적 bal-gul-lyu-jeok; 굴 gul, 구덩이 gu-deong-i

exceed *vt.* 넘다 neom-tta, 초과하다 cho-gwa-ha-da; …보다 뛰어나다 …bo-da ttwi-eo-na-da

exceeding *adj.* 엄청난 eom-cheong-nan, 굉장한 goeng-jang-han

excellent *adj.* 우수한 u-su-han

except *prep.* …을 제외하고 …eul je-oe-ha-go, … 를 제외하고 … reul je-oe-ha-go, …을 빼고 …eul ppae-go, … 를 빼고 … reul ppae-go; ~ **Sundays** 일요일을 빼고 il-yo-il-eul ppae-go; ~ **for certain conditions** 어떤 경우를 제외하고 eo-tteon gyeong-u-reul je-oe-ha-go

exception *n.* 예외 ye-oe; 제외 je-oe

excess *n.* 초과 cho-gwa; 과도 gwa-do; 부절제 bu-jeol-jje

excessive *adj.* 과도한 gwa-do-han, 지나친 ji-na-chin

exchange *n.* 교환 gyo-hwan; *vt.* 교환하다 gyo-hwan-ha-da, 바꾸다 ba-kku-da; ~ **rate** 환율 hwan-nyul; ~ **student** 교환학생 gyo-hwan-hak-saeng

excite *vt.* 자극하다 ja-geu-ka-da; 흥분시키다 heung-bun-si-ki-da

excitement *n.* 흥분 heung-bun; 소동 so-dong

exclaim *vt.* 외치다 oe-chi-da, 고함지르다 go-ham-ji-reu-da

exclamation mark *n.* 느낌표 neu-kkim-pyo

exclude *vt.* 몰아내다 mol-a-nae-da; 제외하다 je-oe-ha-da; 배척하다 bae-cheo-ka-da

exclusive *adj.* 배타적인 bae-ta-jeog-in; 독전적인 dok-jeom-jeog-in

excuse *n.* 변명 byeon-myeong; 사과 sa-gwa; 용서 yong-seo; *vt.* 변명하다 byeon-myeong-ha-da; 용서하다 yong-seo-ha-da; ~ **me** 실례합니다 sil-le-ham-ni-da

execute *vt.* 실행하다 sil-haeng-ha-da; 달성하다 dal-sseong-ha-da; 사형을 집행하다 sa-hyeong-eul ji-paeng-ha-da

executive *n.* 행정부 haeng-jeong-bu; 중역 jung-yeok; *adj.* 행정적인 haeng-jeong-jeog-in

exempt *vt.* 면제하다 myeon-je-ha-da

exemption *n.* 면제 myeon-je

exercise *n.* 운동 un-dong; 연습 yeon-seup; 행사 haeng-sa; ~ **book** 연습장 yeon-seup-jang; *vt.* 운동시키다 un-dong-si-ki-da; 연습시키다 yeon-seup-si-ki-da, 훈련하다 hul-lyeon-si-ki-da; 행사하다 haeng-sa-ha-da

exhale *vi.* 내뿜다 nae-ppum-tta; 발산하다 bal-ssan-si-ki-da; 폭발시키다 pok-bal-si-ki-da

exhaust *n.* 배기 bae-gi; 배기가스 bae-gi-kka-sseu; 배기장치 bae-gi-jang-chi; ~**ed** 지쳐버린 ji-cheo-beo-rin

exhibit *n.* 전시회 jeon-si-hoe; 진열품 jin-yeol-pum; 공시 gong-si; **art** ~ 미술전시회 mi-sul-jeon-si-hoe; *vt.* 전람하다 jeol-lam-ha-da; 진열하다 jin-yeol-ha-da; 나타내다 na-ta-nae-da; **to** ~ **tendencies toward...** ...에 대한 풍조을 나타내다 ...e dae-han pung-jo-eul na-ta-nae-da, ...에 대한 경향을 나타내다 ...e dae-han gyeong-hyang-eul na-ta-nae-da

exile *n.* 망명 mang-myeong; 추방 chu-bang; *vt.* 추방하다 chu-bang-ha-da

exist *vi.* 존재하다 jon-jae-ha-da; 생존하다 saeng-jon-ha-da

existence *n.* 존재 jon-jae; 생존 saeng-jon

exit *n.* 출구 chul-gu; 퇴장 toe-jang, 퇴진 toe-jin; ~ **permit** 출국 허가증 chul-guk heo-ga-jjeung; ~ **visa** 출국비자 chul-guk-bi-ja; *vt.* 퇴장하다 toe-jang-ha-da

exotic *adj.* 외래의 oe-rae-ui; 이국적인 i-guk-jeog-in

expand *vt.* 넓히다 neol-pi-da; 팽창시키다 paeng-chang-si-ki-da; *vi.* 퍼지다 peo-ji-da; 부풀어 오르다 bu-pul-eo o-reu-da

expansion *n.* 팽창 paeng-chang; 신장 sin-jang; 확장 hwak-jang

expect *vt.* 기대하다 gi-dae-ha-da; 예정되어 있다 ye-jeong-doe-eo it-da; 의지하다 ui-ji-ha-da

expectation *n.* 기대 gi-dae; 가능성 ga-neung-sseong

expel *vt.* 쫓아내다 jjoch-a-nae-da; 추방하다 chu-bang-ha-da

expense *n.* 지출 ji-chul; 비용 bi-yong

expensive *adj.* 값비싼 gap-bi-ssan

experience *n.* 경험 gyeong-heom; *vt.* 경험하다 gyeong-heom-ha-da

expert *n.* 전문가 jeon-mun-ga; 명인 myeong-in; 숙련가 sung-nyeon-ga

expire *vi.* 만기가 되다 man-gi-ga doe-da, 기간이 끝나다 gi-gan-i kkeun-na-da

explain *vt.* 분명히 하다 bun-myeong-hi ha-da; 설명하다 seol-myeong-ha-da

explanation *n.* 설명 seol-myeong; 해설 hae-seol

explode *vt.* 폭발시키다 pok-bal-si-ki-da; *vi.* 폭발하다 pok-bal-ha-da

explore *vt.* 탐험하다 tam-heom-ha-da; 탐구하다 tam-gu-ha-da

explosion *n.* 폭발 pok-bal; 폭파음 pok-pa-eum; 폭발적 증가 pok-bal-jjeok jeung-ga

expo *n.* 박람회 bang-nam-hoe

export *n.* 수출 su-chul; 수출품 su-chul-pum; *vt.* 수출하다 su-chul-ha-da

expose *vt.* 노출시키다 no-chul-si-ki-da; 보이다 bo-i-da; 드러내다 deu-reo-nae-da; 발표하다 bal-pyo-ha-da

exposure *n.* 노출 no-chul; 진열 jin-yeol

express *adj.* 명시된 myeong-si-doen; 명백한 myeong-bae-kan; 급행의 geu-paeng-ui; *vt.* 표현하다 pyo-hyeon-ha-da; 표시하다 pyo-si-ha-da; ~ **Mail** 속달우편 sok-dal-u-pyeon, 빠른우편 ppa-reun-u-pyeon; ~ **train** 급행열차 geu-paeng-nyeol-cha; **to** ~ **an opinion** 의견을 표출하다 ui-gyeon-eul pyo-chul-ha-da; **to** ~ **oneself** 생각하는 바를 말하다 saeng-ga-ka-neun ba-reul mal-ha-da

expression *n.* 표현 pyo-hyeon, 말씨 mal-ssi; 표정 pyo-jeong

extend *vt.* 늘이다 neul-i-da; 펴다 pyeo-da; 확대하다 hwak-dae-ha-da; ~**ed family** 대가족 dae-ga-jok

extension *n.* 연장 yeon-jang; 확대 hwak-dae; 증축 jeung-chuk

extent *n.* 넓이 neolb-i; 범위 beom-ui, 정도 jeong-do

exterior *adj.* 외부의 oe-bu-ui; *n.* 외부 oe-bu

external *adj.* 외부의 oe-bu-ui; 표면의 pyo-myeon-ui; 대외적인 dae-oe-jeog-in

extinct *adj.* 꺼진 kkeo-jin, 사멸한 sa-myeol-han; 단절된 dan-jeol-doen

extinguish *vt.* 끄다 kkeu-da, 진화하다 jin-hwa-ha-da; 소멸시키다 so-myeol-si-ki-da; ~**er** 소화기 so-hwa-gi

extra *n.* 여분 yeo-bun; 특별호 teuk-byeol-ho; 엑스트라 ek-seu-teu-ra; *adj.* 여분의 yeo-bun-ui; 특별한 teuk-byeol-han; 임시의 im-si-ui; *adv.* 특별히 teuk-byeol-hi; **~large** 특대 teuk-dae

extract *n.* 발췌 bal-chwe; 추출물 chu-chul-mul; *vt.* 뽑아내다 ppob-a-nae-da, 뽑다 ppop-da; 발췌하다 bal-chwe-ha-da

extradite *vt.* 인도하다 in-do-ha-da

extraordinary *adj.* 비범한 bi-beom-han; 특별한 teuk-byeol-han

extreme *adj.* 과격한 gwa-gyeo-kan; 극단의 geuk-dan-ui; 극도의 geuk-do-ui

eye *n.* 눈 nun; 관찰력 gwan-chal-lyeok; 주시 ju-si; **~liner** 아이라이너 a-i-ra-i-neo

eyeball *n.* 눈알 nun-al; 안구 an-gu

eyebrow *n.* 눈썹 nun-sseop

eyelash *n.* 속눈썹 song-nun-sseop

eyelid *n.* 눈꺼풀 nun-kkeo-pul

eyesight *n.* 시력 si-ryeok

eyewitness *n.* 목격자 mok-gyeok-ja

F

fabric *n.* 직물 jing-mul; 천 cheon

fabulous *adj.* 전설적인 jeon-seol-jjeog-in; 믿어지지 않는 mid-eo-ji-ji an-neun

facade *n.* 정면 jeong-myeon

face *n.* 얼굴 eol-gul; 표면 pyo-myeon; *adj.* **~down** 얼굴을 숙인 eol-gul-eul sug-in; 겉을 밑으로 향한 geot-eul mit-eu-ro hyang-han; **~to~** 정면으로 마주보는 jeong-myeon-eul ma-ju-bo-neun, 직접의 jik-jeob-ui

facial *adj.* 얼굴의 eol-gul-ui; 안면의 an-myeon-ui; ~ **cream** 영양크림 yeong-yang-keu-rim

facilitate *vt.* 손쉽게 하다 son-swip-ge ha-da; 촉진하다 chok-jin-ha-da

facility *n.* 쉬운 swi-um; 솜씨 som-ssi; 편의 pyeon-ui; 설비 seol-bi

facsimile *n.* 팩스 paek-su; 복사 bok-sa, 복제 bok-je

fact *n.* 사실 sa-sil, 진실 jin-sil; **in** ~ 사실은 sa-sil-eun

factor *n.* 요인 yo-in; 원인 won-in, 요소 yo-so

factory *n.* 공장 gong-jang

factual *adj.* 사실의 sa-sil-ui, 실제의 sil-jje-ui

faculty *n.* 능력 neung-nyeok; 재능 jae-neung; 교수진 gyo-su-jin; 학부 hak-bu

fad *n.* 변덕 byeon-deok; 일시적 유행 il-ssi-jeok yu-haeng

fade *vi.* 흐릿해지다 heu-re-tae-ji-da; 사라져가다 sa-ra-jeo-ga-da; 시들다 si-deul-da; **~d** 시든 si-deun; 색이 바랜 saeg-i ba-raen; 쇠퇴한 soe-toe-han

Fahrenheit *adj.* 화씨의 hwa-ssi-ui

fail *vi.* 실패아나 sil-pae-ha-da; 부족하다 bu-jo-ka-da; 쇠하다 soe-ha-da; 못하다 mo-ta-da

failure *n.* 실패 sil-pae; 부족 bu-jok; 실패자 sil-pae-ja

faint *adj.* 어렴풋한 eo-ryeom-pu-tan; 기절할 것 같은 gi-jeol-hal kkeot gat-eun; *vi.* 실신하다 sil-ssin-ha-da, 기절하다 gi-jeol-ha-da

fair *n.* 장 jang; 박람회 bang-nam-hoe; 미인 mi-in; *adj.* 아름다운 a-reum-da-un; *(light-skinned)* 피부가 흰 pi-bu-ga hin; *(light-haired)* 금발의 geum-bal-ui; 맑은 malg-eun; 꽤 많은 kkwae man-eun; *(just, evenhanded)* 공평한 gong-pyeong-han; **church fair** 교회 박람회 gyo-hoe bang-nam-hoe; **county fair** 마을 박람회 ma-eul bang-nam-hoe

fairly *adv.* 공평히 gong-pyeong-hi; 꽤 kkwae

fair play *n.* 페어플레이 pe-eo-peul-le-i

fairy *n.* 요정 yo-jeong; fairy tale 동화 dong-hwa

faith *n.* 신념 sin-nyeom; 신앙 sin-ang; 신뢰 sil-loe; 약속 yak-sok

faithful *adj.* 충실한 chung-sil-han; 징확한 jeong-hwa-kan

fake *n.* 모조품 mo-jo-pum; *adj.* 가짜의 ga-jja-ui; *vt., vi.* 위조하다 wi-jo-ha-da; ...인 체하다 ...in che-ha-da

fall *n.* *(season)* 가을 ga-eul; *(action)* 낙하 na-ka; 쓰러짐 sseu-reo-jim; *vi.* 떨어지다 tteol-eo-ji-da; 내리다 nae-ri-da; 넘어지다 neom-eo-ji-da

false *adj.* 거짓의 geo-jis-ui; 잘못된 jal-mot-doen

falsify *vt.* 위조하다 wi-jo-ha-da; 배신하다 bae-sin-ha-da; **falsified** 위조된 wi-jo-doen

fame *n.* 명성 myeong-seong; 평판 pyeong-pan

familiar *adj.* 친숙한 chin-su-kan; 낯익은 nan-nig-eun

family *n.* 가족 ga-jok; ~ **name** 성 seong; ~ **tree** 가계도 ga-gye-do

famine *n.* 식량부족 sing-nyang-bu-jok, 기근 gi-geun

famous *adj.* 유명한 yu-myeong-han

fan *n.* *(person)* 팬 paen, 광 gwang; 부채 bu-chae; *(appliance)* 선풍기 seon-pung-gi; **opera** ~ 오페라 팬 o-pe-ra paen

fancy *adj.* 공상의 gong-sang-ui; 장식적인 jang-sik-jeog-in; 최상품의 choe-sang-pum-ui

fantastic *adj.* 공상적인 gong-sang-jeog-in, 기이한 gi-i-han, 환상적인 hwan-sang-jeog-in

far *adj.* 먼 meon; *adv.* 멀리 meol-li, 훨씬 hwol-ssin; **He won't go** ~ 그는 그렇게 하지는 않을 것이다 geu-neun geu-reo-ke ha-ji-neun an-eul geoi-da; **by** ~ **the best choice** 지금까지 최상의 선택 ji-geum-kka-ji choe-sang-ui seon-taek; **How** ~ **to the falls** 폭포까지 얼마나 멉니까 pok-po-kka-ji eol-ma-na meom-ni-kka; **It's** ~ **from here** 여기서 좀 먼데요 yeo-gi-seo jom meon-de-yo; **It is** ~ **from easy** 그 건 전혀 안 쉽다 geu geon jeon-hyeo an-swip-da; **so** ~ 지금까지 ji-geum-kka-ji

faraway *adj.* 먼 meon; 꿈꾸는 듯한 kkum-kku-neun deu-tan

fare *n.* 운임 un-im, 통행료 tong-haeng-nyo

farewell *n.* 작별 jak-byeol; 안녕 an-nyeong

farm *n.* 농장 nong-jang; *vi.* 경작하다 gyeong-ja-ka-da, 농사짓다 nong-sa-jit-da

farmer *n.* 농부 nong-bu

farmhouse *n.* 농가 nong-ga

farsighted *adj.* 원시의 won-si-ui, 먼 데를 잘 보는 meon de-reul jal bo-neun; 선견지명이 있는 seon-gyeon-ji-myeong-i in-neun

fart *vi.* 방귀뀌다 bang-gwi-kkwi-da

farther *adv.* 더 멀리 deo meol-li; 더욱이 deo-ug-i

fascinate *vt.* 매혹시키다 mae-hok-si-ki-da; 얼을 빼다 eol-eul ppae-da

fascination *n.* 매혹 mae-hok; 매력 mae-ryeok

fashion *n.* 유행 yu-haeng; 패션 pae-ssyeon; **out of** ~ 유행에 떨어지는 yu-haeng-e tteol-eo-ji-neun; ~ **model** 패션모델 pae-ssyeon-mo-del

fashionable *adj.* 유행의 yu-haeng-ui; 사교계의 sa-gyo-gye-ui

fast *n.* 단식 dan-sik; *adj.* 빠른 ppa-reun; 단단한 dan-dan-han; *vi.* 단식하다 dan-si-ka-da

fast food *n.* 패스트푸드 pae-seu-teu-pu-deu

fasten *vt.* 묶다 muk-da; 죄다 joe-da; 고정하다 go-jeong-ha-da

fat *n.* 지방 ji-bang; *adj.* 뚱뚱한 ttung-ttung-ha-da; 지방이 많은 ji-bang-i man-eun; **low~** 저지방 jeo-ji-bang

fatal *adj.* 치명적인 chi-myeong-jeog-in; 운명적인 un-myeong-jeog-in

fate *n.* 운명 un-myeong; 죽음 jug-eum

father *n.* 아버지 a-beo-ji; 선조 seon-jo; 창시자 chang-si-ja

father-in-law *n.* 시아버님 si-a-beo-nim; 장인어른 jang-in-eo-reun

fatigue *n.* 피로 pi-ro; *vt.* 피곤하게 하다 pi-gon-ha-ge ha-da

fatty *adj.* 지방의 ji-bang-ui

faucet *n.* 수도꼭지 su-do-kkok-ji

fault *n.* 잘못 jal-mot, 과실 gwa-sil; 결점 gyeol-jjeom; 책임 chaeg-im

faulty *adj.* 결점이 많은 gyeol-jjeom-i man-eun

favor *n.* 호의 ho-ui, 친절 chin-jeol; *vt.* 호의를 보이다 ho-ui-reul bo-i-da; 편애하다 pyeon-ae-ha-da

favorite *adj.* 마음에 드는 ma-eum-e deu-neun; 선호하는 seon-ho-ha-neun

favoritism *n.* 편애 pyeon-ae

fax *n.* 팩스 paek-seu; *vt.* 팩스하다 paek-seu-ha-da; ~ **machine** 팩스머신 paek-seu-meo-sin, 팩스기 paek-seu-gi

fear *n.* 두려움 du-ryeo-um, gong-po; geun-sim; *vt.* 두려워하다 du-ryeo-wo-ha-da; 근심하다 geun-sim-ha-da

feasible *adj.* 실행가능한 sil-yeon-ga-neung-han; 그럴싸한 geu-reol-ssa-han

feast *n.* 축제 chuk-je, 향연 hyang-yeon

feather *n.* 깃털 git-teol

feature *n.* 얼굴 생김새 eol-gul saeng-gim-sae; 특징 teunk-jing, 특색 teuk-saek

February *n.* 2월 i-wol-ui

federal *adj.* 연방정부의 yeon-bang-jeong-bu-ui; 연방의 yeon-bang-ui, 연합의 yeon-hab-ui

fee *n.* 요금 yo-geum, 수수료 su-su-ryo

feed *n.* 사육 sa-yuk; 사료 sa-ryo; *vt.* 먹을 것을 주다 meog-eul kkeos-eul ju-da; 부양하다 by-yang-ha-da

feedback *n.* 피드백 pi-deu-baek

feel *n.* 느낌 neu-kkim; 분위기 bun-wi-gi; *vt.* 느끼다 neu-kki-da; 만지다 man-ji-dal; *vi.* 손으로 더듬다 son-eu-ro deo-deum-tta; 감각이 있다 gam-gag-i it-da; …한 생각이 들다 …han saeng-gag-i deul-da

feeling *n.* 촉감 chok-gam; 감각 gam-gak; 감정 gam-jeong

feint *n.* 시늉 si-nyung

fellow *n.* 친구 chin-gu; 동료 dong-nyo; 사람 sa-ram

fellowship *n.* 동료의식 dong-nyo-ui-sik, 친구관계 chin-gu-gwan-gye, 연대감 yeon-dae-gam; 친교 chin-gyo; 협력 hyeom-nyeok; 연구비 yeon-gu-bi; 단체 dan-che, 조합 jo-hap

felt *n.* 펠트 pel-teu

female *n.* 여성 yeo-seong; 암컷 am-keot; *adj.* 여성의 yeo-seong-ui; 암컷의 am-keos-ui

feminine *adj.* 여성의 yeo-seong-ui; 여성스러운 yeo-seong-seu-reo-un

fence *n.* 울타리 ul-ta-ri, 담 dam

fencing *n.* 펜싱 pen-sing

fender *n.* 방호물 bang-ho-mul; 완충장치 wan-chung-jang-chi

ferment *vt.* 발효시키다 bal-hyo-si-ki-da; 들끓게 하다 deul-kkeul-ke ha-da

fern *n.* 고사리 go-sa-ri

Ferris wheel *n.* 페리스 휠 pe-ri-seu-hwil, 회전관람차 hoe-jeon-gwal-lam-cha

ferry *n.* 나루터 na-ru-teo; 나룻배 na-rut-bae; 페리 pe-ri

ferryboat *n.* 나룻배 na-rut-bae, 연락선 yeol-lak-seon

fertile *adj.* 비옥한 bi-o-kan

fertilizer *n.* 비료 bi-ryo

festival *n.* 잔치 jan-chi, 축제 chuk-je; 페스티발 pe-seu-ti-bal

fetch *vt.* 가지고 오다 ga-ji-go o-da, 데리고 오다 de-ri-go o-da; 나오게 하다 na-o-ge ha-da

fetus *n.* 태아 tae-a

fever *n.* 열 yeol; 열중 yeol-jjung; 흥분 heung-bun

few *adj.* 거의 없는 geo-ui eom-neun, 조금은 있는 jo-geum-eun in-neun; *pron.* 소수 so-su, 소수의 사람 so-su-ui sa-ram, 소수의 것 so-su-ui geot; *n.* 소수 so-su

fiance *n.* 약혼자 ya-kon-ja

fiber *n.* 섬유질 seom-yu-jil; 소질 so-jil

fickle *adj.* 변하기 쉬운 byeon-ha-gi swi-un

fiction *n.* 소설 so-seol; 허구 heo-gu

fiddle *n.* 바이올린 ba-i-ol-lin; 사기 sa-gi

fidelity *n.* 충실 chung-sil, 성실 seong-sil

field *n.* 들판 deul-pan; 논밭 non-bat; 경기장 gyeong-gi-jang; 싸움터 ssa-um-teo; 분야 bun-ya

field test *n.* 실제 시험 sil-jje-si-heom

field trip *n.* 연구여행 yeon-gu-yeo-haeng

fieldwork *n.* 현장답사 hyeon-jang-dap-sa, 현장조사 hyeon-jang-jo-sa

fierce *adj.* 사나운 sa-na-un; 맹렬한 maeng-nyeol-han

fifteen *num.* 십오 sib-o; 열다섯 yeol-tta-seot

fifteenth *adj.* 열다섯번째의 yeol-tta-seot-beon-jjae-ui; 제십오회 je sib-o-hoe

fifth *adj.* 다섯번째의 da-seot beon-jjae-ui; 제오회 je-o-hoe

fiftieth *adj.* 오십번째의 o-sip-beon-jjae-ui; 제오십회 je sib-o-hoe

fifty-fifty *adj., adv.* 반반 ban-ban

fifty *num.* 오십 o-sip; 쉰 swin

fig *n.* 무화과 mu-hwa-gwa; 조금 jo-geum; 복장 bok-jang; 형편 hyeong-pyeon

fight *vt., vi.* 싸우다 ssa-u-da; 다투다 da-tu-da; 겨루다 gyeo-ru-da

figure *n.* (number) 숫자 sut-ja; (form) 모양 mo-yang; 인물 in-mul; 그림 geu-rim; 비유 bi-yu; *vt.* (consider) 생각하다 saeng-ga-ka-da; (calculate) 계산하다 gye-san-ha-da; 상징하다 sang-jing-ha-da; *vi.* (appear in) 나타나다 na-ta-na-da; 궁리하다 gung-ni-ha-da

figure skating *n.* 피겨 스케이팅
pi-gyeo-seu-ke-i-ting

filament *n.* 필라멘트 pil-la-men-teu

file *n.* 파일 pa-il; 서류철 seo-ryu-cheol;
줄 jul; *vt.* 정리해 보관하다 jeong-ni-hae
bo-gwan-ha-da; 기록에 남겨두다 gi-rog-e
nam-gyeo-du-da; 기사를 보내다 gi-sa-reul
bo-nae-da; 제출하다 je-chul-ha-da; 줄로
다듬다 jul-lo da-deum-tta; **to ~ one's
nails** 손톱을 다듬다 son-tob-eul
da-deum-tta; **to ~ a folder** 서류를 정리
해 보관하다 seo-ryu-reul jeong-ni-hae
bo-gwan-ha-da

fill *vt.* 가득 채우다 ga-deuk-chae-u-da; 가
득하다 ga-deu-ka-da; 구멍을 메우다
gu-meong-eul me-u-da; 자리를 채우다
ja-ri-reul chae-u-da

filling *n.* *(tooth)* 봉 bong, 필링 pil-ling;
(cooking) 속 sok

film *n.* 필름 pil-leum; 영화 yeong-hwa; 얇
은 막 yalb-eun mak; *vt.* 얇은 막을 덮다
yalb-eun mag-eul deop-da; 영화를 촬영하
다 yeong-hwa-reul chwal-yeong-ha-da; *vi.*
얇게 덮이다 yalp-ge deo-pi-da

filter *n.* 필터 pil-teo; 여과기 yeo-gwa-gi; 여
과지 yeo-gwa-ji

filterate *vt.* 여과하다 yeo-gwa-ha-da

filthy *adj.* 불결한 bul-gyeol-han; 더러운
deo-reo-un

fin *n.* 지느러미 ji-neu-reo-mi; 물갈퀴
mul-gal-kwi

final *adj.* 마지막의 ma-jimmag-ui

finally *adv.* 최후로 choe-hu-ro, 최종적으로
choe-jong-jeog-eu-ro

finance *n.* 재정 jae-jeong; 재원 jae-won

financial *adj.* 재정적인 jae-jeong-jeog-in; 재
정의 jae-jeong-ui

find *n.* 발견 bal-gyeon; 발견물 bal-gyeon-
mul; 횡재 hoeng-jae; *vt.* 발견하다
bal-gyeon-ha-da; 깨닫다 kkae-dat-da

finding *n.* 습득물 seup-deung-mul; 연구결
과 yeon-gu-gyeol-gwa; 발견 bal-gyeon

fine *n.* 벌금 beol-geum; *adj.* 훌륭한
hul-lyung-han; 미세한 mi-se-han; 세련
된 se-ryeon-doen; 날씨가 맑은 nal-ssi-ga
mal-geun; 기분이 좋은 gi-bun-i jo-eun;
~ art 미술품 mi-sul-pum; 미술 mi-sul; **~
print** 작은 글자 jag-eun jeul-jja

finger *n.* 손가락 son-kka-rak; **~ nail** 손톱
son-top

fingerprint *n.* 지문 ji-mun; *vt.* 지문을 채취
하다 ji-mun-eul chae-chwi-ha-da

fingertip *n.* 손끝 son-kkeut

finish *n.* 마무리 ma-mu-ri, 끝손질 kkeut-
son-jil; *(end)* 끝 kkeut, 마지막 ma-ji-mak
(lacquer) 가구의 끝손질 ga-gu-ui
kkeut-son-jil; *vt.* 끝내다 kkeun-nae-da;
마무리하다 ma-mu-ri-ha-da; *vi.* 끝나다
kkeun-na-da; 마치다 ma-chi-da

Finland *n.* 핀란드 pil-laen-deu

fire *n.* 불 bul; 화재 hwa-jae; 열정 yeol-jjeong;
사격 sa-gyeok; *vt.* 불을 붙이다 bul-eul
bu-chi-da; 발사하다 bal-ssa-ha-da; 해고
하다 hae-go-ha-da; **to ~ an employee** 직
원을 해고하다 jig-won-eul hae-go-ha-da;
~ alarm 화재경보 hwa-jae-gyeong-bo;
화재경보기 hwa-jae-gyeong-bo-gi; **~
station** 소방서 so-bang-seo; **~ drill** 소
방연습 so-bang-nyeon-seup, 방화훈련
bang-hwa-hul-lyeon; **~ extinguisher** 소
화기 so-hwa-gi; **~ insurance** 화재보험
hwa-jae-bo-heom

firefly *n.* 반딧불 ban-dit-bul

fireplace *n.* 벽난로 byeong-nal-lo

fireproof *adj.* 방화성의 bang-hwa-sseong-ui,
내화성의 nae-hwa-sseong-ui

firewood *n.* 장작 jang-jak, 땔나무 ttael-la-mu

firework *n.* 불꽃놀이 bul-kkon-nol-i; 불꽃
bul-kkot

firm *n.* 회사 hoe-sa, 상사 sang-sa; *adj.* 확고
한 hwak-go-han; 단단한 dan-dan-han; 안
정된 an-jeong-doen

first *adj.* 첫번째의 cheot-beon-jjae-ui, 최초
의 choi-cho-ui; *adv.* 첫째로 cheot-jjae-ro,
최초로 choe-cho-ro; **at ~** 우선 u-seon; **~
aid** 응급치료 eung-geup-chi-ryo; **~ base**
1루 il-lu; **~ class** 1급 il-tteung-geup, 1종
il-jjong, 최고급 choe-go-geup; **~come-
~served basis** 선착순 seon-chak-sun; **~
lady** 영부인 yeong-bu-in; **~ name** 이름
i-reum

fish *n.* 생선 saeng-seon; 물고기 mul-kko-gi;
vt. 고기를 잡다 go-gi-reul jap-da; 인양하
다 in-yang-ha-da; *vi.* 낚시질하다 nak-si-jil
ha-da; 찾다 chat-da; **~ bowl** 어항 eo-hang;
~ cake 생선전 saeng-seon-jeon

fisherman *n.* 어부 eo-bu; 낚시꾼 nak-si-kkun
fishing *n.* 낚시 nak-si; 어업 eo-eop; **to go ~** 낚시하러 가다 nak-si-ha-reo ga-da
fishy *adj.* 물고기의 mul-kko-gi-ui; 비린내 나는 bi-rin-nae na-neun; 수상한 su-sang-han, 의심스러운 ui-sim-seu-reo-un
fist *n.* 주먹 ju-meok; 움켜 쥠 um-kyeo jwim
fit *n.* 발작 bal-jjak; 경련 gyeong-nyeon; 졸도 jol-tto; 변덕 byeon-deok; *adj.* 알맞은 al-maj-eun; 건강이 좋은 geon-gang-i jo-eun; *vt., vi.* 맞다 mat-da; 적합하다 jeo-ka-pa-da; 어울리다 eo-ul-li-da; **Does it ~ into the slot** 이게 그 구멍에 맞습니까 i-ge geu gu-meong-e mat-seum-ni-kka; **Does the blouse ~** 블라우스가 잘 맞습니끼 beul-la-u-sseu-ga jal mat-seum-ni-kka; **Please ~ me for a dress** 제 드레스를 하나 맞춰 주세요 je deu-re-sseu-reul ha-na mat-chwo ju-se-yo
fitness *n.* 적당 jeok-dang; 적합성 jeo-kap-seong; **~ instructor** 헬스클럽 강사 hel-sseu-keul-leop gang-sa; **physical ~** 신체적 적합성 sin-che-jeok jeo-kap-seong
fitting *adj.* 적당한 jeok-dang-han, 적절한 jeok-jeol-han; *n.* 입어보기 ib-eo-bo-ji; **~ room** 탈의실 tal-ui-sil
five *num.* 오 o, 다섯 da-seot
fix *vt.* 고정시키다 go-jeong-si-ki-da; 찬찬히 보다 chan-chan-hi bo-da; 결정하다 gyeol-Jjeong-ha-da; 고치다 go-chi-da; 준비하다 jun-bi-ha-da; **~ed** 고정된 go-jeong-doen; 결성된 gyeol-jjeong-doen; 고진 go-chin
flag *n.* 기 gi, 깃발 git-bal
flame *n.* 불길 bul-kkil; 정열 jeong-nyeol
flaming *adj.* 불타는 bul-ta-neun, 열렬한 yeol-lyeol-han
flamingo *n.* 플리밍고 peul-la-ming-go
flannel *n.* 면 myeon, 플란넬 peul-lan-nel
flap *n.* 펄럭임 peol-leog-im; 늘어진 것 neul-eo-jin geot; *vi.* 퍼드덕거리다 peo-deu-deok geo-ri-da; 딱 때리다 ttak ttae-ri-da
flare *vi.* 너울거리다 neo-ul-geo-ri-da; 나팔꽃처럼 벌어지다 na-pal-kkot-cheo-reom beol-eo-ji-da
flash *n.* 섬광 seom-gwang; 번쩍임 beon-jjeog-im; 현란함 hyeol-lan-ham; *vi.* 번쩍이다 beon-jjeog-i-da; 번개처럼 스치다 beon-gae-cheo-reom seu-chi-da; **~ card** 플

래시 카드 peul-lae-si ka-deu; **~ light** 플래시 peul-lae-ssi
flat *adj.* 평평한 pyeong-pyeong-han; 단조로운 dan-jo-ro-un; **~ tire** 펑크난 타이어 peong-keu-nan ta-i-eo
flatter *vt.* 아첨하다 a-cheom-ha-da; 우쭐해 하다 u-jjul-hae-ha-da
flavor *n.* 맛 mat; 멋 meot; *vt.* 맛을 내다 mas-eul nae-da; 멋을 곁들이다 meos-eul gyeot-deul-i-da; **orange-~ed** 오렌지맛의 o-ren-ji-mas-ui
flaw *n.* 흠집 heum-jjip; 결점 gyeol-jjeom; 돌풍 dol-pung
flea *n.* 벼룩 byeo-ruk; **~ market** 노천시장 no-cheon-si-jang
flee *vi.* 달아나다 dal-a-na-da; 피하다 pi-ha-da; 사라지다 sa-ra-ji-da
fleece *n.* 양털 yang-teol; 양털모양의 물건 yang-teol-mo-yang-ui mul-geon; 플리스 peul-li-sseu
fleet *n.* 함대 ham-dae; 기단 gi-dan
flesh *n.* 살 sal; 육체 yuk-che
flex *vt.* 관절을 굽히다 gwan-jeol-eul gu-pi-da
flexible *adj.* 구부리기 쉬운 gu-bu-ri-gi swi-un, 유연한 yu-yeon-han
flicker *vi.* 깜빡이다 kkam-ppag-i-da; *n.* 깜빡임 kkam-ppag-im
flight *n.* 비행 pi-haeng; 날아오름 nal-a-o-reum; 도주 do-ju, 탈출 tal-chul; **~ attendant** 객실 승무원 gaek-sil seung-mu-won
flip *vt.* 튀기다 twi-gi-da; 획 던지다 hwik deon-ji-da; 획 뒤집다 hwik dwi-jip-da
flipper *n.* 오리발 o-ri-bal, 고무 물갈퀴 go-mu mul-gal-kkwi
flirt *n.* 바람둥이 ba-ram-dung-i; *vi.* 시시덕 기리다 si-si-deok-geo-ri-da; 훌쩍 날아가다 hul-jjeok nal-a-ga-da; 가지고 놀다 ga-ji-go nol-da
float *vi.* 뜨다 tteu-da; 표류하다 pyo-ryu-ha-da; *vt.* 띄우다 tti-u-da
flock *n.* 무리 mu-ri, 군중 gun-jung; 털뭉치 teol-mung-chi; 짐승의 떼 jim-seung-ui tte
flood *n.* 홍수 hong-su; 범람 beom-nam; 밀물 mil-mul
floor *n.* 마루 ma-ru; 층 cheung; **~ manager** 무대감독 mu-dae-gam-dok; **~ plan** 평면도 pyeong-myeon-do

floppy *adj.* 펄럭거리는 peol-leok-geo-ri-neun, 느슨한 neu-seun-han; 기운없는 gi-un-eom-neun

floral *adj.* 꽃의 kkoch-ui

florist *n.* 꽃장수 kkot-jang-su; 화초 재배자 hwa-cho jae-bae-ja

floss *n.* 플로스 peul-lo-sseu, 치실 chi-sil

flour *n.* 밀가루 mil-kka-ru

flourish *vi.* 번창하다 beon-chang-ha-da, 융성하다 yung-seong-ha-da

flow *n.* 흐름 heu-reum; 유입량 yu-im-nyang; 밀물 mil-mul; 범람 beom-nam; *vi.* 흐르다 heu-reu-da; 경과하다 gyeong-gwa-ha-da

flower *n.* 꽃 kkot; ~ **bed** 화단 hwa-dan; ~ **garden** 꽃밭 kkot-bat, 화원 hwa-won

flowerpot *n.* 화분 hwa-bun

flowershop *n.* 꽃집 kkot-jip, 꽃가게 kkot-ga-ge

flu *n.* 독감 dok-gam

fluctuate *vi.* 변동하다 byeon-dong-ha-da, 오르내리다 o-reu-nae-ri-da

fluent *adj.* 유창한 yu-chang-han

fluffy *adj.* 복슬복슬한 bok-seul-bok-seul-han, 손털의 son-teol-ui; 불분명한 bul-bun-myeong-han; 하찮은 ha-chan-eun

fluid *n.* 유동체 yu-dong-che; 액체 aek-che; *adj.* 유동적인 yu-dong-jeog-in; 변하기 쉬운 byeon-ha-gi swi-un

flunk *vi.* 실패하다 sil-pae-ha-da, 낙제하다 nak-je-ha-da

flush *vi.* 빨개지다 ppal-gae-ji-da, 붉어지다 bulg-eo-ji-da; 쏟아져 나오다 ssod-a-jeo na-o-da; *vt.* 화장실 물을 내리다 hwa-jang-sil mul-eul nae-ri-da; *n.* 홍조 hong-jo; 감격 gam-gyeok; 발랄함 bal-lal-ham; *adj.* 동일평면의 dong-il-pyeong-myeon-ui, 같은 높이의 got-eun nop-i-ui

flute *n.* 플루트 peul-lu-teu

flux *n.* 유동 yu-dong, 흐름 heu-reum

fly *n.* 파리 pa-ri; *vi.* 날다 nal-da; 급히 가다 geu-pi ga-da; 순식간에 사라지다 sun-sik-gan-e sa-ra-ji-da; 도망치다 do-mang-chi-da

flyswatter *n.* 파리채 pa-ri-chae

foam *n.* 거품 geo-pum; ~ **rubber** 거품고무 geo-pum-go-mu, 푸석고무 pu-seok-go-mu

focus *n.* 초점 cho-jjeom; 중심 jung-sim; *vt.* 초점을 맞추다 cho-jjeom-eul mat-chu-da; 집중시키다 jip-jung-si-ki-da; ~ **the camera** 카메라 초점을 맞추세요. ka-me-ra cho-jjeom-eul mat-chu-se-yo. **in** ~ 초점이 맞다 cho-jjeom-i mat-da

foe *n.* 적 jeok, 원수 won-su

fog *n.* 안개 an-gae; 혼미 hon-mi; 흐림 heu-rim

foggy *adj.* 안개가 낀 an-gae-ga kkin; 당황한 dang-hwang-han; 흐린 heu-rin

foil *n.* 호일 ho-il, 은박 eun-bak-ji; *vt.* 은박을 입히다 eun-bag-eul i-pi-da

fold *n.* 주름 ju-reum; 한타래 han-ta-rae; 습곡 seup-gok; 양우리 yang-u-ri; *vt.* 접다 jeop-da; 끼다 kki-da; 안다 an-tta; 싸다 ssa-da

folder *n.* 폴더 pol-deo, 파일 pa-il

folk *n.* 사람들 sa-ram-deul; 가족 ga-jok; ~ **music** 민속음악 min-sog-eum-ak; ~ **tale** 민간설화 min-gan-seol-hwa

follow *vi.* 따라가다 tta-ra-ga-da; 계속하다 gye-so-ka-da; 뒤쫓다 dwi-jjot-da; 이해하다 i-hae-ha-da; 종사하다 jong-sa-ha-da

following *adj.* 다음의 da-eum-ui

follow-up *adj.* 잇따르는 it-tta-reu-neun; *n.* 뒤쫓음 dwi-jjoch-eum

fond *adj.* 좋아하는 jo-a-ha-neun; 다정한 da-jeong-han; **to be ~ of** 좋아하다 jo-a-ha-da

font *n.* 활자 hwal-jja, 폰트 pon-teu

food *n.* 음식 eum-sik, 식품 sik-pum; ~ **chain** 먹이사슬 meog-i-sa-seil; ~ **poisoning** 식중독 sik-jung-dok

fool *n.* 바보 ba-bo

foolish *adj.* 바보스러운 ba-bo-seu-reo-un

foot *n.* *(body part)* 발 bal; *(measurement)* 피트 pi-teu; ~**board** 발판 bal-pan; ~ **ware** 신는 것 sin-neun goet; ~ **print** 발자국 bal-jja-guk

football *n.* 풋볼 put-bol

footprint *n.* 발자국 bal-jja-guk

footstep *n.* 걸음걸이 geol-eum-geol-i; 발자국 bal-jja-guk; 발자국 소리 bal-jja-guk so-ri

footwear *n.* 신발류 sin-bal-lyu

for *prep.* ...을 위하여 ...eul wi-ha-yeo, ...을 위한 ...eul wi-han, ...을 기념하여 ...eul gi-nyeom-ha-yeo, ...에게 주려고 ...e-ge ju-ryeo-go, ...을 향하여 ...eul hyang-ha-yeo, ...을 얻기 위해 ...eul eot-gi-wi-hae, ...에 대비하기 위해 ...e

dae-bi-ha-gi wi-hae, ...용의 ...yong-ui,
...동안 ...dong-an, ...만큼의 ...man-
keum-ui, ...대신에 ...dae-sin-e, ...을 나
타내어 ...eul na-ta-nae-eo, ...와 교환으
로 ...wa gyo-hwan-eu-ro, ...에 대해서
...e dae-hae-seo, ...을 지지하여 ...eul
ji-ji-ha-yeo, ...때문에 ...tta-mun-e, ...에
관해서는 ...e gwan-hae-seo-neun, ...치고
는 ...chi-go-neun, ...에게는 ...e-ge-neun;
conj. 왜냐하면 ...이니까 wae-nya-ha-
myeon ...i-ni-kka, ...이므로 ...i-meu-ro;
There's a fax ~ you 팩스기 왔습니다
paek-seu-ga wat-seum-ni-da; **We had eggs
~ breakfast** 저희는 아침에 계란을 먹었
습니다 jeo-hi-neun a-chim-e gye-ran-eul
meog-eot-seum-ni-da; *(purpose)* **It's used
~ baking** 이건 빵을 구울 때 사용합니다
i-geon ppang-eul gu-ul-ttae sa-yong-ham-
i-da; *(destination or goal)* **the bus ~ the
airport** 공항으로 가는 버스 gong-hang-
eu-ro ga-neun ppeo-sseu; **He left ~ home**
그 분은 집으로 가셨습니다 geu bun-eun
jib-eu-ro ga-syeot-seum-ni-da; **It's all ~
the best** 이것이 최상책입니다 i-geos-i
choe-sang-chaeg-im-ni-da; **thanks ~** ...에
대해 감사드립니다 ...e dae-hae gam-sa-
deu-rim-ni-da; *(on behalf of)* **He works ~
me** 그 분은 저를 위해 일하십니다 geu
bun-eun jeo-reul wi-hae il-ha-sim-ni-da;
(money) **I bought it ~ forty dollars** 저
는 이것을 40달러에 샀습니다 jeo-neun
i-geos-eul sa-sip-gil-deo-e sat-seum-ni-da;
(time) **I was in Kenya ~ two weeks** 나
는 케냐에 2주동안 있었습니다 na-neun
ke-nya-e i-ju-ttong-an iss-eot-sum-ni-da
(with infinitive) **It will be difficult ~ us
to do it that way** 그런 방법으로 이 일
을 하는 것은 어려울 것입니다 geu-reon
bang-beob-eu-ro i il-eul ha-neun geos-eun
eo-ryeo-ul geos-im-ni-da; *(because)* **~ this
reason** 이것 때문에 i-geot tae-mun-e;
**What is the German word ~ 'thank
you'** 'Thank you'를 독일어로 뭐라고 합
니까 ttaeng-kyu-reul dog-il-eo-ro mwo-ra-
go ham-ni-kka
forbid *vt.* 금지하다 geum-ji-ha-da; 방해하
다 bang-hae-ha-da

forbidden *adj.* 금지된 geum-ji-doen
force *n.* 힘 him; 폭력 pong-nyeok; 영향
yeong-hyang; 무력 mu-ryeok; *vt.* 강제하
다 gang-je-ha-da, 억지로 시키다 eok-ji-ro
si-ki-da; 폭행하다 po-kaeng-ha-da; 떠맡기
다 tteo-mat-gi-da; **by ~** 억지로 eok-ji-ro,
강제로 gang-je-ro
forearm *n.* 팔뚝 pal-ttuk
forecast *n.* 예보 ye-bo; 예상 ye-sang
foregoing *adj.* 앞서 말한 ap-seo mal-han, 앞
의 ap-ui
forehead *n.* 이마 i-ma; 앞부분 ap-bu-bun
foreign *adj.* 외국의 oe-gug-ui; 관계없는
gwan-gye-eom-neun
foreigner *n.* 외국인 oe-gug-in; 문외한
mun-oe-han
foremost *adj.* 맨처음의 maen-cheo-eum-ui;
으뜸가는 eu-tteum-ga-neun
foresee *vt.* 예견하다 ye-gyeon-ha-da, 미리
알아차리다 mi-ri al-a-cha-ri-da
foresight *n.* 선견지명 seon-gyeon-ji-myeong;
예지 ye-ji; 예측 ye-cheuk; 깊은 생각
gip-eun saeng-gak
forest *n.* 숲 sup; 임야 im-ya; **rain ~** 열대우
림(지역) yeol-ttae-u-rim(-ji-yeok); **~ fire** 산
불 san-ppul
foretell *vt.* 예언하다 ye-eon-ha-da, 예견하
다 ye-gyeon-ha-da
forever *adv.* 영구히 yeong-gu-hi, 언제나
eon-je-na
foreword *n.* 머리말 meo-rin-mal, 서문
seo-mun
forget *vt., vi.* 잊다 it-da, 잊어버리다
ij-eo-beo-ri-da
forgive *vt.* 용서하다 yong-seo-ha-da
fork *n.* 포크 po keu; 쇠스랑 soe-seu-rang
form *n.* 모양 mo-yang; 형식 hyeong-sik; 용
지 yong-ji; *vt.* 형성하다 hyeong-seong-ha-
da; 구성하다 gu-seong-ha-da
formal *adj.* 정식의 jeong-sig-ui; 표면
적인 pyo-myeon-jeog-in; 형식에 치
우친 hyeong-sig-e chi-u-chin; 모양의
mo-yang-ui
format *n.* 체재 che-je; 구성 gu-seong; 포맷
po-maet
formation *n.* 형성 hyeong-seong; 구조
gu-jo; 대형 dae-hyeong

former *adj.* 이전의 i-jeon-ui

formula *n.* 공식 gong-sik; 구조식 gu-jo-sik; 방식 bang-sik

fort *n.* 성채 seong-chae, 요새 yo-sae

forth *adv.* 밖으로 bakk-eu-ro; 앞으로 ap-eu-ro; 이후 i-hu

forthcoming *adj.* 곧 올 god-ol, 다가오는 da-ga-o-neun

fortieth *adj.* 사십번째의 sa-sip-beon-jjae-ui, 제사십회 je sa-si-poe

fortify *vt.* 요새화하다 yo-sae-hwa-ha-da, 강화하다 gang-hwa-ha-da

fortnight *n.* 2주일간 i-ju-il-gan

fortress *n.* 요새 yo-sae

fortunate *adj.* 운이 좋은 un-i jo-eunl; ~ly 운좋게 un-jo-ke, 다행히도 da-haeng-hi-do

fortune *n.* 운 un; 행운 haeng-un; 재산 jae-san

forty *num.* 사십 sa-sip, 마흔 ma-heun

forward *adv.* 앞으로 ap-eu-ro; 장래 jang-nae

fossil *n.* 화석 hwa-seok

foster *adj.* 양육하는 yang-yu-ka-neun; *vt.* 기르다 gi-reu-da; 육성하다 yuk-seong-ha-da; ~ **child** 수양아들 su-yang-a-deul, 수양딸 su-yang-ttal

foul *n.* 파울 pa-ul, 반칙 ban-chik; *vt.* 더럽히다 deo-reo-pi-da; *adj.* 불결한 bul-gyeol-han, 냄새나는 naem-sae-na-neun, 지저분한 ji-jeo-bun-han

found *vt.* 기초를 두다 gi-cho-reul do-da; 설립하다 seol-li-pa-da; 주조하다 ju-jo-ha-da

foundation *n.* 창설 chang-seol; 기초 gi-cho; 파운데이션 pa-un-de-i-syeon

founder *n.* 설립자 seol-lip-ja

fountain *n.* 샘 saem; 분수 bun-su; ~ **pen** 만년필 man-nyeon-pil

four *num.* 사 sa; 넷 net

fourteen *num.* 십사 sip-sa; 열넷 yeol-let

fourteenth *adj.* 열네번째의 yeol-le-beon-jjae-ui, 제십사회 je-sa-si-poe

fourth *adj.* 네번째의 ne-beon-jjae-ui, 제사회 je-sa-hoe

fowl *n.* 닭 dak; 가금 ga-geum; 들새 deul-ssae

fox *n.* 여우 yeo-u; 교활한 사람 gyo-hwal-han sa-ram

fraction *n.* 파편 pa-pyeon; 분수 bun-su; 소량 so-ryang

fracture *n.* 부서짐 bu-seo-jim, 깨짐 kkae-jim, 부러짐 bu-reo-jim

fragile *adj.* 망가지기 쉬운 mang-ga-ji-gi swi-un; 허약한 heo-ya-kan

fragment *n.* 파편 pa-pyeon

fragrant *adj.* 향기로운 hyang-gi-ro-un, 향긋한hyang-geu-tan; *n.* 방향제 bang-hyang-je

frame *n.* 뼈대 ppyeo-dae; 구조 gu-jo; 체격 che-gyeok; 기분 gi-bun; 틀 teul; 테 te; *vt.* 짜맞추다 jja-mat-chu-da; 고안하다 go-an-ha-da; 테를 두르다 te-reul du-reu-da

framework *n.* 틀구조 teul-gu-jo; 뼈대 ppyeo-dae

France *n.* 프랑스 peu-rang-sseu

franchise *n.* 특권 teuk-gwon; 참정권 cham-jeong-kkwon, 선거권 seon-geo-kkwon; 프랜차이즈 peu-ren-cha-i-jeu

frank *adj.* 솔직한 sol-jji-kan, 명백한 myeong-bae-kan

frantic *adj.* 광란의 gwang-nan-ui; 필사적인 pil-ssa-jeog-in

fraternal *adj.* 형제의 hyeong-je-ui

fraternity *n.* 협동단체 hyeop-dong-dan-che; 친목회 chin-mo-koe; 형제간 hyeong-je-gan

fraud *n.* 사시 sa-si; 부정행위 bu-jeong-haeng-wi; 사기꾼 sa-gi-kkun

freak *n.* 기형 gi-hyeong; 변덕 byeon-deok; 얼룩 eol-luk

free *adj.* 자유로운 ja-yu-ro-un; 한가한 han-ga-han; 무료의 mu-ryo-ui; 고정되어 있지 않은 go-jeong-doe-eo it-ji

freedom *n.* 자유 ja-yu; 해방 hae-bang

free-for-all *adj.* 누구나 참여할 수 있는 nu-gu-na cham-yeo-hal ssu in-neun

freestyle *n.* 자유형 ja-yu-hyeong

freeway *n.* 고속도로 go-seok-do-ro

freeze *vt.* 얼게 하다 eol-ge-ha-da; 간담이 서늘하게 하다 gan-dam-i seo-neul-ha-ge ha-da; 동결하다 dong-gyeol-ha-da; *vi.* 얼다 eol-da; 춥다 chup-da; 등골이 오싹하다 deung-kkol-i o-ssa-ka-da

freezer *n.* 냉동장치 naeng-dong-jang-chi; 냉동실 naeng-dong-sil

freezing *adj.* 매우 추운 mae-u chu-un

freight *n.* 화물 hwa-mul; 화물열차 hwa-mul-lyeol-cha

French *n.* 프랑스사람 peu-rang-sseu-sa-ram; *adj.* 프랑스의 peu-rang-sseu-ui

frequency *n.* 빈도 bin-do; *(time frame)* 빈도
수 bin-do-ssu; 진동수 jin-dong-su; *(radio)*
주파수 ju-pa-su

frequent *adj.* 빈번히 일어나는 bin-beon-hi
il-eo-na-neun

frequently *adv.* 종종 jong-jong

fresh *adj.* 신선한 sin-seon-han; 생기있는
saeng-gi-in-neun; 새로운 sae-ro-un

freshman *n.* 신입생 sin-ip-saeng; 초년생
cho-nyeon-saeng

friction *n.* 마찰 ma-chal; 의견충돌 ui-gyeon-
chung-dol, 알력 al-lyeok

Friday *n.* 금요일 geum-yo-il

fried *adj.* 기름에 튀긴 gi-reum-e twi-gin

friend *n.* 친구 chin-gu; 자기편 ja-gi-pyeon;
지지자 ji-ji-ja

friendly *adj.* 친절한 chin-jeol-han; 마음에
드는 ma-eum-e deu-neun; 친한 chin-han

friendship *n.* 우정 u-jeong; 교우관계
gyo-u-gwan-gye

fright *n.* 공포 gong-po; 경악 gyeong-ak

frighten *vt.* 두려워하게 하다 du-ryeo-wo-
ha-ge ha-da

frightening *adj.* 무서운 mu-seo-un, 두려운
du-ryeo-un

frill *n.* 주름장식 ju-reum-jang-sik

Frisbee *n.* 프리즈비 peu-ri-jeu-bi

frog *n.* 개구리 gae-gu-ri

from *prep.* *(location)* ...에서 ...e-seo, *(time)*
...(으)로부터 ...(eu)-ro-bu-teo, ...부터
...bu-teo; ~ **Russia** 러시아에서 reo-si-a-
e-seo; **a week** ~ **Monday** 월요일부터 일
주일간 wol-yo-il-bu-teo il-jju-il-gan; *(time
and distance)* ~... **to...** ...에서 ...까지
...e-seo ...kka-ji

front *adj.* 정면의 jeong-myeon-ui; 맨 앞의
maen ap-ui; **the ~ door** 앞문 am-mun;
n. 앞 ap; 정면 jeong-myeon; 이마 i-ma;
얼굴 eol-gul; **the ~ of the house** 집앞
jib-ap; **in ~ of** ...의 앞에 ...ui ap-e; ~ **line**
최전선 choe-jeon-seon; ~**page** 제1면
je-il-myeon

frontier *n.* 국경 guk-gyeong; 변방
byeon-bang

frost *n.* 서리 seo-ri; 냉담 naeng-dam

frostbite *n.* 동상 dong-sang

frosting *n.* 프로스팅 peu-ro-seu-ting

frown *n.* 우거지상 u-geo-ji-sang; 불쾌
함 bul-kwae-ham; *vi.* 얼굴을 찡그리다
eol-gul-eul jjing-geu-ri-da; 난색을 표시하
다 nan-saeg-eul pyo-ha-da

frozen *adj.* 언eon; 동상에 걸린 dong-sang-e
geol-lin; 차가운 cha-ga-un; ~ **food** 냉동식
품 naeng-dong-sik-pum

frugal *adj.* 검소한 geom-so-han, 절약하는
jeol-ya-ka-neun

fruit *n.* 과일 gwa-il; 성과 seong-kkwa

fruitful *adj.* 다산의 da-san-ui, 풍작의
pung-jag-ui

frustrate *vt.* 쳐부수다 cheo-bu-su-da; 헛되
게 하다 heot-doe-ge ha-da; 실망시키다
sil-mang-si-ki-da

frustrated *adj.* 실망한 sil-mang-han, 좌절한
jwa-jeol-han

frustration *n.* 좌절 jwa-jeol, 실망 sil-mang

fry *vt.* 튀기다 twi-gi-da, 프라이하다
peu-ra-i-ha-da

frying pan *n.* 프라이팬 peu-ra-i-paen

fuel *n.* 연료 yeol-lyo; *vt.* 연료를 공급하다
yeol-lyo-reul gong-geu-pa-da

fugitive *adj.* 도망치는 do-mang-chi-neun; 일
시적인 il-ssi-geog-in

fulfill *vt.* 이행하다 i-haeng-ha-da, 완료하다
wal-lyo-ha-da

full *adj.* 가득찬 ga-deuk-chan; 충분한
chung-bun-han; ~ **moon** 만월 man wol

fullpage *adj.* 전면에 걸친 jeon-myeon-e
geol-chin

fullscale *adj.* 실물크기의 sil-mul keu-gi-ui

fullservice *n.* 풀서비스 pul-sseo-bi-sseu

fulltime *adj.* 전임의 jeon-im-ui

fully *adv.* 충분히 chung-bun-hi, 완전히
wan-jeon-hi

fume *n.* 연기 yeon-gi, 김 gim; *vi.* 연기가 나
다 yeon-gi-ga na-da; 약이 오르다 yag-i
o-reu-da

fumigate *vt.* 연기가 나게 하다 yeon-
gi-na-ge ha-da, 훈증소독하다
hun-jeung-so-do-ka-da

fun *n.* 즐거움 jeul-geo-um; 장난 jang-nan

function *n.* 기능 gi-neung; 직무 jing-mu; 의
식 ui-sik; *vi.* 작용하다 jag-yong-ha-da;
움직이다 um-jig-i-da; 역할을 다하다
yeo-kal-eul da-ha-da

functional *adj.* 기능의 gi-neung-sang-ui; 직무상의 jing-mu-sang-ui

fund *n.* 펀드 peon-deu, 자금 ja-geum; 축적 chuk-jeok; *vt.* 투자하다 tu-ja-ha-da, 적립하다 jeong-ni-pa-da

fundamental *adj.* 근본적인 geun-bon-jeog-in; 기초적인 gi-cho-jeog-in; 주요한 ju-yo-han

fundraising *n.* 모금활동 mo-geum-hwal-ttong, 자금조달 ja-geum-jo-dal

funeral *n.* 장례식 jang-nye-sik

fungus *n.* 곰팡이균 gom-pang-i-gyun; 곰팡이 gom-pang-i

funny *adj.* 재미있는 jae-mi-in-neun

fur *n.* 모피 mo-pi

furious *adj.* 성난 seong-nan; 맹렬한 maeng-nyeol-han

furnace *n.* 아궁이 a gung-i; 용광로 yong-gwang-no; 난방장치 nan-bang-jang-chi

furnish *vt.* 공급하다 gong-geu-pa-da, 제공하다 je-gong-ha-da

furniture *n.* 가구 ga-gu

further *adv.* 게다가 ge-da-ga, 더욱이 deo-u-gi; 더 멀리 deo meol-li

fury *n.* 격노 gyeong-no, 격분 gyeok-bun

fuse *n.* 퓨즈 pyu-jeu; *vi.* 녹다 nok-da; *vt.* 녹이다 nog-i-da

fuselage *n.* 기체 gi-che

fusion *n.* 용해 yong-hae

fuss *vi.* 야단법석을 떨다 ya-dan-beop-seog-eul tteol-da, 안달을 떨다 an-dal-eul tteol-da

future *n.* 미래 mi-rae, 장차 jang-cha; *adj.* 미래의 mi-rae-ui; 내세의 nae-se-ui

G

gain *n.* 이익 i-ik; 증가 jeung-ga; *vt.* 얻다 eot-da; 도달하다 do-dal-ha-da; 증대하다 jeungdae-ha-da; 이익을 얻다 i-ig-eul eot-da

galaxy *n.* 은하수 eun-ha-su, 은하 eun-ha

gall *n.* 쓸개즙 sseul-gae-jeup; 담낭 dam-nang, 쓸개 sseul-gae; 물집 mul-jip; *vt.* 속태우다 sok-tae-u-da; 피부가 벗겨지다 pi-bu-ga beot-gyeo-ji-da; 성나게 하다 seong-na-ge ha-da; ~ **bladder** 쓸개 sseul-gae, 담낭 dam-nang

gallery *n.* 화랑 hwa-rang, 미술관 mi-sul-gwan; 전시장 jeon-si-jang; 관람석 gwal-lam-seok

gallon *n.* 갤론 gael-lon

gallop *n.* 갤럽 gael-leop, 최대속도 choe-dae-sok-do; *vi.* 질주하다 jil-jju-ha-da; 급히 읽다 geu-pi ik-da; 급속히 진행되다 geup-so-ki jin-haeng-doe-da

gallstone *n.* 담석 dam-seok

gamble *vi.* 노름하다 no-reum-ha-da; 투기하다 tu-gi-ha-da; *n.* 노름 no-reum, 투기 tu-gi

game *n.* *(activity)* 놀이 nol-i, 게임 kke-im; *(wildlife)* 경기 gyeong-gi; 사냥감 sa-nyang-kkam; ~ **room** 오락실 o-rak-sil

gang *n.* 한 떼 han tteo; 일당 il-ttang

Ganges *n.* 갠지스강 gaen-ji-sseu gang

gap *n.* 금 keum; 틈 teum; 간격 gan-gyeok

garage *n.* 차고 cha-go; 자동차 수리소 ja-dong-cha su-ri-so; 비행기 격납고 bi-haeng-gi gyeong-nap-go

garbage *n.* 쓰레기 sseu-re-gi; ~ **can** 쓰레기통 sseu-re-gi-tong; ~ **man** 고물장수 go-mul-jang-su, 넝마주이 neong-ma-ji-i

garden *n.* 뜰 tteul; 공원 gong-won

gardener *n.* 정원사 jeong-won-sa

gargle *vi.* 양치질하다 yang-chi-jil-ha-da

garlic *n.* 마늘 ma-neul

garment *n.* 의복 ui-b, 옷 ot

garnish *n.* 장식물 jang-sing-mul, 장식품 jang-sik-pum; *vt.* 장식하다 jang-si-ka-da, 꾸미다 kku-mi-da; 고명을 얹다 go-myeong-eul eon-tta

gas *n.* 개스 kkae-sseu, 기체 gi-che; 휘발류 hwi-bal-lyu; ~ **cooker** 개스레인지 kkae-sseu-re-in-ji; ~ **station** 주유소 ju-yu-so; ~ **mask** 방독면 bang-dong-myeon

gasoline *n.* 석유 seog-yu, 휘발류 hwi-bal-lyu, 개솔린 gae-sol-lin

gasp *n.* 헐떡거림 heol-tteok-geo-rim; *vi.* 헐떡거리다 heol-tteok-geo-ri-da, 숨이 막히다 sum-i ma-ki-da

gassy *adj.* 개스의 kkae-sseu-ui; 개스를 함유한 kkae-sseu-reul ham-yu-han; 실속없는 sil-ssog-eom-neun

gastric *adj.* 위의 wi-ui, 위장의 wi-jang-ui;
~ **juice** 위액 wi-aek; ~ **ulcer** 위궤양
wi-gwe-yang

gate *n.* 문 mun, 출입구 chul-ip-gu

gather *vi.* 모이다 mo-i-da; 부풀어오르다
bu-pul-eo-o-reu-da

gauge *n.* 표준치수 pyo-jun-chi-ssu, 규격
gyu-gyeok; 척도 cheok-do, 게이지 ge-i-ji;
vt. 재다 jae-da, 측정하다 cheuk-jeong-ha-
da, 평가하다 pyeong-kka-ha-da

gay *adj. (mood)* 명랑한 myeong-nang-han;
화려한 hwa-ryeo-han; *(sexuality)*; 동성연
애의 dong-seong-yeon-ae-ui; *n.* 동성연애
자 dong-seong-yeon-ae-ja

gaze *vt.* 뚫어지게 보다 ttul-eo-ji-ge bo-da,
응시하다 eung-si-ha-da

gear *n.* 기어 gi-eo, 전동상지 jeon-dong-
jang-chi; *vt.* 기어를 넣다 gi-eo-reul neo-ta

gel *n.* 젤 jel, 겔 gel

gelatin *n.* 젤라틴 jel-la-tin

gem *n.* 보석 bo-seok; 귀중품 gwi-jung-pum;
~**stone** 보석 원석 bo-seok won-seok, 준보
석 jun-bo-seok

gender *n.* 성 seong, 성별 seong-byeol

genderneutral *adj.* 성적 구별이 없는
seong-jjeok gu-byeol-i eom-neun

genderspecific *adj.* 성별로 국한된 seong-
byeol-lo gu-kan-doen

gene *n.* 유전자 yu-jeon-ja

general *n.* 장군 jang-gun; 장관 jang-gwan;
adj. 일반의 il-ban-ui; 대체적인 dae-che-
jeog-in; 전반적인 jeon-ban-jeog-in; **in ~**
일반적으로 il-ban-jeog-eu-ro; ~ **hospital**
종합병원 jong-hap-byeong-won

generally *adv.* 일반적으로 il-ban-jeog-eu-ro,
보통 bo-tong

generate *vt.* 발생시키다 bal-ssaeng-si-ki-da;
낳다 na-ta; 야기하다 ya-gi-ha-da

generation *n.* 세대 se-dae; 산출 san-chul,
발생 bal-ssaeng; ~ **gap** 세대차이
se-dae-cha-i

generous *adj.* 관대한 gwan-dae-han; 푸짐한
pu-jim-han

genetic *adj.* 유전적인 yu-jeon-jeog-in

Geneva *n.* 제네바 je-ne-ba

genital *adj.* 생식의 saeng-sig-ui

genitalia *n. pl.* 생식기 saeng-sik-gi

genius *n.* 천재 cheon-jae; 천성 cheon-seong;
특질 teuk-jil

gentle *adj.* 부드러운 bu-deu-reo-un; 점잖은
jeom-jan-eun; 온화한 on-hwa-han; 점진적
인 jeom-jin-jeog-in

gentleman *n.* 신사 sin-sa, 점잖은 사람 jeom-
jan-eun sa-ram

genuine *adj.* 진짜의 jin-jja-ui; 순종의 sun-
jong-ui; 성실한 seong-sil-han

geography *n.* 지리 ji-ri; 지리학 ji-ri-hak

geology *n.* 지질 ji-jil; 지질학 ji-jil-hak

Georgia *n.* 죠지아 jo ji a

germ *n.* 병원균 yeong-won-gyun; 기원 gi-won

German *n.* 독일사람 dog-il-ssa-ram; *adj.* 독
일의 dog-il-ui

Germany *n.* 독일 dog-il

germinate *vi.* 싹이 트다 ssag-i-teu-da; 생겨
나다 saeng-gyeo-na-da

gesture *n.* 몸짓 mom-jjit, 제스처 je-seu-
cheo; 태도 tae-do; *vi.* 몸짓으로 표시하다
mom-jjis-eu-ro pyo-si-ha-da

get *vt.* 얻다 eot-da, 입수하다 ip-su-ha-da; 받
다 bat-da; 잡다 jap-da; *vi.* 이르다 i-reu-da,
도달하다 do-dal-ha-da, 오다 o-da, 가다
ga-da; **to ~ a bill in the mail** 우편으로
청구서를 받다 u-pyeon-eu-ro cheong-
gu-seo-reul bat-da; ~ **me a notepad** 제
게 메모용 노트 하나 좀 가져다 주십시
오 je-ge me-mo-yong no-teu ha-na jom
ga-jyeo-da ju-sip-si-o; **She's got a lot of
money** 그 여자분은 돈을 많이 받았습
니다 geu yeo-Ja-bun-eun don-eul man-i
bad-at-seum-ni-da; **to ~ even** 앙갚음하다
ang-ga-peum-ha-da; **I am ~ting tired** 제가
점점 피곤해 지는군요 je-ga jeom-jeom
pi-gon-hae ji-neun-gun-yo; **They want to ~
this cleaned** 그분들은 이것이 깨끗이 정
리되기를 바라십니다 geu-bun-deul-eun
i-geos-i kkae-kkeus i jeong-ni-doe-gi-reul
ba-ra-sim-ni-da; **The children have got to
stop doing that** 그 아이들은 저런 행동
을 그만두어야 합니다 geu a-i-deul-eun
jeo-reon haeng-dong-eul geu-man-du-
eo-ya ham-ni-da; **to ~ on/off (a mode of
transportation)** 버스나 기차 등을 타다,
버스나 기차 등에서 내리다 beo-sseu-na
gi-cha deung-eul ta-da, beo-sseu-na gi-cha

deung-e-seo nae-ri-da; **to ~ up at seven a.m.** 오전 일곱시에 일어나다 o-jeon il-gop-si-e il-eo-na-da; **to ~ together** 합치다 hap-chi-da, 모으다 mo-eu-da; 합쳐지다 hap-cheo-ji-da, 모이다 mo-i-da; 데이트하다 de-i-teu-ha-da; 의견이 일치하다 ui-gyeon-i il-chi-ha-da; 상담하다 sang-dam-ha-da

Ghana *n.* 가나 ga-na

ghost *n.* 유령 yu-ryeong

giant *n.* 거인 geo-in; *adj.* 거대한 geo-dae-han; 위대한 wi-dae-han

gift *n.* 선물 seon-mul; 재능 jae-neung; 증여 jeung-yeo; *vt.* 선물로 주다 seon-mul-lo ju-da; 재능을 부여하다 jae-neung-eul bu-yeo-ha-da; **~ wrapping** 선물포장 seon-mul-po-jang

gifted *adj.* 재능있는 jae-neung-in-neun

gigabit *n.* 기가비트 gi-ga-bi-teu

gigabyte *n.* 기가바이트 gi-ga-ba-i-teu

gigantic *adj.* 거인 같은 geo-in-gat-eun; 거대한 geo-dae-han

giggle *vi.* 낄낄 웃다 kkil-kkil-ut-da; *n.* 낄낄 웃음 kkil-kkil-us-eum

gild *vt.* 도금하다 do-geum-ha-da; 겉치레하다 geot-chi-re-ha-da

gill *n.* 아가미 a-ga-mi

gilt *n.* 금박 geum-bak, 금가루 geum-kka-ru; 겉치장 geot-chi-jang; *adj.* 금박을 입힌 geum-bag-eul i-pin, 도금한 do-geum-han; 부자의 bu-ja-ui; 귀족의 gwi-jog-ui

gin *n.* 진 jin; 조면기계장치 jo-myeon-gi-gye-jang-chi

ginger *n.* 생강 saeng-gang; *adj.* 생강맛의 saeng-gang-mas-ui

gingko *n.* 은행 eun-haeng

ginseng *n.* 인삼 in-sam

Gipsy *n.* 집시 jip-si

giraffe *n.* 기린 gi-rin

girdle *n.* 거들 geo-deul, 띠 tti; *vt.* 띠로 조르다 tti-ro jo-reu-da

girl *n.* 여자아이 yeo-ja-a-i, 소녀 so-nyeo

girlfriend *n.* 여자친구 yeo-ja-chin-gu

giro *n.* 지로 ji-ro

gist *n.* 요점 yo-jjeom, 요지 yo-ji

give *vt.* 주다 ju-da, 수여하다 su-yeo-ha-da, 지불하다 ji-bul-ha-da, 넘겨주다 neom-gyeo-ju-da; *vi.* 베풀다 be-pul-da;

He gave me a check 그 분이 저에게 수표를 주셨습니다 geu bun-i jeo-e-ge su-pyo-reul ju-syeot-seum-ni-da; **He gave them a ride home** 그 분이 그 사람들을 집까지 태워다 주셨습니다 geu bun-i geu sa-ram-deul-eul jip-kka-ji tae-wo-da ju-syeot-seum-ni-da; **She gave it a try** 그 분은 그 일을 한번 시도해 보셨습니다 geu bun-eun geu il-eul han-beon si-do-hae bo-syeot-seum-ni-da; **to ~ away** 거저주다 geo-jeo-ju-da, 폭로하다 pong-no-ha-da; **to ~ back** 돌려주다 dol-lyeo-ju-da, 응수하다 eung-su-ha-da; **to ~ up** 그만두다 geu-man-du-da, 항복하다 hang-bo-ka-da, 단념하다 dan-nyeom-ha-da; **to ~ in** 제출하다 je-chul-ha-da, 건네다 geon-ne-da; 공표하다 gong-pyo-ha-da, 등록하다 deung-no-ka-da; 항복하다 hang-bo-ka-da, 굴복하다 gul-bo-ka-da; **He gave up smoking** 그분은 담배를 끊었습니다 geu-bun-eun dam-bae-reul kkeun-eot-seum-ni-da; **~ him a chance** 그 사람에게 기회를 좀 주십시오 geu sa-ram-e-ge gi-hoe-reul jom ju-sip-si-o; **~ me a break** 저를 좀 가만히 내버려 두십시오 jeo-reul jom ga-man-hi nae-beo-ryeo du-sip-si-o

give-and-take *n.* 주고받기 ju-go-bat-gi; 의견교환 ui-gyeon-gyo-hwan

giveaway *n.* 포기 po-gi; 폭로 pong-no; 경품 gyeong-pum

given *adj.* 주어진 ju-eo-jin; **~ name** 이름 i-reum

glad *adj.* 기쁜 gi-ppeun

glamour *n.* 아름다움 a-reum-da-um; 매력 mae-ryeok; 마법 ma-beop, 마술 ma-sul

glance *n.* 한번 봄 han-beon bom; 눈짓 nun-jjit; 언급 eon-geup; *vi.* 흘끗 보다 heul-kkeut bo-da; 훑어보다 hult-eo-bo-da; 언급하다 eon-geu-pa-da; 스치다 seu-chi-da

gland *n.* 선 seon

glare *n.* 섬광 seom-gwang; 현란함 hyeol-lan-ham; 날카로운 눈매 nal-ka-ro-un nun-mae; *vi.* 번쩍이다 beon-jjeog-i-da; 노려보다 no-ryeo-bo-da

glass *n.* 유리 yu-ri; 컵 keop; 안경 an-gyeong; **~ware** 유리제품 yu-ri-je-pum

glasses *n.* 안경 an-gyeong

glaze *vt.* 유리를 끼우다 yu-ri-reul kki-u-da; 광택제를 바르다 gwang-taek-je-reul ba-reu-da; *n.* 유리 끼우기 yu-ri kki-u-gi; 광택제 gwang-taek-je

glide *vi.* 미끄러지다 mi-kkeu-reo-ji-da, 활주하다 hwal-jju-ha-da; *n.* 활주 hwal-jju

glimpse *n.* 흘끗 봄 heul-kkeut bom; *vt.* 흘끗 보다 heul-kkeut-bo-da

glitter *vi.* 반짝이다 ban-jjag-i-da; 화려하다 hwa-ryeo-ha-da

global *adj.* 공모양의 gong-mo-yang-ui; 세계적인 se-gye-jeog-in; ~ **warming** 세계적인 온난현상 se-gye-jeog-in on-nan-hyeon-sang; ~ **economy** 세계경제 se-gye-gyeong-je; ~ **village** 지구촌 ji-gu-chon

globe *n.* 지구본 ji-gu-bon; 지구 ji-gu; 공 gong

gloom *n.* 어둠 eo-dum; 우울 u-ul

gloomy *adj.* 어두운 eo-du-un; 우울한 u-ul-han

glory *n.* 영광 yeong-gwang; 명예 myeong-ye; 칭찬 ching-chan

gloss *n.* 광택 gwang-taek; 주석 ju-seok

glove *n.* 장갑 jang-gap; 글러브 geul-reo-beu; ~ **compartment** 글러브 컴파트 geul-leo-beu keom-pa-teu

glow *n.* 백열 baeg-yeol; 달아오름 dal-a-o-reum; 만족감 man-jok-gam; *vi.* 타다 ta-da; 빛을 내다 bich-eul nae-da; 붉어지다 bulg-eo-ji-da

glue *n.* 풀 pul; 아교 a gyo; *vt.* 풀로 붙이다 pul-lo buch-i-da; *vt., vi.* 접합시키다 jeu-pap-si-ki-da, 접힙하다 jeo-pa-pa-da

go *vi.* 가다 ga-da, 향하다 hyang-ha-da, 출발하다 chul-bal-ha-da, 사라지다 sa-ra-ji-da, 죽다 juk da, 무너지다 mu-neo-ji-da, 움직이다 um-jig-i-da, 행동하다 haeng-dong-ha-da, 통용되다 tong-yong-doe-da, 진행되다 jin-haeng-doe-da, 놓이다 no-i-da, 포함되다 po-ham-doe-da, 주어지나 ju-co ji da, 도움이 되다 do-um-i doe-da, 의지하다 ui-ji-ha-da; **They went to Mexico** 그 사람들은 멕시코로 갔습니다 geu sa-ram-deul-eun mek-si-ko-ro gat-seum-ni-da; *(leave)* **I have to ~** 이제 가야 하겠습니다 i-je ga-ya ha-gyet-seum-ni-da; *(become)* **The milk has gone bad** 우유가 상했다 u-yu-ga sang-haet-da; *(with infinitive)* **He was ~ing to call around four** 그분은 4시

경에 전화하려고 했습니다 geu-bun-eun ne-si-gyeong-e jeon-hwa-ha-ryeo-go haet-seum-ni-da; *(up/down)* **He went up the street** 그분은 길을 따라 올라갔습니다 geu-bun-eun gil-eul tta-ra ol-la-gat-seum-ni-da; *(to go on)* **What's ~ing on** 도대체 무슨 일입니까 do-de-che mu-seun il-im-ni-kka; **It went on like that for years** 그것은 몇 년동안 저 상태로 계속되고 있습니다 geu-geos-eun myeon-nyeon-ttong-an jeo sang-tae-ro gye-sok-doe-go it-seum-ni-da; **He just ~es on doing it that way** 그 분은 그 일을 그 방법으로 그저 계속하고 있습니다 geu bun-eun geu il-eul geu-jeo geu bang-beob-eu-ro gye-so-ka-go it-seum-ni-da; **The alarm went off** 경보가 울렸습니다 gyeong-bo-ga ul-lyeot-seum-ni-da; ~ **away** 저리 가 jeo-ri ga, 바보 같은 소리 하지 마 ba-bo-gat-eun so-ri ha-ji ma

goal *n.* 골 gol; 목적 mok-jeok, 목표 mok-pyo; ~**keeper** 골키퍼 g-kkol-ki-peo; ~**post** 골대 kkol-ttae

goat *n.* 염소 yeom-so

Gobi Desert *n.* 고비사막 go-bi-sa-mak

god *n.* 신 sin, 하나님 ha-na-nim, 조물주 jo-mul-jju

godchild *n.* 대자 dae-ja

goddaughter *n.* 대녀 dae-nyeo

goddess *n.* 여신 yeo-sin

godfather *n.* 대부 dae-bu

godmother *n.* 대모 dae-mo

godson *n.* 대사 dae-ja

goggle *vt.* 눈을 부릅뜨다 nun-eul bu-reup-tteu-da; *n.* 눈을 부릅뜸 nun-eul bu-reup-tteum; 가글 ga-geul, 물안경 mul-an-gyeong

gold *n.* 금 geum, 금화 geum-hwa; *adj.* 금빛의 geum-ppich-ui; 금의 geum-ui; ~**fish** 금붕어 geum-bung-eo

golden *adj.* 금빛의 geum-ppich-ui; 귀중한 gwi-jung-han; ~ **age** 전성기 jeon-seong-gi, 황금기 hwang-geum-gi; ~ **rule** 황금률 hwang-geum-nyul

golf *n.* 골프 gol-peu; ~ **ball** 골프공 gol-peu-gong; ~ **club** 골프채 gol-peu-chae

gone *adj.* 지나간 ji-na-gan; 죽은 jug-eun

good *n.* 선 seon; 이익 i-ik; *adj.* 좋은 jo-eun; 친절한 chin-jeol-han; 유능한 yu-neung-

han; 충분한 chung-bun-han; ~ **luck** 행운
haeng-un

good-bye *n.* 고별 go-byeol, 작별 jak-byeol;
안녕 an-nyeong, 안녕히 가십시오 an-
nyeong-hi ga-sip-si-o

good-for-nothing *n.* 쓸모 없는 것sseul-
mo-eom-neun-geot; 쓸모 없는 사람
sseul-mo-eom-neun sa-ram

good-looking *adj.* 잘생긴 jal saeng-gin; 잘
어울리는 jal eo-ul-li-neun

goods *n.* 재산 jae-san; 물건 mul-geon

goose *n.* 거위 geo-wi; ~**flesh** 소름 so-reum

gorgeous *adj.* 호화스러운 ho-hwa-seu-reo-
un, 화려한 hwa-ryeo-han

gospel *n.* 복음 bog-eum; 복음서 bog-eum-
seo; 복음찬송 bog-eum-chan-song

gossip *n.* 잡담 jap-dam; 한담 han-dam; 험담
heom-dam; *vi.* 잡담하다 jap-dam-ha-da;
수군거리다 su-gun-geo-ri-da

gourmet *n.* 미식가 mi-sik-ga

govern *vt., vi.* 통치하다 tong-chi-ha-da;
좌우하다 jwa-u-ha-da; 억제하다
eok-je-ha-da

government *n.* 정부 jeong-bu; 통치 tong-chi

governor *n.* 통치자 tong-chi-ja; 주지사
ju-ji-sa; 총독 chong-dok

gown *n.* 가운 kka-un

grab *v.* 움켜잡다 um-kyeo-jam-da, 부여잡다
bu-yeo-jap-da

grace *n.* 우아 u-a; 은총 eun-chong; 세련
se-ryeon

graceful *adj.* 우아한 u-a-han; 친절한
chin-jeol-han

gracious *adj.* 호의적인 ho-ui-jeog-in; 친절
한 chin-jeol-han

grade *n.* 등급 deung-geup; 성적 seong-
jeok; 학년 hang-nyeon; *vt.* 등급을 메
기다 deung-geub-eul me-gi-da; 채점하
다 chae-jjeom-ha-da; ~ **mark** 품질표시
pum-jil-pyo-si

gradual *adj.* 단계적인 dan-gye-jeog-in; 점차
적인 jeom-cha-jeog-in

graduate *n.* 졸업생 jol-eop-saeng; *vi.* 졸업
하다 jol-eo-pa-da; 자격을 따다 ja-gyeog-
eul tta-da

graduation *n.* 졸업 jol-eop, 졸업식 jol-eop-sik

graft *n.* 접붙이기 jeop-buch-i-gi; 부정이득 bu-
jeong-i-deuk; *vt.* 접목하다 jeom-mo-ka-da;

결합하다 gyeol-ha-pa-da; 부정이익을 취
하다 bu-jeong-i-ig-eul chwi-ha-da

grain *n.* 곡식 gok-sik; 낟알 nod-al; 극소량
geuk-so-ryang

gram *n.* 그램 geu-raem

grammar *n.* 문법 bun-ppeop; 어투 eo-tu

grand *adj.* 웅대한 ung-dae-han; 총괄적인
chong-gwal-jjeog-in; 당당한 dang-dang-
han; 굉장한 goeng-jang-han

grandchildren *n.* *(male)* 손자son-ja, *(female)*
손녀 son-nyeo, 손주 son-ju

granddaughter *n.* 손녀 son-nyeo

grandfather *n.* 할아버지 hal-a-beo-ji

grandmother *n.* 할머니 hal-meo-ni

grandparent *n.* 조부모 jo-bu-mo, 할아버지
와 할머니 hal-a-beo-ji-wa hal-meo-ni

grandslam *n.* 압승 ap-seung

grandson *n.* 손자 son-ja

granite *n.* 화강암 hwa-gang-am

grant *n.* 허가 heo-ga; 양도 yang-do; 보조
금 bo-jjo-geum; *vt.* 주다 ju-da; 승인하다
seung-in-ha-da

grape *n.* 포도 po-do; ~ **juice** 포도주스
po-do-ju-sseu; 비밀 정보망 bi-mil jeong-
bo-mang; 헛소문 heot-so-mun

grapefruit *n.* 자몽 ja-mong

graph *n.* 그래프 geu-rae-peu, 도표 do-pyo

graphic *adj.* 사실적인 sa-sil-jjeog-in; 생생한
saeng-saeng-han; 도표로 표시된 do-pyo-
ro pyo-si-doen; **computer ~s** 컴퓨터 그래
픽스 keom-pu-teo geu-rae-pik-seu

grasp *vt.* 파악하다 pa-a-ka-da; 납득하다
nap-deu-ka-da; 붙잡다 but-jap-da

grass *n.* 잔디 jan-di; 풀 pul

grasshopper *n.* 메뚜기 me-ttu-gi

grateful *adj.* 감사하는 gam-sa-ha-neun

gratitude *n.* 감사 gam-sa

grave *n.* 무덤 mu-deom; 죽음 jug-eum; *adj.*
근엄한 geun-eom-han; 심상치 않은 sim-
sang-chi an-eun; *vt.* 조각하다 jo-ga-ka-da,
새기다 sae-gi-da; ~ **yard** 묘지 myo-ji; ~
stone 비석 bi-seok

gravity *n.* 엄숙함 eom-su-kam; 중대함
jung-dae-ham; 중력 jung-nyeok

gray *adj.* 회색의 hoe-saeg-ui; 흐릿한 heu-ri-
tan; 머리가 희끗한 meo-ri-ga hi-kkeu-tan;
~ **hair** 흰머리 hin-meo-ri; ~ **zone** 회색지
대 hoe-saek-ji-dae

grease *n.* 윤활류 yun-hwal-lyu; 지방 ji-bang; 유성물질 yu-seong-mul-jjil; *vt.* 기름을 바르다 gi-reum-eul ba-reu-da; 뇌물을 주다 noe-mul-eul ju-da

greasy *adj.* 기름이 묻은 gi-reum-i mud-eun; 알랑거리는 al-lang-geo-ri-neun; 미끈거리는 mi-kkeun-geo-ri-neun

great *adj.* 큰 keun, 중대한 jung-dae-han; 거대한 geo-dae-han; 위대한 wi-dae-han

Great Britain *n.* 영국 yeong-guk

great-grandfather *n.* 증조 할아버지 jeung-jo hal-a-beo-ji

great-grandmother *n.* 증조 할머니 jeung-jo hal-meo-ni

great-grandparent *n.* 증조부와증조모 jeung-jo bu wa jeung jo mo, 증조 할아버지와 증조 할머니 Jeung-Jo hal-a-beo-ji-wa jeung-jo hal-meo-ni

Great Lakes *n.* 5대호 o-dae-ho

greatly *adv.* 크게 keu-ge, 심히 sim-hi, 매우 mae-u

greatness *n.* 거대 geo-dae; 대량 dae-ryang; 탁월함 tag-wol-ham

Greece *n.* 그리스 geu-ri-sseu

greedy *adj.* 욕심많은 yok-sim-man-eun; 갈망하는 gal-mang-ha-neun

Greek *n.* 그리스사람 geu-ri-sseu-sa-ram; 그리스어 geu-ri-sseu-eo; *adj.* 그리스의 geu-ri-sseu-ui

green *n.* 파란색 pa-ran-saek, 초록색 cho-rok-saek; 풀밭 pul-bat, 잔디밭 jan-di-bat; 야채 ya-chae; *(lawn)* 골프장 gol-peu-jang; *adj.* 녹색의 nok-saeg-ui; 싱싱한 sing-sing-han; 미숙한 mi-seu-kan; 질투하는 jil-tu-ha-neun; ~ **light** 청신호 cheong-sin-ho, 청색신호 cheong-saek-sin-ho; ~ **tea** 녹차 nok cha

greenbelt *n.* 그린벨트 geu-rin-bel-teu, 녹지대 nok-ji-dae

greencard *n.* 영주권 yeong-ju-kkwon

green-eyed *adj.* 질투가 심한 jil-tu-ga sim-han

greenhouse *n.* 온실 on-sil; ~ **effect** 온실효과 on-sil-hyo-kkwa

Greenland *n.* 그린랜드 geu-in-raen-deu

greet *vt.* 인사하다 in-sa-ha-da; 환영하다 hwan-yeong-ha-da

greeting *n.* 인사 in-sa; 환영 hwan-yeong; ~ **card** 인사장 in-sa-jjang

grief *n.* 슬픔 seul-peum, 비탄 bi-tan

grievance *n.* 불만 bul-man, 불평 bul-pyeong

grieve *vt.* 슬프게 하다 seul-peu-ge ha-da; *vi.* 슬퍼하다 seul-peo-ha-da

grill *n.* 석쇠 seok-soe, 그릴 geu-ril; *vt.* 석쇠에 굽다 seok-soe gup-da, 그릴에 굽다 geu-rile gup-da; 엄하게 심문하다 eom-ha-ge sim-mun-ha-da

grind *vt.* 갈다 gal-da, 가루로 만들다 ga-ru-ro man-deul-da; 깎다 kkak-da; 혹사하다 hok-sa-ha-da

grip *n.* 파악 pa-ak; 손잡이 son-jab-i; 파악력 pa-ang-nyeok; 지배력 ji-bae-ryeok; *vt.* 꽉 쥐다 kkwak jwi-da; 단단히 쥐다 dan-dan-hi jwi-da; 매달리다 mae-dal li da; 끌다 kkeul da; 이해하다 i-hae-ha-da

groan *n.* 신음소리 sin-eum-sso-ri; 불평하는 소리 bul-pyeong-ha-neun so-ri; 삐걱거리는 소리 ppi-geok-geo-ri-neun so-ri; *vi.* 신음하다 sin-eum-ha-da; 번민하다 beon-min-ha-da

grocer *n.* 식료품 상인 sing-nyo-pum sang-in

grocery *n.* 식료품 sing-nyo-pum; 식료품점 sing-nyo-pum-jeom

groin *n.* 샅 sat, 사타구니 sa-ta-gu-ni

gross *adj.* 거친 geo-chin; 천한 cheon-han; 상스러운 sang-seu-reo-un; 커다란 keo-da-ran, 뚱뚱한 ttung-ttung-han; 총체의 chong-che-ui

ground *n.* 땅 ttang; 운동장 un-dong-jang; 기초 gi-cho; 근거 geun-geo; *adj.* 가루로 빻은 ga-ru-ro ppa-eun; 가루의 ga-ru-ui; ~ **pepper** 고추가루 go-chu-kka-ru; 후추가루 hu-chu-kka-ru; ~ **zero** 폭파점 pok-pa-jjeom; 낙하지점 na-ka-ji-jeom

groundwork *n.* 토대 to-dae; 기반 gi-ban; 근거 geun-geo; 기본원리 gi-bon-wol-li

group *n.* 그룹 geu-rup; 단체 dan-che; *vt.* 불러 모으다 bul-leo-mo-eu-da; 분류하다 bul-lyu-ha-da

grow *vt.* 키우다 ki-u-da; 재배하다 jae-bae-ha-da; *vi.* 성장하다 seong-jang-ha-da; 발생하다 bal-ssaeng-ha-da

growl *n.* 으르릉거리는 소리 eu-reu-reong-geo-ri-neun so-ri; *vi.* 으르렁대다 eu-reu-reong-dae-da; 고함치다 go-ham-chi-da; 투덜거리다 tu-deol-geo-ri-da

grown-up *n.* 어른 eo-reun, 성인 seong-in; *adj.* 성숙한 seong-su-kan

growth *n.* 성장 seong-jang; 증대 jeung-dae; 발전 bal-jjeon

grumble *vi.* 투덜거리다 tu-deol-geo-ri-da, 불평하다 bul-pyeong-ha-da

guarantee *n.* 보증 bo-jeung, 개런티 gae-reon-ti; 보증서 bo-jeung-seo; 보증인 bo-jeung-in; *vt.* 보증하다 bo-jeung-ha-da; 장담하다 jang-dam-ha-da; ~d 보증된 bo-jeung-doen

guard *n.* 경계 gyeong-gye; 경호인 gyeong-ho; 방호물 bang-ho-mul; *vt.* 보호하다 bo-ho-ha-da; 지키다 ji-ki-da; 경계하다 gyeong-gye-ha-da

guardian *n.* 보호자 bo-ho-ja, 감시인 gam-si-in

guardrail *n.* 가드레일 ga-deu-re-il, 난간 nan-gan

guerilla *n.* 게릴라 ge-ril-la; 유격병 yu-gyeok-byeong; 비정규군 bi-jeong-gyu-gun; *adj.* 게릴라의 ge-ril-la-ui

guess *n.* 추측 chu-cheuk; *vi.* 추측하다 chu-cheu-ka-da, 짐작하다 jim-ja-ka-da; **a wild** ~ 무모한 추측 mu-mo-han chu-cheuk, 엉터리 추측 eong-teo-ri chu-cheuk

guest *n.* 손님 son-nim; ~ **house** 영빈관 yeong-bin-gwan; 게스트 하우스 ge-seu-teu ha-u-sseu

guide *n.* 가이드 ga-i-deu, 안내자 an-nae-ja, 길잡이 gil-jab-i; 참조기호 cham-jo-gi-ho;

지도원리 ji-do-wol-li; *vt.* ~ **dog** 맹인견 maeng-in-gyeon, 맹도견 maeng-do-gyeon

guidebook *n.* 여행 안내서 yeo-haeng an-nae-seo

guideline *n.* 정책 jeong-chaek, 지침 ji-chim

guilt *n.* 유죄 yu-joe; 죄 joe; 범죄행위 beom-joe-haeng-wi

guilty *adj.* 죄를 범한 joe-reul beom-han; 떳떳치 못한 tteot-tteot-chi mo-tan

guitar *n.* 기타 gi-ta

gulf *n.* 만 man; 큰 간격 keun gan-gyeok

Gulf Stream *n.* 걸프만 geol-peu-man

gulp *vt.* 꿀꺽꿀꺽 마시다 kkul-kkeok-kkul-kkeok ma-si-da; 참다 cham-tta, 억누르다 eong-nu-reu-da

gum *n.* 껌 kkeom; 고무 go-mu; 잇몸 in-mom; **chewing** ~ 추잉껌 chu-ing-kkeom

gun *n.* 총 chong; 대포 dae-po

gunshot *n.* 사격 sa-gyeok

gust *n.* 돌풍 dol-pung; 격정 gyeok-jeong

gutter *n.* 낙수물받이 nak-su-mul-ba-ji; 하수도 ha-su-do; 빈민굴 bin-min-gul

guy *n.* 남자 nam-ja, 녀석 nyeo-seok

gym *n. abbr.* ***gymnasium*** 체육관 che-yuk-gwan

gymnastics *n.* 체조 che-jo

gym suit *n.* 체육복 che-yuk-bok

gynecologist *n.* 산부인과 의사 san-bu-in-kkwa ui-sa

Gypsy *n.* 집시 jip-si

H

habit *n.* 습관 seup-gwan, 버릇 beo-reut; 기질 gi-jil

habitat *n.* 서식지 seo-sik-ji; 거주지 geo-ju-ji

habitual *adj.* 습관적인 seup-gwan-jeog-in, 상습적인 sang-seup-jeog-in

hacker *n.* 해커 hae-keo

Hague *n.* 헤이그 he-i-geu

hail *n.* 우박 u-pak, 싸락눈 ssa-rang-nun; 만세 man-se; *vt.* 환호하며 맞다 hwan-ho-ha-myeo mat-da

hair *n.* 머리 meo-ri; 털 teol; ~**brush** 브러쉬 beu-reo-swi; ~**cut** 머리 자르다 meo-ri ja-reu-da; ~ **dryer** 드라이 deu-ra-I; ~ **net** 헤어네트 he-eo-ne-teu; ~**spray** 스프레이

seu-peu-re-i; ~**dresser** 미용사 mi-yong-sa, 헤어 디자이너 he-eo di-ja-i-neo; ~**raising** 머리털이 곤두서는 meo-ri-teol-i gon-du-seo-neun, 무시무시한 mu-si-mu-si-han, 소름끼치는 so-reum-kki-chi-neun

hairy *adj.* 털이 많은 teol-i man-eun; 섬뜩한 seom-tteu-kan

Haiti *n.* 하이티 ha-i-ti

half *n.* 반 ban; 절반 jeol-ban; *adj.* 절반의 jeol-ban-ui; ~**and**~ 반반의 ban-ban-ui; *n.* 반반 ban-ban

halfway *adj.* 중간의 jung-gan-ui, 중도의 jung-do-ui; *adv.* 중도에서 jung-do-e-seo; 거의 geo-ui

hall *n.* 홀 hol; 현관 hyeon-gwan; 공회당 gong-hoe-dang; 강당 gang-dang

hallway *n.* 현관 hyeon-gwan, 복도 bok-do

ham *n.* 햄 haem; 넓적다리 neop-jeok-da-ri; 아마추어 무선가 a-ma-chu-eo mu-seon-ga

hamburger *n.* 햄버거 haem-beo-geo

hammer *n.* 망치 mang-chi, 해머 hae-meo; *vt., vi.* 망치로 치다 mang-chi-ro chi-da, 두들기다 du-deul-gi-da

hamper *n.* 바구니 ba-gu-ni, 바스켓 ba-seu-ket

hand *n.* 손 son; 일손 il sson; 필적 pil-jjeok; 편 pyeon; *vt.* 건네주다 geon-ne-ju-da; 수교하다 su-gyo-ha-da; **to shake ~s** 악수하다 ak-su-ha-da; **to ~ down** 나눠주다 na-now-ju-da, 돌리다 do-li-da; **to ~ over** 건네주다 geon-ne-ju-da, 양도하다 yang-do-ha-da; **~ me the keys** 키를 제게 건네주십시오 ki-reul je-ge geon-ne ju-sip-si-o

handbag *n.* 핸드백 haen-deu-baek, 손가방 son-kka-bang

handbook *n.* 안내서 an-nae-seo, 편람 pyeol-lam

handcuff *n.* 수갑 su-gap; *vt.* 수갑을 채우다 su-gab-eul chae-u-da

handful *n.* 한웅큼 han-ung-keum, 한줌 han-jum

handgrip *n.* 손잡이 son-jab-i, 자루 ja-ru

handicap *n.* 핸디캡 haen-di-kaep; 불리 bul-li; 장애 jang-ae

handicapped *adj.* 핸디캡이 붙은 haen-di-kaeb-i but-eun; 불리한 입장의 bul-li-han ip-jang-ui

handicraft *n.* 수공업 su-gong-eop, 수세공 su-se-gong

handkerchief *n.* 손수건 son-ssu-geon

handle *n.* 손잡이 son-jab-i, 핸들 haen-deul

handmade *adj.* 손으로 만든 son-eu-ro man-deun, 수공의 su-gong-ui

hand-out *n.* 인쇄물 in-swae-mul; 동냥 dong-nyang

hand-over *n.* 넘겨줌 neom-gyeo-jum, 이양 i-yang

handrail *n.* 난간 nan-gan

handshake *n.* 악수 ak-su

handsome *adj.* 잘생긴 jal-saeng-gin; 단정한 dan-jeong-han

hand-to-mouth *adj.* 그날그날 지내는 geu-nal-geu-nal ji-nae-neun

handy *adj.* 편리한 pyeol-li-han; 능숙한 neung-su-kan; 가까이 있는 ga-kka-i in-neun

hang *vt.* 매달다 mae-dal-da, 매다 mae-da; 목 매달다 mok mae-dal-da; *vi.* 매달리다 mae-dal-li-da; 허공에 뜨다 heo-gong-e tteu-da

hangar *n.* 격납고 gyeong-nap-go; 차고 cha-go

hanger *n.* 양복걸이 yang-bok-geol-i; 교수형 집행자 gyo-su-hyeong ji-paeng-ja; **clothes ~** 옷걸이 ot-geol-i

hang glider *n.* 행글라이더 haeng-geul-la-i-deo

hangover *n.* 잔존물 jan-jon-mul; 유물 yu-mul; 부작용 bu-jag-yong

happen *vi.* 일어나다 il-eo-na-da, 생기다 saeng-gi-da; 우연히 …하다 u-yeon-hi …ha-da

happiness *n.* 행복 haeng-bok, 만족 man-jok, 유쾌 yu-kwae

happy *adj.* 행복한 haeng-bo-kan; 행운의 haeng-un-ui; 기쁜 gi-ppeun

harass *vt.* 괴롭히다 goe-ro-pi-da

harassment *n.* 괴로움 goe-ro-um, 골칫거리 gol-chit-geo-ri

harbor *n.* 항구 hang-gu; 피난처 pi-nan-cheo

hard *adj. (opposite of soft)* 딱딱한 ttak-tta-kan; 거친 geo-chin; 참기 어려운 cham-kki eo-ryeo-un; 근면한 geun-myeon-han; *(difficult)* 어려운 eo-ryeo-un; **~core** 핵심의 haek-sim-ui; 절대적인 jeol-ttae-jeog-in

harden *vi.* 딱딱해지다 ttak-tta-kae-ji-da; 강해지다 gang-hae-ji-da; 무정해지나 mu-jeong-hae-ji-da; 분명해지다 bun-myeong-hae-ji-da

hardheaded *adj.* 완고한 wan-go-han, 고집 센 go-jip sen; 빈틈없는 bin-teum-eom-neun, 실제적인 sil-jje-jeog-in

hardhearted *adj.* 무정한 mu-jeong-han, 냉혹한 naeng-ho-kan

hardly *adv.* 거의 …이 아니다 geo-ui … i a-ni-da, 거의 … 가 아니다 geo-ui … ga a-ni-da; 애써서 ae-sseo-seo, 힘껏 him-kkeot; 심하게 sim-ha-ge, 냉혹하게 naeng-ho-ka-ge

hardness *n.* 견고 gyeon-go, 경도 gyeong-do; 곤란 gol-lan, 난해 nan-hae; 준엄 jun-eom, 가혹 ga-hok; 무정 mu-jeong

hardship *n.* 고난 go-nan; 곤경 gon-gyeong; 학대 hak-dae

hardtime *n.* 불경기 bul-gyeong-gi

hardware *n.* 철물 cheol-mul; 기재설비 gi-jae-seol-bi; **computer** ~ 컴퓨터 하드웨어 keom-pyu-teo ha-deu-we-eo; ~ **store** 철물점 cheol-mul-jeom

hardworking *adj.* 근면한 geun-myeon-han, 열심히 일하는 yeol-ssim-hi il-ha-neun

hardy *adj.* 내구력이 있는 nae-gu-ryeog-i in-neun; 튼튼한 teun-teun-han

hare *n.* 산토끼 san-to-kki; 겁쟁이 geop-jang-i

harm *n.* 해 hae; 손해 son-hae

harmful *adj.* 해로운 hae-ro-un

harmless *adj.* 해가 없는 hae-ga-eom-neun; 악의가 없는 ag-ui-ga eom-neun

harmonic *adj.* 조화하는 jo-hwa-ha-neun, 잘 어울리는 jal eo-ul-li-neun

harmonica *n.* 하모니카 ha-mo-ni-ka

harmony *n.* 조화 jo-hwa, 일치 il-chi, 융화 yung-hwa

harness *n.* 마구 ma-gu; 장치 jang-chi; 평상직무 pyeong-sang-jing-mu; *vt.* 마구를 채우다 ma-gu-reul chae-u-da; 이용하다 i-yong-ha-da; 일상 일을 시키다 il-ssang il-eul si-ki-da

harp *n.* 하프 ha-peu

harsh *adj.* 거친 geo-chin; 사나운 sa-na-un; 가혹한 ga-ho-kan

harvest *n.* 수확 su-hwak; 수확기 su-hwak-gi; 수확물 su-hwang-mul

hassle *n.* 혼란 hol-lan; 말싸움 mal-ssa-um; *vi.* 말다툼하다 mal-da-tum-ha-da

haste *n.* 급속 geup-sok; 성급 seong-geup

hasten *vi.* 서두르다 seo-du-reu-da; *vt.* 서두르게 하다 seo-du-reu-ge ha-da

hasty *adj.* 급한 geu-pan; 조급한 jo-geu-pan, 성급한 seong-geu-pan; ~ **decision** 성급한 결정 seong-geu-pan gyeo-jjeong

hat *n.* 모자 mo-ja

hatch *n.* 부화 bu-hwa; 결말 gyeol-mal; 승강구 seung-gang-gu, 출입문 chul-im-mun; *(doorway)* 해치 hae-chi; *vt.* 부화하다 bu-hwa-ha-da; 음모를 꾸미다 eum-mo-reul

kku-mi-da; *vi.* 알이 깨다 al-i kkae-da; 음모가 꾸며지다 eum-mo-ga kku-myeo-ji-da

hate *n.* 증오 jeung-o, 혐오 hyeom-o; *vt.* 증오하다 jeung-o-ha-da, 미워하다 mi-wo-ha-da

haul *n.* 견인 gyeon-in; 운반 un-ban; 수송물품 su-song-mul-pum; 운반거리 un-ban-geo-ri; *vt.* 끌어당기다 kkeul-eo-dang-gi-da; 운반하다 un-ban-ha-da

haunt *vt.* 빈번히 들르다 bin-beon-hi deul-leu-da; 출몰하다 chul-mol-ha-da; 붙어 따라다니다 but-eo tta-ra-da-ni-da

have *vt.* 가지고 있다 ga-ji-go it-da, 걸리다 geol-li-da, 손에 넣다 son-e neo-ta, 경험하다 gyeong-heom-ha-da, 개최하다 gae-choe-ha-da, 먹다 meok-da, 출산하다 chul-ssan-ha-da; …하게 하다 …ha-ge ha-da, …시키다 …si-ki-da; *(to own or hold)* **I** ~ **a car** 저는 차가 있습니다 jeo-neun cha-ga it-seum-ni-da; *(necessity)* **We** ~ **to be there by eight** 우리는 거기에 8시까지 가야 합니다 u-ri neun geo-gi-e yeo-deol-ssi-kka-ji ga-ya ham-ni-da; *(characteristics)* **He has brown eyes** 그분은 눈이 밤색입니다 geu bun-eun nun-i bam-saeg-im-ni-da; *(to suffer/experience)* **She has a cold** 그 분은 감기에 걸렸습니다 geu bun-eun gam-gi-e geol-lyeot-seum-ni-da; **She had an operation** 그분은 수술을 하셨습니다. geu bun-eun su-sul-eul ha-syeot-seum-ni-da; *(to hold/take part in)* **They will be having a meeting today** 그 사람들은 오늘 만날 겁니다 geu sa-ram-deul-eun o-neul man-nal kkeom-ni-da; *(to partake)* **What will you** ~ 뭘 드시겠습니까 mwol deu-si-get-seum-ni-kka; *(to get something done)* **I want to** ~ **him do it** 저는 그 분이 그 일을 하시게 하고 싶습니다 jeon-neun geu-bun-i geu il-eul ha-si-ge ha-go sip-seum-ni-da; *(in perfect tenses)* **I** ~ **seen it** 저는 그걸 본 적이 있습니다 jeo-neun geu-geol bon jeog-i it-seum-ni-da; *(tag phrases)* **You have already met, ~n't you** 두분은 전에 만나신 적이 있으시지요 du-bun-eun jeon-e man-na-sin jeog-i iss-eu-si-ji-yo; **to** ~ **a baby** 아기를 가지다 a-gi-reul ga-ji-da

Hawaii *n.* 하와이 ha-wa-i

hawk *n.* 매 mae; 사기꾼 sa-gi-kkun; 외야수 oe-ya-su

hay *n.* 건초 geon-cho; ~ **fever** 건초열 geon-cho-yeol

hazard *n.* 우연 u-yeon; 모험 mo-heom; 위험 ui-heom

haze *n.* 아지랑이 a-ji-rang-i; 안개 an-gae; 몽롱함 mong-nong-ham

hazy *adj.* 흐릿한 heu-ri-tan; 안개가 낀 an-gae-ga kkin; 몽롱한 mong-nong-han; 모호한 mo ho han

he *pron.* 그 사람 geu sa-ram, *(hon.)* 그 분 geu bun

head *n.* 머리 meo-ri; 두뇌 du-noe; 정상 jeong-sang; 장 jang; *vt.* 신두에 서다 seon-du-e seo-da; ... 을 향하게 하다 ... eul hyang-ha-ge ha-da, ... 를 향하게 하다 ... reul hyang-ha-ge ha-da; ...의 장이다 ...ui jang-i-da; **He ~s the sales department** 그 분은 판매부 부장님이십니다 geu bun-eun pan-mae-bu bu-jang-nim-i-sim-ni-da

headache *n.* 두통 du-tong; 골칫거리 gol-chit-geo-ri

heading *n.* 제목 je mok, 표제 pyo-je, 방향 bang-hyang; 참수 cham-su; 순치기 sun-chi-gi; 헤딩 he-ding

headlight *n.* 헤드라이트 he-deu-ra-i-teu

headline *n.* 표제 pyo-je, 헤드라인 he-deu-ra-in

headphone *n.* 헤드폰 he-deu-pon

headquarters *n. pl.* 본부 bon-bu; 사령부 san-ryeong-bu; 본사 bon-sa

heal *vt.* 고치다 go-chi-da; 화해시키다 hwa-hae-si-ki-da; 성화시키다 jeong-hwa-si-ki-da; *vi.* 낫다 nat-da; 치류하다 chi-ryo-ha-da

health *n.* 건강geon-gang; 위생 wi-saeng; ~ **center** 보건소 bo-geon-so

healthy *adj.* 건강한 geon-gang-han; 건강에 좋은 geon-gang-e jo-eun

heap *n.* 더미 deo-mi; 덩어리 deong-eo-ri; 많음 man-eum

hear *vt.* 듣다 deut-da; 들리다 deul-li-da

hearing *n.* *(sense)* 청각 cheong-gak; 청력 cheong-nyeok; 들어줌 deul-eo-jum; 들리는 거리 deul-li-neun geo-ri; *(court)* 공판 gong-pan; ~ **aid** 보청기 bo-cheong-gi

heart *n.* 심장 sim-jang; 마음 ma-eum; 기분 gi-bun; 애정 ae-jeong; 열의 yeol-ui; 중심 jung-sim; ~ **attack** 심장마비 sim-jang-ma-bi; ~**burn** 속쓰림 sok-sseu-rim; 가슴앓이 ga-seum-al-i; 질투 jil-tu

heartache *n.* 비탄 bi-tan, 비통 bi-tong

hearth *n.* 난로 nal-lo; 온돌 on-dol; 벽난로 byeong-nal-lo ba-dak

heartless *adj.* 무정한 mu-jeong-han, 냉혹한 naeng-ho-kan

hearty *adj.* 진심의 jin-sim-ui; 마음에서 우러나 ma-eum-e-seo u-reo-nan; 기운찬 gi-un-chan; 원기 왕성한 won-gi wang-seong-han; 배부른 bae-bu-reun

heat *n.* 열 yeol; 더위 deo-wi; 열심 yeol-ssim

heater *n.* 히디 hi-teo, 난방시설 nan-bang-jang-chi

heating *n.* 가열 ga-yeol; 난방장치 nan-bang-jang-chi; **central** ~ 중앙난방장치 jung-ang-nan-bang-jang-chi

heaven *n.* 천국 cheon-guk; 하늘 ha-neul

heavy *adj.* 무거운 mu-geo-un; 대량의 dae-ryang-ui; 힘겨운 him-gyeo-un; 중대한 jung-dae-han

heavyduty *adj.* 아주 튼튼한 a-ju tteun-tteun-han; 격무의 gyeong-mu-ui; 고관세의 go-gwan-sse-ui

hedge *n.* 울타리 ul-ta-ri, 장벽 jang-byeok; 장애 jang-ae; 방지책 bang-ji-chaek

heel *n.* 뒤꿈치 dwi-kkum-chi; 발굽 bal-gup; 뒤축 dwi-chuk

height *n.* 높이nop-I; 키 ki; 고도 go-do; 고지 go-ji; 절정 jeol-jjeong

heir *n.* 상속인 sang-sog-in, 계승자 gye-seung-ja, 후계자 hu-gye-ja

heirloom *n.* 가보 ga-bo; 상속물 sang-song-mul

helicopter *n.* 헬리콥터 hel-li-kop-teo

hell *n.* 지옥 ji-ok; 악귀 ak-gwi; **What the ~** 도대체 무슨 일이지 do-de-che mu-seun il-i-ji

hello *n.* 여보세요 yeo-bo-se-yo; 안녕하세요 an-nyeong-ha-se-yo

helm *n.* 키 ki; 조타장치 jo-ta-jang-chi; 지배 ji-bae

helmet *n.* 헬멧 hel-met; 철모 cheol-mo

help *n.* 도움 do-um; 구조수단 gu-jo-su-dan; 고용인 go-yong-in; *vt.* 돕다 dop-da, 거들

다 geo-deul-da; 조장하다 jo-jang-ha-da; **I cannot ~ you** 도와드릴 수가 없습니다 do-wa-deu-ril ssu-ga eop-seum-ni-da

helper *n.* 조력자 jo-ryeok-ja, 원조자 won-jo-ja; 조수 jo-su

helpful *adj.* 도움이 되는 do-um-i doe-neun, 유용한 yu-yong-han; 편리한 pyeol-li-han

helpless *adj.* 어쩔 수 없는 eo-jjeol ssu eom-neun; 도움없는 do-um-eom-neun; 의지할 데 없는 ui-ji-hal tte eom-neun

Helsinki *n.* 헬싱키 hel-ssing-ki

hem *n.* 가두리 ga-du-ri; 감침질 gam-chim-jil; 경계 gyeong-gye

hemisphere *n.* 반구 ban-gu, 반구체 ban-gu-che

hemoglobin *n.* 헤모글로빈 he-mo-geul-lo-bin

hemophilia *n.* 혈우병 hyeol-u-ppyeong

hemophiliac *n.* 혈우병 환자 hyeol-u-ppyeong hwan-ja; *adj.* 혈우병의 hyeol-u-ppyeong-ui

hemorrhoids *n.* 치질 chi-jil

hen *n.* 암탉 am-tak

hence *adv.* 그러므로 geu-reo-meu-ro, 지금부터 ji-geum-bu-teo

henhouse *n.* 닭장 dak-jang

hepatitis *n.* 간염 gan-yeom

her *adj.* 그 (여자)분의 geu (yeo-ja)-bun-ui; *pron.* 그 (여자)분을 geu (yeo-ja)-bun-eul, 그 (여자)분에게 geu (yeo-ja)-bun-e-ge

herb *n.* 풀 pul, 풀잎 pul-lip; 약초 yak-cho; **~ doctor** 한의사 han-ui-sa; **~ tea** 한약 han-yak

herd *n.* 무리 mu-ri, 떼 tte; 군중 gun-jung

here *adv.* 여기 yeo-gi; **around ~** 이 근처에 i geun-cheo-e; **right ~** 바로 여기에 ba-ro yeo-gi-e

heritage *n.* 세습재산 se-seup-jae-san, 유산 yu-san

hernia *n.* 허니아 heo-ni-a, 탈장 tal-jjang

hero *n.* 영웅 yeong-ung; 남자 주인공 nam-ja ju-in-gong

heroic *adj.* 영웅적인 yeong-ung-jeog-in; 용감한 yong-gam-han

heroine *n.* 여걸 yeo-geol, 여주인공 yeo-ju-in-gong

heron *n.* 왜가리 wae-ga-ri

herring *n.* 청어 cheong-eo

hers *pron.* 그 (여자)분의 것 geu (yeo-ja)-bun-ui kkeot

herself *pron.* 그 (여자)분 자신 geu (yeo-ja)-bun ja-sin

hesitate *vt.* 주저하다 ju-jeo-ha-da, 망설이다 mang-seol-i-da

hesitation *n.* 망설임 mang-seol-im, 주저함 ju-jeo-ham

heterosexual *n.* 이성연애자 i-seong-yeon-ae-ja; *adj.* 이성애의 i-seong-ae-ui; 이성의 i-seong-ui

hiccup *n.* 딸꾹질 ttal-kkuk-jjil; *vi.* 딸꾹질하다 ttal-kkuk-jjil-ha-da

hidden *adj.* 숨은 sum-eun, 숨겨진 sum-gyeo-jin, 숨긴 sum-gin

hide *vt.* 숨기다 sum-gi-da; 덮다 deop-da; 비밀로 하다 bi-mil-lo ha-da; *vi.* 숨다 sum-tta

hide-and-seek *n.* 숨바꼭질 sum-ba-kkok-jil

hideaway *n.* 은신처 eun-sin-cheo, 숨은 곳 sum-eun got

hierarchy *n.* 계급조직 gye-geup-jo-jik

high *adj.* 높은 nop-eun; 고위의 go-wi-ui; 고도의 go-do-ui; 고귀한 go-gwi-han; **~ beam** 헤드라이트 he-deu-ra-i-teu

high-class *adj.* 고급의 go-geub-ui, 1급의 il-geub-ui

high-level *adj.* 상급의 sang-geub-ui, 지위가 높은 ji-wi-ga nop-eun

highlight *n.* 가장 흥미있는 부분 ga-jang heung-mi-in-neun bu-bun, 하이라이트 ha-i-ra-i-teu; *vt.* 강조하다 gang-jo-ha-da, 돋보이게 하다 dot-bo-i-ge ha-da

high-priced *adj.* 값비싼 gap-bi-ssan

high-ranking *adj.* 고위직의 go-wi-jig-ui, 높은 계급의 nop-eun gye-geub-ui

high-rise *n.* 고층빌딩 go-cheung-ppil-ding; *adj.* 고층의 go-cheung-ui

high-speed *adj.* 고속의 go-sog-ui, 고속도의 go-sok-do-ui

high-spirited *adj.* 원기왕성한 won-gi-wang-seong-han, 기운찬 gi-un-chan

high-tech *adj.* 첨단기술의 cheom-dan-gi-seul-ui, 하이테크의 ha-i-te-keu-ui

high school *n.* 고등학교 go-deung-hak-gyo

high season *n.* 전성기 jeon-seong-gi, 성수기 seong-su-gi

highway *n.* 고속도로 go-sok-do-ro

hijack vt. 공중납치하다 gong-jung-nap-chi-ha-da, 강탈하다 gang-tal-ha-da; 강요하다 gang-yo-ha-da; n. 공중납치 gong-jung-nap-chi, 항공기 납치 hang-gong-gi nap-chi

hike n. 하이킹 ha-i-king; vi. 하이킹하다 ha-i-king-ha-da

hiker n. 등산객 deung-san-gaek

hiking n. 하이킹 ha-i-king

hill n. 언덕 eon-deok; 작은 산 jag-eun san

hilly adj. 야산이 많은 ya-san-i man-eun

him pron. 그 (남자)분에게 geu (nam-ja)-bun-e-ge, 그 (남자)분을 geu (nam-ja)-bun-eul

Himalayas n. 히말라야산맥 hi-mal-la-ya-san-maek

himself pron. 그 (남자)분 자신 geu (nam-ja)-bun ja-sin

hinder vt. 방해하다 bang-hae-ha-da, 훼방하다 hwe-bang-ha-da

Hindi n. 힌디어 hin-di-eo

Hindu n. 힌두교도 hin-du-gyo-do; adj. 힌두교의 hin-du-gyo-ui

hinge n. 경첩 gyeong-cheop; 요점 yo-jjeom; vt. 경첩을 달다 gyeong-cheob-eul dal-da; ...에 의해서 정하다 ...e ui-hae-seo jeong-ha-da

hint n. 힌트 hin-teu, 암시 am-si; 주의 ju-i; vi. 넌지시 말하다 neon-ji-si mal-ha-da; 암시하다 am-si-ha-da

hip n. 골반 gol-ban, 엉덩이 eong-deong-i; 찔레열매 jjil-le-yeol-mae; 우물 u-ul

hippo n. 하마 ha-ma

hire vt. 고용하다 go-yong-ha-da; 임대하다 im-dae-ha-da

his pron. 그 (남자)분의 geu (nam-ja)-bun-ui; 그 (남자)분의 것 geu (nam-ja)-bun-ui kkeot

historical adj. 역사상의 yeok-sa-sang-ui; 역사적인 yeok-sa-jeog-in

history n. 역사 yeok-sa; 경력 gyeong-nyeok; 유래 yu-rae

hit n. 타격 ta-gyeok; 적중 jeok-jung; 성공 seong-gong; 명언 myeong-eon; 안타 an-ta

hitchhike vi. 히치하이크하다 hi-chi-ha-i-keu-ha-da

hitchhiker n. 히치하이커 hi-chi-ha-i-keo

hive n. 벌집 beol-jjip; 벌통 beol-tong

hives n. 발진 bal-jjin, 두드러기 du-deu-reo-gi

hoarse adj. 목이 쉰 mog-i swi; 쉰 목소리의 swin mok-so-ri-ui

hobby n. 취미 chwi-mi

hockey n. 하키 ha-ki

hoe n. 괭이 gwaeng-i

hoist vt. 내걸다 nae-geol-da; 끌어올리다 kkeul-eo-ol-li-da

hold n. 파악 pa-ak; 장악 jang-ak; 손잡이 son-jab-i; 예약 ye-yak; 이해 i-hae; 보류 bo-ryu; vt. 갖고있다 gat-go-it-da; 주장하다 ju-jang-ha-da; 생각하다 saeng-ga-ka-da; 유지하다 yu-ji-ha-da; 멈추게 하다 meom-chu-ge ha-da; 열다 yeol-da; 수용하다 su-yong-ha-da

hole n. 구멍 gu-meong, 굴 gul; 함정 ham-jeong; 결함 gyeol-ham; (golf) 홀 hol

holiday n. 휴일 hyu-il; 휴가 hyu-ga

Holland n. 네덜란드 ne-del-lan-deu

hollow adj. 속이 빈 sog-i bin, 우묵한 u-mu-kan; 공허한 gong-heo-han

hologram n. 홀로그램 hol-lo-geu-raem

holy adj. 신성한 sin-seong-han; 경건한 gyeong-geon-han

holy day n. 종교상의 축제일 jong-gyo-sang-ui chuk-je-il

home n. 가정 ga-jeong; 집 jip, 자택 ja-taek; 고향 go-hyang; 본국 bon-guk; at ~ 집에서 jib-e-seo; go ~ 집에 가다 jib-e ga-da; ~made 집에서 만든 jib-eo-seo man-deun; 집에서 만든 것 jib-e-seo man-deun geot

homecoming n. 귀가 gwi-ga, 귀성 gwi-seong, 귀국gwi-guk; 동창회 dong-chang-hoe

home ground n. 홈 그라운드 hom geu-ra-un-deu, 본거지 bon-geo-ji

homeland n. 고국 go-guk, 모국 mo guk, 본국 bon-guk

homeless adj. 집없는 jib-eom-neun

homeowner n. 집주인 jip-ju-in

homepage n. 홈페이지 hom-pe-i-ji

homesick adj. 향수병의 hyang-su-ppyeong-ui

homesickness n. 향수 hyang-su; 향수병 hyang-su-ppyeong

hometown n. 고향마을 go-hyang-ma-eul, 고향도시 go-hyang-do-si

homework n. 숙제 suk-jje

homosexual *n.* 동성연애자 dong-seong-yeon-ae-ja; *adj.* 동성애의 dong-seong-ae-ui; 동성의 dong-seong-ui

honest *adj.* 정직한 jeong-ji-kan; 공정한 gong-jeong-han; 순수한 sun-su-han

honesty *n.* 정직 jeong-jik, 성실 soeng-sil

honey *n.* 벌꿀 beol-kkul

honeymoon *n.* 신혼여행 sin-hon-yeo-haeng; 신혼기간 sin-hon-gi-gan

Hong Kong *n.* 홍콩 hong-kong

honor *n.* 명예 myeong-ye; 체면 che-myeon; 자존심 ja-jon-sim; 경의 gyeong-ui; 우등 u-deung; 정조 jeong-jo; *vt.* 존경하다 jon-gyeong-ha-da; 존중하다 jon-jung-ha-da; 명예롭게 하다 myeong-ye-rop-ge ha-da

hood *n.* 후드 hu-deu

hook *n.* 갈고리 gal-go-ri; 훅 huk; 코바늘 ko-ba-neul; 올가미 ol-ga-mi

hoop *n.* 굴렁쇠 gul-leong-soe; 후프 hu-peu; 테 te

hop *vi.* 깡충 뛰다 kkang-chung-ttwi-da; *vt.* 뛰어넘다 ttwi-eo-neom-tta; *n.* 깡충 뜀 kkang-chung-ttwim; 홉 hop

hope *n.* 희망 hi-mang; 가망 ga-mang; *vt.* 희망하다 hi-mang-ha-da; 기대하다 gi-dae-ha-da

hopeful *adj.* 희망이 있는 hi-mang-i in-neun

hopeless *adj.* 희망이 없는 hi-mang-i eom-neun; 절망적인 jeol-mang-jeog-in

horizon *n.* 수평선 su-pyeong-seon; 지평선 ji-pyeong-seon

horizontal *adj.* 수평의 su-pyeong-ui; 평평한 pyeong-pyeong-han; 가로의 ga-ro-ui

horn *n.* 뿔 ppul; 뿔피리 ppul-pi-ri; 경적 gyeong-jeok; **shoe**~ 신발주걱 sin-bal-jju-geok

horrible *adj.* 무서운 mu-seo-un; 지겨운 ji-gyeo-un

horror *n.* 공포 gong-po; 혐오 hyeom-o

hors-d'oeuvre *n.* 전채요리 jeon-chae-yo-ri

horse *n.* 말 mal; **on ~back** 말을 타고 mal-eul ta-go; **~power** 마력 ma-ryeok; **~ race** 경마 gyeong-ma; **~shoe** 편자 pyeon-ja, 말굽 mal-gup

hose *n.* 호스 ho-seu; 스타킹 seu-ta-king

hospitable *adj.* 호의적인 ho-ui-jeog-in; 극진한 geuk-jin-han

hospital *n.* 병원 byeong-won; 구호소 gu-ho-so

hospitality *n.* 환대 hwan-dae, 후대 hu-dae

host *n.* 주인 ju-in; 주최자 ju-coe-ja; 군중 gun-jung; 성체 seong-che; *vt.* 주최하다 ju-choe-ha-da; 주인노릇하다 ju-in-no-reu-ta-da

hostage *n.* 볼모 bol-mo, 인질 in-jil; 저당물 jeo-dang-mul, 담보 dam-bo; **to hold someone ~** ...을 인질로 잡다 ...eul in-jil-lo jap-da

hostel *n.* 호스텔 ho-seu-tel; **youth ~** 유스호스텔 yu-sseu-ho-seu-tel

hostess *n.* 여주인 yeo-ju-in; 접대부 jeop-dae-bu, 호스테스 ho-seu-te-sseu

hostile *adj.* 적대적인 jeok-dae-jeog-in; 냉담한 naeng-dam-han

hot-tempered *adj.* 성급한 seong-geu-pan, 화를 잘내는 hwa-reul jal-lae-neun

hot *adj.* 뜨거운 tteu-geo-un; 열렬한 yeol-lyeol-han; 격렬한 gyeong-nyeol-han; **~ tub** 온탕 on-tang; **~ dog** 핫도그 hat-do-geu; **~ line** 핫라인 hat-la-in; **~ pepper** 고추 go-chu; **~ spring** 온천 on-cheon

hotel *n.* 호텔 ho-tel; 여관 yeo-gwan

hour *n.* 시간 si-gan; 시 si; **per ~** 한시간에 han-si-gan-e, 시간당 si-gan-dang

house *n.* 집 jip, 주택 ju-taek; 의회 ui-hoe; 회의장 hoe-i-jang

household *n.* 가족 ga-jok; 세대 se-dae; 한집안 han-jib-an

housekeeper *n.* 가정부 ga-jeong-bu; 주부 ju-bu

house-sit *vi.* 집을 봐주다 jib-eul bwa-ju-da

house-to-house *adj.* 집집마다의 jip-jim-ma-da-ui

housewarming *n.* 집들이 jip-deul-i

housewife *n.* 전업주부 jeon-eop-ju-bu

housework *n.* 가사 ga-sa, 집안일 jib-an-nil

how *adv.* 어떻게 eo-tteo-ke, 어떤 방법으로 eo-tteon bang-beob-eu-ro, ...하는 방법 ...ha-neun bang-beop, 어떤 상태로 eo-tteon sang-tae-ro, 어떤 이유로 eo-tteon i-yu-ro, 어느 정도 eo-neu jeong-do, 참으로 cham-eu-ro; 어떻게 해서든지 eo-tteo-ke hae-seo-deun-ji

however *adv.* 아무리 ... 어도 a-mu-ri ...a-do, 아무리 ... 어도 a-mu-ri ... eo-do 그렇지만 geu-reo-chi-man; **I will no**

longer be here, ~ 그렇지만 저는 더이상 여기에 없을 것입니다geu-reo-chi-man jeo-neun deo-i-sang yeo-gi-e eops-eul geos-im-ni-da); *conj.* 어떤 방법으로라 도 eo-tteon bang-beob-eu-ro-ra-do; **We will help ~ we can** 우리가 할 수 있는 것 은 어떤 것이라도 돕겠습니다 u-ri-ga hal ssu in-neun geos-eun eo-tteon geos-i-ra-do dop-get-seum-ni-da

hug *n.* 포옹 po-ong; 껴안기 kkyeo-an-kki; *vt.* 포옹하다 po-ong-ha-da, 껴안다kkyeo-an-tta; 품다 pum-tta; 고집하다 go-ji-pa-da

huge *adj.* 거대한 geo-dae-han

human *adj.* 인간의 in-gan-ui; 인간적인 in-gan-jeog-in; ~ **being** 인간 in-gan, 인류 il-lyu; ~ **rights** 인권 in-kkwon

humane *adj.* 자비로운 ja-bi-ro-un; 우아한 u-a-han; 인문학의 in-mun-hag-ui

humanity *n.* 인류 il-lyu; 인간성 in-gan-sseong; 인간애 in-gan-ae

humble *adj.* 비천한 bi-cheon-han; 초라한 cho-ra-han; 겸손한 gyeom-son-han

humid *adj.* 습도가 높은 seup-do-ga nop-eun; 축축한 chuk-chu-kan

humidity *n.* 습기 seup-gi; 습도 seup-do

humiliate *vt.* 굴욕감을 느끼게 하다 gul-yok-gam-eul neu-kki-ge ha-da, 창피를 주 다 chang-pi-reul ju-da

humor *n.* 유머 yu-meo, 익살 ik-sal, 해학hae-hak; 변덕 byeon-deok; **to have a sense of** ~ 유머가 있다 yu-meo-ga it-da

humorous *adj.* 익살스러운 ik-sal-seu-reo-un, 해학적인 hae-hak-jeog-in, 재미있는 jae-mi-in-neun

hump *n.* 군살 gun-sal; 혹 hok; 난관 nan-gwan

hundred *num.* 백 baek

hundredth *adj.* 백번째의 baek-beon-jjae-ui, 제백회 je-bae-koe-ui

Hungary *n.* 헝가리 heong-ga-ri

hunger *n.* 배고픔 bae-go-peum; 갈망 gal-mang

hungry *adj.* 배고픈 bae-go-peun; 갈망하는 gal-mang-ha-neun

hunt *n.* 사냥 sa-nyang; 수렵대 su-ryeop-dae; 수렵지구 su-ryeop-ji-gu; 수색 su-saek; *vt.* 사냥하다 sa-nyang-ha-da; 추적하다 chu-jeo-ka-da; 찾다 chat-da; **to ~ for** 사냥 하다 sa-nyang-ha-da; 찾아 헤메다 chaj-a he-me-da

hunter *n.* 사냥꾼 sa-nyang-kkun; 사냥개 sa-nyang-kkae; 탐구자 tam-gu-ja

hurray *interj.* 만세 man-se

hurricane *n.* 폭풍 pok-pung, 허리케인 heo-ri-ke-in

hurry *n.* 급함 geu-pam, 서두름 seo-du-reum

hurt *n.* 부상 bu-sang; 상처 sang-cheo; 손 해 son-hae; 고통 go-tong; *vt.* 상처를 내 다 sang-cheo-reul nae-da; 다치게 하다 da-chi-ge ha-da; 감정을 상하게 하다 gam-jeong-eul sang-ha-ge ha-da; *vi.* 아프 다 a-peu-da; 불쾌하다 bul-kwae-ha-da; 다 치다 da-chi-da; **It ~s** 아픕니다 a-peum-ni-da; **Don't ~ him** 그분을 아프게 하 지 마십시오 geu bun-eul a-peu-ge ha-ji ma-sip-si-o

husband *n. (one's own)* 남편 nam-pyeon; *(another's)* 부군 bu-gun

husky *adj.* 껍질의 kkeop-jil-ui; 바짝 마 른 ba-jjak ma-reun; 쉰 목소리의 swin mok-so-ri-ui; 건장한 geon-jang-han, 억 센 eok-sen

hut *n.* 오두막 o-du-mak

hybrid *n.* 잡종 jap-jong, 혼성물 hon-seong-mul

hydrant *n.* 소화전 so-hwa-jeon

hymn *n.* 찬송가 chan-song-ga; 성가 seong-ga

hyphen *n.* 하이픈 ha-i-peun

I

I *pron.* 내가 nae-ga, 나는 na-neun; 제가 je-ga, *(hum.)* 저는 jeo-neun

ice *n.* 얼음 eol-eum; *vt.* 얼리다 eol-li-da; 얼음 으로 식히다 eol-eum-eu-ro si-ki-da, 얼음 으로 덮다 eol-eum-eu-ro deop-da; **~cold** 얼음처럼 차가운 eol-eum-cheo-reom

cha-ga-un; 냉담한 naeng-dam-han; **~d tea** 아이스티 a-i-seu-ti; **to ~ up** 얼음으로 덮 다 eol-eum-eu-ro deop-da; 얼음이 끼다 eol-eum-i kki-da; ~ **hockey** 아이스하키 a-i-seu-ha-ki

ice cream *n.* 아이스크림 a-i-seu-keu-rim

Iceland *n.* 아이스랜드 a-i-seu-lan-deu
ice rink *n.* 실내 스케이트장 sil-lae
  seu-ke-i-teu-jang
ice skate *n.* 스케이트 seu-ke-i-teu
ice water *n.* 얼음물 eol-eum-mul, 찬물
  chan-mul
icicle *n.* 고드름 go-deu-rem
icon *n.* *(religious)* 성상 seong-sang, *(figura-
  tive)* 초상 cho-sang, 상 sang; *(computer)*
  아이콘 a-i-kon
icy *adj.* 얼음의 eol-eum-ui; 차가운 cha-ga-
  un; 쌀쌀한 ssal-ssal-han
idea *n.* 생각 saeng-gak; 관념 gwan-nyeom;
  의식 ui-sik; 인식 in-sik; 의견 ui-gyeon; 계
  획 gye-hoek; 사상 sa-sang
ideal *n.* 이상 i-sang; 관념 gwan-nyeom; *adj.*
  이상의 i-sang-ui; 관념적인 gwan-nyeom-
  jeog-in; 공상적인 gong-sang-jeog-in
identical *adj.* 동일한 dong-il-han; 일치하는
  il-chi-ha-neun
identification *n.* *abbr.* *ID* 동일시 dong-il-si;
  인정 in-jeong; 확인 hwag-in; **photo ~**
  (사진이 붙은) 신분증 (sa-jin-i but-eun)
  sin-bun-jjeung
identify *vt.* 동일시하다 dong-il-si-ha-da; 확
  인하다 hwag-in-ha-da
identity *n.* 신원 sin-won; 동일시 dong-il-si;
  본성 bon-seong
idiom *n.* 숙어 sug-eo, 관용구
  gwan-yong-kku
idiot *n.* 바보 ba-bo, 천치 chon-chi
idle *adj.* 게으른 ge-eu-reun; 한가한 han-ga-
  han; 쓸모없는 sseul-mo-eom-neun
idol *n.* 우상 u-sang
if *conj.* 만약...이면 man-yak...i-myeon, 비
  록...일지라도 bi-rok...il-jji-ra-do, ...할 때
  는 언제나 ...hal ttae-neun eon-je-na, ...인
  지 아닌지 ...in-ji a-nin-ji; **~ so** 만일 그렇
  다면 man-il geu-reo-ta-myeon
ignite *vt.* 불을 붙이다 bul-eul bu-chi-da, 연
  소시키다 yeon-so-si-ki-da
ignition *n.* 점화 jeom-hwa; 연소 yeon-so; 점
  화장치 jeom-hwa-jang-chi
ignorance *n.* 무지 mu-ji
ignorant *adj.* 무지한 mu-ji-han; 모르는
  mo-reu-neun
ignore *vt.* 무시하다 mu-si-ha-da, 묵살하다
  muk-sal-ha-da

ill *adj.* 병든 byeong-deul-da; 나쁜 na-ppeun
illegal *adj.* 불법적인 bul-ppeop-jeog-in
illegible *adj.* 읽기 어려운 il-kki eo-ryeo-un;
  불명료한 bul-myeong-nyo-han
illiterate *adj.* 무식한 mu-si-kan; 문맹의
  mun-maeng-ui
illness *n.* 병 pyeong; 불쾌 bul-kwae
illumination *n.* 조명 jo-myeong; 계몽 gye-
  mong; 해명 hae-myeong
illusion *n.* 환상 hwan-sang; 착각 chak-gak;
  환각 hwan-gak
illustrate *vt.* 설명하다 seol-myeong-ha-da,
  삽화를 넣다 sa-pwa-reul neo-ta
illustration *n.* 삽화 sa-pwa; 실례 sil-lye, 예
  증 ye-jeung
image *n.* 모습 mo-seup; 초상 cho-sang; 닮
  음 dalm-eum; 영상 yeong-sang; 이미지
  i-mi-ji; 상징 sang-jing
imagination *n.* 상상 sang-sang; 상
  상력 sang-sang-nyeok; 창작력
  chang-jang-nyeok
imagine *vt.* 상상하다 sang-sang-ha-da; 추측
  하다 chu-cheu-ka-da
imitate *vt.* 모방하다 mo-bang-ha-da, 흉
  내내다 hyung-nae-nae-da; 모조하다
  mo-jo-ha-da
imitation *n.* 모방 mo-bang; 모조 mo-jo; 모
  조품 mo-jo-pum
immature *adj.* 미숙한 mi-su-kan, 미완성의
  mi-wan-seong-ui
immediate *adj.* 즉각의 jeuk-gag-ui; 직접의
  jik-jeob-ui; 당면한 dang-myeon-han; 아주
  가까운 a-ju ga-kka-un
immediately *adv.* 곧 got, 즉각 jeuk-gak,
  즉시 jeuk-si; 직접 jik-jeop; 인접하여
  in-jeo-pa-yeo
immense *adj.* 막대한 mak-dae-han; 끝이 없
  는 kkeu-chi-eom-neun
immigrant *n.* 이민 i-min, 이주자 i-ju-ja; 외
  래식물 oe-rae-sing-mul
immigrate *vt., vi.* 이주하다 i-ju-ha-da, 이주
  시키다 i-ju-si-ki-da
imminent *adj.* 절박한 jeol-ba-kan, 곧 닥칠
  got dak-chil
immobilize *vt.* 고정시키다 go-jeong-si-ki-da,
  정지시키다 jeong-ji-si-ki-da
immoral *adj.* 비도덕적인 bi-do-deok-jeog-
  in; 음란한 eum-nan-han

immortal *adj.* 죽지 않는 juk-ji-an-neun; 불후의 bul-hu-ui; 영원한 yeong-won-han

immunization *n.* 면역 myeon-yeok, 면역조치 myeon-yeok-jo-chi, 예방접종 ye-bang-jeop-jong

impact *n.* 충돌 chung-dol, 충격 chung-gyeok

impasse *n.* 막다른 골목 mak-da-reun gol-mok; 난국 nan-guk

impatient *adj.* 참을성이 없는 cham-eul-sseong-i eom-neun; 몹시 하고 싶어하는 mop-si ha-go-sip-eo-ha-neun

impending *adj.* 인박한 im-ba-kan, 절박한 jeol-ba-kan

imperfect *adj.* 불완전한 bul-wan-jeon-han; 미완료의 mi-wal-lyo-ui

implant *vt.* 심나 sim-tta; 수입하나 ju-i-pa-da; 박아넣다 bag-a-neo-ta; 이식하다 i-si-ka-da

implement *n.* 도구 do-gu; 수단 su-dan, 방법 bang-beop; *vt.* 도구를 공급하다 do-gu-reul gong-geu-pa-da; 권한을 주다 gwon-han-eul ju-da; 약속을 이행하다 yak-sog-eul i-haeng-ha-da; 조건을 충족하다 jo-kkeon-eul chung-jo-ka-da

implication *n.* 내포 nae-po, 암시 am-si

imply *vt.* 함축하다 ham-chu-ka-da; 의미하다 ui-mi-ha-da; 포함하다 po-ham-ha-da

impolite *adj.* 무례한 mu-rye-han

import *n.* 수입 su-ip; 수입품 su-i-pum; 취지 wi-ji ch; *vt.* 수입하다 su-i-pa-da; 의미를 내포하다 ui-mi-reul nae-po-ha-da; 중요하다 jung-yo-ha-da; ~ **duty** 수입관세 su-ip-gwan-se

importance *n.* 중유성 jung-yo-sseong; 중요한 지위 jung-yo-han ji-wi; 중요한 일 jung-yo-han il; 거느름 삐눔 geo-deu-reum pi-um

important *adj.* 중요한 jung-yo-han; 거드름을 피우는 geo-deu-reum-eul pi-u-neun

impose *vt.* 부과하다 bu-gwa-ha-da; 강요하다 gang-yo-ha-da; 속여팔다 sog-yeo-pal-da

impossible *adj.* 불가능한 bul-ga-neung-han; 믿기 어려운 mit-gi eo-ryeo-un; 참을 수 없는 cham-eul ssu eom-neun

impotent *adj.* 무기력한 mu-gi-ryeo-kan; 허약한 heo-ya-kan

impress *vt.* 감명을 주다 gam-myeong-eul ju-da; 인상을 주다 in-sang-eul ju-da; 도장을 찍다 do-jang-eul jjik-da; 자국을 남기다 ja-gug-eul nam-gi-da

impressive *adj.* 인상적인 in-sang-jeog-in; 감동적인 gam-dong-jeog-in

imprint *vt.* 찍다 jjik-da; 인쇄하다 in-swae-ha-da; 감동을 주다 gam-dong-eul ju-da; 마음에 남기다 ma-eum-e nam-gi-da

imprison *vt.* 감금하다 gam-geum-ha-da; 수용하다 su-yong-ha-da

improper *adj.* 부적당한 bu-jeok-dang-han; 부도덕한 bu-do-deo-kan

improve *vt.* 개선하다 gae-seon-ha-da; 이용하다 i-yong-ha-da; *vi.* 좋아지다 jo-a-ji-da

improvement *n.* 개선 gae-seon; 개선섬 gae-seon-jjeom; 향상 hyang-sang; 이용 i-yong

improvise *vt.* 즉석에서 하다 jeuk-seog-e-seo ha-da

impulse *n.* 추진 chu-jin; 추진력 chu-jin-nyeok; 충격 chung-gyeok; 충동 chung-dong; **on** ~ 충동적으로 chung-dong-jeog-eu-ro

in *prep.* ...안에 ...an-e, ...안에서 ...an-e-seo, ...에 있어서 ...e iss-eo-seo, ...쪽으로 ...jjog-eu-ro, ...쪽에 ...jjog-e, ...을 타고 ...eul ta-go, ...중 ...jung, ...의 상태로 ...ui sang-tae-ro, ...속에서 ...sog-e-seo, ...을 입고 ...eul ip-go, ...동안 ...dong-an, ...사이에 ...sa-i-e, ...지나면 ...ji-na-myeon, ...마다 ...ma-da, ...으로 ...eu-ro, ...을 이루어 ...eul i-ru-eo, ...때문에 ...ttae-mun-e, ...의 목적으로 ...ui mok-jeog-eu-ro, ...하므로 ...ha-meu-ro; *(location)* ~ **the house** 집에서 jib-e-seo; *(time)* ~ **two weeks** 누수농안 du-ju-ttong-an, ~ **summer** 여름에 yeo-reum-e; *(manner)* ~ **French** 프랑스어로 peu-rang-sseu-eo-ro; *(state)* ~ **good condition** 좋은 조건에서 jo-eun jo-kkeon-e-seo, ~ **a mess** 어지럽혀진 상태로 eo-ji-reo-pyeo-jin sang-tae-ro; **Is Mr. Lee** ~ 이선생님 계십니까 i-seon-saeng-nim gye-sim-ni-kka; **Come** ~ 들어오십시오 deul-eo-o-sip-si-o

inability *n.* 무능 mu-neung; 무력 mu-ryeok

inaccessible *adj.* 가까이하기 어려운 ga-kka-i-ha-gi eo-ryeo-un

inactive *adj.* 활발하지 않은 hwal-bal-ha-ji an-eun; 한가한 han-ga-han

inadequate *adj.* 부적절한 bu-jeok-jeol-han; 불충분한 bul-chung-bun-han

inappropriate *adj.* 부적절한 bu-jeok-jeol-han, 온당치 못한 on-dang-chi mo-tan

inaugurate *vt.* 취임식을 거행하다 chwi-im-sig-eul geo-haeng-ha-da; 낙성식을 열다 nak-seong-sig-eul yeol-da; 개관하다 gae-gwan-ha-da

inauguration *n.* 취임식 chwi-im-sik; 낙성식 nak-seong-sik; 개관식 gae-gwan-sik; 취임 chwi-im; 개업 gae-eop; 개시 gae-si

in-between *adj.* 중간적인 jung-gan-jeog-in, 중간의 jung-gan-ui

inborn *adj.* 타고난 ta-go-nan, 천부적인 cheon-bu-jeog-in

inbound *adj.* 귀향하는 gwi-hyang-ha-neun, 본국행의 bon-gu-kaeng-ui; 시내로 가는 si-nae-ro ga-neun

incapable *adj.* 할 수 없는 hal ssu eom-neun, 자격이 없는 ja-gyeog-i eom-neun

incentive *n.* 자극 ja-geuk; 유인 yu-in; 동기 dong-gi; *adj.* 자극적인 ja-geuk-jeog-in, 격려하는 gyeong-nyeo-ha-neun

inch *n.* 인치 in-chi

incident *n.* 일어난 일 il-eo-nan nil, 사건 sa-kkeon; *adj.* 일어나기 쉬운 il-eo-na-gi swi-un, 있기 쉬운 it-gi-swi-un

incidentally *adv.* 부수적으로 bu-su-jeog-eu-ro, 우연히 u-yeon-hi; 말하자면 mal-ha-ja-myeon

inclination *n.* 경사 gyeong-sa; 경향 gyeong-hyang; 선호 seon-ho

incline *n.* 경사 gyeong-sa; 비탈 bi-tal; 케이블카 ke-i-beul-ka; *vi.* 기울이다 gi-ul-i-da; 마음내키게 하다 ma-eum-nae-ki-ge ha-da

include *vt.* 포함하다 po-ham-ha-da; **including** ... 을 포함하여 ... eul po-ham-ha-yeo, ... 를 포함하여 ... reul po-ham-ha-yeo

income *n.* 수입 su-ip, 소득 so-deuk; ~ **tax** 소득세 so-deuk-se

incommunicable *adj.* 말로 할 수 없는 mal-lo hal ssu eom-neun

incomparable *adj.* 비교할 수 없는 bi-gyo-hal ssu eom-neun

incompetent *adj.* 무능력한 mu-neung-nyeo-kan; 부적당한 bu-jeok-dang-han

incomplete *adj.* 불완전한 bul-wan-jeon-han, 불충분한 bul-chung-bun-han

inconceivable *adj.* 상상할 수 없는 sang-sang-hal ssu eom-neun

inconsequence *n.* 모순 mo-sun, 불합리 bul-ham-ni, 부조화 bu-jo-hwa

inconsiderate *adj.* 인정없는 in-jeong-eom-neun; 지각없는 ji-gag-eom-neun

inconsistency *n.* 불일치 bul-il-chi, 모순 mo-sun

inconstant *adj.* 변덕스러운 byeon-deok-seu-reo-un, 신의가 없는 sin-ui-ga eom-neun

inconvenient *adj.* 불편한 bul-pyeon-han, 부자유스러운 bu-ja-yu-seu-reo-un

incorporate *vt.* 통합시키다 tong-hap-si-ki-da, 법인조직을 만들다 beob-in-jo-jig-eul man-deul-da

incorrect *adj.* 부정확한 bu-jeong-hwa-kan; 부적당한 bu-jeok-dang-han

increase *n.* 증가 jeung-ga; 증가액 jeung-ga-aek; 증가물 jeung-ga-mul; *vi.* 늘다 neul-da; 강해지다 gang-hae-ji-da

incredible *adj.* 믿어지지 않는 mid-eo-ji-ji an-neun; 놀라운 nol-la-un

incubator *n.* 인큐베이터 in-kyu-be-i-teo

incurable *adj.* 불치의 bul-chi-ui; 구제불능의 gu-je-bul-leung-ui

indebted *adj.* 부채가 있는 bu-chae-ga in-neun, 빚진 bit-jin

indeed *adv.* 정말로 jeong-mal-lo; 과연 gwa-yeon; 게다가 ge-da-ga

indefinite *adj.* 분명하지 않은 bun-myeong-ha-ji an-eun, 애매한 ae-mae-han, 막연한 mag-yeon-han

independence *n.* 독립 dong-nip; 독립심 dong-nip-sim

independent *adj.* 독립한 dong-ni-pan; 독자적인 dok-ja-jeog-in; 자활할 수 있는 ja-hwal-hal ssu in-neun; 속박되지 않은 sok-bak-doe-ji an-eun

in-depth *adj.* 면밀한 myeon-mil-han, 상세한 sang-se-han, 철저한 cheol-jjeo-han

index *n.* 인덱스 in-dek-seu; 색인 saeg-in; 지표 ji-pyo, 집게손가락 jip-ge son-kka-rak; 지수 ji-su; *vt.* 색인을 붙이다 saeg-in-eul bu-chi-da; 색인에 넣다 saeg-in-e neo-ta

India *n.* 인디아 in-di-a, 인도 in-do

Indian *n.* 인도사람 in-do-ssa-ram; *adj.* 인도의 in-do-ui

Indian Ocean *n.* 인도양 in-do-yang

indicate *vt.* 가리키다 ga-ri-ki-da; 지적하다 ji-jeo-ka-da; 표시하다 pyo-si-ha-da; 암시하다 am-si-ha-da

indicator *n.* 지시자 ji-si-ja; 인디케이터 in-di-ke-i-teo; 지시약 ji-si-yak

indifferent *adj.* 무관심한 mu-gwan-sim-han; 중요치 않은 jung-yo-chi an-eun; 평범한 pyeong-beom-han

indigestion *n.* 소화불량 so-hwa-bul-lyang; 이해부족 i-hae-bu-jok

indignation *n.* 분개 bun-gae, 분노 bun-no

indignity *n.* 경멸 gyeong myeol, 모욕 mo yok; 냉대 naeng-dae

indirect *adj.* 간접의 gan-jeob-ui, 우회적인 u-hoe-jeog-in; 솔직하지 못한 sol-jji-ka-ji mo-tan

indiscipline *n.* 무질서 mu-jil-sseo, 무규율 mu-gyu-yul

indistinctive *adj.* 희미한 hi-mi-han, 흐릿한 heu-ri-tan

individual *n.* 개인 gae-in; 개체 gae-che; *adj.* 개인적인 gae-in-jeog-in; 개인의 gae-in-ui; 독특한 dok-teu-kan

Indonesia *n.* 인도네시아 in-do-ne-si-a

Indonesian *n.* 인도네시아사람 in-do-ne-si-a-ssa-ram; *adj.* 인도네시아의 in-do-ne-si-a-ui

indoor *adj.* 실내의 sil-lae-ui

industrial *adj.* 공업의 gong-eob-ui 공업용의 gong-eom-nyong-ui; 산업의 san-eob-ui; 산업용의 san-eom-nyong-ui

industrious *adj.* 근면한 geun-myeon-han, 부지런한 bu-ji-reon-han

industry *n.* 공업 gong-eop; 산업 san-eop; 공업계 gong-eop-kkye; 산업계 san-eop-kkye; 근면 geun-myeon

inedible *adj.* 먹을 수 없는 meog-eul ssu eom-neun

ineffective *adj.* 효과가 없는 hyo-kkwa-ga eom-neun, 쓸모없는 sseul-mo eom-neun; 무능한 mu-neung-han, 무력한 mu-ryeo-kan

inefficient *adj.* 비능률적인 bi-neung-nyul-jjeog-in; 쓸모없는 sseul-mo-eom-neun

inevitable *adj.* 피할 수 없는 pi-hal ssu eom-neun, 필연적인 pil-yeon-jeog-in; 변함없는 byeon-ham-eom-neun

inexpensive *adj.* 값싼 gap-ssan; 비용이 들지 않는 bi-yong-i deul-ji an-neun

infant *n.* 유아 yu-a; *adj.* 유아의 yu-a-ui; 유치한 yu-chi-han; 초기의 cho-gi-ui

infect *vt.* 감염시키다 gam-yeom-si-ki-da; 영향을 미치다 yeong-hyang-eul mi-chi-da; 나쁜 물을 들이다 na-ppeun mul-eul deul-i-da

infection *n.* 감염 gam-yeom; 나쁜 영향 na-ppeun yeong-hyang; 전염병 jeon-yeom-ppyeong

infectious *adj.* 전염하는 jeon-yeom-ha-neun, 전연성의 jeon-yeom-sseong-ui

inferior *adj.* 하위의 ha-wi-ui; 떨어지는 tteol-eo-ji-neun; 하등의 ha-deung-ui

infinite *adj.* 무한한 mu han han, 끝없는 kkeud-eom-neun

inflamed *adj.* 불타오르는 bul-ta-o-reu-neun; 성난 seong-nan; 염증이 생긴 yeom-jjeung-i saeng-gin

inflammable *adj.* 타기 쉬운 ta-gi swi-un; 흥분하기 쉬운 heung-bun-ha-gi swi-un

inflammation *n.* 점화 jeom-hwa; 연소 yeon-so; 염증 yeom-jjeung

inflatable *adj.* 부풀린 bu-pul-lin; 팽창된 paeng-chang-doen; 과장된 gwa-jang-doen

inflation *n.* 인플레이션 in-peul-le-i-syeon; 팽창 paeng-chang; 과장 gwa-jang

influence *n.* 영향 yeong-hyang; 효과 hyo-kkwa; 세력 se-ryeok

influenza *n.* 독감 dok-gam

inform *vt.* 알리다 al-li-da; 불어넣다 bul eo neo-ta; 정통하다 jeong-tong-ha-da

information *n.* 정보 jeong-bo; 통지 tong-ji; 지식 ji-sik; 안내 an-nae

infringe *vt.* 어기다 eo-gi-da, 위반하다 wi-ban-ha-da; 침해하다 chim-hae-ha-da

ingenious *adj.* 재능이 있는 jae-neung-in-neun; 교묘한 gyo-myo-han, 정교한 jeong-gyo-han

ingredient *n.* 성분 seong-bun; 재료 jae-ryo 요인 yo-in

inhabit *vt.* 살다 sal-da; 서식하다 seo-si-ka-da

inhabitant *n.* 주민 ju-min; 서식동물 seo-sik-dong-mul

inhale *vt.* 빨다 ppal-da; 흡입히다 heub-i-pa-da

inhaler *n.* 흡입자 heub-ip-ja; *(medical)* 흡입기 heub-ip-gi; 호흡용 마스크 ho-heum-nyong ma-seu-keu

inherit *vt.* 상속하다 sang-so-ka-da; 이어받다 i-eo-bat-da; 인계받다 in-gye-bat-da

inheritance *n.* 상속 sang-sok; 유산 yu-san; 유전 yu-jeon

in-house *adj.* 조직 내의 jo-jik nae-ui, 사내의 sa-nae-ui

inhuman *adj.* 몰인정한 mol-in-jeong-han, 잔인한 jan-in-han, 비인간적인 bi-in-gan-jeog-in

initial *n.* 머릿글자 meo-rit-geul-jja, 이니셜 i-nil-syeol; *adj.* 처음의 cheo-eum-ui; 머릿글자의 meo-rit-geul-jja-ui; *vt.* 머릿글자로 서명하다 meo-rit-geul-jja-ro seo-myeong-ha-da; 가조인하다 ga-jo-in-ha-da

initiative *n.* 발의 bal-ui; 솔선 sol-sseon; 창의 chang-ui; 선제 seon-je

inject *vt.* 주사하다 ju-sa-ha-da; 주입하다 ju-i-pa-da; 삽입하다 sab-i-pa-da

injection *n.* 주사 ju-sa; 주입 ju-ip

injure *vt.* 상처를 입히다 sang-cheo-reul i-pi-da; 손해를 끼치다 son-hae-reul kki-chi-da; 기분을 상하게 하다 gi-bun-eul sang-ha-ge ha-da; 명예를 훼손하다 meong-ye-reul hwe-son-ha-da

injured *adj.* 상처입은 sang-cheo-ib-eun; 손해를 본 son-hae-reul bon; 기분이 상한 gi-bun-i sang-han; 명예가 훼손된 myeong-ye-ga hwe-son-doen

injury *n.* 상해 sang-hae; 손해 son-hae; 모욕 mo-yok; 명예훼손 myeong-ye-hwe-son

injustice *n.* 불법 bul-ppeop, 부정 bu-jeong

ink *n.* 잉크 ing-keu; 먹물 meong-mul

inland *n.* 내륙 nae-ryuk; 오지 o-ji; *adj.* 오지의 o-ji-ui; 국내의 gung-nae-ui

in-law *n.* 인척 in-cheok, 친척 chin-cheok

inn *n.* 여관 yeo-gwan, 여인숙 yeo-in-suk

inner *adj.* 내부의 nae-bu-ui; 내적인 nae-jjeog-in; 친밀한 chin-mil-han

innocent *adj.* 순결한 sun-gyeol-han; 결백한 gyeol-bae-kan; 순진한 sun-jin-han; 단순한 dan-sun-han

innovate *vt.* 혁신하다 hyeok-sin-ha-da, 쇄신하다 swae-sin-ha-da

inoculate *vt.* 접붙이다 jeop-bu-chi-da; 예방접종하다 ye-bang-jeop-jong-ha-da; 주입하다 ju-i-pa-da

inoculation *n.* 접목 jeom-mok; 예방접종 ye-bang-jeop-jong; 주입 ju-ip

inordinate *adj.* 과도한 gwa-do-han, 지나친 ji-na-chin; 난폭한 nan-po-kan, 무절제한 mu-jeol-jje-han

input *n.* 입력 im-nyeok; 투입 tu-ip

inquire *vi.* 묻다 mut-da, 문의하다 mun-ui-ha-da

inquiry *n.* 문의 mun-ui; 조사 jo-sa; 연구 yeon-gu

insane *adj.* 미친 mi-chin

inscribe *vt.* 새기다 sae-gi-da; 등록하다 deung-no-ka-da

insect *n.* 벌레 beol-le, 곤충 gon-chung

insecurity *n.* 불안정 bul-an-jeong, 위험 wi-heom

insensible *adj.* 무감각한 mu-gam-ga-kan

insert *n.* 삽입물 sab-im-mul; 삽입광고 sab-ip-gwang-go; 삽입자막 sab-ip-ja-mak; *vt.* 끼워넣다 kki-wo-neo-ta; 적어넣다 jeog-eo-neo-ta; 기사를 게재하다 gi-sa-reul ge-jae-ha-da

inside *n.* 안쪽 an-jjok; 내부 nae-bu; 속사정 sok-sa-jeong; 내심 nae-sim; *adj.* 안쪽의 an-jjog-ui; 비밀의 bi-mil-ui; 내막을 잘 아는 nae-mag-eul jal a-neun

insight *n.* 통찰 tong-chal; 통찰력 tong-chal-lyeok

insignificant *adj.* 대수롭지 않은 dae-su-rop-ji an-eun, 하찮은 ha-chan-eun

insist *vi.* 우기다 u-gi-da; 주장하다 ju-jang-ha-da; 강조하다 gang-jo-ha-da; 강요하다 gang-yo-ha-da

insistence *n.* 주장 ju-jang; 고집 go-jip; 강요 gang-yo

insomnia *n.* 불면증 bul-myeon-jjeung

inspect *vt.* 조사하다 jo-sa-ha-da; 검사하다 geom-sa-ha-da; 검열하다 geom-nyeol-ha-da

inspection *n.* 조사 jo-sa; 검사 geom-sa; 검열 geom-nyeol

inspector *n.* 조사자 jo-sa-ja; 검사자 geom-sa-ja; 검열관 geom-nyeol-gwan

inspiration *n.* 영감 yeong-gam; 착상 chak-sang; 감화 gam-hwa; 들숨 deul-ssum

inspire *vt.* 영감을 주다 yeong-gam-eul ju-da; 불어넣다 bul-eo-neo-ta; 생기를 주다 saeng-gi-reul ju-da

install *vt.* 설치하다 seol-chi-ha-da; 자리에 앉히다 ja-ri-e an-chi-da; 임명하다 im-myeong-ha-da

installation *n.* 임명 im-myeong; 장치 jang-chi

installment *n.* 1회 불입금 il-hoe bul-ip-geum, 분할금 bun-hal-geum

instance *n.* 실례 sil-lye; 사실 sa-sil; 의뢰 ui-roe; 소송절차 so-song-jeol-cha

instant *n.* 순간 sun-gan; 찰나 chal-la; *adj.* 즉시의 jeuk-si-ui; 긴급한 gin-geu-pan; 즉석의 jeuk-seog-ui; 이달의 i-dal-ui; ~ **coffee** 인스턴트 커피 in-seu-tan-teu keo-pi; **in an ~; ~ly** 즉시 jeuk-si, 순식간에 sun-sik-gan-e

instead *adv.* (그) 대신에 (geu) dae-sin-e; **He was going to come but he called ~** 그 사람은 오기로 되어 있었지만 그 대신에 전화를 걸었다 geu sa-ram-eun o-gi-ro doe-eo iss-eot ji-man geu dae-sin-e jeon hwa-reul geol-eot-da; *prep.* ~ **of** ...의 대신에 ...ui dae-sin-e

instep *n.* 발등 bal-tteung; 신발등 sin-bal-tteung

instinct *n.* 본능 bon-neung; 직감 jik-gam; 천성 cheon-seong

institute *n.* 협회 hyeo-poe; 연구소 yeon-gu-so; 대학 dae-hak; 강습회 gang-seu-poe; 관습 gwan-seup; *vt.* 설치하다 seol-chi-ha-da; 조사를 시작하다 jo-sa-reul si-ja-ka-da; 임명하다 im-myeong-ha-da

instruct *vt.* 가르치다 ga-reu-chi-da; 지시하다 ji-si-ha-da; 알리다 al-li-da; 설명하다 seol-myeong-ha-da

instruction *n.* 훈련 hul-lyeon; 교수 gyo-su; 교훈 gyo-hun; 지시 ji-si; 명령 myeong-nyeong

instrument *n.* 기계 gi-gye; 기구 gi-gu; 악기 ak-gi; 방편 bang-pyeon; 증서 jeung-seo

insufficient *adj.* 불충분한 bul-chung-bun-han; 부적당한 bu-jeok-dang-han; 무능력한 mu-neung-nyeo-kan

insulate *vt.* 격리시키다 gyeong-ni-si-ki-da; 절연하다 jeol-yeon-ha-da

insulation *n.* 격리 gyeong-ni, 고립 go-rip; 절연 jeol-yeon; 절연재 jeol-yeon-jae

insulin *n.* 인슐린 in-syul-lin

insult *n.* 모욕 mo-yok; 무례 mu-rye; *vt.* 모욕하다 mo-yo-ka-da; 무례히 굴다 mu-rye-hi gul-da

insurance *n.* 보험 bo-heom; 보험료 bo-heom-nyo; 보험증서 bo-heom-jeung-seo; 보증 bo-jeung; ~ **company** 보험회사 bo-heom-hoe-sa; **travel** ~ 여행보험 yeo-haeng-bo-heom

insure *vt.* 보험을 들다 bo-heom-eul deul-da; 보증하다 bo-jeung-ha-da; 지키다 ji-ki-da; **The car is ~d** 이 차는 보험에 들어 있다 i cha-neun bo-heom-e deul-eo it-da

integrity *n.* 성실 seong-sil, 완전 wan-jeon

intellectual *adj.* 지적인 ji-jjeog-in; 이지적인 i-ji-jeog-in

intelligence *n.* 지능 ji-neung; 지성 ji-seong; 정보 jeong-bo

intelligent *adj.* 지적인 ji-jjeog-in; 영리한 yeong-ni-han; 이해력을 나타내는 i-hae-ryeog-eul na-ta-nae-neun

intend *vt.* ... 을 작정이다 ... eul jak-jeong-i-da, ... 를 작정이다 ... reul jak-jeong-i-da; 예정하다 ye-jeong-ha-da; 의도하다 ui-do-ha-da

intense *adj.* 격렬한 gyeong-nyeol-han; 강렬한 gang-nyeol-han; 긴장된 gin-jang-doen

intensive *adj.* 강한 gang-han, 격렬한 gyeong-nyeol-han; 철저한 cheol-jjeo-han

intent *n.* 의사 ui-sa, 의향 ui-hyang, 의지 ui-ji

intention *n.* 강도 gang-do; 긴장 gin-jang; 노력 no-ryeok

intentional *adj.* 고의의 go-i-ui, 계획된 gye-hoek-doen

interaction *n.* 상호작용 sang-ho-jag-yong

intercept *vt.* 가로채다 ga-ro-chae-da, 가로막다 ga-ro-mak-da

intercom *n.* 인터콤 in-teo-kom, 연락용 통화장치 yeol-lang-nyong tong-hwa-jang-chi

intercontinental *adj.* 대륙간의 dae-ryuk-gan-ui

interest *n.* 흥미 heung-mi; 관심 gwan-sim; 중요성 jung-yo-sseong; 이익 i-ik; 이자 i-ja; *vt.* 흥미를 갖게하다 heung-mi-reul gat-ge-ha-da; 관심을 끌다 gwan-sim-eul kkeul-da; 끌어넣다 kkeul-eo-neo-ta

interesting *adj.* 흥미있는 heung-mi-in-neun; 재미있는 jae-mi-in-neun

interfere *vi.* 방해하다 bang-hae-ha-da; 간섭하다 gan-seo-pa-da; 손상하다 son-sang-ha-da

interior *n.* 인테리어 in-te-ri-eo, 실내장식 sil-lae-jang-sik; 안쪽 an-jjok; 내륙 nae-ryuk; 내정 nae-jeong; 내심 nae-sim; *adj.* 안의 an-ui; 내륙의 nae-ryug-ui; 내적인 nae-jjeog-in; 국내의 gung-nae-ui; 실내의 sil-lae-ui

intermediate *n.* 중간물 jung-gan-mul; *adj.* 중간의 jung-gan-ui

intern *n.* 인턴 in-teon, 수련의 su-ryeon-ui; 실습생 sil-sseup-saeng

internal *adj.* 내부의 nae-bu-ui; 내면적인 nae-myeon-jeog-in; 국내의 gung-nae-ui

internalize *vt.* 내면화하다nae-myeon-hwa-ha-da; 습득하다 seup-deu-ka-da

international *adj.* 국제적인 guk-je-jeog-in; 국제의 guk-je-ui

internet *n.* 인터넷 in-teo-net

interpreter *n.* 통역자 tong-yeok-ja; 해석자 hae-seok-ja

interrupt *vt.* 가로막다 ga-ro-mak-da; 중단시키다 jung-dan-si-ki-da; *vi.* 방해하다 bang-hae-ha-da; 중단하다 jung-dan-ha-da

interruption *n.* 방해 bang-hae; 중단 jung-dan; 불통 bul-tong

intersection *n.* 교차로 gyo-cha-ro, 교차점 gyo-cha-jeom

interval *n.* 간격 gan-gyeok; 틈 teum; 휴지기 hyu-ji-gi; 막간 mak-gan; 격차 gyeok-cha

intervene *vi.* 사이에 끼다 sa-i-e kki-da; 조정하다 jo-jeong-ha-da; 방해하다 bang-hae-ha-da

interview *n.* 인터뷰 in-teo-byu, 면접 myeon-jeop; 회견 hoe-gyeon; *vt.* 면접하다 myeon-jeo-pa-da; 회견하다 hoe-gyeon-ha-da

intestine *n.* 장 jang, 창자 chang-ja

intimate *adj.* 친밀한 chin-mil-han; 깊은 gip-eun; 본질적인 bon-jil-jjeog-in; 내심의 nae-sim-ui; 개인적인 gae-in-jeog-in; *vt.* 암시하다 am-si-ha-da; 공표하다 gong-pyo-ha-da

intimidate *vt.* 협박하다 hyeop-ba-ka-da, 위협하다 wi-hyeo-pa-da

into *prep.* …안에 …an-e, …안으로 …an-eu-ro, …속으로 …sog-eu-ro, …까지 …kka-ji, …으로 …eu-ro, …에 부딪쳐 …e bu-dit-cheo, …을 나누어 …eul na-nu-eo

intolerable *adj.* 참을 수 없는 cham-eul ssu eom-neun

intoxicate *vt.* 취하게 하다 chi-ha-ge ha-da; 흥분시키다 heung-bun-si-ki-da

introduce *vt.* 안으로 들이다 an-eu-ro deul-i-da; 받아들이다 bad-a-deul-i-da; 수입하다 su-i-pa-da; 소개하다 so-gae-ha-da

introduction *n.* 받아들임bad-a-deul-im; 소개 so-gae; 서문 seo-mun; 입문 im-mun; 서곡 seo-guk

intuition *n.* 직관 jik-gwan

invade *vt.* 침입하다 chim-i-pa-da; 침범하다 chim-beom-ha-da; 밀어닥치다 mil-eo-dak-chi-da; 침해하다 chim-hae-ha-da

invaluable *adj.* 값을 헤아릴 수 없는 gaps-eul he-a-ril ssu-eom-neun, 매우 귀중한 mae-u gwi-jung-han

invasion *n.* 침입 chim-ip; 침략 chim-nyak; 침해 chim-hae; 침범 chim-beom

invent *vt.* 발명하다 bal-myeong-ha-da; 날조하다 nal-jjo-ha-da

invention *n.* 발명 bal-myeong; 발명품 bal-myeong-pum; 발명의 재능 bal-myeong-ui jae-neung; 날조 nal-jjo

inventory *n.* 물품 명세서 mul-pum myeon-se-seo; 재산목록 jae-san-mong-nok; 재고품 jae-go-pum; 재고품 명세서 jae-go-pum myeong-se-seo; 인벤토리 in-ben-to-ri

invest *vt.* 투자하다 tu-ja-ha-da

investigate *vt.* 조사하다 jo-sa-ha-da; 연구하다 yeon-gu-ha-da; 취조하다 chwi-jo-ha-da; 심사하다 sim-sa-ha-da

investigation *n.* 조사 jo-sa; 연구 yeon-gu; 취조 chwi-jo; 심사 sim-sa; 조사보고 jo-sa-bo-go

investment *n.* 투자 tu-ja

invisible *adj.* 눈에 보이지 않는 nun-e bo-i-ji an-neun; 눈에 뜨이지 않는 nun-e tteu-i-ji an-neun

invitation *n.* 초대 cho-dae; 권유 gwon-yu; 초대장 cho-dae-jjang; 유인 yu-in

invite *vt.* 초대하다cho-dae-ha-da; 권유하다 gwon-yu-ha-da; 주의를 끌다 ju-i-reul

kkeul-da; 초래하다 cho-rae-ha-da; 요청하
다 yo-cheong-ha-da

invoice *n.* 송장 song-jjang; 송장화물
song-jjang-hwa-mul; *vt.* 송장을 작성하다
song-jjang-eul jak-seong-ha-da; 송장을 제
출하다 song-jjang-eul je-chul-ha-da

involuntarily *adv.* 본의 아니게 bon-ui a-ni-
ge, 부지불식간에 bu-ji-bul-ssik-gan-e

involve *vt.* 말아넣다 mal-a neo-ta; 연관시키
다 yeon-gwan-si-ki-da; 수반하다 su-ban-
ha-da; 몰두시키다 mol-ttu-si-ki-da

Iran *n.* 이란 i-ran

Iraq *n.* 이라크 i-ra-keu

Ireland *n.* 아일랜드 a-il-laen-deu

Irish *n.* 아일랜드사람 a-il-laen-deu-ssa-ram;
아일랜드말 a-il-laen-deu-mal; *adj.* 이일랜
드의 a-il-laen-deu-ui

iron *n.* *(appliance)* 다리미 da-ri-mi; 다림질
da-rim-jil; *(metal)* 철 cheol; 아이언 a-i-eon;
vt. 다림질하다 da-rim-jil-ha-da; 철판을 붙
이다 cheol-pan-eul bu-chi-da; 수갑을 채
우다 su-gab-eul chae-u-da

ironic *adj.* 반어의 ban-eo-ui; 비꼬는 bi-kko-
neun; 풍자적인 pung-ja-jeog-in

irony *n.* 풍자 pung-ja; 비꼬기 bi-kko-gi; 반
어법 ban-eo-ppeop; 뜻밖의 결과 tteut-
bakk-e gyeol-gwa

irrecoverable *adj.* 돌이킬 수 없는 dol-i-kil-
ssu eom-neun

irregular *adj.* 불규칙한 bul-gyu-chi-kan

irrelevant *adj.* 부적절한 bu-jeok-jeol-han,
엉뚱한 eong-ttung-han; 중요하지 않은
jung-yo-ha-ji an-eun

irresponsible *adj.* 책임을 지지 않는
chaeg-im-eul ji-ji an-neun, 책임이 없는
chaeg-im-i eom-neun

irrigate *vt.* 물을 대다 mul-eul dae-da, 관개
하다 gwan-gae-ha-da

irrigation *n.* 물을 댐 mul-eul daem, 관개
gwan-gae

irritate *vt.* 짜증나게 하다 jja-jeung-na-ge
ha-da, 화나게 하다 hwa-na-ge ha-da

Islam *n.* 이슬람교 i-seul-lam-gyo-do, 회
교hoe-gyo; 회교도 hoe-gyo-do; 회교국
hoe-gyo-guk

Islamic *adj.* 회교의 hoe-gyo-ui; 회교도의
hoe-gyo-do-ui

island *n.* 섬 seom; 고립된 지역 go-rip-doen
ji-yeok

isolate *vt.* 격리하다 gyeong-ni-ha-da;
분리하다 bul-li-ha-da; 고립시키다
go-rip-si-ki-da

Israel *n.* 이스라엘 i-seu-ra-el

Israeli *n.* 이스라엘사람 i-seu-ra-el-ssa-ram;
adj. 이스라엘의 i-seu-ra-el-ui

issue *n.* 이슈 i-ssyu; 유출 yu-chul; 발행
bal-haeng; 출구 chul-gu; 논쟁 non-
jaeng, 결과 gyeol-gwa; *vt.* 내다 nae-da;
발행하다 bal-haeng-ha-da; 지급하다
ji-geu-pa-da

Istanbul *n.* 이스탄불 i-seu-tan-bul

it *pron.* 그것은 geu-geos-eun, 그것이
geu-geos-i, 그것을 geu-geos-eul; 술래
sul-lae

Italian *n.* 이태리사람 i-tae-ri-ssa-ram; 이태
리말 i-tae-ri-mal; *adj.* 이태리의 i-tae-ri-ui

italics *n.* 이텔릭체 i-teol-lik-che; 이탈리아어
계 i-tal-li-a-eo-gye

Italy *n.* 이태리 i-tae-ri, 이탈리아 i-tal-li-a

itch *n.* 가려움 ga-ryeo-um; 욕망 yong-mang;
vi. 가려워지다 ga-ryeo-wo-ji-da; 좀
이 쑤시다 jom-i ssu-si-da; 초조해하다
cho-jo-hae-ha-da

item *n.* 항목 hang-mok; 품목 pum-mok; 기
사 gi-sa

its *adj.* 그것의 geu-geos-ui, 그 geu

itself *pron.* 그것 자체를 geu-geot ja-che-reul;
그것 자체에 geu-geot ja-che-e; 바로 그것
ba-ro geu geot

Ivory Coast *n.* 코트디브와르
ko-teu-di-bu-wa-reu

Ivory *n.* 싱아 sang-a; 상아제품 sang-a-je-
pum; 상아색 sang-a-saek

ivy *n.* 담쟁이덩굴 dam-jaeng-i-deong-gul

J

jack *n. (man, guy)* 사나이 sa-na-i, 젊은이 jeolm-eun-i; *(laborer)* 노동자 no-dong-ja; *(tool)* 잭 jaek; 전기 플러그 구멍 jeon-gi peul-leo-geu gu-meong

jacket *n.* 자켓 ja-ket

jade *n.* 옥 ok, 비취 bi-chwi

jail *n.* 교도소 gyo-do-so, 감옥 gam-ok, 구치소 gu-chi-so

jam *n.* 잼 jaem; 혼잡 hon-jap; *vt.* 쑤셔넣다 ssu-syeo-neo-ta, 채워넣다 chae-wo-neo-ta; *vi.* 움직이지 않게 되다 um-jig-i-ji an-ke doe-da; **raspberry ~** 산딸기잼 san-ttal-gi-jjaem

Jamaica *n.* 자메이카 ja-me-i-ka

janitor *n.* 수위 su-wi; 관리인 gwal-li-in

January *n.* 일월 il-wol

Japan *n.* 일본 il-bon

Japanese *n.* 일본사람 il-bon-ssa-ram; 일본어 il-bon-eo; *adj.* 일본의 il-bon-ui

jar *n.* 단지 dan-ji, 항아리 hang-a-ri; 귀에 거슬리는 소리 gwi-e geo-seul-li-neun so-ri; 충격 chung-gyeok

jaundice *n.* 황달 hwang-dal; 질투 jil-tu, 편견 pyeon-gyeon

jaw *n.* 턱 teok

jaywalk *vi.* 무단횡단하다 mu-dan-hoeng-dan-ha-da

jazz *n.* 재즈 jjae-jeu; 소란 so-ran

jealous *adj.* 질투가 많은 jil-tu-ga man-eun; 시샘하는 si-saem-ha-neun; 마음을 쓰는 ma-eum-eul sseu-neun

jealousy *n.* 질투 jil-tu, 시샘 si-saem

jeans *n. pl.* 진 jin, 청바지 cheong-ba-ji

jeep *n.* 지프차 ji-peu-cha

jelly *n.* 젤리 jel-li

jellyfish *n.* 해파리 hae-pa-ri; 의지가 약한 사람 ui-ji-ga ya-kan sa-ram

jerk *n.* 급격한 움직임 geup-gyeo-kan um-jig-im; 경련 gyeon-nyeon; 제조 che-jo; 바보 ba-bo; 포 po; *vt.* 급히 흔들다 geu-pi heun-deul-da; 내뱉듯 말하다 nae-baet-deut mal-ha-da; 포를 만들다 po-reul man-deul-da

jerky *n.* 육포 yuk-po

jersey *n.* 저지 jeo-ji

Jerusalem *n.* 예루살렘 ye-ru-sal-lem

jet *n.* 분출 bun-chul; 분출물 bun-chul-mul; 분출구 bun-chul-gu; 제트기 je-teu-gi; 제트엔진 je-teu-en-jin

jet lag *n.* 제트기 탑승에 따른 피로 je-teu-gi tap-seung-e tta-reun pi-ro

Jew *n.* 유태인 yu-tae-in; 유태교인 yu-tae-gyo-in; 고리대금업자 go-ri-dae-geum-eop-ja; 수전노 su-jeon-no

jewel *n.* 보석 bo-seok; 보석 장신구 bo-seok jang-sin-gu; 귀중품 gwi-jung-pum

jewelry *n.* 보석류 bo-seong-nyu; 장신구 jang-sin-gu; 보석세공 bo-seok-se-gong; **~ store** 보석상 bo-seok-sang

Jewish *adj.* 유태인의 yu-tae-in-ui; 유태인같은 yu-tae-in gat-eun

jigsaw puzzle *n.* 조각그림 퍼즐 jo-gak-geu-rim peo-jeul

jinx *n.* 징크스 jing-keu-sseu

job *n.* 일 il; 의무 ui-mu; 직업 jig-eop; 쥐어박기 jwi-eo-bak-gi; **~hunter** 구직자 gu-jik-ja

jobless *adj.* 실직한 sil-jji-kan; *n.* 실직자 sil-jjik-ja

jockey *n.* 기수 gi-su

jog *n.* 조깅 jo-ging; 자극 ja-geuk; 힌트 hin-teu; 슬쩍밀기 seul-jjeok mil-gi; *vi.* 덜커덕 움직이다 deol-keo-deok um-jig-i-da; 터벅터벅 걷다 teo-beok-teo-beok geot-da; 천천히 달리다 cheon-cheon-hi dal-li-da; **to go ~ging** 조깅하러 가다 jo-ging-ha-reo ga-da

join *vt.* 결합하다 gyeol-ha-pa-da; 합류하다 ham-nyu-ha-da; 합병하다 hap-byeong-ha-da; 가입하다 ga-i-pa-da; 입대하다 ip-dae-ha-da; 맺어주다 maej-eo-ju-da

joint *n.* 이음매 i-eum-mae; 관절 gwan-jeol; 접속부 jeop-sok-bu; **out of ~** 접질리다 jeop-jil-li-da; 뼈가 빠지다 ppyeo-ga ppa-ji-da

joke *n.* 농담 nong-dam; 웃을 일 us-eul lil; 우스운 상황 u-seu-un sang-hwang; *vi.* 농담하다 nong-dam-ha-da; 장난치다 jang-nan-chi-da

joker *n. (playing cards)* 조커 jo-keo; 농담하는 사람 nong-dam-ha-neun sa-ram; 사기 조항 sa-gi-jo-hang

jolly *adj.* 즐거운 jeul-geo-un, 명랑한 myeong-nang-han

Jordan *n.* 요르단 yo-reu-dan

journal *n.* 신문 sin-mun; 잡지 jap-ji; 일지 il-jji

journalist *n.* 기자 gi-ja; 기고가 gi-go-ga; 신문 사주 sin-mun-sa-ju, 잡지사주 jap-ji-sa-ju

journey *n.* 여행 yeo-haeng; 여정 yeo-jeong; *vi.* 여행하다 yeo-haeng-ha-da

joy *n.* 기쁨 gi-ppeum; 행복 haeng-bok; 기쁜 일 gi-ppeun-nil

joyful *adj.* 기쁜 gi-ppeun, 즐거운 jeul-geo-un, 유쾌한 yu-kwae-han

JSA *n. abbr.* **Joint Security Area** 공동경비 구역 gong-dong-gyeong-bi-gu-yeok

judge *n.* 판사 pan-sa; 심판 sim-pan; 감정가 gam-jeong-ga; *vt.* 재판하다 jae-pan-ha-da; 감정하다 gam-jeong-ha-da; 판단하다 pan-dan-ha-da

judgment *n.* 재판 jae-pan; 판결 pan-gyeol; 판단 pan-dan; 견해 gyeon-hae

jug *n.* 주전자 ju-jeon-ja; 맥주잔 maek-ju-jjan

juggle *vt.* 요술을 부리다 yo-sul-eul bu-ri-da; 거짓을 꾸미다 geo-jis-eul kku-mi-da; 속여서 빼앗다 sog-yeo-seo ppae-at-da; 공을 토스하다 gong-eul to-sseu-ha-da

juice *n.* 주스 ju-sseu; 즙 jeup; 정수 jeong-su; 분비액 bun-bi-aek; **orange ~** 오렌지주스 o-ren-ji ju-sseu

juicy *adj.* 수분이 많은 su-bun-i man-eun, 즙이 많은 jeub-i man-eun

July *n.* 7월 chil-wol

jumble *n.* 둥근과자 dung-geun-gwa-ja; 혼잡 hon-jap; 뒤범벅 dwi-beom-beok; 동요 dong-yo; *vt.* 뒤죽박죽을 만들다 dwi-juk-bak-jug-eul man-deul-da, 뒤범벅 해놓다 dwi-beom-beok hae-no-ta

jumbo *adj.* 거대한 geo-dae-han, 아주 큰 a-ju keun

jump *n.* 점프 jeom-peu; 도약 do-yak; 급변 geup-byeon; 급등 geup-deung; *vi.* 점프하다 jeom-peu-ha-da; 뛰어넘다 ttwi-eo-neom-tta; 움찔하다 um-jjil-ha-da; 비약하다 bi-ya-ka-da; 폭등하다 pok-deung-ha-da; 건너뛰다 geon-neo-ttwi-da

jumper *n.* 뛰는 사람 ttwi-neun sa-ram; 잠바 jam-ba

jumper cables *n. pl.* 점퍼 케이블 jeom-peo ke-i-beul

jump rope *n.* 줄넘기 jul-leom-kki

junction *n.* 연합 yeon-hap; 접합 jeo-pap; 접합점 jeo-pap-jeom; 합류점 ham-nyu-jjeom; 환승역 hwan-seung-nyeok; 접속 jeop-sok

June *n.* 6월 yu-wol

jungle *n.* 정글 jeong-geul, 밀림 mil-lim; **~ gym** 정글짐 jeong-geul-jim

junior *n.* 연소자 yeon-so-ja; 소년소녀 so-nyeon-so-nyeo; 후배 hu-bae; 하급자 ha-geup-ja; 3학년 sam-hang-nyeon; *adj.* 손아래의 son-a-rae-ui; 후배의 hu-bae-ui; 3학년의 sam-hang-nyeon-ui; 후순위의 hu-sun-wi-ui; **~ college** 초급대학 cho-geup-dae-hak; **~ high school** 중학교 jung-hak-gyo

junk *n.* 쓰레기 sseu-re-gi; 잡동사니 jap-dong-a-ni; 정크 jeong-keu; **~ mail** 광고 우편물 gwang-go u-pyeon-mul

Jupiter *n.* 목성 mok-seong; 주피터 Ju-pi-teo

jury *n.* 배심원 bae-sim-won; 심사원 sim-sa-won

just *adj.* 올바른 ol-ba-reun; 정당한 jeong-dang-han; 타당한 ta-dang-han; 정확한 jeong-hwa-kan; 적정한 jeok-jeong-han; *adv.* 정확히 jeong-hwa-ki; 방금 bang-geum; 겨우 gyeo-u; 다만 da-man; **He has ~ left** 그분은 방금 떠나셨습니다 geu-bun-eun bal-geum tteo-na-syeot-seum-ni-da

justice *n.* 정의 jeong-i; 공정 gong-jeong; 정당 jeong-dang; 사법 sa-beop; 재판관 jae-pan-gwan

justification *n.* 정당성을 증명함 jeong-dang-sseong-eul jeung-myeong-ham; 정당화 jeong-dang-hwa; 변명 byeon-myeong; 의롭다고 인정됨 ui-rop-da-go in-jeong-doem; 정돈 jeong-don; 조정 jo-jeong

justify *vt.* 정당화하다 jeong-dang-hwa-doe-da; 변명하다 byeon-myeong-ha-da; 죄를 용서하다 joe-reul yong-seo-ha-da; 조정하다 jo-jeong-ha-da

juvenile *n.* 소년소녀 so-nyeon-so-nyeo; 소년소녀용 도서 so-nyeon-so-nyeo-yong do-seo; 어린이역 eo-rin-i-yeok; *adj.* 소년소녀의 so-nyeon-so-nyeo-ui; 소년소녀를 위한 so-nyeon-so-nyeo-reul wi-han; **~ delinquent** 비행소년 bi-haeng-so-nyeon; 소년범죄 so-nyeon-beom-joe

K

kangaroo *n.* 캥거루 kaeng-geo-ru

karaoke *n.* 카라오케 ka-ra-o-ke

karate *n.* 카라테 ka-ra-te, 가라데 ga-ra-de

Kazakhstan *n.* 카작스탄 ka-jak-seu-tan

keel *n.* 석탄 운반선 seok-tan un-ban-seon

keen *adj.* 날카로운 nal-ka-ro-un; 신랄한 sil-lal-han; 예민한 ye-min-han; 열심인 yeol-ssim-in; 격렬한 gyeong-nyeol-han; 강열한 gang-nyeol-han

keep *vt.* 보유하다 bo-yu-ha-da, 보존하다 bo-jon-ha-da, 지키다 ji-ki-da, 따르다 tta-reu-da, 부양하다 bu-yang-ha-da, 두다 du-da, 관리하다 gwal-li-ha-da, 기입하다 gi-i-pa-da, 수호하다 su-ho-ha-da, 계속하다 gye-seo-ka-da, 견디다 gyeon-di-da; *(to retain)* **We'll ~ it** 그건 저희가 보관하겠습니다 geu-geon jeo-hi-ga bo-gwan-ha-get-seum-ni-da; *(to detain)* **What kept you** 왜 늦었어요 wae neuj-eoss-eo-yo; 무슨 일이 있었습니까 mu-seun il-i iss-eot-seum-ni-kka; *(to maintain)* **We ~ it as clean as possible** 그건 저희가 최대한 깨끗하게 보관하고 있습니다 geu-geon jeo-hi-ga choe-dae-han kkae-kkeu-ta-ge bo-gwan-ha-go it-seum-ni-da; *(to stay)* **to ~ still** 가만히 계십시오 ga-man-hi gye-sip-si-o; *(to continue)* **They ~ on doing it** 그 분들은 그 행동을 계속하고 있습니다 geu bun-deul-eun geu haeng-dong-eul gye-so-ka-go it-seum-ni-da; **to ~ up with the news from home** 집으로부터 계속 소식을 듣고 있다 jib-eu-ro-bu-teo gye-sok so-sig-eul deut-go it-da; **to ~ out** 출입금지 chul-ip-geum-ji

keeper *n.* 파수꾼 pa-seu-kkun; 사육자 sa-yuk-ja; 관리인 gwal-li-in; 수비자 su-bi-ja; 제동장치 je-dong-jang-chi

kennel *n.* 개집 gae-jip; 여우굴 yeo-u-gul; 도랑 do-rang; 하수구 ha-su-gu

Kenya *n.* 케냐 ke-nya

kernel *n.* 과일 속 gwa-il ssok; 낟알 nad-al; 핵심 haek-sim

kerosene *n.* 등유 deung-yu; 등불용 석유 deung-ppul-yong seog-yu

ketchup *n.* 케첩 ke-cheop

kettle *n.* 솥 sot

key *n.* 열쇠 yeol-ssoe; 실마리 sil-ma-ri; 해답 hae-dap; 요소 yo-so; 조 jo; 산호초 san-ho-cho; 모래톱 mo-rae-top; **~ ring** 열쇠고리 yeol-ssoe-go-ri; **~ word** 중심어 jung-sim-eo, 키워드 ki-wo-deu

keyboard *n.* 키보드 ki-bo-deu, 자판 ja-pan

key chain *n.* 열쇠 꾸러미 yeol-ssoe kku-reo-mi

keyhole *n.* 열쇠구멍 yeol-ssoe-kku-meong

keypad *n.* 키패드 ki-pae-deu

key word *n.* 키워드 ki-wo-deu, 주요단어 ju-yo-dan-eo

khaki *n.* 카키색 ka-ki-saek; 카키색 군복 ka-ki-saek gun-bok; *adj.* 카키색의 ka-ki-saeg-ui, 황갈색의 hwang-gal-ssaeg-ui

kick *n.* 차기 cha-gi; 반동 ban-dong; 킥 kik; *vt.* 걷어차다 geod-eo-cha-da; 속도를 올리다 sok-do-reul ol-li-da; 공을 골에 차넣다 gong-eul kkol-e cha-neo-ta; 반동을 주다 ban-dong-eul ju-da; **to ~ out** 쫓아내다 jjoch-a-nae-da; *(sports)* **~off** 걷어차다 geod-eo-cha-da; 킥 오프하다 kik o-peu-ha-da; **penalty ~** 패널티킥 pae-neol-ti-kik

kid *n.* *(child)* 아이 a-i; *(goat)* 새끼염소 sae-kki-yeom-so; 조롱 jo-rong; *vt.* 속이다 sog-i-da; *(to tease)* 놀리다 nol-li-da

kidnap *vt.* 유괴하다 yu-goe-ha-da; 채가다 chae-ga-da; **~per** 유괴범 yu-goe-beom, 납치범 nap-chi-beom

kidney *n.* 신장 sin-jang, 콩팥 kong-pat; 성질 seong-jil, 기질 gi-jil

kill *vt.* 죽이다 jug-i-da; 시간을 보내다 si-gan-eul bo-nae-da; 기세를 꺾다 gi-se-reul kkeok-da; 억압하다 eog-a-pa-da; 부결하다 bu-gyeol-ha-da; 삭제하다 sak-je-ha-da

kilogram *n.* 킬로그램 kil-lo-geu-raem

kilometer *n.* 킬로미터 kil-lo-mil-teo

kimchi *n.* 김치 gim-chi

kin *n.* 친척 chin-cheok, 일가 il-ga

kind *n.* 종류 jong-nyu; 종족 jong-jok; 본질 bon-jil; *adj.* 친절한 chin-jeol-han; 정성어린 jeong-seong-eo-rin; **~ of** 일종의 il-jjong-ui; **It is ~ of cold today** 오늘은 좀 추운 편이다 o-neul-eun jom chu-un pyeon-i-da

kindergarten *n.* 유치원 yu-chi-won

kindle *vt.* 불을 지피다 bul-eul ji-pi-da; 밝게하다 bal-kke-ha-da; 선동하다 seon-dong-ha-da

kindness *n.* 친절 chin-jeol; 인정 in-jeong; 친절한 행위 chin-jeol-han haeng-wi

king *n.* *(royalty)* 왕 wang; *(chess/checkers)* 킹 king; 거물 geo-mul

kingdom *n.* 왕국 wang-guk; 왕정 wang-jeong; 신정국가 sin-jeong-guk-ga

king-size *adj.* 특대의 teuk-dae-ui, 최대형의 choe-dae-hyeong-ui, 킹사이즈 king-ssa-i-jeu

kinship *n.* 친척관계 chin-cheok-gwan-gye

kiosk *n.* 정자 jeong-ja; 신문매점 sin-mun-mae-jeom; 공중전화실 gong-jung-jeon-hwa-sil

kiss *n.* 키스 ki-sseu, 입맞춤 im-mat-chum; 가볍게 스침 ga-byeop-ge seu-chim; 가벼운 접촉 ga-byeo-un jeop-chok; *vt.* 키스하다 ki-sseu-ha-da; 가볍게 스치다 ga-byeop-ge seu-chi-da; 가볍게 부딪치다 ga-byeop-ge bu-dit-chi-da

kit *n.* 나무통 na-mu-tong; 장비 jang-bi; 연장그릇 yeon-jang-geu-reut; 여행용구 yeo-haeng-yong-gu; 새끼 고양이 sae-kki go-yang-i

kitchen *n.* 부엌 bu-eok, 주방 ju-bang, 취사장 chwi-sa-jang; ~ **cabinet** 찬장 chan-jang; ~ **sink** 싱크대 ssing-keu-dae

kite *n.* 연 yeon; 솔개 sol-gae; 사기꾼 sa-gi-kkun

kitten *n.* 새끼 고양이 sae-kki go-yang-i; 말괄량이 mal-gwal-lyang-i

kiwi *n.* 키위 ki-wi

Kleenex *n.* 클리넥스 keul-li-nek-seu

knapsack *n.* 배낭 bae-nang

knead *vt.* 반죽하다 ban-ju-ka-da; 혼합하다 hon-ha-pa-da; 도야하다 do-ya-ha-da

knee *n.* 무릎 mu-reup; 무릎관절 mu-reup-wan-jeol; ~**cap** 무릎뼈 mu-reup-ppyeo; 무릎보호대 mu-reup-bo-ho-dae; ~**high** 무릎높이의 mu-reup-nop-i-ui

kneel *vi.* 무릎을 꿇다 mu-reup-eul kkul-ta; **to** ~ **down** 무릎을 꿇다 mu-reup-eul kkul-ta; 굴복하다 gul-bo-ka-da

knife *n.* 나이프 na-i-peu; 식칼 sik-kal

knight *n.* 중세기사 jung-se-gi-sa

knit *vt.* 뜨다 tteu-da; 짜다 jja-da; 찌푸리다 jji-pu-ri-da; 짜맞추다 jja-mat-chu-da; *vi.* 뜨개질하다 tteu-ge-jil-ha-da; 짜맞추어지다 jja-mat-chu-eo-ji-da; 찌푸려지다 jji-pu-ryeo-ji-da; ~**ting needle** 뜨게질 바늘 tteu-ge-jil ba-neul

knob *n.* 손잡이 son-jab-i

knock *n.* 노크 no-keu; 구타 gu-ta, 타격 ta-gyeok; 폭음 pog-eum; 악평 ak-pyeong; *vi.* 치다 chi-da; 두드리다 du-deu-ri-da; 충돌하다 chung-dol-ha-da; 노킹을 일으키다 no-king-eul il-eu-ki-da; **to** ~ **into** ...에 부딪치다 ...e bu-dit-chi-da; ...와 우연히 만나다 ...wa u-yeon-hi man-na-da; 못을 박다 mos-eul bak-da; 억지로 주입시키다 eok-ji-ro ju-ip-si-ki-da; **to** ~ **down** 때려 눕히다 ttae-ryeo-nu-i-da; **to** ~ **out** 때려 내쫓다 ttae-ryeo nae-jjot-da; **a** ~**out** 녹 아웃 nok-a-ut, 압도적인 것 ap-do-jeog-in geot

knot *n.* 매듭 mae-deup; 무리 mu-ri; 혹 hok; 노트 no-teu; *vt.* 매다 mae-da; 결합하다 gyeol-ha-pa-da; 눈살을 찌푸리다 nun-ssal-eul jji-pu-ri-da; 얽히게 하다 eol-ki-ge ha-da; 마디를 만들다 ma-di-reul man-deul-da; **to tie the** ~ 연분을 맺다 yeon-bun-eul maet-da

know *vt.* 알다 al-da; 식별할 수 있다 sik-byeol-hal ssu it-da; 경험이 있다 gyeong-heom-i it-da; *vi.* 알고있다 al-go it-da *(factual)* Does she ~ how to get there 그분은 거기에 어떻게 가는지 알고 계십니까 geu bun-eun geo-gi-e eo-tteo-ke ga-neun-ji al-go gye-sim-ni-kka; *(acquaintance)* Does she ~ you 그분이 선생님을 아십니까 geu bun-i seon-saeng-nim-eul a-sim-ni-kka; *(to inform)* Let me ~ **by Friday** 금요일까지 제게 알려 주십시오 geum-yo-il-kka-ji je-ge al-lyeo ju-sip-si-o; **to** ~ **how to do something** 뭘 어떻게 하는지 안다 mwol eo-tteo-ke ha-neun-ji an-da

know-how *n.* 기술정보 gi-sul-jeong-bo, 노하우 no-ha-u

knowledge *n.* 지식 ji-sik; 학식 hak-sik; 이해 i-hae; 경험 gyeong-heom; 보도 bo-do

known *adj.* 알려진 al-lyeo-jin

knuckle *n.* 손가락 관절 son-kka-rak gwan-jeol; 주먹 ju-meok; 돌쩌귀 dol-jjeo-gwi; 무릎도가니 mu-reup-do-ga-ni

Korea *n.* 한국 han-guk, 대한민국 dae-han-min-guk
Korean *n.* 한국사람 han-guk-sa-ram; 한국말 han-gung-mal; *adj.* 한국의 han-gug-ui; ~ **War** 한국전쟁 han-guk-jeon-jaeng

kosher *adj.* 정결한 jeong-gyeol-han; 적당한 jeok-dang-han; 율법에 맞는 yul-ppeob-e man-neun
kung fu *n.* 쿵후 kung-hu
Kuwait *n.* 쿠웨이트 ku-we-i-teu

L

label *n.* 라벨 ra-bel, 꼬리표 kko-ri-pyo, 레테르 le-te-reu; *vt.* 라벨을 붙이다 ra-bel-eul bu-chi-da
labor *n.* 노동 no-dong; 노동자 no-dong-ja; 고역 go-yeok; 애씀 ae-sseum; 출산 chul-ssan; **go into** ~ 산기가 있다 san-kki-ga it-da, 분만에 들어가다 bun-man-e deul-eo-ga-da; ~**er** 노동자 no-dong-ja, 인부 in-bu
laboratory *n.* 실험실 sil-heom-sil, 랩 laep; 제약소 je-yak-so; 실험 sil-heom
labor camp *n.* 강제 노동 수용소 gang-je no-dong su-yong-so; 이주 노동자 합숙소 i-ju no-dong-ja hap-suk-so
Labor Day *n.* 노동절 no-dong-jeol
labor movement *n.* 노동운동 no-dong-un-dong
labor union *n.* 노동조합 no-dong-jo-hap
labyrinth *n.* 미궁 mi-gung; 미로 mi-ro; 엉클린 사건 eong-keul-lin sa-kkeon
lace *n.* 신발끈 sin-bal-kkeun; 레이스 re-i-sseu; 가장자리 장식 ga-jang-ja-ri jang-sik; *vt.* 끈으로 묶다 kkeun-eu-ro muk-da; 레이스로 장식하다 re-i-sseu-ro jang-si-ka-da
lack *n.* 부족 bu-jok; 부족한 물건 bu-jo-kan mul-geon; *vt.* 모자라다 mo-ja-ra-da
ladder *n.* 사다리 sa-da-ri; 사회적 지위 sa-hoe-jeok ji-wi
ladle *n.* 국자 guk-ja
lady *n.* 숙녀 sung-nyeo; 귀부인 gwi-bu-in; **ladies and gentlemen** 신사숙녀 여러분 sin-sa-sung-nyeo yeo-reo-bun; **ladies' room** 여자 화장실 yeo-ja hwa-jang-sil
ladybug *n.* 무당벌레 mu-dang-beol-le
lag *vi.* 뒤떨어지다 dwi-tteol-eo-ji-da; 천천히 걷다 cheon-cheon-hi geot-da; 관심이 줄다 gwan-sim-i jul-da; 꾸물거리다 kku-mul-geo-ri-da; 투옥하다 tu-o-ka-da; **to ~ behind** 뒤쳐지다 dwi-cheo-ji-da
lake *n.* 호수 ho-su

lamb *n.* 새끼양 sae-kki-yang; 유순한 사람 yu-sun-han sa-ram; 잘 속는 사람 jal song-neun sa-ram; 어린 신도 eo-rin sin-do; ~**skin** 양가죽 yang-ga-juk
lame *adj.* 불구의 bul-gu-ui; 무능력한 mu-neung-nyeo-kan; 불완전한 bul-wan-jeon-han; 서투른 seo-tu-reun; 절름발이의 jeol-leum-bal-i-ui
laminate *vt.* 코팅하다 ko-ting-ha-da
lamp *n.* 등불 deung-ppul, 램프 raem-peu; ~ **shade** 전등 갓 jeon-deung gat
lamppost *n.* 가로등 ga-ro-deung
LAN *n. abbr.* *local area network* 랜 raen
land *n.* *(terrain)* 육지 yuk-ji; 땅 ttang; 토지 to-ji; 국토 guk-to; *(country)* 나라 na-ra; 영역 yeong-yeok; *vt.* 상륙시키다 sang-nyuk-si-ki-da; 착륙시키다 chang-nyuk-si-ki-da; 떨어뜨리다 tteol-eo-tteu-ri-da; 땅으로 끌어올리다 ttang-eu-ro kkeul-eo-ol-li-da; *vi.* 상륙하다 sang-nyu-ka-da; 착륙하다 chang-nyu-ka-da; 떨어지다 tteol-eo-ji-da; 빠지다 ppa-ji-da
landfill *n.* 매립지 mae-rip-ji; 쓰레기 처리장 sseu-re-gi cheo-ri-jang
landing *n.* *(action)* 상륙 sang-nyuk; 착륙 chang-nyuk; *(location)* 상륙장 sang-nyuk-jang; 착륙장 chang-nyuk-jang; *(stairway)* 층계참 cheung-gye-cham
landlord *n.* 지주 ji-ju; 집주인 jip-ju-in
landmark *n.* 경계표 gyeong-gye-pyo; 획기적 사건 hoek-gi-jeok sa-kkeon
landowner *n.* 토지 소유자 to-ji so-yu-ja, 땅주인 ttang-ju-in
landscape *n.* 풍경 pung-gyeong; 전망 jeon-mang; 풍경화 pung-gyeong-hwa
landslide *n.* 산사태 san-sa-tae; 압승 ap-seung
lane *n.* 좁은 길 job-eun gil; 통로 tong-no; 규정항로 gyu-jeong-hang-no; 차선 cha-seon; 레인 re-in

language *n.* 언어 eon-eo, 말 mal; **native ~** 모
국어 mo-gug-eo
lantern *n.* 랜턴 raen-teon; 환등기
hwan-deung-gi
lap *n.* 무릎 mu-reup; 무릎부분 mu-reup-bu-
bun; 한바퀴 han-ba-kkwi; 핥음 halt-eum;
파도소리 pa-do-sso-ri
lapel *n.* 접은 옷깃 jeob-eun ot-git
lapse *n.* 경과 gyeong-gwa; 실책 sil-chaek; 타
락 ta-rak; 소멸 so-myeol; *vi.* 시간이 경과
하다 si-gan-i gyeong-gwa-ha-da; 나쁜길
로 빠지다 na-ppeun-gil-lo ppa-ji-da
laptop *n.* *(computer)* 랩탑 raep-tap
lard *n.* 라아드 ra-a-deu; 돼지기름
dwae-ji-gi-reum
large *n.* 다음 성구로 da-eum seong-kku-ro;
adj. 큰 keun; 꽤 많은 kkwae man-eun; 넓
은 neolb-eun; 대규모의 dae-gyu-mo-ui; 도
랑이 넓은 do-ryang-i neolb-un; *adv.* 크게
keu-ge; 상세히 sang se hi; 과장하여 gwa-
jang-ha-yeo; **~ intestine** 대장 dae-jang;
~-scale *adj.* 대규모의 dae-gyu-mo-ui
larva *n.* 애벌레 ae-beol-le
laryngitis *n.* 후두염 hu-du-yeom
laser *n.* 레이저 re-i-jeo; **~ printer** 레이저 프
린터 re-i-jeo peu-rin-teo
last *adj.* 마지막의 ma-ji-mag-ui; 임종의
im-jong-ui; 바로 전의 ba-ro jeon-ui; 최
근...동안 choe-geun...dong-an; 최근의
choe-geun-ui; 가장...할 것 같지 않은 ga-
jang...hal kkeot gat-ji an-eun; **at ~** 드디어
deu-di-eo, 마침내 ma-chim-nae; *vi.* 계속
하다 gye-so-ka-da; 오래가다 o-rae-ga-da
lasting *adj.* 영속하는 yeong-so-ka-neun, 영
구적인 yeong-gu-jeog-in, 내구력있는
nae-gu-reog-in-neun
last-minute *adj.* 마지막 순간의 ma-ji-mak
sun-gan-ui, 막바지의 mak-ba-ji-ui
last name *n.* 성 seong
latch *n.* 빗장 bit-jang; *vi.* 빗장이 걸리다
bit-jang-i geol-li-da
late *adj.* 늦은 neuj-eun; 말기의 mal-gi-ui; 요
전의 yo-jeon-ui; 최근의 choe-geun-ui; 돌
아가신 dol-a-ga-sin; *adv.* 늦게 neut-ge; 늦
게까지 neut-ge-kka-ji; 전에 jeon-e
lately *adv.* 요즘 yo-jeum, 최근에
choe-geun-e

lathe *n.* 선반 seon-ban; 잘 사용하지 않음
jal sa-yong-ha-ji an-eum; *vt.* 선반에 두다
seon-ban-e du-da
lather *n.* 비누거품 bi-nu-geo-pum; *vi.* 비누
거품을 내다 bi-nu-geo-pum-eul nae-da;
vt. 비누거품을 칠하다 bi-nu-geo-pum-eul
chil-ha-da
Latin *n.* 라틴어 ra-tin-eo; 라틴계사람 ra-
tin-gye sa-ram; *adj.* 라틴어의 ra-tin-eo-ui;
라틴계의 ra-tin-gye-ui; 라틴사람의
ra-tin-ssa-ram-ui
Latin America *n.* 라틴 아메리카 ra tin
a-me-ri-ka
Latin American *adj.* 라틴 아메리카사람
ra-tin a-me-ri-ka-ssa-ram
latitude *n.* 위도 wi-do; 위선 wi-seon; 범위
beom-wi
latrine *n.* 변소 byeon-so
latter *adj.* 뒤쪽의 dwi-jjog-ui; 나중의 na-
jung-ui, 후자의 hu-ja-ui; 말기의 mal-gi-ui;
끝의 kkeut-ui; *pron.* 후자 hu-ja, 마지막 것
ma-ji-mak-geot
laugh *n.* 웃음 us-eum; 웃음소리 us-eum-sso-
ri; *vi.* 웃다 ut-da; 만족하다 man-jo-ka-da;
비웃다 bi-ut-da
laughter *n.* 웃음 us-eum; 웃음소리
us-eum-sso-ri
launch *n.* 진수 ji-su; 발사 bal-ssa; *vt.* 진수하
다 jin-su-ha-da; 발사하다 bal-ssa-ha-da;
내보내다 nae-bo-nae-da; 사업을 시작하
다 sa-eob-eul si-ja-ka-da; 발사하다 bal-
ssa-ha-da; 공격을 가하다 gong-gyeog-eul
ga-ha-da
laundry *n.* 세탁 se-tak; 세탁물 se-tang-
mul; 세탁소 se-tak-so; 세탁실 se-tak sil;
laundromat 세탁장 se-tak-jang; **~ room**
세탁장 se-tak-jang
lava *n.* 용암 yong-am
lavatory *n.* 세면장 se-myeon-jang; 화장실
hwa-jang-sil
lavish *adj.* 아낌없는 a-kkim-eom-neun; 풍
부한 pung-bu-han; 낭비하는 nang-bi-ha-
neun; 사치하는 sa-chi-ha-neun
law *n.* 법 beop; 법학 beo-pak; 법조계 beop-
jo-gye; 소송 so-song; 계율 gye-yul; 관습
gwan-seup; 법칙 beop-chik; **against the ~**
법을 어기다 beob-eul eo-gi-da;

~ **school** 법대 beop-dae; ~ **breaker** 범죄
자 beom-joe-ja

lawful *adj.* 합법의 hap-beob-ui, 합법적인
hap-beop-jeog-in; 정당한jeong-dang-han;
법이 인정하는 beob-i in-jeong-ha-neun;
법에 따라 행동하는 beob-e tta-ra
haeng-dong-ha-neun

lawn *n.* 잔디 jan-di; 잔디밭 jan-di-bat

lawsuit *n.* 소송 so-song; 고소 go-so

lawyer *n.* 법률가 beom-nyul-ga; 변호사
byeon-ho-sa; 법률학자 beom-nyul-hak-ja

laxative *n.* 하제 ha-je, 완화제 wan-hwa-je

lay *vt.* 눕히다 nu-pi-da; 두다 du-da; 알을
낳다 al-eul na-ta; 옆으로 넘어뜨리다
yeop-eu-ro neom-eo-tteu-ri-da; 덧입히다
deon-ni-pi-da; 짐을 지우다 jim-eul ji-u-da;
제출하다 je-chul-ha-da

layer *n.* 층 chung; 칠하기 chil-ha-gi; 계획자
gye-hoek-ja

layoff *n.* 일시적 해고 il-ssi-jeok hae-go; 강제
휴업 gang-je-hyu-eop

layout *n.* 설계 seol-gye

lazy *adj.* 게으른 ge-eu-reun; 활기없는 hwal-
gi-eom-neun; 느린 neu-rin

lead *n.* 선도 seon-do; 안내 an-nae; 리
드 ri-deu; *(metal)* 납 nap; *vt.* 이끌다
i-kkeul-da; 인솔하다 in-sol-ha-da; 지도하
다 ji-do-ha-da; 유인하다 yu-in-ha-da; 지
내다 ji-nae-da; *vi.* 안내하다 an-nae-ha-da;
앞지르다 ap-ji-reu-da; 이르다 i-reu-da;
이끌다 i-kkeul-da; 원인이 되다 won-in-i
doe-da; **to be in the** ~ 지도적 입장에 있
다 ji-do-jeok ip-jang-e it-da, 앞장서고 있
다 ap-jang-seo-go it-da, 리드하고 있다
ri-deu-ha-go it-da

leader *n.* 지도자 ji-do-ja, 수석 su-seok, 리
더 ri-deo

leadership *n.* 지도 ji-do; 지도력 ji-do-ryeok;
지도자의 임무 ji-do-ja-ui im-mu

leading *adj.* 이끄는 i-kkeu-neun; 손꼽히
는 son-kko-pi-neun; *n.* 지도 ji-do, 선도
seon-do; 통솔력 tong-sol-lyeok

leaf *n.* (*pl.* **leaves**) 나뭇잎 na-mun-nip; 잎장
식 ip-jang-sik; 한쪽 문짝 han-jjok mun-jjak

league *n.* 연맹 yeon-maeng, 동맹
dong-maeng

leak *n.* 누설 nu-seol, 샘 saem, 누출 nu-chul;
누출장소 nu-chul-jang-so; 누출량

nu-chul-lyang; *vt.* 새게하다 sae-ge-ha-da;
누출시키다 nu-chul-si-ki-da; 누설시키다
nu-seol-si-ki-da; *vi.* 새다 sae-da; 누설되다
nu-seol-doe-da

lean *adj.* 야윈 ya-win; 기름기가 적은
gi-reum-kki-ga jeog-eun; 내용이 빈약한
nae-yong-i bin-ya-kan; 메마른 me-ma-
reun; 수지가 안맞는 su-ji-ga an-man-
neun; *vt.* 기대게하다 gi-dae-ge ha-da; 구
부리다 gu-bu-ri-da; *vi.* 기대다 gi-dae-da;
기울다 gi-ul-da; 굽히다 gu-pi-da; 의지하
다 ui-ji-ha-da; 쏠리다 ssol-li-da

leap *n.* 도약 do-yak; 비약 bi-yak; 도약점
do-yak-jeom; 도약거리 do-yak-geo-ri; *vi.*
껑충뛰다 kkeong-chung-ttwi-da; 도약하
다 do-ya-ka-da

leap year *n.* 윤년 yun-nyeon

learn *vt.* 배우다 bae-u-da; 기억하다 gi-eo-
ka-da; 알다 al-da; 할수 있게 되다 hal ssu
it-ge doe-da; *vi.* 배우다 bae-u-da; 익히다
i-ki-da; 듣다 deut-da

learner *n.* 학습자 hak-seup-ja; ~**'s permit
(driving)** 가면허증 ga-myeon-heo-jjeung

learning *n.* 학문 hang-mun; 학식 hak-sik; 학
습 hak-seup

lease *n.* 차용 cha-yong; 차용증서 cha-yong-
jeung-seo; 차용권 cha-yong-kkwon; 차
용기간 cha-yong-gi-gan; *vt.* 임대하다
im-dae-ha-da

leash *n.* 개끈 gae-kkeun, 개사슬 gae-sa-seul

least *adj.* 가장 작은 ga-jang jag-eun; 가장
적은 ga-jang jeog-eun; 가장 가치가 없
는 ga-jang ga-chi-ga eom-neun; *adv.* 가
장 적게 ga-jang-jeok-ge; **at** ~ 적어도
jeog-eo-do

leather *n.* 가죽 ga-juk; 가죽제품
ga-juk-je-pum

leave *vt.* 남기고 가다 nam-gi-go ga-da; 둔
채 잊다 dun-chae it-da; 남기고 죽다 nam-
gi-go juk-da; 맡기다 mat-gi-da; 떠나다
tteo-na-da; 그치다 geu-chi-da; 그대로 놔
두다 geu-dae-ro nwa-du-da; … 할 것을 허
용하다 hal kkeos-eul heo-yong-ha-da; *vi.*
떠나다 teo-na-da; 출발하다 chul-bal-ha-
da; 그만두다 geu-man-du-da; **to** ~ **a place**
… 을 떠나다 … eul tteo-na-da; **to** ~ **sth**
…을 방치하다 …eul bang-chi-ha-da; **to**
~ **sb** 을 내버려두다eul nae-beo-ryeo-du-

da; **to ~ behind** ...을 뒤에 남기다 ...eul
dwi-e nam-gi-da
Lebanon *n.* 레바논 re-ba-non
lecture *n.* 강의 gang-ui; 잔소리 jan-so-ri; ~
hall 강당 gang-dang
lecturer *n.* 강연자 gang-yeon-ja; 강사
gang-sa
ledge *n.* 선반 seon-ban; 바위턱 ba-wi-teok;
암초 am-cho
left *adj.* 왼쪽의 oen-jjog-ui; *adv.* 왼쪽에
oen-jjog-e; 왼쪽으로 oen-jjog-eu-ro; **on
the ~ hand side** 왼쪽으로 oen-jjog-eu-ro,
왼쪽에 oen-jjog-e
left-handed *adj.* 왼손잡이의 oen-son-
jab-i-ui; 서투른 seo-tu-reun; 의심스러
운 ui-sim-seu-reo-un; 시부이 맞지 않는
sin-bun-i mat-ji an-neun; 왼쪽으로 가는
oen-jjog-eu-ro gam-neun
leftover *n.* 나머지 na-meo-ji, 찌끼기 jji-kkeo-
gi; *adj.* 나머지의 na-meo-ji-ui, 찌끼기의
jji-kkeo-gi-ui
leftward *adj.* 왼쪽의 oen-jjog-ui; *adv.* 왼쪽
에 oen-jjog-e
leg *n.* 다리 da-ri; 버팀대 beo-tim-ttae; 의
족 ui-jok
legal *adj.* 법률의 beom-nyul-ui; 법정의
beop-jeong-ui; 합법의 hap-beob-ui
legality *n.* 적법 jeok-beop, 합법 hap-beop
legation *n.* 공사관 gong-sa-gwan; 공사관
직원 gong-sa-gwan jig-won; 공사파견
gong-sa-pa-gyeon
legend *n.* 전설 jeon-seol; 범례 beom-nye
legible *adj.* 읽기 쉬운 il-kki swi-un; 명료한
myeong-nyo-han
legislation *n.* 입법 ip-beop; 법령
beom-nyeong
legitimate *adj.* 합법의 hap-beob-ui; 옳은
ol-eun; 이치에 닿는 i-chi-e dan-neun
leisure *n.* 여가 yeo-ga
lemon *n.* 레몬 re-mon
lemonade *n.* 레모네이드 re-mo-ne-i-deu
lend *vt.* 빌려주다 bil-lyeo-ju-da; 제공하다
je-gong-ha-da
length *n.* 길이 gil-i; 세로 se-ro; 키 ki; 거리
geo-ri; 범위 beom-wi; 정도 jeong-do
lengthen *vt.* 길게하다 gil-ge-ha-da, 늘이다
neul-i-da
lengthwise *adj.* 세로의 se-ro-ui, 긴 gin

lens *n.* 렌즈 ren-jeu; 수정체 su-
jeong-che; **contact ~** 콘택트렌즈
kon-taek-teu-ren-jeu
Lent *n.* 사순절 sa-sun-jeol
lentil *n.* 렌즈콩 ren-jeu-kong
lesbian *n.* 동성연애자 dong-seong-yeon-ae-
ja, 레즈비언 re-jeu-bi-eon
lesion *n.* 상해 sang-hae; 손해 son-hae; 장
애 jang-ae
less *adj.* 더 적은 deo jeog-eun; 더 작은 deo
jag-eun; *adv.* 더 적게 deo jeok-ge; **~er**
작은 편의 jag-eun pyeon-ui; 못한 편의
mo-tan pyeon-ui
lessen *vt.* 적게하다 jeok-ge-ha-da, 작게 하다
jak-ge-ha-da
lesson *n.* 학과 hak-gwa; 과 gwa; 수업 su-eop;
교훈 gyo hun
lest *conj.* ...하지 않게 ...ha-ji an-ke, ...하면
인되니까 ...ha-myeon an-doe-ni-kka
let *vt.* ...에게...시키다 ...e-ge...si-ki-da, ...하
게 해주다 ...ha-ge hae-ju-da, 들여보
내다 deul-yeo bo-nae-da, 통과시키다
tong-gwa-si-ki-da, 세놓다 se-no-ta, 일을
주다 il-eul ju-da
letter *n.* 글자 geul-jja; 서체 seo-che; 편지
pyeon-ji
lettuce *n.* 상치 sang-chi, 양상치
yang-sang-chi
level *adj.* 수평 su-pyeong; 수준 su-jun; 평지
pyeong-ji; 동일수준 dong-il-su-jun; 표준
pyo-jun; 수평갱도 su-pyeong-gaeng-do
lever *n.* 지레 ji-re, 레비 re-beo
liability *n.* ...의 경향이 있음 ...ui gyeong-
hyang-i iss-eum; 책임이 있음 chaeg-im-i
iss-eum; 책임액 chaeg-im-aek; 불리한 조
항 bul-li-han jo-hang
liable *adj.* 책임을 져야 할 chaeg-im-eul jeo-
ya-hal; 부과되어야 할 bu-gwa-doe-eo-ya
hal; 의무가 있는 ui-mu-ga in-neun; 자칫
하면...하는 ja-chi-ta-myeon...ha-neun
liaison *n.* 연락 yeol-lak; 섭외 seob-oe; 간통
gan-tong; 연력 yeol-lyeok
liar *n.* 거짓말쟁이 geo-jin-mal-jaeng-i
libel *n.* 명예훼손(죄) myeong-ye-hwe-
son(-jjoe); 모욕이 되는 것 mo-yog-i
doe-neun geot; *vt.* 중상하다 jung-sang-
ha-da; 명예를 훼손하다 myeong-ye-reul
hwe-son-ha-da

liberal *adj.* 자유주의의 ja-yu-ju-i-ui; 민주제의 min-ju-je-ui; 관대한 gwan-dae-han; 자유로운 ja-yu-ro-un; 대범한 dae-beom-han; 풍부한 pung-bu-han

liberty *n.* 자유 ja-yu; 해방 hae-bang; …할 권리 …hal gwol-li

librarian *n.* 도서관 직원 do-seo-gwan jig-won, 사서 sa-seo

library *n.* 도서관 do-seo-gwan; 장서 jang-seo; 수집 su-jip; 문고 mun-go

license *n.* 면허 myeon-heo; 허가증 heo-ga-jjeung; 파격 pa-gyeok; ~ **plate** 자동차 번호판 ja-dong-cha beon-ho-pan; **driver's** ~ 운전면허증 un-jeon-myeon-heo-jjeung; **export** ~ 전문가 면허증 jeon-mun-ga myeon-heo-jjeung

lick *vt.* 핥다 hal-ta; 넘실거리다 neom-sil-geo-ri-da; 매질하다 mae-jil-ha-da

lid *n.* 뚜껑 ttu-kkeong; 눈꺼풀 nun-kkeo-pul; 제한 je-han; 단속 dan-sok

lie *n.* *(falsehood)* 거짓말 geo-jin-mal; 사기 sa-gi; 잘못된 관습 jal-mot-doen gwan-seup; *vi.* 눕다 nup-da; 기대다 gi-dae-da; 묻혀있다 mu-chyeo-it-da; 놓여있다 no-yeo-it-da; 위치하다 wi-chi-ha-da; 거짓말하다 geo-jin-mal-ha-da; 속이다 sog-i-da; **to tell a** ~ 거짓말하다 geo-jin-mal-ha-da

lieutenant *n.* 대위 dae-wi; 중위 jung-wi; 소위 so-wi; 부관 bu-gwan

life *n.* 삶 sam; 생명 saeng-myeong; 수명 su-myeong; 생물 saeng-mul; 생활 saeng-hwal; 인생 in-saeng; 전기 jeon-gi; 활기 hwal-gi

life-and-death *adj.* 생사가 걸린 saeng-sa-ga geol-lin

lifeboat *n.* 구명정 gu-myeong-jeong; 구조선 gu-jo-seon

lifeguard *n.* 수영장 구조원 su-yeong-jang gu-jo-won

life jacket *n.* 구명자켓 gu-myeong-ja-ket

lifeless *adj.* 생명이 없는 saeng-myeong-i eom-neun; 기절한 gi-jeol-han; 활기가 없는 hwal-gi-ga eom-neun

lifelong *adj.* 평생의 pyeong-saeng-ui

lifesavor *n.* 인명구조대 in-myeong-gu-jo-dae

life-size *adj.* 실물크기의 sil-mul-keu-gi-ui

life span *n.* 평균수명 pyeong-gyun-su-myeong, 수명 su-myeong

lifetime *n.* 일생 il-ssaeng; 평생 pyeong-saeng

lift *n.* 올리기 ol-li-gi; 오르기 o-reu-gi; 태우기 tae-u-gi; 승진 seung-jin; *vt.* 들어올리다 deul-eo-ol-li-da; 올리다 ol-li-da; 향상시키다 hyang-sang-si-ki-da; 장애물을 치우다 jang-ae-mul-eul chi-u-da

light *n.* 빛 bit; 햇빛 haet-bit; 교통신호 gyo-tong-sin-ho; 조명 jo-myeong; 광명 gwang-myeong; *adj.* *(color)* 밝은 balg-eun; 엷은 yeot-eun; *(weight)* 가벼운 ga-byeo-un; 경쾌한 gyeong-kwae-han; 손쉬운 son-swi-un; 경미한 gyeong-mi-han; *vt.* 불을 켜다 bul-eul kyeo-da; 밝게하다 bal-kke-ha-da; ~ **bulb** 전구 jeon-gu

lighten *vt.* 밝게하다 bal-kke-ha-da; 가볍게하다 ga-byeop-ge ha-da; 계발하다 gye-bal-ha-da; 명랑하게 하다 myeong-nang-ha-ge ha-da; 색을 여리게 하다 saeg-eul yeo-ri-ge ha-da

lighter *n.* 라이터 ra-i-teo

lighthouse *n.* 등대 deung-dae; ~ **keeper** 등대지기 deung-dae-ji-gi

lighting *n.* 조명 jo-myeong, 조명장치 jo-myeong-jang-chi; 점화 jeom-hwa; 명암 myeong-am

lightning *n.* 번개 beon-gae; ~ **rod** 피뢰침 pi-roe-chim

like *adj.* …와 닮은 …wa dalm-eun; …와 같은 …wa gat-eun; …의 특징을 나타내는 …ui teuk-jing-eul na-ta-nae-neun; …하게 될 것 같은 …ha-ge doel kkeot gat-eun; …다운 …da-un; *adv.* …듯이 …deus-i, …처럼 …cheo-reom; **He is** ~ **his father** 그분은 자기 아버지처럼 생겼습니다 geu bun-eun ja-gi a-beo-ji-cheo-reom saeng-gyeot-seum-ni-da; **It looks** ~ **a good deal** 좋은 거래인 것 같습니다 jo-eun geo-rae-in geot gat-seum-ni-da; *vt.* 좋아하다 jo-a-ha-da; 바라다 ba-ra-da; 체질에 맞다 che-jil-e mat-da

likely *adv.* 아마 a-ma, 십중팔구 sip-jung-pal-gu; …할 것 같은 …hal kkeot gat-eun

likewise *adv.* 똑같이 ttok-ga-chi; 게다가 ge-da-ga

limb *n.* 수족 su-jok; 손발 son-bal; 팔다리 pal-da-ri; 큰 가지 keun ga-ji; 돌출부 dol-chul-bu; 자손 ja-son; 부하 bu-ha; 가장자리 ga-jang-ja-ri

lime *n.* 라임 ra-im; 석회 seo-koe; **~stone** 석회암 seo-koe-am

limit *n.* 한계 han-gye; 경계 gyeong-gye; 제한 je-han; 지정가격 ji-jeong-kka-gyeok; 최대액 choe-dae-aek; 한도 han-do

limited *adj.* 제한된 je-han-doen

limousine *n.* 리무진 ri-mu-jin

limp *n.* 발을 절뚝거림 bal-eul jeol-ttuk-geo-rim; *vi.* 절뚝거리다 jeol-ttuk-geo-ri-da; 느릿느릿 가다 neu-rin-neu-rit ga-da; 운율이 안맞다 un-yul-i an-mat-da

line *n.* 선 seon; 금 geum; 행 haeng; 테두리 te-du-ri; 경계 gyeong-gye; 줄 jul; 노선 no-seon; 끈 kkeun; *vt.* 선을 긋다 seon-eul geut-da; 윤곽을 잡나 yun-gwag-eul jap-da; 정렬시키다 jeong-nyeol-si-ki-da; 주름살을 짓다 ju-reum-ssal-eul jit-da

linen *n.* 린네르 rin-ne-reu; 린네르 제품 rin-ne-reu je-pum

liner *n.* 정기선 jeong-gi-seon; 정기 항공기 jeong-gi hang-gong-gi; 안에 대는 것 an-e dae-neun geot, 안감 an-kkam; 선긋는 기계 seon geun-neun gi-gye, 선긋는 사람 seon geun-neun sa-ram

lineup *n.* 정렬 jeong-nyeol

lining *n.* 안감 an-kkam; 알맹이 al-maeng-i; 내면 nae-myeon; 라이닝 ra-i-ning; 안감대기 an-kkam-dae-gi

link *n.* 고리 go-ri; 코 ko; 한토막 han to mak; 연결자 yeon-gyeol-ja; 링크 ring-keu; 주요단계 ju-yo-dan-gye; *vt.* 연결하다 yeon-gyeol-ha-da; 결합하다 gyeol-ha-pa-da; 팔짱을 끼다 pal-jjang-eul kki-da

lion *n.* 사자 sa-ja; 용감한 사람 yong-gam-han sa-ram; 유명한 사람 yu-myeong-han sa-ram; 라이온즈클럽 회원 ra-i-on-jeu-keul-leop hoe-won

lip *n.* 입술 ip-sul; 입 ip; 말 mal; 식기 가장자리 sik-gi ga-jang-ja-ri; **~stick** 립스틱 rip-seu-tik

liqueur *n.* 리큐르 ri-kyu-reu

liquid *n.* 액체 aek-che; 유동체 yu-dong-che; *adj.* 액체의 aek-che-ui; 유동체의 yu-dong-che-ui; 유창한 y-chang-han; 투명한 tu-myeong-han

liquor *n.* 술 sul; 분비액 bun-bi-aek; 공업용 용액 gong-eom-nyong yong-aek; 물약 mul-lyak

list *n.* 목록 mong-nok; 명부 myeong-bu; 일람표 il-lam-pyo; *vt.* 목록으로 만들다 mong-nog-eu-ro man-deul-da; 명부에 올리다 myeong-bu-e ol-li-da; 목록에 올리다 mong-nog-e ol-li-da; 상장하다 sang-jang-ha-da

listen *vt.* 듣다 deut-da

listener *n.* 듣는 사람 deun-neun sa-ram; 청취자 cheong-chwi-ja

literally *adv.* 글자 그대로 geul-jja geu-dae-ro; 사실상 sa-sil-ssang

literary *adj.* 문학의 mun-hag-ui; 학문의 hang-mun-ui; 문학에 종사하는 mun-hag-e jong-sa-ha-neun; 문학에 통달한 mun-hag-e tong-dal-han

literature *n.* 문학 mun-hag; 문학연구 mun-hang-nyeon-gu; 작가생활 jak-ga-saeng-hwal; 문헌 mun-heon; 저술 jeo-sul

litter *n.* 들것 deul-kkeot; *(puppies)* 깔짚 kkal-jjip; *(trash)* 쓰레기 sseu-re-gi; 혼돈 hon-don

little *pron.* 조금 jo-geum, 소량 so-ryang, 약간 yak-gan, 잠깐 jam-kkan; **~ by ~** 조금씩 조금씩 jo-geum-ssik jo-geum-ssik; *adj.* 작은 jag-eun, 귀여운 gwi-yeo-un, 어린 eo-rin, 사소한 sa-so-han, 초라한 cho-ra-han, 짧은 jjalb-eun, 중요치 않은 jung-yo-chi an-eun; 조금밖에 없는 jo-geum-bakke eom-neun, 조금 있는 jo-geum in-neun; **a ~ bit** 약간 yak-gan; *adv.* 거의 …않다 geo-ui …an-ta, 선혀 …하지 않다 jeon-hyeo …ha-ji an-ta, 약간 yak-gan, 조금은 jo-geum-eun; **It's a ~ dark here** 여기는 좀 어둡다 yeo-gi-neun jom eo-dup-da

live *adj.* 살아있는 sal-a-in-neun; 생생한 saeng-saeng-han; 빛나는 bin-na-neun; 밝은 balg-eun; 움직이고 있는 um-jig-i-go in-neun; 전기가 통하는 jeon-gi-ga tong-ha-neun; *vi.* 살아있다 sal-a-it-da; 살다 sal-da; 생활하다 saeng-hwal-ha-da; 존속하다 jon-so-ka-da

lively *adj.* 생기에 넘친 saeng-gi-ga neom-chin; 약동적인 yak-dong-jeog-in; 생생한 saeng-saeng-han; 아슬아슬한 a-seul-a-seul-han; 상쾌한 sang-kwae-han

liver *n.* 간 gan; 거주자 geo-ju-ja

livestock *n.* 가축 ga-chuk

living *adj.* 살아있는 sal-a-in-neun; 활발한 hwal-bal-han; 현대의 hyeon-dae-ui; *n.* 생활 saeng-hwal, 생계 saeng-gye; ~ **room** 거실 geo-sil; **standard of** ~ 생활수준 saeng-hwal-su-jun

lizard *n.* 도마뱀 do-ma-baem

load *n.* 짐 jim; 적재량 jeok-jae-ryang; 부담 bu-dam; 하중 ha-jung; 장전 jang-jeon; *vt.* 짐을 싣다 jim-eul sit-da; 올려놓다 ol-lyeo-no-ta; 탄환을 재다 tan-hwan-eul jae-da

loaf *n.* 덩어리 deong-eo-ri; **a** ~ **of bread** 빵 한덩어리 ppang han-deong-eo-ri

loan *n.* 대부 dae-bu; 대부금 dae-bu-geum; 대차물 dae-cha-mul; *vt.* 빌려주다 bil-lyeo-ju-da; 대부하다 dae-bu-ha-da; ~**word** 외래어 oe-rae-eo

lobby *n.* 로비 ro-bi; 압력단체 am-nyeok-dan-che

lobster *n.* 바닷가재 ba-dat-ga-jae, 랍스터 rap-seu-teo

local *adj.* 공간의 gong-gan-ui; 지방의 ji-bang-ui; ~ **call** 시내통화 si-nae-tong-hwa; ~ **government** 지방자치단체 ji-bang-ja-chi-dan-che; ~ **time** 현지시각 hyeon-ji-si-gak

localize *vt.* 한 지방에 제한하다 han ji-bang-e je-han-ha-da; 지방화하다 ji-bang-hwa-ha-da

locate *vt.* 위치를 정하다 wi-chi-reul jeong-ha-da; 거처를 정하다 geo-cheo-reul jeong-ha-da

location *n.* 위치선정 wi-chi-seon-jeong; 위치 wi-chi; 로케이션 ro-ke-i-syeon

lock *n.* 자물쇠 ja-mul-ssoe; 수문 su-mun; 교통혼잡 gyo-tong-hon-jap; 제륜장치 je-ryun-jang-chi; *vt.* 자물쇠를 채우다 ja-mul-ssoe-reul chae-u-da; 가두다 ga-du-da; 끌어안다 kkeul-eo-an-tta; 제동시키다 je-dong-si-ki-da; 수문을 설치하다 su-mun-eul seol-chi-ha-da

locker *n.* 로커 ro-keo; 창고지기 chang-kko-ji-gi; ~ **room** 로커룸 ro-keo-rum

locomotive *n.* 기관차 gi-gwan-cha

locust *n.* 메뚜기 me-ttu-gi; 매미 mae-mi

lodge *n.* 오두막집 o-du-mak-jip; 지방지부 ji-bang-ji-bu; 수위실 su-wi-sil; *vi.* 숙박하다 suk-ba-ka-da; 박히다 ba-ki-da; 굴로 도망치다 gul-lo do-mang-chi-da

lodging *n.* 하숙 ha-suk; 셋방 set-bang; 숙박 suk-bak

loft *n.* 다락 da-rak, 지붕밑 방 ji-bung-mit bang; 비둘기장 bi-dul-gi-jang

log *n.* (*lumber*) 통나무 tong-na-mu; 바보 ba-bo; 항해일지 hang-hae-il-jji; 노동시간표 no-dong-si-gan-pyo, 시간기록표 si-gan-gi-rok-pyo; (*computer*) 로그 ro-geu *vt.* 통나무로 자르다 tong-na-mu-ro ja-reu-da, 통나무를 깔다 tong-na-mu-reul kkal-da; 일지를 기입하다 il-jji-reul gi-i-pa-da, 로그하다 ro-geu-ha-da

logic *adj.* 논리 nol-li; 논리학 nol-li-hak; 설득력 seol-tteung-nyeok

logical *adj.* 논리적인 nol-li-jeog-in; 필연의 pil-yeon-ui; 논리상의 nol-li-sang-ui

logo *n.* 로고 ro-go

lollipop *n.* 막대사탕 mak-dae-sa-tang

London *n.* 런던 reon-deon

lone *adj.* 혼자의 hon-ja-ui; 외로운 oe-ro-un; 고립된 go-rip-doen; 외진 oe-jin

lonely *adj.* 외로운 oe-ro-un; 고독한 go-do-kan; 외진 oe-jin; 쓸쓸한 sseul-sseul-han

long *n.* 장시간 jang-si-gan; 장모음 jang-mo-eum; 장음절 jang-eum-jeol; *adj.* 긴 gin; 키가 큰 ki-ga keun; 오랜 o-raen; 다량의 da-ryang-ui; **a** ~ **time** 오랫동안 o-raet-dong-an; ~ **distance** 장거리 전화 jang-geo-ri jeon-hwa; *adv.* 오랫동안 o-raet-dong-an; 내내 nae-nae; *vi.* 간절히 바라다 gan-jeol-hi ba-ra-da; 동경하다 dong-gyeong-ha-da; 그리워하다 geu-ri-wo-ha-da

longevity *n.* 장수 jang-su; 수명 su-myeong

longing *n.* 갈망 gal-mang, 동경 dong-gyeong

longitude *n.* 경도 gyeong-do, 경선 gyeong-seon

long-life *adj.* 수명이 긴 su-myeong-i gin, 오래가는 o-rae-ga-neun

long-run *adj.* 장기흥행의 jang-gi-heung-haeng-ui

long-term *adj.* 장기간의 jang-gi-gan-ui
look *n.* 눈표정 nun-pyo-jeong; 얼굴표정
eol-gul-pyo-jeong; 외관 oe-gwan; 보기
bo-gi; *vi.* 보다 bo-da; 바라보다 ba-ra-
bo-da; 조사하다 jo-sa-ha-da; ...하게
보이다 ...ha-ge boi-da; 예기하다 ye-gi-
ha-da; ... 을 향하다 ... eul hyang-ha-da,
... 를 향하다 ... reul hyang-ha-da; **to ~ at**
보다 bo-da; 고찰하다 go-chal-ha-da; **to
~ for** 찾다 chat-da; 기다리다 gi-da-ri-da;
to ~ out 망보기 mang-bo-gi; 조망대
jo-mang-dae
look-over *vt.* 대충 훑어보다 dae-chung
hult-eo-bo-da
loom *n.* 베틀 be-teul; (노의) 자루 (no-ui)
ja-ru; *vi.* 어렴풋이 나타나다 eo-ryeom-
pus-i na-ta-na-da
loop *n.* 고리 go-ri, 루프 ru-peu
loose *adj.* 풀린 pul-lin; 흐트러진 heu-
teu-reo-jin; 떨어진 tteol-eo-jin; 벗어진
beos-eo-jin; 헐거운 heol-geo-un; 치밀하
지 못한 chi-mil-ha-ji mo-tan; 포장하지 않
은 po-jang-ha-ji an-eun
loosen *vt.* 풀다 pul-da; 놓아주다 no-a-
ju-da; 늦추다 neut-chu-da; 완화하다
wan-hwa-ha-da
lord *n.* 지배자 ji-bae-ja; 군주 gun-ju; 하나
님 ha-na-nim
lose *vt.* 잃다 il-ta; 없애다 eops-ae-da; 낭비
하다 nang-bi-ha-da; 느리다 neu-ri-da; 못
잡다 mot-jap-da; 놓치다 no-chi-da; *vi.* 지
다 ji-da; 감소하다 gam-so-ha-da; 손해보
다 son-hae-bo-da; 쇠하다 soe-ha-da; 늦
다 neut-da
loser *n.* 실패자 sil-pae-ja, 패자 pae-ja
loss *n.* 분실 bun-sil; 상실 sang-sil; 손실
son-sil; 실패 sil-pae; 패배 pae-bae; 사망
sa-mang
lost *adj.* 잃어버린 il-eo-beo-rin; 진 jin; 빼
앗긴 ppae-at-gin; 낭비된 nang-bi-doen;
길을 잃은 gil-eul il-eun; 마음이 팔린
ma-eum-i pal-lin; **We are ~** 우리는 길
을 잃어버렸습니다 u-ri-neun gil-eul
il-eo-beo-ryeot-seum-ni-da; **I ~ the keys**
열쇠를 잃어버렸습니다 yeol-ssoe-reul
il-eo-beo-ryeot-seum-ni-da
lot *n.* 제비 je-bi, 추첨 chu-cheom; 당첨
dang-cheom; 몫 mok; *(property)* 부지

bu-ji, 공지 gong-ji; **a ~ of money** 많은 돈
man-eun don; **a ~ of sense** 이치에 합당함
i-chi-e hap-dang-ham, 사리에 맞음 sa-ri-e
maj-eum
lotion *n.* 로션 ro-syeon
lottery *n.* 복권 bok-gwon; 제비뽑기
je-bi-ppop-gi
loud *adj.* 시끄러운 si-kkeu-reo-un; 목소리가
큰 mok-so-ri-ga keun; 성가신 seong-ga-
sin; 뻔뻔스러운 ppeon-ppeon-seu-reo-un;
야한 ya-han
loudspeaker *n.* 확성기 hwak-seong-gi
lounge *n.* 라운지 ra-un-ji, 로비 ro-bi; 안락의
자 al-lag-ui-ja
love *n.* 사랑 sa-rang; 연애 yeon-ae; 좋아
한 jo-a ham; 애정 ae jeong; 애인 ae-in;
vt. 사랑하다 sa-rang-ha-da; 좋아하다
jo-a-ha-da; 애호하다 ae-ho-ha-da; *vi.* 연
애하고 있다 yeon-ae-ha-go it-da; 사랑하
고 있다 sa-rang-ha-go it-da; **~ letter** 연애
편지 yeon-ae-pyeon-ji; **~ story** 연애소설
yeon-ae-so-seol
lovely *adj.* 사랑스러운 sa-rang-seu-reo-un;
귀여운 gwi-yeo-un; 아름다운 a-reum-da-
un; 멋진 meot-jin; 즐거운 jeul-geo-un; 유
쾌한 yu-kwae-han
lover *n.* 연인 yeon-in; 애인 ae-in; 애호자
ae-ho-ja
lovesickness *n.* 상사병 sang-sa-ppyeong
low *adj.* 낮은 naj-eun; 적은 jeog-eun; 질이
낮은 jil-i naj-eun; 침울한 chim-ul-han; 기
운이 없는 gi-un-i eom-neun; 히층의 ha-
cheung-ui; 상스러운 sang-seu-reo-un; 얕
은 yat-eun; **~ blood pressure** 저혈압 jeo-
hyeol-ap; **~ class** 히층민 ha-cheung-min
lower *vt.* 낮추다 nat-chu-da, 떨어뜨리다
tteol-eo-tteu-ri-da; *vi.* 내려지다 nae ryeo
ji-da; *adj.* 하급의 ha-geub-ui, 아래쪽의
a-rae-jjog-ui
low-pressure *adj.* 저기압의 jeo-gi-ab-ui
low-spirited *adj.* 기운이 없는 gi-un-i eom-
neun, 우울한 u-ul-han, 시들한 si-deul-han
low season *n.* 비수기 bi-su-gi
loyal *adj.* 충성스러운 chung-seong-seu-
reo-un; 성실한 seong-sil-han; 정직한
jeong-ji-kan
lubricate *vt.* 기름을 치다 gi-reum-eul chi-da;
미끄럽게 하다 mi-kkeu-reop-ge ha-da

luck *n.* 운 un; 행운 haeng-un; 요행 yo-
   haeng; **good** ~ 행운 haeng-un
luckily *adv.* 운좋게 un-jo-ke; 요행히도
   yo-haeng-hi-do
lucky *adj.* 행운의 haeng-un-ui; 상서로운
   sang-seo-ro-un
luggage *n.* 수하물 su-ha-mul; 여행가방
   yeo-haeng-kka-bang; ~ **rack** 그물선반
   geu-mul-seon-ban, 선반 seon-ban
lullaby *n.* 자장가 ja-jang-ga
lumber *n.* 잡동사니 jap-dong-sa-ni; 목재
   mok-jae, 재목 jae-mok
lump *n.* 덩어리 deong-eo-ri; 한조각 han-jo-
   gak; 혹 hok; 대다수 dae-da-su
lunar *adj.* 달의 dal-ui; 달 모양의 dal mo-
   yang-ui; 달에 의한 dal-e ui-han; ~ **calendar**
   태음력 tae-eum-nyeok, 음력 eum-nyeok
lunatic *adj.* 미친 mi-chin; 미치광이같은
   mi-chi-gwang-i-gat-eun; 정신병자를 위한
   jeong-sin-ppyeong-ja-reul wi-han

lunch *n.* 점심 jeom-sim; 간단한 식사 gan-
   dan-han sik-sa; **to have** ~ 점심을
   먹다 jeom-sim-eul meok-da; ~ **box**
   도시락 do-si-rak; ~ **time** 점심시간
   jeom-sim-ssi-gan
lung *n.* 폐 pye; 인공호흡장치
   in-gong-ho-heup-jang-chi
Luxembourg *n.* 룩셈부르크
   ruk-sem-bu-reu-keu
luxurious *adj.* 사치스러운 sa-chi-seu-
   reo-un; 사치를 좋아하는 sa-chi-reul
   jo-a-ha-neun; 쾌락을 추구하는
   kwae-rag-eul chu-gu-ha-neun; 방종한
   bang-jong-han
luxury *n.* 사치 sa-chi; 호사 ho-sa; 사치품
   sa-chi-pum; 쾌락 kwae-rak
lye *n.* 잿물 jaen-mul, 알칼리액
   al-kal-li-aek
lynch *vt.* 린치를 가하다 rin-chi-reul
   ga-ha-da

M

macaroni *n.* 마카로니 ma-ka-ro-ni
machine *n.* 기계 gi-gye; 기계장치 gi-gye-
   jang-chi; 기관 gi-gwan
machinery *n.* 기계 gi-gye; 기계장치 gi-gye-
   jang-chi; 기관 gi-gwan
mad *adj.* 열광적인 yeol-gwang-jeog-in; 열
   중한 yeol-jjung-han; 무모한 mu-mo-han;
   (insane) 미친 mi-chin; *(furious)* 광포
   한 gwang-po-han; **He is** ~ **at me** 그분
   은 저한테 화가 났습니다 geu bun-eun
   jeo-han-te hwa-ga nat-seum-ni-da
Madagascar 마다가스카르 ma-da-ga-
   seu-ka-reu
madam *n.* 아씨 a-ssi; 부인 bu-in, 마님 ma-nim
Madeira *n.* 마데이라 ma-de-i-ra
Madrid *n.* 마드리드 ma-deu-ri-deu
mafia *n.* 마피아 ma-pi-a
magazine *n.* 잡지 jap-ji; 병기고 byeong-gi-
   go; 식량창고 sing-nyang-chang-go
magic *n.* 마법 ma-beop; 기술 gi-sul; 매력
   mae-ryeok
magical *adj.* 마법의 ma-beob-ui; 기술의 gi-
   sul-ui; 마법과 같은 ma-beop-gwa gat-eun

magician *n.* 마법사 ma-beop-sa; 요술장이
   yo-sul-jang-i; 기술자 gi-sul-jja
magistrate *n.* 행정장관 haeng-jeong-jang-
   gwan; 치안판사 chi-an-pan-sa
magma *n.* 마그마 ma-geu-ma
magnet *n.* 자석 ja-seok
magnetic *adj.* 자석의 ja-seog-ui; 매력
   있는 mae-ryeog-in-neun; 최면술의
   choe-myeon-sul-ui
magnificent *adj.* 장대한 jang-dae-han; 굉장
   한 goeng-jang-han; 당당한 dang-dang-
   han; 엄청난 eom-cheong-nan
magnify *vt.* 확대하다 hwak-dae-ha-da; 과장
   하다 gwa-jang-ha-da; ~**ing glass** 확대경
   hwak-dae-gyeong, 돋보기 dot-bo-gi
maid *n.* 소녀 so-nyeo; 하녀 ha-nyeo; 미혼여
   성 mi-hon-nyeo-seong
mail *n.* 우편물 u-pyeon-mul; 우편제도 u-
   pyeon-je-do; 우편용차 u-pyeon-nyong-cha
mailbox *n.* 우체통 u-che-tong; 우편함
   u-pyeong-ham
mailman *n.* 우편배달부 u-pyeon-bae-dal-bu,
   집배원 jip-bae-won

mail order *n.* 통신판매 tong-sin-pan-mae

main *adj.* 주요한 ju-yo-han; 최대의 choe-dae-ui

mainland *n.* 본토 bon-to; 대륙 dae-ryuk

mainstream *n.* 주류 ju-ryu, 대세 dae-se; *adj.* 주류의 ju-ryu-ui

maintain *vt.* 지속하다 ji-so-ka-da; 유지하 다 yu-ji-ha-da; 간수하다 gan-su-ha-da; 부양하다 bu-yang-ha-da; 주장하다 ju-jang-ha-da

maintenance *n.* 유지 yu-ji; 지속 ji-sok; 간수 gan-su; 부양 bu-yang; 생계 saeng-gye; ~ man정비공 jeong-bi-gong

majestic *adj.* 장엄한 jang-eom-han; 위엄있 는 wi-eom-in-neun

majesty *n.* 위엄 wi-eom; 권위 gwon-wi; 주권 ju-kkwon; 왕 wang

major *n. (school specialization)* 전공 jeon-gong; *(military)* 소령 so-ryeong; *adj. (greater)* 대다수의 dae-da-su-ui; *(considerable)* 주요한 ju-yo-han; 성년의 seong-nyeon-ui; 전공의 jeon-gong-ui

majority *n.* 대부분 dae-bu-bun; 다수파 da-su-pa; 과반수a-ban-su g; 성년 seong-nyeon; 소령직 so-ryeong-jik

make *n.* 제작법 je-jak-beop, 모양 mo-yang, 지음새 ji-eum-sae, 구조 gu-jo, 구성 gu-seong, 조직 jo-jik, 형식 hyeong-sik, 체격 che-gyeok, 성격 seong-kkyeok, 기질 gi-jil, 제작수량 je-jak-su-ryang, 생산고 saeng-san-go; *vt.* 만들다 man-deul-da, 제작하다 je-ga-ka-da, 창조하다 chang-jo-ha-da, 창 작하다 chang-ja-ka-da, 길들이다 gil-deul-i-da, 발달시키다 bal-ttal-si-ki-da, 준비하 다 jun-bi-ha-da, 구성하다 gu-seong-ha-da, 고안하다 go-an-ha-da, 돈을 벌다 don-eul beol-da, 실행하다 sil-haeng-ha-da, 먹다 meok-da; ...을 ...으로 만들다 ...eul ...eu-ro man-deul-da, ...시키다 ...si-ki-da, 억지 로 ...하게 하다 eok-ji-ro ...ha-ge ha-da

maker *n.* 제작자 je-jak-ja; 제조업자 je-jo-eop-ja; 조물주 jo-mul-jju

make-up *n.* 조립 jo-rip; 짜임새 jja-im-sae, 구 성 gu-seong; 조직 jo-jik; 체질 che-jil; 조판 jo-pan; *(cosmetics)* 화장 hwa-jang

malaria *n.* 말라리아 mal-la-ri-a

Malaysia *n.* 말레이지아 mal-le-i-ji-a

male *n.* 남자의 nam-ja-ui; 수컷의 su-keos-ui

malfunction *n.* 고장 go-jang; *vi.* 고장나다 go-jang-na-da

malignant *adj.* 악의 있는 ag-ui-in-neun; 악 성의 ak-seong-ui

mall *n.* 몰 mol, 상가 sang-ga

malnutrition *n.* 영양실조 yeong-yang-sil-jjo

Malta *n.* 몰타섬 mol-ta-seom

maltreat *vt.* 학대하다hak-dae-ha-da, 혹사하 다 hok-sa-ha-da

mammal *n.* 포유류 po-yu-ryu, 포유동물 po-yu-dong-mul

man *n.* 남자 nam-ja; 사람 sa-ram; 남자다움 nam-ja-da-um

manage *vt.* 다루다 da-ru-da; 처리하다 cheo-ri-ha-da; 관리하다 gwal-li-ha-da; 해 내다 he-nae-da

management *n.* 관리 gwal-li; 경영 gyeong-yeong; 취급chwi-geup; 경영력 gyeong-yeong-nyeok; 경영진 gyeong-yeong-jin

manager *n.* 지배인 ji-bae-in; 경영자 gyeong-yeong-ja

mandatory *adj.* 명령의 myeong-nyeong-ui, 강제의 gang-je-ui

maneuver *vi.* 연습하다 yeon-seu-pa-da; 책 략을 쓰다 chaeng-nyag-eul sseu-da

manhole *n.* 맨홀 maen-hol

manhood *n.* 인격 in-kkyeok; 남자다움 nam-ja-da-um; 성년 seong-nyeon

mania *n.* 열광 yeol-gwang, 마니아 ma-ni-a

manicure *n.* 매니큐어 mae-ni-kyu-eo

manifold *n.* 다양성 da-yang-sseong; 사본 sa-bon, 복사 bok-sa

manipulate *vt.* 교묘히 다루다 gyo-myo-hi da-ru-da; 농간을 부리다 nong-gan-eul bu-ri-da; 속임수를 쓰다 sog-im-su-reul sseu-da

mankind *n.* 인류 il-lyu, 인간 in-gan, 사람 sa-ram

manly *adj.* 남자다운 nam-ja-da-un; 남성적 인 nam-seong-jeog-in

man-made *adj.* 인공적인 in-gong-jeog-in

mannequin *n.* 마네킹 ma-ne-king

manner *n.* 방법 bang-beop; 예절 ye-jeol; 풍 습 pung-seup; 태도 tae-do; 양식 yang-sik; 특징teuk-jing

manpower *n.* 인력자원 il-lyeok-ja-won, 인력 il-lyeok, 총인원 chong-in-won

mansion *n.* 대저택 dae-jeo-taek

man-to-man *adj.* 직접 대면한 jik-jeop dae-myeon-han, 일대일의 il-ttae-il-ui

manual *adj.* 손의 son-ui, 수공의 su-gong-ui; *n.* 소책자 so-chaek-ja, 안내서 an-nae-seo

manufacture *n.* 제조 je-jo; 제조업 je-jo-eop; 제품 je-pum; *vt.* 제조하다 je-jo-ha-da; 말을 꾸며대다 mal-eul kku-myeo-dae-da

manufacturer *n.* 제조업자 je-jo-eop-ja

manure *n.* 거름 geo-reum; 비료 bi-ryo

manuscript *n.* 원고 won-go; 피사본 pi-sa-bon; 사본 sa-bon

many *adj.* 많은 man-eun, 다수의 da-su-ui

map *n.* 지도 ji-do; 설명도 seol-myeong-do; 도해 do-hae

marathon *n.* 마라톤 ma-ra-ton

marble *n.* 대리석 dae-ri-seok; 구슬 gu-seul; 공기돌 gong-gi-ttol

March *n.* 3월 sam-wol; 행진 haeng-jin; 행진곡 haeng-jin-gok; 진보 jin-bo

march *n.* 행진 haeng-jin, 행군 haeng-gun; *vi.* 행진하다 haeng-jin-ha-da; *vt.* 행군시키다 haeng-guk-si-ki-da

mare *n.* 암말 am-mal

margarine *n.* 마가린 ma-ga-rin

margin *n.* 가장자리 ga-jang-ja-ri; 판매수익 pan-mae-su-ik, 이문 i-mun; 여백 yeo-baek; 여유 yeo-yu

marine *n.* 해병대 hae-byeong-dae; 선박 seon-bak; 해병 hae-byeong; 해군 hae-gun; *adj.* 바다의 ba-da-ui; 해상의 hae-sang-ui; 선박의 seon-bag-ui

mark *n.* 표 pyo; 기호 gi-ho; 표적 pyo-jeok; 흔적 heun-jeok; 목표 mok-pyo; 인상 in-sang; 감화 gam-hwa; 점수 jeom-su; 평점 pyeong-jjeom; 표시 pyo-si; 특징 teuk-jing; *vt.* 채점하다 chae-jjeom-ha-da; 표를 붙이다 pyo-reul bu-chi-da; 한계를 정하다 han-gye-reul jeong-ha-da; 주의를 기울이다 ju-i-reul gi-ul-i-da

market *n.* 시장 si-jang; 판로 pal-lo; 수요 su-yo; 거래 jeo-rae; 매매 mae-mae; 시황 si-hwang; 시세 si-se

marketing *n.* 매매 mae-mae; 마케팅 ma-ke-ting

marketplace *n.* 시장 si-jang, 장터 jang-teo

market price *n.* 시세 si-se, 시장가격 si-jang-kka-gyeok

market research *n.* 시장조사 si-jang-jo-sa

marmalade *n.* 마말레이드 ma-mal-le-i-deu

maroon *adj.* 밤색의 bam-saeg-ui

marriage *n.* 결혼 gyeol-hon; 결혼식 gyeol-hon-sik; 부부생활 bu-bu-saeng-hwal

married *adj.* 결혼한 gyeol-hon-han; 부부간의 bu-bu-gan-ui; 굳게 결합한 gut-ge gyeol-ha-pan

marrow *n.* 정수 jeong-su; 영양가 많은 음식 yeong-yang-kka man-eun eum-sik; *(bone marrow)* 골수 gol-ssu

marry *vt.* 결혼하다 gyeol-hon-ha-da; 결혼시키다 gyeol-hon-si-ki-da; 굳게 결합하다 gut-ge gyeol-ha-pa-da

Mars *n.* 화성 hwa-seong

marsh *n.* 습지 seup-ji; 늪 neup; 초지 cho-ji

marshal *n.* 사령관 sa-ryeong-gwan; 경찰서장 gyeong-chal-sseo-jang; 소방서장 so-bang-seo-jang

marshmallow *n.* 마시멜로우 ma-si-mel-lo-u

martial *adj.* 호전적인 ho-jeon-jeog-in, 전쟁의 jeon-jaeng-ui; ~ **art** *n.* 무술 mu-sul, 격투기 gyeok-tu-gi

marvelous *adj.* 불가사의한 bul-ga-sa-ui-han; 놀라운 nol-la-un; 훌륭한 hul-lyung-han

mascara *n.* 마스카라 ma-seu-ka-da

mascot *n.* 마스코트 ma-seu-ko-teu

masculine *adj. (manly)* 남자다운 nam-ja-da-un; *(grammar)* 남성의 nam-seong-ui

mash *vt.* 짓이기다 jin-ni-gi-da; 반하게 하다 ban-ha-ge ha-da

mask *n.* 가면 ga-myeon; 복면 bong-myeon; 가장 ga-jang; 방독면 bang-dong-myeon

mass *adj.* 대량의 dae-ryang-ui; 대중의 dae-jung-ui; *(mass production)* 대량생산 dae-ryang-saeng-san; *n.* 덩어리 deong-eo-ri; 모임 mo-im; 일반대중 il-ban-dae-jung; 부피 bu-pi; 미사 mi-sa; *(the greater part)* 다량 da-ryang, 대량 dae-ryang; **The great ~ of the catch is exported** 수확된 양의 대부분이 수출된다 su-hwak-doen dae-bu-bun-ui yang-i su-chul-doen-da; *(a large body of)* **a great ~ of paper** 많은 분량의 종이 man-eun bul-lyang-ui jong-i; *(religious)* **Sunday ~** 일요미사 il-yo-mi-sa

massage *n.* 마사지 ma-ssa-ji, 안마 an-ma

massive *adj.* 부피가 큰 bu-pi-ga keun; 단단한 dan-dan-han; 무거운 mu-geo-un; 당당한 dang-dang-han; 대량의 dae-ryang-ui; 광범위한 gwang-beom-wi-han

mass communication *n.* 매스컴 mae-seu-keom

mass media *n.* 매스 미디어 mae-ssu mi-di-eo

mast *n.* 돛대 dot-dae, 마스트 ma-seu-teu

master *n.* 주인 ju-in; 장 jang; 선생 seon-saeng; 대가 dae-ga; 승리자 seung-ni-ja

master bedroom *n.* 안방 an-ppang

master key *n.* 마스터 키 ma-seu-teo ki

master plan *n.* 종합계획 jong-hap-gye-hoek, 마스터 플랜 ma-seu-teo-peul-laen

masterpiece *n.* 대표작 dae-pyo-jak, 걸작 geol-jjak, 명작 myeong-jak

mastery *n.* 지배 ji-bae; 우세 u-se; 숙달 suk-dal

mat *n.* 매트 mae-teu; **place** ~ 매트 mae-teu; door ~ 도어매트 do-eo-mae-teu

match *n.* 시합 si-hap; 싹싯기 jjak-jit-gi; 상대 sang-dae; *(as for cigarettes)* 성냥 seong-nyang; *(an equal, counterpart)* 짝 jjak; **He's no ~ for them** 그는 그들의 상대가 되지 않는다 geu-neun geu-deul-ui sang-dae-ga doe-ji an-neun-da; **a soccer ~** 축구시합 chuk-gu-si-hap

matchbox *n.* 성냥갑 seong-nyang-kkap

matchmaker *n.* 중매쟁이 jung-mae-jaeng-i

matchstick *n.* 성냥개비 seong-nyang-kkae-bi

mate *n.* 상대 sang-dae; 짝 jjak; 동료 dong-nyo; *vt.* 짝지어주다 jjak-ji-eo-ju-da; 어울리게 하다 eo-ul-li-ge ha-da; *vi.* 결혼하다 gyeol-hon-ha-da

material *n.* 재료 jae-ryo; 요소 yo-so; 제재 je-jae; 용구 yong-gu

maternity *n.* 모성 mo-seong, 어머니다움 eo-meo-ni-da-um; *adj.* 인신의 im-sin-ui, 임산부의 im-san-bu-ui, 임산부용의 im-san-bu-yong-ui; ~ **leave** *n.* 출산휴가 chul-ssan-hu-ga

mathematics *n.* 수학 su-hak

matter *n.* 물질 mil-jjil; 제재 je-jae; 문제 mun-je; 사건 san-kkeon; 지장 ji-jang; **What's the ~** 무슨 일입니까 mu-seun il-im-ni-kka

mattress *n.* 매트리스 mae-teu-ri-sseu

mature *adj.* 익은 ig-eun; 성숙한 seong-su-kan; 신중한 sin-jung-han

maturity *n.* 성숙 seong-suk; 어음 만기일 eo-eum man-gi-il; 화농 hwa-nong

maxim *n.* 격언 gyeog-eon, 좌우명 jwa-u-myeong

maximize *v.* 최대화하다 choe-dae-hwa-ha-da, 극대화하다 geuk-dae-hwa-ha-da

maximum *n.* 최대 choe-dae; *adj.* 최대의 choe-dae-ui; 최고의 choe-go-ui

May *n.* 5월 o-wol

may *aux.* ...해도 좋다 ...hae-do jo-ta, ...해도 괜찮다 ...hae-do gwaen-chan-ta, ...일지도 모르다 ...il-jji-do mo-reu-da, 아마 ...일 것이다 a-ma ...il kkeos-i-da, ...인지 모르지만 ...in-ji mo-reu-ji-man, ...하기 위하여 ...ha-gi wi-ha-yeo, ...하도록 ...ha-do-rok

maybe *adv.* 어쩌면 eo-jjeo-myeon, 이마 a-ma

mayonnaise *n.* 마요네즈 ma-yo-ne-jeu

mayor *n.* 시장 si-jang

maze *n.* 미로 mi-ro; 흔란 hol-lan; 당황 dang-hwang

me *pron.* 나를 na-reul; 나에게 na-e-ge; *(hum.)* 저를 jeo-reul; 지에게 jeo-e-ge

meadow *n.* 풀밭 pul-bat; 목초지 mok-cho-ji; 초원 cho-won

meager *adj.* 야윈 ya-win; 불충분한 bul-chung-bun-han; 무미건조한 mu-mi-geon-jo-han

meal *n.* 식사 sik-sa; 거칠게 간 곡식 geo-chil-ge gan gok-sik; ~ **ticket** 식권 sik-kkwon; ~**time** 식사시간 sik-sa-si-gan

mean *n.* 중간 gung-gan; 평균치 pyeong-gyun-chi; 수단 su-dan, 방법 bang-beop; 재산 jae-san; *adj.* 보통의 bo-tong-ui; 천한 cheon-ahn; 초라한 cho-ra-han; 상스러운 sang-seu-reo-un; 비열한 bi-yeol-han; 심술궂은 sim-sul-guj-eun; 중간의 jung-gan-ui; 평균의 pyeong-gyun-ui; *vt.* 의미하다 ui-mi-ha-da; 의도하다 ui-do-ha-da

meaning *n.* 의미 ui-mi; 복적 mok-jeok

meaningful *adj.* 의미심장한 ui-mi-sim-jang-han; 의미있는 ui-mi-in-neun

meaningless *adj.* 뜻이 없는 tteus-i eom-neun, 무의미한 mu-ui-mi-han

means *n.* 수단 su-dan; 방법 bang-beop; 기관 gi-gwan; 재력 jae-ryeok

meantime *n.* 그 동안 geu dong-an; *adv.* 그 사이에 geu sa-i-e; 한편 han-pyeon; **in the ~/meanwhile** 그 사이에 geu sa-i-e;

우선 u-seon; 당분간은 dang-bun-gan-eun; 한편 han-pyeon

measure *n.* 치수 chi-ssu; 분량 bul-lyang; 도량단위 do-ryang-dan-wi; 한도 han-do; 수단 su-dan; 도량형기 do-ryang-hyeong-gi; *vt.* 재다 jae-da, 측정하다 cheuk-jeong-ha-da

measuring cup *n.* 계량컵 ge-ryang-keop

meat *n.* 고기 go-gi; 속알맹이 sog-al-maeng-i; 내용 nae-yong; 취미 chwi-mi

Mecca *n.* 메카 me-ka

mechanic *n.* 기계 수리공 gi-gye su-ri-gong

mechanical *adj.* 기계적인 gi-gye-jeog-in, 기계의 gi-gye-ui

medal *n.* 메달 me-dal; 훈장 hun-jang

meddle *vi.* 간섭하다 gan-seo-pa-da, 관여하다 gwan-yeo-ha-da

mediate *vi.* 조정하다 jo-jeong-ha-da, 중재하다 jung-jae-ha-da

medical *adj.* 의학의 ui-hag-ui; 의약의 ui-yag-ui; 내과의 nae-kkwa-ui

medicine *n.* 약 yak; 의학 ui-hak; 내과치료 nae-kkwa-chi-ryo; 주술 ju-sul

medieval *adj.* 중세의 jung-se-ui

meditate *vt.* 명상하다 myeong-sang-ha-da; 묵상하다 muk-sang-ha-da

Mediterranean Sea, the *n.* 지중해 ji-jung-hae

medium *n.* 중간jung-gan; 매개물 mae-gae-mul; 생활환경 saeng-hwal-hwan-gyeong; 무당 mu-dang; *adj.* 중간의 jung-gan-ui; 보통의 bo-tong-ui; **the news media** 뉴스미디어 nyu-sseu-mi-di-eo, **the mass media** 대중매체 dae-jung-mae-che; ~ **cooked** 적당히 익은 jeok-dang-hi ig-eun

medley *n.* 접속곡 jeop-sok-gok; 잡동사니 jap-dong-sa-ni

meet *vt.* 만나다 man-na-da; 마주치다 ma-ju-chi-da; 맞서다 mat-seo-da; 겪다 gyeok-da; *vi.* 만나다 man-na-da; 회합하다 hoe-ha-pa-da; 하나로 합치다 ha-na-ro hap-chi-da; 합의하다 hab-ui-ha-da

meeting *n.* 만남 man-nam; 모임 mo-im; 경기 gyeong-gi; 교차 gyo-cha

mega *adj.* 대규모의 dae-gyu-mo-ui; ~**byte** 메가바이트 me-ga-ba-i-teu

megaphone *n.* 메가폰 me-ga-pon, 확성기 hwak-seong-gi

mellow *adj.* 달콤한 dal-kom-han; 향기로운 hyang-gi-ro-un; 부드럽고 아름다운 bu-deu-reop-go a-reum-da-un; 기름진 gi-reum-jin; 원숙한 won-su-kan

melodicous *adj.* 선율적인 seon-nyul-jjeog-in, 음악적인 eum-ak-jeog-in

melodrama *n.* 멜로드라마 mel-lo-deu-ra-ma

melody *n.* 멜로디 mel-lo-di

melon *n.* 멜론 mel-lon

melt *vi.* 녹다 nok-da; 점차 사라지다 jeom-cha sa-ra-ji-da; 누그러지다 nu-geu-reo-ji-da; 찌는듯이 덥다 jji-neun-deus-i deop-da; *vt.* 녹이다 nog-i-da; 감동시키다 gam-dong-si-ki-da

member *n.* 일원 il-won; 구성부분 gu-seong-bu-bun; 정당지부 jeong-dang-ji-bu

membership *n.* 회원권 hoe-won-kkwon; 회원지위 hoe-won-ji-wi

membrane *n.* 얇은 막 yalb-eun mak; 막피 mak-pi

memo *n.* 메모 me-mo

memoir *n.* 전기 jeon-gi; 연구보고 yeon-gu-bo-go

memorial *n.* 기념관 gi-nyeom-gwan, 기념물 gi-nyeom-mul, 기념비 gi-nyeom-bi; *adj.* 기념의 gi-nyeom-ui

memorize *vt.* 기억하다 gi-eo-ka-da, 암기하다 am-gi-ha-da

memory *n.* 기억 gi-eok; 기억력 gi-eong-nyeok; 회상 hoe-sang; 추억 chu-eok; 기억장치 gi-eok-jang-chi

men's room *n.* 남자 화장실 nam-ja hwa-jang-sil

men's wear *n.* 남성복 nam-seong-bok, 신사복 sin-sa-bok

menace *n.* 위협 wi-hyeop, 협박 hyeop-bak; *vt.* 위협하다 wi-hyeo-pa-da, 협박하다 hyeop-ba-ka-da

mend *vt.* 수선하다 su-seon-ha-da; 개선하다 gae-seon-ha-da; *vi.* 호전하다 ho-jeon-ha-da; 개심하다 gae-sim-ha-da

menopause *n.* 폐경기 pye-gyeong-gi

mental *adj.* 마음의 ma-eum-ui; 정신의 jeong-sin-ui; 지능의 ji-neung-ui; 정신병의 jeong-sin-ppyeong-ui

mentally *adv.* 정신적으로 jeong-sin-jeog-eu-ro

mention *n.* 기재 gi-jae; 언급 eon-geup; *vt.* 언급하다 eon-geu-pa-da; 말하다 mal-ha-da; 이름을 들다 i-reum-eul deul-da

menu *n.* 메뉴 me-nyu, 차림표 cha-rim-pyo; 식단표 sik-dan-pyo

merchandise *n.* 상품 sang-pum; 재고품 jae-go-pum

merchant *n.* 상인 sang-in; 무역상 mu-yeok-sang

merciful *adj.* 자비로운 ja-bi-ro-un; 인정이 많은 in-jeong-i man-eun

merciless *adj.* 무자비한 mu-ja-bi-han; 냉혹한 naeng-ho-kan

mercury *n.* 수은 su-eun; 수성 su-seong

mercy *n.* 자비 ja-bi; 인정 in-jeong; 연민 yeon-min

merely *adv.* 단지 dan-ji, 그저 geu-jeo

merge *vt.* 합병하다 hap-byeong-ha-da; 융합시키다 yung-hap-si-ki-da

merit *n.* 장점 jang-jjeom; 공적 gong-jeok

merry *adj.* 명랑한 myeong-nang-han; 유쾌한 yu-kwae-han; 떠들썩한 tteo-deul sseo kan; ~ **Christmas** 메리 크리스마스 me-ri keu-ri-sseu-ma-sseu

merry-go-round *n.* 회전목마 hoe-jeon-mong-ma

mesh *n.* 망사 mang-sa; 올가미 ol-ga-mi; 그물 geu-mul

mess *n.* 혼란 hol-lan; 뒤죽박죽 dwi-juk-bak-juk; 곤란한 상태 gol-lan-han sang-tae; 더러운 것 deo-reo-un geot; 실수많은 사람 sil-ssu-man-eun sa-ram; *vt.* 망쳐놓다 mang-cheo-no-ta; 뒤죽박죽으로 만들다 dwi-junk-bak-jung-eu-ro man-deul-da, 엉망으로 만들다 eong-mang-eu-ro man-deul-da

message *n.* 메시지 me-ssi-ji; 통신 tong-sin; 교서 gyo-seo; 신탁 sin-tak; 교훈 gyo-hun

messenger *n.* 배달인 bae-dal-in; 심부름꾼 sim-bu-reum-kkun; 메신저 me-ssin-jeo

metabolism *n.* 신진대사 sin-jin-dae-sa

metal *n.* 금속 geum-sok; 주철 ju-cheol

metalwork *n.* 금속 세공품 geum-sok se-gong-pum

meter *n.* *(unit of length)* 미터 mi-teo; *(rhythm in verse)* 보격운율 bo-kkyeok-un-yul; *(instrument for measuring)* 계량기 gye-ryang-gi; **postage/gas** ~ 계량기 gye-ryang-gi; **parking** ~ 미터기 mi-teo-gi

method *n.* 방법 bang-beop; 교수법 gyo-su-ppeop; 순서 sun-seo; 분류법 bul-lyu-ppeop

methodical *adj.* 질서있는 jil-sseo-in-neun; 조직적인 jo-jik-jeog-in

metromome *n.* 메트로놈 me-teu-ro-nom

Mexican *n.* 멕시코사람 mek-si-ko ssa-ram; *adj.* 멕시코의 mek-si-ko-ui

Mexico *n.* 멕시코 mek-si-ko

microphone *n.* 마이크 ma-i-keu

microscope *n.* 현미경 hyeon-mi-gyeong

microwave oven *n.* 전자레인지 jeon-ja re-in-ji

mid *adj.* 중앙의 jung-ang-ui, 가운데의 ga-un-de-ui

midday *n.* 정오 jeong-o, 한낮 han-nat

middle *adj.* 한가운데의 han-ga-un-de-ui; 중류의 jung-nyu-ui; 중세의 jung-se-ui; ~ **Ages** 중세기 jung-se-gi; ~ **age** 중년 jung-nyeon

middle-aged *adj.* 중년의 jung-nyeon-ui

middle class *n.* 중산층 jung-san-cheung, 중류계급 jung-nyu-gye-geup

Middle East *n.* 중동 jung-dong

middleman *n.* 중간상인 jung-gan-sang-in; 중개인 jung-gae-in

middle school *n.* 중학교 jung-hak-gyo

middle-sized *adj.* 중형의 jung-hyeong-ui

midnight *n.* 한밤중 han-bam-jjung; 암흑 am-heuk

midterm *n.* 중간시험 jung-gan-si-heom; 중간기 jung-gan-gi; *adj.* 중간의 jung gan ui

midwife *n.* 산파 san-pa; 조산원 jo-san-won

might *aux.* *(past tense of* **may***)*; *n.* 힘 him, 세력 se-ryeok, 권력 gwol-lyeok; **That shop ~ have what you are looking for** 그 가게에는 아마 선생님이 찾으시는 물건이 있을 겁니다 geu ga-ge-e-neun a-ma seon-saeng-nim-i chaj-eu-si-neun mul-geon-i Iss-eul kkeom-nl-da; **It ~ be a good day tomorrow** 내일은 아마 좋은 날이 될 겁니다 nae-il-eun a-ma jo-eun nal-i doel kkeom-ni-da

mighty *adj.* 강력한 gang-nyeo-kan, 힘센 him-ssen

migrate *vi.* 이주하다 i-ju-ha-da; 이동하다 i-dong-ha-da

microphone *n.* 마이크 ma-i-keu

mild *adj.* 온순한 on-sun-han; 온화한 on-hwa-han; 부드러운 bu-deu-reo-un; 가벼운 ga-byeo-un

mile *n.* 마일 ma-il; 상당한 거리 sang-dang-han geo-ri

milestone *n.* 이정표 i-jeong-pyo; 획기적 사건 hoek-gi-jeog-in sa-kkeon

militant *adj.* 교전하고 있는 gyo-jeon-ha-go in-neun; 호전적인 ho-jeon-jjeog-in

military *n.* 군인 gun-in; 군대 gun-dae; ~ **academy** 사관학교 sa-gwan-hak-gyo; ~ **policeman** 헌병 heon-byeong; ~ **service** 병역 byeong-yeok

milk *n.* 우유 u-yu, 밀크 mil-keu; 젖 jeot

Milky Way *n.* 은하수 eun-ha-su

mill *n.* 맷돌 maet-dol; 물방아간 mul-bang-a-kkan; 풍차간 pung-cha-kkan; 공장 gong-jang; *vt.* 맷돌로 갈다 maet-dol-lo gal-da; 제분하다 je-bun-ha-da

miller *n.* 방앗간 주인 bang-at-gan ju-in; 제분업자 je-bun-eop-ja; 가루 날리는 나방 ga-ru nal-li-neun na-bang

millimeter *n.* 밀리미터 mil-li-mi-teo

million *n.* 백만 baeng-man; 다수 da-su; 민중 min-jung

millionaire *n.* 백만장자 baeng-man-jang-ja, 큰 부자 keun bu-ja

mimic *adj.* 흉내를 잘 내는 hung-nae-reul jal lae-neun; 가짜의 ga-jja-ui; *vt.* 흉내내다 hyung-nae-nae-da, 본뜨다 bon-teu-da

mince *vt.* 잘게 썰다 jal-ge-sseol-da; 조심스레 말하다 jo-sim-seu-re mal-ha-da

mind *n.* 마음 ma-eum; 지성 ji-seong; 의견 ui-gyeon; 의향 ui-hyang; 감정 gam-jeong; 기억 gi-eok; 본정신 bon-jeong-sin; *vt.* 주의를 기울이다 ju-i-reul gi-ul-i-da; 돌보다 dol-bo-da; 신경쓰다 sin-gyeong-sseu-da; 걱정하다 geok-jeong-ha-da; 귀찮게 여기다 gwi-chan-ke yeo-gi-da

mindful *adj.* 주의깊은 ju-i-gip-eun; 정신을 차리는 jeong-sin-eul cha-ri-neun; 잊지 않는 it-ji-an-neun

mindless *adj.* 부주의한 bu-ju-i-han; 정신을 차리지 않는 jeong-sin-eul cha-ri-gi an-neun; 분별없는 bun-byeol-eom-neun; 조심성없는 jo-sim-sseong eom-neun

mind reading *n.* 독심술 dok-sim-sul

mine *n.* 광산 gwang-san; 풍부한 자원 pung-bu-han ja-won; 갱도 gaeng-do; 지뢰 ji-roe; 비밀계략 bi-mil-gye-ryak; *pron.* 나의 것 na-ui kkeot; 나의 가족들 na-ui ga-jok-deul; *(hum.)* 저의 것 jeo-ui kkeot; 저의 가족들 jeo-ui ga-jok-deul

miner *n.* 광부 gwang-bu; 광산업자 gwang-san-eop-ja

mineral *n.* 광물질 gwang-mul-jjil, 광석 gwang-seok

mingle *vi.* 뒤섞이다 dwi-seokk-i-da; 사귀다 sa-gwi-da; 참가하다 cham-ga-ha-da

miniature *n.* 축소물 chuk-so-mul; 세밀화 se-mil-hwa; *adj.* 소형의 so-hyeong-ui

minimize *vt.* 최소화하다 choe-so-hwa-ha-da; 과소평가하다 gwa-so-pyeong-kka-ha-da

minimum *n.* 최소 choe-so, 최저 choe-jeo; ~ **wage** 최소임금 choe-so-im-geum

mining *n.* 광업 gwang-eop; 채광 chae-gwang; 지뢰부설 ji-roe-bu-seol

miniseries *n.* 미니시리즈 mi-ni-ssi-ri-jeu

minister *n.* 성직자 seong-jik-ja; 장관 jang-gwan; 공사 gong-sa

ministry *n.* 성직 seong-jik; 목사 mok-sa; 내각 nae-gak

minor *n.* 미성년자 mi-seong-nyeon-ja; 단조 dan-jjo; 부전공 bu-jeon-gong; *adj.* 보다 작은 bo-da jag-eun, 보다 적은 bo-da jeog-eun; 중요하지 않은 jung-yo-ha-ji an-eun; 손아래의 son-a-rae-ui; 미성년의 mi-seong-nyeon-ui; 단음계의 dan-eum-gye-ui

minority *n.* 소수파 so-su-pa; 소수민족 so-su-min-jok; 미성년자 mi-seong-nyeon-ja

mint *n.* 박하 ba-ka; 조폐소 jo-pye-so; 거액 geo-aek; 근원 geun-won; *adj.* 아직 쓰지 않은 a-jik sseu-ji an-eun, 갓 발행된 gat bal-haeng-doen

minus *prep.* 마이너스 ma-i-neo-sseu; ...을 뺀 ...eul ppaen; **Twenty ~ three is seventeen** 20 빼기 3은 17 i-sip ppae-gi sam-eun sip-chil

minute *n.* 분 bun; 잠깐 jam-kkan; 기록 gi-rok; 의사록 ui-sa-rok; 초고 cho-go; *adj.* 즉석에서 만드는 jeuk-seog-e-seo man-deu-neun; 자디잔 ja-di-jan; 상세한 sang-se-han

miracle *n.* 기적 gi-jeok; 경이 gyeong-i; 불가사의 bul-ga-sa-ui

miraculous *adj.* 기적적인 gi-jeok-jeog-in; 불가사의한 bul-ga-sa-i-han; 놀랄만한 nol-lal-man-han

mirage *n.* 신기루 sin-gi-ru; 아지랑이 a-ji-raeng-i; 망상 mang-sang

mire *n.* 진창 jin-chang, 수렁 su-reong

mirror *n.* 거울 geo-ul; 반사경 ban-sa-gyeong; 본보기 bon-bo-gi

misadventure *n.* 불운 bul-un; 불행 bul-haeng

misbehave *vi.* 못된짓을 하다 mot-doen-jis-eul ha-da, 방탕하다 bang-tang-ha-da

miscalculate *vt., vi.* 계산착오하다 gye-san-chag-o-ha-da

miscarriage *n.* 실패 sil-pae, 과실 gwa-sil; 유산 yu-san

miscellaneous *adj.* 잡다한 jap-da-han, 갖가지의 gat-ga-ji-ui

mischief *n.* 해악 hae-ak; 악영향 ag-yeong-hyang; 곤란한 짐 gol-lan-han jeom

misconceive *vt., vi.* 오해하다 o-hae-ha-da, 질못 생각하다 jal-mo saeng-ga-ka-da

misdeed *n.* 악행 a-kaeng; 비행 bi-haeng; 범죄 beom-joe

miserable *adj.* 불쌍한 bul-ssang-han, 비참한 bi-cham-han; 구질구질한 gu-jil-gu-jil-han; 괘씸한 gwae-ssim-han

misery *n.* 불행 bul-haeng; 비참한 신세 bi-cham-han sin-se; 빈곤 bin-gon

misfortune *n.* 붕운 bul-un; 재난 jae-nan

mishap *n.* 가벼운 사고 ga-byeo-un sa-go, 불상사 bul-ssang-sa

misinform *vt.* 오보를 전하다 o-bo-reul jeon-ha-da

misinterpret *vt.* 오해하다 o-hae-ha-da, 오역하다 o-yeo-ka-da

mislay *vt.* 잘못두다 jal-mot-du-da; 두고 잊다 du-go It-da

misleading *adj.* 현혹하는 hyeon-ho-ka-neun, 오해하게 하는 o-hae-ha ge ha neun

mismatch *n.* 안어울림 an-eo-ul-lim; *vt.* 어울리지 않다 eo-ul-li-ji an-ta

misplace *vt.* 질못 두다 Jal-mot du-da; 둔 곳을 잊다 dun gos-eul it-da; 잘못 주다 jal-mot ju-da

misplay *n.* 실수 sil-ssu, 에러 e-reo; *vt.* 잘못 처리하다 jal-mot cheo-ri-ha-da

Miss *n.* ...양 ...yang, ...씨 ....ssi

miss *n.* 빗맞힘 bit-ma-chim; 놓침 no-chim; 실수 sil-ssu; 누락 nu-rak; 벗어남 beos-eo-nam; 유산 yu-san; *vt.* 빗맞히다

bin-ma-chi-da; 놓치다 no-chi-da; 보지 못하다 bo-ji mo-ta-da; 빠뜨리다 ppa-tteu-ri-da; 까딱 ...을 뻔하다 kka-ttak ...eul ppeon-ha-da; ...이 없는 것을 깨닫다 ...i eom-neun geos-eul kkae-dat-da; ...이 없어서 불편하게 여기다 ...i eops-eo-seo bul-pyeon-ha-ge yeo-gi-ga; **We ~ed the train** 우리는 그 기차를 놓쳤습니다 u-ri-neun geu gi-cha-reul no-cheot-seum-ni-da; **We are ~ing forty dollars** 우리는 40불을 잃어버렸습니다 u-ri-neun sa-sip-bul-eul il-eo-beo-ryeot-seum-ni-da; **He really ~es her** 그분은 그 여자분을 정말 그리워합니다 geu bun-eul geu yeo-ja-beun-eul jeong-mal geu-ri-wo-ham-ni-da

missile *n.* 미사일 mi-sa-il

missing *adj.* 빠진 ppa-jin, 보이지 않는 bo-i-ji-an-neun

mission *n.* 임무 im-mu; 사절단 sa jeol-ttan; 전도 jeon-do; 파견 pa-gyeon; 선교회 seon-gyo-hoe; 사회 구세시설 sa-hoe gu-je-si-seol

Mississippi *n. (river)* 미시시피강 mi-si-sl-pi-gang

mist *n.* 안개 an-gae; 흐릿함 heu-rit-ham; 흐리게 하는 goet

mistake *n.* 실수 sil-ssu; 잘못 jal-mot; 오해 o-hae; *vt.* 실수하다 sil-ssu-ha-da; 틀리다 teul-li-da; 혼동하다 hon-dong-ha-da; 오해히디 o-hae-ha-da

mistaken *adj.* 잘못된 jal-mot-doen; 틀린 teul-lin; 오해하고 있는 o-hae-ha-go in-neun

Mister (Mr.) *n.* ...씨 ...ssi, ...선생님 ...seon-saeng-nim

mistreat *vt.* 학대하다 hak-dae-ha-da, 흑사하다 hok-sa-ha-da

mistress *n.* 여주인 yeo-ju-in; 여지배자 yeo-ji-bae-in; 여류명인 yeo-ryu-myeong-in; 정부 jeong-bu

mistrust *vt.* 불신하다 bul-ssin-ha-da; 의심하다 ui-sim-ha-da

misty *adj.* 안개가 자욱한 an-gae-ga ja-u-kan, 안개가 짙은 an-gae-ga jit-eun; 희미한 hi-mi-han, 분명치 않은 bun-myeong-chi an-eun

misunderstanding *n.* 오해 o-hae; 의견차이 ui-gyeon-cha-i

misuse *vt.* 오용하다 o-yong-ha-da, 혹사하다 hok-sa-ha-da

mitten *n.* 벙어리장갑 beong-eo-ri jang-gap

mix *n.* 혼합 hon-hap; 혼합물 hon-ham-mul; 혼합비 hon-hap-bi; 혼란 hol-lan; *vt.* 섞다 seok-da; 첨가하다 cheom-ga-ha-da; 섞어 만들다 seokk-eo man-deul-da; 교재시키다 gyo-jae-si-ki-da; 교배시키다 gyo-bae-si-ki-da; 결합하다 gyeol-ha-pa-da; ~ed 섞인 seokk-in; 가지각색의 ga-ji-gak-saeg-ui; 잡다한 jap-da-han; 혼란된 hol-lan-doen

mixture *n.* 혼합 hon-hap; 혼합물 hon-ham-mul; 혼방직물 hon-bang-jing-mul

moan *n.* 신음소리 sin-eum-sso-ri; 슬퍼함 seul-peo-ham; *vt.*, *vi.* 신음하다 sin-eum-ha-da; 불평하다 bul-pyeong-ha-da

mobile *adj.* 이동할 수 있는 i-dong-hal ssu in-neun; 움직이기 쉬운 um-jig-i-gi swi-un; 변덕스러운 byeon-deok-seu-reo-un, 변하기 쉬운 byeon-ha-gi swi-un

mobile home *n.* 이동식 주택 i-dong-sik ju-taek, 모빌홈 mo-bil-hom

mode *n.* 양식 yang-sik; 방법 bang-beop; 유행 yu-haeng

model *n.* 모형 mo-hyeong; 모범 mo-beom; 모델 mo-del; 패션모델 pae-ssyeon-mo-del; 설계 seol-gye

modem *n.* 모뎀 mo-dem

modern *adj.* 현대식의 hyeon-dae-sig-ui, 최신의 choe-sin-ui; 근대의 geun-dae-ui, 현대의 hyeon-dae-ui

modernize *vt.* 현대화하다 hyeon-dae-hwa-ha-da; *vi.* 현대화되다 hyeon-dae-hwa-doe-da

modest *adj.* 겸손한 gyeom-son-han; 정숙한 jeong-su-kan; 적당한 jeok-dang-han

modification *n.* 수정 su-jeong; 변경 byeon-gyeong; 조절 jo-jeol; 수식 su-sik

modify *vt.* 수정하다 su-jeong-ha-da; 변경하다 byeon-gyeong-ha-da; 조절하다 jo-jeol-ha-da; 수식하다 su-si-ka-da

modular *adj.* 도량단위의 do-ryang-dan-wi-ui; 기준치수의 gi-jun-chi-ssu-ui; 모듈의 mo-dyul-ui

module *n.* 도량단위 do-ryang-dan-wi; 기준치수 gi-jun-chi-ssu; 모듈 mo-dyul

moist *adj.* 습기있는 seup-gi-in-neun; 축축한 chuk-chu-kan; 비가 많은 bi-ga man-eun; 눈물어린 nun-mul-eo-rin

moisten *vt.* 축축하게 하다 chuk-chu-ka-ge ha-da; *vi.* 축축해지다 chuk-chu-kae-ji-da

moisture *n.* 습기 seup-gi; 수분 su-bun; 수증기 su-jeung-gi

moisturize *vt.* 습기를 주다 seup-gi-reul ju-da, 촉촉하게 하다 chok-cho-ka-ge ha-da

mold *n.* 주형 ju-hyeong; 틀 teul; 특성 teuk-seong; 곰팡이 gom-pang-i; 옥토 ok-to; *vt.* 틀에 넣다 teul-e neo-ta; 틀에 넣어 만들다 teul-e neo-eo-seo man-deul-da; 반죽해서 만들다 ban-ju-kae-seo man-deul-da; 인격을 도야하다 in-kkyeog-eul do-ya-ha-da; 곰팡이가 나다 gom-pang-i-ga na-da

molest *vt.* 괴롭히다 goe-ro-pi-da; 못살게 굴다 mot-sal-ge gul-da

mom(my) *n.* 엄마 eom-ma

moment *n.* 순간 sun-gan; 기회 gi-hoe; 중요성 jung-yo-sseong; 계기 gye-gi; 능률 neung-nyul

monarch *n.* 군주 gun-ju; 독재 정치자 dok-jae jeong-chi-ga; 거물 geo-mul

monarchy *n.* 군주국가 gun-ju-guk-ga; 군주정치 gun-ju-jeong-chi

monastery *n.* 수도원 su-do-won

Monday *n.* 월요일 wol-yo-il

monetary *adj.* 화폐의 hwa-pye-ui, 금전상의 geum-jeon-sang-ui

money *n.* 돈 don; 화폐 hwa-pye; 재산 jae-san

Mongolia *n.* 몽고 mong-go

monitor *n.* 충고자 chung-go-ja; 반장 ban-ajng; 탐지장치 tam-ji-ajng-chi; 모니터장치 mo-ni-teo-jang-chi; *vt.* 감시하다 gam-si-ha-da, 청취하다 cheong-chwi-ha-da; **computer** ~ 컴퓨터 모니터 keom-pu-teo mo-ni-teo

monk *n.* 승려 seung-nyeo, 수사 su-sa

monkey *n.* 원숭이 won-sung-i; 장난꾸러기 jang-nan-kku-reo-gi; 흉내쟁이 hyung-nae-jaeng-i; ~ **business** 기만 gi-man, 사기 sa-gi; 장난 jang-nan, 짓궂은 짓 jit-guj-eun jit

monodrama *n.* 모노드라마 mo-no-deu-ra-ma

monopoly *n.* 독점 dok-jeom; 독점권 dok-jeom-kkwon; 독점판매 dok-jeom-pan-mae; 독점사업 dok-jeom-sa-eop; 독점회사 dok-jeom-hoe-sa

monorail *n.* 모노레일 mo-no-re-il

monotonous *adj.* 단조로운 dan-jo-ro-un; 한결같은 han-gyeol-gat-eun; 지루한 ji-ru-han

monsoon *n.* 몬순 mon-sun, 계절풍 gye-jeol-pung

monster *n.* 괴물 goe-mul; 거대한 사람 geo-dae-han sa-ram; 극악무도한 사람 geug-ang-mu-do-han sa-ram; 무서운 위협 mu-seo-un wi-hyeop

monstrous *adj.* 괴물같은 goe-mul-gat-eun; 거대한 geo-dae-han; 가공할 ga-gong-hal; 터무니없는 teo-mu-ni-eom-neun

montage *n.* 몽타주 mong-ta-ju

month *n.* 달 dal, 월 wol

monthly *adv.* 매달 mae-dal, 한달에 한번 han-dal-e han-beon; *adj.* 매달의 mae-dal-ui; 한달동안 유효한 han-dal-ttong-an yu-hyo-han

monument *n.* 기념비 gi-nyeom-bi, 기념물 gi-nyeom-mul; 금자탑 geum-ja-tap

mood *n.* 기분 gi-bun; 마음가짐 ma-eum-ga-jim; 분위기 bun-wi-gi; 우울 u-ul; **in a bad ~** 기분이 나쁘다 gi-bun-i na-ppeu-da

moody *adj.* 침울한 chim-ul-han, 언짢은 eon-jjan-eun, 시무룩한 si-mu-ru-kan

moon *n.* 달 dal; 위성 wi-seong; **full ~** 보름달 bo-reum-ttal

moonlight *n.* 달빛 dal-ppit

moonrise *n.* 월출 wol-chul, 달이 뜸 dal-i tteum; 달뜨는 시각 dal-tteu-neun si-gak

moonshine *n.* 달빛 dal-ppit; 공상적인 생각 gong-sang-jeog-in saeng-gak

mop *n.* 자루걸레 ja-ru-geol-le; *vt.* 닦다 dak-da; 청소하다 cheong-so-ha-da; 얼굴을 찡그리다 eol-gul-eul jjing-geu-ri-da

moral *n.* 교훈 gyo-hun; 윤리학 yul-li-hak; 도덕 do-deok

morale *n.* 사기 sa-gi; 풍기 pung-gi; 의욕 ui-yok

more *adj.* 더 많은 deo man-eun; 더 큰 deo keun; 여분의 yeo-bun-ui; *adv.* 더 많이 deo man-i, 더 크게 deo keu-ge; 더욱 deo-uk; 한층 더 han-cheung deo; 오히려 o-hi-ryeo; **~ than** ...보다 많은 ...bo-da man-eun; ...뿐만 아니라 ...ppun-man a-ni-ra

moreover *adv.* 그 위에 geu wi-e; 또한 tto-han

morning *n.* 아침 a-chim; 오전 o-jeon; **~ paper** 조간신문 jo-gan-sin-mun

Morocco *n.* 모로코 mo-ro-ko

mortal *adj.* 죽을 운명의 jug-eul un-myeong-ui; 치명적인 chi-myeong-jeog-in; 인간의 in-gan-ui

mortar *n.* 회반죽 hoe-ban-juk; 절구 jeol-gu; 막자사발 mak-jja-sa-bal; *(building material)* 몰타르 mol-ta-reu; *(military)* 박격포 bak-gyeok-po

mortgage *n.* 저당 jeo-dang; 저당권 jeo-dang-kkwon; 저당증서 jeo-dang-jeung-seo; 주택대출 ju-taek-dae-chul; *vt.* 저당잡히다 jeo-dang-ja-pi-da

Moscow *n.* 모스코바 mo-seu-ko-ba

mosque *n.* 모스크 mo-seu-keu, 회교사원 hoe-gyo-sa-won

mosquito *n.* 모기 mo-gi; **~ net** 모기장 mo-gi-jang

moss *n.* 이끼 i-kki

most *adj.* 가장 큰 ga-jang keun, 가장 많은 ga-jang man-eun; 최대의 choe-dae-ui; 대개의 dae-gae-ui; *adv.* 가장 ga-jang; 대단히 dae-dan-hi; **at ~** 많아야 man-a-ya

mostly *adv.* 대개 dae-gae, 주로 ju-ro, 거의 geo-ui, 대부분 dae-bu-bun

motel *n.* 모텔 mo-tel

moth *n.* 나방 na-bang; 좀 jom

mother *n.* 어머니 eo-meo-ni; 대모 dae-mo; 모성애 mo-seong-ae

mother country *n.* 모국 mo-guk, 조국 jo-guk; 본국 bon-guk

motherhood *n.* 모성 mo-seong

mother-in-law *n.* 시어머니 si-eo-meo-ni; 장모님 jang-mo-nim

Mother Nature *n.* 자연 ja-yeon

motif *n.* 주제 ju-je, 모티프 mo-ti-peu; 동기 dong-gi

motion *n.* 운동 un-dong; 운행 un-haeng; 동작 dong-jak; 동의 dong-ui; 명령 myeong-nyeong; 장치 jang-chi

motivate *vt.* 동기를 주다 dong-gi-reul ju-da; 자극하다 ja-geu-ka-da; 움직이다 um-jig-i-da; 유도하다 yu-do-ha-da

motivation *n.* 동기 dong-gi; 자극 ja-geuk; 유도 yu-do; 동기부여 dong-gi-bu-yeo

motive *n.* 동기 dong-gi; 제재 je-jae

motor *n.* 모터 mo-teo, 발동기 bal-ttong-gi; 자동차 ja-dong-cha; 원동력 won-dong-nyeok

motorbike *n.* 오토바이 o-to-ba-i

motorcycle *n.* 오토바이 o-to-ba-i

motto *n.* 좌우명 jwa-u-myeong, 표어 pyo-eo, 모토 mo-to

mount *vt.* 오르다 o-reu-da; 타다 ta-da; 태우다 tae-u-da; 놓다 no-ta; 장치하다 jang-chi-ha-da; *vi.* 오르다 o-reu-da; 쌓이다 ssa-i-da; 늘어나다 neul-eo-na-da

mountain *n.* 산 san; 산맥 san-maek; 다량 da-ryang; ~ **climbing** 등산 deung-san; ~ **range** 산맥 san-maek; ~ **top** 산꼭대기 san-kkok-dae-gi

Mount Everest *n.* 에베레스트산 e-be-re-seu-teu-san

mourn *vt.* 슬퍼하다 seul-peo-ha-da; 애도하다 ae-do-ha-da

mourning *n.* 애도 ae-do; 비탄 bi-tan; 상 sang; 상복 sang-bok

mouse *n.* 생쥐 saeng-jwi; 겁쟁이 geop-jaeng-i; 예쁜이 ye-ppeun-i; *(computer)* 컴퓨터 마우스 keom-pyu-teo ma-u-sseu; ~ **pad** 마우스 패드 ma-u-sseu pae-deu

mousehole *n.* 쥐구멍 jwi-gu-meong

mouse trap *n.* 쥐덫 jwi-deot

mouth *n.* 입 ip; 입구 ip-gu; 주둥이 ju-dung-i; 부양가족 bu-yang-ga-jok

mouthful *adj.* 한입 가득 han-nip ga-deuk

mouthpiece *n.* 마우스피스 ma-u-sseu-pi-sseu; 대변자 dae-byeon-ja; 재갈 jae-gal

mouthwash *n.* 마우스워시 ma-u-sseu-wo-ssi

mouth-watering *adj.* 군침이 도는 gun-chim-i do-neun, 맛있어 보이는 mas-iss-eo bo-i-neun

movable *adj.* 움직일 수 있는 un-jig-il ssu in-neun

move *n.* 움직임 um-jig-im; 행동 haeng-dong; 이사 i-sa; 진행 jin-haeng; *vt.* 움직이다 um-jig-i-da; 진행시키다 jin-haeng-si-ki-da; 흔들다 heun-deul-da; 감동시키다 gam-dong-si-ki-da; *vi.* 움직이다 um-jig-i-da; 행동하다 haeng-dong-ha-da; 이사하다 i-sa-ha-da; 진전하다 jin-jeon-ha-da; 제안하다 je-an-ha-da

movement *n.* 운동 un-dong, 움직임 um-jig-im; 행동 haeng-dong, 동정 dong-jeong; 이동 i-dong, 이사 i-sa

mover *n.* 운송업자 un-song-eop-ja; 이전자 i-jeon-ja; 발기인 bal-gi-in

movie *n.* 영화 yeong-hwa; 영화관 yeong-hwa-gwan

moving *adj.* 움직이는 um-jig-i-neun; 감동적인 gam-dong-jeog-in; 움직이게 하는 um-jig-i-ge ha-neun

moving van *n.* 이삿짐 트럭 i-sat-jim teu-reok

mow *vt.* 풀을 베다 pul-eul be-da; 소탕하다 so-tang-ha-da

Mrs. *n.* ...씨 ...ssi, ...여사 ...yeo-sa

much *adj.* 많은 man-eun, 다량의 da-ryang-ui; ~ **money** 많은 돈 man-eun don; ~ **time** 많은 시간 man-eun si-gan; **too** ~ 너무 많은 neo-mu man-eun; *adv.* 매우 mae-u, 대단히 dae-dan-hi; ~ **earlier** 너무 일찍 neo-mu il-jjik; ~ **happier** 너무 행복하게 neo-mu haeng-bo-ka-ge

mud *n.* 진흙 jin-heuk; 진창 jin-chang; 시시한 것 si-si-han geot; 욕설 yok-seol

muddy *adj.* 진창의 jin-chang-ui, 진흙투성이의 jin-heuk-tu-seong-i-ui; 흐리멍텅한 heu-ri-meong-teong-han

mudpack *n.* 머드팩 meo-deu-paek

muffin *n.* 머핀 meo-pin

muffle *vt.* 싸다 ssa-da; 감아싸다 gam-a-ssa-da; 소음하다 so-eum-ha-da

muffler *n.* 머플러 meo-peul-leo; 목도리 mok-do-ri; 두꺼운 장갑 du-kkeo-un jang-gap

mug *n.* 머그 meo-geu; 컵 keop; ~ **of coffee** 커피머그 keo-pi-meo-geu; *vt.* 수배사진을 찍다 su-bae-sa-jin-eul jjik-da; 주입식으로 공부하다 ju-ip-sig-eu-ro gong-bu-ha-da

muggy *adj.* 무더운 mu-deo-un

multimedia *n.* 멀티미디어 meol-ti-mi-di-eo

multiple *adj.* 복합적인 bo-kap-jeog-in; 다수의 da-su-ui; 배수의 bae-su-ui

multiple-choice *adj.* 사지선다의 sa-ji-seon-da-ui

multiplication *n.* 증가 jeung-ga; 곱셈 gop-sem

multiplication table *n.* 곱셈표 gop-sem-pyo

multiply *vt.* 늘리다 neul-li-da; 번식시키다 beon-sik-si-ki-da; 곱하다 go-pa-da

multipurpose *adj.* 다목적의 da-mok-jeog-ui

mummy *n.* 미이라 mi-i-ra

municipality *n.* 자치제 ja-chi-je; 시당국 si-dang-guk; 전시민 jeon-si-min

murder *n.* 살인 sal-in

murderer *n.* 살인자 sal-in-ja

murmur *vt.* 중얼거리다 jung-eol-geo-ri-da, 투덜거리다 tu-deol-geo-ri-da

muscle *n.* 근육 geu-yuk; 힘줄 him-jjul; 완력 wal-lyeok; 압력 am-nyeok; 주요부분 ju-yo-bu-bun; 기름기 없는 고기 gi-reum-kki-eom-neun go-gi

muscular *adj.* 근육의 geun-yug-ui; 근육이 발달한 geun-yug-i bal-ttal-han; 힘있는 him-eom-neun

museum *n.* 박물관 bang-mul-gwan, 미술관 mi-sul-gwan; ~ **piece** 박물관 소장품 bang-mul-gwan so-jang-pum

mushroom *n.* 버섯 beo-seot; 양송이 yang-song-i

mushy *adj.* 걸죽한 geol-jju-kan; 감상적인 gam-sang-jeog-in

music *n.* 음악 eum-ak; 음악작품 eum-ak-jak-pum; 듣기 좋은 소리 deut-gi jo-eun so-ri; 음감 eum-gam

musical *adj.* 음악적인 eum-ak-jeog-in, 음악의 eum-ag-ui

music hall *n.* 음악회장 eum-a-koe-jang

musician *n.* 음악가 eum-ak-ga; 작곡가 jak-gok-ga

music school *n.* 음악학교 eum-a-kak-gyo

Muslim *n.* 회교도 hoe-gyo-do; *adj.* 회교도의 hoe-gyo-do-ui

mussel *n.* 홍합 hong-hap

must *aux.* ...해야 하다 ...hae-ya ha-da, ...히지 않으면 안되다 ...ha-ji an-eu-myeon an-doe-da, 꼭 ...하여야 하다 kkok ...ha-yeo-ya-ha-da, 반드시 ...하다 ban-deu-si ...ha-da, ...임에 틀림없다 ...im-e teul-lim-eop-da, ...이었음에 틀림없다 ...i-eoss-eum-e teul-lim-eop-da; **You ~ go**

to Pattaya 파타야에 꼭 가셔야 합니다 pa-ta-ya-e kkok ga-syeo-ya ham-ni-da; **You ~ not do that** 그 일을 하셔서는 안됩니다 geu il-eul ha-syeo-seo-neun an-doem-ni-da

mustache *n.* 콧수염 kot-su-yeom

mustard *n.* 겨자 gyeo-ja; 자극물 ja-geung-mul; 열의 yeol-ui

mute *adj.* 무언의 mu-eon-ui; 벙어리의 beong-eo-ri-ui; 발음을 안하는 bal-eum-eul an-ha-neun; 말로 나타내지 않는 mal-lo na-ta-nae-ji an-neun; 묵비권을 행사하는 muk bi kkwon-eul haeng-sa-ha-neun

mutiny *n.* 폭동 pok-dong; 반란 bal-lan

mutter *vt., vi.* 중얼거리다 jung-eol-geo-ri-da, 투덜거리다 tu-deol-geo-ri-da

mutton *n.* 양고기 yang-go-gi; 당면한 문제 dang-myeon-han mun-je

mutual *adj.* 서로의 seo-ro-ui; 공동의 gong-dong-ui

muzzle *n.* 부리 bu-ri; 주둥이 ju-dung-i; 재갈 jae-gal; 총구 chong-gu

my *adj.* 내 nae, *(hum.)* 제 je

myself *pron.* 나 자신 na ja-sin, *(hum.)* 제 자신 je ja-sin

mystery *n.* 신비 sin-bi; 불가사의 bul-ga-sa-ui; 비결 bi-gyeol; 비법 bi-ppeop; 괴기소설 goe-gi-so-seol; **It's a ~ to us** 그건 우리에게는 불가사의다 geu-geon u-ri-e-ge-neun bul-ga-sa-ui-da; **I am reading a murder ~** 저는 살인에 관한 괴기소설을 읽고 있습니다 je-neun sal-in-e gwan-han goe-gi-so-seol-eul il-kko it-seum-ni-da

myth *n.* 신화 sin-hwa; 전설 jeon-seol; 꾸며낸 이야기 kku-myeo-naen i-ya-gi

mythology *n.* 신화 sin-hwa; 신화집 sin-hwa-jip; 신화학 sin-hwa-hak

N

nag *vt., vi.* 성가시게 잔소리하다 seong-ga-si-ge jan-so-ri-ha-da

nagging *adj.* 잔소리 심한 jan-so-ri sim-han, 쨍쨍거리는 jjaeng-jjaeng-geo-ri-neun

nail *n.* *(toe)* 발톱 bal-top; *(finger)* 손톱 son-top; *(fastener)* 못 mot; ~ **file** 손톱줄 son-top-jul; ~ **polish** 메니큐어 me-ni-kyu-eo;

~ **clippers** 손톱깎기 son-top-kkak-gi; *vt.* 못을 박다 mos-eul bak-da; 꼼짝 못하게 하다 kkom-jjak mo-ta-ge ha-da; 붙잡다 but-jap-da; 간파하다 gan-pa-ha-da

naive *adj.* 순진한 sun-jin-han; 천진난만한 cheon-jin-nan-man-han; 고지식한 go-ji-sei-kan; 소박한 so-ba-kan

naked *adj.* 벌거벗은 beol-geo-beos-eun; 껍
질이 없는 kkeop-jil-i eom-neun; 불모의
bul-mo-ui; 무방비의 mu-bang-bi-ui; 적
나나한 jeong-na-na-han; 증거가 없는
jeung-geo-ga eom-neun

name *n.* 이름 i-reum; 명칭 myeong-ching; 명
성 myeong-seong; 유명인 yu-myeong-in;
명목 myeong-mok; 가명 ga-myeong; **first**
~ 이름 i-reum, *(hon.)* 성함 seong-ham;
last ~ 성 seong; *vt.* 이름을 붙이다 i-reum-
eul bu-chi-da; 이름을 짓다 i-reum-eul
jit-da; 지명하다 ji-myeong-ha-da; 이름을
말하다 i-reum-eul mal-ha-da; 고발하다
go-bal-ha-da; 지정하다 ji-jeong-ha-da

namely *adj.* 다시 말하자면 da-si mal-ha-ja-
myeon, 즉 jeuk

nameplate *n.* 명찰 myeong-chal; 문패
mun-pae

nanny *n.* 유모 yu-mo

nap *n.* 낮잠 nat-jam; 보풀 bo-pul; *vi.* 졸다
jol-da; 낮잠자다 nat-jam-ja-da; 방심하다
bang-sim-ha-da; **to take a** ~ 낮잠을 자다
nat-jam-eul ja-da

napkin *n.* 냅킨 naep-kin

narcotic *n.* 마취제 ma-chwi-je; 진정
제 jin-jeong-je; 마취제 중독환자
ma-chwi-je jung-do-kwan-ja; *adj.* 마
취성의 ma-chwi-sseong-ui; 최면성의
choe-myeon-sseong-ui

narrate *vt.* 말하다 mal-ha-da; 서술하다 seo-
sul-ha-da; 이야기를 만들다 i-ya-gi-reul
man-deul-da

narrator *n.* 이야기하는 사람 i-ya-gi-ha-
neun sa-ram; 해설자 hae-seol-jja

narrow *adj.* 좁은 job-eun; 좁아서 답답한
job-a-seo dap-da-pan; 부족한 bu-jo-kan;
빠듯한 ppa-deu-tan; 정밀한 jeong-mil-
han; ~ **minded** 속이 좁은 sog-i job-eun

NASA *n. abbr.* **National Aeronautics and
Space Administration** 미 우주 항공국
mi u-ju hang-gong-guk

nasty *adj.* 불쾌한 bul-kwae-han; 역한
yeo-kan; 불결한 bul-gyeol-han; 성질이 나
쁜 seong-jil-i na-ppeun; 다루기 어려운
da-ru-gi eo-ryeo-un; 심술궂은 sim-sul-guj-
eun; 악취미의 ak-chwi-mi-ui

nation *n.* 국가 guk-ga; 국민 gung-min; 인류
il-lyu; 민족 min-jok; 종족 jong-jok; ~ **wide**

adj. 전국적인 jeon-guk-jeog-in; 전국적
규모의 jeon-guk-jeok gyu-mo-ui; *adv.* 전
국적으로 jeon-guk-jeog-eu-ro

national *n.* 국민의 일원 gung-min-ui il-won;
동포 dong-po; *adj.* 국민의 gung-min-ui;
국가의 guk-ga-ui; 국유의 gug-yu-ui; 전
국적인 jeon-guk-jeog-in; 그 나라 고
유의 geu na-ra go-yu-ui; ~ **park** 국립공
원 gung-nip-gong-won; ~ **anthem** 국가
guk-ga; ~ **cemetery** 국립묘지 gung-nim-
myo-ji; ~ **holidays** 국경일 guk-gyeong-il;
~ **monument** 천연기념물 cheon-yeon-
gi-nyeom-mul, 사적 sa-jeok, 명승지
myeong-seung-ji

nationality *n.* 국적 guk-jeok; 국민 gung-min;
국가 guk-ga; 국가적 독립 guk-ga-jeok
dong-nip; 국민성 gung-min-sseong

nationalization *n.* 국유화 gug-yu-hwa, 국영
gug-yeong; 귀화 gwi-hwa

native *n.* 원주민 won-ju-min; ...태생 ...tae-
saeng; *adj.* 출생의 chul-ssaeng-ui; 출생
지의 chul-ssaeng-ji-ui; 토착의 to chag-ui;
원주민의 won-ju-min-ui; 선천적인 seon-
cheon-jeog-in; ~ **land** 고향 go-hyang; ~
language 모국어 mo-gug-eo

NATO *n. abbr.* **North Atlantic Treaty
Organization** 나토 na-to, 북대서양 조약
기구 buk-dae-seo-yang jo-yak-gi-gu

natural *adj.* 자연의 ja-yeon-ui; 자연계의
ja-yeon-gye-ui; 타고난 ta-go-nan; 자연 그
대로의 ja-yeon geu-rae-ro-ui; 자연스러
운 ja-yeon-seu-reo-un; 당연한 dang-
yeon-han; 천연의 cheon-yeon-ui; 평상의
pyeong-sang-ui; **museum of** ~ **history** 자
연사 박물관 ja-yeon-sa bang-mul-gwan

natural gas *n.* 천연가스 cheon-yeon-kka-sseu

naturalization *n.* 귀화 gwi-hwa

naturally *adj.* 자연스럽게 ja-yeon-seu-reop-
ge; 있는 그대로 in-neun geu-dae-ro; 당연
히 dang-yeon-hi

nature *n.* 자연 ja-yeon; 본바탕 bon-ba-tang

naughty *adj.* 장난꾸러기의 jang-nan-kku-
reo-gi-ui; 버릇없는 beo-reu-deom-neun;
품행이 나쁜 pum-haeng-i na-ppeun

nausea *n.* 멀미 meol-mi; 혐오 hyeom-o; 불
쾌감 bul-kwae-gam

nauseous *adj.* 메스꺼운 me-seu-kkeo-un; 싫
은 sil-eun

Naval Academy *n.* 해군사관학교 hae-gun-sa-gwan-hak-gyo

naval *adj.* 해군의 hae-gun-ui; 군함의 gun-ham-ui

navel *n.* 배꼽 bae-kkop; 중앙 jung-ang; 중심 jung-sim

navigate *vt.* 항해하다 hang-hae-ha-da; 조종하다 jo-jong-ha-da; 진행시키다 jin-haeng-si-ki-da; 통과시키다 tong-gwa-si-ki-da

navigation *n.* 운항 un-hang; 항해 hang-hae; 횡해술 hang-hae-sul, 항공술 hang-gong-sul

navigator *n.* 항공사 hang-gong-sa, 항해사 hang-hae-sa

navy *n.* 해군 hae-gun; 해군력 hae-gun-nyeok

navy blue *n.* 감색 gam-saek, 짙은 청색 jit-eun cheong-saek; *adj.* 감색의 gam-saeg-ui, 짙은 청색의 jit-eun cheong-saeg-ui

Nazi *n.* 나찌 na-jji

near *adj.* 가까운 ga-kka-un; 친한 chin-han; *adv.* 가까이 ga-kka-i, 가깝게 ga-kkap-ge, 거의 geo-ui; **in the ~ future** 가까운 장래에 ga-kka-un jang-nae-e, 곧 got

nearby *adj.* 가까운 ga-kka-un; *adv.* 가까이에 ga-kka-i-e

nearly *adv.* 거의 geo-ui; 긴밀하게 gin-mil-ha-ge; 아주 a-ju; 세밀하게 se-mil-ha-ge; 겨우 gyeo-u

nearsighted *adj.* 근시의 geun-si-ui; 소견이 좁은 so-gyeon-i job-eun

neat *adj.* 깨끗한 kkae-kkeu-tan; 산뜻한 san-tte-tan; 균형잡힌 gyun-hyeong-ja-pin; 적절한 jeok-jeol-han; 순수한 sun-su-han; 훌륭한 hul-lyung-han

necessarily *adv.* 반드시 ban-deu-si; 필연적으로 pil-yeon-jeog-eu-ro

necessary *adj.* 필연적인 pil-yeon-jeog-in; 필요한 pil-yo-han

necessity *n.* 필요 pil-yo; 필수품 pil-ssu-pum; 필연성 pil-yeon-sseong; 궁핍 gung-pip; **basic necessities** 기초 필수품 gi-cho pil-ssu-pum

neck *n.* 목 mok; 옷깃 ot-git; 목부분 mok-bu-bun; 해협 hae-hyeop

necklace *n.* 목걸이 mok-geol-i

necktie *n.* 넥타이 nek-ta-i

need *n.* 필요 pil-yo; 필요한 것 pil-yo-han geot; 결핍 gyeol-pip; 빈곤 bin-gon; *vt.* 필요하다 pil-yo-ha-da; ...할 필요가 있다 ...hal pil-yo-ga it-da

needle *n.* 바늘 ba-neul; 바늘잎 ba-neul-lip; 주사 ju-sa; 짜증 jja-jeung; 걱정 jeok-jeong; 당황 dang-hwang

needless *adj.* 필요없는 pil-yo-eom-neun; **~ly** *adv.* 필요없이 pil-yo-eops-i

needy *adj.* 매우 가난한 mae-u ga-nan-han

negation *n.* 부정 bu-jeong; 거절 geo-jeol; 반대 ban-dae; 존재하지 않음 jon-jae-ha-ji an-eum

negative *n.* 부정 bu-jeong; 거부 geo-bu; 반대 ban-dae; 부정어 bu-jeong-eo; 늠수 eum-su; 음전기 eum-jeon-gi; *(photographic)* 네가티브 ne-ga-ti-beu, 음화 eum-hwa; *adj.* 부정의 bu-jeong-ui; 거부의 geo-bu-ui; 반대의 ban-dae-ui; 소극적인 so-geuk-jeog-in; 음전기의 eum-jeon-gi-ui

neglect *vt.* 게을리하다 ge-eul-li-ha-da; 무시하다 mu-si-ha-da; 방치하다 bang-chi-ha-da

negligent *adj.* 태만한 tae-man-han; 무관심한 mu-gwan-sim-han, 부주의한 bu-ju-i-han

negotiate *vi.* 협상하다 hyeop-sang-ha-da; 매도하다 mae-do-ha-da; 통과하다 tong-gwa-ha-da

negotiation *n.* 협상 hyeop-sang; 교섭 gyo-seop; 양도 yang-do; 극복 geuk-bok

neighbor *n.* 이웃 i-ut; 이웃나라 i-un-na-ra; 동포 dong-po; 동료 dong-nyo

neighborhood *n.* 근처 geun-cheo; 지역 ji-yeok; 지역주민 ji-yeok-ju-min; 동포감 dong-po-gam; 근접 geun-jeop

neither *adj.* 어느 쪽도 아닌 eo-neu jjok-do a-nin; *adv.* ...도 ...도 아니다 ...do... do a-ni-da; **~ will do** 둘 다 안될 겁니다 dul da an-doel geom-ni-da, 둘 다 적합하지 않습니다 dul da jeo-ka-pa-ji an-seum-ni-da

Nepal 네팔 ne-pal

nephew *n.* 조카 jo-ka

nerve *n.* 신경 sin-gyeong; 용기 yong-gi; 뻔뻔스러움 ppeon-ppeon-seu-reo-um; 신경과민 sin-gyeong-gwa-min; 힘줄 him-jjul; 중추 jung-chu

nervous *adj.* 신경의 sin-gyeong-ui; 신경
질적인 sin-gyeong-jil-jjeog-in; 힘찬 him-
chan; 간결한 gan-gyeol-han

nest *n.* 둥지 dung-ji; 보금자리 bo-geum-ja-ri;
은신처 eun-sin-cheo; 찬합 chan-hap; *vi.*
보금자리를 짓다 bo-geum-ja-ri-reul jit-da;
편안히 살다 pyeon-an-hi sal-da; 찬합을
끼우다 chan-hab-eul kki-u-da

net *n.* 그물 geu-mul; 그물조직 geu-mul-jo-
jik; 올가미 ol-ga-mi; 네트 ne-teu; 거미줄
geo-mi-jul; 방송망 bang-song-mang; 정량
jeong-nyang; 순이익 sun-i-ik; 정가 jeong-
kka; *adj.* 에누리없는 e-nu-ri-eom-neun;
정미의 jeong-mi-ui; 순수한 sun-su-han; ~
profit 순이익 sun-i-ik; ~ **total** 순총액, 총
량 sun-chong-aek, chong-nyang; *vt.* 그물
로 잡다 geu-mul-lo jap-da; 수익을 올리
다 su-ig-eul ol-li-da; 올가미에 걸리게
하다 ol-ga-mi-e geol-li-ge ha-da; 그물을
치다 geu-mul-eul chi-da; 뜨다 tteu-da, 짜
다 jja-da

Netherlands, the *n.* 네델란드 ne-del-lan-deu

network *n.* 그물세공 geu-mul-se-gong; 그
물조직 geu-mul-jo-jik; 방송망 bang-
song-mang; *vt.* 그물모양으로 부설하다
geu-mul-mo-yang-eu-ro bu-seol-ha-da; *vi.*
방송망을 설치하다 bang-song-mang-eul
seol-chi-ha-da

neural *adj.* 신경의 sin-gyeong-ui; 신경
계의 sin-gyeong-gye-ui; 신경중추의
sin-gyeong-jung-chu-ui

neuralgia *n.* 신경통 sin-gyeong-tong

neurologist *n.* 신경과 의사 sin-gyeong-kkwa
ui-sa, 신경학자 sin-gyeong-hak-ja

neurosis *n.* 노이로제 no-i-ro-je

neurotic *adj.* 신경의 sin-gyeong-ui; 신
경계의 sin-gyeong-gye-ui; 신경과민
의 sin-gyeong-gwa-min-ui; 신경증의
sin-gyeong-jjeung-ui

neuter *adj.* 중성의 jung-seong-ui; 자동의
ja-dong-ui; 암수구별이 없는 am-su-gu-
byeol-i eom-neun

neutral *adj.* 중립의 jung-lib-ui; 공평한
gong-pyeong-han; 애매한 ae-mae-han;
중성의 jung-seong-ui; 또렷하지 않은
tto-ryeo-ta-ji a-neun; 암수구별이 없는
am-su-gu-byeol-i eom-neun

neutrality *n.* 중립 jung-nip; 중간상태 jung-
gan-sang-tae; 중성 jung-seong

neutralizer *n.* 중화제 jung-hwa-je

never *adv.* 결코 ...지 않다 ...gyeol-ko ji
an-ta; 설마 ...은 아니겠지요 ...seol-ma
eun a-ni-get-ji-yo

never-ending *adj.* 끝없는 kkeud-eom-neun,
영원한 yeong-won-han

nevertheless *adv.* 그럼에도 불구하고
geu-reom-e-do bul-gu-ha-go, 그렇지만
geu-reo-chi-man

new *adj.* 새 sae, 새로운 sae-ro-un; 신식
의 sin-sig-ui; 신품의 sin-pum-ui; 신선한
sin-seon-han; 신임의 sin-im-ui; 경험이 없
는 gyeong-heom-i eom-neun; 새로워진
sae-ro-wo-jin

newborn *n.* 신생아 sin-saeng-a; *adj.* 신생의
sin-saeng-ui; 재생의 jae-saeng-ui

newcomer *n.* 새로온 사람 sae-ro-on sa-ram

New Delhi *n.* 뉴델리 nyu-del-li

new look *n.* 새로운 스타일 sae-ro-un seu-ta-il

newly *adv.* 최근에choe-geun-e, 새로이
sae-ro-i, 다시 da-si

news *n.* 뉴스nyu-sseu; 기사 gi-sa; 소식
so-sik; 신문 sin-mun; **good** ~ 좋은 소식 jo-
eun so-sik; ~**letter** 시사해설 si-sa-hae-seol;
~ **conference** 기자회견 gi-ja-hoe-gyeon;
~ **flash** 뉴스속보 nuy-sseu sok-bo; ~
magazine 시사잡지 si-sa-jap-ji

newspaper *n.* 신문 sin-mun; 신문지 sin-
mun-ji; 신문사 sin-nun-sa

newsstand *n.* 신문잡지 판매점 sin-mun-jap-
ji pan-mae-jeom

New Testament *n.* 신약성서
sin-yak-seong-seo

New Year *n.* 새해 sae-hae, 신년 sin-nyeon;
~**'s Day** 설날 seol-lal; ~**'s Eve** 섣달그믐밤
seot-dal-geu-meum-ppam

New York *n.* 뉴욕 nyu-yok

New Zealand *n.* 뉴질랜드 nyu-jil-laen-deu

next *adj.* 다음의 da-eum-ui; 가장 가까
운 ga-jang-ga-kka-un; 그 다음 가는 geu
da-eum ga-neun; *adv.* 다음에 da-eum-e;
다음으로 da-eum-eu-ro; *prep.* ...의 다
음에 ...ui da-eum-e; ...에서 가장 가까
운 ...e-seo ga-jang ga-kka-un; ~ **week** 다
음주 da-eum-jju; ~ **year** 내년 nae-nyeon;

Who's ~ 다음은 누구십니까 da-eum-eun
nu-gu-sim-ni-kka; **What is** ~ 다음은 뭡니
까 da-eum-eun mwom-ni-kka; ~ **we went**
swimming 그 다음에 우리는 수영하
러 갔습니다 geu da-eum-eun u-ri-neun
su-yeong-ha-reo gat-seum-ni-da; **The** ~
closest shopping center 그 다음으로 가
까운 쇼핑센터 geu da-eum-eu-ro ga-kka-
un syo-ping-ssen-teo; ~ **of kin** 가장 가까
운 친족 ga-jang ga-kka-un chin-jok

next-door *adj.* 이웃집의 i-ut-jib-ui; *adv.* 이웃
집에 i-ut-jib-ui; **her** ~ **neighbor** 그분 옆집
에 사는 이웃 geu-bun yeop-jib-e sa-neun
i-ut; ~ **to** 옆집에 yeop-jib-e

nibble *vt.* 물어뜯다 mul-eo-tteut-da

nice *adj.* 좋은 jo-eun; 말쑥한 mal-ssu-kan;
맛있는 mas-in-neun; 인정많은 in-jeong-
man eun; 점잖은 jeom-jan-eun

nicely *adv.* 훌륭하게 hul-lyung-ha-ge;
정밀하게 jeong-mil-ha-ge; 제대로 잘
je-dae-ro jal

niche *n.* 벽감 byeok-gam; 직소 jeok-so; 활동
범위 hwal-ttong-beom-wi

nickel *n.* 니켈 ni-kel; 5센트 o-ssen-teu

nickname *n.* 별명 byeol-myeong; 약칭
yak-ching

niece *n.* 여자조카 yeo-ja-jo-ka, 조카딸
jo-ka-ttal

Nigeria *n.* 나이지리아 na-i-ji-ri-a

Nigerian *n.* 나이지리아사람 na-i-ji-ri-a-ssa-
ram; *adj.* 나이지리아의 na-i-ji-ri-a-ui

night *n.* 밤 bam; 저녁 jeo-nyeok; 어둠 eo-
dum; 노령 no-ryeong; 죽음 jug-eum

nightclothes *n.* 잠옷 jam-ot

nightclub *n.* 나이트클럽 na-i-teu-keul-leop

nightmare *n.* 악몽 ang-mong; 가위눌림 ga-
wi-nul-lim; 공포상황 gong-po-sang-hwang

nighttime *n.* 야간 ya-gan, 밤 bam

Nile *n.* 나일강 na-il-gang

nimble *adj.* 재빠른 jae-ppa-reun; 영리
한 yeong-ni-han; 유통이 빠른 yu-tong-i
ppa-reun

nine *num.* 아홉 a-hop; 구 gu

nineteen *num.* 열아홉 yeol-a-hop; 십구 sip-gu

nineteenth *adj.* 열아홉번째의 yeol-a-hop-
beon-jjae-ui; 제십구회 je sip-gu-hoe

ninety *num.* 아흔 a-heun; 구십 gu-sip

ninth *adj.* 아홉번째의 a-hop-beon-jjae-ui; 제
구회 je-gu-hoe

nitrogen *n.* 질소 jil-sso

no *adj.* 조금의 -도 없는 jo-geum-ui -do
eom-neun; 거의 –않는 geo-ui -an-neun;
~ **good** 쓸모없는 sseul-mo-eom-neun,
무가치한 mu-ga-chi-han; *adv.* 아니오
a-ni-o, *(opp. of yes)* 아니 a-ni; ~ **parking**
주차금지 ju-cha-geun-ji; ~ **way** 절대로
아니다 jeol-ttae-ro a-ni-da, 절대로 안된
다 jeol-ttae-ro an-doen-da, 조금도 –않
다 jo-geum-do-an-ta; *n.* 쓸모없는 것
sseul-mo-eom-neun geot, 쓸모없는 사람
sseul-mo-eom-neun sa-ram

noble *n.* 귀족 gwi-jok; 양반 yang-ban; *adj.* 귀
족의 gwi-jog-ui; 고상한 go-sang-han; 숭
고한 sung-go-han

Nobel prize *n.* 노벨상 no-bel-ssang

nobody *pron.* 아무도 ...않다 ...a-mu-do an-ta

nocturnal *adj.* 밤의 bam-ui; 야행성의
ya-haeng-sseong-ui

nod *vi.* 끄덕이다 kkeu-deog-i-da; 인사하다
in-sa-ha-da; 졸다 jol-da

node *n.* 매듭 mae-deup, 마디 ma-di

noise *n.* 소리 so-ri; 소음 so-eum; 잡음
jab-eum

noisy *adj.* 떠들썩한 tteo-deul-sseo-kan; 시끄
러운 si-kkeu-reo-un; 야한 ya-han; 화려한
hwa-ryeo-han

nomadic *adj.* 유목의 yu-mog-ui; 유목민의
yu-mog-min-ui; 방랑의 bang-nang-ui

nominate *vt.* 지명하다 ji-myeong-ha-da;
임명하다 im-myeong-ha-da; 지정하다
ji-jeong-ha-da

nomination *n.* 지명 ji-myeong; 임명 im-
myeong; 지정 ji-jeong

nonabrasive *adj.* 거슬리지 않는 geo-seul-li-
ji an-neun, 불쾌하지 않은 bul-kwae-ha-ji
an-eun; 닳지 않는 dal-chi-an-neun

none *pron.* 아무도 ...않다 ...a-mu-do an-ta;
아무것도 ...않다 ...a-mu-geot-do an-ta;
조금도 ...않다 ...jo-geum-do an-ta

nonessential *adj.* 비본질적인
bi-bon-jil-jjeog-in

nonfiction *n.* 논픽션 non-pik-syeon

nonflammable *adj.* 불연성의 bul-yeon-
sseong-ui, 불에 타지 않는 bul-e
ta-ji-an-neun

noninterference *n.* 불간섭 bul-gan-seop
nonmember *n.* 비회원 bi-hoe-won
nonpolitical *adj.* 비정치적인 bi-jeong-chi-jeog-in
nonprofessional *adj.* 비전문적인 bi-jeon-mun-jeog-in
nonprofit *adj.* 비영리의 bi-yeong-ni-ui
nonresident *n.* 비거주자 bi-geo-ju-ja, 부재지주 bu-jae-ji-ju; *adj.* 거주하지 않는 geo-ju-ha-ji an-neun
nonsense *n.* 무의미 mu-ui-mi; 넌센스 non-ssen-sseu; 허튼말 heo-teun mal; 허튼짓 heo-teun jit
nonstick *adj.* 들러붙지 않는 deul-leo-but-ji an-neun
nonstop *adj.* 직행의 ji-kaeng-ui; 연속의 yeon-sog-ui; *adv.* 직행으로 ji-kaeng-eu-ro, 연속적으로 yeon-sok-jeog-eu-ro
noodle *n.* 국수 guk-su
noon *n.* 정오 jeong-o; 한낮 han-nat; 전성기 jeon-seong-gi
no one *pron.* 아무도 a-mu-do
nor *conj.* ...도 또한 ...지 않다 ...do tto-han ...ji an-ta; ...도 아니다 ...do a-ni-da
norm *n.* 표준 pyo-jun, 규범 gyu-beom
normal *adj.* 보통의 bo-tong-ui; 정상의 jeong-sang-ui; 표준의 pyo-jun-ui; 규정의 gyu-jeong-ui
normality *n.* 정상상태 jeong-sang-sang-tae
normally *adv.* 보통은 bo-tong-eun; 정상적으로 jeong-sang-jeog-eu-ro; 평소대로 pyeong-so-dae-ro
north *n.* 북쪽 buk-jjok; 북부지방 buk-bu-jji-bang; *adj.* 북쪽의 buk-jjog-ui; 북쪽에서의 buk-jjog-e-seo-ui; **~bound**북행의 bu-kaeng-ui
North American 북아메리카사람 bug-a-me-ri-ka-ssa-ram
North America *n.* 북아메리카 bug-a-me-ri-ka
northeast *n.* 북동쪽 buk-dong-jjog; *adj.* 북동쪽의 buk-dong-jjog-ui; 북동쪽에서의 buk-dong-jjog-e-seo-ui
northern *adj.* 북쪽에 있는 buk-jjog-e in-neun; 북으로부터 오는 bug-eu-ro-bu-teo o-neun; 북부 독자적인 buk-bu dok-ja-jeog-in
North Korea *n.* 북한 bu-kan
North Pole *n.* 북극 buk-geuk

North Sea *n.* 북극해 buk-geu-kae
northward *adj.* 북쪽을 향한 buk-jjog-eul hyang-han; *adv.* 북쪽을 향하여 buk-jjog-eul hyang-ha-yeo
northwest *n.* 북서쪽 buk-seo-jjok; *adj.* 북서쪽의 buk-seo-jjog-ui; 북서쪽에서의 buk-seo-jjog-e-seo-ui
Norway *n.* 노르웨이 no-reu-we-i
nose *n.* 코 ko; 후각 hu-gak; 돌출부 dol-chul-bu; **~bleed** 코피 ko-pi
no-show *n.* 불참 bul-cham
nostalgia *n.* 향수 hyang-su
nostril *n.* 콧구멍 kot-gu-meong
not *adv.* 아니다 a-ni-da, 않다 an-ta; ...이 아니라 ...i a-ni-ra
notable *adj.* 주목할 만한 ju-mo-kal-man-han
notably *adv.* 현저하게 hyeon-jeo-ha-ge, 특히 teu-ki
notarize *vt.* 공증하다 gong-jeung-ha-da
notary public *n.* 공증인 gong-jeung-in
note *n.* 노트 no-teu; 각서 gak-seo; 문서 mun-seo; 주 ju; 지폐 pi-pye; 중대성 jung-dae-sseong; 기호 gi-ho; 음표 eum-pyo; 어조 eo-jo; *vt.* 적어두다 jeog-eo-du-da; 주석을 달다 ju-seog-eul dal-da; 주목하다 ju-mo-ka-da; 가리키다 ga-ri-ki-da
notebook *n.* 공책 gong-chaek, 노트 no-teu; 수첩 su-cheop; 약속어음 yak-sog-eo-eum
noteworthy *adj.* 주목할만한 ju-mo-kal-man-han
nothing *pron.* 아무것도 아니다 a-mu-geot-do a-ni-da
notice *n.* 주목 ju-mok; 통지 tong-ji; 예고 ye-go; 공고 gong-go; *vt.* 알아채다 al-a-chae-da; 주의하다 ju-i-ha-da; 통지하다 tong-ji-ha-da; 인사하다 in-sa-ha-da; 정중히 다루다 jeong-jung-hi da-ru-da; 언급하다 eon-geu-pa-da; 소개하다 so-gae-ha-da
noticeable *adj.* 눈에 띄는 nun-e tti-neun; 주목할 만한 ju-mo-kal man-han
notification *n.* 통지 tong-ji; 신고서 sin-go-seo; 공고문 gong-go-mun; 통지표 tong-ji-pyo
notify *vt.* 통지하다 tong-ji-ha-da; 통고하다 tong-go-ha-da; 신고하다 sin-go-ha-da
notion *n.* 관념 gwan-nyeom; 생각 saeng-gak; 이해력 i-hae-ryeok

notorious *adj.* 유명한 yu-myeong-han,
이름난 i-reum-nan, 악명높은
ang-myeong-nop-eun

noun *n.* 명사 myeong-sa

nourish *vt.* 영양분을 주다 yeong-yang-bun-eul ju-da; 육성하다 yuk-seong-ha-da; 희망
을 품다 hi-mang-eul pum-tta

nourishing *adj.* 영양분이 있는 yeong-yang-bun-i in-neun

nourishment *n.* 영양분 yeong-yang-bun; 음
식물 eum-sing-mul; 양육 yang-yuk; 영양
상대 yeong-yang-sang-tae

novel *n.* 소설 so-seol; *adj.* 신기한 sin-gi-han;
새로운 sae-ro-un; 기발한 gi-bal-han

novelty *n.* 신기함 sin-gi-ham; 새로운 것
sae-ro-un geot; 신세품 sin-je-pum

November *n.* 11월 sib-il-wol

novice *n.* 풋내기 pun-nae-gi; 초신자 cho-sin-ja

now *adv.* 지금 ji-geum; 현재 hyeon-jae; 이제
부터 i-je-bu-teo; 방금 bang-geum; until ~
지금까지 ji-geum-kka-ji

nowadays *adv.* 현재에는 hyeon-jae-e-neun

nowhere *adv.* 아무데도 없다 a-mu-de-do
eop-da

no-win *adj.* 승산이 없는 seung-san-i
eom-neun

noxious *adj.* 유해한 yu-hae-han; 불건전한
bul-geon-jeon-han

nozzle *n.* 파이프 주둥이 pa-i-peu ju-dung-i

nuance *n.* 색조 saek-jo; 미묘한 차이 mi-myo-han cha-i; 뉘앙스 nwi-ang-sseu

nuclear *adj.* 핵의 haeg-ui; 원자핵의 won-ja-haeg-ui; 중심의 jung-sim-ui; ~ **energy**
핵에너지 haeg-e-neo-ji; ~ **bomb** 핵폭탄
haek-pok-tan; ~ **fuel** *n.* 핵연료 haeg-yeol-lyo; ~ **power** *n.* 핵무기 보유국 haeng-mu-gi bo-yu-guk; 원자력 won-ja-ryeok; ~ **test**
n. 핵실험 haek-sil-heom

nucleus *n.* 핵 haek; 핵심 haek-sim; 토대
to-dae

nude *adj.* 벌거벗은 beol-geo-beos-eun; 수목
이 없는 su-mog-i eom-neun; 장식이 없는
jang-sig-i eom-neun; 무상의 mu-sang-ui;
털이 없는 teol-i eom-neun

nudity *n.* 벌거숭이 beol-geo-sung-i; 나체상
na-che-sang

nuisance *n.* 폐 pye; 성가심 seong-ga-sim; 귀
찮은 것 gwi-chan-eun geot

null *adj.* 효력이 없는 hyo-ryeog-i eom-neun;
특징이 없는 teuk-jing-i eom-neun; 존재
하지 않는 jon-jae-ha-ji an-neun; ~ **and**
void 무효의 mu-hyo-ui

nullify *vt.* 무효로하다 mu-hyo-ro-ha-da; 폐
기하다 pye-gi-ha-da

numb *adj.* 감각을 잃은 gam-gag-eul il-eun;
언 eon; 마비된 ma-bi-doen

number *n.* 수 su; 숫자 sut-ja; 번호 beon-ho;
다수 da-su; *vi.* 세다 se-da, 계산하다 gye-san-ha-da; *vt.* 번호를 메기다 beon-ho-eul
me-gi-da, 번호로 구별하다 beon-ho-ro
gu-byeol-ha-da; **without** ~ 수없이 su-eops-i; **beyond** ~ 무수한 mu-su-han, 헤
아릴 수 없을 정도의 he-a-ril su eops-eul
jeong-do-ui; **in** ~ 합계 hap-gye, 모두 mo-du; 숫자상으로 sut-ja-sang-eu-ro; ~ **one** *n.*
일인자 il-in-ja; 소변 so-byeon; ~ **two** *n.* 이
인자 i-in-ja; 대변 dae-byeon

numeral *n.* 숫자 sut-ja; *adj.* 숫자의 sut-ja-ui

numerous *adj.* 다수의 da-su-ui; 운율적인
un-yul-jjeog-in

nun *n.* 수녀 su-nyeo

nurse *n.* 간호원 gan-ho-won; 유모 yu-mo;
양성소 yang-seong-so; *vt.* 아이를 돌보
다 a-i-reul dol-bo-da; 양육하다 yang-yu-ka-da; 마음에 품다 ma-eum-e pum-tta;
간호하다 gan-ho-ha-da; 주의하여 다루
다 ju-i-ha-yeo da-ru-da; 기분을 맞추다
gi-bun-eul mat-chu-da

nursery *n.* 아이방 a-i-bang; 탁아소 tag-a-so;
종묘원 jong-myo-won; 양어장 yang-eo-jang; 양성소 yang-seong-so; ~ **rhyme** 동
요 dong-yo; ~ **tale** 동화 dong-hwa

nursing *n.* 수유 su-yu; 양육 yang-yuk; 병
구안 byeong gu-wan; ~ **home** 양로
원 yang-no-won; ~ **school** 간호학교
gan-ho-hak-gyo

nut *n.* 견과류 gyeon-gwa-ryu; 어려운 것 eo-ryeo-un-geot; 고정나사 go-jeong-na-sa; 조
리개 jo-ri-gae; 미치광이 mi-chi-gwang-I;
~**shell** 견과류 껍질 gyeon-gwa-ryu kkeop-jil *(literal)*

nutrition *n.* 영양 yeong-yang; 영양분
yeong-yang-bun; 영양학 yeong-yang-hak

nutritious *adj.* 영양분이 있는 yeong-yang-bun-i in-neun; 영양의 yeong-yang-ui

O

o'clock *adv.* ...시 ...si

oak *n.* 오크나무 o-keu-na-mu

oar *n.* 노 no; 노젓는 사람 no-jeon-neun sa-ram

oasis *n.* 오아시스 o-a-si-sseu

oat *n.* 귀리 gwi-ri

oath *n.* 맹세 maeng-se; 저주 jeo-ju; 욕설 yok-seol

oatmeal *n.* 오트밀 o-teu-mil

obedience *n.* 복종 bok-jong; 순종 sun-jong; 귀의 gwi-ui

obedient *adj.* 순종하는 sun-jong-ha-neun; 말 잘듣는 mal jal-deun-neun

obese *adj.* 지나치게 살찐 ji-na-chi-ge sal-jjin

obesity *n.* 비만 bi-man, 비대 bi-dae

obey *vt.* 순종하다 sun-jong-ha-da; 복종하다 bok-jong-ha-da; 반응하다 ban-eung-ha-da

object *n.* 물건 mul-geon; 목적 mok-jeok; 대상 dae-sang; 목적어 mok-jjeog-eo; *vi.* 반대하다 ban-dae-ha-da; 항의하다 hang-i-ha-da; 불평을 품다 bul-pyeong-eul pum-tta; 싫어하다 sil-eo-ha-da

objection *n.* 반대 ban-dae; 반감 ban-gam; 난점 nan-jjeom; 결함 gyeol-ham

objective *adj.* 객관적인 gaek-gwan-jeog-in; 편견이 없는 pyeon-gyeon-i eom-neun; 물질적인 mul-jjil-jeog-in; 목적의 mok-jeog-ui

obligation *n.* 의무 ui-mu; 책임 chaeg-im; 계약 gye-yak; 증권 jeung-kkwon; 의리 ui-ri

obligatory *adj.* 의무적인 ui-mu-jeog-in; 필수의 pil-ssu-ui

oblige *vt.* 강제하다 gang-je-ha-da; 은혜를 베풀다 eun-hye-reul be-pul-da

oblong *n.* 타원형 ta-won-hyeong; *adj.* 타원형의 ta-won-hyeong-ui

obscene *adj.* 외설의 oe-seol-ui; 추잡한 chu-ja-pan

obscure *adj.* 어두운 eo-du-un; 불명료한 bul-myeong-nyo-han; 확실하지 않은 hwak-sil-ha-ji an-eun; 눈에 띄지 않는 nun-e tti-ji an-neun; 알려지지 않은 al-lyeo-ji-ji an-eun; *vt.* 어둡게 하다 eo-dup-ge ha-da; 덮어 감추다 deop-eo gam-chu-da; 빛을 가리다 bich-eul ga-ri-da; 불명료하게 하다 bul-myeong-nyo-ha-ge ha-da

observation *n.* 관찰 gwan-chal; 주목 ju-mok; 관찰력 gwan-chal-lyeok; 관찰결과 gwan-chal-gyeol-gwa; 의견 ui-gyeon; 발언 bal-eon

observatory *n.* 천문대 cheon-mun-dae; 기상대 gi-sang-dae; 관측소 gwan-cheuk-so; 전망대 jeon-mang-dae

observe *vt.* 관습을 지키다 wan-seub-eul ji-ki-da; 명절을 축하하다 myeong-jeol-eul chu-ka-ha-da; 의식을 거행하다 ui-sig-eul geo-haeng-ha-da; 관찰하다 gwan-chal-ha-da; 인지하다 in-ji-ha-da; 진술하다 jin-sul-ha-da

obsessive *adj.* 강박관념의 gang-bak-gwan-nyeom-ui; 망상의 mang-sang-ui; 도를 지나친 do-reul ji-na-chin

obstacle *n.* 장애물 jang-ae-mul; 방해 bang-hae; 고장 go-jang

obstetrician *n.* 산부인과 의사 san-bu-in-kkwa ui-sa

obstinate *adj.* 완고한 wan-go-han; 끈질긴 kkeun-jil-gin; 완강한 wan-gang-han; 고치기 힘든 go-chi-gi him-deun

obstruct *vt.* 막다 mak-da; 차단하다 cha-dan-ha-da; 방해하다 bang-hae-ha-da

obstruction *n.* 차단 cha-dan; 방해 bang-hae; 저지 jeo-ji; 장해물 jang-hae-mul; 방해물 bang-hae-mul

obtain *vt.* 얻다 eot-da; 획득하다 hoek-deu-ka-da

obtainable *adj.* 얻을 수 있는 eod-eul ssu in-neun; 손에 넣을 수 있는 son-e neo-eul ssu in-neun

obvious *adj.* 명백한 myeong-bae-kan; 빤한 ppan-han; 두드러진 du-deu-reo-jin

occasion *n.* 경우 gyeong-u; 기회 gi-hoe; 행사 haeng-sa; 이유 i-yu

occasional *adj.* 가끔의 ga-kkeum-ui; 임시의 im-si-ui; 우연한 u-yeon-han; 특별한 경우를 위한 teuk-byeol-han gyeong-u-reul wi-han; ~**ly** 이따금 i-tta-geum, 가끔 ga-kkeum

occult *adj.* 신비로운 sin-bi-ro-un; 초자연적인 cho-ja-yeon-jeog-in; 마술적인 ma-sul-jjeog-in

occupancy *n.* 점유 jeom-yu; 점령 jeom-nyeong; 점유기간 jeom-yu-gi-gan

occupation n. 직업 jig-eop; 점유 jeom-yu; 점령 jeom-nyeong; 거주 geo-ju; 거주권 geo-ju-kkwon; 거주기간 geo-ju-gi-gan; 종사 jong-sa; 임기 im-gi

occupy vt. 차지하다 cha-ji-ha-da; 점령하다 jeom-nyeong-ha-da; 거주하다 geo-ju-ha-da; 점유하다 jeom-yu-ha-da; 종사시키다 jong-sa-si-ki-da; 마음을 사로잡다 ma-eum-eul sa-ro-jap-da

occur vi. 일어나다 il-eo-na-da; 나타나다 na-ta-na-da; 떠오르다 tteo-o-reu-da

occurrence n. 사건 sa-kkeon; 발생 bal-ssaeng; 산출 san-chul; 존재 jon-jae

ocean n. 대양 dae-yang; 바다 ba-da

octagon n. 팔각형 pal-ga-kyeong

October n. 10월 si-wol

octopus n. 문어 mun-eo; 낙지 nak-ji

odd adj. (not even) 홀수의 hol-ssu-ui; (strange) 기묘한 gi-myo-han

oddity n. 기이함 gi-i-ham; 괴짜 goe-jja

odor n. 냄새 naem-sae; 향기 hyang-gi; 향료 hyang-nyo; 기색 gi-saek; 평판 pyeong-pan

odorless adj. 냄새가 안나는 naem-sae-ga an-na-neun

of prep. ...의 ui, ...에 속하는 ...e so-ka-neun; ...(이)라고 하는 ...(i)-ra-go ha-neun; ...(으)로 만든 (eu-)ro man-deun; ...(으)로 부터 ...(eu-)ro-bu-teo; **three ~ them** 그들 중 셋 geu-deil jung set; **a package ~ cookies** 쿠키 한봉지 ku-ki han-bong-ji; **It was very kind ~ you** 정말 친절하시군요 jeong-mal chin-jeol-ha-si-gun-yo

off adv. 떨어져서 tteol-eo-jeo-seo, 분리되어 bul-li-doe-eo, 벗어나서 beos-eo-na-seo; (canceled) **the meeting is ~** 모임이 끝났습니다 mo-im-i kkeun-nat-seum-ni-da, 모임이 취소됐습니다 mo-im-i chwi-so-dwaet-seum-ni-da; **The lights are ~** 등(불)이 꺼졌습니다 deung(-ppul)-i kkeo-jeot-seum-ni-da; prep. ...에서 떨어져서e-seo tteol-eo-jeo-seo; ...(으)로부터 떨어져서eu-ro-bu-teo tteol-eo-jeo-seo; **~ duty** 쉬는 날인 swi-neun nal-in, 비번의 bi-beon-ui; **~ the beaten track** 별난 byeol-lan, 생소한 saeng-so-han, 상도를 벗어난 sang-do-reul beos-eo-nan, 별난 byeol-lan, 독특한 dok-teu-kan; **It fell ~ the table** 그 것이 식탁에서 떨어졌습니다 geu-geos-i

sik-tag-e-seo tteol-eo-jeot-seum-ni-da; adj. 벗어난 beos-eo-nan, 잘못된 jal-mot-doen, 틀린 teul-lin

off-center adj. 중심을 벗어난 jung-sim-eul beos-eo-nan, 균형을 잃은 gyun-hyeong-eul il-eun, 불안정한 bul-an-jeong-han

offend vt. 성나게 하다 seong-na-ge ha-da; 불쾌하게 하다 bul-kwae-ha-ge ha-da; 위반하다 wi-ban-ha-da; 죄를 범하게 하다 joe-reul beom-ha-ge ha-da

offense n. 위반 wi-ban; 화냄 hwa-naem; 화가 나는 원인 hwa-ga na-neun won-in; 공격 gong-gyeok; 장애 jang-ae

offensive adj. 불쾌한 bul-kwae-han; 무례한 mu-rye-han; 공격적인 gong-gyeok-jeog-in; 더러운 deo-reo-un

offer n. 제언 je-eon; 신청 sin-cheong; 바침 ba-chim; 기부 gi-bu; 매매제의 mae-mae-je-ui; vt. 권하다gwon-ha-da; 제공하다 je-gong-ha-da; 바치다 ba-chi-da; 감사를 표현하다 gam-sa-reul pyo-hyeon-ha-da; 제출하다 je-chul-ha-da; 말하다 mal-ha-da; 야기하다 ya-gi-ha-da

office n. 임무 im-mu; 직책 jik-chaek; 관공서 gwan-gong-seo; 사무소 sa-mu-so; 직원 jig-won; 진찰실 jin-chal-sil; 연구실 yeon-gu-sil, **hours** 근무시간 geun-mu-ssi-gan

officer n. 장교 jang-gyo; 경관 gyeong-gwan; 공무원 gong-mu-won; 일원 im-won

official n. 공무원 gong-mu-won; adj. 공무의 gong-mu-won-ui; 직무상의 jing-mu-sang-ui; 관직에 있는 gwan-jig-e in-neun; 직권에 의한 jik-gwon-e ui-han

off-line adj. 오프라인의 o-peu-ra-in-ui; adv. 오프라인으로 o-peu-ra-in-eu-ro

off-price adj. 할인의 hal-in-ui

off-season adj. 비수기의 bi-su-gi-ui, 오프시즌 o-peu-ssi-jeun

offset vt. 상쇄하다 sang-swae-ha-da; 오프셋 인쇄로 하다 o-peu-set in-swae-ro ha-da; 단을 짓다 dan-eul jit-da

offspring n. 자손 ja-son, 자식 ja-sik

off-stage adj. 무대 뒤의 mu-dae dwi-ui; 사생활의 sa-saeng-hwal-ui; 비공식의 bi-gong-sig-ui

off-the-record adj. 비공식의 bi-gong-sig-ui, 기록을 남기지 않는 gi-rog-eul nam-gi-ji an-neun; *adv.* 비공식으로 bi-gong-sig-eu-ro, 기록을 남기지 않고 girog-eul nam-gi-ji an-ko

often *adv.* 종종 jong-jong; 가끔 ga-kkeum

oil *n.* 기름 gi-reum; 석유 seog-yu; 유화물감 yu-hwa-mul-kkam; 유화 yu-hwa; **cooking ~** 식용류 sig-yong-nyu; **heating ~** 난방용 기름 nan-bang-nyong gi-reum; **~ filter** 기름필터 gi-reum-pil-teo; **~ well** 유정 yu-jeong; **~ field** 유전 yu-jeon; **~ painting** 유화 yu-hwa; **~ tanker** 석유 수송차 seog-yu su-song-cha

oily *adj.* 기름의 gi-reum-ui; 기름칠한 gi-reum-chil-han; 말솜씨가 좋은 mal-ssom-ssi-ga jo-eun

ointment *n.* 연고 yeon-go; 고약 go-yak

OK *interj. (also* **okay)** 좋습니다 jo-sseum-ni-da; 됐습니다 dwaet-seum-ni-da; 승인하다 seung-in-ha-da; *adj.* 훌륭한 hul-lyung-han, 만족스러운 man-jok-seu-reo-un; *adv.* 잘 jal, 틀림없게 teul-lim-eop-ge; *vt.* ...에 **OK**라고 쓰다 ...e o-ke-i-ra-go sseu-da, ...을 승인하다 ...eul seung-in-ha-da, ...을 찬성하다 ...eul chan-seong-ha-da; *n.* 승인 seung-in, 시인 si-in, 허가 heo-ga

old *adj.* 나이든 na-i-deun; 노년의 no-nyeon-ui; 낡은 nalg-eun; 이전의 i-jeong-ui; 예로부터의 ye-ro-bu-teo-ui; 친한 chin-han; 노후한 no-hu-han; 노련한 no-ryeon-han

old age *n.* 노령 no-ryeong, 노년 no-nyeon

old boy *n.* 정정한 노인 jeong-jeong-han no-in; 졸업생 jol-eop-saeng, 교우 gyo-u

old-fashioned *adj.* 구식의 gu-sig-ui; 유행에 뒤진 yu-haeng-e dwi-jin

old lady *n.* 노부인 no-bu-in

old maid *n.* 노처녀 no-che-nyeo, 올드미스 ol-deu-mi-sseu

old man *n.* 노인 no-in

Old Testament *n.* 구약성서 gu-yak-seong-seo

old-time *adj.* 옛날의 yeon-nal-ui, 옛날부터의 yen-nal-bu-teo-ui

olive *n.* 올리브 ol-li-beu; **~ green** 올리브색 ol-li-beu-saek; **~ oil** 올리브 오일 ol-li-beu o-il

Olympic *adj.* 올림픽 경기의 ol-lim-pik gyeong-gi-ui; **~ Games** 올림픽 게임 ol-lim-pik kke-im

omelet(te) *n.* 오믈렛 o-meul-let; **ham-and-cheese ~** 햄하고 치즈를 넣은 오믈렛 haem-ha-go chi-jeu-reul neo-eun o-meul-let

omission *n.* 생략 saeng-nyak; 탈락 tal-lak; 소홀 so-hol

omit *vt.* 빼다 ppae-da; 빠뜨리다 ppa-tteu-ri-da; 게을리하다 ge-eul-li-ha-da

on *prep.* ...의 표면에 ...ui pyo-myeon-e, ...에 붙여서 ...e bu-cheo-seo, ...(으)로 ...(eu-)ro, ...에 접하여 ...e jeo-pa-yeo, ...에 입각해서 ...e ip-ga-kae-seo, ...의 도중에 ...ui do-jung-e, ...하자 곧 ...ha-ja got, ...에 대해서 ...e dae-hae-seo, ...(으)로 ...(eu-)ro; *adv.* 위에 wi-e, 입고서 ip-go-seo, 끊임없이 kkeun-im-eops-i, 행하여져서 haeng-ha-yeo-jeo-seo; **~ duty** 당번인dang-beon-in, 당직인 dang-jig-in; **~ schedule** 일정에 맞는 il-jjeong-e man-neun

onboard *adj.* 기내에 장착된 gi-nae-e jang-chak-doen

once *adv.* 한번 han-beon; 이전에 i-jeon-e; 언제 한번 eon-je han-beon; **at ~** 한번 han-beon; **~ in a while** 가끔 한번씩 ga-kkeum han-beon-ssik

oncoming *adj.* 접근하는 jeop-geun-ha-neun, 다가오는 da-ga-o-neun, 장래의 jang-nae-ui

one *num.* 하나 ha-na, 한사람 han-sa-ram, 한개 han-gae; *adj.* 하나의 ha-na-ui, 일 il; 어떤 eo-tteon; 한쪽의 han-jjog-ui

one-dimensional *adj.* 일차원의 il-cha-won-ui; 깊이가 없는 gip-i-ga eom-neun, 피상적인 pi-sang-jeog-in

one-piece *n.* 원피스 won-pi-sseu

oneself *pron.* 몸소 mom-so, 자기자신을 ja-gi-ja-sin-eul, 자기자신에게 ja-gi-ja-sin-e-ge

one-sided *adj.* 한쪽으로 치우친 han-jjog-eu-ro chi-u-chin; 일방적인 il-bang-jeog-in

onetime *adj.* 한때의 han-ttae-ui

one-to-one *adj.* 일대일의 il-ttae-il-ui

one-way *adj.* 한쪽의n-jjog-ui h, 편도의 pyeon-do-ui, 일방통행의 il-bang-tong-haeng-ui

ongoing *adj.* 전진하는 jeon-jin-ha-neun, 진행중인 jin-haeng-jung-in

onion *n.* 양파 yang-pa

on-line *adj.* 온라인의 ol-la-in-ui; *adv.* 온라인으로 ol-la-in-eu-ro; 온라인에 ol-la-in-e

only *adj.* 유일한 yu-il-han; 비할바 없는 bi-hal-ppa eom-neun; 최상의 choe-sang-ui; *adv.* 오직 o-jik; 겨우 gyeo-u

on-screen *adj.* 영화의 yeong-hwa-ui; *adv.* 영화에서 yeong-hwa-e-seo

on-stage *adj.* 무대 위의 mu-dae wi-ui; *adv.* 무대 위에서 mu-dae wi-e-seo

on-street *adj.* 노상의 no-sang-ui

opaque *adj.* 불투명한 bul-tu-myeong-han, 통과시키지 않는 tong-gwa-si-ki-ji an-neun; 광택이 없는 gwang-taeg-i eom-neun; 분명치 않은 bun-myeong-chi an-eun; 칙칙한 chik-chi-kan

open *adj.* 열린 yeol-lin; 광활한 gwang-hwal-han; 비어있는 bi-eo-in-neun; 공개된 gong-gae-doen; 공공연한 gong-gong-yeon-han; 솔직한 sol-jji-kan; 노출되어 있는 no-chul-doe-eo-in-neun; *vt.* 열다 yeol-da; 개간하다 gae-gan-ha-da; 개시하다 gae-si-ha-da; 개방하다 gae-bang-ha-da; 털어놓다 teo-eo-no-ta; 계발하다 gye-bal-ha-da; *vi.* 열리다 yeol-li-da; 꽃이 피다 kkoch-i pi-da; 터지다 teo-ji-da; 통하다 tong-ha-da; 시작하다 si-ja-ka-da; 전개하다 jeon-gae-ha-da; 눈을 뜨다 nun-eul tteu-da

open-air *adj.* 옥외의 og-oe-ui, 야외의 ya-oe-ui

open door *n.* 기회균등 gi-hoe-gyun-deung, 개방정책 gae-bang-jeong-chaek

open-ended *adj.* 제한이 없는 je-han-i eom-neun, 자유로운 ja-yu-ro-un

opener *n.* 병따개 pyeong-tta-gae

open-eyed *adj.* 빈틈없는 bin-teum-eom-neun; 눈이 휘둥그레진 nun-i hwi-dung-geu-re-jin, 놀란 nol-lan

open-handed *adj.* 손이 빈 son-i bin; 후한 hu-han, 관대한 gan-dae-han

open-hearted *adj.* 솔직한 sol-jji-kan, 진정한 jin-jeong-han, 관대한 gwan-dae-han

open house *n.* 오픈하우스 o-peun-ha-u-sseu, 집들이 jip-deul-i

opening *n.* 개방 gae-bang; 열린구멍 yeol-lin-gu-meong; 통로 tong-no; 빈터 bin-teo; 개시 gae-si; 취직자리 chwi-jik-ja-ri; 초장 cho-jang

openly *adv.* 공공연하게 gong-gong-yeon-ha-ge

open-minded *adj.* 편견이 없는 pyeon-gyeon-i eom-neun

open-mouthed *adj.* 입을 벌린 ib-eul beol-lin; 얼빠진 eol-ppa-jin

open sea *n.* 공해 gong-hae, 먼바다 meon-ba-da

opera *n.* 오페라 o-pe-ra; ~ **house** 가극장 ga-geuk-jang

operate *vt.* 조작하다 jo-ja-ka-da; 운영하다 un-yeong-ha-da, 밀으기다 il-eu-ki-da, 결정하다 gyeol-jjeong-ha-da; *vi.* 움직이다 um-jig-i-da; 작용하다 jag-yong-ha-da; 수술하다 su-sul-ha-da; 작전하다 jak-jeon-ha-da; 효과를 나타내다 hyo-kkwa-reul na-ta-nae-da

operating *adj.* 수술에 쓰는 su-sul-e sseu-neun; 경영상의 gyeong-yeong-sang-ui

operating system *n.* 운영체제 un-yeong-che-gye

operation *n.* 가동 ga-dong; 효력 hyo-ryeok; 조작 jo-jak; 운영 un-yeong; 수술 su-sul; 군사행동 gun-sa-haeng-dong

operator *n.* 조작자 jo-jak-ja; 기사 gi-sa; 교환수 gyo-hwan-su; 수술의사 su-sul-ui-sa; 중매인 jung-mae-in

opinion *n.* 의견 ui-gyeon, 견해 gyeon-hae; 평가 pyeong-kka; 전문가의 의견 jeon-mun-ga-ui ui-gyeon

opium *n.* 이편 a-pyeon

opponent *n.* 적 jeok; 상대 sang-dae; 대항자 dae-hang-ja; 반대자 ban-dae-ja

opportunity *n.* 기회 gi-hoe; 행운 haeng-un; 가망 ga-mang

oppose *vt.* 반대하다 ban-dae-ha-da; 저지하다 jeo-ji-ha-da; 대비시키다 dae-bi-si-ki-da; 손가락을 맞내다 son-kka-rag-eul mat-dae-da

opposite *n.* 반대자 ban-dae-ja; 반댓말 ban-daen-mal; 상대자 sang-dae-ja; *adj.* 맞은편의 maj-eun-pyeon-ui; 정반대의 jeong-ban-dae-ui; 마주나는 ma-ju-na-neun

opposition *n.* 반대 ban-dae; 방해 bang-hae; 대립 dae-rip; 이의신청 i-ui-sin-cheong

oppress *vt.* 압박하다 ap-ba-ka-da; 학대하다 hak-dae-ha-da; 답답하게 하다 dap-da-pa-ge ha-da; 무겁게 덮치다 mu-geop-ge deop-chi-da

oppression *n.* 압박 ap-bak; 억압 eog-ap; 압제 ap-je; 중압감 jung-ap-gam; 무기력 mu-gi-ryeok; 고난 go-nan; 직권남용죄 jik-gwon-nam-yong-jjoe

oppressive *adj.* 압제적인 ap-je-jeog-in; 답답한 dap-da-pan; 숨막힐듯한 sum-ma-kil tteu-tan

optical *adj.* 눈의 nun-ui; 시각의 si-gag-ui; 시력을 돕는 si-ryeog-eul dom-neun; 광학의 gwang-hag-ui

optician *n.* 광학기계상 gwang-hak-gi-gye-sang; 안경상 an-gyeong-ang

optimist *n.* 낙천주의자 nak-cheon-ju-i-ja

optimistic *adj.* 낙천적인 nak-cheon-jeog-in; 낙관적인 nak-gwan-jeog-in; 낙천주의의 nak-cheon-ju-i-ui

option *n.* 선택권 seon-taek-gwon; 선택과목 seon-taek-gwa-mok; 선택매매 seon-taeng-mae-mae

optional *adj.* 임의의 im-i-ui; 선택의 seon-taeg-ui

optometrist *n.* 검안사 geom.-an-sa; 시력 측정자 si-ryeok cheuk-jeong-ja

or *conj.* 또는 tto-neun, 즉 jeuk, 그렇지 않으면 geu-reo-chi an-eu-myeon

oral *adj.* 구두의 gu-du-ui; 입의 ib-ui

orange *n.* 오렌지 o-ren-ji; 오렌지색 o-ren-ji-saek; *adj.* 오렌지색의 o-ren-ji-saeg-ui; ~ **juice** 오렌지주스 o-ren-ji-ju-sseu; ~ **peel** 오렌지 껍질 o-ren-ji kkeop-jil

orbit *n.* 궤도 gwe-do; 활동범위 hwal-ttong-beom-ui

orchard *n.* 과수원 gwa-su-won; 과수 gwa-su

orchestra *n.* 오케스트라 o-ke-seu-teu-ra, 교향악단 gyo-hyang-ak-dan

order *n.* 명령 myeong-nyeong; 주문 ju-mun; 규칙 gyu-chik; 순서 sun-seo; 정돈 jeong-don; 상태 sang-tae; 이치 i-chi; 서열 seol-yeol; 계급 gye-geup; *vt.* *(command)* 명령하다 myeong-nyeong-ha-da; *(purchase)* 주문하다 ju-mun-ha-da; 배열하다 bae-yeol-ha-da; 지시하다 ji-si-ha-da; 정하다 jeong-ha-da; **in** ~ 차례대로 cha-rye-dae-ro; **out of** ~ 고장나다 go-jang-na-da; **in** ~ **to**

...하기 위해서 ...ha-gi wi-hae-seo; **money** ~ 송금환 song-geum-hwan; **postal order** 우편소액환 u-pyeon-so-ae-kwan

order form *n.* 주문용지 ju-mun-nyong-ji

orderly *adj.* 순서바른 sun-seo-ba-reun; 규율있는 gyu-yul-in-neun; 순종하는 sun-jong-ha-neun; 명령의 myeong-nyeong-ui

ordinary *adj.* 보통의 bo-tong-ui; 평범한 pyeong-beom-han; 관할권이 있는 gwan-hal-kkwon-i in-neun

ore *n.* 광석 gwang-seok; 원광 won-gwang

organ *n.* *(instrument)* 오르간 o-reu-gan; 기관 gi-gwan; *(body part)* 기관지 gi-gwan-ji

organic *adj.* 유기체의 yu-gi-che-ui; 유기적 yu-gi-jeok; 고유의 go-yu-ui; 기관의 gi-gwan-ui; ~ **food** 자연식품 ja-yeon-sik-pum, 유기농 식품 yu-gi-nong sik-pum

organization *n.* 조직 jo-jik; 기구 gi-gu; 조직체 jo-jik-che; 생물체 saeng-mul-che

organize *vt.* 조직하다 jo-ji-ka-da; 체계화하다 che-gye-hwa-ha-da; 창립하다 chang-ni-pa-da; 노동조합을 만들다 no-dong-jo-hab-eul man-deul-da

oriental *adj.* 동양의 dong-yang-ui

orientation *n.* 방위 bang-wi; 지향 ji-hyang, 귀소본능 gwi-so-bon-neung; 적응 jeog-eung, 예비교육 ye-bi-gyo-yuk

origin *n.* 기원 gi-won; 태생 tae-saeng; 원점 won-jjeom; 유래 yu-rae; 가문 ga-mun

original *n.* 원형 won-hyeong; 원본 won-bon; 기인 gi-in; *adj.* 최초의 choe-cho-ui; 원본의 won-bon-ui; 독창적인 dok-chang-jeog-in; 색다른 saek-da-reun

originally *adv.* 원래 wol-lae; 최초에 choe-cho-e; 최초부터 choe-cho-bu-teo

originate *vt.* 시작하다 si-ja-ka-da; 창작하다 chang-ja-ka-da; *vi.* 비롯하다 bi-ro-ta-da, 시발하다 si-bal-ha-da

ornament *n.* 장식 jang-sik; 장식품 jang-sik-pum; *vt.* 꾸미다 kku-mi-da

orphan *n.* 고아 go-a

orphanage *n.* 고아원 go-a-won

orthodox *adj.* 정통파의 jeong-tong-pa-ui, 정교회의 jeong-gyo-hoe-ui

oscillate *vi.* 진동하다 jin-dong-ha-da; 동요하다 dong-yo-ha-da; 왕복하다 wang-bo-ka-da; 변동하다 byeon-dong-ha-da

Oslo *n.* 오슬로 o-seul-lo

ostracism *n.* 추방 chu-bang; 배척 bae-cheok

other *adj.* 다른 또 하나의 da-reun tto ha-na-ui, 그 밖의 geu bakk-ui, 다른 da-reun; *pron.* 그밖의 것 geu-bakk-ui geot

otherwise *adv.* 딴 방법으로 ttan bang-beob-eu-ro; 그렇지 않으면 geu-reo-chi an-eu-myeon

ouch *interj.* 아야 a-ya

ounce *n.* 온스 on-sseu

our *adj.* 우리의 u-ri-ui, *(hum.)* 저희의 jeo-hi-ui

ours *pron.* 우리의 것 u-ri-ui keot, *(hum.)* 저희의 것 jeo-hi-ui geot

ourselves *pron.* 우리 자신을 u-ri ja-sin-eul; 우리 자신에게 u-ri ja-sin-e-gye; *(hum.)* 저희 자신을 jeo-hi ja-sin-eul; 저회 자신에게 jeo-hi ja-sin-e-ge

out *adv.* 밖에 bakk-e, 밖으로 bakk-eu-ro; 튀어 나와서 twi eo na-wa-seo, 나타나서 na-ta-na-seo; 피어서 pi-eo-seo; 큰 소리로 keun so-ri-ro; 마지막까지 ma-ji-mak-kka-ji; 벗어나서 beos-eo-na-seo

outbound *adj.* 외국행의 oe-gu-kaeng-ui, 시외행의 si-oe-haeng-ui

outbreak *n.* 발발 bal-bal

outburst *n.* 폭발 pok-bal

outcast *n.* 추방당한 사람 chu-bang-dang-han sa-ram; 집없는 사람 jib-eom-neun sa-ram; 부랑자 bu-rang-ja; 폐물 pye-mul

outcome *n.* 결과 gyeol gwa; 성과 seong-kkwa

outdated *adj.* 구식의 gu-sig-ui, 시대에 뒤떨어진 si-dae-e dwi-tteol-eo-jin

outdoor *adj.* 집밖의 jip-bakk-ui; 야외의 ya oe ui; 사회시설 외의 sa-hoe-si-seol oe-ui; *adv.* 문밖에서 mun-bakk-e-seo; 야외에서 ya-oe-e-seo

outer *adj.* 밖의 bakk-ui; 외부의 oe-bu-ui; 객관적인 gaek-gwan-jeog-in; ~ **space** 우주 공간 u-ju-gong-gan

outfit *n.* 의상 한벌 ui-sang-han-beol; 도구 한벌 do-gu han-beol

outflow *n.* 유출 yu-chul, 유출물 yu-chul-mul

outgoing *adj.* 나가는 na-ga-neun, 떠나가는 tteo-na-ga-neun; 사임하는 sa-im-ha-neun; 사교적인 sa-gyo-jeog-in

outlet *n.* 출구 chul-gu, 방수구 bang-su-gu; 배출구 bae-chul-gu; 소매점 so-mae-jeom

outline *n.* 윤곽 yun-gwak; 개요 gae-yo; 약도 yak-do; *vt.* 윤곽을 그리다 yun-gwag-eul geu-ri-da; 밑그림을 그리다 mit-geu-rim-eul geu-ri-da; 개설하다 gae-seol-ha-da; 개요를 말하다 gae-yo-reul mal-ha-da; 약도를 그리다 yak-do-reul geu-ri-da

outlook *n.* 조망 jo-mang; 예측 ye-cheuk; 견해 gyeon-hae

outmoded *adj.* 유행에 뒤진 yu-haeng- dwi-jin

outmost *adj.* 가장 먼 ga-jang-meon, 가장 바깥쪽의 qa-jang-ba-kkat-jjog-ui

out-of-bounds *adj.* 필드 밖의 pil-deu bakk-ui; 엉뚱한 eong-ttung-han

out-of-date *adj.* 구식의 gu-sig-ui, 낡은 nalg-eun

output *n.* 생산 saeng-san; 생산고 saeng-san-go; 출력 chul-lyeok; *vt.* 출력하다 chul-lyeo-ka-da

outrageous *adj.* 잔인한 jan-in-han; 무법의 mu-beob-ui; 엉뚱한 eong-ttung-han

outside *n.* 바깥쪽 ba-kkat-jjok; 외관 oe-gwan; 외부 oe-bu; 극단 geuk-dan; *adj.* 바깥쪽의 ba-kkat-jjog-ui; 외면의 oe-myeon-ui; 외부의 oe-bu-ui; 표면상의 pyo-myeon-sang-ui; 극단의 geuk-dan-ui; *adv.* 밖에 bakk-e; 밖으로 bakk-eu-ro; *prep.* …의 밖으로 …ui bakk-eu-ro; …이상으로 …i-sang-eu-ro; …을 세외하고 …eul je-oe-ha-go

outsider *n.* 문외한 mun-oe-han; 외부인 oe-bu-in

outskirts *n.* 변두리 byeon-du-ri; 교외 gyo-oe

outspoken *adj.* 거침없이 말하는 geo-chim-eops-i mal-ha-neun, 노골적인 no-gong-jjeog-in

outstanding *adj.* 탁월한 tag wol han; 눈에 띄는 nun-e tti-neun; 돌출한 dol-chul-han; 미해결의 mi-hae-gyeol-ui

oval *n.* 다원체 ta-won-che; *adj.* 타원형의 ta-won-hyeong-ui

oven *n.* 오븐 o-beun

over *adv.* 위에 wi-e, 멀리 떨어진 곳에 meol-li-tteol-eo-jin gos-e, 뒤집어서 dwi-jib-eo-seo, 끝나서 kkeun-na-seo, 처음부터 끝까지 cheo-eum-bu-teo kkeut-kka-ji, 되풀이해서 doe-pul-i-hae-seo, 넘쳐서 neom-cheo-seo; *prep.* 위쪽에 wi-jjog-e,

전면에 jeon-myeon-e, ...을 너머 ...eul
neo-meo, ...을 넘어서 ...eul neom-eo-
seo, ...을 지배하여 ...eul ji-bae-ha-yeo,
...하는 사이 ...ha-neun sa-i, ...하면서
...ha-myeon-seo

overall *adj.* 전부의 jeon-bu-ui; 일체를 포함
한 il-che-reul po-ham-han; *adv.* 전체적으
로 jeon-che-jeog-eu-ro

overalls *n.* 작업용 바지 jag-eom-nyong ba-ji

overcast *adj.* 흐린 heu-rin; 음침한 eum-
chim-han; *vt.* 구름으로 덮다 gu-reum-eu-
ro deop-da

overcharge *vt.* 지나치게 돈을 받다 ji-na-
chi-ge don-eul bat-da; 지나치게 충전하다
ji-na-chi-ge chung-jeon-ha-da

overcome *vt.* 극복하다 geuk-bo-ka-da; 이기
다 i-gi-da

overcooked *adj.* 너무 익은 neo-mu ig-eun

overdo *vt.* 지나치게 하다 ji-na-chi-ge ha-da;
과장하다 gwa-jang-ha-da; 지나치게 쓰다
ji-na-chi-ge sseu-da

overdue *adj.* 기한이 지난 gi-han-i ji-nan; 늦
은 neunj-eun; 연착한 yeon-cha-kan

overflow *vt.* 넘치다 neom-chi-da; 가득차다
ga-deuk-cha-da; *n.* 범람 beom-nam; 과다
gwa-da, 과잉 gwa-ing; 배수로 ba-su-ro, 배
수관 ba-su-gwan

overhead projector *n.* 오에이치피 o-e-i-chi-
pi, 프로젝터 peu-ro-jek-teo

overlap *vt.* 겹치다 gyeop-chi-da; 중복되다
jung-bok-doe-da

overlook *vt.* 바라보다 ba-ra-bo-da; 내려
다보다 nae-ryeo-da-bo-da; 감시하다
gam-si-ha-da; 눈감아주다 nun-gam-a-ju-
da; 노려보다 no-ryeo-bo-da **The cliff ~s
the sea** 그 절벽은 바다를 내려다 보고
있습니다 geu jeol-byeog-eun ba-da- reul
nae-ryeo-da-bo-go it-seum-ni-da; **We ~ed
his mistake** 우리는 그사람의 실수를 눈
감아 주었습니다 u-ri-neun geu sa-ram-ui
sil-ssu-reul nun-gam-a ju-eot-seum-ni-da)

overnight *adv.* 밤새껏 bam-sae-kkeot; 하룻
밤 사이에 ha-rut-bam sa-i-e

overpass *n.* 고가도로 go-kka-do-ro, 육교
yuk-gyo

over-ride *vt.* 무시하다 mu-si-ha-da; 번복하
다 beon-bo-ka-da, 무효로 하다 mu-hyo-ro
ha-da

overseas *adj.* 해외의 hae-oe-ui; 해외로부
터의 hae-oe-ro-bu-teo-ui; 해외로 가는
hae-oe-ro ga-neun; *adv.* 해외로 hae-oe-ro;
해외에 hae-oe-e; 해외에서 hae-oe-e-seo

overtake *vt.* 따라잡다 tta-ra-jap-da; 갑자기
덮쳐오다 gap-ja-gi deop-cheo-o-da

over-the-counter *adj.* 장외 거래의 jang-oe
geo-rae-ui; 처방전 없이 살 수 있는 cheo-
bang-jeon eops-i sal ssu-in-neun

overtime *n.* 초과근무 cho-gwa-geun-mu; 초
과근무 수당 cho-gwa-geun-mu su-dang;
연장경기 yeon-jang-gyeong-gi

overweight *adj.* 중량이 초과된 jung-nyang-i
cho-gwa-doen; 너무 무거운 neo-mu
mu-geo-un

overwork *vt.* 과로시키다 gwa-ro-si-ki-da; *vi.*
과로하다 gwa-ro-ha-da

owe *vt.* 빚지고 있다 bit-ji-go it-da; 은혜를
입고 있다 eun-hye-reul ip-go it-da; 의무
를 지고 있다 ui-mu-reul ji-go it-da

owl *n.* 올빼미 ol-ppae-mi; 점잔빼는 사람
jeom-jan-ppae-neun sa-ram; 밤에 일하는
사람 bam-e il-ha-neun sa-ram

own *adj.* 자기 자신의 ja-gi ja-sin-ui; 고유한
go-yu-han; 직접의 jik-jeob-ui; 자신의 것
ja-sin-ui geot; *vt.* 소유하다 so-yu-ha-da;
인정하다 in-jeong-ha-da; **He wrecked
his ~ car** 그분은 자기 차를 망가뜨
렸습니다 geu bun-eun ja-gi cha-reul
mang-ga-tteu-ryeot-seum-ni-da

owner *n.* 주인 ju-in; 소유권자 so-yu-kkwon-
ja; **owner-driver** *n.* 자가 운전자 ja-ga
un-jeon-ja

ownership *n.* 소유권 so-yu-kkwon

ox *n.*, **oxen** *pl.* 수소 su-sso; 소 so

oxygen *n.* 산소 san-so; **~ mask** 산소 마스크
san-so ma-seu-keu

oyster *n.* 굴 gul; 입이 무거운 사람 ib-i
mu-geo-un sa-ram; **~ farm** 굴 양식장 gul
yang-sik-jang

ozone *n.* 오존 o-jon; **~ layer** 오존층
o-jon-cheung

P

p.m. *adj. abbr.* **post meridiem (after noon)**
오후의 o-hu-ui; **7:30** ~ 오후 일곱시 삼십
분 o-hu il-gop-si sam-sip-bun

pace *n.* 한걸음 han-geol-eum; 걸음걸이
geol-eum-geol-i; 걷는 속도 geon-neun-
sok-do; 페이스 pe-i-sseu; *vt.* 걷다 geot-da,
걸어다니다 geo-eo-da-ni-da; 보측하다
bo-cheu-ka-da

pacemaker *n.* 보조 조정자 bo-jo jo-jeong-ja;
(medical device) 페이스 메이기 pe-i-sseu
me-i-keo

Pacific Ocean *n.* 태평양 tae-pyeong-nyang

pacifier *n.* 고무 젖꼭지 go-mu jeot-kkok-ji

pack *vt.* 꾸러미 kku-reo-mi; 팩 paek; 통조림
출하량 tong-jo-rim chul-ha-ryang; 한 떼
han tteo; 한 벌 han beol; 한 갑 han-gap;
vi. 짐을 꾸리다 jim-eul kku-ri-da; 포장되
나 po-jang-doe-da; 굳어지다 gud-eo-ji-da;
떼를 짓다 tte-reul jit-da; 한곳으로 몰리
다 han-gos-eu-ro mol-li-da; **to** ~ **up** 짐을
꾸리다 jim-eul kku-ri-da

package *n.* 짐꾸리기 jim-kku-ri-gi; 포장
po-jang; 꾸러미 kku-reo-mi; 소포 so-po; ~
tour 패키지 투어 pae-ki-ji tu-eo

packed *adj.* 꽉찬 kkwak-chan, 만원의
man-won-ui

packet *n.* 한묶음 han-mukk-eum

packing *n.* 짐꾸리기 jim-kku-ri-gi; 포장
po-jang; 포장재료 po-jang-jae-ryo; 패킹
pae-king; ~ **material** 포장재료 po-jang-
jae-ryo; ~ **slip/list** 포장내역 명세서
po-jang-nae-yeok myeong-se-seo

pad *n.* 패드 pae-deu; 받침 bat-chim; 발사대
bal-ssa-dae; 종이철 jong-i-cheol; *vt.* 덧대
다 deot-dae-da; 받침을 대다 bat-chim-eul
dae-da; 군말을 하다 gun-mal-eul ha-da;
허위조작하다 heo-wi-jo-ja-ka-da; **~ded**
envelope 패드를 댄 봉투 pae-deu-reul
daen bong-tu, 버블봉투 beo-beul-bong-tu

paddleboat *n.* 노젓는 배 no-jeon-neun bae

pagan *n.* 이교도 i-gyo-do; 무종교자 mu-
jong-gyo-ja; *adj.* 이교도의 i-gyo-do-ui; 무
종교의 mu-jong-gyo-ui

page *n.* 페이지 pe-i-ji, 쪽 jjok; 역사적 사건
yeok-sa-jeok sa-kkeon; 역사적 시기 yeok-
sa-jeok si-gi; 책 chaek, 문서 mun-seo

paid *adj.* 유급의 yu-geub-ui; 지불이 끝난
ji-bul-I kkeun-nan

pail *n.* 바께쓰 ba-kke-sseu, 물통 mul-tong;
그릇 geu-reut, 용기 yong-gi

pain *n.* 고통 go-tong; 노력 no-ryeok; *vt.*
괴롭히다 goe-ro-pi-da; 고통을 주
다 go-tong-eul ju-da; 걱정시키다
geok-jeong-si-ki-da

painful *adj.* 아픈 a-peun; 괴로운 goe-ro-
un; 에처러운 ae-cheo-reo-un; 힘드는
him-deu-neun

painkiller *n.* 진통제 jin-tong-je

painless *adj.* 아프지 않은 a-peu-ji an-eun; 무
통의 mu-tong-ui; 힘들지 않은 him-deul-ji
an-eun

paint *n.* 그림물감 geu-rim-mul-kkam;
페인트 pe-in-teu; *vt.* 페인트를 칠하다
pe-in-teu-reul chil-ha-da; 물감으로
칠하다 mul-kkam-eu-ro chil-ha-da;
바르다 ba-reu-da; 생생하게 묘사하다
saeng-saeng-ha-ge myo-sa-ha-da; *vi.* 페
인트를 칠하다 pe-in-teu-reul chil-ha-da;
그림을 그리다 geu-rim-eul geu-ri-da;
그림으로 그려지다 geu-rim-eu-ro
geu-ryeo-ji-da

painter *n.* 화가 hwa-ga; 도장공
do-jang-gong

painting *n.* 그림 geu-rim; 그림 그리기 geu-
rim geu-ri-gi; 채색 chae-saek; **acrylic** ~ 아
크릴화 a-keu-ril-hwa; **oil** ~ 유화 yu-hwa;
watercolor ~ 수채화 su-chae-hwa

pair *n.* 한 쌍 han ssang; 한 벌 han beol; 부부
bu-bu; **a** ~ **of shoes** 신발 한켤레 sin-bal
han-kyeol-le

pajamas *n. pl.* 파자마 pa-ja-ma, 짐옷 jam-ot

Pakistan *n.* 파키스탄 pa-ki-seu-tan

pal *n.* 동아리 dong-a-ri; 친구 chin-gu; 동료
dong-nyo

palace *n.* 궁전 gung-jeon; 대저택 dae-jeo-
taek; 호화건물 ho-hwa-geon-mul

pale *adj.* 창백한 chang-bae-kan; 엷은 yeolb-
eun; 어슴푸레한 eo-seum-pu-re-han; 가
날픈 ga-nyal-peun; ~ **blue** 엷은 청색
yeolb-eun cheong-saek; ~ **in the face** 창백
한 얼굴 chang-bae-kan eol-gul

Palestine *n.* 팔레스타인 pal-le-seu-ta-in

palette *n.* 팔레트 pal-le-teu; 독특한 색채 dok-teu-kan saek-chae

pall *n.* 관덮는 보 gwan-deop-neun bo; 휘장 hwi-jang

pallet *n.* 팔레트 pal-le-teu, 조색판 jo-saek-pan

palm *n.* 야자나무 ya-ja-na-mu; 승리 seung-ni; *(of the hand)* 손바닥 son-ppa-dak; ~ **tree**야자나무 ya-ja-na-mu

palpitation *n.* 박동 bak-dong; 떨림 teol-lim; 고동 go-dong; **heart ~s** 심장박동 sim-jang-bak-dong

pamphlet *n.* 팜플렛 pam-peul-let

pan *n.* 남비 nam-bi; *(skillet)* 프라이팬 peu-ra-i-paen

Panama *n.* 파나마 pa-na-ma

Panama Canal *n.* 파나마 운하 pa-na-ma un-ha

pancake *n.* 팬케이크 paen-ke-i-keu

panda *n.* 팬더 paen-deo

panel *n.* 판벽널 pan-byeong-neol; 위원회 wi-won-hoe; 화판 hwa-pan; 패널 pae-neol; ~ **discussion** 공개 토론회 gong-gae to-ron-hoe

panelist *n.* 토론자 to-ron-ja, 해답자 hae-dap-ja

pan-fry *vt.* 튀기다 twi-gi-da

panic *n.* 공포 gong-po; 당황 dang-hwang; ~ **attack** 공포스러운 공격 gong-po-seu-reo-un gong-gyeok

panorama *n.* 파노라마 pa-no-ra-ma; 개관 gae-gwan

pant *vi.* 숨차다 sum-cha-da; 두근거리다 du-geun-geo-ri-da; 그리워하다 geu-ri-wo-ha-da; 증기를 뿜다 jeung-gi-reul ppum-tta

panties *n. pl.* 팬티 paen-ti

pantomime *n.* 무언극 mu-eon-geuk, 팬터마임 paen-teo-ma-im

pantry *n.* 식료품 창고 sing-nyo-pum chang-go; 식기실 sik-gi-sil

pants *n. pl.* 바지 ba-ji

pantyhose *n.* 팬티스타킹 paen-ti-seu-ta-king

paper *n.* 종이 jong-i; 도배지 do-bae-ji; 신문 sin-mun; 서류 seo-ryu; 논문 non-mun; 시험 답안지 si-heom dab-an-ji; ~ **bag** 종이가방 jong-i-ga-bang; **copy** ~ 복사지 bok-sa-ji; **recycled** ~ 재생종이 jae-saeng-jong-i; **wrapping** ~ 포장지 po-jang-ji; ~**clip** 종이클립 jong-i-keul-lip; ~ **money** 지폐 ji-pye; ~**work** 서류사무 seo-ryu-sa-mu, 사무처리 sa-mu-cheo-ri

paperback *n.* 종이표지책 jong-i-pyo-ji-chaek; 염가 문고본 yeom-kka mun-go-bon; *adj.* 종이표지의 jong-i-pyo-ji-ui; 염가본의 yeom-kka-bon-ui

Papua New Guinea *n.* 파푸아 뉴기니아 pa-pu-a nyu-gi-ni-a

parachute *n.* 낙하산 na-ka-san; *vt., vi.* 낙하산으로 떨어뜨리다 na-ka-san-eu-ro tteol-eo-tteu-ri-da

parade *n.* 퍼레이드 peo-re-i-deu, 시가행진 si-ga-haeng-jin; 열병식 yeol-byeong-sik; 과시 gwa-si; *vt.* 행진하다 haeng-jin-ha-da; 열병하다 yeol-byeong-ha-da; 과시하다 gwa-si-ha-da

paradise *n.* 천국 cheon-guk; 낙원 nag-won; 극락 geung-nak

paragraph *n.* 절 jeol, 단락 dal-lak, 패러그래프 pae-reo-geu-rae-peu

parallel *adj.* 평행의 pyeong-haeng-ui; 나란한 na-ran-han; 같은 방향의 gat-eun bang-hyang-ui; 같은 경향의 gat-eun gyeong-hyang-ui; 같은 종류의 gat-eun jong-nyu-ui

paralysis *n.* 마비 ma-bi; 활동불능 hwal-ttong-bul-leung; 마비생태 ma-bi-sang-tae

paralyze *v.* 마비시키다 ma-bi-si-ki-da; 무력하게 하다 mu-ryeo-ka-ge ha-da

paraphrase *vt., vi.* 바꾸어 말하다 ba-kku-eo mal-ha-da, 의역하다 ui-yeo-ka-da

parasite *n.* 기생충 gi-saeng-chung; 기식자 gi-sik-ja

parasitic *adj.* 기생하는 gi-saeng-ha-neun; 기생충에 의한 gi-saeng-chung-e ui-han; 기식하는 gi-si-ka-neun

parasol *n.* 양산 yang-san, 파라솔 pa-ra-sol

parcel *n.* 소포 so-po; 꾸러미 kku-reo-mi

parchment *n.* 양피지 yang-pi-ji, 양피지 문서 yang-pi-ji mun-seo; 졸업증서 jol-eop-jeung-seo, 증서 jeung-seo

pardon *n.* 용서 yong-seo; 관대 gwan-dae; 사면 sa-myeon; *vt.* 용서하다 yong-seo-ha-da; 관대히 대하다 gwan-dae-hi dae-ha-da; 사면하다 sa-myeon-ha-da

parent *n.* 부모님 bu-mo-nim; 조상 jo-sang; 근원 geun-won

parenting *n.* 양육 yang-yuk, 육아 yug-a

Paris 파리 pa-ri

parish *n.* 본당 bon-dang; 교구 gyo-gu; 지역 교회 ji-yeok-gyo-hoe; 한 교회 신도 han gyo-hoe sin-do

park *n.* 공원 gong-won; 주차장 ju-cha-jang; 운동장 un-dong-jang; ~**ing light** 주차 등 ju-cha-deung; ~**ing ticket** 주차위반 티켓 ju-cha-wi-ban ti-ket, 교통위반 딱 지 gyo-tong-wi-ban ttak-ji; ~**ing meter** 파킹미터 pa-king-mi-teo; ~**ing lot** 주 차장 ju-cha-jang *vt.* 공원으로 만들다 gong-won-eu-ro man-deul-da; 주차하다 ju-cha-ha-da; 두고 가다 du-go ga-da; *vi.* 주차하다 ju-cha-ha-da;

parliament *n.* 의회 ui-hoe; 국회 gu koe

parliamentary *n.* 의회의 ui-hoe-ui; 의회에 서 제정된 ui-hoe-e-seo je-jeong-doen; 정 중한 Jeong-Jung-han

parrot *n.* 앵무새 aeng-mu-sae

parsley *n.* 파슬리 pa-seul-li

part *n.* 부분 bu-bun; 자질 ja-jil; 부품 bu-pum; 직분 jik-bun; 지역 ji-yeok; 편 pyeon; **spare** ~ 예비부품 ye-bi-bu-pum; *vi.* 갈라 지다 gal-la-ji-da; 헤어지다 he-eo-ji-da; 손 을 떼다 son-eul tte-da; 내어놓다 nae-eo-no-ta; 떠나다 tteo-na-da

partial *adj.* 부분적인 bu-bun-jeog-in; 불 공평한 bul-gong-pyeong-han; 편파적인 pyeon-pa-jeog-in

participate *vt.* 참가하다 cham-ga-ha-da; 관 여히다 gwan-yeo-ha-da

particle *n.* 미립자 mi-rip-ja; 극소량 geuk-so-ryang; 불변화사 bul-byeon-hwa-sa; 조 한 jo-hang

particular *adj.* 특별한 teuk-byeol-han; 특정 한 teuk-jeong-han; 각별한 gak-byeol-han; 상세한 sang-se-han; 개개의 gae-ga-ui; 꼼 꼼한 kkom-kkom-han

particularly *adv.* 특히 teu-ki; 자세히 ja-se-hi

partition *n.* 분할 bun-hal; 구분 gu-bun; 구 획 gu-hoek; 구획선 gu-hoek-seon; 간막 이 gan-mag-i

partly *adv.* 부분적으로 bu-bun-jeog-eu-ro; 어느 정도는 eo-neu jeong-do-neun

partner *n.* 협동자 hyeop-dong-ja; 배우자 bae-u-ja; 상대 sang-dae; **domestic** ~ 동거 커플 dong-geo-keo-peul

partnership *n.* 공동 gong-dong, 협력 hyeom-nyeok

part-time *adj.* 파트타임의 pa-teu-ta-im-ui

party *n.* 모임 mo-im, 파티 pa-ti; 정당 jeong-dang; 일행 il-haeng; 당사자 dang-sa-ja

pass *n.* 통행 tong-haeng; 통과 tong-gwa; 합격 hap-gyeok; 통로 tong-no; 산길 san-kkil; *vt.* 지나가다 ji-na-ga-da; 통과하다 tong-gwa-ha-da; 건너다 geon-neo-da; 통과시키다 tong-gwa-si-ki-da; 보 내다 bo-nae-da; 넘겨주다 neom-gyeo-ju-da; 넌다 neom tta; 가결하다 ga gyeol-ha-da; 합격하다 hap-gyeo-ka-da; **no** ~**ing** 통행금지

passage *n.* 통행 tong-haeng; 통과 tong-gwa; 경과 gyeong-gwa; 분반 un-ban; 여행 yeo-haeng; 한구절 han-gu-jeol

passenger *n.* 승객 seung-gaek; 여객 yeo-gaek; 통행인 tong-haeng-in; ~ **car** 객차 gaek-cha; ~ **seat** 객식 gaek-seok

passerby *n.*, **passersby** *pl.* 지나가는 사람 ji-na-ga-neun sa-ram; 행인 haeng-in

passion *n.* 열정 yeol-jjeong; 흥분 heung-bun; 열애 yeol-ae; 열망하는 것 yeol-mang-ha-neun geot

passionate *adj.* 열렬한 yeol-lyeol-han; 강렬한 gang-nyeol-han; 정열의 jeong-nyeol-ui

passive *adj.* 수동적인 su-dong-jeog-in; 무 저항의 mu jeo hang-ui; 활발히지 못한 hwal-bal-ha-ji mo-tan

passport *n.* 여권 yeo-kkwon; 통행 허가증 tong-haeng-heo-ga-jjeung; ~ **control** 어 권발급,관리규정 yeo-kkwon-bal-geup gwal-li-gyu-jeong; 여권 검사대 yeo-kkwon geom-sa-dae

password *n.* 비밀번호 bi-mil-beon-ho, 패스 워드 pae-sseu-wo-deu

past *n.* 과거 gwa-geo; *adj.* 과거의 gwa-geo-ui; 지나간 ji-na-gan, 이전의 i-jeon-ui

paste *n.* 반죽 ban-juk; 반죽해서 만든 물건 ban-ju-kae-seo man-deun mul-geon; 반죽 한 식품 ban-ju-kan sik-pum; *vt.* 풀로 붙이 다 pul-lo bu-chi-da

pastel *n.* 파스텔 pa-seu-tel

pasteurized *adj.* 저온살균된 jeo-on-sal-gyun-doen

pastime *n.* 기분전환 gi-bun-jeon-hwan; 소일 거리 so-il-kkeo-ri

pastor *n.* 사제 sa-je, 목사 mok-sa

pastry *n.* 페이스트리 pe-i-seu-teu-ri

pat *vt.* 톡톡치다 tok-tok-chi-da, 가볍게 두드 리다 ga-byeop-ge du-deu-ri-da, 쓰다듬다 sseu-da-deum-tta; *n.* 절편 jeol-pyeon; 작 은 조각 jag-eun jo-gak

patch *n.* 헝겊조각 heong-geop-jo-gak; 판 자조각 pan-ja-jjo-gak; 고약 go-yak; 부스 러기 bu-seu-reo-gi; 밭 bat; *vt.* 헝겊을 대 다 heong-geob-eul dae-da; 주워 맞추다 ju-wo mat-chu-da; 미봉책으로 수습하다 mi-bong-chaeg-eu-ro su-seu-pa-da

patent *n.* 특허 teu-keo; 특허권 teu-keo-kkwon; 특허증 teu-kkeo-jjung; 특허품 teu-kkeo-pum

paternal *adj.* 아버지의 a-beo-ji-ui, 아버지 같은 a-beo-ji-gat-eun; 부계의 bu-gye-ui

path *n.* 작은 길 jag-eun gil; 통로 tong-no; 행로 haeng-no; 방침 bang-chim; 방향 bang-hyang; ~**way** 오솔길 o-sol-kkil, 좁은 길 job-eun gil

pathetic *adj.* 애처로운 ae-cheo-ro-un; 감상적인 gam-sang-jeog-in; 어울리 지 않는 eo-ul-li-ji an-neun; 형편없는 hyeong-pyeon-eom-neun, 가치없는 ga-chi-eom-neun

patience *n.* 인내력 in-nae-ryeok, 인내심 in-nae-sim; 인내 in-nae

patient *n.* 환자 hwan-ja; *adj.* 인내심이 강 한 in-nae-sim-i gang-han; 잘 견디는 jal gyeon-di-neun; 부지런한 bu-ji-reon-han

patriot *n.* 애국자 ae-guk-ja, 우국지사 u-guk-ji-sa

patriotic *adj.* 애국적인 ae-guk-jeog-in, 우국 의 u-gug-ui

patrol *n.* 순찰 sun-chal; 정찰 jeong-chal; 순 찰대 sun-chal-ttae; 정찰대 jeong-chal-ttae; 순경 sun-gyeong; ~ **car** 순찰차 sun-chal-cha; *vi.* 순찰하다 sun-chal-ha-da 행진하 다 haeng-jin-ha-da;

patron *n.* 보호자 bo-ho-ja; 후원자 hu-won-ja; 단골손님 dan-gol-sson-nim

pattern *n.* 모범 mo-beom; 양식 yang-sik; 경향 gyeong-hyang; 도안 do-an; 견본 gyeon-bon

paunch *n.* 배 bae; 위 wi

pause *n.* 휴지 hyu-ji; 중지 jung-ji; *vt.* 중단하 다 jung-dan-ha-da; *vi.* 잠시 멈추다 jam-si meom-chu-da; 한숨 돌리다 han-sum dol-li-da; 머뭇거리다 meo-mut-geo-ri-da

pave *vt.* 도로를 포장하다 do-ro-reul po-jang-ha-da; ...을 덮다 ...eul deop-da

pavement *n.* 포장도로 po-jang-do-ro; 포장 재료 po-jang-jae-ryo; 차도 cha-do

pavilion *n.* 큰 천막 keun cheon-mak; 누각 nu-gak; 정자 jeong-ja; 병동 byeong-dong; 별관 byeol-gwan

paw *n.* 동물의 발 dong-mul-ui bal

pawn *n.* 전당 jeon-dang; 전당물 jeon-dang-mul; 인질 in-jil; 체스의 졸 che-sseu-ui jol; ~**broker** 전당포 업자 jeon-dang-po eop-ja; ~**shop** 전당포 jeon-dang-po; *vt.* 전당잡히다 jeon-dang-ja-pi-da; 목숨 을 걸고 맹세하다 mok-sum-eul geol-go maeng-se-ha-da

pay *n.* 지불 ji-bul; 봉급 bong-geup; 보상 bo-sang; *vt.* 갚다 gap-da; 지불하다 ji-bul-ha-da; 이익을 주다 i-ig-eul ju-da; 관심을 보이다 gwan-sim-eul bo-i-da; 경 의를 표하다 gyeong-i-reul pyo-ha-da; **to ~ for** 지불하다 ji-bul-ha-da; **to ~ attention to** ...에 주의하다 ...e ju-i-ha-da; ...에 경의를 표하다 ...e gyeong-i-reul pyo-ha-da; **to ~ a bill** 요금을 내다 yo-geum-eul nae-da

payback *n.* 환불 hwan-bul, 자본회수 ja-bon-hoe-su

paycheck *n.* 급료지불용 수표 geum-nyo-ji-bul-lyong su-pyo

payday *n.* 월급날 wol-geum-nal; 지불일 ji-bul-il

payment *n.* 지불 ji-bul; 지불금액 ji-bul-geum-aek; 상환 sang-hwan; 보수 bo-su; 보상 bo-sang

payoff *n.* 급료지불 geum-nyo-ji-bul; 청산 cheong-san

pay slip *n.* 임금 명세서 im-geum myeong-se-seo, 급료 명세서 geum-nyo myeong-se-seo

pea *n.* 완두콩 wan-du-kong

peace *n.* 평화 pyeong-hwa; 치안 chi-an; 화 친 hwa-chin; 평정 pyeong-jeong

peaceful *adj.* 평화로운 pyeong-hwa-ro-un; 온화한 on-hwa-han

peacetime *adj.* 평화시의 pyeong-hwa-si-ui, 평시의 pyeong-si-ui

peach *n.* 복숭아 bok-sung-a; 복숭아색 bok-sung-a-saek; *vi.* 밀고하다 mil-go-ha-da

peacock *n.* 공작 gong-jak; 겉치레꾼 geot-chi-re-kkun

peak *n.* 첨단 cheom-dan; 산꼭대기 san-kkok-dae-gi; 피크 pi-keu; *(highest level)* 정점 jeong-jjeom; *(summit)* 정상 jeong-sang; 극치 geuk-chi; *vi.* 뾰족해지다 ppyo-jo-kae-ji-da; 우뚝 솟다 u-ttuk-sot-da; 수척해지다 su-cheo-kae-ji-da

peanut *n.* 피넛 pi-neot, 땅콩 ttang-kong; ~ **butter** 피넛버터 pi-neot-beo-teo

pear *n.* 배 bae; ~ **tree** 배나무 bae-na-mu

pearl *n.* 진주 jin-ju; 자개 ja-gae; 귀중한 물건 gwi-jung-han mul-geon

peasant *n.* 농부 nong-bu; 시골사람 si gol-ssa-ram

pebble *n.* 조약돌 jo-yak-dol, 자갈 ja-gal; 수정 su-jeong

peck *vt.* 쪼다 jjo-da, 쪼아먹다 jjo-a-meok da

peculiar *adj.* 독특한 dok-teu-kan, 고유의 go-yu-ui, 특별한 teuk-byeol-han

pedal *n.* 페달 pe-dal

pedestrian *n.* 보행자 bo-haeng-ja; 보도여행자 bo-do-yeo-haeng-ja; ~ **crossing** 횡단보도 hoeng-dan-bo-do

pediatrician *n.* 소아과 의사 so-a-kkwa-ui-sa

pee *vi.* 오줌누다 o-jum-nu-da

peek *vi.* 살짝 들여다보다 sal-jjak deul-yeo-da-bo-da, 엿보다 yeot-bo-da

peel *n.* 껍질 kkeop-jil; *vt.* 껍질을 벗기다 kkeop-jil-eul beot-gi-da; 까다 kka-da

peephole *n.* 틈구멍 teum-kku-meong

peer *n.* 동료 dong-nyo; *vi.* 자세히 들여다보다 ja-se-hi deul-yeo-da-bo-da, 응시하다 eung-si-ha-da; 보이기 시작하다 bo-i-gi si-ja-ka-da; ~ **group** 동료집단 dong-nyo-jip-dan

peg *n.* 나무못 na-mu-mot; 나무마개 na-mu-ma-gae; 빨래집게 ppal-lae-jjip-gae; 계기 gye-gi

pelvis *n.* 골반 gol-ban

pen *n.* 펜 pen; 볼펜 bol-pen; 문체 mun-che; 작가 jak-ga; 축사 chuk-sa, 우리 u-ri

penalize *vt.* 벌을 주다 beol-eul ju-da, 벌칙을 적용하다 beol-chig-eul jeog-yong-ha-da

penalty *n.* 벌금 beol-geum; 형벌 hyeong-beol; 재앙 jae-ang; 페널티 pe-neol-ti; 벌점 beol-jjeom; 악조건 ak-jo-kkeon

pencil *n.* 연필 yeon-pil; 샤프 sya-peu; ~ **sharpener** 연필깎이 yeon-pil-kkakk-i; ~ **case** 필통 pil-tong

pendant *n.* 펜던트 pen-dan-teu

pending *adj.* 미결의 mi-gyeol-ui, 현안의 hyeon-an-ui; 절박한 jeol-ba-kan, 임박한 im-ba-kan

penetrate *vi.* 통과하다 tong-gwa-ha-da; 스며들다 seu-myeo-deul-da; 가파하다 gan-pa-ha-da

penicillin *n.* 페니실린 pe-ni-sil-lin

peninsula *n.* 반도 ban-do; **Korean** ~ 한반도 han-ban-do

penis *n.* 음경 eum-gyeong, 페니스 pe-ni-sseu, 고추 go-chu

penknife *n.* 주머니칼 ju-meo-ni-kal

penniless *adj.* 무일푼의 mu-il-pun-ui, 매우 가난한 mae-u ga-nan-han

penny *n.* 페니 pe-ni; 센트 ssen-teu; 푼돈 pun-tton; ~ **pincher** 구두쇠 gu-du-soe

pen pal *n.* 펜팔 pen-pal

pension *n.* 연금 yeon-geum

pentagon *n.* 오각형 o-ga-kyeong; 펜타곤 pen-ta-gon

people *n.* 사람들 sa-ram-deul; 국민 gung-min; 민족 min-jok; 수민 ju-min; 서민 seo min

pepper *n.* 고추 go-chu; 후추 hu-chu; 자극성 ja-geuk-seong; 실랄함 sil-lal-ham; **green** ~ 파란피망 pa-ran-pi-mang, 파란고추 pa-ran go-chu; **black** ~ 후추 hu-chu; **red** ~ 붉은피망 bulg-eun pi-mang, 붉은고추 bulg-eun go-chu; ~ **mill** 후추 분쇄기 hu-chu bun-swae-gi

peppermint *n.* 페퍼민트 pe-peo-min-teu, 박하 ba-ka

per *prep.* ... 에 대하여 e dae-ha-yeo, ...에 의하여 e ui-ha-yeo, ... 마다 ma-da

perceive *vt.* 감지하다 gam-ji-ha-da; 인식하다 in-ji-ha-da; 파악하다 pa-a-ka-da

percent *n.* 퍼센트 peo-sen-teu; 백분율 baek-bun-nyul

perception *n.* 지각 ji-gak; 인식 in-sik; 취득 chwi-deuk

perch *n.* 횃대 hwaet-dae; 높은 지위 nop-eun ji-wi; 마부석 ma-bu-seok; 야구장 좌석 ya-gu-jang jwa-seok; 직물 검사대 jing-nul geom-sa-dae

percussion *n.* 충격 chung-gyeok, 충돌 chung-dol; 진동 jin-dong; 타악기 ta-ak-gi

perfect *adj.* 완전한 wan-jeon-han; 우수한 u-su-han; 정확한 jeong-hwa-kan; *vt.* 완성하다 wan-seong-ha-da, 완전하게 하다 wan-jeon-ha-ge ha-da

perfectly *adv.* 완전히 wan-jeon-hi, 이상적으로 i-sang-jeog-eu-ro; 몹시 mop-si, 굉장히 goeng-jang-hi

perform *vi.* 실행하다 sil-haaeng-ha-da; 행하다 haeng-ha-da; 공연하다 gong-yeon-ha-da; 연기하다yeon-gi-ha-da; 연주하다 yeon-ju-ha-da

performance *n.* 실행 sil-haeng; 작업 jag-eop; 성능 seong-neung; 성과 seong-kkwa; 공적 gong-jeok; 연기 yeon-gi; 공연 gong-yeon

perfume *n.* 향기 hyang-gi; 향료 hyang-nyo; 향수 hyang-su

perhaps *adv.* 아마 a-ma; 어쩌면 eo-jjeo-myeon; 혹시 hok-si

peril *n.* 위험 wi-heom; 모험 mo-heom

period *n.* 수업시간 su-eop-si-gan; 종결 jong-gyeol; *(punctuation mark)* 마침표 ma-chim-pyo; *(segment of time)* 기간 gi-gan; 시대 si-dae; *(a woman's period)* 생리 saeng-ni

periodic *adj.* 주기적인 ju-gi-jeog-in; 정기적인 jeong-gi-jeog-in

periodical *n.* 정기간행물 jeong-gi-gan-haeng-mul; 잡지 jap-ji

perish *vi.* 죽다 juk-da, 멸망하다 myeol-mang-ha-da; *vt.* 말려죽이다 mal-lyeo-jug-i-da; 몹시 괴롭히다 mop-si goe-ro-pi-da

perishable *adj.* 썩기 쉬운 sseok-gi-swi-un; 말라죽는 mal-la-jung-neun; 죽을 운명의 jug-eul un-myeong-ui

perm *vt., vi.* 파마하다 pa-ma-ha-da

permanence *n.* 영구 yeong-gu; 영속성 yeong-sok-seong; 불변 bun-byeon; 내구성 nae-gu-sseong

permanent *adj.* 영구의 yeong-gu-ui; 영속하는 yeong-so-ka-neun; 상설의 sang-seol-ui; ~ **press** 영구처리가공 yeong-gu-cheo-ri-ga-gong, 퍼머넌트프레스 가공 peo-meo-neon-teu-peu-re-ssu ga-gong

permission *n.* 허가 heo-ga; 면허 myeon-heo; 허용 heo-yong; 인가 in-ga

permit *n.* 면허장 myeon-heo-jjang; 허가장 heo-ga-jjang; 증명서 jeung-myeong-seo; *vt.* 허락하다 heo-ra-ka-da; 허가하다 heo-ga-ha-da; 내버려두다 nae-beo-ryeo-du-da; 용납하다 yong-na-pa-da

perpendicular *adj.* 수직의su-jig-ui; 깎아지른 kkakk-a-ji-reun; 절벽의 jeol-byeog-ui

Persian Gulf *n.* 페르시아만 pe-reu-si-a-man

persist *vi.* 고집하다 go-ji-pa-da; 주장하다 ju-jang-ha-da; 지속하다 ji-so-ka-da

person *n.* 사람 sa-ram; 인간 in-gan; 인물 in-mul; 신체 sin-che

person-to-person *adv.* 개인대 개인으로 gae-in-dae gae-in-eu-ro

personal *adj.* 개인의 gae-in-ui; 본인 스스로의 bon-in seu-seu-ro-ui; 개인에 관한 gae-in-e gwan-han; 인격적인 in-kkyeok-jeog-in; 신체의 sin-che-ui

personality *n.* 개성 gae-seong; 성격 seong-kkyeok; 인격 in-kkyeok; 인간성 in-gan-sseong; 인물 in-mul

personally *adv.* 개인적으로 gae-in-jeog-eu-ro; 직접 jik-jeop

personnel *n.* 직원 jig-won; 인원 in-won

perspective *n.* 원근법 won-geun-ppeop; 조망 jo-mang; 전망 jeon-mang; 가망 ga-mang

perspiration *n.* 발한작용 bal-han-jag-yong; 땀 ttam; 노력 no-ryeok

perspire *vi.* 땀을 흘리다 ttam-eul heul-li-da; 증발하다 jeung-bal-ha-da; 분비하다 bun-bi-ha-da; 땀나게 노력하다 ttam-na-ge no-ryeo-ka-da

persuade *vt.* 설득하다 seol-tteu-ka-da; 납득시키다 nap-deuk-si-ki-da, 확인시키다 hwag-in-si-ki-da

persuasion *n.* 설득 seol-tteuk; 확신 hwag-in; 신조 sin-jo

Peru 페루 pe-ru

pessimist *n.* 비관론자 bi-gwan-non-ja; 염세가 yeom-se-ga

pessimistic *adj.* 비관적인 bi-gwan-jeog-in; 염세적인 yeom-se-jeog-in

pest *n.* 해충 hae-chung; 골칫거리 gol-chit-geo-ri; 페스트 pe-seu-teu

pester *vt.* 괴롭히다 goe-ro-pi-da; 고통을 주다 go-tong-eul ju-da

pesticide *n.* 구충제 gu-chung-je, 살충제 sal-chung-je

pet *n.* 애완동물 ae-wan-dong-mul; 마음에 드는 것 ma-eum-e deu-neun geot; *vt.* 귀여워하다 gwi-yeo-wo-ha-da; 껴안다 kkyeo-an-tta

petal *n.* 꽃잎 kkon-nip

petition *n.* 탄원 tan-won, 청원 cheong-won; *vt.* 청원하다 cheong-won-ha-da, 탄원하다 tan-won-ha-da

petrol *n.* 가솔린 ga-sol-lin; 경유 gyeong-yu

petroleum *n.* 석유 seog-yu; 바셀린 ba-sel-lin; ~ **jelly** 바셀린 ba-sel-lin

petty *adj.* 사소한 sa-so-han; 마음이 좁은 ma-eum-i job-eun; 소규모의 so-gyu-mo-ui

phantom *n.* 환영 hwan-yeong; 환각 hwan-gak; 영상 yeong-sang

pharmaceutical *adj.* 조제학의 jo-je-hag-ui; 제약의 je-yag-ui

pharmacist *n.* 약사 yak-sa

pharmacology *n.* 약리학 yang-ni-hak; 약물학 yang-mul-hak

pharmacy *n.* 약국 yak-guk; 약학 ya-kak; 제약업 je-yag-eop

phase *n.* 국면 gung-myeon; 단계 dan-gye; 년 myeon; 상 sang; *vt.* 실행하다 sil-haeng-ha-da; 조정하다 jo-jeong-ha-da; 예정하다 ye-jeong-ha-da; 위상에 맞추다 wi-sang-e mat-chu-da

pheasant *n.* 꿩 kkwong

phenomenon *n.*, **phenomena** *pl.* 현상 hyeon-sang; 사건 sa-kkeon

Philippines 필리핀 pil-li-pin

philosophy *n.* 철학 cheol-hak; 철학체계 cheol-hak-che-gye; 철학책 cheol-hak-chaek; 철학사상 cheol-hak-sa-sang; 철학정신 cheol-hak-jeong-sin

phlegm *n.* 담 dam; 냉담 naeng-dam; 무기력 mu-gi-ryeok

phobia *n.* 공포증 gong-po-jjeung

phone *n.* 전화 jeon-hwa; 전화기 jeon-hwa-gi; 수화기 su-hwa-gi; 단음 dan-eum; 음성 eum-seong; *vt.*, *vi.* 전화걸다 jeon-hwa-geol-da

phone book *n.* 전화번호부 jeon-hwa-beon-ho-bu

phone booth *n.* 공중전화박스 gong-jung-jeon-hwa-ppak-sseu

phone card *n.* 전화카드 jeon-hwa-ka-deu

phone number *n.* 전화번호 jeon-hwa-beon-ho

phonetic *adj.* 음성의 eum-seong-ui; 음성학의 eum-seong-hag-ui

phonetics *n. pl.* 음성학 eum-seong-hak

phony *adj.* 가짜의 ga-jja-ui, 허위의 heo-wi-ui

photo(graph) *n.* 사진 sa-jin

photocopier *n.* 복사기 bok-sa-gi

photocopy *n.* 복사 bok-sa; *vt.* 복사하다 bok-sa-ha-da

photograph *vt.* 사진을 찍다 sa-jin-eul jjik-da, 촬영하다 chwal-yeong-ha-da; *n.* 사진 sa-jin

photographer *n.* 사진기사 sa-jin-gi-sa

photography *n.* 사진술 sa-jin-sul; 사진촬영 sa-jin-chwal-yeong

phrase *n.* 구절 gu-jeol; 관용구 gwan-yong-kku; 말씨 mal-ssi; ~ **book** 숙어집 sug-eo-jip; 관용구집 gwan-yong-kku-jip; *vt.* 말로 표현하다 mal-lo-pyo-hyeon-ha-da; 진술하다 jin-sul-ha-da

physical *adj.* 육체의 yuk-che-ui; 물질의 mul-jjil-ui; 물리학의 mul-li-hag-ui; 실제의 sil-jje-ui; 자연의 ja-yeon-ui; ~ **education** 체육 che-yuk

physically *adv.* 물리학적으로 mul-li-hak-jeog-eu-ro; 물질적으로 mul-jjil-jeog-eu-ro; 육체적으로 yuk-che-jeog-eu-ro

physician *n.* 의사 ui-sa; 내과의사 nae-kkwa-ui-sa

physicist *n.* 물리학자 mul-li-hak-ja

physics *n.* 물리학 mul-li-hak

piano *n.* 피아노 pi-a-no

pick *n.* 곡괭이 gok-gwaeng-i; 채굴기 chae-gul-gi; 선택권 seon-taek-gwon; 정수 jeong-su; 선택된 것 seon-taek-doen geot; *vt.* 따다 tta-da; 뜯다 tteut-da; 골라잡다 gol-la-jap-da; 소매치기하다 so-mae-chi-gi-ha-da; 붙잡다 but-jap-da; 계기를 만들다 gye-gi-reul man-deul-da; ~ **[out] the one you like** 좋아하는 것으로 고르십시오 jo-a-ha-neun geos-eul go-reu-sip-si-o

They ~ed apples 그분들은 사과를 땄
습니다 geu bun-deul-eun sa-gwa-reul
ttat-seum-ni-da; **I'll ~ you up after work.**
일을 끝낸 후에 제가 모시러 가겠습니
다 il-eul kkeun-naen hu-e je-ga mo-si-reo
ga-gyet-seum-ni-da

picked *adj.* 선발된 seon-bal-doen, 정선된
jeong-seon-doen; 잡아뜯은 jab-a-tteud-
eun; 곱게 다듬은 gop-ge da-deum-eun

picket *n.* 말뚝 mal-ttuk; 피켓 pi-ket

pickle *n.* 피클 pi-keul; 곤경 gon-gyeong; 장
난꾸러기 jang-nan-kku-reo-gi; *vt.* 말뚝
을 박다 mal-ttug-eul bak-da; 울타리를 치
다 ul-ta-ri-reul chi-da; 경계병을 배치하다
gyeong-gye-byeong-eul bae-chi-ha-da; 말
뚝을 매다 mal-ttug-eul mae-da; 감시원을
두다 gam-si-won-eul du-da

pickpocket *n.* 소매치기 so-mae-chi-gi

picky *adj.* 까다로운 kka-da-ro-un

picnic *n.* 피크닉 pi-keu-nik, 소풍 so-pung; *vi.*
소풍가다 so-pung-ga-da

picture *n.* 그림 geu-rim; 사진 sa-jin; 경
치 gyeong-chi; 심상 sim-sang; 영상
yeong-sang; 화면 hwa-myeon; *vt.* 그리
다 geu-ri-da; 상상하다 sang-sang-ha-da;
묘사하다 myo-sa-ha-da; **~ book** 그림책
geu-rim-chaek

picturesque *adj.* 그림과 같은 geu-rim-gwa
gat-eun; 생생한 saeng-saeng-han; 재미있
는 jae-mi-in-neun

pie *n.* 파이 pa-i

piece *n.* 조각 jo-gak; 단편 dan-pyeon; 부분
bu-bun; 부분품 bu-bun-pum

pier *n.* 부두 bu-du; 방파제 bang-pa-je

pierce *vt.* 관통하다 gwan-tong-ha-da, 꿰뚫
다 kkwe-ttul-ta; 구멍을 내다 gu-meong-
eul nae-da, 구멍을 뚫다 gu-myeong-eul
ttul-ta; 돌파하다 dol-pa-ha-da; 간파하다
gan-pa-ha-da; 찌르다 jji-reu-da; 스며들다
seu-myeo-deul-da

pig *n.* 돼지 dwae-ji; 돼지새끼 dwae-ji-sae-
kki; 돼지고기 dwae-ji-go-gi; 탐욕스러운
사람 tam-yok-seu-reo-un sa-ram

pigeon *n.* 비둘기 bi-dul-gi

piggy bank *n.* 돼지 저금통 dwae-ji
jeo-geum-tong

pigtail *n.* 따은 머리 tta-eun meo-ri

pike *n.* 창 chang; 도로요금 징수소 do-ro-
yo-geum jing-su-so; 통행요금 tong-haeng-
nyo-geum; 유료도로 u-ryo-do-ro

pile *n.* 더미 deo-mi; 장작더미 jang-jak-deo-
mi; 대량 dae-ryang; 솜털 som-teol; 보풀
bo-pul; *vt.* 쌓아올리다 ssa-a-ol-li-da; 축
적하다 chuk-jeo-ka-da; 모으다 mo-
eu-da; *vi.* 쌓이다 ssa-i-da; 몰려들어가
다 mol-lyeo-deul-eo-ga-da; 몰려나오다
mol-lyeo-na-o-da

pilgrim *n.* 순례자 sul-lye-ja; 성지 참배자
seong-ji cham-bae-ja; 방랑자 bang-nang-
ja; 필그림 pil-geu-rim

pilgrimage *n.* 순례여행 sul-lye-yeo-haeng;
긴여행 gin yeo-haeng; 인생행로 in-
saeng-haeng-no, 생애 saeng-ae

pill *n.* 알약 al-lyak; 싫은 일 sil-eun nil

pillar *n.* 기둥 gi-dung; 대들보 dae-deul-ppo

pillow *n.* 베개 be-gae; 쿠션 ku-ssyeon

pillowcase *n.* 베갯잇 be-gaen-nit

pilot *n.* 수로 안내인 su-ro an-nae-in; 조종
사 jo-jong-sa

pimple *n.* 여드름 yeo-deu-reum; 뾰루지
ppyo-ru-ji

PIN *abbr.* **personal identification number**
주민등록번호 ju-min-deung-nok-beon-ho

pin *n.* 핀 pin; 브로치 beu-ro-chi; **bobby**
~ 바비핀 ba-bi-pin; **safety ~** 안전핀
an-jeon-pin

pincers *n. pl.* 뻰찌 ppen-jji; 족집게 jjok-jjip-
ge; 집게발 jip-ge-bal

pinch *n.* 꼬집음 kko-jib-eum; 조금 jo-geum;
고통 go-tong; 위기 wi-gi; *vt.* 꼬집다
kko-jip-da; 집다 jip-da; 잘라내다 jal-la-
nae-da; 괴롭히다 goe-ro-pi-da; 훔치다
hum-chi-da

pine *n.* 솔 sol; 소나무 목재 so-na-mu mok-
jae; **~ tree** 소나무 so-na-mu; **~ cone** 솔방
울 sol-ppang-ul; *vi.* 그리워하다 geu-ri-wo-
ha-da, 갈망하다 gal-mang-ha-da

pineapple *n.* 파인애플 pa-in-ae-peul

ping-pong *n.* 탁구 tak-gu, 핑퐁 ping-pong

pinhole *n.* 바늘구멍 ba-neul-kku-meong

pink *adj.* 연분홍색의 yeon-bun-hong-saeg-
ui; 흥분한 heung-bun-han; 붉은 물이 든
bulg-eun mul-i deun

pinkie *n.* 새끼손가락 sae-kki-son-kka-rak

pinpoint *n.* 핀 끝 pin kkeut; 하찮은 것 ha-chan-eun geot; 소량 so-ryang; *vt.* 위치를 정확하게 지적하다 wi-chi-reul jeong-hwa-ka-ge ji-jeo-ka-da; 정밀폭격하다 jeongmil-pok-gyeo-ka-da

pint *n.* 파인트 pa-in-teu

pinwheel *n.* 바람개비 ba-ram-gae-bi; 회전불꽃 hoe-jeon-bul-kkot

pioneer *n.* 개척자 ga-cheok-ja; 선구자 seon-gu-ja

pious *adj.* 신앙심이 깊은 sin-ang-sim-i gip-eun; 경건한 gyeong-geon-han; 종교적인 jong-gyo-jeog-in; 종교를 빙자한 jong-gyo-reul bing-ja-han; 칭찬할만한 ching-chan-hal-man-han

pipe *n.* 파이프 pa-i-peu; 관 gwan; 담뱃대 dam-baet-dae; 관악기 gwan-ak-gi

pipeline *n.* 수송관로 su-song-gwan-no, 보급선 bo-geup-seon; 경로 gyeong-no, 루트 ru-teu

piper *n.* 피리부는 사람 pi-ri-bu-neun sa-ram; 숨가쁜 말 sum-ga ppeun mal

pirate *n.* 해적 hae-jeok; 해적선 hae-jeok-seon; 표절자 pyo-jeol-jja; *vt.* 약탈하다 yak-tal-ha-da; 저작권을 침해하다 jeo-jak-kkwon-eul chim-hae-ha-da; 표절하다 pyo-jeol-ha-da

pistol *n.* 권총 gwon-chong, 피스톨 pi-seu-tol

piston *n.* 피스톤 pi-seu-ton

pit *n.* 구덩이 gu-deong-i; 갱 gaeng; 겨드랑이 gyeo-deu-rang-i; 함정 ham-jeong; 무덤 mu-deom; *(hole)* 구멍 gu-meong; *(kernel of fruit)* 씨 ssi

pitcher *n.* 포석 po-seok; *(container)* 피처 pi-cheo; *(baseball)* 투수 tu-su, 피처 pi-cheo

pitfall *n.* 함정 ham-jeong, 유혹 yu-hok

pity *n.* 동정 dong-jeong; 유감스런 일 yu-gam-seu-reon il; *vi.* 동정을 느끼다 dong-jeong-eul neu-kki-da, 불쌍히 여기나 bul-ssang-hi yeo-gi-da; 애석하게 여기다 ae-seo-ka-ge yeo-gi-da

pizza *n.* 피자 pi-ja

placard *n.* 플래카드 peul-lae-ka-deu, 벽보 byeok-bo, 포스터 po-seu-teo

place *n.* 장소 jang-so; 부분 bu-bun; 지방 ji-bang; 지위 ji-wi; 공간 gong-gan; 좌석 jwa-seok; ~ **of birth** 출생지 chul-ssaeng-ji; **to take** ~ 개최되다 gae-choe-doe-da; 생

기다 saeng-gi-da; *vt.* 두다 du-da; 놓다 no-ta; 걸다 geol-da; 임명하다 im-myeong-ha-da; 투자하다 tu-ja-ha-da; 평가하다 pyeong-kka-ha-da

placement *n.* 배치 bae-chi; 직업소개 jig-eop-so-gae; ~ **test** 반편성 시험 ban-pyeon-seong si-heom

plagiarize *vt.* 표절하다 pyo-jeol-ha-da

plague *n.* 전염병 jeon-yeom-ppyeong; 재앙 jae-ang; 귀찮은 일 gwi-chan-eun il; *vt.* 애태우다 ae-tae-u-da; 괴롭히다 goe-ro-pi-da; 성가시게 하다 seong-ga-si-ge ha-da; 병에 걸리게 하다 byeong-e geol-li-ge ha-da; 재앙이 들게 하다 jae-ang-i deul-ge ha-da

plain *n.* 평지 pyeong-ji, 평원 pyeong-won; *adj.* 분명한 bun-myeong-han; 명백한 myeong-bae-kan; 솔직한 sol-jji-kan; 무지한 mu-ji-han; 보통의 bo-tong-ui; 검소한 geom-so-han; 판판한 pan-pan-han

plan *n.* 계획 gye-hoek; 설계도 seol-gye-do; 모형 mo-hyeong; 방식 bang-sik; *vt.* 계획하다 gye-hoe-ka-da; 설계하다 seol-gye-ha-da; 마음먹다 ma-eum-meok-da; *vi.* 계획하다 gye-hoe-ka-da

plane *n.* *(airplane)* 비행기 bi-haeng-gi; *(geometry term)* 평면 pyeong-myeon; 수준 su-jun; *(tool)* 대패 dae-pae; *vt.* 대패로 밀다 dae-pae-ro mil-da

planet *n.* 혹성 hok-seong; 중요인물 jung-yo-in-mul; 중대사 jung-dae-sa

plank *n.* 두꺼운 판자 du-kkeo-un pan-ja; 생선 구이판 saeng-seon-gu-i-pan

plant *n.* 식물 sing-mul; 공장 gong-jang; 모종 mo-jong; 농작물 nong-jang-mul; 건물 geon-mul; 설비 seol-bi; *vt.* 심다 sim tta; 주입하다 ju-i-pa-da; 수립하다 su-ri-pa-da; 배치하다 bae-chi-ha-da; 찌르다 jji-reu-da; 심다 sim-tta, 씨를 뿌리다 ssi-reul ppu-ri-da; 이식하다 i-si-ka-da; 주입하다 ju-i-pa-da, 가르치다 ga-reu-chi-da; 창립하다 chang-ni-pa-da, 건설하다 geon-seol-ha-da; 찌르다 jji-reu-da, 때려박다 ttae-ryeo-bak-da

plasma *n.* 플라즈마 peul-la-jeu-ma, 혈장 hyeol-jjang

plaster *n.* 회반죽 hoe-ban-juk; 반창고 ban-chang-kko; 고약 go-yak

plastic *n.* 플라스틱 peul-la-seu-tik; 플라스틱 제품 peul-la-seu-tik je-pum; *adj.* 플라스틱의 peul-la-seu-tig-ui; 플라스틱으로 만든 peul-la-seu-tig-eu-ro man-deun; 유연한 yu-yeon-han

plate *n.* 접시 jeop-si; 식기류 sik-gi-ryu; ~ **glass** 판유리 pan-nyu-ri; *vt.* 도금하다 do-geum-ha-da

platform *n.* 연단 yeon-dan; 플랫폼 peul-laet-pom; 승강단 seung-gang-dan; 강령 gang-nyeong

platinum *n.* 백금 baek-geum; 플라티늄 peul-la-ti-nyum

play *n.* 연극 yeon-geuk; 놀이 nol-i; 솜씨 som-ssi; 장난 jang-nan; 내기 nae-gi; 활동 hwal-ttong; *vt.* 게임을 하다 kke-im-eul ha-da; 돈을 걸다 don-eul geol-da; 상연하다 sang-yeon-ha-da; 연주하다 yeon-ju-ha-da; *vi.* 놀다 nol-da; 자유로이 움직이다 ja-yu-ro-i um-jig-i-da; 장난치다 jang-nan-chi-da; 게임을 즐기다 kke-im-eul jeul-gi-da; 상연하다 sang-yeon-ha-da; **The children ~ in the garden** 아이들이 정원에서 놉니다 a-i-deul-i jeong-won-e-seo nom-ni-da; **The children ~ the violin** 아이들이 바이올린을 연주합니다 a-i-deul-i ba-i-ol-lin-eul yeon-ju-ham-ni-da; **They ~ soccer** 그 사람들이 축구를 합니다 geu sa-ram-deul-I chuk-gu-reul ham-ni-da; **She ~s an important role** 그 여자분은 중요한 역할을 맡았습니다 geu yeo-ja-bun-eun jung-yo-han yeo-kal-eul mat-at-seum-ni-da

player *n.* **sports** ~ 경기자 gyeong-gi-ja; 선수 seon-su; *(actor)* 배우 bae-u; 자동연주장치 ja-dong-yeon-ju-jang-chi; **a CD ~** 씨디 플레이어 ssi-di-peul-le-i-eo

playground *n.* 운동장 un-dong-jang; 놀이터 nol-i-teo

playing field *n.* 경기장 gyeong-gi-jang

play-off *n.* 플레이오프 peul-le-i-o-peu

plaza *n.* 대광장 dae-gwang-jang, 플라자 peul-la-ja; 쇼핑센터 syo-ping-ssen-teo

plea *n.* 탄원 tan-won; 청원 cheong-won; 변명 byeon-myeong; **a guilty ~** 유죄인정 yu-joe-in-jeong

plead *vi.* 변론하다 byeol-lon-ha-da; 탄원하다 tan-won-ha-da; **to ~ innocent** 결

백함을 탄원하다 gyeol-bae-kam-eul tan-won-ha-da

pleasant *adj.* 즐거운 jeul-geo-un; 날씨가 좋은 nal-ssi-ga jo-eun; 호감이 가는 ho-gam-i ga-neun

please *vt.* 기쁘게 하다 gi-ppeu-ge ha-da, 만족시키다 man-jok-si-ki-da; *adv.* 제발 je-bal, 아무쪼록 a-mu-jjo-rok; ~ **come in** 어서 오십시오 eo-seo o-sip-si-o

pleasure *n.* 기쁨 gi-ppeum; 만족 man-jok; 즐거운 일 jeul-geo-un il

pledge *n.* 담보 dam-bo; 보증 bo-jeung; 맹세 maeng-se

plenty *n.* 많음 man-eum; 가득함 ga-deu-kam; 충분함 chung-bun-ham

pliers *n. pl.* 집게 jip-ge; 뻰찌 ppen-jji

plot *n.* 음모 eum-mo; 줄거리 jul-geo-ri; 소구획 so-gu-hoek; *(of a novel)* 줄거리 jul-geo-ri; *vt.* 계획하다 gye-hoe-ka-da; 구분하다 gu-bub-ha-da; 도면을 만들다 do-myeon-eul man-deul-da

plow *n.* 쟁기 jaeng-gi; 제설기 je-seol-gi; 농업 nong-eop; 경작지 gyeong-jak-ji; *vt.* 쟁기로 갈다 jaeng-gi-ro gal-da; 주름살을 짓다 ju-reum-ssal-eul jit-da; 헤치고 나가다 he-chi-go na-ga-da

plug *n.* 마개 ma-gae; 플러그 peul-leo-geu; *vt.* 막다 mak-da; 채우다 chae-u-da; 밀어넣다 mil-eo-neo-ta; 플러그를 끼우다 peul-leo-geu-reul kki-u-da; **to ~ sth. in** 뭔가를 안에 채우다 mwon-ga-reul an-e chae-u-da

plum *n.* 플럼 peul-leom, 자두 ja-du; 짙은 보라색 jit-eun bo-ra-saek, 자두색 ja-du-saek

plumber *n.* 배관공 bae-gwan-gong

plume *n.* 깃털 git-teol; 깃털장식 git-teol-jang-sik

plump *adj.* 부푼 bu-pun; 불룩한 bul-lu-kan, 토실토실한 to-sil-to-sil-han; 대단한 dae-dan-han; 노골적인 no-gol-jjeog-in; 정직한 jeong-ji-kan; 퉁명스러운 tung-myeong-seu-reo-un; *vi.* 털썩 떨어지다 teol-sseok tteol-eo-ji-da, 갑자기 뛰어들다 gap-ja-gi ttwi-eo-deul-da

plunge *vi.* 뛰어들다 ttwi-eo-deul-da; 돌진하다 dol-jjin-ha-da; 착수하다 chak-su-ha-da

plural *n.* 복수 bok-su; 복수형 bok-su-hyeong; *adj.* 복수의 bok-su-ui

plus *n.* 양수 yang-su; 여분 yeo-bun; 더하기 기호 deo-ha-gi gi-ho; *prep.* ...을 더하여 ...eul-reul deo-ha-yeo; ...에 덧붙여서 ...e deot-bu-chyeo-seo; **Seven ~ eleven is eighteen** 칠 더하기 십일은 십팔이다 chil deo-ha-gi sib-il-eun sip-pal-i-da; **~ tax** 세금을 포함해서 se-geum-eul po-ham-hae-seo; *conj.* ...을 더한 ...eul deo-han, ...을 더하여 ...eul deo-ha-yeo

pneumonia *n.* 폐렴 pye-ryeom

pocket *n.* 포켓 po-ket, 호주머니 ho-ju-meo-ni; 한부대 han-bu-dae; 옴폭한 땅 om-po-kan ttang; **~book** 문고판 mun-go-pan; 수첩 su-cheop; 돈지갑 don-ji-gap

pod *n.* 꼬투리 kko-tu-ri; 누에고치 nu-e-go-chi

poem *n.* 시 si

poet *n.* 시인 si-in

poetry *n.* 시 si; 시집 si-jip; 시작법 si-jak-beop; 시적재능 si-jjeok-jae-neung; 시적 요소 si-jjeok yo-so

pogo stick *n.* 포고스틱 po-go-seu-tik

point *n.* 첨단 cheom-dan; 끝 kkeut; 점 jeom; 촉 chok; 득점 deuk-jeom; 평정 pyeong-jeong; 요점 yo-jjeom; 목표 mok-pyo; 효과 hyo-kkwa; 점촉점 jeop-chok-jeom; *(of land)* 곶 got; *(a sharp end, as on an arrow)* 촉 chok; *(in a game or sport)* 점수 jeom-su; **That's a good ~** 그건 좋은 지적입니다 geu-geon jo-eun ji-jeog-im-ni-da; **a ~ in time or place** 시점 si-jjeom, 순간 sun-gan; 지점 ji-jeom, 장소 jang-so; **What is the ~ of . . .** ...의 요점이 뭡니까 ... ui yo-jjeom-i mwom-ni-kka; **to be to the ~** 적절한 jeok-jeol-han, 요령있는 yo-ryeong-in-neun; **beside the ~** 겨냥이 빗나간 gyeo-nyang-i bin-na-gan, 짐작이 틀린 jim-jag-i teul-lin; *vt.* 뾰족하게 하다 ppyo-jo-ka-ge ha-da; 끝을 붙이다 kkeu-cheul bu-chi-da; 자극하다 ja-geu-ka-da; 점을 찍다 jeom-eul jjik-da; 강조하다 gang-jo-ha-da; ... 을 향하게 하다 eul hyang-ha-ge ha-da, ... 를 향하게 하다 reul hyang-ha-ge ha-da; 지적하다 ji-jeo-ka-da; 지시하다 ji-si-ha-da; *vi.* 가리키다 ga-ri-ki-da; 지시하다 ji-si-ha-da; 경향이 있다 gyeong-hyang-

i it-da; 지목하다 ji-mo-ka-da; **to ~ out** 지시하다 ji-si-ha-da; 지적하다 ji-jeo-ka-da

poison *n.* 독 dok; 독약 dog-yak; 해독 hae-dok, 폐해 pye-hae; **~ gas** 독가스 dok-kka-sseu

poisonous *adj.* 유독한 yu-do-kan; 유해한 yu-hae-han; 악의의 ag-i-ui; 불쾌한 bul-kwae-han

poke *vt.* 찌르다 jji-reu-da; 구멍을 내다 gu-meong-eul nae-da

poker-faced *adj.* 무표정한 mu-pyo-jeong han

Poland *n.* 폴란드 pol-lan-deu

polar *adj.* 남극의 nam-geug-ui, 북극의 buk-geug-ui, 극지의 geuk-ji-ui; 정반대의 jeong-ban-dae-ui; **~ bear** 북극곰 buk-geuk-gom

pole *n.* 막대기 mak-dae-gi; 장대 jang-ttae; 기둥 gi-dung; 극 geuk; 극지 geuk-ji; 전극 Jeon-geuk; 극단 geuk-dan

police *n.* 경찰 gyeong-chal, 경찰관 gyeong-chal-gwan; 치안 chi-an; *vt.* 치안을 유지하다 chi-an-eul yu-ji-ha-da, ...을 단속하다 ...eul dan-so-ka-da; **~ car** 경찰차 gyeong-chal-cha; **~man** 경찰 gyeong-chal; **~ station** 경찰서 gyeong-chal-sseo

policy *n.* 정책 jeong-chaek; 방침 bang-chim; 방책 bang-chaek; 수단 su-dan; 보험증권 bo-heom-jeung-kkwon; **insurance ~** 보험 약관 bo-heom-yak-gwan

polish *n.* 광택 gwang-taek; 광택재료 gwang-taek-jae ryo; 세련 se-ryeon; **furniture ~** 가구 광택제 ga-gu gwang-taek-je; **shoe ~** 구두약 gu-du-yak; *vt.* 닦다 dak-da; 윤을 내다 yun-eul nae-da; 품위있게 하다 pum-wi-it-ge ha-da; 퇴고하다 toe-go-ha-da; 마멸시키다 ma-myeol-si-ki-da

Polish *n.* 폴란드말 pol-lan-deu-mal; 폴란드 사람 pol-lan-deu-ssa-ram; *adj.* 폴란드의 pol-lan-deu-ui; 폴란드 사람의 pol-lan-deu ssa-ram-ui

polite *adj.* 공손한 gong-son-han; 예의바른 ye-ui-ba-reun; 세련된 se-ryeon-doen; 우아한 u-a-han

political *adj.* 정치의 jeong-chi-ui; 정치에 관한 jeong-chi-e gwan-han

politician *n.* 정치가 jeong-chi-ga

politics *n. pl.* 정치학 jeong-chi-hak; 정치 jeong-chi; 정략 jeong-nyak

poll *n.* 투표 tu-pyo; 머리 meo-ri; 투표소 tu-pyo-so; 선거인 명부 seon-geo-in myeong-bu; 여론조사 yeo-ron-jo-sa; *vi.* -에게 투표하다 e-ge tu-pyo-ha-da; *vt.* 표를 획득하다 pyo-reul hoek-deu-ka-da

pollen *n.* 꽃가루 kkot-ga-ru

pollute *vt.* 더럽히다 deo-reo-pi-da; 오염시키다 o-yeom-si-ki-da; 모독하다 mo-do-ka-da; 타락시키다 ta-rak-si-ki-da

polluted *adj.* 술취한 sul-chwi-han; 오염된 o-yeom-doen

pollution *n.* 오염 o-yeom; 공해 gong-hae; 모독 mo-dok; 타락 ta-rak

Polynesia *n.* 폴리네시아 pol-li-ne-si-a

polytail *n.* 땋은 머리 tta-eun meo-ri

pond *n.* 연못 yeon-mot; 양어장 yang-eo-jang; 늪 neup

pony *n.* 조랑말 jo-rang-mal; 작은말 jag-eun mal; 소형차 so-hyeong-cha

pool *n.* 물웅덩이 mul-ung-deong-i; 저수지 jeo-su-ji; 풀장 pul-jang; 합동자금 hap-dong-ja-geum; 공동계산 gong-dong-gye-san; 집결소 jip-gyeol-sso; pool table 당구대 dang-gu-dae

poor *adj.* 부족한 bu-jo-kan; 서투른 seo-tu-reun; 열등한 yeol-tteung-han; *(in wealth)* 가난한 ga-nan-han; *(unfortunate)* 불쌍한 bul-ssang-han

pop *vi.* 뻥 터지다 ppeong teo-ji-da, 펑 소리나다 peong so-ri-na-da; 갑자기 움직이다 gap-ja-gi um-jig-i-da; 튀어나오다 twi-eo-na-o-da; *n.* 대중음악 dae-jung-eum-ak, 유행가 yu-haeng-ga

popcorn *n.* 팝콘 pap-kon

pope *n.* 로마교황 ro-ma-gyo-hwang; 희랍정교회 교구성직자 hi-rap-jeong-gyo-hoe gyo-gu-seong-jik-ja

pop music *n.* 팝송 pap-song; 대중음악 dae-jung-eum-ak

popular *adj.* 민중의 min-jung-ui; 대중적인 dae-jung-jeog-in; 인기있는 in-kki-in-neun

popularity *n.* 인기 in-kki; 유행 yu-haeng

population *n.* 인구 in-gu; 주민 ju-min; 주민수 ju-min-ssu

porcelain *n.* 자기 ja-gi; 자기제품 ja-gi-je-pum

porch *n.* 현관 hyeon-gwan; 입구 ip-gu

pore *n.* 털구멍 teol-kku-meong; 기공 gi-gong; 흡수공 heup-su-gong; *vt.* 숙고하다 suk-go-ha-da

pork *n.* 돼지고기 dwae-ji-go-gi

porridge *n.* 죽 juk

port *n.* 항구 hang-gu; 항구도시 hang-gu-do-si; 공항 gong-hang

portable *adj.* 휴대용의 hyu-dae-yong-ui; 운반할 수 있는 un-ban-hal ssu in-neun

porter *n.* 짐꾼 jim-kkun; 포터 po-teo; 운반기구 un-ban-gi-gu

portfolio *n.* 포트폴리오 po-teu-pol-li-o; 서류철 seo-ryu-cheol; 손가방 son-kka-bang; 장관직 jang-gwan-jik

portion *n.* 일부 il-bu, 몫 mok; 일인분 il-in-bun; 분배재산 bun-bae-jae-san; 운명 un-myeong; *vt.* 분할하다 bun-hal-ha-da

portrait *n.* 초상화 cho-sang-hwa; 인물사진 in-mul-sa-jin; 인물묘사 in-mul-myo-sa

Portugal *n.* 포르투갈 po-reu-tu-gal

Portuguese *n.* 포르투갈 사람 po-reu-tu-gal ssa-ram; 포르투갈 말 po-reu-tu-gal mal; *adj.* 포르투갈의 po-reu-tu-gal-ui; 포르투갈 사람의 po-reu-tu-gal ssa-ram-ui

pose *n.* 자세 ja-se; *vi.* 자세를 취하다 ja-se-reul chwi-ha-da

position *n.* 위치 wi-chi; 장소 jang-so; 처지 cheo-ji; 지위 ji-wi; 태도 tae-do; 상태 sang-tae

positive *adj.* 확신하는 hwak-sin-ha-neun; 단정적인 dan-jeong-jeog-in; 명확한 myeong-hwa-kan; 긍정적인 geung-jeong-jeog-in; 완전한 wan-jeon-han

possess *vt.* 소유하다 so-yu-ha-da; 자격을 갖추다 ja-gyeog-eul gat-chu-da; 능통하다 neung-tong-ha-da; ...에게 알리다 ...e-ge al-li-da; ...을 지배하다 ...eul-reul ji-bae-ha-da

possession *n.* 소유 so-yu; 소유물 so-yu-mul; 재산 jae-san; 속지 sok-ji; 사로잡힘 sa-ro-ja-pim

possessive *adj.* 소유의 so-yu-ui; 소유욕이 강한 so-yu-yog-i gang-han

possibility *n.* 가능성 ga-neung-sseong, 가망 ga-mang

possible *adj.* 가능한 ga-neung-han; 할 수 있는 hal ssu-in-neun; 있음직한

iss-eum-ji-kan; 그런대로 괜찮은 geu-reon-dae-ro gwaen-chan-eun

post *n.* 우체국 u-che-guk; 우체통 u-che-tong; *(a pole or stake)* 기둥 gi-dung; 푯말 pyon-mal; 말뚝 mal-ttuk; *(the mail)* 우편 u-pyeon; *(station, task or position to which one is appointed)* 지위 ji-wi; 직 jik; 직장 jik-jang; 부서 bu-seo; 담당구역 dam-dang-gu-yeok; *vt.* 정보를 알리다 jeong-bo-reul al-li-da; 게시물을 붙이다 ge-si-mul-eul bu-chi-da; 게시하다 ge-si-ha-da; 임명하다 im-myeong-ha-da; *(to station sb. somewhere)* 배치하다 bae-chi-ha-da; *(to mail)* 우송하다 u-song-ha-da; **Keep me ~ed** 계속 정보를 보내주십시오 gye-sok jeong-bo-reul bo-nae-ju-sip-si-o

postage *n.* 우편요금 u-pyeon-nyo-geum; **~ stamp** 우표 u-pyo

postcard *n.* 우편엽서 u-pyeon-nyeop-seo

poster *n.* 포스터 po-seu-teo

posterity *n.* 자손 ja-son; 후세 hu-se

postmark *n.* 소인 so-in; *vt.* 소인을 찍다 so-in-eul jjik-da

post office *n.* 우체국 u-che-guk

post-office box *n.* 사서함 sa-seo-ham

postpone *vt.* 연기하다 yeon-gi-ha-da, 미루다 mi-ru-da

pot *n.* 냄비 nam-bi; 단지 dan-ji; 항아리 hang-a-ri

potato *n.* 감자 gam-ja

potential *adj.* 가능한 ga-neung-han; 잠재하는 jam-jae-ha-neun, 잠재적인 jam-jae-jeog-in

potentiality *n.* 가능성 ga-neung-sseong

pothole *n.* 수직동굴 su-jik-dong-gul; 움푹 패인곳 um-puk pae-in-got

potion *n.* 일회분 il-hoe-bun

pottery *n.* 도기 do-gi; 도기 제조법 do-gi je-jo-ppeop; 도기 제조소 do-gi je-jo-so

potato chip *n.* 포테이토칩 po-te-i-to-chip, 감자칩 gam-ja-chip

pouch *n.* 주머니 ju-meo-ni; 우편행낭 u-pyeon-haeng-nang

poultry *n.* 가금류 ga-geum-nyu

pound *n.* 파운드 pa-un-deu; 울타리 ul-ta-ri; 우리 u-ri; 유치장 yu-chi-jang; 타격 ta-gyeok; 강타 gang-ta; *vt.* 울에 넣다 ul-e neo-ta; 구류하다 gu-ryu-ha-da; 계속 치다 gye-sok chi-da; 맹공격하다 maeng-gong-gyeo-ka-da; *vi.* 연타하다 yeon-ta-ha-da; 두근거리다 du-geun-geo-ri-da; 꾸준히 노력하다 kku-jun-hi no-ryeo-ka-da

pour *vt.* 따르다 tta-reu-da; 쏟다 ssot-da; 퍼붓다 peo-but-da; *vi.* 흐르다 heu-reu-da; 쇄도하다 swae-do-ha-da; 퍼붓다 peo-but-da; 연발하다 yeon-bal-ha-da

poverty *n.* 가난 ga-nan, 빈곤 bin-gon

POW *n. abbr.* *prisoner of war* 전쟁포로 jeon-jaeng-po-ro

powder *n.* 가루 ga-ru; 가루제품 ga-ru-je-pum; 화약 hwa-hak; 흙먼지 heung-meon-ji

power *n.* 힘 him; 체력 che-ryeok; 동력 dong-nyeok; 효력 hyo-ryeok; 능력 neung-nyeok; 권력 geol-lyeok; 권력자 gwol-lyeok-ja; 강국 gang-guk

powerful *adj.* 강한 gang-han; 강력한 gang-nyeo-kan; 유력한 yu-ryeo-kan; 우세한 u-se-han; 감동시키는 gam-dong-si-ki-neun

power plant *n.* 발전소 bal-jjeon-so

practical *adj.* 실제의 sil-jje-ui; 실용적인 sil-yong-jeog-in; 경험있는 gyeong-heom-in-neun; 사실상의 sa-sil-ssang-ui

practically *adv.* 실제적으로 sil-jje-jeog-eu-ro; 사실상 sa-sil-ssang

practice *n.* 실행 sil-haeng; 실습 sil-sseup; 연습 yeon-seup; 버릇 beo-reut; 습관 seup-gwan; **medical ~** 임상의료실습 im-sang-ui-ryo-sil-sseup; *vt.* 실행하다 sil-haeng-ha-da; 연습하다 yeon-seu-pa-da; 훈련하다 hul-lyeon-ha-da; *vi.* 연습하다 yeon-seu-pa-da; 익히다 i-ki-da; 개업하다 gae-eo-pa-da; 습관적으로 하다 seup-gwan-jeog-eu-ro ha-da

praise *n.* 칭찬 ching-chan; 찬미 chan-mi; 숭배 sung-bae; *vt.* 칭찬하다 ching-chan-ha-da; 찬미하다 chan-mi-ha-da; 숭배하다 sung-bae-ha-da

praiseworthy *adj.* 칭찬할만한 ching-chan-hal-man-hab; 기특한 gi-teu-kan

prawn *n.* 참새우 cham-sae-u

pray *vi.* 기원하다 gi-won-ha-da; 기도하다 gi-do-ha-da; 빌다 bil-da

prayer *n.* 기도하는 사람 gi-do-ha-neun sa-ram; 기도 gi-do; 소원 so-won

preach *vt.*, *vi.* 전도하다 jeon-do-ha-da; 설교하다 seol-gyo-ha-da; 타이르다 ta-i-reu-da; 장려하다 jang-nyeo-ha-da

precarious *adj.* 불확실한 bul-hwak-sil-han; 불안정한 bul-an-jeong-han; 위험한 wiheom-han; 근거없는 geun-geo-eom-neun

precaution *n.* 조심 jo-sim, 예방조치 ye-bang-jo-chi

precede *vt.* 선행하다 seon-haeng-ha-da, 앞서다 ap-seo-da; 선도하다 seon-do-hada; 우선하다 u-seon-ha-da; 전제하다 jeon-jae-ha-da

precious *adj.* 귀중한gwi-jung-han, 값비싼 gap-bi-ssan

precise *adj.* 정밀한 jeong-mil-han; 정확한 jeong-hwa-kan; 꼼꼼한 kkom-kkom-han

predator *n.* 약탈자 yak-tal-jja, 포획자 po-hoek-ja

predetermine *vt.* 미리 결정하다 mi-ri gyeol-jjeong-ha-da

predict *vt.* 예언하다 ye-eon-ha-da; 예보하다 ye-bo-ha-da

predominent *adj.* 우세한 u-se-han, 탁월한 tag-wol-han; 두드러진 du-deu-reo-jin

preface *n.* 서문 seo-mun; 전제 jeon-je, 발단 bal-ttan

prefer *vt.* 좋아하다 jo-a-ha-da; 선호하다 seon-ho-ha-da; 발탁하다 bal-ta-ka-da

preference *n.* 선호 seon-ho; 편애 pyeon-ae; 더 좋아하는 것 deo jo-a-ha-neun geot; 우선권 u-seon-kkwon

prefix *n.* 접두사 jeop-du-sa; 경칭 gyeong-ching

pregnant *adj.* 임신한 im-sin-han; 가득찬 ga-deuk-chan; 의미심장한 ui-mi-sim-jang-han; 풍부한 pung-bu-han

prehistoric *adj.* 유사 이전의 yu-sa-i-jeon-ui

prejudice *n.* 편견 pyeon-gyeon; 선입관 seon-ip-gwan; 침해 chim-hae

prelude *n.* 전주곡 jeon-ju-gok

premature *adj.* 조산의 jo-san-ui; 시기상조의 si-gi-sang-jo-ui

premium *n.* 할증금 hal-jjeung-geum; 상금 sang-geum; 보험료 bo-heom-nyo, 수수료 su-su-ryo; 사례금 sa-rye-geum

preoccupy *vt.* 선취하다 seon-chwi-ha-da; 몰두하게 하다 mol-ttu-ha-ge ha-da

preparation *n.* 준비 jun-bi; 각오 gag-o; 조제 jo-je

prepare *vt.* 준비시키다 jun-bi-si-ki-da; 각오시키다 gag-o-si-ki-da; *vi.* 준비하다 jun-bi-ha-da; 채비하다 chae-bi-ha-da; 각오하다 gag-o-ha-da

preposition *n.* 전치사 jeon-chi-sa

pre-requisite *adj.* 필수의 pil-ssu-ui, 전제가 되는 jeon-je-ga doe-neun; *n.* 필요조건 pil-yo-jo-kkeon

preschool *n.* 유치원 yu-chi-won, 유아원 yu-a-won

prescribe *vt.* 규정하다 gyu-jeong-ha-da; 처방하다 cheo-bang-ha-da; 권하다 gwon-ha-da; 지시하다 ji-si-ha-da

prescription *n.* 명령 myeong-nyeong; 법규 beop-gyu; 처방 cheo-bang; 처방전 cheo-bang-jeon

present *n.* 현재 hyeon-jae, 오늘날 o-neul-lal; 선물 seon-mul; *adj.* 있는 in-neun, 출석하는chul-sseo-ka-neun; 지금의 ji-geum-ui, 현재의 hyeon-jae-ui; 당면한 dang-myeon-han; *vt.* 선물하다 seon-mul-ha-da; 증정하다 jeung-jeong-ha-da; 주다 ju-da; 제출하다 je-chul-ha-da; 소개하다 so-gae-ha-da; 제공하다 je-gong-ha-da

presentation *n.* 증정 jeung-jeong, 수여 su-yeo; 선물 seon-mul; 소개 so-gae; 발표 bal-pyo; 공연 gong-yeon

presently *adv.* 이내 i-nae, 곧got

preservation *n.* 보존 bo-jon, 보호 bo-ho; 보존상태 bo-jon-sang-tae

preserve *n.* 잼 jjaem; 과일 통조림 gwa-il tong-jo-rim; 사냥금지구역 sa-nyang-geum-ji-gu-yeok; 양어장 yang-eo-jang; 개인영역 gae-in-yeong-yeok; **nature** ~ 자연보호구역 ja-yeon-bo-ho-gu-yeok; **strawberry ~s** 딸기잼 ttal-gi-jjaem; *vt.* 유지하다 yu-ji-ha-da; 보존하다 bo-jon-ha-da; 저장식품을 만들다 jeo-jang-sik-pum-eul man-deul-da; 보호하다 bo-ho-ha-da

president *n.* 대통령 dae-tong-nyeong; 회장 hoe-jang; 의장 ui-jang; 총재 chong-jae; 사장 sa-jang

press *n.* 누름 nu-reum; 인쇄기 in-swae-gi; 신문 sin-mun; 보도기관 bo-do-gi-gwan; 기자 gi-ja; 혼잡 hon-jap; ~ **conference** 기자

회견 gi-ja-hoe-gyeon; ~ **release** 보도자료 bo-do-ja-ryo; *vt.* 누르다 nu-reu-da; 눌러 펴다 nul-leo pyeo-da; 움켜잡다 um-kyeo-jap-da; 좁을 짜다 jeub-eul jja-da; 강조하다 gang-jo-ha-da; 강요하다 gang-yo-ha-da; 압박하다 ap-ba-ka-da

pressure *n.* 압력 am-nyeok; 압축 ap-chuk; 압박 ap-bak; 곤란 gol-lan; 긴급 gin-geup

prestige *n.* 위신 wi-sin; 명성 myeong-seong

presumably *adv.* 아마 a-ma

presume *vt.* 가정하다 ga-jeong-ha-da, 추정하다 chu-jeong-ha-da

pretend *vt.* …인체 하다…in-che-ha-da, …인 척 하다…in-cheo-ka-da

pretty *adj.* 예쁜 ye-ppeun; 귀여운 gwl-yeo-un; 멋진 meot-jin; 꽤 많은 kkwae man-eun; *adv.* 꽤 kkwae; 비교적 bi-gyo-jeok; 아주 a-ju; ~ **hot** 아주 뜨겁다 a-ju tteu-geop-da

prevailing *adj.* 우세한 u-se-han; 유력한 yu-ryeo-kan; 효과적인 hyo-kkwa-jeog-in; 유행하는 yu-haeng-ha-neun; 일반적인 il-ban-jeog-in

prevent *vt.* 막다 mak-da; 방해하다 bang-hae-ha-da; 예방하다 ye-bang-ha-da; 보호하다 bo-ho-ha-da; 회피하다 hoe-pi-ha-da

prevention *n.* 방지 bang-ji; 예방 ye-bang; 예방법 ye-bang-ppeop; 방해 bang-hae

preventive *adj.* 예방의 ye-bang-ui; 예방하는 ye-bang-ha-neun; 방지하는 bang-ji-ha-neun; ~ **medicine** 예방약 ye-bang-nyak

preview *n.* 시사회 si-sa-hoe, 시연 si-yeon; 방송예고 bang-song-ye-go; 사전검토 sa-jeon-jeom-geom

previous *adj.* 앞의 ap-ui; 이전의 i-jeon-ui; 사전의 sa-jeon-ui; 앞서의 ap-seo-ui

prey *n.* 먹이 meog-i; *vi.* 잡아먹다 jab-a-meok-da; 약탈하다 yak-tal-ha-da

price *n.* 가격 ga-gyeok; 대가 daet-ga; 시세 si-se; 물가 mul-kka; 보상 bo-sang; 값 gap; *vt.* 값을 매기다 gaps-eul me-gi-da; 평가하다 pyeong-kka-ha-da; 값을 묻다 gaps-eul mut-da; ~ **tag** 가격표 ga-gyeok-pyo

priceless *adj.* 대단히 귀중한 dae-dan-hi gwi-jung-han; 돈으로 살 수 없는 don-eu-ro sal ssu eom-neun

pride *n.* 자존심 ja-jon-sim; 자랑 ja-rang; 자만심 ja-man-sim; 자랑거리 ja-rang-kkeo-ri

priest *n.* 성직자 seong-jik-ja; 목사 mok-sa; 사제 sa-je

primary *adj.* 첫째의 cheot-jjae-ui; 주요한 ju-yo-han; 최초의 choe-cho-ui; 근원적인 geun-won-jeog-in; 초등의 cho-deung-ui; ~ **school** 초등학교 cho-deung-hak-gyo

prime *adj.* 첫째의 cheot-jjae-ui; 가장 중요한 ga-jang jung-yo-han; 최초의 choe-cho-ui; 기초적인 gi-cho-jeog-in; 일류의 il-lyu-ui; 훌륭한 hul-lyung-han; ~ **minister** 국무총리 gung-mu-chong-ni

primitive *adj.* 원시의 won-si-ui, 원시적인 won-si-jeog-in; 초기의 cho-gi-ui; 근본의 geun-bon-ui

prince *n.* 왕자 wang-ja; 제후 je-hu

princess *n.* 공주 gong-ju; 왕지비 wang-ja-bi

principal *n.* 장관 jang-gwan; 교장 gyo-jang; 회장 hoe-jang; 주동자 ju-dong-ja; *adj.* 주요한 ju-yo-han; 원금의 won-geum-ui

principle *n.* 원리 wol-li, 원칙 won-chik; 근본방침 geun-bon-bang-chim; 행동원리 haeng-dong-wol-li; 법칙 beop-chik

print *vt.* 인쇄하다 in-swae-ha-da; 출판하다 chul-pan-ha-da; 찍다 jjik-da; 인상을 주다 in-sang-eul ju-da; 인화하다 in-hwa-ha-da

printer *n.* 프린터 peu-rin-teo; 인쇄업자 in-swae-eop-ja; 인쇄기계 in-swae-gi-gye

printing *n.* 인쇄 in-swae; 인쇄술 in-swae-sul; 인쇄부수 in-swae-bu-ssu; 인쇄물 in-swae-mul

prior *adj.* 이전의 i-jeon-ui; …보다 중요한…bo-da jung-yo-han

priority *n.* 우선권 u-seon-kkwon; 앞섬 ap-seom; 보다 중요함 bo-da jung-yo-ham

prism *n.* 프리즘 peu-ri-jeum

prison *n.* 교도소 gyo-do-so, 감옥 gam-ok, 구치소 gu-chi-so; 감금 gam-geum

prisoner *n.* 죄수 joe-su; 포로 po-ro

privacy *n.* 사생활 sal-saeng-hwal; 개인적 자유 gae-in-jeok ja-yu; 비밀 bi-mil

private *adj.* 사적인 sa-jjeog-in, 개인의 gae-in-ui; 비밀의 bi-mil-ui; 사립의 sa-rib-ui; *(military rank)* 사병 sa-byeong; ~ **school** 사립학교 sa-ri-pak-gyo

privilege *n.* 특권 teuk-gwon; 특전 teuk-jeon; 특별취급 teuk-byeol-chwi-geup

prize *n.* 상품 sang-pum; 상 sang; 현상금 hyeon-sang-geum; 당첨 dang-cheom;

전리품 jeol-li-pum; ~**winner** 수상자 su-sang-ja

pro *n. abbr.* **professional** 프로 peu-ro, 전문가 jeon-mun-ga, 직업선수 jig-eop-seon-su; *adj.* 직업의 jig-eob-ui, 프로의 peu-ro-ui; *adv.* 찬성하여 chan-seong-ha-yeo

probable *adj.* 있음직한 iss-eum-ji-kan; 사실같은 sa-sil-gat-eun; 예상되는 ye-sang-doe-neun;

probably *adv.* 아마 a-ma; 대개 dae-gae

problem *n.* 문제 mun-je; 의문 ui-mun; 귀찮은 일 gwi-chan-eun il

procedure *n.* 순서 sun-seo; 절차 jeol-cha; 진행 jin-haeng

proceed *vi.* 나아가다 na-a-ga-da; 진행되다 jin-haeng-doe-da; 계속하다 gye-so-ka-da; 착수하다 chak-su-ha-da; 처리하다 cheo-ri-ha-da; ~**s** *n.* 수익 su-ik; 매상 mae-sang; 결과 gyeol-gwa

process *n.* 진행 jin-haeng; 경과 gyeong-gwa; 과정 gwa-jeong; 진전 jin-jeon; 작용 jag-yong; *vt.* 처리하다 cheo-ri-ha-da; 작성하다 jak-seong-ha-da; 조사분류하다 jo-sa-bul-lyu-ha-da; 가공처리하다 ga-gong-cheo-ri-ha-da; 현상하다 hyeon-sang-ha-da

proclaim *vt.* 선언하다 seon-eon-ha-da, 공포하다 gong-po-ha-da

produce *vt.* 산출하다 san-chul-ha-da; 낳다 na-ta; 생산하다 saeng-san-ha-da; 일으키다 il-eu-ki-da; 제시하다 je-si-ha-da; 연출하다 yeon-chul-ha-da; *vi.* 만들어내다 man-deul-eo-nae-da; 산출하다 san-chul-ha-da; 창작하다 chang-ja-ka-da

product *n.* 생산품 saeng-san-pum; 제작물 je-jang-mul; 창작품 chang-jak-pum; 결과 gyeol-gwa; 성과 seong-kkwa

production *n.* 생산 saeng-san; 제품 je-pum; 연출 yeon-chul; 영화제작소 yeong-hwa-je-jak-so

productive *adj.* 생산적인 saeng-san-jeog-in; 다산의 da-san-ui; 비옥한 bi-o-kan

profession *n.* 전문직업 jeon-mun-jig-eop; 고백 go-baek

professional *adj.* 전문적인 jeon-mun-jeog-in; 전문직업상의 jeon-mun-jig-eop-sang-ui; 직업의 jig-eob-ui

professor *n.* 교수 gyo-su

proficient *adj.* 익숙한 ik-su-kan, 능숙한 neung-su-kan

profile *n.* 옆모습 yeom-mo-seup; 윤곽 yun-gwak; 측면도 cheung-myeon-do

profit *n.* 이익 i-ik; 수익 su-ik; 득 deuk; 덕 deok; *vi.* 이익을 보다 i-ig-eul bo-da; 소득을 얻다 so-deug-eul eot-da; 덕을 입다 deog-eul ip-da; 득이 되다 deug-i-doe-da

profound *adj.* 깊은 gip-eun; 뜻깊은 ttet-gip-eun; 정중한 jeong-jung-han

program *n.* 프로그램 peu-ro-geu-raem; 상연종목 sang-yeon-jong-mok; 계획 gye-hoek; 예정표 ye-jeong-pyo; 학과과정 hak-gwa-gwa-jeong; **computer** ~ 컴퓨터 프로그램 keom-pyu-teo peu-ro-geu-raem; **television** ~ 텔레비전 프로그램 tel-le-bi-jeon peu-ro-geu-raem; *vt.* 프로그램을 짜다 peu-ro-geu-raem-eul jja-da; 계획을 세우다 gye-hoeg-eul se-u-da

programmer *n.* 프로그래머 peu-ro-geu-rae-meo, 프로그램 작성자 peu-ro-geu-raem jak-seong-ja

progress *n.* 전진 jeon-jin; 진보 jin-bo; 경과 gyeong-gwa; *vi.* 전진하다 jeon-jin-ha-da; 진보하다 jin-bo-ha-da; 진척되다 jin-cheok-doe-da

progressive *adj.* 전진하는 jeon-jin-ha-neun; 진보적인 jin-bo-jeog-in; 점진적인 jeom-jin-jeog-in

prohibit *vt.* 금지하다 geum-ji-ha-da; 방해하다 bang-hae-ha-da

prohibition *n.* 금지 geum-ji

project *n.* 안 an, 계획 gye-hoek; 계획사업 gye-hoek-sa-eop; 연구계획 yeon-gu-gye-hoek

projector *n.* 설계자 seol-gye-ja; 계획자 gye-hoek-ja; 투사기 tu-sa-gi; 영사기 yeong-sa-gi

promenade *n.* 무도회 mu-do-hoe; 산보 san-ppo; 산책길 san-chaek-gil

prominent *adj.* 두드러진 du-deu-reo-jin; 현저한 hyeon-jeo-han, 유명한 yu-myeong-han

promise *n.* 약속 yak-sok; 계약 gye-yak; 기대 gi-dae; *vt., vi.* 약속하다 yak-so-ka-da; 가망이 있다 ga-mang-i it-da; 기대하다 gi-dae-ha-da; 단언하다 dan-eon-ha-da

promote *vt.* 승진시키다 seung-jin-si-ki-da; 장려하다 jang-nyeo-ha-da, 촉진하다 chok-jin-ha-da

prompt *adj.* 신속한 sin-so-kan, 즉시의 jeuk-si-ui; *vt.* 자극하다 ja-geu-ka-da; 생각나게 하다 saeng-gang-na-ge ha-da

promptly *adv.* 재빨리 jae-ppal-li, 즉시 jeuk-si

pronoun *n.* 대명사 dae-myeong-sa

pronounce *vt.* 발음하다 bal-eum-ha-da; 소리내어 읽다 so-ri-nae-eo ik-da; 선언하다 seon-eon-ha-da; 단언하다 dan-eon-ha-da

pronunciation *n.* 발음 bal-eum; 발음법 bal-eum-ppeop

proof *n.* 증명 jeung-myeong; 증거 jeung-geo; 증거서류 Jeung-geo-seo-ryu

propaganda *n.* 선전 seon-jeon; 선전활동 seon-jeon-hwal-ttong; 선전내용 seon-jeon-nae-yong; 선전기관 seon-jeon-gi-gwan

propel *vt.* 추진하다 chu-jin-ha-da; 몰아대다 mol-a-dae-da

propeller *n.* 프로펠러 peu-ro-pel-leo, 추진기 chu-jin-gi; 추진자 chu-jin-ja

proper *adj.* 적당한 jeok-dang-han; 타당한 ta-dang-han; 올바른 ol-ba-reun; 예의바른 ye-I-ba-reun; 고유의 go-yu-ui; 본래의 bol-lae-ui

properly *adv.* 적당히 jeok-dang-hi, 마땅히 ma-ttang-hi

property *n.* 재산 jae-san; 소유물 so-yu-mul; 소유지 so-yu-ji; 소유권 so-yu-kkwon; 고유성 go-yu-sseong, 성질 seong-jil; ~ **tax** 재산세 jae-san-sse

prophecy *n.* 예언 ye-eon; 예언능력 ye-eon-neung-nyeok

proportion *n.* 비율 bi-yul, 비 bi; 균형 gyun-hyeong, 조화 jo-hwa; 몫 mok, 부분 bu-bun

proposal *n.* 신청 sin-cheong; 제안 je-an; 계획 gye-hoek; 결혼신청 gyeol-hon-sin-cheong

propose *vt.* 신청하다 sin-cheong-ha-da; 제안하다 je-an-ha-da; 기도하다 gi-do-ha-da; 추천하다 chu-cheon-ha-da; 청혼하다 cheong-hon-ha-da

proposition *n.* 제안 je-an; 계획 gye-hoek

proprietor *n.* 소유자 so-yu-ja; 경영자 gyeong-yeong-ja

prose *n.* 산문 san-mun; 단조로운 이야기 dan-jo-ro-un i-ya-gi

prospect *n.* 전망 jeon-mang; 예상 ye-sang; 경치 gyeong-chi

prospective *adj.* 예기되는 ye-gi-doe-neun; 장래의 jang-nae-ui

prosper *vi.* 번영하다 beon-yeong-ha-da; 성공하다 seong-gong-ha-da; 잘 되다 jal doe-da

prosperity *n.* 번영 beon-yeong; 성공 seong-gong; 행운 haeng-un

prosperous *adj.* 번영하는 beon-yeong-ha-neun; 성공한 seong-gong-han; 부유한 bu-yu-han; 순소로운 sun-jo-ro-un

prostate *n.* 전립선 jeol-lip-seon

prostitute *n.* 매춘부 mae-chun-bu; *vt.* 몸을 팔다 mom eul pal-da

protect *vt.* 보호하다 bo-ho-ha-da, 지키다 ji-ki-da; 막다 mak-da; 안전장치를 하다 an-jeon-jang-chi-reul ha-da; 주의신호를 내리다 ju-i-sin-ho-reul nae-ri-da

protection *n.* 보호 bo-ho; 후원 hu-won; 두둔 du-dun; 보호장비 bo-ho-jang-bi

protein *n.* 단백질 dan-baek-jil

protest *n.* 항의 hang-ui; 주장 ju-jang; *vt.*, *vi.* 항의하다 hang-ui-ha-da; 주장하다 ju-jang-ha-da

Protestant *n.* 신교도 sin-gyo-do; *adj.* 신교의 sin-gyo-ui; 신교도의 sin-gyo-do-ui; a ~ **church** 개신교교회 gae-sin-gyo-gyo-hoe; a ~ **minister** 개신교 성직자 gae-sin-gyo seong-jik-ja

Protestantism *n.* 신교 sin-gyo; 신교교리 sin-gyo-gyo-ri; 신교도 sin-gyo-do; 신교교회 sin-gyo-gyo-hoe

proud *adj.* 거만한 geo-man-han; 자존심이 있는 ja-jon sim-i in-neun; 자랑으로 여기는 ja-rang-eu-ro yeo-gi-neun; 사랑할 만한 sa-rang-hal-man-han

prove *vt.* 증명하다 jeung-myeong-ha-da; 시험하다 si-heom-ha-da; 검증하다 eom-jeung-ha-da

proverb *n.* 속담 sok-dam; 격언 gyeog-eon

provide *vt.* 준비하다 jun-bi-ha-da; 대비하다 dae-bi-ha-da; 공급하다 gong-geu-pa-da;

규정하다 gyu-jeong-ha-da; ~d that ...을
조건으로 ...eul jo-kkeon-eu-ro; 만약
...(이)면man-yak ...(i-)myeon

provident *adj.* 신중한 sin-jung-han, 선견
지명이 있는 seon-gyeon-ji-myeong-i
in-neun; 검약한 geom-ya-kan

province *n.* 지방 ji-bang; 지역 ji-yeok; 범위
beom-wi; 분야 bun-ya

provoke *vt.* 화나게 하다 hwa-na-ge ha-da;
자극시키다 ja-geuk-si-ki-da

proxy *n.* 대리 dae-ri, 대리투표 dae-ri-tu-pyo,
대리인 dae-ri-in; 위임 wi-im

prudent *adj.* 신중한 sin-jung-han; 세심
한 se-sim-han; 총명한 chong-myeong-
han; 공손한 gong-son-han; 빈틈없는
bin-teum-eom-neun

prune *n.* 자두 ja-du; 짙은 자주색 jit-eun
ja-ju-saek; ~ **juice** 자두주스 ja-du-ju-sseu

psychiatrist *n.* 정신병 의사 jeong-sin-
ppyeong ui-sa; 정신병 학자 jeong-sin-
ppyeong hak-ja

psycho *n.* 정신병자 jeong-sin-ppyeong-ja;
adj. 정신병의 jeong-sin-ppyeong-ui

psychological *adj.* 심리학의 sim-ni-hag-ui;
정신적인 jeong-sin-jeog-in

psychologist *n.* 심리학자 sim-ni-hak-ja

psychology *n.* 심리학 sim-ni-hak; 심리상태
sim-ni-sang-tae; 심리 sim-ni

pub *n.* 술집 sul-jjip; 여인숙 yeo-in-suk

public *adj.* 공중의 gong-jung-ui; 공공의
gong-gong-ui; 공립의 gong-nib-ui; 공개
의 gogn-gae-ui; 공공연한 gong-gong-
yeon-han; 공공적인 gong-gong-jeog-in;
~ **opinion** 여론 yeo-ron; ~ **school** 공립학
교 gong-ni-pak-gyo; ~ **service** 공공사업
gong-gong-sa-eop, 공공기업 gong-gong-
gi-eop; ~ **speaking** 연설 yeon-seol

publication *n.* 발표 bal-pyo; 출판 chul-pan;
출판물 chul-pan-mul; 저서 jeo-seo

publicity *n.* 널리 알려짐 neol-li al-lyeo-jim;
명성 myeong-seong; 평판 pyeong-pan; 선
전 seon-jeon, 광고 gwang-go

publish *vt.* 발표하다 bal-po-ha-da; 공표하다
gong-pyo-ha-da; 출판하다 chul-pan-ha-da

publisher *n.* 출판업자 chul-pan-eop-ja; 발행
자 bal-haeng-ja

pudding *n.* 푸딩 pu-ding

puddle *n.* 웅덩이 ung-deong-i

puff *n.* 훅 불기 huk bul-gi; 담배 한모금
dam-bae han-mo-geum; 퍼프 peo-peu; 부
풀은 것 bu-pul-eun geot; *vt., vi.* 훅 불다
huk bul-da

pull *vt.* 당기다 dang-gi-da; 끌어 당기다
kkeul-eo dang-gi-da; 끌고가다 kkeul-go
ga-da; 떼어놓다 tte-eo-no-ta; 뽑다
ppop-da; *vi.* 잡아당기다 jab-a-dang-gi-da;
배를 젓다 bae-reul jeot-da; 나아가다
na-a-ga-da; 끌리다 kkeul-li-da

pulley *n.* 도르레 do-reu-re

pullover *n.* 풀오버 스웨터 pul-o-beo
seu-we-teo

pulp *n.* 과육 gwa-yuk, 펄프 peol-peu

pulse *n.* 맥박 maek-bak; 의향 ui-hyang; 경향
gyeong-hyang

pump *n.* 펌프 peom-peu; 유도심문 yu-do-
sim-mun; *vt.* 펌프로 푸다eom-peu-ro
pu-da; 퍼내다 peo-nae-da; 퍼붓다 peo-
but-da; 펌프로 공기를 넣다 peom-peu-ro
gong-gi-reul neo-ta; 주입하다 ju-i-pa-da;
짜내다 jja-nae-da

pumpkin *n.* 호박 ho-bak, 귀여운 아이
gwi-yeo-un a-i; 보기 흉한 것 bo-gi-hung-
han geot

punch *n.* 펀치 peon-chi; 타격 ta-gyeok; *vt.*
구멍을 뚫다 gu-meong-eul ttul-ta; 주먹으
로 치다 ju-meog-eu-ro chi-da; 막대기로
찌르다 mak-dae-gi-ro jji-reu-da

punching bag *n.* 펀칭백 peon-ching-baek

punctual *adj.* 시간을 잘 지키는 si-gan-eul
jal ji-ki-neun; 세심한 se-sim-han

punctuate *vt.* 구둣점을 찍다 gu-dut-jeom-
eul jjik-da; 강조하다 gang-jo-ha-da; 중단
시키다 jung-dan-si-ki-da

punctuation *n.* 구둣점 gu-dut-jeom; 구둣법
gu-dut-beop

puncture *n.* 찌르기 jji-reu-gi; 구멍
gu-meong; 빵꾸 ppang-kku; *vt.* 찌르다
jji-reu-da; 구멍을 뚫다 gu-meong-eul
ttul-ta; 빵꾸내다 ppang-kku-nae-da; 망쳐
놓다 mang-cheo-no-ta

punish *vt.* 벌주다 beol-ju-da; 혼내주다
hon-nae-ju-da; 마구먹다 ma-gu-meok-da;
강타하다 gang-ta-ha-da

punishment *n.* 벌 beol, 처벌 cheo-beol; 징
계 jing-gye; 혹사 hok-sa, 학대 hak-dae; 강
타 gang-ta

pupil *n.* *(student)* 학생 hak-saeng; 제자 je-ja; *(of the eye)* 눈동자 nun-ttong-ja, 동공 dong-gong

puppet *n.* 작은 인형 jag-eun in-hyeong; 꼭 두각시 kkok-du-gak-si

puppy *n.* 강아지 gang-a-ji; 건방진 애송이 geon-bang-jin ae-song-i

purchase *n.* 구입 gu-ip; 구입품 gu-i-pum; 획득 hoek-deuk; 매수 mae-su; *vt.* 사다 sa-da; 매수하다 mae-su-ha-da; 획득하다 hoek-deu-ka-da

pure *adj.* 순수한 sun-su han; 깨끗한 kkae kkeu-tan; 청순한 cheong-sun-han; 순결한 sun-gyeol-han; 맑은 malg-eun

purification *n.* 세정 se-jeong; 정화의식 jeong-hwa-ui-sik; **water ~ tablets** 물 세정제 mul se-jeong-je

purify *vt.* 깨끗이하다 kkae-kkeus-i-ha-da; 순 화하다 sun-hwa-ha-da; 정화하다 jeong-hwa-ha-da; 세련하다 se-ryeon-ha-da; 제거하다 je-geo-ha-da

purple *adj.* 자줏빛의 ja-jut-bich-ui

purpose *n.* 목적 mok-jeok; 의지 ui-ji; 용도 yong-do; 요점 yo-jjeom; 취지 chwi-ji; **on ~** 일부러 il-bu-reo; 의도적으로 ui-do-jeog-eu-ro

purse *n.* 지갑 ji-gap; 핸드백 han-deu-baek

pursue *vt.* 뒤쫓다 dwi-jjot-da; 추구하다 chu-gu-ha-da; 속행하다 so-kaeng-ha-da

pus *n.* 고름 go-reum

push *n.* 밀기 mil-gi; 추진 chu-jin; 박력 bang-nyeok; 분발 bun-bal; 추천 chu-cheon, 후원 hu-won; 공격 gong-gyeok; 급박 geup-bak, 위기 wi-gi; *vt.* 밀다 mil-da; 확장 하다 hwak-jang-ha-da; 추구하다 chu-gu-ha-da; 재촉하다 jae-cho-ka-da; 강요하다 gang-yo-ha-da; 뻗다 ppeot-da; 후원하다 hu-won-ha-da, *vi.* 밀다 mil-da, 공격하다 gong-gyeo-ka-da; 노력하다 no-ryeo-ka-da; 나오다 na-o-da

push-up *n.* 팔 굽혀펴기 al-gu-pyeo-pyeo-gi

put *vt.* 놓다 no-ta, 가지고 가다 ga-ji-go ga-da, 붙이다 bu-chi-da; 표현하다 pyo-hyeon-ha-da; *vi.* 전진하다 jeon-jin-ha-da, 흘러가다 heul-leo-ga-da

puzzle *n.* 퍼즐 peo-jeul; 난세 nan-je; 낭 황 dang-hwang; *vt.* 당황하게 하다 dang-hwang-ha-ge ha-da; 머리 아프게 하 다 meo-ri a-peu-ge ha-da; 문제를 풀다 mun-je-reul pul-da

pyramid *n.* 피라미드 pi-ra-mi-deu, 금자탑 geum-ja-tap

Q

quack *n.* 돌팔이의사 dol-pal-i-ui-sa, 가 짜의사 ga-jja-ui-sa *(doctor)*; 사기꾼 sa-gi-kkun; 소음 so-eum; *vi.* 꽥꽥거리다 kkwaek-kkwaek-geo-ri-da; 시끄럽게 떠들 다 si-kkeu-reop-ge tteo-deul-da

quail *n.* 메추라기 me-chu-ra-gi; *vi.* 풀죽다 pul-juk-da, 겁내다 geom-nae-da, 움찔하 다 um-jjil-ha-da

quaint *adj.* 기묘한 gi-myo-han; 색다른 saek-da-reun; 옛스러운 yet-seu-reo-un

quake *vi.* 흔들리다 heun-deul-li-da; 덜덜 떨 다 deol-deol-tteol-da; *n.* 지진 ji-jin; 흔들림 heun-deul-lim

qualification *n.* 자격부여 ja-gyeok-bu-yeo; 자격 ja-gyeok; 자격 증명서 ja-gyeok jeung-myeong-seo; 제한조건 je-han-jo-kkeon

qualified *adj.* 사격이 있는 ja-gyeog-i in-neun; 적당한 jeok-dang-han; 제한된 je-han-doen

qualify *vi.* 자격을 따다 ja-gyeog-eul tta-da; 예선을 통과하다 ye-seon-eul tong-gwa-ha-da; 선서하다 seon-seo-ha-da; **to ~ for** 자격을 얻다 ja-gyeog-eul eot-da

quality *n.* 품질 pum-jil; 성질 seong-jil; 특성 teuk-seong; 양질 yang-jil; 음색 eum-saek

quality control *n.* 품질관리 pum-jil-gwal-li

qualm *n.* 현기증 hyeon-gi-jjeung; 구역질 gu-yeok-jil; 걱정 geok-jeong; 의심 ui-sim; 가책 ga-chaek

quantity *n.* 양 yang, 다수 da-su; 음량 eum-nyang

quarantine *n.* 격리 gyeong-ni; 검역기간 geom-yeok-gi-gwan; 검역소 geom-yeok-so; 절교 jeol-gyo

quarrel *n.* 말다툼 mal-da-tum; 불평 bul-pyeong; 불화 bul-hwa; *vi.* 싸우다 ssa-u-da; 불화하게 되다 bul-hwa-ha-ge doe-da; 불평하다 bul-pyeong-ha-da

quarry *n.* 채석장 chae-seok-jang; 원천 won-cheon; 출처 chul-cheo; 사냥감 sa-nyang-kkam; 추구의 대상 chu-gu-ui dae-sang

quart *n.* 쿼트 kwo-teu; 카드 4장 한패 ka-deu ne-jang han-pae

quarter *n.* 1/4 sa-bun-ui il; 15분 sib-o-bun; 4분기 sa-bun-gi; 25센트 i-sib-o-ssen-teu; 방면 bang-myeon; 지역 ji-yeok; **a ~ of an hour** 15분 sib-o-bun

quarterly *adj.* 연4회의 yeon sa-hoe-ui; 철마다의 cheol-ma-da-ui; 4등분한 sa-deung-bun-han; *adv.* 철마다 cheol-ma-da; *(four times per year)* 연4회 yeon sa-hoe

quartz *n.* 석영 seog-yeong; **~ crystal** 크리스탈 keu-ri-seu-tal, 수정 su-jeong

quasi *adj.* 의사의 ui-sa-ui, 유사한 yu-sa-han

queasy *adj.* 느글거리는 neu-geu-geo-ri-neun; 역겨운 yeok-gyeo-un; 불안한 bul-an-han; 소심한 so-sim-han; 불쾌한 bul-kwae-han; 까다롭게 구는 kka-da-rop-ge gu-neun

queen *n.* 여왕 yeo-wang; 왕비 wang-bi; 여신 yeo-sin; 연인 yeon-in; 퀸 kwin; **~ size** 퀸사이즈 kwin-ssa-i-jeu

queen mother *n.* 황태후 hwang-tae-hu, 대비 dae-bi

queer *adj.* 이상한 i-sang-han; 기묘한 gi-myo-han; 수상한 su-sang-han; 어지러운 eo-ji-reo-un; 머리가 돈 meo-ri-ga don

query *n.* 질문 jil-mun; 의문 ui-mun; 물음표 mul-eum-pyo; *vt.* 질문하다 jil-mun-ha-da; 캐어묻다 kae-eo-mut-da

quest *n.* 탐색 tam-saek, 추구 chu-gu

question *n.* 질문 jil-mun; 의문 ui-mun; 문제 mun-je; *vt.* 묻다 mut-da; 신문하다 sin-mun-ha-da; 의문으로 여기다 ui-mun-eu-ro yeo-gi-da

question mark *n.* 물음표 mul-eum-pyo

questionnaire *n.* 질문사항 jil-mun-sa-hang, 설문조사 seol-mun-jo-sa, 앙케이트 ang-ke-i-teu

queue *n.* 땋아늘인 머리 tta-a-neul-in meo-ri; 열 yeol; 꼬리 kko-ri

quick *adj.* 빠른 ppa-reun; 민감한 min-gam-han; 영리한 yeong-ni-han; 성미 급한 seong-mi-geu-pan; 눈치빠른 nun-chi-ppa-reun

quickly *adv.* 빨리 pal-li, 급히 geu-pi

quickstep *n.* 속보 sok-bo, 빠른걸음 ppa-reun-geol-eum

quiet *n.* 고요 go-yo; 평정 pyeong-jeong; *adj.* 조용한 jo-yong-han; 정숙한 jeong-su-kan; 온화한 on-hwa-han; 숨겨진 sum-gyeo-jin; 수수한 su-su-han; 한산한 han-san-han

quilt *n.* 누비이불 nu-bi-i-bul, 퀼트 qil-teu

quit *vi.* 그만두다 geu-man-du-da; 떠나다 tteo-na-da; 버리고 가다 beo-ri-go ga-da; 빚을 갚다 bij-eul gap-da

quite *adv.* 완전히 wan-jeon-hi; 아주 a-ju; 확실히 hwak-sil-hi; 사실상 sa-sil-ssang

quiz *n.* 퀴즈 kwi-jeu; 질문 jil-mun; 놀림 nol-lim; *vt.* 질문하다 jil-mun-ha-da; 놀리다 nol-li-da; 빤히 보다 ppan-hi-bo-da; **~ show** 퀴즈프로 kwi-jeu-peu-ro

quota *n.* 몫 mok; 할당 hal-ttang; 분담액 bun-dam-aek

quotation *n.* 인용 in-yong; 인용구 in-yong-kku; 시세 si-se; 가격표 ga-gyeok-pyo; **~ mark** 인용부호 in-yong-bu-ho

quote *n.* 인용구 in-yong-kku; 인용부호 in-yong-bu-ho; *vt.* 인용하다 in-yong-ha-da; 예시하다 ye-si-ha-da; 시세를 부르다 si-se-reul bu-reu-da; 인용부호를 두르다 in-yong-bu-ho-reul du-reu-da; **stock (market) ~** 주식시장 시세 ju-sik-si-jang-si-se

R

rabbit *n.* 집토끼 jip-to-kki; 토끼 to-kki; 연한 갈색 yeon-han-gal-ssaek

rabies *n.* 광견병 gwang-gyeon-ppyeong, 공수병 gong-su-ppyeong; ~ **shot** 광견병 예방주사 gwang-gyeon-ppyeong ye-bang-ju-sa

race *n.* 경주 gyeong-ju, 레이스 re-i-sseu; 경마 gyeong-ma; 경쟁 gyeong-jaeng; 생애 saeng-ae; 시간의 경과 si-gan-ui gyeong gwa, 급류 geum-ryu, 인종 in-jong; 민족 min-jok; 혈통 hyeol-tong; 종족 jong-jok; **auto** ~ 자동차 경주 ja-dong-cha gyeong-ju; ~**track** 경주장 gyeong-ju-jang; **the human** ~ 인종 in-jong; ~**horse** 경주마 gyeong-ju-ma

racial *adj.* 인종의 in-jong-ui; 종족의 jong-jog-ui

rack *n.* 선반 seon-ban; 분류상사 bul-lyu-sang-ja; 조각구름 jo-gak-gu-reum; 겨보 gyeong-bo; 파괴 pa-goe; 황폐 hwang-pye; *vt.* 고문하다 go-mun-ha-da, 괴롭히다 goe-ro-pi-da, 착취하다 chak-chwi-ha-da

racket *n.* 라켓 ra-ket, 채 chae; 야단법석 ya-dan-beop-seok, 소음 so-eum; 시련 si-ryeon; 사기 sa-gi; **tennis** ~ 테니스 라켓 te-ni-sseu ra-ket; *(noise, uproar)* **to raise a** ~ 소음이 더 심해지다 so-eum-i deo sim-hae-ji-da; *(scheme)* **They have a** ~ **going** 사람들은 흥청망청 놀고 있습니다 geu sa-ram-deul-eun heung-cheong-mang-cheong nol-go iss-eum-ni-da

radar *n.* 레이더 re-i-deo; 전파탐지기 jeon-pa-tam-ji-gi

radial *adj.* 광선의 gwang-seon-ui, 방사상의 bang-sa-sang-ui

radiator *n.* 라디에이터 ra-di-e-i-teo, 냉각장치 naeng-gak-jang-chi

radical *adj.* 근본적인 geun-bon-jeog-in; 급진적인 geup-jin-jeog-in

radio *n.* 라디오 ra-di-o; 무선통화 mu-seon-tong-hwa

radioactive *adj.* 방사성의 bang-sa-sseong-ui; 방사능의 bang-sa-neung-ui; ~ **waste** 방사선 bang-sa-seon

radish *n.* 무우 mu-u

radius *n.* 반경 ban-gyeong; 범위 beom-wi; **within a** ~ **of** … 의 반경안에 … ui ban-gyeong-an-e

raffle *n.* 제비뽑기 je-bi-ppop-gi, 추첨 chu-cheom; 추첨판매 chu-cheom-pan-mae; 잡동사니 jap-dong-sa-ni; *vt.* 제비를 뽑다 je-bi-reul ppop-da, 추첨하다 chu-cheom-ha-da; 추첨식으로 팔다 chu-cheom-sig-eu-ro pal-da

raft *n.* 뗏목 tten-mok; 부유물 bu-yu-mul; 부교 bu-gyo; 다수 da-su

rag *n.* 넝마 neong-ma; 누더기옷 nu-deo-gi-ot; 속지 sok-ji; 석회암 seo-koe-am

rage *n.* 격노 gyeong-no; 격정 gyeok-jeong; 사나움 sa-na-um; 대유행 dae-yu-haeng

ragged *adj.* 누덕누덕한 nu-deok-nu-deo-kan; 텁수룩한 teop-su-ru-kan; 거친 geo-chin; 울퉁불퉁한 ul-tung-bul-tung-han; 기진맥진한 gi-jin-maek-jin-han

raid *n.* 습격 seup-gyeok; 수색 su-saek; 투매 tu-mae; *vt.* 급습하다 geup-seu-pa-da; 수색하다 su-sae-ka-da; 어지럽히다 eo-ji-reo-pi-da

rail *n.* 가로대 ga-ro-dae; 난간 nan-gan; 레일 re-il; 철도 cheol-tto

railing *n.* 난간 nan-gan; 난간재료 nan-gan-jae-ryo

railroad *n.* 철도 cheol-tto; 궤도 gwe-do

railway *n.* 철도 cheol-tto; ~ **line** 철도 cheol-lo, 철도노선 cheol-tto-no-seon

rain *n.* 비 bi; 소나기 so-na-gi; 장마 jang-ma; *vi.* 비가 오다 bi-ga o-da; 비오듯 쏟아지다 bi-o-deut ssod-a-ji-da; 비를 내리다 bi-reul nae-ri-da; **It looks like** ~ 비가 올 것 같습니다 bi-ga ol-kkeot gat-seum-ni-da; ~**coat** 비옷 bi-ot; ~**drop** 빗방울 bit-bang-ul; ~**storm** 폭풍우 pok-pung-u; ~ **check** 레인체크 re-in-che-keu, 물품제공 보증권 mul-pum-je-gong bo-jeung-kkwon; **It is ~ing** 비가 옵니다 bi-ga om-ni-da

rainbow *n.* 무지개 mu-ji-gae

rain cloud *n.* 비구름 bi-gu-reum

rainfall *n.* 강우 gang-u, 강수량 gang-su-ryang

rainy *adj.* 비오는 bi-o-neun; 비올듯한 bi-ol-tteu-tan; 비에 젖은 bi-e jeoj-eun

raise *vt.* 올리다 ol-li-da; 끌어올리다 kkeul-eo-ol-li-da; 일으켜 세우다 il-eu-kyeo se-u-da; 승진시키다 seung-jin-si-ki-da; 불러 일으키다 bul-leo il-eu-ki-da; 세우다 se-u-da; 기르다 gi-reu-da; 모금하다 mo-geum-ha-da; **to ~ standards** 기준을 강화하다 gi-jun-eul gang-hwa-ha-da; **to ~ salaries** 월급을 올리다 wol-geub-eul ol-li-da; **to ~ a family** 가족을 돌보다 ga-jog-eul dol-bo-da; **I was ~d in England** 저는 영국에서 자랐습니다 jeo-neun yeong-gug-e-seo ja-rat-seum-ni-da; **They ~ horses and/or sheep** 그 사람들은 말이나 양같은 것들을 기릅니다 geu sa-ram-deul-eun mal-i-na yang-gat-eun geot-deul-eul gi-reum-ni-da

raisin *n.* 건포도 geon-po-do

rake *n.* 갈퀴 gal-kwi; 부지깽이 bu-ji-kkaeng-i; 방탕자 bang-tang-ja; *vt.* 갈퀴로 긁다 gal-kwi-ro jeuk-da; 샅샅이 찾아보다 sat-sa-chi chaj-a-bo-da; 들추어 밝히다 deul-chu-eo bal-ki-da; 죽 훑어보다 jjuk hult-eo-bo-da; 방탕하다 bang-tang-ha-da

rally *n.* 집결 jip-gyeol, 모임 mo-im; 회복 hoe-bok; 복구 bok-gu; 연달아 쳐 넘기기 yeon-dal-a cheo neom-gi-da; *vt.* 다시 모으다 da-si mo-eu-da; 불러 모으다 bul-leo mo-eu-da; 집중시키다 jip-jung-si-ki-da; *vi.* 다시 모이다 da-si mo-i-da; 참가하다 cham-ga-ha-da; 회복하다 hoe-bo-ka-da; 시세를 회복하다 si-se-reul hoe-bo-ka-da; 공을 연속해 쳐서 넘기다 gong-eul yeon-so-kae cheo neom-gi-da

ram *n.* 숫양 sun-nyang; 램 ram; *vt.* 때려박다 ttae-ryeo-bak-da; 쑤셔박다 ssu-syeo-bak-da

ramble *vi.* 거닐다 geo-nil-da; 만연히 이야기하다 man-yeon-hi i-ya-gi-ha-da; 덩굴이 퍼지다 deong-gul-I peo-ji-da; 굽이치다 gub-i-chi-da

ramification *n.* 나뭇가지 na-mut-ga-ji; 분지법 bun-ji-ppeop; 분파 bun-pa; 결과 gyeol-gwa

ramp *n.* 경사로 gyeong-sa-ro; 비탈길 bi-tal-kkil; 사기 sa-gi; 폭리 pong-ni

ranch *n.* 대목장 dae-mok-jang; 농장 nong-jang

rancid *adj.* 썩은 냄새가 나는 sseog-eun name-sae-ga na-neun; 불쾌한 bul-kwae-han; 썩은 sseog-eun

random *adj.* 엉터리의 eong-teo-ri-ui; 되는대로의 doe-neun-dae-ro-ui; 임의의 im-i-ui; 일정치 않은 il-jjeong-chi an-eun; **~ access memory** 임의추출 기억장치 im-i-chu-chul gi-eok-jang-chi; **~ sampling** 임의추출법 im-i-chu-chul-ppeop

range *n.* 열 yeol; 줄 jul; 산맥 san-maek; 목장 mok-jang; 분포구역 bun-po-gu-yeok; 범위 beom-wi; 레인지 re-in-ji; **electric ~** 전자 레인지 jeon-ja-re-in-ji; **a ~ of options** 선택의 범위 seon-taeg-ui beom-wi; *(camera)* **~ finder** 사진용 거리계 sa-jin-nyong geo-ri-ge; **mountain ~** 산맥 san-maek

ranger *n.* 방랑자 bang-nang-ja; 산림 경비대 sal-lim gyeong-bi-dae

rank *n.* 열 yeol; 계급 gye-geup; 지위 ji-wi; 가로줄 ga-ro-jul; *vt.* 나란히 세우다 na-ran-hi se-u-da; 위치를 정하다 wi-chi-reul jeong-ha-da; 등급짓다 deung-geup-jit-da; 평가하다 pyeong-kka-ha-da

ranking *n.* 순위 sun-wi, 등급을 매김 deung-geub-eul mae-gim

ransack *vt.* 샅샅이 찾다 sat-sa-chi chat-da; 찾아 돌아다니다 chaj-a dol-a-da-ni-da; 약탈하다 yak-tal-ha-da

ransom *n.* 몸값 mom-kkap, 배상금 bae-sang-geum; 속전 sok-jeon; 공갈 gong-gal, 협박 hyeop-bak; *vt.* 몸값을 치르고 되찾다 mom-kkaps-eul chi-reu-go doe-chat-da; 몸값을 받고 석방하다 mom-kkaps-eul bat-go seok-bang-ha-da

rape *n.* 강탈 gang-tal; 강간 gang-gan; *vt.* 강탈하다 gang-tal-ha-da; 강간하다 gang-gan-ha-da

rapid *adj.* 빠른 ppa-reun; 조급한 jo-geu-pan; 서두르는 seo-du-reu-neun; 가파른 ga-pa-reun

rap music *n.* 랩뮤직 raem-nyu-jik

rare *adj.* 드문 deu-mun, 진기한 jin-gi-han; 유례없는 yu-re-eom-neun; 희박한 hi-ba-kan; 어이없는 eo-i-eom-neun; 덜 구워진 deol gu-wo-jin, 설익은 seol-ig-eun

rarely *adv.* 드물게 deu-mul-ge, 좀처럼 jom-cheo-reom

rash *n.* 발진 bal-jjin; 뾰루지 ppyo-ru-ji; *adj.* 분별없는 bun-byeol-eom-neun; 경솔한 gyeong-sol-han; **heat ~** 열꽃 yeol-kkot; **a ~ of burglaries** 가는 곳마다 벌어지는 강도사건 ga-neun gon-ma-da beol-eo-ji-neun gang-do-sa-kkeon

raspberry *n.* 산딸기 san-ttal-gi, 레스베리 re-seu-be-ri

rat *n.* 쥐 jwi; 변절자 byeon-jeol-jja; **~ race** 과당경쟁 gwa-dang-gyeong-jaeng; **~ trap** 쥐덫 jwi-deot; 절망적인 상황 jeol-mang-jeog-in sang-hwang, 낙국 nan-guk

rate *n.* 비율 bi-yul; 가격 ga-gyeok; 요금 yo-geum; 속도 sok-do; 등급 deung-geup; **at any ~** 하여튼 ha-yeo-teun, 여하간 yeo-ha-gan; 적어도 jeog-eo-do; **exchange ~** 환율 hwan-nyul; **at a ~ of X euros to the dollar** 달러당 x유로의 비율로 dal-leo-dang ek-sseu-yu-ro-ui bi-yul-lo; **~ of speed** 속도비 sok-do-bi

rather *adv.* 오히려 o-hi-ryeo; 보다 정확히 말하자면 bo-da jeong-mil-hi mal-ha-ja-myeon; 그렇고 말고 geu-reo-ko mal-go; 물론 mul-lon

ratification *n.* 비준 bi-jun, 재가 jae-ga; 실증 sil-jjeung, 확증 hawk-jjeung

ratify *vt.* 비준하다 bi-jun-ha-da, 재가하다 jae-ga-ha-da; 확증하다 hawk-jeung-ha-da, 실증하다 sil-jjeung-ha-da

ratio *n.* 비 bi, 비율 bi-yul

ration *n.* 정액 jeong-aek, 정량 jeong-nyang; 배급량 bae-geum-nyang, 할낭량 hal-ttang-nyang; *vt.* 배급하다 bae-geu-pa-da; 급식하다 geup-si-ka-da; 소비를 제한하다 so-bi-reul je-han-ha-da

rational *adj.* 이성이 있는 i-seong-i in-neun; 이성적인 i-seong-jeog-in; 합리적인 ham-ni-jeog-in; 온당한 on-dang-han

rattan *n.* 등나무 deung-na-mu; 등나무 줄기 deung-na-mu Jul-gi

rattle *vi.* 덜컥거리다 deol-keok-geo-ri-da, 덜컥 움직이다 deol-keok um-jig-i-da; *n.* 딸랑이 ttal-lang-i

ravine *n.* 협곡 hyeop-gok; 계곡 gye-gok, 산골짜기 san-kkol-jja-gi

raw *adj.* 날것의 nal-geos-ui; 가공하지 않은 ga-gong-ha-ji an-eun; 무경험의 mu-gyeong-heom-ui; 얼얼한 eol-eol-han;

으스스 추운 eu-seu-seu chu-un; 원색의 won-saeg-ui; 노골적인 no-gol-jjeog-in; **~ material** 원료 wol-lyo, 소재 so-jae

ray *n.* 광선 gwang-seon; 번득임 beon-deug-im; 가오리 ga-o-ri

razor *n.* 면도칼 myeon-do-kal; 전기 면도기 jeon-gi myeon-do-gi; **~ blade** 안전 면도날 an-jeon-myeon-don-nal

reach *n.* 손을 내뻗침 son-eul nae-ppeot-chim; 발돋움 bal-dod-um; 손발이 닿는 범위 son-bal-i dan-neun beom-wi; 유효범위 yu-hyo-beom-wi; *vt.* 도착하다 do-cha-ka-da, 도달하다 do-dal-ha-da; 마음을 움직이다 ma-eum-eul um-jig-i-da; 뻗치다 ppeot-chi-da, 내밀다 nae-mil-da; 건네주다 geon-nae-ju-da; **to ~ a destination** 목적지에 다다르다 mok-jeok-ji-e da-da-reu-da; **to ~ a person** 어떤 사람에게 연락이 닿다 eo-tteon sa-ram-e-ge yeol-lag-i dat-da; **within ~** 가까이에 ga-kka-i-e

react *vi.* 반작용하다 ban-jag-yong-ha-da; 반대하다 ban-dae-ha-da; 반응을 나타내나 ban-eung-eul na-ta-nae-da; 되돌아가다 doe-dol-a-ga-da

reaction *n.* 반응 ban-eung; 반작용 ban-jag-yong; 반동 ban-dong; 복고 bok-go; **his ~** 그분의 반응 geu-bun-ui ban-eung; **chemical ~** 화학반응 hwa-hak-ban-eung; **chain ~** 연쇄작용 yeon-swae-jag-yong

read *vt.* 읽다 ik-da; 읽어주다 ilg-eo-ju-da; 판독하다 pan-do-ka-da; 해독하다 hae-do-ka-da; 해석하다 hae-seo-ka-da; 표시하다 pyo-si-ha-da; 읽어서 알다 ilg-eo-seo al-da

reader *n.* 독자 dok-ja; 독서가 dok-seo-ga; 독본 dok-bon; 교정원 gyo-jeong-won; 낭독자 nang-dok-ja

reading *n.* 독시 dok-seo; 학식 hak-sik; 낭독회 nang-do-koe; 읽을거리 ilg-eul kkeo-ri; **a poetry ~** 시낭송회 si-nang-song-hoe; **~ lamp** 독서용 스탠드 dok-seo-yong seu-ten-deu; **~ glasses** 확대경, 독서용 안경 dok-seo-yong an-gyeong; **~ room** 도서 열람실 do-seo yeol-lam-sil, 독서실 dok-seo-sil

ready *adj.* 준비가 된 jun-bi-ga doen; ...금방 ...을 것 같은 ...geum-bang ...eul kkeot gat-eun; 재빠른 jae-ppa-reun; 즉시 쓸 수 있는 jeuk-si sseul ssu in-neun

ready-made *adj.* 기성품의 gi-seong-pum-ui; 개성이 없는 gae-seong-i eom-neun; *n.* 기성품 gi-seong-pum

real *adj.* 진실의 jin-sil-ui, 진짜의 jin-jja-ui; 현실의 hyeon-sil-ui, 실제의 sil-jje-ui; 부동산의 bu-dong-san-ui; ~ **estate** 부동산 bu-dong-san; ~ **life** 실생활 sil-ssaeng-hwal; ~ **time** 실시간의 sil-ssi-gan-ui

realistic *adj.* 현실적인 hyeon-sil-jjeog-in, 현실주의의 hyeon-sil-ju-i-ui; 사실주의의 sa-sil-ji-ui

reality *n.* 진실 jin-sil; 사실 sa-sil; 현실 hyeon-sil; 실재 sil-jjae; 실물 그대로 sil-mul geu-dae-ro

realize *vt.* 실현하다 sil-hyeon-ha-da; 여실히 보이다 yeo-sil-hi bo-i-da; 실감하다 sil-gam-ha-da; 얻다 eot-da, 벌다 beol-da; 현금으로 바꾸다 hyeon-geum-eu-ro ba-kku-da

really *adv.* 실제로 sil-jje-ro, 정말로 jeong-mal-lo

realm *n.* 왕국 wang-guk; 범위 beom-wi, 영역 yeong-yeok

realtor *n.* 부동산업자 bu-dong-san-eop-ja

ream *n.* 연 yeon; **a ~ of paper** 종이 한연 jong-i han-nyeon; 다량의 종이 da-ryang-ui jong-i

reap *vt.* 수확하다 su-hwa-ka-da, 거둬들이다 geo-dwo-deul-i-da; 획득하다 hoek-deu-ka-da

reappear *vi.* 다시 나타나다 da-si na-ta-na-da; 재발하다 jae-bal-ha-da

rear *n.* 뒤 dwi; 후미 hu-mi; 배후 bae-hu; *adj.* 뒤의 dwi-ui; 뒤에 있는 dwi-e in-neun; **~view mirror** 백미러 ppaeng-mi-reo

rearward *adj.* 후미의 hu-mi-ui, 제일 뒤의 je-il dwi-ui; *adv.* 후방에 h-bang-ui, 배후에 bae-hu-e

reason *n.* 이유 i-yu; 도리 do-ri; 이성 i-seong; 본정신 bon-jeong-sin; *vi.* 추론하다 chu-ron-ha-da; 설득하다 seol-tteu-ka-da; **the ~ for sth.** 어떤것에 대한 이유 eo-tteon geos-e dae-han i-yu; **the ability to ~** 설득할 수 있는 능력 seol-tteu-kal ssu in-neun neung-nyeok

reasonable *adj.* 분별있는 bun-byeol-in-neun; 이치에 맞는 i-chi-e man-neun; 온

당한 on-dang-han; 비싸지 않은 bi-ssa-ji an-eun

reassure *vt.* 재보증하다 jae-bo-jeung-ha-da; 안심시키다 an-sim-si-ki-da

rebate *n.* 환불 hwan-bul; 리베이트 ri-be-i-teu; 어음할인 eo-eum-hal-in

rebel *n.* 반역자 ban-yeok-ja; 배반자 bae-ban-ja; *vi.* 배반하다 bae-ban-ha-da; 반항하다 ban-hang-ha-da; 조화하지 못하다 jo-hwa-ha-ji mo-ta-da; 소름끼치다 so-reum-kki-chi-da

rebellion *n.* 모반 mo-ban; 반란 bal-lan; 폭동 pok-dong; 반항 ban-hang; 배반 bae-ban

rebound *vi.* 되튀다 doe-twi-da; 되돌아오다 doe-dol-a-o-da; 다시 일어서다 da-si il-eo-seo-da

rebuff *vt.* 딱잘라 거절하다 ttak-jal-la geo-jeol-ha-da; 저지하다 jeo-ji-ha-da

rebuild *vt.* 재건하다 jae-geon-ha-da, 개조하다 gae-jo-ha-da

recall *vt.* 생각해내다 saeng-ga-kae-nae-da; 기억을 불러 일으키다 gi-eog-eul bul-leo il-eu-ki-da; 소환하다 so-hwan-ha-da; 리콜하다 ri-kol-ha-da; 취소하다 chwi-so-ha-da; 되살아나게 하다 doe-sal-a-na-ge ha-da

receipt *n.* 수취 su-chwi, 수령 su-ryeong; 영수증 yeong-su-jeung; 수령액 su-ryeong-aek

receive *vt.* 받다 bat-da; 들어주다 deul-eo-ju-da; 인정하다 in-jeong-ha-da; 받치다 bat-chi-da; 맞이하다 maj-i-ha-da; 수용하다 su-yong-ha-da

receiver *n.* 수취인 su-chwi-in; 수상기 su-sang-gi; *(radio)* 수신기 su-sin-gi; *(telephone)* 수화기 su-hwa-gi

recent *adj.* 최근의 choe-geun-ui; 새로운 sae-ro-un

recently *adv.* 최근 choe-geun; 얼마전에 eol-ma-jeon-e

reception *n.* 받아들임 bad-a-deul-im; 응접 eung-jeop; 환영회 hwan-yeong-hoe; 가입 ga-ip; 반응 ban-eung; 시인 si-in; 이해력 i-hae-ryeok: ~ **desk** 접수처 jeop-su-cheo, 프런트 데스크 peu-reon-teu de-seu-keu; ~ **room** 응접실 eung-jeop-sil; 대합실 dae-hap-sil

receptionist *n.* 접수원 jeop-su-won

recess *n.* 휴게 hyu-ge, 휴회 hyu-hoe; 휴가 hyu-ga; 후미진 곳 hu-mi-jin got

recession *n.* 후퇴 hu-toe; 불경기 bul-gyeong-gi

recharge *n.* 재충전 jae-chung-jeon; 재습격 jae-seup-gyeok

recipe *n.* 처방 cheo-bang; 조리법 jo-ri-ppeop; 비결 bi-gyeol

recipient *n.* 수령인 su-ryeong-in

reciprocity *n.* 상호성 sang-ho-sseong; 상호관계 sang-ho-gwan-gye; 상호이익 sang-ho-i-ik, 교환 gyo-hwan

recital *n.* 리사이틀 ri-ssa-i-teul, 독주회 dok-ju-hoe, 독창회 dok-chang-hoe; 낭독회 nang-do-koe

recite *vt.* 암송하다 am-song-ha-da; 낭송하다 nang-song-ha-da; 이야기하다 i-ya-gi-ha-da

reckon *vt.* 세다 se-da; 간주하다 gan-ju-ha-da; 셈하다 sem-ha-da; 생각하다 saeng-ga-ka-da

reclamation *n.* 교정 gyo-jeong; 길들임 gil-deul-im; 교화 gyo-hwa; 개척 gae-cheok; 개간 gae-gan; 재생이용 jae-saeng-i-yong

recline *vt.* 기대게 하다 gi-dae-ge ha-da, 눕히다 nu-pi-da; *vi.* 기대다 gi-dae-da, 눕다 nup-da

reclining chair *n.* 안락의자 al-lag-ui-ja

recognition *n.* 인시 in-ji; 승인 seung-in; 인정 in-jeong; 감사 gam-sa; 인식 in-sik

recognize *vt.* 알아보다 al-a-bo-da; 인정하다 in-jeong-ha-da; 감사하나 gam-sa-ha-da; 승인하다 seung-in-ha-da

recollect *vt.* 회상하다 hoe-sang-ha-da; 다시 모으다 da-si mo-eu-da, 진정시키다 jin-jeong-si-ki-da; *vi.* 기억나다 gi-eong-na-da

recollection *n.* 회상 hoe-sang, 기억 gi-eok, 기억력 gi-eong-nyeok

recommend *vt.* 추천하다 chu-cheon-ha-da; 충고하다 chung-go-ha-da; 위탁하다 wi-ta-ka-da

recommendation *n.* 추천 chu-cheon; 추천서 chu-cheon-seo; 충고 chung-go; 장점 jang-jjeom

recompense *n.* 보수 bo-su; 보상 bo-sang; 배상 bae-sang; *vt.* 보답하다 bo-da-pa-da; 보상하다 bo-sang-ha-da

reconcile *vt.* 화해시키다 hwa-hae-si-ki-da; 조화시키다 jo-hwa-si-ki-da; 만족하게 하다 man-jo-ka-ge ha-da; 단념하게 하다 dan-nyeom-ha-ge ha-da

reconciliation *n.* 조정 jo-jeong; 화해 hwa-hae; 복종 bok-jong; 단념 dan-nyeom; 조화 jo-hwa; 일치 il-chi

reconsider *vt.* 재고하다 jae-go-ha-da

reconstruct *vt.* 재건하다 jae-geon-ha-da; 개조하다 gae-jo-ha-da; 재현하다 jae-hyeon-ha-da; 재구성하다 jae-gu-seong-ha-da

record *n.* 기록문서 gi-rong-mun-seo; 경력 gyeong-nyeok; 경기기록 gyeong-gi-gi-rok; ~ **of information** 기록 gi-rok, 정보 jeong-bo; **music** ~ 레코드 re-ko-deu; ~ **breaker** 기록 경신자 gi-rok gyeong-sin-ja; ~ **breaking** 기록을 경신함 gi-rog-eul gyeong-sin-ham; *vt.* 기록하다 gi-ro-ka-da; 녹음하다 nog-eum-ha-da; 표시하다 pyo-si-ha-da; 표시되다 pyo-si-doe-da; 기록문서 gi-rong-mun-seo

recording *n.* 녹음 nog-eum, 녹화 no-kwa; 녹음된 것 nog-eum-doen geot, 녹화된 것 no-kwa-doen geot

recover *vi.* 원상태로 되다 won-sang-tae-ro doe-da; 회복하다 hoe-bo-ka-da; 복구하다 bok-gu-ha-da; ~**y room** 회복실 hoe-bok-sil

recreation *n.* 레크리에이션 re-keu-ri-e-i-syeon; 휴양 hyu-yang; ~ **center** 레크리에이션 센터 re-keu-ri-e-i-syeon ssen-teo

recruit *n.* 보충병 bo-chung-byeong; 신병 sin-byeong; 신참자 sin-cham-ja; 초심자 cho-sim-ja; *vt.* 새회원을 모집하다 sae-hoe-won-eul mo-ji-pa-da; 보강하다 bo-gang-ha-da; 보충하다 bo-chung-ha-da

rectangle *n.* 직사각형 jik-sa-ga-kyeong

rectangular *adj.* 직사각형의 jik-sa-ga-kyeong-ui; 직각의 jik-gag-ui

recuperate *vi.* 회복하다 hoe-bo-ka-da; 만회하나 man-hoe-ha-da

recurrence *n.* 재기 jae-gi; 재현 jae-hyeon; 재발 jae-bal; 반복 ban-bok; 순환 sun-hwan; 회상 hoe-sang; 추억 chu-eok

recurring *adj.* 되풀이하여 일어나는 doe-pul-i-ha-yeo il-eo-na-neun; 순환하는 sun-hwan-ha-neun

recycle *vt.* 재생하여 이용하다 jae-sang-ha-yeo i-yong-ha-da, 리사이클

하다 ri-ssa-i-keul-ha-da, 재활용하다
jae-hwal-yong-ha-da

recycling *n.* 재생이용 jae-saeng-i-yong, 재활
용 jae-hwal-yong, 리사이클 ri-ssa-i-keul

red *adj.* 빨간 ppal-gan, 붉은 bulg-eun; 피에
물든 pi-e mul-deun; 잔학한 jan-ha-kan;
공산주의의 gong-san-ju-i-ui; ~ **alert** 공
습경보 gong-seup-gyeong-bo; ~ **blood
cell** 적혈구 jeok-hyeol-gu; ~ **light** 적신호
jeok-sin-ho; ~ **pepper** 붉은 고추 bulg-eun
go-chu

Red Cross *n.* 적십자사 jeok-sip-ja-sa

redeem *vt.* 되사다 doe-sa-da, 되찾다
doe-chat-da

redness *n.* 붉음 bulg-eum; 적색 jeok-saek; 불
그레함 bul-geu-re-ham

Red Sea *n.* 홍해 hong-hae

reduce *vt.* 축소하다 chuk-so-ha-da; 격하시
키다 gyeo-ka-si-ki-da; 떨어뜨리다 tteol-
eo-tteu-ri-da; 쇠약하게 하다 soe-ya-ka-ge
ha-da; 진압하다 jin-a-pa-da; 간단히 하다
gan-dan-hi ha-da; 할인하다 hal-in-ha-da

reduction *n.* 감소 gam-so; 절감 jeol-gam; 할
인 hal-in; 환원 hwan-won; 영락 yeong-
nak; 정복 jeong-bok; 진압 jin-ap; 분류
bul-lyu

redundant *adj.* 여분의 yeo-bun-ui; 장황한
jang-hwang-han; 잉여의 ing-yeo-ui

reed *n.* 갈대 gal-ttae; 갈대밭 gal-ttae-bat; 리
드 ri-deu

reef *n.* 암초 am-cho; 광맥 gwang-maek

reel *n.* 릴 ril; 얼레 eol-le; 물레 mul-le;
비틀걸음 bi-teul-geol-eum; 현기증
hyeon-gi-jjeung

refer *vt.* 위탁하다 wi-ta-ka-da; 돌리다 dol-li-da

referee *n.* 심판원 sim-pan-won, 레퍼리
re-peo-ri

reference *n.* 문의 mun-ui; 신용조회처
sin-yong-jo-hoe-cheo; 신용조회장 sin-
yong-jo-hoe-jjang; 참조 cham-jo; 참고문
cham-go-mun; 언급 eon-geup; 관련 gwal-
lyeon; **in ~ to** ...에 관하여 ...e gwan-ha-
yeo; ~ **book** 참고서적 cham-go-seo-jeok;
personal ~s 참고인 cham-go-in, **letter of
~** 신용조회서 sin-yong-jo-hoe-seo, 신원
증명서 sin-won-jeung-myeong-seo

refill *vt.* 다시 채우다 da-si chae-u-da; 보충
하다 bo-chung-ha-da

refine *vt.* 정제하다 jeong-je-ha-da; 세련하다
se-ryeon-ha-da; 품위있게 하다 pum-wi-
it-ge ha-da

refinery *n.* 정제소 jeong-je-so; 정제시설
jeong-je-si-seol

refit *vt.* 수리하다 su-ri-ha-da; 재장비하다
jae-jang-bi-ha-da

reflect *vi. vt.* 반사하다 ban-sa-ha-da; 반영하
다 ban-yeong-ha-da; 반성하다 ban-seong-
ha-da; 초래하다 cho-rae-ha-da

reflector *n.* 반사기 ban-sa-gi; 반사물 ban-sa-
mul; 반사경 ban-sa-gyeong

reform *vi.* 개혁하다 gae-hyeo-ka-da;
수습하다 su-seu-pa-da; 교정하다
gyo-jeong-ha-da

refresh *vt.* 상쾌하게 하다 sang-kwae-ha-ge
ha-da; 맑게하다 mal-kke-ha-da; 새롭게
하다 sae-rop-ge ha-da; 새로 공급하다
sae-ro gong-geu-pa-da

refreshment *n.* 원기회복 won-gi-hoe-bok;
다과 da-gwa

refrigerate *vt.* 냉각하다 naeng-ga-ka-da;
냉장하다 naeng-jang-ha-da; 차게하다
cha-ge-ha-da

refrigerator *n.* 냉장고 naeng-jang-go; 냉장
장치 naeng-jang-jang-chi

refuge *n.* 피난 pi-nan; 피난처 pi-nan-cheo;
위안물 wi-an-mul; 도피구 do-pi-gu

refugee *n.* 피난민 pi-nan-min; 망명자 mang-
myeong-ja; 도피자 do-pi-ja; ~ **camp** 피난
민촌 pi-nan-min-chon; ~ **status** 망명자 신
분 mang-myeong-ja sin-bun

refund *n.* 반환 ban-hwan; 상환 sang-hwan;
vt. 반환하다 ban-hwan-ha-da; 상환하다
sang-hwan-ha-da

refusal *n.* 거절 geo-jeol; 거부 geo-bu; 사
퇴 sa-toe

refuse *n.* 폐물 pye-mul; 찌꺼기 jji-kkeo-gi; 허
접쓰레기 heo-jeop-sseu-re-gi; *vt.* 거절하
다 geo-jeol-ha-da; 거부하다 geo-bu-ha-da;
사퇴하다 sa-toe-ha-da

regal *adj.* 제왕다운 je-wang-da-un, 당당한
dang-dang-han

regard *n.* 주목 ju-mok; 주의 ju-ui; 고려 go-
ryeo; 관심 gwan-sim; 존중 jon-jung; 호의
ho-ui; 인사 in-sa; 관계 gwan-gye; *vt.* 주목
해 보다 ju-mo-kae-bo-da; 감정을 가지고
대하다 gam-jeong-eul ga-ji-go dae-ha-da;

중시하다 jung-si-ha-da; 고려하다 go-ryeo-ha-da; …로 여기다 …ro yeo-gi-da; …에 관계하다 …e gwan-gye-ha-da

regarding *prep.* …에 관하여 e gwan-ha-yeo; …의 점에서는 ui jeom-e-seo-neun

regardless *prep.* 부주의한 bu-ju-i-han, 관심 없는 gwan-sim-eom-neun

regeneration *n.* 재건 jae-geon, 부흥 bu-heung, 부활 bu-hwal; 개혁 gae-hyeok, 혁신 hyeok-sin

regime *n.* 정권 jeong-kkwon; 정부 jeong-bu; 사회조직 sa-hoe-jo-jik

region *n.* 지방 ji-bang; 지역 ji-yeok; 층 cheung; 영역 yeong-yeok; 범위 beom-wi; 부분 bu-bun

regional *adj.* 지방의 ji-bang-ui; 지역적인 ji-yeok-jeog-in; 국부의 guk-bu-ui

register *n.* 등록부 deung-nok-bu, 등기부 deung-gi-bu; 자동 등록기 ja-dong deung-nok-gi; *vt.* 기재하다 ji-jae-ha-da, 기명하다 gi-myeong-ha-da; 등기로 보내다 deung-gi-ro bo-nae-da; ~ed mail 등기우편 deung-gi-u-pyeon; to ~ mail 편지를 등기로 보내다 pyeon-ji-reul deung-gi-ro bo-nae-da

registration *n.* 기재 gi-jae, 등기 deung-gi; 등기우편 deung-gi-u-pyeon; 등록자 수 deung-nok-ja su, 등록건수 deung-nok-kkeon-ssu; ~ number 등록번호 deung-nok-beon-ho; registry office 등기소 deung-gi-so

regret *n.* 유감 yu-gam; 후회 hu-hoe; 슬픔 seul-peum; 낙담 nak-dam; *vt.* 후회하다 hu-hoe-ha-da; 유감으로 생각하다 yu-gam-eu-ro saeng-ga-ka-da; 슬퍼하다 seul-peo-ha-da; 아쉬워하다 a-swi-wo-ha-da

regular *adj.* 규칙적인 gyu-chik-jeog-in; 정기적인 jeong-gi-jeog-in; 일상의 il-ssang-ui; 보통의 bo-tong-ui; 정규의 jeong-gyu-ui

regulation *n.* 규칙 gyu-chik; 규정 gyu-jeong; 조절 jo-jeol; 단속 dan-sok; 제한 je-han

rehabilitation *n.* 복원하다 bog-won-ha-da; 회복시키다 hoe-bok-si-ki-da; 복권하다 bok-gwon-ha-da

rehearsal *n.* 연습 yeon-seup, 리허설 ri-heo-seol, 예행연습 ye-haeng-nyeon-seup

rehearse *vt.* 연습하다 yeon-seu-pa-da; 예행연습하다 ye-haeng-nyeon-seu-pa-da

reimburse *vt.* 갚다 gap-da; 상환하다 sang-hwan-ha-da; 변상하다 byeon-sang-ha-da

rein *n.* 고삐 go-ppi; 구속 gu-sok; 행동의 자유 haeng-dong-ui ja-yu; ~s 신장 sin-jang, 콩팥 kong-pat

reinforce *vt.* 강화하다 gang-hwa-ha-da; 보강하다 bo-gang-ha-da; 보상하다 bo-sang-ha-da

reject *vt.* 거절하다 geo-jeol-ha-da; 사절하다 sa-jeol-ha-da; 거부하다 geo-bu-ha-da; 토해내다 to-hae-nae-da

rejection *n.* 거절 geo-jeol; 부결 bu-gyeol, 기토 gu-to; 폐기물 pye-gi-mul

relapse *n.* 재발 jae-bal; 되돌아감 do-dol-a-gam

relate *vt.* 관계시키다 gwan-gye-si-ki-da; 결부시키다 gyeol-bu-si-ki-da; …와 이어져있다 …wa i-eo-ejo-it-da; 이야기하다 i-ya-gi-ha-da

relation *n.* 관계 gwan-gye; 관련 gwal-lyeon; 사이 sa-i; 연고 yeon-go; 진술 jin-sul

relationship *n.* 친족관계 chin-jok-gwan-gye; 연고관계 yeon-go-gwan-gye

relative *n.* 친척 chin-cheok; 인척 in-cheok; 관계사항 gwan-gye-sa-hang; *adj.* 비교상의 bi-gyo-sang-ui; 상대적인 sang-dae-jeog-in; 상호의 sang-ho-ui; …나름의 … na-reum-ui; 관계있는 gwan-gye-in-neun

relatively *adv.* 상대적으로 sang-dae-jeog-eu-ro, 비교적 bi-gyo-jeok

relax *vi.* 느슨해지나 neu-seun-hae-ji-da; 누그러지다 nu-geu-reo-ji-da; 마음을 풀다 ma-eum-eul pul-da; 진정하다 jin-jeong-ha-da

relaxation *n.* 이완 i-wan; 완화 wan-hwa; 휴양 hyu-yang; 경감 gyeong-gam

relay *n.* 교대자 gyo-dae-ja; 릴레이 ril-le-i, 계주 gye-ju

release *n.* 해방 hae-bang; 석방 seok-bang; 면제 myeon-je; 발사 bal-ssa; 개봉 gae-bong; 발매 bal-mae; *vt.* 풀어놓다 pul-eo-no-ta; 해방하다 hae-bang-ha-da; 면제하다 myeon-je-ha-da; 발사하다 bal-ssa-ha-da; 개봉하다 gae-bong-ha-da; 발매하다 bal-mae-ha-da

relevant *adj.* 관련된 gwal-lyeon-doen, 적절한 jeok-jeol-han

reliable *adj.* 의지가 되는 ui-ji-ga doe-neun; 확실한 hawk-sil-han

relic *n.* 유물 yu-mul, 유품 yu-pum; 잔재 jan-jae

relief *n.* 경감 gyeong-gam; 안심 an-sim; 구원 gu-won, 구제 gu-je; 교체 gyo-che; 증원 jeung-won

relieve *vt.* 경감하다gyeong-gam-ha-da; 안도케하다 an-do-ke-ha-da; 구원하다 gu-won-ha-da; 해임하다 hae-im-ha-da; 돋보이게 하다 dot-bo-i-ge ha-da; **to feel ~d** 안도감을 느끼다 an-do-gam-eul neu-kki-da

religion *n.* 종교 jong-gyo; 신앙 sin-ang; 신앙심 sin-ang-sim; 귀중한 의무 gwi-jung-han-ui-mu

religious *adj.* 종교의 jong-gyo-ui; 종교적인 jong-gyo-jeog-in; 양심적인 yang-sim-jeog-in; 교단의 gyo-dan-ui

relocate *vt.* 재배치하다 jae-bae-chi-ha-da, 이전시키다 i-jeon-si-ki-da

reluctant *adj.* 마음내키지 않는 ma-eum nae-ki-gi an-neun

rely *vi.* 의지하다 ui-ji-ha-da; 신뢰하다 sil-loe-ha-da; **to ~ on** …을 의지하다 …eul ui-ji-ha-da

remain *vi.* 남다 nam-tta; 머무르다 meo-mu-reu-da; 남아있다 nam-a-it-da; …한 대로 이다 …han dae-ro-i-da; …의 수중에 있다 …ui su-jung-e it-da; *n.* 잔고 jan-go, 나머지 na-meo-ji, 잔재 jan-jae; 잔존자 jan-jon-ja

remaining *adj.* 남아있는 nam-a-in-neun, 남은 nam-eun

remark *n.* 주의 ju-i; 관찰 gwan-chal; 소견 so-gyeon; 비평 bi-pyeong; *vi.* 의견을 말하다 ui-gyeon-eul mal-ha-da; 비평하다 bi-pyeong-ha-da; **to ~ on** …에 대해 의견을 말하다 …e dae-ha ui-gyeon-eul mal-ha-da

remarkable *adj.* 주목할 만한 ju-mo-kal man-han; 비범한 bi-beom-han

remarkably *adv.* 두드러지게 du-deu-reo-ji-ge

remedy *n.* 치료 chi-ryo; 구제 gu-je; 교정 gyo-jeong; 배상 bae-sang; *vt.* 고치다 go-chi-da; 치료하다 chi-ryo-ha-da; 개선하다 gae-seon-ha-da; 배상하다 bae-sang-ha-da

remember *vt.* 생각해내다 saeng-ga-kae-nae-da; 기억하고 있다 gi-eo-ka-go it-da;

vi. 기억나다 gi-eong-na-da; 생각나다 saeng-gang-na-da

remind *vt.* 생각나게 하다 saeng-gang-na-ge ha-da; 깨닫게 하다 kkae-dat-ge ha-da; **to ~ sb. of sth.** 어떤 사람에게 어떤 것을 생각나게 하다 eo-tteon sa-ram-e-ge eo-tteo geos-eul saeng-gang-na-ge ha-da

reminder *n.* 생각나게 하는 것 saeng-gang-na-ge ha-neun geot; 주의 ju-i

remit *vt.* 보내다 bo-nae-da; 우송하다 u-song-ha-da; 조회하다 jo-hoe-ha-da; 원상태로 돌이키다 won-sang-tae-ro dol-i-ki-da; 면제하다 myeon-je-ha-da; 누그러뜨리다 nu-geu-reo-tteu-ri-da

remittance *n.* 송금 song-geum; 송금액 song-geum-aek

remodel *vt.* 개조하다 gae-jo-ha-da, 개축하다 gae-chu-ka-da

remorse *n.* 후회 hu-hoe; 양심의 가책 yang-sim-ui ga-chaek

remote *adj.* 먼 meon; 외딴 oe-ttan; 관계가 적은 gwan-gye-ga jeog-eun; **television ~ control**텔레비전 리모콘 tel-le-bi-jeon ri-mo-kon; **a ~ place** 먼 곳 meon got

removable *adj.* 이동 가능한 i-dong ga-neung-han; 제거할 수 있는 je-geo-hal ssu in-neun; 면직 가능한 myeon-jik ga-neung-han

remove *vt.* 옮기다 om-gi-da; 움직이다 um-jig-i-da, 이동하다 i-dong-ha-da; 제거하다 je-geo-ha-da, 치우다 chi-u-da; 물러나게 하다 mul-leo-na-ge ha-da

render *vt.* …하게 하다 …ha-ge ha-da, …이 되게하다 …i doe-ge ha-da; 주다 ju-da, 보답하다 bo-da-pa-da

renew *vt.* 새롭게 하다 sae-rop-ge ha-da; 되찾다 doe-chat-da; 되풀이하다 doe-pul-i-ha-da; 기한을 연장하다 gi-han-eul yeon-jang-ha-da; 신품과 교환하다 sin-pum-gwa gyo-hwan-ha-da

renewal *n.* 새롭게 함 sae-rop-ge ham; 회복 hoe-bok; 재생 jae-saeng; 재개시 jae-gae-si; **~ notice** 기한연장 통지 gi-han-yeon-jang tong-ji

renounce *vt.* 포기하다 po-gi-ha-da; 부인하다 bu-in-ha-da; 관계를 끊다 gwan-gye-reul kkeun-tta

renovate *vt.* 새롭게 하다 sae-rop-ge ha-da; 개선하다 gae-seon-ha-da; 회복하다 hoe-bo-ka-da

renovation *n.* 혁신 hyeok-sin; 수선 su-seon; 원기회복 won-gi-hoe-bok

rent *n.* 집세 jip-se; 소작료 so-jang-nyo; 임대료 im-dae-ryo; *vt.* 빌리다 bil-li-da; 세놓다 se-no-ta; *vi.* 세놓아지다 se-no-a-ji-da; **~a-car** 렌터카 ren-teo-ka

reorganize *vt.* 재편성하다 jae-pyeon-seong-ha-da; 개혁하다 gae-hyeo-ka-da; 개조하다 qae-jo-ha-da

repair *n.* 수리 su-ri, 수선 su-seon; 수리상태 su-ri-sang-tae; 수리작업 su-ri-jag-eop; *vt.* 수리하다 su-ri-ha-da, 수선하다 su-seon-ha-da; 치료하다 chi-ryo-ha-da; 회복하다 hoe-bo-ka-da; 정정하다 jeong-jeong-ha-da; 배상하다 bae-sang-ha-da; **~man** 수리공 su-ri-gong

repeat *n.* 반복 ban-bok; 반복무늬 ban-bong-mu-ni; 반복기호 ban-bok-gi-ho; 재주문 jae-ju-mun; 재방송 jae-bang-song; 재연주 jae-yeon-ju; *vi.* 되풀이하여 말하다 doe-pul-i-ha-yeo mal-ha-da; 먹은 것이 넘어오다 meog-eun geos-i neom-eo-o-da; 순환하다 sun-hwan-ha-da

repel *vt.* 쫓아버리다 jjoch-a-beo-ri-da; 저항하다 jeo-hang-ha-da; 거절하다 geo-jeol-ha-da; 반발하다 ban-bal-ha-da; 혐오감을 주다 hyeom-o-gam-eul ju-da

repertoire *n.* 레퍼터리 re-peo-teo-ri, 연주목록 yeon-ju-mong-nok

repetition *n.* 반복 ban-bok; 재현 jae-hyeon; 암송 am-song; 사본 sa-bon

replace *vt.* 되돌리다 doe-dol-li-da; 돌려주다 dol-lyeo-ju-da; 복직시키다 bok-jik-si-ki-da; …을 대신하다 …eul dae-sin-ha-da; 바꾸다 ba-kku-da

reply *n.* 내답 dae-dap; 보답 bo-dap; 응수 eung-su; *vi.* 대답하다 dae-da-pa-da; 응수하다 eung-su-h-da; 메아리치다 me-a-ri-chi-da; **to ~ to** …에 대답하다 …e dae-da-pa-da; …에 응수하다 …e eung-su-ha-da

report *n.* 보고 bo-go; 기사 gi-sa; 성적표 seong-jeok-pyo; 소문 so-mun; *vt., vi.* 보고하다 bo-go-ha-da; 신고하다 sin-go-ha-da; 기사를 쓰다 gi-sa-reul sseu-da; 고자질하다 go-ja-jil-ha-da; **~ card** 성적표 seong-jeok-pyo

reporter *n.* 보고자 bo-go-ja; 보도기자 bo-do-gi-ja

reporting *n.* 보도 bo-do, 보고 bo-go

represent *vt.* 묘사하다 myo-sa-ha-da; 상상하다 sang-sang-ha-da; 말하다 mal-ha-da; 표시하다 pyo-si-ha-da; 대표하다 dae-pyo-ha-da; 납득시키다 nap-deuk-si-ki-da

representative *n.* 대표자 dae-pyo-ja; 대리인 dae-ri-in; 대의원 dae-ui-won; 견본 gyeon-bon; *adj.* 대표적인 dae-pyo-jeog-in; 대리하는 dae-ri-ha-neun; 표시하는 pyo-si-ha-neun

repression *n.* 억제 eok-je; 진압 jin-ap; 저지 jeo-ji

reprimand *n.* 징계 jing-gye; 비난 bi-nan; 질책 jil-chaek; *vt.* 징계하다 jing-gye-ha-da; 호되게 꾸짖다 ho-doe-ge kku-jit-da

reprint *vt.* 재판을 내다 jae-pan-eul nae-da; *vi.* 재판되다 jae-pan-doe-da

reprisal *n.* 앙갚음 ang-ga-peum; 보복 bo-bok

reproduce *vt.* 재생하다 jae-sang-ha-da; 재현하다 jae-hyeon-ha-da; 복사하다 bok-sa-ha-da; 모조하다 mo-jo-ha-da; 번식시키다 beon-sik-si-ki-da

reproduction *n.* 재생 jae-saeng; 재현 jae-hyeon; 재생산 jae-saeng-san; 복제물 bok-je-mul; 복사 bok-sa; 생식 saeng-sik

reptile *n.* 파충류 pa-chung-nyu; 비열한 사람 bi-yeol-han sa-ram

republic *n.* 공화국 gong-hwa-guk; 공화정치 gong-hwa-jeong-chi

republican *n.* 공화주의자 gong-hwa-ju-i-ja; 공화당원 gong-hwa-dang-won; *adj.* 공화정의 gong-hwa-jeong-ui; 공화국의 gong-hwa-gug-ui; 공화주의의 gong-hwa-ju-i-ui

reputation *n.* 평판 pyeong-pan; 명성 myeong-seon, 신망 sin-mang

request *n.* 요구 yo-gu; 의뢰 ui-roe; 수요 su-yo; *vt.* 신청하다 sin-cheong-ha-da; 부탁하다 bu-ta-ka-da

require *vt.* 요구하다 yo-gu-ha-da; 필요로 하다 pil-yo-ro ha-da

requirement *n.* 요구 yo-gu, 필요 pil-yo; 필요한 것 pil-yo-han geot; 필요조건 pil-yo-jo-kkeon

rerun vt. 재상영하다 jae-sang-yeong-ha-da, 재연하다 jae-yeon-ha-da

reschedule vt. 일정을 재조절하다 il-jjeong-eul jae-jo-jeol-ha-da

rescue n. 구조 gu-jo; 구제 gu-je; vt. 구조하다 gu-jo-ha-da; 보호하다 bo-ho-ha-da

research n. 연구 yeon-gu; 조사 jo-sa; 탐색 tam-saek; vt. 연구하다 yeon-gu-ha-da; 조사하다 jo-sa-ha-da

resemblance n. 유사성 yu-sa-sseong; 유사점 yu-sa-jjeom; 닮은 얼굴 dalm-eun eol-gul

resemble vt. ...하고 닮았다 ha-go dalm-at-da; ...와 공통점이 있다 wa gong-tong-jjeom-i it-da

resent vt. 화내다 hwa-nae-da; 원망하다 won-mang-ha-da

reservation n. 보류 bo-ryu; 제한 je-han; 사양 sa-yang; *(arrangement, e.g. booking)* 예약 ye-yak; *(doubt/misgiving)* 의심 ui-sim; 비밀 bi-mil; 은폐 eun-pye

reserve n. 비축 bi-chuk; 예비 ye-bi; 예비군 ye-bi-gun; 보류 bo-ryu; vt. 비축하다 bi-chu-ka-da; 준비해두다 jun-bi-hae-du-da; 예약하다 ye-ya-ka-da; 유보하다 yu-bo-ha-da; 연기하다 yeon-gi-ha-da; **army** ~ 예비군 ye-bi-gun

reserved adj. 보류된 bo-ryu-doen; 예약된 ye-yak-doen; 예비의 ye-bi-ui; 수줍어하는 su-jub-eo-ha-neun

reservoir n. 저장소 jeo-jang-so; 저수지 jeo-su-ji; 축적 chuk-jeok; 저장 jeo-jang

reset vt. 고쳐놓다 go-cheo-no-ta, 다시 짜다 da-si jja-da, 바꿔놓다 ba-kkwo-no-ta

reside vi. 살다 sal-da; 존재하다 jon-jae-ha-da; ...에 귀속하다 ...e gwi-so-ka-da

residence n. 주택 ju-taek; 거주 geo-ju; 주재 ju-jae; 소재 so-jae; ~ **permit** 거주허가 geo-ju-heo-ga

resident n. 거주자 geo-ju-ja; 외지주재 사무관 oe-ji-ju-jae sa-mu-gwan; 텃새 teot-sae; 레지던트 re-ji-deon-teu; adj. 거주하는 geo-ju-ha-neun; 주재하는 ju-jae-ha-neun; 고유의 go-yu-ui, 내재하는 nae-jae-ha-neun; 이주하지 않는 i-ju-ha-ji an-neun

residue n. 나머지 na-meo-ji; 찌꺼기 jji-kkeo-gi; 잔유물 jan-yu-mul; **chemical** ~ 화학 잔유물 hwa-hak jan-yu-mul

resign vi. 사임하다 sa-im-ha-da; 포기하다 po-gi-ha-da; 복종하다 bok-jong-ha-da

resignation n. 사직 sa-jik; 사표 sa-pyo; 포기 po-gi; 체념 che-nyeom; 감수 gam-su

resin n. 송진 song-jin

resist vt. 저항하다 jeo-hang-ha-da; 방해하다 bang-hae-ha-da; 견디다 gyeon-di-da; 영향을 받지 않다 yeong-hyang-eul bat-ji-an-ta

resistance n. 저항 jeo-hang; 저항력 jeo-hang-nyeok; 레지스탕스 re-ji-seu-tang-sseu; 지하저항운동 ji-ha-jeo-hang-un-dong

resistant adj. 저항하는 jeo-hang-ha-neun; 저항력이 있는 jeo-hang-nyeog-i in-neun

resolution n. 결의 gyeol-ui, 결심 gyeol-ssim

reasoning n. 추리 chu-ri, 추리력 chu-ri-ryeok

resort n. 리조트 ri-jo-teu, 유흥지 yu-heung-ji; 의지 ui-ji; 수단 su-dan, 방책 bang-chaek; **last** ~ 마지막 수단 ma-ji-mak su-dan; **vacation** ~ 리조트 ri-jo-teu, 유흥지 yu-heung-ji

resource n. 자원 ja-won, 물자 mul-jja; 수단 su-dan; 기략 gi-ryak

respect n. 존경 jon-gyeong; 경의 gyeong-ui; 존중 jon-jung; 관심 gwan-sim; 점 jeom; 관계 gwan-gye; vt. 존중하다 jon-jung-ha-da; 존경하다 jon-gyeong-ha-da; 고려하다 go-ryeo-ha-da; 관여하다 gwan-yeo-ha-da

respectively adv. 각각 gak-gak, 저마다 jeo-ma-da, 제각기 je-gak-gi

respirator n. 마스크 ma-seu-keu; 방독면 bang-dong-myeon; 인공호흡장치 in-gong-ho-heup-jang-chi

respond vi. 응답하다 eung-da-pa-da; 반응하다 ban-eung-ha-da; 책임을 다하다 chaeg-im-eul da-ha-da

response n. 응답 eung-dap; 반응 ban-eung

responsible adj. 책임있는 chaeg-im-in-neun; 원인이 되는 won-in-i doe-neun; 신뢰할 수 있는 sil-loe-hal ssu in-neun; 책임이 무거운 chaeg-im-i mu-geo-un; 의무이행 능력이 있는 ui-mu-i-haeng-neung-nyeog-i in-neun

rest n. 휴식 hyu-sik; 안정 an-jeong; 수면 su-myeon; 죽음 jug-eum; 정지 jeong-ji; 나머지 na-meo-ji; 준비금 jun-bi-geum; vi. 쉬

다 swi-da; 자다 ja-da; 죽다 juk-da;
안심하다 an-sim-ha-da; 정지하다
jeong-ji-ha-da; 놓여있다 no-yeo-it-da;
의지하다 ui-ji-ha-da; 기초를 두다
gi-cho-reul du-da; 여전히 ...한 대로이다
...yeo-jeon-hi han dae-ro-i-da; ~ **home**
요양소 yo-yang-so

restaurant *n.* 음식점 eum-sik-jeom, 식당
sik-dang

restless *adj.* 침착하지 못한 chim-cha-ka-ji
mo-tan; 끊임없는 kkeun-im-eom-neun; 쉬
지 못하는 swi-ji mo-ta neun

restore *vt.* 되돌리다 doe-dol-li-da; 되찾다
doe-chat-da; 복원하다 bog-won-ha-da; 복
귀시키다 bok-gwi-si-ki-da; 회복시키다
hoe-bok-si-ki-da

restrain *vt.* 제지하다 je-ji-ha-da; 억누르다
eong-nu-reu-da; 구속하다 gu-so-ka-da

restrict *vt.* 제한하다 je-han-ha-da, 한정하다
han-jeong-ha-da

restricted *adj.* 제한된 je-han-doen, 통제
된 tong-je-doen; ~ **area** 출입통제구역
chul-ip-tong-je-gu-yeok

restriction *n.* 제한 je-han, 한정 han-jeong;
구속 gu-sok; 사양 sa-yang

restroom *n.* 화장실 hwa-jang-sil

result *n.* 결과 gyeol-gwa; 성과 seong-kkwa;
결정 gyeol-jjeong; 성적 seong-jeok; *vi.*
결과로 일어나다 gyeol-gwa-ro il-eo-
na-da; 귀착하다 gwi-cha-ka-da, 끝나다
kkeun-na-da; **to ~ in** ...로 끝나다 ...ro
kkeun-na-da

résumé *n.* 이력서 i-ryeok-seo; 적요 jeog-yo;
요약 yo-yak

resume *vt.* 다시 차지하다 da-si cha-ji-ha-da;
되찾다 doe-chat-da; 다시 시작하다 da-si
si-ja-ka-da; 요약하다 yo-ya-ka-da

retail *n.* 소매 so-mae; *vt.* 소매하다 so-mae-
ha-da; 소문을 퍼뜨리다 so-mun-eul
peo-tteu-ri-da; **to sell at** ~ 소매로 팔
다 so-mae-ro pal-da; ~ **trade** 소매업
so-mae-eop

retailer *n.* 소매상인 so-mae-sang-in

retain *vt.* 보류하다 bo-ryu-ha-da; 고용하다
go-yong-ha-da; 존속시키다 jon-sok-si-ki-
da; 잊지않고 있다 it-ji-an-ko it-da

retarded *adj.* 성장 발달이 늦은 seong-jang-
bal-ttal-i neuj-eun

retina *n.* 망막 mang-mak

retire *vi.* 물러가다 mul-leo-ga-da; 자다
ja-da; 은퇴하다 eun-toe-ha-da; 퇴각하다
toe-ga-ka-da

retired *adj.* 은퇴한 eun-toe-han; 사양 잘
하는 sa-yang jal-ha-neun; 은둔하는
eun-dun-ha-neun

retirement *n.* 은퇴 eun-toe, 퇴직 toe-jik; ~
pension 퇴직연금 toe-jing-yeon-geum

retreat *n.* 퇴각 toe-gak; 피난처 pi-nan-cheo,
은거처 eun-geo-cheo; 묵상회 muk-sang-
hoe; *vi.* 물러서다 mul leo seo da; 은거하
다 eun-geo-ha-da

retribution *n.* 보답 bo-dap; 천벌 cheon-
beol; 보복 bo-bok

retroactive *adj.* 소급하는 so-geu-pa-neun

retrospect *n.* 회고 hoe-go; *vt.* 회고하다
hoe-go-ha-da

return *n.* 돌아옴 dol-a-om; 복귀 bok-gwi; 재
발 jae-bal; 반환 ban-hwan; 보답 bo-dap;
대답 dae-dap; *vt.* 돌려주다 dol-lyeo-ju-da;
보답하다 bo-da-pa-da; 대답하다 dae-da-
pa-da; *vi.* 되돌아가다 doe-dol-a-ga-da;
재발하다 jae-bal-ha-da; 말대꾸하다
mal-dae-kku-ha-da; ~ **flight** 돌이기는 비
행기 dol-a-ga-neun bi-haeng-gi

reunion *n.* 재결합 jae-gyeol-hap; 재회 jae-
hoe, 동창회 dong-chang-hoe

reunite *vt.* 다시 결합시키다 da-si gyeol-hap-
si-ki-da; 화해시키다 hwa-hae-si-ki-da; 재
회시키다 jae-hoe-si-ki-da

reusable *adj.* 재사용 가능한 jae-sa-yong
ga-neung-han

reveal *vt.* 드러내다 deu-reo-nae-da; 나타내
다 na-ta-nae-da

revelation *n.* 폭로 pong-no; 발각 bal-gak; 묵
시 muk-si

revenge *n.* 복수 bok-su; 원한 won-han; 설욕
의 기회 seol-yog-ui gi-hoe

revenue *n.* 소득 so-deuk; 재원 jae-won; 세입
se-ip; 국세청 guk-se-cheong; ~ **stamp** 수
입인지 su-ip-in-jji

reverend *n.* 목사님 mok-sa-nim, 성직자
seong-jik-ja; *adj.* 목사님의 mok-sa-nim-ui,
성직자의 seong-jik-ja-ui

reverse *n.* 반대 ban-dae; 뒷면 dwin-myeon;
역전 yeok-jeon; 불운 bul-un; *adj.* 반대
의 ban-dae-ui; 거꾸로의 geo-kku-ro-ui;

뒤로 향한dwi-ro hyang-han; 역전하는
yeok-jeon-ha-neun; 배후의 bae-hu-ui; *vt.*
뒤집다 dwi-jip-da; 바꾸어 놓다 ba-kku-eo
no-ta; 번복하다 beom-bo-ka-da; 파기하
다 pa-gi-ha-da

reverse *n.* 역 yeok, 뒤 dwi, 후진 hu-jin, 역
전 yeok-jeon; *adj.* 거꾸로의 geo-kku-ro-ui,
상반되는 sang-ban-doe-neun; *vt.* 거꾸
로 하다 geo-kku-ro ha-da, 전환시키다
jeon-hwan-si-ki-da; 역전시키다 yeok-jeon-
si-ki-da; ~ **gear** 후진기어 hu-jin-gi-eo

reversely *adv.* 반대로 ban-dae-ro; 또 한편으
로 tto han-pyeon-eu-ro

review *n.* 재검토 jae-geom-to; 조사 jo-sa; 관
찰 gwan-chal; 복습 bok-seup; 회고 hoe-
go; *vt.* 재검토하다 jae-geom-to-ha-da; 조
사하다 jo-sa-ha-da; 관찰하다 gwan-chal-
ha-da; 복습하다 bok-su-pa-da; 회고하다
hoe-go-ha-da

reviewer *n.* 평론가 pyeong-non-ga, 비평가
bi-pyeong-ga

revise *vt.* 개정하다 gae-jeong-ha-da; 수정하
다 su-jeong-ha-da; 재조사하다 jae-jo-
sa-ha-da; 의견을 바꾸다 ui-gyeon-eul
ba-kku-da

revive *vt.* 소생시키다 so-saeng-si-ki-da; 회
복시키다 hoe-bok-si-ki-da; 재상영하
다 jae-sang-yeong-ha-da; *vi.* 소생하다
so-saeng-ha-da; 기운이 나다 gi-un-i na-da;
되살아나다 doe-sal-a-na-da; 재유행하다
jae-yu-haeng-ha-da

revocation *n.* 폐지 pye-ji; 취소 chwi-so

revoke *vt.* 폐지하다 pye-ji-ha-da; 취소하다
chwi-so-ha-da; 해약하다 hae-ya-ka-da

revolt *n.* 반란 bal-lan; 폭동 pok-dong; 반항
심 ban-hang-sim; 불쾌감 bul-kwae-gam;
vi. 반란을 일으키다 bal-lan-eul il-eu-ki-
da; 배반하다 bae-ban-ha-da; 비위에 거슬
리다 bi-wi-e geo-seul-li-da; 반감을 품다
ban-gam-eul pum-tta

revolution *n. (political)* 혁명 hyeong-
myeong; 변혁 byeon-hyeok; *(rotation)* 순
환 sun-hwan, 회전 hoe-jeon

revolve *vt.* 회전하다 hoe-jeon-ha-da; 자전
하다 ja-jeon-ha-da; 공전하다 gong-jeon-
ha-da; 순환하다 sun-hwan-ha-da; 맴돌
다 maem-dol-da; **revolving door** 회전문
hoe-jeon-mun; 공전 gong-jeon

reward *n.* 보수 bo-su; 현상금 hyeon-sang-
geum; 사례금 sa-rye-geum; 보답 bo-dap;
보복 bo-bok; *vt.* 보답하다 bo-da-pa-da;
보수를 주다 bo-su-reul ju-da; 상을 주다
sang-eul ju-da; 보복하다 bo-bo-ka-da

rewind *vt.* 다시 감다 da-si gam-tta

rheumatism *n.* 류머티즘 ryu-meo-ti-jeum

Rhine *n.* 라인강 ra-in-gang

rhombus *n.* 마름모꼴 ma-reum-mo-kkol

rhyme *n.* 압운 ab-un; 각운 gag-un

rhythm *n.* 리듬 ri-deum; 주기적 반복 ju-gi-
jeog ban-bok; 운율 un-yul

rib *n.* 갈비 gal-bi; 갈빗대 gal-bit-dae; 늑골
neuk-gol

ribbon *n.* 리본 ri-bon; 띠 tti

rice *n.* 쌀 ssal; 밥 bap; 벼 byeo

rich *adj.* 부자의 bu-ja-ui; 부유한 bu-yu-han;
풍부한 pung-bu-han; 비옥한 bi-o-kan; 값
진 gap-jin; 영양분이 많은 yeong-yang-
bun-i man-eun; 선명한 seon-myeong-han

rickety *adj.* 곱사등의 gop-sa-deung-ui; 구루
병에 걸린 gu-ru-ppyeong-e geol-lin; 쓰러
질듯한 sseu-reo-jil-tteu-tan

ridden *adj.* 지배된 ji-bae-doen, 고통받은
go-tong-bad-eun

riddle *n.* 수수께끼 su-su-kke-kki; 어려운 문
제 eo-ryeo-un mun-je

ride *n.* 탐 tam; 타고 감 ta-go gam; 태움
tae-um; 타는 시간 ta-neun si-gan; 승마
여행 seung-ma-yeo-haeng; 승마도로
seung-ma-do-ro; *vt.* 타다 ta-da; 타고가
다 ta-go-ga-da; 태우다 tae-u-da; 뜨다
tteu-da; 걸리다 geol-li-da; 정박시키다
jeong-bak-si-ki-da

rider *n.* 타는 사람 ta-neun sa-ram; 첨
부서류 cheom-bu-seo-ryu; 추가조항
chu-ga-jo-hang

ridge *n.* 산마루 san-ma-ru, 산등성이 san-
tteung-seong-i; 융기 yung-gi; 이랑 i-rang

ridiculous *adj.* 우스운 u-seu-un; 어리석은
eo-ri-seog-eun; 엉뚱한 eong-ttung-han

riding *n.* 승마 seung-ma, 승차 seung-cha

riffle *n.* 물살이 빠른 곳 mul-ssal-I ppa-reun
got; 잔물결 jan-mul-kkyeol; 트럼프 섞는
법 teu-reom-peu seng-neun beop; *vi.* 페이
지를 넘기다 pe-i-ji-reul neom-gi-da; 잔물
결이 일다 jan-mul-kkyeol-i il-da; *vt.* 트럼
프를 섞다 teu-reom-peu-reul seok-da

rifle *n.* 라이플총 ra-i-peul-chong; 소총 so-chong; ~ **range** 사격장 sa-gyeok-jang

right *n.* 정의 jeong-ui; 권리 gwol-li; 정확함 jeong-hwa-kam; 진상 jin-sang; 오른쪽 o-reun-jjok; 보수파 bo-su-pa; *adj.* 올바른 ol-ba-reun; 정확한 jeong-hwa-kan; 진정한 jin-jeong-han; 곧은 god-eun; 적절한 jeok-jeol-han; 정상적인 jeong-sang-jeog-in; 제정신의 je-jeong-sin-ui; 부수적인 bu-su-jeog-in; *(correct)* 올바른 ol-ba-reun; *(opp. of left)* 오른쪽의 o-reun-jjog-ui; *adv.* 바르게 ba-reu-ge; 정확히 jeong-hwa-ki; 적절히 jeok-jeol-hi; 바로 ba-ro; 우측으로 u-cheug-eu-ro; **Turn** ~ 오른쪽으로 돌다 o-reun-jjog-eu-ro dol-da; ~ **of way** 통행권 tong-haeng-kkwon; 부선권 u-seon-kkwon, 우선 통행권 u-seon tong-haeng-kkwon; 진행허가 jin-haeng-heo-ga; **on the** ~ 오른쪽에 o-reun-jjog-e; ~ **arm** 오른팔 o-reun-pal; 심복 sim-bok; ~ **wing** 우익 u-ik, 보수파 bo-su-pa

right-handed *adj.* 오른손잡이의 o-reun-son-jab-i-ui; 오른손용의 o-reun-son-nyong-ui; 오른쪽으로 도는 o-reun-jjog-eu-ro do-neun

rightly *adv.* 바르게 ba-reu-ge, 정확히 jeong-hwa-ki; 마땅히 ma-ttang-hi

rigid *adj.* 단단한 dan-dan-han; 완고한 wan-go-han; 엄격한 eom-kkyeo-kan; 엄밀한 eom-mil-han

rigorous *adj.* 엄한 eom-han, 엄격한 eom-kkyeo-kan; 엄밀한 eom-mil-han, 정밀한 jeong-mil-han

rim *n.* 가장자리 ga-jang-ja-ri; 테 te; 수면 su-myeon

rind *n.* 껍질 kkeop-jil; 외견 oe-gyeon

ring *n.* 고리 go-ri; 반지 ban-ji; 원형 won-hyeong; 나이테 na-i-te; 경기장 gyeong-gi-jang; 동맹 dong-maeng; 울리는 소리 ul-li-neun so-ri; 울림 ul-lim; *vt.* 둘러싸다 dul-leo-ss-da; 고리를 끼우다 go-ri-reul kki-u-da; 고리모양으로 깎다 go-ri-mo-yang-eu-ro kkak-da; 원을 그리며 돌다 won-eul geu-ri-myeo dol-da; 울리다 ul-li-da; 음향을 내다 eum-hyang-eul nae-da; 부르다 bu-reu-da; *vi.* 둥글게 되다 dung-geul-ge doe-da; 날아오르다 nal-a-o-reu-da; 빙빙돌다 bing-bing-dol-da; 울리다 ul-li-da; 울려퍼지다 ul-lyeo-peo-ji-da

rink *n.* 실내 스케이트장 sil-lae seu-ke-i-teu-jang, 실내 경기장 sil-lae jyeong-gi-jang

rinse *n.* 헹구기 heng-gu-gi; 씻어내기 ssis-eo-nae-gi; *vt.* 헹구다 heng-gu-da; 씻어내다 ssis-eo-nae-da

riot *n.* 폭동 pok-dong; 소동 so-dong; 혼잡 hon-jap; 방탕 bang-tang; *vi.* 폭동을 일으키다 pok-dong-eul il-eu-ki-da; 방탕히다 bang-tang-ha-da; 빠져들다 ppa-jeo-deul-da

rip *n.* 찢음 jjij-eum; 찢어짐 jjij-eo-jim; 찢어진 곳 jjij-eo-jin got; 늙은 말 neulg-eun mal; 불량배 bul-lyang-bae; 거센 파도 geo-sen pa-do; *vt.* 쪼개다 jjo-gae-da; 찢다 jjit-da; 벗겨내다 beot-gyeo-nae-da; 폭로하다 pong-no-ha-da; 거칠게 말하다 geo-chil-ge mal-ha-da

ripe *adj.* 익은 ig-eun; 숙성한 suk-seong-han; 원숙한 won-su-kan; 고령의 go-ryeong-ui; 기회가 무르익은 gi-hoe-ga mu-reu-ig-eun

ripen *vi.* 익다 ik-da; 원숙해지다 won-su-kae-ji-da; 기회가 무르익다 gi-hoe-ga mu-reu-ik-da

ripple *n.* 잔물결 jan-mul-kkyeol, 파문 pa-mun; *vt.* 파문을 일으키다 pa-mun-eul il-eu-ki-da; 곱슬곱슬하게 하다 gop-seul-gop-seul-ha-ge ha-da; *vi.* 잔물결이 일다 jan-mul-kkyeol-i il-da; ~ **effect** 파급효과 pa-geu-pyo-kkwa

rise *n.* 상승 sang-seung; 증가 jeung-ga; 고조 go-jo; 진보 jin-bo; 고지대 go-ji-dae; 반란 bal-lan; 떠오름 tteo-o-reum; 기원 gi-won; 회생 hoe-saeng; *vt.* 올리다 ol-li-da; 높이다 no-pi-da

rising *adj.* 올라가는 ol-la-ga-neun, 떠오르는 tteo-o-reu-neun; *n.* 상승 sang-seung; 기립 gi-rip; 소생 so-saeng

risk *n.* 위험 wi-heom; 모험 mo-heom; 위험율 wi-heom-nyul; *vt.* 위험에 내맡기다 wi-heom-e nae-mat-gi-da; 위험을 무릅쓰다 wi-heom-eul mu-reup-sseu-da

risky *adj.* 위험한 wi-heom-han; 아슬아슬한 a-seul-a-seul-han

ritual *adj.* 의례적인 ui-rye-jeog-in, 의식적
인 ui-sik-jeog-in; *n.* 종교적인 의식 jong-
gyo-jeok ui-sik; 의식적 행사 ui-sik-jeok
haeng-sa

rival *n.* 경쟁자 gyeong-jaeng-ja, 라이벌
ra-i-beol, 적수 jeok-su; *adj.* 경쟁자의
gyeong-jaeng-ja-ui; 서로 싸우는 seo-ro
ssa-u-neun

rivalry *n.* 경쟁 gyeong-jaeng, 대항 dae-hang

river *n.* 강 gang; 다량의 흐름 da-ryang-ui
heu-rum; **~bank** 강둑 gang-ttuk; **~side** 강
변 gang-byeon, 강기슭 gang-kki-seuk

road *n.* 길 gil, 도로 do-ro; 진로 jil-lo; 통로
tong-no; **~block** 방책 bang-chaek; 장애물
jang-ae-mul; **~ map** 도로지도 do-ro-ji-do
~side 길가 gil-kka; **~ test** 운전 실기시험
un-jeon-sil-gi-si-heom; **~way** 도로 do-ro; **~
work** 도로공사 do-ro-gong-sa

roar *n.* 고함소리 go-ham-sso-ri; 으르렁거리
는 소리 eu-reu-reong-geo-ri-neun so-ri;
vi. 으르렁거리다 eu-reu-reong-geo-ri-da;
고함치다 go-ham-chi-da; 크게 웃다
keu-ge ut-da; 큰소리를 내다 keun-so-ri-
reul nae-da

roast *n.* 불고기 bul-go-gi; 불고기용 고기
bul-go-gi-yong go-gi; 굽기 gup-gi; 볶기
bok-gi; *adj.* 구운 gu-un; 볶은 bokk-eun;
vt. 굽다 gup-da; 볶다 bok-da; 그을리다
geu-eul-li-da; 녹이다 nog-i-da; **~ beef** 불
고기 bul-go-gi; **~ turkey** 터어키 구이
teo-eo-ki-gu-i

roasting *adj.* 타는듯한 ta-neun-deu-tan, 찌
는듯한 jji-neun-deu-tan, 몹시 더운 mop-si
deo-un

rob *vt.* 훔치다 hum-chi-da; 빼앗다 ppae-at-
da; 유린하다 yu-rin-ha-da

robber *n.* 도둑 do-duk; 강도 gang-do; 약탈
자 yak-tal-jja

robbery *n.* 강도 gang-do; 약탈 yak-tal

robe *n.* 예복 ye-bok; 로브 ro-beu

robin *n.* 울새 ul-ssae, 로빈 ro-bin

robot *n.* 로보트 ro-bo-teu, 인조인간 in-jo-in-
gan; 자동장치 ja-dong-jang-chi

rock *n.* 바위 ba-wi; 암초 am-cho; 난관 nan-
gwan; 지주 ji-ju; 흔들림 heun-deul-lim; 동
요 dong-yo; *vt.* 돌로 치다 dol-lo chi-da; 돌
을 던지다 dol-eul deon-ji-da; 진동시키다

jin-dong-si-ki-da; 흔들다 heun-deul-da

rock-climbing *n.* 암벽등반 am-byeok-
deung-ban, 바위타기 ba-wi-ta-gi, 록클라
이밍 rok-keul-la-i-ming

rocket *n.* 로케트 ro-ke-teu; 봉화 bong-hwa

rocking chair *n.* 흔들의자 heun-deul ui-ja

rock music *n.* 록음악 rog-eum-ak

rocky *adj.* 바위로 된 ba-wi-ro doen; 바위같
은 ba-wi-gat-eun; 부동의 bu-dong-ui; 완
고한 wan-go-han; 냉혹한 naeng-ho-kan;
불안정한 bul-an-jeong-han; 현기증나는
hyeon-gi-jjeung-na-neun

Rocky Mountains 록키산맥 ro-ki-san-maek

rod *n.* 장대 jang-ttae; 낚싯대 nak-sit-dae; 작
은 가지 jag-eun ga-ji; 지팡이 ji-pang-i; 회
초리 hoe-cho-ri; 가늠자 ga-neum-ja; 홀
hol; 피뢰침 pi-roe-chim

role *n.* 배역 bae-yeok; 역할 yeo-kal; **to play
a ~** ...의 역을 담당하다 ...ui yeo-kal-
eul dam-dang-ha-da; **~ model** 역할모
델 yeo-kal-mo-del; **~ playing** 역할연기
yeo-kal-yeon-gi

roll *n.* 회전 hoe-jeon; 기복 gi-bok; 출석부
chul-sseok-bu; 두루마리 du-ru-ma-ri; 롤
러 rol-lro; 롤 rol; 울림 ul-lim; *(bread)* 롤
빵 rol-ppang; *vt.* 굴리다 gul-li-da; 굽이치
게 하다 gub-i-chi-ge ha-da; 동그랗게 말
다 dong-geu-ra-ke mal-da; 판판하게 하다
pan-pan-ha-ge ha-da; 조작하다 jo-ja-ka-da;
둥둥 울리다 dung-dung-ul-lu-da; *vi.* 구르
다 gu-reu-da; 회전하다 hoe-jeon-ha-da;
진행하다 jin-haeng-ha-da; 굽이치다
gub-i-chi-da; 천둥이 울리다 cheon-dung-i
ul-li-da; 북이 울리다 bug-i ul-li-da; 동그래
지다 dong-geu-rae-ji-da

roller *n.* 롤러 rol-leo; **~ coaster** 롤러 코스터
rol-leo-ko-seu-teo; **~ skate** 롤러스케이트
rol-leo-seu-ke-i-teu

Roman Catholic *n.* 카톨릭교 ka-tol-lik-gyo;
카톨릭교도 ka-tol-lik-gyo-do; *adj.* 카
톨릭교의 ka-tol-lik-gyo-ui, 천주교의
cheon-ju-gyo-ui

romance *n.* 가공적인 이야기 ga-gong-
jeog-in i-ya-gi; 연애이야기 yeon-ae-i-
ya-gi; 로맨스 ro-maen-sseu; 서정음악
seo-jeong-eum-ak

Romania *n.* 루마니아 ru-ma-ni-a

romantic *adj.* 로맨틱한 ro-maen-ti-kan; 가공의 ga-gong-ui; 공상적인 gong-sang-jeog-in; 낭만주의의 nang-man-ji-i-ui

Rome *n.* 로마 ro-ma

roof *n.* 지붕 ji-bung; 정상 jeong-sang, 꼭대기 kkok-dae-gi

rookie *n.* 신병 sin-byeong, 풋내기 pun-nae-gi

room *n.* 방 bang; 장소 jang-so; 공간 gong-gan; 여유 yeo-yu; 기회 gi-hoe; ~ **service** 룸서비스 rum-sseo-bi-sseu; ~ **temperature** 방안 온도 bang-an on-do, 실내온도 sil-lae-on-do

roommate *n.* 룸메이트 rum-me-i-teu

rooster *n.* 수탉 su-tak; 잘난척 하는 사람 jal-lan-cheok ha-neun sa-ram

root *n.* 뿌리 ppu-ri; 밑동 mit-dong; 근원 geun-won; 기초 gi-cho; 밑바닥 mit-ba-dak; 조상 jo-sang

rope *n.* 새끼 sae kki, 밧줄 bat-jul, 로프 ro-peu; 올가미줄 ol-ga-mi-jul; 한두름 han-du-reum; 측량줄 cheung-nyang-jjul

rosary *n.* 염주 yeom-ju, 묵주 muk-ju, 로사리오 ro-sa-ri-o; 장미원 jang-mi-won

rose *n.* 장미 jang-mi; 장미무늬 jang-mi-mu-ni; 장미빛 jang-mi-ppit; 미인 mi-in; 장미향료 jang-mi-hyang-nyo; *adj.* 장미의 jang-mi-ui; 장미빛의 jang-mi-ppich-ui; 장미로 둘러싸인 jang-mi-ro dul-leo-ssa-in

rosebush *n.* 장미덩굴 jang-mi-deol-gul

roster *n.* 근무명부 geun-mu-myeong-bu; 등록부 deung-nok-bu

rot *vi.* 썩음 sseog-eum; 말라죽음 ml-la-jug-eum; 타락 ta-rak; *vt.* 썩이다 kkeog-i-da, 타락시키다 ta-rak-si-ki-da; *n.* 타락 ta-rak, 썩음 sseog-eum; 부패물 bu-pae-mul

rotate *vi.* 회전하다 hoe-jeon-ha-da, 지전하다 Ja-jeon-ha-da; 교내하나 gyo-dae-ha-da; *vt.* 회전시키다 hoe-jeon-si-ki-da; 교대시키다 gyo-dae-si-ki-da

rotten *adj.* 썩은 sseog-eun; 부패한 bu-pae-han; 더러운 deo-reo-un; 취약한 chwi-ya-kan

rouge *n.* 루즈 ru-jeu; 스크럼 seu-keu-reom

rough *adj.* 거친 geo-chin; 텁수룩한 teop-su-ru-kan; 험악한 heom-a-kan; 가공되지 않은 ga-gong-doe-ji an-eun; 난폭한 nan-po-kan; 고된 go-doen; 대강의 dae-gang-ui; 날림의 nal-lim-ui

roughly *adv.* 거칠게 geo-chil-ge; 대충 dae-chung, 개략적으로 gae-ryak-jeog-eu-ro

round *adj.* 둥근 dung-geun; 원형의 won-hyeong-ui; 살찐 sal-jjin; 왕복의 wang-bog-ui; 우수리 없는 u-su-ri eom-neun; 상당한 sang-dang-han; 원숙한 won-su-kan; ~ **trip** 왕복여행 wang-bog-yeo-haeng, 일주여행 il-jju-yeo-haeng; ~ **table** 원탁 won-tak; ~**up** 몰이 mol-i; 검거 geom.-geo; 총괄 chong-gwal; 반올림 ban-ol-lim

route *n.* 길 gil, 노정 no-jeong, 루트 ru-teu, 항로 hang-no

routine *n.* 판에박힌 일 pan-e ba-kin nil; 일상의 과정 il-ssang-ui gwa-jeong; 기계적인 순서 gi-gye-jeog-in sun-seo; *adj.* 일상의 il-ssang-ui; 판에 박힌 pan-e ba-kin

row *n.* 열 yeol, 줄 jul; 노젓기 no-jeot-gi; 노젓는 거리 no-jeon-neun geo-ri; 법석 beop-seok, 소동 so-dong; 말다툼 mal-da-tum; *vt., vi.* 노를 젓다 no-reul jeot-da; 보트 레이스를 하다 bo-teu re-i-sseu-reul ha-da; 말다툼하다 mal-da-tum-ha-da, 소란을 피우다 so-ran-eul pi-u-da; ~ **of seats** 좌석 줄 jwa-seok jul; ~**boat** 노젓는 배 no-jeon-neun bae

royal *adj.* 왕족의 wang-jog-ui; 왕립의 wang-nib-ui; 당당한 dang-dang-han; 보증된 bo-jeung-doen; 호화로운 ho-hwa-ro-un; ~ **jelly** 로얄젤리 ro-yal-jel-li; ~ **road** 왕도 wang-do, 쉬운 방법 swi-un bang-beop, 지름길 ji-reum-kkil

royalty *n.* 왕위 wang-wi, 왕권 wang-kkwon; 왕족 wang-jok; 특허권 사용료 teu-keo-kkwon sa-yong-nyo, 저작권 사용료 jeo-jak-gwon sa-yong-nyo

rub *vt.* 문지르다 mun-ji-reu-da; 닦다 dak-da; 안달하다 an-dal-ha-da; 바르다 ba-reu-da; 탁본하다 tak-bon-ha-da; ~**bing alcohol** 소독용 알코올 so-dong-nyong al-kol

rubber *n.* 고무 go-mu; 고무세품 go-mu-je-pum; 안마사 an-ma-sa; ~ **band** 고무줄 go-mu-jul

ruby *n.* 루비 ru-bi; 루비색깔 ru-bi-saek-kkal

rucksack *n.* 배낭 bae-nang; 룩색 ruk-saek

rudder *n.* 방향타 bang-hyang-ta; 지침 ji-chim; 지도자 ji-do-ja; 꽁지깃 kkong-ji-kkit

rude *adj.* 버릇없는 beo-reud-eom-neun; 무례한 mu-rye-han; 무뚝뚝한 mu-ttuk-ttu-kan;

미가공의 mi-ga-gong-ui; 조잡한 jo-ja-pan; 건장한 geon-jang-han

rug *n.* 깔개 kkal-gae; 양탄자 yang-tan-ja

ruin *n.* 파멸 pa-myeol; 몰락 mol-lak; 황폐 hwang-pye; 타락 ta-rak; 무너짐 mu-neo-jim; 폐허 pye-heo; 화근 hwa-geun; *vt.* 파괴하다 pa-goe-ha-da; 황폐시키다 hwang-pye-si-ki-da; 망쳐놓다 mang-cheo-no-ta; 타락시키다 ta-rak-si-ki-da

rule *n.* 규칙 gyu-chik; 법칙 beop-chik; 통례 tong-nye; 지배 ji-bae; 자 ja; *vt.* 다스리다 da-seu-ri-da; 지도하다 ji-do-ha-da; 억제하다 eok-je-ha-da; 규정하다 gyu-jeong-ha-da; 판결하다 pan-gyeol-ha-da; 구별하다 gu-byeol-ha-da

ruler *n.* *(straight edge)* 자 ja; *(political)* 통치자 tong-chi-ja; 지배자 ji-bae-ja

rum *n.* 럼주 reom-ju

rumble *n.* 우르릉 소리 u-reu-reung sso-ri; 마차 조수석 ma-cha jo-su-seok; *vi.* 우르릉 울리다 u-reu-reung ul-li-da; 덜컥거리며 가다 deol-keok-geo-ri-myeo ga-da

rumor *n.* 소문 so-mun, 풍문 pung-mun

rumple *n.* 구김살 gu-gim-ssal; *vt.* 구기다 gu-gi-da

run *n.* 달림 dal-lim; 드라이브 deu-ra-i-beu; 주행거리 ju-haeng-geo-ri; 노선 no-seon; 폭락 pong-nak; 작업량 jag-eom-nyang; 흐름 heu-reum; 연속 yeon-sok; 형세 hyeong-se; **a ~ of bad results** 나쁜 결과의 계속 na-ppeun gyeol-gwa-ui gye-sok, **the average ~ of applicants** 평년수준 인원의 지원자 pyeong-nyeon-su-jun in-won-ui ji-won-ja **a press ~** 인쇄작업 in-swae-jag-eop; **a ~ in the park** 공원에서 달리기 gong-won-e-seo dal-li-gi; **a ~away** 도망자 do-mang-ja; 도망친 do-mang-chin; **~way** 활주로 hwal-jju-ro; *vi.* 달리다 dal-li-da; 헤매다 he-mae-da; 달아나다 dal-a-na-da; 세월이 흐르다 se-wol-i heu-reu-da; 기사화되다 gi-sa-hwa-doe-da; 입후보하다 i-pu-bo-ha-da; 움직이다 um-jig-i-da; 영업하다 yeong-eo-pa-da; 계속하다 gye-so-ka-da; **to ~ in a race** 경주에

서 달리다 gyeong-ju-e-seo dal-li-da; **to ~ a business** 사업을 하다 sa-eob-eul ha-da; **to ~ a machine** 기계를 돌리다 gi-gye-reul dol-li-da; **I ran into her downtown** 저는 그 여자분을 시내에서 만났습니다 jeo-neun geu yeo-ja-bun-eul si-nae-e-seo man-nat-seum-ni-da

runner *n.* *(a person who runs)* 경주자 gyeong-ju-ja; 도망자 do-mang-ja; *(blade on a skate)* 활주부 hwal-jju-bu; *(on a sliding door)* 롤러 rol-leo; *(a narrow rug)* 기다란 융단 gi-da-ran yung-dan; 러너 reo-neo; *(of a plant)* 덩굴 deong-gul

running *adj.* 달리는 dal-li-neun; 흐르는 heu-reu-neun; 연속적인 yeon-sok-jeog-in; **~ mate** 러닝메이트 reo-ning-me-i-teu; **~ water** 수도물 so-don-mul

rural *adj.* 시골의 si-gol-ui, 전원의 jeon-won-ui

rush *n.* 돌진 dol-jjin; 쇄도 swae-do; 분망 bun-mang; 러시 reo-si; *vt.* 몰아대다 mol-a-dae-da; 급히 해치우다 geu-pi hae-chi-u-da; 장애물을 돌파하다 jang-ae-mul-eul dol-pa-ha-da; 돌진하다 dol-jjin-ha-da; **~ hour** 러시아워 reo-si-a-wo

Russia *n.* 러시아 reo-si-a

Russian *n.* 러시아사람 reo-si-a-ssa-ram; 러시아말 reo-si-a-mal; *adj.* 러시아의 reo-si-a-ui

rust *n.* 녹 nok; 고동색 go-dong-saek; *vt.* 녹슬게 하다 nok-seul-ge ha-da; 둔하게 하다 dun-ha-ge ha-da; 못쓰게 하다 mot-sseu-ge ha-da

rustic *adj.* 시골의 si-gol-ui; 단순한 dan-sun-han; 교양없는 gyo-yang-eom-neun; 거칠게 만든 geo-chil-ge man-deun

rusty *adj.* 녹슨 nok-seun; 녹에서 생긴 nog-e-seo saeng-gin; 낡은 nalg-eun; 못쓰게 된 mot-sseu-ge doen; 목이 쉰 mog-i swin; 썩어가는 sseog-eo-ga-neun; 고집이 센 go-jib-i sen; 부루퉁한 bu-ru-tung-han

rye *n.* 호밀 ho-mil; **~ bread** 호밀빵 ho-mil-ppang

S

sabotage *n.* 사보타지 sa-bo-ta-ji, 파괴행위 pa-goe-haeng-wi; *vt.* 고의로 방해하다 go-ui-ro bang-hae-ha-da, 고의로 파괴하 다 go-ui-ro pa-goe-ha-da

saccharine *n.* 사카린 sa-ka-rin

sack *n.* 자루 ja-ru; 봉지 bong-ji; 헐렁한 웃 옷 heol-leong-han od-ot

sacred *adj.* 신성한 sin-seong-han; 종교적 인 jong-gyeo-jeog-in; 신성불가침의 sin-seong bul ga chim ui; 비쳐진 ba-cheo-jin

sacrifice *n.* 희생 hi-saeng, 제물 je-mul; 헌 신 heon-sin; 속죄기도 sok-joe-gi-do; *vt.* 희생하다 hi-saeng-ha-da; 단념하다 dan-nyeom-ha-da; *vi.* 산제물을 바치다 san-je-mul-eul ba-chi-da

sad *adj.* 슬픈 seul-peun; 슬퍼할 seul-peo-hal; 색이 칙칙한 saeg-i chik-chi-kan

sadden *vi.* 슬프게 하다 seul peu-ge ha-da; 칙칙한 색으로 하다 chik-chi-kan saeg-eu-ro ha-dah

saddle *n.* 안장 an-jang; 등부분 deung-bu-bun; *vt.* 안장을 놓다 an-jang-eul no-ta; ...에게 짊어 시우다 ...e-ge jilm-eo-ji-u-da

sadism *n.* 변태성욕 byeon-tae-seong-yok, 극 단적 잔학성 geuk-dan-jeok jan-hak-seong

sadness *n.* 슬픔 seul-peum, 비애 bi-ae; 슬픈 안색 seul-peun an-saek

safari *n.* 사파리 ssa-pa-ri; ~ **park** 사파리 공 원 ssa-pa-ri gong-won

safe *adj.* 안전한 an-jeon-han; 무사히 mu-sa-hi; 신중한 sin-jung-han; 믿을 수 있는 mid-eul ssu-in-neun; 확실한 hawk sil-han; *n.* 금고 geum-go

safeguard *n.* 부호 bo-ho; 보호물 bo-ho-mul; 보장조항 bo-jang-jo-hang; 호위병 ho-wi-byeong; 안선통행증 an-jeon-tong-haeng-jjeung

safety *n.* 안전 an-jeon; 무해 mu-hae; 안전 장치 an-jeon-jang-chi; ~ **pin** 안전핀 an-jeon-pin; ~ **belt** 구명대 gu-myeong-dae; ~ **first** 안전제일 an-jeon-je-il; ~ **zone** 안 전지대 an-jeon-ji-dae; ~ **check** 안전점검 an-jeon-jeom-geom

saggy *adj.* 아래로 처진 a-rae-ro cheo-jin, 축 늘어진 chuk neul-eo-jin

Sahara Desert *n.* 사하라 사막 sa-ha-ra sa-mak

sail *n.* 돛 dot; 돛단배 dot-dan-bae; 항해 hang-hae; 풍차 날개 pung-cha-nal-gae; *vt.* 항해하다 hang-hae-ha-da; 배를 띄 우다 bae-reul tti-u-da; *vi.* 항해하다 hang-hae-ha-da; 날다 nal-da; 점잖게 걷 다 jeom-jan-ke geot-da; 힘있게 일을 시작 하다 him-it-ge il-eul si-ja-ka-da; 공격하다 gong-gyeo-ka-da

sailboat *n.* 돛단배 dot-dan-bae, 범선 bom-seon

sailor *n.* 뱃사람 baet-sa-ram, 선원 seon-won; 수병 su-byeong

saint *n.* 성인 seong-in; 덕이 높은 사람 deog-i no-peun sa-ram; 천사 cheon-sa; ~ **John** 성 요한 seong yo-han

sake *n.* 목적 mok-jeok; 이유 i-yu; **for the ~ of** ...을 위해 ...eul wi-hae

salable *adj.* 팔기에 적당한 pal-gi-e jeok-dang-han; 값이 적당한 gaps-i jeok-dang-han; 수요가 많은 su-yo-ga man-eun

salad *n.* 샐러드 ssael-leo-deu; 생채요리 saeng-chae-yo-ri; ~ **dressing** 샐러드 드레 싱 ssael-leo-deu deu-re-ssing

salary *n.* 봉급 bong-geup, 월급 wol-geup

sale *n.* 판매 pan-mae; 매상 mae-sang; 세일 sse-il; 경매 gyeong-mae; **for ~** 팔려고 내 놓은 pal-lyeo-go nae-no-eun; **on ~** 판매중 인 pan-mae-jung-in

sales department *n.* 판매부

salesman *n.* 점원 jeom-won, 판매원 pan-mae-won

sales representative *n.* 외판원 oe-pan-won

sales tax *n.* 세금 se-geum

salmon *n.* 연어 yeon-eo; 연어고기 yeon-eo-go-gi; 연어색 yeon-eo-saek; **smoked ~** 훈 제연어 hun-je yeon-eo

salon *n.* 살롱 ssal-long; 상류사회 sang-nyu-sa-hoe; 미술전람회장 mi-sul jeol-lam-hoe-jang

salt *n.* 소금 so-geum; 짠맛 jjan-mat; *vt.* 소 금을 치다 so-geum-eul chi-da; 간을 맞추 다 gan-eul mat-chu-da; 절이다 jeol-i-da; 흥미를 돋우다 heung-mi-reul dod-u-da;

~ **water** 바닷물ba-dan-mul; 소금물 so-geum-mul

salty *adj*. 짠 jjan; 재치있는 jae-chi-in-neun; 상스러운 sang-seu-reo-un; 기운찬 gi-un-chan

salted *adj*. 소금에 절인 so-geum-e jeol-in, 소금으로 간을 한 so-geum-eu-ro gan-eul han

salute *vt*. …에게 경례하다 …e-ge gyeong-nye-ha-da; 맞이하다 maj-i-ha-da; *vi*. 인사 하다 in-sa-ha-da; 예포를 쏘다 ye-po-reul sso-da

salvation *n*. 구조 gu-jo, 구제 gu-je; 구조 gu-jo-ja, 구조수단 gu-jo-su-dan; 구원 gu-won; 구세주 gu-se-ju; ~ **Army** 구세군 gu-se-gun

salve *n*. 연고 yeon-go; 위안 wi-an

same *adj*. 같은 gat-eun; 마찬가지의 ma-chan-ga-ji-ui; 다름없는 da-reum-i eom-neun; 바로 그 ba-ro geu; 단조로운 dan-jo-ro-un

sample *n*. 견본 gyeon-bon; 표본 pyo-bon; 실례 sil-lye; *vt*. 견본을 뽑다 gyeon-bon-eul ppop-da; 견본이 되다 gyeon-bon-i doe-da; 시식하다 si-si-ka-da, 시음하다 si-eum-ha-da

sanctuary *n*. 거룩한 장소 geo-ru-kan jang-so; 성당 seong-dang; 신전 sin-jeon; 교회 gyo-hoe; 사원 sa-won; 성역 seong-yeok

sand *n*. 모래 mo-rae; 사막 sa-mak; 모래밭 mo-rae-bat; 모래색깔 mo-rae-saek-kkal

sandal *n*. 샌들 ssaen-deul

sandbag *n*. 샌드백 ssaen-deu-baek, 모래자루 mo-rae-jja-ru

sandbox *n*. 모래 놀이터 mo-rae nol-i-teo

sandcastle *n*. 모래성 mo-rae-seong

sandglass *n*. 모래시계 mo-rae-si-gye

sandpaper *n*. 사포 sa-po, 샌드페이퍼 ssaen-deu-pe-i-peo

sandwich *n*. 샌드위치 ssaen-deu-wi-chi

sane *adj*. 제정신의 je jeong-sin-ui; 건전한 geon-jeon-han

sanitary *adj*. 위생의 wi-saeng-ui; 위생적인 wi-saeng-jeog-in; 균이 없는 gyun-i eom-neun; ~ **napkin** *n*. 생리대 saeng-ni-dae

sanity *n*. 제정신 je-jeong-sin; 건전 geon-jeon

sap *n*. 수액 su-aek; 체액 che-aek; 활력 hwal-lyeok; *vt*. 수액을 짜내다 su-aeg-eul jja-nae-da

sapphire *n*. 사파이어 ssa-pa-i-eo

sarcastic *adj*. 빈정대는 bin-jeong-dae-neun, 비꼬는 bi-kko-neun, 풍자적인 pung-ja-jeog-in

sardine *n*. 정어리 jeong-eo-ri

satellite *n*. 위성 wi-seong; 인공위성 in-gong-wi-seong; 위성국 wi-seong-guk; 위성도시 wi-seong-do-si; 보조비행장 bo-jo-bi-haeng-jang; ~ **dish** 위성방송 수신기 wi-seong-bang-song su-sin-gi; ~ **TV** 위성 텔레비전 wi-seong tel-le-bi-jeon; ~ **broadcasting** 위성방송 wi-seong-bang-song

satisfaction *n*. 만족 man-jok; 변제 byeon-je; 배상 bae-sang; 의무이행 ui-mu-i-haeng

satisfactory *adj*. 만족한 man-jo-kan, 더할나위 없는 deo-hal-la-wi eom-neun

satisfied *adj*. 만족한 man-jo-kan, 흡족한 heup-jo-kan; 확신한 hawk-sin-han, 납득한 nap-deu-kan

satisfy *vt*. 만족시키다 man-jok-si-ki-da; 납득시키다 nap-deuk-si-ki-da; 변제하다 byeon-je-ha-da; 의무를 이행하다 ui-mu-reul i-haeng-ha-da

Saturday *n*. 토요일 to-yo-il

Saturn *n*. 토성 to-seong

sauce *n*. 소스 sso-sseu; 양념 yang-nyeom

saucepan *n*. 냄비 nam-bi

saucer *n*. 받침접시 bat-chim-jeop-si, 컵받침 keop-bat-chim

Saudi Arabia *n*. 사우디 아라비아 ssa-u-di a-ra-bi-a

sausage *n*. 소시지 sso-si-ji

savage *n*. 야만인 ya-man-in; 잔인한 사람 jan-in-han sa-ram; 버릇없는 사람 beo-reu-deom-neun sa-ram; *adj*. 야만의 ya-man-ui; 미개인의 mi-gae-in-ui; 잔혹한 jan-ho-kan; 황량한 hwang-nyang-han

save *vt*. 구하다 gu-ha-da; 지키다 ji-ki-da; 떼어두다 tte-eo-du-da; 절약하다 jeol-ya-ka-da; 모으다 mo-eu-da; 덜다 deol-da, 적게하다 jeok-ge ha-da

saving *n*. 절약 jeol-yak; 저금 jeo-geum; 구제 gu-je; ~s 저금 jeo-geum, 저축 jeo-chuk; ~s

account 보통예금구좌 bo-tong-ye-geum gu-jwa

savior *n.* 구조자 gu-jo-ja; 구세주 gu-se-ju

savor *n.* 맛 mat; 풍미 pung-mi; 기미 gi-mi; 흥미 heung-mi; *vt.* ...에 맛을 내다 ...e mas-eul nae-da; ...한 맛이 나다 ...han mas-i na-da; ...한 기미가 있다 ...han gi-mi-ga it-da

savory *adj.* 맛좋은 mat-jo-eun; 향기로운 hyang-gi-ro-un; 짭짤한 jjap-jjal-han; 기분 좋은 gi-bun-jo-eun; 평판이 좋은 pyeong-pan-i jo-eun

saw *n.* 톱 top; 격언 gyeog-eon; *vt.* 톱으로 자르다 tob-eu-ro ja-reu-da; 앞뒤로 움직이다 ap-dwi-ro um-jig-i-da

sawdust *n.* 톱밥 top-bap

sawmill *n.* 제제소 je-je-so

say *vt.* 말하다 mal-ha-da; 표현하다 pyo-hyeon-ha-da; ...라고 씌어져 있다 ...ra-go ssi-eo-jeo it-da; 전하다 jeon-ha-da; 암송하다 am-song-ha-da; ...라고 가정한다면 ...ra-go ga-jeong-han-da-myeon; 명령하다 myeong-nyeong-ha-da; *vi.* 말하다 mal-ha-da

saying *n.* 말하기 mal-ha-gi; 속담 sok-dam, 격언 gyeog-eon

scab *n.* 딱지 ttak-ji; 피부병 pi-bu-ppyeong; 비조합원 bi-jo-hab-won

scaffold *n.* 발판 bal-pan; 교수대 gyo-su-dae; 골격 gol-gyeok, 뼈대 ppyeo-dae; 야외무대 ya-oe-mu-dae

scald *n.* 화상 hwa-sang; 썩음 sseog-eum; 변색 byeon-saek; *vt.* 화상을 입히다 hwa-sang-eul i-pi-da; 데치다 de-chi-da; 끓이다 kkeul-i-da

scale *n.* 눈금 nun-kkeum; 자 ja; 축척 chuk-cheok; 비율 bi-yul; 규모 gyu-mo; 등급 deung-geup; 천칭접시 cheon-ching-jeop-si; 비늘 bi-neul; 물때 mul-ttae; 꼬투리 kko-tu-ri; ~s 양팔저울 yang-pal-jeo-ul, 천칭 cheon-ching

scallop *n.* 가리비 ga-ri-bi

scan *vt.* 자세히 조사하다 ja-se-hi jo-sa-ha-da; 운율을 고르다 un-yul-eul go-reu-da; 대충 훑어보다 dae-chung hult-eo-bo-da; 레이다로 탐지하다 re-i-da-ro tam-ji-ha-da

scandal *n.* 스캔들 seu-kaen-deul, 추문 chu-mun; 불명예 bul-myeong-ye; 물의 mul-ui; 악평 ak-pyeong

scandalous *adj.* 명예롭지 못한 myeong-ye-rop-ji mo-tan; 괘씸한 gwae-ssim-han; 욕을 하는 yog-eul ha-neun

Scandinavia *n.* 스칸디나비아 seu-kan-di-na-bi-a

Scandinavian *n.* 스칸디나비아 사람 seu-kan-di-na-bi-a ssa-ram; 스칸디나비아 말 seu-kan-di-na-bi-a mal; *adj.* 스칸디나비아의 seu-kan-di-na-bi-a-ui

scanner *n.* (*medical; computer*) 스캐너 seu-kae-neo

scar *n.* 흉터 hyung-teo; 자국 ja-guk; 상처 sang-cheo

scarce *adj.* 결핍한 gyeol-pi-pan, 불충분한 bul-chung-bun-han; 드문 deu-mun, 회귀한 hi-gwi-han

scarcely *n.* 간신히 gan-sin-hi, 가까스로 ga-kka-seu-ro; 거의 ...이 아니다 geo-i ...i a-ni-da

scare *vt.* 위협하다 wi-hyeo-pa-da; 놀라게 하다 nol-la-ge ha-da; 위협해서 쫓아내다 wi-hyeo-pae-seo jjoch-a-nae-da

scarecrow *n.* 허수아비 heo-su-a-bi; 허세 heo-se

scaredy-cat *n.* 겁쟁이 geop-jaeng-i

scarf *n.* 스카프 seu-ka-peu; 목도리 mok-do-ri; 덮개 deop-gae; 이음조각 i-eum-jjo-gak

scarlet *adj.* 주홍색의 ju-hong-saeg-ui; 주홍색 옷을 입은 ju-hong-saek os-eul ib-eun; 음란한 eum-nan-han

scatter *vt.* 흩어버리다 heut-eo-beo-ri-da; 쫓아버리다 jjoch-a-beo-ri-da; 뿌리다 ppu-ri-da; 흩뜨려 놓다 heut-tteu-ryeo no-ta; 낭비하다 nang-bi-ha-da; *vi.* 흩어지다 heut-eo-ji-da; 사라지다 sa-ra-ji-da

scenario *n.* 시나리오 si-na-rI-o, 영화각본 yeong-hwa-gak-bon

scene *n.* 장면 jang-myeon; 무대장치 mu-dae-jang-chi; 광경 gwang-gyeon, 경치 gyeong-chi; 현장 hyeon-jang

scenery *n.* 무대장면 mu-dae-jang-myeon; 배경 bae-gyeong; 풍경 pung-gyeong

scent *n.* 냄새 name-sae; 향기 hyang-gi; 후각 hu-gak; 센스 ssen-sseu; 냄새의 자취

name-sae-ui ja-chwi; 단서 dan-seo; 향수 hyang-su

schedule *n.* 시간표 si-gan-pyo; 예정표 ye-jeong-pyo; 일람표 il-lam-pyo; *vt.* 예정 하다 ye-jeong-ha-da; ...에 기재하다 ...e gi-jae-ha-ad

scheme *n.* 계획 gye-hoek; 설계 seol-gye; 책략 chaeng-nyak; 조직 jo-jik; 일람표 il-lam-pyo; 개요 gae-yo

scholar *n.* 학자 hak-ja; 장학생 jang-hak-saeng

scholarship *n.* 학식 hak-sik; 장학금 jang-hak-geum; 장학생의 자격 jang-hak-saeng-ui ja-gyeok

school *n.* 학교 hak-gyo; 수업 su-eop; 학부 hak-bu; 학계 hak-gye; 학파 hak-pa; 물고기 떼 mul-kko-gi-tte; **at** ~ 수업 중에 su-eop-jung-e; 학교에서 hak-gyo-e-seo; 등교하여 deung-gyo-ha-yeo; **to** ~ 학교에 hak-gyo-e; 학교로 hak-gyo-ro; ~ **bus** 학교버스 hak-gyo-ppeo-sseu, 스쿨버스 seu-kul-ppeo-sseu; ~ **age** 취학연령 chwi-hag-yeol-lyeong; 의무교육 연한 ui-mu-gyo-yuk yeon-han; ~ **district** 학구 hak-gu, 학군 hak-gun

schoolbook *n.* 교과서 gyo-gwa-seo

schoolchild *n.* 학생 hak-saeng

schoolmate *n.* 동창 dong-chang, 교우 gyo-u

schoolteacher *n.* 선생님 seon-saeng-nim

science *n.* 과학 gwa-hak; 과학분야 gwa-hak-bun-ya; 과학적 지식 gwa-hak-jeok-ji-sik; 기술 gi-sul

scientific *adj.* 과학적인 gwa-hak-jeog-in; 과학의 gwa-hag-ui; 학술상의 hak-sul-sang-ui; 과학연구에 종사하는 gwa-hag-yeon-gu-e jong-sa-ha-neun; 과학적으로 생각하는 gwa-hak-jeog-eu-ro saeng-ga-ka-neun

scientist *n.* 과학자 gwa-hak-ja; 자연과학자 ja-yeon-gwa-hak-ja

scissors *n. pl.* 가위 ga-wi

scold *vt.* 꾸짖다 kku-jit-da; 잔소리하다 jan-so-ri-ha-da

scoop *n.* 국자 guk-ja, 큰 숟가락 keun sut-ga-rak; 떠냄 tteo-naem; *vt.* 푸다 pu-da, 뜨다 tteu-da

scooter *n.* 스쿠터 seu-ku-teo

scope *n.* 범위 beom-wi, 영역 yeong-yeok; 기회 gi-hoe; 여지 yeo-ji; 의도 ui-do; 지역 ji-yeok

score *n.* 득점 deuk-jeom; 성적 seong-jeok; ~ **of people** 다수의 사람들 da-su-ui sa-ram-deul; ~ **of a game** 경기의 득점 gyeong-gi-ui deuk-jeom; **musical** ~ 악보 ak-bo; *vt.* 기록하다 gi-ro-ka-da; 채점하다 chae-jjeom-ha-da; 득점하다 deuk-jeom-ha-da; 악보를 쓰다 ak-bo-reul sseu-da; *vi.* 득점을 매기다 deuk-jeom-eul mae-gi-da; 이기다 i-gi-da; 성공하다 seong-gong-ha-da

scoreboard *n.* 스코어보드 seu-ko-eo-bo-deu, 득점 게시판 deuk-jeom ge-si-pan

scorecard *n.* 채점표 chae-jjeom-pyo

scorn *n.* 경멸 gyeong-myeol; 웃음거리 us-eum-kkeo-ri; *vt.* 경멸하다 gyeong-myeol-ha-da; 수치로 여기다 su-chi-ro yeo-gi-da

scorpion *n.* 전갈 jeon-gal; 음흉한 남자 eum-hung-han nam-ja

Scotch tape *n.* 스카치 테이프 seu-ka-chi-te-i-peu

Scotland *n.* 스코틀랜드 seu-ko-teul-laen-deu

scour *vt.* 문질러 닦다 mun-jil-leo dak-da; 비벼 빨다 bi-byeo-ppal-da; 씻어 없애다 ssis-eo eops-ae-da; 일소하다 il-sso-ha-da; 씻어내다 ssis-eo-nae-da

scout *n.* 정찰 jeong-chal; 정찰병 jeong-chal-byeong; 정찰기 jeong-chal-gi; 소년 소녀단원 so-nyeon-so-nyeo-dan-won; 신인 발굴자 sin-in bal-gul-ja; *vt.* 정찰하다 jeong-chal-ha-da; 수색하다 su-sae-ka-da; 스카우트하다 seu-ka-u-teu-ha-da; 제의를 뿌리치다 je-i-reul ppu-ri-chi-da

scrabble *vt.* 갈겨쓰다 gal-gyeo-sseu-da, 낙서하다 nak-seo-ha-da

scramble *vi.* 기어 오르다 gi-eo o-reu-da; 다투다 da-tu-da, 서로 빼앗다 seo-ro ppae-at-gi-da; 휘저어 익히다 hwi-jeo-eo i-ki-da

scrap *n.* 작은 조각 jag-eun jo-gak; 찌꺼기 jji-kkeo-gi; 발췌 bal-chwe

scrape *vt.* 문지르다 mun-ji-reu-da; 면도하다 myeon-do-ha-da; 문질러 지우다 mun-jil-leo ji-u-da; 문질러 없애다 mun-jil-leo eops-ae-da; 삐걱거리게 하다 ppi-geok-geo-ri-ge ha-da; 긁어 모으다 geulg-eo mo-eu-da; 긁어내다 geulg-eo-nae-da

scratch *vt.* 할퀴다 hal-kwi-da; 긁다 geuk-da; 휘갈겨 쓰다 hwi-gal-gyeo sseu-da; 지워 없애다 ji-wo eops-ae-da; 긁어 모으

다 geulg-eo mo-eu-da; ~ **paper** 메모용지 me-mo-yong-ji

scream *vt.* 큰 소리로 외치다 keun so-ri-ro oe-chi-da, 절규하다 jeol-gyu-ha-da; *vi.* 소리치다 so-ri-chi-da; 비명을 지르다 bi-myeong-eul ji-reu-da; 깔깔대다 kkal-kkal-dae-da; 앙앙울다ang-ang-ul-da; 기적이 울리다 gi-jeog-i ul-li-da; 바람이 씽씽 불다 ba-ram-i ssing-ssing-bul-da

screen *n.* 방충망 bang-chung-mang; **standing/partition** ~ 간막이 gan-mag-i; **movie/computer** ~ 스크린 seu-keu-rin; *vt.* 가리다 ga-ri-da; 가로막다 ga-ro-mak-da; 체로 치다 che-ro chi-da; 선발하다 seon-bal-ha-da; 영사하다 yeong-sa-ha-da; 촬영하다 chwal-yeong-ha-da

screening *n.* 심사 sim-sa, 선발 seon-bal; 상영 sang-yeong, 영사 yeong-sa

screw *n.* 나사 na-sa; 스크루 seu-keu-ru; 나선부 na-seon-bu; 병따개 byeong-tta-gae; 비틀기 bi-teul-gi; *vt.* 나사로 죄다 na-sa-ro joe-da; 돌리다 dol-li-da; 찡그리다 jjing-geu-ri-da; 긴장시키다 gin-jang-si-ki-da; 쥐어짜다 jwi-eo-jja-da; 괴롭히다 goe-ro-pi-da

screwdriver *n.* 스크루 드라이버 seu-keu-ru deu-ra-i-beo

scribble *vt.* 갈겨쓰다 gal-gyeo-sseu-da, 낙서하다 nak-seo-ha-da

script *n.* 손으로 쓴 것 son-eu-ro sseun geot; 필적 pil-jjeok; 대본 dae-bon, 각본 gak-bon

scroll *n.* 두루마리 du-ru-ma-ri

scrub *vt.* 비벼빨다 bi-byeo-ppal-da; 북북 문지르다 buk-buk mun-ji-reu-da; 제거하다 je-geo-ha-da

scruple *n.* 망설임 mang-seol-im; 사양 sa-yang; 양심의 가책 yang-sim-ui ga-chaek

scrupulous *adj.* 빈틈없는 bin-teum-eom-neun, 꼼꼼한 kkom-kkom-han; 양심적인 yang-sim-jeog-in, 신중한 sin-jung-han

scrutiny *n.* 음미 eum-mi; 자세히 봄 ja-se-hi bom; 투표 재검사 tu-pyo jae-geom-sa

sculpt *vi.* 조각하다 jo-ga-ka-da; 조각으로 장식하다 jo-gag-eu-ro jang-si-ka-da; 침식하다 chim-si-ka-da

sculptor *n.* 조각가 jo-gak-ga

sculpture *n.* 조각 jo-gak; 조각술 jo-gak-sul; 조각작품 jo-gak-jak-pum

scum *n.* 찌끼 jji-kki

scythe *n.* 큰 낫 keun nat

sea *n.* 바다 ba-da; 파도 pa-do; 다량 da-ryang; ~ **horse** 해마 hae-ma; ~ **level** 해수면 hae-su-myeon

seacoast *n.* 해안 hae-an, 바닷가 ba-dat-ga, 연안 yeon-an

seafood *n.* 해산물 hae-san-mul

seagull *n.* 갈매기 gal-mae-gi

seal *n.* 서약 seo-yak; 잔시우표 jang-sig-u-pyo; *(animal)* 바다표범 ba-da-pyo-beom, 물개 mul-kkae; *(something that secures or closes)* 봉인 bong-in; 보증인 bo-jeung-in; *vt.* 바다표범을 사냥하다 ba-da-pyo-beom-eul sa-nyang-ha-da; 날인하다 nal-in-ha-da; 봉인하다 bong-in-ha-da; 검인하다 geom-in-ha-da; 봉하다 bong-ha-da; 가두다 ga-du-da; 막다 mak-da; 비밀을 엄수하다 bi-mil-eul eom-su-ha-da

sealant *n.* 밀폐제 mil-pye-je, 봉합제 bong-hap-je

seam *n.* 솔기 sol-gi; 이음매 i-eum-mae; 접합선 jeo-pap-seon; 갈라진 틈 gal-la-jin teum; 주름 ju-reum

seaport *n.* 항구 hang-gu; 항구도시 hang-gu-do-si

search *n.* 탐색 tam-saek, 수색 su-saek; 추구 chu-gu; 조사 jo-sa, 검사 geom-sa; *vt.* 찾다 chat-da, 탐색하다 tam-sae-ka-da; 수색하다 su-sae-ka-da; 살펴보다 sal-pyeo bo-da; *vi.* 찾다 chat-da; 조사하다 jo-sa-ha-da

seashell *n.* 조개 jo-gae, 조가비 jo-ga-bi

seashore *n.* 해변 hae-byeon, 해안 hae-an

seasick *adj.* 뱃멀미가 난 bae-meol-mi-ga nan; 뱃멀미의 bae-meol-mi-ui

seasickness *n.* 뱃멀미 bae-meol-mi

season *n.* 계절 gye-jeol; 시절 si-jeol; 시기 si-gi; 한창때 han-chang-ttae; **in** ~ 때 맞춘 ttae mat-chun, 제철의 je-cheol-ui; **out of** ~ 철지난 cheol-ji-nan; ~ **ticket** 정기 입장권 jeong-gi ip-jang-kkwon

seasonal *adj.* 계절의 gye-jeol-ui; 주기적인 ju-gi-jeog-in

seasoned *adj.* 양념한 yang-nyeom-han; 잘 마른 jal ma-reun; 경험이 많은

gyeong-heom-i man-eun, 노련한 no-ryeon-han

seasoning *n.* 양념 yang-nyeom, 조미료 jo-mi-ryo

seat *n.* 자리 ja-ri, 좌석 jwa-seok; 왕권 wang-kkwon; 소재지 so-jae-ji; **Is this ~ free** 여기 자리 있습니까 yeo-gi ja-ri it-seum-ni-kka

seatbelt *n.* 안전벨트 an-jeon-bel-teu

seawater *n.* 바닷물 ba-dan-mul, 해수 hae-su

seaweed *n.* 해초 hae-cho; 바닷말 ba-dan-mal

seclusion *n.* 격리 gyeong-ni; 은퇴 eun-toe; 은둔 eun-dun

second *n.* 두번째 du-beon-jjae; 제2세대 je-i-se-dae; 대리자 dae-ri-ja; 보조자 bo-jo-ja; *adj.* 제2의 je-i-ui; 두번째의 du-beon-jjae-ui; 다음 가는 da-eum-ga-neun; 보조의 bo-jo-ui; 또 하나의 tto-ha-na-ui; **~ best** 차선책 cha-seon-chaek

secondary *adj.* 제2의 je-i-ui; 버금가는 beo-geum-ga-neun; 종속적인 jong-sok-jeog-in; 중등교육의 jung-deung-gyo-yug-ui; **~ school** 중등학교 jung-deung-hak-gyo

second-class *adj.* 제2종의 je-i-jong-ui; 2등급의 i-deung-geub-ui

second-degree *adj.* 2급의 i-geub-ui, 2도의 i-do-ui

second-generation *adj.* 2세의 i-se-dae-ui

secondhand *adj.* 중고의 jung-go-ui; 간접의 gan-jeob-ui

secret *n.* 비밀 bi-mil; 비결 bi-gyeol; 해결의 열쇠 hae-gyeol-ui yeol-ssoe; *adj.* 비밀의 bi-mil-ui; 은밀한 eun-mil-han; 눈에 보이지 않는 nun-e bo-i-ji an-neun; 으슥한 eu-seu-kan; 비밀을 지키는 bi-mil-eul ji-ki-neun; 신비스러운 sin-bi-seu-reo-un; **~ agent** 첩보원 cheop-bo-won, 간첩 gan-cheop; **~ service** 첩보기관 cheop-bo-gi-gwan

secretary *n.* 비서 bi-seo; 비서관 bi-seo-gwan; 사무관 sa-mu-gwan; 장관 jang-gwan

section *n.* 절단 jeol-ttan; 단면 dan-myeon; 단면도 dan-myeon-do; 구분 gu-bun; 당파 dang-pa; 부 bu

secular *adj.* 현세의 hyeon-se-ui; 비종교적인 bi-jong-gyo-jeog-in, 세속의 se-sog-ui

secure *adj.* 확실한 hawk-sil-han; 안전한 an-jeon-han; 견고한 gyeon-go-han; 확신하는 hawk-sin-ha-neun; *vt.* 안전하게 하다 an-jeon-ha-ge ha-da; 확고히 하다 hawk-go-hi ha-da; 보증하다 bo-jeung-ha-da; 보호하다 bo-ho-ha-da; 확보하다 hawk-bo-ha-da; 붙잡다 but-jap-da; 단단히 잠그다 dan-dan-hi jam-geu-da

security *n.* 안전 an-jeon; 보안 bo-an; 보증 bo-jeung; 유가증권 yu-kka-jeung-kkwon; **~ guard** 경비원 gyeong-bi-won

sedate *vt.* 진정시키다 jin-jeong-si-ki-da, 안정시키다 an-jeong-si-ki-da; *adj.* 침착한 chim-cha-kan; 진지한 jin-ji-han

sedated *adj.* 진정된 jin-jeong-doen, 차분해진 cha-bun-hae-jin, 침착해진 chim-cha-kae-jin

sedative *n.* 진정제 jin-jeong-je; 진정시키는 것 jin-jeong-si-ki-neun geot

seduce *vt.* 부추기다 bu-chu-gi-da; 유혹하다 yu-ho-ka-da

seduction *n.* 유혹 yu-hok; 매력 mae-ryeok

see *vt.* 보다 bo-da; 관찰하다 gwan-chal-ha-da; 만나보다 man-na-bo-da; 방문하다 bang-mun-ha-da; 데이트하다 de-i-teu-ha-da; 목격하다 mok-gyeo-ka-da; 인정하다 in-jeong-ha-da; 깨닫다 kkae-dat-da; 검사하다 geom-sa-ha-da; 생각해보다 saeng-ga-kae-bo-da; 배웅하다 bae-ung-ha-da; 원조를 주다 won-jo-reul ju-da; 마음을 쓰다 ma-eum-eul sseu-da; 묵인하다 mug-in-ha-da; *vi.* 보다 bo-da; 이해하다 i-hae-ha-da; 조사하다 jo-sa-ha-da; 생각해보다 saeng-ga-kae-bo-da; **to ~ about/to** 지켜보다 ji-kyeo-bo-da

seed *n.* 씨앗 ssi-at; 자손 ja-son; 알 al; 알뿌리 al-ppu-ri; 근원 geun-won, 원인 won-in; **~ money** 출발기금 chul-bal-gi-geum, 종자돈 jong-ja-tton

seedless *adj.* 씨가 없는 ssi-ga eom-neun

seek *vt.* 찾다 chat-da; 시도하다 si-do-ha-da; ...에 가고 싶어하다 ...e ga-go sip-eo-ha-da

seem *vi.* ...으로 보이다 ...eu-ro bo-i-da; ...으로 생각되다 ...eu-ro saeng-gak-doe-da; ...인 것 같다 ...in geot gat-da

seemingly *adv.* 겉으로는 geot-eu-ro-neun, 표면상으로는 pyo-myeon-sang-eu-ro-neun

seesaw *n.* 시소 si-so; 동요 dong-yo, 변동 byeon-dong

see-through *adj.* 비치는 bi-chi-neun; *n.* 비치
는 옷 bi-chi-neun ot

segment *n.* 단편 dan-pyeon; 부분 bu-bun; 구
획 gu-hoek

seize *vt.* 붙잡다 but-jap-da; 빼앗다 ppae-
at-da; 파악하다 pa-a-ka-da; 엄습하다
eom-seu-pa-da; 체포하다 che-po-ha-da;
몰수하다 mol-ssu-ha-da; 잡아매다
jab-a-mae-da

seizure *n.* 붙잡기 but-jap-da; 압류 am-nyu;
점령 jeom-nyeong; 발작 bal-jjak

seldom *adv.* 드물게 deu-mul-ge; 좀처
럼 ...하지 않는 jom-che-reom ...ha-ji
an-neun

select *vt.* 선택하다 seon-tae-ka-da; 발췌하다
bal chwe ha da; 선발하다 seon-bal-ha-da

selection *n.* 선발 seon-bal; 선정 seon-jeong;
발췌 bal-chwe

self *adj.* 지기 ja-gi, 지신 ja-sin; 본성 bon-
seong, 진수 jin-su

self-centered *adj.* 자기 중심적인 ja-gi jung-
sim-jeog-in, 이기적인 i-gi-jeog-in

self-control *n.* 자제심 ja-je-sim, 극기심
geuk-gi-sim

self-defense *n.* 자기 방어 ja-gi bang-eo; 정
당방위 jeong-dang-bang-wi

selfish *adj.* 이기적인 i-gi-jeog-in, 제멋대로
하는 je-meot-dae-ro ha-neun

self-service *adj.* 셀프 서비스의 ssel-peu
sseo-pi-sseu-ui

sell *vt.* 팔다 pal-da; 배반하다 bae-ban-ha-da;
판매를 촉진하다 pan-mae-reul chok-jin-
ha-da; 납득시키다 nap-deuk-si-ki-da

seller *n.* 판매인 pan-mae-in; 팔리는 상품
pal-li-neun sang-pum

sellout *n.* 매진 mae-jin, 대만원
dae-man-won

semester *n.* 한학기 han-hak-gi

semiannual *adj.* 반년마다의 ban-nyeon-ma-
da-ui, 일년에 두번의 il-lyeon-e du-beon-ul

semicolon *n.* 세미콜론 sse-mi-kol-lon

semiconductor *n.* 반도체 ban-do-che

semifinal *n.* 준결승 jun-gyeol-sseung

seminar *n.* 세미나 sse-mi-na

semiprecious *adj.* 준보석의 jun-bo-seog-ui

senate *n.* 상원 sang-won; 입법부 ip-beop-bu;
의회 ui-hoe

senator *n.* 상원의원 sang-won-ui-won

send *vt.* 보내다 bo-nae-da; 파견하다 pa-
gyeon-ha-da; 송신하다 song-sin-ha-da; 송
전하다 song-jeon-ha-da; 차례로 돌리다
cha-rye-ro dol-li-da; 발사하다 bal-ssa-ha-
da; 내몰다 nae-mol-da; ...의 상태가 되게
하다 ...ui sang-tae-ga doe-ge ha-da; **to ~
back** 돌려주다 dol-lyeo-ju-da; 반환하다
ban-hwan-ha-da; **to ~ for** ...을 가지러 보
내다 ...eul ga-ji-reo bo-nae-da; ...을 부르
러 보내다 ...eul bu-reu-reo bo-nae-da; **to
~ off** 배웅하다 bae-ung-ha-da; 발송하다
bal-ssong-ha-da; 여기를 내다 yeon-gi-reul
nae-da; 쫓아내다 jjoch-a-nae-da

sender *n.* 발송인 bal-ssong-in, 보내는 사람
bo-nae-neun sa-ram; 발신기 bal-ssin-gi; 송
신기 song-sin-gi

Senegal *n.* 세네갈 sse-ne-gal

senior *n.* 연장자 yeon-jang-ja; 선배 seon-
bae; 상사 sang-sa; 4학년 sa-hang-nyeon;
adj. 손위의 son-wi-ui; 연상의 yeon-
sang-ui; 선배의 seon-bae-ui; 최상급의
choe-sang-kkeub-ui; **~ citizen** 노인 no-in

sensation *n.* 감각 gam-gak; 마음 ma-eum; 감
동 gam-dong; 센세이션 ssen-sse-i-syeon

sensational *adj.* 선풍적인 seon-pung-jeog-
in; 선정적인 seon-jeong-jeog-in; 지각의
ji-gag-ui

sense *n.* 감각 gam-gak; 오감 o-gam; 느낌
neu-kkim; 감수성 gam-su-sseong; 의견
ui-gyeon; 의미 ui-mi; 이치에 맞음 i-chi-e
maj-eum

senseless *adj.* 무감각한 mu-gam-ga-kan;
몰상식한 mol-ssang-si-kan; 뜻없는
tteud-eom-neun

sensitive *adj.* 민감한 min-gam-han; 느끼
기 쉬운 neu-kki-gi swi-un; 감수성이 강
한 gam-su-sseong-i gang-han; 신경과민
의 sin-gyeong-gwa-min-ui; 화를 잘 내
는 hwa-reul jal nae-neun; 걱정하는 jeok-
jeong-ha-neun; 감도가 좋은 gam-do-ga
jo-eun

sensor *n.* 감지기 gam-ji-gi, 센서 ssen-sseo

sentence *n.* 판정 pan-jeong; *(grammar)* 문장
mun-jang; *(prison)* 판결 pan-gyeol; *vt.* 판
결을 내리다 pan-gyeol-eul nae-ri-da; 형을
선고하다 hyeong-eul seon-go-ha-da

sentimental *adj.* 감상적인 gam-sang-jeog-in;
감정적인 gam-jeong-jeog-in

separate *adj*. 분리된 bul-li-doen; 따로따로의 tta-ro-tta-ro-ui; 독립된 dong-nip-doen; 별거하는 byeol-geo-ha-neun; *vt*. 분리하다 bul-li-ha-da; 떼어놓다 tte-eo-no-ta; 구별하다 gu-byeol-ha-da; 분류하다 bul-lyu-ha-da; *vi*. 분리하다 bul-li-ha-da; 독립하다 dong-ni-pa-da; 교제를 끊다 gyo-je-reul kkeun-ta; 별거하다 byeol-geo-ha-da; 헤어지다 he-eo-ji-da

separation *n*. 분리 bul-li; 이별 i-byeol; 별거 byeol-geo; 이직 i-jik

September *n*. 9월 gu-wol

septic *adj*. 부패시키는 bu-pae-si-ki-neun; 부패에 의한 bu-pae-e ui-han; ~ **tank** 오수 정화조 o-su jeong-hwa-jo; **to become** ~ 부패되다 bu-pae-doe-da

sequel *n*. 후편 hu-pyeon; 결과 gyeol-gwa; 귀착점 gwi-chak-jeom

sequence *n*. 연속 yeon-sok; 귀결 gwi-gyeol

sequential *adj*. 연속하는 yeon-so-ka-neun; 결과로 일어나는 gyeol-gwa-ro il-eo-na-neun

sergeant *n*. 하사관 ha-sa-gwan; 경사 gyeong-sa

serial number *n*. 일련번호 il-lyeon-beon-ho

series *n. pl*. 일련 il-lyeon; 연속 yeon-sok; 시리즈 ssi-ri-jeu

serious *adj*. 진지한 jin-ji-han; 엄숙한 eom-su-kan; 중대한 jung-dae-han; 심상치 않은 sim-sang-chi an-eun; 딱딱한 ttak-tta-kan

sermon *n*. 설교 seol-gyo; 잔소리 jan-so-ri

serum *n*. 장액 jang-aek; 혈청 hyeol-cheong; 임파액 im-pa-aek

servant *n*. 고용인 go-yong-in; 하인 ha-in; 부하 bu-ha; 공무원 gong-mu-won

serve *vt*. 섬기다 seom-gi-da; 주문을 받다 ju-mun-eul bat-da; 음식을 차리다 eum-sig-eul cha-ri-da; 편의를 제공하다 pyeon-ui-reul je-gong-ha-da; 도움이 되다 do-um-i doe-da; 기한을 채우다 gi-han-eul chae-u-da; 서브하다 sseo-beu-ha-da

service *n*. 봉사 bong-sa; 공헌 gong-heon; 도움 do-um; 일 il; 고용 go-yong; 서비스 sseo-bi-sseu; 운항 un-hang; 공공사업 gong-gong-sa-eop; 부문 bu-mun; 병역 byeong-yeok; 예배 ye-bae; ~ **charge** 봉사료 bong-sa-ryo; **The ~ is not included** 서

비스가 포함되지 않았습니다 sseo-bi-sseu-ga po-ham-doe-ji an-at-seum-ni-ta; ~ **area** 가시청 구역 ga-si-cheong gu-yeok, 유효범위 yu-hyo-beom-wi, 공급구역 gong-geup-gu-yeok; 서비스 에어리어 sseo-bi-sseu e-eo-ri-eo

sesame *n*. 참깨 cham-kkae; ~ **oil** 참기름 cham-gi-reum

session *n*. 개회중 gae-hoe-jung; 회기 hoe-gi; 학기 hak-gi; 활동기간 hwal-ttong-gi-gan

set *n*. 해 지는 시각 hae ji-neun si-gak; 해 짐 hae jim; 한벌 han-beol; 한세트 han-sse-teu; 수상기 su-sang-gi; 모양새 mo-yang-ae; 자세 ja-se; 경향 gyeong-hyang; *adj*. 고정된 go-jeong-doen; 결심한 gyeol-ssim-han; 정규의 jeong-gyu-ui; **a ~ price** 정찰가 jeong-chal-kka; *vt*. 두다 du-da, 놓다 no-ta; 앉히다 an-chi-da; 심다 sim-tta; 배치하다 bae-chi-ha-da; 준비하다 jun-bi-ha-da; 붙이다 bu-chi-da; 향하다 hyang-ha-da; ...하게 하다 ...ha-ge ha-da; 정하다 jeong-ha-da; 고정하다 go-jeong-ha-da; *vi*. 저물다 jeo-mul-da; 기울다 gi-ul-da; 굳어지다 gud-eo-ji-da; 모양이 잡히다 mo-yang-i ja-pi-da; 어울리다 eo-ul-li-da; 종사하다 jong-sa-ha-da; 움직이기 시작하다 um-jig-i-gi si-ja-ka-da; **to ~ something down** 적어두다 jeog-eo-du-da; 규정하다 gyu-jeong-ha-da; **Allow it to ~ in the refrigerator** 그것을 냉장고 안에서 굳도록 한다 geu-geos-eul naeng-jang-go an-eo-seo gut-do-rok han-da
; **to ~ a bone** 접골하다 jeop-gol-ha-da

setting *n*. 놓음 no-eum; 일몰 il-mol; 보석세팅 bo-seok-sse-ting; 배경 bae-gyeong, 환경 hwan-gyeong; 무대장치 mu-dae-jang-chi; 식기류 sik-gi-ryu

settle *vt*. 놓다 no-ta; 안정시키다 an-jeong-si-ki-da; 앉히다 an-chi-da; 자리잡게 하다 ja-ri-jap-ge ha-da; ...에 거주하다 ...e geo-ju-ha-da; 진정시키다 jin-jeong-si-ki-da; 가라앉히다 ga-ra-an-chi-da; 결정하다 gyeol-jjeong-ha-da; 정리하다 jeong-ni-ha-da; 물려주다 mul-lyeo-ju-da; *vi*. 앉다 an-tta; 자리잡다 ja-ri-jap-da; 안정하다 an-jeong-ha-da; 결심하다 gyeol-ssim-ha-da; 가라앉히다 ga-ra-an-chi-da; *(fall* *to the bottom)* 가라앉다 ga-ra-an-tta; **to ~ down** 앉다 an-tta; 이주하다 i-ju-ha-da; 안정하다 an-jeong-ha-da

settlement *n.* 이민 i-min; 생활의 안정 saeng-hwal-ui an-jong; 정리 jeong-ni; 해결 hae-gyeol; *(habitation)* 정착 jeong-chak; 거류지 geo-ryu-ji; *(legal)* 양도 yang-do

seven *num.* 일곱 il-gop; 칠 chil

seventeen *num.* 열일곱 yeol-il-gop; 십칠 sip-chil

seventeenth *adj.* 열일곱번째의 yeol-il-gop-beon-jjae-ui; 제십칠회 je-sip-chil-hoe

seventh *adj.* 일곱번째의 il-gop-beon-jjae-ui; 제칠회 je-chil-hoe

seventy *num.* 일흔 il-heun; 칠십 chil-ssip

several *adj.* 몇몇의 myeon-myeos-ui; 여러가지의 yeo-reo-ga-ji-ui

severe *adj.* 엄한 eom-han; 엄격한 eom-kkyeo-kan; 심한 sim-han; 힘드는 him-deu-neun; 엄밀한 eom-mil-han; 엄숙한 eom-su-kan

sew *vt.* 꿰매다 kkwe-mae-da; 제본하다 je-bon-ha-da; *vi.* 바느질하다 ba-neu-jil-ha-da; 재봉틀로 박다 jae-bong-teul-lo bak-da

sewage *n.* 하수 ha-su, 하수도 ha-su-do

sewer *n.* 재봉사 jae-bong-sa; 하수구 ha-su-gu

sewerage *n.* 하수설비 ha-su-seol-bi, 하수도 ha-su-do; 하수처리 ha-su-cheo-ri

sewing *n.* 재봉 jae-bong; 재봉업 jae-bong-eop; 바느질감 ba-neu-jil-kkam; **~ needle** 바늘 ba-neul

sewing machine *n.* 재봉틀 jae-bong-teul

sex *n.* 성 seong; 성별 seong-byeol; 성욕 seong-yok; 성교 seong-gyo; **~ appeal** 성적 매력 seong-jjeong-mae-ryeok; **~ education** 성교육 seong-gyo-yuk; **~ ratio** 성비 seong-bi; **~ role** 성역할 seong-yeo-kal

sexism *n.* 성차별 seong-cha-byeol, 남성상위주의 nam-seong-sang-wi-ju-i

sexual *adj.* 성적인 seong-jjeog-in; 성의 seong-ui; **~ orientation** 성적성향 seong-jjeok seong-hyang; **~ assault** 성폭행 seong-po-kaeng, 강간 gang-gan

sexuality *n.* 성별 seong-byeol; 성욕 seong-yok

shabby *adj.* 초라한 cho-ra-han; 해어진 hae-eo-jin; 추레한 chu-re-han; 비열한 bi-yeol-han

shade *n.* 그늘 geu-neul; 땅거미 ttang-kkeo-mi; 음양 eum-yang; 미묘한 차이 mi-myo-han cha-i; 아주 조금 a ju jo-geum; 어두운 기색 eo-du-un gi-saek; *(of a tree)* 나무그늘 na-mu geu-neul; **lamp ~** 차양 cha-yang; **window ~** 차광막 cha-gwang-mak

shadow *n.* 그림자 geu-rim-ja; 어두움 eo-du-um; 슬픔 seul-peum; 영상 yeong-sang; 자취 ja-chwi

shady *adj.* 그늘의 geu-neul-ui; 의심스러운 ui-sim-seu-reo-un; 떳떳하지 못한 tteot-tteo-ta-ji mo-tan

shaft *n.* 자루 ja-ru; 끌채 kkeul-chae; 샤프트 sya-peu-teu

shaggy *adj.* 털북숭이의 teol-buk-sung-i-ui; 머리가 덥수룩한 meo-ri-ga deop-su-ru-kan; 우둘두툴한 u-tul-du-tul-han

shake *vt.* 흔들다 heun-deul-da; 휘두르다 hwi-du-reu-da; 줄어들게 하다 jul-eo-deul-ge ha-da; 동요시키다 dong-yo-si-ki-da; *vi.* 흔들리다 heun-deul-li-da; 떨다 tteol-da; 뚝뚝 떨어지다 ttuk-ttuk tteol-eo-ji-da

shaker *n.* 셰이커 sy-i-keo

shaky *adj.* 흔들리는 heun-deul-li-neun; 떨리는 tteol-li-neun; 불안정한 bul-an-jeong-han

shall *aux.* ...일까요 ...il-kka-yo, ...할까요 ...hal-kka-yo; ...하지 않으시겠습니까 ...ha-ji an-eu-si-get-seum-ni-kka; ...하여 주겠다 ...ha-yeo ju-get-da, 반드시 ...하다 ban-deu-si...ha-da

shallow *adj.* 얕은 yat-eun; 천박한 cheon-ba-kan; 피상적인 pi-sang-jeog-in

sham *n.* 속임 sog-im; 가짜 ga-jja; 사기꾼 sa-gi-kkun; 꾀병쟁이 kkoe-byeong-jaeng-i; 침대덮개 chim-dae-deop-gae

shaman *n.* 샤먼 sya-meon, 무당 mu-dang

shame *n.* 부끄러움 bu-kkeu-reo-um, 수치 su-chi; **What a ~** 이게 무슨 창피한 일이지 i-ge mu-seun chang-pi-han il-i-ji

shameful *adj.* 부끄러운 bu-kkeu-reo-un, 창피스러운 chang-pi-seu-reo-un

shameless *adj.* 파렴치한 pa-ryeom-chi-han, 뻔뻔스러운 ppeon-ppeon-seu-reo-un

shampoo n. 샴푸 syam-pu

shape n. 모양 mo-yang; 생김새 saeng-gim-sae; 형태 hyeong-tae; 상태 sang-tae; 형식 hyeong-sik; vt. 모양짓다 mo-yang-jit-da; 구체화하다 gu-che-hwa-ha-da; 맞추다 mat-chu-da

share n. 역할 yeo-kal; 공헌 gong-heon; *(a portion)* 분담 bun-dam; 몫 mok; *(of a company)* 주식 ju-sik, 증권 jeung-kkwon; vt. 분배하다 bun-bae-ha-da; 공유하다 gong-yu-ha-da; vi. 할당받다 hal-ttang-bat-da; 공동부담하다 gong-dong-bu-dam-ha-da

shareholder n. 주주 ju-ju

shark n. 상어 sang-eo; 탐욕스러운 사람 tam-yok-su-reo-un sa-ram; 고리대금업자 go-ri-dae-geum eop-ja

sharp adj. 날카로운 nal-ka-ro-un; 격렬한 gyeong-nyeol-han; 예민한 ye-min-han; 명확한 myeong-hwa-kan; ~ **eyed** 눈이 날카로운 nun-i nal-ka-ro-un; 통찰력이 예리한 tong-chal-lyeog-i e-ri-han; ~ **tongued** 말이 신랄한 mal-i sil-lal-han, 독설을 내뱉는 dok-seol-eul nae-baen-neun

sharpen vt. 날카롭게 하다 nal-ka-rop-ge ha-da; 뾰족하게 하다 ppyo-jo-ka-ge ha-da; 격심하게 하다 gyeok-sim-ha-ge ha-da; 또렷하게 하다 tto-ryeo-ta-ge ha-da

shave vt., vi. 깎다 kkak-da; 면도하다 myeon-do-ha-da; 스치다 seu-chi-da

shaving n. 면도 myeon-do; ~ **brush** 면도용 솔 myeon-do-yong sol; ~ **cream** 면도용 크림 myeon-do-yong keu-rim, 셰이빙 크림 sye-i-bing keu-rim

shawl n. 쇼올 syo-ol

she pron. 그 여자분이 geu yeo-ja-bun-i; 그 여자분은 geu yeo-ja-bun-eun; 그 여자분을 geu-yeo-ja-bun-eul

sheaf n., **sheaves** pl. 단 dan, 묶음 mukk-eum

shear n. 큰 가위 keun ga-wi; 전지가위 jeon-ji-ga-wi; 양털깎기 yang-teol-kkak-gi; 깎아낸 양털 kkakk-a-naen yang-teol; 털깎는 횟수 teol-kkang-neun hoet-su; ~**s** 큰 가위 keun ga-wi; 전지가위 jeon-ji-ga-wi; vt. 잘라내다 jal-la-nae-da; 치다 chi-da; 빼앗다 ppae-at-da

shed n. 헛간 heot-gan; 가축우리 ga-chug-u-ri; 작업장 jag-eop-jang; 격납고 gyeong-nap-go; 창고 chang-go; vt. 뿌리다 ppu-ri-da; 흘리다 heul-li-da; 떨어뜨리다 tteol-eo-tteu-ri-da; 벗어버리다 beos-eo-beo-ri-da; 발산하다 bal-ssan-ha-da; 결별하다 gyeol-byeol-ha-da; 영향을 주다 yeong-hyang-eul ju-da

sheep n. 양 yang; 양가죽 yang-ga-juk; 온순한 사람 on-sun-han sa-ram; 신자 sin-ja

sheer adj. 얇은 yalb-eun; 섞이지 않은 seok-i-ji an-eun; 순전한 sun-jeon-han; 험준한 heom-jun-han

sheet n. 시트 si-teu, 홑이불 hon-ni-bul; 얇은 판 yalb-eun pan; 장 jang

shelf n., **shelves** pl. 선반 seon-ban; 여울목 yeo-ul-mok; 암초 am-cho

shell n. 조가비 jo-ga-bi; 껍질 kkeop-jil; 어패류 eo-pae-rye; 조개 jo-gae; 포탄 po-tan; 외관 oe-gwan; ~**ed** 껍질을 깐 kkeop-jil-eul kkan

shellfish n. 어패류 eo-pae-ryu; 조개 jo-gae; 새우 sae-u; 게 ge

shelter n. 은신처 eun-sin-cheo; 엄호물 eom-ho-mul; 보호 bo-ho; 피난 pi-nan

shelve vt. 선반에 얹다 seon-ban-e eon-tta; 보류하다 bo-ryu-ha-da; 해고하다 hae-go-ha-da; 완만히 경사지다 wan-man-hi gyeong-sa-ji-da

shepherd n. 양치기 yang-chi-gi, 목자 mok-ja; 목사 mok-sa

sheriff n. 군 보안관 gun bo-an-gwan

shield n. 방패 bang-pae; 보호물 bo-ho-mul; 보호자 bo-ho-ja; 보호 bo-ho

shift n. 변천 byeon-cheon; 변화 byeon-hwa; 교체 gyo-che; 교대 gyo-dae; 임시변통 im-si-byeon-tong; vt. 위치를 옮기다 wi-chi-reul om-gi-da; 변경하다 byeon-gyeong-ha-da; 바꾸다 ba-kku-da; vi. 이동하다 i-dong-ha-da; 방향을 바꾸다 bang-hyang-eul ba-kku-da; 변화하다 byeon-hwa-ha-da; 변속하다 byeon-so-ka-da; 변통하다 byeon-tong-ha-da

shimmer vi. 희미하게 반짝이다 hi-mi-ha-ge ban-jjag-i-da

shin n. 정강이 jeong-gang-i

shine vt. 빛나게 하다 bin-na-ge ha-da; 닦다 dak-da; vi. 빛나다 bin-na-da; 비치다 bi-chi-da; 두드러지다 du-deu-reo-ji-da

ship *n.* 배 bae; 우주선 u-ju-seon; *vt.* 수송하
다 su-song-ha-da; 적재하다 jeok-jae-ha-
da; 배에 설비하다 bae-e seol-bi-ha-da;
선원으로 고용하다 seon-won-eu-ro
go-yong-ha-da

shipwreck *n.* 난파 nan-pa; 파멸 pa-myeol,
파괴 pa-goe

shirt *n.* 와이셔츠 ya-i-syeo-cheu; 셔츠
syeo-cheu

shiver *vi.* 와들와들 떨다 wa-deul-wa-
deul tteol-da; 돛이 펄럭이다 doch-i
peol-leog-i-da

shock *n.* 충격 chung-gyeok; 타격 ta-gyeok;
진동 jin-dong; **electric** ~ 전기충격 jeon-
gi-chung-gyeok; *vt.* 부딪치다 bu-dit-chi-
da; 놀라다 nol-la-da

shocked *adj.* 충격을 받은 chung-gyeog-eul
bad-eun, 얼떨떨한 eol-tteol-tteol-han

shoe *n.* 신 sin, 신발 sin-bal; 구두 gu-du; ~
polish 구두약 gu-du-yak

shoebrush *n.* 구둣솔 gu-dut-sol

shoehorn *n.* 구둣주걱 gu-dut-ju-geok

shoelace *n.* 신발끈 sin-bal-kkeun; 구두끈
gu-du-kkeun

shoot *vt.* 쏘다 sso-da, 발사하다 bal-ssa-ha-
da; 던지다 deon-ji-da; 연발하다 yeon-bal-
ha-da; 사살하다 sa-sal-ha-da

shooting range *n.* 사격장 sa-gyeok-jang

shooting star *n.* 유성 yu-seong

shop *n.* 가게 ga-ge; 공장 gong-jang; 작업장
jag-eop-jang; *vi.* 물건을 사다 mul-geon-
eul sa-da, 쇼핑하다 syo-ping-ha-da

shopkeeper *n.* 가게주인 ga-ge-ju-in

shopping *n.* 쇼핑 syo-ping, 물건사기 mul-
geon-sa-gi; ~ **bag** 쇼핑백 syo-ping-ppaek;
~ **center** 쇼핑센터 syo-ping-ssen-teo; ~
mall 쇼핑몰 syo-ping-mol

shore *n.* 바닷가 ba-dat-ga, 해안 hae-an; 지
주 ji-ju, 버팀대 beo-tim-ttae

short *adj.* 짧은 jjalb-eun; 간결한 gan-gyeol-
han; 키가 작은 ki-ga jag-eun; 불충분
한 bul-chung-bun-han; ~ **circuit** 누전
nu-jeon; ~ **list** 선발 후보자 명단 seon-bal
hu-bo-ja myeong-dan; ~ **story** 단편소설
dan-pyeon-so-seol

shortage *n.* 부족 bu-jok; 결핍 gyeol-pip; 부
족량 bu-jong-nyang; 결함 gyeol-ham, 결
점 gyeol-jjeom

shortcoming *n.* 결점 gyeol-jjeom, 단점
dan-jjeom

shortcut *n.* 지름길 ji-reum-kkil; 손쉬운 방법
son-swi-un bang-beop

shorten *vt.* 짧게 하다 jjalp-ge ha-da; 짧게 보
이다 jjalp-ge bo-i-da; 삭감하다 sak-gam-
ha-da; 생략하다 saeng-nya-ka-da; 줄이
다 jul-i-da

shortening *n.* 짧게함 jjalp-ge-ham, 단축
dan-chuk; 쇼트닝 syo-teu-ning

shorthanded *adj.* 일손이 모자라는 il-sson-I
mo-ja-ra-neun

shortly *adv.* 곧 got; 잠시 jam-si; 간단히 gan-
dan-hi; 냉랭하게 naeng-naeng-ha-ge

shorts *n. pl.* 반바지 ban-ba-ji

shortsighted *adj.* 근시안의 geun-si-an-
ui, 근시의 geun-si-ui; 근시안적인
geun-si-an-jeog-in

short-term *adj.* 단기간의 dan-gi-gan-ui

shot *n.* 발포 bal-po, 발사 bal-ssa, 포성 po-
seong; 탄환 tan-hwan

should *aux.* ...일 것이다 ...il goes-i-sa; ...하
여야 하다 ...ha-yeo-ya ha-da; ...하다
니 ...ha-da-ni; ...하지 않으면 안되다
...ha-ji an-eu-myeon an-doe-da; 다름아
닌 da-reum-a-nin; 반드시...일 것이다
ban-deu-si ...il geos-i-da; 만일 ...이라면
man-il ...i-ra-myeon

shoulder *n.* 어깨 eo-kkae; 어깨관절 eo-kkae-
gwan-jeol; 어깨부분 eo-kkae-bu bun

shout *vi.* 외치다 oe-chi-da, 큰 소리를 내
다 keun so-ri-reul nae-da; 소리를 지르다
so-ri-reul ji-reu-da; *n.* 외침 oe-chim, 환호
hwan-ho, 갈채 gal-chae

shove *vt.* 밀치다 mil-chi-da; *vi.* 밀다 mil-da;
밀고가다 mil-go-ga-da

shovel *n.* 부삽 bu-sap, 삽 sap; 큰숟갈
keun-sut-gal

show *n.* 보이기 bo-i-gi; 과시 gwa-si;
표시 pyo-si; 구경거리 gu-gyeong-
kkeo-ri; 징후 jing-hu; 외관 oe-gwan;
TV ~ 텔레비전 프로 tel-le-bi-jeon
peu-ro; **talk** ~ 토크쇼 to-keu-ssyo;
vt. 보이다 bo-i-da; 지적하다 ji-jeo-ka-da;
나타내다 na-ta-nae-da; 제시하다
je-si-ha-da; 설명하다 seol-myeong-ha-
da; 안내하다 an-nae-ha-da; 진열하다
jin-yeol-ha-da

show business *n.* 연예업 yeon-ye-eop, 연예계 yeon-ye-gye

showcase *n.* 진열장 jin-yeol-jjang, 윈도우 win-do-u

shower *n.* 소나기 so-na-gi; 쏟아짐 ssod-a-jim; 축하선물 chu-ka-seon-mul; *vi.* 소나기가 오다 so-na-gi-ga o-da; 빗발치듯 쏟아지다 bit-bal-chi-deut ssod-a-ji-da

showmanship *n.* 흥행수완 heung-haeng-su-wan; 연출솜씨 yeon-chul-som-ssi

showroom *n.* 진열실 jin-yeol-sil, 전시실 jeon-si-sil

shred *n.* 조각 jo-gak, 파편 pa-pyeon; 소량 so-ryang; *vt.* 조각조각 찢다 jo-gak-jo-gak jjit-da

shrewd *adj.* 빈틈없는 bin-teum-eom-neun; 기민한 gi-min-han

shrimp *n.* 작은 새우 jag-eun sae-u; 왜소한 사람 wae-so-han sa-ram

shrine *n.* 사당 sa-dang; 납골당 nap-gol-ttang

shrink *vt.* 수축시키다 su-chuk-si-ki-da; 축소시키다 chuk-so-si-ki-da; *vi.* 줄어들다 jul-eo-deul-da; 작아지다 jag-a-ji-da

shuffle *vt.* 발을 끌다 bal-eul kkeul-da; 이리저리 움직이다 i-ri-jeo-ri um-jig-i-da; 되는대로 입다 doe-neun-dae-ro ip-da; 얼버무리다 eol-beo-mu-ri-da; *(cards)* 카드를 섞다 ka-deu-reul seok-da

shut *vt.* 닫다 dat-da; 눈을 감다 nun-eul gam-tta; 폐쇄하다 pye-swae-ha-da; 막다 mak-da

shutdown *n.* 일시휴업 il-ssi-hyu-eop, 조업정지 jo-eop-jeong-ji

shutoff *n.* 마개 ma-gae, 차단장치 cha-dan-jang-chi; 정지 jeong-ji, 차단 cha-dan

shutter *n.* 덧문 deon-mun; 뚜껑 ttu-kkeong; *(window)* 셔터 syeo-teo; **camera ~** 카메라 셔터 ka-me-ra syeo-teo; **~ speed** 셔터속도 syeo-teo-sok-do

shuttle *n.* 셔틀 syeo-teul; 북 buk; *vt., vi.* 앞뒤로 움직이다 ap-dwi-ro um-jig-i-da; 왕복하다 wang-bo-ka-da; **~ service** 왕복운행 wang-bog-un-haeng; 셔틀서비스 syeo-teul-sseo-bi-sseu

shy *adj.* 소심한 so-sim-han; 조심성 많은 jo-sim-sseong man-eun; 잘 놀라는 jal nol-la-neun

Siberia *n.* 시베리아 si-be-ri-a

sibling *n.* 형제자매 hyeong-je-ja-mae

sick *adj.* 병에 걸린 byeong-e geol-lin; 환자의 hwan-ja-ui; 느글거리는 neu-geul-geo-ri-neun; 신물나는 sin-mul-lan-neun; 그리워하는 geu-ri-wo-ha-neun; 좋지 않은 jo-chi-an-eun

sickness *n.* 병 byeong; 멀미 meol-mi, 구역질 gu-yeok-jil

side *n.* 쪽 jjok, 측면 cheung-myeon; 산중턱 san-jung-teok; 가장자리 ga-jang-ja-ri; 변두리 byeon-du-ri; 옆구리 yeop-gu-ri; 옆 yeop; 편 pyeon; 면 myeon; **~ effect** 부작용 bu-jag-yong

sidewalk *n.* 보도 bo-do, 인도 in-do

sideways *adj.* 옆으로 향한 yeop-eu-ro hang-han; *adv.* 옆으로 yeop-eu-ro

sieve *n.* 체 che; 조리 jo-ri; 입이 가벼운 사람 ib-i ga-byeo-un sa-ram

sift *vt.* 체로 치다 che-ro chi-da; 거르다 geo-reu-da; 가려내다 ga-ryeo-nae-da; 면밀히 조사하다 myeon-mil-hi jo-sa-ha-da; 손가락으로 빗다 son-kka-rag-eu-ro bit-da

sigh *n.* 한숨 han-sum; 탄식 tan-sik; 산들거리는 소리 san-deul-geo-ri-neun so-ri; *vi.* 한숨 쉬다 han-sum-swi-da; 탄식하다 tan-si-ka-da; 그리워 한탄하다 geu-ri-wo han-tan-ha-da; 바람에 살랑거리다 ba-ram-e sal-lang-geo-ri-da

sight *n.* 시각 si-gak; 시력 si-ryeok; 목격 mok-gyeok; 시계 si-gye; 견해 gyeon-hae; 조망 jo-mang; 구경거리 gu-gyeong-kkeo-ri; 조준 jo-jun

sign *n.* 기호 gi-ho; 신호 sin-ho; 암호 am-ho; 손짓 son-jjit; 표지 pyo-ji; 조짐 jo-jim; 흔적 heun-jeok; *vi.* 서명하다 seo-myeong-ha-da; 신호하다 sin-ho-ha-da; 표지를 달다 pyo-ji-reul dal-da

signal *n.* 신호 sin-ho; 암호 am-ho; 신호기 sin-ho-gi; 징후 jing-hu; 계기 gye-gi

signature *n.* 서명 seo-myeong; 기호 gi-ho

significance *n.* 의의 ui-i; 의미심장 ui-mi-sim-jang; 중요성 jung-yo-sseong

signify *vt.* 의미하다 ui-mi-ha-da; 표시하다 pyo-si-ha-da; 알리다 al-li-da; 조짐이 되다 jo-jim-i doe-da

sign language *n.* 수화 su-hwa; **American ~** 미국식 수화 mi-guk-sik su-hwa

silence *n.* 침묵 chim-muk; 무소식 mu-so-sik; 비밀엄수 bi-mil-eom-su; 묵살 muk-sal; 망

각 mang-gak; 고요함 go-yo-ham; vt. 침
묵시키다 chim-muk-si-ki-da; 가라앉히다
ga-ra-an-chi-da; 억누르다 eong-nu-reu-da

silent adj. 침묵하는 chim-mu-ka-neun; 말
없는 mal-eom-meun; 기록되어 있지 않
은 gi-rok-doe-eo it-ji an-eun; 무소식의
mu-so-sig-ui; 잠잠한 jam-jam-han; 알리지
않은 al-li-ji an-eun

silk n. 비단 bi-dan, 견직물 gyeon-jing-mul

sill n. 토대 to-dae; 문지방 mun-jji-bang, 문
턱 mun-teok

silly adj. 어리석은 eo-ri-seog-eun; 바보같은
ba-bo-gat-eun; 어이없는 eo-i-eom-neun;
기절한 gi-jeol-han

silver n. 은 eun; 은제품 eun-je-pum; 은화
eun-hwa; 은색 eun-saek

silverware n. 은그릇 eun-geu-reut

similar adj. 유사한 yu-sa-han, 비슷한
bi-su-tan

similarity n. 유사성 yu-sa-sseong, 닮은 점
dalm-eun-jeom

simmer vi. 부글부글 끓다 bu-geul-bu-geul
kkeul-ta; 푹푹거리다 puk-puk-geo-ri-da;
속을 끓이다 sog-eul kkeul-i-da; 지그시 참
다 ji-geus-i cham-tta

simple adj. 하나의 ha-na-ui; 단순한
dan-sun-han; 간소한 gan-so-han; 순박한
sun-ba-kan; 순전한 sun-jeon-han; 무조건
의 mu-jo-kkeon-ui; 하찮은 ha-chan-eun

simplify vt. 단순화하다 dan-sun-hwa-ha-da;
간단히 하다 gan-dan-hi ha-da; 수수하게
하다 su-su-ha-ge ha-da

simply adv. 솔직이 sol-jjig-i; 소박히게
so-ba-ka-ge; 순진하게 sun-jin-ha-ge; 알기
쉽게 al-gi-swip-ge; 간단히 gan-dan-hi; 단
순히 dan-sun-hi

simulate vt. 가장하다 ga-jang-ha-da; 흉내내
다 hung-nae-nae-da; 분장하다 bun-jang-
ha-da; 모의실험을 하다 mo-ui-sil-heom-
eul ha-da

simulation n. 가장 ga-jang; 모의실험
mo-ui-sil heom; 흉내 hung-nae; 꾀병
kkoe-byeong

sin n. 죄 joe; 과실 gwa-sil; 위반 wi-ban; 어
리석은 일 eo-ri-seog-eun il; vi. 죄를 짓
다 joe-reul jit-da; 예의에 어긋나다 ye-i-e
eo-geun-na-da

since adv. 종종 jong-jong, 그때 이래 geu-
ttae- i-rae; prep. ...이래 ...i-rae; conj. ...이
래 ...i-rae; ...이므로 ...i-meu-ro

sincere adj. 성실한 seong-sil-han; 성심성의
의 seong-sim-seong-i-ui

sincerity n. 성실 seong-sil; 성의 seong-i; 순
수함 sun-su-ham

sinew n. 근육 geun-yuk; 체력 che-ryeok; 정
력 jeong-nyeok; 지지자 ji-ji-ja; 원동력
won-dong-nyeok

sing vt., vi. 노래하다 no-rae-ha-da; 새가
지저귀다 sae-ga ji-jeo-gwi-da; 크게
기뻐하다 keu-ge gi-ppeo-ha-da; 노래로
부르다 no-rae-ro bu-reu-da; 귀가 울다
gwi-ga ul-da

Singapore n. 싱가포르 ssing-ga-po-reu

singer n. 가수 ga-su; 성악가 seong-ak-ga

singing n. 노랫소리 no-raet-so-ri; 노래하기
no-rae-ha-gi; 지저귐 ji-jeo-gwim; 귀울림
gwi-ul-lim

single adj. 단 하나의 dan ha-na-ui; 일인용
의 il-in-nyong-ui; 혼자의 hon-ja-ui; 독신
의 dok-sin-ui; 외로운 oe-ro-un; 한결같은
han-gyeol-gat-eun; 단결된 dan-gyel-doen;
~ **room** 일인용 침실 il-in-nyong chim-sil;
I am ~ 저는 독신입니다 jeo-neun
dok-sin-im-ni-da

sinister adj. 불길한 bul-gil-han; 인상이 나
쁜 In-sang-i na-ppeun; 사악한 sa-a-kan; 불
행한 bul-haeng-han

sink n. 싱크 ssing-keu; 수채 su-chae; 하수
구 ha-su-gu; 웅덩이 ung-deong-i; vt. 가
라앉다 ga-ra-an-tta; 침몰하다 chim-mol-
ha-da; 해가 지다 hae-ga ji-da; 기울다
gi-ul-da; 내려앉다 nae-ryeo-an-tta; 수그
러시나 su-geu-reo-ji-da; 쑥 늘어가다 ssuk
deul-eo-ga-da; 풀썩 주저앉다 pul-sseok
ju-jeo-an-tta; 풀이 죽다 pul-i juk-da

sip n. 한모금 han-mo-geum; vt. 한모금 마시
다 han-mo-geum ma-si-da

sir n. (hon.) 선생님 seon-saeng-nim

sister n. 여자형제 yeo-ja-hyeong-je; (of a
female) 언니 eon-ni, (of a male) 누나
nu-na

sister-in-law n. 형수 hyeong-su; 동서
dong-seo; 시누이 si-nu-i; 올케 ol-ke; 처형
cheo-hyeong; 처제 cheo-je

sit *vi.* 앉다 an-tta; 앉아있다 anj-a-it-da; 개
회하다 gae-hoe-ha-da; 자세를 취하다
ja-se-reul chwi-ha-da; 위치하다 wi-chi-
ha-da; **to ~ down** 앉다 an-tta; 자리잡다
ja-ri-jap-da; 포위하다 po-wi-ha-da; 착수하
다 chak-su-ha-da

site *n.* 위치 wi-chi; 장소 jang-so; 부지 bu-ji;
유적 yu-jeok

situation *n.* 위치 wi-chi; 환경 hwan-gyeong;
입장 ip-jang; 사정 sa-jeong; 정세 jeong-
se; 상태 sang-tae; 국면 gung-myeon; 지
위 ji-wi

six *num.* 여섯 yeo-seot; 육 yuk

sixteen *num.* 열여섯 yeol-yeo-seot; 십육
sim-nyuk

sixteenth *adj.* 열여섯번째의 yeol-yeo-seot-
beon-jjae-ui; 제십육회 je-sim-nyu-koe

sixth *adj.* 여섯번째의 yeo-seot-beon-jjae-ui;
제육회 je-yu-koe

sixty *num.* 예순 ye-sun; 육십 yuk-sip

size *n.* 크기 keu-gi; 넓이 neob-i; 치수 chi-ssu;
부피 bu-pi; 양 yang; 규모 gyu-mo

skate *n.* 스케이트 seu-ke-i-teu; *vi.* 스케이트
를 타다 seu-ke-i-teu-reul ta-da; 미끄러지
듯 달리다 mi-kkeu-reo-ji-deut dal-li-da; 약
간 손대다 yak-gan son-dae-da

skeleton *n.* 골격 gol-gyeok; 해골 hae-gol; 뼈
대 ppyeo-dae; 윤곽 yun-gwak; 골자 gol-jja

sketch *n.* 스케치 seu-ke-chi; 약도 yak-do;
밑그림 mit-geu-rim; 개요 gae-yo; 단편
dan-pyeon; *vt.*, *vi.* 스케치하다 seu-ke-
chi-ha-da; 약도를 그리다 yak-do-reul
geu-ri-da; 개략을 진술하다 gae-ryag-eul
jin-sul-ha-da; 윤곽을 그리다 yun-gwag-
eul geu-ri-da

ski *n.* 스키 seu-ki; 추진장치 chu-jin-jang-chi;
~ resort 스키 리조트 seu-ki ri-jo-teu; *vi.*
스키를 타다 seu-ki-reul ta-da

skid *vi.* 미끄러지다 mi-kkeu-reo-ji-da

skill *n.* 숙련 sung-nyeon; 능숙함 neung-su-
kam; 솜씨 som-ssi; 기술 gi-sul

skillful *adj.* 능숙한 neung-su-kan; 숙련된
sung-nyeon-doen

skim *vt.* 찌끼를 걷어내다 jji-kki-reul geod-
eo-nae-da; 스쳐 지나가다 seu-cheo ji-na-
ga-da; 스쳐 날리다 seu-cheo nal-li-da; 대
충 훑어보다 dae-chung hult-eo-bo-da;

얇은 막으로 덮다 yalb-eun mag-eu-ro
deop-da; **~ milk** 탈지우유 tal-ji-u-yu

skin *n.* 피부 pi-bu; 가죽 ga-juk; 껍질 kkeop-
jil; **~ lotion** 스킨로숀 seu-kin-ro-syon

skinny *adj.* 바짝 여윈 ba-jjak yeo-win; 가죽
모양의 ga-juk mo-yang-ui

skip *vi.* 가볍게 뛰다 ga-byeop-ge ttwi-da; 뛰
기며 나아가다 twi-gi-myeo na-a-ga-da;
줄넘기하다 jul-leom-kki-ha-da; 이리저
리 바뀌다 i-ri-jeo-ri ba-kkwi-da; 빠뜨리다
ppa-tteu-ri-da; 월반하다 wol-ban-ha-da;
급히 떠나다 geu-pi tteo-na-da

skirt *n.* 스커트 seu-keo-teu; 치마 chi-ma; 옷
자락 ot-ja-rak; 가장자리 ga-jang-ja-ri

skull *n.* 두개골 du-gae-gol; 머리 meo-ri, 두
뇌 du-noe

sky *n.* 하늘 ha-neul; 기후 gi-hu; 날씨 nal-ssi;
하늘빛 ha-neul-ppit

slack *adj.* 느슨한 neu-seun-han; 부주의한
bu-ju-i-han; 꾸물거리는 kku-mul-geo-ri-
neun; 기운없는 gi-un-eom-neun; 침체된
chim-che-doen

slam *vt.* 꽝 닫다 kkwang dat-da; 팽개치다
paeng-gae-chi-da; 때리다 ttae-ri-da; 혹평
하다 hok-pyeong-ha-da

slang *n.* 속어 sog-eo, 은어 eun-eo

slant *n.* 경사 gyeong-sa; 빗면 bin-myeon; 경
향 gyeong-hyang; 관점 gwan-jjeom; 곁눈
질 gyeon-nun-jil; *vi.* 경사지다 gyeong-sa-
ji-da; 기대다 gi-dae-da; …은 경향이 있다
…eun gyeong-hyang-i it-da; 비스듬히 가
다 bi-seu-deum-hi ga-da

slap *n.* 손바닥으로 때림 son-ppa-dag-eu-ro
ttae-rim; 손바닥으로 치는 소리 son-ppa-
dag-eu-ro chi-neun so-ri; 모욕 mo-yok; 거
절 geo-jeol

slash *vt.* 휘 베다 hwi be-da; 난도질하
다 nan-do-jil-ha-da; 채찍으로 치다
chae-jjig-eu-ro chi-da; 터놓다 teo-no-ta;
대폭 깎다 dae-pok kkak-da; 크게 개정하
다 keu-ge gae-jeong-ha-da; 깎아내리다
kkakk-a-nae-ri-da

slate *n.* 슬레이트 seul-le-i-teu; 석판 seok-
pan; 석판색 seok-pan-saek; 공인 후보자
명단 gong-in hu-bo-ja myeong-dan

slave *n.* 노예 no-ye; …에 빠진 사람 …e
ppa-jin sa-ram

slavery *n.* 노예상태 no-ye-sang-tae; 노예신
분 no-ye-sin-bun; 맹종 maeng-jong; 노예
제도 no-ye-je-do; 고역 go-yeok; 천한 일
cheon-han il

sled *n.* 썰매 sseol-mae

sleep *vi.* 잠자다 jam-ja-da; 묻혀있다
mu-chyeo-it-da; 활동하지 않다 hwal-
ttong-ha-ji an-ta; 마비되어 있다 ma-bi-
doe-eo it-da

sleeping bag *n.* 슬리핑백 seul-li-ping-ppaek,
침낭 chim-nang

sleeping car *n.* 침대차 chim-dae-cha

sleeping pill *n.* 수면제 su-myeon-je

sleepy *adj.* 졸린 jol-lin; 조는 jo-neun; 머리
가 멍한 meo-ri-ga meong-han; 활기없는
hwal-gi-eom-neun

sleeve *n.* 소매 so-mae, 소맷자락
so-maet-ja-rak

slender *adj.* 홀쭉한 hol-jju-kan; 가느다란
ga-neu-da-ran; 날씬한 nal-ssin-han;
얼마 안되는 eol-ma an-doe-neun; 미
덥지 못한 mi-deop-ji mo-tan; 빈약한
bin-ya-kan

slice *n.* 한조각 han-jo-gak; 부분 bu-bun; 얇
은 칼 yalb-eun kal; *vt.* 얇게 썰다 yalp-ge
sseol-da; 나누다 na-nu-da; 헤치듯 나아
가다 he-chi-deut na-a-ga-da; 깎아치다
kkakk-a-chi-da

slide *n.* 활주 hwal-jju; 슬라이딩 seul-la-i-
ding; 비탈길 bi-tal-kkil; 미끄럼틀 mi-kkeu-
reom-teul; 사태 sa-tae; *(movement)* 미
끄러짐 mi-kkeu-reo-jim; *(transparency)*
슬라이드 seul-la-i-deu; *vi.* 미끄러지
다 mi-kkeu-reo-ji-da; 미끄럼을 타다
mi-kkeu-reom-eul ta-da; 슬라이딩하
다 seul-la-i-ding-ha-da; 부지중에 빠지
다 bu-ji-jung-e ppa-ji-da; 살짝 달아나다
sal-jjak dal-a-na-da

slim *adj.* 호리호리한 ho-ri-ho-ri-han; 가냘
픈 ga-nyal-peun; 얼마 안되는 eol-ma
an-doe-neun; 빈약한 bin-ya-kan

sling *n.* 투석기 tu-seok-gi; 새총 sae-chong;
투석 tu-seok; 삼각붕대 sam-gak-bung-
dae; 슬링 seul-ling

slip *n.* 과실 gwa-sil; 빠뜨림 ppa-tteu-rim;
저하 jeo-ha; 하락 ha-rak; 가느다란 조
각 ga-neu-da-ran jo-gak;탈주 tal-jju; 단
층 dan-cheung; *(movement)* 미끄러짐

mi-kkeu-reo-jim; *(article of clothing)* 슬립
seul-lip; ~ **of the tongue** 말실수 mal-sil-
ssu; *vi.* 미끄러지다 mi-kkeu-reo-ji-da; 헛
디디다 heot-di-di-da; 가만히 떠나다 ga-
man-hi tteo-na-da; 몰래 들어가다 mol-lae
deul-eo-ga-d; 벗겨지다 beot-gyeo-ji-da;
무심코 입밖에 내다 mu-sim-ko ip-bakk-e
nae-da; 지나가 버리다 ji-na-ga beo-ri-da;
미끄러지듯 달리다 mi-kkeu-reo-ji-deut
dal-li-da

slipper *n.* 슬리퍼 seul-li-peo, 실내화
sil-lae-hwa

slippery *adj.* 미끄러운 mi-kkeu-reo-un; 반
들반들한 ban-deul-ban-deul-han; 믿을
수 없는 mid-eul ssu eom-neun; 불안정한
bul-an-jeong-han

slogan *n.* 슬로건 seul-lo-geon, 표
어 pyo-eo; 외침 oe-chim; 선전문구
seon-jeon-mun-kku

slope *n.* 경사면 gyeong-sa-myeon, 비
탈 bi-tal; 기울기 gi-ul-gi; 경기하강
gyeong-gi-ha-gang

sloppy *n.* 묽은 mulg-eun; 질퍽거리는 jil-
peok-geo-ri-neun; 단정치 못한 dan-jeong-
chi-mo-tan; 간결하지 못한 gan-gyeol-ha-ji
mo-tan; 깊이가 없는 gip-i-ga eom-neun;
엉성한 eong-seong-han

slot *n.* 홈 hom; 동전구멍 dong-jeon-kku-
meong; 지위 ji-wi; 발자국 bal-jja-guk

Slovakia *n.* 슬로바키아 seul-lo-ba-ki-a

slow *adj.* 느린 neu-rin; 가벼운 ga-byeo-un;
화력이 약한 hwa-ryeog-i ya-kan; 효과
가 늦은 hyo-kkwa-ga neuj-eun; 침체
한 chim-che-han; 이해가 늦은 i-hae-ga
neuj-eun; 따분한 tta-bun-han; *vt.* 더디
게 하다 deo-di-ge ha-da; 속력을 낮추다
song-nyeog-eul nat-chu-da; *vi.* 느리게 되
다 neu-ri-ge doe-da; 속력이 떨어지다
song-nyeog-i tteol-eo-ji-da

slug *n.* 민달팽이 min-dal-paeng-i; 느
린 사람 neu-rin-sa-ram, 게으름뱅이
ge-eu-reum-baeng-il

sluggish *adj.* 게으른 ge-eu-reun; 느린
neu-rin; 완만한 wan-man-han; 활발치 못
한 hwal-bal-chi mo-tan

sluice *n.* 수문 su-mun, 보 bo; 봇물 bon-
mul; 인공수로 in-gong-su-ro; 배출구
bae-chul-gu

slum *n*. 빈민굴 bin-min-gul, 슬럼가 seul-leom-ga

small *adj*. 작은 jag-eun; 비좁은 bi-job-eun; 소규모의 so-gyu-mo-ui; 얼마 안되는 eol-ma an-doe-neun; 사소한 sa-so-han; 인색한 in-sae-kan; 부끄러운 bu-kkeu-reo-un; 가는 ga-neun; 약한 ya-kan

smart *adj*. 영리한 yeong-ni-han; 쿡쿡 쑤시는 kuk-kuk ssu-si-neun; 날카로운 nal-ka-ro-un; 날렵한 nal-lyeo-pan; 빈틈없는 bin-teum-eom-neun; 약아빠진 yag-a-ppa-jin; 스마트한 seu-ma-teu-han

smash *vt*. 분쇄하다 bun-swae-ha-da; 박살내다 bak-sal-lae-da; 충돌시키다 chung-dol-si-ki-da; 깨뜨리다 kkae-tteu-ri-da; 타파하다 ta-pa-ha-da; 세게 때리다 se-ge ttae-ri-da; 파산시키다 pa-san-si-ki-da

smell *n*. 냄새 naem-sae; 향기 hyang-gi; 후각 hu-gak; 악취 ak-chwi; 킴새 kkim-sae; *vt*. 냄새를 맡다 naem-sae-reul mat-da; 냄새를 느끼다 naem-sae-reul neu-kki-da; 알아채다 al-a-chae-da; *vi*. 냄새가 나다 naem-sae-ga na-da; 냄새를 풍기다 naem-sae-reul pung-gi-da; 수상하다 su-sang-ha-da

smile *n*. 미소 mi-so; 웃는 얼굴 un-neun eol-gul; 조소 jo-so; 호의 ho-i; 길조 gil-jjo; *vi*. 미소짓다 mi-so-jit-da, 생글거리다 saeng-geul-geo-ri-da; 경치가 환하다 gyeong-chi-ga hwan-ha-da; 운이 트이다 un-i teu-i-da

smith *n*. 대장장이 dae-jang-jang-i, 금속 세공장 geum-sok sae-gong-jang

smog *n*. 스모그 seu-mo-geu

smoggy *adj*. 스모그가 많은 seu-mo-geu-ga man-eun

smoke *n*. 연기 yeon-gi; 담배연기 dam-bae-yeon-gi; ~ **detector** 화재 탐지기 hwa-jae tam-ji-gi; *vt*. 연기나게 하다 yeon-gi-na-ge ha-da; 훈제하다 hun-je-ha-da; 연기로 소독하다 yeon-gi-ro so-do-ka-da; 담배를 피우다 dam-bae-reul pi-u-da; **no smoking** 금연 geum-yeon

smoky *adj*. 연기나는 yeon-gi-na-neun; 연기가 자욱한 yeon-gi-ga ja-u-kan; 그을은 geu-eul-eun

smooth *adj*. 매끄러운 mae-kkeu-reo-un; 반반한 ban-ban-han; 부드러운 bu-deu-reo-un; 순조로운 sun-jo-ro-un; 유창한 yu-chang-han; 윤이 나는 yun-i na-neun; 잘 섞인 jal seokk-in; 입에 당기는 ib-e dang-gi-neun; 호감을 주는 ho-gam-eul ju-neun; 민숭민숭한 min-sung-min-sung-han

smuggle *vt*. 밀수하다 mil-ssu-ha-da; 숨기다 sum-gi-da; 살짝 넘기다 sal-jjak neom-gi-da

smuggler *n*. 밀수업자 mil-ssu-eop-ja

smuggling *n*. 밀수 mil-ssu

snack *n*. 간식 gan-sik; 가벼운 식사 ga-byeo-un sik-sa; 한입 han-nip; ~ **bar** 스낵바 seu-naek-ba

snail *n*. 달팽이 dal-paeng-i; 빈둥거리는 사람 bin-dung-geo-ri-neun sa-ram

snake *n*. 뱀 baem; 음흉한 사람 eum-hyung-han sa-ram

snapshot *n*. 스냅사진 seu-naep-sa-jin; 함부로 쏘아대기 ham-bu-ro sso-a-dae-gi

snarl *vi*. 으르렁거리다 eu-reu-reong-geo-ri-da; 호통치다 ho-tong-chi-da; 고함치다 go-ham-chi-da

sneakers *n. pl*. 운동화 un-dong-hwa

sneeze *n*. 재채기 jae-chae-gi; *vi*. 재채기하다 jae-chae-gi-ha-da; 코웃음치다 ko-us-eum-chi-da

snob *n*. 속물 song-mul; 건방진 사람 geon-bang-jin sa-ram

snobbish *adj*. 속물의 song-mul-ui

snore *vi*. 코를 골다 ko-reul gol-da

snorkel *n*. 스노클 seu-no-keul

snort *vi*. 콧방귀를 뀌다 kot-bang-gwi-reul kkwi-da; 코를 씨근거리다 ko-reul ssi-geun-geo-ri-da; 증기를 내뿜다 jeung-gi-reul nae-ppum-tta; 씩씩거리며 말하다 ssik-ssik-geo-ri-myeo mal-ha-da

snout *n*. 돼지코 dwae-ji-ko; 주둥이 ju-dung-i; 호스 끝 ho-seu kkeut

snow *n*. 눈 nun; 적설 jeok-seol; *vi*. 눈이 내리다 nun-i nae-ri-da; 눈처럼 내리다 nun-cheo-reom nae-ri-da

snowflake *n*. 눈송이 nun-ssong-i

snowstorm *n*. 눈보라 nun-bo-ra

snub *vt*. 윽박지르다 euk-bak-ji-reu-da; 냉대하다 naeng-dae-ha-da; 급히 멈추

다 geu-pi meom-chu-da; 펭펭히 하다 paeng-pang-hi ha-da; 담배를 비벼끄다 dam-bae-reul bi-byeo-kku-da

so *adv.* 그와 같이 geu-wa ga-chi, 그러하여 geu-reo-ha-yeo, 정말로 jeong-mal-lo, ...와 마찬가지로 ...wa ma-chan-ga-ji-ro, 그 때 문에 geu ttae-mun-e; 그만큼 geu-man-keum, ...만큼은 ...man-keum-eun, 대단 히 ...해서 dae-dan-hi...hae-seo; *conj.* 그 래서 geu-rae-seo, ...하기 위하여...ha-gi wi-ha-yeo

soak *vt.* 적시다 jeok-si-da; 적셔서 빨아 내다 jeok-syeo-seo ppal-a-nae-da; 스며 들다 seu-myeo-deul-da; 빨아들이다 ppal-a-deul-i-da; *vi.* 젖다 jeot-da; 스미다 seu-mi-da

soaking *adj.* 흠뻑 젖는 heum-ppeok jeon-neun; *adv.* 흠뻑 젖어서 heum-ppeok jeoj-eo-seo

soap *n.* 비누 bi-nu; *vt.* 비누로 씻다 bi-nu-ro ssit-da; 비누칠하다 bi-nu-chil-ha-da

soar *vi.* 높이 날다 nop-i nal-da; 기류를 타 고 날다 gi-ryu-reul ta-go nal-da; 물가가 급등하다 mul-kka-ga geup-deung-ha-da; 희망이 부풀다 hi-mang-i bu-pul-da; 솟 다 sot-da

sob *vi.* 흐느끼다 heu-neu-kki-da; 쉭쉭 소리 를 내다 swik-swik so-ri-reul nae-da

social *adj.* 사회적인 sa-hoe-jeog-in; 사교적인 sa-gyo-jeog-in; 사교계의 sa-gyo-gye-ui; 교 제를 좋아하는 gyo-je-reul jo-a-ha-neun; 사회주의적인 sa-hoe-ju-i-jeog-in

socialism *n.* 사회주의 sa-hoe ju-i, 사회주의 운동 sa-hoe-ju-i un-dong

socialist *n.* 사회주의자 sa-hoe-ju-i-ja; *adj.* 사 회주의적인 sa-hoe-ju-i-jeog-in

sock *n.* 짧은 양말 jjalb-eun yang-mal; 구두 인창 gu-du an-chang; 타격 ta-gyeok; 성공 적인 연극 seong-gong-jeog-in yeon-geuk

socket *n.* 소켓 so-ket; **electric ~** 전기소켓 jeon-gi-so-ket

soda *n.* 탄산음료수 tan-san-eum-nyo-su

sodium *n.* 나트륨 na-teu-ryum

sofa *n.* 소파 sso-pa

soft *adj.* 부드러운 bu-deu-reo-un; 매끄 러운 mae-kkeu-reo-un; 촉감이 좋은 chok-gam-i jo-eun; 차분한 cha-bun-han;

온화한 on-hwa-han; **~ drink** 청량음료 cheong-nyang-eum-nyo

software *n.* 소프트웨어 so-peu-teu-we-eo

soil *n.* 흙 heuk; 토양 to-yang; 토질 to-jil; 땅 ttang; 나라 na-ra; 국토 guk-to

solar *adj.* 태양의 tae-yang-ui; 태양광선의 tae-yang-gwang-seon-ui; **~ panels** 태양 전 지판 tae-yang-jeon-ji-pan

soldier *n.* 군인 gun-in

sole *n.* 발바닥 bal-ppa-dak; *(of a shoe)* 신발 바닥 sin-bal-ppa-dak; *(fish)* 가자미 ga-ja-mi, 넙치 neop-chi; *adj.* 유일한 yu-il-han; 독점적 dok-jeom-jeok

solid *n.* 고체 go-che; *adj.* 고체의 go-che-ui; 딱딱한 ttak-tta-kan; 견고한 gyeon-go-han; 충실한 chung-sil-han; 건실한 gyeon-sil-han; 단결한 dan-gyeol-han; 한결같은 han-gyeol-gat-eun; 연속된 yeon-sok-doen

solution *n.* 용해 yong-hae; 용해상태 yong-hae-sang-tae; 용액 yong-aek; 분해 bun-hae; 해결 hae-gyeol; 해법 hae-ppeop

solve *vt.* 풀다 pul-da; 해결하다 hae-gyeol-ha-da

solvent *n.* 지급능력이 있는 ji-geum-neung-nyeog-i in-neun; 용해력이 있는 yong-hae-ryeog-i in-neun; 누그러지게 하 는 nu-geu-reo-ji-ge ha-neun; 약화시키는 ya-kwa-si-ki-neun

somber *adj.* 어둠침침한 eo-dum-chim-chim-han; 음침한 eum-chim-han; 우울한 u-ul-han; 칙칙한 chik-chi-kan

some *adj.* 얼마간의 eol-ma-gan-ui, 무언 가의 mu-eon-ga-ui; *pron.* 어떤 사람들 eo-tteon sa-ram-deul

somebody *pron.* 어떤 사람 eo-tteon sa-ram; 누군가 nu-gun-ga; *n.* 상당한 인물 sang-dang-han in-mul, 대단한 사람 dae-dan-han sa-ram

somehow *adv.* 어떻게든지 eo-tteo-ke-deun-ji; 어쨌든 eo-jjaet-deun; 어쩐지 eo-jjeon-ji; 아무래도 a-mu-rae-do

someone *pron.* 누군가 nu-gun-ga; 어떤 사람 eo-tteon sa-ram

someplace *adv.* 어딘가에 eo-din-ga-e; 어딘가로 eo-din-ga-ro; 어딘가에서 eo-din-ga-e-seo

something *pron.* 무언가 mu-eon-ga; 어떤 것 eo-tteon geot; 어느 정도 eo-neu jeong-do; *n.* 가치있는 물건 ga-chi-in-neun mul-geon; 뛰어난 것 ttwi-eo-nan geot

sometime *adv.* 언젠가 eon-jen-ga; **sometimes** 가끔 ga-kkeum

somewhat *adv.* 얼마간 eol-ma-gan; 어느 정도 eo-neu jeong-do

somewhere *adv.* 어딘가에 eo-din-ga-e; 어딘가에서 eo-din-ga-e-seo; 어디론가 eo-di-ron-ga; 대략 dae-ryak

son *n.* 아들 a-deul; 자손 ja-son

son-in-law *n.* 사위 sa-wi

song *n.* 노래 no-rae; 시 si

soon *adv.* 곧 got; 급히 geu-pi; 이르게 i-reu-ge; 자진하여 ja-jin-ha-yeo; **as ~ as** 가능한 한 빨리 ga-neung-han-han ppal-li

sore *n.* 헌데 heon-de; 종기 jong-gi; 상처 sang-cheo; *adj.* 아픈 a-peun; 염증의 yeom-jjeung-ui; 슬픈 seul-peun; 쓰라린 sseu-ra-rin; 울화가 치미는 ul-hwa-ga chi-mi-neun; 성난 seong-nan; **~ throat** 후두염 hu-du-yeom

sorrow *n.* 슬픔 seul-peum; 아쉬움 a-swi-um; 유감 yu-gam; 후회 hu-hoe

sorry *adj.* 슬픈 seul-peun; 유감스러운 yu-gam-seu-reo-un; 가엾은 ga-yeops-eun; 미안합니다 mi-an-ham-ni-da; **to be ~ for sth.** …이 딱하다 …i tta-ka-da

sort *n.* 종류 jong-nyu; 성질 seong-jil; 양식 yang-sik; 인품 in-pum; *vt.* 분류하다 bul-lyu-ha-da; 가려내다 ga-ryeo-nae-da; 구분하다 gu-bun-ha-da

soul *n.* 영혼 yeong-hon; 생기 saeng-gi; 정신 jeong-sin; 마음 ma-eum; 생명 saeng-myeong; 전형 jeon-hyeong; 중심인물 jung-sim-in-mul

sound *n.* 소리 so-ri; 음 eum; 음향 eum-hyang; 울림 ul-lim; 어감 eo-gam; 음성 eum-seong; **~ track** 사운드 트랙 ssa-un-deu teu-raek, 녹음대 nog-eum-dae; *adj.* 건전한 geon-jeon-han; 확실한 hwak-sil-han; 단단한 dan-dan-han; 철저한 cheol-jjeo-han; 충분한 chung-bun-han; *vi.* 소리가 나다 so-ri-ga na-da; 소리를 내다 so-ri-reul nae-da; 울리다 ul-li-da; …하게 들리다 …ha-ge deul-li-da; 전해지다 jeon-hae-ji-da; …로 발음되다 …ro

bal-eum-doe-da; **The idea ~s interesting** 그 생각은 참 흥미롭습니다 geu saeng-gag-eun cham heung-mi-rop-seum-ni-da; **It ~s like fun** 그것 참 재미있겠네요 geu-geot cham jae-mi-it-gen-ne-yo

soup *n.* 수프 su-peu, 국물 gung-mul

sour *adj.* 시큼한 si-keum-han; 시어진 si-eo-jin; 불쾌한 bul-kwae-han; 표준 이하의 pyo-jun i-ha-ui; 까다로운 kka-da-ro-un; 산성의 san-seong-ui

source *n.* 수원 su-won; 원천 won-cheon; 근원 geun-won; 출처 chul-cheo; 소식통 so-sik-tong

south *n.* 남쪽 nam-jjok; 남부 nam-bu; 남부지방 nam-bu-jji-bang; **the ~** 남쪽 nam-jjok; *adj.* 남쪽의 nam-jjog-ui; 남부의 nam-bu-ui; 남쪽을 향한 nam-jjog-eul hyang-han; **the ~ entrance** 남쪽 입구 nam-jjok ip-gu; *adv.* 남쪽에 nam-jjog-e; 남쪽으로 nam-jjog-eu-ro; **fly ~** 남쪽으로 날아가다 nam-jjog-eu-ro nal-a-ga-da

South Africa *n.* 남아프리카 nam-a-peu-ri-ka

South African *n.* 남아프리카 사람 nam-a-peu-ri-ka sa-ram; *adj.* 남아프리카의 nam-a-peu-ri-ka-ui

South America *n.* 남아메리카 nam-a-me-ri-ka

South American *n.* 남아메리카 사람 nam-a-me-ri-ka sa-ram; *adj.* 남아메리카의 nam-a-me-ri-ka

southeast *n.* 남동쪽 nam-dong-jjok; 남동부 nam-dong-bu; *adj.* 남동쪽의 nam-dong-jjog-ui; 남동부의 nam-dong-bu-ui; 남동으로부터의 nam-dong-eu-ro-bu-teo-ui

southeastern *adj.* 남동의 nam-dong-ui; 남동쪽에 있는 nam-dong-jjog-e in-neun; 남동에서의 nam-dong-e-seo-ui; 남동향의 nam-dong-hyang-ui

southern *adj.* 남쪽의 nam-jjog-ui; 남쪽에 있는 nam-jjog-e in-neun; 남쪽으로의 nam-jjog-eu-ro-ui; 남향의 nam-hyang-ui

South Korea *n.* 남한 nam-han, 대한민국 dae-han-min-guk

South Pole *n.* 남극 nam-geuk

southwest *n.* 남서쪽 nam-seo-jjok; 남서부 nam-seo-bu; *adj.* 남서쪽의 nam-seo-jjog-ui; 남서부의 nam-seo-bu-ui; 남서로부터의 nam-seo-ro-bu-teo-ui

southwestern *adj.* 남서의 nam-seo-ui; 남서쪽에 있는 nam-seo-jjog-e in-neun; 남서에서의 nam-seo-e-seo-ui; 남서향의 nam-seo-hyang-ui

souvenir *n.* 기념품 gi-nyeom-pum; 선물 seon-mul

sovereign *adj.* 주권자 ju-kkwon-ja; 군주 gun-ju; 독립국 dong-nip-guk

sow *n.* 암퇘지 am-twae-ji; 큰 주형 keun ju-hyeong

soy *n.* 간장 gan-jang

soybean *n.* 콩 kong

space *n.* 공간 gong-gan; 우주 u-ju; 장소 jang-so; 여지 yeo-ji; 자리 ja-ri; 지면 ji-myeon; 간격 gan-gyeok; 기간 gi-gan

spade *n.* *(tool)* 삽 sap, 가래 ga-rae; *(cards)* 스페이드 seu-pe-i-deu

Spain *n.* 스페인 seu-pe-in

Spaniard *n.* 스페인 사람 seu-pe-in ssa-ram

Spanish *n.* 스페인말 seu-pe-in-mal; 스페인 사람 seu-pe-in ssa-ram; *adj.* 스페인의 seu-pe-in-ui

spare part *n.* 예비부품 ye-bi-bu-pum

spark *n.* 불꽃 bul-kkot; 광채 gwang-chae; 생기 saeng-gi; 스파크 seu-pa-keu; ~ **plug** 스빠크 플러그 seu-pa-keu peul-leo-geu, 점화전 jeom-hwa-jeon *vt.* 발화시키다 bal-hwa-si-ki-da; 북돋다 buk-dot-da; 생기를 띠게하다 saeng-gi-reul tti-ge-ha-da; 불꽃이 튀다 bul-kkoch-i twi-da; 격려하다 gyeong-nyeo-ha-da

sparkle *vi.* 불꽃을 튀기다 bul-kkoch-eul twi-gi-da; 번쩍이다 beon-jjeog-i-da; 생기가 있다 saeng-gi-ga it-da; 재치가 뛰어나다 jae-chi-ga ttwi-eo-na-da; 거품이 일다 geo-pum-i il-da

sparrow *n.* 참새 cham-sae

spatial *adj.* 공간의 gong-gan-ul; 공간적인 gong-gan-jeog-in; 장소의 jang-so-ui

speak *vt.* 말하다 mal-ha-da; 이야기하다 i-ya-gi-ha-da; 증명하다 jeung-myeong-ha-da; 나타내다 na-ta-nae-da; 말을 걸다 mal-eul geol-da; *vi.* 이야기하다 i-ya-gi-ha-da; 이야기를 걸다 i-ya-gi-reul geol-da; 연설하다 yeon-seol-ha-da; 전달하다 jeon-dal-ha-da

speaker *n.* 강연자 gang-yeon-ja; *(person)* 의장 ui-jang; 연설자 yeon-seol-jja; *(audio)* 스피커 seu-pi-keo

special *adj.* 특별한 teuk-byeol-han; 독특한 dok-teu-kan; 전용의 jeon-yong-ui; 전문의 jeon-mun-ui; 임시의 im-si-ui; 유별난 yu-byeol-lan

specialist *n.* 전문가 jeon-mun-ga

specify *vt.* 지정하다 ji-jeong-ha-da; 상술하다 sang-sul-ha-da; 명세서에 기입하다 myeong-se-seo-e gi-i-pa-da

specimen *n.* 견본 gyeon-bon; 표본 pyo-bon; 실례 sil-lye; 검사자료 geom-sa-ja-ryo; 괴짜 goe-jja

spectator *n.* 구경꾼 gu-gyeong-kkun; 관객 gwan-gaek; 관찰사 gwan-chal-jja; 목격자 mok-gyeok-ja

speech *n.* 강연 gang-yeon; *(oration)* 연설 yeon-seol; 화법 hwa-ppeop; *(faculty of)* 말 mal, 언어 eon-eo; 이야기 i-ya-gi; ~ **impediment** 언어장애 eon-eo-jang-ae

speed *n.* 속도 sok-do; 신속 sin-sok; 변속장치 byeon-sok-jang-chi; ~ **limit** 속도제한 sok-do-je-han; *vi.* 급히 가다 geu-pi-ga-da; 스피드를 내다 seu-pi-deu-reul nae-da; 일이 진행되다 il-i jin-haeng-oe-da

speedometer *n.* 속도계 sok-do-gye

spell *vt.* 철자를 말하다 cheol-jja-reul mal-ha-da; 뜯어보다 tteud-eo-bo-da; -라고 읽다 ra-go ik-da; 의미하다 ui-mi-ha-da; **How do you ~ that word** 그 단어를 어떻게 씁니까 geu dan-eo-reul eo-tteo-ke sseum-ni-kka

spend *vt.* 쓰다 sseu-da, 소비하다 so-bi-ha-da; 보내다 bo-nae-da; 낭비하다 nang-bi-ha-da; 지치게 하다 ji-chi-ge ha-da

sphere *n.* 구형 gu-hyeong; 천체 cheon-che; 지구의 ji-gu-ui; 활동영역 hwal-ttong-yeong-yeok; 신분 sin-bun

spice *n.* 양념 yang-nyeom; 짜릿한 맛 jja ri tan mat; ...한 기미 ...han gi-mi

spicy *adj.* 향긋한 hyang-geu-tan; 멋신 meot-jin; 야비한 ya-bi-han; 기운찬 gi-un-chan

spider *n.* 거미 geo-mi

spider web *n.* 거미줄 geo-mi-jul, 거미집 geo-mi-jip

spill *n.* 엎지름 eop-ji-reum; 엎지른 자국 eop-ji-reun ja-guk; 떨어짐 tteol-eo-jim; *vt.* 엎지르다 eop-ji-reu-da; 흩뜨리다 heut-tteu-ri-da; 내동댕이치다

nae-dong-daeng-i-chi-da; 누설하다 nu-
seol-ha-da; 낭비하다 nang-bi-ha-da

spin *vi.* 방적하다 bang-jeo-ka-da; 실을 내
다 sil-eul nae-da; 장황하게 이야기하다
jang-hwang-ha-ge i-ya-gi-ha-da; 오래 질
질 끌다 o-rae jil-jil kkeul-da; 회전시키다
hoe-jeon-si-ki-da

spinach *n.* 시금치 si-geum-chi

spine *n.* 등뼈 deung-ppyeo, 척추 cheok-chu;
가시 ga-si

spiral *adj.* 나선모양의 na-seon-mo-yang-ui;
소용돌이의 so-yong-dol-i-ui; ~ **bound** 나
선제본 na-seon-je-bon, 스파이럴제본
seu-pa-i-reol-je-bon

spire *n.* 뾰족탑 ppyo-jok-tap; 원추형
won-chu-hyeong; 절정 jeol-jjeong; 정
상 jeong-sang; 나선 na-seon; 소용돌이
so-yong-dol-i

spirit *n.* 정신 jeong-sin; 마음 ma-eum; 영혼
yeong-hon; 유령 yu-ryeong; 활기 hwal-gi;
용기 yong-gi; 기분 gi-bun; 성품 seong-
pum; 풍조 pung-jo

spiritual *adj.* 정신적인 jeong-sin-jeog-in; 정
신의 jeong-sin-ui; 영적인 yeong-jjeog-in;
신의 sin-ui; 신성한 sin-seong-han

spit *vt.* 침을 뱉다 chim-eul baet-da; 내뱉
듯 말하다 nae-baet-deut mal-ha-da; 점
화하다 jeom-hwa-ha-da; *vi.* 침을 뱉다
chim-eul baet-da; 비가 후두둑 오다 bi-ga
hu-du-duk o-d; 지글지글 타다 ji-geul-ji-
geul ta-da

spite *n.* 악의 ag-ui; 심술 sim-sul; 원한
won-han; 앙심 ang-sim; **in ~ of** ... 에도 불
구하고 e-do bul-gu-ha-go, ...을 무릅쓰고
...eul mu-reup-sseu-go

splash *n.* 물을 튀기다 mul-eul ttwi-gi-da; 물
이 튀어 오르다 mul-i twi-eo o-reu-da; 첨
벙거리다 cheom-beong-geo-ri-da; *vi.* 튀
다 twi-da; 물보라치다 mul-bo-ra-chi-da;
첨벙거리며 가다 cheom-beong-geo-ri-
meo ga-da; 첨벙 떨어지다 cheom-beong
tteol-eo-ji-da

splint *n.* 얇은 널조각 yalb-eun neol-jjo-gak;
접골용 부목 jeop-gol-lyong bu-mok; 비
골 bi-gol

splinter *n.* 부서진 조각 bu-seo-jin jo-gak; 파
편 pa-pyeon; 나무의 가시 na-mu-ui ga-si

spoil *vt.* 망쳐놓다 mang-cheo-no-ta; 못쓰게
만들다 mot-sseu-ge man-deul-da; 버릇없
게 기르다 beo-reud-eop-ge gi-reu-da; 썩
게 하다 sseok-ge ha-da; *vi.* 못쓰게 되다
mot-sseu-ge doe-da; 썩다 sseok-da; 열망
하다 yeol-mang-ha-da

spoke *n.* 바퀴살 ba-kwi-ssal, 스포크 seu-
po-keu; 디딤대 di-dim-ttae; 바퀴 멈춤대
ba-kwi meom-chum-ttae

sponge *n.* 해면 hae-myeon; 스펀지 seu-
peon-ji; 식객 sik-gaek

sponsor *n.* 보증인 bo-jeung-in; 후원자
hu-won-ja; 스폰서 seu-pon-seo, 광고주
gwang-go-ju; 대부모 dae-bu-mo; *vt.* 후원
하다 hu-won-ha-da; 보증하다 bo-jeung-
ha-da; 광고주가 되다 gang-go-ju-ga
doe-da; 신임회원을 소개하다 sin-i-poe-
won-eul so-gae-ha-da

spontaneous *adj.* 자발적인 ja-bal-jjeog-in;
자연적인 ja-yeon-jeog-in; 자동적인
ja-dong-jeog-in; 자생의 ja-saeng-ui; 자연
스러운 ja-yeon-seu-reo-un

spool *n.* 실패 sil-pae, 실꾸리 sil-kku-ri

spoon *n.* 숟가락 sut-ga-rak

sport *n.* 스포츠 seu-po-cheu, 운동경기
un-dong-gyeong-gi; 운동회 un-dong-hoe;
위안 wi-an, 즐거움 jeul-geo-um

sports car *n.* 스포츠카 seu-po-cheu-ka

sportsman *n.* 스포츠맨 seu-po-cheu-man,
운동 애호가 un-dong ae-ho-ga

spot *n.* 반점 ban-jeom, 얼룩 eol-luk;
부스럼 bu-seu-reom; 오점 o-jjeom;
장소 jang-so; 점찍기 jeom-jjik-gi; *vt.*
점을 찍다 jeom-eul jjik-da; 얼룩지게
하다 eol-luk-ji-ge ha-da; 손상시키다
son-sang-si-ki-da; 얼룩을 빼다 eol-lug-eul
ppae-da; 알아내다 al-a-nae-da; 배치하다
bae-chi-ha-da; 위치를 관측하다 wi-chi-
reul gwan-cheu-ka-da; ...에 스포트라이
트를 비추다 ...e seu-po-teu-ra-i-teu-reul
bi-chu-da

spout *n.* 주전자 주둥이 ju-jeon-ja ju-dung-i;
물꼭지 mul-kkok-ji; 분수공 bun-su-gong;
분출 bun-chul; 물기둥 mul-kki-dung; *vt.*
내뿜다 nae-ppum-tta; 분출하다 bun-chul-
ha-da; 막힘없이 말하다 ma-kim-eops-i
mal-ha-da

sprain *n.* 삠 ppim, 접질림 jeop-jil-lim; *vt.* 삐다 ppi-da, 접질리다 jeop-jil-li-da; **a ~ed ankle** 접질린 발목 jeop-jil-lin bal-mok, 삔 발목 ppin bal-mok

spray *n.* 물보라 mul-bo-ra; 물안개 mul-an-gae; 스프레이 seu-peu-re-i; 분무기 bun-mu-gi; *vt.* 물보라를 날리다 mul-bo-ra-reul nal-li-da; 뿌리다 ppu-ri-da; 끼얹다 kki-eon-tta

spread *n.* 퍼짐 peo-jim; 넓이 neolb-i; 뻗음 ppeod-eum; 보급 bo-geup; 만연 man-yeon; 확장 hwak-janq; 전성 jwon-seong; 식탁보 sik-tak-bo; 침대시트 chim-dae-si-teu; 스프레드 seu-peu-re-deu; 특집기사 teuk-jip-gi-sa; 겉치장 geot-chi-jang; **~sheet** 스프레드 시트 seu peu re deu si-teu, 매트릭스 정신표 mae-teu-rik-seu jeong-san-pyo; *vt.* 펼치다 pyeol-chi-da; 벌리다 beol-li-da; 얇게 바르다 yalp-ge ba-reu-da; 늘어놓다 neul-eo-no-ta; 살포하다 sal-po-ha-da; 연기하다 yeon-gi-ha-da; 소문을 퍼뜨리다 so-mun-eul peo-tteu-ri-da; 상에 차려놓다 sang-e cha-ryeo-no-ta; 납작하게 하다 nap-ja-ka-ge ha-da; *vi.* 퍼지다 peo-ji-da; 펼쳐지다 pyeol-cheo-ji-da; 가지를 뻗다 ga-ji-reul ppeot-da; 멀리 미치다 meol-li mi-chi-da; 걸치다 geol-chi-da; 전개되다 jeon-gae-doe-da; 얇게 늘어나다 yalp-ge neul-eo-na-da; 번지다 beon-ji-da; 흩어지다 heut-eo-ji-da

spring *n.* 성장기 seong-jang-gi, 초기 cho-gi; 튀어오름 twi-eo-o-reum; 샘 saem; 광천지 gwang-cheon-ji; 근원 geun-won; 원동력 won-dong-nyeok; 탄성 tan-seong; 뒤틀림 dwi-teul-lim; *(season)* 봄 bom; *(mechanical)* 스프링 seu-peu-ring, 용수철 yong su cheol; *vi.* 튀다 twi-da; 도약하다 do-ya-ka-da; 갑자기 움직이다 gap-ja-gi um-jig-i-da; 솟아 오르다 sos-a o-reu-da; 발생하다 bal-ssaeng-ha-da; 싹트다 ssak-teu-da; 우뚝 솟다 u-ttuk sot-da; 뒤틀리다 dwi-teul-li-da

sprinkle *vt.* 뿌리다 ppu-ri-da; 끼얹다 kki-eon-tta; 섞다 seok-da

sprinkler *n.* 스프링클러 seu-peu-ring-keul-leo; 살수장치 sal-ssu-jang-chi; 물뿌리개 mul-ppu-ri-gae

sprint *vi.* 역주하다 yeok-ju-ha-da

sprout *n.* 싹 ssak, 눈 nun; 봉오리가 벌어짐 bong-o-ri-ga beol-eo-jim, 발아 bal-a; **wheat ~** 밀싹 mil-ssak; **bamboo ~** 대나무순 dae-na-mu-sun; *vi.* 싹이 트다 ssag-i teu-da; 발육하다 bal-yu-ka-da

spur *n.* 박차 bak-cha; 자극 ja-geuk, 격려 gyeong-nyeo; 동기 dong-gi

spy *n.* 간첩 gan-cheop, 스파이 seu-pa-i; 탐정 tam-jeong; 정찰 jeong-chal; *vi.* 스파이가 되다 seu-pa-i-ga doe-da; 감시하다 gam-si-ha-da; 몰래 조사하다 mol-lae jo-sa-ha-da

square *n.* *(shape)* 정사각형 jeong-sa-ga-kyeong; **town ~** 광장 gwang-jang; 구획 gu-hoek; *adj.* 정사각형의 jeong-sa-ga-kyeong-ui; 직각을 이루는 jik-gag-eul i-ru-neun; 수평을 이루는 su-pyeong-eul i-ru-neun; 동등한 dong-deung-han; 셈이 끝난 sem-i kkeun-nan; 가지런한 ga-ji-reon-han; 공명정대한 gong-myeong-jeong-dae-han; 단호한 dan-ho-han

squash *n.* 과즙음료 gwa-jeub-eum-nyo; 붐빔 bum-bim; 군중 gun-jung; *(vegetable)* 호박 ho-bak; *(sport)* 스쿼시 seu-kwo-si; *vt.* 으깨다 eu-kkae-da; 쑤셔넣다 ssu-syeo-neo-ta; 억누르다 eong-nu-reu-da; 진압하다 in-a-pa-da; 윽박지르다 euk-bak-ji-reu-da

squint *vi.* 사팔눈이다 sal-pal-lun-i-da; 곁눈질로 보다 gyeon-nun-jil-lo bo-da; 틈으로 들여다보다 teum-eu-ro deul-yeo-da-bo-da; 기울다 gi-ul-da

squirrel *n.* 다람쥐 da-ram-jwi

stable *n.* 마구간 ma-gu-kkan, 가축우리 ga-chug-u-ri; 경마말 관리인 gyeong-ma-mal gwal-li-in; *adj.* 안정된 an-jeong-doen; 영속적인 yeong-sok-jeog-in; 견실한 gyeon-sil-han; 착실한 chak-sil-han

stadium *n.* 스타디움 seu-ta-di-um, 육상 경기장 yuk-sang-gyeong-gi-jang

staff *n.* 막대기 mak-dae-gi, 지팡이 ji-pang-i; 지휘봉 ji-hwi-bong; 측량대 cheung-nyang-dae; 깃대 git-dae; 참모 cham-mo; 부원 bu-won, 직원 jig-won

stage *n.* 무대 mu-dae; 연단 yeon-dan; 활동무대 hwal-ttong-mu-dae; 발판 bal-pan; 여정 yeo-jeong; 단계 dan-gye, 시기 si-gi

stain *n.* 더러움 deo-reo-um; 얼룩 eol-luk; 오점 o-jjeom; 착색 chak-saek; 색소 saek-so;

~ **remover** 얼룩 제거제 eol-luk je-geo-je; *vt.* 더럽히다 deo-reo-pi-da; 채색하다 chae-sae-ka-da; *vi.* 더러워지다 deo-reo-wo-ji-da; 얼룩이 지다 eol-lug-i ji-da; ~**ed glass** 스테인드 글라스 seu-te-in-deu gel-la-sseu, 색유리 saeg-yu-ri

stainless *n.* 스텐 seu-ten, 스텐레스 seu-ten-re-sseu; ~ **steel**스테인레스강 seu-te-in-re-sseu-gang

stair *n.* 계단 gye-dan

staircase *n.* 계단 gye-dan

stake *n.* 말뚝 mal-ttuk, 막대기 mak-dae-gi; 내기 nae-gi; 상금 sang-geum; 이해관계 i-hae-gwan-gye

stale *adj.* 상한 sang-han; 김빠진 gim-ppa-jin; 신선미가 없는 sin-seon-mi-ga eom-neun; 곰팡내 나는 gom-pang-nae na-neun; 생기가 없는 saeng-gi-ga eom-neun

stalk *n.* 줄기 jul-gi; 가느다란 버팀 ga-neu-da-ran beo-tim; 성큼성큼 걷기 seong-keum-seong-keum geot-gi; 추적 chu-jeok; *vt.* 살그머니 접근하다 sal-geu-meo-ni jeop-geun-ha-da; *vi.* 활보하다 hwal-bo-ha-da; 만연하다 man-yeon-ha-da; 몰래 추적하다 mol-lae chu-jeo-ka-da

stall *n.* 축사 chuk-sa; 성직자석 seong-jik-ja-seok; 성가대석 seong-ga-dae-seok; 골무 gol-mu; 구실 gu-sil

stammer *n.* 말더듬기 mal-deo-deum-kki; *vi.* 말을 더듬다 mal-eul deo-deum-tta

stamp *n.* 스탬프 seu-taem-peu, 도장 do-jang; 인지 in-jji; 각인 gag-in; 검인 geom-in; 특징 teuk-jing, 종류 jong-nyu; 발구르기 bal-gu-reu-gi; **postage** ~ 우표 u-pyo; **airmail** ~ 항공우편 스탬프 hang-gong-u-pyeon seu-tam-peu; *vt.* 우표를 붙이다 u-pyo-reyl bu-chi-da; 도장을 찍다 do-jang-eul jjik-da; 각인하다 gag-in-ha-da; 무늬를 내다 mu-ni-reul nae-da; 인상을 지우다 in-sang-eul ji-u-da; 틀로 찍어내다 teul-lo jjig-eo-nae-da; 짓밟다 jit-bal-tta; 발을 구르다 bal-eul gu-reu-da

stand *n.* 정지 jeong-ji; 섬 seom; 위치 wi-chi; 입장 ip-jang; 저항 jeo-hang; 스탠드 seu-ten-deu; 노점 no-jeom, 노점상 no-jeom-sang; 진열대 jin-yeol-ttae; 정류장 jeong-nyu-jang; 증인대 jeung-in-dae; **a fruit** ~ 과일 노점상, 진열대gwa-il

no-jeom-sang/jin-yeol-ttae; **a souvenir** ~기념품 노점상gi-nyeom-pum no-jeom-sang; *vt.* 세우다 se-u-da; 놓다 no-ta; 견디다 gyeon-di-da; 저항하다 jeo-hang-ha-da; 고집하다 go-ji-pa-da; 한턱내다 han-teong-nae-da; 비용이 들다 bi-yong-i deul-da; 당번을 맡다 dang-beon-eul mat-da; *vi.* 일어서다 il-eo-seo-da; 멈춰서다 meom-chwo-seo-da; 위치하다 wi-chi-ha-da; ...한 상태에 있다 ...han sang-tae-e it-da; 오래가다 o-rae-ga-da; 정체되어 있다 jeong-che-doe-eo it-da

standard *n.* 표준 pyo-jun; 규범 gyu-beom; 규격 gyu-gyeok; 도량형 do-ryang-hyeong; 등급 deung-geup; *adj.* 표준의 pyo-jun-ui; 모범적인 mo-beom-jeog-in; 우수한 u-su-han; 권위있는 gwon-wi-in-nwun; 받침이 달린 bat-chim-i dal-lin; ~ **of living** 생활수준 saeng-hwal-su-jun

standing *adj.* 서 있는 seo in-neun; 움직이지 않는 um-jig-i-ji an-neun; 변하지 않는 byeon-ha-ji an-neun; 고정된 go-jeong-doen; 일정한 il-jjeong-han; ~ **order** 의사규칙 ui-sa-gyu-chik; 내무규정 nae-mu-gyu-jeong

staple *n.* 주요산물 ju-yo-san-mul; 주성분 ju-seong-bun; 원료 wol-lyo; 스테이플 seu-te-i-peul; ~ **remover** 스테이플 제거기 seu-te-i-peul je-geo-gi; *adj.* 중요한 jung-yo-han; 대량생산의 dae-ryang-saeng-san-ui; 널리 거래되는 neol-li geo-rae-doe-neun; *vt.* 분류하다 bul-lyu-ha-da; 선별하다 seon-byeol-ha-da

stapler *n.* 스테이플러 seu-te-i-peul-leo, 호치키스 ho-chi-ki-sseu; 양털상 yang-teol-ssang

star *n.* 별 byeol; 스타 seu-ta, 인기인 in-kki-in; 훈장 hun-jang; 운수 un-su

starboard *n.* 우현 u-hyeon, 우측 u-cheuk

starch *n.* 전분 jeon-bun, 녹말 nong-mal; 풀 pul; 전분이 많은 음식 jeon-bun-i man-eun eum-sik; 거북함 geo-bu-kam; *vt.* 풀을 먹이다 pul-eul meog-i-da; 거북하게 하다 geo-bu-ka-ge ha-da

stare *vi.* 응시하다 eung-si-ha-da; 눈을 동그랗게 뜨다 nun-eul dong-geu-ra-ke tteu-da; 눈에 띄다 nun-e tti-da; 털이 곤두서다 teol-i gon-du-seo-da

starfish *n*. 불가사리 bul-ga-sa-ri

start *n*. 출발 chul-bal, 스타트 seu-ta-teu; 출발점 chul-bal-jjeom; 출발신호 chul-bal-sin-ho; 펄쩍 뜀 peol-jjeok ttwim; 깜짝 놀람 kkam-jjak nol-lam; 시동 si-dong; 개시 gae-si; *vt*. 출발시키다 chul-bal-si-ki-da; 내보내다 nae-bo-nae-da; 시작하게 하다 si-ja-ka-ge ha-da; 시작하다 si-ja-ka-da; 시동을 걸다 si-dong-eul geol-da; 가동하다 ga-dong-ha-da; 착수하다 chak-su-ha-da; 깜짝 놀라게 하다 kkam-jjak nol-la-ge ha-da; 선도하다 seon-do-ha-da; *vi*. 출발하다 chul-bal-ha-da; 시작되다 si-jak-doe-da; 돌발하다 dol-bal-ha-da; 나타나다 na-ta-na-da; 움찔하다 um-jjil-ha-da; 갑자기 늠식이나 gap-ja-gi um-jig-i-da

starter *n*. 출발자 chul-bal-jja, 개시자 gae-si-ja; 시초 si-cho, 개시 gae-si; 경주 참가자 gyeong-ju cham-ga-ja; 스타트 신호계 seu-ta-teu sin-ho-gye; 원인 won-in; *(auto)* 시동장치 si-dong-jang-chi

starvation *n*. 굶주림 gum-ju-rim, 기아 gi-a; 아사 a-sa

state *n*. 상태 sang-tae; 지위 ji-wi, 신분 sin-bun; 위엄 wi-eom; 의식 ul-sik; 국가 guk-ga; 주 ju; *vt*. 진술하다 jin-sul-ha-da; 주장하다 ju-jang-ha-da; 지정하다 ji-jeong-ha-da

statement *n*. 성명 seong-myeong; 성명서 seong-myeong-seo; 진술 jin-sul; 진술문 jin-sul-mun; 신고서 sin-go-seo; 명세서 myeong-se-seo; **bank** ~ 은행 거래 명세서 eun-haeng-geo-rae myeong-se-seo

statesman *n*. 정치가 jeong-chi-ga

station *n*. 정거장 jeong-geo-jang, 역 yeok; 소방서 so-bang-seo, 경찰서 gyeong-chal-sseo; 방송국 bang-song-guk; 주둔지 ju-dun-ji, 근거지 geun-geo-ji; 위치 wi-chi; 부서 bu-seo; **radio** ~ 라디오 방송국 ra-di-o bang-song-guk; **TV** ~ 텔레비전 방송국 tel-le-bi-jeon bang-song-guk; **train** ~ 기차역 gi-cha-yeok; *vt*. 주둔시키다 ju-dun-si-ki-da; 배치하다 bae-chi-ha-da

stationary *adj*. 움직이지 않는 um-jig-i-ji an-neun; 변화하지 않는 byeon-hwa-ha-ji an-neun; 고정시킨 go-jeong-si-kin; 상비의 sang-bi-ui

stationery *n*. 문구용품 mun-gu-yong-pum; 편지지 pyeon-ji-ji; 무료 입장권 mu-ryo-ip-jang-kkwon

statistic *n*. 통계량 tong-gye-ryang; 통계치 tong-gye-chi

statistical *adj*. 통계상의 tong-gye-sang-ui; 통계학의 tong-gye-hag-ui

statue *n*. 상 sang, 동상 dong-sang

status *n*. 상태 sang-tae; 지위 ji-wi; 자격 ja-gyeok; 신분 sin-bun; ~ **quo** 이전의 상태 i-jeon-uinsang-tae

statutory *adj*. 법령의 beom-nyeong-ui; 법정의 beop-jeong-ui; 법에 걸리는 beob-e geol-li-neun

stay *n*. 체재 che-jae, 체류 che-ryu; 체제기간 che-je-gi-gan; *vi*. 미무르다 meo-mu-reu-da, 체재하다 che-jae-ha-da; 멈춰서다 meom-chwo-seo-da; 기다리다 gi-da-ri-da; …인 채로 있다 …in chae-ro it-da; 지탱하다 ji-aeng-ha-da; 견디다 gyeon-di-da

steady *adj*. 고정된 go-jeong-doen; 확고한 hwak-go-han; 안정된 an-jeong-doen; 착실한 chak-sil-han; 동요되지 않는 dong-yo-doe-ji an-neun

steak *n*. 불고기 bul-go-gi; 스테이크 seu-te-i-keu

steal *vt*. 훔치다 hum-chi-da; 가로채다 ga-ro-chae-da; 독점하다 dok-jeom-ha-da; 몰래 …하다 mol-lae…ha-da; *vi*. 도둑질하다 do-duk-jil-ha-da; 졸음이 엄습하다 jol-eum-i eom-seu-pa-da; 도루하다 do-ru-ha-da

steam *n*. 증기 jeung-gi, 스팀 seu-tim, 수증기 su-jeung-gi; 놀 nol; 안개 an-gae; 힘 him, 원기 won-gi, 정력 jeong-nyeok

steamship *n*. 증기선 jeung-gi-seon, 기선 gi-seon

steel *n*. 강철 gang-cheol; 칼 kal; 버팀대 beo-tim-ttae; 강철제품 gang-cheol-je-pum; ~ **mill** 제강소 je-gang-so; ~ **wool** 강철솜 gang-cheol-ssom

steer *vt*. 조종하다 jo-jong-ha-da; 방향을 돌리다 bang-hyang-eul dol-li-da; *vi*. 키를 잡다 ki-reul jap-da; 향하다 hyang-ha-da; 처신하다 cheo-sin-ha-da; 조종되다 jo-jong-doe-da

steering wheel *n*. 타륜 ta-ryun, 핸들 haen-deul

stem *n.* 줄기 jul-gi, 대 dae; 종족 jong-jok; 어간 eo-gan; 자루 ja-ru; 제동 je-dong

step *n.* 걸음 geol-eum, 보행 bo-haeng; 걸음걸이 geol-eum-geol-i, 보조 bo-jo; 발소리 bal-sso-ri; 발자국 bal-jja-guk; 한걸음 han-geol-eum; 계단 gye-dan; 단계 dan-gye; 조치 jo-chi; *vi.* 걷다 geot-da; 밟다 bal-tta; 급히 서두르다 geu-pi seo-du-reu-da; ...의 상태로 되다 ...ui sang-tae-ro doe-da

stepbrother *n.* 이복형제 i-bo-kyeong-je

stepdaughter *n.* 의붓딸 ui-but-ttal

stepfather *n.* 새아버지 sae-a-beo-ji, 계부 gye-bu

stepmother *n.* 새어머니 sae-eo-meo-ni, 계모 gye-mo

stepparent *n.* 새아버지와 새어머니 sae-a-beo-ji-wa sae-eo-meo-ni, 계부와 계모 gye-bu-wa gye-mo

stepsister *n.* 이복자매 i-bok-ja-mae

stepson *n.* 의붓아들 ui-bu-da-deul

stereo *n.* 입체음향 ip-che-eum-hyang, 스테레오 seu-te-re-o; **in ~** 스테레오로 seu-te-re-o-ro

stereotype *n.* 선입관 seon-ip-gwan; 상투수단 sang-tu-su-dan; 상투어구 sang-tu-eo-kku

sterile *adj.* 메마른 me-ma-reun; 불모의 bul-mo-ui; 불임의 bul-im-ui; 단조로운 dan-jo-ro-un; 빈곤한 bin-gon-han; 살균한 sal-gyun-han; 열매를 맺지 않는 yeol-mae-reul mat-ji an-neun

sterilize *vt.* 불모케 하다 bul-mo-ke ha-da; 불임케 하다 bul-im-ke ha-da; 빈약하게 하다 bin-ya-ka-ge ha-da; 살균소독하다 sal-gyun-so-do-ka-da; 철거하다 cheol-geo-ha-da

stern *n.* 고물 go-mul, 선미 seon-mi; 후부 hu-bu; 동물의 엉덩이 dong-mul-ui eong-deong-i; *adj.* 엄격한 eom-kkyeo-kan; 단호한 dan-ho-han; 엄숙한 eom-su-kan; 준엄한 jun-eom-han

stethoscope *n.* 청진기 cheong-jin-gi

stew *n.* 스튜 seu-tyu; 근심 geun-sim; 당황 dang-hwang; 초조 cho-jo; 양어장 yang-eo-jang, 양식장 yang-sik-jang

steward *n.* 청지기 cheong-ji-gi; 지배인 ji-bae-in; 사무장 sa-mu-jang; 스튜어드 seu-tyu-eo-deu, 승무원seung-mu-won

stewardess *n.* 스튜어디스 seu-tyu-eo-di-sseu, 여승무원 yeo-seung-mu-won

stick *n.* 막대기 mak-dae-gi; 지팡이 ji-pang-i; 채찍질 chae-jjik-jil; 등신 deung-sin, 밥통 bap-tong; *vt.* 막대기로 버티다 mak-dae-gi-ro beo-ti-da; 식자하다sik-ja-ha-da

sticky *adj.* 끈끈한 kkeun-kkeun-han; 완고한 wan-go-han; 귀찮은 gwi-chan-eun; 서투른 seo-tu-reun; 습기가 많은 seup-gi-ga man-eun

stiff *adj.* 뻣뻣한 ppeot-ppeo-tan; 뻐근한 ppeo-geun-han; 팽팽한 paeng-paeng-han; 고착된 go-chak-doen; 딱딱해진 ttak-tta-kae-jin; 완강한 wan-gang-han; 강경한 gang-gyeong-han; 어려운 eo-ryeo-un; 엄청난 eom-cheong-nan

stiffen *vt.* 뻣뻣하게 하다 ppeot-ppeo-ta-ge ha-da; 뻐근하게 하다 ppeo-geun-ha-ge ha-da; 강경하게 하다 gang-gyeong-ha-ge ha-da; 딱딱하게 하다 ttak-tta-ka-ge ha-da; 진하게 하다 jin-ha-ge ha-da; *vi.* 뻣뻣해지다 ppeot-ppeo-tae-ji-da; 굳어지다 gud-eo-ji-da; 바람이 세어지다 ba-ram-i se-eo-ji-da; 고집이 세어지다 go-jib-i se-eo-ji-da; 딱딱해지다 ttak-tta-kae-ji-da; 진해지다 jin-hae-ji-da; 비싸지다 bi-ssa-ji-da

still *adj.* 정지한 jeong-ji-han; 소리가 없는 so-ri-gan eom-neun; 조용한 jo-yong-han; 평화로운 hyeong-hwa-ro-un; 거품이 일지 않는 geo-pum-i il-ji an-neun; *adv.* 아직도 a-jik-do; 그럼에도 geu-reom-e-do; 더욱 deo-uk

stimulant *n.* 흥분제 heung-bun-je; 알코올 음료 al-kol-eum-nyo; 자극물 ja-geung-mul

stimulate *vt.* 자극하다 ja-geu-ka-da; 기운을 북돋다 gi-un-eul buk-dot-da; 흥분시키다 heung-bun-si-ki-da

sting *n.* 찌르기 jji-reu-gi; 쏘기 sso-gi; 찔린 상처 jjil-lin sang-cheo; 쑤시는 아픔 ssu-si-neun a-peum; 자극 ja-geuk; 실랄함 sil-lal-ham; 빈정댐 bin-jeong-daem; 고통 go-tong; *vt.* 찌르다 jji-reu-da; 따끔따끔하게 하다 tta-kkeum-tta-kkeum-ha-ge ha-da; 괴롭히다 goe-ro-pi-da; 자극하다 ja-geu-ka-da; *vi.* 쏘다 sso-da; 찌르다 jji-reu-da; 따끔따끔하다 tta-kkeum-tta-kkeum-ha-da; 고통을 주다 go-tong-eul ju-da; 고통을 느끼다 go-tong-eul neu-kki-da

stir *vt.* 움직이다 um-jig-i-da; 휘젓다 hwi-jeot-da; 분발시키다 bun-bal-si-ki-da; 감동시키다 gam-dong-si-ki-da; 자극하다 ja-geu-ka-da

stirrup *n.* 등자 deung-ja; 등자 가죽끈 deung-ja ga-juk-kkeun; 등골 deung-kkol

stitch *n.* 한바늘 han-ba-neul; 바늘땀 ba-neul-ttam; 솔기 sol-gi; 바느질 솜씨 ba-neu-jil-ssom-ssi; 헝겊조각 heong-geop-jjo-gak; 조금 jo-geum; 통증 tong-jjeung

stock *n.* 주식 ju-sik, 증권 jeung-kkwon; 줄기 jul-qi; 자루 ja-ru; 혈통 hyeol-tong; 종족 jong-jok; 저장 jeo-jang; 저축 jeo-chuk; 재고품 jae-go-pum; 재료 jae-ryo; *(in a company)* 주식 ju-sik, 증권 jeung-kkwon; **exchange** 증권거래소 jeung-kkwon-geo-rae-so; 증권 브로커 조합 jeung-kkwon beu-ro-keo jo-hap; ~ **market** 증시 jeung-si, 증권시장 jeung-kkwon-si-jang; ~ **option** 스톡옵션 seu-toq-op-syeon; **in** ~ 재고가 남은 jae-go-ga nam-eun; **out of** ~ 품절된 pum-jeol-doen; *vt.* 자루를 달다 ja-ru-reul dal-da; 비축하다 bi-chu-ka-da; 씨를 뿌리다 ssi-reul ppu-ri-da; 구입하다 gu-i-pa-da

stockbroker *n.* 증권 브로커 jeung-kkwon-beu-ro-keo, 증권 중개인 jeung-kkwon jung-gae-in

Stockholm *n.* 스톡홀름 seu-to-kol-leum

stocking *n.* 스타킹 seu-ta-king; 긴 양말 gin-nyang-mal

stomach *n.* 위 wi, 위장 wi-jang; 식욕 sig-yok, 욕망 yong-mang; ~ **cramps** 위경련 wi-gyeong-nyeon

stomachache *n.* 위통 wi-tong, 복통 bok-tong

stone *n.* 돌 dol, 돌멩이 dol-meng-I; 비석 bi-seok; 맷돌 maet-dol; 결석 gyeol-sseok

stool *n.* 걸상 geol-ssang; 발판 bal-pan; 변기 byeon-gi; 대변 dae-byeon; 그루터기 geu-ru-teo-gi; 끄나풀 kkeu-na-pul; 창문지방 chang-mun-jji-bang

stop *n.* 멈춤 meom-chum; 정지 jeong-ji; 끝 kkeut; 정류장 jeong-nyu-jang, 정거장 jeong-geo-jang; 착륙장 chang-nyuk-jang; 방해물 bang-hae-mul; *vt.* 멈추다 meom-chu-da; 붙잡다 but-jap-da; 방해하다 bang-hae-ha-da; 중지하다 jung-ji-ha-da; 막다 mak-da; 정지하다 jeong-ji-ha-da; *vi.*

멈추다 meom-chu-da; 들르다 deul-leu-da; 서다 seo-da; 막히다 ma-ki-da; *(imperative)* 서십시오 seo-sip-si-o, 그만두십시오 geu-man-du-sip-si-o

storage *n.* 저장 jeo-jang; 창고 chang-kko; 보관료 bo-gwan-nyo; 수용력 su-yong-nyeok; 기억장치 gi-eok-jang-chi

store *n.* 저축 jeo-chuk; 비축 bi-chuk; 대비 dae-bi; 가게 ga-ge, 상점 sang-jeom; *vt.* 저축하다 jeo-chu-ka-da; 저장하다 jeo-jang-ha-da; 공급하다 gong-geu-pa-da; 보관하다 bo-gwan-ha-da; ...을 여지를 가지다 ...eul yeo-ji-reul ga-ji-da; 기억하다 gi-eo-ka-da

storeroom *n.* 저장실 jeo-jang-sil, 광 gwang

stork *n.* 황새 hwang-sae

storm *n.* 폭풍우 pok-pung-u, 폭풍 pok-pung; 격정 gyeok-jeong; 소동 so-dong

stormy *adj.* 폭풍우의 pok-pung-u-ui; 격렬한 gyeong-nyeol-han; 소란스러운 so-ran-seu-reo-un; 난폭한 nan-po-kan; 논쟁하기 좋아하는 non-jaeng-ha-gi jo-a-ha-neun

story *n.* 이야기 i-ya-gi; 소설 so-seol; 기사 gi-sa; 줄거리 jul-geo-ri; 내력 nae-ryeok; 소문 so-mun; *(of a building)* 층 cheung; **to tell a** ~ 이야기하다 i-ya-gi-ha-da

stout *n.* 흑맥주 heung-maek-ju; 뚱뚱보 ttung-ttung-bo; 치수가 큰 옷 chi-ssu-ga keun ot; *adj.* 단단한 dan-dan-han; 견고한 gyeon-go-han; 난호한 dan-ho-han; 용감한 yong-gam-han; 완강한 wan-gang-han, 뚱뚱한 ttung-ttung han; 실속있는 sil-ssog-in-neun

stove *n.* 스토브 seu-to-beu, 난로 nal-lo; 건조실 geon-jo-sil

straight *adj.* 곧은 god-eun; 일직선의 il-jjik-seon-ui; 수직의 su-jig-ui; 수평의 su-pyeong-ui; 평행의 pyeong-haeng-ui; 정면으로부터의 jeong-myeon-eu-ro-bu-teo-ui; 솔직한 sol-jji-kan; 공정한 gong-jeong-han; 믿을 수 있는 mid-eul ssu in-neun; 일관된 il-gwan-doen; 잇따른 it-tta-reun; 철저한 cheol-jjeo-han

strain *vt.* 잡아당기다 jab-a-dang-gi-da; 긴장시키다 gin-jang-si-ki-da; 무리하게 사용하다 mu-ri-ha-ge sa-yong-ha-da; 접질리다 jeop-jil-li-da; 뒤틀리게 하다 dwi-teul-li-ge ha-da; 곡해하다 go-kae-ha-da; 남용하

다 nam-yong-ha-da; 무리한 요구를 하다 mu-ri-han yo-gu-reul ha-da

strainer *n.* 잡아당기는 사람 jab-a-dang-gi-neun sa-ram; 팽팽히 하는 도구 paeng-paeng-hi ha-neun do-gu; 여과기 yeo-gwa-gi; 체 che

strand *n.* 물가 mul-kka, 해안 hae-an; 밧줄 가닥 bat-jul ga-dak; 섬유 seom-yu; *(of hair)* 머리숱 meo-ri-sut

strange *adj.* 이상한 i-sang-han; 낯선 nat-seon; 생소한 saeng-so-han; 서먹서먹한 seo-meok-seo-meo-kan

stranger *n.* 낯선사람 nat-seon-sa-ram; 외국 인 oe-gug-in; 경험이 없는 사람 gyeong-heom-i eom-neun sa-ram

strangle *vt.* 질식시키다 jil-ssik-si-ki-da; 억누르다 eong-nu-reu-da; 묵살하다 muk-sal-ha-da

strap *n.* 가죽끈 ga-juk-kkeun, 혁대 hyeok-dae; 가죽 손잡이 ga-juk son-jab-i; 띠 tti; 견장 gyeon-jang; 피대 pi-dae

straw *n.* 짚 jip, 밀짚 mil-jjip; 스트로우 seu-teu-ro-u; 밀짚모자 mil-jjim-mo-ja; 하 찮은 물건 ha-chan-eun mul-geon; 조금 jo-geum

strawberry *n.* 딸기 ttal-gi

streak *n.* 줄 jul; 줄무늬 jul-mu-ni; 광 맥 gwang-maek; 연속 yeon-sok; 경향 gyeong-hyang; 단기간 dan-gi-gan; *vi.* 줄 이 지다 jul-i ji-da; 질주하다 jil-jju-ha-da; 스트리킹을 하다 seu-teu-ri-king-ha-da, 벌 거벗고 달리다 beol-geo-beot-go dal-li-da

stream *n.* 시내 si-nae, 개울 gae-ul; 연속 yeon-sok; 경향 gyeong-hyang; 흐름 heu-reum; 물결 mul-kkyeol; 유출 yu-chul

street *n.* 거리 geo-ri; 차도 cha-do; 중심가 jung-sim-ga

strength *n.* 세기 se-gi; 힘 him; 체력 che-ryeok; 정신력 jeong-sin-nyeok; 도의심 do-ui-sim; 힘이 되는 것 him-i doe-neun goet; 저항력 jeo-hang-nyeok, 내구력 nae-gu-ryeok; 강도 gang-do; 농도 nong-do; 효 과 hyo-kkwa; 설득력 seol-tteung-nyeok

strengthen *vt.* 강하게 하다 gang-ha-ge ha-da; 튼튼하게 하다 teun-teun-ha-ge ha-da; 힘을 돋우다 him-eul dod-u-da; 증원하다 jeung-won-ha-da

strep throat *n.* 패혈성 인후염 pae-hyeol-sseong in-hu-yeom

stress *n.* 압박 ap-bak; 시련 si-ryeon; 긴장 gin-jang, 스트레스 seu-teu-re-sseu; 압 력 am-nyeok; 강조 gang-jo; *vt.* 강조하다 gang-jo-ha-da; 압박하다 ap-pa-ka-da; 압 력을 가하다 am-nyeog-eul ga-ha-da; ~ed out 스트레스를 받다 seu-teu-re-sseu-reul bat-da

stretch *vt.* 뻗치다 ppeot-chi-da; 늘이다 neul-i-da; 잡아당기다 jab-a-dang-gi-da; 펴 다 pyeo-da; 내밀다 nae-mil-da; 크게 벌리 다 keu-ge beol-li-da; 과장하다 gwa-jang-ha-da; 왜곡하다 wae-go-ka-da

stretcher *n.* 들것 deul-kkeot; 펴는 사람 pyeo-neun sa-ram, 펴는 도구 pyeo-neun do-gu

strict *adj.* 엄격한 eom-kkyeo-kan; 정밀한 jeong-mil-han; 진정한 jin-jeong-han; 완전 한 wan-jeon-han

strike *n.* 때리기 ttae-ri-gi; 스트라이크 seu-teu-ra-i-keu; 파업 pa-eop; to go on ~ 파업 하다 pa-eo-pa-da

striking *adj.* 현저한 hyeon-jeo-han; 인상적 인 in-sang-jeog-in; 공격하는 gong-gyeo-ka-neun; 파업중인 pa-eop-jung-in

string *n.* 끈 kkeun, 줄 jul; 꿰미 kkwe-mi; 일 련 il-lyeon; 현악기 hyeon-ak-gi; 섬유 seom-yu

strip *n.* 길고 가는 조각 gil-go ga-neun jo-gak; 좁고 긴 땅 jop-go gin ttang

stripe *n.* 줄무늬 jul-mu-ni

striped *adj.* 줄무늬가 있는 jul-mu-ni-ga in-neun

stroke *n.* 한번 치기 han-beon chi-gi; 한번 젓기 han-beon jeot-gi; 젓는 법 jeon-neun beop; 타격법 ta-gyeok-beop; 수영법 su-yeong-ppeop; *(of a pen)* 필법 pil-ppeop; 자획 ja-hoek; *(of the heart)* 뇌일혈 noe-il-hyeol; **heat** ~ 일사병 il-ssa-ppyeong

stroller *n.* 유모차 yu-mo-cha; 우유배달용 손수레 u-yu-bae-dal-yong son-su-re

strong *adj.* 강한 gang-han; 유력한 yu-ryeo-kan; 튼튼한 teun-teun-han; 완강한 wan-gang-han; 확고한 hwak-go-han; 강렬한 gang-nyeol-han; 강경한 gang-gyeong-han

structure *n.* 구조 gu-jo; 조직 jo-jik; 구조물 gu-jo-mul; 건축물 geon-chung-mul

struggle *n.* 버둥거림 beo-dung-geo-rim; 노력 no-ryeok; 싸움 ssa-um; *vi.* 버둥거리다 beo-dung-geo-ri-da; 헤치고 나아가다 he-chi-go na-a-ga-da; 노력하다 no-ryeo-ka-da; 싸우다 ssa-u-da

stub *n.* 그루터기 geu-ru-teo-gi; 동강 dong-gang; 꽁초 kkong-cho; *(of a ticket)* 원부 won-bu, 서류 한쪽 seo-ryu han-jjok

stubborn *adj.* 완고한 wan-go-han; 완강한 wan-gang-han; 다루기 어려운 da-ru-gi eo-ryeo-un; 잘 녹지 않는 jal nok-ji an-neun

student *n.* 학생 hak-saeng; 연구생 yeon-gu-saeng; 장학생 jang-hak-saeng

study *n.* 학문 hang-mun; 학과 hak-gwa; 연구사항 yeon-gu-sa-hang; *(room)* 서재 seo-jae; **a ~ of something** 공부 gong-bu; 연구 yeon-gu; 조사 jo-sa; *vt.* 배우다 bae-u da; 연구하다 yeon gu ha da; 공부하다 gong-bu-ha-da; 조사하다 jo-sa-ha-da; 살피다 sal-pi-da; *vi.* 공부하다 gong-bu-ha-da; 연구하다 yeon-gu-ha-da; 고찰하다 go-chal-ha-da

stuff *n.* 재료 jae-ryo; 자료 ja-ryo; 자질 ja-jil; 소지품 so-ji-pum; 지식 ji-sik; 기술 gi-sul; 작품 jak-pum; *vt.* 채워넣다 chae-wo-neo-ta, 가득 채우다 ga-deuk chae-u-da; *vi.* 배부르게 먹다 bae-bu-reu-ge meok-da; **~ed animal** 봉제 동물인형 bong-je dong-mul in-hyeong; **~ed pepper** 속을 넣은 피망요리 sog-eul neo-eun pi-mang-yo-ri

stumble *vi.* 넘어지다 neom-eo-ji-da; 마주치다 ma-ju-chi-da; 비틀거리다 bi-teul-geo-ri-da; 실수하다 sil-ssu-ha-da; 더듬거리다 deo eum geo ri da

stun *vt.* 기절시키다 gi-jeol-si-ki-da; 깜짝 놀라게 하다 kkam-jjak nol-la-ge ha-da; 귀를 멍멍하게 하다 gwi-reul meong-meong-ha-ge ha-da

stupid *adj.* 어리석은 eo-ri-seog-eun, 비보같은 ba-bo-gat-eun; 하찮은 ha-chan-eun; 무감각한 mu gam ga kan

style *n.* 문체 mun-che; 어조 eo-jo; 유파 yu-pa; 방법 bang-beop; 생활양식 saeng-hwal-lyang-sik; 스타일 seu-ta-il; 차림새 cha-rim-sae

stylish *adj.* 현대식의 hyeon-dae-sig-ui; 유행의 yu-haeng-ui

subdue *vt.* 정복하다 jeong-bo-ka-da; 가라앉히다 ga-ra-an-chi-da; 뿌리뽑다 ppu-ri-ppop-da; 차분하게 하다 cha-bun-ha-ge ha-da

subject *n.* 국민 gung-min; 학과 hak-gwa; 주어 ju-eo; 주관 ju-gwan; 환자 hwan-ja; 실험대상 sil-heom-dae-sang; *(area of discussion or study)* 주제 ju-je

subjective *adj.* 주관의 ju-gwan-ui; 주관적인 ju-gwan-jeog-in; 사적인 sa-jjeog-in; 내성적인 nae-seong-jeog-in

submarine *n.* 잠수함 jam-su-ham; 해저 동식물 hae-jeo dong-sing-mul

submit *vt.* 복종시키다 bok-jong-si-ki-da; 제출하다 je-chul-ha-da; 의견을 진술하다 ui-gyeon-eul jin-sul-ha-da; *vi.* 복종하다 bok-jong-ha-da; 항복하다 hang-bo-ka-da; 감수하다 gam-su-ha-da

subscribe *vi.* 기부하다 gi bu ha da; 동의하다 dong-ui-ha-da; 예약하다 ye-ya-ka-da; 정기구독하다 jeong-gi-gu-do-ka-da; 서명하다 seo-myeong-ha-da; **to ~ to a magazine** 잡지를 정기구독하다 jap-ji-reul jeong-gi-gu-do-ka-da

subscription *n.* 기부신청 gi-bu-sin-cheong; 응모 eung-mo; 가입 ga-ip; 예약금 ye-yak-geum; 구독예약 gu-dog-ye-yak; 예약 ye-yak; 서명승낙 seo-myeong-seung-nak; 권유판매 gwon-yu-pan-mae

subsidy *n.* 국가 보조금 guk-ga-bo-jo-geum; 장려금 jang-nyeo-geum

substance *n.* 생존 saeng-jon; 생계 saeng-gye; 실재 sil-jje; 존재 jon-jae

substantial *adj.* 실질적인 sil-jjil-jeog-in; 내용이 풍부한 nae yong i pung bu han; 실속있는 sil-ssog-in-neun; 대폭적인 dae-pok-jeog-in; 풍부한 pung-bu-han; 신용있는 sin-yong-in-neun; 견실한 gyeon-sil-han; 실체의 sil-che-ui

substitute *adj.* 대리의 dae-ri-ui; 대체의 dae-che-ui; 예비의 ye-bi-ui; 대용의 dae-yong ui; *vt.* 대용하다 dae-yong-ha-da; 대신하다 dae-sin-ha-da; **~ worker** 대리 근로자 dae-ri geul-lo-ja

substitution *n.* 대리 dae-ri; 대용 dae-yong; 대체 dae-che; 교환 gyo-hwan

subtitle *n.* 부제 bu-je; 대사자막 dae-sa-ja-mak

subtle *adj.* 미묘한 mi-myo-han; 희박한 hi-ba-kan; 희미한 hi-mi-han; 예민한 ye-min-han; 교활한 gyo-hwal-han; 부지불식간의 bu-ji-bul-ssik-gan-ui

subtract *vt.* 빼다 ppae-da; 공제하다 gong-je-ha-da

suburb *n.* 교외 gyo-oe, 근교 geun-gyo

subway *n.* 지하철 ji-ha-cheol

succeed *vi.* 성공하다 seong-gong-ha-da; 번창하다 beon-chang-ha-da; 계속되다 gye-sok-doe-da; 상속하다 sang-so-ka-da

success *n.* 성공 seong-gong; 합격 hap-gyeok; 출세 chul-sse

such *adj.* 그런 geu-reon; 그와 같은 geu-wa gat-eun; ...할 만큼 ...hal man-keum; ~ **as** ...와 같은 ...wa gat-eun

suck *vt.* 빨다 ppal-da; 핥다 hal-tta; 흡수하다 heup-su-ha-da; 휩쓸어 넣다 hwip-sseul-eo neo-ta

sudden *adj.* 돌연한 dol-yeon-han, 별안간의 byeol-an-gan-ui, 갑작스러운 gap-jak-seu-reo-un

suddenly *adv.* 갑자기 gap-ja-gi; 졸지에 jol-jji-e

suede *n.* 세무 sse-mu; 세무 가죽용품 sse-mu ga-jug-yong-pum

Suez Canal *n.* 수에즈 운하 su-e-jeu un-ha

suffer *vi.* 고통을 경험하다 go-tong-eul gyeong-heom-ha-da; 견디다 gyeon-di-da, 참다 cham-tta; 내버려 두다 nae-beo-ryeo du-da

suffice *vi.* 족하다 jo-ka-da, 충분하다 chung-bun-ha-da

sufficient *adj.* 충분한 chung-bun-han, 족한 jo-kan

suffix *n.* 접미사 jeom-mi-sa; 추가물 chu-ga-mul

sugar *n.* 설탕 seol-tang; 당 dang; 감언 gam-eon; ~ **bowl** 설탕그릇 seol-tang-kkeu-reut; 슈거볼 경기장 syu-geo-bol gyeong-gi-jang; **low blood ~** 저혈당 jeo-hyeol-ttang

suggest *vt.* 암시하다 am-si-ha-da; 시사하다 si-sa-ha-da; 제안하다 je-an-ha-da; 연상시키다 yeon-sang-si-ki-da

suggestion *n.* 암시 am-si; 연상 yeon-sang; 제안 je-an; 유발 yu-bal; 기색 gi-saek

suicide *n.* 자살 ja-sal; 자살자 ja-sal-jja; **to commit ~** 자살을 시도하다 ja-sal-eul si-do-ha-da

suit *n.* 소송 so-song; 청원 cheong-won; 구혼 gu-hon; 한벌 han-beol; *(of clothes)* 옷 한벌 ot han-beol; *(of cards)* 카드 한벌 ka-deu han-beol; **a law~** 소송 so-song; *vt.* 적합하게 하다 je-ka-pa-ge ha-da; 일치시키다 il-chi-si-ki-da; 적합하다 jeo-ka-pa-da; 마음에 들다 ma-eum-e deul-da; ...에 편리하다 ...e pyeol-li-ha-da; 옷을 입히다 os-eul i-pi-da

suitable *adj.* 적당한 jeok-dang-han; 어울리는 eo-ul-li-neun; 알맞은 al-maj-eun

suitcase *n.* 여행용 가방 yeo-haeng-nyong ga-bang

suite *n.* 일행 il-haeng, 수행원 su-haeng-won; *(in a hotel)* 스위트 seu-wi-teu

suitor *n.* 제소인 je-so-in, 원고 won-go; 청원자 cheong-won-ja

sullen *adj.* 무뚝뚝한 mu-ttuk-ttu-kan; 음침한 eum-chim-han; 육중한 yuk-jung-han; 찌푸린 jji-pu-rin

sum *n.* 총계 chong-gye; 절정 jeol-jjeong; 개요 gae-yo; 금액 geum-aek; 계산 gye-san; *vt.* 합계하다 hap-gye-ha-da; 요약하다 yo-ya-ka-da; **to ~ up** 요약하다 yo-ya-ka-da; 총계하다 chong-gye-ha-da

summary *n.* 요약 yo-yak; 대략 dae-ryak; 일람 il-lam

summer *n.* 여름 yeo-reum; 한창때 han-chang-ttae; ~ **school** 여름학교 yeo-reum-hak-gyo; ~ **vacation** 여름방학 yeo-reum-ppang-hak, 여름휴가 yeo-reum-hyu-ga

summit *n.* 정상 jeong-sang, 꼭대기 kkok-dae-gi; 절정 jeol-jjeong, 극치 geuk-chi; 최고 수뇌부 choe-go su-noe-bu

sun *n.* 태양 tae-yang; 해 hae; 햇빛 haet-bit; 햇볕 haet-byeot

sunbathe *vi.* 일광욕을 하다 il-gwang-yog-eul ha-da

sunburn *n.* 햇볕에 탐 haet-byeot-e tam; 햇볕에 탄 자국 haet-byeot-e tan ja-guk

Sunday *n.* 일요일 il-yo-il

sunflower *n.* 해바라기 hae-ba-ra-gi; ~ **seed** 해바라기 씨 hae-ba-ra-gi ssi

sunglasses *n. pl.* 선글라스 sseon-geul-la-sseu

sunny *adj.* 양지바른 yang-ji-ba-reun, 해가 잘 드는 hae-ga jal deu-neun; 명랑한 myeong-nang-han, 쾌활한 kwae-hwal-han

sunrise *n.* 해돋이 hae-do-ji; 동틀녘 dong-teul-lyeok; 해뜨는 쪽 hae-tteu-neun jjok; 초년 cho-nyeon

sunroof *n.* 선루프 sseon-ru-peu

sunscreen *n.* 선스크린 sseon-seu-keu-rin; 선크림 sseon-keu-rim

sunset *n.* 일몰 il-mol; 해질녘 hae-jil-lyeok; 해지는 쪽 hae-ji-neun jjok; 말년 mal-lyeon

sunshine *n.* 햇빛 haet-bit; 양지 yang-ji; 맑은 날씨 malg-eun nal-ssi; 명랑한 사람 myeong-nang-han sa-ram

sunstroke *n.* 일사병 il-ssa-ppyeong

suntan *n.* 선탠 sseon-taen; ~ **lotion** 선탠로션 sseon-taen-ro-syeon

superficial *adj.* 표면의 pyo-myeon-ui; 얕은 yat-eun; 면적의 myeon-jeog-ui; 피상적인 pi-sang-jeog-in; 영향이 적은 yeong-hyang-i jeog-eun

superior *adj.* 상위의 sang-wi-ui; 뛰어난 ttwi-eo-nan; 우세한 u-se-han; ...을 초월한 ....eul cho-wol-han; 거만한 geo-man-han

supermarket *n.* 슈퍼마켓 syu-peo-ma-ket

superstitious *adj.* 미신적인 mi-sin-jeog-in; 미신에 의한 mi-sin-e ui-han; 미신에 사로잡힌 mi-sin-e sa-ro-ja-pin

supervise *vt.* 관리하다 gwal-li-ha-da; 감독하다 gam-do-ka-da; 지도하다 ji-do-ha-da

supervisor *n.* 관리자 gwal-li-ja; 감독관 gam-dok-gwan; 지도교수 ji-do-gyo-su

supper *n.* 저녁식사 jeo-nyeok-sik-sa

supplement *n.* 부충 chu-ga; *vt.* 보충하다 bo-chung-ha-da; 추가하다 chu-ga-ha-da; 부록을 달다 bu-rog-eul dal-da

supply *n.* 공급 gong-geup; 배급 bae-geup; 재고품 jae-go-pum; 공급품 gong-geu-pum; *vt.* 공급하다 gong-geu-pa-da; 배급하다 bae-geu-pa-da; 보완하다 bo-wan-ha-da

support *n.* 버팀 beo-tim; 지지물 ji-ji-mul; 지지자 ji-ji-ja; 원조 won-jo; 부양 bu-yang; *vt.* 지탱하다 ji-taeng-ha-da; 지지하다 ji-ji-ha-da; 원조하다 won-jo-ha-da; 찬성하다 chan-seong-ha-da; 부양하다 bu-yang-ha-da; 지원하다 ji-won-ha-da; 입증하다 ip-jeung-ha-da

supporter *n.* 지지자 ji-ji-ja; 원조자 won-jo-ja; 후원자 hu-won-ja; 지지물 ji-ji-mul; 버팀 beo-tim

suppose *vi.* 가정하다 ga-jeong-ha-da; 추측하다 chu-cheu-ka-da

suppository *n.* 좌약 jwa-yak

suppress *vt.* 억압하다 eog-a-pa-da; 진압하다 jin-a-pa-da; 억누르다 eong-nu-reu-da; 참다 cham-tta; 금하다 geum-ha-da

surcharge *n.* 과중 gwa-jung; 과충전 gwa-chung-jeon; 부당청구 bu-dang-cheong-gu; 추가요금 chu-ga-yo-geum; 추징금 chu-jing-geum; 부당지출 배상액 bu-dang-ji-chul bae-sang-aek

sure *adj.* 틀림없는 teul-lim-eom-neun; 안전한 an-jeon-han; 믿을 수 있는 mid-eul ssu-in-neun; 확신하는 hwak-sin-ha-neun; **to make ~ of something** 어떤 일을 확인하다 eo-tteon il-eul hwag-in-ha-da; 어떤 것을 손에 넣다 eo-tteon-geos-eul son-e neo-ta

surety *n.* 보증 bo-jeung; 담보 dam-bo; 저당물 jeo-dang-mul; 보증물 bo-jeung-mul; 담보물 dam-bo-mul

surf *n.* 파도 pa-do; *vi.* 파도를 타다 pa-do-reul ta-da

surface *n.* 표면 pyo-myeon; 외부 oe-bu; 외관 oe-gwan

surfboard *n.* 서핑보드 sseo-ping-bo-deu

surgeon *n.* 외과의사 oe-kkwa-ui-sa

surgery *n.* 수술 su-sul; 외과병원 oe-kkwa-byeong-won; 수술실 su-sul-sil

surly *adj.* 무뚝뚝한 mu-ttuk-ttu-kan; 퉁명스러운 tung-myeong-seu-reo-un; 험악한 heom-a-kan

surname *n.* 성 seong

surpass *vt.* ...을 능가하다 ...eul neung-ga-ha-da; 뛰어나다 ttwi-eo-na-da; 초월하다 cho-wol-ha-da

surplus *n.* 나머지 na-meo-ji; 잔여 jan-yeo; 과잉 gwa-ing; 초과액 cho-gwa-aek; 잉여물 ing-yeo-mul

surprise *n.* 놀람 nol-lam; 경악 gyeong-ak; 놀라운 일 nol-la-un il; 기습 gi-seup; *vt.* 놀라게 하다 nol-la-ge ha-da; 놀라다 nol-la-da; 불시에 덮치다 bul-ssi-e deop-chi-da; 기습하다 gi-seu-pa-da; 알아채다 al-a-chae-da

surrender *vt.* 인도 in-do; 양도 yang-do; 항복 hang-bok; 자수 ja-su; 보험해약 bo-heom-hae-yak; *vi.* 항복하다 hang-bo-ka-da; 골몰하다 gol-mol-ha-da; 감정에 빠지다 gam-jeong-e ppa-ji-da

surround *vt.* 에워싸다 e-wo-ssa-da; 포위하
다 po-wi-ha-da

surrounding *adj.* 주위의 ju-wi-ui; 부근의
bu-geun-ui

surroundings *n. pl.* 주위환경 ju-wi-hwan-
gyeong; 주위상황 ju-wi-sang-hwang; 주위
사람 ju-wi-ssa-ram

survive *vi.* 살아남다 sal-a-nam-tta; 잔존하
다 jan-jon-ha-da

survivor *n.* 생존자 saeng-jon-ja; 유족 yu-jok;
유물 yu-mul

suspect *vi.* 의심하다 ui-sim-ha-da; 혐의를
두다 hyeom-ui-reul du-da

suspend *vt.* 매달다 mae-dal-da; 중지하다
jung-ji-ha-da; 연기하다 yeon-gi-ha-da;
정지시키다 jeong-ji-si-ki-da; 뜨게 하다
tteu-ge ha-da; 불안하게 하다 bul-an-ha-
ge ha-da

suspenders *n. pl.* 바지 멜빵 ba-ji mel-ppang;
매다는 물건 mae-da-neun mul-geon

suspense *n.* 미정 mi-jeong, 어중간한 상태
eo-jung-gan-han sang-tae; 걱정 geok-
jeong, 불안 bul-an; 긴장감 gin-jang-gam,
서스펜스 sseo-seu-pen-sseu

suspicion *n.* 혐의 hyeom-ui; 의심 ui-sim; 낌
새 kkim-sae; 극소량 geuk-so-ryang

suspicious *adj.* 의심스러운 ui-sim-seu-reo-
un, 수상쩍은 su-sang-jjeog-eun; 의심 많
은 ui-sim-man-eun

sustain *vt.* 떠받치다 tteo-bat-chi-da; 유지하
다 yu-ji-ha-da; 부양하다 bu-yang-ha-da;
손해를 입다 son-hae-reul ip-da; 참고 견
디다 cham-kko gyeon-di-da; 확증하다
hwak-jeung-ha-da

swallow *n.* 삼킴 sam-kim, 마심 ma-sim; 식도
sik-do; 수채구 su-chae-gu; 제비 je-bi; *vt.*
들이키다 deul-i-ki-da; 삼키다 sam-ki-da;
그대로 받아들이다 geu-dae-ro bad-a-
deul-i-da; 참다 cham-tta; 가슴에 묻어두
다 ga-seum-e mud-eo-du-da

swamp *n.* 늪 neup; 습지 seup-ji

swan *n.* 백조 baek-jo; 훌륭한 사람 hul-
lyung-han sa-ram

swarm *n.* 떼tte, 무리 mu-ri; 군중 gun-jung,
다수 da-su

swear *vt.* 맹세하다 maeng-se-ha-da; 증언하
다 jeung-eon-ha-da; 단언하다 dan-eon-
ha-da; 선서시키다 seon-seo-si-ki-da; 맹

세시키다 maeng-se-si-ki-da; *vi.* 맹세하다
maeng-se-ha-da; 보증하다 bo-jeung-ha-
da; 욕설하다 yok-seol-ha-da

sweat *n.* 땀 ttam; 발한 bal-han; 습기 seup-gi;
물기 mul-kki; 어려운 일 eo-ryeo-un il; 불
안 bul-an, 초조 cho-jo; **~band** 스웻밴드
seu-wet-ben-deu, 땀받이띠 ttam-ba-ji-tti;
모자 속테 mo-ja sok-te; *vi.* 땀을 흘리다
ttam-eul heul-li-da; 땀이 배다 ttam-i bae-
da; 습기가 서리다 seup-gi-ga seo-ri-da; 물
이 스며나오다 mul-i seu-myeo-na-o-da;
땀 흘리며 일하다 ttam heul-li-myeo
il-ha-da

sweater *n.* 스웨터 sseu-we-teo; 발한제 bal-
han-je; 악덕 고용주 ak-deok go-yong-ju

sweatshirt *n.* 스웻셔츠 seu-wet-sye-cheu

Swede *n.* 스웨덴 사람 seu-we-den ssa-ram

Sweden *n.* 스웨덴 seu-we-den

Swedish *adj.* 스웨덴의 seu-we-den-ui; 스웨
덴 사람의 seu-we-den ssa-ram-ui

sweep *vt.* 청소하다 cheong-so-ha-da; 쓸다
sseul-da; 일소하다 il-sso-ha-da; 스쳐 지
나가다 seu-cheo ji-na-ga-da; 연승하다
yeon-seung-ha-da; 압승하다 ap-seung-ha-
da; 옷이 끌리다 os-i kkeul-li-da

sweet *n.* 단맛 dan-mat; 단것 dan-geot; 사
탕 sa-tang; 유쾌한 경험 yu-kwae-han
gyeong-heom; *adj.* 단 dan; 향기로운
hyang-gi-ro-un; 맛좋은 mat-jo-eun; 듣
기 좋은 deut-gi jo-eun; 유쾌한 yu-kwae-
han; 상냥한 sang-nyang-han; 애교있는
ae-gyo-in-neun

sweeten *vt.* 달게 하다 dal-ge-ha-da; 향기롭
게 하다 hyang-gi-rop-ge ha-da; 듣기좋
게 하다 deut-gi-jo-ke ha-da; 유쾌하게 하
다 yu-kwae-ha-ge ha-da; 온화하게 하다
on-hwa-ha-ge ha-da

swell *n.* 팽창 paeng-chang; 부어오름 bu-eo-
o-reum; 큰 파도 keun pa-do; 증대 jeung-
dae, 확대 hwak-dae; 거물 geo-mul; *vi.* 부
풀다 bu-pul-da; 솟아오르다 sos-a-o-reu-
da; 부어오르다 bu-eo-o-reu-da; 증대하다
jeung-dae-ha-da; 격해지다 gyeo-kae-ji-da;
부글부글 끓다 bu-geul-bu-geul kkeul-ta;
(ocean) 밀물 mil-mul

swelling *n.* 팽창 paeng-chang; 종기 jong-gi;
혹 hok; 융기 yung-gi; 돌출부 dol-chul-bu;
언덕 eon-deok

swift *adj.* 빠른 ppa-reun; 순식간의 sun-sik-gan-ui; 즉각적인 jeuk-gak-jeog-in; ...하기 쉬운 ...ha-gi swi-un

swim *vi.* 수영하다 su-yeong-ha-da; 떠서 움직이다 tteo-seo um-jig-i-da; 물에 잠기다 mul-e jam-gi-da; 현기증이 나다 hyeon-gi-jjeung-i na-da

swimmer *n.* 수영하는 사람 su-yeong-ha-neun sa-ram

swimming *n.* 수영 su-yeong; 현기증 hyeon-gi-jjeung; **to go ~** 수영하러 가다 su-yeong-ha-reo ga-da; **~ pool** 수영장 su-yeong-jang

swindle *vt.* 사취하다 sa-chwi-ha-da, 사기치다 sa-gi-chi-da

swindler *n.* 사기꾼 sa-gi-kkun

swing *n.* 그네 geu-ne; 그네타기 geu-ne-ta-gi; 휘두름 hwi-du-reum; 흔들림 heun-deul-lim; 변동 byeon-dong; *vt.* 흔들다 heun-deul-da; 휘두르다 hwi-du-reu-da; 회전시키다 hoe-jeon-si-ki-da; 매달다 mae-dal-da; 방향을 바꾸다 bang-hyang-eul ba-kku-da; *vi.* 흔들리다 heun-deul-li-da; 매달리다 mae-dal-li-da; 그네뛰다 geu-ne-ttwi-da; 빙돌다 bing-dol-da

Swiss *n.* 스위스 사람 seu-wi-sseu sa-ram; *adj.* 스위스의 seu-wi-sseu-ui; 스위스 사람의 seu-wi-sseu sa-ram-ui

switch *n.* 스위치 seu-wi-chi; 바꿈 ba-kkum, 변경 byeon-gyeong; 회초리 hoe-cho-ri; **electric ~** 전기 스위치 jeon-gi seu-wi-chi; *vt.* 전등을 켜다 jeon-deung-eul kyeo-da; 전화를 연결하다 jeon-hwa-reul yeon-gyeol-ha-da; 전류를 끊다 jeol-lyu-reul kkeun-ta; 바꾸다 ba-kku-da, 전환하다 jeon-hwan-ha-da; 휘두르다 hwi-du-reu-da; 회초리로 때리다 hoe-cho-ri-ro ttae-ri-da; **to ~ on** 켜다 kyeo-da; **to ~ off** 끄다 kkeu-da; 연결하다/끊다 yeon-gyeol-ha-da/kkeun-ta

Switzerland *n.* 스위스 seu-wi-sseu

sword *n.* 검 geom, 칼 kal; 무력 mu-ryeok, 병력 byeong-nyeok; 통수권 tong-su-kkwon; 전쟁 jeon-jaeng

syllable *n.* 음절 eum-jeol; 한마디 han-ma-di

symbol *n.* 상징 sang-jing; 기호 gi-ho

symbolic *adj.* 상징적인 sang-jing-jeog-in; 상징하는 sang-jing-ha-neun; 기호의 gi-ho-ui

sympathetic *adj.* 동정적인 dong-jeong-jeog-in; 공감을 나타내는 gong-gam-eul na-ta-nae-neun; 호의적인 ho-ui-jeog-in; 마음에 맞는 ma-eum-e man-neun

sympathize *vi.* 동정하다 dong-jeong-ha-da; 조의를 표하다 jo-ui-reul pyo-ha-da; 공감하다 gong-gam-ha-da

sympathy *n.* 동정 dong-jeong; 문상 mun-sang; 위문 wi-mun; 호의 ho-ui; 찬성 chan-seong; 일치 il-chi, 조화 jo-hwa

symphony *n.* 교향곡 gyo-hyang-gok, 심포니 ssim-po-ni

symptom *n.* 증상 jeung-sang; 징후 jing-hu; 조짐 jo-jim, 전조 jeon-jo

synagogue *n.* 유태교 회당 yu-tae-gyo hoe-dang; 유태인 집회 yu-tae-in ji-poe

synonym *n.* 동의어 dong-ui-eo, 비슷한 말 bi-seu-tan mal

syntax *n.* 통사론 tong-sa-ron, 구문론 gu-mun-non

synthetic *adj.* 종합적인 jong-hap-jeog-in; 합성의 hap-seong-ui; 인조의 in-jo-ui

Syria *n.* 시리아 si-ri-a

syringe *n.* 주사기 ju-sa-gi; 관장기 gwan-jang-gi; 세척기 se-cheok-gi

syrup *n.* 시럽 si-reop

system *n.* 시스템 ssi-seu-tem; 체계 che-gye; 계통 gye-tong; 신체 sin-che; 조직 jo-jik, 제도 je-do; 방식 bang-sik, 빙법 bang-beop; **the metric ~** 미터법 mi-teo-ppeop

systematic *adj.* 체계적인 che-gye-jeog-in; 질서있는 jil-sseo-in-neun; 규칙적인 gyu-chik-jeog-in; 계획적인 gye-hoek-jeog-in

T

table *n.* 탁자 tak-ja, 테이블 te-i-beul; 식탁 sik-tak; 표 pyo; 목록 mong-nok

tablecloth *n.* 식탁보 sik-tak-bo

tablespoon *n.* 테이블 스푼 te-i-beul seu-pun, 큰술 keun-sul

table tennis *n.* 탁구 tak-gu, 핑퐁 ping-pong

tablet *n*. 명판 myeong-pan; 패 pae; *(esp. medical use)* 정제 jeong-je

tack *n*. 압정 ap-jeong; 가봉 ga-bong; 접착성 jeop-chak-seong; 정책 jeong-chaek; **thumb~** 압정 ap-jeong

tact *n*. 재치 jae-chi; 요령 yo-ryeong; 박자 bak-ja

tactful *adj*. 재치있는 jae-chi-in-neun; 약삭빠른 yak-sak-ppa-reun; 솜씨좋은 som-ssi-jo-eun

tactics *n. pl* 전술 jeon-sul; 책략 chaeng-nyak; 작전 jak-jeon

tag *n*. 꼬리표 kko-ri-pyo; 정가표 jeong-kka-pyo; 늘어뜨린 부분 neul-eo-tteu-rin bu-bun; 술래잡기 sul-lae-jap-gi

tail *n*. 꼬리 kko-ri; 끄트머리 kkeu-teu-meo-ri; 하단여백 ha-dan-nyeo-ba다; ~ **light** 후미등 hu-mi-deung, 뒷전등 dwit-jeon-deung;

taillight *n*. 미등 mi-deung, 테일라이트 te-il-la-i-teu

tailor *n*. 재봉사 jae-bong-sa; 재단사 jae-dan-sa; 양복직공 yang-bok-jik-gong; *vt*. 양복을 만들다 yang-bog-eul man-deul-da; 맞추어 만들다 mat-chu-eo man-deul-da

tailored *adj*. 양복점에서 만든 yang-bok-jeom-e-seo man-deun; 남자옷처럼 만든 nam-ja-ot-cheo-reom man-deun; 주문에 따라 만든 ju-mun-e tta-ra man-deun

take *vt*. 손에 잡다 son-e jap-da; 붙잡다 but-jap-da; 빼앗다 ppae-at-da; 손에 넣다 son-e neo-ta; 매혹시키다 mae-hok-si-ki-da; 가지고 가다 ga-ji-go ga-da; 데리고 가다 de-ri-go ga-da; 받다 bat-da; 받아들이다 bad-a-deul-i-da; 선택하다 seon-tae-ka-da; ~ **it with you** 이거 가져가세요 i-geo ga-jyeo-ga-se-yo; consume; **Do you ~ sugar in your tea** 차에 설탕 넣으세요 cha-e seol-tang neo-eu-se-yo; time; **It ~s a week** 일주일은 걸리겠는데요 il-jju-il-eun geol-li-gen-neun-de-yo; **Let's ~ a taxi** 택시를 타지요 taek-si-reul ta-ji-yo; **We ~ most credit cards** 저희는 대부분 모든 카드를 다 받습니다 jeo-hi-neun dae-bu-bun mo-deun ka-deu-reul da bat-sum-ni-da; **to ~ an exam** 시험을 보다 si-heom-eul bo-da; **to ~ something apart** 분해하다 bun-hae-ha-da; 분석하다 bun-seo-ka-da; 혼내주다 hon-nae-ju-da; ~ **it away** 방송시작 bang-song-si-jak; 이거 치우세요 i-geo chi-u-se-yo; **to ~ over (a company, etc.)** (회사를) 인수하다 (hoe-sa-reul) in-su-ha-da; **to ~ on work** 일을 맡다 il-eul mat-da; *(clothing)* **to ~ off** 벗다 beot-da; 제거하다 je-geo-ha-da; 옮기다 om-gi-da; 할인하다 hal-in-ha-da; 베끼다 be-kki-da; 흉내내다 hung-nae-nae-da; 마셔버리다 ma-syeo-beo-ri-da; 죽이다 jug-i-da; 이륙하다 i-ryu-ka-da; 떠나가다 tteo-na-ga-da; **to ~ it easy** 마음 편하게 가지세요 ma-eum pyeon-ha-ge ga-ji-se-yo; ~ **out a bottle of wine** 와인 한병을 꺼내다 wa-in han-byeong-eul kkeo-nae-da; **to ~ to sth.** 가지고 가다 ga-ji-go ga-da; **to ~ to sb.** 데리고 가다 de-ri-go ga-da; **to ~ down the details** 세부사항을 적어두다 se-bu-sa-hang-eul jeog-eo-du-da

talc *n*. 활석 hwal-sseok; 운모 un-mo

talent *n*. 재주 jae-ju, 재능 jae-neung; 재주있는 사람 jae-ju-in-neun sa-ram, 인재 in-jae; 탤런트 tal-len-teu, 연예인 yeon-ye-in

talented *adj*. 재주있는 jae-ju-in-neun, 재능있는 jae-neung-in-neun

talk *n*. 이야기 i-ya-gi; 의논 ui-non; 연설 yeon-seol; 소문 so-mun; 화제 hwa-je; 말투 mal-tu; *vi*. 말하다 mal-ha-da; 의논하다 ui-non-ha-da; 소문을 내다 so-mun-eul nae-da; 불평하다 bul-pyeong-ha-da

talkative *adj*. 수다스러운 su-da-seu-reo-un, 말이 많은 mal-i man-eun

tall *adj*. 키가 큰 ki-ga keun; 높은 nop-eun; 긴 gin; 엄청난 eom-cheong-nan; 과장된 gwa-jang-doen; **five feet eight inches** ~ 오 피트 육인치 높이 o-pi-teu yug-in-chi no-pi; 키 오피트 육인치 ki o-pi-teu yug-in-chi

tame *adj*. 길든 gil-deun; 재배된 jae-bae-doen; 무기력한 mu-gi-ryeo-kan; 단조로운 dan-jo-ro-un; *vt*. 길들이다 gil-deul-i-da; 복종시키다 bok-jong-si-ki-da; 무기력하게 하다 mu-gi-ryeo-ka-ge ha-da; 억누르다 eong-nu-reu-da; 부드럽게 하다 bu-deu-reop-ge ha-da

tamper *vt*. 간섭하다 gan-seo-pa-da; 함부로 변경하다 ham-bu-ro byeon-gyeong-ha-da; 매수하다 mae-su-ha-da

tampon *n*. 탬폰 taem-pon

tan *adj.* 황갈색의 hwang-gal-ssaeg-ui; *vt.* 무
두질하다 mu-du-jil-ha-da; 햇볕에 태우
다 haet-byeot-e tae-u-da; 타닌을 먹이
다 ta-nin-eul meog-i-da; 때리다 ttae-ri-da;
vi. 부드러워지다 bu-deu-reo-wo-ji-da; 볕
에 타다 byeot-e ta-da; ~**ned** 햇볕에 탄
haet-byeot-e tan; ~**ning lotion** 선탠로션
sseon-taen-ro-syeon

tangerine *n.* 감귤 gam-gyul, 귤 gyul

tangle *vt.* 엉키게 하다 eong-ki-ge ha-da; 혼
란시키다 hol-lan-si-ki-da; 함정에 빠뜨리
다 ham-jeong-e ppa-tteu-ri-da; **to become**
~**d** 엉키다 eong-ki-da

tank *n.* 물탱크 mul-taeng-keu; 가스탱크
kka-sseu-tang-keu; 저수지 jeo-su-ji; 탱크
taeng-keu; **oil** ~ 석유탱크 seog-yu-taeng-
keu; **gas** ~ 가스탱크 kka-sseu-taeng-keu;
fill the ~ 탱크를 채우다 taeng-keu-reul
chae-u-da

tanker *n.* 유조선 yu-jo-seon; 급유 비행기
geub-yu bi-haeng-gi; **oil** ~ 유조선 yu-jo-seon

Tanzania *n.* 탄자니아 tan-ja-ni-a

tap *n.* 주둥이 ju-dung-i; 꼭지 kkok-ji; 마개
ma-gae; 술집 sul-jjip; 탭 taep; *vt.* 가볍게
두드리다 ga-byeop-ge du-deu-ri-da; 박자
를 맞추다 bak-ja-reul mat-chu-da; 구두
창을 갈다 gu-du-chang-eul gal-da; 꼭지
를 달다 kkok-ji-reul dal-da; 꼭지를 따다
kkok-ji-reul tta-da; 꼭지로 따르다 kkok-ji-
ro tta-reu-da; 접속시키다 jeop-sok-si-ki-
da; 엿듣다 yeot-deut-da; *vi.* 가볍게 치다
ga-byeop-ge chi-da; 다진하다 ta-jin-ha-da

tape *n.* 끈 kkeun; 테이프 te-i-peu; *vt.* ...을 달
다 ...eul dal-da; ...로 묶다 ...ro muk-da; 테
이프를 감다 te-i-peu-reul gam-tta; 줄자로
재다 jul-ja-ro jae-da; 데이프를 치다 te-i-
peu-reul chi-da; 녹음하다 nog-eum-ha-da

tape recorder *n.* 녹음기 nog-eum-gi

tapered *adj.* 점점 가늘어지는 jeom-jeom
ga-neul-eo-ji-neun, 점점 약해지는 jeom-
jeom ya-kae-ji-neun

tapestry *n.* 타피스트리 ta-pi-seu-teu-ri, 벽걸
이용 융단 byeok-geol-i-yong yung-dan

tar *n.* 콜타르 kol-ta-reu; 선원 seon-won

target *n.* 과녁 gwa-nyeok, 표적 pyo-jeok; 목
표 mok-pyo; 목적물 mok-jeong-mul; *vt.* 목
표로 정하다 mok-pyo-ro jeong-ha-da; 목
적으로 하다 mok-jeog-eu-ro ha-da

tariff *n.* 관세표 gwa-sse-pyo; 운임표 un-im-
pyo; 요금표 yo-geum-pyo

tart *adj.* 시큼한 si-keum-han; 신랄한
sil-lal-han

task *n.* 임무 im-mu; 작업 jag-eop; 노역
no-yeok; 타스크 ta-seu-keu

taste *n.* 미각 mi-gak; 맛 mat; 시식 si-sik;
경험 gyeong-heom; 눈치 nun-chi; 취
미 chwi-mi; 스타일 seu-ta-il; *vt.* 맛을 보
다 mas-eul bo-da; 맛을 느끼다 mas-eul
neu-kki-da; 경험하다 gyeong-heom-ha-da;
이해하다 i-hae-ha-da; *vi.* 맛이 나다 mas-i
na-da; 맛을 보다 mas-eul bo-da; 기미가
있다 gi-mi-ga it-da; 경험하다 gyeong-
heom-ha-da; **This** ~**s good** 이건 맛이 좋
네요 i-geon mas-i jon-ne-yo

tasty *adj.* 맛있는 mas-in-neun; 재미있는
jae-mi-in-neun; 점잖은 jeom-jan-eun

tavern *n.* 선술집 seon-sul-jjip; 여인숙
yeo-in-suk

tax *n.* 세금 se-geum; 부담 bu-dam; 회비
hoe-bi; ~ **return** 납세 신고서 nap-se
sin-go-seo; ~ **free** 면세 myeon-se

taxi *n.* 택시 taek-si

tea *n.* 차 cha; ~ **bag** 티백 ti-baek; ~ **cup** 찻잔
chat-jan; **a cup/pot of** ~ 차 한잔/한주전
자 cha han-jan/han-ju-jeon-ja; **black** ~ 홍
차 hong-cha; **green** ~ 녹차 nok-cha

teach *vt.* 가르치다 ga-reu-chi-da; 훈련하다
hul-lyeon-ha-da; 교육하다 gyo-yu-ka-da;
깨닫게 하다 kkae-dat-ge ha-da; *vi.* 가르
치다 ga-reu-chi-da

teacher *n.* 선생님 seon saeng nim, 교사
gyo-sa

teakettle *n.* 차끓이는 솥 cha-kkeul-i-neun
sot

team *n.* 팀 tim, 조 jo; 한 떼 han-tte

teapot *n.* 찻주전자 chat-ju-jeon-ja

tear *n.* 눈물 nun-mul; 슬픔 seul-peum; 물방
울 mul-ppang-ul; *vt.* 찢다 jjit-da; 잡아뜯다
jab-a-tteut-da; 상처내다 sang-cheo-nae-
da; 세게 당기다 se-je dang-gi-da; 분열시
키다 bun-yeol-si-ki-da; **You have torn a**
ligament 인대가 찢어지셨군요 in-dae-ga
jjij-eo-ji-syeot-gun-yo

tease *n.* 괴롭히기 goe-ro-pi-gi; 조롱 jo-rong;
괴롭히는 사람 goe-ro-pi-neun sa-ram; 조

롱하는 사람 jo-rong-ha-neun sa-ram; vt.
괴롭히다 goe-ro-pi-da; 놀리다 nol-li-da;
조르다 jo-reu-da

teaspoon n. 티스푼 ti-seu-pun, 찻숟가락
chat-sut-ga-rak

technical adj. 기술적인 gi-sul-jjeog-in; 전문
의 jeon-mun-ui; 공업의 gong-eob-ui

teenager n. 10대 sip-dae, 틴에이저
tin-e-i-jeo

telegram n. 전보 jeon-bo, 전신 jeon-sin

telephone n. 전화 jeon-hwa; 전화기
jeon-hwa-gi; ~ **directory** 전화번호부
jeon-hwa-beon-ho-bu; vt. 전화를 걸다
jeon-hwa-reul geol-da; 전화로 말하다
jeon-hwa-ro mal-ha-da

telescope n. 망원경 mang-won-gyeong

television n. 텔레비전 방송 tel-le-bi-jeon
bang-song; (broadcast) 텔레비전 방송
tel-le-bi-jeon; (physical apparatus) 텔
레비전 수상기 tel-le-bi-jeon su-sang-gi;
cable ~ 케이블 텔레비전 ke-i-beul tel-
le-bi-jeon; **to watch** ~ 텔레비전을 보다
tel-le-bi-jeon-eul bo-da

tell vt. 말하다 mal-ha-da, 이야기하다
i-ya-gi-ha-da; 알리다 al-li-da; 가르쳐주다
ga-reu-chyeo-ju-da; 명령하다 myeong-
nyeong-ha-da; 분간하다 bun-gan-ha-da

temper n. 기질 gi-jil; 기분 gi-bun; 짜증 jja-
jeung; 첨가물 cheom-gmul; 조절 jo-jeol

temperate adj. 온화한 on-hwa-han; 알맞은
al-maj-eun; 절제하는 jeol-jje-ha-neun

temperature n. 온도 on-do; 기온 gi-on; 체
온 che-on

temple n. (place of worship) 신전 sin-jeon;
성당 seong-dang; 절 jeol; 사원 sa-won;
(part of forehead) 관자놀이 gwan-ja-nol-i

temporary adj. 일시의 il-ssi-ui, 잠시의
jam-si-ui

tempt vt. 마음을 끌다 ma-um-eul kkeul-da;
유혹하다 yu-ho-ka-da; 부추기다 bu-chu-
gi-da; 돋우다 dod-u-da

temptation n. 유혹 yu-hok; 유혹함 yu-
ho-kam; 유혹됨 yu-hok-doem; 유혹물
yu-hong-mul

ten num. 십 sip; 열 yeol

tenacious adj. 고집하는 go-ji-pa-neun;
집요한 jeb-yo-han; 참을성이 강한

cham-eul-sseong-i gang-han; 끈끈한
kkeun-kkeun-han; 좀처럼 잊지 않는
jom-cheo-reom it-ji-an-neun

tenant n. 소작인 so-jag-in; 세든 사람
se-deun sa-ram

tend vi. 향하다 hyang-ha-da; 도달하다
do-dal-ha-da; 공헌하다 gong-heon-
ha-da; **to ~ to** …하기 쉽다 …ha-gi
swip-da, …하는 경향이 있다 …ha-neun
gyeong-hyang-i it-da; …을 돌보다 …eul
dol-bo-da

tendency n. 경향 gyeong-hyang; 성
향 seong-hyang; 추세 chu-se; 취향
chwi-hyang

tender adj. 부드러운 bu-deu-reo-un; 연
한 yeon-han; 부서지기 쉬운 bu-seo-ji-gi
swi-un; 다루기 힘든 da-ru-gi him-deun; 다
정다감한 da-jeong-da-gam-han; 상냥한
sang-nyang-han

tendon n. 힘줄 him-jjul, 건 geon

tennis n. 테니스 te-ni-sseu, 정구 jeong-gu

tenor n. 방침 bang-chim; 진로 jil-lo; 취지
chwi-ji; 테너 te-neo

tense n. 시제 si-je; adj. 팽팽한 paeng-paeng-
han; 긴장한 gin-jang-han

tension n. 긴장 gin-jang; 긴장상태 gin-jang-
sang-tae; 장력 jang-nyeok

tent n. 텐트 ten-teu, 천막 cheon-mak

tentacle n. 촉수 chok-su

tentative adj. 시험적인 si-heom-jeog-in; 임
시의 im-si-ui

tenth adj. 열번째의 yeol-ppeon-jjae-ui; 제십
회 je si-poe

tenuous adj. 희박한 hi-ba-kan; 엷은 yeolb-
eun; 미세한 mi-se-han; 빈약한 bin-ya-kan

tepid adj. 미지근한 mi-ji-geun-han; 열성이
없는 yeol-sseong-i eom-neun

term n. 기간 gi-gan; 임기 im-gi; 학기 hak-gi;
기한 gi-han; 조건 jo-kkeon; 말 mal, 용어
yong-eo

terminate vt. 끝내다 kkeun-nae-da; 그만두
다 geu-man-du-da; 한정하다 han-jeong-
ha-da; 종결시키다 jong-gyeol-si-ki-da

termite n. 흰개미 hin-gae-mi

terrace n. 테라스 te-ra-sseu; 계단모양 광장
gye-dan-mo-yang gwang-jang; 전망도로
jeon-mang-do-ro

terrestrial *adj.* 지구상의 ji-gu-ang-ui; 뭍에
사는 mut-e sa-neun; 지상의 ji-sang-ui; 현
세의 hyeon-se-ui

terrible *adj.* 무서운 mu-seo-un; 심한sim-
han; 지독한 ji-do-kan

terribly *adv.* 무섭게 mu-seop-ge; 몹시 mop-
si; 굉장히 goeng-jang-han

terrific *adj.* 무서운 mu-seo-un; 지독한
ji-do-kan; 훌륭한 hul-lyung-han

territory *n.* 영토 yeong-to; 지역 ji-yeok; 세
력권 se-ryeok-kkwon; 영역 yeong-yeok; 담
당구역 dam-dang-gu-yeok

terror *n.* 공포 gong-po; 공포의 원인 gong-
po-ui won-in; 테러 te-reo; 성가신 사람
seong-ga-sin sa-ram

test *n.* 시험 si-heom, 테스트 te-seu-teu,
검사 geom-sa; 시련 si-ryeon; 분석
bun-seok; *vt.* 검사하다 geom-sa-ha-
da; 조사하다 jo-sa-ha-da; 테스트하다
te-seu-teu-ha-da; 확인하다 hwag-
in-ha-da

testify *vi.* 증명하다 jeung-myeong-ha-da;
증언하다 jeung-eon-ha-da; 증거가 되다
jeung-geo-ga doe-da

testimony *n.* 증언 jeung-eon; 성명 seong-
myeong; 증거 jeung-geo

text *n.* 본문 bon-mun; 원문 won-mun; 화
제 hwa-je

textbook *n.* 교과서 gyo gwa seo

textile *n.* 직물 jing-mul; 옷감 ot-gam; 직물
원료 jing-mul-wol-lyo

Thailand *n.* 타이 ta-i, 타일랜드
ta-il-laen-deu

than *conj.* ...보다(도) ...bo-da(-do), ...밖
에는 ...bakk-e-neun; *prep.* ...보나(노)
...bo-da(-do)

thank *vt.* 감사하다 gam-sa-ha-da; 사례하
다 sa-rye-ha-da; 사의를 표하다 sa-ui-reul
pyo-ha-da; ~ **you (very much) for X** X에
대해 (대단히) 감사합니다 X-e dae-hae
(dae-dan-hi) gam-sa-ham-ni-da

thankful *adj.* 고마워하는 go-ma-wo-ha-
neun; 감사하는 gam-sa-ha-neun

thankfulness *n.* 감사 gam-sa; 사의 sa-ui; 사
례 sa-rye

thanks *n. pl.* 감사 gam-sa; 사의 sa-ui; 사례
sa-rye

that *adj.* 저 jeo, 그 geu; *pron.* 그것 geu-geot,
저것 jeo-geot; *adv.* 그만큼 geu-man-
keum, 그렇게 geu-reo-ke, 그렇게까지
geu-reo-ke-kka-ji; *conj.* ...이라는 것은
...i-ra-neun geos-eun; ...하므로 ...ha-meu-
ro, ...한 것은 ...han geos-eun; ...하는 것은
...ha-neun geos-eun

thaw *vt.* 녹이다 nog-i-da; 따뜻하게 하다
tta-tteu-ta-ge ha-da; 풀리게 하다 pul-li-ge
ha-da; *vi.* 녹다 nok-da; 따뜻해지다 tta-
tteu-tae-ji-da; 풀리다 pul-li-da

the *art.* 그 geu; ...이라는 것 ...i-ra-neun
geot; *adv.* 그만큼 geu-man-keum; ~
more ~ more ...하면 할수록 ...ha-myeon
hal-ssu-rok

theater *n.* 극장 geuk-jang; 연극 yeon-geuk,
현장 hyeon-jang; 연기 yeon-gi; 계단식 강
당 gye-dan-sik gang-dang

their *pron.* 그 사람들의 geu sa-ram-deul-
ui; 저 사람들의 jeo sa-ram-deul-ui; 그
것들의 geu-geot-deul-ui; 저것들의
jeo-geot-deul-ui

them *pron.* 그 사람들을 geu sa-ram-deul-
eul; 그 사람들에게 geu sa-ram-deul-e-ge;
그것들을 geu-geot-deul-eul; 그것들에
geu-geot-deul-e

theme *n.* 주제 ju-je; 제목 je-mok; 작문 jang-
mun; 테마 te-ma

themselves *pron.* 그 사람들 자신 geu
sa-ram-deul ja-sin; 그 사람들 자신을 geu
sa-ram-deul ja-sin-eul; 그 사람들 자신에
게 geu sa-ram-deul ja-sin-e-ge

then *adv.* 그때 geu-ttae; 그 다음에 geu
da-eum-e; 그 위에 geu-wi-e; 그렇다면
geu-reo-ta-myeon

theology *n.* 신학 sin-hak; 종교 심리학
jong-gyo-sim-ni-hak

theoretical *adj.* 신학의 sin-hag-ui; 신학상의
sin-hak-sang-ui

theory *n.* 학설 hak-seol; 이론 i-ron; 원리
wol-li; 의견 ui-gyeon

therapeutic *adj.* 치료의 chi-ryo-ui; 치료학의
chi-ryo-hag-ui

therapist *n.* 요법학자 yo-ppeo-pak-ja; 임상
의사 im-sang-ui-sa; **physical ~** 물리치료
사 mul-li-chi-ryo-sa

therapy *n.* 치료 chi-ryo; 요법 yo-ppeop

there *adv.* 그곳에 geu-gos-e, 그곳으로 geu-gos-eu-ro, 그곳에서 geu-gos-e-seo; *interj.* 거봐 geo-bwa, 저런 jeo-reon

therefore *adv.* 그러므로 geu-reo-meu-ro; 그 결과로 geu gyeol-gwa-ro

thermometer *n.* 온도계 on-do-gye; 체온계 che-on-gye

thermos *n.* 보온병 bo-on-byeong

thermostat *n.* 온도조절장치 on-do-jo-jeol-jang-chi

these *pron.* 이것들 i-geot-deul; 이 사람들 i sa-ram-deul

thesis *n.* 논문주제 non-mun-ju-je; 제목 je-mok; 논문 non-mun

they *pron.* 그 사람들 geu sa-ram-deul; 그것들 geu-geot-deul; 사람들 sa-ram-deul

thick *adj.* 두꺼운 du-kkeo-un; 굵은 gulg-eun; 진한 jin-han; 어둠이 깊은 eo-dum-i gip-eun; 빽빽한 ppaek-ppae-kan; 목이 쉰 mog-i swin; 혼잡한 hon-ja-pan; 우둔한 u-dun-han; 친밀한 chin-mil-han

thicken *vt.* 두껍게 하다 du-kkeop-ge ha-da; 굵게 하다 gul-kke-ha-da; 진하게 하다 jin-ha-ge ha-da; 빽빽하게 하다 ppaek-ppae-ka-ge ha-da; 강하게 하다 gang-ha-ge ha-da; 심하게 하다 sim-ha-ge ha-da; 흐리게 하다 heu-ri-ge ha-da; 복잡하게 하다 bok-ja-pa-ge ha-da; 불명료하게 하다 bul-myeong-nyo-ha-ge ha-da; *vi.* 두꺼워지다 du-kkeo-wo-ji-da; 굵어지다 gulg-eo-ji-da; 진해지다 jin-hae-ji-da; 빽빽해지다 ppaek-ppae-kae-ji-da; 강해지다 gang-hae-ji-da; 심해지다 sim-hae-ji-da; 흐려지다 heu-ryeo-ji-da; 복잡해지다 bok-ja-pae-ji-da; 불명료해지다 bul-myeong-nyo-hae-ji-da

thickness *n.* 두께 du-kke; 굵기 gul-kki; 농도 nong-do; 조밀도 jo-mil-tto; 무성 mu-seong; 불명료 bul-myeong-nyo; 혼탁 hon-tak; 우둔 u-dun; 빈번 bin-beon

thief *n.*, **thieves** *pl.* 도둑 do-duk, 좀도둑 jom-tto-duk

thigh *n.* 넓적다리 neop-jjeok-da-ri, 대퇴부 dae-toe-bu

thimble *n.* 골무 gol-mu; 마찰 방지용 고리 ma-chal bang-ji-yong go-ri

thin *adj.* 얇은 yalb-eun; 가는 ga-neun; 야윈 ya-win; 성긴 seong-gin; 희박한 hi-ba-kan; 가냘픈 ga-nyal-peun

thing *n.* 물건 mul-geon; 물체 mul-che; 도구 do-gu; 문물 mun-mul; 것 geot; 일 il

think *vi.* 생각하다 saeng-ga-ka-da; 기대하다 gi-dae-ha-da; 예기하다 ye-gi-ha-da

third *adj.* 세번째의 se-beon-jjae-ui; 제삼회 je-sam-hoe

thirst *n.* 갈증 gal-jjeung; 갈망 gal-mang

thirsty *adj.* 목마른 mong-ma-reun; 갈망하는 gal-mang-ha-neun; 술마시고 싶은 sul-ma-si-go si-peun; 건조한 geon-jo-han

thirteen *num.* 열셋 yeol-sset; 십삼 sip-sam

thirteenth *adj.* 열세번째의 yeol-sse-beon-jjae-ui; 제십삼회 je-sip-sam-hoe

thirty *num.* 서른 seo-reun; 삼십 sam-sip

this *adj.* 이 i; 지금의 ji-geum-ui; 이번의 i-beon-ui; *pron.* 이것 i-geot; 후자 hu-ja; 바로 지금 ba-ro ji-geum; 여기 yeo-gi; 이곳 i-got

thorn *n.* 가시 ga-si; 가시나무 ga-si-na-mu; 고통 근심의 원인 go-tong geun-sim-ui won-in

thorough *adj.* 철저한 cheol-jjeo-han; 완전한 wan-jeon-han; 면밀한 myeon-mil-han; 전적인 jeon-jjeog-in

thoroughfare *n.* 통로 tong-no; 주요도로 ju-yo-do-ro; 통행 tong-haeng; 통과 tong-gwa; 수로 su-ro

those *pron.* 그것들 geu-geot-deul; 그 사람들 geu sa-ram-deul; 사람들 sa-ram-deul

though *conj.* …이지만 …i-ji-man; 비록 …일지라도 bi-rok …il-jji-ra-do

thought *n.* 사색 sa-saek; 생각 saeng-gak; 고려 go-ryeo; 사고력 sa-go-ryeok; 착상 chak-sang; 의도 ui-do; 사상 sa-sang

thoughtful *adj.* 생각이 깊은 ssaeng-gag-i gip-eun; 주의깊은 ju-ui-gi-peun; 인정 있는 in-jeong-in-neun; 생각에 잠기는 saeng-gag-e jam-gi-neun

thousand *num.* 천 cheon

thousandth *adj.* 천번째의 cheon-beon-jjae-ui; 제천회 je-cheon-hoe-ui

thread *n.* 실 sil; 섬유 seom-yu; 줄거리 jul-geo-ri; 맥락 maeng-nak; 가냘픈 의지 ga-nyal-peun ui-ji; 여명 yeo-myeong

threat *n.* 으름장 eu-reum-jjang; 협박 hyeop-bak; 징조 jing-jo

threaten *vt.* 협박하다 hyeop-ba-ka-da; 위협
하다 wi-hyeo-pa-da; 임박하다 im-ba-ka-
da; 징후를 보이다 jing-hu-reul bo-i-da
three *num.* 셋 set, 삼 sam
threshold *n.* 문지방 mun-jji-bang; 문간
mun-kkan; 발단 bal-ttan; 역치 yeok-chi
thrift *n.* 검약 geom-yak; 검소 geom-so; 번성
beon-seong
thrifty *adj.* 검소한 geom-so-han; 무성한
mu-seong-han; 번영하는 beon-yeong-
ha-neun
thrive *vi.* 번창하다 beon-chang-ha-da; 잘 자
라다 jal ja-ra-da; 성공하다 seong-gong-
ha-da; 무성하다 mu-seong-ha-da
throat *n.* 목구멍 mok-gu-meong; 목청
mok-cheong; 숨통 sum-tong; 좁은 두루
job-eun do ro; 협류 hyeom nyu
throb *vi.* 고동 go-dong; 맥박 maek-bak; 진
동 jin-dong; 흥분 heung-bun
throne *n.* 왕좌 wang-jwa; 왕권 wang-
kkwon; 왕위 wang-wi; 교황성좌
gyo-hwang seong jwa
throttle *n.* 조절판 jo-jeol-pan; 목구멍
mok-gu-meong
through *adj.* ...을 통하여 ...eul tong-ha-
yeo, 두루 du-ru, ...동안 내내 ...dong-an
nae-nae, ...을 거쳐서 ...eul geo-cheo-seo,
...에 의하여 ...e ui-ha-yeo, ...으로 인하
여 ...eu-ro in-ha-yeo; *adv.* 통과하여
tong-gwa-ha-yeo, 처음부터 끝까지
cheo-eum-bu-teo kkeut-kka-ji, 죽 juk, 내
내 nae-nae; 완전히 wan-jeon-hi, 미치고
ma-chi-go
throughout *adv.* 처음부터 끝까지
cheo-eum-bu-teo kkeut-kka-ji; 철두철미
cheol-ttu-cheol-mi; 어디든지 eo-di-deun-ji;
모든 점에서 mo-deun jeom-e-seo
throw *n.* 던지기 deon-ji-gi; 발사 bal-ssa; 사
정거리 sa-jeong-geo-ri; *vt.* 던지다 deon-
ji-da; 내동댕이치다 nae-dong-daeng-
i-chi-da; 힘있게 움직이다 him-it-ge
um-jig-i-da; 발사하다 bal-ssa-ha-da; 배치
하다 bae-chi-ha-da; *vi.* 던지다 deon-ji-da;
발사하다 bal-ssa-ha-da; 팽개치다 paeng-
gae-chi-da; **to ~ away** 낭비하다 nang-bi-
ha-da; 버리다 beo-ri-da; 잃다 il-ta; **to ~ up**
던져올리다 deon-jeo-ol-li-da; 밀어올리다
mil-eo-ol-li-da; 그만두다 geu-man-du-da;

포기하다 po-gi-ha-da; 토하다 to-ha-da;
두드러지게 하다 du-deu-reo-ji-ge ha-da;
급조하다 geup-jo-ha-da
thumb *n.* 엄지손가락 eom-ji son-kka-rak
thunder *n.* 천둥 cheon-dung, 우뢰 u-roe
thunderstorm *n.* 뇌우 noe-u
Thursday *n.* 목요일 mog-yo-il
thyme *n.* 사향 sa-hyang, 타임 ta-im
Tibet *n.* 티벳 ti-bet
ticket *n.* 표 pyo, 입장권 ip-jang-kkwon; 정
찰표 jeong-chal-pyo; 교통위반딱지 gyo-
tong-wi-ban-ttak-ji; 자격증명서 ja-gyeok
jeung-myeong-seo; 전표 jeon-pyo
tickle *vt.* 간질이다 gan-jil-i-da; 따끔거리
게 하다 tta-kkeum-geo-ri-ge ha-da; 기쁘
게 하다 gi-ppeu-ge ha-da; 가볍게 움직이
다 ga byeop ge um jig i da; *vi.* 간지럽다
gan-ji-reo-pi-da
tide *n.* 조수 jo-su, 조류 jo-ryu; 흥망성
쇠 heung-mang-seong-soe; 시대풍조
si-dae-pung-jo
tidy *adj.* 말쑥한 mal-ssu-kan; 산뜻한 san-
tteu-tan; 상당한 sang-dang-han
tie *n.* 끈 kkeun; 넥타이 nek-ta-i; 연분
yeon-bun; 속박 sok-bak; 이음 i-eum;
(bond) 유대 yu-dae; 결속 gyeol-ssok;
(score) 동점 dong-jjeom; *(knot)* 매듭
mae-deup; **neck~** 넥타이 nek-ta-i; *vt.*
묶다 muk-da; 매다 mae-da; 구속하다
gu-so-ka-da; 결합하다 gyeol-ha-pa-da;
결혼시키다 gyeol-hon-si-ki-da; 동점
이 되다 dong-jjeom-i doe-da; 연결하다
yeon-gyeol-ha-da
tiger *n.* 호랑이 ho-rang-i, 범 beom; 잔인한
사람 jan-in-han sa-ram
tight *n.* 타이츠 ta-i-cheu; *(clothing)* **~s** 다이
츠 ta-i-cheu; *adj.* 단단한 dan-dan-han; 팽
팽한 paeng-paeng-han; 긴장한 gin-jang-
han; 견고한 gyeon-go-han; 빈틈없는
bin-teum-eom-neun; 감감한 gap-ga-pan;
꽉찬 kkwak-chan; 곤란한 gol-lan-han; 돈
이 딸리는 don-i ttal-li-neun; 막상막하의
mak-sang-ma-ka-ui
tighten *vt.* 죄다 joe-da; 팽팽하게 하다
paeng-paeng-ha-ge ha-da; 엄하게 하다
eom-ha-ge ha-da
tile *n.* 타일 ta-il; 기와 gi-wa; 토관 to-gwan;
마작 패 ma-jak pae

tilt *vi.* 기울다 gi-ul-da, 경사지다 gyeong-sa-ji-da; 창으로 찌르다 chang-eu-ro jji-reu-da; 공격하다 gong-gyeo-ka-da; 상하로 움직이다 sang-ha-ro um-jig-i-da

timber *n.* 재목 jae-mok; 수목 su-mok, 삼림 sam-nim; 대들보 dae-deul-ppo

time *n.* 시간 si-gan; 때 ttae; 여가 yeo-ga, 틈 teum; 기간 gi-gan; 시각 si-gak; 시기 si-gi; 시대 si-dae; 일생 il-ssaeng; 번 beon

timetable *n.* 시간표 si-gan-pyo; 예정표 ye-jeong-pyo

tin *n.* 주석 ju-seok; 함석 ham-seok; 양철깡통 yang-cheol-kkang-tong; ~ **can** 통조림 깡통 tong-jo-rim kkang-tong

tingle *vi.* 따끔따끔 아프다 tta-kkeum-tta-kkeum a-peu-da; 귀가 울리다 gwi-ga ul-li-da; 흥분하다 heung-bun-ha-da; 안절부절하다 an-jeol-bu-jeol-ha-da; 진동하다 jin-dong-ha-da

tint *n.* 엷은빛깔 yeolb-eun bit-gal; 색의 농담 saeg-ui nong-dam; 담색배경 dam-saek-bae-gyeong; 기미 gi-mi; 모발용 염료 mo-bal-lyong yeom-nyo; *vt.* 색을 칠하다 saeg-eul chil-ha-da; 기미를 띠게 하다 gi-mi-reul tti-ge ha-da

tiny *adj.* 작은 jag-eun, 조그마한 jo-geu-ma-han

tip *n.* 첨단 cheom-dan; 끝 kkeut; 꼭대기 kkok-dae-gi; 팁 tip; 비밀정보 bi-mil-jeong-bo; 비결 bi-gyeol; *vt.* 끝을 달다 kkeut-eul dal-da; 끄트머리에 씌우다 kkeu-teu-meo-ri-e ssi-u-da; 끝을 자르다 kkeut-eul ja-reu-da; 기울이다 gi-ul-i-da; 뒤집어엎다 dwi-jib-eo-eop-da; 쓰러뜨리다 sseu-reo-tteu-ri-da; 살짝 알리다 sal-jjak al-li-da; *vi.* 기울다 gi-ul-da; 뒤집히다 dwi-ji-pi-da; 팁을 주다 tib-eul ju-da; 정보를 제공하다 jeong-bo-reul je-gong-ha-da

tiptoe *n.* 발끝 bal-kkeut; *vi.* 발끝으로 걷다 bal-kkeu-teu-ro geot-da

tire *n.* 타이어 ta-i-eo, 바퀴 ba-kkwi; **to change a** ~ 타이어를 교환하다 ta-i-eo-reul gyo-hwan-ha-da; *vt.* 피곤하게 하다 pi-gon-ha-ge ha-da; 싫증나게 하다 sil-jjeung-na-ge ha-da

tired *adj.* 피로한 pi-ro-han; 지친 ji-chin; 싫증난 sil-jjeung-nan; 참을 수 없는 cham-eul ssu eom-neun; 낡은 nalg-eun

tiredness *n.* 피로 pi-ro; 싫증 sil-jjeung

tireless *n.* 지칠줄 모르는 ji-chil-jjul mo-reu-neun; 싫증내지 않는 sil-jjeung-nae-ji an-neun; 꾸준한 kku-jun-han

tiresome *adj.* 지치는 ji-hi-neun; 지루한 ji-ru-han; 싫증나는 sil-jjeung-na-neun; 성가신 seong-ga-sin

tissue *n.* 직물 jing-mul; 티슈 ti-ssyu; *(of the body)* 조직 jo-jik; **bathroom** ~ 화장지 hwa-jang-ji

title *n.* 표제 pyo-je; 직함 ji-kam; 권리 gwol-li; 선수권 seon-su-kkwon; 타이틀 ta-i-teul

to *prep.* ...쪽으로 ...jjog-eu-ro, ...으로 ...eu-ro, ...하게도 ...ha-ge-do, ...까지 ...kka-ji, ...을 위하여 ...eul wi-ha-yeo, ...을 마주보고 ...eul ma-ju-bo-go, ...에 대하여 ...e dae-ha-yeo, ...에 맞추어서 ...e mat-chu-eo-seo, ...에 비하여 ...e bi-ha-yeo; ...하는 일 ...ha-neun il, ...하기 위한 ...ha-gi wi-han, ...하기 위하여 ...ha-gi wi-ha-yeo

toad *n.* 두꺼비 du-kkeo-bi; 징그러운 것 jing-geu-reo-un geot

tobacco *n.* 담배 dam-bae

today *adv.* 오늘 o-neul; 현재 hyeon-jae

toe *n.* 발가락 bal-kka-rak; 발끝 bal-kkeut; 발앞부분 bal ap-bu-bun; 언저리 eon-jeo-ri

together *adv.* 함께 ham-kke, 같이 ga-chi; 합쳐져서 hap-cheo-jeo-seo; 계속하여 gye-seo-ka-yeo; 동시에 dong-si-e; 협력하여 hyeom-nyeo-ka-yeo

toil *vi.* 수고 su-go, 노고 no-go, 고생 go-saeng

toilet *n.* 화장실 hwa-jang-sil; 몸단장 mom-dan-jang; 화장도구 hwa-jang-do-gu

token *n.* 토큰 to-keun; 표 pyo; 기념품 gi-nyeom-pum; 증거품 jeung-geo-pum

Tokyo *n.* 토쿄 to-kyo, 도꾜 do-kkyo

tolerance *n.* 관용 gwan-yong, 아량 a-ryang; 내성 nae-seong

tolerate *vt.* 관대히 다루다 gwan-dae-hi da-ru-da; 묵인하다 mug-in-ha-da; 참다 cham-tta, 견디다 gyeon-di-da; 내성이 있다 nae-seong-i it-da

toll *n.* 통행료 tong-haeng-nyo; 사용료 sa-yong-nyo; 장거리 전화료 jang-geo-ri jeon-hwa-ryo; 희생 hi-saeng; 종소리 jong-sso-ri; 종 울리기 jong ul-li-gi

tomato *n.* 토마토 to-ma-to; ~ **sauce** 토마토 소스 to-ma-to sso-sseu; ~ **juice** 토마토 주스 to-ma-to ju-sseu

tomb *n.* 무덤 mu-deom, 묘 myo; 묘비 myo-bi

tomorrow *adv.* 내일 nae-il; 가까운 장래 ga-kka-un jang-nae

ton *n.* 톤 ton

tone *n.* 음질 eum-jil; 어조 eo-jo; 색조 saek-jo; 기풍 gi-pung; 정상상태 jeong-sang-sang-tae

tongs *n. pl.* 집게 jip-ge; 부젓가락 bu-jeot-ga-rak

tongue *n.* 혀 hyeo; 말 mal, 언어 eon-eo; 언어능력 eon-eo-neung-nyeok; 말투 mal-tu

tonnage *n.* 톤수 ton-ssu; 총톤수 chong-ton-ssu; 톤세 ton-sse

tonsils *n. pl.* 편도선 pyeon-do-seon

too *adv.* 또한 tto-han, 너무 neo-mu, ...하기에는 너무나 ...ha-gi-e-neun neo-mu-na

tool *n.* 도구 do-gu, 연장 yeon-jang; 앞잡이 ap-jab-i

tooth *n.* 이 i; 기호 gi-ho; 위력 wi-ryeok; 결 gyeol

toothache *n.* 치통 chi-tong

toothbrush *n.* 칫솔 chit-sol

toothpaste *n.* 치약 chi-yak

top *adj.* 정상 jeong sang; 꼭대기 kkok-dae-gi; 절정 jeol-jjeong; 최고위 choe-go-wi; 선두 seon-du; 최전성기 choe-jeon-seong-gi; 지붕 ji-bung; 뚜껑 ttu-kkeong; 마개 ma-gae; 팽이 paeng-i

topic *n.* 화제 hwa-je; 제목 je-mok; 총론 chong-non; 일반론 il-ban-non

topical *adj.* 화제의 hwa-je-ui; 시사문제의 si-sa-mun-je-ui; 총론적인 chong-non-jeog-in; 국부적인 guk-bu-jeog-in; *(esp. in medical sense)* 국소의 guk-so-ui

torch *n.* 햇불 hwaet-bul; 빛 bit; 토치램프 to-chi-raem-peu

torment *n.* 고통 go-tong; 고뇌 go-noe; 고문 go-mun; 고통거리 go-tong-kkeo-ri; *vt.* 괴롭히다 goe-ro-pi-da; 고문하다 go-mun-ha-da; 귀찮게 굴다 gwi-chan-ke gul-da

torrent *n.* 급류 geum-nyu; 억수 eok-su; 연발 yeon-bal

torture *n.* 고문 go-mun; 고통 go-tong; *vt.* 고문하다 go-mun-ha-da; 괴롭히다 goe-ro-pi-da; 억지로 비틀다 eok-ji-ro bi-teul-da; 곡해하다 go-kae-ha-da

toss *vt.* 던지다 deon-ji-da; 던져 올리다 deon-jeo ol-li-da; 뒤로 젖히다 dwi-ro jeo-chi-da; 흔들다 heun-deul-da; 철저히 논하다 cheol-jjeo-hi non-ha-da; 뒤섞다 dwi-seok-da; 단숨에 들이키다 dan-sum-e deul-i-ki-da

total *n.* 합계 hap-gye; 총수 chong-su; *adj.* 전체의 jeon-che-ui; 합계의 hap-gye-ui; 완전한 wan-jeon-han; 총력적인 chong-nyeok-jeog-in; *vt.* 합계하다 hap-gye-ha-da; 합치다 hap-chi-da; 합이 ...이 되다 hab-i ...i doe-da

totalitarian *adj.* 전체주의의 Jeon-che-Ju-i-ui

totally *adv.* 전혀 jeon-hyeo; 완전히 wan-jeon-hi; 모조리 mo-jo-ri

touch *n.* 접촉 jeop-chok; 연락 yeol-lak; 감촉 gam-chok; 수법 su-ppeop; 필치 pil-chi; 가필 ga-pil; 특징 teuk-jing; 기운 gi-un; *vt.* ...에 닿다 ...e da-ta; 손을 대다 son-eul dae-da; 만지다 man-ji-da; 인접하다 in-jeo-pa-da; ...에 이르다 ...e i-reu-da; 마음을 움직이다 ma-eum-eul um-jig-i-da; 붙이다 bu-chi-da; 수정하다 su-jeong-ha-da

touching *adj.* 감동시키는 gam-dong-si-ki-neun; 애처로운 ae-cheo-ro-un

touchy *adj.* 성미가 까다로운 seong-mi-ga kka-da-ro-un; 다루기 힘든 da-ru-gi him-deun; 위험한 wi-heom-han

tough *adj.* 강인한 gang-in-han; 튼튼한 teun-teun-han; 끈기있는 kkeun-gi-in-neun; 곤란한 gol-lan-han; 지독한 ji-do-kan; 어려운 eo-ryeo-un

toughen *vt.* 강인하게 하다 gang-in-ha-ge ha-da; 튼튼하게 하다 teun-teun-ha-ge ha-da; 끈기있게 하다 kkeun-gi-it-ge ha-da

toughness *n.* 강인함 gang-in-ham; 튼튼함 teun-teun-ham; 끈기 kkeun-gi

tour *n.* 관광 gwan-gwang; 여행 yeo-haeng; 순회공연 sun-hoe-gong-yeon; 순회 sun-hoe; *vt.* 여행하다 yeo-haeng-ha-da; 걸어 돌아다니다 geol-eo dol-a-da-ni-da; 순회공연하다 sun-hoe-gong-yeon-ha-da

tourism *n.* 관광여행 gwan-gwang-yeo-haeng; 관광사업 gwan-gwang-sa-eop

tourist *n.* 여행자 yeo-haeng-ja; 관광객 gwan-gwang-gaek; *adj.* 여행자의 yeo-haeng-ja-ui; 관광객을 위한 gwan-gwang-gaeg-eul wi-han

tournament *n.* 경기대회 gyeong-gi-dae-hoe, 토너먼트 to-neo-meon-teu

tow *vt.* 끌다 kkeul-da; 끌고가다 kkeul-go-ga-da

toward *prep.* ...쪽으로 ...jjog-eu-ro; ...가까이 ...ga-kka-i; ...을 위해서 ...eul wi-hae-seo; ...에 대해서 ...e dae-hae-seo

towel *n.* 타월 ta-wol, 수건 su-geon

tower *n.* 탑 tap, 망루 mang-nu; 철탑 cheol-tap; 철도 신호소 cheol-tto sin-ho-so; 고층건물 go-cheung-geon-mul; 요새 yo-sae

town *n.* 읍 eup; 마을 ma-eul; 도시 do-si

toy *n.* 장난감 jang-nan-kkam

trace *n.* 발자국 bal-jja-guk; 자취 ja-chwi; 영향 yeong-hyang; 기운 gi-un; 도형 do-hyeong; *vt.* 자국을 더듬다 ja-gug-eul deo-deum-tta; 추적하다 chu-jeo-ka-da; 출처를 조사하다 chul-cheo-reul jo-sa-ha-da; 흔적을 발견하다 heun-jeog-eul bal-gyeon-ha-da; 길을 따라가다 gil-eul tta-ra-ga-da; 선을 긋다 seon-eul geut-da; 도안을 그리다 do-an-eul geu-ri-da; 베끼다 be-kki-da

trachea *n.* 기관 gi-gwan; 도관 do-gwan

track *n.* 지나간 자국 ji-na-gan ja-guk; 통로 tong-no; 인생행로 in-saeng-haeng-no; 진로 jil-lo; 단서 dan-seo; 궤도 gwe-do; 트랙 teu-raek; **railroad ~s** 기찻길 gi-chat-gil; *vt.* 뒤를 쫓다 dwi-reul jjot-da; 탐지하다 tam-ji-ha-da; 발자국을 내다 bal-jja-gug-eul nae-da; 선로를 깔다 seol-lo-reul kkal-da; 앞의 자국을 따르다 ap-ui ja-gug-eul tta-reu-da; 끌다 kkeul-da; 능력별로 편성하다 neung-nyeok-byeol-lo pyeon-seong-ha-da

traction *n.* 끌기 kkeul-gi; 견인 gyeon-in; 견인력 gyeon-in-nyeok; 마찰 ma-chal; 수축 su-chuk

tractor *n.* 트랙터 teu-raek-teo; 견인차 gyeon-in-cha; 견인식 비행기 gyeon-in-sik bi-haeng-gi; 끄는 사람 kkeu-neun sa-ram

trade *n.* 매매 mae-mae; 무역 mu-yeok; 직업 jig-eop; 소매업자 so-mae-eop-ja; 타협 ta-hyeop; *vt.* 매매하다 mae-mae-ha-da; 팔아버리다 pal-a-beo-ri-da; 교환하다 gyo-hwan-ha-a; *vi.* 장사하다 jang-sa-ha-da; 무역여행을 하다 mu-yeog-yeo ha-da; 화물을 운송하다 hwa-mul-eul un-song-ha-da; 물건을 사다 mul-geon-eul sa-da; 팔리다 pal-li-da; 뒷거래하다 dwit-geo-rae-ha-da

trader *n.* 상인 sang-in; 무역업자 mu-yeog-eop-ja; 상선 sang-seon

tradition *n.* 전설 jeon-seol; 전통 jeon-tong; 관습 gwan-seup

traditional *adj.* 전통의 jeon-tong-ui; 전통적인 jeon-tong-jeog-in; 관습의 gwan-seub-ui

traffic *n.* 교통 gyo-tong; 수송 su-song; 부정한 거래 bu-jeong-han geo-rae; 매매 mae-mae; *vi.* 장사하다 jang-sa-ha-da; 거래하다 geo-rae-ha-da; 무역하다 mu-yeo-ka-da; 교제하다 gyo-je-ha-da; 돌아다니다 dol-a-da-ni-da

tragedy *n.* 비극 bi-geuk; 비극적 이야기 bi-geuk-jeok i-ya-gi; 비극적 사건 bi-geuk-jeok sa-kkeon

tragic *adj.* 비극의 bi-geug-ui; 비참한 bi-cham-han

trail *n.* 늘어진 것 neul-eo-jin geot; 자국 ja-guk; 오솔길 o-sol-kkil; 여파 yeo-pa; *vi.* 질질 끌리다 jil-jil kkeul-li-da; 덩굴이 뻗다 deong-gul-i ppeot-da; 꼬리를 끌다 kko-ri-reul kkeul-da; 발을 끌며 가다 bal-eul kkeul-myeo ga-da; 추적하다 chu-jeo-ka-da; **to ~ behind** 뒤를 추적하다 dwi-reul chu-jeo-ka-da

trailer *n.* 끄는 사람 kkeu-neun sa-ram; 트레일러 teu-re-il-leo

train *n.* 기차 gi-cha; 행렬 haeng-nyeol; 연속 yeon-sok; 뒤에 끌리는 것 dwi-e-seo kkeul-li-neun geot; 수행원 su-haeng-won; 도화선 do-hwa-seon; 절차 jeol-cha; *vt.* 가르치다 ga-reu-chi-da; 훈련하다 hul-lyeon-ha-da; 단련시키다 dal-lyeon-si-ki-da; 길들이다 gil-deul-i-da

trainer *n.* 훈련자 hul-lyeon-ja; 지도자 ji-do-ja; 코치 ko-chi; 연습용 기구 yeon-seum-nyong gi-gu; **physical ~** 체력 단련사 che-ryeok dal-lyeon-sa

training *n.* 훈련 hul-lyeon; 연습 yeon-seup; 양성 yang-seong; **job ~** 직업훈련 jig-eop-hul-lyeon; 직업연수 jig-eop-seon-su

trait *n.* 특색 teuk-saek; 얼굴 생김새 eol-gul saeng-gim-sae; 붓글씨 솜씨 but-geul-ssi som-ssi

traitor *n.* 배반자 bae-ban-ja, 반역자 ban-yeok-ja

tram *n.* 궤도전차 gwe-do jeon-cha; 전기궤도 jeon-gi-gwe-do; 석탄 운반차 seok-tan un-ban-cha; 조정기 jo-jeong-gi

tramp *n.* 짓밟음 jit-balb-eum; 짓밟는 소리 jit-bam-neun so-ri; 방랑자 bang-nang-ja; 장거리 도보여행 jang-geo-ri do-bo-yeo-haeng; 스파이크 seu-pa-i-keu; 부정기 화물선 bu-jeong-gi hwa-mul-sseon

trance *n.* 황홀 hwang-hol; 열중 yeol-jjung; 혼수상태 hon-su-sang-tae

transaction *n.* 취급 chwi-geup; 거래 geo-rae; 처리 cheo-ri; 보고서 bo-go-seo

transfer *n.* 이동 i-dong; 양도 yang-do; 갈아타기 gal-a-ta-gi; 갈아타는 지점 gal-a-ta-neun ji-jeom; 갈아타는 표 gal-a-ta-neun pyo; 대체 dae-che; 명의변경 myeong-ui-byeon-gyeong; 융통 yung-tong; 이적자 i-jeok-ja; 전학 jeon-hak; *vt.* 옮기다 om-gi-da; 전학시키다 jeon-hak-si-ki-da; 운반하다 un-ban-ha-da; 양도하다 yang-do-ha-da; 책임을 전가하다 chaeg-im-eul jeon-ga-ha-da; 전하다 jeon-ha-da

transit *n.* 통과 tong-gwa; 운송 un-song; 변천 byeon-cheon, 운송로 un-song-no

translate *vt.* 번역하다 beon-yeo-ka-da; 해석하다 hae-seo-ka-da; 쉽게 다시 표현하다 swip-ge da-si pyo-hyeon-ha-da; 다른 형식으로 바꾸다 da-reun hyeong-sig-eu-ro ba-kku-da; 다른 장소로 옮기다 da-reun jang-so-ro om-gi-da

translation *n.* 번역 beon-yeok; 통역 tong-yeok; 번역서 beon-yeok-seo; 해석 hae-seok

translator *n.* 번역자 beon-yeok-ja; 통역 tong-yeok; 번역기 beon-yeok-gi

transmission *n.* 트렌스미션 teu-raen-seu-mi-ssyeon, 변속장치 byeon-sok-jang-chi; 송달 song-dal; 전달 jeon-dal; 양도 yang-do; 유전 yu-jeon; 전도 jeon-do; 전송 jeon-song; 전동 jeon-dong

transmit *vt.* 보내다 bo-nae-da; 방송하다 bang-song-ha-da; 도전하다 do-jeon-ha-da; 물려주다 mul-lyeo-ju-da; 유전하다 yu-jeon-ha-da; 병을 옮기다 byeong-eul om-gi-da; 전달하다 jeon-dal-ha-da

transport *n.* 수송 su-song, 운송 un-song; 수송선 su-song-seon; 수송기 su-song-gi; 도취 do-chwi; 열중 yeol-jjung; 유형수 yu-hyeong-su; *vt.* 수송하다 su-song-ha-da, 운반하다 un-ban-ha-da; 도취하게 하다 do-chwi-ha-ge ha-da; 열중하게 하다 yeol-jjung-ha-ge ha-da; 추방하다 chu-bang-ha-da

transporter *n.* 운송자 un-song-ja; 운반장치 un-ban-jang-chi

trap *n.* 올가미 ol-ga-mi; 함정 ham-jeong; 속임수 sog-im-su; 트랩 teu-raep; 들창 deul-chang; 표적 날리개 pyo-jeok nal-li-gae; 휴대품 hyu-dae-pum; *vt.* 올가미로 잡다 ol-ga-mi-ro jap-da; 방취장치를 하다 bang-chwi-jang-chi-reul ha-da; 함정문을 달다 ham-jeong-mun-eul dal-da; 말장식을 달다 mal-jang-sig-eul dal-da

trash *n.* 쓰레기 sseu-re-gi; 잡동사니 jap-dong-sa-ni; 객담 gaek-dam; 졸작 jol-jjak

travel *n.* 여행 yeo-haeng; 여행담 yeo-haeng-dam; 교통량 gyo-tong-nyang; 진행 jin-haeng; 순환운동 sun-hwan-un-dong; *vi.* 여행하다 yeo-haeng-ha-da; 이동하다 i-dong-ha-da; 순회판매하다 sun-hoe-pan-mae-ha-da; 교제하다 gyo-je-ha-da; 빨리 움직이다 ppal-li um-jig-i-da; 운송에 적합하다 un-song-e jeo-ka-pa-da

traveler *n.* 여행자 yeo-haeng-ja; 외무원 oe-mu-won; 이동 기중기 i-dong gi-jung-gi

tray *n.* 쟁반 jaeng-ban; 높이가 낮은 상자 nop-i-ga naj-eun sang-ja

treason *n.* 반역죄 ban-yeok-joe; 배신 bae-sin; 국사범 guk-sa-beom

treasure *n.* 보물 bo-mul; 귀중품 gwi-jung-pum; 소중한 것 so-jung-han geot

treasurer *n.* 회계원 hoe-gye-won; 출납계원 chul-lap-gye-won; 귀중품 보관자 gwi-jung-pum bo-gwan-ja

treasury *n.* 국고 guk-go; 기금 gi-gum; 재무성 jae-mu-seong; 보고 bo-go

treat *n.* 한턱냄 han-teong-nam; 큰기쁨 keun-gi-ppeum; 특별한 즐거움

teuk-byeol-han jeul-geo-um; 위안회
wi-an-hoe; *vt.* 대우하다 dae-u-ha-da; 간주
하다 gan-ju-ha-da; 다루다 da-ru-da; 치료
하다 chi-ryo-ha-da; 처리하다 cheo-ri-ha-
da; 대접하다 dae-ejo-pa-da; 한턱내다
han-teong-nae-da

treatise *n.* 논문 non-mun; 보고서 bo-go-seo

treatment *n.* 취급 chwi-geup; 대우 dae-u;
처리법 cheo-ri-ppeop; 치료법 chi-ryo-
ppeop

treaty *n.* 조약 jo-yak; 약정 yak-jeong

tree *n.* 나무 na-mu; 목제물건
mok-je-mul-geon

tremble *vi.* 떨다 tteol-da; 진동하다 jin-
dong-ha-da; 흔들리다 heun-deul-li-da; 조
바심하다 jo-ba-sim-ha-da

trench *n.* 도랑 do-rang; 해구 hae-gu; 참호
cham-ho

trend *n.* 방향 bang-hyang; 동향 dong-hyang;
추세 chu-se; 유행 yu-haeng

trespass *vi.* 침입하다 chim-i-pa-da; 침해하
다 chim-hae-ha-da; 방해하다 bang-
hae-ha-da; 끼어들다 kki-eo-deul-da; 편
승하다 pyeon-seung-ha-da; 위법하다
wi-beo-pa-da

trial *n.* 공판 gong-pan; 시도 si-do; 시련
si-ryeon; 골칫거리 gol-chit-geo-ri; **to go to**
~ 재판에 회부되다 jae-pan-e hoe-bu-
doe-da, 공판에 불려나가다 gong-pan-e
bul-lye-na-ga-da

triangle *n.* 삼각형 sam-ga-kyeong; 트라이앵
글 teu-ra-i-aeng-geul; 삼각관계 sam-gak-
gwan-gye; 삼각자 sam-gak-ja

triangular *adj.* 삼각형의 sam-ga-kyeong-
ui; 삼자간의 sam-ja-gan-ui; 삼국
간의 sam-guk-gan-ui; 삼각관계의
sam-gak-gwan-gye-ui

tribe *n.* 부족 bu-jok; 종족 jong-jok; 족 jok

tribute *n.* 공물 gong-mul; 강제로 징수된 물
건 gang-je-ro jing-su-doen mul-geon; 감
사를 나타내는 선물 gam-sreul na-ta-nae-
neun seon-mul

trick *n.* 묘기 myo-gi; 기술 gi-sul; 비결 bi-
gyeol; 책략 chaeng-nyak; 장난 jang-nan;
착각 chak-gak; *vt.* 속이다 sog-i-da; 기대
에 어긋나다 gi-dae-e eo-geun-na-da; 예
상을 뒤엎다 ye-sang-eul dwi-eop-da; 장
식하다 jang-si-ka-da

trickle *n.* 똑똑 떨어짐 ttok-ttok tteol-eo-jim;
졸졸 흐름 jjol-jjol heu-reum; 물방울 mul-
ppang-ul; 개울 gae-ul; *vi.* 똑똑 떨어지다
ttok-ttok tteol-eo-ji-da; 졸졸 흐르다 jol-jol
heu-reu-da; 조금씩 새다 jo-geum-ssik sae-
da; 드문드문 오다 deu-mun-deu-mun o-da

tricycle *n.* 세발 자전거 se-bal ja-jeon-geo;
삼륜차 sam-nyun-cha; 삼륜 오토바이
sam-nyun o-to-ba-i

trifle *n.* 하찮은 일 ha-chan-eun il; 소량 so-
ryang; 땜납 ttaem-nap; 소품 so-pum

trigger *n.* 방아쇠 bang-a-soe; 제동기
je-dong-gi; 제륜장치 je-ryun-jang-chi; *vt.*
방아쇠를 당기다 bang-a-soe-reul dang-
gi-da; ...의 계기가 되다 ...ui gye-gi-ga
doe-da; 행동을 개시하다 haeng-dong-eul
gae-si-ha-da

trimester *n.* 삼개월 sam-gae-wol; 삼학기제
sam-hak-gi-je

triumph *n.* 승리 seung-ni; 대성공 dae-
seong-gong; 위업 wi-eop; 승리의 기쁨
seung-ni-ui gi-peum; *vi.* 승리를 거두다
seung-ni-reul geo-du-da; 의기 양양해하
다 ui-gi yang-nyang-hae-ha-da

trivia *n.* 사소한일 sa-so-han-nil; 하찮은 것
ha-chan-eun goet; ~ **game** 상식퀴즈게임
sang-sik-kwi-jeu-kke-im

trivial *adj.* 하찮은 ha-chan-eun; 사소한
sa-so-han; 경박한 gyeong-ba-kan

troop *n.* 떼 tte, 무리 mu-ri; 군대 gun-dae; 병
력 byeong-nyeok; ~**s** 군대 gun-dae; 병력
byeong-nyeok

tropical *adj.* 열대지방의 yeol-ttae-ji-bang-ui;
열대성의 yeol-ttae-sseong-ui; 열정적인
yeol-jjeong-jeog-in

tropics *n. pl.* 회귀선 hoe-gwi-seon; 열대지
방 yeol-ttae-jji-bang

trouble *n.* 고생 go-saeng; 근심 geun-sim;
두통거리 go-tong-kkeo-ri; 수고 su-go;
폐 pye; 시끄러운 일 si-kkeu-reo-un il;
고장 go-jang; 병 byeong; *vt.* 괴롭히다
goe-ro-pi-da; 걱정시키다 geok-jeong-si-
ki-da; 폐를 끼치다 pye-reul kki-chi-da; 고
통을 주다 go-tong-eul ju-da; 어지럽히다
eo-ji-reo-pi-da

troublesome *adj.* 골치아픈 gol-chi-a-peun;
귀찮은 gwi-chan-eun; 다루기 힘든 da-ru-
gi him-deun

trout *n.* 송어 song-eo

trowel *n.* 흙손 heuk-son; 모종삽 mo-jong-sap

truant *n.* 게으름뱅이 ge-eu-reum-baeng-i; 무단 결석자 mu-dan-gyeol-sseok-ja; *adj.* 게으름 피우는 ge-eu-reum pi-u-neun; 무단 결석하는 mu-dan gyeol-sseo-ka-neun; 빈들빈들 노는 bin-deul-bin-deul no-neun

truck *n.* 트럭 teu-reok, 화물 자동차 hwa-mul ja-dong-cha; 손수레 son-su-re; 운반차 un-ban-cha; 교환 gyo-hwan; 교역품 gyo-yeok-pum; 물품에 의한 임금지급 mul-pume ui-han im-geum-ji-geup; 잡동사니 jap-dong-sa-ni; 허튼소리 heo-teun-so-ri; 잠꼬대 jam-kko-dae

true *adj.* 정말의 jeong-mal-ui, 진실한 jin-sil-han; 해당되는 hae-dang-doe-neun; 진짜의 jin-jja-ui; 성실한 seong-sil-han; 정확한 jeong-hwa-kan; 실물 그대로의 sil-mul geu-dae-ro-ui; 정당한 jeong-dang-han

truly *adv.* 참으로 cham-eu-ro, 진실로 jin-sil-lo; 올바르게 ol-ba-reu-ge; 확실히 hwak-sil-hi; 정확하게 jeong-hwa-ka-ge; 충실히 chung-sil-hi; 성실히 seong-sil-hi; 정직하게 jeong-ji-ka-ge; 사실은 sa-sil-eun

trump *n.* 최고의 패 choe-go-ui pae; 호남아 ho-nam-a; 최후수단 choe-hu-su-dan; *vt.* 트럼프를 치다 teu-reom-peu-reul chi-da; 으뜸패를 내놓다 eu-tteum-pae-reul nae-no-ta; 비방을 쓰다 bi-bang-eul sseu-da; 나팔을 불다 na-pal-eul bul-da; *(cards)* 트럼프 teu-reom-peu

trunk *n.* 나무줄기 na-mu-jul-gi; 몸통 mom-tong; 본체 bon-che; 중앙부분 jung-ang-bu-bun; 트렁크 teu-reong-keu; 여행용 가방 yeo-haeng-nyong ga-bang; 간선 gan-seon; 중계선 jung-gye-seon; 코끼리 고 ko-kki-ri ko; 운동팬츠 un-dong pae-cheu

trust *n.* 신뢰 sil-loe; 신용받는 사람 sin-yong-ban-neun sa-ram; 확신 hwak-sin; 기대 gi-dae; 책임 chaeg-im; 신탁품 sin-tak-pum; *vt.* 신뢰하다 sil-loe-ha-da; 안심하고 맡기다 an-sim-ha-go mat-gi-da; 위탁하다 wi-ta-ka-da; 기대하다 gi-dae-ha-da; 비밀을 털어놓다 bi-mil-eul teol-eo-no-ta; 신용대부하다 sin-yong-dae-bu-ha-da

trustworthy *adj.* …신뢰할 수 있는 …sil-loe-hal ssu in-neun; 확실한 hwak-sil-han

truth *n.* 진리 jil-li; 진실성 jin-sil-sseong; 사실 sa-sil; 성실 seong-sil; 정확성 jeong-hwak-seong

truthful *adj.* 정직한 jeong-ji-kan; 진실한 jin-sil-han; 올바른 ol-ba-reun; 정말의 jeong-mal-ui

try *n.* 시험 si-heom; 시도 si-do; 노력 no-ryeok; *vt.* 해보다 hae-bo-da, 시도하다 si-do-ha-da; 시험하다 si-heom-ha-da; 재판에 부치다 jae-pan-e bu-chi-da; 시련을 겪게 하다 si-ryeon-eul gyeok-ge ha-da; *vi.* 시험해보다 si-heom-hae-bo-da; 노력하다 no-ryeo-ka-da; **to ~ something on** 입어보다 ib-eo-bo-da; 시험삼아 해보다 si-heom-sam-a hae-bo-da

tube *n.* 관 gwan, 통 tong, 튜브 tyu-beu; 진공관 jin-gong-gwan; **inner ~ (of a car tire)** (자동차의) 타이어 안쪽의 고무튜브 (ja-dong-cha-ui) ta-i-eo an-jjog-ui go-mu-tyu-beu; **test ~** 시험관 si-heom-gwan

tubing *n.* 배관 bae-gwan; 관 조직 gwan jo-jik; 관 재료 gwan jae-ryo; 관류 gwan-nyu; 관의 한토막 gwan-ui han-to-mak; *(sport)* 튜빙게임 tyu-bing-kke-im

Tuesday *n.* 화요일 hwa-yo-il

tug *n.* 세게 당김 se-ge dang-gim; 잡아당김 jab-a-dang-gim; 노력 no-ryeok; 분투 bun-tu; 경쟁 gyeong-jaeng; 예인선 ye-in-seon; *vi.* 잡아당기다 jab-a-dang-gi-da; 노력하다 no-ryeo-ka-da; 분투하다 bun-tu-ha-da

tugboat *n.* 예인선 ye-in-seon

tulip *n.* 튤립 tyul-lip

tumor *n.* 종기 jong-gi; 종양 jong-yang

tune *n.* 곡 gok, 곡조 gok-jo; 가락 ga-rak; 기분 gi-bun; 조화 jo-hwa; *vt.* 연주하다 yeon-ju-ha-da; 조율하다 jo-yul-ha-da; 동조시키다 dong-jo-si-ki-da; 파장을 맞추다 pa-jang-eul mat-chu-da

Tunisia *n.* 튀니지 twi-ni-ji

tunnel *n.* 터널 teo-neol; 지하도 ji-ha-do; 갱도 gaeng-do; 굴 gul

turbine *n.* 터빈 teo-bin

Turkey 터어키 teo-eo-ki

turkey *n.* 칠면조 chil-myeon-jo; 터어키 teo-eo-ki

Turkish *n.* 터어키어 teo-eo-ki-eo; 터어키사람 teo-eo-ki-eo; *adj.* 터어키의 teo-eo-ki-ui
turmoil *n.* 소란 so-ran; 혼동 hon-dong
turn *n.* 회전 hoe-jeon; 방향전환 bang-hyang-jeon-hwan; 모퉁이 mo-tung-i; 변화 byeon-hwa; 변화점 byeon-hwa-jjeom; 새로운 견해 sae-ro-un gyeon-hae; 순번 sun-beon; 성향 seong-hyang; *vt.* 돌리다 dol-li-da; 켜다 kyeo-da; 잠그다 jam-geu-da; 감아올리다 gam-a-ol-li-da; 뒤엎다 dwi-eop-da; 향하게 하다 hyang-ha-ge ha-da; 딴데로 돌리다 ttan-de-ro dol-li-da; 변화시키다 byeon-hwa-si-ki-da; *vi.* 순회하다 sun-hoe-ha-da; 돌다 dol-da; 회전하다 hoe-jeon-ha-da; 향하다 hyang-ha-da; ...으로 변하다 ...eu-ro byeon-ha-da; 뒤엎어지다 dwi-eo-peo-ji-da; 역전하다 yeok-jeon-ha-da
turtle *n.* 바다거북 ba-da-geo-buk
tweezers *n. pl.* 족집게 jjok-jip-ge, 핀셋 pin-set
twelfth *adj.* 열두번째의 yeol-ttu-beon-jjae-ui; 제십이회 je-sib-i-hoe
twelve *num.* 열둘 yeol-ttul; 십이 sib-i
twentieth *adj.* 스무번째의 seu-mu-beon-jjae-ui; 제이십회 je-i-si-poe
twenty *num.* 스물 seu-mul; 이십 i-sip
twice *adv.* 두번 du-beon; 두배로 du-bae-ro
twig *n.* 잔가지 jan-ga-ji; 지맥 ji-maek; 지선 ji-seon; 점치는 막대기 jeom-chi-neun mak-dae-gi
twilight *n.* 땅거미 ttang-kkeo-mi, 황혼 hwang-hon; 여명기 yeo-myeong-gi; 희미한 빛 hi-mi-han bit

twin *n.* 쌍둥이 ssang-dong-i; 한쌍 han-ssang
twinge *n.* 쑤시는 듯한 아픔 ssu-si-neun de-tan a-peum; 양심의 가책 yang-sim-ui ga-chaek
twinkle *vi.* 반짝반짝 빛나다 ban-jjak-ban-jjak bin-na-da; 어른거리다 eo-reun-geo-ri-da; 눈을 깜빡이다 nun-eul kkam-ppag-i-da
twist *n.* 비틂 bi-teum; 꼬임 kko-im; 꼬인 것 kko-in-geot; 묘한 성격 myo-han seong-kkyeok; 회전 hoe-jeon; 굴곡 gul-gok; *vt.* 비틀다 bi-teul-da; 꼬다 kko-da; 얽히게 하다 eol-ki-ge ha-da; 얼굴을 찡그리다 eol-gul-eul jjing-geu-ri-da; 접질리다 jeop-jil-li-da, 삐다 ppi-da; 왜곡하다 wae-go-ka-da
two *num.* 둘 dul; 이 i
type *n.* 유형 yu-hyeong; 전형 jeon-hyeong; 표상 pyo-sang; 활자 hwal-jja; 혈액형 hyeol-ae-kyeong; *vt.* 대표하다 dae-pyo-ha-da; 전형을 이루다 jeon-hyeong-eul i-ru-da; ...의 형을 조사하다 ...ui hyeong-eul jo-sa-ha-da; 타이프로 치다 ta-i-peu-ro chi-da; *vi.* 타이프를 치다 ta-i-peu-reul chi-da; **typing paper** 타자용지 ta-ja-yong-ji
typewriter *n.* 타이프라이터 ta-i-peu-ra-i-teo, 타자기 ta-ja-gi
typhoon *n.* 태풍 tae-pung
typical *adj.* 전형적인 jeon-hyeong-jeog-in; 대표적인 dae-pyo-jeog-in; 특유의 teug-yu-ui; 특징적 teuk-jing-jeok
typist *n.* 타이피스트 ta-i-pi-seu-teu, 타자수 ta-ja-su

U

UFO *n. abbr.* **unidentified flying object** 비행접시 bi-haeng-eop-si, 유에프오 yu-e-peu-o
ugly *adj.* 못생긴 mot-saeng-gin; 추악한 chu-a-kan; 험악한 heom-a-kan
UHF *n. abbr.* **ultrahigh frequency** 극초단파 geuk-cho-dan-pa
ulcer *n.* 궤양 gwe-yang; 종기 jong-gi; 병폐 byeong-pye

ultra *adj.* 과도한 gwa-do-han, 극단적인 geuk-dan-jeog-in, 과격한 gwa-gyeo-kan
ultrasound *n.* 초음파 cho-eum-pa
ultraviolet *adj.* 자외선의 ja-oe-seon-ui; ~ **rays** 자외선 ja-oe-seon
umbilical cord *n.* 탯줄 taet-jul
umbrella *n.* 우산 u-san; 양산 yang-san; 산하 san-ha; 핵우산 haeg-u-san; ~ **stand** 우산꽂이 u-san-kkoj-i

umpire *n.* 심판 sim-pan; *vt., vi.* 심판을 보다 sim-pan-eul bo-da

UN *n. abbr.* United Nations 국제연합 guk-je-yeon-hap, 유엔 yu-en

unable *adj.* ...할 수 없는 ...hal ssu eom-neun; 연약한 yeon-ya-kan; 무력한 mu-ryeo-kan

unacceptable *adj.* 받아들이기 어려운 bad-a-deul-i-gi eo-ryeo-un; 마음에 안드는 ma-eum-e an deu-neun

unaccountable *adj.* 설명할 수 없는 seol-myeong-hal ssu eom-neun, 까닭을 알 수 없는 kka-dalg-eul al ssu eom-neun; 책임이 없는 chaeg-im-I eom-neun

unanimous *adj.* 만장일치의 man-jang-il-chi-ui; 합의의 hab-i-ui

unarmed *adj.* 무장하지 않은 mu-jang-ha-ji an-eun; 맨손의 maen-son-ui

unauthorized *adj.* 권한 외의 gwon-han oe-ui; 공인되지 않은 gong-in-doe-ji an-eun; 독단의 dok-dan-ui

unavoidable *adj.* 피할 수 없는 pi-hal ssu eom-neun; 무효로 할 수 없는 mu-hyo-ro hal ssu eom-neun

unaware *adj.* 눈치채지 못하는 nun-chi-chae-ji mo-ta-neun; 방심하는 bang-sim-ha-neun

unbearable *adj.* 참을 수 없는 cham-eul ssu eom-neun

uncertain *adj.* 불확실한 bul-hwak-sil-han; 변덕스러운 byeon-deok-seu-reo-un

uncle *n.* 삼촌 sam-chon; 외삼촌 oe-sam-chon; 고모부 go-mo-bu; 이모부 i-mo-bu

uncomfortable *adj.* 불편한 bul-pyeon-han; 불쾌한 bul-kwae-han; 귀찮은 gwi-chan-eun

unconscious *adj.* 의식이 없는 ui-sig-i eom-neun; 무의식의 mu-ui-sig-ui; 모르는 mo-reu-neun; 인사불성의 in-sa-bul-sseong-ui

uncover *vt.* 폭로하다 pong-no-ha-da; 뚜껑을 열다 ttu-kkeong-eul yeol-da; 모자를 벗다 mo-ja-reul beot-da; 무방비상태에 두다 mu-bang-bi-sang-tae-e du-da

undamaged *adj.* 손해를 당하지 않은 son-hae-reul dang-ha-ji an-eun, 손해를 입지 않은 son-hae-reul ip-ji an-eun

undecided *adj.* 미정의 mi-jeong-ui; 우유부단한 u-yu-bu-dan-han; 분명치 않은 bun-myeong-chi an-eun

under *adv.* ...아래에 ...a-rae-e, ...아래로 ...a-rae-ro; *prep.* ...의 아래에 ...ui a-rae-e, ...중인 ...jung-in, ...에 속하는 ...e so-ka-neun, ...미만으로 ...mi-man-eu-ro

underage *adj.* 미성년의 mi-seong-nyeon-ui

underestimate *vt.* 낮게 어림잡다 nat-ge eo-rim-jap-da, 과소평가하다 gwa-so-pyeong-kka-ha-da

undergo *vi.* 받다 bat-da; 경험하다 gyeong-heom-ha-da; 견디다 gyeon-di-da

undergraduate *n.* 대학생 dae-hak-saeng; *adj.* 대학생의 dae-hak-saeng-ui

underground *adj.* 지하의 ji-ha-ui; 숨은 sum-eun; 비밀의 bi-mil-ui

underline *vt.* 밑줄을 긋다 mit-jul-eul geut-da; 강조하다 gang-jo-ha-da; 예고하다 ye-go-ha-da

underneath *prep.* ...의 아래에 ...ui a-rae-e; ...의 지배하에 ...ui ji-bae-ha-e; ...의 형태로 ...ui hyeong-tae-ro

underpants *n. pl.* 속옷 sog-ot, 내의 nae-ui; 팬티 pan-ti

underpass *n.* 지하도 ji-ha-do

undersea *adj.* 해저의 hae-jeo-ui, 바다속의 ba-da-ssog-ui

undershirt *n.* 속옷 sog-ot, 내의 nae-ui; 러닝셔츠 reon-ning-syeo-cheu

undersign *vt., vi.* ...의 아래에 서명하다 ...ui a-rae-e seo-myeong-ha-da

understand *vt.* 이해하다 i-hae-ha-da; 알아듣다 al-a-deut-da; 추측하다 chu-cheu-ka-da; *vi.* 이해력이 있다 i-hae-ryeog-i it-da; 들어서 알고있다 deul-eo-seo al-go it-da

understanding *n.* 이해 i-hae; 지식 ji-sik; 이해력 i-hae-ryeok; 분별 bun-byeol; 의사소통 ui-sa-so-tong; 협정 hyeop-jeong

undertake *vt.* 떠맡다 tteo-mat-da; 보증하다 bo-jeung-ha-da; 맡아서 돌보다 mat-a-seo dol-bo-da; 착수하다 chak-su-ha-da

under-the-counter *adj.* 밀수의 mil-ssu-ui; 불법의 bul-ppeob-ui, 위법의 wi-beob-ui

under-the-table *adj.* 밀수의 mil-ssu-ui; 불법의 bul-ppeob-ui, 위법의 wi-beob-ui

underwater *adj.* 물속의 mul-ssog-ui

underwear *n.* 내의 nae-ui; 속옷 sog-ot

undesirable *adj.* 탐탁치 않은 tam-tak-chi an-eun, 불쾌한 bul-kwae-han

undeveloped *adj.* 미개발의 mi-gae-bal-ui, 미발달의 mi-bal-ttal-ui; 현상되지 않은 hyeon-sang-doe-ji an-eun

undigested *adj.* 소화 안되는 so-hwa an-doe-neun, 어설픈 eo-seol-peun, 조잡한 jo-ja-pan

undo *vi.* 원상태로 돌리다 won-sang-tae-ro dol-li-da; 파멸시키다 pa-myeol-si-ki-da; 풀다 pul-da; 끄르다 kkeu-reu-da

uneasiness *n.* 불안 bul-an; 걱정 geok-jeong; 불쾌 bul-kwae; 거북함 geo-bu-kam

uneasy *adj.* 불안한 bul-an-han; 거북한 geo-bu-kan; 어색한 eo-sae-kan

uneducated *adj.* 교육을 받지 못한 gyo-yug-eul bat-ji mo-tan; 무지한 mu-ji-han

unemployed *adj.* 직업이 없는 jig-eob-i eom-neun; 쓰이지 않는 sseu-i-ji an-neun; 한가한 han-ga-han

unemployment *n.* 실업 sil-eop; 실직 sil-jjik

unending *adj.* 끝이 없는 kkeu-chi eom-neun; 영원한 yeong-won-han

unequal *adj.* 동등하지 않은 dong-deung-ha-ji an-eun; 불공평한 bul-gong-pyeong-han; 한결같지 않은 han-gyeol-gat-eun; 불충분한 bul-chung-bun-han

unfair *adj.* 불공평한 bul-gong-pyeong-han; 부정직한 bu-jeong-ji-kan

unfamiliar *adj.* 생소한 saeng-so-han; 익숙치 못한 ik-suk-chi mo-tan; 낯선 nat-seon

unfasten *vt.* 늦추다 neut-chu-da; 벗기다 beot-gi-da; 풀다 pul-da; 헐거워지다 heol-geo-wo-ji-da; 풀리다 pul-li-da; 벗겨지다 beot-gyeo-ji-da

unformed *adj.* 미발달의 mi-bal-ttal-ui, 미숙한 mi-su-kan; 형성되지 않은 hyeong-seong-doe-ji an-eun

unfortunate *adj.* 불행한 bul-haeng-han; 한심스러운 han-sim-seu-reo-un; 잘못된 jal-mot-don; ~ly 불행하게도 bul-haeng-ha-ge-do

unfriendly *adj.* 불친절한 bul-chin-jeol-han; 적의가 있는 jeog-i-ga in-neun; 나쁜 na-ppeun

unfurnished *adj.* 가구가 없는 ga-gu-ga eom-neun, 비품이 없는 bi-pum-i eom-neun

ungrammatical *adj.* 비문법적인 bi-mun-ppeop-jeog-in

unguarded *adj.* 부주의한 bu-ju-i-han, 방심한 bang-sim-han; 지키지 않는 ji-ki-ji an-neun, 수비하지 않는 su-bi-ha-ji an-neun

unhappy *adj.* 불행한 bul-haeng-han; 부적당한 bu-jeok-dang-han

unhealthy *adj.* 건강하지 못한 geon-gang-ha-ji mo-tan; 건강에 좋지 않은 geon-gang-e jo-chi an-eun; 불건전한 bul-geon-jeon-han

uniform *n.* 제복 je-bok; 유니폼 yu-ni-pom; *adj.* 한결같은 han-gyeol-gat-eun; 획일적인 hoeg-il-jjeog-in; 변화하지 않는 byeon-hwa-ha-ji an-neun; 균등한 gyun-deung-han

unimportant *adj.* 중요하지 않은 jung-yo-ha-ji an-eun; 대수롭지 않은 dae-su-rop-ji an-eun

unintentional *adj.* 고의가 아닌 go-ui-ga a-nin; 우연한 u-yeon-han

uninvited *adj.* 초청받지 않은 cho-cheong-bat-ji an-eun; 쓸데없이 참견하는 sseul-tte-eops-i cham-gyeon-ha-neun

union *n.* 결합 gyeol-hap; 합일 hab-il; 단결 dan-gyeol; 결혼 gyeol-hon; 조합 jo-hap; 클럽 keul-leop; 연합 yeon-hap; **labor** ~ 노동조합 no-dong-jo-hap

unique *adj.* 유일한 yu-il-han; 진기한 jin-gi-han

unisex *adj.* 남녀공용의 nam-nyeo-gong-yong-ui; 남녀공통의 nam-nyeo-gong-tong-ui

unit *n.* 단위 dan-wi; 학점 hak-jeom; 부대 bu-dae; 한개 han-gae; 한세트 han-sse-teu

unite *vt.* 결합하다 gyeol-ha-pa-da; 결혼시키다 gyeol-hon-si-ki-da; 겸비하다 gyeom-bi-ha-da

United Arab Emirates *n.* 아랍 에미레이트 a-rap e-mi-re-i-teu

United Kingdom *n.* 영국 yeong-guk

United Nations *n.* 유엔 yu-en, 국제연합 guk-je-yeon-hap

United States of America *n.* 미국 mi-guk, 아메리카 합중국 a-me-ri-ka hap-jung-guk

unity *n.* 통일 tong-il; 일관성 il-gwan-sseong; 조화 jo-hwa; 개체 gae-che; 단일성 dan-il-sseong; 공유 gong-yu

universal *adj.* 우주의 u-ju-ui; 전세계의 jeon-se-gye-ui; 보편적인 bo-pyeon-jeog-in;

일반의 il-ban-ui; 광범위한 gwang-beom-wi-han; 만능의 man-neung-ui; 포괄적인 po-gwal-jjeog-in

universe *n.* 우주 u-ju; 삼라만상 sam-na-man-sang; 전세계 jeon-se-gye; 분야 bun-ya

university *n.* 대학교 dae-hak-gyo; 대학당국 dae-hak-dang-guk; 대학팀 dae-hak-tim

unknown *adj.* 알려지지 않은 al-lyeo-ji-ji an-eun; 알 수 없는 al ssu-eom-neun; 셀 수 없는 sel-ssu eom-neun

unlawful *adj.* 불법의 bul-ppeob-ui, 비합법적인 bi-hap-beop-jeog-in

unless *conj.* ...하지 않는 한 ...ha-ji an-neun han; ... 이 아니면 ... i a-ni-myeon, ... 가 아니면 ... ga a-ni-myeon

unlike *adj.* 닮지 않은 dam-jji an-eun; ...답지 않은 ...dap-ji an-eun

unlikely *adj.* 있음직하지 않은 iss-eum-ji-ka-ji an-eun; 가망없는 ga-mang-eom-neun; 마음에 들지 않는 ma-eum-e deul-ji an-neun

unlimited *adj.* 끝없는 kkeud eom neun, 제한없는 je-han-eom-neun

unload *vt.* 짐을 내리다 jim-eul nae-ri-da; 근심을 덜다 geun-sim-eul deol-da; 총알을 빼내다 chong-al-eul ppae-nae-da; 주식을 매각하다 ju-sig-eul mae-ga-ka-da

unlucky *adj.* 불행한 bul-haeng-han; 불길한 bul-gil-han; 성공못한 seong-gong-mo-tan; 운이 나쁜 un-i na-ppeun

unmanned *adj.* 무인의 mu-in-ui, 승무원이 타지 않은 seung-mu-won-i ta-ji an-eun

unmarked *adj.* 무표의 mu-pyo-ui, 눈에 띄지 않는 nun-e tti-ji an-neun, 표가 없는 pyo-ga eom-neun

unmarried *adj.* 미혼의 mi-hon-ui, 독신의 dok-sin-ui

unmask *vt., vi.* 가면을 벗기다 ga-myeon-eul beot-gi-da, 정체를 드러내다 jeong che reul deu-reo-nae-da

unnecessary *adj.* 불필요한 bul-pil-yo-han; 무익한 mu-i-kan

unofficial *adj.* 비공식적인 bi-gong-sik-jeog-in; 무허가인 mu-heo-ga-in

unpack *vi.* 짐을 풀다 jim-eul pul-da; *vt.* 꺼내다 kkeo-nae-da; 빼내다 ppae-nae-da; 털어놓다 teol-eo-no-ta

unpleasant *adj.* 불유쾌한 bul-yu-kwae-han, 기분나쁜 gi-bun-na-ppeun

unpopular *adj.* 인기가 없는 in-kki-ga eom-neun; 평판이 나쁜 pyeong-pan-i na-ppeun; 유행하지 않는 yu-haeng-ha-ji an-neun

unrest *n.* 불안 bul-an; 침착하지 못함 chim-cha-ka-ji mo-tam

unsafe *adj.* 불안전한 bul-an-jeon-han; 불안한 bul-an-han

unsatisfactory *adj.* 마음에 차지 않는 ma-eum-e cha-ji an-neun; 불충분한 bul-chung-bun-han

unskilled *adj.* 숙련되지 않은 sung-nyeon-doe-ji an-eun; 숙련을 요하지 않는 sung-nyeon-eul yo-ha-ji an-neun

unstable *adj.* 불안정한 bul-an-jeong-han; 변하기 쉬운 byeon-ha-gi swi-un; 분해하기 쉬운 bun-hae-ha-gi swi-un; 침착하지 않은 chim-cha-ka-ji an-eun

unsuccessful *adj.* 성공하지 못한 seong-gong-ha-ji mo-tan; 불운의 bul-un-ui

untie *vt.* 풀다 pul-da; 끄르다 kkeu-reu-da; 자유롭게 하다 ja-yu-rop-ge ha-da

until *prep.* ...까지 ...kka-ji; ~ **further notice** 추후 통지가 있을 때까지 chu-hu tong-ji-ga iss-eul ttae-kka-ji; ~ **tomorrow** 내일까지 nae-il-kka-ji

untrue *adj.* 거짓의 geo-jis-ui; 불성실한 bul-sseong-sil-han; 부성확한 bu-jeong-hwa-kan

unwell *adj.* 기분이 좋지 않은 gi-bun-i jjo-chi an-eun; 찌뿌드드한 jji-ppu-deu-deu-han; 불쾌한 bul-kwae-han

unwrap *vt.* 포장을 풀다 po-jang-eul pul-da

up *adv.* 위쪽으로 wi jjog eu-ro, 위로 wi-ro, 보다 높은 데로 bo-da nop-eun de-ro, 몸을 일으켜서 mom-eul il-eu-kyeo-seo, 북으로 bug-eu-ro, 기세좋게 gi-se-jo-ke, 올라 ol-la; *prep.* ...의 위로 ...ui wi-ro, ...의 위에 ...ui wi-e; *adj.* 위로 가는 wi-ro ga-neun, 올라가는 ol-la-ga-neun; *n.* 상승 sang-seung, 향상 hyang-sang, 오르막길 o-reu-mak-gil; **The sun is** ~ 해가 떴습니다 hae-ga tteot-seum-ni-da; **The children are** ~ 아이들이 일어났습니다 a-i-deul-i il-eo-nat-seum-ni-da; **to give** ~ 포기하다 po-gi-ha-da; ~ **until now** 현재까

지 hyeon-jae-kka-ji; ~ **the stairs** 계단 위에 gye-dan wi-e

upkeep *n.* 유지 yu-ji; 유지비 yu-ji-bi; 수리비 su-ri-bi

upon *prep.* ...의 표면에 ...ui pyo-myeon-e, ...에 붙여서 ...e bu-cheo-seo, ...으로 ...eu-ro, ...에 접하여 ...e jeo-pa-yeo, ...에 입각해서 ...e ip-ga-kae-seo, ...의 도중에 ...ui do-jung-e, ...하자 곧 ...ha-ja got, ...에 대해서 ...e dae-hae-seo

upper *adj.* 위쪽의 wi-jjog-ui; 소리가 높은 so-ri-ga nop-eun; 상위의 sang-wi-ui; 상류의 sang-nyu-ui

uproar *n.* 소란 so-ran; 소음 so-eum

upset *n.* 전복 jeon-bok; 혼란 hol-lan; 당황 dang-hwang; 불화 bul-hwa; *vt.* 뒤집어 엎다 dwi-jib-eo eop-da; 망쳐버리다 mang-cheo-beo-ri-da; 타도하다 ta-do-ha-da; 당황케하다 dang-hwang-ke-ha-da

upsetting *adj.* 뒤집어 엎는 dwi-jib-eo eom-neun

upside down *adv.* 거꾸로 geo-kku-ro; 뒤집혀 dwi-ji-pyeo; 혼란되어 hol-lan-doe-eo; 엉망으로 eong-mang-eu-ro; *adj.* 거꾸로 된 geo-kku-ro deon; 뒤집힌 dwi-ji-pin; 혼란된 hol-lan-doen; 엉망이 된 eong-mang-i doen

upstairs *adj.* 2층의 i-cheung-ui; 위층의 wi-cheung-ui; *adv.* 2층에 i-cheung-e; 높은 지 위에 nop-eun jji-wi-e; 고공에 go-gong-e

upstream *adj.* 상류로 향하는 sang-nyu-ro hyang-ha-neun; 흐름에 거슬러 올라가는 heu-reum-e geo-seul-leo ol-la-ga-neun; 상류에 있는 sang-nyu-e in-neun; *adv.* 상류로 sang-nyu-ro; 흐름에 거슬러 올라가 heu-reum-e geo-seul-leo ol-la-ga

up-to-date *adj.* 최신의 choe-sin-ui; 최근의 choe-geun-ui; 현대적인 hyeon-dae-jeog-in; 첨단적인 cheom-dan-jeog-in; 현재까지의 hyeon-jae-kka-ji-ui

upward *adv.* 위를 향한 wi-reul hyang-han; 상승하는 sang-seung-ha-neun

urban *adj.* 도시의 do-si-ui; 도회지에 사는 do-hoe-ji-e sa-neun; 도시풍의 do-si-pung-ui; 도시에 있는 do-si-e in-neun

urge *n.* 충동 chung-dong; 강한 자극 gang-han ja-geuk; 몰리는 느낌 mol-li-neun neu-kkim; *vt.* 재촉하다 jae-cho-ka-da; 격

려하다 gyeong-nyeo-ha-da; 몰아대다 mol-a-da-da; 주장하다 ju-jang-ha-da

urgency *n.* 긴급 gin-geup; 절박 jeol-bak; 긴급한 일 gin-geu-pan il; 집요 jib-yo

urgent *adj.* 긴급한 gin-geu-pan; 재촉하는 jae-cho-ka-neun

urinary *adj.* 오줌의 o-jum-ui; 비뇨기의 bi-nyo-gi-ui

urinate *v.* 소변을 보다 so-byeon-eul bo-da

urine *n.* 소변 so-byeon, 오줌 o-jum

urn *n.* 항아리 hang-a-ri; 납골단지 nap-gol-dan-ji; 묘 myo; 커피 주전자 keo-pi ju-jeon-ja

urologist *n.* 비뇨기과 의사 bi-nyo-gi-kkwa ui-sa; 비뇨기과 학자 bi-nyo-gi-kkwa hak-ja

us *pron.* 우리들을 u-ri-deul-ui; 우리들에게 u-ri-deul-e-ge

usage *n.* 용법 yong-ppeop; 관습 gwan-seup; 대우 dae-u; 취급법 chwi-geup-beop

use *n.* 사용 sa-yong; 용도 yong-do; 쓸모 sseul-mo; 습관 seup-gwan; *vt.* 쓰다 sseu-da, 사용하다 sa-yong-ha-da; 대우하다 dae-u-ha-da; 이용하다 i-yong-ha-da; **It's of no ~ (to us)** 그건 우리한테 쓸모가 없습니다 geu-geon u-ri-han-te sseul-mo-ga eop-seum-ni-da; **I ~ it everyday** 저는 그걸 매일 사용합니다 jeo-neun geu-geol mae-il sa-yong-ham-ni-da; **~d to** ...곤 하다 ...gon ha-da; **to ~ up** 다 써버리다 da sseo-beo-ri-da

used *adj.* ...에 익숙한 ...e ik-su-kan; ...곤 하다 ...gon ha-da; **to be ~ to** ...에 익숙해져 있다 ...e ik-su-kae-jyeo-it-da; **He is ~ to air-conditioning** 그분은 에어컨 사용에 익숙해져 있습니다 geu-bun-eun e-eo-kon sa-yong-e ik-su-kae-jyeo it-seum-ni-da

useful *adj.* 쓸모있는 sseul-mo-in-neun; 유익한 yu-i-kan; 편리한 pyeol-li-han

useless *adj.* 쓸모없는 sseul-mo-eom-neun, 쓸데없는 sseul-tte-eom-neun; 무익한 mu-i-kan

user *n.* 사용자 sa-yong-ja; 수요자 su-yo-ja

usher *n.* 안내인 an-nae-in; 수위 su-wi

usual *adj.* 보통의 bo-tong-ui; 평소의 pyeong-so-ui; 평범한 pyeong-beom-han

usually *adv.* 보통 bo-tong

utensil *n.* 기구 gi-gu; 도구 do-gu; **kitchen ~s** 부엌용품 bu-eong-nyong-pum

uterus *n.* 자궁 ja-gung
utility *n.* 유용 yu-yong; 실용 sil-yong; 실
  용품 sil-yong-pum; 전기 수도 가스사업
  jeon-gi su-do kka-sseu-sa-eop; 전기 수도
  가스사업 설비 jeon-gi su-do kka-sseu-sa-
  eop seol-bi; **electric ~** 전기설비 jeon-gi
  seol-bi; **~ room** 보일러실 bo-il-leo-sil
utilize *vt.* 활용하다 hwal-yong-ha-da; 쓰다
  sseu-da

utmost *adj.* 최대한의 choe-dae-han-ui; 극단
  의 geuk-dan-ui; 극도의 geuk-do-ui; 맨 끝
  의 maen kkeut-ui
utter *adj.* 전적인 jeon-jjeog-in; 완전한
  wan-jeon-han; 무조건의 mu-jo-kkeon-ui;
  절대적인 jeol-ttae-jeog-in; *vt.* 소리를 내
  다 so-ri-reul nae-da; 말을 하다 mal-eul
  ha-da; 공표하다 gong-pyo-ha-da; 유통시
  키다 yu-tong-si-ki-da

V

vacancy *n.* 공허 gong-heo; 틈 teum; 공석
  gong-seok; 빈방 bin-bang; 공터 gong-teo;
  방심 bang-sim
vacant *adj.* 공허한 gong-heo-han; 비어있
  는 bi-eo-in-neun; 공석중인 gong-seok-
  jung-in; 한가한 han ga han; 멍청한
  meong-cheong-han
vacation *n.* 휴가 hyu-ga; 방학 bang-hak; 휴
  일 hyu-il; 사직 sa-jik
vaccinate *vt.* 예방접종을 하다 ye-bang-
  jeop-jong-eul ha-da
vaccination *n.* 예방접종 ye-bang-jeop-jong
vaccine *n.* 백신 baek-sin
vacuum *n.* 진공 jin-gong; 공백 gong-baek;
  공허 gong-heo; **~ cleaner** 진공청소기 jin-
  gong-cheong-so-gi, 청소기 cheong-so-gi
vacuum *vt.* 청소기로 청소하다 cheong-
  so-gi-ro cheong-so-ha-da; 청소하다
  cheong-so-ha-da
vague *adj.* 어렴풋한 eo-ryeom-pu-tan; 애
  매한 ae-mae-han; 분명치 않은 bun-
  myeong-chi an-eun; 흐릿한 heu ri tan; 모
  호한 mo-ho-han; 넋나간 neong-na-gan
vain *adj.* 쓸데없는 sseul-tte-eom-neun;
  하찮은 ha-chan-eun; 허영심이 강한
  heo-yeong-sim-i gang-han; **in ~** 헛되이
  heot-doe-i, 쓸데없이 sseul-tte-eops-i
valet *n.* 시종 si-jong, 도우미 do-u-mi
valiant *adj.* 용감한 yong-gam-han; 영웅적
  인 yeong-ung-jeog-in
valid *adj.* 정당한 jeong-dang-han; 유효한
  yu-hyo-han; 타당한 ta-dang-han
validity *n.* 정당성 jeong-dang-sseong; 타당
  성 ta-dang-sseong; 유효성 yu-hyo-seong;
  효력 hyo-ryeok

valley *n.* 골짜기 gol-jja-gi, 계곡 gye-gok
valuable *n.* 귀중품 gwi-jung-pum; *adj.* 귀중
  한 gwi-jung-han; 값비싼 gap-bi-ssan; 가치
  있는 ga-chi-in-neun
value *n.* 가치 ga-chi; 가격 ga-gyeok; 평가
  pyeong-kka; 가치기준 ga-chi-gi-jun; *vt.*
  평가하다 pyeong-kka-ha-da; 존중하다
  jon-jung-ha-da
valve *n.* 밸브 bael-beu; 막이판 mag-i-pan;
  판막 pan-mak; 진공관 jin-gong-gwan
van *n.* 밴 baen, 봉고차 bong-go-cha
vanilla *n.* 바닐라 ba-nil-la
vanish *vi.* 사라지다 sa-ra-ji-da, 없어지다
  eops-eo-ji-da; 희미해지다 hi-mi-hae-ji-da
vapor *n.* 증기 jeung-gi, 수증기 su-jeung-gi;
  공상 gong-sang
variable *n.* 변하는 것 byeon-ha-neun geot;
  변하기 쉬운 것 byeon-ha-gi swi-un geot;
  변수 byeon-su; *adj.* 변하기 쉬운 byeon-
  ha-gi swi-un; 일정치 않은 il-jjeong-chi
  an-eun; 변경될 수 있는 byeon-gyeong-hal
  ssu in-neun
variation *n.* 변화 byeon-hwa; 변화량 byeon-
  hwa-ryang; 변형물 byeon-hyeong-mul; 변
  주곡 byeon-ju-gok; 변종 byeon-jong; 편
  차 pyeon-cha
variety *n.* 변화 byeon-hwa; 불일치 bul-il-chi;
  가지각색의 것 ga-ji-gak-saeg-ui kkeot; 종
  류 jong-nyu; 다양성 da-yang-sseong
various *adj.* 여러가지의 yeo-reo-ga-ji-ui, 다
  양한 da-yang-han; 변화가 많은 byeon-
  hwa-ga man-eun; 각 개인의 gak gae-in-ui;
  몇사람 myeot-sa-ram, 몇 개 myeot-gae
varnish *n.* 니스 ni-sseu, 광택제 gwang-taek-
  je; 겉치레 geot-chi-re; 눈가림 nun-ga-rim;

vt. 니스를 칠하다 ni-sseu-reul chil-ha-da; 광을 내다 gwang-eul nae-da

vary *vt.* 변화를 주다 byeon-hwa-reul ju-da; 변경하다 byeon-gyeong-ha-da; *vi.* 변화하다 byeon-hwa-ha-da; 서로 다르다 seo-ro da-reu-da; 벗어나다 beos-eo-na-da; 변이하다 byeon-i-ha-da

vase *n.* 꽃병 kkot-byeong; 항아리 hang-a-ri, 단지 dan-ji

Vaseline *n.* 바셀린 ba-sel-lin; *(brand name)* 바셀린로션 ba-sel-lin ro-syeon

Vatican *n.* 바티칸 ba-ti-kan

vault *n.* 둥근 천장 dung-geun cheon-jang; 지하 납골당 ji-ha nap-gonl-ttang; 지하 감옥 ji-ha-gam-ok; *(bank)* 은행 금고실 eun-haeng geum-go-sil; *(funeral)* 납골당 nap-gol-ttang

VCR *n. abbr.* **videocassette recorder** 비디오 bi-di-o

veal *n.* 송아지 고기 song-a-ji go-gi

vegetable *n.* 야채 ya-chae, 채소 chae-so; 식물 sing-mul; 활기가 없는 사람 hwal-gi-ga eom-neun sa-ram; 식물인간 sing-mul-in-gan

vegetarian *n.* 채식주의자 chae-sik-ju-i-ja; *adj.* 채식주의자의 chae-sik-ju-i-ja-ui; 야채만의 ya-chae-man-ui

vegetation *n.* 식물 sing-mul; 한 지방 특유의 식물 han ji-bang teug-yu-ui sing-mul; 식물의 생장 sing-mul-ui saeng-jang; 무위도식 생활 mu-wi-do-sik saeng-hwal

vehement *adj.* 격렬한 gyeong-nyeol-han; 열심인 yeol-ssim-in, 열성적인 yeol-sseong-jeog-in

vehicle *n.* 차량 cha-ryang; 매개물 mae-gae-mul; 전달수단 jeon-dal-su-dan

veil *n.* 베일 be-il; 면사포 myeon-sa-po; 덮개 deop-gae; 핑계 ping-gye

vein *n.* 정맥 jeong-maek; 혈관 hyeol-gwan; 엽맥 yeom-maek; 광맥 gwang-maek; 기질 gi-jil; 기분 gi-bun

Velcro *n.* 벨크로 bel-keu-ro, *(trademark)* 찍찍이 jjik-jjig-i

velvet *n.* 벨벳 bel-bet, 우단 u-dan

venerate *vt.* 존경하다 jon-gyeong-ha-da, 공경하다 gong-gyeong-ha-da

venereal *adj.* 성교의 seong-gyo-ui; 성교에서 오는 seong-gyo-e-seo o-neun; 성병에 걸린 seong-ppyeong-e geol-lin; 성병치료의 seong-ppyeong-chi-ryo-ui; ~ **disease** 성병 seong-ppyeon

Venezuela *n.* 베네수엘라 be-ne-su-el-la

vengeance *n.* 복수 bok-su, 앙갚음 ang-ga-peum

venom *n.* 독 dok; 독물 dong-mul; 악의 ag-ui; 독설 dok-seol; 비방 bi-bang

vent *n.* 구멍 gu-mong; 공기구멍 gong-gi-kku-meong; 배출구 bae-chul-gu; *vt.* ...에 구멍을 내다 ...e gu-meong-eul nae-da; 구멍에서 빼내다 gu-meong-e-seo ppae-nae-da; 배출구를 터주다 bae-chul-gu-reul teo-ju-da; 터뜨리다 teo-tteu-ri-da

ventilate *vt.* 환기하다 hwan-gi-ha-da; 공기를 정화하다 gong-gi-reul jeong-hwa-ha-da; 통풍설비를 하다 tong-pung-seol-bi-reul ha-da; 자유롭게 토의하다 ja-yu-rop-ge to-ui-ha-da

ventilation *n.* 통풍 tong-pung; 환기 hwan-gi; 통풍장치 tong-pung-jang-chi; 논의 non-ui

ventilator *n.* 통풍기 tong-pung-gi; 통풍구멍 tong-pung-gu-meong, 환기창 hwan-gi-chang

ventricle *n.* 뇌실 noe-sil; 심실 sim-sil; **left** ~ 좌심실 jwa sim-sil; **right** ~ 우심실 u-sim-sil

venture *n.* 모험 mo-heom; 모험적 사업 mo-heom-jeok sa-eop; 투기 tu-gi; 투기 대상물 to-gi dae-sang mul; **joint** ~ 합작투자 hap-jak-tu-ja, 합작기업 hap-jak-gi-eop, 합작시공 hap-jak-si-gong

verb *n.* 동사 dong-sa

verbal *adj.* 말의 mal-ui; 말뿐인 mal-ppun-in; 축어적인 chug-eo-jeog-in; 동사의 dong-sa-ui

verdict *n.* 평결 pyeong-gyeool; 답신 dap-sin; 판단 pan-dan; 결정 gyeol-jjeong

verge *n.* 가장자리 ga-jang-ja-ri; 모서리 mo-seo-ri; 경계 gyeong-gye; 한계 han-gye; 권장 won-jang; **on the** ~ **of** ... 가 되려고 하여 ... ga doe-ryeo-go ha-yeo, ...이 되려고 하여 ...i doe-ryeo-go ha-yeo; ...에 직면하여 ...e jing-myeon-ha-yeo

verification *n.* 확인 hwag-in-ha-da; 입증 ip-jeung; 증명 jeung-myeong

verify *vt.* 입증하다 ip-jeung-ha-da; 확
인하다 hwag-in-ha-da; 증명하다
jeung-myeong-ha-da

versatile *adj.* 재주가 많은 jae-ju-ga man-
eun; 변하기 쉬운 byeon-ha-gi swi-un; 용
도가 다양한 yong-do-ga da-yang-han; 자
유로 방향이 바뀌는 ja-yu-ro bang-hyang-
i ba-kkwi-neun

verse *n.* 시 si; 시구 si-kku; 절 jeol

version *n.* 번역 beon-yeok; 번역문; beon-
yeong-mun 변형 byeon-hyeong; 판 pan;
해석 hae-seok

versus *prep.* ...대 ...dae; ...와 대비하여
...wa dae-bi-ha-yeo; **nature ~ nurture** 유
전 대 환경 yu-jeon dae hwan-gyeong

vertebra *n.* 척추골 cheok-chu-gol, 추
골 chu gol; *(pl.)* 척추 cheok-chu, 등뼈
deung-ppyeo

vertical *adj.* 수직의 su-jig-ui, 세로의 se-ro-
ui; 꼭대기의 kkok-dae-gi-ui; 세로로 연결
한 se-ro-ro yeon-gyeol-han

very *adv.* 아주 a ju, 무척 mu-cheok, 대단히
dae-dan-hi

vessel *n.* *(container)* 용기 yong-gi, 그릇 geu-
reut; *(ship)* 배 bae; 비행선 bi-haeng-seon;
(blood) 혈관 hyeol-gwan; 관 gwan

vest *n.* *(garment)* 조끼 jo-kki

veteran *n.* 고참병 go-cham-byeong; 퇴역군
인 toe-yeok-gun-in; 노련가 no-ryeon-ga,
베테랑 be-te-rang; *adj.* 전투경력을 쌓은
jeon-tu-gyeong-nyeog-eul ssa-eun; 노련한
no-ryeon-han; 특유한 teug-yu-ui

veterinarian *n.* 수의사 su-ui-sa

veterinary *adj.* 가축병 치료의 ga-chuk-
byeong chi-ryo-ui, 수의의 su-i-ui

VHF *n. abbr.* **very high frequency** 브이에이
치에프 beu-i-e-i-chi-e-peu

via *prep.* ...경유로 ...gyeong-yu-ro, ...을
거쳐 ...eul geo-cheo; ...에 의하여 ...e
ui ha yeo, ...을 통해 ...eul tong-hae; **to
go from London to Washington ~ New
York** 런던에서 뉴욕을 경유하여 워싱
턴으로 가다 reon-deon-e-seo nyu-yog-eul
gyeong-yu-ha-yeo wo-sing-teon-eu-ro
ga-da; **information sent ~ a computer
network** 컴퓨터망을 통해 보내는 정보
keom-pyu-teo-mang-eul tong-hae bo-nae-
neun jeong-bo

vial *n.* 유리병 yu-ri-byeong

vibrate *vi.* 진동하다 jin-dong-ha-da; 소리
가 울리다 so-ri-ga ul-li-da; 감동하다 gam-
dong-ha-da; 혼미해지다 hon-mi-hae-ji-da

vibration *n.* 진동 jin-dong; 동요 dong-yo; 전
율 jeon-nyul; 불안 bul-an

vice *n.* 악덕 ak-deok; 부도덕 bu-do-deok; 악
습 ak-seup; 결함 gyeol-ham; 병 byeong;
나쁜 버릇 na-ppeun beo-reut; 부회장
bu-hoe-jang; 부총장 bu-chong-jang; 대리
자 dae-ri-ja

vice president *n.* 부회장 bu-hoe-jang; 부사
장 bu-sa-jang; 무총상 bu-chong-jang; 부
통령 bu-tong-nyeong

vicinity *n.* 근접 geun-jeop; 부근 bu-geun

vicious *adj.* 사악한 sa-a-kan; 악의있는 aq-
i-in-neun; 심술궂은 sim-sul-guj-eun; 버릇
나쁜 beo-reun-na-ppeun; 나쁜 na-ppeun,
옳지않은 ol-chi-an-eun; 타락시키는
ta-rak-si-ki-neun; 심한 sim-han

victim *n.* 희생자 hi-saeng-ja; 피해자 pi-hae-ja

victory *n.* 승리 seung-ni; 정복 jeong-bok; 극
복 geuk-bok

video *n.* 비디오 bi-di-o; **~ game** 비디오 게임
bi-di-o kke-im

videocassette *n.* 비디오 카세트 bi-di-o
ka-se-teu

videotape *n.* 비디오 테이프 bi-di-o te-i-peu;
~ recorder 비디오 bi-di-o, 브이씨알
beu-i-ssi-al

Vienna *n.* 비엔나 bi-en-na

Vietnam *n.* 베트남 be-teu-nam

view *n.* 전망 jeon-mang; 시야 si-ya; 경치
gyeong-chi; 시력 si-ryeok; 일견 il-gyeon;
관찰 gwan-chal; 견해 gyeon-hae; 의도
ui-do; 개관 gae-gwan; *vt.* 바라보다 ba-
ra-bo-da; 조사하다 jo-sa-ha-da; 간주하다
gan-ju-ha-da; 시청하다 si-cheong-ha-da

viewfinder *n.* 파인더 pa-in-deo

vigor *n.* 활기 hwal-gi; 정력 jeong-nyeok; 생
기 saeng-gi; 강도 gang-do; 구속력 gu-
song-nyeok; 유효성 yu-hyo-sseong

villa *n.* 별장 byeol-jjang; 별장식 주택 byeol-
jjang-sik ju-taek

village *n.* 마을 ma-eul; 마을사람
ma-eul-ssa-ram

vine *n.* 덩굴 deong-gul; 포도나무
po-do-na-mu

vinegar *n.* 식초 sik-cho; 찡그린 얼굴 jjing-geu-rin eol-gul

vineyard *n.* 포도원 po-do-won, 포도밭 po-do-bat

vintage *n.* 포도 수확기 po-do su-hwak-gi; 포도 수확량 po-do su-hwang-nyang; 제조연도 je-jo-nyeon-do; 수명 su-myeong

violate *vt.* 어기다 eo-gi-da; 모독하다 mo-do-ka-da; 방해하다 bang-hae-ha-da; 폭행을 가하다 po-kaeng-eul ga-ha-da

violation *n.* 위반 wi-ban; 방해 bang-hae; 모독 mo-dok; 폭행 po-kaeng; 강간 gang-gan; **traffic** ~ 교통위반 gyo-tong-wi-ban

violence *n.* 격렬 gyeong-nyeol; 폭력 pong-nyeok; 불경 bul-gyeong; 곡해 go-kae

violent *adj.* 격렬한 gyeong-nyeol-han; 극단적인 geuk-dan-jeog-in; 강력한 gang-nyeo-kan; 폭력적인 pong-nyeok-jeog-in; 폭력에 의한 pong-nyeog-e ui-han; 무리한 mu-ri-han

violet *n.* 제비꽃 je-bi-kkot; 보라빛 bo-ra-ppit; 신경질적인 사람 sin-gyeong-jil-jjeog-in sa-ram; 수줍어하는 사람 su-jub-eo-ha-neun sa-ram; *adj.* 보라색의 bo-ra-saeg-ui

violin *n.* 바이올린 ba-i-ol-lin

violoncello *n.* 첼로 chel-lo

viral *adj.* 바이러스의 ba-i-reo-sseu-ui, 바이러스성의 ba-i-reo-sseu-sseong-ui; ~ **infection** 바이러스 감염 ba-i-reo-sseu-gam-yeom

virgin *n.* 처녀 cheo-nyeo; 아가씨 a-ga-ssi; 성모 마리아 seong-mo ma-ri-a; 동정녀 dong-jeong-nyeo

virtual *adj.* 실질적인 sil-jjil-jeog-in, 사실상의 sa-sil-ssang-ui; 가상의 ga-sang-ui; 효과적인 hyo-kkwa-jeog-in; ~**ly** 사실상 sa-sil-ssang, 실질적으로 sil-jjil-jeog-eu-ro

virtue *n.* 미덕 mi-deok; 정조 jeong-jo; 장점 jang-jjeom; 효력 hyo-ryeok

virus *n.* 바이러스 ba-i-reo-sseu; 병균 byeong-gyun; 해독 hae-dok

visa *n.* 비자 bi-ja

visibility *n.* 가시도 ga-si-do; 시계 si-gye; 볼 수 있음 bol-ssu iss-eum; 알아볼수 있음 al-a-bol-ssu iss-eum

visible *adj.* 보이는 bo-i-neun; 명백한 myeong-bae-kan; 뚜렷한 ttu-ryeo-tan; 면회할 수 있는 myeon-hoe-hal ssu in-neun; 현존의 hyeon-jon-ui

vision *n.* 시력 si-ryeok; 상상력 sang-sang-nyeok; 상상도 sang-sang-do; 환상 hwan-sang; 일견 il-gyeon

visit *n.* 방문 bang-mun; 구경 gu-gyeong; 시찰 si-chal; 왕진 wang-jin; 잡담 jap-dam; *vt.* 방문하다 bang-mun-ha-da; 시찰하다 si-chal-ha-da; 왕진하다 wang-jin-ha-da; 엄습하다 eom-seu-pa-da; 생각이 떠오르다 saeng-gag-i tteo-o-reu-da

visitor *n.* 손님 son-nim; 관광객 gwan-gwang-gaek

visor *n.* 챙 chaeng; 복면 bong-myeon; 마스크 ma-seu-keu; 차양 cha-yang; 변장 byeon-jang; **sun** ~ 챙 chaeng; 차양 cha-yang; 해가리개 hae-ga-ri-gae

visual *adj.* 시각의 si-gag-ui; 눈에 보이는 nun-e bo-i-neun; 보기 위한 bo-gi wi-han

vital *adj.* *(life related)* 생명의 saeng-myeong-ui; *(lively, fresh)* 생생한 saeng-saeng-han; *(fatal, mortal)* 치명적인 chi-myeong-jeog-in; *(necessary)* 절대로 필요한 jeol-ttae-ro pil-yo-han; ~ **signs** 살아있는 증거 sal-a-in-neun jeung-geo

vitality *n.* 생명력 saeng-myeong-nyeok; 활기 hwal-gi; 지속력 ji-song-nyeok

vitamin *n.* 비타민 bi-ta-min; ~ **C** 비타민 씨 bi-ta-min-ssi

vivid *adj.* 생생한 saeng-saeng-han; 선명한 seon-myeong-han; 명확한 myeong-hwa-kan

vocabulary *n.* 어휘 eo-hwi; 단어집 dan-eo-jip; 표현형식 pyo-hyeon-nyang-sik

vocal *adj.* 목소리의 mok-so-ri-ui; 잔소리가 심한 jan-so-riga sim-han

voice *n.* 목소리 mok-so-ri; 발언 bal-eon; 의견 ui-gyeon; 발언권 bal-eon-kkwon; *vt.* 말로 나타내다 mal-lo na-ta-nae-da; 조율하다 jo-yul-ha-da

voice mail *n.* 음성녹음 eum-seong-nog-eum, 보이스메일 bo-i-sseu-me-il

void *adj.* 빈 bin; 공석인 gong-seog-in; 없는 eom-neun; 무효의 mu-hyo-ui; 무익한 mu-i-kan

volcano *n.* 화산 hwa-san

volt *n.* 볼트 bol-teu; 회전 hoe-jeon

voltage *n.* 전압 jeon-ap; 전압량 jeon-am-nyang, 볼트수 bol-teu-ssu

volume *n.* *(book)* 책 chaek; 권 gwon; 용적 yong-jeok; *(bulk, mass)* 양 yang; 대량 dae-ryang; 음량 eum-nyang; 볼륨 bol-lyum; 거래량 geo-rae-ryang

voluntary *adj.* 자발적인 ja-bal-jjeog-in; 기부로 경영되는 gi-bu-ro gyeong-yeong-doe-neun; 자유의지를 가진 ja-yu-ui-ji-reul ga-jin; 고의적인 go-ui-jeog-in

volunteer *n.* 지원자 ji-won-ja; 독지가 dok-ji-ga

vomit *vi.* 토하다 to-ha-da; 분출하다 bun-chul-ha-da

vote *n.* 투표 tu-pyo; 지지 ji-ji; 투표권 tu-pyo-kkwon; 결의사항 gyeol-ui-sa-hang; *vi.* 투표하다 tu-pyo-ha-da; 제안하다 je-an-ha-da

voter *n.* 투표자 tu-pyo-ja; 유권자 yu-kkwon-ja

voucher *n.* 보증인 bo-jeung-in; 증거물 jeung-geo-mul; 증서 jeung-seo

vow *n.* 맹세 maeng-se; 서원 seo-won; *vt.* 맹세하다 maeng-se-ha-da; 서원하다 seo-won-ha-da

vowel *n.* 모음 mo-eum

voyage *n.* 항해 hang-hae; 우주여행 u-ju-yeo-haeng; 항해기 hang-hae-gi; *vi.* 항해하다 hang-hae-ha-da; 우수녀행을 하다 u-ju-yeo-haeng-eul ha-da

vulgar *adj.* 저속한 jeo-so-kan; 통속적인 tong-sok-jeog-in; 대중적인 dae-jung-jjeog-in

W

wad *n.* 속뭉치 som-mung-chi; 패킹 pae-king

wade *vi.* 걸어서 건너다 geol-eo-seo geon-neo-da; 힘들여 걸어가다 him-deul-yeo geol-eo-ga-da; 힘차게 달려들다 him-cha-ge dal-lyeo-ga-da

wag *vt.* 흔들어 움직이다 him-deul-yeo un-jig-i-da; *vi.* 흔들리다 heun-deul-li-da; 계속 움직이다 gye-seok um-jig-i-da; 비틀비틀 걷다 bi-teul-bi-teul geot-da

wages *n.* 임금 im-geum, 급료 geum-nyo

wagon *n.* 수레 su-re; 짐차 jim-cha; 포장마차 po-jang-ma-cha

waist *n.* 허리 heo-ri; 동체 중앙부 dong-che jung-ang-bu

wait *n.* 기다리기 gi-da-ri-gi; 기다리는 시간 gi-da-ri-neun si-gan; *vi.* 기다리다 gi-da-ri-da; 준비되어 있다 jun-bi-doe-eo it-da; 잠시 미루다 jam-si mi-ru-da; 시중을 들다 si-jung-eul deul-da; **to ~ on (sb.)** (누구를) 시중들다 (nu-geu-reul) si-jung-deul-da; 방문하다 bang-mun-ha-da

waiter *n.* 웨이터 we-i-teo

waiting room *n.* 대기실 dae-gi-sil; 대합실 dae-hap-sil

waitress *n.* 웨이트레스 we-i-teu-re-sseu

waiver *n.* 포기 bo-gi; 기권 gi-kkwon; 면제 myeon-je

wake *n.* 지나간 자국 ji-na-gan ja-guk; *(before a funeral)* 철야제 cheol-ya-je, 밤샘 bam-saem; *vt.* 깨우다 kkae-u-da; 눈뜨게 하다 nun-tteu-ge ha-da; *vi.* *(to wake up)* 일어나다 il-eo-na-da; 깨어있다 kkae-eo-it-da; 눈뜨다 nun-tteu-da; 되살아나다 doe-sal-a-na-da

Wales *n.* 웨일즈 we-il-jeu

walk *n.* 산책 san-chaek; 걸음걸이 geol-eum-geol-i; 보행거리 bo-haeng-geo-ri; 보도 bo-do; *vt.* 걸어가다 geol-eo-ga-da; 동행하다 dong-haeng-ha-da; 걷게하다 geot-ge-ha-da; 데리고 가다 de-ri-go ga-da; *vi.* 걸어가다 geol-eo-ga-da; *(to take a walk)* 산책하다 san-chae-ka-da; **I'm going to ~ the dog** 저는 개를 데리고 좀 걷겠습니다 jeo-neun gae-reul de-ri-go jom geot-get-seum-ni-da; **a pleasant ~** 기분좋은 산책 gi-bun-jo-eun san-chaek

walker *n.* *(pedestrian)* 보행자 bo-haeng-ja; *(walking aid)* 보행기 bo-haeng-gi

wall *n.* 벽 byeok; 담 dam; 장애 jang-ae; 성벽 seong-byeok

wallet *n.* 지갑 ji-gak

walnut *n.* 호두 ho-du; 호두색 ho-du-saek

wand *n.* 막대기 mak-dae-gi; 마술지팡이 ma-sul-ji-pang-i; 지휘봉 ji-hwi-bong

wander *vi.* 돌아다니다 dol-a-da-ni-da; 빗나가다 bin-na-ga-da; 오락가락하다 o-rak-g-ra-ka-da

want *n.* 결핍 gyeol-pip; 필요 pil-yo; 가난 ga-nan; 욕망 yong-mang; *vt.* 탐내다 tam-nae-da; …고 싶다 …go sip-da; 필요로 하다 pil-yo-ro ha-da; … 이 없다 … I eop-da, … 가 없다 … ga eop-da

war *n.* 전쟁 jeon-jaeng, 싸움 ssa-um; 불화 bul-hwa; 적의 jeog-i

wardrobe *n.* 옷장 ot-jang; 의류 ui-ryu

ware *n.* 상품 sang-pum; 용품 yong-pum

warehouse *n.* 창고 chang-go; 도매상점 do-mae-sang-jeom

warm *adj.* 따뜻한 tta-tteu-tan; 화끈거리는 hwa-kkeun-geo-ri-neun; 다정한 da-jeong-han; 열렬한 yeol-lyeol-han; 활발한 hwal-bal-han

warmth *n.* 따뜻함 tta-tteu-tam; 온정 on-jeong; 흥분 heung-bun

warn *vt.* 경고하다 gyeong-go; 훈계하다 hun-gye-ha-da; 알리다 al-li-da

warning *n.* 경고 gyeong-go; 훈계 hun-gye; 예고 ye-go

warrant *n.* 근거 geun-geo; 권리 gwol-li; 보증 bo-jeung; 가망 ga-mang; 보증서 bo-jeung-seo; 영장 yeong-jjang; 허가증 heo-ga-jjeung

warranty *n.* 담보dam-bo; 보증서 bo-jeung-seo; 근거 geun-geo

Warsaw *n.* 바르샤바 ba-reu-sya-ba

wart *n.* 사마귀 sa-ma-gwi; 혹 hok

wary *adj.* 주의깊은 ju-i-gip-eun; 세심한 se-sim-han

wash *vt.* 씻다 ssit-da; 빨다 ppal-da; 적시다 jeok-si-da; 씻어내리다 ssis-eo-nae-ri-da

washable *adj.* 세탁할 수 있는 se-ta-kal ssu in-neun; 물로 씻어지는 mul-li ssis-eo-ji-neun

washer *n.* *(dish washer)* 식기 세척기 sik-gi se-cheok-gi; *(a machine part)* 워셔 wo-ssyeo; 세탁기 se-tak-gi

washing machine *n.* 세탁기 se-tak-gi

Washington, D.C. *(D.C. abbr. District of Columbia)* 워싱턴 디씨 wo-sing-teon di-ssi

wasp *n.* 말벌 mal-beol; 까다로운 사람 kka-da-ro-un sa-ram

waste *n.* 낭비 nang-bi; 쓰레기 sseu-re-gi; 황무지 hwang-mu-ji; 쇠퇴 soe-toe; *vt.* 낭비하다 nang-bi-ha-da; 기회를 놓치다 gi-hoe-reul no-chi-da; 황폐하게 하다 hwang-pye-ha-ge ha-da; 약화시키다 ya-kwa-si-ki-da

waste basket *n.* 휴지통 hyu-ji-tong

wasteful *adj.* 낭비하는 nang-bi-ha-neun; 헛된 heot-doen

watch *n.* 조심 jo-sim; *(timepiece)* 손목시계 son-mok-si-gye; 불침번 bul-chim-beon; *vt.* 지켜보다 ji-kyeo-bo-da; 망보다 mang-bo-da; 돌보다 dol-bo-da; 기회를 엿보다 gi-hoe-reul yeot-bo-da; *vi.* 대기하다 dae-gi-ha-da; 불침번을 서다 bul-chim-beon-eul seo-da; **to ~ out** 조심하세요 jo-sim-ha-se-yo

watchband *n.* 손목시계줄 son-mok-si-gye-jjul

watchful *adj.* 조심스러운 jo-sim-seu-reo-un; 경계하는 gyeong-gye-ha-neun

watchman *n.* 경비원 gyeong-bi-won; 야경 ya-gyeong

water *n.* 물 mul; 바다 ba-da; 수심 su-sim; 용액 yong-aek; *vt.* 물을 주다 mul-eul ju-da; 물을 타다 mul-eul ta-da; 물결무늬를 넣다 mul-kkyeol-mu-ni-reul neo-ta; **fresh ~** 신선한 물 sin-seon-han mul; 담수 dam-su; **running ~** 수도물 su-don-mul; **salt ~** 바닷물 ba-dan-mul; 짠물 jjan-mul

watercolor *n.* 그림물감 geu-rim-mul-kkam; 수채화 su-chae-hwa; *adj.* 수채화의 su-chae-hwa-ui

waterfall *n.* 폭포 pok-po

waterfront *n.* 부두 bu-du; 선창 seon-chang; 해안통 hae-an-tong

watermelon *n.* 수박 su-bak

waterproof *adj.* 방수의 bang-su-ui; 물이 새지 않는 mul-i sae-ji an-neun

water-ski *n.* 수상스키 su-sang-seu-ki; *vi.* 수상스키를 타다 su-sang-seu-ki-reul ta-da

watery *adj.* 물기가 많은 mul-kki-ga man-eun; 축축한 chuk-chu-kan; 눈물어린nun-mul-eo-rin; 묽은 mulg-eun; 약한 ya-kan

watt *n.* 와트 wa-teu

wattage *n.* 와트수 wa-teu-ssu; **What is the**
~ 와트수가 얼마입니까 wa-teu-ssu-ga
eol-ma-im-ni-kka

wave *n.* 파도 pa-do; 파동 pa-dong; 파 pa; 물
결모양 mul-kkyeol-mo-yang; *vt.* 흔들다
heun-deul-da; 휘두르다 hwi-du-reu-da; 물
결모양으로 하다 mul-kkyeol-mo-yang-
eu-ro ha-da

wavelength *n.* 파장 pa-jang

waver *vi.* 흔들리다 heun-deul-li-da; 망
설이다 mang-seol-i-da; 동요되다
dong-yo-doe-da

wax *n.* 왁스 wak-seu; 귀지 gwi-ji; *vt.* 왁스를
바르다 wak-seu-reul ba-reu-da; 왁스로 닦
다 wak-seu-ro dak-da; 결정적으로 이기다
gyeol-jjeong-jeog eu ro i gi da; **hair - ing**
탈모 tal-mo, 제모 je-mo

way *n.* 길 gil, 도로 do-ro; 방법 bang-beop;
진행 jin-haeng; 방향 bang-hyang; 습관
seup-gwan; 사항 sa-hang; **to be in the** ~
방해하다 bang-hae-ha-da; **by the** ~ 그런
데 geu-reon-de; **to get out of the** ~ 피하
다 pi-ha-da, 비키다 bi-ki-da; **in a** ~ 보기에
따라서는 bo-gi-e tta-ra-seo-neun; 어느 정
도 eo-neu jeong-do; **to lose one's** ~ 길을
잃다 gil-eul il-ta; **a one-~ street** 일방통행
로 il-bang-tong-haeng-no

wayward *adj.* 제멋대로 하는 je-
meot-dae-r ha-neun; 변덕스러운
byeon-deok-seu-reo-un

we *pron.* 우리가 u-ri-ga, 우리는 u-ri-neun;
(hum.) 저희가 jeo-hi-ga, 저희는 Jeo-hi-neun

weak *adj.* 약한 ya-kan; 열등한 yeol-tteung-
han; 묽은 mulg-eun; 서소한 jeo-jo-han

weaken *vt.* 약하게 하다 ya-ka-ge ha-da, 약
화시키다 ya-kwa-si-ki-da

weakness *n.* 약점 yak-jeom; 약함 ya-kam; 우
유부단 u-yu-bu-dam

wealth *n.* 부유 bu-yu; 재산 jae-san; 부자
bu-ja; 풍부 pung-bu

wealthy *adj.* 부유한 bu-yu-han; 넉넉한
neong-neo-kan; 풍부한 pung-bu-han

weapon *n.* 무기 mu-gi; 공격수단
gong-gyeok-su-dan

wear *vt.* 입다 ip-da; 신다 sin-tta; 쓰다
sseu-da; 몸에 지니다 mom-e ji-ni-da; 닳게
하다 dal-ke-ha-da; 지치게 하다 ji-chi-ge
ha-da; *vi.* 오래가다 o-rae-ga-da; 낡아서

해지다 nalg-a-seo hae-ji-da; **to ~ out** 해지
다 hae-ji-da; 해지게 하다 hae-ji-ge ha-da;
지치게 하다 ji-chi-ge ha-da

weary *adj.* 피로한 pi-ro-han; 싫증난 sil-
jjeung-nan; 지치게 하는 ji-chi-ge ha-neun

weather *n.* 날씨 nal-ssi, 기후 gi-hu; ~ **report**
기상통보 gi-sang-tong-bo; 일기예보
il-gi-ye-bo

weave *vt.* 짜다 jja-da, 뜨다 tteu-da; 엮다
yeok-da; 종합하다 jong-ha-pa-da; 구성하
다 gu-seong-ha-da

weaver *n.* 직공 jik-gong

web *n.* 직물 jing-mul; 거미집 geo-mi-jip; 물
갈퀴 mul-gal-kkwi

website *n.* 웹사이트 wep-ssa-i-teu

wedding *n.* 결혼식 gyeol-hon-sik; 융합
yung-hap; ~ **reception** 결혼식 피로연
gyeol-hon-sik pi-ro-yeon; ~ **ring** 결혼반지
gyeol-hon-ban-ji

wedge *n.* 쐐기 sswae-gi; V자형 beu-i-jja-
hyeong; 방해 bang-hae; **a ~ of cheese** 치
즈 한조각 ch-jeu han-jjo-gak

Wednesday *n.* 수요일 su-yo-il

weed *n.* 잡초 jap-cho; 담배 dam-bae; 호리
호리한 말 ho-ri-ho-ri-han mal; *vt.* 잡초
를 뽑다 jap-cho-reul ppop-da; 제거하다
je-geo-ha-da; **to ~ the garden** 정원의 잡
초 jeong-won-ui jap-cho

week *n.* 주 ju; 일주간 il-jju-gan; **per** ~ 일주
일에 il-jju-il-e, 주당 ju-dang

weekday *n.* 평일 pyeong-il

weekend *n.* 주말 ju-mal

weep *vi.* 울다 ul-da; 불방울을 떨어뜨리다
mul-ppang-ul-eul tteol-eo-tteu-ri-da; 가지
를 늘어뜨리다 ga-ji-reul neul-eo-tteu-ri-da

weigh *vt.* 무게를 달다 mu-ge reul dal-da;
체중을 달다 che-jung-eul dal-da; 신중
하게 고려하다 sin jung-ha-ge go-ryeo-
ha-da; 무게로 내리누르다 mu-ge-ro
nae-ri-nu-reu-da

weight *n.* 무게 mu-ge; 체중 che-jung; 부
담 bu-dam; 아령 a-ryeong; 중요함 jung-
yo-ham; **~s** *(for exercise; for weighing)*
아령 a-ryeong; **to gain** ~ 체중이 늘다
che-jung-i neul-da

weird *adj.* 수상한 su-sang-han; 섬뜩한
seom-tteu-kan; 이상한 i-sang-han

welcome *n.* 환영 hwan-yeong; 환영인사
hwan-yeong-in-sa; *vt.* 환영하다

hwan-yeong-ha-da; ~ **to** ...에 오
신걸 환영합니다 ...e o-sin-geol
hwan-yeong-ham-ni-da

weld *vt.* 용접하다 yong-jeo-pa-da; 접착
시키다 jeop-chak-si-ki-da; 결합시키다
gyeol-hap-si-ki-da

welding *n.* 용접 yong-jeop

welfare *n.* 복지 bok-ji; 복지사업
bok-ji-sa-eop

well *n.* 우물 u-mul; 샘 saem; 변호인석
byeon-ho-in-seok; *adj.* 건강한 geon-gang-
han; 좋은 jo-eun; 적당한 jeok-dang-han;
adv. 잘 jal; 능숙히 neung-su-ki; 충분히
chung-bun-hi; *interj.* 그런데 geu-reon-de;
어머 eo-meo; 이것 참 i-geot cham; **He
did it** ~ 그분은 그걸 잘 하셨습니다 geu
bun-eun geu-geol jal ha-syeot-seum-ni-da;
as ~ **as** ...뿐만 아니라 ...도 ...ppun-man
a-ni-ra ...do; **as** ~ 게다가 ge-da-ga; 또
한 tto-han; **I am** ~ 저는 잘 있습니다
jeo-neun jal it-seum-ni-da, 저는 건강합니
다 jeo-neun geon-gang-ham-ni-da; **~-to-do**
유복한 yu-bo-kan, 부유한 bu-yu-han, 잘
사는 jal-sa-neun; 부유층 bu-yu-cheung;
~, **let me see** 어디 좀 볼까요 eo-di jom
bol-kka-yo

west *n.* 서쪽 seo-jjok; 서부 seo-bu; 서양 seo-
yang; 서부지방 seo-bu-jji-bang; *adj.* 서쪽
의 seo-jjog-ui; 서양의 seo-yang-ui; *adv.* 서
쪽에 seo-jjog-e; 서쪽으로 seo-jjog-eu-ro;
in the ~ 서쪽에서 seo-jjog-e-seo; **a** ~
wind 서풍 seo-pung; **They went** ~ 그분들
은 서쪽으로 가셨습니다 geu-bun-deul-
eun seo-jjog-eu-ro ga-syeot-seum-ni-da

West Africa *n.* 서아프리카 seo-a-peu-ri-ka

western *adj.* 서쪽의 seo-jjog-ui; 서양의 seo-
yang-ui; 서부지방의 seo-bu-jji-bang-ui

West Indies *n.* 서인도제도 seo-in-do-je-do

wet *vt.* 축이다 chug-i-da; 술을 마시며 축
하하다 sul-eul ma-si-myeo chu-ka-ha-da;
adj. 축축한 chuk-chu-kan; 비내리는
bi-nae-ri-neun

whale *n.* 고래 go-rae; 거장 geo-jang

wharf *n.* 부두 bu-du, 선창 seon-chang

what *adj. pron.* ~ **color** 무슨 색깔 mu-seun
saek-kkal; ~ **time** 몇 시 myeot-si; ~ **a
mess** 뭘 이렇게 어질렀지 mwol i-reo-ke
eo-jil-leot-ji; ~ **is this** 이게 뭐지요 i-ge

mwo-ji-yo; **That is** ~ **they say** 그게 바로
그분들이 말하는 겁니다 geu-ge ba-ro
geu-bun-deul-i mal-ha-neun geom-ni-da

whatever *adv.* 어떠한 ...이라도 eo-tteo-han
...i-ra-do, 얼마간의 ...이라도 eol-ma-
gan-ui ...i-ra-do; 설사 ...이라도 seol-ssa
...i-ra-do; *pron.* ...하는 것은 무엇이든
...ha-neun geos-eun mu-eos-i-deun; 무
엇을 ...하든지 mu-eos-eul ...ha-deun-ji;
도대체 무엇을 do-de-che mu-eos-eul; ~
happens 무슨 일이 일어나든지 mu-seun
il-i il-eo-na-deun-ji

wheat *n.* 밀 mil

wheel *n.* 수레바퀴 su-re-ba-kwi; 핸들 haen-
deul; 자전거 ja-jeon-geo; 회전 hoe-jeon

wheelbarrow *n.* 외바퀴 손수레 oe-ba-kwi
son-su-re

wheeze *n.* 헐떡이는 소리 heol-tteog-i-neun
so-ri; 삽입대사 sab-ip-dae-sa; 맞장구 mat-
jang-gu; *vi.* 씨근거리다 ssi-geun-geo-ri-da

when *adv.* 언제 eon-je, ...하는 때 ...ha-neun
ttae, 그때에 geu-ttae-e; ~ **will you return**
언제 돌아오실 겁니까 eon-je dol-a-o-sil
geom-ni-kka; *conj.* ...할 때에 ...hal ttae-e,
...으면 ...eu-myeon, ...인데도 ...in-de-do;
~ **the flight arrives** 비행기가 도착할 때
bi-haeng-gi-ga do-cha-kal ttae

whenever *conj.* ...할때는 언제나 ...hal-ttae-
neun eon-je-na; 언제 ...하든지 eon-je
...ha-deun-ji; *adv.* 도대체 언제 do-de-che
eon-je

where *adv.* 어디에 eo-di-e, 어디로 eo-di-ro,
어디를 eo-di-reul, 어디에서 eo-di-e-seo,
...하는 ...ha-neun, 그리고 거기에서 geu-
ri-go geo-gi-e-seo, ...하는 곳 ...ha-neun
got; ~ **are you going** 어디 가십니까 eo-di
ga-sim-ni-kka; *conj.* ...하는 곳에 ...ha-
neun gos-e, ...하는 곳으로 ...ha-neun
gos-eu-ro, ...하는 곳을 ...ha-neun gos-eul,
...하는데 ...ha-neun-de; **stay** ~ **you
are** 지금 있는 곳에 계십시오 ji-geum
in-neun gos-e gye-sip-si-o

wherever *adv.* 대체 어디로 dae-che eo-di-ro,
대체 어디에서 dae-che eo-di-e-seo; *conj.*
어디든지 eo-di-deun-ji, 어디로든지
eo-di-ro-deun-ji

which *adj.* 어느 eo-neu, 어떤 eo-tteon, 어느
쪽의 eo-neu-jjog-ui; 어느 ...이든 eo-neu

...i-deun; *pron.* 어느쪽 eo-neu-jjok, 어
느것 eo-neu-geot; ...하는 것 ...ha-neun
geot, ...하는 일 ...ha-neun il; 그리고 그
것을 geu-ri-go geu-geos-eul

whichever *adj.* 어느 것의 ...이든지 eo-neu
geos-ui ...i-deun-ji, 어느 쪽이 ...이든지
eo-neu jjog-i ...i-deun-ji; *pron.* 어느 쪽이
든지 eo-neu jjog-i-deun-ji, 어느 쪽을 ...하
든지 eo-neu jjog-eul ...ha-deun-ji, 도대체
어느 것을 do-de-che eo-neu geos-eul

while *n.* 동안 dong-an, 잠깐 jam-kkan, 잠
시 jam-si; *conj.* ...하는 동안 ...ha-neun
dong-an, ...하지만 ...ha-ji-man; **It is
worth your ~** 그것은 해볼만한 가치가
있습니다 geu-geos-eun hae-bol-man-han
ga-chi-ga It-seum-ni-da; **stay a ~** 잠깐만
계십시오 jam-kkan-man gye-sip-si-o; **You
had a call ~ you were out** 외출하신 동안
전화가 왔습니다 oe-chul-ha-sin dong-an
jeon-hwa-ga wat-seum-ni-da

whip *vt.* 채찍질하다 chae-jjik-jil-ha-da; 격
려하다 gyeong-nyeo-ha-da; 강요하
다 gang-yo-ha-da; 휘저어 거품을 내다
hwi-jeo-eo geo-pum-eul nae-da; 잡아채다
jab-a-chae-da; 꿰매다 kkwe-mae-da; **~ped
cream** 생크림 saeng-keu-rim

whirl *vi.* 빙빙돌다 bing-bing-dol-da; 현기
증나다 hyeon-gi-jjeung-na-da; 질주하다
jil-jju-ha-da

whirlpool *n.* 소용돌이 so-yong-dol-i;
~ bath 와류욕 wa-ryu-yok, 와류욕조
wa ryu yok jo

whisk *n.* 솔 sol; 거품기 geo-pum-gi; 털어
냄 teol-eo-nam; *vt.* 털다 teol-da; 채가다
chae-ga-da; 휘젓다 hwi-jeot-da; 거품을
내다 geo-pum-eul nae-da

whisker *n.* 구레나루 gu-ren-na-ru; 수염
su-yeom

whiskey, whisky *n.* 위스키 wi-seu-ki

whisper *n.* 속삭임 sok-sag-im; 소문 so-mun;
기미 gi-mi; *vi.* 속삭이다 sok-sag-i-da; 밀
담을 하다 mil-ttam-eul ha-da; 살랑거리
다 sal-lang-geo-ri-da

whistle *n.* 휘파람 hwi-pa-ram; 호각 ho-gak;
경적 gyeong-jeok; *vi.* 휘파람을 불다
hwi-pa-ram-eul bul-da; 호각을 불다
ho-gag-eul bul-da

white *adj.* 흰색의 hin-saeg-ui; 무색의
mu-saeg-ui; 백인의 baeg-in-ui; 눈덮
인 nun-deop-in; 핏기를 잃은 pit-gi-reul
il-eun; 결백한 gyeol-bae-kan

whiten *vt.* 희게하다 hi-ge-ha-da; 표백하다
pyo-bae-ka-da

who *pron.* 누가 nu-ga; 누구를 nu-gu-reul

whoever *pron.* ...하는 누구든지 ...ha-neun
nu-gu-deun-ji; 누가 ...하더라도 nu-ga
...ha-deo-ra-do

whole *adj.* 전부의 jeon-bu-ui; ...중 내내
...jung nae-nae; 완전한 wan-jeon-han; 건
전한 geon-jeon-han; **~ grain** 통곡물 tong-
gong-mul; 정미하지 않은 곡물 jeong-mi-
ha-ji an-eun gong- mul; **~ milk** 전지우유
jeon-ji-u-yu, **~ wheat** 통밀 tong-mil

wholesale *adj.* 도매의 do-mae-ui; 대규모의
dae-gyu-mo-ui; 대강의 dae-gang-ui

wholesome *adj.* 건강에 좋은 geon-gang-e
jo-eun; 건전한 geon-jeon-han

whom *pron.* 누구를 nu-gu-reul; 누구에게
nu-gu-e-ge

whose *adj.* 누구의 nu-gu-ui

why *adv.* 왜 wae; **~ is it so** 그게 왜 그렇습
니까 geu-ge wae geu reot seum ni kka;
conj. ...한 이유 ...han i-yu; 왜 ...은지
wae ...eun-ji; **I know ~ they're late** 그분
들이 왜 늦었는지 제가 그 이유를 압니
다 geu-bun-deul-i wae neuj-eon-neun-ji
je-ga geu i-yu-reul am-ni-da

wick *n.* 양초심지 yang-cho-sim-ji

wicked *adj.* 사악한 sa-a-kan; 심술궂은
sim-sul-guj-eun; 성질이 거친 seong-jil-i
geo-chin; 싫은 sil-eun

wicker *n.* 버들가지 beo-deul-ga-ji; 고리버들
세공 go-ri-beo-deul-se-gong; **~ basket** 고
리버들 바구니 go-ri-beo-deul ba-gu-ni

wide *adj.* 넓은 neolb-eun; 폭넓은 pong-
neolb-eun; 광범위한 gwang-beom-wi-han;
헐렁한 heol-leong-han; 크게 열린 keu-ge
yeol-lin; 동떨어진 dong-tteol-eo-jin; 빈틈
없는 bin-teum-eom-neun

widen *vt.* 넓히다 neol-pi-da; 넓게되다
neol-kke-doe-da

widespread *adj.* 널리 보급된 neol-li bo-
geup-doen; 넓게 펼친 neol-kke pyeol-chin

widow *n.* 과부 gwa-bu, 미망인 mi-mang-in

widower *n.* 홀아비 hol-a-bi

width *n.* 폭 pok, 나비 na-bi, 넓이 neolb-i

wield *vt.* 휘두르다 hwi-du-reu-da; 지배하다 ji-bae-ha-da

wife *n.* 아내 a-nae, 집사람 jip-sa-ram, *(one's own)* 처 cheo; *(somebody else's)* 부인 bu-in

wig *n.* 가발 ga-bal; 머리장식 meo-ri-jang-sik

wild *adj.* 야생의 ya-saeng-ui; 야만의 ya-man-ui; 황량한 hwang-nyang-han; 거친 geo-chin; 사나운 sa-na-un; 열광적인 yeol-gwang-jeog-in; 난폭한 nan-po-kan; 엉터리같은 eong-teo-ri-gat-eun

wilderness *n.* 황야 hwang-ya; 황폐한 곳 hwang-pye-han got

wildlife *n.* 야생생물 ya-saeng-dong-mul

will *n.* 의지 ui-ji; 의도 ui-do; 결의 gyeol-ui; 태도 tae-do; 유언 yu-eon; *vi.* 바라다 ba-ra-da; **free ~** 자유의지 ja-yu-ui-ji; **~ and testament** 유언과 유언장 yu-eon-gwa yu-eon-jjang; *aux.* ...할 것이다 ...hal geos-i-da, ...할 작정이다 ...hal jak-jeong-i-da, ...하기를 원하다 ...ha-gi-reul won-ha-da, ...하는 법이다 ...ha-neun beob-i-da, ...일 것이다 ...il geos-i-da, 곧 잘 ...하다 got-jal ...ha-da; **We ~ accept it** 저희가 그걸 받아들이겠습니다 jeo-hi-ga geu-geol bad-a-deul-i-get-seum-ni-da

willing *adj.* 기꺼이 ...하는 ...gi-kkeo-i ...ha-neun; 자발적인 ja-bal-jjeog-in; **~ly** 기꺼이 gi-kkeo-i, 자진해서 ja-jin-hae-seo

willow *n.* 버드나무 beo-deu-na-mu

win *n.* 승리 seung-ni; 이득 i-deuk; *vt.* 이기다 i-gi-da; 획득하다 hoek-deu-ka-da; 확보하다 hwak-bo-ha-da; 얻다 eot-da; 설득하다 seol-tteu-ka-da; *vi.* 이기다 i-gi-da; 다다르다 da-da-reu-da; 영향력을 미치다 yeong-hang-nyeog-eul mi-chi-da

wind *n.* 바람 ba-ram; 풍문 pung-mun; 예감 ye-gam; 동향 dong-hyang; 관악기 wan-ak-gi; *vt.* 악기를 불다 ak-gi-reul bul-da; 바람을 쐬다 ba-ram-eul ssoe-da; 낌새를 채다 kkim-sae-reul chae-da; 숨을 돌리게 하다 sum-eul dol-li-ge ha-da; 비뚤어지다 bi-ttul-eo-ji-da; 구부러지다 gu-bu-reo-ji-da; 휘감기다 hwi-gam-gi-da

windmill *n.* 풍차 pung-cha

window *n.* 창문 chang-mun; 진열창 jin-yeol-jjang; 창구 chang-gu; 매표소 mae-pyo-so

windowsill *n.* 창턱 chang-teok; 창받침 chang-bat-chim

windshield *n.* 자동차 앞유리 ja-dong-cha am-nyu-ri; 바람막이 창 ba-ram-mag-i chang

windy *adj.* 바람이 센 ba-ram-i sen; 바람을 세게 맞는 ba-ram-eul se-ge man-neun; 공허한 gong-heo-han; 헛배부른 heot-bae-bu-reun

wine *n.* 와인 wa-in, 포도주 po-do-ju; 과실주 gwa-sil-jju; 포도주색 po-do-ju-saek; **white ~** 백포도주 baek-po-do-ju

wing *n.* 날개 nal-gae; 무대 양옆 mu-dae yang-nyeop

wink *n.* 윙크 wing-keu; 눈짓 nun-jjit; 반짝임 ban-jjag-im; 순간 sun-gan; *vi.* 눈을 감빡이다 nun-eul kkam-ppag-i-da; 윙크하다 wing-keu-ha-da; 눈짓하다 nun-jji-ta-da; 반짝이다 ban-jjag-i-da; 못본척 하다 mot-bon-cheok ha-da

winner *n.* 승자 seung-ja, 승리자 seung-ni-ja; 수상자 su-sang-ja

winter *n.* 겨울 gyeo-ul

wipe *vt.* 닦다 dak-da; 지우다 ji-u-da; 말소하다 mal-sso-ha-da; 씻어버리다 ssis-eo-beo-ri-da; 문지르다 mun-ji-reu-da; **baby ~s** 아기용 물수건 a-gi-yong mul-ssu-geon

wire *n.* 철사 cheol-ssa; 전선 jeon-seon; 전신 jeon-sin; 철망 cheol-mang; *vt.* 철사로 고정하다 cheol-ssa-ro go-jeong-ha-da; 전선을 끌어넣다 jeon-seon-eul kkeul-eo-neo-ta; 덫으로 잡다 deoch-eu-ro jap-da; 전보로 통지하다 jeon-bo-ro tong-ji-ha-da

wireless *adj.* 무선의 mu-seon-ui; 무선전신의 mu-seon-jeon-sin-ui

wisdom *n.* 지혜 ji-hye; 현명함 hyeon-myeong-ham; 금언 geun-eon; 현인 hyeon-in

wise *adj.* 지혜로운 ji-hye-ro-un; 정통한 jeong-tong-han; 박식한 bak-si-kan; 교활한 gyo-hwal-han

wish *n.* 소원 so-won; 호의 ho-ui; 요청 yo-cheong; 바라는 것 ba-ra-neun geot; *vt.* ...기를 바라다 ...gi-reul ba-ra-da; ...고 싶다 ...go sip-da; ...으면 좋겠다고 생각하다 ...eu-myeon jo-ket-da-go saeng-ga-ka-da; ...기를 빌다 ...gi-reul bil-da

wit *n.* 위트 wi-teu, 재치 jae-chi; 지혜 ji-hye; 제정신 je-jeong-sin

witch *n.* 마녀 ma-nyeo; 추한 노파 chu-han no-pa; 매력적인 여자 mae-ryeok-jeog-in yeo-ja

with *prep.* ... 을 가지고 ... eul ga-ji-go, ... 를 가지고 ... reul ga-ji-go; ...하고 ...ha-go; ...(으)로 ...(eu)-ro; ...에 대하여 ...e dae-ha-yeo; **I wrote it ~ a pencil** 저는 이것을 연필로 썼습니다 jeo-neun i-geos-eul yeon-pil-lo sseot-seum-ni-da; **a man ~ black hair** 머리가 까만 남자분 meo-ri-ga kka-man nam-ja-bun

withdraw *vt.* 움츠리다 um-cheu-ri-da; 회수하다 hoe-su-ha-da; 인출하다 in-chul-ha-da; 철회하다 cheol-hoe-ha-da; 박탈하다 bak-tal-ha-da; *vi.* 물러나다 mul-leo-na-da; 철수하다 cheol-ssu-ha-da; 탈퇴하다 tal-toe-ha-da; 그만두다 geu-man-du-da; *(to retreat)* 후퇴하다 hu-toe-ha-da; *(in banking)* 돈을 인출하다 don-eul in-chul-ha-da

withdrawal *n.* 움츠림 um-cheu-rim; 회수 hoe-su; 철수 cheol-ssu; 취소 chwi-so; ~ **slip** 출금표 chul-geum-pyo, 출금신청서 chul-geum-sin-cheong-seo

withhold *vt.* 보류하다 bo-ryu-ha-da; 억누르다 eong-nu-reu-da

within *adv.* 안에 an-e; 안으로 an-eu-ro; 마음속으로 ma-eum-sog-eu-ro; *prep.* ...의 안쪽에 ...ui an-jjog-e; ...의 안쪽으로 ...ui an-jjog-eu-ro; ...이내에 ...i-nae-e; ...의 범위 안에 ...ui beom-wi-an-e; ~ **reason** 합당한 범위 내에서 hap-dang-han beom-wi-nae-e-seo

without *adv.* 밖에 bakk-e; 외부에 oe-bu-e; 겉으로는 geot-eu-ro-neun; *prep.* ...없이 ...eops-i; ...없이는 ...eops-i-neun; ...하지 않고 ...ha-ji an-ko; ...의 밖에 ...ui bakk-e

withstand *vt.* 저항하다 jeo-hang-ha-da; 잘 견디다 jal gyeon-di-da

witness *n.* 증인 jeung-in; 증언 jeung-eon; 입회인 i-poe-in; 증거 jeung-geo; *vt.* 목격하다 mok-gyeo-ka-da; 증언하다 jeung-eon-ha-da; 입회하다 i-poe-ha-a

witty *adj.* 재치있는 jae-chi-in-neun

wolf *n.* 이리 i-ri, 늑대 neuk-dae; 잔인한 사람 jan-in-han sa-ram

woman *n.* 여자 yeo-ja, 여성 yeo-seong, 부인 bu-in; 여자다움 yeo-ja-da-um

womb *n.* 자궁 ja-gung

wonder *vi.* 놀라다 nol-la-da; 의아하게 생각하다 ui-a-ha-ge saeng-ga-ka-da

wonderful *adj.* 놀라운 nol-la-un; 이상한 i-sang-han; 훌륭한 hul-lyung-han

wood *n.* 나무 na-mu; 목재 mok-jae; *(forest)* 숲 sup; 땔나무 ttael-la-mu; 목관악기 mok-gwan-ak-gi;

wool *n.* 양털 yang-teol; 털실 teol-sil; 모직물 mo-jing-mul

woolen *adj.* 양털의 yang-teol-ui; 모직의 mo-jig-ui

word *n.* 말 mal; 낱말 nan-mal; 이야기 i-ya-gi; 한마디 말 han-ma-di mal; 약속 yak-sok; 논쟁 non-jaeng; 소식 so-sik; 지시 ji si; - **for** - 축어적인 chug-eo-jeog-in, 직역의 jig-yeog-ui, 축어적으로 chug-eo-jeog-eu-ro, 직역하면 jig-yeo-ka-myeon; **He repeated it ~ for ~** 그분은 그것을 단어 하나하나 반복했습니다 geu-bun-eun geu-geos-eul dan-eo ha-na-ha-da ban-bo-kaet-seum-ni-da

word processing *n.* 워드 프로세싱 wo-deu peu-ro-sse-ssing

word processor *n.* 워드 프로세서 wo-deu peu-ro-sse-sseo

work *n.* 일 il; 노동 no-dong; 공부 gong-bu; 노력 no-ryeok; 연구 yeon-gu; 솜씨 som-ssi; 행위 haeng-wi; 작품 jak-pum; 일자리 il-jja-ri; 공장 gong-jang; *vi.* 일하다 il-ha-da; 노력하다 no-ryeo-ka-da; 공부하다 gong-bu-ha-da; 근무하다 geun-mu-ha-da; 작동하다 jak-dong-ha-da; 움직이다 um jig i da; 영향을 미치다 yeong-hyang-eul mi-chi-da; ~**day** 일하는 날 il-ha-neun nal; ~ **of art** 예술작품 ye-sul-jak-pum, 미술작품 mi-sul-jak-pum; ~ **permit** 노동허가서 no-dong-heo-ga-seo; ~**place** 직장 jik-jang, 일터 il-teo

worker *n.* 일하는 사람 il-ha-neun sa-ram; 공부하는 사람 gong-bu-ha-neun sa-ram; 일손 il-sson; 노동자 no-dong-ja; 직공 jik-gong

workshop *n.* 일터 il-teo; 작업장 jag-eop-jang; 직장 jik-jang; 워크샵 wo-keu-shap

world *n.* 세계 se-gye; 지구 ji-gu; 세상 se-sang; 현세 hyeon-se

World Bank *n.* 세계은행 se-gye-eun-haeng

World Health Organization *n.* 세계보건기구 se-gye-bo-geon-gi-gu

worldwide *adj.* 세계적인 se-gye-jeog-in

worm *n.* 벌레 beol-le; 지렁이 ji-reong-i; 회충 hoe-chung; 벌레같은 인간 beol-le-gat-eun in-gan

worn out *adj.* 닳아빠진 dal-a-ppa-jin; 기진맥진한 gi-jin-maek-jin-han; 진부한 jin-bu-han

worried *adj.* 난처한 nan-cheo-han; 딱한 tta-kan; 걱정스러운 geok-jeong-seu-reo-un

worry *n.* 걱정 geok-jeong; 고생 go-saeng; *vi.* 걱정하다 geok-jeong-ha-da; 고민하다 go-min-ha-da; 간신히 타개하다 gan-sin-hi ta-gae-ha-da

worse *adj.* 보다 나쁜 bo-da na-ppeun; 악화된 a-kwa-doen; *adv.* 더 나쁘게 deo na-ppeu-ge

worship *n.* 예배 ye-bae; 참배 cham-bae; 숭배 sung-bae; 존경 jon-gyeong; *vt., vi.* 예배하다 ye-bae-ha-da; 참배하다 cham-bae-ha-da; 숭배하다 sung-bae-ha-da; 존경하다 jon-gyeong-ha-da; **~per** 예배자 ye-bae-ja; 참배자 cham-bae-ja; 숭배자 sung-bae-ja

worst *adj.* 최악의 choe-ag-ui; 가장 심한 ga-jang sim-han; *adv.* 가장 나쁘게 ga-jang na-ppeu-ge

worth *adj.* ...의 가치가 있는 ...ui ga-chi-ga in-neun; ...의 만큼의 재산을 가지고 ...ui man-keum-ui jae-san-eul ga-ji-go; **It's ~ seeing** 그건 볼 가치가 있습니다 geu-geon bol ga-chi-ga it-seum-ni-da

worthless *adj.* 가치 없는 ga-chi eom-neun; 쓸모 없는 sseul-mo eom-neun

worthwhile *adj.* ...할 보람이 있는 ...hal bo-ram-i in-neun; 시간을 들일 만한 si-gan-eul del-il man-han

wound *n.* 부상 bu-sang; 상처 sang-cheo; 고통 go-tong; 타격 ta-gyeok; *vt.* 상처를 입히다 sang-cheo-reul i-pi-da; 감정을 상하다 gam-jeong-eul sang-ha-da

wrap *vt.* 감싸다 gam-ssa-da; 둘러싸다 dul-leo-ssa-da; 포함하다 ho-ham-ha-da; **~ping paper** 포장지 po-jang-ji

wrath *n.* 격노 gyeong-no; 노여움 no-yeo-um; 천벌 cheon-beol

wreath *n.* 화관 hwa-gwan; 화환 hwa-hwan; 소용돌이 so-yong-dol-i

wreck *n.* 난파 nan-pa; 파괴 pa-goe; 난파선 nan-pa-seon; 조난화물 jo-nan-hwa-mul; 난파잔해 nan-pa-jan-hae; *vt.* 난파시키다 nan-pa-si-ki-da; 파괴하다 pa-goe-ha-da; 파멸로 이끌다 pa-myeol-lo i-kkeul-da

wrench *n.* 비틂 bi-teum; 접질림 jeop-jil-lim; 렌치 ren-chi; 고통 go-tong; 왜곡 wae-gok; **monkey ~** 멍키스패너 meong-ki-seu-pae-neo, 렌치 ren-chi, 장애물 jang-ae-mul

wrestle *vt.* 레슬링하다 re-sseul-ling; 맞붙어 싸우다 mat-but-eo ssa-u-da

wrestler *n.* 레슬링 선수 re-sseul-ling seon-su; 씨름꾼 ssi-reum-kkun

wrinkle *n. (skin)* 주름살 ju-reum-ssal; *(fabric)* 구김 gu-gim; *vi.* 주름이 지다 ju-reum-i ji-da; 구겨지다 gu-gyeo-ji-da

wrist *n.* 손목 son-mok; 손재주 son-jjae-ju

wristwatch *n.* 손목시계 son-mok-si-gye

write *vt.* 쓰다 sseu-da; 기록하다 gi-ro-ka-da; 써 보내다 sseo bo-nae-da; 새겨넣다 sae-gyeo-neo-ta; 명백히 나타내다 myeong-baek-i na-ta-nae-da

writer *n.* 저자 jeo-ja; 작가 jak-ga; 서기 seo-gi; 필기자 pil-gi-ja

writing *n.* 집필 jip-pil; 저술업 jeo-sul-eop; 문서 mun-seo; 필적 pil-jjeok; **in ~** 쓴 sseun; 써 있는 sseo in-neun; 서면으로 seo-myeon-eu-ro; 써서 sseo-seo

wrong *adj.* 잘못된 jal-mot-doen; 부적당한 bu-jeok-dang-han; 부정한 bu-jeong-han; 상태가 나쁜 sang-tae-ga na-ppeun; 고장난 go-jang-nan; 반대쪽의 ban-dae-jjog-ui

X

xenophobia *n.* 외국인을 싫어함 oe-gug-in-eul sil-eo-ham
xenophobic *adj.* 외국인을 싫어하는 oe-gug-in-eul sil-eo-ha-neun
Xerox *n.* *(copy machine)* 복사기 bok-sa-gi; *vt., vi.* *(copy)* 복사하다 bok-sa-ha-da
Xmas *n.* *abbr.* **Christmas** 크리스마스 keu-ri-sseu-ma-sseu

X-rated *adj.* 성인용의 seong-in-nyong-ui, 미성년자 관람 불가의 mi-seong-nyeon-ja gwal-lam bul-ga-ui; 금지된 geum-ji-doen; 외설적인 oe-seol-jjeog-in; ~ **film** 성인용 영화 seong-in-nyong yeong-hwa
X-ray *vt.* 엑스레이를 찍다 ek-seu-re-i-reul jjik-da; *n.* 엑스레이 ek-seu-re-i
xylophone *n.* 실로폰 sil-lo-pon

Y

yacht *n.* 요트 yo-teu; 개인용 유람선 gae-in-nyong yo-ram-seon
yam *n.* 고구마 go-gu-ma
Yangtze River *n.* 양쯔강 yang-jjeu-gang
yank *vt.* 확 잡아덩기다 hawk jab-a-dang-gi-da
Yankee *n.* 미국사람 mi-guk-sa-ram; 뉴잉글랜드사람 nyu-ing geul laen deu ssa ram
yard *n.* 안마당 an-ma-dang; 구내 gu-nae; 작업장 jag-eop-jang; 조차장 jo-cha-jang; 야드 ya-deu; 막대 mak-dae; **back~** 뒷마당 dwin-ma-dang; **three ~s of cloth** 옷감 3야드 ot-gam sam-ya-deu; ~ **sale** 중고 가정용품 세일 jung-go ga-jeong-nyong-pum sse-il; ~ **stick** 야드자 ya-deu-ja, 판단기준 pan-dan-gi-jun
yarn *n.* 실 sil; 털실 teol-sil; 허풍 heo-pung
yawn *n.* 하품 ha-pum; 틈 teum; *vi.* 하품하다 ha-pum-ha-da; 입이 크게 벌어지다 ib-i keu-ge beol-eo-ji-da
year *n.* 년 nyeon, 해 hae; 연령 yeol-lyeong, 나이 na-i; 학년 hang-nyeon; 연도 yeon-do; ~**book** 연감 yeon-gam, 연부 yeon-bo; ~**end** 연말의 yeon-mal-ui
yearlong *adj.* 일년에 걸친 il-lyeon-e geol-chin
yearly *adj.* 매년의 mae-nyeon-ui; 일년간의 il-lyeon-gan-ui
yearn *vi.* 그리워하다 geu-ri-wo-ha-da; 갈망하다 gal-mang-ha-da; 동정하다 dong-jeong-ha-da
year-round *adj.* 연간 계속되는 yeon-gan gye-seok-doe-neun
yeast *n.* 이스트 i-seu-teu; 자극 ja-geuk; 소동 so-dong

yell *n.* 고함 go-ham; 부르짖음 bu-reu-jij-eum; *vi.* 고함치다 go-ham-chi-da; 폭소하다 pok-so-ha-da
yellow *adj.* 노란 no-ran; 노란색의 no-ran-saeg-ui; 질투심이 많은 jil-tu-sim-i man-eun; 겁이 많은 geob-i man-eun; 선정적인 seon-jeong-jeog-in; ~ **card** 옐로우카드 yel-lo-u ka-deu; ~ **line** 황색선 hwang-saek-seon; ~ **Pages** 업종별 전화번호부 eop-jong-byeol jeon-hwa-beon-ho-bu, 업종별 기업 안내 eop-jong-byeol gi-eob-an-nae
Yellow River *n.* 황하강 hwang-ha-gang
Yellow Sea *n.* 황해 hwang-hae
yes *adv.* 네 ne, 응 eung; ~**man** 예스맨 ye-sseu-maen
yesterday *n.* 어제 eo-je
yet *adv.* 아직 a-jik; 이미 i-mi, 벌써 beol-sseo; *conj.* 그래도 geu-rae-do
yield *n.* 산출물 san-chul-mul; 이익배딩 i-ik-bae-dang; 양보 yang-bo; *vt.* 산출하다 san-chul-ha-da; 양보하다 yang-bo-ha da
yin and yang *n.* 음과 양 eum-gwa-yang, 음양 eum-yang
yodel *n.* 요들송 yo-deul-ssong
yoga *n.* 요가 yo-ga
yogurt *n.* 요구르트 yo-gu-reu-teu
yoke *n.* 멍에 meong-e; 지배 ji-bae; 연결 yeon-gyeol; 인연 in-yeon; 요크 yo-keu
yolk *n.* 노른자위 no-reun-ja-wi; 양모지 yang-mo-ji
yonder *adv.* 저쪽에 jeo-jjog-e
you *pron.* 당신은 dang-sin-eun, 너는 neo-neun; 당신이 ang-sin-i, 네가 ne-ga; *(hon.)*

선생님은 seon-saeng-nim-eun; 선생님이
seon-saeng-nim-i

young *n.* 젊은이들 jeolm-eun-i-deul; 새끼
sae-kki; ~ **lady** 숙녀 sung-nyeo; ~ **man** 청
년 cheong-nyeon

youngest *n.* 막내 mang-nae

your *pron.* 당신의 dang-sin-ui, 너의 neo-ui,
(hon.) 선생님의 seon-saeng-nim-ui

yours *pron.* 당신의 것 dang-sin-ui geot, 너
의 것 neo-ui goet, *(hon.)* 선생님의 것
seon-saeng-nim-ui geot

yourself *pron.* 당신 자신을 dang-sin
ja-sin-eul, 너 자신을 neo ja-sin-eul; 당신
자신에게 dang-sin ja-sin-e-ge, 너 자신에
게 neo ja-sin-e-ge; *(hon.)* 선생님 자신을

seon-saeng-nim ja-sin-eul; 선생님 자신에
게 seon-saeng-nim ja-sin-e-ge

youth *n.* 젊음 jeolm-eum; 청년시대
cheong-nyeon-si-dae; 청년남녀cheong-
nyeon-nam-nyeo; ~ **hostel** 유스호스텔
yu-sseu-ho-seu-tel

youthful *adj.* 젊은 jeolm-eun; 발랄한 bal-
lal-han; 청년의 cheong-nyeon-ui; 초기의
cho-gi-ui

yo-yo *n.* 요요 yo-yo; *adj.* 오르내리는 o-reu-
nae-ri-neun, 변동하는 byeon-dong-ha-neun

yucky *adj.* 맛이 없는 mas-i eom-neun; 몹시
싫은 mop-si sil-eun

yummy *adj.* 맛있는 mas-in-neun; 기분 좋은
gi-bun jo-eun

Z

Zaire *n.* 자이레 ja-i-re; 자이레강 ja-i-re-gang

Zambia *n.* 잠비아 jam-bi-a

zany *n.* 익살광대 ik-sal-gwang-dae; *adj.* 익
살스러운 ik-sal-seu-reo-un

zap *vt., vi.* 재빨리 하다 jae-ppal-li ha-da; 죽
이다 jug-i-da; 쏘다 sso-da

zeal *n.* 열의 yeol-ui; 열심 yeol-ssim; 열정
yeol-jjeong; **show ~ for** ...에 열의를 나타
내다 ...e yeol-ui-reul na-ta-nae-da; **with ~**
열의를 가지고yeol-ui-reul ga-ji-go

zealot *n.* 열광자 yeol-gwang-ja

zealous *adj.* 열심인 yeol-ssim-in; 열광
적인 yeol-gwang-jeog-in; 열성적인
yeol-sseong-jeog-in

zebra *n.* 얼룩말 eol-lung-mal; *adj.* 얼룩말 무
늬의eol-lung-mal mu-ni-ui

Zen *n.* 선seon; ~ **Buddhism** 선종seon-jeong

zenith *n.* 천정 cheon-jeong; 정점 jeong-
jjeom; 절정 jeol-jjeong; 전성기 jeon-
seong-gi; **at one's ~** ...의 전성기에 ...ui
jeon-seong-gi-e; **at the ~ of** ...의 절정에
...ui jeol-jjeong-e

zero *num.* 제로 je-ro; 영 yeong; 공 gong; ~ **in
on** ...을 겨냥하다 ...eul gyeo-nyang-ha-
da; ...에 노력을 집중하다...e no-ryeog-
eul jip-jung-ha-da; ~ **defects** 완전무결
wan-jeon-mu-gyeol; ~ **gravity** 무중력상태
mu-jung-nyeok-sang-tae

zest *n.* 풍미 pung-mi; 맛 mat; 풍취pung-
chwi; 풍미를 더하는 것 pung-mi-reul
deo-ha-neun geot; 맛을 더하는 것 mas-
eul deo-ha-neun geot; 열의 yeol-ui; 열정
yeol-jjeong; **add some ~ to** ...에 풍미를
더하다 ...e pung-mi-reul deo-ha-da; **with
~** 열심히 yeol-ssim-hi; 맛있게 mas-it-ge;
vt. ...에 풍미를 더하다 ...e pung-mi-reul
deo-ha-da, ...에 풍취를 더하다 ...e pung-
chwi-reul deo-ha-da

zestful *adj.* 풍미가 있는 pung-mi-ga in-neun;
풍취가 있는 pung-chwi-ga in-neun; 묘미
가 있는 myo-mi-ga in-neun; 열의가 있는
yeol-ui-ga in-neun

Zeus *n.* 제우스신 je-u-sseu-sin

zigzag *n.* 지그재그 ji-geu-jae-geu; Z자형
ji-jja-hyeong; *adj.* 지그재그의 ji-geu-jae-
geu-ui; Z자형의 ji-jja-hyeong-ui; *adv.* 지
그재그로 ji-geu-jae-geu-ro; Z자형으로
ji-jja-hyeong-eu-ro; *vt.* 지그재그 모양으로
하다 ji-geu-jae-geu mo-yang-eu-ro ha-da;
vi. 지그재그 모양으로 걷다 ji-geu-jae-
geu mo-yang-eu-ro geot-da; 갈짓자로 걷
다 gal-jit-ja-ro geot-da

zillion *n.* 억만 eong-man; 엄청난 수 eom-
cheong-nan su; *adj.* 억만의 eong-man-ui;
엄청난 수의 eom-cheong-nan su-ui

zillionaire *n.* 억만장자 eong-man-jang-ja

Zimbabwe *n.* 짐바브웨 jim-ba-beu-we

zinc *n.* 아연 a-yeon; *vt.* 아연으로 도금하다 a-yeon-eu-ro do-geum-ha-da; 아연을 입히다 a-yeon-eul i-pi-da

Zion *n.* 시온산 si-on-san; 예루살렘 시 ye-ru-sal-lem si; 이스라엘 백성 i-seu-ra-el baek-seong; 천국 cheon-guk, 이상향 i-sang-hyang

Zionism *n.* 시온주의 si-on-ju-i

zip *n.* 지퍼 ji-peo; 원기 won-gi, 정기 jeong-gi; *vi.* 지퍼를 닫다 ji-peo-reul dat-da, 지퍼를 열다 ji-peo-reul yeol-da; 기운차게 날아가다 gi-un-cha-ge nal-a-ga-da; *vt.* 지퍼로 잠그다 ji-peo-ro jam-geu-da; **to ~ up one's jacket** 자켓의 지퍼를 짐그다 ja-kes-ui ji-peo-reul jam-geu-da; 빠르게 하다 ppa-reu-ge ha-da; 활기를 주다 hwal-gi-reul ju-da; 활발히 하다hwal-bal-hi ha-da; **to ~ across the horizon** 갑자기 유명해지다 gap-ja-gi yu-myeong-hae-ji-da

zip code *n.* 우편번호 u-pyeon-beon-ho; *vt.* ...에 우편번호를 써 넣다 ...e u-pyeon-beon-ho-reul sseo neo-ta

zipper *n.* 지퍼 ji-peo; 지퍼 달린 장화 ji-peo dal-lin jang-hwa; *vi.* 지퍼로 열리다 ji-peo-ro yeol-li-da, 지퍼로 채워지다ji-peo-ro chae-wo-ji-da; *vt.* ...을 지퍼로 열다 ...eul ji-peo-ro yeol-da, ... 지퍼로 채우다 ...reul ji-peo-ro chae-u-da

zodiac *n.* 점성술 jeom-seong-sul; 12궁 sib-i-gung; 12궁 일람도 sib-i-gung il-lam-do; **signs of the ~** 12궁 sib-i-gung; 점성술의 12가지 유형 jeom-seong-sul-ui yeol-ttu-ga-ji yu-hyeong

zombie *n.* 좀비 jom-bi; 죽은 사람을 살리는 초자연적인 힘 jug-eun sa-ram-eul sal-li-neun cho-ja-yeon-jeog-in him; 마법으로 살아난 시체 ma-beob-eu-ro sal-a-nan si-che

zonal *adj.* 띠의 tti-ui; 띠모양의 tti-mo-yang-ui; 토양대의 to-yang-dae-ui

zone *n.* 지대 ji-dae; 지역 ji-yeok; 지방 ji-bang; 지구 ji-gu; 구역gu-yeok; **tropical ~** 열대지방yeol-ttae-ji-bang; **safety ~** 안전지대 an-jeon-ji-dae; **occupied ~** 점령지구 jeom-nyeong-ji-gu; **time ~** 시간대 si-gan-ttae; **postal delivery ~** 우편배달구역 u-pyeon-bae-dal-gu-yeok; **~ defense** 지역방어 ji-yeok bang-eo; *vi.* 띠모양을 이루다 tti-mo-yang-eul i-ru-da; 띠모양이 되다 tti-mo-yang-i doe-da; *vt.* ...을 띠모양으로 두르다 ...eul tti-mo-yang-eu-ro du-reu-da; 지역으로 구분하다 ji-yeog-eu-ro gu-bun-ha-da; 구획하다 gu-hoe-ka-da

zoo *n.* 동물원 dong-mul-won

zoological *adj.* 동물학의 dong-mul-hag-ui; 동물에 관한 dong-mul-e gwan-han

zoologist *n.* 동물학자 dong-mul-hak-ja

zoology *n.* 동물학 dong-mul-hak

zoom *n.* 줌 jum; 급상승 geup-sang-seung; 급등 geup-deung; *vi.* (비행기가)급상승하다 (bi-haeng-gi-ga) geup-sang-seung-ha-da; (가격이)급등하다 (ga-gyeog-i) geup-deung-ha-da; *vt.* 급상승시키다 geup-sang-seung-si-ki-da; 급등시키다 geup-deung-si-ki-da; **~ in** 화면을 감자기 확대시키다 hwa-myeon-eul gap-ja-gi hwak-dae-si-ki-da; **~ out** 화면을 감자기 축소시키다 hwa-myeon-eul gap-ja-gi chuk-so-si-ki-da; **to ~ in on** 영상을 급격히 확대하다 yeong-sang-eul geup-gyeo-ki hwak-dae-ha-da; **~ lens** 줌렌즈 jum-ren-jeu

zucchini *n.* 호박 ho-bak

Zurich *n.* 취리히 jjwi-ri-hi

KOREAN-INTEREST TITLES FROM HIPPOCRENE BOOKS

Beginner's Korean with 2 Audio CDs
Jeyseon & Kangjin Lee

The Beginner's series offers basic language instruction, presenting grammar, vocabulary, and common phrases in clear, concise lessons. Review questions and exercises accompany each lesson. Historical and cultural material gives insight into customs and everyday situations. This introduction to Korean is designed for both classroom use and self-study. The 12 lessons combine dialogues with easy-to-follow grammatical explanations, and include vocabulary, cultural material, and exercises that reinforce the material covered. Each lesson builds upon the previous one, allowing the student to gain confidence and mastery over the language. The audio CDs complement the dialogue and vocabulary sections of the book, helping the student to understand the language as spoken.

520 pages · 2 Audio CDs · 5½ x 8½ · ISBN-10: 0-7818-7092-2 · $32.00p

Korean-English/English-Korean Dictionary and Phrasebook
Jeyseon & Kangjin Lee

Over 63 million people speak Korean worldwide, and the Korean peninsula has become one of the globe's most important business and financial centers. This guide, with its bilingual dictionary and practical-minded phrasebook, is an essential too for students, travelers, and businesspeople.

- More than 5,000 total dictionary entries
- Korean words presented in Hangul script with Romanized pronunciation
- Easy-to-use pronunciation guide
- Special section devoted to Korean grammar

5,000 entries · 312 pages · 3¾ x 7½ · ISBN-10: 0-7818-1029-9 · $14.95p

Korean-English/English-Korean Handy Dictionary
Thomas Eccardt

- A comprehensive English-Korean section with all the words and phrases listed alphabetically according to the main word in the expression

- All the Korean words and phrases you will meet in stores, on signs and menus, or hear as standard replies, conveniently arranged in subject areas to help you recognize and understand them when they occur

- Pronunciation, whenever it presents a problem

- The basics of Korean grammar, clearly presented for rapid reference

194 pages · 5 x 8 · ISBN-10: 0-7818-0082-X · $8.95p

Korean-English/English-Korean Practical Dictionary
Si-sa-yong-o-sa

This pocket-sized dictionary is specially designed for the traveler. Over 8,500 entries are supplemented with phrases addressing practicalities such as buying a ticket, customs, and immigration.

8,500 entries · 368 pages · 4⅜ x 8¼ · ISBN-10: 0-87052-092-X · $19.95p

Korea: An Illustrated History from Ancient Times to 1945
David Rees

Koreans call their country *Choson,* which is familiarly translated as "The Land of the Morning Calm." From the time of the legendary Tan-Gun in the third millennium B.C. until the middle of the twentieth century, however, Korea was forced to weather many military and political storms. This volume concisely depicts these political and social events, as well as Korea's profound spiritual and cultural heritage – a panoramic view that is complemented by more than fifty illustrations and maps.

b/w illustrations · 170 pages · 5 x 7 · ISBN-10: 0-7818-0873-1 · $12.95p

OTHER ASIAN LANGUAGE TITLES FROM HIPPOCRENE BOOKS

Beginner's Korean with Two Audio CDs
510 pages · ISBN 978-0-7818-1092-0 · $35.00p

Japanese-English/English-Japanese Concise Dictionary
Romanized
8,000 entries · 235 pages · 4 x 6 · ISBN-10: 0-7818-0162-1 · $11.95p

Japanese-English/English Japanese Dictionary & Phrasebook
2,300 entries · 231 pages · 3¾ x 7½ · ISBN-10: 0-7818-0814-6 · $12.95p

Beginner's Chinese with Two Audio CDs, Second Edition
360 pages · 2 Audio CDs · 5½ x 8½ · ISBN-10: 0-7818-1257-7 · $32.00p

Intermediate Chinese with Audio CD
320 pages · 1 Audio CD · 5½ x 8½ · ISBN-10: 0-7818-0992-4 · $21.95p

Chinese (Mandarin)-English/English-Chinese (Mandarin) Dictionary & Phrasebook
4,000 entries · 314 pages · 3¾ x 7½ · ISBN-10: 0-7818-1135-X · $13.95p

Chinese-English/English-Chinese Practical Dictionary
15,000 entries · 487 pages · 4⅜ x 7 · ISBN-13: 978-0-7818-1236-8 · $19.95p

Beginner's Vietnamese with 2 Audio CDs
262 pages · 5½ x 8½ · ISBN-13: 978- 0-7818-1265-8 · $29.95p

Vietnamese-English/English-Vietnamese Dictionary & Phrasebook
3,000 entries · 248 pages · 3¾ x 7 · ISBN-10: 0-7818-0991-6 · $13.95p

Vietnamese-English/English-Vietnamese Standard Dictionary
23,000 entries · 889 pages · 5 ½ x 8 · ISBN-10: 0-87052-924-2 · $29.95p

Vietnamese-English/English-Vietnamese Practical Dictionary
15,000 entries · 248 pages · 4⅜ x 7 · ISBN-13: 978-0-7818-1244-3 · $19.95p

Mongolian-English/English-Mongolian
Dictionary & Phrasebook
3,500 entries · 259 pages · 4 x 7½ · ISBN-10: 0-7818-0958-4 · $14.95p

All prices are subject to change without prior notice.
TO ORDER HIPPOCRENE TITLES: contact your local bookstore, call (212) 685-4373, visit www.hippocrenebooks.com or write to: Hippocrene Books. 171 Madison Avenue. New York, NY 10016.